WAR OFFICE, *31st July, 1914.*   [*Crown Copyright Reserved.*]

By Authority.

THE
MONTHLY
ARMY LIST
FOR
AUGUST, 1914.

Under the provisions of the Army Act, 1881, Section 163D, this Army List is evidence of the status and rank of the Officers mentioned in it.

SCHEDULE OF ARRANGEMENT.

I.—The KING, H.M. Aides-de-Camp, Equerries, Hon. Physicians, Hon. Surgeons, and Hon. Chaplains.

II.—Foreign Sovereigns who are Colonels-in-Chief, &c., of regiments.

III.—Army Council, &c.

IV.—Inspector-General of the Home Forces.

V.—Inspector-General of the Oversea Forces.

VI.—Military Attachés to Embassies and Legations at Foreign Courts.

VII.—Commands of the Army:—
1. Home:—(*a.*) Aldershot, Eastern, Irish, London District, Northern, Scottish, Southern, and Western Commands. (*b.*) Channel Islands.
2. India.
3. Mediterranean.
4. Dominions, Colonies, and Protectorates.

VIII.—Egyptian Army and Sudan Administration.

IX.—Field - Marshals; General Officers, Colonels and Brevet Colonels, Officers, not shewn in any Regiment or Corps, extra Regimentally employed.

X.—Officers unemployed, by ranks.

XI.—1. Royal Flying Corps.
2. Aeronautical Inspection Department.
3. Indian Central Flying School.

XII.—Regimental Lists:—
1. Cavalry (Regular Troops and Special Reserve).
   " (Irish Horse and King Edward's Horse — Special Reserve).
   " (Yeomanry, Territorial Force.)

2. Royal Regiment of Artillery.
   (*a*) Regulars (Royal Horse, Royal Field, and Royal Garrison Artillery).
   (*b*) Royal Field and Royal Garrison Artillery, Special Reserve.
   (*c*) Territorial Force (Honourable Artillery Company, Royal Horse, Royal Field, and Royal Garrison Artillery).
   (*d*) Royal Malta Artillery.
   (*e*) Bermuda Militia Artillery.

3. Royal Engineers (Regular Troops, Special Reserve, Militia, and Territorial Force).

4. Foot Guards (Regular Troops and Special Reserve.)

5. Infantry (Regular Troops, Special Reserve, Territorial Force, and 7 V.B. Liverpool Regiment.)

6. Army Service Corps (Regular Troops, Special Reserve and Territorial Force).

7 and XV. (3) & (4). Army Medical Service. Royal Army Medical Corps (Regular Troops, Special Reserve, Territorial Force, and *late* Volunteers).

8. Army Veterinary Service. Army Veterinary Corps (Regular Troops, Special Reserve and Territorial Force), and Indian Civil Veterinary Dept.

(*continued on page* ii.)

,904. 14,868/918. 12,000. 8/14. J. J. K. & Co., Ltd.

A

Schedule of Arrangement—*(continued)*.

XIII.—1. Army Chaplains' Department.
2. Staff for Royal Engineer Services.
3. Queen Alexandra's Imperial Military Nursing Service.
4. Territorial Force Nursing Service.
5. Army Ordnance Department.
6. Army Pay Department.
7. Army Schools.

XIV.—1. West African Regiment.
2. Corps of Military Police.
3. Eastern Telegraph Reserve.
4. Channel Islands Militia.
5. The King's Own Malta Regiment of Militia.
6. Bermuda Volunteer Rifle Corps.
7. Unattached list.
8. Officers Training Corps.
9. Officers of the late Volunteer Force doing duty with Cadet units.
10. Officers holding Volunteer Commissions under former Cadet Regns., not doing duty with Cadet units.

XV.—1. Indian Army.
  (a) General List.
  (b) Unattached List.
  (c) Supernumerary List.
  (d) Native Indian Land Forces.
  (e) Indian Units.
2. Indian Medical Service.
3. Indian Army Departments.

XVI.—1. Royal Marines.
2. Naval Ordnance Department.

XVII.—Warrant Officers.

XVIII.—1. Reserve of Officers.
2. Army Medical Reserve.
3. Territorial Force Reserve.

XIX.—List of Units of the Territorial Force.

XX.—Territorial Force Associations.

XXI.—Cadetships at the Royal Military College, Sandhurst.

XXII.—Establishments :—
1. Educational and Training.
2. Manufacturing.
3. Miscellaneous.

XXIII.—Special Lists :—
1. Officers attached to Egyptian Army.
2. West African Frontier Force.
3. King's African Rifles.
4. Officers interchanged between the British and Indian Armies and the Military Forces of the British Dominions beyond the seas.
5. Officers holding Military and other Appointments not remunerated out of Army funds.
6. Officers now serving who are Staff College Graduates.
7. Officers now serving who are qualified for Staff Employment in consequence of Service on the Staff in the Field.
8. Officers now serving who have qualified in a course of instruction at the London School of Economics.
9. Officers now serving who have passed the final examination of the Advanced Class, Ordnance College.
10. Officers now serving who have passed the first year's course at the Ordnance College.
11. Officers now serving who have obtained a 1st Class Certificate in the Long Course of Gunnery or Gunnery Staff Course prior to 1906, or have obtained the Certificate of the Gunnery Staff Course subsequent to 1905.
12. Officers now serving who have qualified as Interpreters in Modern Foreign Languages.
13. Officers undergoing a course of study in the Chinese, Japanese or Russian Language.
14. Officers granted Local, Temporary, or Honorary Rank.
15. Officers who have been selected for Rewards.

XXIV.—1. Promotions, &c., gazetted during preceding month.
2. List of Deaths.
3. Soldiers' Balances Unclaimed.

XXV.—Index (Active List and Reserve of Officers).

To which the following unindexed lists will be added in the issues for January, April, July and October :—

I.—Officers of the Regular Army, &c., retired from the Active List, in receipt of a retired allowance; and Officers on the Unemployed Supernumerary List (arranged alphabetically).

II.—Yeomen of the Guard, Gentlemen-at-Arms, and the King's Body Guard for Scotland.

III.—Victoria Cross, Orders of Knighthood, Distinguished Service Order, Imperial Service Order, Royal Red Cross, and Foreign Orders (arranged alphabetically within the Divisions of each Order).

IV.—Medallists (arranged alphabetically).

(iii)

TABLE OF CONTENTS.

	COL.
Abbottabad Brigade	69
Abbreviations	xxxiv
Aberdeen, City of, Batts., R. F. A.	674
———— Fortress R. E.	847
———— Terr. Force Assocn.	2424
———— Terr. Force Assocn.	2424
———— University Contgt., O.T.C.	1878
Aberdeenshire Militia, Royal	1471
Aberystwith Univ. Coll. Contgt., O.T.C.	1893
Abyssinia, Offr. empld. in	2522
Academy, Royal Mil., Woolwich	2486
Accountants and Chief Accountants, War Office	13
Accounts, Army, Director of	13
Active List, Officers on the	328
Aden Brigade	77
Adjutant-General to the Forces	5, 9
Advisory Board, Army Medical	2494
———— Commee. on Motor Cyclists	2502
———— Voluntary Aid	2502
———— Council, T. F. Nurs. Serv.	2503
Aeronautical Inspection Dept.	385
Aeronautics, Military, Dir.-Gen. of	15
Africa, East and Central	81, 2524
———— South	81, 2527
———— West	84
African Rifles, King's	2518
———— West, Frontier Force	2511
———— Regiment	1832
Agents, Army	xxxiv
Agricultural Coll., R., Contgt., O.T.C.	1891
Agriculture and Fisheries, Board of, Offrs. Empld. under	2528
Ahmednagar Brigade	75
Aides-de-Camp General to the King	1
———— Personal, to the King	1
———— to the King	1
Aircraft Factory, Royal	2492
Aldenham Sch. Contgt., O.T.C.	1894
Alderney, Guernsey and, District	64
———— Militia, Royal	1841
Aldershot Command	17
Alexander Memorial Medallists	*2878
Alexandra, Pss. of Wales's Own (York. Hrs.)	498
Alexandra, Pss. of Wales's Own (York. R.)	1073
Allahabad Brigade	72

	COL
Allan's School Cadet Unit	939
All Hallows Sch. Contgt., O.T.C.	1894
Alphabetical List of Regiments	xxxvii
Alterations, Notice regarding	xxxiv
Ambala (Cavalry) Brigade	70
Ampleforth Coll. Contgt., O.T.C.	1894
Anglesey, Carnarvonshire and, Bn., R. W. Fus.	1120
———— R. E., Royal	808
———— Terr. Force Assocn.	2425
Angus & Dundee Bn., R. Highrs.	1286
Antrim Militia, Royal	1491
———— R. G. A.	651
Appointments, Promotions, &c.	2708
Ardeer Co., R. Sc. Fus.	1100
Ardingly College Contgt., O.T.C.	1894
Ardwick Bn., Manch. R.	1409
Argyll and Sutherland Highlanders	1513
———— Inf. Brig.	45
———— Terr. Force Assocn.	2425
Argyllshire Bn., Arg. & Suth'd Highrs.	1522
———— (Mtn.) Batt., R. G. A.	748
Armagh Militia	1500
Army Accounts, Director of	13
———— Agents	xxxiv
———— Chaplains' Department	1789
———— Clothing Factory, Royal	2492
———— Council	5
———— Department, Govt. of India	65
———— Medical Advisory Board	2494
———— College, Royal	2488
———— Corps, R.	1678
———— Spec. Res.	1705
———— Terr. Force	1714
———— Training Estabt.	20, 2488
———— Wt. Offrs.	2289
———— Reserve	2385
———— Service	1678
———— Dir.-Gen.	9
———— Ordnance Corps	1811, 1822, 2291
———— Department	1811
———— Services, Inspr. of	10
———— Pay Corps	2295
———— Department	1823
———— Postal Services, Director of	808
———— Purchase Commission	2494
———— Sanitation, School of	20, 2488
———— School of Cookery	2487
———— Schools	1831

* Published in January, April, July and October issues only.

Table of Contents.

	COL.		COL.
Army Service Corps	1633	Bablake School (Coventry) Cadet Co.	954
—— Inspr. of	10	Bahamas	86
—— Spec. Res.	1645	Bandmasters (Wt. Offrs.) ... 2279,	2299
—— Terr. Force	1654	Banff and Donside Bn. (Gord. Highrs.)	1475
—— Training Estabt.	2487	—— Terr. Force Assocn.	2426
—— Wt. Offrs.	2283	Bangalore Brigade	76
—— Signal School, Aldershot ...20,	2487	Bangor Univ. Coll. Contgt., O.T.C.	1893
—————— Bulford ...53,	2487	Bannu Brigade	72
—————— Service	805	Barbados ...86,	2523
—— Signals, Director of (Home Defence)	831	Bareilly Brigade	71
—— Veterinary Corps	1778	Barrack Construction, Director of...	11
—————— Spec. Res.	1781	Barracks, Military Detention	2498
—————— Terr. Force	1781	Bath, Order of the	*2823
—————— Wt. Offrs.	2289	Beaumont College Contgt., O.T.C.	1895
—————— School ...20,	2488	Beccles Cadet Corps, R.F.A.	671
—————— Service	1778	Bedford Grammar Sch. Contgt., O.T.C.	1895
—————— Dir.-Gen.	10	—— Modern Sch. Contgt., O.T.C.	1895
Arnold House School Cadet Corps...	1330	—— Militia	1051
Arrangement, Schedule of	i	—— Terr. Force Assocn.	2427
Artillery Company, Honourable	655	Bedfordshire Regiment	1049
—— Director of	11	—— Yeomanry	446
—— Field, Committee	2495	Belfast Univ. Contgt., O.T.C.	1878
—— Royal ...514,	590	Belgaum Brigade	75
—————— Inspr. of	16	Bengal, Governor of	65
—————— Spec. Res.	574	Berkhamsted Sch. Contgt., O.T.C.	1895
—————— Terr. Force	667	Berks Militia, Royal	1343
—— Garrison, Royal ...542,	618	—— Terr. Force Assocn.	2427
—————— Inspr. of	16	—— Yeomanry	447
—————— Spec. Res.	651	Berkshire Regiment, Royal...	1341
—————— Terr Force	747	—————— 4 Bn., 1st Cadet Co.	1348
—— Horse, Royal ...514,	582	—— R.H.A.	659
—————— Inspr. of	16	Bermuda	86
—————— Terr. Force	659	—— Cadet Corps	1845
—— Institution, R., Medallists	*2877	—— Militia Artillery	779
—— Malta, Royal	779	—— Volunteer Rifle Corps	1842
—— Militia, Bermuda	779	Berwick, North, Cadet Corps	903
—— Royal, Committee	2499	—— Terr. Force Assocn.	2428
—— Regiment of	506	Birkenhead Cadet Corps, 1st	1105
—— Terr. Force	659	Birmingham Univ. Contgt., O.T.C.	1879
—— Wt. Offrs.	2265	Black Watch Inf. Brig.	43
Artists Rifles (Lond. R.)	1607	—————— Sig. Sect.	840
Assistant Financial Secretary ... 6,	13	—————— (R. Highrs.)	1281
—— Military Secretary	6	Blackheath and Woolwich Bn. (Lond. R.)	1600
—— Principals, War Office 12, 13, 14,	15	Bloxham Sch. Contgt., O.T.C.	1896
—— Secretary of the War Office 6,	14	Blundell's Sch. Contgt., O.T.C.	1896
Associations, Territorial Force	2424	Blythswood Bn. (High. L.I.)	1449
Attachés, Military	16a	Body Guard for Scotland	*2818
Australia, Commonwealth of 85, 2522,	2523	Bolton Artillery	687
Ayr and Wigtown Militia, Royal...	1095	Bombay, Governor of	65
—— Terr. Force Assocn.	2426	—— Brigade	75
Ayrshire Batts., R. F. A.	709		
Ayrshire R. H. A.	659		
—— Yeomanry	445		

* Published in January, April, July and October issues only.

(v)

Table of Contents.

	COL.
Border Bn. (K. O. Sco. Bord.) ...	1137
——— Regiment	1217
Borderers, Scottish, King's Own ...	1133
———————— Militia	1135
———————— South Wales	1125
———————————— Mila., Royal	1127
Bournemouth Sch. Contgt., O.T.C.	1897
Bradfield Coll. Contgt., O.T.C. ...	1897
Bradford Postal Tel. Messengers' Cadet Corps...	1035
Brecknock Terr. Force Assocn. ...	2428
Brecknockshire Bn. (S. Wales Bord.)	1129
Bridgnorth Cadet Co.	1372
Bridlington Grammar Sch. Contgt., O.T.C.	1898
Brierley Hill Cadet Corps	1252
Brigade, Cavalry, 1st	18
——————— 2nd	48
——————— 3rd	29
——————— 4th	22, 32
——————— 5th	23, 36
——— Infantry, 1st, 2nd, 3rd ...	18
——————— 4th (Ft. Gds.) ...	19, 32
——————— 5th, 6th	19
——————— 7th, 8th, 9th ...	48
——————— 10th, 11th, 12th...	22
——————— 13th, 14th, 15th...	29
——————— 16th, 17th ...	30
——————— 18th	30, 36
——————— Malta	80
Brigades, Indian ...see under Title of each	
——————— Territorial see under Title of each	
Brighton Brigade, Sussex Cadets ...	679
——— Coll. Contgt., O.T.C. ...	1898
——— Preparatory Schools Cadet Corps	1230
Bristol, City of, Bn. (Glouc. R.) ...	1165
Bristol Grammar Sch. Contgt., O.T.C.	1898
Bristol Univ. Contgt., O.T.C. ...	1879
British Guiana 86,	2523
——— Honduras	86
——— Red Cross Society	2494
——— South Africa Co.	2523
Bromsgrove Sch. Contgt., O.T.C....	1898
Buchan and Formartin Bn. (Gord. Highrs.)	1474
Buckingham Terr. Force Assocn. ...	2429
Buckinghamshire Bn. (Oxf. and Bucks. L.I.)	1299
——————— Oxf. and, Lt. Inf.	1293
——————— Yeomanry ...	448
Buffs (East Kent Regt.)	917
Building Works Dept., Woolwich Arsenal	2492

	COL.
Burford Grammar Sch. Cadet Corps	1298
Burma Division	77
Bury Grammar Sch. Contgt., O.T.C.	1899
Bute Terr. Force Assocn.	2429
Buteshire (Mtn.) Batt., R.G.A. ...	749
Cadet Corps, Bermuda	1845
Cadet Units affiliated to units of the Territorial Force :—	
Allan's School Cadet Unit ...	939
Arnold House Sch. Cadet Corps	1330
Bablake School (Coventry) Cadet Co.	954
Beccles Cadet Corps, R.F.A. ...	671
Berks. Regt., Royal, 4 Bn., 1st Cadet Co.	1348
1st Birkenhead Cadet Corps ..	1105
Bradford Postal Tel. Messengers' Cadet Corps	1035
Bridgnorth Cadet Co.	1372
Brierley Hill Cadet Corps ...	1252
Brighton Brigade, Sussex Cadets	679
Brighton Preparatory Schools Cadet Corps	1230
Burford Grammar Sch. Cadet Corps	1298
Chatham House (Ramsgate) Cadet Corps	922
1st Cadet (Chatham) Co., R.M.L.I.	1356
Chelmsford King Edward VI. Sch. Cadet Corps	1307
Cheshire Regt., 1st Cadet Bn.	1108
Christ's College Cadet Co. ...	1380
2nd (Civil Service) Cadet Bn., Lond. R.	1593
Colchester R. Grammar Sch. Cadets	1307
Collegiate Sch. Cadet Co., Hastings	822
Coopers' Company's Sch. Cadet Corps	1578
Cornwall, "A" Co. 1st Cadet Bn. of	1202
Cowley Cadet Corps	1298
Dartmouth Cadet Co.	1012
Depôt, R. Mar. Cadet Corps ...	922
Dunoon Grammar Sch. Cadet Corps	1523
Ealing Cadet Co.	1381
Eng., R., Cadets (2 Lond. Div.)	826
Essex Regt., 1st Cadet Bn. ...	1309
Exeter Cathedral Sch. Cadet Co.	1006
Frimley and Camberley Cadet Corps	916
Fus., R., 1st Cadet Bn. ...	965
1st (Glasgow Highland) Cadet Co., High. L.I.	1456

A 3

Table of Contents.

	COL.
Cadet Units affiliated to units of the Territorial Force—*contd.*	
Glouc. Regt., 6 Bn., 1st and 2nd Cadet Cos.	1168
Haddington Cadet Corps	903
Haltwhistle Cadets	937
Harrow Cadet Co.	1382
Haytor (Newton Abbot) Cadet Corps	1007
Herne Bay College Cadet Corps	922
2nd Hertfordshire (Watford Scouts) Cadet Co.	1612
3rd Hertfordshire Cadets (Stortford School)	1612
4th Hertfordshire Cadets (St. George's School)	1612
1st Home Cos. Brig., R.F.A., 1st Cadet Bn. (Imperial Service Cadet Corps)	679
Hutcheson's Grammar School Cadet Corps	1150
Kensington and Hammersmith Navy League Boys' Brigade	1590
Kent (Fort.) R.E., Cadet Bn.	854
Kilburn Grammar School Cadet Co.	1382
King's R. Rif. C., 1st Cadet Bn.	1390
King's Sch., Peterborough, Cadet Corps	1340
Kirkby Lonsdale Cadet Co.	1223
Lan. Fus., 8 Bn., 1st Cadet Co.	1088
Leeds Postal Tel. Messengers' Cadet Co.	842
Lond. R., 6 Bn., 1st Cadet Co.	1578
———— 2nd (Civil Service) Cadet Bn.	1593
Macclesfield Grammar Sch. Cadet Corps	1112
———— Industrial Sch. Cadet Corps	1112
Manchester Regt., 2nd Cadet Bn.	1412
Manor Park Cadet Co.	1306
Monmouthshire Regt., 1st Cadet Bn.	1562, 1563, 1564
Morpeth Grammar Sch. Cadet Co.	940
New Brighton, 1st Cadet Corps	1105
New College (Herne Bay) Cadet Corps	922
Newport Cadet Corps, R.F.A.	742
Norfolk Artillery, Cadet	668
North Berwick Cadet Corps	903
Northampton School Cadet Corps	1340
Ongar Grammar School Cadets	1306
Palmer's School Cadet Corps	1309
Peter Symonds School Cadet Corps	1238
No. 2 (Plymouth) Cadet Co., Devon (Fort.) R.E.	849
Plymouth Lads' Brigade Cadet Corps	1007

	COL.
Cadet Units affiliated to units of the Territorial Force—*contd.*	
1st Poulton Cadet Co.	1105
Prestonpans Cadet Corps	903
Queen's Westminster Cadet Corps	1595
Richmond County Sch. Cadet Corps	1196
St. Peter's Cadet Co.	1590
St. Thomas's (Wandsworth) Cadet Corps	1604
Scots Fus., R., 1st Cadet Bn.	1098, 1100
Settle Cadet Bn.	1211
South London Cadets	1602
Southend High Sch. Cadet Corps	1309
Southport Cadet Corps	977
Steyne School Cadet Corps	679
Sunbury House Sch. Cadet Co.	1382
G. and H. (Surrey) Cos., 1st Cadet Bn. of Hampshire	916
Surrey Yeo., "E" Cadet Sqdn.	491
Tollington Sch. Cadet Co.	1380
Tranent Industrial School Cadet Corps	903
Univ. Sch. Cadet Co., Hastings	822
Ventnor Cadet Co.	1243
Warley Garrison Cadets	1306
Warwickshire Regt. Royal, 1st Cadet Bn.	956
Warwickshire Regt., Royal, 2nd Cadet Bn.	954
West Croydon Cadets	914
Westerham and Chipstead Cadet Corps	1355
1st Woolwich Cadet Corps	698
No. 1 (Yealmpton) Cadet Co., Devon (Fort.) R.E.	849
Yorkshire Sqdn., Impl. Cadet Yeo.	498
Cadet Units, Offrs. of the late Vol. Force doing duty with	1938
Cadet Units, Offrs. holding Vol. Commns. under former Cadet Regns., not doing duty with	1940
Cadetships at the R. Mil. Coll.	2478
Caithness, Suth'd and, Highland Bn. (Sea. Highrs)	1462
———— Terr. Force Assocn.	2430
Camberley Staff College	2480
Cambridge and County Sch. Contgt., O.T.C.	1899
———— I. of Ely T.F. Assocn.	2430
———— Univ. Contgt., O.T.C.	1879
Cambridgeshire Regiment	1561
Camel Corps Sch. (Egypt)	78
Cameron Highlanders	1481
———— Seaforth and, Inf. Brig.	44
Cameronians (Scottish Rifles)	1141
Campbell Coll. Contgt., O.T.C.	1899
Canada, Dominion of	86, 2528
Canadians, Royal (Leins. R.)	1518
Cape of Good Hope District	83
Carabiniers (6th Dragoon Guards)	400
———— Hampshire Yeo.)	459

(vii)

Table of Contents.

	COL.
Cardigan Terr. Force Assocn.	2431
Cardiganshire Batt., R. F. A.	738
Carmarthen Terr. Force Assocn.	2431
Carnarvon Terr. Force Assocn.	2432
Carnarvonshire and Anglesey Bn. (R. W. Fus.)	1120
Carnarvonshire R. G. A. (Heavy)	758
Carriage Factory, Royal	2492
Castlemartin (Pembroke Yeo.)	483
Cavalry	386
——— Brigade, 1st	18
——— ——— 2nd	48
——— ——— 3rd	29
——— ——— 4th	22, 32
——— ——— 5th	23, 36
——— Committee	2495
——— Depôts	437
——— Indian	2021
——— Records, Cols. i/c	392
——— Inspector of	16
——— School, Netheravon	2482
——— ——— Saugor	2482
——— Warrant Officers	2265
Cavan Militia	1502
Central Africa	81
——— Bn., King's Afr. Rif.	2518
——— Flying School	379
——— ———, Indian	385
Ceylon	87, 2523
Channel Islands	64
——— Militia	1834
Chaplain-General	14
Chaplains Dept., Army	1789
——— Terr. Force	1793
Chaplains, Honorary, to the King	3
Charterhouse Sch. Contgt., O.T.C.	1899
Chatham, 1st Cadet Co., R.M.L.I.	1356
Chatham House (Ramsgate) Cadet Corps	922
Chelmsford King Edward VI. Sch. Cadet Corps	1307
Chelsea, Royal Hospital	2500
Cheltenham Coll. Contgt., O.T.C.	1900
Chemical Branch, Research Dept.	2496
Cheshire Batts., R. F. A.	739
——— Brig. R.F.A.	739
——— Brig. Co., A.S.C.	1675
——— Field Co., R. E.	475
——— Infantry Brigade	59
——— Lancashire &, R. G. A.	772
——— Militia, Royal	1103
——— Regiment	1101
——— Yeomanry	449
Chester Terr. Force Assocn.	2432
Chestnut Troop, R. H. A.	582
Chief Accountants, War Office	13
——— Inspector of Works	1797
——— of the Imperial General Staff	5, 7
——— Paymaster, War Office	13

	COL.
Chigwell Sch. Contgt., O.T.C.	1900
Chile, Offr. empld. in	2524
China	87, 2524
Christ's College Cadet Co.	1380
——— Hospital Contgt., O.T.C.	1900
Churcher's College Contgt., O.T.C.	1901
Cinque Ports Ammn. Col., R.F.A.	682
——— Bn. (R. Suss. R.)	1230
——— Brig., R.F.A.	681
——— Fortress R.E.	847
City of Aberdeen Batts., R.F.A.	674
——— Fortress R.E.	847
——— T.F. Assocn.	2424
——— Bristol Bn. (Glouc. R.)	1165
——— Dundee Batt., R.F.A.	676
——— Bn. (R. Highrs.)	1285
——— Fortress R.E.	849
——— T.F. Assocn.	2437
——— Edinburgh Batts. R.F.A.	707
——— Fortress R.E.	850
——— R.G.A. (Heavy)	755
——— T.F. Assocn.	2439
——— Glasgow Batts., R.F.A.	710, 711
——— Bns. (High. L.I.)	1446, 1448
——— T.F. Assocn.	2443
——— London Batts., R.F.A.	696
——— Bns. (Lond. R.)	1569 to 1581
——— Brig. R. F. A.	695
——— Field Ambulances	1728, 1729
——— Horse Art.	655
——— Gen. Hospitals	1744 to 1746
——— Regt. (R. Fus.)	957
——— Sanitary Co.	1766
——— Sch. Contgt., O.T.C.	1901
——— T.F. Assocn.	2455
——— Yeomanry	469
Civil Member of the Army Council	5, 6, 12
——— Service Rifles (Lond. R.)	1592
2nd (Civil Service) Cadet Bn., Lond. R.	1593
Clackmannan Terr. Force Assocn.	2433
Clearing Hospitals	1770
Clifton College Contgt., O.T.C.	1901
Clothing, Dress and, Asst. Dir.	10
——— Factory, Army, Royal	2492
Clyde R.G.A.	759
Coast Bn., R.E.	805
Coast Defences :—	
Eastern	23
Harwich	23
North Eastern	37
North Irish	30
North Western	55
Scottish	43
South Eastern	24
South Irish	30
South Western	49
Southern	49
Western	55

(viii)

Table of Contents.

	COL.
Colchester R. Grammar Sch. Cadets	1307
Coldstream Guards	871
College, Army Medical, Royal	2488
——— Military, Royal, Sandhurst	2485
——— of Surgeons, Royal, in Ireland, Contgt., O.T.C.	1892
——— Ordnance	2483
——————— Offrs. passed	2577, 2583
——— Staff, Camberley	2480
——————— Graduates	2533
——————— Quetta	2481
Colonels	336
Colonies, Protectorates, etc. :—	
Africa	81
Australia	85
Bahamas	86
Barbados	86
Bermuda	86
British Guiana	86
——— Honduras	86
Canada	86
Cape of Good Hope	83
Central Africa	81
Ceylon	87
China	87
Cyprus	78
East Africa	81
Egypt	78
Falkland Islands	88
Fiji Islands	88
Gambia	84
Gibraltar	79
Gold Coast	84
Hong Kong	87
Jamaica	89
Leeward Islands	89
Malta	80
Mauritius	89
Mediterranean	78
Newfoundland	96
New South Wales	85
New Zealand	90
Nigeria	84
Nyasaland	81
Orange Free State	83
Papua	85
Queensland	85
St. Helena	90
Seychelles	90
Sierra Leone	84
Somaliland	81
South Africa	81
South Australia	85
Straits Settlements	90

	COL.
Colonies, Protectorates, etc.—*contd.*	
Tasmania	85
Tobago	90
Trinidad	90
Uganda	81
Victoria	85
Wei-Hai-Wei	87
West Africa	84
Western Australia	85
Windward Islands	90
Commander-in-Chief in India	66
Commands of the Army:—	
Dominions, Colonies and Protectorates	81
East Indies	65
Mediterranean	78
United Kingdom	17
Commands (United Kingdom):—	
Aldershot	17
Channel Islands (Dist. Comds.)	64
Eastern	21
Irish	28
London District	32
Northern	36
Scottish	42
Southern	47
Western	54
Committees :—	
Cavalry	2495
Establishments and Equipment	2495
Field Artillery	2495
Imperial Defence	2528
Motor Cyclists (Technical Res.)	2502
Overseas Defence	2528
Royal Artillery	2499
Royal Engineer	2500
Small Arms	2502
Voluntary Aid (Technical Res.)	2502
Composite Regiment of Household Cavalry	22, 32
Comptroller of Lands	12
Connaught Rangers	1505
Contracts, Director of	13
Convalescent Home, Osborne	Cover
Cookery, Army School of	2487
Coopers' Company's Sch. Cadet Corps	1578
Cork Grammar Sch. Contgt., O.T.C.	1902
——— R.G.A.	653
——— South, Mila.	1541
Cornwall, "A" Co. 1st Cadet Bn. of	1202
——— Devon and, Brig. Co., A.S.C.	1677
——————— Inf. Brig.	53
——— Fortress R.E.	847
——— Rangers Mila., Royal	1199
——— R.G.A.	760
——— Terr. Force Assocn.	2433

(ix)

Table of Contents.

	COL.
County of Durham Brigs., R.F.A.	726,728
———— London Batts., R.F.A.	697 to 706
———— Bns. (Lond. R.)	1582 to 1608
———— Yeomanry	470 to 472
Cowley Cadet Corps	1298
Cranbrook College (Ilford) Cadets	1306
———— Sch. Contgt., O.T.C.	1902
Cranleigh Sch. Contgt., O.T.C.	1902
Cromarty, Ross & (Mtn.) Batt., R.G.A.	749
Cumberland and Westmorland Bn. (Bord. R.)	1221
———— Artillery	688
———— Batts., R.F.A.	689
———— Bn. (Bord. R.)	1223
———— Militia, Royal	1219
———— Terr. Force Assocn.	2434
———— Westmorland &, Yeo.	494
Cyclist Battalions 905, 992, 1009, 1020, 1047, 1232, 1244, 1277, 1311, 1606, 1613,	1617
Cyclists, Motor, Advisory Commee. on	2502
Cyprus	78
Dartford Grammar Sch. Contgt., O.T.C.	1902
Dartmouth Cadet Co.	1012
Dean Close Sch. Contgt., O.T.C.	1902
Deaths	2727
Deeside Highland Bn. (Gord. Highrs.)	1477
Dehra Dun Brigade	71
Denbigh & Flint Militia, Royal	1115
———— Terr. Force Assocn.	2434
Denbighshire Bn. (R. W. Fus.)	1117
———— Yeomanry	450
Denstone College Contgt., O.T.C.	1903
Depôt, R.Mar. Cadet Corps.	922
Deputy Judge Advocate	14
Derajat Brigade	72
Derby Militia	1315
———— Notts. and, Brig. Co., A.S.C.	1670
———— ———— Inf. Brig.	41
———— ———— Mtd. Brig.	40
———— ———— Ammn.Col.	664
———— ———— Fd. Amb.	1716
———— ———— T.&S.Col.	1656
———— School Contgt., O.T.C.	1903
———— Terr. Force Assocn.	2435
Derbyshire Batts., R.F.A.	716,717
———— Notts. and, Regt.	1313
———— Yeomanry	451
Detention Barracks and Prisons, Military	2498
Devon and Cornwall Brig. Co., A.S.C.	1677
———— ———— Inf. Brig.	53
———— Militia	1003
———— Terr. Force Assocn.	2435
———— Yeomanry, Royal 1st	452

	COL
Devon Yeomanry, Royal North	453
Devonshire Batts., R.F.A.	748,749
———— Fortress R.E.	848
———— Regiment	1001
———— R.G.A.	761
Director of Army Accounts	13
———— Postal Services	808
———— Signals (Home Defence)	831
———— Artillery	11
———— Barrack Construction	11
———— Contracts	13
———— Equipmt. & Ord. Stores	10
———— Financial Services	13
———— Fortifications and Works	11
———— Military Operations	7
———— Military Training	8
———— Mobilization	9
———— Personal Services	9
———— Recruiting and Orgn.	9
———— Remounts	10,438
———— Staff Duties	8
———— Supplies and Quartering	10
———— Transport and Movements	10
Director-Gen., Army Med. Service	9
———— Army Vety., Service	10
———— Military Aeronautics	15
———— Terr. Force	12
Discharge Depôt, Gosport	51
Distinguished Service Order	*2848
———— ———— Rewards	2679
District No. 1.	43
———— 2	44
———— 3	55
———— 4	56
———— 5	37
———— 6	38
———— 7 & 8	50
———— 9 & 10	24
———— 11 & 12	31
Division (British) 1st	18
———— 2nd	19, 23, 32
———— 3rd	48
———— 4th	22
———— 5th	29
———— 6th	30, 36
———— (Indian) 1st (Peshawar)	68
———— 2nd (Rawal Pindi)	69
———— 3rd (Lahore)	70
———— 4th (Quetta)	73
———— 5th (Mhow)	74
———— 6th (Poona)	74
———— 7th (Meerut)	71
———— 8th (Lucknow)	71
———— 9th (Secunderabad)	75
———— Burma	77

* Published in January, April, July and October issues only.

(z)

Table of Contents.

	COL.
Divisional R. E. (T.F.)	819
Divisions, Territorial—see under Title of each	
Dollar Institution Contgt., O.T.C	1903
Dominions, Colonies and Protectorates	81
Donside, Banff &, Bn. (Gord. Highrs.)	1475
Dorchester Grammar Sch. Contgt., O.T.C.	1903
Dorset Militia (Dorset R.)	1255
———— Terr. Force Assocn.	2436
———— Yeomanry	454
Dorsetshire Batt., R.F.A.	746
———————— Fortress R.E.	849
———————— Regiment	1253
———————— R.G.A.	763
Dover College Contgt., O.T.C.	1904
Down North, Militia, Royal	1493
———— South, Militia, Royal	1495
Downside Sch. Contgt., O.T.C.	1904
Dragoon Guards, 1st (King's)	392
———————————— 2nd (Queen's Bays)	394
———————————— 3rd (P. of Wales's)	396
———————————— 4th (Royal Irish)	398
———————————— 5th (Pss. Charlotte of Wales's)	399
———————————— 6th (Carabiniers)	400
———————————— 7th (Pss. Royal's)	401
Dragoons, 1st (Royal)	403
———————— 2nd (Royal Scots Greys)	405
———————— 6th (Inniskilling)	411
Dress and Clothing, Asst. Dir.	10
Dublin City Mila., Royal	1549
———— County Mila.	1551
———— Fusiliers, Royal	1545
———— Recruiting Area	31
———— Univ. Contgt., O.T.C.	1882
Duke of Albany's (Seaforth Highrs.)	1457
———— Cambridge's Hrs.	470
———————————— Own Lrs. (17th)	431
———————————— (Midd'x R.)	1373
———— Connaught's Own Bn. (Hamps. R.)	1239
———————————— (R.E. Kent Yeo.)	461
———— Cornwall's Light Inf.	1197
———————————— R.G.A.	760
———— Edinburgh's (Wilts. R.)	1393
———— Lancaster's Own Yeo.	466
———— Wellington's (W. Rid. R.)	1205
———— York's Royal Mil. School	2489
———————————— Own Loyal Suff. Hrs.	490
Dulwich College Contgt., O.T.C.	1904
Dumbarton Terr. Force Assocn.	436
Dumbartonshire Bn. (Arg. & Suth'd Highrs.)	1523

	COL.
Dumfries & Galloway Bn. (K. O. Sco. Bord.)	1139
Dumfries Terr. Force Assocn.	2437
Duncan Prize Essay Gold Medallists	*2877
Dundee, Angus &, Bn. (R. Highrs.)	1286
———— City of, Batt., R.F.A.	676
———————— Bn. (R. Highrs.)	1285
———————— Fortress R.E.	849
———————— T.F. Assocn.	2437
Duncon Grammar Sch. Cadet Corps	1523
Durham Batts., R.F.A.	727 to 729
———— County of, Brigs., R.F.A.	726, 728
———— Fortress R.E.	850
———— Lt. Inf.	1429
———— Brig.	38
———— Co., A.S.C.	1673
———— Militia	1431, 1433
———— R.G.A.	763
———— Terr. Force Assocn.	2438
———— Univ. Contgt., O.T.C.	1883
———— York and, Brig. Co., A.S.C.	1673
———————————— Inf. Brig.	38
Ealing Cadet Co.	1381
Earl of Carrick's Own (Ayr. Yeo.)	445
———— Chester's Bn. (Ches. R.)	1106
———————— Yeo.	449
East Africa Bn., King's Afr. Rif.	2519
———— Protectorate	81, 2524
———— Anglian Brigs., R.F.A.	667 to 673
———————— Clearing Hospital	1770
———————— Division	25
———————— Divl. R.E.	819
———————— Sig. Co.	831
———————— T.& S. Col.	1658
———————— Fd. Ambs.	1718 to 1722
———————— R.G.A. (Heavy)	751
———— Indies	65
———— Kent Militia	919
———————— Regiment	917
———————— Yeomanry, Royal	461
———— Lancashire Brigs., R.F.A.	684 to 689
———————— Clearing Hospital.	1770
———————— Division	57
———————— Divl. R.E.	823
———————— Sig. Co.	834
———————— T.&S. Col.	1663
———————— Fd. Ambs.	1725, 1726
———————— Inf. Brig.	57
———————— Regiment	1181
———— Middlesex Mila., Royal	1378
———— Midland Brig. Co., A.S.C.	1659
———————— Inf. Brig.	25
———— Riding Batts., R.F.A.	725
———————— Fortress R.E.	857
———————— of Yorkshire Yeo.	499

* Published in January, April, July and October issues only.

(xi)

Table of Contents.

	COL.
East Riding R.G.A.	765
—— Surrey Regiment	1189
—— York Mila. (E. York R.)	1043
—— Yorkshire Regiment	1041
Eastbourne Coll. Contgt., O.T.C.	1904
Eastern Cavalry Depôt	437
—— Coast Defences	23
—— Command	21
—— General Hospitals	1742, 1743
—— Mounted Brig.	25
—————— Ammn. Col.	661
—————— Fd. Amb.	1714
—————— Sig. Troop	499
—————— T. & S. Col.	1654
—— Telegraph Reserve	1833
Economics, London Sch. of, Offrs. qualified in course at	2571
Edinburgh Academy Contgt., O.T.C.	1905
—— City of, Batts., R.F.A.	707
—————— Fortress R.E.	850
—————— R.G.A. (Heavy)	755
—————— T.F. Assocn.	2439
—— Light Inf. Mila.	896
—— Recruiting Area	44
—— Rifles, Queen's (R.Scots)	897, 898
—— Univ. Contgt., O.T.C.	1883
Educational & Training Estabts.	2480
Egypt, Force in	78
—— Offrs. empld. in	2524
Egyptian Army, Hd.-Qrs. Staff	93
—————— Offrs. attached to	2506
Electric Lighting, Schools of	2483
—— Lights, Inspector of	11
Electrical R.E. (T.F.)	855
Elgin Terr. Force Assocn.	2439
Elizabeth Coll. (Guernsey) Contgt., O.T.C.	1905
Ellesmere Coll. Contgt., O.T.C.	1905
Elstow Sch. Contgt., O.T.C.	1905
Elthorne Militia, Royal (Midd'x R.)	1377
Emanuel Sch. Contgt., O.T.C.	1905
Embarkation Staff (Southampton)	51
Embodied Militia Service	xxxviii
Empress of India's Lancers (21st)	437
Enfield Lock, Inspection Staff	2496
—————— Small Arms Factory	2492
Engineer and Railway Staff Corps	859
—— Committee, Royal	2500
—— Services, Royal, Staff for	1797
—— Stores, Royal, Inspn. Staff	2496
Engineering, Mechanical, Dept., Woolwich Arsenal	2492
—————— Military, School of	2483
Engineers, Royal	783
—————— Cadets (2 Lond. Div.)	826
—————— Coast Bn.	805

	COL.
Engineers, Royal, Inspr. of	16
—————— Militia	811
—————— Spec. Res.	808
—————— Terr. Force	819
—————— Wt. Offrs.	2271
Epsom College Contgt., O.T.C.	1906
Equerries	2, 2523, 2528
Equipment and Ordnance Stores, Director of	10
Equipment and Stores, Chief Inspector of	1820
Essex and Suffolk R.G.A.	766
—— Batts., R.F.A.	669
—— Brig. Co. A.S.C.	1659
—— Fortress R.E.	851
—— Infantry Brigade	25
—— Regiment	1301
—— Rifles Mila.	1303
—— R.G.A. (Heavy)	751
—— R.H.A.	660
—— Terr. Force Assocn.	2440
—— Yeomanry	455
Establishments :—	
Educational and Training	2480
Manufacturing	2492
Miscellaneous	2494
Establishments and Equipmt. Commee.	2495
Eton College Contgt., O.T.C.	1906
Exeter Cathedral School Cadet Co.	1906
—— School Contgt., O.T.C.	1906
Experimental Staff	2495
Extra Regtly. Empld. Officers, not shewn in any Regt. or Corps	368
Factories :—	
Aircraft, Royal	2492
Army Clothing, Royal	2492
Gun and Carriage, Royal	2492
Gunpowder and Small Arms, Royal	2492
Ordnance	2492
Falkland Islands	88
Felstead School Contgt., O.T.C.	1907
Fermanagh Mila.	1157
Ferozepore Brigade	70
Fettes College Contgt., O.T.C	1907
Field Ambulances	1705, 1714, 1718
—— Artillery Committee	2495
—————— Royal	514, 590
—————— Inspr. of	16
—————— Spec. Res.	574
—————— Terr. Force	667
—— Marshals	328

(xii)

Table of Contents.

	COL.
Fife and Forfar Yeomanry	456
—— Bn. (R. Highrs.)	1290
—— Terr. Force Assocn.	2441
Fifeshire Batt., R.F.A.	676
—————— R.G.A. (Heavy)	751
Fiji Islands	88
Finance Member of the Army Council	5, 6, 13
Financial Secretary	5, 6, 13
——Services, Director of	13
Finsbury Rifles (Lond. R .)	1585
Flint, R. Denbigh and, Mila.	1115
—— Terr. Force Assocn.	2441
Flintshire Bn. (R. W. Fus.)	1118
Flying Corps, Royal	379
—————— Wt. Offrs.	2275
—— School, Central	379
—————— Indian Central	385
Foot Guards	863
—————— Brigade	19, 32
—————— Wt. Offrs.	2275
Foreign Languages, Interpreters in	2605
—— Orders	*2863
—— Sovereigns who are Cols.-in-Chief or Hon.-Cols. of Regts.	4
Forest Sch. (Walthamstow) Contgt., O.T.C.	1907
Forfar, Fife and, Yeomanry	456
—— Terr. Force Assocn.	2442
Forfarshire Batt., R.F.A.	675
Formartin, Buchan and, Bn. (Gord. Highrs.)	1474
Forth R.G.A.	767
Fortifications and Works, Director of	11
Fortress R.E. (T.F.)	843
Framlingham Coll. Contgt., O.T.C.	1907
Frimley and Camberley Cadet Corps	916
Fusiliers, Dublin, Royal	1545
—— Inniskilling, Royal	1153
—— Irish, Royal	1497
—— Lancashire	1081
—— Munster, Royal	1537
—— Royal	957
—— Scots, Royal	1093
—— Welsh, Royal	1113
Fyzabad Brigade	72
Galloway, Dumfries and, Bn. (K.O. Sco. Bord.)	1139
Galway Mila.	1507
Gambia	84
—— Co., W.A.F.F.	2517
Garhwal Brigade	71
Garrison Artillery, Royal	542, 618
—————— Insp. of	16
—————— Spec. Res.	651
—————— Terr. Force	747

	COL.
Garter, Order of the	*282
General Hospitals	174
—————— Staff, Imperial, Chief of the	5,
Generals	32
Gentlemen-at-Arms, Hon. Corps of	*281
George Heriot's Sch. Contgt., O.T.C.	1908
—————— Watson's Boys' Coll. Contgt., O.T.C.	1908
Gibraltar	79
Giggleswick Sch. Contgt., O.T.C.	1908
Glamorgan Batts., R.F.A.	736 to 738
—————— Bn. (Welsh R.)	1275
—————— Fortress R.E.	851
—————— Mila., Royal	1271
—————— R.G.A.	768
—————— R.H.A.	661
—————— Terr. Force Assocn.	2442
—————— Yeomanry	457
Glasgow Academy Contgt., O.T.C.	1908
—————— City of, Batts., R.F.A.	710, 711
—————— Bns. (High.L.I.)	1446, 1448
—————— Terr. Force Assocn.	2443
—————— High Sch. Contgt., O.T.C.	1909
—————— Highland Bn. (High. L.I)	1452
—————— Cadet Co., 1st	1456
—————— Univ. Contgt., O.T.C.	1885
1st (Glasgow Highland) Cadet Co., High. L.I.	1456
Glenalmond College Contgt., O.T.C.	1909
Gloucester and Worcester Brig. Co., A.S.C.	1671
—————— Inf. Brig.	51
—————— South, Mila., Royal	1163
—————— Terr. Force Assocn.	2444
Gloucestershire Batts., R.F.A.	718
—————— Brigade, R.F.A.	717
—————— Regiment	1161
—————— 1st and 2nd Cadet Cos.	1168
—————— Yeomanry	458
Gold Coast Colony	84, 2524
—————— Regiment	2516
Gordon Brig. Co., A.S.C.	1661
—————— Highlanders	1469
—————— Infantry Brigade	45
Grammar Sch., R. (High Wycombe) Contgt., O.T.C.	1923
—————— (Lancaster) Contgt., O.T.C.	1923
—————— (Newcastle-on-Tyne) Contgt., O.T.C.	1923
—————— (Worcester) Contgt., O.T.C.	1924
—————— of King Ed. VI. (Guildford) Contgt. O.T.C.	1924

* Published in January, April, July and October issues only.

Table of Contents.

	COL.
Grenadier Guards	863
Gresham's School Contgt., O.T.C	1909
Grimsby Municipal Coll. Contgt. O.T.C.	1909
Guards, Brigade of	32
——— Depôt	887
——— Dragoon	392
——— Foot	863
——— Horse, Royal	390
——— Life	386, 388
Guernsey and Alderney District	64
——— Militia, Royal	1838
Guiana, British	86, 2523
Gun and Carriage Factories, Royal	2492
Gunnery, School of	2482
——— Staff Course, Offrs. passed	2587
——— Students	647
Gunpowder Factory, Royal	2492
Gymnasia	2487
——— Inspector of	20, 2487
Hackney (10th) County of London Bn., London Regt.	1584
Haddington Cadet Corps	903
——— Terr. Force Assocn.	2444
Haileybury College Contgt., O.T.C.	1910
Half-pay List	380
Hallamshire Bn. (York & Lanc. R.)	1425
Haltwhistle Cadets	937
Hampshire Batts., R.F.A.	742 to 745
——— Brig. Co., A.S.C.	1677
——— Fortress R.E.	852
——— Infantry Brigade	53
——— Militia	1237
——— Regiment	1235
——— 1st Cadet Bn,	916, 1240
——— R.G.A.	769
——— (Heavy)	758
——— R.H.A.	662
——— Terr. Force Assocn.	2467
——— Yeomanry	459
Handsworth Grammar Sch. Contgt., O.T.C.	1910
Harrow Cadet Co.	1382
——— School Contgt., O.T.C.	1910
Harwich Coast Defences	23
Haytor (Newton Abbot) Cadet Corps	1007
Hereford Cathedral School Contgt., O.T.C.	1910
——— Terr. Force Assocn.	2445
Herefordshire Regiment	1613
Herne Bay College Cadet Corps	922
Hertford Grammar School Contgt., O.T.C.	1911
——— Mila.	1053
——— Terr. Force Assocn.	2445
Hertfordshire Batts. R.F.A.	672
——— Regiment	1609

	COL.
Hertfordshire Cadet Cos.	1612
Herts Yeomanry	460
Hibernian Military School, Royal	2490
Highgate School Contgt., O.T.C.	1911
Highland Borderers Mila.	1516
——— Brigs., R.F.A.	673 to 678, 747
——— Clearing Hospital	1770
——— Cyclist Bn	1617
——— Deeside, Bn. (Gord. Highrs.)	1477
——— Division	44
——— Divl. R.E.	820
——— Sig. Co.	832
——— T. & S. Col.	1660
——— Field Ambulances	1722, 1723
——— Glasgow, Bn. (High. L.I.)	1452
——— Light Inf.	1441
——— Brig.	46
——— Co., A.S.C.	1669
——— (Light Inf.) Mila.	1484
——— (Mtn.) Brig. R.G.A.	747
——— Mtd. Brig.	44
——— Ammn. Col.	663
——— Fd. Amb.	1714
——— Sig. Troop	499
——— T. & S. Col.	1654
——— (Rifle) Mila.	1459
——— Ross, Bn. (Sea. Highrs.)	1461
——— R.G.A. (Heavy)	751
——— Suth'd & Caithness, Bn. (Sea. Highrs.)	1462
Highlanders, Argyll & Sutherland	1513
——— Bn. (R. Scots)	903
——— Cameron	1481
——— Gordon	1469
——— Royal	1281
——— Seaforth	1457
Hillhead High Sch. Contgt., O.T.C.	1911
Home Counties Brigs., R.F.A.	678 to 684
——— 1st Cadet Bn.	679
——— Clearing Hospital	1770
——— Division	22
——— Divl. R.E.	821
——— Sig. Co.	833
——— T. & S. Col.	1666
——— Field Ambulances	1724, 1725
——— R.G.A. (Heavy)	752
——— Forces, Inspr.-Gen. of the	16
——— Office, Offr. empld. under	2528
Honduras, British	86
Hong Kong	87
Hong Kong-Singapore Bn., R.G.A.	647
Honorary Chaplains to the King	3
——— Physicians to the King	3
——— Rank	xxxviii, 2653
——— Surgeons to the King	3
Honourable Artillery Company	655
Horse Artillery, Royal	514, 582

(xiv)

Table of Contents.

	COL.
Horse Artillery, Royal, Inspr. of ...	16
———————— Terr.Force...	659
———— Guards, Royal...	390
Hospital, King Edward VII.'s ...	Cover
————— Queen Alexandra Mil., Hon. Consulting Staff...	2488
————— Royal, Chelsea	2500
————— Royal, Kilmainham ...	2501
————— Victoria, Royal, Netley ...	51
Household Cavalry, Composite Regiment of	22, 32
Hungerford Yeomanry (Berks.) ...	447
Huntingdon Militia	1391
———————— Terr. Force Assocn. ...	2446
Huntingdonshire Cyclist Bn. ...	1617
Hurstpierpoint Coll. Contgt., O.T.C.	1911
Hussars, 3rd (King's Own)	407
———— 4th (Queen's Own) ...	409
———— 7th (Queen's Own) ...	413
———— 8th (King's Royal Irish) ...	415
———— 10th (P. of Wales's Own R.)	419
———— 11th (Prince Albert's Own)	421
———— 13th	425
———— 14th (King's)	426
———— 15th (The King's)	427
———— 18th (Queen Mary's Own)	432
———— 19th (Queen Alexandra's Own Royal)	434
———— 20th	436
Hutcheson's Grammar School Cadet Corps	1150
Hymers College Contgt., O.T.C. ...	1911
Hythe, School of Musketry	2483
Imperial Defence, Commee. of ...	2528
———— General Staff, Chief of the	5, 7
———— Military Nursing Service, Queen Alexandra's	1799
———— Service Cadet Corps, Eastbourne	681
———— Service Coll. Contgt., O.T.C.	1912
———— Service Order	*2858
India, Army Department	65
———— Commander-in-Chief in ...	66
———— Headquarters Staff	66
———— Northern Army	68
———— Offrs. empld. in	2524
———— Schools of Musketry ...	2483
———— Southern Army	73
———— Star of, Order of	*2833
———— Viceroy of	65
Indian Army	1941
——————— Departments	2237
——————— Remount Dept. ...	2005
——————— Supernumerary List...	2017
——————— Unattached List ...	2005

	COL.
Indian Army Units	2021
——————— Cavalry	2021
——————— Central Flying School ...	385
——————— Civil Veterinary Dept. ...	1787
——————— Empire, Order of	*2840
——————— Infantry	2073
——————— Medical Service	2209
——————— Mountain Batteries	2061
——————— Native, Land Forces... ...	2017
——————— Sappers and Miners	2065
——————— Subordinate Med. Dept. ...	2233
Infantry	893
———— Indian	2073
———— Brigade, 1st, 2nd, 3rd ...	18
——————————— 4th (Ft. Gds.) ...	19, 32
——————————— 5th, 6th	19
——————————— 7th, 8th, 9th ...	48
——————————— 10th, 11th, 12th	22
——————————— 13th, 14th, 15th	29
——————————— 16th, 17th	30
——————————— 18th	30, 36
——————————— Malta	80
———— Brigades, Territorial—see under Title of each	
———— Inspector of	16
———— Wt. Offrs.	2275
Inland Revenue, Board of, Offr. Empld. under	2528
Inniskilling Dragoons (8th) ...	411
——————— Fusiliers, Royal ...	1153
Inns of Court O.T.C.	1609
Inspection and Experimental Staff	2496
Inspection Dept., Aeronautical ...	385
——————— Staff, A.O. Dept. ...	1520
Inspector-Gen. of the Home Forces	16
——————— Oversea Forces	16
Inspector of Army Ord. Services ...	10
——————— Army Service Corps ...	10
——————— Cavalry	16
——————— Electric Lights ...	11
——————— Gymnasia	20, 2847
——————— Infantry	16
——————— Medical Services ...	9
——————— Mil. Equipmt. & Clothing under Ind.Govt...	1820
——————— Regimental Colours ...	1820
——————— R.E.	16
——————— R.G.A.	16
——————— R.H. and R.F.A. ...	16
Inspectors of Army Schools ...	1821
——————— Mech. Transport ...	1646
——————— Ord. Machinery ...	1820
——————— Remounts	438
——————— Subsidized Transport Vehicles	1646
——————— Works	1797

* Published in January, April, July and October issues only.

(xv)

Table of Contents.

	COL.
Interchanged Officers	2522
Interpreters List	2605
Inverness Terr. Force Assocn.	2446
Inverness-shire R.H.A.	663
Ipswich School Contgt., O.T.C.	1912
Ireland	28
Irish Bn. (L'pool R.)	977
—— Cavalry Depôt	437
—— Coast Def., North & South	30
—— Command	28
—— Dragoon Guards, Royal (4th)	398
—— Fusiliers, Royal	1497
—— Guards	887
—— Horse	441
—— Hussars, King's Royal (8th)	415
—— Lancers, Royal (5th)	410
—— London, Rifles (Lond. R.)	1597
—— Regiment, Royal	1065
—— Rifles, Royal	1489
Isle of Man Vol. Bn. (L'pool R.)	981
—— Wight Rifles (Hamps. R.)	1242
Jamaica	89, 2525
Jersey District	64
—— Militia, Royal	1834
Jhansi Brigade	74
Jhelum Brigade	69
Jubbulpore Brigade	74
Judge Advocate-General	14
Jullundur Brigade	70
Karachi Brigade	73
Kelly College Contgt., O.T.C.	1912
Kelvinside Acad. Contgt., O.T.C.	1912
Kensington and Hammersmith Navy League Boys' Brigade	1590
—————— Bn. (Lond. R.)	1588
Kent Batts., R.F.A.	682, 683
—— Brig. Co., A.S.C.	1662
—— Cyclist Bn.	1617
—— East, Militia	919
———— Regiment	917
———— Yeomanry, Royal	461
—— Fortress R.E.	853
———— Cadet Bn.	854
—— Infantry Brigade	26
—— R.G.A.	771
—— (Heavy)	752
—— Terr. Force Assocn.	2447
—— Weald of, Bn. (E. Kent. R.)	923
—— West, Militia	1351
———— Regt., Royal	1349
———— 1st Cadet Bn.	1356
———— Yeomanry	462
Kerry Militia	1539
Kilburn Grammar School Cadet Co.	1382

	COL.
Kildare Militia	1547
Kilkenny Militia	1069
Kilmainham, Royal Hospital	2501
Kincardine Terr. Force Assocn.	2448
King, Aides-de-Camp General to the	1
—— Aides-de-Camp to the	1
—— Alfred's Sch. (Wantage) Contgt. O.T.C.	1912
—— Chaplains, Honorary, to the	3
—— Edward VII.'s Hospital	Cover
—— Edward VII. Sch. (Sheffield) Contgt., O.T.C.	1912
—— Edward's Grammar Sch.(Bury St.Edmund's) Contgt.,O.T.C.	1913
—— Edward's Horse (The King's Oversea Dominions Regt.)	443
—— Edward's Sch. (Bath) Contgt., O.T.C.	1913
—— Edward's Sch. (Birmingham) Contgt., O.T.C.	1918
—— Equerries to the	2
—— Personal Aides-de-Camp to the	1
—— Physicians, Honorary, to the	3
—— Surgeons, Honorary, to the	3
—— William's College (I. of Man) Contgt., O.T.C.	1914
King's African Rifles	2518
—— Body Guards	*2816 to *2818
—— Coll. (Taunton) Contgt. O.T.C.	1914
—— Coll. Sch. (Wimbledon) Contgt., O.T.C.	1914
—— County Mila.	1531
—— Dragoon Guards (1st)	392
—— Hussars (14th)	426
—— (15th)	427
—— Liverpool Regiment	969
—— Own Hussars (3rd)	407
—————— Malta Regt. of Mila	1842
—————— (R. Lanc. R.)	925
—————— Royal Regt. (Norf. Yeo.)	477
—————— R.Tower Ham. Mila.	1560
—————— Scottish Borderers	1133
—————— Stafford Mila.	1247, 1249, 1415, 1417
—————— (Yorks. L.I.)	1357
—— Royal Irish Hussars (8th)	415
—— Royal Rifle Corps	1385
—— Sch. (Bruton) Contgt., O.T.C.	1914
———— (Canterbury) Contgt., O.T.C.	1914
———— (Grantham) Contgt., O.T.C.	1915
—— Peterborough, Cadet Corps	1340

*Published in January, April, July and October issues only.

(xvi)

Table of Contents.

	COL.
King's Sch. (Rochester) Contgt., O.T.C.	1915
———— (Warwick) Contgt., O.T.C.	1915
———— (Worcester) Contgt., O.T.C.	1915
———— (Shropshire Light Inf.)	1365
Kinross Terr. Force Assocn.	2448
Kirkby Lonsdale Cadet Co.	1223
Kirkcaldy High Sch. Contgt., O.T.C.	1915
Kirkcudbright Terr. Force Assocn...	2449
Kirkcudbrightshire Batt., R.F.A.	709
Kneller Hall, School of Music	2489
Kohat Brigade...	72
Laboratory, R., Woolwich Arsenal	2492
Lahore Division	70
Lanark Bn. (High. L.I.)	1450
———— Mila., Royal ... 1143, 1145, 1444, 1445	
———— Terr. Force Assocn.	2449
Lanarkshire Yeomanry	...463, 464
Lancashire, and Cheshire R.G.A.	772
———— Batts. R.F.A.	684 to 689
———— Brig., R.G.A. (Heavy)	753
———— East, Brigs., R.F.A.	684 to 689
———— Division	57
———— Divl. R.E.	823
———— T. & S. Col.	1663
———— Fd. Ambs.	1725, 1726
———— Inf. Brig.	57
———— Regiment	1181
———— Fortress R.E.	855
———— Fusiliers	1081
———— 8 Bn., 1st Cadet Co.	1088
———— Brig.	57
———— Co., A.S.C.	1663
———— Hussars Yeomanry	465
———— Militia, Royal 927, 971, 973, 1083, 1084. 1183, 1263, 1327, 1403, 1405	
———— North, Brig. Co., A.S.C.	1665
———— Inf. Brig.	56
———— Regiment, Loyal	1325
———— R.G.A. (Heavy)	753
———— South, Brig. Co., A.S.C.	1665
———— Inf. Brig.	56
———— Regiment	1261
———— Terr. Force Assocns.	2450
———— West, Brigs., R.F.A.	689 to 695
———— Division	56
———— Divl. R.E.	824
———— T. & S. Col.	1664
———— Fd. Ambs.	1727, 1728
Lancaster Regiment, Royal	925
———— York and, Regiment	1421
Lancaster's, Duke of, Own Yeomanry	466
Lancers, 5th (Royal Irish)	410

	COL.
Lancers, 9th (Queen's Royal)	417
———— 12th (P. of Wales's R.)	423
———— 16th (The Queen's)	429
———— 17th (D. of Cambridge's Own)	431
———— 21st (Empress of India's)	437
Lancing College Contgt., O.T.C.	1916
Land Agent and Valuer	12
Lands, Comptroller of	12
Language Students, Chinese, Japanese and Russian	2643
Languages, Foreign, Interpreters in	2605
Leeds Grammar Sch. Contgt., O.T.C.	1916
———— Postal Tel. Messengers' Cadet Co.	842
———— Rifles (West Yorkshire Regt.)	1035
———— University Contgt., O.T.C.	1886
Leeward Islands	89
Leicester, Lincoln and, Brig. Co., A.S.C.	1670
———— Inf. Brig.	41
———— Terr. Force Assocn.	2451
Leicestershire Mila.	1059
———— Regiment	1057
———— R.H.A.	663
———— Yeomanry	467
Leinster Regiment	1529
Leys School Contgt., O.T.C.	1916
Lieutenant-Generals	328
Life Guards	386, 388
Limerick County Mila., Royal	1543
Lincoln and Leicester Brig. Co., A.S.C.	1670
———— Inf. Brig.	41
———— North, Mila. Royal	995
———— Terr. Force Assocn.	2455
Lincolnshire Batts., R.F.A.	712, 712
———— Regiment	993
———— Yeomanry	468
Linlithgow Terr. Force Assocn.	2452
Liverpool Brig. Co., A.S.C.	1665
———— College Contgt., O.T.C.	1916
———— Infantry Brigade	56
———— Institute Contgt., O.T.C.	1917
———— Recruiting Area	55
———— Regiment	969
Local Temp. and Hon. Rank	2653
London Bns., London Regt.	1569 to 1608
———— Brig., R.G.A. (Heavy)	754
———— Brigs., R.F.A.	695 to 706
———— City of, Batts., R.F.A.	696
———— Bns., Lond. R.	1569 to 1581
———— Brig., R.F.A.	695
———— Fd. Ambs.	1728, 1729
———— General Hospitals	1744
———— Horse Artillery	655
———— Regiment	957

(xvii)

Table of Contents.

	COL.
London, City of, Sanitary Co.	1766
——————— Terr. Force Assocn.	2455
——————— Yeomanry	469
——— 1st & 2nd Clearing Hospitals	1771
——— County of, Batts., R.F.A.	697 to 706
——————— Bns., Lond. R.	1582 to 1608
——————— Yeomanry	470 to 472
——— District	32
——— Signal Cos., R.E.	839
——— Divisions, 1st and 2nd	33, 34
——— Divl. R.E.	824, 825
——— Sig. Cos.	835, 836
——— T. & S. Cols.	1665, 1666
——— Electrical R.E.	855
——— Field Ambulances	1728 to 1731
——— General Hospitals	1744 to 1748
——— Infantry Brigades	33, 34, 35
——— Irish Rifles (Lond. R.)	1597
——— Militia, Royal	964
——— Mtd. Brig.	33
——————— Ammn. Col.	655
——————— Fd. Amb.	1715
——————— Sig. Troop	499
——————— T. & S. Col.	1654
——— Recruiting Area	33
——— Regiment	1569
——— Rif. Brig. (Lond. R.)	1577
——— R.G.A. (Heavy)	754
——— Sanitary Cos.	1766, 1768
——— Scottish (Lond. R.)	1590
——— Terr. Force Assocn.	2453
——— Univ. of, Contgt., O.T.C.	1886
Loretto School Contgt., O.T.C.	1917
Lothian Infantry Brigade	43
——————— Sig. Sect.	839
——— Regiment (Royal Scots)	893
Lothians and Border Horse	473
Louth School Contgt., O.T.C.	1917
Lovat's Scouts Yeomanry	474, 475
Lowland Brigs., R.F.A.	707 to 712
——— Clearing Hospital	1771
——— Division	46
——— Divl. R.E.	826
——— Sig. Co.	836
——— T. & S. Col.	1668
——— Field Ambulances	1731, 1732
——— Mtd. Brig.	45
——————— Ammn. Col.	659
——————— Fd. Amb.	1715
——————— Sig. Troop	499
——————— T. & S. Col.	1655
——— R.G.A. (Heavy)	755
Lucknow Brigades	71, 72
——— Division	571
Macclesfield Grammar School Cadet Corps	1112

	COL.
Macclesfield Industrial School Cadet Corps	1112
Machinery Department	2498
——————— Ordnance, Inspectors of	1820
Madras, Governor of	65
Maidstone Grammar School Contgt., O.T.C.	1917
Major-Generals	332
Malay States Guides	2525
——— Officers empld. in	2525
Malta	80
——— Artillery, Royal	779
——— Div., R.E. Mila.	811
——— Infantry Brigade	80
——— Militia	1842
Malvern College Contgt., O.T.C.	1917
Manchester Artillery	685
——————— Brig. Co., A.S.C.	1664
——————— Grammar School Contgt., O.T.C.	1918
——————— Infantry Brigade	57
——————— Recruiting Area	55
——————— Regiment	1401
——————— Univ. Contgt., O.T.C.	1888
Mandalay Brigade	77
Manor Park Cadet Co.	1306
Manufacturing Establishments	2492
Marines, Royal	2241
——— Warrant Officers	2299
Marlborough College Contgt., O.T.C.	1918
Master-General of the Ordnance	5, 11
Master Gunners, Royal Artillery	2265
Mauritius	89
Meath Mila., Royal	1535
Mechanical Branch, Research Dept.	2496
——— Engineering Dept., Woolwich Arsenal	2492
——— Transport, Inspectors of	1646
Medallists, Alexander Memorial	*2878
——— Parkes Memorial	*2879
——— R.A. Inst.	*2877
——— R. United Service Inst.	*2878
——— Worshipful Company of Musicians	*2879
Medical Advisory Board, Army	2494
——— College, Army, R.	2488
——— Corps, Army, R.	1678
——————— Spec. Res.	1705
——————— Terr. Force	1714
——————— Training Estabt.	20, 2488
——————— Wt. Offrs.	2289
——— Reserve, Army	2385
——— Service, Army	1678
——————— Dir.-Gen.	9
——————— Ret. Offrs. empld.	1702

* Published in January, April, July and October issues only.

Table of Contents.

	COL.
Medical Service, Indian	2209
———— Services, Inspector of	9
Mediterranean Command	78
Meerut (Cavalry) Brigade	71
———— Division	71
Merchant Taylors' Sch. Contgt., O.T.C.	1918
Merchiston Castle Sch. Contgt., O.T.C.	1919
Merioneth and Montgomery Bn. (R. W. Fus.)	1121
———— Terr. Force Assocn.	2455
Merit, Order of	*2832
Mhow Division	74
Middlesex Brig. Co., A.S.C.	1662
———— D. of Cambridge's Hrs.	470
———— East, Militia, Royal	1378
———— Infantry Brigade	27
———— Militia, 2nd, Royal	1392
———— Regiment	1373
———— South, Militia, Royal	963
———— Terr. Force Assocn.	2456
Midlothian Batt., R.F.A.	708
———— Terr. Force Assocn.	2456
Military Academy, Royal, Woolwich	2486
———— Aeronautics, Dir.-Gen. of	15
———— and other Appointments not remunerated out of Army funds	145
———— Attachés	16a
———— College, Royal, Sandhurst	2485
———— Detention Barracks and Prisons	2498
———— Engineering, School of	2483
———— Hospital, Queen Alexandra, Hon. Consulting Staff	2488
———— Knights of Windsor	2504
———— Operations, Director of	7
———— Police, Corps of	1833
———— Provost Staff Corps	2295
———— School, D. of York's Royal	2489
———— ———— Hibernian, Royal	2490
———— ———— of Music, Royal	2489
———— Sec. to the Sec. of State for War	6
———— Training, Director of	8
———— Wing, Royal Flying Corps	379, 383
Militia Artillery, Bermuda	779
———— Channel Islands	1834
———— Malta, Regt. of	1842
———— R.E., Malta Div.	811
———— Service, Embodied	xxxviii
Mill Hill School Contgt., O.T.C.	1919
Miners, Sappers and, Indian	2065
Miscellaneous Establishments	2494

	COL.
Mobilization, Director of	9
Monkton Combe Sch. Contgt., O.T.C.	1919
Monmouth Terr. Force Assocn.	2457
Monmouthshire Batts., R.F.A.	741
———— Regiment	1561
———— R.E., Royal	809
Montgomery, Merioneth and, Bn. (R. W. Fus.)	1121
———— Terr. Force Assocn.	2457
Montgomeryshire Yeomanry	476
Morayshire Bn. (Sea. Highrs.)	1463
Morpeth Grammar School Cadet Co.	940
Morrison's Academy Contgt., O.T.C.	1919
Motor Cyclist Section, R.E. Spec. Res.	808
———— Cyclists, Advisory Commee. on	2502
Mountain Batteries, Indian	2061
———— Brig., R.G.A. (T.F.)	747
———— Div., R.G.A.	618
Mounted Brigades, Territorial, see under Title of each.	
Movements, Transport and, Dir. of	10
Munich, Offr. empld. at	2525
Munster Fusiliers, Royal	1537
Music, Military School of, Royal	2489
Musicians, Worshipful Company of, Medallists	*2879
Musketry, School of, Hythe	2483
———— Schools of, India	2483
Nairn Terr. Force Assocn.	2458
Nasirabad Brigade	74
Native Indian Land Forces	2017
Naval Air Service, Royal	379, 380
———— Ordnance Dept.	2257
———— Wing, Royal Flying Corps	379, 380
Netheravon, Cavalry School	2482
Netley, Royal Victoria Hospital	51
New Brighton, 1st, Cadet Corps	1105
New College (Herne Bay) Cadet Corps	922
New South Wales	85
New Zealand, Dominion of	90, 2525
Newcastle Divl. Tel. Co., R.E.	831
———— Field Cos., R.E.	831
Newcastle-under-Lyme High School Contgt., O.T.C.	1920
Newfoundland	90
Newport Cadet Corps, R.F.A.	742
Nigeria	84, 2526
———— Regiment	2511
Non-Effective List	*2710
Norfolk and Suffolk Brig. Co., A.S.C.	1659
———— Artillery, Cadet	668
———— Inf. Brig.	25
———— Batts., R.F.A.	667, 668

* Published in January, April, July and October issues only.

Table of Contents.

	COL.
Norfolk Militia	988
——— Regiment	985
——— Terr. Force Assocn.	2458
——— Yeomanry	477
North Berwick Cadet Corps	903
——— China	87
——— Devon Yeomanry, Royal	453
——— Down Mila., Royal	1493
——— Eastern Coast Defences	37
——— County Sch. Contgt., O.T.C.	1920
——— Irish Coast Defences	30
——— Horse	441
——— Lancashire Brig. Co., A..C.	1665
——— Inf. Brig.	56
——— Regt., Loyal	1325
——— Lincoln Mila., Royal	995
——— Midland Brigs., R.F.A.	712 to 717
——— Clearing Hospital	1772
——— Division	41
——— Divl. R.E.	827
——— Sig. Co.	837
——— T. & S. Col.	1669
——— Fd. Ambs.	1733, 1734
——— Mtd. Brig.	40
——— Ammn.Col.	663
——— Fd. Amb.	1716
——— Sig. Troop	499
——— T. & S. Col.	1655
——— R.G.A. (Heavy)	755
——— Riding Batt., R.F.A.	726
——— Fortress R.E.	858
——— R.G.A. (Heavy)	756
——— Scottish R.G.A.	775
——— Somerset Yeomanry	487
——— Staffordshire Regiment	1413
——— Tipperary Militia	1067
——— Wales Brig. Co., A.S.C.	1676
——— Infantry Brigade	59
——— Western Coast Defences	55
Northampton and Rutland Militia	1335
——— School Cadet Corps	1340
——— Terr. Force Assocn.	2459
Northamptonshire Batt., R.F.A.	673
——— Regiment	1333
——— Yeomanry	478
Northern Army, India	68
——— Cavalry Depôt	437
——— Command	36
——— Signal Cos., R.E.	841
——— Cyclist Bn.	1613
——— General Hospitals	1749 to 1753
Northumberland Batts., R.F.A.	723, 724
——— Brig. Co., A.S.C	1672
——— Fusiliers	933

	COL.
Northumberland Infantry Brigade	38
——— Militia	935
——— Terr. Force Assocn.	2459
——— Yeomanry	479
Northumbrian Brigs., R.F.A.	723 to 729
——— Clearing Hospital	1772
——— Division	38
——— Divl. R.E.	829
——— Sig. Co.	838
——— T. & S. Col.	1672
——— Field Ambulances	1736, 1737
——— R.G.A. (Heavy)	756
Nottingham High School Contgt., O.T.C.	1920
——— Terr. Force Assocn.	2460
——— Univ.Coll.Contgt.,O.T.C.	1889
Nottinghamshire R.H.A.	664
——— Yeomanry	480, 481
Notts. & Derby Brig. Co., A.S.C.	1670
——— Inf. Brig.	41
——— Mtd. Brig.	40
——— Ammn.Col.	664
——— Fd. Amb.	1716
——— Sig. Troop	500
——— T. & S. Col.	1656
——— Regiment	1313
Nowshera Brigade	68
Nursing Board	2498
——— Service, Impl. Mil., Queen Alexandra's	1799
——— Terr. Force	1808
——— Advisory Council	2503
Nyasaland Protectorate	81, 2526
Oakham School Contgt., O.T.C.	1920
Officers Training Corps:—	
Contingents of Senior Div.	1878
——— Junior Div.	1894
Inns of Court	1609
Ongar Grammar School Cadets	1306
Oratory School, Edgbaston, Contgt. O.T.C.	1920
Orders :—	
Bath	*2823
Foreign	*2863
Distinguished Service	*2848
Garter	*2821
Imperial Service	*2858
Indian Empire	*2840
Merit	*2832
St. Michael & St. George	*2835
St. Patrick	*2822
Star of India	*2833
Thistle	*2822
Victorian, Royal	*2843

* Published in January, April, July and October issues only.

(xx)

Table of Contents.

	COL.
Ordnance Board	2499
———— College	2483
———— Officers passed	2577, 2583
———— Corps, Army	1811, 1822, 2291
———— Department, Army	1811
———— Naval	2257
———— Factories	2492
———— Machinery, Insprs. of	1820
———— Master-General of the	5, 11
———— Services, Army, Inspr. of	10
———— Stores, Equipmt. and, Dir. of	10
———— Survey, Offrs. empld.	2528
Organization, Recruiting and, Dir. of	10
Orkney R.G.A.	774
———— Terr. Force Assocn.	2460
Osborne Convalescent Home	p. 3 of Cover
Oundle School Contgt., O.T.C.	1921
Oversea Forces, Inspr.-Gen. of the	16
Overseas Defence Commee.	2528
Oxford Mila.	1295
———— Terr. Force Assocn.	2461
———— University Contgt., O.T.C.	1889
Oxfordshire and Bucks. Lt. Inf.	1293
———— Yeomanry	482
Palmer's School Cadet Corps	1309
Papua	85
Parkes Memorial Medallists	*2879
Parliamentary Under Sec. of State for War	5, 6, 12
Pay Corps, Army	2295
———— Department, Army	1823
Paymaster, Chief, War Office	13
Paymaster-General's Department	2499
Peebles Terr. Force Assocn.	2461
Peking Legation Guard	646
Pembroke R.G.A.	775
———— Terr. Force Assocn.	2462
———— Yeomanry	483
Perse School Contgt., O.T.C.	1921
Personal Aides-de-Camp to the King	1
———— Services, Director of	9
Perth Mila., Royal	1283
———— Terr. Force Assocn.	62
Perthshire Bn. (R. Highrs.)	1288
Peru, Officer empld. in	2526
Peshawar Division	68
———— Infantry Brigade	68
Peter Symonds School Cadet Corps	1238
Physicians, Honorary, to the King	3
Pinckard's Remount Depôt	438
Plymouth Cadet Co.	849

	COL.
Plymouth College Contgt., O.T.C.	1921
———— Lads' Brigade Cadet Corps	1007
Police, Military, Corps of	1833
Poona Division	74
———— Infantry Brigade	75
Poplar and Stepney Rif. (Lond. R.)	1596
Portsmouth Grammar Sch. Contgt., O.T.C.	1921
Post Office Rifles (Lond. R.)	1580
Postal Section, R. E. Spec. Res.	808
———— Services, Army, Director of	808
Potchefstroom District	83
Poulton Cadet Co.	1105
Precedence Lists :—	
Artillery, Royal, Cos. and Batts.	626
———— (Spec. Res.)	651
———— (Terr. Force)	659, 759
Engineers, Royal (Spec. Res.)	808
———— (Terr. Force)	819
Infantry (Terr. Force)	892
Yeomanry (Terr. Force)	445
Presidency Brigade	72
Prestonpans Cadet Corps	903
Pretoria District	82
Prince Albert's Own Hussars (11th)	421
———— (Leic. Yeo.)	467
———— (Som. L.I.)	1021
———— Consort's Own (Rif. Brig.)	1553
———— of Wales's Bn. (Devon. R.)	1006
———— Dragoon Gds. (3rd)	396
———— Leins. R.	1529
———— (N. Staff. R.)	1413
———— Own, Civil Service Rif. (Lond. R.)	1592
———— R. Hrs. (10th)	419
———— R. Regt. (R. Wilts Yeo.)	495
———— (W. York R.)	1029
———— Royal Lrs. (12th)	423
———— Vols. (S. Lan. R.)	1261
Princess Beatrice's, I. of Wight Rif. (Hamps. R.)	1242
———— Charlotte of Wales's Dragoon Gds. (5th)	399
———— Charlotte of Wales's (R. Berks. R.)	1341
———— Louise's (Arg. & Suth'd Highrs.)	1513
———— of Wales's Own, Alexandra (York R.)	1073
———— Royal's Dragoon Gds. (7th)	401
———— Victoria's (R. Ir. Fus.)	1497
Principals, War Office	13, 14
———— Assistant, War Office	12, 13, 14

* Published in January, April, July and October issues only.

(xxi)

Table of Contents.

	COL.
Prisons, Military	2498
Promotions, Appointments, &c.	2708
Protectorates, Dominions, Colonies and	81
Proof and Experimental Staff	2496
Purchase Commission, Army	2494
Purfleet and Rainham Rifle Ranges	33
Qualified for Staff employment	2567
Quartering, Supplies and, Dir. of	10
Quarter-Master-General to the Forces	5, 10
Queen Alexandra Mil. Hosp., Hon. Consulting Staff	2488
——— Mil. Hosp., Officers' Wards	Cover
——— Alexandra's Impl. Mil. Nursing Service	1799
——— Alexandra's Own R. Hrs (19th)	434
Queen Mary's Grammar Sch. (Walsall) Contgt., O.T.C.	1921
——— Own Hussars (18th)	432
——— Regiment (Surrey Yeo.)	491
——— Victoria School	2491
——— Victoria's R. (Lond. R.)	1582
Queen's Bays (2 D.G.)	394
——— County Mila.	1533
——— Edinburgh Rifles (R. Scots)	897, 898
——— Lancers (16th)	429
——— (London Regt.)	1602, 1605
——— Own Cameron Highrs.	1481
——— (Dorset Yeomanry)	454
——— Hussars (4th)	409
——— (7th)	413
——— Oxford Hrs.	482
——— R. Glasgow Yeo.	464
——— Royal Regt. (Staff. Yeo.)	489
——— R. Tower Ham. Mila.	1559
——— (R. W. Kent R.)	1349
——— (W. Kent Yeo.)	462
——— Worcester Hrs.	496
——— (Yorks. Dns.)	497
——— Royal Lancers (9th)	417
——— (Royal West Surrey Regt.)	909
——— Westminster Cadet Corps	1595
——— Rif. Lond. R.	1594
Queensland	85
Quetta Division	73
——— Infantry Brigades	73
——— Staff College	2481
Radley College Contgt., O.T.C.	1922
Radnor Terr. Force Assocn.	2463
Railway, Engineer and, Staff Corps	859
Rangers (Lond. R.)	1587
Rangoon Brigade	77

	COL.
Rawal Pindi Division	69
——— Infantry Brigade	69
Reading School Contgt., O.T.C.	1922
——— Univ. Coll. Contgt., O.T.C.	1891
Records, Officers in charge of :—	
A. Ord. Dept.	1811
A. Pay Dept.	1823
A. S. C.	1633
A. V. C.	1778
Cavalry	392
Corps of Army Schoolmasters	1831
Corps of Mil. Police	1833
Infantry	891
Military Provost Staff Corps	2498
Rifle	1385, 1553
R. A. M. C.	1678
R. E.	783
R. Flying Corps (Mil. Wing)	383
R. G. A.	542
R. H. and R.F.A.	514
Recruiting and Organization, Dir. of	9
——— Area, Dublin	31
——— Edinburgh	44
——— Liverpool	55
——— London	33
——— Manchester	55
——— Sheffield	37
——— Depôt, Central	33
——— Duties, Ret. Offrs. empld. on	31, 37, 38, 43, 50, 56
Red Cross, Royal	*2859
——— Society, British	2494
Regiments, Alphabetical List of	xxxvii
Reigate Grammar School Contgt., O.T.C.	1922
Remount Service	438
Remounts, Director of	10, 438
Renfrew Militia, Royal	1517
——— Terr. Force Assocn.	2463
Renfrewshire Batts., R.F.A.	677
——— Bns., Arg. & Suth'd Highrs.	1518, 1519
——— Fortress R.E.	856
——— Small Arms Section Ammn. Col.	678
Repton School Contgt., O.T.C.	1922
Research Department	2496
Reserve, Army Medical	2385
——— of Officers	2301
——— R. Flying Corps	384
——— Territorial Force	2385

* Published in January, April, July and October issues only.

Table of Contents.

	COL.
Retired Officers	*2710
———— empld. on Recruiting Duties	31, 37, 38, 43, 50, 56
Rewards for Distinguished and Meritorious Service	2679
Rhodesia, Offrs., empld. in	2526
Richmond County Sch. Cadet Corps	1196
Riding Establishment, Woolwich	586
Rifle Bn., Liverpool Regiment	975
—— Brigade	1553
—— Corps, King's Royal	1385
—— Depôt	1385, 1553
Risalpur Cavalry Brigade	68
Robin Hood Bn., Notts. & Derby. R.	1320
Roscommon Militia	1509
Ross & Cromarty (Mtn.) Batt., R.G.A.	749
———————— Terr. Force Assocn.	2464
—— Highland Bn., Sea. Highrs.	1461
Rossall School Contgt., O.T.C.	1923
Ross-shire Buffs (Seaforth Highrs.)	1457
Rough Riders City of Lond. Yeo.)	469
Roxburgh Terr. Force Assocn.	2464
Roysse's School Contgt. O.T.C.	1924
Rugby School Contgt., O.T.C.	1924
Rutland, Northampton and, Mila.	1335
—— Terr. Force Assocn.	2465
St. Albans Sch. Contgt., O.T.C.	1924
St. Andrews Coll. Contgt., O.T.C.	1925
St. Andrews Univ. Contgt., O.T.C.	1893
St. Bees School Contgt., O.T.C.	1925
St. Columbus' Coll. Contgt., O.T.C.	1925
St. Dunstan's Coll. (Catford) Contgt., O.T.C.	1925
St. Edmund's Sch. (Canterbury) Contgt., O.T.C.	1925
St. Edward's Sch. (Oxford) Contgt., O.T.C.	1926
St. Helena	90
St. Helens Divl. Tel. Co., R.E.	824
———— Fd. Cos., R.E.	824, 825
St. John's Sch. (Leatherhead) Contgt., O.T.C.	1926
St. Lawrence Coll. (Ramsgate) Contgt., O.T.C.	1926
St. Leonard's Collegiate School Cadet Co.	681
St. Michael and St. George, Order of	*2835
St. Pancras Bn. (Lond. R.)	1598
St. Patrick, Order of	*2822
St. Paul's Sch. Contgt., O.T.C.	1926
St. Peter's Cadet Co.	1590
———— Sch. (York) Contgt., O.T.C.	1926
St. Thomas's (Wandsworth) Cadet Corps	1604

	COL.
Salop Terr. Force Assocn.	2466
Sandhurst, Royal Military College	2485
Sanitary Service, Terr. Force	1766
Sanitation, Army, School of	20, 2488
Sappers and Miners, Indian	2065
School, Army Signal, Aldershot	20, 2487
———— Bulford	53, 2487
———— Veterinary, Aldershot	20, 2488
———— Camel Corps, Egypt	78
———— Cavalry, Netheravon	2482
———— Saugor	2482
———— Duke of York's Royal Military	2489
———— Flying, Central	379
———— Indian Central	385
———— Queen Victoria	2491
———— Royal Hibernian Military	2490
School of Army Sanitation	20, 2488
———— Cookery, Army	2487
———— Economics, London, Offrs. qualified in course at	2571
———— Gunnery	2482
———— Instn. for Offrs. of T.F.	35
———— Military Engineering	2483
———— Music, Royal Military	2489
———— Musketry, Hythe	2483
Schoolmasters	2259 to 2264, 2299
Schools, Army	1831
———— of Electric Lighting	2483
———— Instn., R.A.M.C., T. F.	1774
———— Musketry, India	98
———— recommending candidates for nomination to Cadetships at the R. Mil. Coll.	2478
Scotland, King's Body Guard for	*2818
Scots Fusiliers, Royal	1093
—— Greys, Royal (2nd Dragoons)	405
—— Guards	879
—— Royal (Lothian Regiment)	893
Scottish Bn., Liverpool Regiment	979
———— Borderers, King's Own	1133
———— Borderers Militia	1135
———— Cavalry Depôt	437
———— Coast Defences	43
———— Command	42
———— Signal Cos., R.E	843
———— General Hospitals	1753 to 1757
———— Horse	484
———— North, R.G.A.	775
———— Rifle Brigade	46
———— Co., A.S.C.	1669
———— Rifles (The Cameronians)	1141
———— South, Infantry Brigade	46

*Published in January, April, July and October issues only.

Table of Contents.

	COL.
Seaforth and Cameron Inf. Brig.	44
——— Highlanders	1457
Secretary of State for War	5, 6
——————— the Army Council	5
——————— War Office	6, 14
——————— Assistant	6, 14
Secunderabad Brigades	76
——————— Division	75
Sedbergh School Contgt., O.T.C.	1927
Selection Board	6, 2501
Selkirk Terr. Force Assocn.	2465
Settle Cadet Bn.	1211
Seychelles	90
Sharpshooters (3 Co. of Lond. Yeo.)	472
Sheffield, Univ. of, Contgt., O.T.C.	1893
Sherborne School Contgt., O.T.C.	1927
Sherwood Foresters (Notts. & Derby. R.)	1313
——————— Mila., Royal	1317
——————— Rangers (Notts. Yeo.)	480
Shetland Cos., Gord. Highrs.	1479
Shoeburyness, School of Gunnery	2482
Shrewsbury School Contgt., O.T.C.	1927
Shropshire Light Infantry	1365
——————— Militia	1367
——————— R.H.A.	665
——————— Terr. Force Assocn.	2466
——————— Yeomanry	486
Sialkot Brigade	69
Sidcup Hall School Contgt., O.T.C.	1928
Sierra Leone	84, 2527
——————— Bn., W.A.F.F.	2517
——————— Co., R.G.A.	647
Signal Cos. (Army Troops) R.E. (T.F.)	839
——————— School, Army, Aldershot	20, 2487
——————— Bulford	53, 487
——————— Service, Army	785, 805
——————— T.F.	839
Signals, Army, Director of (Home Defence)	831
Singapore, Hong-Kong—, Bn., R.G.A.	647
Sirhind Brigade	70
Sir Roger Manwood's School Contgt., O.T.C.	1928
Skinners' School Contgt., O.T.C.	1928
Small Arms Committee	2502
——————— Factory	2492
——————— Inspection Staff	2496
Soldiers' Balances Unclaimed	2729
Solihull Grammar Sch. Contgt., O.T.C.	1928

	COL.
Somaliland Ind. Contgt., K. Afr. Rif.	2520
——————— Protectorate	81, 2527
Somerset Light Infantry	1021
——————— Militia	1023
——————— North, Yeomanry	487
——————— R.H.A.	665
——————— Terr. Force Assocn.	2466
——————— West, Yeomanry	488
South Africa	81, 2527
——————— Remount Service	438
——————— Sch. of Musketry	98
——————— Australia	85
——————— China	88
——————— Cork Militia	1541
——————— Down Militia, Royal	1495
——————— Eastern Coast Defences	24
——————— Mtd. Brig.	26
——————— Ammn.Col.	656
——————— Fd. Amb.	1714
——————— Sig. Troop	500
——————— T.&S.Col.	1656
——————— Gloucester Militia, Royal	1163
——————— Irish Coast Defences	30
——————— Horse	442
——————— Lancashire Brig. Co., A.S.C.	1665
——————— Inf. Brig.	56
——————— Regiment	1261
——————— London Cadets	1602
——————— Middlesex Mila., Royal	963
——————— Midland Brigs., R.F.A.	717 to 722
——————— Clearing Hospital	1772
——————— Division	51
——————— Divl. R.E.	828
——————— Sig. Co.	837
——————— T. & S. Col.	1670
——————— Fd. Ambs.	1734, 1735
——————— Inf. Brig.	52
——————— Mtd. Brig. Ammn. Cols.	660, 666
——————— Fd.Ambs.	1717, 1718
——————— T. & S.Cols.	1655
——————— Mtd.Brigs.,1st & 2nd	51
——————— Sig. Troops	500
——————— R.G.A. (Heavy)	756
——————— Notts. Hrs. (Notts. Yeo.)	481
——————— Scottish Infantry Brigade	46
——————— Staffordshire Regiment	1245
——————— Wales Borderers	1125
——————— Mila., Royal	1127
——————— Inf. Brig.	59
——————— Sig. Sect.	842

Table of Contents.

	COL.
South Wales Mtd. Brig.	58
——————— Ammn. Col.	662
——————— Fd. Amb.	1719
——————— Sig. Troop	501
——————— T. & S. Col.	1656
—— Western Brig. Co., A.S.C.	1677
——————— Coast Defences	49
——————— Inf. Brig.	53
——————— Mtd. Brig. Ammn. Cols.	662, 666
——————— Fd. Ambs.	1720
——————— T.&S. Cols.	1657
——————— Mtd. Brigs., 1st & 2nd	52
Sig. Troops	501
Southampton Terr. Force Assocn.	2467
Southend High Sch. Cadet Corps	1309
Southern Army, India	73
——————— Brigade (India)	76
——————— Cavalry Depôt	437
——————— Coast Defences	49
——————— Command	47
——————— Signal Cos. R.E.	844
——————— General Hospitals	1758 to 1763
Southport Cadet Corps	977
Special Lists	2506
——————— Reserve, A.S.C.	1645
——————— A.V.C.	1781
——————— Cavalry	391, &c.
——————— E. Tel. Res.	1833
——————— Ft. Gds.	870, 878, 885, 890
——————— Infantry	895, &c.
——————— Irish Horse	441
——————— King Edward's Horse	441
——————— R.A.M.C.	1705
——————— R.E.	808
——————— R.F.A.	574
——————— R. Flying Corps	385
——————— R.G.A.	651
——————— Unattd. List	1846
——————— Warrant Officers	2295
Staff College, Camberley	2480
——————— Graduates	2533
——————— Quetta	2481
—— Duties, Director of	8
—— Emplt., Offrs. qualified for	2567
—— for Royal Engineer Services	1797
—— Inspection and Experimental	2496
Stafford Militia	1247, 1249, 1415, 1416
——————— Terr. Force Assocn.	2468

	COL.
Staffordshire Batts., R.F.A.	714, 715
——————— Brig. Co., A.S.C.	1670
——————— Infantry Brigade	41
——————— North, Regiment	1413
——————— R.G.A. (Heavy)	755
——————— South, Regiment	1245
——————— Yeomanry	489
Star of India, Order of	*2833
Stepney, Poplar &, Rifles (Lond. R.)	1596
Steyne School Cadet Corps	679
Stirling Terr. Force Assocn.	2469
Stonyhurst Coll. Contgt., O.T.C.	1928
Stores, Equipment and, Chief Inspector of	1820
—— Ordnance, Equipment and, Director of	10
Straits Settlements	90, 2527
Students, Chinese, Japanese and Russian Languages	2643
Subordinate Med. Dept., Ind.	2233
Sudan Govt., Offrs. empld. under	94
Suffolk Batts., R.F.A.	671
—— Essex and, R.G.A.	766
—— Norfolk and, Brig. Co., A.S.C.	1659
—— Inf. Brig.	25
—— Regiment	1013
—— Terr. Force Assocn.	2469
—— West, Militia	1015
—— Yeomanry	490
Sunbury House School Cadet Co.	1382
Supernumerary List, Indian Army	2017
Supplies and Quartering, Director of	10
Supply Reserve Depôt, Woolwich Dockyard	27
Surgeon-Generals	328, 336
Surgeons, Honorary, to the King	3
Surrey Brig. Co., A.S.C.	1662
——————— Cos., 1 Cadet Bn., Hamps. R.	916
——————— East, Regiment	1189
——————— Infantry Brigade	26
——————— Militia, Royal	912, 1191, 1193
——————— Rifles (Lond. R.)	1601
——————— Terr. Force Assocn.	2470
——————— West, Cadets	916
——————— Regt., Royal	911
——————— Yeomanry	491
——————— "E" Cadet Sqdn.	491
Sussex Batts., R.F.A.	678 to 681
—— Fortress R.E.	858
—— Militia, Royal	1227
—— Regiment, Royal	1225
—— R.G.A.	777
—— Terr. Force Assocn.	2470

* Published in January, April, July and October issues only.

(xxv)

Table of Contents.

	COL.
Sussex Yeomanry	492
Sutherland and Caithness Highland Bn., Sea. Highrs.	1462
——— Argyll and, Highrs.	1513
——————— Inf. Brig.	45
——— Terr. Force Assocn.	2471
Tasmania	85
Taunton School Contgt., O.T.C.	1928
Technical Reserve Advisory Committees:—	
Motor-Cyclists	2502
Voluntary Aid	2502
Telegraphic Addresses, Registered	xxviii, xxxiii, xxxiv, 2424 to 2477
Temporary Rank	2653
Territorial Divisions and Brigades	25, 33, 38, 44, 51, 56
——— Force, A. S. C.	1654
——————— A. V. C.	1781
——————— Associations	2424
——————— Chaplains Dept	1793
——————— Dir.-Gen. of the	12
——————— Hon. Art. Co.	665
——————— Infantry	897, &c.
——————— List of Units	2417
——————— Nursing Service	1808
————————————— Advisory Council	2503
——————— Reserve	2395
——————— R.A.M.C.	1714
——————— R.E.	819
——————— R.H.A.	659
——————— R.F.A.	667
——————— R.G.A.	747
——————— School of Instn.	35
——————— Unattd. List	1848
——————— Yeomanry	445
Thistle, Order of the	*2822
Tipperary, North, Militia	1067
Tobago	90
Tollington School Cadet Co.	1380
Tonbridge School Contgt., O.T.C.	1929
Tower Hamlets Mila., Royal	1559, 1560
——— of London	2503

	COL.
Training and Educational Estabts.	2480
——— Establishment, A.S.C.	2487
————————— R.A.M.C.	2488
——— Military, Director of	8
Tranent Industrial School Cadet Corps	903
Transport and Movements, Director of	10
——— Vehicles, Subsidized, Inspectors of	1646
Trent College Contgt., O.T.C.	1929
Trinidad	90
Turkish Empire, Offrs. empld. in	2527
Tyne Electrical R.E.	860
Tynemouth R.G.A.	778
Tyrone Militia, Royal	1155
Uganda Bn., King's Afr. Rif.	2520
——— Protectorate	81, 2527
Unattached List	1846
——————— Indian Army	2005
Under Secretary of State for War	5, 6, 12
Unemployed Officers on Active List	372
United Service Institution, Royal, Medallists	*2878
University Coll. Sch. Contgt., O.T.C.	1929
——— of London Contgt., O.T.C.	1886
——— Sheffield Contgt., O.T.C.	1893
——— Wales Contgt., O.T.C.	1893
——— Sch. Cadet Co., Hastings	822
Uppingham School Contgt., O.T.C.	1930
Ventnor Cadet Co.	1243
Veterinary Coll., R. (Dick), Edinburgh Contgt., O.T.C.	1892
——— Coll., R., of Ireland Contgt., O.T.C.	1892
——— Corps, Army	1778
——————— Spec. Res.	1781
——————— Terr. Force	1781
——————— Wt. Offrs.	2289
——— Department, Ind.Civil	1787
——— School, Army	20, 2488
——— Service, Army	1778
——————— Dir.-Gen.	10
Victoria	85
——— Coll. (Jersey) Contgt., O.T.C.	1930

* Published in January, April, July and October issues only.

Table of Contents.

	COL.
Victoria Cross	*2819
———— Hospital, Royal, Netley	51
Victorian Order, Royal	*2843
Voluntary Aid, Advisory Commee. on	2502
Volunteer Bn., Isle of Man	981
———— Commns. held under former Cadet Regns.	1940
———— Force, Offrs. of the late, doing duty with Cadet units	1938
———— Rif. Corps, Bermuda	1842
Wales, North, Brig. Co., A.S.C.	1676
———— ———— Infantry Brigade	59
———— South, Borderers	1125
———— ———— ————Mila., Royal	1127
———— ———— Inf. Brig.	59
———— ———— Mtd. Brig.	58
———— ———— ———— Ammn.Col.	662
———— ———— ———— Fd. Amb.	1719
———— ———— ———— T.& S. Col.	1656
———— Univ. of, Contgt., O.T.C.	1893
Waltham Abbey, Royal Gunpowder Factory	2492
War Office	6
———— Secretary of State for	5, 6
———— Under Secretary of State for	5, 6, 12
Warley Garrison Cadets	1306
Warrant Officers	2259
Warwick Militia	948, 949
———— Terr. Force Assocn.	2472
Warwickshire Batts., R.F.A.	720 to 722
———— ———— Brig. Co., A.S.C.	1671
———— ———— Infantry Brigade	51
———— ———— Regiment, Royal	945
———— ———— R.G.A. (Heavy)	756
———— ———— R.H.A.	666
———— ———— Yeomanry	493
Weald of Kent Bn. (E. Kent R.)	923
Wei-hai-Wei	87
Wellingborough Grammar School Contgt., O.T.C.	1930
Wellington College (Berks) Contgt., O.T.C.	1931
———— ———— (Salop) Contgt., O.T.C.	1931
———— School, Somerset, Contgt., O.T.C.	1931
Welsh Border Brig. Co., A.S.C.	1676
———— ———— Inf. Brig.	59
———— ———— Mtd. Brig.	58
———— ———— ———— Ammn. Col.	665
———— ———— ———— Fd. Amb.	1721
———— ———— ———— Sig. Troop	501
———— ———— ———— T. & S. Col.	1657

	COL.
Welsh Brigs., R.F.A.	736 to 742
———— Clearing Hospital	1773
———— Division	58
———— Divl. R.E.	831
———— ———— Sig. Co.	839
———— ———— T. & S. Col.	1675
———— Field Ambulances	1739, 1740
———— Fusiliers, Royal	1113
———— Regiment	1269
———— R.G.A. (Heavy)	758
Wessex Brigades, R.F.A.	742 to 750
———— Clearing Hospital	1773
———— Division	53
———— Divl. R.E.	833
———— ———— Sig. Co.	841
———— ———— T. & S. Col.	1676
———— Field Ambulances	1740, 1741
———— R.G.A. (Heavy)	758
West Africa	84
———— African Frontier Force	2511
———— Regiment	1832
———— Buckland School Contgt., O.T.C.	1932
———— Croydon Cadets	914
———— India Regiment	1629
———— Kent Militia	1351
———— ———— Regiment, Royal	1349
———— ———— Yeomanry	462
———— Lancashire Brigs., R.F.A.	689 to 695
———— ———— Clearing Hospital	1771
———— ———— Division	56
———— ———— Divl. R.E.	823
———— ———— ———— Sig. Co.	835
———— ———— ———— Fd. Ambs.	1727, 1728
———— Riding Batts., R.F.A.	730 to 735
———— ———— Brigs., R.F.A.	729 to 736
———— ———— Clearing Hospital	1773
———— ———— Division	39
———— ———— Divl. R.E.	830
———— ———— ———— Sig. Co.	838
———— ———— ———— T. & S. Col.	1673
———— ———— Field Ambulances	1737, 1738
———— ———— Infantry Brigades	39, 40
———— ———— Regiment	1205
———— ———— R.G.A. (Heavy)	757
———— ———— R.H.A.	664
———— Somerset Yeomanry	488
———— Suffolk Militia	1015
———— Surrey Regiment, Royal	909

* Published in January, April, July and October issues only.

Table of Contents.

	COL.
West York Militia	1031, 1032, 1075, 1207, 1359, 1423
—— Yorkshire Regiment	1029
Westerham and Chipstead Cadet Corps	1355
Western Australia	85
—————— Cavalry Depôt	437
—————— Coast Defences	55
—————— Command	54
—————— Signal Cos. R.E.	845
—————— General Hospitals	1763 to 1765
Westminster Dns. (2 Co. of Lond. Yeo.)	471
—————— Militia, Royal	962
—————— Rifles, Queen's (Lond. R.)	1594
—————— School Contgt., O.T.C.	1932
Westmorland & Cumberland Yeo.	494
—————— Cumberland &, Bn., Bord. R.	1221
—————— Terr. Force Assocn.	2473
Whitgift Grammar School Contgt., O.T.C.	1932
Wigtown, R. Ayr and, Mila.	1095
—————— Terr. Force Assocn.	2473
Wilson's Sch. (Camberwell) Contgt., O.T.C.	1932
Wilts Terr. Force Assocn.	2474
Wiltshire Batt., R.F.A.	746
—————— Fortress R.E.	849
—————— Militia, Royal	1395
—————— Regiment	1393
—————— Yeomanry, Royal	495
Winchester College Contgt., O.T.C.	1933
Windsor Castle	2504
—————— Military Knights of	2504
Windward Islands	90, 2527
Wolverhampton Grammar School Contgt., O.T.C.	1933
Woodbridge School Contgt., O.T.C	1933
Woolwich, A.S.C. Offs. with Hd.-Qrs. at	27
—————— Arsenal	2492, 2496
—————— Blackheath and, Bn. (Lond. R.)	1600
Woolwich, 1st, Cadet Corps.	698
—————— Ordnance College	2483
—————— Riding Estabt.	586
—————— Royal Carriage Factory	2492
—————— Royal Gun Factory	2492
—————— Royal Military Academy	2486
Worcester, Gloucester &, Brig. Co., A.S.C	1671
—————— Inf. Brig.	51
—————— Militia	1173, 1174
—————— Terr. Force Assocn.	2474
Worcestershire Batts., R.F.A.	719, 720
—————— Regiment	1169
—————— Yeomanry	496
Works, Chief Inspector of	1787
—————— Fortifications and, Director of	11
Worksop College Contgt., O.T.C.	1933
Yealmpton Cadet Co.	849
Yeomanry	445
Yeomen of the Guard	*2816
York & Durham Brig. Co., A.S.C.	1673
—————— Inf. Brig.	38
—————— Lancaster Regt.	1421
—————— East, Militia	1043
—————— (East Riding) T. F. Assocn.	2475
—————— (North Riding) T. F. Assocn.	2475
—————— West, Militia	1031, 1032, 1075, 1207, 1359, 1423
—————— (West Riding) T. F. Assocn.	2476
Yorkshire Dragoons Yeomanry	497
—————— East, Regiment	1041
—————— East Riding of, Yeomanry	499
—————— Hussars Yeomanry	498
—————— Light Infantry	1357
—————— Mtd. Brig.	38
—————— Ammn. Col.	665
—————— Fd. Amb.	1721
—————— Sig. Troop	501
—————— T. & S. Col.	1657
—————— Regiment	1073
—————— Sqdn., Impl. Cadet Yeo.	498
—————— West, Regiment	1029
Zanzibar, Officers employed in	2527
Zetland Terr. Force Assocn.	2477

* Published in January, April, July and October issues only.

(xxviii)

Registered Telegraphic Addresses.

REGISTERED TELEGRAPHIC ADDRESSES.

The Registered Telegraphic Address at Stations Abroad are shown on page xxxiii, those of the Army Agents on page xxxiv, and those of the Secretaries of County Associations on pages 2424 to 2477.

The following addresses have been registered and will be used in official telegrams.

The addresses are **not to be used for any places except those detailed in the 3rd column**, which indicates the place or places at which each abbreviated address is registered.

This list does not contain certain addresses which have been registered for local use.

When telegrams are addressed to Officers or Departments not shown in the List, all unnecessary words in the designation of the addresses will be omitted.

THE WAR OFFICE AND THE STAFFS OF THE INSPECTOR-GENERAL OF THE HOME FORCES AND OF THE INSPECTOR-GENERAL OF THE OVERSEA FORCES, &c.

Title of Officer. (Arranged Alphabetically.)	Code Word.	Telegraph Office at which registered.
Adjutant-General to the Forces	Adulatory	
Assistant Adjutant-General for Recruiting	Timoleon	
Assistant Financial Secretary	Polytlas	
Chaplain-General	Meekness	
Chief of the Imperial General Staff	Chief	
Comptroller of Lands	Landlord	
Director of Artillery	Fusibility	
Director of Barrack Construction	Brickbat	
Director of Contracts	Army Contracts	
Director of Equipment and Ordnance Stores	Gunshot	
Director of Fortifications and Works	Exemptible	
Director of Military Operations	Heeltool	
Director of Military Training	Dehiscence	
Director of Mobilization	Dirmobize	
Director of Personal Services	Seemliness	
Director of Recruiting and Organization	Forcedly	
Director of Remounts	Remounting	
Director of Staff Duties	Broadness	
Director of Supplies and Quartering	Jauntiness	
Director of Transport and Movements	Packsaddle	
Director-General, Army Medical Service	Dehorted	
Director-General, Army Veterinary Service	Nudation	
Director-General of Military Aeronautics	Adastral	
Director-General of the Territorial Force	Terrifor	London.
Financial Secretary	Ephialtes	
Inspector-General of the Home Forces	Sidonius	
Inspector-General of the Oversea Forces and General Officer Commanding-in-Chief in the Mediterranean	Picked	
Inspector of Army Ordnance Services	Strephonic	
Inspector of Cavalry	Trottable	
Inspector of Infantry	Inspentry	
Inspector of Medical Services	Enhance	
Inspector of Royal Engineers	Enginology	
Inspector of Royal Garrison Artillery	Guncase	
Inspector of Royal Horse and Royal Field Artillery	Gunlock	
Inspector of the Army Service Corps	Kit	
Judge Advocate General	Judvocate	
Master-General of the Ordnance	Assaults	
Matron-in-Chief, Territorial Force Nursing Service and Secretary, Territorial Force Nursing Service Advisory Council	Terrnurse	
Military Secretary	Military Secretary	
Quarter-Master-General to the Forces	Fessitude	
Secretary of State for War	Proemial	
Secretary of the War Office	Troopers	
Secretary, Territorial Force Nursing Service Advisory Council, see Matron-in-Chief.		

(xxix)

Registered Telegraphic Addresses.

STAFF, &c., IN THE HOME COMMANDS.

Title of Officer.	Code Word.	Telegraph Offices at which registered.
General Officer Commanding-in-Chief	Commandeth	Aldershot, Chester, Dublin, Edinburgh, London, Salisbury, York.
General Officer Commanding, London District	Usted	London.
General Officer Commanding Division	General	*Aldershot, Bulford Camp, Cork, Curragh Camp, Exeter, Hounslow, Lichfield, Perth, Richmond (Yorks.), Shrewsbury, Warwick, Woolwich, York.
General Officer Commanding { Lowland Division	Genlow	Glasgow.
West Lancashire Division	Genwesla	Liverpool.
1st London Division	Genfirlo	London.
2nd London Division	Genseclo	London.
East Lancashire Division	Geneasla	Manchester.
East Anglian Division	Territorial	Warley Common (for Warley).
General Officer Commanding	General	Guernsey, Jersey.
General Officer Commanding Coast Defences	Defensible	Chatham, Devonport, Portsmouth.
Officer Commanding Coast Defences	Defensible	Dover, Edinburgh, Harwich, Liverpool, Londonderry, Newcastle-on-Tyne, Pembroke Dock, Queenstown.
Maj.-Gen. or Brig.-Gen. i/c Administration	Practician	Aldershot, Chester, Dublin, Edinburgh, London, Salisbury, York.
Brigade Commander	Brigadier	Aberdeen, *Aldershot, Ayr, Bedford, Belfast, Bordon, Bulmer (for Sudbury, Suffolk), Canterbury, Cardiff, Carmarthen, Cheltenham, Chester, Colchester, Cork, Devonport, Dover, Dublin, Dundee, Durham, Fermoy, Grantham, Lancaster, Leicester, Lichfield, Malton, Newcastle-on-Tyne, Norwich, Portsmouth, Preston, Salisbury, Sheffield, Shorncliffe Camp, Skipton, Southampton, Stafford, Stirling (Sudbury, Suffolk, see Bulmer), Taunton, Tonbridge, Wrexham, Brentwood.
Brigade Commander { Essex Infantry Brigade	Brigsex	Brentwood.
14th Infantry Brigade	Brigadier	Curragh Camp.‡
3rd Cavalry Brigade	Brigadier Cavalry	Curragh Camp.
Lothian Infantry Brigade	Brigadier	Edinburgh.
Lowland Mounted Brigade	Brigadier Mounted	Edinburgh.
Devon & Cornwall Inf. Brig.	Brigadier	Exeter.
2nd S. Western Mtd. Brig.	Brigadier Mounted	Exeter.
Highland Light Infantry Brig.	Brigadier Hilin	Glasgow.
Scottish Rifle Brigade	Brigadier Rifle	Glasgow.
Seaforth & Cameron Inf. Brig.	Brigadier	Inverness.
Highland Mounted Brigade	Brigadier Mounted	Inverness.
Liverpool Infantry Brigade	Brigadier	Liverpool.
South Lancashire Inf. Brig.	Brigadier Solan	Liverpool.
London Mounted Brigade	Brigadier Mounted	London.
Middlesex Inf. Brig.	First Brigadier	London.
1st London Inf. Brig.	Brigadier Firlon	London.
2nd London Inf. Brig.	Second Brigadier	London.
3rd London Inf. Brig.	Third Brigadier	London.
4th London Inf. Brig.	Fourth Brigadier	London.
5th London Inf. Brig.	Fifth Brigadier	London.
6th London Inf. Brig.	Sixth Brigadier	London.
South Eastern Mtd. Brigade	Brigadier Semobri	London.
Surrey Inf. Brig.	Brigsurr	London.
East Lancashire Inf. Brig.	Brigelan	Manchester.
Manchester Inf. Brig.	Terrifor	Manchester.
Notts. & Derby. Inf. Brig.	Brigadier	Nottingham.
Notts. & Derby. Mtd. Brigade	Brigadier Mounted	Nottingham.
2nd S. Midland Mtd. Brigade	Brigadier	Oxford.
South Midland Inf. Brigade	Brigadier Southmid	Oxford.
Welsh Border Mtd. Brig.	Mounted	Shrewsbury.
Welsh Border Inf. Brig.	Welsbor	Shrewsbury.
7th Infantry Brigade	Brigadier	Tidworth.
2nd Cavalry Brigade	Brigadier Cavalry	Tidworth.
1st S. Midland Mtd. Brigade	Brigadier	Warwick.
Warwickshire Inf. Brigade	Brigwar	Warwick.
5th Cavalry Brigade	Brigadier Cavalry	York.
1st West Riding Inf. Brigade	Brigadier	York.
Yorkshire Mounted Brigade	Brigadier Mounted	York.

*In the case of Aldershot the number of the Division or Infantry Brigade must be added to the code word and in the case of Brigade Commander of Cavalry the word "Cavalry" must be added.

(xxx)

Registered Telegraphic Addresses.

STAFF, &c., IN THE HOME COMMANDS—*contd.*

Title of Officer.	Code Word.	Telegraph Offices at which registered.
Commanding Royal Artillery (Divisional Troops)	Brigadier	Bulford Camp, Kempsey, Mallow, Nantwich, Newbridge, Richmond (Yorks.), Shrewsbury.
Commanding Royal Artillery (Divisional Troops) { 1st Division	Brigadier Artillery	Aldershot.
2nd Division	Brigadier Gunnery	Aldershot.
Highland Division	Brigadier Artillery	Dundee.
Wessex Division	Brigadier Artillery	Exeter.
Lowland Division	Brigadier Gunnery	Glasgow.
West Lancashire Division	Brigadier Welansion	Liverpool.
1st London Division	Brigadier Artillery	London.
2nd London Division	Brigadier Guns	London.
N. Midland Division	Brigadier Artillery	Stafford.
East Anglian Division	Brigadier Artillery	Warley Common (for Warley).
4th Division	Brigadier	Woolwich.
Home Counties Division	Brigadier Homeco	Woolwich.
West Riding Division	Brigadier Artillery	York.
Chief Engineer (except London District)	Engerto	Aldershot, Chatham, Chester, Devonport (for Plymouth), Dublin, Edinburgh, London, (*Plymouth*, see *Devonport*), Portsmouth, Salisbury, York.
Chief Engineer, London District	Achromatic	London.
Comdg. Royal Engineer, Sub-District	Empowering	Belfast, Chatham, Colchester, Cork, Devonport (for Plymouth), Dover, Dublin, Edinburgh, Exeter, Gosport, ‡Gravesend, Liverpool, Newcastle-on-Tyne, Pembroke Dock, Perth, (*Plymouth*, see *Devonport*), (*Portsea*, see *Portsmouth*), Portsmouth (for Portsea), Ryde, Sheerness, Shoeburyness, Weymouth, Woolwich, York.
Comdg. Royal Engineer, Lands Sub-District	Farming	Aldershot.
Comdg. Royal Engineers { 1st Divn.	Empowering First	Aldershot.
2nd Divn.	Empowering Second	Aldershot.
3rd Divn.	Empowering	Bulford Camp.
5th Divn.	Empowering	Curragh Camp.
6th Divn.	Empowering	Fermoy.
Assistant Director of Supplies and Transport (except London District)	Suppleons	Aldershot, Chester, Dublin, Edinburgh, London, Salisbury, York.
Assistant Director of Supplies and Transport, London District	Duellum	London.
Deputy Director of Medical Services (except London District)	Nerves	Aldershot, Chester, Dublin, Edinburgh, London, Salisbury, York.
Officer in Charge, Royal Victoria Hospital, Netley	Nerves	Netley Abbey.
Deputy Director of Medical Services, London District	Nervincent	London.
Assistant Director of Medical Services	Jatrophic	Belfast, Bordon, Chatham, Colchester, Cork, Devonport, Dover, Dublin, Portsmouth, Tidworth Barracks, Woolwich.
Senior Medical Officer	Jatrophic	Guernsey, Jersey.
Assistant Director of Ordnance Stores	Guncotton	Aldershot, Chester, Dublin, Edinburgh, London, Salisbury, York.
Deputy Director of Ordnance Stores	Guncotton	Woolwich.
Chief Ordnance Officer (except Southampton)	Ordnance	Aldershot, Belfast, Bordon, Burscough Bridge, Carrickfergus, Chatham, Chester, Colchester, Cork (for Haulbowline), Curragh Camp, Devonport, Dover, Dublin, Edinburgh, Guernsey, (*Haulbowline*, see *Cork*), Jersey, London, Pembroke Dock, Portsmouth, Purfleet, Stirling, Tidworth, Weedon, Woolwich, York.
Chief Ordnance Officer, Southampton	Mobilization	Southampton.

‡ On mobilization

(xxxi)

Registered Telegraphic Addresses.

STAFF, &c., IN THE HOME COMMANDS—contd.

Title of Officer.	Code Word.	Telegraph Offices at which registered.
Local Auditor	Aphelion	Aldershot, Chester, Dublin, Edinburgh, London, Salisbury, York.
Officer Commanding District (except No. 11 District).	Group	Cork, Exeter, Hamilton, Hounslow, Lichfield, Perth, Preston, Shrewsbury, Warley Common (for Warley), Warwick, York.
Officer Commanding No. 11 District	Grouping	Dublin.
Officer Commanding Rifle Depôt	Group	Winchester.
Officer Commanding the Troops, Warley	General	Warley Common (for Warley).
Officer in charge of Cavalry Records	Attest	Canterbury, ‡ York.
Officer in charge of R.H. & R.F.A. Records	Attest	Woolwich Dockyard.
Officer in charge of R.G.A. Records	Attest	Dover.
Officer in charge of R.E. Records	Attest	Chatham.
Officer in charge of Infantry Records	Attest	Dublin, Cork, Exeter, Hamilton, Hounslow, Lichfield, Perth, Preston, Shrewsbury, Warley Common (for Warley), Warwick, Winchester, ‡ York.
Officer in charge of A.S.C. Records	Attest Commissariat	Woolwich Dockyard.
Officer in charge of R.A.M.C. Records	Attest	Aldershot.
Officer in charge of A.V.C. Records	Attest Veterinary	Woolwich.
Officer in charge of Army Ordnance Corps Records and Commanding Army Ordnance Corps	Okore	Woolwich.
Assistant Director of Veterinary Services	Vetleder	Aldershot, Curragh Camp, Dublin, London, Salisbury, York.
Senior Veterinary Officer	Veterinus	Bordon, Bulford Camp, Chatham, Colchester, Edinburgh, Portsmouth, Woolwich.
Officer Commanding A.S.C.	Commissariat	Aldershot, Belfast, Bordon, Bulford Camp, Chatham, Chester, Colchester, Cork, Curragh Camp, Devonport, Dover, Dublin, Edinburgh, Guernsey, Jersey, London, Portsmouth, Woolwich, York.
A.S.C. Officer in charge of Norwich Sub-Dist.	Commissariat	Norwich.
A.S.C. Officer in charge of Warwick Sub-Dist.	Commissariat	Warwick.

OFFICERS, &c., NOT INCLUDED IN THE FOREGOING TABLES.
Educational Establishments.

	Title	Code Word	Telegraph Office
Commandant	Army Service Corps Training Establishment, Aldershot.	Micrometer	Aldershot.
	Army Signal School, Aldershot	Signals	Aldershot.
	Army Signal School, Bulford	Signals	Bulford Camp.
	Royal Military College, Sandhurst.	Training	Camberley.
	Staff College, Camberley	Tactics	Camberley.
	School of Military Engineering, Chatham.	Training	Chatham.
	Duke of York's Royal Military School	Dukeyites	Dover
	Royal Hibernian Military School	Hiberboys	Dublin.
	Queen Victoria School	Queenvic	Dunblane.
	Royal Military School of Music	Kneller	Hounslow.
	School of Musketry, Hythe	Musketry	Hythe.
	Royal Army Medical College, Millbank, Grosvenor Rd., S.W.	Jaspage	London.
	Cavalry School, Netheravon	Riding	Netheravon.
	School of Gunnery, Shoeburyness.	Gunnery	Shoeburyness.
	Central Flying School	Speedy	Upavon.
	Ordnance College, Woolwich	College	Woolwich.
	Royal Military Academy, Woolwich.	Training	Woolwich.
Officer in charge, Queen Alexandra Military Hospital, Millbank, S.W.		Afflicted	London.

‡ In the case of "Attest, York" the arm of the Service must be added to the code word.

Registered Telegraphic Addresses.

OFFICERS, &c., NOT INCLUDED IN THE FOREGOING TABLES—*contd.*

Title of Officer.	Code Word.	Telegraph Offices at which registered.
Ordnance Factories Officers; Inspection Staff; and Committees		
Chief Inspector of Small Arms, Armoury Road, Small Heath, Birmingham.	Inspection	Birmingham.
Superintendent, Royal Small Arms Factory, Enfield Lock	Small Arms	} Enfield Lock.
Chief Inspector of Small Arms, Enfield Lock	Inspection	
Chief Ordnance Officer, Royal Army Clothing Department, Grosvenor Road, S.W.	Centrally	
Chief Inspecting Officer, Royal Army Clothing Department, Grosvenor Road, S.W.	Clothcraft	} London
Inspector of Steel, Sheffield	Steeliness	Sheffield.
Superintendent of Experiments, Shoeburyness	Experiments	Shoeburyness.
Superintendent, Royal Aircraft Factory	Ballooning	South Farnborough.
Superintendent, Royal Gunpowder Factory, Waltham Abbey	Powder	Waltham Abbey.
Secretary, Royal Artillery Committee, Woolwich	Artillery	
Superintendent, Building Works, Royal Arsenal, Woolwich	Construct	
Chief Superintendent Ordnance Factories, Woolwich	Factories	
Chief Inspector, Inspection Staff, Woolwich	Inspection	} Woolwich.
Inspector, Royal Engineer Stores	Iris	
Superintending Engineer and Constructor of Shipping, Woolwich	Machinery	
Superintendent, Research Dept., Woolwich	Research	
Chief Inspector of Equipment and Stores, Woolwich	Scrutiny	
Secretary, Ordnance Board, Woolwich	Secretary	
Recruiting and Discharge Depôt Officers.		
Chief Recruiting Staff Officer, Central Recruiting Depôt, Whitehall, S.W.	Recruiting	London.
Recruiting Staff Officer	Recruiting	Edinburgh, Manchester, Sheffield, Woolwich.
Retired Officer employed on Recruiting Duties	Recruiting	Belfast, Birmingham, Bristol, Cardiff, Cork, Dublin, Dundee, Glasgow, Leeds, Liverpool, Middlesbrough, Nottingham, Stoke-on-Trent, Sunderland, Wolverhampton.
Commandant, Discharge Depôt, Fort Brockhurst, Gosport	Discharge	Gosport.
Regimental Headquarters.		
Grenadier Guards	Guardroom	
Coldstream Guards	Coldblast	} London.
Scots Guards	Guardhouse	
Irish Guards	Patness	
Supply and Transport Officers.		
Embarkation Commandant, Southampton	Embarking	Southampton.
Transport Officer, Weedon	Transport	Weedon.
Officer in Charge, Supply Reserve Depôt, Royal Dockyard, Woolwich	Reserves	} Woolwich.
Assistant Director of Military Transport, Royal Arsenal, Woolwich	Transport	
Miscellaneous.		
Officer Commanding Royal Army Medical Depôt, Aldershot	Medcor	Aldershot.
Officer Commanding, Training Depôt, Royal Engineers, Aldershot.	Redep	Aldershot.
Secretary Royal Engineer Institute, Chatham.	Sapper	Chatham.
Officer Commanding K Telegraph Company R.E., Aldborough House, Dublin	Telegraph Battalion	Dublin.
Remount Depôts (Nos. I., II., III. and IV.)	Remounts	Dublin, Woolwich, Melton Mowbray, Arborfield Cross.
Officer Commanding Lowland Divl. T. & S. Col.	Serviceable	Glasgow.
Director of Army Signals, Home Defence	Home Signals	
Secretary, Royal Hospital, Chelsea	Pensionize	} London.
Assistant Adjutant and Quartermaster-General, London District, Great Scotland Yard, Whitehall, S.W.	Withholder	
Range Commandant, Purfleet Rifle Range	Musketry	Purfleet.
Officer Commanding, Detachment Royal Flying Corps, Lark Hill, Salisbury.	Aeronautics	Salisbury.
Director-General, Ordnance Survey, Southampton	Ordnance Survey	Southampton
Officer Commanding, Royal Flying Corps, Military Wing, South Farnborough	Aeronautics	South Farnborough.
Chief Inspector, Aeronautical Inspection Department, South Farnborough	Inspection	South Farnborough

(xxxiii)

Registered Telegraphic Addresses.

REGISTERED TELEGRAPHIC ADDRESSES AT STATIONS ABROAD.

(*For Telegraphic Addresses of Stations at Home see pages* xxviii *to* xxxii.)

The following addresses have been registered, and will be used in official telegrams.

This list does not contain certain addresses which have been registered for local use.

When telegrams are addressed to Officers or Departments abroad not shewn in the list, all unnecessary words in the designation of the addresses will be omitted.

Title of Officer and Station.		Telegraphic Address.
BERMUDA.	General Officer Commanding-in-Chief	General, Bermuda.
CEYLON.	Officer Commanding, Ceylon	General, Colombo.
CHINA.	Officer Commanding, North China	Praebebo, Tientsin.
	General Officer Commanding, South China	Fervour, Hong-Kong.
	Military Attaché, Peking	Machin, Peking.
EAST INDIES.	Commander-in-Chief	Chief, India.
	Military Secretary to Commander-in-Chief	Repellam, Simla (*or* Delhi).
	Chief of the General Staff	Hablistas, Simla (*or* Delhi).
	Adjutant-General	Adulatress, Simla (*or* Delhi).
	Quartermaster-General	Haliotidae, Simla (*or* Delhi).
	Director, Medical Services	Jatrophic, Simla (*or* Delhi).
	General Officer Commanding, Northern Army	Gulosior, Murree.
	General Officer Commanding, Southern Army	Diaxylon, Ootacamund.
EGYPT, ETC.	Inspector-General of the Oversea Forces and General Officer Commanding-in-Chief in the Mediterranean	Picked, Egypt.
	General Officer Commanding	Superflux, Cairo.
	General Staff Officer	Alert, Cairo.
	A.A.G., Cairo	Adultness, Cairo.
	D.A.A. & Q.M.G., Cairo	*Daglock, Cairo.
	Officer Commanding Royal Artillery	Chattels, Cairo.
	Chief Engineer	Chattering, Cairo.
	Officer Commanding Army Service Corps	Chieftain, Cairo.
	Principal Medical Officer	Jatrophic, Cairo.
	Chief Ordnance Officer	Marmorean, Cairo.
	Command Paymaster, Cairo	Seawolf, Cairo.
	Officer Commanding Troops, Alexandria	Ferial, Alexandria.
	EGYPTIAN ARMY.	
	Sirdar, Egyptian Army	Sirdar, Khartoum.
	Adjutant-General, Egyptian Army	Lewa, Khartoum.
	Assistant Adjutant-General, Egyptian Army	Naib, Khartoum.
GIBRALTAR.	Inspector-General of the Oversea Forces and General Officer Commanding-in-Chief in the Mediterranean	Picked, Gibraltar.
	General Officer Commanding-in-Chief	Chief, Gibraltar.
	Assist. Adjt. and Quar.-Mr.-Gen.	Practician, Gibraltar.
JAMAICA.	Officer Commanding Jamaica	General, Jamaica.
JAPAN.	Military Attaché, Tokio	Majap, Tokio.
MALTA.	Inspector-General of the Oversea Forces and General Officer Commanding-in-Chief in the Mediterranean	Picked, Malta.
	General Officer Commanding-in-Chief	Commandeth, Malta.
	Asst. Adjt. and Qr.-Mr.-General	Practician, Malta.
	Local Auditor	Aphelion, Malta.
SOUTH AFRICA	General Officer Commanding-in-Chief	Chebec, Pretoria.
	Major-General in charge of Administration	Mica, Pretoria.
	Local Auditor	Aphelion, Pretoria.
	Officer Comdg. Pretoria District	Ingot, Pretoria.
	Officer Comdg. Cape of Good Hope District	Chowder, Cape Town.
	Officer Comdg. Potchefstroom District	Brig., Potchefstroom.
STRAITS SETTLEMENTS.	General Officer Commanding	General, Singapore.
	D.A.A. & Q.M.G.	Aduncous, Singapore
WEST AFRICA.	General Officer Commanding	General, Sierra Leone.

* Telegrams intended for the Q.M.G.'s Department *only* should be addressed "Daglock," All telegrams for the Adjutant General's Branch should be addressed "Adultness."

(xxxiv)

ARMY AGENTS.

Messrs. Cox & Co., Charing Cross, S.W. [*Telegraphic Address*—"Coxis, London."] and Hornby Rd., Bombay. [*Telegraphic Address*—"Coxis, Bombay."]

Messrs. Holt & Co., 3, Whitehall Place, S.W. [*Telegraphic Address*—"Mensarius, London."]

Sir Charles R. McGrigor, Bt., & Co., 39, Panton Street, Haymarket, S.W. [*Telegraphic Address*—"Dhream, London."]

ALTERATIONS.

Communications from Officers of the Special Reserve and Auxiliary Forces regarding the entry in this publication (a) of letters denoting military qualifications, and (b) of the symbol ✕, denoting War Service*, should be forwarded *through the usual official channels*. Other communications regarding alterations, errors, or omissions, should be addressed direct as follows:—

THE SECRETARY OF THE WAR OFFICE,
Army List.
War Office,
London, S.W.

Officers who succeed to peerages, baronetcies, or courtesy titles, are responsible for immediately notifying the same to the Secretary of the War Office, in order that the necessary alterations may be made in the Army List and in the official records of the War Office.

No Army List except this and the Quarterly is authorised by the War Office.

EXPLANATIONS OF ABBREVIATIONS.

NOTE.—Where the conditions qualifying for a symbol have varied from time to time, the present conditions, only, are indicated.

(A)	..	‡Passed the prescribed examination in Artillery.
(a)	..	‡Obtained a Certificate in Supply Duties, Army Service Corps Training Establishment, Aldershot.
a.d.	..	Airship Detachment (Royal Flying Corps).
𝔄.𝔇.ℭ.	..	Aide-de-Camp General to the King.
A.D.C.	..	Aide-de-Camp to the King.
a.p.	..	Aircraft Park (Royal Flying Corps).
a.s.	..	Serving with Army Service Corps.
(b)	..	‡Obtained a Certificate in Transport Duties at the Army Service Corps Training Establishment, Aldershot, or at the Army Service Corps Transport Classes, Woolwich and Manchester.
[B.C.]	..	Baptist and Congregationalist (Chaplain, Territorial Force).
ℭ.	..	Served in the Crimean Campaign.
c.f.s.	..	Central Flying School (Royal Flying Corps).
c.o.	..	Serving under Colonial Office or under a Colonial Government.
c.l.	..	Student, Chinese Language.
[C.S.]	..	Church of Scotland (Chaplain.)
d.	..	On the strength of the Depôt.
(d)	..	Serving with Details.
[E.]	..	Protestant Episcopalian Chaplain.
e.	..	Qualified in a course of instruction at the London School of Economics.
e.a	..	Attached to Egyptian Army.
[E.P.]	..	Presbyterian, Church of England (Chaplain, Territorial Force).
Eq.	..	Equerry to the King.
[F]	..	Signifies that the Officer's name appears in the "Foreign Orders" list, published quarterly, on pages 2635 to 2648.
f.	..	Passed Firemasters' Class, Ordnance College.
f.c.	..	Belonging or attached to the Royal Flying Corps.
f.c.r.	..	Belonging to the Royal Flying Corps Reserve.
f.o.	..	Serving under Foreign Office.
g.	..	Obtained a 1st Class Certificate in the Long Course of Gunnery or Gunnery Staff Course prior to 1906, or the Certificate of the Gunnery Staff Course subsequent to 1905.
(g)	..	‡Officer who has undergone the one month's course of instruction, and is qualified to superintend the Physical Training of Recruits.
(H)	..	Officer of the Special Reserve of Officers, Militia, Territorial Force, or Volunteers qualified at a School of Musketry
h.o.	..	Serving under Home Office.
h.p.	..	Half Pay.
i.	..	Holding an extra regimental appointment in India.
(I)	..	‡Qualified for post of Instructor of Artillery.
i.a.	..	Serving with Indian Army.
Ind. Pens.	..	Indian Pension.
(Ind. Sup. List.)		On the Indian Supernumerary List.
I. of A.	..	Instructor of Artillery.
I. of M.	..	Regimental Instructor of Musketry.
i.v.	..	Serving with Indian Volunteers.
[J]	..	Jewish Chaplain (Territorial Force).
j.l.	..	Student, Japanese Language.
K.H.C.	..	Hon. Chaplain to the King.
K.H.P.	..	Hon. Physician to the King.
K.H.S.	..	Hon. Surgeon to the King.
k.s.	..	Kite Section (Royal Flying Corps).
[L]	..	Qualified as 1st Class Interpreter in a Modern Foreign Language.
[l]	..	Qualified as 2nd Class Interpreter in a Modern Foreign Language.

* *Vide* also page 2204 of the Quarterly Army List, in the January issue of which book statements of War Service appear.

‡Qualification gained prior to 1 July 09, since which date the grant of this symbol has been discontinued.

(xxxv)

EXPLANATIONS OF ABBREVIATIONS—contd.

₥.	..	Served in the Indian Mutiny Campaign.
m.	..	In Regtl. Lists denotes that Officer is serving with Militia.
m.a.	..	Attached to the Royal Military Academy.
m.c.	..	Attached to the Royal Military College.
m.c.c.	..	Certificate, Senior Department, Royal Military College.
m.p.	..	Seconded (or an extra Captain allowed in the case of a Major), placed on half-pay, or not immediately available on mobilization, as Member of Parliament.
o.	..	Passed the Ordnance Course.
o.c.	..	Under instruction at Ordnance College.
o.d.	..	Serving with Army Ordnance Department.
[P]	..	Presbyterian Chaplain.
(P)	..	‡Passed full course in Submarine Mining.
p.	..	‡Subaltern or Captain who holds Certificate of Proficiency (or is otherwise qualified as Proficient) for rank of Field Officer.
p.	..	‡Subaltern or Captain who holds Certificate of Proficiency (or is otherwise qualified as Proficient) for rank of Captain; or Field Officer who is (similarly) qualified for rank of Field Officer; or Quarter-Master or Veterinary Officer who holds a Certificate of Proficiency (or is otherwise qualified as Proficient) as such; or Medical Officer who holds a Certificate of Proficiency as such.
(p)	..	‡Subaltern's Certificate of Proficiency.
p.a.c.	..	Passed the final examination of the Advanced Class Ordnance College.
P.c.	..	‡Subaltern of the Special Reserve of Officers, Militia, Territorial Force or Volunteers who has attended the Cavalry Officers' Pioneer Class, Chatham.
p.d.	..	Serving with Army Pay Department.
prov.	..	Provisional.
P.s.	..	‡Passed final examination in defence electric lighting.
p.s.	..	‡Subaltern or Captain (other than of Artillery) who has passed School of Instruction for rank of Field Officer, or, in the case of Infantry, has been attached to Regular Forces and obtained a satisfactory report for rank of Field Officer; or Medical Officer who has obtained a satisfactory report after 14 days' attendance at the Depôt, R.A.M.C., or at a selected Military Hospital; or Veterinary Officer who has obtained a satisfactory report after 14 days' attendance at a Veterinary School, or attachment to a Mounted Unit of the Regular Forces.
p.s.	..	‡Officer of Artillery who has passed School of Instruction; or Subaltern or Captain (other than of Artillery) who has passed School of Instruction for rank of Captain; or, in the case of Infantry, has been attached to Regular Forces and obtained a satisfactory report for rank of Captain; or Field Officer (other than of Artillery) who has passed School of Instruction for rank of Field Officer; or, in the case of Infantry, has been attached to Regular Forces and obtained a satisfactory report for rank of Field Officer.
(p.s.)	..	‡Subaltern of Yeomanry who holds School Certificate; or other Subaltern who has passed School of Instruction for rank of Lieutenant, or, in the case of Infantry, has been attached to Regular Forces and obtained a satisfactory report for rank of Lieutenant.
p.s.c.	..	Staff College Graduate.
p.v.c.	..	‡Officer who has attended satisfactorily a course at the Veterinary School, Aldershot.
(Q)	..	Officer of the Special Reserve of Officers, Militia, Territorial Force or Volunteers, qualified in each of the sub-heads of subject (d) (Captains), vide Appendix XI. King's Regulations.
(q)	..	Officer of the Special Reserve of Officers, Militia, Territorial Force or Volunteers, qualified in each of the sub-heads of subject (d) (Lieutenants) vide Appendix XI. King's Regulations.
q.s.	..	Officer qualified for Staff Employment in consequence of service on the Staff in the Field.
r.	..	In Regtl. Lists denotes an Officer of the Regular Forces serving in the Special Reserve as Adjutant or Quarter-Master.
[R]	..	Reward for Distinguished and Meritorious Service.
[R.C.]	..	Roman Catholic Chaplain.
r.d.	..	Recruit Depôt (Royal Flying Corps).
r.e.	..	Officer on Regular Establishment attached to a Special Reserve Battalion other than as Adjutant or Quarter-Master.
(Res. list)	..	On the Reserved List.
r.f.p.	..	Retired on full pay.
r.l.	..	Student, Russian Language.
R.R.C.	..	Royal Red Cross.
s.	..	On Staff.
ⓢ	..	Officer of the Special Reserve of Officers, Militia, Territorial Force or Volunteers qualified as Instructor in Army Signalling.
s.c.	..	Staff College Student.
[S.E.]	..	Scottish Episcopal Chaplain.
S.O.P.	..	Staff Officer of Pensioners.
s.s.	..	Employed with Army Signal Service.
sp. emp.	..	Specially employed.
t.	..	In Regtl. Lists denotes an Officer of the Regular Forces or Special Reserve of Officers serving with the Territorial Force.

‡Qualification gained prior to 1 July 09, since which date the grant of this symbol has been discontinued

(xxxvi)

EXPLANATIONS OF ABBREVIATIONS—*contd.*

[T]	.. ..	Officer of the Special Reserve of Officers, Militia, Territorial Force, or Volunteers who obtained Special Mention in Examination in Tactics laid down for Captains in the Army before 1 January, 1890.
	.. ..	Officer of the Special Reserve of Officers, Militia, Territorial Force or Volunteers qualified in sub-head (1) of subject (d) (Captains), *vide* Appendix XI, King's Regulations.
(T)	.. ..	Officer of the Special Reserve of Officers, Militia, Territorial Force or Volunteers who obtained Special Mention in Examination in Tactics laid down for Lieutenants in the Army before 1 January, 1890.
(t)	.. ..	Officer of the Special Reserve of Officers, Militia, Territorial Force or Volunteers qualified in sub-head (1) of subject (d) (Lieutenants), *vide* Appendix XI, King's Regulations.
t.a.	.. ..	Secretary of a Territorial Force Association.
TD	.. ..	Territorial Decoration.
[U.F.C.]	..	United Free Church of Scotland (Chaplain).
u.s.l.	.. ..	Unemployed Supernumerary List.
V.B.	.. ..	Volunteer Battalion.
VC	.. ..	Victoria Cross.
VD	.. ..	Volunteer Officers' Decoration.
V.R.C.	..	Volunteer Rifle Corps.
[W]	.. ..	Wesleyan (Chaplain, Territorial Force).
w.a.	.. ..	Serving with West African Regiment.
[W.C.M.]	..	Welsh Calvinistic Methodist (Chaplain, Territorial Force).
*	.. ..	Temporary Rank.
✕	.. ..	Officer serving with Special Reserve of Officers, Territorial Force, Reserve of Officers, &c., who has War Service.

The words subscribed to the titles of Regiments, as "Peninsula," "Waterloo," &c., denote the Honorary Distinctions permitted to be borne by such Regiments on their Standards or Colours, or, in the case of Regiments having no Standards or Colours on their Appointments, in commemoration of their Services.

The words "Imperial Service" shown at the head of a unit of the Territorial Force denote that 90 per cent. of the establishment of that unit accept liability for service abroad. (*Vide* Army Order No. 3 of 1910).

Officers whose names are printed in *Italics* are on the Supernumerary or Seconded Lists.

In Regimental Lists an Officer's Battalion is indicated by a number against his name; a number enclosed in brackets denotes that the Officer is *attached* and not posted.

ORDERS.

K.G.	.. ..	Knight of the Garter.
K.T.	.. ..	Knight of the Thistle.
K.P.	.. ..	Knight of St. Patrick.
G.C.B.	..	Knight Grand Cross ⎫
K.C.B.	..	Knight Commander ⎬ of the Bath.
C.B.	.. ..	Companion ⎭
O.M.	.. ..	Member of the Order of Merit.
G.C.S.I.	..	Knight Grand Commander ⎫ of the
K.C.S.I.	..	Knight Commander ⎬ Star of
C.S.I.	..	Companion ⎭ India.
G.C.M.G.	..	Knight Grand Cross ⎫
K.C.M.G.	..	Knight Commander ⎬ of St. Michael and St. George.
C.M.G.	..	Companion ⎭

G.C.I.E.	..	Knight Grand Commander ⎫ of the Indian
K.C.I.E.	..	Knight Commander ⎬ Empire.
C.I.E.	..	Companion ⎭
G.C.V.O.	..	Knight Grand Cross ⎫ of the
K.C.V.O.	..	Knight Commander ⎬ Royal
C.V.O.	..	Commander ⎬ Victorian
M.V.O.	..	Member of the 4th or 5th Class ⎭ Order.
D.S.O.	..	Companion of the Distinguished Service Order.
C.I.	..	Lady of the Imperial Order of the Crown of India.
I.S.O.	..	Companion of the Imperial Service Order.

(xxxvii)

ALPHABETICAL LIST OF REGIMENTS.

BY THE TITLES DIRECTED TO BE USED IN OFFICIAL CORRESPONDENCE.

Regiment.	Army List Abbreviations.	Regtl. Dist.	Regiment.	Army List Abbreviations.	Regtl. Dist.
Coldstream Guards	C. Gds.	—	Munster Fusiliers, Royal	R. Muns. Fus.	101
Grenadier Guards	G. Gds.	—	Norfolk Regiment	Norf. R.	9
Irish Guards	I. Gds.	—	Northamptonshire Regiment	North'n R.	48
Scots Guards	S. Gds.	—	Northumberland Fusiliers	North'd Fus.	5
			Nottinghamshire and Derbyshire Regiment	Notts. & Derby. R.	45
			Oxfordshire and Buckinghamshire Light Infantry	Oxf. & Bucks. L. I.	43
Argyll and Sutherland Highlanders	Arg. & Suth'd Highrs.	91	Rifle Brigade	Rif. Brig.	—
			Royal Fusiliers	R. Fus.	7
Bedfordshire Regiment	Bedf. R.	16	Royal Highlanders	R. Highrs.	42
Berkshire Regiment, Royal	R. Berks. R.	49	Scots, Royal	R. Scots	1
Border Regiment	Bord. R.	34	Scots Fusiliers, Royal	R. Sc. Fus.	21
Cameron Highlanders	Cam'n Highrs.	79	Scottish Borderers, King's Own	K. O. Sco. Bord.	25
Cheshire Regiment	Ches. R.	22	Scottish Rifles	Sco. Rif.	26
Connaught Rangers	Conn. Rang.	88	Seaforth Highlanders	Sea. Highrs.	72
Cornwall's Light Infantry, Duke of	D. of Corn. L.I.	32	Shropshire Light Infantry	Shrops. L. I.	53
			Somerset Light Infantry	Som. L. I.	13
Devonshire Regiment	Devon. R.	11	Staffordshire Regiment, North	N. Staff. R.	64
Dorsetshire Regiment	Dorset. R.	39	Staffordshire Regiment, South	S. Staff. R.	38
Dublin Fusiliers, Royal	R. Dub. Fus.	102	Suffolk Regiment	Suff. R.	12
Durham Light Infantry	Durh. L.I.	68	Surrey Regiment, East	E. Surr. R.	31
			Surrey Regiment, Royal West	R. W. Surr. R.	2
Essex Regiment	Essex R.	44	Sussex Regiment, Royal	R. Suss. R.	35
Gloucestershire Regiment	Glouc. R.	28	Wales Borderers, South	S. Wales Bord.	24
Gordon Highlanders	Gord. Highrs.	75	Warwickshire Regiment, Royal	R. War. R.	6
Hampshire Regiment	Hamps. R.	37	Welsh Fusiliers, Royal	R. W. Fus.	23
Highland Light Infantry	High. L. I.	71	Welsh Regiment	Welsh R.	41
Inniskilling Fusiliers, Royal	R. Innis. Fus.	27	West Riding Regiment	W. Rid. R.	33
Irish Fusiliers, Royal	R. Ir. Fus.	87	Wiltshire Regiment	Wilts. R.	62
Irish Regiment, Royal	R. Ir. Regt.	18	Worcestershire Regiment	Worc. R.	29
Irish Rifles, Royal	R. Ir. Rif.	83	York and Lancaster Regiment	York & Lanc. R.	65
Kent Regiment, East	E. Kent R.	3	Yorkshire Light Infantry	Yorks. L.I.	51
Kent Regiment, Royal West	R.W. Kent R.	50	Yorkshire Regiment	York. R.	19
King's Royal Rifle Corps	K. R. Rif. C.	—	Yorkshire Regiment, East	E. York. R.	15
Lancashire Fusiliers	Lan. Fus.	20	Yorkshire Regiment, West	W. York. R.	14
Lancashire Regiment, East	E. Lan. R.	30			
Lancashire Regiment, Loyal North	N. Lan. R.	47	Army Medical Corps, Royal	R.A.M.C.	—
			Army Service Corps	A.S.C.	—
Lancashire Regiment, South	S. Lan. R.	40	Army Veterinary Corps	A.V.C.	—
Lancaster Regiment, Royal	R. Lanc. R.	4	Cambridgeshire Regiment	Camb. R.	—
Leicestershire Regiment	Leic. R.	17	Herefordshire Regiment	Hereford R.	—
Leinster Regiment	Leins. R.	100	Hertfordshire Regiment	Herts. R.	—
Lincolnshire Regiment	Linc. R.	10	Highland Cyclist Battalion	Highl. Cyclist Bn.	—
Liverpool Regiment	L'pool R.	8	Huntingdonshire Cyclist Battalion.	Hunts. Cyclist Bn.	—
Manchester Regiment	Manch. R	63	Kent Cyclist Battalion	Kent Cyclist Bn.	—
Middlesex Regiment	Midd'x R.	57	London Regiment	Lond. R.	—
			Monmouthshire Regiment	Mon. R.	—
			Northern Cyclist Battalion	N. Cyclist Bn.	—
			West African Regiment	W. Afr. R.	—
			West India Regiment	W.I.R.	—

A 4

HONORARY RANK IN THE ARMY

held by Officers of the Special Reserve of Officers in virtue of

EMBODIED MILITIA SERVICE.

An Officer of the Special Reserve of Officers, who belongs to any of the undermentioned Special Reserve units, and who was serving on the last day of the (first or second) embodiment of the corresponding Militia unit, holds honorary rank in the Army equivalent to the Militia regimental rank he then held. The periods of embodiment of the corresponding Militia units are given in the appended Table.

Special Reserve Unit.	Former Militia Unit.	Embodied. From.	Embodied. To.	Special Reserve Unit.	Former Militia Unit.	Embodied. From.	Embodied. To.
Royal Garrison Artillery.				*Infantry* —contd.			
Antrim	Antrim	8May00	6Nov.00	3 Bn. Norf. R.	3 Bn. Norf. R.	25Jan.00	11Apr.02
Cork	Cork	9May00	6Nov.00	3 Bn. Linc. R.	3 Bn. Linc. R.	9May00 / 17Feb.02	5July01 / 8Oct.02
				3 Bn. Devon. R.	4 Bn. Devon. R.	11May00	16July01
				3 Bn. Suff. R.	3 Bn. Suff. R.	4Dec.99 / 24Feb.02	3July01 / 27Sept.02
Royal Engineers.				3 Bn. Som. L.I.	3 Bn. Som. L.I.	15May00	4Dec.00
R. Anglesey	R. Anglesey	7May00	13Oct.00	3 Bn. W. York.R.	3 Bn.W. York.R.	4May00	1Oct.02
R. Monmouthshire	R. Monmouthshire	1May00	31Oct.00	4 Bn. W. York.R.	4 Bn.W. York.R.	11Dec.99	25Mar.02
				3 Bn. E. York. R.	3 Bn. E. York, R.	4May00 / 17Feb.02	4Dec.00 / 10Oct.02
Infantry.				3 Bn. Bedf. R.	3 Bn. Bedf. R.	8May00	4Dec.00
3 Bn. R. Scots	3 Bn. R. Scots	5Dec.99	28May02				
3 Bn. R.W. Surr. R.	3 Bn. R.W. Surr. R.	4Dec.99	1Apr.02	4 Bn. Bedf. R.	4 Bn. Bedf. R.	16Jan.00	11June02
3 Bn. E. Kent R.	3 Bn. E. Kent R.	18Jan.00	17July02	3 Bn. Leic. R.	3 Bn. Leic. R.	20Feb.00 / 24Feb.02	5Dec.00 / 4Oct.02
3 Bn. R. Lanc. R.	3 Bn. R. Lanc. R.	23Jan.00	5Feb 02	3 Bn. R. Ir. Regt	4 Bn. R. Ir. Regt.	2May00	5July01
3 Bn. North'dFus.	5 Bn. North'dFus.	12Dec.99	8July01				
3 Bn. R. War. R.	5 Bn. R. War. R.	23Jan.00 / 2Dec.01	18Oct.00 / 29Sept.02	4 Bn. R. Ir. Regt.	5 Bn. R. Ir. Regt.	14May00	6July01
				3 Bn. York. R.	3 Bn. York. R.	14Dec.99	14May02
4 Bn. R. War. R.	6 Bn. R. War. R.	14Dec.99	3June02	3 Bn. Lan. Fus.	5 Bn. Lan. Fus.	19Feb.00 / 6May01	17Oct.00 / 25July02
5 Bn. R.Fus.	5 Bn. R. Fus.	18Dec.99 / 6May01	16Oct.00 / 26July02	4 Bn. Lan. Fus.	6 Bn. Lan. Fus.	13Dec.99	14Oct.01
5 Bn. R Fus.	7 Bn. R. Fus.	14May00	15Oct.00				
6 Bn. R. Fus.	6 Bn. R. Fus.	1May00	18Oct.00	3 Bn. R. Sc. Fus.	3 Bn. R. Sc. Fus.	8Dec.99	4Dec.00
3 Bn. L'pool R	3 Bn. L'pool R.	23Jan.00 / 2Dec.01	16Oct.00 / 15Sept.02	3 Bn. Ches. R.	3 Bn. Ches. R.	1May00 / 6Jan.02	4Dec.00 / 4Oct.02
4 Bn. L'pool R.	4 Bn. L'pool R.	3May00 / 6Jan.02	1Nov.00 / 15Sept.02	3 Bn. R. W. Fus.	3 Bn. R. W. Fus.	8Dec.99	5July01

(xxxix)

Militia Embodiments.

Special Reserve Unit.	Former Militia Unit.	Embodied. From.	Embodied. To.	Special Reserve Unit.	Former Militia Unit.	Embodied. From.	Embodied. To.
Infantry —contd.				*Infantry* —contd.			
3 Bn. S. Wales Bord.	3 Bn. S. Wales Bord.	23Jan.00	25Mar.02	5 Bn. K. R.Rif.C.	5 Bn. K. R.Rif.C.	2May00	4Dec.00
3 Bn. K. O. Sco. Bord.	3 Bn. K. O. Sco. Bord.	25Jan.00	18June02	6 Bn. K. R.Rif.C.	7 Bn. K. R.Rif.C.	8May00	15Oct.00
3 Bn. Sco. Rif. ...	3 Bn. Sco. Rif. ...	3May00	15July02	3 Bn. Wilts. R...	3 Bn. Wilts. R...	16Jan.00	11Sept.02
4 Bn. Sco. Rif. ...	4 Bn. Sco. Rif. ...	12Dec.99	27June01	3 Bn. Manch. R.	5 Bn.Manch.R.	3May00 6May01	20Oct.00 28July02
3 Bn. R. Innis. Fus.	4 Bn. R. Innis. Fus.	2May00	18Oct.00	4 Bn. Manch. R.	6 Bn.Manch.R.	4May00 6Jan.02	15Oct.00 30Sept.02
4 Bn. R. Innis. Fus.	3 Bn. R. Innis. Fus	5Dec.99	16Oct.00	3 Bn. N. Staff. R	3 Bn.N.Staff.R.	2May00 10Feb.02	15Oct.00 23Sept.02
3 Bn. Glouc. R...	3 Bn. Glouc. R...	15May00	13July01	4 Bn. N. Staff. R.	4 Bn. N. Staff. R.	24Jan.00	11June02
5 Bn. Worc. R...	5 Bn. Worc. R...	7May00	15Oct.00	3 Bn. York & Lanc. R.	3 Bn. York & Lanc. R.	13Dec.99 9Dec.01 23Jan.00	4Dec.00 28Sept.02 4Dec.00
6 Bn. Worc. R...	6 Bn. Worc. R.	8May00 9Dec.01	19Oct.00 10Oct.02	3 Bn. Durh. L.I.	4 Bn.Durh.L.I.	6Jan.02	30Oct.02
3 Bn. E. Lan. R.	3 Bn. E. Lan. R.	24Jan.00	25Mar. 02	4 Bn. Durh. L. I.	3 Bn. Durh. L. I.	5Dec.99	12June01
3 Bn. E. Surr. R.	3 Bn. E Surr. R.	12May00 6May01	15Oct.00 26July02	3 Bn. High. L. I.	3 Bn. High.L.I.	6Dec.99 9Dec.01	20Oct.00 25Sept.02
4 Bn. E. Surr. R.	4 Bn. E. Surr. R.	4Dec.99 24Feb.02	13July01 25Sept.02	4 Bn. High. L.I.	4 Bn. High. L. I	2May00	15Oct.00
3 Bn. D. of Corn. L.I.	3 Bn. D. of Corn. L.I.	5Dec.99	4Dec.00	3 Bn.Sea.Highrs.	3 Bn.Sea.Highrs.	13Dec.99	11June01
3 Bn. W. Rid. R.	3 Bn. W. Rid. R.	17Jan.00	10May02	3 Bn. Gord. Highrs.	3 Bn. Gord. Highrs.	6Dec.99	6July01
3 Bn. Bord. R. ..	3 Bn. Bord. R. ..	18Dec.99	1Nov.00	3 Bn. Cam'n Highrs.	3 Bn. Cam'n Highrs.	6Dec.99	4Dec.00
3 Bn. R. Suss. R.	3 Bn. R. Suss. R.	11Dec.99	11Sept.02	3 Bn. R. Ir. Rif.	4 Bn. R. Ir. Rif.	10May00	1Nov.00
3 Bn. Hamps. R.	3 Bn. Hamps. R.	24Jan.00	4Dec.00	4 Bn. R. Ir. Rif.	3 Bn. R. Ir. Rif.	14May00	19Oct.00
3 Bn. S. Staff. R.	3 Bn. S. Staff. R.	3May00 6May01	16Oct.00 19July02	5 Bn. R. Ir. Rif.	5 Bn. R. Ir. Rif.	10May00	24July02
4 Bn. S. Staff. R.	4 Bn. S. Staff. R.	5Dec.99	12Aug. 01	3 Bn. R. Ir. Fus.	3 Bn. R. Ir. Fus.	14May00	4Dec.00
3 Bn. Dorset. R.	3 Bn. Dorset. R.	14Dec.99	13July01	4 Bn. R. Ir. Fus.	4 Bn. R. Ir. Fus.	5Dec.99	19Oct.00
3 Bn. S. Lan. R.	3 Bn. S. Lan. R.	13Dec.99	3Aug.01	3 Bn. Conn.Rang.	4 Bn. Conn.Rang.	7May00	17Oct.00
3 Bn. Welsh R..	3 Bn. Welsh R...	4Dec.99	8Mar.02	4 Bn. Conn.Rang.	3 Bn. Conn.Rang.	6Dec.99	5July01
3 Bn. R. Highrs.	3 Bn. R. Highrs.	14Dec.99	4Dec.00	3 Bn. Arg. & Suth'd Highrs.	3 Bn. Arg. & Suth'dHighrs.	23Jan.00 6Jan.02	4Dec.00 23Sept.02
3 Bn. Oxf. & Bucks. L.I.	4 Bn. Oxf. L.I. ..	1May00	3July01	4 Bn. Arg. & Suth'd Highrs.	4 Bn. Arg. & Suth'dHighrs.	5Dec.99	6Aug.01
3 Bn. Essex R. ..	3 Bn. Essex R.	11Dec.99 10Mar.02	20Oct.00 8Oct.02	3 Bn. Leins. R. ...	3 Bn. Leins. R...	18Jan.00	26May02
3 Bn. Notts. and Derby R.	3 Bn. Notts and Derby. R.	23Jan.00	4Dec.00	4 Bn. Leins. R...	4 Bn. Leins.R...	8May00	6July01
4 Bn. Notts. and Derby, R.	4 Bn. Notts. and Derby. R.	11Dec.99	10May01	5 Bn. Leins. R...	5 Bn. Leins.R...	2May00	19Oct.00
3 Bn. N. Lan. R.	3 Bn. N. Lan. R.	13Dec.99	15Mar. 02	3 Bn. R. Muns. Fus.	4 Bn. R. Muns. Fus.	4May00	18Oct.00
3 Bn. North'n R.	3 Bn. North'n R.	4Jan.00 17Mar.02	5Dec.00 28Sept.02	4 Bn. R. Muns. Fus.	3 Bn. R. Muns. Fus.	5Dec.99	31Mar.02
3 Bn. R. Berks.R.	3 Bn. R. Berks.R.	19Feb.00	13July01	5 Bn. R. Muns. Fus.	5 Bn. R. Muns. Fus.	10May00	8Oct.01
3 Bn. R.W. Kent R.	3 Bn. R.W. Kent R.	11Dec.99	10June01	3 Bn. R.Dub,Fus.	3 Bn. R.Dub.Fus.	4May00	18Oct.00
3 Bn. Yorks. L I.	3 Bn. Yorks. L.I.	5May00 6May01	17Oct.00 2Apr.02	4 Bn. R. Dub. Fus.	4 Bn. R. Dub. Fus.	3May00 10Mar. 02	4Dec.00 4Oct.02
3 Bn.Shrops. L.I.	3 Bn. Shrops. L.I.	4May00	11July01	5 Bn. R.Dub.Fus.	5 Bn. R.Dub.Fus.	5Dec.99	25Feb.02
5 Bn.Midd'x R.	5 Bn.Midd'x R.	4May00 6Jan.02	15Oct.00 18Sept.02	5 Bn. Rif. Brig...	5 Bn. Rif. Brig.	1May00 9Dec.01	20Oct.00 3Oct.02
6 Bn.Midd'x R.	6 Bn. Midd'x R.	13Dec.99	1Apr.00	6 Bn. Rif. Brig...	7 Bn. Rif. Brig...	4May00	18Oct.00

B

(1)

The KING

Field-Marshal - - 7May10.

PERSONAL AIDES-DE-CAMP TO THE KING.

Field-Marshal *H.R.H.* Arthur W. P. A. *Duke of* Connaught and Strathearn, *K.G.*, *K.T.*, *K.P.*, *G.C.B.*, *G.C.S.I.*, *G.C.M.G.*, *G.C.I.E.*, *G.C.V.O.*
Bt. Maj. *H.R.H. Prince* Arthur F. P. A. *of* Connaught, *K.G.*, *K.T.*, *G.C.V.O.*, 2 Dns.
Gen. *H.R.H. Prince* Frederic Christian Charles Augustus *of* Schleswig-Holstein, *K.G.*, *G.C.V.O.*
Hon. Col. *H.H.* Adolphus C. A. A. E. G. P L. L., *Duke of* Teck, *G.C.B.*, *G.C.V.O.*, *C.M.G.*, 8 Bn. Lond. R., Bt. Lt.-Col. 1 L.G.

AIDES-DE-CAMP GENERAL TO THE KING.

Scallon, Lt.-Gen. *Sir* R. I., *K.C.B.*, *K.C.I.E.*, *D.S.O.*, Ind. Army.
Haig, Lt.-Gen. *Sir* D., *K.C.B.*, *K.C.I.E.*, *K.C.V.O.*, Col. 17 Lrs., *p.s.c.*
Duff, Gen. *Sir* B., *G.C.B.*, *K.C.S.I.*, *K.C.V.O.*, *C.I.E.*, Ind Army, *p.s.c.*
Hamilton, Gen. *Sir* I. S. M., *G.C.B.*, *D.S.O.*, Col. Cam'n Highrs., *q s.*
Douglas, Gen. *Sir* C. W. H., *G.C.B.*, Col. Gord. Highrs., *q.s.*
Grierson, Lt.-Gen. *Sir* J. M., *K.C.B.*, *C.V.O.*, *C.M.G.*, *p.s.c.* [L]

AIDES-DE-CAMP TO THE KING.

Cavendish, Col. J. C., vD, 6 Bn. Notts. and Derby. R.
Northumberland, Col. *Rt. Hon.* H. G., *Duke of, K.G.*, vD, 3 Bn. North'd Fus.
Haddington, Col. G., *Earl of, K.T.*, TD, Loth. and Border Horse Yeo.(*King's Body Gd. for Scotland*).
Richmond and Gordon, Col. C. H., *Duke of, K.G.*, *G.C.V.O.*, *C.B.*, 3 Bn. R. Suss. R. (*King's Body Gd. for Scotland*).
Stevenson, Col. J., *C.B.*, vD, 8 Bn. High. L.I.
Wood-Martin, Col. W. G., *late* Sligo R.G.A. (Mila).
Montrose, Col. D. B. M. R., *Duke of, K.T., late* 3 Bn. Arg. & Suth'd Highrs.
Clarendon, Col. *Rt. Hon.* E. H., *Earl of, G.C.B.*, *G.C.V.O.*, TD, Herts. Yeo.
Harewood, Col. H. U., *Earl of* K.C.V.O., TD, *late* Yorks. Hrs. Yeo.
Galway, Col. G. E. M., *Visct.*, *C.B.*, TD, Notts. (Sherwood Rangers) Yeo.
Londonderry, Col. *Rt. Hon.* C. S., *Marq. of, K.G.*, *G.C.V.O.*, *C.B.*, vD, 3 Northbn. Brig. R.F.A.
Brownlow, Col. *Rt. Hon.* A. W. B., *Earl*, vD, 1 Bn. Herts. R.
Beaufort, Col. H. A. W. F., *Duke of*, TD, Glouc. Yeo.
Kilmorey, Col. F. C., *Earl of, K.P., late* Shrops. Impl. Yeo.
Clifford, Col. L. H. H. *Lord*, vD, Wessex Divl. T. & S. Col., A.S.C.
Crichton, Col. *Hon. Sir* H. G.L., *K.C.B.*, TD, Hamps. Yeo. and 5 Bn. Hamps.R. (Hon. Lt.-Col. ret. pay).
Scarbrough, Col. A. F. G. B., *Earl of*, K.C.B., TD, York. Dns. Yeo. and W. Rid. Divl. T. & S. Col.
Percy, Col. *Lord* A. M. A., *late* 3 Bn. North'd Fus.
Munro, Col. *Sir* W., *Bt.*, 3 Bn. Sea. Highrs.
Villiers, Col. E., vD, 21 Bn. Lond. R.
Stradbroke, Col. G. E. J. M., *Earl of, C.V.O.*, *C.B.*, vD, 8 E. Anglian (Howr.) Brig., R.F A.
Leicester, Col. T. W., *Earl of, G.C.V.O.*, *C.M.G.*, ret. pay, *late* Lt.-Col. Norf. R.G.A. (Mila.).
Kintore, Col. *Rt. Hon.* A. H. T., *Earl of*, K.C.M.G., *late* 3 Bn. Gord. Highrs. [F]
Breadalbane, Col. *Rt. Hon.* G., *Marq. of, K.G.*, Highl. Cyclist Bn. (*King's Body Gd. for Scotland*).
Fortescue, Col. H. F., *Earl*, K.C.B., TD, R. N. Devon Yeo.
Salisbury, Col. *Rt. Hon.* J. E. H., *Marq. of, G.C.V.O.*, *C.B.*, TD, 4 Bn. Bedf. R.
Albemarle, Col. (*Hon. Lt.-Col. in Army*) A. A. C., *Earl of, K.C.V.O.*, *C.B.*, vD, 5 Bn. Norf. R.
Le Mottée, Col. J. E., *late* R. Guernsey Mila.
Mitford, Col. W. K., *C.M.G.*, *late* Midd'x Impl. Yeo. (*Gent.-at-Arms*).
Barton, Col. B. J., *late* 5 Bn. R. Innis. Fus.
Cooke-Collis, Col. W., *C.M.G.*, *late* 9 Bn. K. R. Rif. C., *q.s.*
O'Callaghan-Westropp, Col. G., Res. of Off.
Stanton, Col. (*temp. Brig.-Gen.*) H. E., *C.B.*, *D.S.O.*, *p.s.c.*
McKenna, Col. P. A., *D.S.O.*
Fitton, Col. (*temp. Brig.-Gen.*) H. G., *C.B.*, *D.S.O.*, *p.s.c.* [L]
Forestier-Walker, Col. (*temp. Brig.-Gen.*) G. T., *p.s.c.* [L]
Harrington, Col. C. A., *Earl of*, Ches. Yeo.
McGough, Col. (*temp. Brig.-Gen.*) J. E., *C.M.G.*, *p.s.c.*
Heneker, Bt. Col. W. C. G., *D.S.O.*, N. Staff. R.
Barclay, Col. H. A., *C.V.O.*, TD, *late* Norf. Yeo.

(*Continued on page 2.*)

Aides-de-Camp to The King—*continued*.

Bedford, Col. H. A., *Duke of, K.G., late* 3 Bn. Bedf. R.
Harris, Col. G. R. C., *Lord, G.C.S.I., G.C.I.E.,* TD, *late* R. E. Kent Yeo.
Stewart, Col. J. M., *C.B.,* Ind. Army.
Lovat, Col. S. J., *Lord, K.C.V.O., C.B., D.S.O.,* 1 & 2 Lovat's Scouts Yeo. and 4 Bn. Gord. Highrs.
Nugent, Col. O. S. W., *D.S.O.,* h.p., *p.s.c.* [*l*]
Buckland, Col. R. U. H.
Essex, Col. (*Hon. Maj. in Army*) G. D. de V., *Earl of,* TD, *late* Herts. Yeo.
Marchant, Col. 2nd Comdt. A. E., *C.B.,* R. Mar.
Dobell, Col. (*temp. Brig.-Gen.*) C. M., *D.S.O., p.s.c.* [*l*]
Westmorland, Col. A. M. J., *Earl of,* 3 Bn. North'n R.
Norie, Col. E. W. M., *p.s.c.*
Hardinge, Col. (*Hon. Lt.-Col. in Army*) H. C., *Visct., C.B., late* 6 Bn. Rif. Brig.
Moncreiffe, Col. *Sir* R. D., *Bt.,* VD, 6 Bn. R. Highrs.
Denbigh and Desmond, Col. R.R.B.A.A., *Earl of, C.V.O.,* TD, Hon. Art. Co.
Goodwin, Col. F., *C.I.E.,* VD, Ind. Vols.
Aston, Col. 2nd Comdt. *Sir* G. G., *K.C.B.,* R. Mar. Art., *p.s.c.*
Godfray, Hon. Brig.-Gen. J. W., *C.V.O., C.B.,* ret. pay, *p.s.c.* (A.A.G., R. Mila. of Island of Jersey).
Ewart, Col. R. H., *C.I.E., D.S.O.,* Ind. Army.
Mercer, Col. (*temp. Brig.-Gen.*) H. F., *C.B.*
Cobbe, Col. A. S., *D.S.O.,* 32 Pioneers, *p.s.c.*
Knight, Bt. Col. W. C., *D.S.O.,* Ind. Army, *p.s.c.* [L].
Kenyon, Col. L., *Lord, K.C.V.O.,* TD, *late* Shrops. Yeo.
Burn, Col. C. R., 2 Co. of Lond. Yeo., Lt.-Col. ret. pay (*Gent.-at-Arms*).
Gordon, Bt. Col. W. E., Gord. Highrs.
Roberts, Col. C. F., *C.M.G., late* C'wealth Mil. Forces (*Honorary*).
Hon. Maj. Gen. *H.H. Sir* Madho Rao Scindia, *Bahadur, Maharaja of* Gwalior, *G.C.S.I., G.C.V.O.*, (*Honorary*).
Hon. Maj.-Gen. *H.H. Maharaja Sir* Pratap Singh, *Bahadur, Regent of* Jodhpur, *G.C.S.I., G.C.V.O., K.C.B.* (*Honorary*)
Hon. Col. *Nawab Sir* Muhammad Aslam Khan, *Sardar Bahadur, K.C.I.E., K.C.V.O.* (*Honorary*).
Hon. Col. *H.H. Maharaja Raj Rajeshwar Siromani Sri Sir* Gunga Singh, *Bahadur, of* Bikaner, *G.C.S.I., G.C.I.E.* (*Honorary*).
Hon. Col. *H. H. Nawab Sir* Muhammad Hamid Ali Khan, *Bahadur, of* Rampur, *G.C.I.E., G.C.V.O.* (*Honorary*).

EQUERRIES TO THE KING.

Grafton, Hon. Gen. A. C. L., *Duke of, K.G., C.B.,* ret. pay (*Honorary*).
Wentworth-Fitzwilliam, Capt. *Hon. Sir* W. C., *K.C.V.O., late* R.H.G. (*Crown Equerry*).
Legge, Hon. Col. *Hon. Sir* H. C., *K.C.V.O.,* ret. pay.
Ponsonby, Bt. Lt.-Col. *Sir* F. E. G., *K.C.V.O., C.B.,* ret. pay (*Maj. Res. of Off.*) (*Asst. Private Secretary*).
Nairne, Maj. *Lord* C. M., *M.V.O.,* 1 Dns. [*l*]
Wigram, Maj. C., *C.S.I., M.V.O.,* 18 Lrs., *p.s.c.* (*Asst. Private Secretary*).
Beresford, *Lord* M. T. De la P., *C.V.O., late* 7 Hrs. (*Extra*).
Bor, Gen. J. H., *C.B., C.M.G.,* R. Mar. Art. (*Extra*).
Campbell, Lt.-Col. C. F., *C.I.E.,* ret. Ind. Army (*Gent.-at-Arms*) (*Extra*).
Carington, Lt.-Col. *Rt. Hon. Sir* W. H. P., *G.C.V.O., K.C.B., late* G. Gds. (*Keeper of Privy Purse*) (*Extra*).
Crichton, Maj. H. W., *Visct., M.V.O., D.S.O.,* R.H.G. (*Extra*).
Davidson, Bt. Col. *Sir* A., *K.C.B., K.C.V.O.,* ret. pay (*Extra*).
Dugdale, Lt.-Col. F., *C.V.O.,* TD, War. Yeo. (*Extra*).
Ewart, Maj.-Gen. *Sir* H. P., *Bt., G.C.V.O., K.C.B.,* ret. pay, Col. 7 D.G. (*Extra*).
Gleichen, Col. (*temp. Brig.-Gen.*) A. E. W., *Count K.C.V.O., C.B., C.M.G., D.S.O., p.s.c.* [L] (*Extra*).
Greville, Hon. Lt.-Col. *Hon.* A. H. F., *M.V.O., late* War. Impl. Yeo. (*Extra*).
Grimston, Col. (*temp. Brig.-Gen*) *Sir* R. E., *K.C.V.O., C.I.E.,* Ind. Army (*Extra*).
Holford, Bt. Lt.-Col. *Sir* G. L., *K.C.V.O., C.I.E.,* ret. pay (*Extra*).
Probyn, Gen. *Rt. Hon. Sir* D. M., *G.C.B., G.C.S.I., G.C.V.O., I.S.O.,* u.s.l. Ind. Army (*Extra*).
Stamfordham, Lt.-Col. *Rt. Hon.* A. J., *Lord, G.C.I.E., G.C.V.O., K.C.B., K.C.S.I., K.C.M.G., I.S.O.* ret. pay (*Private Secretary*) (*Extra*).
Streatfeild, Bt. Col. H., *C.V.O., C.B.,* ret. pay (*Extra*).
Ward, *Hon.* J. H., *C.V.O., late* 2nd Lt. Worc. Yeo. (*Extra*).
Watson, Lt.-Col. H. D., *C.I.E., M.V.O.,* 9 Gurkha Rif. (*Extra*).
Haig, Hon. Lt.-Col. A. B., *C.V.O., C.M.G.,* ret. pay (*Extra*).
Keppel, Hon. Lt.-Col. *Hon. Sir* D. W. G., *K.C.V.O., C.M.G., C.I.E.,* VD., *late* 12 Midd'x. V.R.C. (*Master of the Household*) (*Extra*.)

HONORARY PHYSICIANS TO THE KING.

꧅. Bradshaw, Surg.-Maj.-Gen. *Sir* A. F., *K.C.B.*, ret.
Taylor, Surg.-Gen. *(ranking as Lt.-Gen.) Sir* W., *K.C.B., M.D.*, ret.
Henderson, Col. R. S. F., *M.B.*
Macpherson, Surg.-Gen. W. G., *C.M.G., M.B., Dep. Dir.-Gen., Army Medical Service.*
Corker, Surg.-Gen. T. M., *M.D.*
Leishman, Bt. Col. *Sir* W.B., *Knt., F.R.S., M.B., F.R.C.P.*, R.A.M.C.
Kinnear, Col. W., *M.D.*, VD.
Oliver, Col. C. P., *M.D.*, TD.

Indian Military Forces.

Pinkerton, Surg.-Maj.-Gen. J., *M.D.*, ret.
McVittie, Surg.-Gen. C. E., *F.R.C.S.I.*, ret.
Franklin, Surg.-Gen. *Sir* B., *K.C.I.E.*, ret.
McLeod, Hon. Col. K., *M.D.*, Lt.-Col. ret.
Cunningham, Hon. Col. D. D., *C.I.E., M.B.*, Brig.-Surg.-Lt.-Col. ret.
Bannerman, Surg.-Gen. W. B., *C.S.I., M.D.*, Ind. Med. Serv.

HONORARY SURGEONS TO THE KING.

꧅. ꧅. Reade, Surg.-Maj.-Gen. *Sir* J. B. C., *K.C.B.*, ret.
Stevenson, Hon. Surg.-Gen. W. F., *C.B., M.B.*, ret.
Sloggett, Surg.-Gen. *(ranking as Lt.-Gen.) Sir* A. T., *Knt., C.B., C.M.G. (Director-General, Army Medical Service).*
Hickson, Col. S., *M.B.*
Bull, Col. W. H., *F.R.C.S. Edin.*, VD.
Jones, Col. J. A., *M.D.*, VD.
꧅꧅. Babtie, Surg.-Gen. W., *C.B., C.M.G., M.B.*
Gibbard, Bt. Col. T. W., *M.B.*, R.A.M.C.

Indian Military Forces.

Cleghorn, Surg.-Gen. J., *C.S.I., M.D.*, ret.
Turnbull, Surg.-Maj.-Gen. P. S., *M.D.*, ret.
Hooper, Hon. Col. *Sir* W. R., *K.C.S.I.*, ret.
Spencer, Surg.-Gen. *Sir* L. D., *K.C.B., M.D.*, ret.
Lukis, Surg.-Gen. *Sir* C. P., *K.C.S.I., M.D., F.R.C.S.*, Ind. Med. Serv.
Crefts, Surg.-Gen. A. M., *C.I.E.*, ret.

HONORARY CHAPLAINS TO THE KING.

Edghill, *Rev.* J. C., *D.D.*, Chaplain-General, ret. pay.
Bullock, *Rev.* R. H., *D.C.L.*, Chaplain to the Forces (*1st Class*) ret. pay.
Goodwin, *Rev.* E. H., *B.A.*, Chaplain to the Forces (*1st Class*) ret. pay.
Wirgman, *Ven. Archdeacon* A. T., *D.D.*, VD, Chaplain *(Hon. Lt.-Col.)* Cape Colonial Forces.
Raymond, *Rev.* P. F., *M.A.*, Chaplain to the Forces (*1st Class*) ret. pay.
Wickins, *Ven. Archdeacon* W. J., *M.A.*, Senior Chaplain, Indian Ecclesiastical Establt.
Simms, *Rev.* J. M., *D.D.*, Chaplain to the Forces (*1st Class*).

FOREIGN SOVEREIGNS who are Colonels-in-Chief or Honorary Colonels of Regiments.

Field-Marshal *His Imperial Majesty* Francis Joseph I, EMPEROR OF AUSTRIA and KING OF HUNGARY, K.G.
Colonel-in-Chief, 1st Dragoon Guards.

Field-Marshal *His Majesty* William II., GERMAN EMPEROR KING OF PRUSSIA, K.G., G.C.V.O.
Colonel-in-Chief, 1st Dragoons.

His Imperial Majesty Nicholas II., EMPEROR OF RUSSIA, K.G.,
Colonel-in-Chief, 2nd Dragoons.

General *His Majesty* Alfonso XIII., KING OF SPAIN K.G., G.C.V.O.
Colonel-in-Chief, 16th Lancers.

His Majesty Haakon VII., KING OF NORWAY, K.G., G.C.B., G.C.V.O.
Honorary Colonel, Norfolk Yeomanry.

His Majesty Christian X., KING OF DENMARK, K.G., G.C.B., G.C.V.O.
Colonel-in-Chief, East Kent Regiment.

ARMY COUNCIL.

The Rt. Hon. H. H. ASQUITH, *K.C., M.P.,*
SECRETARY OF STATE FOR WAR.

GENERAL *Sir* C. W. H. DOUGLAS, *G.C.B.,* Col. Gord. Highrs., *q.s.,* A.D.C.,
CHIEF OF THE IMPERIAL GENERAL STAFF *(First Military Member)*

LIEUTENANT-GENERAL *Sir* H. C. SCLATER, *K.C.B.,*
ADJUTANT-GENERAL TO THE FORCES *(Second Military Member).*

MAJOR-GENERAL *Sir* J. S. COWANS, *K.C.B., M.V.O., p.s.c.,*
QUARTER-MASTER-GENERAL TO THE FORCES *(Third Military Member).*

COLONEL *(local and temp. Maj.-Gen.) Sir* S. B. VON DONOP, *K.C.B., g.,*
MASTER-GENERAL OF THE ORDNANCE *(Fourth Military Member).*

The Rt. Hon. H. J. TENNANT, *M.P.,*
PARLIAMENTARY UNDER SECRETARY OF STATE FOR WAR
(Civil Member).

H. T. BAKER, *Esq., M.P.,*
FINANCIAL SECRETARY *(Finance Member).*

Secretary.

Sir R. H. BRADE, *K.C.B.*

WAR OFFICE.

Secretary of State for War.

The Rt. Hon. H. H. ASQUITH, K.C., M.P.

Principal Private Secretary .. H. J. Creedy, *Esq., M.V.O.*
Private Secretary .. .. Capt. *Hon.* A. M. Henley, 5 Lrs., *p.s.c.*

Military Secretary to the Secretary of State for War, and Secretary of the Selection Board

Lt.-Gen. *Sir* W. E. Franklyn, *K.C.B.*, Col. York. R., *p.s.c.* ... ... 6 Oct. 11
Assistant Military Secretary.. Col. E. W. M. Norie, *p.s.c., A.D.C.* 8Sept.12

Parliamentary Under Secretary of State for War.

The Rt. Hon. H. J. TENNANT, *M.P.*

Private Secretary .. .. .. W. H. Schlich, *Esq.*
Parliamentary Private Secretary.. J. I. Macpherson, *Esq., M.P. (unpaid).*

Financial Secretary.

H. T. BAKER, *Esq., M.P.*
Private Secretary .. .. .. J. A. Dale, *Esq.*

Assistant Financial Secretary
Sir C. Harris, *K.C.B.*
Private Secretary.. F. C. Bovenschen, *Esq.*

Secretary of the War Office.

Sir R. H. BRADE, *K.C.B.*

Private Secretaries .. .. { H. C. Gordon, *Esq.*
                              { E. B. Charteris, *Esq. (unpaid).*

Assistant Secretary of the War Office.
B. B. Cubitt, *Esq., C.B.*

(7)

War Office—(continued).

DEPARTMENT
OF THE
CHIEF OF THE IMPERIAL GENERAL STAFF.

Chief of the Imperial General Staff	GEN. *Sir* C. W. H. DOUGLAS, *G.C.B.*, Col. Gord. Highrs., *q.s.*, 𝔄.𝔇.ℭ.	6Apr.14
Private Secretaries	{ H. W. Mogridge, *Esq.* { Capt. P. R. Laurie, 2 Dns	
Director of Military Operations	.. Maj.-Gen. H. H. Wilson, *C.B.*, *D.S.O.*, *p.s.c.*	1Aug.10
General Staff Officers, 1st grade	Col. G. M. Harper, *D.S.O.*, *p.s.c.* [*l*] .. Col. A. G. Dallas, *p.s.c.* [*l*] .. Col. W. C. Hedley .. .. .. Col. H. S. Sloman, *D.S.O.*, *p.s.c.* [L] .. Col. G. M. W. Macdonogh, *p.s.c.* [L]	23June11 20Sept.11 20Sept.11 { 21Sept.12 { 3May11 { 30Oct.12 { 27Oct.06
General Staff Officers, 2nd grade ..	Maj. H. S. de Brett, *D.S.O.*, R.A., *p.s.c.* [L] .. Maj. A. G. Stuart, 40 Pathans, *p.s.c.* .. Maj. H. W. Studd, *D.S.O.*, C. Gds., *p.s.c.* [*l*] Maj. W. Gillman, *D.S.O.*, R.A., *p.s.c.* .. Maj. C. B. Thomson, R.E., *p.s.c.* [L] Bt. Lt.-Col. A. B. Lindsay, 2 Gúrkha Rif., *p.s.c.* [L] Maj. P. P. de B. Radcliffe, R.A., *p.s.c.* [L] .. Maj. E. M. Jack, R.E. .. .. .. Maj. B. W. B. Bowdler, R.E., *p.s.c.* [L] .. Maj. M. C. P. Ward, R.A., *p.s.c.* [*l*] .. Maj. R. M. Johnson, R.A., *p.s.c.*	20Sept.10 { 1Feb.12 { 23Feb.11 1Apr.12 { 28Apr.12 { 14Aug.10 { 27 Feb.13 { 16Oct 11 { 16June13 { 14Nov.12 { 20Sept.13 { 15Oct.11 { 1Oct.13 { 22Jan.13 { 27Nov.13 { 22Mar.10 { 17Mar.14 { 17Nov.11 { 1May14 { 1Apr.11
Attached.	Maj.J.V.Forrest,*M.B.*,R.A.M.C.[L](*Dep.-Asst.-Dir.-Gen.*)	29Dec.13
General Staff Officers, 3rd grade ..	Capt. N. P. Brooke, Leins. R. [L] .. .. .. Capt. W. V. Nugent, R.A. .. .. .. Maj. L. R. Vaughan, 7 Gúrkha Rif., *p.s.c.* .. Capt. E. W. Cox, R. E. [L] .. .. .. Capt. E. FitzG. Dillon, R. Muns. Fus., *p.s.c.* [L] Capt. A. P. Wavell, R. Highrs., *p.s.c.* [L] .. 𝔇ℭCapt. L. A. E. Price-Davies, *D.S.O.*, K.R. Rif. C., *p.s.c.* Bt.-Maj. W. M. St. G. Kirke, R.A., *p.s.c.* .. .. Maj. F. W. Gosset, R.A., *p.s.c.* .. .. .. Capt. W. E. Davies, Rif. Brig., *p.s.c.* .. .. Capt. F. W. L. S. H. Cavendish, 9 Lrs., *p.s.c.* .. Capt. H. C. Johnson, K.R. Rif. C., *D.S.O.*, *p.s.c.* .. Maj. S. E. Hollond, Rif. Brig., *p.s.c.* .. .. Capt. A. S. Redman, R.E. .. .. .. Bt. Maj. B, T. Buckley, North'd Fus., *p.s.c.* [L] Capt. H. E. R. R. Braine, R. Muns. Fus., *p.s.c.* .. Capt. H. D. Goldsmith, D. of Corn. L. I., *p.s.c.* [*l*] .. Lt. O. E. Wynne, R.E. .. .. .. Capt. F. S. G. Piggott, R.E. [L] .. .. .. Capt. C. P. Deedes, *D.S.O.*, Yorks. L.I., *p.s.c.* ..	7Oct.10 22Jan.11 1Feb.12 1May12 13May12 { 21Sept.12 { 1Apr.12 { 23Sept.12 { 1Nov.10 24Sept.12 6Jan.13 { 7Jan.13 { 1Jan.11 27Feb.13 27Mar.13 { 29July13 { 4Nov.11 13Oct.13 27Nov.13 { 1Dec.13 { 24Sept.12 8Mar.14 16Mar.14 { 5May14 { 1Apr.12

[*Continued on page* 8.]

(8)

War Office—(continued.)

Department of the Chief of the Imperial General Staff—contd.

Director of Staff Duties	Maj.-Gen. F. J. Davies, C.B., p.s.c. [l]	9Oct.1:
General Staff Officers, 1st grade {	Col. W. H. Bowes, p.s.c. [L] Col. R. D. Whigham, D.S.O., p.s.c. [l]	5Jan.1 16Apr.1
General Staff Officers, 2nd grade {	Maj. R. W. Hare, D.S.O., Norf. R., p.s.c., q.s. Capt. C. F. Aspinall, R. Muns. Fus., p.s.c. Capt. I. L. B. Vesey, R. W. Surr. R., p.s.c.	8Oct.1: 23Apr.1: 12Mar.1(12Apr.1(29Aug.1]
General Staff Officers, 3rd grade {	Lt. H. C. L. Howard, 16 Lrs., p.s.c. Maj. W. H. Bartholomew, R.A., p.s.c. Capt. B. P. Lefroy, D.S.O., R. War. R., p.s.c.	16Apr.1! 20Oct.1: 1Nov.1: 14Apr.14
Dominion Section. Attached {	Lt.-Col. (local Lt.-Col. in Army) P. E. Thacker, Lord Strathcona's Horse, p.s.c. Lt.-Col. (local Lt.-Col. in Army) J. G. Legge, C.M.G., C'wealth Mil. Forces Maj. (local Maj. in Army) G. S. Richardson, N.Z. Staff Corps, p.s.c.	1Apr.1: 22July1: 22Dec.1:
Director of Military Training	Maj.-Gen. Sir W. R. Robertson, K.C.V.O., C.B., D.S.O., p.s.c. [L]	9Oct.1:
General Staff Officers, 1st grade {	Col. F. S. Maude, C.M.G., D.S.O., p.s.c. Col. A. L. Lynden-Bell, C.M.G., p.s.c. [L]	1Feb.1(19Feb.1(
General Staff Officers, 2nd grade {	Bt. Maj. R. E. H. James, N. Lan. R., p.s.c. Maj. B. T. Pell, D.S.O., R. W. Surr. R., p.s.c. Bt. Maj. R. S. May, R. Fus., p.s.c. [l] Maj. P. W. Game, R.A., p.s.c. Bt. Lt.-Col. Hon. J. F. Gathorne-Hardy, G. Gds., p.s.c. [l]	1June1! 13Apr.1: 28Mar.1: 20Aug.1! 24Apr.1! 7Sept.1: 31Dec.1(1Apr.1(9 June1:
Attached	Lt.-Col. H. E. R. James, C.B., F.R.C.S., ret. pay	1Apr.0
General Staff Officers, 3rd grade {	Maj. C. G. Fuller, R.E., p.s.c. [L] Capt. E. G. Wace, R.E., p.s.c. [L] Capt. H. A. Ramsay, R.A., p.s.c., g. Capt. A. T. Paley, Rif. Brig., p.s.c. Maj. G. N. Cory, D.S.O., R. Dub. Fus., p.s.c. Maj. P. D. FitzGerald, D.S.O., 11 Hrs., p.s.c. [l] Maj. J. G. Dooner, R.A., p.s.c. Capt. H. F. L. Grant, R.A., p.s.c. [l] Capt. R. F. S. Grant, M.V.O., D.S.O., Rif. Brig., p.s.c. [l]	13Mar.1: 11Oct.1: 13Apr.1: 10June1: 8Sept.1: 10ct.1: 2Apr.1: 1Apr.14 1Apr.14 2)Apr.14 1May14

(9)

War Office—*(continued).*

DEPARTMENT

OF THE

ADJUTANT-GENERAL TO THE FORCES.

Adjutant-General to the Forces	LT.-GEN. *Sir* H. C. SCLATER, *K.C.B.*	9Apr.14
Private Secretary	K. Lyon, *Esq.*	
Director of Recruiting and Organization	Col. *(temp. Brig.-Gen.)* H. G. Fitton, *C.B., D.S.O., p.s.c.* [L] A.D.C.	8Sept.13
Assistant Adjt.-Gens.	Col. F. L. Banon, *p.s.c.* [*l*]	14July10
	Col. R. J. Strachey, *p.s.c.*	1June11
	Col. G. P. Wyndham, *C.B., M.V.O., p.s.c.* [*l*]	19Nov.13
	Col. R. S. Curtis, *C.M.G., D.S.O.*	1Apr.13
	Lt.-Col. M. Peake, *C.M.G.,* R.A.	16May14
Dep. Asst. Adjt.-Gens.	Maj. C. M. A. Wood, North'd Fus., *p.s.c.*	{ 1June11 / 1Dec.10
	Maj. A. B. Gosset, Ches. R. (*also C.R.S.O., Lond. Dist.*)	19Mar.14
Staff Captains	Maj. P. E. Lewis, R.A., *p.s.c.*	1Apr.12
	Capt. B. J. Curling, K.R. Rif. C., *p.s.c.*	{ 2Apr.12
Director of Personal Services	Maj.-Gen. *Sir* C. F. N. Macready, *K.C.B.*	1June10
Assistant Adjt.-Gens.	Col. H. C. Sutton	28Oct.13
	Lt.-Col. J. W. G. Roy	26Feb.14
	Col. R. S. Curtis, *C.M.G., D.S.O.*	1Apr.13
	Lt.-Col. M. Peake, *C.M.G.,* R.A.	16May14
Dep. Asst. Adjt.-Gen.	Bt. Maj. B. E. W. Childs, R. Ir. Regt.	{ 13Apr.14 / 15Feb.11
Staff Captains	Capt. W. H.-E. Segrave, *D.S.O.,* High. L.I., *p.s.c* [*l*]	1Jan.14
	Capt. M. R. Walsh, Worc. R., *p.s.c.*	18Apr.14
Director of Mobilization	Col. *(temp. Brig.-Gen.)* E. M. Woodward, *p.s.c.*	9May13
Dep. Asst. Adjt.-Gen.	Bt. Maj. G. R. Frith, R. E., *p.s.c.*	{ 1June12 / 21Oct.11
Staff Captain	Capt. J. B. Wells, *D.S.O.,* N. Lan. R., *p.s.c.*	1June12
Director-General, Army Medical Service	Surg.-Gen. *(ranking as Lt.-Gen.) Sir* A. T. Sloggett, *Knt., C.B., C.M.G., K.H.S.*	1June14
Deputy Director-General	Surg.-Gen. W. G. Macpherson, *C.M.G., M.B., K.H.P.*	6Mar.14
Asst. Director-General	Lt.-Col. C. H. Burtchaell, *M.B.,* R.A.M.C.	1June10
Dep. Asst. Director-Generals	Lt.-Col. G. B. Stanistreet, *M.B.,* R.A.M.C.	20Jan.13
	Maj. W. R. Blackwell, R.A.M.C.	1Apr.14
	Maj. H. P. W. Barrow, R.A.M.C.	1May14
Inspector of Medical Services	Hickson, Col. S., *M.B., K.H.S.* (*Horse Guards, S. W.*)	23Apr.14

(10)

War Office—*(continued).*

DEPARTMENT

OF THE

QUARTER-MASTER-GENERAL TO THE FORCES.

Quarter-Master-General to the Forces	MAJ.-GEN. Sir J. S. COWANS, K.C.B., M.V.O., p.s.c.	8June1!
Private Secretary	L. G. S. Reynolds, *Esq.*	
Director of Transport and Movements	Maj.-Gen. F. W. B. Landon, C.B.	{1Apr.1! / 4Jan.1!
Assistant Director of Movements	Lt.-Col. Hon. A. R. Montagu-Stuart-Wortley, D.S.O., p.s.c. [L]	1Apr.1
Staff Captain for Railway Transport	Capt. H. O. Mance, D.S.O., R.E.	2Dec.1!
Deputy Assistant Director of Transport	Maj. F. W. Stringer, A.S.C.	1Feb.1
Staff Captain	Capt. R. M. Campbell, A.S.C.	1Oct.1!
Director of Remounts	Maj.-Gen. W. H. Birkbeck, C.B., C.M.G., p.s.c.	12Sept.1!
Assistant Director of Remounts		
Deputy Assistant Director	Bt. Lt.-Col. G. F. MacMunn, D.S.O., R.A., p.s.c., q.s.	7Mar.12
Staff Captain	Capt. L. R. G. Bell	{1Apr.0! / 1Apr.0!
Director of Supplies and Quartering	Col. (*temp. Brig.-Gen.*) S. S. Long, C.B.	{1Apr.1! / 9Jan.1!
Assistant Director of Supplies	Col. St. J. W. T. Parker	9Jan.1!
Dep. Asst. Dir. of Quartering	Maj. C. F. Moores, D.S.O., A.S.C., p.s.c., e. [l]	20Apr.11
Dep. Asst. Dir. of Supplies	Maj. W. K. Tarver, A.S.C., e.	1Nov.1
Director of Equipment and Ordnance Stores	Maj.-Gen. (*hon.*) T. P. Battersby, A. Ord. Dept.	1Apr.1!
Assistant Directors	Col. E. H. Seymour, A. Ord. Dept., f.	21Sept.0!
	Lt.-Col. R. K. Scott, D.S.O., A. Ord. Dept., f.	
Assistant Director (Dress and Clothing)	Col. H. A. Anley, A. Ord. Dept., f.	25Feb.1
Deputy Assistant Directors	Maj. R. T. Russell, A. Ord. Dept., p.a.c.	9Sept.1!
	Maj. M. W. H. McCheane, A. Ord. Dept., e.,f.	23May1!
Director-General, Army Veterinary Service	Maj.-Gen. (*hon.*) R. Pringle, C.B., D.S.O., A.V.S. (16, *Victoria St., S.W.*)	15Oct.1(
Asst. Director-General	Maj. A. G. Todd, A.V.C.	1Apr.14
Inspector of the Army Service Corps	Col. (*temp. Brig.-Gen.*) T. D. Foster, C.B., M.V.O., e. (*Horse Guards, S.W.*)	15Aug.1!
Inspector of Army Ordnance Services	Col. (*temp. Brig.-Gen.*) R. T. H. Law, A. Ord. Dept. (*Horse Guards, S.W.*)	1Apr.1!

(11)

War Office—*(continued).*

DEPARTMENT
OF THE
MASTER-GENERAL OF THE ORDNANCE.

Master-General of the Ordnance	COL.(*local and temp.Maj.-Gen.*) Sir S.B.VON DONOP, K.C.B., *g*...	8Feb.13
Private Secretary	A. Earl, *Esq.*	
Director of Artillery	Col. (*temp. Brig.-Gen.*) H. G. Smith, *C.B., g.*	25 Mar.13
Assistant Directors	Col. C. S. Meeres, *p.a.c.* Col. T. E. Carte Col. *Hon.* F. R. Bingham	21Oct.12 6Dec.12 3Sept.13
Deputy Assistant Director	Maj. H. J. A. Banks, *D.S.O.*, A, Ord. Dept., *o.*	28Dec.11
Staff Captains	Maj. H. E. T. Kelly, R.A., *g.* Capt. A. C. S. Ward-Simpson, R.A., *p.a.c.* Capt. E. F. Creswell, R.A., *g*... Capt. C. E. T. Rolland, R.A., *p.a.c.*	19Feb.12 1Apr.12 10Aug.12 1Apr.14 30Nov.10
Director of Fortifications and Works	Maj.-Gen. G. K. Scott-Moncrieff, *C.B., C.I.E.*	7Sept.11
Assistant Directors	Col. A. M. Stuart. Col. E. H. Hemming Col. W. R. Stewart	10Sept.10 1Oct.12 12Jan.16
Inspector of Electric Lights	Maj. A. H. Dumaresq, R.E.	6Sept.12
Inspector of Iron Structures (*graded as Staff Captain*)	Capt. R. Oakes, R.E.	1Oct.13
Staff Captains	Maj. R. L. B. Thompson, R.E. Capt. A. L. C. Neame, R.E. Maj. B. H. O. Armstrong, R.E. Capt. J. J. H. Nation, R.E. Capt. M. St. L. Simon, R.E. Maj. R. H. Lewis, R.E. Capt. G. L. Hall, R.E. Capt. C. W. Biggs, R.E.	7Sept.10 1Feb.11 1Apr.11 1July11 29July11 25July13 1Sept.13 1Oct.13
Director of Barrack Construction	H. B. Measures, *Esq., M.V.O., F.R.I.B.A.*, 80, *Pall Mall, S.W.*	1July04
Assistant Director (Surveyor)	T. Ivor-Moore, *Esq., F.S.I., A.I.E.E., Assoc. M. Inst. C.E.*	20Mar.05
Assistant Directors (Architects)	C. W. Maplesden, *Esq.* S. S. Reay, *Esq., F.R.I.B.A.*	1Apr.09 1Sept.12
Chief Technical Examiner for Works Services	Col. S. Davidson (54 *Victoria St., S.W.*)	9July13
Technical Examiner	Hon. Maj. A. Gregory, *F.S.I.*	1Oct.13

DEPARTMENT

OF THE

CIVIL MEMBER OF THE ARMY COUNCIL.

Parliamentary Under-Secretary of State for War (Civil Member) } *The Rt. Hon.* H. J. TENNANT, *M.P.*

    Private Secretary .. .. .. W. H. Schlich, *Esq.*

    Parliamentary Private Secretary .. J. I. Macpherson, *Esq., M.P.* (*unpaid*).

Director General of the Territorial Force } Lt.-Gen. E. C. Bethune, *C.V.O., C.B.,* Col. 4 D.G., *p.s.c.* .. 3 June 12

    Assistant Directors ... ... { Col. E. Satterthwaite, *C.B.,* VD, Unattd. List (T.F.) .. 23 Feb.12
Col. E. St. G. Pratt, *D.S.O., p.s.c.* [J] .. .. .. 28 July 13

    Assistant Principal .. .. G. K. King, *Esq., M.V.O.*

    Staff Captain .. .. .. Capt. R. F Riley, *D.S.O.,* Yorks. L.I., *p.s.c.* .. .. { 3 Jan.12
1 Dec.10

Comptroller of Lands .. .. E. H. Coles *Esq.*

    Assistant Principal .. .. H. E. Davies, *Esq.*

    Land Agent and Valuer .. .. H. C. Cole, *Esq., F.S.I.*

Non-effective Votes .. .. *Administered through the Assistant Financial Secretary.*

War Office—*(continued)*.

DEPARTMENT

OF THE

FINANCE MEMBER OF THE ARMY COUNCIL.

Financial Secretary (Finance Member) } H. T. BAKER, *Esq., M.P.*

    Private Secretary .. .. J. A. Dale, *Esq.*

Assistant Financial Secretary .. .. Sir C. Harris, *K.C.B.*

    Private Secretary .. .. .. F. C. Bovenschen, *Esq.*

Director of Army Accounts.   Director of Financial Services.
J. A. Flynn, *Esq., C.B.*   W. P. Perry, *Esq., C.B.*

PRINCIPALS.

G. P. Wight, *Esq.*
J. M. Bull, *Esq.*
J. G. Ashley, *Esq.*
W. A. Bland, *Esq.*
J. A. Corcoran, *Esq.*
S. Dannreuther, *Esq.*

Assistant Principals.

A. F. Major, *Esq.*
J. B. Crosland, *Esq.*
R. J. G. C. Paterson, *Esq.*
B. E. Holloway, *Esq.*
A. E. Widdows, *Esq., C.B.*
. T. Clark, *Esq.*

CHIEF PAYMASTER.

Col. J. T. Carter, A.P. Dept.

CHIEF ACCOUNTANTS.

J. S. Ross, *Esq.*
H. J. Edwards, *Esq., I.S.O.*
C. W. Cooper, *Esq. (acting*

Accountants.

J. M. Spaight, *Esq.*
R. N. Bradley, *Esq.*
W. Round, *Esq. (acting).*

Director of Contracts .. .. .. H. D. De la Bère, *Esq., C.B.*
    Assistant Director of Contracts N. F. B. Osborn, *Esq.*

    Assistant Principals .. .. { B. M. Draper, *Esq.*
                                 { E. J. Riley, *Esq.*

DEPARTMENT

OF THE

SECRETARY OF THE WAR OFFICE.

Secretary ... ... *Sir* R. H. BRADE, *K.C.B.*

Private Secretaries .. { H. C. Gordon, *Esq.*
E. B. Charteris, *Esq.*, (*unpaid*).

Assistant Secretary of the War Office.
B. B. Cubitt, *Esq.*, *C.B.*

PRINCIPALS .. .. .. { H. H. Fawcett, *Esq.*
H. W. W. McAnally, *Esq.*
A. C. Pedley, *Esq.*, *I.S.O.*

Assistant Principals .. { A. C. Strange, *Esq.*
L. D. Holland, *Esq.*
E. V. Fleming, *Esq.*
C. F. Watherston, *Esq.*
A. E. Turner, *Esq.* (*Attached to the Dir.-Gen. of Military Aeronautics*).
H. J. Creedy, *Esq.*, *M.V.O.*
B. R. T. Grindle, *Esq.* (*acting*).

CHAPLAIN GENERAL

Rt. Rev. Bishop J. Taylor Smith, *C.V.O., D.D.* .. .. 1 Nov. 01

JUDGE ADVOCATE GENERAL

Sir T. Milvain, *Knt., C.B., K.C.* (68, *Victoria Street, S.W.* .. .. 1 Aug. 05

Deputy Judge-Advocate.

J. G. S. Mellor, *Esq.* .. .. 11 Oct. 11

(**15**)

War Office—(*continued*).

DIRECTOR-GENERAL OF MILITARY AERONAUTICS.

Director-General of Military Aeronautics	Col. (*temp. Brig.-Gen.*) *Sir* D. Henderson, *K.C.B.*, *D.S.O.*, *p.s.c.*, *f.c.r.*	18Sept.13 1July12
Assistant Director	Col. W. MacAdam	25Sept.13
General Staff Officer, 2nd grade..	Maj. W. S. Brancker, R.A., *p.s.c.*, *f.c.r.*	3Oct.13 1Apr.13
General Staff Officers, 3rd grade	Capt. W. G. H. Salmond, R.A., *p.s.c.* [*l*] *f.c.r.* .. Maj. B. D. Fisher, 17 Lrs., *p.s.c.*	3l July13 1Oct.13
Staff Captain	Capt. J. T. Dreyer, R.A.	7July13

Attached from Secretary's Department.

Assistant Principal .. .. .. A. E. Turner, *Esq.*

INSPECTOR-GENERAL OF THE HOME FORCES.

(Horse Guards, S.W.)

Private Secretary

Aides-de-Camp

Staff Officer to the Inspr.-Gen. of the Home Forces (Brig.- Gen., Gen. Staff) — Col. *(temp. Brig.-Gen.)* J. P. Du Cane, *C.B.* .. 1July12

Inspector of Cavalry	Maj.-Gen. E. H. H. Allenby, *C.B.*, Col. 5 Lrs., *p.s.c.* [L]	25Apr.10
Inspector of Royal Horse and Royal Field Artillery	Col. *(temp. Brig.-Gen.)* H. S. Horne, *C.B.*	1May12
Staff Captain..	Capt. C. R, Woodroffe, R.A. [*l*]	29Jan.14
Inspector of Royal Garrison Artillery	Col. *(temp. Brig.-Gen.)* E. G. Nicolls, *C.B., g…*	1Mar.13
Staff Captain..	Lt. K. F. Dunsterville, R.A., *g.*	18June14
Inspector of Royal Engineers	Col. *(temp. Brig.-Gen.)* G. H. Fowke	1Apr.13
Inspector of Infantry	Maj.-Gen. T. Capper, *C.B., D.S.O., p.s.c,*	1Feb.14

INSPECTOR-GENERAL OF THE OVERSEA FORCES.

Assistant Military Secretary

Aide-de-Camp

Staff Officer to the Inspr.-Gen. of the Oversea Forces (Brig.- Gen., Gen. Staff) — Col. *(temp. Brig.-Gen.)* G. F. Ellison, *C.B., p.s c.* .. 1June11

MILITARY ATTACHÉS TO EMBASSIES AND LEGATIONS AT FOREIGN COURTS.

(General Staff Officers.)

Russell, Maj. *(temp. Lt.-Col.)* Hon. A. V. F., *M.V.O.*, G. Gds., p.s.c. [L]	{ Berlin / Stockholm }	20Mar.10
Somerville, Maj. *(temp. Lt.-Col.)* J. A. C., R. Suss. R. [*l*]	Tokyo	10Feb.11
Granet, Col. E. J., *C.B.*, p.s.c. [L]	{ Rome / Berne }	23Feb.11
Grogan, Maj. *(temp. Lt.-Col.)* Sir E. I. B., *Bt.*, Rif. Brig., p.s.c. [L]	{ Buenos Ayres / Rio de Janeiro / Santiago / Lima / Monte Video / Asuncion }	3Mar.11
Knox, Maj. *(temp. Lt.-Col.)* A. W. F., 58 Rif., p.s.c. [L]	St. Petersburg	3May11
Robertson, Capt. *(temp. Maj.)* D. S., R. Sc. Fus., p.s.c. [L]	Peking	9 Feb.12
Yarde-Buller, Col. *Hon.* H., *M.V.O.*, *D.S.O.*, p.s.c. [*l*]	{ Paris / Madrid / Lisbon }	29June12
Gage, Maj. *(temp. Lt.-Col.)* M. F. 5 D.G., p.s.c.	{ Washington / Mexico }	12July12
Cuninghame, Capt. *(temp. Maj.)* Sir T. A. A. M., *Bt.*, *D.S.O.*, Rif. Brig., p.s.c.	{ Vienna / Cettinje }	2Aug.12
FitzGerald, Maj. O. A. G., 18 Lrs., p.s.c.	Cairo	19Sept.12
Plunkett, Maj. *(temp. Lt.-Col.)* E.A., Linc. R., p.s.c. [L]	{ Bucharest / Sofia / Belgrade / Athens }	15Aug.13
Cunliffe Owen, Maj. *(temp. Lt.-Col.)* F., R.A., p.s.c. [L]	Constantinople	26Nov.13
Steel, Maj. R. A., 17 Cav., p.s.c. [*l*]	Tehran	3Dec.13
Fairholme, Col. W. E., *C.M.G.*, *M.V.O.*, p.s.c. [L]	{ Brussels / The Hague / Copenhagen / Christiania }	10Mar.14
Calthorp, Maj. E. F., R.A., p.s.c. [L]	Tokyo	—

COMMANDS OF THE ARMY (UNITED KINGDOM).
(Arranged alphabetically.)

ALDERSHOT COMMAND. From the Railway Station at Liss, north-eastward along the South-Western Railway (but omitting the three small Portions of Sussex lying to the north of the railway, and the portions of the parishes of Artington, St. Nicholas and Stoke-next-Guildford to the west of the railway), through Woking to the Eastern boundary of Woking Parish, thence northward following the eastern boundaries of the Parishes of Woking, Horsell and Chobham to the Wokingham and Reading Railway, thence westward along that railway as far as the River Loddon ; thence southwards along the River Loddon and the road leading from Reading to Liss Railway Station, through Odiham, Alton, Alton Butts and Selbourne ; but inclusive also of the portions of the Parishes of Alton and Chawton lying west of that road.

Head-Quarters—Aldershot.

GENERAL OFFICER COMMAND-ING-IN-CHIEF	Haig, Lt.-Gen. *Sir* D., K.C.B., K.C.I.E., K.C.V.O., Col. 17 Lrs.,*p.s.c.*, 亞,旦,℃.	1Mar.12
Assistant Military Secretary	Charteris, Capt. J., R.E., *p.s.c.*,	1Mar.12
Aide-de-Camp	Baird, Capt. H. B. D., 12 Cav., *p.s.c.*	1Mar.12
General Staff.		
Brigadier-General	旦℃,Gough,Col.(*temp.Brig.-Gen.*) J. E.,C.M.G.,*p.s.c.*,A.D.C.	9Oct.13
General Staff Officer, 2nd grade		
General Staff Officer, 3rd grade	Hinde, Maj. A., R.A. *p.s.c.*	1Oct.13
Attached to the General Staff.		
Major, graded as Brigade-Major	Festing, Capt. F. L., North'd Fus.	1Oct.12
Administrative, Technical and Departmental Staff.		
Major-General in charge of Administration	Hamilton Gordon, Maj.-Gen. A., C.B., *p.s.c.*	1July14
Dep. Asst. Adjt.-Gen.	Clarke, Maj. T. E., R. Innis. Fus.	1Jan.12
Asst. Qr.-Mr.-Gen.	Marker, Lt.-Col. R. J., D.S.O., *p.s.c.*, *q.s.*	29Nov.13
Dep. Asst. Qr.-Mr.-Gen.	Harding Newman, Capt. J. C., Essex R., *p.s.c.*	{ 23Nov.11 / 8Nov.10
Staff Officer for R.H. & F.A.	Drake, Col. B. F.	3May12
Chief Engineer	Fell, Col. (*temp. Brig.-Gen.*) S. R., C.B.	8Sept.11
Staff Officer, Royal Engineers	Grubb, Maj. A. H. W., D.S.O., R.E.	
Asst. Dir. of Supplies and Transport	Sargent, Col. H. N., D.S.O.	15Dec.13
Dep. Asst. Dir. of Supplies and Transport	Young, Maj. J. M., A.S.C., *e.*	1Jan.14
Dep. Dir. of Medical Services	Woodhouse, Surg.-Gen. T. P.	
Dep.-Asst. Dir. of Medical Services	Fell, Maj. M. H. G., R.A.M.C.	
Asst. Dir. of Veterinary Services	Moore, Col. J., F.R.C.V.S.	
Asst. Director of Ordnance Stores	Perry, Col. H. W., A. Ord. Dept.	
Command Paymaster	Gaussen, Col. J. S., A. P. Dept.	
Deputy Assistant Director of Remounts	McLaughlin, Lt.-Col. H. J., D.S.O., Res. of Off.	{ 1Apr.14 / 27Apr.05
District Barrack Officer	Lynn, Bt.·Col. S. H., ret. pay.	

Department of the Finance Member of the Army Council
(*detached from the War Office for duty at Head-Quarters of the Command*),

Local Auditor	King, J. A., *Esq.*
Assistant Local Auditor	Edwards, J. A., *Esq.*

At Aldershot.
Chief Ordnance Officer .. .. Watts, Lt.-Col. C. D. R., A. Ord. Dept., *e., f.*

At Bordon.
Asst. Dir. of Medical Services .. Cree, Lt.-Col. G., R.A.M.C.
Garrison Adjutant(graded Staff Capt.) Savile, Capt. L. W., R.A. 1Apr.12

Army Service Corps.	Army Service Corps—contd.	Army Service Corps—contd.	Army Veterinary Corps.
1 Transpt. Depôt Co.	31 Co.	60 (M.T.) Co.	
7 Co.	35 Co.	61 (M.T.) Co.	
9 Co.	36 Co.	"A" (Depôt) Co.	1 and 2 Sections.
10 Co.	52 (M.T.) Depôt Co.	"C" Co.	
13 Co. (*Bordon*).	53 (M.T.) Co.	Royal Army Medical Corps.	
16 Co.	54 (M.T.) Co.	1 Co.	Army Ordnance Corps.
20 Co.	57 (M.T.) Co.	2 Co.	
26 Co.	58 (M.T.) Co.	5 Co.	
27 Co.	59 (M.T.) Co.	"A" "B" and "C" Cos. (Depôt)	1 and 4 Cos.
28 Co.			

(18)

Commands (United Kingdom).

Aldershot Command—contd.

FIELD TROOPS (REGULARS).

1st CAVALRY BRIGADE. *Aldershot.*

Brigade Commander	Briggs, Col. *(temp. Brig.-Gen.)* C. J., C.B.	11May13
Brigade-Major	Cawley, Maj. J. S., 20 Hrs., p.s.c. [*l*]	16Apr.13

2 D.G.   5 D.G.   11 Hrs.   1 Signal Troop R.E.

Attached:—
IV. Brig., R.H.A., "J" Batt.
VII. Brig., R.H.A. { "I" Batt. }   1 Fd. Squadron R.E.
{ "L" Batt. }

1st DIVISION. *Aldershot.*

General Officer Commanding	Lomax, Maj.-Gen. S. H., *p.s.c.*	7Aug.10
Aide-de-Camp	Giffard, Lt. R., R.A.	7Aug.10
General Staff Officer, 1st grade	Fanshawe, Col. R., *D.S.O., p.s.c.* [*l*]	25Oct.11
Dep. Asst. Adjt. and Qr.-Mr.-Gen.	Gordon, Maj. A. F., *D.S.O.*, Gord. Highrs., *p.s.c.*	{ 21Jan.14 / 6June13 }

1st Infantry Brigade. *Aldershot.*

Brigade Commander	Maxse, Col. *(temp. Brig.-Gen.)* F. I., *C.V.O., C.B., D.S.O., q.s.* [L]	1Aug.10
Brigade-Major	Corkran, Maj. C. E., G. Gds., *p.s.c.*	1Oct.11

1 Bn. C. Gds.   1 Bn. R. Highrs.
1 Bn. S. Gds.   2 Bn. R. Muns. Fus.

2nd Infantry Brigade. *Blackdown.*

Brigade Commander	Bulfin, Col. *(temp. Brig.-Gen.)* E. S., *C.V.O., C.B., q s.*	{ 30June13 / 1June11 }
Brigade-Major	Cooke, Maj. B. H. H., Rif. Brig., *p.s.c.* [L]	{ 1Jan.14 / 1Nov.11 }

2 Bn. R. Suss. R. *(Woking)*.   1 Bn. North'n R. *(Blackdown)*.
1 Bn. N. Lan. R. *(Aldershot)*.   2 Bn. K. R. Rif. C. *(Blackdown)*.

3rd Infantry Brigade *Bordon.*

Brigade Commander	Landon, Col. *(temp. Brig.-Gen.)* H. J. S., *C.B.*	7Aug.10
Brigade-Major	Jenkinson, Capt. J. B., Rif. Brig., *p.s.c.*	{ 2Apr.13 / 1Oct.12 }

1 Bn. R. W. Surr. R.   1 Bn. Glouc. R.
1 Bn. S. Wales Bord.   2 Bn. Welsh R.

Divisional Troops.
Royal Artillery. *Aldershot.*

Commanding Royal Artillery	Findlay, Col. *(temp. Brig.-Gen.)* N. D., *C.B., p.s.c.* [*l*]	14July10
Brigade Major	Street, Maj. H. E., R.A., *p.s.c.*	1Dec.13

XXV. Brig. R.F.A. { 113 Batt. / 114 Batt. / 115 Batt. } *(Deepcut)*.   XXXIX. Brig. R.F.A. { 46 Batt. / 51 Batt. / 54 Batt. } *(Bordon)*.

XXVI. Brig. R.F.A. { 116 Batt. / 117 Batt. / 118 Batt. } *(Aldershot)*.   XLIII. (Howr.) Brig. R.F.A. { 30 Batt. / 40 Batt. / 57 Batt. } *(Deepcut)*.

For Heavy Battery, R.G.A. *see* Southern Command, page 48.

Royal Engineers. *Aldershot.*

Commanding Royal Engineers	Schreiber, Lt.-Col. A. L., *D.S.O.*, R.E.

23 Fd. Co. *(Aldershot)*.   1 Signal Co. *(Aldershot)*.
26 Fd. Co. *(Bordon)*.

[Continued on page 19]

(19)
Commands of the Army.

Aldershot Command—contd.

2nd DIVISION. *Aldershot.*

General Officer Commanding	.. .. Murray, Maj.-Gen. *Sir* A. J., *K.C.B., C.V.O., D.S.O., p.s.c.* [*l*]	1Feb.14
Aide-de-Camp	.. .. Rothwell, Capt. W. E., R. Innis. F.	1Feb.14
General Staff Officer, 1st grade	.. .. Gordon, Col. *Hon.* F., *D.S.O., p.s.c.*	10Aug.11
Dep. Asst. Adjt. and Qr.-Mr.-Gen. ..	.. White, Bt. Lt.-Col. W. A., Conn. Rang., *p.s.c.* [*l*] ..	23Jan;11

For 4th Infantry Brigade, see London District, page 32.

5th Infantry Brigade. *Aldershot.*

Brigade Commander	.. .. Haking, Col. (*temp. Brig.-Gen.*) R. C. B., *C.B., p.s.c.*	28Sept.11
Brigade-Major	.. .. Gilkison, Capt. D. S., Sco. Rif., *p.s.c.*	{ 1Aug.13 29Apr.12

| 2 Bn. Worc. R. | 2 Bn. High. L.I. |
| 2 Bn. Oxf. & Bucks. L.I. | 2 Bn. Conn. Rang. |

6th Infantry Brigade. *Aldershot.*

Brigade Commander	.. .. Davies, Col. (*temp. Brig.-Gen. in Army*) R. H., *C.B.,* N. Z. Staff Corps	16Oct.10
Brigade-Major	.. .. Maxwell-Scott, Capt. W. J., Sco. Rif., *p.s.c.* .. {	1Dec.13 16Oct.11

| 1 Bn. L'pool R. | 1 Bn. R. Berks. R. |
| 2 Bn. S. Staff. R. | 1 Bn. K. R. Rif. C. |

Divisional Troops.
Royal Artillery. *Aldershot.*

Commanding Royal Artillery	.. .. Perceval, Col. (*temp. Brig.-Gen.*) E. M., *D.S.O., p.s.c.*	1Apr.14
Brigade Major	.. .. Chenevix-Trench, Capt. F. M., R.A., *p.s.c.* [L] ..	1Aug.13

XXXIV. Brig., R.F.A. ..{ 22 Batt.
50 Batt.
70 Batt. }(*Aldershot*). XLI. Brig., R.F.A. .. { 9 Batt.
16 Batt.
17 Batt. } (*Bordon*).

XXXVI. Brig., R.F.A. ..{ 15 Batt.
48 Batt.
71 Batt. }(*Ewshott*,) For Howitzer Brigade, see Eastern Command, page 23.
For Heavy Battery R.G.A., see Southern Command. page 48.

Royal Engineers. *Aldershot.*

Commanding Royal Engineers .. .. Boys, Lt.-Col. R. H. H., *D.S.O.*, R.E.

| 5 Fd. Co. | 11 Fd. Co. | 2 Signal Co. |

ARMY TROOPS.
Royal Engineers.

| "A" Signal Co. | 1 Bridging Train. |

Royal Flying Corps (Military Wing).

Hd.-Qrs.
Airship Detachment.
Kite Section.
1, 5, 6 & 7 Squadrons.
Aircraft Park. } (*South Farnboroguh*).

OTHER TROOPS IN THE COMMAND.

Cavalry.	Royal Engineers.	Infantry.
Regular Troops.	*Regular Troops.*	*Regular Troops.*
15 Hrs. (*Longmoor*).	Training Depôt for Field Units.	Mil. Foot Police (Hd.-Qrs.)
Mil. Mtd. Police Hd.-Qrs.	8 Co. (Ry.) (*Longmoor, East Liss*).	
	10 Co. (Ry.) (*Longmoor, East Liss*).	
	1 Signal Squadron (*Longmoor, East Liss*).	

(20)

Commands (United Kingdom).

Aldershot Command—contd.

SCHOOLS OF INSTRUCTION, ETC.

Inspector of Gymnasia	Couper, Col. V. A.		1Apr.10
Assistant Inspector of Gymnasia	Wright, Maj. W. C., North'd Fus.		{ 23Apr.12 10Dec.11
Instructor	de Joux, Capt. J. S. N., S. Staff. R. [L]		15Apr.13
Master-at-Arms	Betts, Hon. Lt. J., Qr.-Mr.		3Apr.07

Army Signal School—

Commandant	Fowler, Lt.-Col. J. S., *D.S.O.*, R.E., p.s.c. [l]		Apr.13
Chief Instructor	Newbigging, Maj. W. P. E., *D.S.O.*, Manch. R.		{ 3July12 16Apr.12
Instructors	French, Maj. A. H., R. Mar.		5Sept.12
	Smith, Capt. H. C., R.E.		1Feb.13
	Frost, Capt. O. M, T., Dorset R.		3Feb.13
	Salmond, Capt. H. A. B., York. & Lanc. R.		7Apr.13
	Powell, Capt. R. M., R.A.		1May1

Royal Army Medical Corps Training Establishment—

Commandant (and O.C. Depôt, R.A.M.C.)	Sutton, Lt.-Col. A. A., *D.S.O.*, R.A.M.C.		20Sept.13
Instructor, Training School	Morgan, Maj. C. K., *M.B.*, R.A.M.C.		29Oct.10
Assistant Instructor, Training School	Wright, Capt. T. J., R.A.M.C.		15June12

School of Army Sanitation—

Instructor (and Sanitary Officer, Aldershot Comd., ex-officio)	Fawcus, Maj. H. B., *M.B.*, R.A.M.C.		1Mar.1
Assistant Instructor (and Assistant Sanitary Officer, Aldershot Comd.)	Smallman, Maj. A. B., *M.D.*, R.A.M.C. [l]		3Mar.1

Army Veterinary School—

Commandant	Martin, Maj. E. E.. *F.R.C.V.S.*, A.V.C.		1Apr.14
Instructor	McKenzie, Capt. K. McL., A.V.C.		—

Camp Quarter-Master	Dixon, Hon. Maj. C. J., Qr.-Mr.		19Jan.07
Quarter-Master	Crook, Hon. Lt. A., Qr.-Mr. (*Supdt., Fire Brigade*)		11Oct.05
Provost Marshal (graded Staff Capt.)	Terry, Maj. R. J. A., *M.V.O.*, R. Suss. R. (*Comdt., Corps of Mtd. Police*)		8Nov.10
Assistant Provost Marshal	Gale, Hon. Lt. A. W., Qr.-Mr. Mil. Police Corps		{ 29May06 16Nov.04

(21)

Commands of the Army.

EASTERN COMMAND.—The Counties of Northamptonshire, Cambridgeshire, Norfolk, Suffolk, Essex (except Purfleet and Rainham Rifle Range), Huntingdonshire, Bedfordshire, Hertfordshire, Middlesex, Kent, Surrey (except the portion included in the Aldershot Command), Sussex and Woolwich (exclusive of the Territorial Troops quartered therein).

Head-Quarters.—Horse Guards, Whitehall, S.W.

GENERAL OFFICER COMMANDING-IN-CHIEF	Grierson, Lt.-Gen. *Sir* J. M., *K.C.B , C.V.O., C.M.G.,* p.s.c. [L] 𝔄.𝔅.ℭ.	4Apr.12
Assistant Military Secretary	Fraser, Maj. H. F., 21 Lrs., *e.*	4Apr.12
Aide-de-Camp	Banbury, Capt. C. W., C. Gds.	4Apr.12

General Staff.

Brigadier-General	Fortescue, Col., *(temp. Brig.-Gen.) Hon.* C. G.,*C.B.,C.M.G., D.S.O., p.s.c.*	28Apr.12
General Staff Officer, 2nd grade	𝔈ℭReed, Bt. Lt.-Col. H. L., R.A., *p.s.c.* [l]	20Sept.13
General Staff Officer, 3rd grade	Walcot, Capt. B., R.E., *p.s c.*	20May13
Attached to the General Staff.		
Captain, graded as Brigade-Major	Humphreys, Capt. E. T., Lan. Fus., *p.s.c.* [l]	27Sept.11

Administrative, Technical and Departmental Staff

Major-General in charge of Administration	Adye, Maj.-Gen. J., *C.B., p.s.c.*	1Oct.12
Asst. Adjt.-Gen.	Hamilton, Col. L. A. H., *p.s.c.*	8Sept.13
Asst. Qr.-Mr.-Gen.	Wanless-O'Gowan, Col. R.	27Apr.14
Staff Captain	Alexander, Capt. H. L., Dorset R.,*p.s.c.*	10Nov.11
Chief Engineer	Anderson, Col. *(temp. Brig.-Gen.)* F. J...	12Jan.13
Staff Officer, Royal Engineers	Hammond, Capt. F. D., R.E.	
Asst. Director of Supplies and Transport.	Boyce, Col. W. G. B., *D.S.O.*	Dec.13
Dep. Asst. Director of Supplies and Transport	James, Maj. M. R. de B., A.S.C.	1Nov.10
Dep. Dir. of Medical Services	Whitehead, Surg.-Gen. H. R., *C.B., F.R.C.S.*	
Dep.-Asst. Dir. of Med. Services	Shanahan, Lt.-Col. D. D., R.A.M.C.	
Asst. Dir. of Veterinary Services	Butler, Col. E. R. C., *F.R.C.V.S.*	
Asst. Director of Ordnance Stores	Wrigley, Lt.-Col. C. C., A. Ord. Dept.,*p.a.c.*	
Command Paymaster	Smith, Col. G. B., A. P. Dept. (2, *Duke Street, Adelphi, W.C.*	
Dep. Asst. Dirs. of Remounts ⎧ No. 1 Circle	Richardson, Maj. F. J., *D.S.O.,* 4 Bn. Arg. & Suth'd Highrs., Capt. ret. pay *(Res. of Off.)*	31July11
⎨ No. 2 Circle	Matcham, Capt. W. E., *D.S.O.,* ret. pay *(Res. of Off.)*	10Apr.12
⎩ No. 3 Circle	Adye, Col. W., *C.B.,* ret. pay, *p.s.c.*	1Apr.14
District Barrack Officer	Wyncoll, Bt. Col. C. E., ret. pay.	

Department of the Finance Member of the Army Council
(detached from the War Office for duty at Head-Quarters of the Command).

Local Auditor	Beavis, A. B., *Esq.*	
Assistant Local Auditor	Piper, G., *Esq*	

Officer in charge of Time-Expired Men, etc.†	Grattan, Bt. Col. O'D. C., *D.S.O.,* ret. pay *(Holm Lodge, Lexden, Colchester.)*	

At Woolwich.

Garrison Adjutant (graded Staff Capt.)	Cavendish, Capt. H. C., R.A.	1Feb.14
Asst. Dir. of Medical Services	Faunce, Col. C, E.	
Senior Veterinary Officer	Williams, Maj. G. M., A.V. C.	
Chief Ordnance Officer	Harter, Maj. O. B., A. Ord. Dept., *p.a.c.*	

At Dover.

Garrison Adjutant (graded Staff Capt.)	Gordon, Maj. W. F. L., Norf. R.	16July12
Asst. Dir. of Medical Services	Birrell, Col. W. G., *M.B.*	
Chief Ordnance Officer	Oldfield, Maj. A. R., A. Ord. Dept., *o.*	

At Colchester.

Garrison Adjutant (graded Staff Capt.)	Commings, Capt. P. R. C., S. Staff. R.	22Jan,11
Asst. Dir. of Medical Services	Jencken, Col. F. J., *M.B*	
Chief Ordnance Officer	Stewart, Maj. J. A., A. Ord. Dept., *o.*	

At Chatham.

Asst. Dir. of Medical Services	Reilly, Col. C. C.	
Chief Ordnance Officer	Bainbridge, Maj. N. B., *D.S.O.,* A. Ord. Dept., *o.*	

At Shorncliffe.

Garrison Adjutant (graded Staff Capt.)	Stewart, Maj. A. F., Midd'x R.	1Apr.12

At Canterbury.

Garrison Adjutant	Norman, Capt. E. C., E. Kent. R.	17Oct.12

† Deals also with Recruits enlisted in the Aldershot Command.

(22)

Commands (United Kingdom).

Eastern Command—contd.

Army Service Corps.

2 (Depôt) Co. (*Woolwich*).
5 Co. (*Woolwich*).
14 Co. (*Woolwich*).
25 Co. (*Woolwich*).
32 Co. (*Shorncliffe*).
38 Co. (*Dover*).
46 (M.T.) Co. (*Woolwich*).
47 (M.T.) Co. (*Woolwich*).
65 (M.T.) Co. (*Chatham*).
"AA" Co. (*Woolwich*).
"E" Co. (*Woolwich*).

Royal Army Medical Corps.

9 Co. (*Colchester*).
10 Co. (*Chatham*).
11 Co. (*Shorncliffe*).
12 Co. (*Woolwich*).
34 Co. (*Woolwich*).

Army Veterinary Corps.

3 & 4 Sections (*Woolwich*)
11 Section (*Colchester*).
Det. (*Shorncliffe*).

Army Ordnance Corps.

6 Co. { Chatham Section.
       Colchester Section.
       Dover Section.

7 & 8 Cos. (Woolwich Depôt).

FIELD TROOPS (REGULARS).

4th CAVALRY BRIGADE. *Canterbury.*

Brigade Commander	.. Bingham, Col. (*temp. Brtg.-Gen.*) Hon. C. E., *C.V.O.*, *C.B.* ..	11Nov.10
Brigade-Major	.. Durand, Maj. H. M., 9 Lrs., *p.s.c.* ..	1Feb.13

3 Hrs. (*Shorncliffe*). 6 D.G. (*Canterbury*). 4 Signal Troop R.E. (*Canterbury*).

For Composite Regiment of Household Cavalry, *see* London District, page 32.

Attached:—
19 Hrs. (*Hounslow*).
X. Brig., R.H.A. { "P" Batt. } (*Woolwich*).
                 { "R" Batt. }
II. Brig., R.H.A. "C" Batt. (*Canterbury*).

Special Reserve.
King Edward's Horse (*London*).

4th DIVISION. *Woolwich.*

General Officer Commanding	.. Snow, Maj.-Gen. T. D'O., *C.B.*, *p.s.c.*	.. 12May11
Aide-de-Camp	.. Allfrey, Capt. H. I. R., Som. L.I.	.. 12May11
General Staff Officer, 1st grade	.. Edmonds, Col. J. E., *C.B.*, *p.s.c.* [L]	.. 1Mar.11
Dep. Asst. Adjt. and Qr.-Mr.-Gen.	.. Burnett-Hitchcock, Capt. B. F., Notts. & Derby. R. *p.s.c.* [L]	{ 27Mar.12 { 25Nov.10

10th Infantry Brigade. *Shorncliffe.*

Brigade Commander	.. Haldane, Col. (*temp. Brig.-Gen.*) J. A. L., *C.B.*, *D.S.O.*, *p.s.c.* [*l*]	28Apr.12
Brigade-Major	.. Wilson, Maj. A. H. H., Wilts. R., *p.s.c.* [*l*]	.. 26Jan.11

1 Bn. R. War. R. (*Shorncliffe*). | 1 Bn. R. Ir. Fus. (*Shorncliffe*).
2 Bn. Sea. Highrs. (*Shorncliffe*). | 2 Bn. R. Dub. Fus. (*Gravesend*).

11th Infantry Brigade. *Colchester.*

Brigade Commander	.. Hunter-Weston, Col. (*temp. Brig.-Gen.*) A.G., *C.B.*,*D.S.O.*, *p.s.c.* [L]..	1Feb.14
Brigade-Major	.. Boyd, Capt. G. F., *D.S.O.*, Leins. R., *p.s.c.*	21Sept.12

1 Bn. Som. L. I. | 1 Bn. Hamps. R.
1 Bn. E. Lan. R. | 1 Bn. Rif. Brig.

12th Infantry Brigade. *Dover.*

Brigade Commander	.. Wilson, Col. (*temp. Brig.-Gen.*) H. F. M., *C.B.*	.. 7June12
Brigade-Major	.. Davies, Capt. C. M., Rif. Brig., *p.s.c.*	.. 30Mar.12

1 Bn. R. Lanc. R. (*Dover*). | 2 Bn. R. Innis. Fus. (*Dover*).
2 Bn. Lan. Fus. (*Dover*). | 2 Bn. Essex R. (*Chatham*).

[*Continued on page* 23]

(23)

Commands of the Army.

Eastern Command—contd.
4th *Division*—contd.

Divisional Troops.
Royal Artillery.
Woolwich.

Commanding Royal Artillery	.. .. Milne, Col. temp. Brig.-Gen.) G. F., C.B., D.S.O., p.s.c. [l]		1Oct.13
Brigade Major	.. .. Leggett, Capt. E, H, G,, R.A., g.		{ 23July13 22Jan.11

| XIV, Brig., R.F.A. | ..{ 39 Batt.
68 Batt.
88 Batt. }(*Colchester*). | XXXII, Brig., R.F.A. | { 27 Batt.
134 Batt.
135 Batt. }(*Woolwich*). |
| XXIX, Brig., R.F.A. | ..{ 125 Batt.
126 Batt.
127 Batt. }(*Shorncliffe*). | XXXVII. (Howr.) Brig., R.F.A. | { 31 Batt.
35 Batt.
55 Batt. }(*Woolwich*). |

Heavy Battery R.G.A., shown under "Other Regular Field Units."

Royal Engineers.
Woolwich.

Commanding Royal Engineers.. .. Jones, Lt.-Col. H, B,, R.E.
7 Fd. Co. (*Shorncliffe*) | 4 Signal Co. (*Woolwich*) (*temp.*)
9 Fd. Co. (*Woolwich*),

5th CAVALRY BRIGADE (*part of*).
Lrs. (*Norwich*). | 20 Hrs. (*Colchester*).
Attached 5th Cavalry Brigade :—
V. Brig. R.H.A. .. ..{ "G" Batt.
"O" Batt. }(*Ipswich*).

2nd DIVISION (*part of*).
XLIV.(Howr.) Brig.,R.F.A.{ 47 Batt.
56 Batt.
60 Batt. }(*Brighton*).

OTHER REGULAR FIELD UNITS.
Royal Artillery.
XXXV. Brig. R.F.A. ..{ 12 Batt.
25 Batt.
58 Batt. }(*Woolwich*).

2 Heavy
Brig.,
R.G.A. { 24 Batt. (*part of 6th Div.*)
31 Batt. (*part of 4th Div.*)
48 Batt. (*part of 3rd Div.*) }(*Woolwich*).

Royal Engineers.
29 Works, L. of C. Co. (*Chatham*).
54 Co. (Fd.) (*Chatham*)
2 Bridging Train (*Chatham*).
1 Printing Co. (*Chatham*).

Infantry.
1 Bn. G. Gds. (*Warley*).
1 Bn. Midd'x R. (*Woolwich*).

COAST DEFENCES.
EASTERN COAST DEFENCES.
Defended ports of the Medway and the Thames (including Shoeburyness).

General Officer Commanding	Maxwell, Maj.-Gen. R. C., C.B. .. .. Chatham	17Dec.11
Aide-de-Camp	Maitland, Lt. R. C. F., R.A.	30Jan.12
General Staff Officer, 2nd grade	Pollard, Maj. J. H.-W., R. Sc. Fus., p.s.c, [l] ..	23Sept.11
Dep. Asst. Adjt. and Qr.-Mr.-Gen... ..	Clarke, Maj. J. L. J., E. York. R., p.s.c. ..	1June13
Chief Instructor in Gunnery	Mullins, Col. A. J., g.	{ 31May13 1Apr.13
Captain Instructor in Gunnery	Edmeades, Capt. W. A., R.A., g.	23Aug.12
Staff Captain, Royal Artillery	Barne, Capt. W. B. G., R.A., p.s.c.	5Feb.13
Chief Engineer	Jones, Col. L.	8May12
Staff Officer, Royal Engineers..	Robertson, Maj. W., R.E., p.s.c.	
Senior Medical Officer	Haines, Lt.-Col. H. A., M.D., R.A.M.C.	

Royal Garrison Artillery.
Regulars.
2, 18, 19 & 22 Cos. Sheerness).
14 Co. (*Shoeburyness*).

Territorial.
Essex and Suffolk (2 Cos.)
Kent (2 Cos,)

Royal Engineers.
Regulars.
39 Co. (Fortress) (*Sheerness*).

Territorial.
Kent (Fortress).

HARWICH COAST DEFENCES.
Defended port of Harwich.

Officer Commanding (*ex officio*) .. .. Buckle, Lt.-Col. (*local Col.*) C. R., D.S.O., R.G.A. Harwich.

General Staff Officer, 3rd grade .. .. Martin, Capt. G. H., K, R. Rif. C., p.s.c. 8Jan.13

Royal Garrison Artillery.
Regulars.
13 Co.

Territorial.
Essex and Suffolk (2 Cos.)

Royal Engineers'
Regulars.
21 Co. (Fortress).

Territorial.
Essex (Fortress).

Commands (United Kingdom).

Eastern Command— contd.

SOUTH EASTERN COAST DEFENCES.
Defended ports of Dover and Newhaven.

Officer Commanding	Crampton, Col. F. H... ... ... *Dover*	4Jan.14
General Staff Officer, 2nd grade	Marriott-Dodington, Maj. W., Oxf. & Bucks. L.I., *p.s.c.*	16July12
Captain Instructor in Gunnery	Beattie, Capt. M. A., R.A., *g.* [*l*]	1July 13
Senior Medical Officer	O'Callaghan, Lt.-Col. D. M., R.A.M.C.	

Royal Garrison Artillery.	Royal Engineers.
Regulars.	*Regulars.*
40 & 46 Cos.	3 Co. (Fortress).
Territorial.	*Territorial.*
Kent (1 Co.)	Sussex (Fortress).
Sussex (2 Cos.)	Cinque Ports (Fortress).

No. 9 DISTRICT.

Comprising the Counties of Norfolk, Cambridgeshire, Suffolk, Bedfordshire, Hertfordshire, Huntingdonshire, Essex, and Northamptonshire.

Officer Commanding	Travers, Col. J. H. du B. ... *Warley*	16May14
Staff Captain	Denne, Capt. W. H., Bedf. R.	1Apr.12

Regulars.	Special Reserve.
Royal Artillery.	*Infantry.*
4 Depôt, R.G.A. (*Great Yarmouth*).	3 Bn. Norf. R.
	3 Bn. Suff. R.
Infantry.	3 & 4 Bns. Bedf. R.
Depôts.	3 Bn. Essex R.
Norf. R. (*Norwich*).	3 Bn. North'n R.
Suff. R. (*Bury St. Edmunds*).	
Bedf. R. (*Bedford*).	
Essex R. (*Warley*).	
North'n R. (*Northampton*).	

No. 10 DISTRICT.

Comprising the Counties of Surrey, Kent, Middlesex, and Sussex, and Woolwich exclusive of Territorial troops.

Officer Commanding	O'Donnell, Col. H., *p.s.c.* ... *Hounslow*	14May14
Staff Captain	Miller, Capt. W., Midd'x R.	1Apr 12

Regulars.	*Regulars*—contd.	Special Reserve.
Cavalry.	*Infantry.*	*Infantry.*
1 Depôt.	*Depôts.*	3 Bn. R.W. Surr. R.
5 and 12 Lrs.		3 Bn. E. Kent R.
9 and 21 Lrs. (*Woolwich*).	R.W. Surr. R. (*Guildford*).	5 & 6 Bns. R. Fus.
16 and 17 Lrs.	E. Kent R. (*Canterbury*).	3 & 4 Bns. E. Surr. R.
	R. Fus. (*Hounslow*).	3 Bn. R. Suss. R.
Royal Artillery.	E. Surr. R. (*Kingston*).	3 Bn. R.W. Kent R.
Depôt, R.H.A. (*Woolwich*).	R. Suss. R. (*Chichester*).	5 & 6 Bns. Midd'x R.
IV. Res. {142 Batt.} (*Woolwich*).	R. W. Kent R. (*Maidstone*)	
Brig. {143 Batt.}	Midd'x R. (*Mill Hill*).	
R.F.A.		
4 Depôt, R.F.A (*Woolwich*).		
1 Depôt, R.G.A. (*Newhaven*).		

[*Continued on page* 25.]

(25)

Commands of the Army.

Eastern Command—contd.

OTHER REGULAR AND SPECIAL RESERVE TROOPS IN THE COMMAND.

Regulars.	Regulars—contd.	Special Reserve.
Royal Artillery.	*Royal Engineers.*	*Cavalry.*
R.A. Riding Establishment	A, B, C, D E, F, G, L and M Depôt Cos.	King Edward's Horse. (*attd. 4 Cav. Brig.*)
R.A. Band.		
Adjutant's Detachment (*Shoeburyness*)		

TERRITORIAL DIVISIONS AND BRIGADES.

(Territorial troops allotted to Coast Defences are shewn with the Regulars)

EASTERN MOUNTED BRIGADE. *Belchamp Hall, Sudbury, Suffolk.*

Brigade Commander	.. .. ..	Hodgson, Col. H. W., C.V.O, ...	1Apr.12
Brigade-Major	.. ..	Gibbs, Capt. W., 7 Hrs.	10Mar.13
Suff. Yeo.	Norf. Yeo.	Essex Yeo. Essex R.H.A. (Batt. & Ammn. Col.)	
		E. Mtd. Brig. T. & S. Col. A.S.C.	
		E. Mtd. Brig. Fd. Amb., R.A.M.C.	
Attached for Training :—			
Herts. Yeo.		Bedf. Yeo.	North'n Yeo.

EAST ANGLIAN DIVISION. *Warley.*

General Officer Commanding	Inglefield, Maj.-Gen. F. S., *C.B., D.S.O., p.s.c.* [L] ..	7June13
Gen. Staff Officer, 2nd grade ..	Stirling, Maj. C., R. A., *p.s.c., c., q.s.*	8Mar.13
Dep. Asst. Adjt. and Qr.-Mr.-Gen. ..	Evans, Maj. E., *D.S.O.,* Wilts. R.	4Jan.12
Asst. Dir. of Medical Services..	Hoyland, Col.S.S., *M.D.,* VD.(53, *Woodbridge Road, Ipswich*)	1Apr.12
Dep.-Asst. Dir. of Medical Services ..	Freeman, Maj. E. C., *M.D.,* ret. pay (*Res. of Off.*)	
Sanitary Officer	Fremantle, Maj. F. E., *M.B.*	1Apr.08
Asst. Dir. of Veterinary Services ..	Clarke, Maj. (*temp. Lt.-Col. Terr. Force*) A. E., ret. pay (*Res. of Off.*)	25June13

Norfolk and Suffolk Infantry Brigade.

18a, Prince of Wales Road, Norwich.

Brigade Commander	.. .. ..	Bayard, Col. R., *D.S.O.*		9Oct.11
Brigade-Major	.. ..	Swan, Capt. N. E., York. R., *p.s.c.*		5Sept.13
4 Bn. Norf. R.	5 Bn. Norf. R.	4 Bn. Suff. R.	5 Bn. Suff. R.	

East Midland Infantry Brigade. *The Shire Hall, Bedford.*

Brigade Commander	.. ..	de Winton, Col. C.		21Aug.11
Brigade-Major	.. ..	Hay, Capt. S., Cam'n. Highrs		12Feb.13
5 Bn. Bedf. R.	4 Bn. North'n R.	1 Bn. Camb. R.	Bn. Herts. R.	

Essex Infantry Brigade. *Drill Hall, Brentwood (temp.)*

Brigade Commander	.. ..	Lawford, Col. S. T. B.		30June13
Brigade-Major	.. ..	Fargus, Maj. H., *D.S.O.,* D. of Corn. L.I. ..	..	11Mar.12
4 Bn. Essex R.	5 Bn Essex R.	6 Bn. Essex R.	7 Bn. Essex R.	

Commands (United Kingdom).

Eastern Command—contd.
Territorial Divisions and Brigades—East Anglian Division—contd.

Divisional Troops.

Royal Artillery.   Claremont House, Warley.

Commanding Royal Artillery .. .. Biddulph, Col. G. W., *g.* 1Jan.13
Staff Captain.. .. .. .. Jameson, Capt. W. K. E., R.A. [*l*] 1Jan.11

1 E. Anglian Brig., R.F.A. { 1 Norf. Batt. / 2 Norf. Batt. / 3 Norf. Batt. / 1 E. Anglian Ammn. Col.

2 E. Anglian Brig., R.F.A. { 1 Essex Batt. / 2 Essex Batt. / 3 Essex Batt. / 2 E. Anglian Ammn. Col.

3 E. Anglian (Howr.) Brig., R.F.A. { 1 Suff. Batt. / 2 Suff. Batt. / 3 E. Anglian Ammn. Col.

4 E. Anglian Brig., R.F.A. { 1 Herts. Batt. / 2 Herts. Batt. / North'n Batt. / 4 E. Anglian Ammn. Col.

E. Anglian R.G.A.

Royal Engineers.   Ashburnham Road, Bedford.

Commanding Royal Engineers .. .. Wells, Lt.-Col. G. H., E. Anglian Divl. R.E.

1 E. Anglian Fd. Co.   2 E. Anglian Fd. Co.   E. Anglian Divl. Signal Co.

Army Service Corps.	Royal Army Medical Corps.
E. Anglian Divl. T. & S. Col. { Divl. Co. (H.Q.) / Norf. & Suff. Brig. Co. / E. Midland Brig. Co. / Essex Brig. Co.	1 E. Anglian Fd. Amb. / 2 E. Anglian Fd. Amb. / 3 E. Anglian Fd. Amb.

SOUTH EASTERN MOUNTED BRIGADE.   43, *Russell Square, W.C.*

Brigade Commander .. .. .. Brown, Col. H. C. 11May13
Brigade-Major .. .. .. Cecil, Maj. R. E., 21 Lrs. 1Apr.14

Kent Yeo.   W. Kent Yeo.   Suss. Yeo.

For R.H.A. Batt. & Ammn. Col., see Lond. Mtd. Brig., page 33.

S.E. Mtd. Brig. T. & S. Col., A.S.C.

S.E. Mtd. Brig. Fd. Amb., R.A.M.C.

Attached for training :—Surrey Yeo.

HOME COUNTIES DIVISION.   *Hounslow.*

General Officer Commanding .. .. Young, Maj.-Gen. J. C., Col. R. Suss. R., p.s.c. 25Oct.12
Gen. Staff Officer, 2nd grade .. Atkinson, Maj. B., R.A., p.s.c., *g.* [L] 16Jan.13
Dep. Asst. Adjt. and Qr.-Mr.-Gen. .. Grubb, Capt. H. W., Bord. R., *p.s.c.* .. .. { 1Apr.12 / 1Apr.12
Asst. Dir. of Medical Services .. Oliver, Col. C. P., *M.D., K.H.P.*, TD, (*The Gables, Maidstone*) 1Apr.12
Dep. Asst. Dir. of Medical Services .. Wight, Lt.-Col. E. O., ret. pay.
Sanitary Officer .. .. .. Greenwood, Maj. A., San. Serv., R.A.M.C. (T.F.) 20Aug.13
Asst. Dir. of Veterinary Services .. Sullivan, Maj. (*temp. Lt.-Col. Terr. Force*) H. A., ret. pay (Res. of Off.) 26Oct.1

Surrey Infantry Brigade.   *Caxton House, Westminster, S.W.*

Brigade Commander .. .. .. Marriott, Col. J., *M.V.O., D.S.O.* 1Apr.13
Brigade-Major .. .. .. Young, Maj. E. D., Devon. R. [L] 20Aug.12

4 Bn. R. W. Surr. R.   5 Bn. R. W. Surr. R.   6 Bn. E. Surr. R.   6 Bn. E. Surr. R.

Kent Infantry Brigade.   1, *Bank Street, Tonbridge.*

Brigade Commander .. .. .. Bunbury, Col. V. T., *C.B., D.S.O.* 1July11
Brigade-Major .. .. .. Thicknesse, Maj. J. A., Som. L.I. 1Apr.12

4 Bn. E. Kent R.   5 Bn. E. Kent R.   4 Bn. R. W. Kent R.   5 Bn. R. W. Kent R.

[*Continued on page* 27]

(27)

Commands of the Army.

Eastern Command—contd.
Territorial Divisions and Brigades.—Home Counties Division.—contd.

Middlesex Infantry Brigade.   15, *Pall Mall East, S.W.*

Brigade Commander	.. .. .. Clifford, Col. W. R.	.. ..	26Dec.12
Brigade-Major	.. .. .. Thomson, Maj. E. P., R. Muns. Fus.	.. .. ..	29Apr.12

7 Bn. Midd'x R.   8 Bn. Midd'x R.   9 Bn. Midd'x R   10 Bn. Midd'x R.

Divisional Troops.

Royal Artillery.   14, *Nightingale Place, Woolwich.*

Commanding Royal Artillery	.. .. Caulfeild, Col. C. T.	1Oct.13
Staff Captain	.. .. .. Nixon, Capt. *Sir* C. W., *Bt.*, R.A.	1Apr.12

1 Home Counties Brig., R.F.A. { 1 Sussex Batt. / 2 Sussex Batt / 3 Sussex Batt. / 1 Home Counties Ammn. Col.

2 Home Counties Brig. R.F.A. { 4 Sussex Batt / 5 Sussex Batt. / 6 Sussex Batt. / 2 Home Counties Ammn. Col.

3 Home Counties Brig., R.F.A. { 2 Kent Batt. / 3 Kent Batt. / 3 Home Counties Ammn. Col.

4 Home Counties (Howr.) Brig., R.F.A. { 4 Kent Batt. / 5 Kent Batt. / 4 Home Counties Ammn. Col.

Home Counties R.G.A.

Royal Engineers.   *Ordnance Yard, Eastbourne.*

Commanding Royal Engineers .. .. Cheesewright, Lt.-Col. W. F., Home Cos. Divl. R.E.

1 Home Counties Fd. Co.   2 Home Counties Fd. Co.   Home Counties Divl. Signal Co.

Army Service Corps.
Home Counties Divl. T. & S. Col. { Divl. Co. (H.Q.) / Surrey Brig. Co. / Kent Brig. Co. / Midd'x Brig. Co.

Royal Army Medical Corps.
1 Home Counties Fd. Amb.
2 Home Counties Fd. Amb.
3 Home Counties Fd. Amb.

ARMY TROOPS ATTACHED HOME COUNTIES DIVISION.

Infantry.

4 Bn. R. Suss. R. | 5 Bn. R. Suss. R.

OTHER TERRITORIAL TROOPS IN THE COMMAND.

Cyclists.

6 Bn. Norf. R.
6 Bn. Suff. R.
6 Bn. R. Suss. R.
8 Bn. Essex R.
Kent Cyclist Bn.
Hunts. Cyclist Bn.

Royal Army Medical Corps

1 E. Gen. Hosp.
2 E. Gen. Hosp.
E. Ang. Clearing Hosp.
Home Counties Clearing Hosp.

OFFICERS HAVING THEIR HEADQUARTERS AT WOOLWICH, BUT NOT FORMING PART OF THE EASTERN COMMAND.

Assistant Director of Military Transport	King, Col. *Sir* C. W., *Knt.*, *M.V.O.* ..	*Woolwich Arsenal (including Purfleet)*	1Aug.12
Deputy Director of Ordnance Stores ..	Butcher, Col. (*temp. Brig.-Gen.*) G. J., *C.B., C.M.G.*	*Woolwich Arsenal (including Purfleet)*	
Officer in charge Supply Reserve Depôt	Ryan, Lt.-Col. C. M., *D.S.O.*, A.S.C.	*Woolwich Dockyard*	

(28)

Commands (United Kingdom).

IRELAND.

LIEUTENANT-GENERAL AND GENERAL GOVERNOR } Aberdeen, Rt. Hon. J.C., Earl of, K.T., G.C.M.G., G.C.V.O.
Dublin Castle.

Aides-de-Camp ..
{ Warner, Lt. E. C. T., S. Gds. 22Aug.10
Forbes, Capt. Hon. D. A., M.V.O., R.A. 7Feb.11
Bellingham, Lt. R. C. N., R.F.A. Spec. Res. .. 8Nov.12
Hope, Lt. W. E., I. Gds. Spec. Res. .. .. .. 1Dec.12 }

IRISH COMMAND.

Head-Quarters.—Parkgate, Dublin.

GENERAL OFFICER COMMANDING-IN-CHIEF THE FORCES IN IRELAND } Paget, Gen. Rt. Hon. Sir A. H., G.C.B., K.C.V.O. .. 10May12
Assistant Military Secretary .. Kincaid-Smith, Maj. K. J., D.S.O., R.A. 10May12
Aides-de-Camp .. { Mackintosh, Lt. A. A., R.H.G. 22Sept.13

General Staff.
Brigadier-General .. .. .. Forestier-Walker, Col. (temp. Brig. Gen.) G. T., p.s.c. [L]
 A.D.C. 22Oct.12
General Staff Officer, 2nd grade .. Williams, Col. H. B., D.S.O., p.s.c. [L] .. { 15Apr.14
 3Jan.12

Attached to the General Staff.
Captain, graded as Brigade-Major .. Baring, Capt. T. E., Rif. Brig., e... .. .. .. 8Feb.12
Major, graded as Brigade-Major .. Carter, Maj. A. J., D.S.O., N. Lan. R. 1Jan.14

Administrative, Technical and Departmental Staff.
Major-General in charge of Administration } Friend, Maj.-Gen. L. B., C.B. 2Jan.13
Asst. Adjt.-Gen. .. .. De Gex, Col. F. J., C.B. 3Jan.14
Staff Captain .. Costeker, Capt. J. H. D., D.S.O., p.s.c., R. War. R. .. 13May14
Asst. Inspr. of Recg. (graded Staff Captain) } Kinsman, Capt. W. A. C., D.S.O. .. .. { 1Apr.12
Asst. Quarter-Master-Gen. .. Hickie, Col. W. B., C.B., p.s.c. [l] 12Mar.13
Dep. Asst. Qr.-Mr. Gen. .. Romer, Bt. Lt.-Col. C. F., R Dub. Fus., p.s.c. .. 1Apr.12
Chief Engineer .. Sandbach,Col. (temp. Brig.-Gen.) A. E., C.B., D.S.O., p.s.c. 7Oct 10
Staff Officer, Royal Engineers .. Traill, Maj. W. S., R.E.
Asst. Director of Supplies and Transport .. Moore, Col. J. S... .. .. 1Apr.14
Dep. Asst. Director of Supplies and Transport } Delavoye, Maj. A. E., A.S.C., e. 10Oct.10
Dep. Dir. of Medical Services .. Anderson, Surg.-Gen. L. E., C.B.
Dep.-Asst. Dir. of Medical Services .. Connor, Lt-Col. J. C., M.B., R.A.M.C.
Asst. Dir. of Veterinary Services .. Taylor, Lt.-Col. E., A.V.C.
Asst. Director of Ordnance Stores .. Hale, Col. T. W., A. Ord. Dept.
Command Paymaster .. .. Magee, Col. A. H.
Dep. Asst. Dirs. of Remounts { *No. 2 Circle* .. Gartside-Spaight, Maj. C. W., ret. pay .. { 24July12
 1May10
 No. 1 Circle .. King, Capt. W. H., ret. pay (Capt. 3 Bn. Conn. Rang.) .. 4Dec.12
 Head-Quarters .. Fowle, Col. J., C.B., ret. pay (Res. of Off.) 20June14
District Barrack Officer .. .. Collard, Col. A. W., ret. pay

Department of the Finance Member of the Army Council
(detached from the War Office for duty at Head-Quarters of the Command).
Local Auditor .. .. .. Goligher, H. G., Esq. (Lower Castle Yard, Dublin)
Assistant Local Auditor .. .. Toplis, J., Esq.

Officer in charge of Time-Expired men, etc... Higgins, Hon. Maj. J. T., Qr.-Mr. ret. pay (1, Park Place, Dublin).

At Dublin.
Garrison Adjutant (graded Staff Captain) .. Hollins, Capt. C. E., Linc. R. 22Jan.14
Asst. Dir. of Medical Services .. .. Sawyer, Col. R. H. S., M.B., F.R.C.S.I, [L]
Chief Ordnance Officer .. .. Keddie, Maj. H. W. G., A. Ord. Dept., e., f.

At Curragh.
Asst. Dir. of Veterinary Services .. ..

At Cork.
Asst. Dir. of Medical Services .. .. Trevor, Col. H. O.

At Haulbowline.
Chief Ordnance Officer .. .. Howard, Maj. H. M., A. Ord. Dept., e. o.

At Belfast.
Garrison Adjutant (graded Staff Captain) Trevor, Maj. W. H., E. Kent R. [L] 9Mar.14
Asst. Dir. of Medical Services .. .. Sloggett, Col. H. M.
Chief Ordnance Officer .. .. Greer, Maj. MacG., A. Ord. Dept., p.s.c.

[*Continued on page* 29]

Commands of the Army.

Irish Command—contd.

Army Service Corps.

4 Co. (*Dublin*).
6 Co. (*Curragh*).
17 Co. (*Cork*).
19 Co. (*Dublin*).
23 Co. (*Curragh*).
33 Co. (*Belfast*).
37 Co. (*Curragh*).
48 (M. T.) Co. (*Dublin*).
49 (M. T.) Co. (*Curragh*).
50 (M. T.) Co. (*Fermoy*).
51 (M. T.) Co. (*Curragh*).

Army Service Corps—contd.
"D" Co. (*Curragh*)
"BB" Co. (*Dublin*).
"CC" Co. (*Lusk*).
"DD" Co. (*Dublin*).

Royal Army Medical Corps.

14 Co. (*Dublin*).
15 Co. (*Belfast*).
16 Co. (*Cork*).
17 Co. (*Curragh*).

Army Veterinary Corps.

7 and 8 Sections (*Curragh*).
Det. (*Newbridge*).
Det. (*Kildare*).

Army Ordnance Corps.

3 Co. { Dublin Section.
 Curragh Section.
 Haulbowline Section.

FIELD TROOPS (REGULARS).
3rd CAVALRY BRIGADE.   *Curragh.*

Brigade Commander	.. Gough, Col. (*temp. Brig.-Gen.*) H. De la P., C.B.,p.s.c. [l]	1Jan.11
Brigade-Major	.. Kearsley, Maj. R. H., 5 D.G., p.s.c.	4Oct.13
16 Lrs. (*Curragh*).	4 Hrs. (*Curragh*). 5 Lrs. (*Dublin*). 3 Signal Troop R.E.	(*Curragh*).
Attached—		
III. Brig. R.H.A. .. { "D" Batt. "E" Batt. } (*Newbridge*).	4 Fd. Troop, R.E.	.. (*Curragh*).

5th DIVISION.   *Curragh.*

General Officer Commanding	.. Fergusson, Maj.-Gen. *Sir* C., *Bt.*, C.B., M.V.O., D.S.O.	4Feb.13
Aide-de-Camp	.. Graham, Lt. *Lord* D. M., R.A. [l]	4Feb.13
General Staff Officer, 1st grade	.. Wolley-Dod, Col. O. C., D.S.O., p.s.c. [l]	1Feb.14
Dep. Asst. Qr.-Mr. Gen.	.. Anderson, Maj. N, G., D.S.O., A.S.C., p.s.c.	16Jan.13
Staff Captain	.. Dunlop, Capt. F. P., Worc. R., p.s.c. [L]	{ 1Apr.12

13th Infantry Brigade.   *Dublin.*

Brigade Commander	.. Cuthbert, Col. (*temp. Brig.-Gen.*) G. J., C.B.	2Feb.14
Brigade-Major	.. Currie, Capt. R. A. M., Sem. L.I., p.s.c.	18June12
2 Bn. K. O. Sco. Bord. 2 Bn. W. Rid. R.	1 Bn. R. W. Kent R. 2 Bn. Yorks. L. I.	

14th Infantry Brigade.   *Curragh.*

Brigade Commander	.. Rolt, Col. (*temp. Brig.-Gen.*) S. P., C.B.	30Nov.12
Brigade-Major	.. Wethered, Capt. J. R., Glouc. R., p.s.c.	{ 30May13 15July11
2 Bn. Suff. R. (*Curragh*). 1 Bn. E. Surr. R. (*Dublin*).	1 Bn. D. of Corn. L. I. (*Curragh*). 2 Bn. Manch. R. (*Curragh*).	

15th Infantry Brigade.   *Belfast.*

Brigade Commander	.. Gleichen, Col. (*temp. Brig.-Gen.*) A. E. W., *Count*, K.C.V.O., C.B., C.M.G., D.S.O., p.s.c. [L] Eq.	1Aug.11
Brigade-Major	.. Weatherby, Capt. J. T., Oxf. & Bucks. L.I.,p.s.c.	{ 1May14 23Sept.12
1 Bn. Norf. R. (*Holywood*). 1 Bn. Bedf. R. (*Mullingar*).	1 Bn. Ches. R. (*Londonderry*). 1 Bn. Dorset R. (*Belfast*).	

Divisional Troops.
Royal Artillery.   *Newbridge.*

Commanding Royal Artillery	.. Headlam, Col. (*temp. Brig.-Gen.*) J. E. W., C.B., D.S.O.,g.	1Oct.13
Brigade Major	.. Tallyour, Maj. G. H. F., R.A.	{ 23July13 22Jan.12
VIII. (Howr.) Brig. R.F.A. { 37 Batt. 61 Batt. 65 Batt. } (*Kildare*).	XXVII. Brig. R.F.A. { 119 Batt. 120 Batt. 121 Batt. } (*Newbridge*).	
XV. Brig. R.F.A. { 11 Batt. 52 Batt. 80 Batt. } (*Kildare*).	XXVIII. Brig. R.F.A. { 122 Batt. 123 Batt. 124 Batt. } (*Dundalk*).	

For Heavy Battery, R.G.A. see Southern Command, page 48[2].

Royal Engineers.   *Curragh.*

Commanding Royal Engineers	.. Tulloch, Lt.-Col. J. A. S., R.E., p.s.c. [l]	
7 Fd. Co.	(*Curragh*). 5 Signal Co.	(*Carlow*) (*temp.*)
59 Fd. Co.	(*Curragh*).	

(30)

Commands (United Kingdom).

Irish Command—contd.

6th DIVISION.   *Cork*

General Officer Commanding	Keir, Maj.-Gen. J. L., *C.B., p.s.c., g.*	—
Aide-de-Camp	Brooke, Lt. W. H., Yorks. L.I.	—
General Staff Officer, 1st grade	Furse, Col. W. T., *D.S.O., p.s.c.* [L]	1Oct.13
Dep. Asst. Adjt. and Qr.-Mr. Gen.	Dundas, Maj. F. C., Arg. & Suth'd Highrs., *p.s.c.* [*l*]	21Feb.12

16th Infantry Brigade.   *Fermoy.*

Brigade Commander   Ingouville-Williams, Col. *(temp. Brig.-Gen.)* E. C., *C.B., D.S.O., q.s.*   } 18 June 12

Brigade-Major   Mangles, Capt. R. H., *D.S.O.,* R.W. Surr. R., *p.s.c.*   { 9Mar.12 / 15Oct.10

1 Bn. E. Kent R. (*Fermoy*). | 1 Bn. Shrops. L.I. (*Tipperary*).
1 Bn. Leic. R. (*Fermoy*). | 2 Bn. York & Lanc. R. (*Limerick*).

17th Infantry Brigade.   *Cork.*

Brigade Commander   Doran, Col. *(temp. Brig.-Gen.)* W. R. B., *C.B., D.S.O., p.s.c.*   8Apr.12

Brigade-Major   Green, Maj. A. D., *D.S.O.,* Worc. R., *p.s.c.*   28June11

1 Bn. R. Fus. (*Kinsale*). | 2 Bn. Leins. R. (*Cork*).
1 Bn. N. Staff. R. (*Buttevant*). | 3 Bn. Rif. Brig. (*Cork*).

For 18th Infantry Brigade, *see* Northern Command, page 36.

Divisional Troops.
Royal Artillery.   *Mallow.*

Commanding Royal Artillery   Paget, Col. *(temp. Brig.-Gen.)* W. L. H., *C.B., M.V.O.*   12Sept.10

Brigade-Major   Farquhar, Maj. J., R.A., *p.s.c.*   { 23July13 / 1Oct.12

II. Brig., R.F.A. { 21 Batt. / 42 Batt. / 53 Batt. } (*Cahir*.)   XXIV. Brig., R.F.A. { 110 Batt. / 111 Batt. / 112 Batt. } (*Ballincollig*).

XII. (Howr.) Brig., R.F.A. { 43 Batt. (*Fethard*). / 86 Batt. (*Clonmel*). / 87 Batt. (*Kilkenny*). }   XXXVIII. Brig., R.F.A. { 24 Batt. / 34 Batt. (*Fermoy*). / 72 Batt. (*Waterford*). }

For Heavy Battery, R.G.A., *see* Eastern Command, page 23.

Royal Engineers.   *Fermoy.*

Commanding Royal Engineers   Kemp, Lt.-Col. G. C., R.E. [*l*]

12 Fd. Co.   (*Moore Park*).   6 Signal Co.   (*Limerick*) (*temp.*)
38 Fd. Co.   (*Cork*).

ARMY TROOPS.
Royal Engineers.
" B " Signal Company.   (*Limerick*.)

COAST DEFENCES.
NORTH IRISH COAST DEFENCES.
Defended ports of Lough Swilly and Belfast.

Officer Commanding (ex-officio)	Eyre, Lt.-Col. (*local Col.*) M. S., R.G.A. *Londonderry*	
General Staff Officer, 3rd grade	Hamilton, Maj. C. L. C., R.A., *p.s.c.*	3Mar.12
Senior Medical Officer	Daly, Lt.-Col. J. H., R.A.M.C.	

Royal Garrison Artillery.
15 Co.
Special Reserve.
Antrim.

SOUTH IRISH COAST DEFENCES.
Defended ports of Queenstown Harbour and Berehaven.

Officer Commanding	Hill, Col. (*temp. Brig.-Gen.*) C.,	*Queenstown* 4July14
General Staff Officer, 2nd grade	Davie, Maj. K. M., Glouc. R., *p.s.c.* [*l*]	1Jan.14
Captain Instructor in Gunnery	Dean, Capt. A. C. H., R.A., *g.*	30Jan.14
Senior Medical Officer	Morris, Lt.-Col. A. E., *M.D.,* R.A.M.C.	

Royal Garrison Artillery.   **Royal Engineers.**
10, 43 & 49 Cos.   33 Co. (Fortress).
Special Reserve.
Cork.

[*Continued on page* 31]

(31)

Commands of the Army.

Irish Command—contd.

No. 11 DISTRICT.

Comprising the Counties of Londonderry, Antrim, Donegal, Tyrone, Down, Fermanagh, Armagh, Monaghan, Louth, Cavan, Dublin, Kildare, Wicklow and Carlow.

Officer Commanding	.. Napier, Col. H. E.	*Dublin*	25June14
Staff Captain	.. Cooke Collis, Capt. W. J. N., R. Ir. Rif., e.		15Nov.11

Regulars.	Regulars—contd.	Special Reserve.
Cavalry.	*Infantry.*	*Infantry.*
2 Depôt.	*Depôts.*	3 & 4 Bns. R. Innis. Fus.
4 and 8 Hrs. } (*Dublin*).	R. Innis. Fus. (*Omagh*).	3, 4 & 5 Bns. R. Ir. Rif.
11 and 13 Hrs. }	R. Ir. Rif. (*Belfast*).	3 & 4 Bns. R. Ir. Fus.
	R. Ir. Fus. (*Armagh*).	3, 4 & 5 Bns. R. Dub. Fus.
	R. Dub. Fus. (*Naas*).	

Dublin Recruiting Area.

Medical Officer .. .. Crawford, Maj. G. S., *M.D.*, R.A.M.C.

Retired Officers employed on Recruiting { Ward, Hon. Maj. J., Qr.-Mr. ret. pay .. (*Dublin*)   29Dec.13
Duties   Drage, Hon.Maj.G.T., Qr.-Mr. ret. pay (*Res. of Off.*)
                                                           (*Belfast*)   18Apr.14

No. 12 DISTRICT.

Comprising the Counties of Sligo, Leitrim, Mayo, Roscommon, Longford, Meath, Westmeath, Galway, King's County, Queen's County, Clare, Tipperary, Kilkenny, Wexford, Limerick, Waterford, Kerry and Cork.

Officer Commanding	.. Scrase-Dickins, Col. S. W.	*Cork*	29July12
Staff Captain	.. Wickham, Capt. C. G., *D.S.O.*, Norf. R.		16Apr.14

Regulars.	Regulars—contd.	Special Reserve.
Royal Artillery.	*Infantry.*	*Infantry.*
V. Res. } 144 Batt. } (*Athlone*).	*Depôt.*	3 & 4 Bns. R. Ir. Regt.
Brig., } 145 Batt }	R. Ir. Regt. (*Clonmel*).	3 & 4 Bns. Conn. Rang.
R.F.A. }	Conn. Rang. (*Galway*).	3, 4 & 5 Bns. Leins. R.
5 Depôt, R.F.A. (*Athlone*).	Leins. R. (*Birr*).	3, 4 & 5 Bns. R. Muns. Fus.
	R. Muns. Fus. (*Tralee*).	

Retired Officer employed on Recruiting } Dundas, Hon. Capt. W., Qr.-Mr. ret. pay .. *Cork* ..   1Apr.09
Duties

OTHER TROOPS IN THE COMMAND.

Cavalry.	Royal Engineers.
Special Reserve	"K" Signal Co. (*Aldborough House, Dublin*).
N. Irish Horse } (*attd. 3 Cav. Brig.*)	14 Co. (Surrey) (*Dublin*).
S. Irish Horse }	

(32)

Commands (United Kingdom).

LONDON DISTRICT.—The County of London, the Guards' Depôt at Caterham, Purfleet, Rainham Rifle Range, and (for Regular troops) Windsor. For purposes of training, the camp at Pirbright is included in the London District. Woolwich (exclusive of the Territorial troops quartered therein) is under the command of the General Officer Commanding-in-Chief Eastern Command.

Head-Quarters—Horse Guards, Whitehall, S.W.

General Officer Commanding	Lloyd, Maj.-Gen. *Sir* F., *K.C.B., C.V.O., D.S.O.*	.. 3Sept.13
Aide-de-Camp	Gort, Lt. J. S. S. P. V., *Visct., M.V.O.*, G. Gds.	.. 3Sept.13

General Staff.

General Staff Officer, 2nd grade ..	Windsor Clive, Maj. G., C. Gds., *p.s.c.*	.. 1Mar.14
Attached to the General Staff.		
Captain, graded as Brigade-Major	Alston, Capt,. F. G., S. Gds.	.. 3Feb.11

Administrative, Technical and Departmental Staff.

Asst. Adjt. and Qr.-Mr.-Gen.	Lambton, Col. *Hon.* W., *C.M.G., M.V.O., D.S.O., p.s.c.*	1Jan.13
Chief Engineer	Russell, Col. W.	{ 7Mar.13 / 8Aug.10
Staff Officer, Royal Engineers ..	Hoysted, Maj. D. M. Fitz G., R.E.	
Asst. Director of Supplies and Transport	Atkins, Lt.-Col. A.R.C., A.S.C.	
Dep. Dir. of Medical Services	Lynden-Bell, Col. E. H. L., *M.B.*	
Asst. Dir. of Veterinary Services	The Asst. Dir. of Veterinary Services, Eastern Command.	
Chief Ordnance Officer		
Command Paymaster	Minchin, Col. W. C., A.P. Dept. (91, *York Street, Westminster, S.W.*)	
Deputy Assistant Director of Remounts..	Elwes, Maj. W. V. J. C., ret. pay (*Res. of Off.*) ..	.. 28Apr.14

Department of the Finance Member of the Army Council
(*detached from the War Office for duty at Head-Quarters of the Command*).

Local Auditor	Beavis, A. B., *Esq.*	
Assistant Local Auditor	Piper, G., *Esq.*	

Officer in charge of Time-Expired Men, etc. Grattan, Bt. Col. O'D.C., *D.S.O.*, ret. pay (*Holm Lodge, Lexden, Colchester.*)

Commandant and Division Officer, Purfleet and Rainham Rifle Ranges.. { Boynton, Hon. Lt.-Col. (*temp. Col. in Army*) F., *M.Inst.C.E.*, late R. Anglesey R. Res. E., Maj. ret.

Army Service Corps.	Royal Army Medical Corps
11 Co. (*Kensington Barracks*).	18 Co. (*Rochester Row, S.W.*)
18 Co. (*Kensington Barracks*).	35 Co. (*Grosvenor Road, S.W.*)

Brigade-Major (Brigade of Guards) .. Hore Ruthven, Maj. *Hon.* W. P. (*Master of Ruthven*) *D.S.O.*, S. Gds., *p.s.c., e.* 3Feb.12

FIELD TROOPS (REGULARS).

4th CAVALRY BRIGADE (*part of*)

Composite Regiment of Household Cavalry:—
1 L.G.   2 L.G.   R.H.G.

2nd DIVISION (*part of*).

4th Infantry Brigade (Foot Guards).

2 Bn. G. Gds. (*London*).   2 Bn. C. Gds. (*Windsor*).   3 Bn. C. Gds. (*London*).   1 Bn. I. Gds. (*London*).

[*Continued on page* 33]

Commands of the Army.

London District—contd.

OTHER TROOPS IN THE DISTRICT.

Cavalry.	Royal Artillery.	Infantry.	Infantry—contd.
Regular Troops.	*Regular Troops.*	*Regular Troops.*	*Special Reserve.*
1 L. G. 2 L. G. (*Windsor*.) R. H. G.	IV. Brig., R.H.A., "F" Batt. Dist. Establt., R.G.A.	3 Bn. G. Gds. 2 Bn. S. Gds. Gds. Depôt.	7 Bn. R. Fus.

London Recruiting Area.

(*Administered, for Recruiting purposes, direct from the War Office.*)

(Central Recruiting Depôt, Whitehall, S.W.)

Chief Recruiting Staff Officer	Gossett, Maj. A. B., Ches. R. (*D.A.A.G., War Office*)	
Recruiting Staff Officers (Class II)	Whiffen, Capt. T. W.	25Feb.11
	Anwyl-Passingham, Capt. A. M. O. A., Midd'x R. [*l*]	21Feb.13
	Price, Maj. G. D., W. York. R. (*Woolwich*)	1Oct.13
Senior Medical Officer and Medical Inspector of Recruits, London District	Yarr, Lt.-Col. M. T., *F.R.C.S.I.*, R.A.M.C.	
Medical Examiners of Recruits	Langstaff, Maj. J. W., R.A.M.C.	
	Dennis, Maj. B. R., *M.B.*, R.A.M.C.	
	Siberry, Maj. E. W., R.A.M.C.	
	Barbour, Maj. J. H., *M.B.*, R.A.M.C.	
	Baker, Maj. W. L., R.A.M.C.	
	Scott, Lt.-Col. B. H., R.A.M.C.	
Retired Officers employed on Recruiting Duties	Birch, Hon. Maj. C., Qr.-Mr. ret. pay.	1May13
	Daw, Hon. Maj. T., Qr.-Mr. ret. pay	7July14

TERRITORIAL DIVISIONS AND BRIGADES.
LONDON MOUNTED BRIGADE.

Duke of York's Headquarters, Chelsea, S.W.

Brigade Commander	Taylor, Col. A. H. M., *D.S.O.*	25May14
Brigade-Major	Rome, Capt. C. S., 11 Hrs.	24Nov.11

City of Lond. Yeo.   1 Co. of Lond. Yeo.   3 Co. of Lond. Yeo.   Hon. Art. Co. (A. Batt. and Ammn. Col.)

Lond. Mtd. Brig. T. & S. Col., A.S.C.

Lond. Mtd. Brig. Fd. Amb., R.A.M.C.

Attached for training:—

2 Co. of Lond. Yeo.   Hon. Art. Co. (B. Batt. and Ammn. Col.)
(part of S. E. Mtd. Brig.)

1st LONDON DIVISION.

Friar's House, New Broad Street, E.C.

General Officer Commanding	Fry, Maj.-Gen. W., *C.V.O., C.B.* (Col. W. York. R.)	22Feb.12
Gen. Staff Officer, 2nd grade	Boyce, Maj. H. A., R.A., *p.s.c.* [L]	12Dec.13
Dep. Asst. Adjt. and Qr.-Mr.-Gen.	Steele, Maj. J. McC., C. Gds.	1Apr.12
Asst. Dir. of Medical Services	Harper, Col. J., *M.D.*	1Apr.12
Dep.-Asst. Dir. of Medical Services	Gubbin, Lt.-Col. G. F., ret. pay	
Sanitary Officer	Copeman, Lt.-Col. S. A. M., *M.D., F.R.S.*, TD, p.	1Apr.08

1st London Infantry Brigade.

Friar's House, New Broad Street, E.C.

Brigade Commander	Lucan, Col. (Terr. Force) G. C., *Earl of*, Capt. ret.	9Dec.12
Brigade-Major	Legge, Maj. R. F., Leins. R., *e*.	17May12

1 Bn. Lond. R.   2 Bn. Lond. R.   3 Bn. Lond. R.   4 Bn. Lond. R.

(34)

Commands (United Kingdom).

London District—contd.

Territorial Divisions and Brigades—1st London Division—contd.

2nd London Infantry Brigade.   Buckingham Gate, S.W.

Brigade Commander	.. .. ..	Scott-Kerr, Col. R., *C.B., M.V.O., D.S.O. (Officer comdg. G. Gds.)*
Brigade-Major	.. ..	Gregson, Capt. L. M., G. Gds. *(Regtl. Adjt., G. Gds.)*
5 Bn. Lond. R.	6 Bn. Lond. R.	7 Bn. Lond. R. 8 Bn. Lond. R.

3rd London Infantry Brigade.   Buckingham Gate, S.W.

Brigade Commander	.. .. ..	Monck, Col. C. S. O., *p.s.c. (Officer comdg. C. Gds.)*
Brigade-Major	.. ..	Crawfurd, Capt. R. B. J., C. Gds. *(Regtl. Adjt., C. Gds.)*
9 Bn. Lond. R.	10 Bn. Lond. R.	11 Bn. Lond. R. 12 Bn. Lond. R.

Divisional Troops.

Royal Artillery.   Friar's House, New Broad Street, E.C.

Commanding Royal Artillery ..	.. Duffus, Col. G. S.	.. ..	29July12
Staff Captain	.. .. McLay, Capt. W. J., R.A.	.. ..	1Nov.12

1 Lond. Brig. R.F.A.	{ 1 City of Lond. Batt. 2 City of Lond. Batt. 3 City of Lond. Batt. 1 Lond. Ammn. Col.	3 Lond. Brig. R.F.A.	{ 7 Co. of Lond. Batt. 8 Co. of Lond. Batt. 9 Co. of Lond. Batt. 3 Lond. Ammn. Col.
2 Lond. Brig. R.F.A.	{ 4 Co. of Lond. Batt. 5 Co. of Lond. Batt. 6 Co. of Lond. Batt. 2 Lond. Ammn. Col.	4 Lond. (Howr.) Brig. R.F.A.	{ 10 Co. of Lond. Batt. 11 Co. of Lond. Batt. 4 Lond. Ammn. Col.

1 Lond. R.G.A.

Royal Engineers.   10, *Victoria Park Square.*

Commanding Royal Engineers ..   .. Walters, Lt.-Col. G. W., TD, 1 Lond. Divl. R.E.

1 Lond. Fd. Co.	2 Lond. Fd. Co.	1 Lond. Divl. Signal Co.

Army Service Corps.		*Royal Army Medical Corps.*
1 Lond. Divl. T. & S. Col.	{ Divl. Co. (H.-Q.) 1 Lond. Brig. Co. 2 Lond. Brig. Co. 3 Lond. Brig. Co.	1 Lond. Fd. Amb. 2 Lond. Fd. Amb. 3 Lond. Fd. Amb.

ARMY TROOPS ATTACHED 1st LONDON DIVISION.

Royal Engineers.	*Infantry.*
Lond. Wireless Signal Co. Lond. Cable Signal Co. Lond. Air Line Signal Co.	Hon. Art. Co. (Inf.)

2nd LONDON DIVISION.

Duke of York's Headquarters, Chelsea, S.W.

General Officer Commanding ..	.. Monro, Maj.-Gen. C. C., *C.B., p.s.c.*	31Mar.12
Gen. Staff Officer, 2nd grade	.. Thwaites, Bt. Lt.-Col. W., R.A., *p.s.c.* [*l*]	17Feb.12
Dep. Asst. Adjt. and Qr.-Mr.-Gen. ..	de la Fontaine, Maj. H.V.M., E. Surr. R., *p.s.c.* [L] ..	2Oct.11
Asst. Dir. of Medical Services	.. Harrison, Col. C. E., *C.V.O., M.B., F.R.C.S.*, Bt. Col., Brig- Surg. Lt.-Col. ret. pay	1Apr.12
Dep.-Asst. Dir. of Medical Services	Butt, Col. E., *F.R.C.S.I.*, ret. pay	
Sanitary Officer	Smith, Maj. P. C., *M.D.*	2July13
Asst. Dir. of Veterinary Services ..	Walker, Maj. *(temp. Lt.-Col. Terr. Force)* W. R., ret. pay *(Res. of Off.)*	8June12

4th London Infantry Brigade.   Buckingham Gate, S.W.

Brigade Commander	.. ..	Heyworth, Col. F. J., *D.S.O.,(Officer comdg. S. Gds.)*
Brigade-Major	.. ..	Tempest, Capt. R. S., S. Gds. *(Regtl. Adjt., S. Gds.)*
13 Bn Lond. R.	14 Bn. Lond. R.	15 Bn. Lond. R. 16 Bn. Lond. R.

[*Continued on page 35*].

(85)

Commands of the Army.

London District—contd.

Territorial Divisions and Brigades—2nd London Division—contd.

5th London Infantry Brigade. *Buckingham Gate, S.W.*

Brigade Commander	ℭℭ, FitzClarence, Col. C., *p.s.c. (Officer comdg. I. Gds.)*	
Brigade-Major	Reid, Capt. P. L., I. Gds.	9Sept.11
17 Bn. Lond. R.	18 Bn. Lond. R.	19 Bn. Lond. R.	20 Bn. Lond. R.

6th London Infantry Brigade. *Duke of York's Headquarters, Chelsea, S.W.*

Brigade Commander	Heathcote-Drummond-Willoughby, Col. *(Terr. Force)* Hon. C. S., Maj. ret. pay *(Res. of Off.)*	11Apr.12
Brigade-Major	Kentish, Capt. R. J., R. Ir. Fus.	24Feb.13
21 Bn. Lond. R.	22 Bn. Lond. R.	23 Bn. Lond. R.	24 Bn. Lond. R.

Divisional Troops.

Royal Artillery.   *Duke of York's Headquarters, Chelsea, S.W.*

Commanding Royal Artillery ..	Wray, Col. *(Terr. Force)* J. C., *M.V.O. (Maj. Res. of Off.)* (Yeo. of Gd.)	1Apr.12
Staff Captain	Burton, Capt. F. C. D., R.A.	1Dec.12

5 Lond. Brig. R.F.A.	{ 12 Co. of Lond. Batt. 13 Co. of Lond. Batt. 14 Co. of Lond. Batt. 5 Lond. Ammn. Col.	7 Lond. Brig. R.F.A.	{ 18 Co. of Lond. Batt. 19 Co. of Lond. Batt. 20 Co. of Lond. Batt. 7 Lond. Ammn. Col.
6 Lond. Brig. R.F.A.	{ 15 Co. of Lond. Batt. 16 Co. of Lond. Batt. 17 Co. of Lond. Batt. 6 Lond. Ammn. Col.	8 Lond. (Howr.) Brig. R.F.A.	{ 21 Co. of Lond. Batt. 22 Co. of Lond. Batt. 8 Lond. Ammn. Col.

2 Lond. R.G.A.

Royal Engineers.   *Duke of York's Headquarters, Chelsea, S.W.*

Commanding Royal Engineers .. Taylor, Lt.-Col. H. H., TD 2 Lond. Divl. R.E. *(Capt. Res. of Off.)*
3 Lond. Fd. Co.   4 Lond. Fd. Co.   2 Lond. Divl. Signal Co.

Army Service Corps.		*Royal Army Medical Corps.*
2 Lond. Divl. T. & S. Col.	{ Divl. Co. (H.-Q.) 4 Lond. Brig. Co. 5 Lond. Brig. Co. 6 Lond. Brig. Co.	4 Lond. Fd. Amb. 5 Lond. Fd. Amb. 6 Lond. Fd. Amb.

ARMY TROOPS ATTACHED 2nd LONDON DIVISION.

Infantry.
28 Bn. Lond. R.

OTHER TERRITORIAL TROOPS IN THE DISTRICT.

Royal Engineers. Lond. Elec. Eng. *Cyclists.* 25 Bn. Lond. R.	*Royal Army Medical Corps.* 1 Lond. Gen. Hosp. 2 Lond. Gen. Hosp. 3 Lond. Gen. Hosp. 4 Lond. Gen. Hosp.	*Royal Army Medical Corps*—contd. 1 Lond. San. Co. 2 Lond. San. Co. 1 Lond. Clearing Hosp. 2 Lond. Clearing Hosp.

SCHOOL OF INSTRUCTION FOR OFFICERS OF THE TERRITORIAL FORCE.

(Chelsea Barracks).

Commandant	Longueville, Capt. E. C. Gds.	1May11
Adjutant	Egerton-Warburton, Lt. J. S. Gds.	1Dec.10

(36)
Commands (United Kingdom).

NORTHERN COMMAND.—Berwick-on-Tweed (except Regulars and Special Reserve), and the Counties of Northumberland, Durham, Yorkshire, Lincolnshire, Nottinghamshire, Derbyshire, Staffordshire, Leicestershire and Rutland.

Head-Quarters—York.

GENERAL OFFICER COMMANDING-IN-CHIEF	Plumer, Lt.-Gen. *Sir* H. C.O., *K.C.B., p.s.c.*	10Nov.11
Assistant Military Secretary	Harding Newman, Maj. E., R.A., *g.*	10Nov.11
Aide-de-Camp	Jones-Bateman, Capt. L.N., Norf. R.	10Nov.11

General Staff.

General Staff Officer, 1st grade	Chapman, Col. A. J., *C.B., p.s.c.*	10Oct.12
General Staff Officer, 3rd grade	Holland, Capt. L., Sea. Highrs., *p.s.c.*	{ 1Aug.13 / 1Apr.12
Attached to the General Staff. *Captain, graded as Brigade-Major*	de Putron, Capt. C., Lan. Fus. [*l*]	1Dec.13

Administrative, Technical and Departmental Staff.

Brigadier-General in charge of Administration	Cole, Col. (*temp. Brig.-Gen.*) A. W. G. L., *C.B., D.S.O., p.s.c.*	16Oct.12
Dep. Asst. Adjt.-Gen.	Freeth, Bt. Lt.-Col. G. H. B., *D.S.O.*, Lan. Fus., *p.s.c.*	31Oct.11
Asst. Quarter-Master-Gen.	Ludlow, Col, E. R. O., *p.s.c.*	4Nov.10
Chief Engineer	Petrie, Col. R. D.	8Mar.12
Staff Officer, Royal Engineers	Falcon, Maj. C. G., R.E.	
Asst. Dir. of Supplies and Transport	Master, Lt.-Col. A. G., A.S.C.	
Dep. Dir. of Medical Services	Ford, Surg.-Gen. R. W., *D.S.O.*	
Dep.-Asst. Dir. of Medical Services	Bewley, Lt.-Col. A. W., R.A.M.C.	
Asst. Dir. of Veterinary Services	Sawyer, Lt.-Col. H. T., A.V.C.	
Asst. Director of Ordnance Stores	Blunt, Lt.-Col, C. J., A. Ord. Dept., *f.*	
Command Paymaster	Hill, Col. F. W., A.P. Dept.	
Dep. Asst. Dirs. of Remounts { *No. 3 Circle*	Hood, Capt. E. T. F., Linc. Yeo. (Lt. ret. pay)	31July11
No. 2 Circle	Nevile, Capt. M. M. H., 3 Bn. York R. (Capt. ret. pay)	{ 23July12 / 17Apr.12
No. 1 Circle	Dowell, Maj. G. W., ret. pay (*Res. of Off.*)	6Dec.12
Head-Quarters	Anderson-Pelham, Capt. C. H., Res. of Off.	10Dec.12
District Barrack Officer	Hill, Bt. Col. R. E., ret. pay (*Res. of Off.*)	

Department of the Finance Member of the Army Council.
(*detached from the War Office for duty at Head-Quarters of the Command*).

Local Auditor	Gaul, W. M., *Esq.*
Assistant Local Auditor	Sutherland, C. R., *Esq.*

Officer in charge of Time-Expired men, etc. } Edye, Col. M. W. J., ret. pay (*Govt. House, Bootham, York*).

At York.
Chief Ordnance Officer .. .. Low, Maj. C. F. G., A. Ord. Dept., *o.*

Army Service Corps.	Royal Army Medical Corps.	Army Ordnance Corps.
(Depôt) Co. (*Bradford*). 24 Co. (*York*).	8 Co. (*York*).	5 Co. (York Section).

FIELD TROOPS (REGULARS).

5th CAVALRY BRIGADE.   York.

Brigade Commander	Chetwode, Col. (*temp. Brig.-Gen.*) *Sir* P. W., *Bt., D.S.O.*	15May14
Brigade-Major	Howard-Vyse, Capt. G. H., R.H.G., *p.s.c.*	4May14
2 Dns. (*York*).	5 Signal Troop, R.E. (*York*).	

For other units of this Brigade, *see* Eastern Command, page 23.

6th DIVISION (*part of*).

18th Infantry Brigade.   Lichfield.

Brigade Commander	*V.C.* Congreve, Col. (*temp. Brig.-Gen.*) W.N., *C.B., M.V.O.*	6Dec.11
Brigade-Major	Wallace, Capt. R. F. H., R. Highrs., *p.s.c.*	{ 6Oct.13 / 26Nov.11

1 Bn. W. York. R. (*Lichfield*)	2 Bn. Notts. and Derby R. (*Sheffield*).
1 Bn. E. York. R. (*York*).	2 Bn. Durh. L.I. (*Lichfield*).

[*Continued on page* 37]

(87)

Commands of the Army.

Northern Command—contd.

OTHER REGULAR TROOPS.

Royal Artillery.

XXXI.Brig.R.F.A. ..{ 131 Batt. 132 Batt. 133 Batt. }(*Sheffield*).

XLV. Brig. R.F.A. ..{ 1 Batt. 3 Batt. 5 Batt. }(*Leeds*).

Royal Engineers.

13 Co. (Survey)   (*York.*)

COAST DEFENCES.
NORTH EASTERN COAST DEFENCES.
Defended Ports of the Tyne, the Tees, Hartlepool, and the Humber.

Officer Commanding (ex-officio)	Baylay, Lt.-Col. (*local Col.*) F., R.E.	*Newcastle-on-Tyne.*
General Staff Officer, 3rd grade ..	Newman, Maj. C. R., R.A., *p.s.c.*	15Mar.12
Captain Instructor in Gunnery ..	Hardinge, Capt. T. S. N., R.A., *g.*	{ 1Apr.13 11Jan.13
Senior Medical Officer	Brown, Lt.-Col. H. H., *M.B.*, R.A.M.C.	

Royal Garrison Artillery.
Regulars.
12 and 47 Cos. (*Tynemouth*).
Territorial.
Tynemouth.
East Riding.
Durham.

Royal Engineers.
Regulars.
16 Co. (Coast Bn.)
Territorial.
North Riding (Fortress).
Durham (Fortress).
East Riding (Fortress).
Tyne Electrical Eng.

No. 5 DISTRICT.
Comprising the Counties of Northumberland, Durham and Yorkshire, and Berwick-on-Tweed (except Regulars and Special Reserve).

Officer Commanding ..	Watson, Col. J. E., *C.B.*	York	24June11
Staff Captain	Ainsworth, Capt. W. J., *D.S.O.*, Durh. L.I.		6June11

Regulars.

Cavalry.
3 *Depôt.*
10 and 18 Hrs. }(*Scarborough*).
14 and 20 Hrs.

Royal Artillery.
I. Res. Brig. { 136 Batt. }(*Newcastle*).
R.F.A.   { 137 Batt.
1 Depôt, R.F.A. (*Newcastle-on-Tyne*)

Regulars—contd.

Infantry.
Depôts.
North'd Fus. (*Newcastle*).
W. York. R. (*York*).
E. York. R. (*Beverley*).
York. R. (*Richmond*).
W. Rid. R. (*Halifax*).
Yorks. L.I. (*Pontefract*).
York. & Lanc. R. (*Pontefract*).
Durh. L.I. (*Newcastle*).

Special Reserve.

Infantry.
3 Bn. North'd Fus.
3 & 4 Bns. W. York. R.
3 Bn. E. York. R.
3 Bn. York. R.
3 Bn. W. Rid. R.
3 Bn. Yorks. L.I.
3 Bn. York & Lanc. R.
3 & 4 Bns. Durh. L.I.

Sheffield Recruiting Area.
Recruiting Staff Officer (Class II.)   ..   Harris, Capt. *Hon.* A. F. W. 28Aug.13

Retired Officers employed on Recruiting Duties { Byrne, Hon. Maj. J. M., Qr.-Mr. ret. pay (*Sunderland*). 18Apr.05
Rance, Hon. Maj. G., Qr.-Mr. ret. pay (*Res. of Off.*) (*Middlesbrough*)   .. { 19May11
1Oct.08
Kelly, Hon. Capt. J., Qr.-Mr. ret. pay (*Leeds*) 4Mar.14

(38)

Commands (United Kingdom).

Northern Command —contd.

No. 6 DISTRICT.
Comprising the Counties of Lincolnshire, Leicestershire, Rutland, Staffordshire, Nottinghamshire and Derbyshire.

Officer Commanding	.. .. .. Churchward, Col. P. R. S., *C.B.*	Lichfield	26 Dec. 12
Staff Captain	.. .. .. Liddell, Capt. C. G., Leic. R.	..	1 Apr. 12

Regulars.	Special Reserve.
Infantry.	*Infantry.*
Depôts,	3 Bn. Linc. R.
Linc. R. (*Lincoln*).	3 Bn. Leic. R.
Leic. R. (*Leicester*).	3 & 4 Bns. S. Staff. R.
S. Staff. R. (*Lichfield*).	3 & 4 Bns. Notts. & Derby. R.
Notts. & Derby. R. (*Derby*).	3 & 4 Bns. N. Staff. R.
N. Staff. R. (*Lichfield*).	

Retired Officers employed on Recruiting Duties	Pearson, Maj. W., ret. pay (*Res. of Off.*) (*Wolverhampton*)	..	{ 1 Apr. 12 18 Apr. 07
	McGuire, Hon. Capt. M., Qr.-Mr. ret. pay (*Nottingham*).	..	11 July 07
	Wall, Hon. Capt. M., Qr.-Mr. ret. pay (*Stoke-on-Trent*).	..	9 June 10

TERRITORIAL DIVISIONS AND BRIGADES.
(Territorial troops allotted to Coast Defences are shewn with the Regulars.)

YORKSHIRE MOUNTED BRIGADE.
9, St. Leonards, York.

Brigade Commander	.. .. .. Nickalls, Col. N. T.	1 Feb. 12
Brigade-Major	.. .. .. Fryer, Maj. J., 7 Hrs.	5 Jan. 12

York. Hrs. Yeo.   York. Dns. Yeo.   E. Rid. of Yorks. Yeo.
W. Rid. R.H.A. (Batt. & Ammn. Col.).
Yorks. Mtd. Brig. T. & S. Col., A.S.C.
Yorks. Mtd. Brig. Fd. Amb., R.A.M.C.
Attached for training:—Northumberland Yeo.

NORTHUMBRIAN DIVISION. *Frenchgate, Richmond, Yorks.*

General Officer Commanding	.. .. Burton, Maj.-Gen. B., *C.B.*	1 Mar. 12
General Staff Officer, 2nd grade	.. Hume-Spry, Maj. L., *D.S.O.*, W. York. R., *p.s.c.* ..	16 Mar. 12
Dep. Asst. Adjt. and Qr.-Mr.-Gen.	Wallace, Capt. A. W. B., Durh. L.I.	1 Apr. 12
Asst. Dir. of Medical Services	Rutherford, Col. J. V. W., TD.	1 Apr. 12
Dep.-Asst. Dir. of Medical Services	MacKenzie, Maj. T. C., *D.S.O.*, R.A.M.C.	5 Nov. 13
Sanitary Officer	.. .. .. Hill, Maj. T. E., *M.B.*	24 June 08

Northumberland Infantry Brigade. *6, Eldon Square, Newcastle-on-Tyne.*

Brigade Commander	.. .. Riddell, Col. J. F.	3 July 11
Brigade-Major	.. .. Moore, Capt. F. H., R. Berks. R., *p.s.c.*	6 Dec. 13

4 Bn. North'd Fus.   5 Bn. North'd Fus.   6 Bn. North'd Fus.   7 Bn. North'd Fus.

York and Durham Infantry Brigade. *12, Castlegate, Malton.*

Brigade Commander	.. .. Bush, Col. J. E.	18 June 11
Brigade-Major	.. .. Guy, Capt. R. F., Wilts. R.	9 Sept. 12

4 Bn. E. York. R.   4 Bn. York. R.   5 Bn. York. R.   5 Bn. Durh. L.I.

Durham Light Infantry Brigade. *Old Elvet, Durham.*

Brigade Commander	.. .. Sears, Col. J. W.	30 Mar. 13
Brigade-Major	.. .. Clayton, Capt. E. R., Oxf. & Bucks. L.I., *p.s.c.* ..	12 Oct. 10

6 Bn. Durh. L.I.   7 Bn. Durh. L.I.   8 Bn. Durh. L.I.   9 Bn. Durh. L.I.

[*Continued on page* 39]

(39)

Commands of the Army.

Northern Command—contd.
Territorial Divisions and Brigades.—Northumbrian Division—contd.

Divisional Troops.

Royal Artillery.   Frenchgate, Richmond, Yorks.

Commanding Royal Artillery	.. .. Hussey, Col. A. H., ...	1Oct.13
Staff Captain	.. Thomson, Capt. R. G., R.A. [L]	1Jan.11

1 North'bn Brig. R.F.A. { 1 North'd Batt. / 2 North'd Batt. / 3 North'd Batt. / 1 North'bn Ammn. Col.

2 North'bn Brig. R.F.A. { 1 E. Riding Batt. / 2 E. Riding Batt. / 3 N. Riding Batt. / 2 North'bn Ammn. Col.

3 North'bn Brig. R.F.A. { 1 Durham Batt. / 2 Durham Batt. / 3 Durham Batt. / 3North'bn Ammn. Col.

4 North'bn (Howr.) Brig. R.F.A. .. .. { 4 Durham Batt. / 5 Durham Batt. / 4 North'bn Ammn. Col.

North'bn R.G.A.

Royal Engineers.   Barras Bridge, Newcastle-on-Tyne.

Commanding Royal Engineers .. .. Crawford, Lt.-Col. and Hon. Col. F. S., VD. 1Apr.08
1 North'bn Fd. Co.   2 North'bn Fd. Co.   North'bn Div. Signal Co.

Army Service Corps.   *Royal Army Medical Corps.*

North'bn Divl. T. & S. Col. { Divl. Co. (H.-Q.) / North'd Brig. Co. / York. & Durh. Brig. Co. / Durh. L.I. Brig. Co.

1 North'bn Fd. Amb.
2 North'bn Fd. Amb.
3 North'bn Fd. Amb.

WEST RIDING DIVISION.

9, St. Leonards, York.

General Officer Commanding	Baldock, Maj.-Gen. T. S., *C.B.*, *p.s.c.*	19Sept.11
General Staff Officer, 2nd grade ..	Wilkins, Maj. H. St. C., R. W. Surr. R., *p.s.c.* [*l*] ..	4Sept.13
Dep. Asst. Adjt. and Qr.-Mr.-Gen.	Pratt, Bt. Maj. A. G., Essex R.	{ 1Oct.13 / 25May 10
Asst. Dir. of Medical Services ..	Lee, Col. E., VD, (*Red House, Marygate, York*)	1Apr.12
Dep.-Asst. Dir. of Medical Services	Hyde, Maj. D. O., *M.B.*, R.A M.C.	1Apr.11
Sanitary Officer	Kaye, Lt.-Col. J. R., *M.B.*	10June08

1st West Riding Infantry Brigade.

3, Tower Street, York.

Brigade Commander	MacFarlan, Col. F. A.	.. 25Nov.13
Brigade-Major	Pope-Hennessy, Maj. L. H. R., *D.S.O.*, Oxf. & Bucks. L. I., *p.s.c.* [*l*]	.. 13May12

5 Bn. W. York. R.   6 Bn. W. York. R.   7 Bn. W. York. R.   8 Bn. W. York. R.

2nd West Riding Infantry Brigade. *Drill Hall, Skipton-in-Craven.*

Brigade Commander	Brereton, Col. E. F., *D.S.O.*	.. 11May12
Brigade-Major	North, Maj. E. B., R. Fus. [*l*]	24Apr.12

4 Bn. W. Rid. R.   Bn. W. Rid.R.   6 Bn. W. Rid. R.   7 Bn. W. Rid. R

(40)

Commands (United Kingdom).

Northern Command—contd.

Territorial Divisions and Brigades—West Riding Division—contd.

3rd West Riding Infantry Brigade. 7, *Bank Court Chambers, Sheffield.*

Brigade Commander .. .. ,..	Dawson, Col. R.		1Apr.12
Brigade-Major	Pickering, Capt. C. J., W. Rid. R., *e.*		18Nov.12

4 Bn. Yorks. L.I.   5 Bn. Yorks. L.I.   4 Bn. York & Lanc. R.   5 Bn. York & Lanc. R.

Divisional Troops.

Royal Artillery.   *Red House, Marygate, York.*

Commanding Royal Artillery .. .. Browne, Col. S. D. 1Jan.13
Staff Captain .. .. .. Lewer, Capt. L. W., R.A., *g.* 26Apr.12

1 W. Rid. Brig. { 1 W. Rid. Batt.
R.F.A.   { 2 W. Rid. Batt.
                 { 3 W. Rid. Batt.
                 { 1 W. Rid. Ammn. Col.

3 W. Rid. Brig. { 7 W. Rid. Batt.
R.F.A.   { 8 W. Rid. Batt.
                 { 9 W. Rid. Batt.
                 { 3 W. Rid. Ammn. Col.

2 W. Rid. Brig. { 4 W. Rid. Batt.
R.F.A.   { 5 W. Rid. Batt.
                 { 6 W. Rid. Batt.
                 { 2 W. Rid. Ammn. Col.

4 W. Rid. (Howr.) { 10 W. Rid. Batt.
Brig. R.F.A.   { 11 W. Rid. Batt.
                   { 4 W. Rid. Ammn. Col.

W. Rid. R.G.A.

Royal Engineers.   *Glossop Road, Sheffield.*

Commanding Royal Engineers .. .. Bingham, Lt.-Col. A. E., VD, W. Rid. Divl. R.E.
1 W. Rid. Fd. Co.   2 W. Rid. Fd. Co.   W. Rid. Div. Signal Co.

Army Service Corps.   *Royal Army Medical Corps.*
                 { Divl. Co. (H.-Q.)   1 W. Rid. Fd. Amb.
1 W. Rid. Divl. { 1 W. Rid. Brig. Co.   2 W. Rid. Fd. Amb.
T. & S. Col.   { 2 W. Rid. Brig. Co.   3 W. Rid. Fd. Amb.
                 { 3 W. Rid. Brig. Co.

ARMY TROOPS ATTACHED WEST RIDING DIVISION.

Royal Engineers.
N. Wireless Signal Co.
N. Cable Signal Co.
N. Air Line Signal Co.

NOTTS. & DERBY MOUNTED BRIGADE. *Derby Road, Nottingham.*

Brigade Commander	V℃Kenna, Col. P. A., *D.S.O., A.D.C.*		1Apr.12
Brigade-Major	Franks, Maj. G. D., 19 Hrs.		10Mar.14

Notts. Yeo.   S. Notts. Hrs. Yeo.   Derby. Yeo.   Notts. R.H.A. (Batt. & Ammn. Col.)
Notts. & Derby Mtd. Brig. T. & S. Col., A.S.C.
Notts. & Derby Mtd. Brig. Fd. Amb., R.A.M.C.

NORTH MIDLAND MOUNTED BRIGADE. 7, *Magazine Square, Leicester.*

Brigade Commander	Williams, Col. C.		18Sept.11
Brigade-Major	Knowles, Maj. J., 1 Hrs., *p.s.c.* [*l*]		15Aug.12

Staffs. Yeo.   Leic. Yeo.   Linc. Yeo.   Leic. R.H.A. (Batt. & Ammn. Col.)
N. Mid. Mtd. Brig. T. & S. Col., A.S.C.
N. Mid. Mtd. Brig. Fd. Amb. R.A.M.C.

[*Continued on page* 41]

(41)

Commands of the Army.

Northern Command—contd.
Territorial Divisions and Brigades—contd.

NORTH MIDLAND DIVISION. *Lichfield.*

General Officer Commanding ..	Montagu-Stuart-Wortley, Maj.-Gen. *Hon.* E. J., *C.B., C.M.G., M.V.O., D.S.O., q.s.*	1June14
Gen. Staff Officer, 2nd grade	Weber Maj. W. H. F., R.A., *p.s.c.,* [*l*] ..	17Mar.14
Dep. Asst. Adjt. & Qr.-Mr.-Gen. ..	Dansey, Capt. F. H., Wilts. R., *s.*	1Oct.13
Asst. Dir. of Medical Services	Clarke,Col. A. V., *M.D.*(91, *Siddals Road, Derby*)	10May13
Dep.-Asst. Dir. of Medical Services	Beevor, Lt.-Col. W. C., *C.M.G., M.B.,* ret. pay	
Sanitary Officer	Reid, Maj. G., *M.D.* ..	10Aug.08
Asst. Dir. of Veterinary Services	McDougall, Maj.(*temp. Lt.-Col. Terr. Force*) W. A., *F.R.C.V.S.,* ret. pay (*Res. of Off.*)	24Sept.13

Lincoln & Leicester, Infantry Brigade. *Culverthorpe, Grantham.*

Brigade Commander ..	.. ..	Taylor, Col. A. W.	.. ..	9Aug.13
Brigade-Major ..	.. ..	Adlercron, Maj. R. L., Cam'n Highrs.	.. ..	28Sept.11
4 Bn. Linc. R.	5 Bn. Linc. R.	4 Bn. Leic. R.	5 Bn. Leic. R.	

Staffordshire Infantry Brigade. *Market Square, Stafford.*

Brigade Commander..	.. ..	Bromilow, Col. W. ..	.. ..	10Oct.12
Brigade-Major ..	.. ..	Abadie, Capt. R. N., K. R. Rif. C. ..	.. ..	1Nov.12
5 Bn. S. Staff. R.	6 Bn. S. Staff. R.	5 Bn. N. Staff. R.	6 Bn. N. Staff. R.	

Notts. & Derby Infantry Brigade. *The Drill Hall, Derby Road, Nottingham.*

Brigade Commander ..	.. ..	Shipley, Col. C. T. ..	.. ..	9Sept.11
Brigade-Major ..	.. ..	Morris, Maj. E. M., Devon. R.	.. ..	5July11
5 Bn. Notts. & Derby. R.	6 Bn. Notts. & Derby. R.	7 Bn. Notts. & Derby. R.	8 Bn. Notts. & Derby. R.	

Divisional Troops.

Royal Artillery. 5, *Market Square, Stafford.*

Commanding Royal Artillery ..	Campbell, Col. H. M., *h.p.*		
Staff Captain	Budge, Capt. P. P., R.A.		21July13

1 N. Mid. Brig. R.F.A.	{ 1 Linc. Batt. 2 Linc. Batt. 3 Linc. Batt. 1 N. Mid. Ammn. Col.	3 N. Mid. Brig. R.F.A.	{ 4 Staff. Batt. 5 Staff. Batt. 6 Staff. Batt. 3 N. Mid. Ammn. Col.
2 N. Mid. Brig. R.F.A.	{ 1 Staff. Batt. 2 Staff. Batt. 3 Staff. Batt. 2 N. Mid. Ammn. Col.	4 N. Mid. (Howr.) Brig. R.F.A.	{ 1 Derby. Batt. 2 Derby. Batt. 4 N. Mid. Ammn. Col.

N. Mid. R.G.A.

Royal Engineers. *Norton Hall, Norton Canes, Cannock.*

Commanding Royal Engineers ..	Harrison, Lt.-Col. W. E., N. Mid. Divl. R.E.	
1 N. Mid. Fd. Co.	2 N. Mid. Fd. Co.	N. Mid. Divl. Signal Co.

Army Service Corps.	*Royal Army Medical Corps.*
N. Mid. Divl. T. & S. Col. { Divl. Co. (H.-Q.) Linc. & Leic. Brig. Co. Staff. Brig. Co. Notts. & Derby. Brig. Co.	1 N Mid. Fd. Amb. 2 N Mid. Fd. Amb. 3 N Mid. Fd. Amb.

OTHER TERRITORIAL TROOPS IN THE COMMAND.

Cyclists.	*Royal Army Medical Corps*—contd.
5 Bn. E. York. R. N. Cyclist Bn.	3 N. Gen. Hosp. 4 N. Gen. Hosp. 5 N. Gen. Hosp. North'bn Clearing Hosp. W. Rid. Clearing Hosp. N. Mid. Clearing Hosp.
Royal Army Medical Corps.	
1 N. Gen. Hosp. 2 N. Gen. Hosp.	

(42)

Commands (United Kingdom).

SCOTTISH COMMAND.—Scotland and Berwick-on-Tweed (so far as regards Regulars and Special Reserve only).

Head-Quarters—Edinburgh.

GENERAL OFFICER COMMANDING-IN-CHIEF	Ewart, Lt.-Gen. *Sir* J. S., K.C.B., p.s.c.	5May14
Assistant Military Secretary	Browne, Maj. A. N. E., High. L I.	4July14
Aide-de-Camp	Nicholson, Lt. A. S., Cam'n. Highrs.	13May14

General Staff.

General Staff Officer, 1st grade	Kerr, Col. F. W., D.S.O., p.s.c.	29May13
General Staff Officer, 3rd grade	Douglas, Capt. W. S., R.E., p.s.c. [L]	29May14

Attached to the General Staff.

Captain, graded as Brigade-Major	Tudor, Capt. L. H., S. Wales Bord.	1Feb.13

Administrative, Technical and Departmental Staff.

Brigadier-General in charge of Administration	Wintour, Col. (*temp. Brig.-Gen.*) F., C.B., p.s.c.	10Oct.12
Dep. Asst. Adjt.-Gen.	Marshall, Maj. F. J., Sea. Highrs., p.s.c.	4Feb.14
Asst. Inspr. of Recg. (graded Staff Capt.)	Scott, Capt. J. C., Arg. & Suth'd Highrs.	23Apr.14
Asst. Qr.-Mr.-Gen.	Campbell, Col. W., D.S.O., p.s.c. [l]	20Dec.11
Chief Engineer	Huskisson, Col. W.	23Feb.12
Staff Officer, Royal Engineers	Walker, Maj. R. S., R.E., [L]	
Asst. Director of Supplies and Transport	Conway-Gordon, Lt.-Col. G., A.S.C., e.	
Dep. Dir. of Medical Services	Thompson, Col. H.N., D.S.O., M.B.	
Asst. Dir. of Veterinary Services	The Asst. Dir. of Veterinary Services, Northern Command.	
Asst. Dir. of Ordnance Stores	Bernard, Maj. J. F., A. Ord. Dept., e., f., g. [L]	
Command Paymaster	Lowry, Col. J., A. P. Dept.	
Deputy Asst. Dirs. of Remounts. { No. 2 Circle / No. 1 Circle & Head-Quarters }	Bridge, Capt. W. B. C., ret. pay (*Res. of Off.*)	2Dec.12
	Cadell, Lt.-Col. J. F., ret. pay (*Res. of Off.*) p.s.c.	1Apr.14
District Barrack Officer	Welch, Col. G. O., C.B., ret. pay (*Res. of Off.*)	

Department of the Finance Member of the Army Council
(*detached from the War Office for duty at Head-Quarters of the Command*).

Local Auditor	Neylan, D., *Esq.*	
Assistant Local Auditor	Moir, C. R., *Esq.*	

Acting Chaplain in charge of Time Expired men, etc.	Mackay, Rev. P. R., D.D. (11, *Cumin Place, Edinburgh*).	

At Glasgow.

Garrison Adjutant	Follett, Lt. (D.O.) J. E. G., R.F.A.	25May14

At Stirling.

Chief Ordnance Officer	Exham, Maj. F. S., A.O. Dept., e., o.	

Army Service Corps.	Royal Army Medical Corps.	Army Ordnance Corps.
8 Co. (*Edinburgh*).	13 Co. (*Edinburgh*).	5 Co. (Stirling Section)

ARMY TROOPS.
Royal Flying Corps (Military Wing).
2 Squadron (*Montrose*).

OTHER REGULAR FIELD TROOPS.

Royal Artillery.	Infantry.
1 Brig. R.F.A. { 13 Batt. / 67 Batt. / 69 Batt. } (*Edinburgh*).	1 Bn. Sco. Rif. (*Glasgow*). 1 Bn. Cam'n Highrs. (*Edinburgh*). 2 Bn. Arg. & Suth'd Highrs. (*Fort George*).

[*Continued on page* 43]

(48)

Commands of the Army.

Scottish Command—contd.

COAST DEFENCES.

SCOTTISH COAST DEFENCES.

Defended ports of the Forth, the Clyde, the Tay, and Aberdeen.

Officer Commanding	Heath-Caldwell, Maj.-Gen. F. C., *C.B., p.s.c., Edinburgh*	15Aug.13
General Staff Officer, 2nd grade	Marindin, Maj. A. H., R. Highrs., *p.s.c.* [L]	7Nov.13
Dep. Asst. Adjt. & Qr.-Mr. Gen.	Sandilands, Capt. J. W., *D.S.O.*, Cam'n Highrs., *p.s.c.* [l]	1May14
Chief Instructor in Gunnery	Scott, Col. C. D.	1Apr.13
Major Instructor in Gunnery	Lewes, Maj. P. K., R.A., *g.* *Broughty Ferry*	1Apr.13 / 21May11
Senior Medical Officer	O'Halloran, Lt.-Col. M., *M.D.*, R.A.M.C. *Edinburgh*	

Royal Garrison Artillery.	Royal Engineers.
Regulars.	*Regulars.*
21 Co.	49 Co. (Coast Bn.)
Territorial.	*Territorial.*
Forth.	City of Aberdeen (Fortress).
Clyde.	Renfrew (Fortress).
North Scottish.	City of Edinburgh (Fortress).
Orkney.	City of Dundee (Fortress).

Infantry.
Territorial.

Lothian Infantry Brigade.   23, *Rutland Square, Edinburgh.*

Brigade Commander	Kays, Col. H. F.	1Oct.13
Brigade-Major	Neilson, Capt. W. G., *D.S.O.*, Arg. and Suth'd Highrs.	12July12
4 Bn. R. Scots.	5 Bn. R. Scots. 8 Bn. R. Scots. 9 Bn. R. Scots.	
6 Bn. R. Scots.	*Attached Lothian Infantry Brigade.* 7 Bn. R. Scots. 8 Bn. High. L.I.	

Black Watch Infantry Brigade.

Drill Hall, Bell Street, Dundee.

Brigade Commander	McKerrell, Col. A. de S., *C.B.*	1Apr.12
Brigade Major	Laird, Capt. K. M., Arg. & Suth'd Highrs., *p.s.c.*	25Mar.14
4 Bn. R. Highrs.	5 Bn. R. Highrs. 6 Bn. R. Highrs. 7 Bn. R. Highrs.	
	Attached Black Watch Infantry Brigade. 5 Bn. Arg. & Suth'd Highrs.	

No. 1 DISTRICT.

Comprising the Counties of Perthshire, Forfarshire, Fifeshire, Orkney, Shetland, Caithness, Sutherland, Ross and Cromarty, Elgin, Nairn, Aberdeenshire, Banffshire, Kincardine, Inverness-shire, Argyll, Bute, Kinross, Clackmannan, Stirlingshire, Dumbartonshire and Renfrewshire.

Officer Commanding	Mackintosh, Col. G., *C.B.* [l] *Perth*	1Apr.12
Staff Captain	Buchanan, Capt. K.G., Sea. Highrs.	16Apr.12

Regulars.	Regulars—contd.	Special Reserve.
Royal Artillery.	*Infantry.*	*Infantry.*
	Depôts.	3 Bn. R. Highrs.
VI.Res.Brig. { 146 Batt. } (*Glasgow*).	R. Highrs. (*Perth*).	3 Bn. Sea. Highrs.
R.F.A. { 147 Batt. }	Sea. Highrs. (*Fort George*).	3 Bn. Gord. Highrs.
	Gord. Highrs. (*Aberdeen*).	3 Bn. Cam'n Highrs.
6 Depôt, R. F. A. (*Glasgow*).	Cam'n Highrs. (*Inverness*).	3 & 4 Bns. Arg. & Suth'd Highrs.
	Arg. & Suth'd Highrs. (*Stirling*).	

Retired Officer employed on Recruiting Duties } Carnegie, Hon. Maj. M. L., Qr.-Mr. ret. pay. (*Dundee*) 12May13

(44)

Commands (United Kingdom).

Scottish Command—contd.

No. 2 DISTRICT.

Comprising the Counties of Linlithgow, Edinburgh, Haddington, Peebles, Ayrshire, Wigtownshire, Berwickshire, Berwick-on-Tweed (so far as regards the Regulars and Special Reserve only), Roxburgh, Selkirk, Dumfries, Kirkcudbright and Lanarkshire.

Officer Commanding	..	..	.. Paterson, Col. S.	Hamilton 27July12
Staff Captain	..	..	.. Pack-Beresford, Maj. H. J., High.L.I. ..	.. .. 1Apr.12

Regulars.	Special Reserve.
Cavalry.	
6 *Depôt.*	*Infantry.*
1 & 5 D. G. } Dunbar.	3 Bn. R. Scots.
1 & 2 Dns. }	3 & 4 Bns. Sco. Rif.
	3 & 4 Bns. High. L. I.
Infantry.	3 Bn. R. Sc. Fus.
Depôts.	3 Bn. K. O. Sco. Bord.
R. Scots. (*Glencorse, Milton Bridge, N.B.*).	
R. Sc. Fus. (*Ayr*).	
K.O. Sco. Bord. (*Berwick-on-Tweed*).	
Sco. Rif. (*Hamilton*).	
High. L. I. (*Hamilton*).	

Edinburgh Recruiting Area.

Recruiting Staff Officer (Class II.) .. ᵁℂRobertson, Hon. Capt. W., Qr.-Mr. Gord. Highrs. .. 13Dec.07

Retired Officer employed on Recruiting } Ross, Hon. Capt. W., Qr.-Mr. ret. pay (*Res. of Off.*)
Duties .. .. } (*Glasgow*) 1Apr.14

TERRITORIAL DIVISIONS AND BRIGADES.

(Territorial troops allotted to Coast Defences are shewn with the Regulars.)

HIGHLAND MOUNTED BRIGADE. *Academy Street, Inverness.*

Brigade Commander .. .. .. Tyndale-Biscoe, Col. J. D. T.	1Jan.13
Brigade-Major .. .. .. Cape, Maj. H. A., 5 Lrs.	15Jan.12

Fife & Forfar Yeo. 1 Lovat's Scouts Yeo. 2 Lovat's Scouts Yeo. Inverness. R.H.A. (Batt. & Ammn. Col.)
Highl. Mtd. Brig. T. & S. Col., A.S.C.
Highl. Mtd. Brig. Fd. Amb., R.A.M.C.

HIGHLAND DIVISION. 2, *Charlotte Street, Perth.*

General Officer Commanding ..	Mackenzie, Maj.-Gen. C. J., *C.B., p.s.c.* [*l*] ..	..	..	3Mar.14
General Staff Officer, 2nd grade ..	Moir, Maj. A. J. G., R. Scots, *p.s.c.*	..	..	1Apr.12
Dep. Asst. Adjt. & Qr.-Mr.-Gen. ..	Nicholson, Capt. W. N., Suff. R., *p.s.c.*	..	..	{ 1°Mar.14 / 22June12
Asst. Dir. of Medical Services ..	Kinnear, Col. W., *M.D., K.H.P.,* vD	..	..	1Apr.12
Dep.-Asst. Dir. of Medical Services	Keble, Maj. A. E. C., R.A.M.C. ..	..	..	3June12
Sanitary Officer	Dewar, Lt.-Col. T. F., *M.D.,* TD. ..	..	..	1Apr.08

Seaforth and Cameron Infantry Brigade. *The Drill Hall, Margaret Street, Inverness.*

Brigade Commander .. .. .. Macfarlane, Col. D. A., *D.S.O.*	9May11
Brigade-Major .. .. .. Booth, Capt. T. M., Gord. Highrs. [L]	12Aug.11

4 Bn. Sea. Highrs.   5 Bn. Sea. Highrs.   6 Bn. Sea. Highrs.   4 Bn. Cam'n Highrs.

[*Continued on page 45*]

(45)

Commands of the Army.

Scottish Command—contd.

Territorial Divisions and Brigades—Highland Division—contd.

Gordon Infantry Brigade.
Territorial Barracks, Fonthill Road, Aberdeen.

Brigade Commander .. .. .. Stockwell, Col. G, C. I., D.S.O., p.s.c. [l]	..	.. .. 22Jan,12
Brigade-Major .. .. .. Arbuthnot, Maj. K. W., Sea. Highrs.	..	.. .. 12Oct.11

Bn. Gord. Highrs.   5 Bn. Gord. Highrs.   6 Bn. Gord. Highrs.   7 Bn. Gord. Highrs.

Argyll and Sutherland Infantry Brigade.   *Princes Street, Stirling.*

Brigade Commander .. .. .. Burton, Col. St. G. E. W.	.. .. ..	1June11
Brigade-Major .. .. .. Thomson, Maj. N. A., Sea. Highrs., e.	.. ..	11Nov.12

6 Bn. Arg. & Suth'd Highrs.   7 Bn. Arg. & Suth'd Highrs.   8 Bn. Arg. & Suth'd Highrs.   9 Bn. Arg. & Suth'd Highrs.

Divisional Troops.

Royal Artillery.   *Dudhope Drill Hall, Dundee.*

Commanding Royal *Artillery*   ..   Brendon, Col. (*Terr.Force*) H. A., Lt.-Col. ret. pay (*Res. of Off.*) 15May13
Staff Captain   ..   ..   Wynne, Maj. H, E. S., R.A. 9Feb.11

1 Highl. Brig. R.F.A.
   { 1 City of Aberdeen Batt.
     2 City of Aberdeen Batt.
     3 City of Aberdeen Batt.
     1 Highl. Ammn. Col.

3 Highl. (Howr.) Brig. R.F.A.

4 Highl. (Mtn.) Brig. R.G.A.

2 Highl. Brig. R.F.A.
   { Forfar Batt.
     Fife Batt.
     City of Dundee Batt.
     2 Highl. Ammn. Col.

{ 1 Renfrew Batt.
  2 Renfrew Batt.
  3 Highl. Ammn. Col.
  Renfrew S. A. Section Ammn. Col.

{ Argyll. Batt.
  Ross and Cromarty Batt.
  Bute Batt.
  4 Highl. Ammn. Col.

Highl. R.G.A.

Royal Engineers.   80, *Hardgate, Aberdeen.*

Commanding Royal Engineers ..   ..   ..   Cornwall, Lt.-Col. G, A., VD, Highl. Divl. R.E.

2 Highl. Fd. Co. | Highl. Divl. Signal Co.

Army Service Corps.   *Royal Army Medical Corps.*

Highl. Divl. T. & S. Col.
   { 1 (H.-Q.) Co.
     2 Co.
     3 (Gordon Brig.) Co.
     4 Co.

1 Highl. Fd. Amb.
2 Highl. Fd. Amb.
3 Highl. Fd. Amb.

ARMY TROOPS ATTACHED HIGHLAND DIVISION.

Infantry.

Attached Gordon Infantry Brigade.
The Shetland Cos., Gord. Highrs.

LOWLAND MOUNTED BRIGADE.   10, *Dublin Street, Edinburgh.*

Brigade Commander .. .. Lee, Col. F. [L]	.. ..	27June14
Brigade-Major .. .. .. McNeile, Maj. H. D., 1 Dns.	.. .. ..	5Aug.11

Ayr. Yeo.   Lanark. Yeo.   Loth. & Bord. Horse Yeo.   Ayr. R.H.A. (Batt. & Ammn. Col.
                         Low. Mtd. Brig. T. & S. Col., A.S.C.
                         Low. Mtd. Brig. Fd. Amb., R.A.M.C.
Attached for training:—Lanark, (R. Glasgow) Yeo.

(46)

Commands (United Kingdom).

Scottish Command—contd.

Territorial Divisions and Brigades—contd.

LOWLAND DIVISION. 7, West George Street, Glasgow.

General Officer Commanding	.. .. Egerton, Maj.-Gen. G. G. A., C.B.	21Mar.14
General Staff Officer, 2nd grade	.. .. Walshe, Maj. F. W. H., R.A., p.s.c.	19Feb.14
Dep. Asst. Adjt. & Qr.-Mr.-Gen.	.. .. Maclean, Bt. Maj. C. A. H., Arg. & Suth'd Highrs. ..	10Sept.10
Asst. Dir. of Medical Services	.. .. MacKintosh, Col. D. J., M.V.O., M.B. (Yorkhill Parade, Yorkhill, Glasgow)	1Apr.12
Dep.-Asst. Dir. of Medical Services	.. Thom, Maj. G. St. C., M.B., R.A.M.C.	13Dec.13
Sanitary Officer	.. .. .. Chalmers, Lt.-Col. A. K., M.D., TD	1Apr.08

South Scottish Infantry Brigade. 7, Wellington Square, Ayr.

Brigade Commander	.. .. .. Erskine, Col. J. F., M.V.O.	19May11
Brigade-Major	.. .. .. Mudie, Capt. T. C., R. Scots, p.s.c.	2June11

4 Bn. R. Sc. Fus.   5 Bn. R. Sc. Fus.   4 Bn. K.O. Sco. Bord.   5 Bn. K.O. Sco. Bord.

Scottish Rifle Brigade. 34, Robertson Street, Glasgow.

Brigade Commander	.. .. .. Hare, Col. S. W.	20Aug.12
Brigade-Major	.. .. .. Girdwood, Capt. E. S., Sco. Rif.	{ 29June11 22June11

5 Bn. Sco. Rif.   6 Bn. Sco. Rif.   7 Bn. Sco. Rif.   8 Bn. Sco. Rif.

Highland Light Infantry Brigade. 34, Robertson Street, Glasgow.

Brigade Commander..	.. .. .. Hendry, Col. P. W., VD, Capt. ret. (Q)	8June11
Brigade-Major	.. .. .. Armstrong, Maj. E., High. L.I.	27Nov.11

5 Bn. High. L.I.   6 Bn. High. L.I.   7 Bn. High. L.I.   9 Bn. High. L.I.

Divisional Troops.
Royal Artillery.   Newton Terrace, Charing Cross, Glasgow.

Commanding Royal Artillery	.. .. Johnstone, Col. F. B., D S.O...	1Apr.13
Staff Captain	.. .. Cossart, Capt. A. R. B., R.A...	27Sept.13

1 Low. Brig. R.F.A. {	1 City of Edin. Batt. 2 City of Edin. Batt. Midlothian Batt. 1 Low. Ammn. Col.	3 Low. Brig. R.F.A. {	1 City of Glasgow Batt. 2 City of Glasgow Batt. 3 City of Glasgow Batt. 3 Low. Ammn. Col.
2 Low. Brig. R.F.A. {	1 Ayr. Batt. 2 Ayr. Batt. Kirkcudbright Batt. 2 Low. Ammn. Col.	4Low.(Howr.)Brig. { R.F.A.	4 City of Glasgow Batt. 5 City of Glasgow Batt. 4 Low. Ammn. Col.

Low. R.G.A.
Royal Engineers.   Drill Hall, Rutherglen.

Commanding Royal Engineers .. .. Symington, Lt.-Col. T., Low. Divl. R.E.	
1 Low. Fd. Co. 2 Low. Fd. Co.	Low Divl. Signal Co.
Army Service Corps.	Royal Army Medical Corps.
Low. Divl. T. & S. Col. {	1 (H.-Q.) Co. 2 Co. 3 (Sco. Rif. Brig.) Co. 4 (High. L.I. Brig.) Co.	1 Low. Fd. Amb. 2 Low. Fd. Amb. 3 Low. Fd. Amb.

ARMY TROOPS ATTACHED LOWLAND DIVISION.

Royal Engineers.

Sco. Wireless Signal Co.   Sco. Cable Signal Co.   Sco. Air Line Signal Co.
Attached :—1 Highl. Fd. Co.

OTHER TERRITORIAL TROOPS IN THE COMMAND.

Yeomanry.	Cyclists.	Royal Army Medical Corps.
Sco. Horse.	10 Bn. R. Scots. Highl. Cyclist Bn.	1 Sco. Gen. Hosp. 2 Sco. Gen. Hosp. 3 Sco. Gen. Hosp. 4 Sco. Gen. Hosp. High. Clearing Hosp. Low. Clearing Hosp.
Infantry. Ardeer Co. R. Sc. Fus.		

(47)

Commands of the Army.

SOUTHERN COMMAND.—The Counties of Warwickshire, Worcestershire, Gloucestershire, Oxfordshire, Buckinghamshire, Berkshire (except Windsor for Regular troops and that portion of the County included in the Aldershot Command), Cornwall, Devonshire, Somersetshire, Dorsetshire, Wiltshire and Hampshire (except that portion included in the Aldershot Command).

Head-Quarters—Salisbury.

GENERAL OFFICER COMMANDING-IN-CHIEF	Smith-Dorrien, Gen. Sir H. L., G.C.B., D.S.O., Col. Notts & Derby. R., p.s.c.	1 Mar.12
Assistant Military Secretary	Johnstone, Maj. H., R. A., g., f.	1 Mar.12
Aide-de-Camp	Bowly, Capt. W. A. T., Dorset R.	20 Dec.13
General Staff.		
Brigadier-General	Montgomery, Col. (*temp. Brig.-Gen.*) R. A. K., C.B., D.S.O., p.s.c., g...	16 Oct.11
General Staff Officer, 2nd grade	Shoubridge, Bt. Lt.-Col. T. H., D.S.O., North'd Fus., p.s.c.	5 Sept.12
Attached to the General Staff.		
Captain, graded as Brigade-Major	Walford, Capt. G. H., Suff. R., p.s.c.	1 Apr.14
Administrative Technical and Departmental Staff.		
Major-General in charge of Administration	Altham, Maj.-Gen. E, A., C.B., C.M.G. p.s.c.	17 Dec.11
Asst. Adjt.-Gen.	Cavendish, Col. A. E, J., C.M.G., p.s.c.	9 May13
Asst Inspr. of Recg. (graded Staff Captain)	Hill, Capt. G. E. M., E. Lan. R.	1 Apr.14
Asst. Qr.-Mr.-Gen.	Rycroft, Col. W. H., C.B., p.s.c.	22 Oct.12
Staff Captains	Wroughton, Maj. J. B., R. Suss. R., e.	14 Jan.12
	Henvey, Maj. R., R.A., p.s.c. [1]	29 Apr.12
Chief Engineer	Glubb, Col. (*temp. Brig.-Gen.*) F. M., C.B., D.S.O.	8 Mar.12 / 25 Feb.09
Staff Officer, Royal Engineers	Reid, Capt. A. W., R.E.	
Asst. Director of Supplies and Transport	Long, Col. A., D.S.O.	16 Oct.13 / 14 July13
Dep. Asst. Director of Supplies and Transport	Davies, Maj. P. M., A.S.C.	15 Dec.13
Dep. Dir. of Medical Services	MacNeece, Surg.-Gen. J. G., C.B.	
Dep.-Asst. Dir. of Medical Services	Russell, Lt.-Col. J. J., M.B., R.A.M.C.	
Asst. Dir. of Veterinary Services	Rutherford, Col. C., C.B., C.M.G., F.R.C.V.S.	
Asst. Director of Ordnance Stores	Mathew, Col. C. M., C.B., D.S.O., A. Ord. Dept.	
Command Paymaster	Bray, Col. C. A., C.B., C.M.G., A.P. Dept.	
	Head-Quarters Fair, Lt.-Col. J. G., D.S.O., ret. pay (*Res. of Off.*)	31 July11
	No. 1 Circle Norton, Lt. (*temp. Capt.*) J. H., Res. of Off.	18 Aug.11
Dep. Asst. Dirs. of Remounts	No. 2 Circle Shaw, Capt. F. S. K., ret. pay (*Res. of Off.*)	1 Dec.11
	No. 3 Circle Sandars, Maj. E. C., ret. pay (*Res. of Off.*)	18 Dec.12 / 29 Dec.11
	No. 4 Circle Hankey, Capt. S. R. A., S. Irish Horse	11 Dec.12
District Barrack Officer	Phelps, Lt.-Col. A.	18 Dec.13

Department of the Finance Member of the Army Council
(detached from the War Office for duty at Head-Quarters of the Command).

Local Auditor	McArthur, W. L., Esq.
Assistant Local Auditor	Arnold, F. J., Esq.

Officer in charge of Time-Expired Men, etc. — Jones, Hon, Maj. O. G., Qr.-Mr. ret. pay, late A.S.C. (33, *Castle Road, Salisbury*)

At Tidworth.
Asst. Dir. of Medical Services	Jones, Lt.-Col. F. W. C., M.B., R.A.M.C.
Chief Ordnance Officer	Bush, Maj. H. S., A. Ord. Dept., e., o.

At Devonport.
Asst. Dir. of Medical Services	Geddes, Col. R. J., D.S.O., M.B.
Chief Ordnance Officer	Forbes, Lt.-Col. A., A. Ord. Dept., e., f.

At Portsmouth.
Asst. Dir. of Medical Services	Westcott, Col. S., C.M.G.
Chief Ordnance Officer	Baker, Lt.-Col. A. S., A. Ord. Dept., p.a.c.

Army Service Corps.
12 Co. (*Portsmouth*).
15 Co. (*Bulford*).
21 Co. (*Devonport*).
22 Co. (*Bulford*).
29 Co. (*Portsmouth*).
30 Co. (*Devonport*).
34 Co. (*Cosham*).
45 (M.T.) Co. (*Devonport*).
55 (M.T) Co. (*Bulford*).
56 (M.T.) Co. (*Bulford*).
62 (M.T.) Co. (*Portsmouth*).

Army Service Corps—contd.
63 (M.T.) Co. (*Bulford*).
64 (M.T.) Co. (*Bulford*).
"B" Co. (*Gosport*)

Royal Army Medical Corps.
4 Co. (*Netley*).
5 Co. (*Netley*).
6 Co. (*Cosham*).
7 Co. Devonport
20 Co. (*Tidworth*).
21 Co. (*Netley*)

Army Veterinary Corps.
5 & 6 Sections (*Bulford*).

Army Ordnance Corps.
2 Co. { Portsmouth Section. Tidworth Section. Devonport Section. }

(48)

Commands (United Kingdom).

Southern Command—contd.

FIELD TROOPS (REGULARS).
2nd CAVALRY BRIGADE.　　　　　　　　　*Tidworth.*

Brigade Commander	De Lisle, Col. (*temp. Brig.-Gen.*) H. De B., C.B., D.S.O., p.s.c. [l]..	5Aug.11
Brigade-Major	Hamilton-Grace, Capt. R. S., 13 Hrs., p.s.c. [l]	8June14 / 29Nov.11

4 D.G.　　　　9 Lrs.　　　　18 Hrs.　　　　2.Signal Troop R.E.

Attached:—

VI. Brig., R.H.A. { H Batt. (*Trowbridge*). / K Batt. (*Christchurch*).

3rd DIVISION.　　　　　　　　　*Bulford.*

General Officer Commanding	Hammick, Maj.-Gen. H. I. W., C.V.O., C.B., D.S.O., p.s.c.	1June14
Aide-de-Camp	Hammick, Lt. R. T., R.A.	1June14
Gen. Staff Officer, 1st grade ..	Boileau, Col. F. R. F., p.s.c. [t]	1July10
Dep. Asst. Adjt. and Qr.-Mr.-Gen.	Farmar, Maj. G. J., Worc. R., p.s.c.	1Nov.12

7th Infantry Brigade.　　　　　　　　　*Tidworth.*

Brigade Commander	McCracken, Col. (*temp. Brig.-Gen.*) F. W. N., C.B., D.S.O., p.s.c.	2Oct.12
Brigade-Major	Hildyard, Capt. R. J. T., R. W. Kent R., p.s.c. ..	10Oct.13 / 10Oct.11

3 Bn. Worc. R.　　　　　　　　1 Bn. Wilts. R.
2 Bn. S. Lan. R.　　　　　　　　2 Bn. R. Ir. Rif.

8th Infantry Brigade.　　　　　　　　　*Devonport.*

Brigade Commander	Doran, Col. (*temp. Brig.-Gen.*) B. J. C., C.B., q.s.	3May12
Brigade-Major	Butler, Maj. Hon. L. J. P., I. Gds., p.s.c. ..	27Jan.13

2 Bn. R. Scots (*Plymouth*).　　　　4 Bn. Midd'x R. (*Devonport*).
2 Bn. R. Ir. Regt. (*Devonport*).　　　1 Bn. Gord. Highrs. (*Plymouth*).

9th Infantry Brigade.　　　　　　　　　*Portsmouth.*

Brigade Commander	Shaw, Col. (*temp. Brig.-Gen.*), F.C., C.B. ..	21May13
Brigade-Major	Stevens, Capt. R. W. M., R. Ir. Rif., p.s.c. ..	1Nov.12

1 Bn. North'd Fus. (*Portsmouth*).　　　1 Bn. Linc. R. (*Portsmouth*).
4 Bn. R. Fus. (*Parkhurst*).　　　　　1 Bn. R. Sc. Fus. (*Gosport*).

Divisional Troops.
Royal Artillery.　　　　　　　　　*Bulford Camp.*

Commanding Royal Artillery ..	Wing, Col. (*temp. Brig.-Gen.*) F. D. V., C.B. ..	16Jan.13
Brigade Major	Mackworth, Capt. F. J. A., R.A., p.s.c. ..	20Oct.13

XXIII. Brig. R.F.A. { 107 Batt. / 108 Batt. / 109 Batt. }　　XL. Brig. R.F.A. { 6 Batt. / 23 Batt. / 49 Batt. }

XXX. (Howr.) Brig. R.F.A. { 128 Batt. / 129 Batt. / 130 Batt. }　　XLII. Brig. R.F.A. { 29 Batt. / 41 Batt. / 45 Batt. }

For Heavy Battery, R.G.A., *see* Eastern Command, page 23.

Royal Engineers.

Commanding Royal Engineers ..	Wilson, Lt.-Col. C. S., R.E.	*Bulford.*

56 Fd. Co.　　　　　　　　3 Signal Co.
57 Fd. Co.

ARMY TROOPS.
Royal Flying Corps (Military Wing.)
3 & 4 Squadrons (*Salisbury Plain.*)

OTHER REGULAR FIELD TROOPS.

Royal Artillery.	Infantry.
XXXIII. Brig., R.F.A. { 32 Batt. / 53 Batt. / 36 Batt. } (*Exeter*).	2 Bn. R.W. Fus. (*Portland*).

1 Heavy Brig., R.G.A. { 26 Batt. (*part of 1st Div.*) / 35 Batt. (*part of 2nd Div.*) / 108 Batt. (*part of 5th Div.*) } (*Fareham*).

[*Continued on page 49*]

(49)

Commands of the Army.

Southern Command—contd.

COAST DEFENCES.
SOUTHERN COAST DEFENCES.
Defended ports of Portsmouth and Portland.

General Officer Commanding	.. Blewitt, Maj.-Gen. W. E., *C.B., C.M.G., g.* (*Portsmouth*)	24July11
Aide-de-Camp	.. Blewitt, Capt. G., Oxf. & Bucks. L.I.	24July11
General Staff Officer, 2nd grade..	.. Traill, Capt. W. H., E. Lan. R., *p.s.c.*	4Nov.13
Dep. Asst. Adjt. and Qr.-Mr.-Gen.	.. Dawson, Maj. D'O. B., S. Lan. R.	27Mar.14
Commanding Royal Artillery	.. Kelly, Col. (*temp. Brig.-Gen.*) R. M, B. F., *C.B., D.S.O., g.*	18Aug.10
Staff Captain, Royal Artillery ..	.. Gillett, Capt. C. R., R.A., *g.*	2Apr.12
Chief Instructor in Gunnery	.. Benson, Lt.-Col. (*temp. Col.*) R. P., R.A. (*Golden Hill*)	4Jan.14
		1Apr.13
Major Instructor in Gunnery	.. Moultrie, Maj. H. C., R.A., *g.* (*Golden Hill*)	2Feb 12
		1Apr.13
Captain Instructor in Gunnery	.. Niven, Capt. O. C., R.A., *g.*	28Jan.11
Chief Engineer ..	.. Godby, Col. C.	7Mar.13
Staff Officer, Royal Engineers	.. Walker, Capt. R., R.E.	
Senior Medical Officer ..	.. Meek, Lt.-Col. J., *M.D.,* R.A.M.C.	

Royal Artillery.

Regulars.
III. Res. Brig. { 140 Batt. } (*Hilsea*).
R.F.A. { 141 Batt. }
3½Depôt, R.F.A. (*Hilsea*).
23 (Siege) Co., R.G.A (*Fort Grange, Gosport*).
37 & 42 Cos., R.G.A. (*Inner Defences, Portsmouth*).
29 & 67 Cos., R.G.A. (*Outer Defences, Portsmouth*).
11 & 33 Cos., R.G.A. (*Western Forts, Isle of Wight*).
32 & 34 Cos., R.G.A. (*Culver, Isle of Wight*).
16, 28 & 30 Cos., R.G.A. (*Weymouth*).
2*Depôt, R.G.A. (*Fort Rowner, Gosport*).

Territorial.
Hampshire.
Dorsetshire.

Royal Engineers.

Regulars.
4 Co. (Fortress)
6 Co. (Fortress)
22 Co. (Fortress)
42 Co. (Fortress)

Territorial.
Hampshire (Fortress)
Wiltshire (Fortress)
Dorsetshire (Fortress)

SOUTH-WESTERN COAST DEFENCES.
Defended ports of Plymouth and Falmouth.

General Officer Commanding	.. Penton, Maj.-Gen. A. P., *O.V.O., C.B., p.a.c.* (*Devonport*)	19Apr.12 / 10Oct.08
Aide-de-Camp	.. Lock, Capt. R. F., R.A., *g.*	19Apr.12 / 24Oct.08
General Staff Officer, 2nd grade..	.. Fuller, Maj. F. G., R.E., *p.s.c.* [*l*]	10Oct.13
Dep. Asst. Adjt. and Qr.-Mr.-Gen.	.. Uniacke, Maj. R. F., R. Innis. Fus., *p.s.c.* [*l*]	15May14
Commanding Royal Artillery .	.. Nelson, Col. (*temp. Brig.-Gen.*) E. F., *g., f.*	5Jan.14
Staff Captain, Royal Artillery ..	.. Dwyer, Capt. G. T. C., R.A.	13Apr.13
Chief Instructor in Gunnery	.. Duhan, Col. W. W. T., *g.*..	18May12
		1Apr.13
Major Instructor in Gunnery	.. Barron, Maj. N. G., R.A., *g.* (*Plymouth*)	24July13
Captain Instructor in Gunnery	.. Leggett, Capt. W. N., R.A., *g.* (*Plymouth*)..	29Jan.14
Chief Engineer ..	.. Painter, Col. A. C.	4July14
Staff Officer, Royal Engineers	.. King, Capt. W. A. de C., R.E.	
Senior Medical Officer ..	.. Macleod, Lt.-Col. R. L. R., *M.B.,* R.A.M.C.	

Royal Garrison Artillery.

Regulars.
39 & 107 Cos. (Siege Artillery Brig.)
36 & 45 Cos. (*Eastern Section*).
38 & 41 Cos. (*Western Section*).
3 Depôt (*Plymouth*).

Territorial.
Devonshire.
Cornwall.

Royal Engineers.

Regulars.
18 Co. (Fortress)
20 Co. (Fortress)
30 Co. (Fortress)

Territorial.
Devon (Fortress)
Cornwall (Fortress)

‡ *Railway Station for Recruits for No. 3 Depôt R.F.A.* "*Cosham.*"
 Postal Address "*Hilsea.*"
* *Railway Station for Recruits for No. 2 Depôt R.G.A.,* "*Fort Brockhurst*" (*L. & S. W.*)
 Postal and Telegraphic Address—O.C. *No. 2 Depôt, R.G.A., Fort Rowner, Gosport.*

(50)

Commands (United Kingdom).

Southern Command—contd.

No. 7 DISTRICT.

Comprising the Counties of Warwickshire, Gloucestershire, Worcestershire, Oxfordshire, Buckinghamshire and Berkshire.

Officer Commanding	Hacket-Thompson, Col. F., *C.B.*	*Old Barracks, Warwick* 21Apr.11
Staff Captain	Hill, Capt. C. G., *D.S.O.*, R. Berks. R.	1Apr.12

Regulars.	*Regulars*—contd.	Special Reserve.
Cavalry	Infantry.	Infantry.
	Depôts.	3 & 4 Bns. R. War. R.
5 *Depôt.*	R. War. R. (*Warwick*).	3 Bn. Glouc. R.
3 and 7 Hrs. } (*Bristol*)	Glouc. R. (*Bristol*).	5 & 6 Bns. Worc. R.
15 and 19 Hrs. }	Worc. R. (*Worcester*).	3 Bn. Oxf. & Bucks. L.I.
	Oxf. & Bucks. L.I. (*Oxford*).	3 Bn. R. Berks. R.
	R. Berks. R. (*Reading*).	

Retired Officers employed on Recruiting Duties { Carr, Hon. Maj. J., Qr.-Mr. ret. pay (*Bristol*) 1July11
{ Floyd, Hon. Capt. H., Qr.-Mr. ret. pay (*Res. of Off.*)(*Birmingham*) 1Apr.14

No. 8 DISTRICT.

Comprising the Counties of Devonshire, Somersetshire, Cornwall, Hampshire, Dorsetshire and Wiltshire.

Officer Commanding	Western, Col. W.G.B., *C.B., p.s.c.* [L]. ..	.. *Exeter*	7Feb.11
Staff Captain	Wetherell, Capt. R. M., D. of Corn. L.I. ..	.. ..	1Apr.12

Regulars.	Special Reserve.
Infantry.	*Infantry.*
Depôts.	3 Bn. Devon R.
Devon R. (*Exeter*).	3 Bn. Som. L.I.
Som. L.I. (*Taunton*).	3 Bn. D. of Corn. L.I.
D. of Corn. L.I. (*Bodmin*).	3 Bn. Hamps. R.
Hamps. R. (*Winchester*).	3 Bn. Dorset R.
Dorset R. (*Dorchester*).	3 Bn. Wilts R.
Wilts R. (*Devizes*).	

OTHER REGULAR AND SPECIAL RESERVE TROOPS IN THE COMMAND.

Regulars.	Special Reserve.
Royal Engineers.	*Infantry.*
19 Co. (Survey).	5 and 6 Bns. K. R. Rif C. (*Winchester*)
Infantry.	5 and 6 Bns. Rif. Brig. (*Winchester*).
Rifle Depôt (*Winchester*).	

[*Continued on page* 51]

Commands of the Army.

Southern Command—contd.

Assistant Provost Marshal (*Tidworth*)	.. Innes, Hon. Capt. C., Qr.-Mr. Mil. Police Corps	.. 21Apr.04
Discharge Depôt (*Fort Brockhurst, Gosport*).		
Commandant	.. Brunker, Col. C. M., *D.S.O.*	.. 27Aug.12
Adjutant	.. Evans, Capt. J., R. Innis. Fus.	.. 3Sept.13
Paymaster	.. Constable, Maj. J. G., A. P. Dept.	
Quarter-Master	.. Fletcher, Hon. Maj. C. W., Qr.-Mr. ..	.. 28Sept.11
Embarkation Staff (*Southampton*).		
Embarkation Commandant (*A.Q.M.G.*)	.. Hamilton, Col. A. B., *p.s.c.*	..{ 10Oct,13 21Mar,11
Embarkation Medical Officer ..	.. Anderson, Maj. J. B., R.A.M.C.	.. 10Nov,10
Paymaster	.. Regtl. Paymaster, Netley.	
Royal Victoria Hospital, Netley.		
Officer in Charge	..	
Registrar and Secretary	.. Chopping, Maj. A., R.A.M.C.	
Paymaster	.. Strong, Maj. F. L. H., A. P. Dept., *e.*	

TERRITORIAL DIVISIONS AND BRIGADES.

(Territorial Troops allotted to Coast Defences are shewn with the Regulars.)

1st SOUTH MIDLAND MOUNTED BRIGADE.
St. John's, Warwick.

Brigade Commander	.. Wiggin, Col. (*Terr. Force*) E. A., Bt. Lt.- Col., ret. pay (*Maj. Res. of Off.*)	.. 27June14
Brigade-Major	.. Darell, Capt. L. E.-H. M., 1 L.G.	.. 11Dec.13
War. Yeo. Glouc. Yeo. Worc. Yeo. War. R.H.A. (Batt. & Ammn. Col.)		
1 S. Mid. Mtd. Brig. T. & S. Col., A.S.C.		
1 S. Mid. Mtd. Brig. Fd. Amb., R.A.M.C.		

2nd SOUTH MIDLAND MOUNTED BRIGADE. 12 *Lonsdale Road, Oxford.*

Brigade Commander	.. Longford, Col. T., *Earl of, K.P., M.V.O.* ..	.. 1Apr.12
Brigade-Major	.. Watkin, Maj. H. G., 4 Hrs., *p.s.c.* ..	..{ 23May11 10Apr.11
Bucks. Yeo. Berks. Yeo. Oxford Hrs. Yeo. Berks. R.H.A. (Batt. & Ammn. Col.)		
2 S. Mid. Mtd. Brig. T. & S. Col., A.S.C.		
2 S. Mid. Mtd. Brig. Fd. Amb., R.A.M.C.		

SOUTH MIDLAND DIVISION.   *The Old Barracks, Warwick.*

General Officer Commanding	.. Graham, Maj.-Gen. E. R. C., *C.B., p.s.c.* (Col. Ches. R.)	—
Gen. Staff Officer, 2nd grade ..	.. Clarke, Capt. A. L. C., Arg. & Suth'd Highrs., *p.s.c.* [L]	4Mar.14
Dep. Asst. Adjt. & Qr.-Mr.-Gen. ..	.. Law, Capt. W. H. P., A.S.C.	.. 26Feb,13
Asst. Dir of Medical Services ..	.. Bull, Col. W. H., *F.R.C.S. Edin., K.H.S.,* VD.	.. 1Apr.12
Dep.-Asst. Dir. of Medical Services	.. Haywood, Lt.-Col. L., *M.B.*, ret. pay.	
Sanitary Officer	..	
Asst. Dir. of Veterinary Services	.. Harris, Maj. (*temp. Lt.-Col., Terr. Force*) C. B. M., *D.S.O., F.R.C.V.S.*, ret. pay (*Res. of Off.*) ..	.. 11May12

Warwickshire Infantry Brigade.   *The Old Barracks, Warwick.*

Brigade Commander	.. James, Col. C. H. L.	1June11
Brigade-Major	.. Higginson, Maj. H. W., R. Dub. Fus. ..	1May14
5 and 6 Bns. R. War. R.	7 Bn. R. War. R.	8 Bn. R. War. R.

Gloucester and Worcester Infantry Brigade.   *Charlecote, Battledown, Cheltenham.*

Brigade Commander	.. Daubeney, Col. E. K., *D.S.O.*	.. 7Dec.10
Brigade-Major	.. Haig, Capt. C. H., Leic. R.	.. 18May13
4 Bn. Glouc. R.	6 Bn. Glouc. R. 7 Bn. Worc. R.	8 Bn. Worc. R.

(52)

Commands (United Kingdom).

Southern Command—contd.

Territorial Divisions and Brigades.—South Midland Division—contd.

South Midland Infantry Brigade. 20, *Magdalen Street, Oxford.*

Brigade Commander	.. McClintock, Col. W. K.	1July11
Brigade-Major	.. Nunn, Capt. T. H. C., *D.S.O.*, R.W.Kent R., *p.s.c*..,	2Nov.11

5 Bn. Glouc. R.   4 Bn. Oxf. & Bucks. L.I.   Bucks. Bn., Oxf. & Bucks. L.I.   4 Bn. R. Berks. R.

Divisional Troops.

Royal Artillery.   *Draycott Lodge, Kempsey, Worcester.*

Commanding Royal Artillery .. .. .. Butler, Col. H. H. 18July14
Staff Captain ... . Hill, Maj. H. B., ret. pay (*Res. of Off.*) *g* .. . 2Oct.09

1 S. Mid. Brig. R.F.A.	{ 1 Glouc. Batt. 2 Glouc. Batt. 3 Glouc. Batt. 1 S. Mid. Ammn. Col.	3 S. Mid. Brig. R.F.A.	{ 1 War. Batt. 2 War. Batt. 3 War. Batt. 3 S. Mid. Ammn. Col.
2 S. Mid. Brig R.F.A.	{ 1 Worc. Batt. 2 Worc. Batt. 3 Worc. Batt. 2 S. Mid. Ammn. Col.	4 S. Mid. (Howr.) Brig. R.F.A.	{ 4 War. (Howr.) Batt. 5 War. (Howr.) Batt. 4 S. Mid. Ammn. Col.

S. Mid. R.G.A.

Royal Engineers.   32, *Park Row, Bristol.*

Commanding Royal Engineers .. .. .. Sinnott, Lt.-Col. (*Hon. Lt. in Army*) E. S., *M. Inst. C.E.*, VD,
S. Mid. Divl. R.E.

1 S. Mid. Fd. Co.   2 S. Mid. Fd. Co.   S. Mid. Divl. Signal Co.

Army Service Corps.   *Royal Army Medical Corps.*

S. Mid. Divl. T. & S. Col. { Divl. Co. (Hd.-Qrs.)
War. Brig. Co.
Glouc. and Worc. Brig. Co.
S. Mid. Brig. Co. | 1 S. Mid. Fd. Amb.
2 S. Mid. Fd. Amb.
3 S. Mid. Fd. Amb.

ARMY TROOPS ATTACHED SOUTH MIDLAND DIVISION.

S. Wireless Signal Co.   S. Cable Signal Co.   S. Air Line Signal Co.

1st SOUTH WESTERN MOUNTED BRIGADE. 28a, *Butcher Row, Salisbury.*

Brigade Commander .. .. .. Shaftesbury, Col. (*Terr. Force*) A. A. C., *Earl of*, K.P.,
K.C.V.O., Hon. Col. N. Irish Horse & Hon. Col.
Antrim R.G.A. 1Jan.13
Brigade-Major .. .. Hill-Whitson, Maj. T. E. L., 14 Hrs., *p.s.c.* 1June11

R. Wilts. Yeo.   N. Som. Yeo.   Hamps. Yeo.   Hamps. R.H.A. (Batt. & Ammn. Col.)
1 S.W. Mtd. Brig. T. & S. Col., A.S.C.
1 S.W. Mtd. Brig. Fd. Amb., R.A.M.C.
Attached for training :—Dorset Yeo.

2nd SOUTH WESTERN MOUNTED BRIGADE. *Lennards Buildings, Goldsmith Street, Exeter.*

Brigade Commander .. .. .. Hoare, Col. R. 1Apr.12
Brigade-Major .. .. Lascelles, Capt. E. H. W., 3 D. G. 19Dec.11

Devon Yeo.   R. N. Devon Yeo.   W. Som. Yeo.   Som. R.H.A. (Batt. & Ammn. Col.)
2 S.W. Mtd. Brig. T. & S. Col., A.S.C.
S.W. Mtd. Brig. Fd. Amb., R.A.M.C.

[*Continued on page* 53]

(53)

Commands of the Army.

Southern Command—contd.
Territorial Divisions and Brigades—contd.

WESSEX DIVISION.   19, *Cathedral Close, Exeter.*

General Officer Commanding	Donald. Maj.-Gen. C. G., C.B.,	10Feb.11
General Staff Officer, 2nd grade	Buzzard Maj. F. A., R.A. p.s.c., g.	8May14
Dep. Asst. Adjt. & Qr.-Mr.-Gen.	Mudge, Maj. A., R.W. Surr. R.	19Apr.12
Asst. Dir. of Medical Services	Mackay, Col. H. J., M.D., TD	1Apr.12
Dep.-Asst. Dir. of Medical Services	T.C. Inkson, Maj. E. T., R.A.M.C.	25Apr.14
Sanitary Officer	Burnet, Maj. R., M.B., San. Serv., R.A.M.C. (T.F.)	26Feb.13
Asst. Dir. of Veterinary Services	England, Maj. *(temp. Lt.-Col. Terr. Force)* A., ret. pay (*Res. of Off.*)	8Oct.13

Devon and Cornwall Infantry Brigade.   *Lennards Buildings, Goldsmith Street, Exeter.*

Brigade Commander	Pinney, Col. R. J., p.s.c.	16July13
Brigade-Major	Howard, Capt. C. A., K.R. Rif. C.	30June12

4 Bn. Devon R.   5 Bn. Devon R.   4 Bn. D. of Corn. L. I.   5 Bn. D. of Corn. L. I.

South Western Infantry Brigade.   *County Territorial Hall, Taunton.*

Brigade Commander	Elliot, Col. G. S. McD...	16Jan.14
Brigade-Major	Fisher, Capt. H. B., Wilts. R.	8Apr.14

4 Bn. Som. L.I.   5 Bn. Som. L.I.   4 Bn. Dorset R.   4 Bn. Wilts. R.

Hampshire Infantry Brigade.   30, *Carlton Place, Southampton.*

Brigade Commander	Nicholson, Col. G. H.	14Feb.14
Brigade-Major	Kenrick, Maj. G. E. R., D.S.O., R. W. Surr. R., p.s.c.	25Aug.13

4 Bn. Hamps. R.   5 Bn. Hamps. R.   6 Bn. Hamps. R.   7 Bn. Hamps. R.

Divisional Troops.
Royal Artillery.   *Lennards Buildings, Goldsmith Street, Exeter.*

Commanding Royal Artillery	Fanshawe, Col. E. A.	1Oct.13
Staff Captain	Thomson, Capt. A. F., R.A.	28June11

1 Wessex Brig. R.F.A. { 1 Hamps. Batt. / 2 Hamps. Batt. / 3 Hamps. Batt. / 1 Wessex Ammn. Col.   3 Wessex Brig. R.F.A. { 6 Hamps. Batt. / Dorset Batt. / Wilts. Batt. / 3 Wessex Ammn. Col.

2 Wessex (Howr.) Brig. R.F.A. { 4 Hamps. Batt. / 5 Hamps. Batt. / 2 Wessex Ammn. Col.   4 Wessex Brig. R.F.A. { 1 Devon Batt. / 2 Devon Batt. / 3 Devon Batt. / 4 Wessex Ammn. Col.

Wessex R.G.A.

Royal Engineers.   The *Drill Hall, Upper Bristol Road, Bath.*

Commanding Royal Engineers	Lt.-Col. S. Keen, TD.	1Apr.06

1 Wessex Fd. Co.   2 Wessex Fd. Co.   Wessex Divl. Signal Co.

Army Service Corps.   *Royal Army Medical Corps.*

Wessex Divl. T. & S. Col. { Divl. Co. (H.-Q.) / Devon and Corn. Brig. Co. / S.W. Brig. Co. / Hamps. Brig. Co.   1 Wessex Fd. Amb. / 2 Wessex Fd. Amb. / 3 Wessex Fd. Amb.

ARMY TROOPS ATTACHED WESSEX DIVISION.
Infantry.
6 Bn. Devon R.

OTHER TERRITORIAL TROOPS IN THE COMMAND.

Infantry.
8 Bn. Hamps. R.

Cyclists
7 Bn. Devon R.
9 Bn. Hamps.

Royal Army Medical Corps.
1 S. Gen. Hosp.
2 S. Gen. Hosp.
3 S. Gen. Hosp.
4 S. Gen. Hosp.
5 S. Gen. Hosp.
S. Mid. Clearing Hosp.
Wessex Clearing Hosp.

ARMY SIGNAL SCHOOL.
(Bulford.)

Commandant	Barker, Capt. E. F. W., Yorks. L. I.	11Feb.13
Instructor	Crocker, Capt. H. E., Essex R. [*l*]	1Oct.13

(54)

Commands (United Kingdom).

WESTERN COMMAND.—Wales and the Counties of Cheshire, Shropshire, Herefordshire, Monmouthshire, Lancashire, Cumberland and Westmorland, and the Isle of Man.

Head-Quarters—Chester.

GENERAL OFFICER COMMANDING-IN-CHIEF	Mackinnon, Gen. *Sir* W. H., *K.C.B., K.C.V.O.*	31Oct.10
Assistant Military Secretary	Peck, Maj. H. R., R.A.	31Oct.16
Aide-de-Camp	Pilcher, Lt. W. S., G. Gds.	1Nov.12

General Staff.

General Staff Officer, 1st grade	Bainbridge, Col. E. G. T., *C.B., p.s.c., q.s.*	16Mar.12
General Staff Officer, 3rd grade	Place, Capt. C. O., *D.S.O., R.E., p.s.c.* [L]	1Apr.12

Attached to the General Staff.

Captain, graded as Brigade-Major	Marsden, Capt. C. H., York. R.	1Apr.14

Administrative, Technical and Departmental Staff.

Brigadier-General in charge of Administration	Caunter, Col. (*temp.* Brig.-Gen.) J. E., *C.B., p.s.c.*	28Oct.13
Dep. Asst. Adjt.-Gen.	Tyndall, Maj. W. E. M., *D.S.O.*, W. Rid R., *p.s.c.*	13May14
Asst. Inspr. of Recog. (graded Staff Captain)	Allen, Maj. P., North'n R.	1Apr.14
Asst. Qr.-Mr.-Gen.	Koe, Col. F. W. B., *C.B.*	21Sept.12
Chief Engineer	Huleatt, Col. H. [L]	17Oct.12
Staff Officer, Royal Engineers	Smith, Maj. G. E., *C.M.G.*, R.E.	
Asst. Director of Supplies and Transport	Thring, Lt.-Col. E. C., A.S.C.	
Dep. Dir. of Medical Services	Swan, Lt.-Col. W. T., *M.B.*, R.A.M.C.	
Asst. Dir. of Veterinary Services	The Asst. Dir. of Veterinary Services, Northern Command.	
Asst. Director of Ordnance Stores	Moore-Lane, Lt.-Col. W., A. Ord. Dept.	
Command Paymaster	Newland, Col. E. W., A. P. Dept.	
Dep. Asst. Dirs. of Remounts No. 2 Circle	Hine-Haycock, Capt. V. R., *D.S.O.*, ret. pay (*Res. of Off.*)	25Nov.10
No. 3 Circle	Wilson, Capt. H. S., ret. pay (*Res. of Off.*)	2Aug.11
No. 1 Circle	Goring, Maj. A., ret. pay (*Res. of Off.*)	3Aug.11
No. 4 Circle	Urquhart, Maj. E. W. L., ret. pay (*Res. of Off.*)	31Dec.12
District Barrack Officer	Roberts, Bt. Col. A. N., ret. pay (*Lt.-Col. Res. of Off.*)	

Department of the Finance Member of the Army Council
(detached from the War Office for duty at Head-Quarters of the Command)

Local Auditor	Bownas, F. O., Esq.	
Assistant Local Auditor	Goffin, S. F. H., Esq.	

Officer in charge of Time-Expired Men, etc. Pesare, Hon. Capt. T., Qr.-Mr., ret. pay (*Cabra House, Newton Lane, Chester*

At Burscough.
Chief Ordnance Officer .. .. Gregson, Maj. H. G. F. S., A, Ord. Dept., *e., o.*

At Pembroke Dock.
Chief Ordnance Officer .. .. Fisher, Capt. A. J., A. Ord. Dept., *e., o,*

Royal Army Medical Corps.	Army Ordnance Corps.
19 Co. (*Chester*).	5 Co. (Burscough Section).

REGULAR FIELD TROOPS.
Infantry.
2 Bn. Bord. R. (*Pembroke Dock*).

[*Continued on page* 55]

(55)

Commands of the Army.

Western Command—contd.

COAST DEFENCES.

NORTH-WESTERN COAST DEFENCES.

Defended ports of the Mersey and Barrow.

Officer Commanding (ex-officio)	Edwards, Lt.-Col. (local Col.) R. F.,R.E.14,Elliott Street,Liverpool.	
General Staff Officer, 3rd grade	de Watteville, Capt. H. G., R.A., p.s.c. [L]	22 Jan.12
Senior Medical Officer	Daly, Lt.-Col. T., R.A.M.C.	

Royal Garrison Artillery.	Royal Engineers.
Regulars. District Estabt.	*Regulars.* Det. 35 Co. (Fortress).
Territorial. Lancs. & Ches.	*Territorial.* Lancs. (Fortress).

WESTERN COAST DEFENCES.

Defended ports of Milford Haven, Cardiff, Barry and Swansea.

Officer Commanding	Triscott, Col. (temp. Brig.-Gen.) C. P., C.B., D.S.O., q.s., { Pembroke Dock .. .. {	7Aug.12 1Apr.11
General Staff Officer, 2nd grade	Armstrong, Bt. Lt.-Col. St. G. B., R. Mar., p.s.c. [L] ..	3Nov.13
Capt. Instructor in Gunnery	Ridout, Capt. J. Y. H., R.A., g.	8Apr.13
Senior Medical Officer	Jones, Maj. T. P., M.B., R.A.M.C.	

Royal Garrison Artillery.	Royal Engineers.
Regulars. 44 & 57 Cos.	*Regulars.* 35 Co. (Fortress).
Territorial. Glamorgan. Pembroke.	*Territorial.* Glamorgan (Fortress).

No. 3 DISTRICT.

Comprising the Counties of Cumberland, Westmorland, and Lancashire (except the 40th Regimental District and the Isle of Man.

Officer Commanding	Tudway, Col. R. J., C.B., D.S.O. ..	Preston ..	5Sept.11
Staff Captain	Browne, Capt. A. D. M., R. Lanc. R. ..	.. ..	1 Apr.12

Regulars.	Regulars—contd.	Special Reserve.
	Infantry.	*Infantry.*
	Depôts.	3 Bn. R. Lanc. R.
Royal Artillery.	R. Lanc. R. (*Lancaster*).	3 & 4 Bns. L'pool R.
	L'pool R. (*Seaforth*).	3 & 4 Bns. Lan. Fus.
I. Res. Brig., { 138 Batt. } (*Preston*).	Lan. Fus. (*Bury*).	3 Bn. E. Lan. R.
R.F.A. { 139 Batt. }	E. Lan. R. (*Preston*).	3 Bn. Bord. R.
2 Depôt, R.F.A (*Preston*.)	Bord. R. (*Carlisle*).	3 Bn. N. Lan. R.
	N. Lan. R. (*Preston*).	3 & 4 Bns. Manch. R.
	Manch. R. (*Ashton-under-Lyne*)	

Liverpool Recruiting Area,			
Medical Officer	Whitty, Lt.-Col. M. J., M.D., ret. pay		25Aug.06
Manchester Recruiting Area,			
Recruiting Staff Officer (Class II.)	Lowe, Capt. P. E. H., W. York. R.		11Aug 10
Medical Officer	Rowney, Lt.-Col. W., M.D., ret. pay		31Oct.08

Retired Officer employed on Recruiting Duties .. .. } Finch, Hon. Capt. B. J., Qr.-Mr. ret. pay (*Liverpool*) .. { 1Mar.12

(56)

Commands (United Kingdom).

Western Command—contd.

No. 4 DISTRICT.

Comprising the Counties of Cheshire, Flintshire, Denbighshire, Anglesey, Carnarvonshire, Merionethshire, Montgomeryshire, Radnorshire, Cardiganshire, Brecknockshire, Monmouthshire, Pembrokeshire, Carmarthenshire, Glamorganshire, Herefordshire, Shropshire, and that portion of Lancashire in the 40th Regimental District.

Officer Commanding	.. .. .. Evans, Col. H. J., *p.s.c.* [*l*] ..	*Shrewsbury* ..	18Feb.13
Staff Captain	.. .. .. Jones, Maj. L. M., *D.S.O.*, L'pool R.	.. ..	17Nov.12

Regulars.	Special Reserve.
Cavalry.	
4 *Depôt.*	*Royal Engineers.*
2 D.G. and 6 Dns. ⎫	R. Anglesey.
3 and 6 D.G. ⎬ (*Newport, Mon.*)	R. Monmouth.
4 and 7 D.G. ⎭	
Infantry.	
Depôts.	*Infantry.*
Ches. R. (*Chester*).	3 Bn. Ches. R.
R. W. Fus. (*Wrexham*).	3 Bn. R. W. Fus.
S. Wales Bord. (*Brecon*).	3 Bn. S. Wales Bord.
S. Lan. R. (*Warrington*).	3 Bn. S. Lan. R.
Welsh R. (*Cardiff*).	3 Bn. Welsh R.
Shrops. L.I. (*Shrewsbury*).	3 Bn. Shrops. L.I.

Retired Officer employed on Recruiting Duties .. Lucas, Maj. T. L. W., ret. pay (*Cardiff*) 2May07

TERRITORIAL DIVISIONS AND BRIGADES.

(Territorial troops allotted to Coast Defences are shewn with the Regulars.)

WEST LANCASHIRE DIVISION. 21, *Islington, Liverpool.*

General Officer Commanding	.. Lindsay, Maj.-Gen. W. F. L., *C.B., D.S.O., g.*	3June12
General Staff Officer, 2nd grade	.. Buckley, Maj. E. J., R. Innis. Fus., *p.s.c.*	19Feb.14
Dep. Asst. Adjt. and Qr.-Mr. Gen.	.. McClintock, Capt. A. G., 5 Lrs.	21Apr.14
Asst. Dir. of Medical Services	.. Jackson. Col. R., *M.B.* TD,(3, *Fraser Street. Liverpool*)..	19Mar 13
Dep. Asst. Dir. of Medical Services	.. Macpherson, Maj. J. D. G., *M.B.*, R.A.M.C.	29Jan.14
Sanitary Officer	.. Smart, Lt.-Col. D., *M.B.*, VD, R.A.M.C.(T.F.).. ..	9Mar.13

North Lancashire Infantry Brigade. 16, *Castle Park, Lancaster.*

Brigade Commander	.. .. Hibbert, Col. G. L., *D.S.O.*	.. .. ..	17Feb.13
Brigade-Major ..	.. .. Bruce, Maj. G. D., 61 Pioneers, *p.s.c.*	.. .. ..	19Oct.10

4 Bn. R. Lanc. R.   5 Bn. R. Lanc. R.   4 Bn. N. Lan. R.   5 Bn. N. Lan. R.

Liverpool Infantry Brigade. 73, *Shaw St., Liverpool.*

Brigade Commander	.. .. Gilbert, Col. A. R., *D.S.O.*	.. .. ..	11May12
Brigade-Major ..	.. .. Fulton, Maj. H. A., Worc. R. ..	.. .. ..	22June12

5 Bn. L'pool R.   6 Bn. L'pool R.   7 Bn. L'pool R.   8 Bn. L'pool R.

South Lancashire Infantry Brigade. 21, *Victoria Street, Liverpool.*

Brigade Commander	.. .. Macfie, Col. (*Terr. Force*) A. L., VD. (Q)..	.. ..	3Oct.11
Brigade-Major ..	.. .. Bellamy, Capt. R., *D.S.O.*, R. Suss. R. ..	.. ..	3Oct.11

9 Bn. L'pool R.   10 Bn. L'pool R.   4 Bn. S. Lan. R.   5 Bn. S. Lan. R.

(*Continued on page 57*)

(57)

Commands of the Army.

Western Command—contd.

Territorial Divisions and Brigades—West Lancashire Division—contd.

Divisional Troops.

Royal Artillery.   Derby Buildings, 24, Fenwick Street, Liverpool.

Commanding Royal Artillery	.. .. Gay, Col. A. W., D.S.O., p.s.c. [l]	1Apr.14
Staff Captain .. .. Benson, Capt. R., R.A.	18June14

1 W. Lanc. Brig. R.F.A.	{ 1 Lanc. Batt. 2 Lanc. Batt. 3 Lanc. Batt. 1 W. Lanc. Ammn. Col	3 W. Lanc. Brig. R.F.A. { 12 Lanc. Batt. 13 Lanc. Batt. 14 Lanc. Batt. 3 W. Lanc. Ammn. Col.
2 W. Lanc. Brig. R.F.A.	{ 9 Lanc. Batt. 10 Lanc. Batt. 11 Lanc. Batt. 2 W. Lanc. Ammn. Col.	4 W. Lanc. (Howr.) Brig. R.F.A. { 7 Lanc. Batt. 8 Lanc. Batt. 4 W. Lanc. Ammn. Col.

1 Lanc. R.G.A.

Royal Engineers.   Engineer Drill Hall, Cropper's Hill, St. Helens.

Commanding Royal Engineers .. .. Sayce, Lt.-Col. G. E., TD, W. Lanc. Divl. R.E.
1 W. Lanc. Fd. Co.   2 W. Lanc. Fd. Co.   W. Lanc. Divl. Signal Co.

Army Service Corps.   Royal Army Medical Corps.
W. Lanc. Divl. { Divl. Co. (H.-Q.),   1 W. Lanc. Fd. Amb.
T. & S. Col. { N. Lanc. Brig. Co.   2 W. Lanc. Fd. Amb.
{ L'pool Brig. Co.   3 W. Lanc. Fd. Amb.
{ S. Lanc. Brig. Co.

ARMY TROOPS ATTACHED WEST LANCASHIRE DIVISION.

Royal Engineers.
W. Wireless Signal Co.
W. Cable Signal Co.
W. Airline Signal Co.
Attached to West Lancashire Division.
7 V.B. L'pool R.

EAST LANCASHIRE DIVISION.   *National Buildings, St. Mary's Parsonage, Manchester.*

General Officer Commanding	.. .. Douglas, Maj.-Gen. W., C.B.,D.S.O. p.s.c. ..	5May13
General Staff Officer, 2nd grade	.. Tufnell, Capt. A. W., R. W. Surr. R., p.s.c, [l]	1Apr.12
Dep. Asst. Adjt. & Qr.-Mr.-Gen.	.. Allen, Capt. R. S., Hamps. R., p.s.c.	1Jan.11
Asst. Dir. of Medical Services	.. Mann, Col. J. B., TD	1Apr.12
Dep.-Asst. Dir. of Medical Services	.. Rawnsley, Lt.-Col. G. T., R.A.M.C.	1Mar.11
Sanitary Officer	.. Sergeant, Maj. E.	19June08

Lancashire Fusiliers Brigade.   5, *Chapel Street, Preston.*

Brigade Commander	.. .. Frith, Col. H. C. [L]	30May14
Brigade-Major	.. .. Allardyce, Bt. Maj. A. J., Lan. Fus.	11Oct.12

5 Bn. Lan. Fus.   6 Bn. Lan. Fus.   7 & 8 Bns. Lan. Fus.

East Lancashire Infantry Brigade.   15, *Piccadilly, Manchester.*

Brigade Commander	.. .. Prendergast, Col. D. G., h.p.	—
Brigade-Major	.. .. Hickie, Maj. C. J., R. Fus.	1Apr.13

4 Bn. E. Lan. R.   5 Bn. E. Lan. R.   9 Bn. Manch. R.   10 Bn. Manch. R.

Manchester Infantry Brigade.   3, *Stretford Road, Manchester.*

Brigade Commander	.. .. Lee, Col. (Terr. Force) N., VD. (Q)	1Sept.11
Brigade-Major	.. .. Knight, Maj. H. L., R. Ir. Fus., p.s.c.	16Apr.12

5 Bn. Manch. R.   6 Bn. Manch. R.   7 Bn. Manch. R.   8 Bn. Manch. R.

(58)

Commands (United Kingdom).

Western Command—contd.
Territorial Divisions and Brigades—East Lancashire Division—contd.

Divisional Troops.

Royal Artillery. Artillery Head-Quarters, Nantwich, Cheshire.

Commanding Royal Artillery			
Staff Captain	... Cockcraft, Capt. L. W. La T., R.A.		10Jan.11

1 E. Lanc. Brig. R.F.A.	4 Lanc. Batt. 5 Lanc. Batt. 6 Lanc. Batt. 1 E. Lanc. Ammn. Col.	3 E. Lanc. Brig. R.F.A.	18 Lanc. Batt. 19 Lanc. Batt. 20 Lanc. Batt. 3 E. Lanc. Ammn. Col.
2 E. Lanc. Brig. R.F.A.	15 Lanc. Batt. 16 Lanc. Batt. 17 Lanc. Batt. 2 E. Lanc. Ammn. Col.	4 E. Lanc. (Howr.) Brig. R.F.A.	1 Cumb. Batt. 2 Cumb. Batt. 4 E. Lanc. Ammn. Col.

2 Lanc. R.G.A.

Royal Engineers. 73, Seymour Grove, Old Trafford, Manchester.

Commanding Royal Engineers ... Newton, Lt.-Col. C. E., *M. Inst. C.E.*, E. Lanc. Divl. R.E.
1 E. Lanc. Fd. Co.   2 E. Lanc. Fd. Co.   E. Lanc. Div. Signal Co.

Army Service Corps.   *Royal Army Medical Corps.*

E. Lanc. Divl. T. & S. Col.
- Divl. Co. (H.-Q.)
- Lanc. Fus. Brig. Co.
- E. Lanc. Brig. Co.
- Manch. Brig. Co.

1 E. Lanc. Fd. Amb.
2 E. Lanc. Fd. Amb.
3 E. Lanc. Fd. Amb.

ARMY TROOPS ATTACHED EAST LANCASHIRE DIVISION.

Infantry.
4 Bn. Bord. R.
5 Bn. Bord. R.

OTHER TROOPS ATTACHED EAST LANCASHIRE DIVISION.

Special Reserve.

Royal Army Medical Corps.
No. 18 Fd. Amb.

WELSH BORDER MOUNTED BRIGADE. 15, *High Street, Shrewsbury.*

Brigade Commander	... Herbert, Col. E. A., *M.V.O.*	4Apr.12
Brigade-Major	... Burt, Maj. A., 3 D.G.	1Apr.12
Shrops. Yeo.	Ches. Yeo. Denbigh Yeo. Shrops. R.H.A. (Batt. & Ammn. Col.) Welsh Bord. Mtd. Brig. T. and S. Col., A.S.C. Welsh Bord. Mtd. Brig. Fd. Amb., R.A.M.C.	

Attached for training :—
D. of Lanc. Own Yeo.   West. & Cumb. Yeo.   Lanc. Hrs. Yeo.

SOUTH WALES MOUNTED BRIGADE. *The Barracks, Carmarthen.*

Brigade Commander	... Fryer, Col. F. A. B.	1Jan.13
Brigade-Major	... Haag, Maj. E. C., 18 Hrs., *p.s.c.* [L]	20July13
Pemb. Yeo.	Montgom. Yeo. Glam. Yeo. Glam. R.H.A. (Batt. & Ammn. Col.) S. Wales Mtd. Brig. T. & S. Col., A.S.C. S. Wales Mtd. Brig. Fd. Amb., R.A.M.C.	

WELSH DIVISION. 3, *Belmont, Shrewsbury.*

General Officer Commanding	... Lindley, Maj.-Gen. *Hon.* J. E., Col. 1 Dns., *p.s.c.*	14Oct.13
General Staff Officer, 2nd grade	... Williams, Maj. W. de L., *D.S.O.*, Hamps. R., *p.s.c.*	29Sept.13
Dep. Asst. Adjt. and Qr.-Mr.-Gen.	... Derry, Capt. A., *D.S.O.*, Welsh R.	1Apr.12
Asst. Dir. of Medical Services	... Jones, Col. J. A., *M.D., K.H.S.,* VD. (128, *Abbey Foregate, Shrewsbury*)	18Jan.11
Dep.-Asst. Dir. of Medical Services	... Turner, Lt.-Col. W., ret. pay	
Sanitary Officer	... Averill, Lt.-Col. C., *M.D.,* VD.	20May11
Asst. Dir. of Veterinary Servicer	... Meredith, Vety.-Maj. *(temp. Lt.-Col. Terr. Force)* J. A., *F.R.C.V.S.,* ret. pay *(Res. of Off.)*	15May12

[*Continued on page 59*]

Commands of the Army.

Western Command—contd.
Territorial Divisions and Brigades—Welsh Division—contd.

Cheshire Infantry Brigade. *Drill Hall, Chester.*

Brigade Commander	.. Cowans, Col. E. A.,	25June14
Brigade-Major	.. Crookenden, Capt. A., Ches. R., p.s.c. [L]	19Apr.11

4 Bn. Ches. R.   5 Bn. Ches. R.   6 Bn. Ches. R.   7 Bn. Ches. R.

North Wales Infantry Brigade. *Barracks, Wrexham.*

Brigade Commander	.. Lloyd, Col. F. C.	26July12
Brigade-Major	.. Berners, Maj. R. A., R.W. us.	1June11

4 Bn. R. W. Fus.   5 Bn. R. W. Fus.   6 Bn. R. W. Fus.   7 Bn. R. W. Fus.

Welsh Border Infantry Brigade. 15, *High Street, Shrewsbury.*

Brigade Commander	.. Hume, Col. J. J. F.	1July10
Brigade-Major	.. Solly-Flood, Capt. R. E., Rif. Brig.	16Apr.14

1 Bn. Mon. R.   2 Bn. Mon. R.   3 Bn. Mon. R.   1 Bn. Hereford R.

Divisional Troops.

Royal Artillery.   15, *High Street, Shrewsbury.*

Commanding Royal Artillery	.. McLeod, Col. W. K.	12Aug.12
Staff Captain	.. Oldham, Capt. F. H. L., R.A.	1Apr.12

1 Welsh (Howr.) Brig. R.F.A. { 1 Glam. Batt. / 2 Glam. Batt. / 1 Welsh Ammn. Col.   Ches. Brig. R.F.A.   { 1 Ches. Batt. / 2 Ches. Batt. / 3 Ches. Batt. / 3 Ches. Ammn. Col.

2 Welsh Brig. R.F.A. { 3 Glam. Batt. / 4 Glam. Batt. / Card. Batt. / 2 Welsh Ammn. Col.   4 Welsh Brig. R.F.A.   { 1 Mon. Batt. / 2 Mon. Batt. / 3 Mon. Batt. / 4 Welsh Ammn. Col.

Welsh R.G.A.

Royal Engineers.   59, *Charles Street, Cardiff.*

Commanding Royal Engineers .. Hutchison, Lt.-Col. (Hon. Lt. in Army) R.L., Welsh Divl. R.E.

Cheshire Fd. Co.   Welsh Fd. Co.   Welsh Div. Signal Co.

Army Service Corps.
Welsh Divl. T. & S. Col. { Divl. Hd.-Qrs. Co. / Ches. Brig. Co. / N. Wales Brig. Co. / Welsh Bord. Brig. Co.

Royal Army Medical Corps.
1 Welsh Fd. Amb.
2 Welsh Fd. Amb.
3 Welsh Fd. Amb.

ARMY TROOPS ATTACHED WELSH DIVISION.

Infantry.

South Wales Infantry Brigade. 29, *Windsor Place, Cardiff.*

Brigade Commander	.. Campbell, Col. D.	16May14
Brigade-Major	.. Ready, Maj. B. T., Welsh R.	12June12

Brecknock Bn. S. Wales Bord.   4 Bn. Welsh R.   5 Bn. Welsh R.   6 Bn. Welsh R.

Attached Welsh Border Infantry Brigade.
4 Bn. Shrops. L. I.

OTHER TERRITORIAL TROOPS IN THE COMMAND.

Cyclists.
7 Bn. Welsh R.

Royal Army Med. Corps.
1 W. Gen. Hosp.
2 W. Gen. Hosp.

Royal Army Med. Corps—contd.
3 W. Gen. Hosp.
W. Lan. Clearing Hosp.
E. Lan. Clearing Hosp.
Welsh Clearing Hosp.

Commands (United Kingdom).

CHANNEL ISLANDS.

(Arranged alphabetically.)

GUERNSEY AND ALDERNEY DISTRICT.

LT.-GOVERNOR & COMMANDING THE TROOPS   Lawson, Maj.-Gen. H. M., *C.B.*, *p.s.c.* .. 8Apr.14
Administrative, Technical and Departmental Staff (*Head-Quarters, Guernsey*).

Deputy Assistant Adjutant-General	Craig-Brown.Capt.E.,Cam'n Highrs., *p,s,c., e.* 4Feb.14
Officer Commanding Royal Engineers	Bigge, Maj. G. O., R.E.
Officer Commanding Army Service Corps	Crawley, Capt. R. P., *M.V.O.*, A.S.C., *s.*
Senior Medical Officer	Mosse, Lt.-Col. C. G. D., *F.R.C.S.I.*, ret. pay.
Chief Ordnance Officer	Dudley, Capt. G. de S., A. Ord. Dept., *e., o.*

TROOPS QUARTERED IN COMMAND.

Royal Garrison Artillery.
Regular Troops.
17 Co.
Militia.
R. Guernsey Art. & Eng.
R. Alderney Art. & Eng.

Royal Engineers.
34 (Fortress) Co.

Infantry.
Regular Troops.
2 Bn. York. R.

Militia.
1 Bn. R. Guernsey L.I.
2 Bn. R. Guernsey L.I.

Army Service Corps.
Detachment.

Royal Army Medical Corps.
6 Co. (Det.)

Army Ordnance Corps.
Detachment.

JERSEY DISTRICT.

LT.-GOVERNOR & COMMANDING THE TROOPS   Rochfort,Maj.-Gen.*Sir* A.N.,*K.C.B.,C.M.G*, 16June10
Administrative, Technical and Departmental Staff.

Deputy Assistant Adjutant-General	Riddell, Maj. E. V. D., R.A., *p.s.c.* .. 22July11
Officer Commanding Royal Engineers	Fleming, Capt. J. G., R.E.
Officer Commanding Army Service Corps	Morris, Capt. J. H., A.S.C.
Senior Medical Officer	Gordon, Lt.-Col. P. C. H., R.A.M.C.
Chief Ordnance Officer	Hill, Capt. F. W. R., *D.S.O.*, A. Ord. Dept., *o.*

TROOPS QUARTERED IN THE COMMAND.

Royal Garrison Artillery.
Regular Troops.
20 Co.
Militia.
R. Jersey Art.(and Eng. Co.)

Royal Engineers.
Detachment 34 (Fortress) Co.

Infantry.
Regular Troops.
1 Bn. Devon. R.

Militia.
1 Bn. R. Jersey L.I.
2 Bn. R. Jersey L.I.
3 Bn. R. Jersey L.I.
Medical Corps Section.

Army Service Corps.
Detachment.

Royal Army Medical Corps.
6 Co. (Det.)

Army Ordnance Corps.
Detachment.

Commands of the Army.

EAST INDIES.

VICEROY AND GOVERNOR-GENERAL	Hardinge, *Rt. Hon.* C., *Lord,* *G.C.B.*, *G.C.M.G.*, *G.C.V.O.*, *I.S.O.*	
Military Secretary	Maxwell, Maj. *(temp. Lt.-Col.)* F. A., *C.S.I.*, *D.S.O.*, 18 Lrs., *p.s.c.*	23Nov.10
Aides-de-Camp	Tod, Capt. A. A., Rif. Brig.	13Mar.12
	Muir, Capt. W. W., 15 Sikhs	15Apr.12
	Benson, Lt. R. L., 9 Lrs.	25Apr.13
	Stephens, Capt. R., Oxf. & Bucks. L. I.	22Mar.14

ARMY DEPARTMENT, GOVERNMENT OF INDIA.

MEMBER OF COUNCIL IN CHARGE ... Duff, Gen. *Sir* B., *G.C.B.*, *K.C.S.I.*, *K.C.V.O.*, *C.I.E.*, Ind. Army, *p.s.c.*, A・D・C.

Secretary.

Birdwood, Maj.-Gen. W. R., *C.B.*, *C.S.I.*, *C.I.E.*, *D.S.O.*, Ind. Army, *q.s.* 17Nov.12

Deputy Secretary.

Holloway, Col. B., Ind. Army, *p.s.c.* [L] 1Apr.12

Assistant Secretaries. (3).

Spence, Maj. A. H. O., 39 Horse [*l*]	22Apr.09
Graham, Maj. R. B., 33 Punjabis	1Nov.12
Chitty, Maj. A. W., 126 Inf., *p.s.c.*	1Apr.13

Director-General, Indian Medical Service.

Lukis, Surg.-Gen. *Sir* C. P., *K.C.S.I.*, *M.D.*, *F.R.C.S.*, *K.H.S.*, Ind. Med. Serv. 1Jan.10

MADRAS.

GOVERNOR	Pentland, *Rt. Hon.* J., *Lord,* *G.C.I.E.*	
Military Secretary	Allanson, Capt. C. J. L., 6 Gúrkha Rif., *p.s.c.*	30Oct.12
Aides-de-Camp	Butchart, Capt. J. A., R.A.	30Oct.12
	Colmore, Capt. H., 7 Hrs.	15Nov.12
	Cavendish, Lt. R. H. V., *M.V.O.*, G. Gds. *(extra)*	—

BOMBAY.

GOVERNOR	Willingdon, F., *Lord,* *G.C.I.E.*	
Military Secretary	Greig, Maj. J. G., *C.I.E.*, 121 Pioneers	5Apr.13 / 18Oct.07
Aides-de-Camp	Goldie, Capt. K. O., 10 Horse	5Apr.13
	Egerton, Lt. E. B., 17 Lrs. *(extra)*	—

BENGAL.

GOVERNOR	Carmichael, T. D., *Lord,* *G.C.I.E.*, *K.C.M.G.*	
Military Secretary	Bateman-Champain, Maj. H. F., 9 Gúrkha Rif.	2Apr.12 / 1Jan.12
Aides-de-Camp	Vaux, Lt. H G. ..	2Apr.12
	Robertson, Capt. K., 2 Lrs.	3Nov.11
		19Oct.13
	Douglas-Pennant, Lt. *Hon.* A. G. S., h.p. *(extra)*	1Apr.14

(66)

Commands (East Indies).

HEAD QUARTERS STAFF OF THE ARMY IN INDIA

COMMANDER-IN-CHIEF	... ...	Duff, Gen. *Sir* B., *G.C.B.,K.C.S.I., K.C.V.O., C.I.E*, Ind. Army, 🕮, *p.s.c., Simla* 8Mar.14
Military Secretary	.. ..	Scott, Lt.-Col. *(temp.Col.)* T. E., *C.I.E., D.S.O.,* Ind.Army 8Mar.14
Asst. Mil. Secretary and Interpreter	..	Reichwald, Capt. W. F., R.A. [L] 8Mar.14
Aides-de-Camp	.. .. ..	Vernon, Capt. H. A., K.R. Rif. C. .. .. .. 8Mar.14 Bruce, Capt. G. E., 53 Sikhs 8Mar.14

GENERAL STAFF BRANCH.

Chief of the General Staff ...	...	Lake, Lt.-Gen. *Sir* P. H. N., *K.C.M.G., C.B.,* Col. E. Lan. R., *p.s.c.*.. .. .. 21Feb.12
Director of Military Operations	..	Kirkpatrick, Col. *(temp. Brig.-Gen.)* G. M., *C B., p.s.c.*... 1June14
General Staff Officers, 1st grade	..	Bingley, Col. A. H., *C.I.E.,* Ind. Army .. .. .. 10Nov.11 Hoghton, Col. F. A., Ind. Army .. .. .. 30June13 Tod, Lt.-Col. J. K., Ind. Army, *p.s.c.* [L] 1Apr.14
General Staff Officers, 2nd grade	..	Battine, Maj. R. St. C., 21 Cav., *p.s.c.* [L] .. .. 19Feb.11 Wagstaff, Capt. C. M., R.E., *p.s.c.* .. .. .. 10Ct.11 Stockley, Maj. H. R., *C.I.E.,* R.E. .. .. .. 1Mar.12 Pryce, Maj. H. E. ap R., 18 Inf., *p.s.c.* .. .. 11Nov.12 Stokes, Maj. C.B., 3 Horse, *p.s.c.* .. .. .. 15Nov.12 Holman, Bt. Lt.-Col. H. C., *D.S.O.,* 16 Cav., *p.s.c.* [L] 1July13 Norman, Maj. C. L., *M.V.O.,* Corps of Guides, *p.s.c.* { 17Sept.13 1Feb.13 Kaye, Maj. C., *C.I.E.,* 20 Inf. .. .. .. 10Ct.13 Macmullen, Capt. C. N., 15 Sikhs .. .. ..{ 4Dec.13 7Jan.13 Talbot, Capt. F. E. G., 14 Sikhs, *p.s.c.* 20Mar.14
General Staff Officers, 3rd grade	..	Finlay, Capt. R. F., 58 Rif. .. .. 23Sept.11 Stoney, Capt. P. S., 26 Punjabis, *p.s.c.*... .. 27Nov.11 Keen, Capt. P. H., 56 Rif. .. .. 14June12 Rowlandson, Capt. M. G. D., 38 Dogras, *p.s.c.* [L] 1Nov.12 Moens, Capt. A. W. H. M., 52 Sikhs, *p.s.c.* .. 4Feb.13 Jeffery, Capt. W. H., *C.I.E.,* 73 Inf. .. .. 1July13 Wigram, Maj. K., 2 Gúrkha Rif., *p.s.c.* .. .. 15Nov.13 Cromble, Capt. D. C., 23 Cav., *p.s.c.* 4Dec.13
Director of Staff Duties and Military Training	..	Shore, Col. *(temp. Brig. Gen.),* O, B, S, F., *C.B., D.S.O.,* Ind. Army, *p.s.c.* [L] 3Apr.13
General Staff Officers, 1st grade	..	Powell, Col. S. H. *[l]* .. .. 21Oct.10 Knight, Bt.Col. W. C., *D.S.O.,* Ind.Army, *p.s.c.* [L]*A.D.C.* 22July12 Crowe, Col. J. H. V., *p.s.c.* [L] .. .. .. 7Oct.13 Knox, Maj. H. H. S., North'n R., *p.s.c.* 19Feb.11
General Staff Officers, 2nd grade	..	Charles, Bt. Maj. J. R. E., *D.S.O.,* R.E., *p.s.c.* .. { 29Sept.12 26Nov.10 Price, Maj. T. R. C., 11 Lrs., *p.s.c.* 16June13

Attached.

Inspector of Cavalry	.. ..	Rimington, Maj.-Gen. M, F., *C.V.O., C.B.,* Col. 6 Dns. .. 18Mar.11
Inspector of Royal Horse and Royal Field Artillery	}	Mercer, Col. *(temp. Brig.-Gen.)* H. F., *C.B., A.D.C.* ..{ 20Nov.12 20Oct.10
Inspector of Royal Garrison Artillery		Cockburn, Col. *(temp. Brig.-Gen.)* W, F., *g.* 1June12
Inspector of Volunteers	..	Lean, Col. *(temp. Brig.-Gen.)* K. E., *O.B.* 28Apr.12

ADJUTANT-GENERAL'S BRANCH.

Adjutant-General	.. .. ..	Aylmer, Maj.-Gen. F. J., *C.B.* 25Mar12
GENERAL SECTION.		
Deputy Adjutant-General	.. ..	Walter, Col. *(temp. Brig.-Gen.)* J. MacN., *D.S.O., p.s.c.,* 5Sept.13
Asst. Adjt.-Gens.	.. ..	Delamain, Col. W. S., *C.B., D.S.O.,* Ind. Army .. 17Nov.12 Rich, Col. H. H., R.A. .. .. 14Mar.13 O'Leary, Col. W. E., *p.s.c.* [L] 5Nov.13
Dep. Asst. Adjt.-Gen.	.. ..	Jones, Bt. Lt.-Col. L. C., *M.V.O.,* 5 Cav., *p.s.c.* *[l]* 16Mar.12
Dep. Asst. Adjt.-Gen., R.E.	..	Lesslie. Maj. W. B., R.E. 21Feb.12
Brigade-Major, R.A.	..	Luke, Maj. T. M., *D.S.O.,* R.A. 6Jan.14
Dir. of Mil. Prisons & Detention Barracks		Morse, Lt.-Col. C. J. .. .. —
RECRUITING SECTION.		
Staff Officer	.. .. ..	Harrison, Maj. A. H. P., 33 Punjabis 12Mar.12

[*Continued on page 67*]

D

Commands of the Army.

EAST INDIES—*contd.*
India Headquarters Staff—contd.
Adjutant General's Branch—*contd.*

JUDGE ADVOCATE GENERAL'S SECTION.

Judge Advocate General	Caruana, Lt.-Col. A. J., Ind. Army	1May1.
Assistant Judge Advocate General	Nicholas, Maj. S. H. E., 95 Inf.	1May1?

QUARTERMASTER-GENERAL'S BRANCH.

Quartermaster-General	Bunbury, Maj.-Gen. W. E., *C.B.*, Ind. Army, *p.s.c.*	7Nov.1.

MOVEMENTS, QUARTERINGS, AND CANTONMENTS SECTION.

Deputy Quarter-Master-General	Stanton, Col., *(temp. Brig.-Gen.)* H. E., *C.B.,D.S.O.,p.s.c.*, A.D.C.	4May1?
Dep. Asst. Quarter-Master-General	Rice, Maj. S. M., 64 Pioneers, *p.s.c.*	1June1!
Staff Captain	Orr, Maj. G. M., 11 Lrs., *p.s.c.*	22Oct.10

SUPPLY AND TRANSPORT SECTION.

Director of Supplies and Transport	Williams, Col. *(temp. Brig.-Gen.)* A.B.C.,C.B.,Ind.Army	1Sept.1!
Dep. Director of Supplies	Thomas, Col. F. H. S., Ind. Army	1Sept.1!
Dep. Director of Transport	Barry, Lt.-Col. J. F., Ind. Army	18Mar.1!
Dep. Asst. Director of Supplies	Muscroft, Bt. Lt.-Col. W. St. C., Ind. Army	1Apr.1!
Dep. Asst. Director of Transport	Walter, Capt. E., Ind. Army	1Apr.1?

REMOUNT SECTION.

Director-General, Army Remount Dept.	Broome, Maj.-Gen. R. C., *C.I.E.*, Ind. Army	1Apr.0!
Staff Veterinary Officer and Personal Assistant to the Dir.-Gen., Army Remount Dept.	Gillett, Capt. E. S., A.V.C.	20Nov.1!

FARMS SECTION.

Director of Military Farms	Hallowes, Lt.-Col. F. W., Ind. Army	1Apr.1?

VETERINARY SECTION.

Principal Veterinary Officer in India	Hazelton, Col. E. H., *F.R.C.V.S.*	12Mar.1!
Assistant Principal Veterinary Officer	Glasse, Capt. M. St. G., A. V.C.	1Oct.1!

CLOTHING SECTION.

Director of Army Clothing	O'Meara, Maj. C. A. E., Ind. Army	21Apr.10

MEDICAL BRANCH.

Director, Medical Services	B.C. Babtie, Surg.-Gen. W., *C.B., C.M.G., M.B., K.H.S.*	22Mar.14
Deputy Director, Medical Services	Hendley, Col. H., *M.D.*, Ind. Med. Serv.	8Aug.1!
Assistant Director, Medical Services (British Service)	Blenkinsop, Lt.-Col. A. P., R.A.M.C.	9May1!
Assistant Director, Medical Services (Indian Service)	Granger, Bt. Lt.-Col. T. A., *M.B.*, Ind. Med. Serv.	22May1!

ORDNANCE BRANCH.

Director-General of Ordnance	Stuart, Col. *(temp. Maj.-Gen.)* R. C. O., *f.*	8May1!
Dep. Dir.-Gen. of Ordnance		
Asst. Dir.-Gen. of Ordnance	Palmer, Maj. C. C., R.A., *p.a.c.*	4Apr.12
Dir. of Ordnance Stores	Jennings, Lt.-Col. *(temp. Col.)* H. A K., R.A., *f.*	—
Dep. Dir. of Ordnance Stores	Woods, Maj. G. G., R.A.	9Apr.1!

MILITARY WORKS BRANCH.

Director-General of Military Works	Williams, Col. *(temp. Maj.-Gen.)* G.	6Apr.1
Dep. Dir.-Gen. of Military Works	Nanton, Col. H. C.	1Dec.1!
Asst. Dirs.-Gen. of Military Works	{ Hingston, Maj. G. B., R.E.	13Nov.10
	{ Ogilvie, Maj. D., R.E.	29Sept.1!
Inspector of Machinery	Nugent, Maj. C. H. H., R.E.	17Feb.11
Dep. Asst. Dirs.-Gen. of Mil. Works	{ Stace, Capt. R. E., R.E.	28Oct.11
	{ Evans, Capt. W. H., R.E.	29Sept.12

(68)

Commands (East Indies).

EAST INDIES—*contd*,

STAFF OF ARMIES.

NORTHERN ARMY.

Head-Quarters—Murree.

GENERAL OFFICER COMMANDING..	Willcocks, Lt.-Gen. *Sir* J., *K.C.B., K.C.S.I., K.C.M.G., D.S.O., q.s.,*	6Oct.10
Asst. Mil. Sec. and Aide-de-Camp	Tomkins, Maj. H. L., *D.S.O.,* 28 Punjabis.	6Oct.10
Aide-de-Camp	Willcocks, Lt. J. L., R. Highrs.	13July13
General Staff.		
Brigadier-General..	Hudson, Col. *(temp.Brig.-Gen.)*H.,*C.B.,C.I.E.,* Ind.Army	1Oct.12
General Staff Officer, 2nd grade	Vincent, Maj. B., 6 Dns., *p.s.c.*	11Feb.13
Deputy Judge-Advocate-General	Beatson Bell, Lt.-Col. J., Ind. Army	{ 1Nov.10 { 14Jan.08
Inspector of Physical Training	Urquhart, Capt. E. F. M., R. Highrs.	19Mar.13
Superintendent of Physical Training	Wallace, Lt. R., E. York. R.	8July12

1st (PESHAWAR) DIVISION. *Cherat.*

Commander	Blomfield, Maj.-Gen. C. J., *C.B., D.S.O.,* Col. Lan.Fus.	{ 30Oct.12 { 3Mar.11
Aide-de-Camp	Wilson, Lt. H. M., 24 Punjabis	{ 30Oct.12 { 3Mar.11
General Staff Officer, 1st grade	Rice, Lt.-Col. G. B. H., Ind. Army, *p.s.c.*	22Jan.14
General Staff Officer, 2nd grade	Wilkinson, Maj. H. B. Des. V., Durh. L. I., *p.s.c., q.s.*	29Mar.12
Dep. Asst. Adjt.-Gen.	Bradshaw, Maj. C. R., 9 Gúrkha Rif., *p.s.c.* [*l*]	18Nov.12
Asst.Qr.-Mr. Gen.	Tidswell, Col. E. C., *D.S.O.*	18Sept.13
Commanding Royal Artillery	Stokes, Col. *(temp. Brig.-Gen.)* A., *D.S.O., g.*	22Dec.11
Asst. Dir. of Ord. Stores	Douglas, Maj. A. P., R.A.	6June14
Asst. Dir. of Medical Services	Firth, Col. R. H., *F.R.C.S.*	

Peshawar Infantry Brigade. *Peshawar.*

Brigade Commander	Young, Maj.-Gen. C. F. G., Ind. Army	{ 16May13 { 20June12
Brigade-Major	Keen, Maj. F. S., 45 Sikhs, *p.s.c.*	6Apr 12

Nowshera Brigade. *Nowshera.*

Brigade Commander	Cox, Col. *(temp. Brig.-Gen.)* H.V., *C.B.,C.S.I.,*Ind.Army (*Col. on Staff*)	{ — { 11Jan.12
Brigade-Major	Twiss, Capt. W. L. O., 9 Gúrkha Rif., *p.s.c.* [L]	1Apr.13

Risalpur Cavalry Brigade. *Risalpur.*

Brigade Commander	Turner, Maj.-Gen J.G., *C.B.,* Ind. Army	{ 17Nov.12 { 5Jan 11
Brigade-Major	Moir, Capt. J. E., 10 Lrs., *p.s.c,*	1May12

BRITISH TROOPS IN THE DIVISION.

Royal Artillery.
VIII. Brig. R.H.A. M. Batt.
III. Brig. R.F.A. 75 Batt.
  89 Batt.
XVI. Brig. R.F.A. { 90 Batt.
  { 91 Batt.
1 Ammn. Col., R.F.A.
72 Batt. R. G. A.

Infantry.
2 Bn. L'pool R.
1 Bn. R. Suss. R.
1 Bn. Durh. L. I.

(69)

Commands of the Army.

EAST INDIES—contd.

Northern Army—contd.

2nd (RAWAL PINDI) DIVISION. *Murree.*

Commander	Kitson, Maj.-Gen. *Sir* G. C., *K.C.V.O., C.B., C.M.G., p.s.c.,*	4May 12
Aide-de-Camp		
General Staff Officer, 1st grade	Campbell, Col. A. A. E., Ind. Army	29Sept.13
General Staff Officers, 2nd grade	O'Dowda, Maj. J. W., R.W. Kent R., *p.s.c.*	3Sept.13
	Deane, Maj. D., 12 Cav., *p.s.c.* [*l*]	1Mar.14
Dep. Asst. Adjt.-Gen.	Abbott, Maj. L. H., 11 Rajputs, *p.s.c.*	25Feb.12
Asst. Qr.-Mr.-Gen.	Lecky, Col. R. St. C.	19May.13
Commanding Royal Artillery	Smith, Col. *(temp. Brig.-Gen.)* G. B.	21Dec.11
Asst. Dir. of Ord. Stores	Douglas, Maj. A. P., R.A.	6June14
Dep. Dir. of Medical Services		

Rawal Pindi Infantry Brigade. *Rawal Pindi.*

Brigade Commander	Townshend, Maj.-Gen. C. V. F., *C.B., D.S.O.*	30June13
Brigade Major	Catty, Capt. T. C., 69 Punjabis, *p.s.c.*	1Oct.11

Jhelum Brigade. *Jhelum.*

Brigade Commander	Macintyre, Maj.-Gen. D. C. F., *C.B.,* Ind. Army	15Apr.12
Brigade-Major	Calvert, Maj. R.T.C., 120 Inf., *p.s.c.*	3Oct.11

Abbottabad Brigade. *Abbottabad.*

Brigade Commander	Loch, Col. *(temp. Brig. Gen.)* H. F., Ind. Army, *p.s.c.* (Col. on Staff)	20June12
Brigade-Major	Loveday, Capt. F. W., R.A., *p.s.c.*	1Nov.12

Sialkot Brigade. *Sialkot.*

Brigade Commander	Leader, Col. *(temp. Brig.-Gen.)*H.P., *C.B.*	1June11
Brigade-Major	Rivett-Carnac, Maj. J. S., 14 Lrs., *p.s.c.*	11Nov.11

BRITISH TROOPS IN THE DIVISION

Cavalry.	Royal Artillery—contd.	Infantry.
7 Lrs.	VII. Brig., R.F.A. { 4 Batt. 38 Batt. 78 Batt.	1 Bn. York R.
21 Lrs.		4 Bn. K. R. Rif. C.
	2 Ammn. Col., R.F.A.	2 Bn N. Staff. R.
		2 Bn. Rif. Brig.

Royal Artillery.	
VIII. Brig. R.H.A., Q Batt.	1, 6 and 9 Mtn.Batts. R.G.A
A. and B. Ammn. Cols., R.H.A.	68 and 94 Cos., R.G.A.
	104 Batt., R.G.A.

(70)

Commands (East Indies).

EAST INDIES—*contd.*

Northern Army—contd.

3rd (LAHORE) DIVISION. *Dalhousie.*

Commander	Watkis, Lt.-Gen. H. B. B., *C.B.*, Ind. Army, *p.s.c.*	{ 30Oct.12 6May12
Aide-de-Camp	Watkis, Lt. H. L., 31 Punjabis..	25Oct.13
General Staff Officer, 1st grade	O'Leary, Col. T. E., *C.B.*	14Mar.13
General Staff Officers, 2nd grade	{ King, Maj. S. W., 17 Inf., *p.s.c.* [l] Hart-Synnot, Maj. A. H. S., *D.S.O.*, E.Surr.R.,*p.s.c.* [L]	26May11 27Oct.13
Dep. Asst. Adjt.-Gen.	Lukin, Maj. R. C. W., 9 Horse	25Mar.13
Asst. Qr.-Mr.-Gen.	Hodson, Col. G. B., *C.B.*, *D.S.O.*, Ind. Army	6Nov.12
Commanding Royal Artillery	Johnson, Col. (*temp. Brig.-Gen.*) F.E., *D.S.O.*	{ 13Oct.11 17May11
Asst. Dir. of Medical Services	Lyons, Surg.-Gen. R. W. S., *M.D.*, Ind. Med. Serv.	

Jullundur Brigade. *Dalhousie*

Brigade Commander	Carnegy, Maj.-Gen.P. M., *C.B.*, Ind. Army..	{ 20June12 14Nov.10
Brigade-Major	Hill, Maj. H., *M.V.O.*, R. W. Fus., *p.s.c.*	1Oct.12
Staff Captain	Alexander, Capt. R. G., 11 Lrs.	22Dec.12

Sirhind Brigade. *Kasauli.*

Brigade Commander	Brunker, Maj.-Gen. J. M. S.	31Dec.11
Brigade-Major	Ridgeway, Capt. D. G., 3 Gúrkha Rif. *p.s.c.*	1May12

Ambala (Cavalry) Brigade. *Kasauli.*

Brigade Commander	Pirie, Maj.-Gen. C. P. W., Ind. Army	{ 1July12 11Apr.10
Brigade-Major	Cheyne, Maj. R. E., 8 Cav.	5Sept.10

Ferozepore Brigade. *Ferozepore.*

Brigade Commander	Egerton, Col. (*temp. Brig.-Gen.*) R. G., *C.B.*, Ind. Army *(Col. on Staff)*	4Nov.11
Brigade-Major	Sangster, Maj. P. B., 2 Lrs.	29Mar.12

BRITISH TROOPS IN THE DIVISION.

Cavalry.

8 Hrs.

Royal Artillery.

I. Brig. R.H.A. { "A" Batt.
"B" Batt.

C. and I. Ammn. Cols.,R.H.A.

Royal Artillery—contd.

III. Brig., R.F.A. .. { 16 Batt.
62 Batt.

XVIII. Brig., R.F.A. .. { 59 Batt.
93 Batt.
94 Batt.

3 Ammn. Col.,R.F.A.

2 and 5 Mtn.Batts.,R.G.A

82 Co.and 86 Batt.,R.G.A.

Royal Engineers.

H. Co.

Infantry.

2 Bn. North'd Fus.
1 Bn. W. Rid. R.
2 Bn. R. W. Kent. R.
1 Bn. Manch. R.
1 Bn. High. L.I.
1 Bn. Conn. Rang.
4 Bn. Rif. Brig.

(71)

Commands of the Army.

EAST INDIES—contd.

Northern Army—contd.

7th (MEERUT) DIVISION. *Mussoorie.*

Commander	Anderson, Lt.-Gen. C. A., C.B.	21Aug.1
Aide-de-Camp	Brock, Capt. B. de L., 126 Inf.	21Aug.1
General Staff Officer, 1st grade	Jacob, Col. C. W., Ind. Army	28Sept.1
General Staff Officer, 2nd grade	Davies, Maj. W. P. L., R.A., p.s.c.	7Jan.1
Dep. Asst. Adjt.-Gen.		
Asst. Qr.-Mr. Gen.	Lindesay, Col. A. L.	8June1
Commanding Royal Artillery.		
Asst. Dir. of Medical Services	Treherne, Col. F. H., F.R.C.S. Edin.	—

Meerut (Cavalry) Brigade. *Meerut.*

Brigade Commander	Edwards, Col. (temp. Brig.-Gen.) Fitz J. M., Ind. Army, D.S.O., p.s.c. (Col. on Staff)	29Sept.1
Brigade-Major	Muspratt, Maj. V. E., 30 Lrs., p.s.c. [l]	5Jan.1

Bareilly Brigade. *Ranikhet.*

Brigade Commander	Macbean, Maj.-Gen. F., C.V.O., C.B.	Sept.1
Brigade-Major	Glasgow, Maj. A. E., R. Suss. R.	1Mar.1
Staff Captain	Hamer, Capt. M. A., 129 Baluchis, p.s.c.	7Feb 1

Dehra Dun Brigade. *Dehra Dun.*

Brigade Commander	Johnson, Col. (temp. Brig.-Gen.) C. E., Ind. Army (Col. on Staff)	17Nov.1
Brigade-Major	Walker, Maj. H. A., R. Fus., p.s.c.	15Sept.1

Garhwal Brigade. *Lansdowne.*

Brigade Commander	Keary, Maj.-Gen. H. D'U., C.B., D.S.O., Ind. Army	{ 14Nov.1 20Jan.1
Brigade-Major	Young, Capt. A., 1 Gúrkha Rif., p.s.c.	1June1

BRITISH TROOPS IN THE DIVISION.

Cavalry.
6 Dns.
13 Hrs.

Royal Artillery.
XII. Brig., R.H.A. { V. Batt.
W. Batt.
F. Ammn. Col., R.H.A.

Royal Artillery—contd.
VI. Brig., R.F.A., 77 Batt.
IX. Brig., R.F.A. { 19 Batt.
20 Batt.
28 Batt.

7 Ammn. Col., R.F.A.
59, 73, 74 and 81 Cos., R.G.A.
91 Batt., R. G. A.

Infantry.
2 Bn. Leic. R.
2 Bn. E. Surr. R.
1 Bn. Welsh R.
2 Bn. R. Highrs.
3 Bn. K. R. Rif. C.
1 Bn. Sea. Highrs.

8th (LUCKNOW) DIVISION. *Jalapahar.*

Commander	Scallon, Lt.-Gen; Sir R. I., K.C.B., K.C.I.E., D.S.O., Ind. Army, 豆.卫.C.	{ 16Aug.1 11Feb.1
Aide-de-Camp	Daniell, Capt. W. R., 123 Rif.	{ 16Aug.1 6May1
General Staff Officer, 1st grade	Woodyatt, Col. N. G., Ind. Army	6July1
General Staff Officer, 2nd grade	Marjoribanks, Bt. Maj. R. D., 107 Pioneers, p.s.c.	19Feb.1
Dep. Asst. Adjt.-Gen.	Tyler, Capt. R. M., Durh. L. I., p.s.c.	17Apr.1
Asst. Qr.-Mr. Gen.	Iggulden, Col. H. A.	5Oct.1
Dep. Dir. of Medical Services	Hathaway, Surg.-Gen. H. G., C.B.	

Lucknow Cavalry Brigade. *Lucknow.*

Brigade Commander	Cookson, Maj.-Gen. G. A., C.B., Ind. Army	{ 16Oct.1 16Aug.0
Brigade-Major	Torrie, Capt. T. G. J., 27 Lt. Cav., p.s.c.	1Apr.1

(72)
Commands (East Indies).

EAST INDIES—*contd.*
Northern Army—contd.

8th (Lucknow) Division—contd.

Lucknow Infantry Brigade. *Lucknow.*

Brigade Commander	.. Wilson, Maj.-Gen. A., *C.B.*	.. 22Oct.11
Brigade-Major	.. Howard, Maj. T. N. S. M., W. York. R. ..	.. 9July11

Fyzabad Brigade. *Fyzabad.*

Brigade Commander... ...	... Kavanagh, Col. (*temp.Brig.-Gen.*) C. T. McM., *C.V.O., C.B., D.S.O.*	.. 5Jan.14
Brigade-Major	.. Cloete, Capt. L. B., 87 Dogras, *p.s.c.*	.. 29Oct.12

Allahabad Brigade. *Allahabad.*

Brigade Commander ...	... Cowper, Col. (*temp. Brig.-Gen.*) M., *C.I.E.,* Ind. Army (*Col. on Staff*)	.. 7Jan.13
Brigade-Major	.. Russell, Maj. F. D., 1 Lrs., *p.s.c.* [L]	..{ 28June12 1June11
Staff Captain	.. Pepys, Capt. G. L., 57 Rif., *p.s.c.* (L)	.. 28June12

Presidency Brigade. *Calcutta.*

Brigade Commander ..	.. May, Maj.-Gen. E. S., *C.B., C.M.G.* [I]	.. 25May13
General Staff Officer, 2nd grade	.. Hocken, Maj. C. A. F., 35 Horse, *p.s.c.* [L] ..	.. 11Mar.12
Dep. Asst. Adjt. & Qr.-Mr.-Gen.	..	
Garrison Quarter-Master ..	.. Gillies, Capt. H., 1 Lrs.	—

BRITISH TROOPS IN THE DIVISION.

Cavalry.	Royal Artillery—contd.	Infantry.
1 D.G.		1 Bn. R. Scots.
Royal Artillery.	XVII. Brig. R.F.A. { 10. Batt. 26 Batt. 92 Batt.	2 Bn. R. Lanc. R. 2 Bn. R. Fus. 3 Bn. R. Fus.
XI. Brig.,R.H.A., U. Batt.		1 Bn. K. O. Sco. Bord.
G. Ammn. Col., R.H.A.	8 Ammn. Col., R.F.A.	3 Bn. Midd'x R.
V. Brig., R.F.A., { 63 Batt. 64 Batt. 73 Batt.	51 & 62 Cos., R.G.A.	1 Bn. Arg. & Suth'd Highrs. 1 Bn. Leins. R.

KOHAT BRIGADE. *Fort Lockhart, Samana.*

Brigade Commander ..	.. Campbell, Maj.-Gen. F., *C.B., D.S.O.*, Ind. Army	..{ 17Nov.12 20June06
General Staff Officer, 2nd grade	.. Peck, Maj. A. W., 25 Cav.	29Sept.12
Dep. Asst. Adjt. & Qr.-Mr.-Gen.	.. Duncan, Capt. H. C., 9 Gúrkha Rif., *p.s.c.* ..	.. 1Feb.14

BANNU BRIGADE. *Bannu.*

Brigade Commander ..	.. O'Donnell, Maj.-Gen. H., *C.B., D.S.O.,* Ind. Army	..{ 1Apr.12 1Jan.11
General Staff Officer, 2nd grade	.. Loch, Maj. S. G., *D.S.O.*, R.E., *p.s.c.*	..{ 15Sept.13 10Oct.11
Dep. Asst. Adjt. & Qr.-Mr.-Gen.	.. Tyrrell, Capt. A. C. L., 25 Cav., *p.s.c.*	13May11

DERAJAT BRIGADE. *Sheikh Budin.*

Brigade Commander ..	.. Younghusband, Maj. Gen. *Sir* G. J., *K.C.I.E., C.B.,* Ind. Army, *p.s.c.*	{ 1June11 16Feb.08
General Staff Officer, 2nd grade	.. Tarver, Maj. A. L., *D.S.O.*, 124 Inf., *p.s.c.* ..	12Mar.13
Dep. Asst. Adjt. & Qr.-Mr.-Gen.	.. Hay, Capt. C. J. B., Corps of Guides, *p.s.c.* [L]	.. 28May12

Commands of the Army.

EAST INDIES—*contd.*

SOUTHERN ARMY.

Head-Quarters—Ootacamund.

GENERAL OFFICER COMMANDING	Nixon, Gen. *Sir* J. E., *K.C.B.*	11Oct.1:
Asst. Mil. Sec.	Beach, Maj. W. H., R.E.	11Oct.1:
Aide-de-Camp	Nixon, Lt. E. J., R.A.	11Oct.1:
General Staff.		
Brigadier-General	Money, Col. (*temp. Brig.-Gen.*) A. W., *C.B., p.s.c.*	27Nov.1:
General Staff Officer, 2nd grade	Gregory, Maj. C. L., 19 Lrs., *p.s.c.*	18Nov.1:
Deputy Judge-Advocate General	Brownlow, Maj. d'A. C., Ind. Army	{ 1May1: 1Nov.1(
Inspector of Physical Training	Hayne, Capt. S. S., North'n R.	{ 5Mar.1: 1May1:
Superintendent of Physical Training	Bacon, Lt. R. G., 124 Inf.	30Apr.1:

4th (QUETTA) DIVISION. *Quetta.*

Commander	Grover, Lt.-Gen. *Sir* M. H. S., *K.C.B., K.C.I.E.*, Ind. Army [L]	17Nov.1:
Aide-de-Camp	Elton, Lt. G. D. G., 2 Bn. R. Ir. Fus.	15Apr.1(
General Staff Officer, 1st grade	Taylor, Col. E. T., *p.s.c.*	29Aug.1:
General Staff Officers, 2nd grade	{ ♥℃ Colvin, Maj. J. M. C., R. E., *p.s.c., q.s.* { Deverell, Capt. C. J., W. York. R., *p.s.c.*	1June1: 7Feb.1:
Dep. Asst. Adjt.-Gen.	Norman, Maj. W. H., 11 Lrs., *p.s.c.*	29Dec.1:
Asst. Qr.-Mr.-Gen.	Hardy, Col. T. H., Ind. Army	20Jan.14
Commanding Royal Artillery	Scott, Col. (*temp. Brig.-Gen.*) A. B., *C.B., D.S.O.*	22Dec.1:
Asst. Dir. of Medical Services	Henderson, Col. R. S. F., *M.B., K.H.P.*	—

1st Quetta Infantry Brigade. *Quetta.*

Brigade Commander	Sitwell, Col. (*temp. Brig.-Gen.*) W. H., *C.B., D.S.O., p.s.c.*	7Nov.1:
Brigade-Major	Lakin, Capt. J. H. F., 7 Gūrkha Rif., *p.s.c.*	8June1:

2nd Quetta Infantry Brigade. *Quetta.*

Brigade Commander	♥℃Melliss, Maj.-Gen. C. J., *C.B.*, Ind. Army [L]	{ 11Apr 1: 25Jan.1(
Brigade-Major	Moberly, Maj. H. S., 66 Punjabis, *p.s.c.*	{ 7Feb.1: 11June1:

Karachi Brigade. *Karachi.*

Brigade Commander	Shaw, Maj. Gen. D. G. L., Ind. Army	{ 23Feb.1: 16Oct.1
General Staff Officer, 2nd grade	Dickson, Maj. W. E. R., R. E. [l]	28Oct.1
Dep. Asst. Adjt. & Qr.-Mr.-Gen.	Winter, Maj. C. B., 112 Inf. [L]	10Feb.1:

BRITISH TROOPS IN THE DIVISION.

Royal Artillery.

XXI. Brig., R.F.A. { 101 Batt.
 102 Batt.
 103 Batt.

4 Ammn. Col., R.F.A.
3, 4 and 8 Mtn. Batts., R.G.A.
60, 69 and 101 Cos., R.G.A.

Infantry.

2 Bn. Som. L.I.
1 Bn. Lan. Fus.
1 Bn. S. Lan. R.
2 Bn. R. Ir. Fus.

(74)

Commands (East Indies).

EAST INDIES—*contd.*

Southern Army—contd.

5th (MHOW) DIVISION. *Mhow.*

Commander	Payne, Maj.-Gen. R. L., *C.B., D.S.O.,* Col. Som. L.I.	30Oct.12
Aide-de-Camp		
General Staff Officer, 1st grade	Brooking, Col. H. T., *C.B.,* Ind. Army	{ 29Oct.11 / 11Sept.11
General Staff Officer, 2nd grade	Godwin, Maj. C. A. C., 23 Cav., *p.s.c.*	{ 25Jan.13 / 28May11
Dep. Asst. Adjt.-Gen.	Stirling, Maj. *Sir* G. M. H., *Bt., D.S.O.,* Essex R.	13Jan.11
Asst. Qr.-Mr.-Gen.	Skinner, Col. F. St. D., *p.s.c.*	{ 6Mar.12 / 9Mar.09
Asst. Dir. of Medical Services	Grainger, Col. T., *C.B., M.D.,* Ind. Med. Serv.	

Nasirabad Brigade. *Mount Abu.*

Brigade Commander	Davison, Maj.-Gen. K. S., *C.B.,* Ind. Army	{ 5Jan.11 / 1May08
Brigade-Major	Dickinson, Maj. A. T. S., 51 Sikhs, *p.s.c.* [L]	{ 22Nov.13 / 25Feb.12
Staff Captain	Glynton, Capt. G. M., 3 Gúrkha Rif., *p. .c.*	22Nov.13

Jubbulpore Brigade. *Pachmarhi.*

Brigade Commander	Fanshawe, Maj.-Gen. H. D., *C.B.*	{ 25May13 / 16Dec.10
Brigade-Major	Mackenzie, Capt. J. H., R. Scots, *p.s.c.*	6June11
Staff Captain	Humphreys, Maj. D. W. H., *D.S.O.,* 8 Gúrkha Rif., *p.s.c.*	24Jan.12

Jhansi Brigade. *Jhansi.*

Brigade Commander	Kemball, Maj.-Gen.G. V., *C.B., D.S.O. p.s.c., g.*	20Apr.14
Brigade-Major	Hope, Maj. J. W., R.A., *p.s.c.*	2Oct.13

BRITISH TROOPS IN THE DIVISION.

Cavalry.	Royal Artillery—contd.	Infantry.
14 Hrs.	XI. Brig., R.F.A. .. { 83 Batt. / 84 Batt. / 85 Batt.	2 Bn. E. York R.
		1 Bn. R. Ir. Regt.
Royal Artillery.	XIX. Brig., R.F.A. 95 Batt.	2 Bn. Ches. R.
XIII. Brig., R.H.A. { X Batt. / Y Batt.		2 Bn. Hamps. R.
E. Ammn. Col., R.H.A.	XX. Brig., R.F.A. .. { 98 Batt. / 99 Batt. / 100 Batt.	2 Bn. R. Berks. R.
		1 Bn, York & Lanc. R.
VI. Brig., R.F.A. .. { 74 Batt. / 79 Batt.	5,11 & 12 Ammn.Cols.,R.F.A. 71 & 90 Batts., R. G. A.	

6th (POONA) DIVISION. *Poona.*

Commander	Barrett, Lt.-Gen. *Sir* A. A., *K.C.B., K.C.V.O.,* Ind. Army	21Feb.12
Aide-de-Camp		
General Staff Officer, 1st grade	Gamble, Col. R. N., *D.S.O., p.s.c.* [l]	4May12
General Staff Officer, 2nd grade	Sanders, Maj. G. A. F., R.E., *p.s.c.*	21Feb.12
Dep. Asst. Adjt.-Gen.	Davie, Maj. J. H. M., 34 Horse	19Nov.10
Asst. Qr.-Mr.-Gen.	Shakespear, Col. L. W., Ind. Army	30Sept.13
Commanding Royal Artillery	Smith, Col. *(temp. Brig.-Gen.)* S. C. U., *g.* [l]	22Dec.14
Asst Dir. of Medical Services	Hehir, Col. P., *M.D., F.R.C.S. Edin.,* Ind. Med. Serv.	

[*Continued on page 75*]

(75)

Commands of the Army.

EAST INDIES—*contd.*

Southern Army—contd.

6th (Poona) Division—*contd.*

Poona Infantry Brigade.   *Poona.*

Brigade Commander..	.. .. Aitken,Col.(*temp,Brig-Gen.*) A,E.,Ind.Army (*Col. on Staff*)	{ 19June13 15Nov.11
Brigade-Major ..	.. .. Holdich, Maj. H. A., 5 Gúrkha Rif., *p.s.c.* ..	.. 20May11

Belgaum Brigade.   *Belgaum.*

Brigade Commander	.. .. Fry, Maj.-Gen. C. I., Ind. Army ..	..{ 7Jan.13 1June11
Brigade-Major ..	.. .. Dunn, Capt. E. G., R. Ir. Rif., *p.s.c.*	.. 4Mar.12

Bombay Brigade.   *Deolali (temp.)*

Brigade Commander	.. .. Gorringe, Maj.-Gen. G. F., *C.B., C.M.G., D.S.O.,* q.s.	.. 1May12
General Staff Officer, 2nd grade ..	Browne, Maj. H. J. P., 5 Gúrkha Rif., *p.s.c.* ..	.. 23June13
Dep. Asst. Adjt. & Qr.-Mr.-Gen. ...	Cummins, Maj. H. A. V., 24 Punjabis, *p.s.c.* ..	.. 6July11

Ahmednagar Brigade.   *Ahmednagar.*

Brigade Commander	.. .. Dobbie, Col. (*temp., Brig.-Gen.*) W. H., *C.B.,* Ind. Army (*Col. on Staff*)	{ 19June13 12Apr.12
Brigade-Major	.. Lloyd, Maj. J. H., 6 Gúrkha Rif.	.. 10Nov.10
Staff Captain	.. Yates, Capt. J. A., 103 Lt. Inf.	.. 19Feb.13

BRITISH TROOPS IN THE DIVISION.

Royal Artillery.

D. Ammn. Col., R.H.A.

X. Brig.,R.F.A. ..{ 76 Batt.
81 Batt.
82 Batt.
XIX. Brig., R.F.A.   96 Batt.

8 Ammn. Col., R.F.A.

52, 77, 79 and 85 Cos., R.G.A.

Infantry.

2 Bn. Norf. R.
2 Bn. Dorset R.
1 Bn. Oxf. & Bucks. L.I.
1 Bn. Notts. & Derby. R
2 Bn. Cam'n Highrs.
1 Bn. R. Ir. Rif. (Det.)

9th (SECUNDERABAD) DIVISION.   *Ootacamund.*

Commander	.. Phayre, Maj.-Gen. A., *C.B.,* Ind. Army	.. 15June14
Aide-de-Camp	.. Hemsley, Capt. C., 64 Pioneers	.. 7June13
General Staff Officer, 1st grade..	Strange, Col. R. G.	..{ 19May13 13Oct.11
General Staff Officers, 2nd grade	{ Cassells, Maj. G. R., 35 Sikhs, *p.s.c.* .. .. Julius, Capt. S. de V. A., R. Suss.tR., *p.s.c.* [l] ..	.. 8Nov.12 .. 28Feb.14
Dep. Asst. Adjt.-Gen. ..	.. McCulloch, Capt. A. J., 7 D.G., *p.s.c.*	9Oct.13
Asst. Qr.-Mr.-Gen. ..	.. Fowler, Col. F. J., *D.S.O.,* Ind. Army	.. 19Dec.18
Dep. Dir. of Medical Service ..	Corker, Surg.-Gen. T. M., *M.D., K.H.P.*	

(76)
Commands (East Indies).

EAST INDIES—contd.

Southern Army—contd.

9th (Secunderabad) Division—contd.

Secunderabad (Cavalry) Brigade. *Belarum.*

Brigade Commander	Wadeson, Col. (*temp. Brig.-Gen.*) F. W. G., Ind. Army (*Col. on Staff*)	7Jan.13
Brigade-Major	Williams, Capt. A. F. C., *D.S.O.*, 31 Lrs., *p.s.c.*	9July12

Secunderabad 1st (Infantry) Brigade. *Secunderabad.*

Brigade Commander	Wilkinson, Maj.-Gen. P. S., *C.B., C.M.G.*	17Nov.13
Brigade-Major	Battye, Maj. I. U., Corps of Guides	5Apr.13

Secunderabad 2nd (Infantry) Brigade. *Secunderabad.*

Brigade Commander	Rodwell, Col. (*temp. Brig-Gen.*) E. H., *C.B.*, Ind. Army, *p.s.c.* (*Col. on Staff*)	28Nov.10
Brigade-Major	Shuttleworth, Capt. D. I., 8 Gúrkha Rif., *p.s.c.*	14Feb.10

Bangalore Brigade. *Bangalore.*

Brigade Commander	Wapshare, Col. (*temp. Brig.-Gen.*) R., Ind. Army (*Col. on Staff*)	{ 7Jan.13 1July12
Brigade-Major	O'Grady, Maj. H. de C., 59 Rif., *p.s.c.*	8June11

Southern Brigade. *Wellington.*

Brigade Commander	Hamilton, Col. (*temp. Brig. Gen.*) W. G., *D.S.O., p.s.c.*	5Sept.13
Brigade-Major	de Gourcy, Capt. *Hon.* M. W. R., 32 Pioneers	6Apr.13

BRITISH TROOPS IN THE DIVISION.

Cavalry.

7 D.G.
7 Hrs.

Royal Artillery.

IX. Brig., R.H.A. { N. Batt.
S. Batt.
H. Ammn. Col., R.H.A.

Royal Artillery—contd.

IV. Brig., R.F.A. { 7 Batt.
14 Batt.
66 Batt.
XIII. Brig. R.F.A. { 2 Batt.
8 Batt.
44 Batt.
XIX. Brig., R.F.A. 97 Batt.
9 & 10 Ammn. Cols., R.F.A.

Infantry.

2 Bn. E. Kent R.
1 Bn. R. Innis. Fus.
2 Bn. N. Lan. R.
2 Bn. Shrops. L.I.
1 Bn. R. Dub. Fus.

Commands of the Army.

EAST INDIES—*contd.*

Southern Army—contd.

BURMA DIVISION. *Maymyo.*

Commander	Pilcher, Maj.-Gen. T.D., *C.B.*, Col. Bedf. R., *p.s.c.* [L]	{ 16Aug.13 22Jan.12
Aide-de-Camp	Baker, Capt. St. J. V., 11 Lrs.	25July13
General Staff Officer, 1st grade	Walker, Col. H. B., *D.S.O.*	1Apr.12
General Staff Officer, 2nd grade	Taylor, Maj. E. M., 22 Cav., *p.s.c.*	16Feb.12
Dep. Asst. Adjt.-Gen.	Clarkson, Maj. B. St. J., Dorset R.	16June12
Asst. Qr.-Mr.-Gen.	Stewart, Col. J. M., *C.B.*, Ind. Army, *A.D.C.*	2July12
Asst. Dir. of Medical Services	Dyson, Col. T. E., *M.B.*, Ind. Med. Serv.	

Rangoon Brigade. *Rangoon.*

Brigade Commander	Johnstone, Col. (*temp. Brig.-Gen.*) A. A. J., Ind. Army (*Col. on Staff*)	12Apr.13
Brigade-Major	Buchanan, Maj. F. E., R. Sc. Fus.	{ 1Nov.13 1Oct.10

Mandalay Brigade. *Maymyo (temp.).*

Brigade Commander	Raitt, Maj.-Gen. H. A., *C.B.*	3May13
Brigade-Major	Nangle, Maj. M. C., 92 Punjabis, *p.s.c.*	{ 1Nov.13 17Feb.12

BRITISH TROOPS IN THE DIVISION.

Royal Artillery.	Infantry.
84 and 75 Cos., R.G.A.	4 Bn. Worc. R.
	1 Bn. Bord. R.
	1 Bn. R. Muns. Fus.

ADEN BRIGADE. *Aden.*

Brigade Commander	{ Bell, Maj.-Gen. *Sir* J. A., *K.C.V.O.*, Ind. Army (*Political Resident, Aden*) { *A.D.C. to Political Resident, Aden*— { Perram, Lt. G. T. C., R.A.	14Nov.1 15Jan.1
General Staff Officer, 2nd grade	Basevi, Maj. W. H. F., 91 Punjabis.	{ 1June1 14Aug.1
Dep. Asst. Adjt. & Qr.-Mr.-Gen.	Sprague, Capt. L. C., R. Ir. Rif., *p.s.c.* [L]	31Oct.1

BRITISH TROOPS IN THE BRIGADE.

Royal Artillery.	Infantry
61, 70, and 76 Cos. R.G.A.	1 Bn. R. Ir. Rif.

(78)

Commands (Mediterranean).

MEDITERRANEAN.

GENERAL OFFICER COMMANDING-IN-CHIEF.

Assistant Military Secretary
Aide-de-Camp

General Staff.
Brigadier-General .. .. .. Ellison, Col. (*temp. Brig.-Gen.*) G. F., C.B., p.s.c. 1June11

CYPRUS.

High Commissioner and Commander-in-Chief Goold-Adams, Maj. Sir H. J., G.C.M.G., C.B. ret. pay *Nicosia*
Aide-de-Camp
(*For troops stationed in Cyprus see note at the foot of this page.*)

FORCE IN EGYPT.

General Officer Commanding	Byng, Maj.-Gen. *Hon.* J. H. G., C.B., M.V.O., Col. 3 Hrs., p.s.c.	30Oct.12
Aide-de-Camp	Annesley, Capt. *Hon.* A., 10 Hrs.	8Nov.12

General Staff.
General Staff Officer, 2nd grade .. .. Blair, Maj. A., *D.S.O.*, K. O. Sco. Bord. p.s.c. .. { 27Sept.12 / 9Mar.12

Administrative, Technical and Departmental Staff.

Asst. Adjt. and Qr.-Mr.-Gen.	Little, Col. C. B.	28Sep .13
Dep. Asst. Adjt. and Qr.-Mr.-Gen.	McNalty, Capt. A. G. P., A.S.C.	30Nov.12
Chief Engineer	Buckland, Col. R. U. H., *A.D.C.*	1Apr.13
Asst. Dir. of Supplies and Transport	Ward, Lt.-Col. E. I., A.S.C.	
Dep. Dir. of Medical Services	Manders, Col. N.	
Dep. Asst. Dir. of Veterinary Services	Tatam, Maj. W. J., A.V.C.	
Chief Ordnance Officer	Woodifield, Lt.-Col. A. H., A. Ord. Dept., *e., o.*	
Command Paymaster	Collings, Col. G. D., *D.S.O.*, A. P. Dept.	

Department of the Finance Member of the Army Council
(*detached from the War Office*). *Malta*

Local Auditor .. .. .. Richardson, B. H., *Esq.*
Assistant Local Auditor .. .. Beard, J. J., *Esq.*

Camel Corps School,
(*Abbassia, Cairo.*)
Commandant .. .. .. Broadbent, Capt. E.N., K.O. Sco. Bord. 19May11
Adjutant .. .. .. Davidson, Lt. E. H., Gord. Highrs. 11July14

TROOPS.

Cavalry.	Engineers.	Army Service Corps.	Army Veterinary Corps.
3 D.G.	2 Co. (Field).	41 Co.	
Mil. Mtd. Police (Det.)			Detachment.
	Infantry.		
Artillery.	Regular Troops.	Royal Army Medical Corps.	Army Ordnance Corps.
XI. Brig. R.H.A. "T" Batt	2 Bn. Devon R.		
7 Mtn Batt. R.G.A.	1 Bn. Worc. R.	33 Co.	9 Co. (Egypt Section).
	2 Bn. North'n R.		
	2 Bn. Gord. Highrs.		

NOTE.—The 1 Bn. Suff. R. and a detachment of the R.G.A., A.S.C. and R.A.M.C are stationed at Khartoum, under the command of the Governor-General of the Anglo-Egyptian Sudan. Detachments of the A.S.C. and R.A.M.C., together with half a Co. of the 1 Bn. Suff R., are stationed at Cyprus.

(79)
Commands of the Army.

Mediterranean Command—contd.

GIBRALTAR.

Governor and Commander-in-Chief	Miles, Lt.-Gen. *Sir* H. S. G., *G.C.B., C.V.O.,* Col. R. Muns. Fus., *p.s.c.* [R] ..	15Aug.13
Assistant Military Secretary	Jackson, Capt. T.D., *M.V.O., D.S.O.,* R. Lanc. R.	{19Aug.13 / 30Sept.10}
Aides-de-Camp ..	Greville, Lt. C. H., G. Gds.	15Aug.13

General Staff.

General Staff Officer, 2nd grade ..	Stanton, Maj. F. H. G., R.A., *p.s.c.* [l]	23Feb.12

Administrative, Technical and Departmental Staff.

Asst. Adjt. & Qr.-Mr.-Gen. ..	Morrison, Col. C. G., *p.s.c., e.*	11Oct.12
Dep. Asst. Adjt. & Qr.-Mr.-Gen.	Legge, Maj. W. K., Essex R.' *p.s.c.*	{24Jan.14 / 30Nov.11}
Garrison Adjutant and Quarter-Master	Bankes, Hon. Capt E., Qr-Mr. ..	20June13
Commanding Royal Artillery ..	Johnston, Maj.-Gen. J. T., *C.B., p.s c., g.* [L]	5Aug.13
Brigade-Major (for R.A.) ..	Green, Capt. A. F. U., R.A. *p.s.c.*	24Nov.11
Major Instructor in Gunnery	Bond, Capt. E. L., R.A., *g.*	{1Apr.13 / 1Jan.13}
Chief Engineer ..	Grant, Col A.	7Apr.11
Staff Officer, Royal Engineers	Roberts, Maj. G. B., R.E.	
Officer Commanding Army Service Corps	Black, Lt.-Col. J. C. L., A.S.C.	
Dep. Dir. of Medical Services ..	Maher, Col J.	
Assistant Director of Ordnance Stores ..	Angell, Col. F. J., A. Ord. Dept.	
Command Paymaster ..	Haynes, Lt.-Col. A., A P. Dept.	

TROOPS IN THE COMMAND.

Royal Garrison Artillery.
6, 9, 54 & 55 Cos.(*Northern Section*)
4, 7 & 8 Cos. (*Southern Section*)

Engineers.
1, 15, 32, & 45 Cos. (*Fortress*).

Infantry
2 Bn. R. Sc. Fus
2 Bn. Wilts. R.

Army Service Corps.
39 Co.

Royal Army Medical Corps.
28 Co.

Army Ordnance Corps.
9 Co. (Gibraltar Section).

(80)

Commands (Mediterranean).

Mediterranean Command—contd.

MALTA AND ITS DEPENDENCIES.

Governor and Commander-in-Chief	Rundle, Gen. *Sir* H. M. L., *G.C.B., G.C.M.G., G.C.V.O., D.S.O.,* Col. Comdt. R.A., *q.s.*	21Sept.09
Assistant Military Secretary	Finlay, Maj. F. D., Wilts. R., *p.s.c.*	1Nov.12
Aide-de-Camp	Darell, Capt. G. M., C. Gds.	9Feb.13
Colonial Aide-de-Camp	Teuma Castelletti, Capt. (*local Capt. in Army*) Contino, *M.V.O.*, K. O. Malta Regt. of Mila.	30Sept.09

General Staff.

General Staff Officer, 2nd grade	V.C. Halliday, Maj. L. S. T., *C.B.*, R. Mar., *p.s.c.*, [*l*]	7May14
General Staff Officer, 3rd grade	Howard, Capt. G. W., *D.S.O.*, Essex R., *p.s.c.*	25Apr.14

Administrative, Technical and Departmental Staff.

Asst. Adjt. and Qr.-Mr.-Gen.	Shekleton, Col. H. P., *C.B., p.s.c.*	13Mar.12
Dep. Asst. Adjt. & Qr.-Mr.-Gen.	Ogston, Capt. C., Gord. Highrs., *p.s.c.*	3Aug.12
Commanding Royal Artillery	Barker, Maj.-Gen. J.S.S., *C.B., p.s.c*	6Apr.12
Brigade-Major (for R.A.)	Blount, Capt. G. P. C., R.A., *g.*	4June12
Major Instructor in Gunnery	Jacob, Maj. W. H. B., R.A., *g., f.* [*l*]	{ 1Apr.13 13Sept.11
Chief Engineer	Horniblow, Col. F. H.	7Sept.10
Staff Officer, Royal Engineers	Butterworth, Capt. R. F. A., R.E.	
Asst. Director of Supplies and Transport	Bramhall, Col. E. A.	6Nov.10
Dep. Dir. of Medical Services	Russell, Col. M. W.	
Asst. Director of Ordnance Stores	Bunny, Col. F. W. McT., A. Ord. Dept.	
Command Paymaster	Fitton, Col. G. W., A. P. Dept.	

Department of the Finance Member of the Army Council
(*detached from the War Office for duty at Head-Quarters of the Command*).

Local Auditor	Richardson, B. H., *Esq.*
Assistant Local Auditor	Beard, J. J., *Esq.*

Infantry Brigade.

Brigade Commander	Adam, Col. (*temp. Brig.-Gen.*) F. A., *C.B.*	15Feb.13
Brigade-Major	Renny, Capt. L. F., R. Dub. Fus., *p.s.c.*	10Jan.12

TROOPS IN THE COMMAND.

Royal Garrison Artillery.	Engineers.	Infantry.	Army Service Corps.
1 & 102 Cos.(*Eastern Dist.*) 63 & 65 Cos.(*Central Dist.*) 5, 96, 99 & 100Cos.(*Western Dist.*)	24 & 28 Cos. (Fortress).	2 Bn. R. War. R. 2 Bn. W. York. R. 1 Bn. R. W. Fus. 2 Bn. Sco. Rif. 2 Bn. Midd'x R.	40 Co. **Royal Army Medical Corps.** 30 Co.
R. Malta Art.	*Militia.* Malta Division	*Militia.* K.O.Malta Regt. of Mila.	**Army Ordnance Corps.** Co. (Malta Section).

(81)

Commands of the Army.

DOMINIONS, COLONIES AND PROTECTORATES.
(Arranged Alphabetically.)

AFRICA.

EAST AND CENTRAL AFRICA.

EAST AFRICA PROTECTORATE.

Governor and Commander-in-Chief and High Commissioner for the Zanzibar Protectorate	Belfield, *Sir* H. C., *K.C.M.G.*		*Nairobi.*
Aide-de-Camp	Smith, Lt. B. W., S. Gds		Aug.13

NYASALAND PROTECTORATE.

Governor and Commander-in-Chief	Smith, G., *Esq., K.C.M.G.*		*Zomba.*
Aide-de-Camp	Caldecott, Lt. J. L., R.A.		7Aug.13

SOMALILAND PROTECTORATE

Commissioner and Commander in-Chief	Archer, G. F., *Esq., C.M.G.*		*Berbera.*

UGANDA PROTECTORATE.

Governor and Commander-in-Chief	Jackson, *Sir* F. J., *K.C.M.G., C.B.*		*Entebbe.*
Aide-de-Camp			

UNION OF SOUTH AFRICA.

GOVERNOR-GENERAL AND COMMANDER-IN-CHIEF OF THE UNION OF SOUTH AFRICA, AND HIGH COMMISSIONER FOR SOUTH AFRICA	Gladstone, *Rt. Hon.* H. J., *Visct., G.C B., G.C.M.G., Pretoria.*		
Assistant Secretary for Military Affairs	Paget, Capt. G. M., C. Gds.		2Dec.13 / 30Apr.10
Aides-de-Camp	Carruthers, Capt. J., *M.V.O.,* R.A.		25Apr.12

SOUTH AFRICA.

GENERAL OFFICER COMMANDING-IN-CHIEF	Murray, Lt.-Gen. *Sir* J. W., *K.C.B., p.s.c.* [L] *Pretoria.*		18Apr.14 / 9Dec.13
Assistant Military Secretary	Tovey, Maj. G. S., R.A.		18Apr.14
Aide-de-Camp	Sutherland, Lt. A. H. C., R. Highrs.		18Apr.14
General Staff			
Brigadier-General	Heath, Col. (*temp. Brig.-Gen.*) G. M., *D.S.O., p.s.c., e.*		16Mar.22
General Staff Officer, 2nd grade	Stewart, Bt. Maj. I., Sco. Rif., *p.s.c.* [*l*]		27Sept.12 / 18May11

(82)

Commands (Dominions, etc.).

AFRICA, SOUTH—*contd.*

Administrative, Technical and Departmental Staff.

Major-General in Charge of Administration	Clayton, Maj.-Gen. F. T., *C.B.*	4Feb.11
Dep. Asst. Adjt.-Gen.	Fowle, Lt.-Col. T. E., p.s.c. [*l*]	1Apr.11
Dep. Asst. Qr.-Mr.-Gen.	Mears, Maj. T. I. N., A.S.C.	1Mar.14
Chief Engineer	Roper, Col. A. W., *C.B.*	29July11
Staff Officer, Royal Engineers	Cusins, Maj. A. G. T., *R.E.*	
Asst. Director of Supplies and Transport	Jack, Col. H. R. H., *C.M.G.*	14Jan.11
Dep. Asst. Director of Supplies and Transport		
Dep. Dir. of Medical Services	Bedford, Surg.-Gen. W. G. A., *C.M.G., M.B.*	
Dep.-Asst. Dir. of Medical Services	Delap, Maj. G. G., *D.S.O.*, R.A.M.C.	
Asst. Dir. of Veterinary Services	Nuthall, Col. C. E.	
Assistant Director of Ordnance Stores	Parsons, Col. H. D. E., *C.M.G.*, A. Ord. Dept.	
Command Paymaster	Dorling, Col. L., *D.S.O.*, A. P. Dept.	
Dep. Asst. Dir. of Remounts	Findlay, Bt. Maj. H., E. Kent R.	18Mar.11

Department of the Finance Member of the Army Council
(detached from the War Office for duty at Head-Quarters of the Command.

Local Auditor	Huggett, J., *Esq.*
Assistant Local Auditor	Thomas, W. H., *Esq.*

At Pretoria.

Chief Ordnance Officer .. Bainbridge, Lt.-Col. P. A., A. Ord. Dept., p.a.c.

At Capetown.

Chief Ordnance Officer .. Acworth, Maj. L. E., A. Ord. Dept., e. o.

PRETORIA DISTRICT.

Officer Commanding	Murray, Col. (*temp. Brig.-Gen.*) W. H. E., *C.B.* Roberts' Heights, Transvaal	9Sept.11
Brigade-Major	James, Capt. G. M., E. Kent R., p.s.c.	7Sept.12

TROOPS IN THE DISTRICT

Royal Artillery.
XXII. Brig., R.F.A., 104 & 106 Batts.

Royal Engineers.
55 (Fd.) Co.
7 Signal Co.

Infantry.
Bn. R. W. Surr. R
2 Bn. Bedf. R.
1 Bn. S. Staff. R. (*Pietermaritzburg*).
1 Bn. Essex R. (2 Cos.) (*Pretoria.*)

Army Service Corps.
42 Co.
43 Co. (Det.) (*Tempe*).

Royal Army Medical Corps.
26 Co.

Army Veterinary Corps.
9 Section.

Army Ordnance Corps.
9 Co. Pretoria Section.

Commands of the Army.

AFRICA, SOUTH—*contd.*

POTCHEFSTROOM DISTRICT.

Garrison Adjutant (graded Staff Captain).. Atkinson, Capt. W. H. J. St. L., 1 Dns. 28May13

TROOPS IN THE DISTRICT.

Cavalry.	Royal Artillery. XXII. Brig., R.F.A. 105 Batt.	Royal Army Medical Corps. Detachment.
1 Dns.		
10 Hrs.	Army Service Corps. 43 Co.	Army Veterinary Corps. 10 Section.

CAPE OF GOOD HOPE DISTRICT.

Officer Commanding	Thompson, Col. *(temp. Brig.-Gen.)* C. W., C.B., D.S.O. [l] *Capetown* 21June13
General Staff Officer, 2nd grade..	Greathed, Maj. R. N. R.A., *p.s.c.* [L] 28Mar.14

Administrative and Technical Staff.

Garrison Adjutant (graded Staff Captain)	Gordon, Capt. E. I. D., R. Sc. Fus., *p.s.c.*	{ 10Nov.13 { 7Nov.11
Captain Instructor in Gunnery ..	Greig, Capt.H. I., R.A., *g.*	1Apr.13

TROOPS IN THE DISTRICT

Royal Garrison Artillery. 84 Co. 97 Co. (*Simonstown*).	Infantry. 2.Bn. E, Lan. R. (*Wynberg*).	Royal Army Medical Corps. 22 Co. (*Wynberg*).
Royal Engineers (Fortress) Co. (*Simonstown*)	Army Service Corps Detachment.	Army Ordnance Corps. ε Co. (Capetown Section).

(84)

Commands (Dominions, etc.)

WEST AFRICA.

GAMBIA

Governor and Commander-in-Chief	.. Cameron, E. J., *Esq.*, C.M.G.	.. Bathurst.
Aide-de-Camp	.. Wall, Lt. T L., 5 Lrs. ..	1Apr.14

GOLD COAST COLONY.

Governor and Commander-in-Chief .. Clifford, *Sir* H. C., K.C.M.G. .. .. *Accra*

Aide-de-Camp

NIGERIA.

Governor-General and Commander-in-Chief, Lugard, Bt. Col. *Sir* F. J. D., G.C.M.G., C.B., D.S.O., ret. pay .. .. Zungeru

Aide-de-Camp

SIERRA LEONE.

Governor and Commander-in-Chief	.. Merewether, *Sir* E. M., K.C.V.O., C.M.G., ..	Freetown
Aide-de-Camp	.. Meyer-Griffith, Maj. H. W. G., Unattd. List (T.F.) (*Capt. Res. of Off.*) [*l*] ..	11Feb.14

General Officer Commanding	.. Daniell, Maj.-Gen. J. F., R. Mar., *p.s.c*	3June14
Aide-de-Camp	.. Roberts, Lt. H. W., R.A.[*l*	3June14

General Staff.

General Staff Officer, 2nd grade ..

Administrative, Technical and Departmental Staff.

Dep. Asst. Adjt. and Qr.-Mr. Gen.	.. Bird, Capt. M. H. C., R.A., *p.s.c.*, *g.* [L] ..	1Aug.12
Officer Commanding Royal Artillery		
Officer Commanding Royal Engineers	.. Bonham, Maj. C.B., R.E. [*l*]	
Officer Commanding Army Service Corps	Burne, Maj. R. O., A.S.C.	
Senior Medical Officer	.. Gerrard, Lt.-Col. J. J., M.B., R.A.M.C.	
Chief Ordnance Officer	.. Fisher, Capt. C. T., A. Ord. Dept., *e., o.*	
Command Paymaster	.. Smith, Maj. C. G. R., A. P. Dept.	

TROOPS IN THE COMMAND

Royal Garrison Artillery.	Royal Engineers.	Infantry.	Royal Army Medical Corps. Detachment.
50 Co. Sierra Leone Co.	36 Co. (Fortress).	1 Bn. W. I. R. W. Afr. R.	Army Ordnance Corps. Detachment.

Commands of the Army.

COMMONWEALTH OF AUSTRALIA.

GOVERNOR-GENERAL AND COMMANDER-IN-CHIEF	Munro-Ferguson, *Rt. Hon. Sir* R. C., *G.C.M.G.*	*Melbourne*
Military Secretary	Hamilton-Temple-Blackwood, Capt. *Lord* F. T., D.S.O., ret. pay (*Res. of Off.*)	10Apr.14
Aides-de-Camp	Curwen, Lt. W. J. H., 2 Bn. Lond. R.	1Jan.13
	Anstruther, Lt. J. A., 6 D.G. [*l*]	15Apr.14

NEW SOUTH WALES.

Governor	Strickland, *Sir* G., *G.C.M.G.*	*Sydney.*
Aides-de-Camp	Wallis, Lt. H. J. F., Wilts. R.	9Mar.14
	Wakeman, Lt. O., Res. of Off.	24July14

QUEENSLAND.

Governor	MacGregor, *Sir* W., *G.C.M.G.*, *C.B.*	*Brisbane.*
Aide-de-Camp	Talbot, Lt. H. E., 11 Hrs.	20Dec.13 / 31Jan.13

SOUTH AUSTRALIA.

Governor	Galway, Lt.-Col. *Sir* H. L., *K.C.M.G.*, *D.S.O.*, ret. pay (*Res. of Off.*)	*Adelaide.*
Aide-de-Camp	Hopwood, Lt. R. G., Rif. Brig.	13Mar.14

TASMANIA.

Governor	Ellison-Macartney, *Rt. Hon. Sir* W.G., *K.C.M.G. Hobart.*	
Aide-de-Camp	Richardson, Capt. H. S. C., Rif. Brig.	4Mar.14

VICTORIA.

Governor	Stanley, *Hon. Sir* A. L., *K.C.M.G.*	*Melbourne*
Aides-de-Camp	Gale, Capt. F. H., Bedf. R.	20Jan.14
	Wilson, Lt. C. B., Res. of Off.	20Jan.14

WESTERN AUSTRALIA.

Governor	Barron, Maj.-Gen. *Sir* H., *K.C.M.G.*, *C.V.O.*, ret. pay, *g.*	*Perth.*
Aide-de-Camp	Lindsell, Lt. W. G., R.A.	20Aug.13 / 18Nov.10

PAPUA.

Lieutenant-Governor	Murray, J. H. P., *Esq.*, *C.M.G.*	*Port Moresby.*

(86)

Commands (Dominions, etc.).

BAHAMAS.

Governor and Commander-in-Chief	..	Haddon-Smith, G. B., *Esq., C.M.G.,*	Nassau.
Aide-de-Camp	..	Haddon-Smith, Lt. W. B., R. W. Surr. R.	3Mar.13

BARBADOS, &c.

Governor and Commander-in-Chief of Barbados and its Dependencies } Probyn, *Sir* L., *K.C.M.G.* .. .. Bridgetown.

Aide-de-Camp ..

BERMUDA.

Governor and Commander-in-Chief ..	Bullock. Lt.-Gen. *Sir* G. M., *K.C.B.*, Col. Devon. R. .. .. Hamilton	11May12
Aide-de-Camp	Lawrence, Lt. P. R. B., C. Gds.	19Oct.12

General Staff.

General Staff Officer, 2nd grade ..	.. Jervis, Maj. S J., S. Staff R., *p.s.c.* [*l*]	5Oct.12

Administrative, Technical and Departmental Staff.

Dep. Asst. Adjt. & Qr.-Mr.-Gen. ..	.. Nugent, Maj. G. R. H., R.A., *p.s.c.* [L]	15Nov.11
Officer Commanding Royal Artillery	.. Saltren-Willett, Lt.-Col. A. J., R.G.A., *St. George's*.	
Commanding Royal Engineer ..	.. Clayton, Lt.-Col. H. E. G., R.E.	
Officer Commanding Army Service Corps	.. Liddell, Maj. A. R., A.S.C., *e*.	
Senior Medical Officer	.. Hall, Lt.-Col. R. H., *M.D.*, R.A.M.C.	
Chief Ordnance Officer	.. Hamilton, Lt.-Col. R. S., A. Ord. Dept., *e., f.*	
Command Paymaster	.. Whitmarsh, Maj. J. F. V. S., A.P. Dept.	

TROOPS IN THE COMMAND.

Royal Garrison Artillery.	Infantry.	Royal Army Medical Corps.
8 & 95 Cos.	2 Bn. Linc. R.	25 Co.
Bermuda Militia Artillery.		Army Ordnance Corps.
Royal Engineers.	Army Service Corps.	Detachment.
27 Co. (Fortress).	Detachment.	Bermuda V.R.C.

BRITISH GUIANA.

Governor and Commander-in-Chief	.. Egerton, *Sir* W., *K.C.M.G.*	.. Georgetown.	
Aide-de-Camp	.. Napier, Lt. M. M., N. Staff. R. ..	.. .. ..	19June12

BRITISH HONDURAS.

Governor and Commander-in-Chief ..	Collet, W., *Esq., C.M.G.*... .. .. .. Belize.
Aide-de-Camp	

DOMINION OF CANADA.

GOVERNOR-GENERAL AND COMMANDER-IN-CHIEF	Field-Marshal *H.R.H.* Arthur W. P. A., *Duke of* Connaught and Strathearn, *K.G., K.T., K.P., G.C.B., G.C.S.I., G.C.M.G., G.C.I.E., G.C.V.O.*, Col. G. Gds. and A.S.C., and Col.-in-Chief 6 Dns., High.L. I., R. Dub. Fus. and Rif. Brig., *Personal A.D.C. to the King.* *Ottawa*.

Military Secretary	.. Farquhar, Maj.(*temp.Lt.-Col.*) F.D.,*D.S.O.*,C.Gds.,*p.s.c.*[*l*]	6Oct.13
Aides-de-Camp	.. { Buller Capt. H. C., Rif.Brig.	6Oct.11
	{ Boscawen, Lt. (*temp. Capt.*)*Hon.* G. E., R.A.	6Dec.12
	{ Graham, Lt. (*temp. Capt.*) A. C. D., 9 Lrs.	6Oct.13
Medical Officer	.. Worthington, Maj. *Sir* E. S., *Knt., M.V.O.*, R.A.M.C.	

(87)

Commands of the Army.

CEYLON.

Governor and Commander-in-Chief	.. Chalmers, Sir R., K.C.B. .. .. .. Colombo.	
Aides-de-Camp	.. { Chalmers, Lt. R., Suff. R., ...	2Sept.13
	{ Payne, 2nd Lt. L. G. S., Suff. R., Spec. Res.	23Jan.14
Aides-de-Camp (extra) ..	.. { Smith, Capt. F. C., Ceylon Planters Rif. Corps Reserve	—
	{ Frazer, Maj. G., vD, Ceylon Lt. Inf. (*hon.*)	—
	{ Greer, Capt. H. F. V., R.G.A., Spec. Res. (*hon.*)	—

Officer Commanding .. .. .. Malcolm, Col. (*temp, Brig.-Gen.*) H. H. L., C.B., D.S.O. { 8May13
28Oct.11

Administrative, Technical and Departmental Staff.

Dep. Asst. Adjt. & Qr.-Mr.-Gen. ..	.. Halford, Maj. M. F. York & Lanc. R., *p.s.c.* [*l*]	.. 6Apr.12
Officer Commanding Royal Artillery ..		
Commanding Royal Engineer ..	.. Paul, Lt.-Col. E. M., R.E. [L].	
Officer Commanding Army Service Corps ..	Lord, Maj. F. B., A.S.C., *e*.	
Senior Medical Officer		
Chief Ordnance Officer	Fisher, Maj. C. A., A. Ord. Dept., *e.*, *o*.	
Command Paymaster	Harris, Lt.-Col. C. S., A. Pay Dept.	
Garrison Adjutant	Mills, Lt. H. P. F., R.G.A.	23Jan 14

TROOPS IN THE COMMAND.

Royal Garrison Artillery.	Infantry.	Royal Army Medical Corps.
93 Co.	4 Rajputs.	26 Co.
Royal Engineers	Army Service Corps.	Army Ordnance Corps.
31 Co. (Fortress).	Detachment.	Detachment.

CHINA.

HONG KONG AND ITS DEPENDENCIES.

Governor and Commander-in-Chief	.. May, Sir F. H., K.C.M.G.	Victoria. .. 29Nov.12
Aide-de-Camp	.. { Alison, Lt. G. N., Sea. Highrs.	..
	.. { Hatfield, 2nd Lt. R. B., 8 Bn. Lond. R.	.. 9Apr.14

WEI-HAI-WEI.

Commissioner .. .. .. Lockhart, Sir J. H. S., K.O.M.G.

FORCES IN CHINA.

NORTH CHINA (*including Wei-Hai-Wei*).

Officer Commanding .. .. .. Barnardiston, Col. (*temp, Brig.-Gen.*) N. W., M.V.O., *p.s.c.*	Tientsin 1May14
General Staff.	
General Staff Officer, 2nd grade .. .. Pringle, Maj. H. G., R.A., *p.s.c.* [*l*]	.. 13Sept.13

Administrative, Technical and Departmental Staff.

Dep. Asst. Adjt. & Qr.-Mr.-Gen. ..	.. Moore, Capt. C. D. H., R. War. R., *p.s.c.* 4Dec.12
Commanding Royal Engineer ..	.. Cochrane, Maj. T. H., M.V.O., R.E.
Officer Commanding Army Service Corps ..	Airey, Maj. R. B., A.S.C., *e*.
Senior Medical Officer	MacDonald, Lt.-Col. C. J., M.D., R.A.M.C.
Chief Ordnance Officer	Hill, Capt. B. A., A. Ord. Dept., *p.a.c.*
Provost Marshal	Chauncy, Maj. C.H.K., 124 Inf.
Command Paymaster	Bliss, Maj. T. G. C., A.P. Dept.

(88)

Commands (Dominions, etc.).

CHINA, NORTH—*contd.*

TROOPS QUARTERED IN THE COMMAND.

Royal Artillery.	Army Service Corps.	Indian Supply and Transport Corps.
Detachment.	Detachment.	Detachment.
		Indian Army Hospital Corps.
Infantry.		Detachment.
2 Bn. S. Wales Bord.	Royal Army Medical Corps.	Army Ordnance Corps.
2 Bn. Glouc. R.	Detachment.	Detachment.
36 Sikhs.		

SOUTH CHINA.

General Officer Commanding	.. Kelly, Maj.-Gen. F. H., *C.B.*	.. ..	Hong Kong 13June13
Aide-de-Camp	.. .. ..		

General Staff.

General Staff Officer, 2nd grade	.. McHardy, Maj. A. A., *D.S.O.*, R.A., *p.s.c.*	.. ..	12July13
General Staff Officer, 3rd grade	.. Crosse, Capt. R. M., R.A., *g.* (*l*) ..	.. ..	12June12

Administrative, Technical and Departmental Staff.

Dep. Asst. Adjt. and Qr.-Mr.-Gen.	Stewart, Maj. R. S., L'pool R., *p.s.c.* [L].. .. .. 14Aug.12
Officer Commanding Royal Artillery	Iles, Lt.-Col. H. W., R.G.A., *g.*
Major Instructor in Gunnery	Sargeaunt, Maj. H. G., R.A., *g.* 22Oct.13
Captain Instructor in Gunnery	Mead, Lt. S., R A., *g.* 30June14
Chief Engineer	Brown, Col. W. B. 29Nov.13
Staff Officer, Royal Engineers	de Fonblanque, Lt. P., R.E.
Officer Commanding Army Service Corps	Fitzwilliams, Maj. E. C. L., A.S.C.
Dep. Dir. of Medical Services	Irwin, Col. J. M., *M.B.*
Chief Ordnance Officer	Smith, Lt.-Col. W. H. U., *D.S.O.*, A. Ord. Dept., *p.a.c.*
Command Paymaster	O'Hara, Col. J., A. P. Dept.

TROOPS IN THE COMMAND.

Royal Garrison Artillery.	Infantry.	Royal Army Medical Corps.
83, 87 & 88 Cos.	2 Bn. D. of Corn. L.I.	27 Co.
1, 2 & 3 Cos. Hong Kong—Singapore Bn.	8 Rajputs.	
24 Hazara Mtn. Batt.	25 Punjabis.	Indian Supply and Transport Corps.
	26 Punjabis.	Detachment.
Royal Engineers.	0 Pathans.	
25 Co. (Fortress).	Army Service Corps.	Army Ordnance Corps.
40 Co. (Fortress).	Detachment.	Detachment.

CYPRUS.
See page 78.

FALKLAND ISLANDS AND THEIR DEPENDENCIES.

Governor and Commander-in-Chief	.. Allardyce, W. L., *Esq.*, *C.M.G.*	.. Stanley

FIJI ISLANDS.

Governor and Commander-in-Chief and High Commissioner and Consul General for the Western Pacific	} Sweet-Escott, Sir E. B., *K.C.M.G.* ..	.. Suva.
Aide-de-Camp		

GIBRALTAR.
See page 79.

(89)

Commands of the Army.

JAMAICA.

Captain General and Governor-in-Chief..	Manning, Hon. Brig.-Gen. *Sir* W. H. *K.C.M.G., C.B.,* ret. Ind. Army .. .. *Kingston.*	
Aides-de-Camp	{ St. John, Lt. *Hon.* R. T., Durh. L.I.	22Feb.13
	{ Dennistoun, Capt. I. O., *M.V.O.,* G. Gds. (*extra*) ..	22Mar.13

Inspector of the West Indian Local Forces and Officer Commanding	Dalrymple-Hay, Col. (*temp.* Brig.-Gen.) J. R. M., *C.B., D.S.O.*	19Aug.10

Administrative, Technical and Departmental Staff.

Dep. Asst. Adjt. and Qr.-Mr.-Gen. ..	Thomson, Capt. H. G. A., R. War. R., *p.s.c.* [l]	4Feb.12
Commanding Royal Engineer	Burnaby, Lt.-Col. C. G., R.E.	
Officer Commanding Army Service Corps	Grose, Maj. D. C. E., A.S.C., *e.*	
Senior Medical Officer	Wilson, Lt.-Col. J. B., *M.D.,* R.A.M.C.	
Chief Ordnance Officer	Leslie, Capt S. G., R. Mar. Art., *p.a.c.*	
Command Paymaster	Lang, Capt. E. A., A. P. Dept	
Garrison Adjutant	Nicholson, Capt. T. B., W.I.R.	16May12

TROOPS IN THE COMMAND.

Royal Garrison Artillery.	Infantry.	Royal Army Medical Corps.
66 Co.	2 Bn. W. I. R.	29 Co.
Royal Engineers.	Army Service Corps.	Army Ordnance Corps.
44 Co. (Fortress).	Detachment.	Detachment.

LEEWARD ISLANDS.

Governor and Commander-in-Chief ..	Bell, *Sir* H. H. J., *K.C.M.G.* ..	*St. John's, Antigua.*
Aide-de-Camp		

MALTA.

See page 80.

MAURITIUS.

Governor and Commander-in-Chief ..	Chancellor, Maj. *Sir* J. R., *K.C.M.G., D.S.O.,* R.E.,*p.s.c.* [L] *Port Louis.*	
Aide-de-Camp	Irvine, Lt. J. L. G., Arg. & Suth'd Highrs.	24Feb.12

General Officer Commanding ..	Simpson, Maj.-Gen. C. R., *C.B.,* Col. Linc. R., *p.s.c.* [L]..	20Jan.12
Aide-de-Camp	Boys, Capt. E. J. de C., Linc. R.	—
General Staff.		
General Staff Officer, 2nd grade ..	Birch, Maj. E. M., *D.S.O.,* R. A., *p.s.c.*	1July11

Administrative, Technical and Departmental Staff.

Officer Commanding Royal Artillery ..	
Commanding Royal Engineer . ..	Mair, Lt.-Col. R. J. B., R.E.
Officer Commanding Army Service Corps	Striedinger, Maj. O., A.S.C., *e.*
Senior Medical Officer	Lawson, Maj. D., R.A.M.C.
Chief Ordnance Officer	Ensor, Capt. F. C. C., R.A., *p.a.c., g.*
Command Paymaster	Duxbury, Lt.-Col. S. H., A.P. Dept.

TROOPS IN THE COMMAND.

Royal Garrison Artillery.	Infantry.	Royal Army Medical Corps.
56 Co. 4 Co.Hong Kong—Singapore Bn.	1 Bn. Essex R. (Hd.-Qrs. & 2 Cos.)	21 Co.
Royal Engineers.	Army Service Corps.	Army Ordnance Corps.
48 Co. (Fortress)	Detachment.	Detachment.

(90-92)

Commands (Dominions, etc.).

NEWFOUNDLAND.

Governor and Commander-in-Chief	..	Davidson, W. E., Esq., K.C.M.G.	St. John's.
Aide-de-Camp	.. ..	Moore, Lt. L. G., K.R. Rif. C.	.. .. .. 4June14

DOMINION OF NEW ZEALAND.

GOVERNOR AND COMMANDER-IN-CHIEF	{ Liverpool, Lt.-Col. A. W. de B. S., *Earl of,* G.C.M.G., M.V.O., 8 Bn. Lond. R., Maj. ret. pay (*Res. of Off.*) Wellington.
Military Secretary	Shawe, Capt. C., ret. pay (*Res. of Off.*) .. .. .. { 1July13 / 13Nov.12
Aides-de-Camp	{ Eastwood, Lt. T. R., Rif. Brig. .. .. .. { 1July13 / 6Nov.12 { Hutton, Capt. G. F., R.W. Fus. .. .. .. { 26Nov.13 / 18Dec.12

ST. HELENA.

Governor and Commander-in-Chief.. .. Cordeaux, Maj. H. E. S., O.B., C.M.G., ret. Ind. Army
Jamestown.

SEYCHELLES.

Governor and Commander-in Chief .. .. O'Brien, Bt.Lt.-Col.C.R.M., C.M.G., ret.pay (*Res. of Off.*)
Mahé.

STRAITS SETTLEMENTS.

Governor and Commander-in-Chief of the Straits Settlements and their Dependencies, High Commissioner for the Protected States in the Malay Peninsula and Brunei, and British Agent for the States of North Borneo and Sarawak	Young, Sir A. H., K.C.M.G., late Capt. R. Innis. Fus. Singapore.
Aide-de-Camp	Crofton, Lt. R., R.A. 2Sept.11
Extra Aides-de-Camp	{ Carver, Capt. G. S., Singapore Vol. Inf. (*hon.*) 6Oct.11 { Swettenham, Capt. J. P., Malay States Vol. Rif. (*hon.*) 6Dec.12 { Elim Din, Subadar, Malay States Guides (*hon.*) 6Dec.12
General Officer Commanding..	Reade, Maj.-Gen. R. N. R., C.B., p.s.c. [L] 6May14
Aide-de-Camp	Torr, Lt. W. W. T., W. York. R. 6May14

General Staff.

General Staff Officer, 2nd grade .. .. Pearless, Maj. C. W., S. Wales Bord., p.s.c. [L]

Administrative, Technical and Departmental Staff.

Dep. Asst. Adjt. & Qr.-Mr.-Gen.	Bingham, Maj. C. H. M., A.S.C., p.s.c., e. 6Dec.11
Officer Commanding Royal Artillery.. ..	Brownlow, Lt.-Col. C. W., R.G.A.
Captain Instructor in Gunnery ..	Sanders, Capt. W.O. S., R.A., g. 1Apr.13
Commanding Royal Engineer	Ridout, Lt.-Col. D. H., R.E.
Officer Commanding Army Service Corps ..	Mears, Maj. E. L., A.S.C.
Senior Medical Officer	Ferguson, Lt.-Col. J. D., D.S.O., R.A., M.C.
Chief Ordnance Officer	McVittie, Maj. R. H., A. Ord. Dept., e., o.
Command Paymaster	Owen, Lt.-Col. I. T., A. P. Dept.

TROOPS IN THE COMMAND.

Royal Garrison Artillery.	Infantry.	Royal Army Medical Corps.
78 & 80 Cos. 5 Co. Hong Kong-Singapore Bn.	1 Bn. Yorks. L.I. 3 Brahmans.	32 Co.
Royal Engineers. 41 Co. (Fortress).	Army Service Corps. Detachment.	Army Ordnance Corps. Detachment.

TRINIDAD AND TOBAGO.

Governor and Commander-in-Chief	Le Hunte, Sir G. R., G.C.M.G. .. ..*Port of Spain*.
Aides-de-Camp	{ Boyle, Lt. C. R. C., Oxf. & Bucks. L.I. 20Nov.12

WINDWARD ISLANDS.

Governor and Commander-in-Chief ..	Hayes-Sadler, Lt.-Col. Sir J., K.C.M.G., C.B., ret. Ind. S.C. .. .. .. *St. George, Grenada.*
Aide-de-Camp	

EGYPTIAN ARMY.

Head Quarters Staff.

SIRDAR .. .. Wingate, Gen. Sir F. R., *G.C.B.,G.C.V,O., K.C.M.G., D.S.O.,* q.s.[L]
    Private Secretary .. .. Symes, Capt. G. S., *D.S.O.*, Hamps.R.
    Military Secretary .. .. Rees-Mogg, Capt. R. J., R. Ir. Regt.
    Aides-de-Camp .. .. { Kennedy, Capt. J., Arg. & Suth'd Highrs.

Adjutant-General .. .. .. Drake, Bt. Lt.-Col. W. H., h.p.

Assistant Adjutant-Generals ..
   { Garsia, Lt.-Col. H. G. A., *D.S.O.*, h.p.
    Palmer, Maj. C. E., *D.S.O.*, R.A. (*G.S.O.*. 2nd grade).
    Mackintosh, Capt. E. E. B., R.E. (*G.S.O.*, 3rd grade).
    Kenny, Capt. W. D., R. Innis. Fus.

Dep. Asst. Adjt. Generals ..
   { Kennedy, Capt. J., Arg. & Suth'd Highrs.
    Kyrke, Capt. H. V. V., R.W. Fus.
    Poston, Capt. W. J. L., R.A.
    Irwin, Lt. G. V. C., R. Innis. Fus.
    Webb-Bowen, Capt. H. I., R. W. Fus.

Director of Supplies .. .. Blunt, Maj. C. E. G., ret. pay (*Res. of Off.*)
Director of Military Works .. Grant, Maj. P. G., R.E. [L]
Director of Stores .. .. Anderson, Hon. Maj. G. W., Qr.-Mr. ret. pay.
Principal Medical Officer .. Bray, Maj. (*local Lt.-Col.*) H. A., R.A.M.C.
Principal Veterinary Officer .. Carr, Maj. F. U., A.V.C.

1st Class Military Districts.

Fellden, Maj. R. M., ret pay (*Res. of Off.*) .. .. .. *Bahr-el-Ghazal.*
.. .. .. *Berber.*
.. .. .. *Blue Nile.*
Herbert, Maj. E. S., h.p. .. *Cairo.*
Jackson, Bt. Col. H. W., *C.B.*, ret. pay (*Lt.-Col. Res. of Off.*) .. *Dongola.*

Townsend, Capt. C. H., ret. pay (*Res. of Off.*)
V.C. Smyth, Col. N. M. .. .. *Kassala.*
Savile, Capt. R. V., ret. pay (*Res. of Off.*) .. .. *Khartoum.*
Owen, Capt. R. C. R. *C.M.G.*, ret. pay (*Res. of Off.*) .. *Kordofan.*
Wilson, Capt. R. S., ret. pay (*Res, of Off.*) .. *Mongalla.*
.. *Nuba Mountains.*
Woodward, Capt. F.W., *D.S.O.*, N.Lan.R. *Upper Nile*

2nd Class Military Districts.

Midwinter, E. C., *C.B., C.M.G., D.S.O.*, late Capt. R.E. .. .. *Atbara.*

Wilson, Bt. Maj. C. E., ret. pay (*Capt. Res. of Off.*) .. *Red Sea.*
Logan, Capt. M. H., W. York. R. .. *Sobat-Pibor.*

Officer Comdg. Cavalry .. .. .. Kelly, Maj. P. J. V., 3 Hrs.
Officer Comdg. Artillery .. .. .. Crawford, Col. A., *p.s.c.* [*l*]
Officer Comdg. Came Corps .. .. Romilly, Capt. B. H. S., *D.S.O.*, S. Gds.
Comdt. Military School, Cairo .. .. Herbert, Maj. E. S., h.p.
Comdt. Military School, Khartoum .. Pattisson, Capt. J. H., Essex R.

SUDAN ADMINISTRATION.

GOVERNOR-GENERAL	Wingate, Gen. *Sir* F. R., *G.C.B., G.C.V.O., K.C.M.G., D.S.O., q.s.*[L]
Private Secretary	Symes, Capt. G. S., *D.S.O.*, Hamps. R.
Assistant Private Secretary	Keown-Boyd, A. W., *Esq.*
Military Secretary	Rees-Mogg, Capt. R. J., R. Ir. Regt.
Inspector-General	von Slatin, *Pasha*, Hon. Maj.-Gen. *Sir* R., Baron, *G.C.V.O., K.C.M.G., C.B.*
Civil Secretary	Stack, Maj. L. O. Fitz M., *C.M.G.*, ret. pay (*Res. of Off.*)
Assistant Civil Secretary	Wheatley, Capt. M. J., Dorset R.
Assistant Civil Secretary	Stoney, Capt, G. B., K. O. Sco. Bord.
Dir. of Intell. and Sudan Agent	Clayton, Capt. G. F., ret. pay, (*Res. of Off.*)
Legal Secretary	Bonham-Carter, E., *Esq., C.M.G*
Financial Secretary	Bernard, Bt. Col. E. E., *C.M.G.*, ret. pay (*Res. of Off.*) *q.s.* [L]
Director, Agriculture and Forests	Wilkinson, Maj. E. B., ret. pay (*Res. of Off.*) *q.s.*
Director of Customs	
Director of Education	
Director-General, Med. Dept.	Bray, Maj. (*local Lt.-Col.*) H. A., R.A.M.C.
Director of Posts and Telegraphs	Moir, Maj. J. P., *D.S.O.*, R.E.
Director of Public Works	Kennedy, Capt. M. R., *C.M.G., D.S.O.*, ret. pay (*Res. of Off.*)
Director, Repression of Slave Trade	Ravenscroft, Hon. Lt.-Col. H. V., 3 Bn. Bord. R. (Maj. ret. pay).
Director of Steamers	
Director of Stores and Prisons	Coutts, Maj. M., ret. pay (*Res. of Off.*)
Director of Surveys	Pearson, Maj. H. D., R.E.
Director, Veterinary Dept.	Carr, Maj. F. U., A.V.C.
General Manager, Sudan Govt. Rlys.	Midwinter, E. C., *C.B., C.M.G., D.S.O., late* Capt. R.E.
Staff Offr., Camel Corps Training School, Khartoum	Herring-Cooper, Capt. W. W., *D.S.O.*, A.S.C.

Governors of Provinces.

Feilden, Maj. R. M., ret. pay (*Res. of Off.*)	*Bahr-el-Ghazal.*
Browne, C. P., *Esq.*	*Berber.*
Iles, G. E., *Esq.*	*Blue Nile.*
Jackson, Bt. Col. H. W., *C.B.*, ret. pay (Lt.-Col. *Res. of Off.*)	*Dongola.*
Lyall, C. E., *Esq.*	*Halfa.*
Townsend, Capt. C. H., ret. pay (*Res. of Off.*)	*Kassala.*
More, R. E., *Esq.*	*Khartoum.*
Savile, Capt. R. V., ret. pay (*Res. of Off.*)	*Kordofan.*
Owen, Capt. R. C. R., *C.M.G*, ret. pay (*Res. of Off.*)	*Mongalla.*
Wilson, Capt. R. S., ret. pay (*Res. of Off.*)	*Nuba Mountains.*
Wilson, Bt. Maj. C. E.. ret. pay (*Res. of Off*)	*Red Sea.*
Cameron, Maj. A., ret. pay (*Res. of Off.*)	*Sennar.*
Woodward, Capt. F. W., *D.S.O.*, N. Lan. R.	*Upper Nile.*
Struvé, K. C. P., *Esq.*	*White Nile.*

OFFICERS OF THE ARMY ON THE ACTIVE LIST.

FIELD-MARSHALS.

ᵾC. ₥.ROBERTS, Rt. Hon. F. S., Earl, K.G., K.P., G.C.B., O.M., G.C.S.I., G.C.I.E., VD, Col. Comdt.
 R. A., Col. I. Gds. [R] [F]
His Majesty WILLIAM II., GERMAN EMPEROR, KING OF PRUSSIA, K.G., G.C.V.O., Col.-in-Chief 1 Dns. .. 25May95
His Royal Highness Arthur W. P. A., Duke of CONNAUGHT and STRATHEARN, K.G., K.T., K.P., 27Jan.01
 G.C.B., G.C.S.I., G.C.M.G., G.C.I.E., G.C.V.O., Col. G. Gds. and A.S.C., and Col.-in-Chief 6 Dns.,
 High. L.I., R. Dub. Fus. and Rif. Brig., Personal A.D.C. to the King [F]
ᵾC. ₵. ₥. WOOD, Sir H. E., G.C.B., G.C.M.G., Col. R.H.G., p.s.c. [R] [F] (Constable of the Tower 26June02
 of London)
His Imperial Majesty FRANCIS JOSEPH I., Emperor of AUSTRIA and King of HUNGARY, K.G., 8Apr.03
 Col.-in-Chief 1 D.G.
GRENFELL, Rt. Hon. F. W., Lord, G.C.B., G.C.M.G., Col. 1 L.G., Col. Comdt. K. R. Rif. C., q.s. 1Sept.08
 [R] [F]
BROWNLOW, Sir C. H., G.C.B., Ind. Army [R] 11Apr.08
KITCHENER OF KHARTOUM, H. H., Earl., K.P., G.C.B., O.M., G.C.S.I., G.C.M.G., G.C.I.E., 20June08
 Col. Comdt. R.E., q.s. [F]
METHUEN, P. S., Lord, G.C.B., G.C.V.O., C.M.G., Col. S. Gds. [R] [F] 10Sept.09
NICHOLSON, W. G., Lord, G.C.B. (late R.E.), q.s. [R] [F] 19June11
FRENCH, Sir J. D. P., G.C.B., G.C.V.O., K.C.M.G., Col. 19 Hrs. and Col.-in-Chief R. Ir. Regt. [R] 3June13

GENERALS.

H.R.H. Prince Frederic Christian Charles Augustus of Schleswig-Holstein, K.G., G.C.V.O., Personal A.D.C. to the King 10Oct.77	Hamilton, Sir I. S. M., G.C.B., D.S.O., Col. Cam'n Highrs. q.s. [F] ᵾ₤.Ɖ.₵. 24Oct.07	Duff, Sir B., G.C.B., K.C.S.I., K.C.V.O., C.I.E., Ind. Army, p.s.c. [R] ᵾ.₤.₵. (C.-in-C. East Indies) 3June13	Hamilton, Sir B. M., K.C.B., K.C.V.O., p.s.c. 3June13 Mackinnon, Sir W. H., K.C.B., K.C.V.O. [R] 6Oct.13
H.R.H. E. A. W. A. G. F., Duke of Cumberland and Teviotdale, K.G. 14Dec.96	Barrow, Sir E. G., G.C.B., Ind. Army [R] [F] (Mil. Sec., India Office) 27July09	Adair, Sir W. T., K.C.B., R.Mar., p.s.c. [F] 22Feb.12 Eagles, H. C., R. Mar. [R] 11Apr.12	Wingate, Sir F. R., G.C.B., G.C.V.O., K.C.M.G., D.S.O. (late R.A.), q.s. [L] [R] [F] e.a. 5Nov.13
His Majesty Alfonso XIII., King of Spain, K.G., G.C.V.O., Col.-in-Chief 16 Lrs. 17May05	Rundle, Sir H.M.L., G.C.B., G.C.M.G., G.C.V.O., D.S.O., Col. Comdt. R.A., q.s. [F] s. 10Sept.09	Smith-Dorrien, Sir H. L., G.C.B., D.S.O., Col. Notts and Derby R., p.s.c. [R] [F] s. 10Aug.12	Nixon, Sir J. E., K.C.B., Ind. Army [R] s. 4May14 V₵Hart, Sir R. C., K.C.B. K.C.V.O. (late R.E.) p.s.c. [F] [F] 16May14
Hunter, Sir G., G.C.B., G.C.V.O., D.S.O., Col. R. Lanc. R. [R] [F] 8Dec.05	Douglas, Sir C. W. H., G.C.B., Col. Gord.Highrs., q.s. [R] ᵾ.₤.₵. Chief of the Impl.Gen.Staff (1st Mil. Member, Army Council) 31Oct.10	Grant, Sir H. F., G.C.V.O., K.C.B., p.s.c. [R] [F] 4Sept.12 Paget, Rt. Hon. Sir A. H., G.C.B., K.C.V.O. [R] 5 Mar.13	Nicholls, Sir W. C., K.C.B., R. Mar. Art. [R] s. 6June14 Bor, J.H., C.B., C.M.G., R. Mar. Art., Eq. 6June14

LIEUTENANT-GENERALS.

‡Willcocks, Sir J., K.C.B., K.C.S.I., K.C.M.G., D.S.O., q.s. [R] s. 16July08	Franklyn, Sir W. E., K.C.B.,Col.York R., p.s.c. (Mil. Sec. to S. of S. for War) 31Aug.10	Sclater, Sir H. C., K.C.B. (late R.A.) [F] Adjt.-Gen. to the Forces (2nd Mil. Member, Army Council) 23June11	Grover, Sir M. H. S., K.C.B., K.C.I.E., Ind. Army [L] [R] s. 21Sept.12 Codrington, Sir A. E., K.C.V.O., C.B., [R] [F] s. 3June13
Plumer, Sir H. C. O., K.C.B., p.s.c. [R] [F] s. 4Nov.08	Haig, Sir D., K.C.B., K.C.I.E., K.C.V.O., Col. 17 Lrs., p.s.c. ᵾ.Ɖ.₵., s. 31Oct.11	Scallon, Sir R. I., K.C.B., K.C.I.E., D.S.O., Ind. Army, [R] ᵾ.Ɖ.₵., s. 3Oct.11	Campbell, W. P., C.B. 6Oct.13
Murray, Sir J. W., K.C.B. (late R.A.) p.s.c. [L] s. 1Apr.09	Gatliff, A. F., R.Mar. p.s.c. [R] 22Jan.11 Lake, Sir P.H.N., K.C.M.G.,	Barrett, Sir A. A., K.C.B., K.C.V.O., Ind. Army, [R] s. 5Oct.11	Bethune, E. C., C.V.O., C.B., Col. 4 D.G., p.s.c., (Dir-Gen. of the Terr. Force) 5Nov.13
Miles, Sir H. S. G., G.C.B., C.V.O., Col. R. Mnns. Fus., p.s.c. [R] s. 20Aug.09	C.B., Col. E. Lan. R., p.s.c. [R] s. 19Mar.11 Pearson, Sir A. A., K.C.B., Ind.Army[R] [F] 3May11	Wylde, E. A., R. Mar. [R] 11Apr.12	Woollcombe, C. L., C.B., Col. K. O. Sco. Bord. 3Dec.13
Stopford, Hon. Sir F. W., K.C.M.G., K.C.V.O., C.B., p.s.c. [F] (Lt. of the Tower) 10Sept.09	Woon, Sir J. B., K. C. B., Ind. Army [R] 3 June 11 Bullock, Sir G. M., K.C.B., Col. Devon R., p.s.c., s. 19June11	Maxwell, Sir J. G., K.C.B., C.V.O., C.M.G., D.S.O., (Col. R.Highrs.) [R] [F] 8Aug.12	Watkis, H. B. B., C.B., Ind.Army, p.s.c., s. 4May14 Anderson, C. A., C.B. (late R.A.) s. 12May14
Grierson, Sir J. M., K.C.B., C.V.O., C.M.G. (late R.A.) p.s.c. [L] [R] [F] ᵾ.Ɖ.₵., s. 7May10	Ewart, Sir J. S., K.C.B., p.s.c. [F] s. 19June11	Mahon, Sir B.T., K.C.V.O., C.B., D.S.O., Col. 8 Hrs. [F] 4Sept.12	Eastman, W. I., R. Mar. Art., p.s.c. 6June14

SURGEON-GENERAL.
(Ranking as Lieutenant-General.)

Sloggett, Sir A. T., Knt., C.B., C.M.G., K.H.S., [F], (Dir.-Gen. Army Medical Service) .. 1June14

‡ Promoted for distinguished service.

Officers of the Army on the Active List.

MAJOR-GENERALS.

Stephenson, T. E., *C.B.*,
  p.s.c. [L] [R]   14May06
Alderson, E. A. H.,
  C.B., p.s.c. [R]   1Dec.06
Blomfield. C. J., *C.B.*,
  D.S.O., Col. Lan. Fus
  s.   3Feb.07
Lawson, H. M., *C.B.*
  (late *R.E.*) p.s.c.
  [R] [F] (*Lt.-Gov.*,
  Guernsey)   12Feb.07
Pilcher, T. D., *C.B.*,
  Col. Bedf. R., p.s.c.
  [L] [R] s.   18Feb.07
Heath, C.E., *C.V.O.*,*C.B.*
  (late *A.S.C.*)   1 Mar.07
Rochfort,*Sir*A.N.,*K.C.B.*,
  C.M.G. (late *R.A.*)
  (*Lt.-Gov., Jersey*)10June07
Kitson,*Sir*G.C.,*K.C.V.O.*,
  C.B., *C.M.G.*, p.s.c.,
  s.   3Oct.07
Payne, R. L., *C.B.*,
  D.S.O., Col. Som.
  L.I., s.   7Nov.07
Powell, C. H., *C.B.*,
  Ind.Army [L]   15Nov.07
Hastings, E. S., *C.B.*,
  D.S.O., Ind. Army
  15Nov.07
Forster, J. B.   31Mar.08
Phayre, A., *C.B.*, Ind.
  Army, s.   7Apr.08
Lomax, S. H., p.s.c.,s.
  28Apr.08
Mackenzie-Kennedy,
  E. C, W., *C.B.*, Ind.
  Army   9June08
Fergusson, *Sir* C., *Bt.*,
  C.B., *M.V.O.*, *D.S.O.*,
  s. [F]   28Sept.08
Crutchley, *Sir* C.,
  K.C.V.O., q.s. [F]
  (*Lt.-Gov. and Sec. R.*
  Hosp., Chelsea)   9Dec.08
Pulteney, W. P., *C.B.*,
  D.S.O.   1Jan.09
Bannatine-Allason, R.,
  C.B. (late *R.A.*) [F]
  1Jan.09
Ɐ Aylmer, F. J., *C.B.*,
  (late *R.E.*), s.   19Feb.09
Robb, *Sir* F. S., *K.C.V.O.*,
  C.B., p.s.c.   24Mar.09
Byng, Hon. J. H. G.,
  C.B.,*M.V.O.*, Col. 3
  Hrs., p.s.c., s.   1Apr.09
Clayton, F. T., *C.B.*
  (late *A.S.C.*)   2Apr.09
Barker, J. S., *C.B.*
  (late *R.A.*) p.s.c., s.
  8May09
Rawlinson,*Sir* H.S.,
  Bt., *C.V.O.*, *C.B.*,
  p.s.c., [F]   10May09
Hamilton, H. I. W.,
  C.V.O.,*C.B.*,*D.S.O.*,
  s.   2June09

Keir, J. L., *C.B.* (late
  R.A.) p.s.c., g., s.   7July09
Drummond, *Sir* F. H. R.,
  K.C.I.E.,*C.B.*,Ind.Army
  27July09
Maxwell, R. C., *C.B.*
  (late *R.E.*) s.   28July09
Barter, C. St. L., *C.V.O.*,
  C.B., p.s.c. [L]   14Aug.09
Allenby, E. H. H.,
  p.s.c. [L] (*Inspr.*
  of Cav.)   10Sept.09
Donald,C.G., *C.B.*,s.5Nov.09
Kelly, F, H., *C.B.* (late
  R.E.) s.   4Dec.09
Lloyd, *Sir* F., *K.C.B.*,
  C.V.O., *D.S.O.*, s.   7Dec.09
Penton, A. P., *C.V.O.*,
  C.B. (late *R.A.*)
  p.a.c., s.   7Dec.09
Baldock, T. S., *C.B.*
  (late *R.A.*) p.s.c., s.
  1Jan.10
Young, J. C., Col. R.
  Suss. R.,p.s.c., s.   4Feb.10
Cowans, *Sir* J. S., *K.C.B.*,
  M.V.O., p.s.c., *Q.M.G.*
  (3rd Mil. Member, *Army*
  Council)   21Mar.10
Snow, T. D'O., *C.B.*,
  s.   31Mar.10
Hadden, *Sir* C. F. *K.C.B.*
  (late *R.A.*) p.a.c.
  (*President Ord.Board*)
  6Apr.10
Hammersley, F., *C.B.*,
  p.s.c. [F]   7May10
McCausland, E. L.,
  R. Mar.[R]   19May10
Ferrier, J. A., *C.B.*, *D.S.O.*
  (late *R.E.*) [l]   15June10
Brunker, J. M. S. (late
  R.A.) s.   22June10
Murray, *Str* A. J., *K.C.B.*,
  C.V.O., *D.S.O.*, Col. R.
  Innis. Fus., p.s.c. [l]
  s.   13July10
Mackenzie, C. J., *C.B.*,
  p.s.c. [l] s.   16July10
Altham, E. A., *C.B.*,
  C.M.G., p.s.c., s. 31Aug.10
Rimington, M. F., *C.V.O.*,
  C.B., Col. 5 Dns., s.
  7Sept.10
Lindley, Hon. J. E., Col.
  1 Dns., p.s.c., s.   10Oct.10
Mullaly, H., *C.B.*, *C.S.I.*
  (late *R.E.*)   9Oct.10
Money, H. C.,*C.B.*, R.
  Mar.   12Oct.10
Monro, C. C., *C.B.*,
  p.s.c.,s.   31Oct.10
Macready, *Sir* C. F. N.,
  K.C.B.,(*Dir.of Per-*
  sonal Services)   31Oct.10
Cotter, F. G., R. Mar.
  [R]   21Nov.10

Robertson, *Sir* W. R.,
  K.C.V.O., *C.B.*, *D.S.O.*,
  p.s.c. [L] (*Dir. of*
  Mil. Training)   26Dec.10
May,E.S., *C.B.*,*C.M.G.*
  (late *R.A.*) [l] s.   7Jan.11
Johnstone,J.R.,R.Mar.
  [R]   22Jan.11
Macbean, F., *C.V.O.*,
  C.B., s.   19Mar.11
Wilson, A., *C.B.* s.   1May11
Wallace, A., *C.B.*, Ind.
  Army   3May11
Bell, *Sir* J A., *K.C.V.O.*,
  Ind. Army, s.   6May11
Davison, K. S., *C.B.*,
  Ind. Army, s.   3June11
Adye, J.,*C.B.* (late *R.A.*)
  p.s.c. [F] s.   19June11
Townshend, C. V, F.,
  C.B., *D.S.O.*, s.   19June11
Simpson, C. R., *C.B.*,
  Col. Linc. R. p.s.c.
  [L] s.   23June11
Campbell, F., *C.B.*, *D.S.O.*,
  Ind. Army, s.   29June11
Blewitt, W. E., *C.B.*,
  C.M.G. (late *R.A.*)
  g., s.   24July11
Fry, W., *C.V.O.*, *C.B.*,
  (Col. W. York. R.)
  s.   25Aug.11
Younghusband, *Sir* G.
  J., *K.C.I.E.*, *C.B.*, Ind.
  Army, p.s.c.,s,   29Aug.11
Gorringe, G.F., *C.B.*,
  O.M.G., *D.S.O.* (late
  R.E.) q.s.[F] s.   6Sept.11
Birdwood, W. R., *C.B.*,
  C.S.I., *C.I.E.*, *D.S.O.*,
  Ind. Army, p.s.c.,s. 30Sept.11
Cookson, G. A., *C.B.*,
  Ind. Army, s.   23Oct.11
Keary, H. D'U., *C.B.*,
  D.S.O., Ind. Army, s.
  1Dec.11
Burton, B., *C.B.*,
  (late *R.A.*) s.   17Dec.11
Graham, E.R.C., *C.B.*,
  p.s.c. (Col. Ches.
  R.) s.   3Feb.12
Lindsay, W.F.L., *C.B.*,
  D.S.O. (late *R.A.*) g.,
  s.   7Feb.12
Inglefield, F. S., *C.B.*,
  p.s.c. [L] s.
  7Mar.12
Ɐ Melliss, C. J.,
  C.B.,Ind.Army[L]
  [F] s.   19Mar.12
O'Donnell, H., *C.B.*,
  D.S.O.,Ind.Army,s 1Apr.12
Daniell, J. F.,
  R.Mar., p.s.c.[R], s.
  11Apr.12
Bunbury, W. E.,
  C.B., Ind. Army,
  p.s.c., s.   1May12
Friend, L. B., *C.B.*
  (late *R.E.*) s. [F] 3June12
Hanbury-Williams,
  Sir J., *K.C.V.O.*,
  C.M.G. [F]   10July12
Reade, R. N. R.,
  C.B., p.s.c. [L] s. 16July12

Wilkinson, P, S.,
  C.B., *C.M.G.*, s.   8Aug.12
Douglas, W., *C.B.*,
  D.S.O., p.s.c., s. 10Aug.12
Carnegy, P, M., *C.B.*,
  Ind. Army, s.   1Sept.12
Raitt, H. A., *C.B.*, s. 4Sept12
Young, C. F. G., Ind.
  Army, s.   21Sept.12
Scott-Moncrieff,
  G. K., *C.B.*, *C.I.E.*
  (late *R.E.*) (*Dir.*
  of Fortns.& Works)
  1Oct.12
Broome, R. C.,
  C.I.E., s.   12Oct.12
Egerton, G. G. A.,
  C.B., s.   10Dec.12
Hamilton Gordon,
  A., *C.B.*,(late *R.A.*)
  p.s.c., s.   22Jan.13
Drummond, L. G., *C.B.*,
  M.V.O.   15Feb.13
Montagu-Stuart-Wortley,
  Hon. E, J., *C.B.*, *C.M.G.*,
  M.V.O., *D.S.O.*, p.s.c.,
  q.s. [F] s.   5Mar.13
Morland, T. L. N.,
  C.B., *D.S.O.*, p.s.c.
  30Mar.13
Landon, F. W. B.,
  C.B. (late *A.S.C.*)
  (*Dir. of Transport*
  and Movements) 1Apr.13
Davies, F. J., *C.B.*,
  p.s.c. [L] (*Dir. of*
  Staff Duties)   18May13
Johnston, J. T.,
  C.B., (late *R.A.*)
  p.s.c., g.[L] s.   19May13
Hickman, H. F.,
  (late *R.A.*) g.   3June13
Birkbeck, W. H.,
  C.B., *C.M.G.*,
  p.s.c. (*Dir. of*
  Remounts) [F]   25Sept.13
Fanshawe, H. D.,
  C.B., s.   6Oct.13
Wilson, H. H.,
  C.B.,*D.S.O.*,p.s.c.
  (*Dir.of Mil. Opns.*)
  5Nov.13
Heath, H. N. C., *C.B.*,
  p.s.c. [L]   3Dec.13
Pirie, C. P. W., Ind.
  Army, s.   30Jan.14
Turner, J. G., *C.B.*,
  Ind. Army, s.   5Feb.14
Fry, C.J., Ind. Army
  [F] s.   11Mar.14
Shaw, D. G. L., Ind.
  Army, s.   20Mar.14
Kemball, G.V., *C.B.*,
  D.S.O. (late *R.A.*)
  p.s.c., g., s.   8Apr.14
Hunter-Blair, W.C.
  (late *R.A.*)   22Apr.14
Macintyre, D. C. F.,
  C.B., s.   4May14
Capper, T., *C.B.*,
  D.S.O., p.s.c. (*Inspr. of*
  Inf.)   12May14
Pease, L. T., R. Mar. Art.
  p.s.c. [R]   6June14
Heath-Caldwell, F, C.,
  C.B. (late *R.E.*)
  s.   11July14

Officers of the Army on the Active List.

SURGEON-GENERALS.

(Ranking as Major-Generals.)

Whitehead, H. R.,
C.B., F.R.C.S. 21Jan.09
Lukis,*Sir* C.P., *K.C.S.I.,
M.D., F.R.C.S., K.H.S.,*
Ind. Med. Serv. [R]
(*Dir. Gen., Ind. Med.
Serv.*) 1Jan.10
MacNeece, J. G.,
C.B. [F] 23Apr.10

Bannerman, W. B.,
C.S.I.,M.D.,K.H.P..
IndMed.Serv.[R]26July11
Corker, T. M., *M.D.,
K.H.P.* 11Dec.11
DGBabtie, W., *C.B.,
C.M.G., M.B., K.H.S.* 11Dec.11

Bruce,*Sir* D.,*Knt.,C.B.,
F.R.S., M.B.,F.R.C.P.* 1Apr.12
Anderson,L.E.,*C.B.*4May12
Hathaway, H. G.,
C.B. 15Oct.12
Bedford, W. G. A.,
C.M.G., M.B. 1Jan.14

Lyons, R. W. S.,
M.D., Ind. Med.
Serv. 11Jan.14
Ford, R. W., *D.S.O.* 1June14
Woodhouse, T. P. 14July14
Macpherson, W. G.,
C.M.G., M.B., K.H.P.,
[F] s, 14July14

COLONELS.

(With the honorary rank of Major-General.)

Pringle, R., *C.B., D.S.O. (Dir.-Gen., Army
Veterinary Service)* 11Dec.06
Col. ranking as Maj.-Gen. }
       Maj.-Gen. (hon.) } 15Oct.10

Battersby, T. P. *(Dir. of Equipment and Ord.
Stores)* 2Nov.04
Col. ranking as Maj.-Gen. }
       Maj -Gen.(hon.) } 1Apr.13

COLONELS FROM CAVALRY, ROYAL ARTILLERY, ROYAL ENGINEERS, INFANTRY AND ARMY SERVICE CORPS.

Crole Wyndham, W. G.,
O.B., p.s.c. *(Cav.
Records)* 7Sept.02

Sandbach, A. E., *C.B.,
D.S.O.* (late *R.E.*)
p.s.c, *(temp, Brig.-Gen.)* 10Feb.04

McKerrell, A. de S. *C.B.,*
[F], s, 10Feb.04

Lumley, *Hon.* O. V. G.
A. h.p. 10Feb.04

Hacket-Thompson,
F., *C.B.* [F]
*(No. 7 Dist. and
Record Office,
Warwick)* 9Mar.04

Western, W. G. B.,
C.B., p.s.c. [L]
*(No. 8 Dist. and
Record Office,
Exeter)* 9Apr.04

Sitwell, W. H.,*C.P.,
D.S.O.,* p.s.c*(temp.
Brig.-Gen.)* s, 2July04

Landon, H. J. S., *C.B.,
(temp.Brig.-Gen.)* s. 13July04

Granet, E J.,
C.B., (late *R.A.*)
p.s.c. [L] *(Mil.
Attaché)* 31July04

Koe, F. W. B., *C.B.*
(late *A.S.C.*) s. 3Aug.04

Dairymple-Hay, J. R. M.,
*C.B., D.S.O. (temp.
Brig.-Gen.)* s. 28Oct.04

Tudway, R. J., *C.B.,
D.S.O.* [F] *(No. 3
Dist. and Record
Office, Preston)* 16Nov.04

Shekleton, H.P.,*C.B.,*
p.s.c. [F] s. 16Nov.04

Pink, F. J., *C.B.,
C.M.G., D.S.O.,*
h.p., q.s. 16Nov.04

Wilson, H. F. M.,*C.B.*
[F] *(temp,Brig.-Gen.)*
s, 18Nov.04

Cooper, E. J.,*C.B.,
M.V.O., D.S.O.,*
h.p. 28Nov.04

McGrigor, C. R. R.,
C.B.. h.p., p.s.c
[l] [F] 30Dec.04

Maxse, F. I.,
*C.V.O., C.B.,
D.S.O.,* q.s. [L] *(temp.
Brig.-Gen.)* s. 20Jan.05

Thomson, A. G.,
C.B., h.p. (late
R.E.) 8Feb.05

McCracken,F.W.N.,
C.B., D.S.O., p.s.c.
(temp, Brig.-Gen.)
s. 13Feb.05

Godley, A. J.,
K.C.M.G., C.B.,
p.s.c. *(temp. Maj.-
Gen.)* 13Feb.05

Nicholson, J. S.,
*C.B., C.M.G.,
D.S.O.,* h.p. 16Feb.05

V&Phipps-Hornby,
E. J., *C.B.,* h.p.
(late *R.A.*) 22Mar.05

Rolt, S. P.,*C.B.*(temp.
Brig.-Gen.) s. 31Mar.05

Malcolm, H. H. L.,*C.B.,
D.S.O. (temp. Brig.-
Gen.)* s. 3Apr.05

Kiggell, L. E.,*C.B.,*
p.s.c*(temp.Brig.-
Gen.)* s. 28Apr.05

Watson, J. E., *C.B.
(No. 5 Dist. and
Record Office,
York)* 3May05

Peyton, W.E., *C.V.O.,
C.B., D.S.O.,* h.p.,
p.s.c. [F] 5May05

Doran,W.R. B., *C.B.
D.S.O.,* p.s.c.
(*temp. Brig.-
Gen.)* s. 29May05

V&Congreve, W. N.,
C.B.,M.V.O.,(temp.
Brig. Gen.) s. 4June05

Haking, R. C. B.,
C.B., p.s.c.(temp.
Brig.-Gen.) s. 19June05

Bainbridge, E. G. T.,
C.B., p.s.c.,q.s. [F] s.
20June05

Leader,H.P.,*C.B.,
(temp. Brig.-Gen.)*
s. 28June05

Gilpin, F. C. A.,
C.B., h.p. *(late
A.S.C.)* 2July05

Lean, K. E., *C.B.
(temp. Brig.-Gen.)*
s. 2July05

Fortescue, *Hon.* C. G.,
C.B., C.M.G., D.S.O.,
p.s.c., *(temp. Brig.-
Gen.)* s. 8July05

Armitage, E. H.,
*C.B.,*h.p. (late *R.A.*),
g. 8July05

Cuthbert, G. J., *C.B.
(temp. Brig.-Gen.)*
s, 4Aug.05

Kavanagh, C. T.
McM., *C.V.O.,C.B.,
D.S.O., (tempBrig.-
Gen.)* s. 18Aug.05

Montgomery, R. A. K.,
*C.B., D.S.O. (late
R.A.)* p.s.c., g.
(temp. Brig.-Gen.)
s, 22Aug.05

Officers of the Army on the Active List.

COLONELS FROM CAVALRY, ROYAL ARTILLERY, ROYAL ENGINEERS, INFANTRY AND ARMY SERVICE CORPS—*contd.*

Headlam, J.E.W., C.B., D.S.O.,(late R.A.), g.,(temp. Brig.-Gen.) s. 22Aug.05

Money, A. W., C.B., (late R.A.), p.s.c., (temp. Brig.- Gen.) s. 10Sept.05

Hill, F. F., C.B., D.S.O., h.p. 14Sept.05

Mercer, H. F., C.B. (late R.A.) A.D.C. (temp.Brig.-Gen.)s.1Oct.05

Murray, W. H. E., C.B. (temp.Brig.-Gen.)s. 6Oct.05

Ellison, G. F., C.B., p.s.c.(temp.Brig.- Gen.) s. 13Oct.05

Wintour, F., C.B., p.s.c.,(temp. Brig.- Gen.) s. 15Oct.05

Du Cane, H. J., C.B., M.V.O., h.p. (late R.A.) p.s.c. [L] 15Oct.05

Findlay, N. D., C.B. (late R.A.) p.s.c. [l] (temp. Brig. Gen.) s. 15Oct.05

Fortescue, F. A. C.B., p.s.c. [F] (Rif. Depôt and Record Office) 15Oct.05

Smith, G. R. F., C.V.O., C.B.,h.p., p.s.c. 16Oct.05

Doran, B. J. C., C.B., q.s. (temp. Brig. Gen.) s. 18Oct.05

Cole, A. W. G. L., C.B., D.S.O., p.s.c. (temp. Brig.-Gen.) s. 27Oct.05

Wyndham, G. P., C.B., M.V.O., p.s.c. [l] s. 29Oct 05

Paget, W. L. H., C.B., M.V.O. (late R.A.) (temp. Brig.-Gen.) s. 3Nov.05

Nicolls, E. G., C.B. (late R.A.),g.(temp. Brig.-Gen.)(Inspr. of R.G.A.) 3Nov.05

Milne, G. F., C.B., D.S.O. (late R.A). p.s.c. [l] (temp. Brig.-Gen.) s. 8Nov.05

Henderson, Sir D., K.C.B., D.S.O., p.s.c.,(temp.Brig.- Gen.)(Dir.-Gen.of Mil.Aeronautics) f.c.r. 22Nov.05

Thompson, C. W., C.B., D.S.O.,p.s.c. [l] (temp. Brig.- Gen.) s. 4Dec.05

Ingouville-Williams, E. C., C.B., D.S.O., q.s.(temp. Brig.-Gen.) s. 25Dec.05

Haldane, J. A. L., C.B., D.S.O., p.s.c. [l] [F] (temp. Brig.-Gen.) s. 11Jan.06

Williams, C., s. 21Jan.06

Scott, A. B., C.B., D.S.O.(late R.A.) (temp. Brig.- Gen.) s. 22Jan.06

Capper, J E., C.B. (late R.E.) s. 28Jan.06

Rice, S. R., C.B. (late R.E.)(temp. Brig.-Gen.) 12Feb.06

Mackintosh, G., C.B. [l] (No. 1 Dist. and Record Office, Perth) 5Mar.06

Glubb, F. M., C.B., D.S.O. (late R.E.) (temp. Brig.-Gen.)16Apr.06

Kelly, R. M. B. F., C.B., D.S.O. (late R.A.) g. (temp. Brig.-Gen.), s. 1May06

Pinney, R. J., p.s.c., s. 3May06

von Donop, Sir S. B., K.C.B. (late R.A.) g. (local and temp. Maj.-Gen.) (4th Mil. Member, Army Council) 13May06

Horne, H. S., C.B. (late R.A.) (temp. Brig.-Gen.)(Inspr. of R.H. & R.F.A.) 23May06

Wing, F.D.V., C.B. (late R.A.) (temp. Brig.-Gen.) s. 23May06

Carter, C. H. P., C.B., C.M.G., (Comdt., Nig. R.) 4June06

Churchward, P. R. S., C.B. (No. 6 Dist. and Record Office, Lichfield) 8June06

Gough, H. De la P., C.B., p.s.c. [l] (temp. Brig. Gen.) s. 11June06

Paterson, S. (No. 2 Dist. and Record Office, Hamilton) 27June06

Triscott, C. P., C.B., D.S.O. (late R.A.) q.s. (temp. Brig.-Gen.), s. 15July06

Smith, H. G., C.B., (late R.A.), g.(temp. Brig.-Gen.) (Dir. of Art.) 20July06

Adam, F. A., C.B. (temp. Brig.-Gen.) s. 28July06

Fanshawe, E. A. (late R.A.) s. 29July06

Roper, A. W., C.B. (late R.E.) 31July06

Shaw, F. C., C.B. (temp. Brig.-Gen.) s. 6Aug.06

Skinner, F. St. D., p.s.o.[F] s. 12Aug.06

Elliot, G. S. McD. (late R.E.) [L] [F] s. 13Aug.06

De Lisle, H. De B., C.B., D.S.O., p.s.c. [l] (temp. Brig.- Gen.) s. 22Aug.06

Briggs, C. J., C.B. (temp. Brig.-Gen.) s. 7Sept.06

Kirkpatrick, G. M., C.B. (late R.E.), p.s.c. (temp. Brig.-Gen.) s. 12Oct.06

Gleichen, A. E. W., Count, K.C.V.O., C.B., C.M.G., D.S.O., p.s.c. [L] [F] (temp. Brig.- Gen.) s., Eq. 15Oct.06

Daubeney, E. K., D.S.O., s. 16Oct.06

Caunter, J. E., C.B., p.s.c. (temp. Brig.- Gen.) s. 28Oct.06

Bulfin, E. S., C.V.O C.B., q.s. (temp. Brig.-Gen.), s. 17Nov.06

Du Cane, J. P., C.B. (late R.A.)(temp. Brig.-Gen.)s. 27Nov.06

Hunter-Weston, A. G., C.B., D.S.O. (late R.E.) p.s.c. [L] [F] (temp. Brig.- Gen.) s. 29Nov.06

O'Leary, T. E., C.B., s. 29Nov.06

St. John, G. F. W., C.B., h.p. (late R.A.) 29Nov.06

Cowie, C. H. (late R.E.) 29Nov.06

Bingham, Hon. C. E., C.V.O., C.B., [F], (temp. Brig.- Gen.) s. 29Nov.06

V& Brown-Synge-Hutchinson, E. D., h.p. 29 Nov.06

Biddulph, G. W. (late R.A.), g., s. 29Nov.06

Stewart, W. R. (late R.E.) s. 29Nov.06

Hickie, W. B., C.B., p.s.c., [l] s. 29Nov.06

Renny-Tailyour,T.F.B. C.S.I. (late R.E.) 29Nov.06

Foster, T. D., C.B., M.V.O. (late A.S.C.) e. (Inspr. of A.S.C.) (temp. Brig.-Gen.) 29Nov.06

De Gex,F.J.,C.B.,s. 1Dec.06

Stanton, H. E., C.B., D.S.O., A.D.C. (temp. Brig.-Gen.) s. 1Dec.06

V&Kenna, P. A., D.S.O. A.D.C., s. 1Dec

Officers of the Army on the Active List.

COLONELS FROM CAVALRY, ROYAL ARTILLERY, ROYAL ENGINEERS, INFANTRY AND ARMY SERVICE CORPS—*contd.*

Long, S. S., *C.B.* (late *A.S.C.*)(*temp. Brig.-Gen.*) (*Dir. of Supplies and Quartering*) 13Dec.06

Browne, C. A. R., (*late R.E.*) 3Jan.07

Fairholme, W. E., *C.M.G.*, *M.V.O.* (late *R.A.*), *p.s.c.* [L] *Mil. Attaché* 19Jan.07

Nanton, H. C. (*late R.E.*) s. .. 1Feb.07

Fitton, H. G., *C.B.*, *D.S.O.*, *p.s.c.* [L] [F] *A.D.C.* (*temp. Brig.-Gen.*) (*Dir. of Recg. and Organization*) 12Feb.07

Scott-Kerr, R., *C.B.*, *M.V.O.*, *D.S.O.*, G. Gds. and Regtl. Dist. 14Feb.07

Chapman, A. J., *C.B.*, *p.s.c.*, s. 15Feb.07

Evans, H. J., *p.s.c.* [l] (*No. 4 Dist. and Record Office, Shrewsbury*) 17Feb.07

Forestier-Walker, G. T. (*late R.A.*) *p.s.c.* [L] *A.D.C.* (*temp. Brig.-Gen.*) s. 18Feb.07

Dawkins, C. T., *C.M.G.*, h.p. 19Feb.07

Curtis, R. S., *C.M.G.*, *D.S.O.* (late *R.E.*) [F] s. 20Feb.07

Hamilton, W. G., *D.S.O.*, *p.s.c.*(*temp. Brig.-Gen.*) s. 12Mar.07

Williams, G. (*late R.E.*) (*temp. Maj.- Gen.*) s. 14Mar.07

Macfarlane, D. A., *D.S.O.*, s. 1Apr.07

Huskisson, W. (*late R.E.*) 4Apr.07

Stuart, R. C. O. (*late R.A.*) *f.* (*temp. Maj.-Gen.*) 3June07

Anderson, F. J. (*late R.E.*) (*temp. Brig.-Gen.*) s. 21June07

Herbert, E. A., *M.V.O.*, s. 2July07

Minchin, F. F. (*late R.A.*) *p.a.c.* (*Ind. Ord. Dept.*) 13July07

Jackson, H. K., *D.S.O.*, h.p. (*late R.A.*) 5Aug.07

Barnardiston, N. W., *M.V.O.*, *p.s.c.*, (*temp. Brig.-Gen.*) s. 8Aug.07

McGough, J. E., *C.M.G.*, *p.s.c.*, *A.D.C.*, s. 14Aug.07

Riddell, J. F., s. 15Aug.07

Heath, G. M., *D.S.O.* (late *R.E.*) *p.s.c.*, s. (*temp. Brig.-Gen.*) s. 20Aug.07

McClintock, W. K., s. 29Aug.07

Stopford, L. A. M., *p.s.c.* [l] (*temp. Brig. Gen.*) m.c. 10Sept.07

Horniblow, F. H., (late *R.E.*) 20Sept.07

Rycroft, W. H., *C.B.*, *p.s.c.* [F] s. 29Sept.07

Bushe, T. F., *C.M.G.* (late *R.A.*) *p.a.c.*, s. 1Oct 07

Smith, S. C. U., (late *R.A.*) *g.* [l] *temp. Brig.-Gen.*) s. 14Oct.07

Smith, G. B., (late *R.A.*) (*temp.Brig.- Gen.*) s. 7Nov.07

Burrard, S. G., *K.C.S.I.*, (late *R.E.*) 15Nov.07

Gwatkin, W. G., 20Nov 07

Nelson, E. F. (late *R.A.*) *g.*, *f.* (*temp. Brig.-Gen.*) s. 22Nov.07

St. John, C. W. R., h.p. (*late R.E.*) 10Dec.07

Scrase-Dickins, S. W. (*No. 12 Dist. and Record Office, Cork*) 18Dec.07

Fanshawe, R., *D.S.O.*, *p.s.c.* [l] s. 5Mar.08

Russell, W. (late *R.E.*) s. 29Mar.08

Hobbs, P. E. F., *C.M.G.*, h.p. (late *A.S.C.*) 2Apr.08

Travers, J. H. du B. (*No. 9 Dist. and Record Office, Warley*) 10Apr.08

Dallas, J. (*late R.E.*) 22Apr.08

Prinsep, D. G., (late *R.A.*) *g.*, (*Col. i/o R.H. & R.F.A. Records*) 23Apr.08

Gordon, Hon. F., *D.S.O.*, *p.s.c.*, s. 30Apr.08

Stuart, A. M. (late *R.E.*) s. 6May08

Hoare, R., s. 13May08

Gardiner, H. L. (late *R.A.*) *g.*, s. 13June08

Dundee, W. J. D., *C.I.E.* (late *R.E.*) 16July08

Grant, A. (late *R.E.*) 12Aug.08

Huleatt, H., (late *R.E.*) [L] [F] 12Aug.08

Maclagan, R. S., *C.B.*, *C.S.I.* (*late R.E.*) 12Aug.08

Lawford, S. T. B., s. 22Aug.08

Fowke, G. H., (late *R.E.*) [F] (*temp. Brig.-Gen.*) (*Inspr. of R.E.*) 22Aug.08

Bramhall, E. A., (late *A.S.C.*) 3Sept.08

Thackwell, O. M. R. (*late R.E.*) 4Oct.08

Taylor, E. T., *p.s.c.*, s. 12Oct.08

Ludlow, E. R. O. (late *A.S.C.*) *p.s.c.*, s. 15Oct.08

Baddeley, C. E. (late *R.E.*) 22Oct.08

Stokes, A., *D.S.O.*, (late *R.A.*) *g.*, (*temp. Brig.-Gen.*) s. 14Nov.08

Perceval, E. M., *D.S.O.* (late *R.A.*) *p.s.c.* (*temp. Brig.-Gen.*) s. 14Nov.08

Barlow, Sir H. W. W., *Bt.*, *C.B.* (late *R.A.*) (*Ord. Fact.*) *p.a.c.* 14Nov.08

Holland, A. E. A., *M.V.O.*, *D.S.O.* (late *R.A.*) *q.s.*, *g.* (*temp. Brig.-Gen.*) m.a. 14Nov.08

Hill, C. (late *R.E.*) (*temp. Brig.-Gen.*) s. 22Nov.08

James, C. H. L., s. 23Nov.08

Couper, V. A., s. 1Dec.08

Petrie, R. D. (late *R.E.*) 5Dec.08

Johnson, F. E., *D.S.O.* (late *R.A.*) (*temp. Brig.-Gen.*) s. 20Dec.08

Banon, F. L., *p.s.c.* [l] s. 23Dec.08

King, Sir C. W., *Knt.*, *M.V.O.* (late *A.S.C.*) 1Jan.09

Strange, R. G., (late *R.A.*), s. 15Jan.09

Braithwaite, W. P., *C.B.*, *p.s.c.* [l] (*temp. Brig.-Gen.*) s. 16Jan.09

Hume, J. J. F., s. 8Feb.09

Edmonds, J. E., *C.B.*(late *R.E.*) *p.s.c.* [L] s. 13Feb.09

Delmé-Radcliffe, C., *C.V.O.*, *C.B.*, *C.M.G.*, h.p., *p.s.c.* [L] [F] 8Mar.09

Boileau, F. R. F., (late *R.E.*)p.s.c. [l] s. 31Mar.09

Glanville, F., *D.S.O.* (late *R.E.*) 1Apr.09

Ellis, W. M. (late *R.E.*) 1Apr.09

Erskine, J. F., *M.V.O.*, s. 25Apr.09

Jack, H. R. H., *C.M.G.*, (late *A.S.C.*) 7May09

Burton, St. G.E.W., s. 24May09

Campbell, H.M., h.p. (late *R.A.*), s. 8June09

Nugent, O. S. W., *D.S.O.*, h.p., *p.s.c.* [l] *A.D.C.* 23June09

Brunker, C. M., *D.S.O.*, Disch. Depôt 24June09

Goold-Adams, H. E. F., *C.M.G.* (late *R.A.*) *g.* (*Member, Ord. Board*) 17July09

Hemming, E. H. (late *R.E.*) s. 18July09

Walton, E. W. (late *R.E.*) 25July09

Blackden, L. S., h.p. 26July09

Officers of the Army on the Active List.

COLONELS FROM CAVALRY, ROYAL ARTILLERY, ROYAL ENGINEERS, INFANTRY AND ARMY SERVICE CORPS—contd.

Jones, L. (late R.E.) s. 5Aug.09
Iggulden, H. A., s. 11Aug.09
Craster, S. L. (late R.E.) 13Aug.09
Longford,T.,Earl of, K.P., M.V.O., s. 14Aug.09
Bush, J. E.,s. 15Aug.09
Bowes, W. H., p.s.c. [L] s. 25Aug.09
Fuller, R. W., D.S.O., h.p. (late R.A.) 11Sept.09
Bythell,W.J.(late R.E. 25Sept.09
Dawson, R., s. 29Sept.09
Ward, B. R. (late R.E.) [L] (R.E. Record Office) 1Oct.09
Walter, J. MacN., D.S.O., p.s.c. (temp. Brig.-Gen.), s. 2Oct.09
Sargent, H. N., D.S.O. (late A.S.C.) 27Oct.09
Lambton, Hon. W., C.M.G., M.V.O., D.S.O.,p.s.c., s. 28Oct.09
Buckland, R. U. H. (late R.E.) A.D.C. [F] s. 28Oct.09
Bunbury, V. T., C.B., D.S.O. [F] s. 11Nov.09
Dobell, C. M., D.S.O., p.s.c. [l] A.D.C. (temp. Brig.-Gen.) 4Nov.10
Norie, E. W. M., p.s.c.,A.D.C., s. 21Mar.11
Milner, G. F., D.S.O. (Oaz. Record;, 19July11
Cockburn, W. F. (late R.A.), g. (temp.Brig.-Gen.), s. 19July11
Campbell, W., D.S.O. p.s.c. [l] s. 19July11
Harper,G.M.,D.S.O. (late R.E.) p.s.c. [l] s. 19July11
Chamier, G. D., C.M.G.(late R.A.) g. (Col. t/c R.G.A. Records) 19July11

Godby, C., (late R.E.) [F] s. 19July11
Scaife, H. B., h.p. 19July11
Bayard, R., D.S.O., s. 19July11
Drake, B. F. (late R.A.) s. 19July11
de Winton, C., s. 19July11
Davidson, S., (late R.E.) s. 19July11
Shipley, C. T., s. 19July11
Gamble, R. N., D.S.O., p.s.c. [l] [F] s. 19July11
Strachey, R. J., p.s.c, s. 19July11
Brereton, E. F., D.S.O., s. 19July11
Kent, H. V., h.p. (late R.E.) 19July11
Houston, E. (late R.E.) 19July11
Woodward, E. M., p.s.c. (temp. Brig.-Gen.), s. 19July11
Maude, F.S.,C.M.G., D.S.O., p.s.c., s. 19July11
Yarde-Buller, Hon. H., M.V.O., D.S.O., p.s.c. [l] Mil. Attaché 19July11
Dallas, A. G., p.s.c. [l] s. 19July11
Cavendish,A.E.J., C.M.G., p.s.c., s. 30Aug.11
Ruggles-Brise, H. G., M.V.O.,p.s.c., s. [l] s. 30Aug.11
Gilbert,A.R., D.S.O., s. 30Aug.11
Brown, W. B. (late R.E.) 30Aug.11
Little, C. B., s. 30Aug.11
Nickalls, N. T., s. 30Aug.11
Napier, H. E. (No. 11 Dist. and Record Office, Dublin) 30Aug.11

Stockwell, G. C. I., D.S.O., p.s.c [l] s. 30Aug.11
Tidswell, E. C., D.S.O., s. 30Aug.11
Painter, A. C. (late R.E.) s. 30Aug.11
Du Boulay, N.W.H., h.p. (late R.A.)p.s.c. 30Aug.11
Carte, T. E. (late R.A.) s. 30Aug.11
Oxley, R. S., p.s.c. [l] s. 30Aug.11
Crowe, J. H. V., (late R.A.) p.s.c. [L] s. 30Aug.11
Short, A. H., (late R.A.) 30Aug.11
Parker St. J.W. T. (late A.S.C.), s. 4Oct.11
Furse, W. T., D.S.O., (late R.A.) p.s.c. [L] s. 4Oct.11
Chetwode, Sir P W. Bt., D.S.O., (temp. Brig.-Gen.) s. 4Oct.11
Montagu, E., h.p., p.s.c. [L] 4Oct.11
Hamilton, A. B., p.s.c., s. 4Oct.11
McLeod, W. K. (late R.A.) s. 4Oct.11
Johnstone, F. B., D.S.O. (late R.A.) 4Oct.11
Morrison, C. G., p.s.c., e., s. 4Oct.11
Crampton, P. H., s. 4Oct.11
Long, A., D.S.O. (late A.S.C.) 4Oct.11
Whigham, R. D., D.S.O., p.s.c. [l] s. 4Oct.11
Wolley-Dod, O. C., D.S.O., p.s.c. [l] s. 4Oct.11
Heard, E. S., p.s.c. 4Oct.11
Baldwin,A.H., h.p. 4Oct.11
O'Donnell, H., p.s.c., (No. 10 Dist. and Record Office, Hounslow) 4Oct.11
Bromilow, W., s. 4Oct.11
Hodgson, H. W., C.V.O., s. 10Oct.11
Heyworth, F. J., D.S.O., S. Gds. & Regtl. Dist. 6Dec.11
Rose, C. S. (late R.E.) 6Dec.11

Nugent, G. C., M,V,O., s. 6Dec.11
Vaughan, J., D.S.O., p.s.c. [l] s. 6Dec.11
Browne, S. D, (late R.A.), s. 6Dec.11
Martel, C. P. (late R.A.) p.a.c., s. 6Dec.11
Meeres, C. S. (late R.A.) p.a.c., s. 6Dec.11
Hamilton, L. A. H., p.s.c., s. 6Dec.11
Wynne, J. G. E. (late R.A.) g., s. 7Mar.12
Walker, H. B., D.S.O., s. 7Mar.12
Fryer, F. A. B., s. 7Mar.12
Jeudwine, H. S. (late R.A.) g., 7Mar.12
Williams, H. B., D.S.O. (late R.E.) p.s.c. [L] s. 7Mar.12
Kerr, F. W. D.S.O., p.s.c., s. 7Mar.12
Lynden-Bell, A. L., C.M.G., p.s.c. [L] s. 7Mar.12
Morton, W. R., (late R.E.) [L] 7May 12
Duffus, G. S. (late R.E.) 7Mar.12
Gibbon, J. A., h.p. (late R.E.) 7Mar.12
Caulfeild, C. T. (late R.A.), s. 7Mar.12
Hare, S. W., s. 7Mar.12
Brown, H. C., s. 7Mar.12
Reynolds, A. R., h.p. (late R.E.) 7Mar.12
Pery, C. C. J., h.p. (late R.E.) 6June12
Monck, C. S. O., C. Gds. and Regtl. Dist., p.s.c. 6June12
Hussey, A. H. (late R.A.), s. 6June12
Clifford,W. R., s. 6June12
Tyndale-Biscoe, J, D. T., s. 6June12
James, W. R. W., h.p. (late R.A.) g. 6June12
Wright, H.B.H., h.p. (late R.E.) 6June12

E

Officers of the Army on the Active List.

COLONELS FROM CAVALRY, ROYAL ARTILLERY, ROYAL ENGINEERS, INFANTRY AND ARMY SERVICE CORPS—contd.

LLoyd, F. C. s. 6June12	Boyce, W. G. B.,	MacMahon, J. J.,	Bingham, Hon. F.R.
Lecky, R. St. C.	D.S.O.(lateA.S.C.) 30Oct.12	h.p. (late R.A.)	(late R.A.) s. 2June
(late R.A.) s. 6June12	Marriott, J., M.V.O.,	Campbell, D., s. 4Dec.12	Chichester, A. A.,
Rimington, J. C.	D.S.O., s. 30Oct.12	Butler, H. H.	D.S.O., h.p., p.s.c. 2June
(late R.E.) 6June12	Macdonogh, G. M.	(late R.A.) s. 4Dec 12	van Straubenzee,
O'Leary, W. E.,	W., p.s.c. [L] (late	Parker, F. J., h.p. 4Dec.12	C. H. C., h.p. 2June
p.s.c. [L] [F] s. 6June12	R.E.) s. 30Oct.12	MacAdam, W. (late	Haggard, H., h.p. 2June
Roe,C.H.(lateR.E.)6 June12	Mullins, A. J. (late	R.E.) s. 4Dec.12	Cayley, W. de S., h.p.
Moore, J. S. (late	R.A.) g., s. 30Oct.12	Taylor, A. H. M.,	2June
A.S.C.) s.	Taylor, A. W., s. 30Oct.12	D.S.O., s. 2Jan.13	Maxwell, R. P., h.p., 2June
Humphrys, C. V. 6June12	Gay, A. W., D.S.O,	Scott, C. D. (late	Shute, C. D., h.p.,
Hibbert, G. L., D.S.O.,	(late R.A.) p.s.c. [l]	R.A.) s. 6Mar.13	p.s.c. 2June
s. 6June12	s. 30Oct.12	ⓌⒸ, FitzClarence, C.,	Prendergast, D. G.,
Renny, S.M., C.I.E.	Brewin, J. P.	I. Gds. and Regtl.	h.p., s. 2June
(late R.A.) 6June12	(late R.E.) 30Oct.12	Dist., p.s.c. 6Mar.13	Everett, H. J., h.p.,
Duhan, W. T.	MacFarlan, F. A.	Boyle, R. C., h.p. 6Mar.13	p.s.c. [l] 16Dec.
(late R.A.) g., s. 6June12	[F] s. 30Oct.12	Wanless-O'Gowan,	Carleton, L. R.,
Kays, H.F., s. 6June12	Crawford, A. (late	R., s. 6Mar.13	D.S.O., p.s.c. 16Dec.
Close, C. F., C.M.G.	R.A.) p.s.c. [l] [F]	Powell, S. H. [l] (late	Hedley, W. C. (late
(late R.E.) (Dir.	e.a. 4Dec.12	R.E.), s. 2June13	R.E.) s. 16Dec.
Gen., Ord. Survey)6June12	Heffernan, N. B. (late	Frith, H. C. [L]	Fisher, F. T. (late
Sloman, H. S., D.S.O.,	R.A.) p.a.o.,g. (Mem-	[F], s. 2June13	R.A.), p.a.c., s. 16Dec.
p.s.c. [L] [F] 21Sept.12	ber Ord. Board) 4Dec.12	Cowans, E. A., s. 2June13	Pratt, E. St. G.,
Sears, J.W., s. 30Oct.12	Rich, H. H. (late	Daniell, F. F. W.,	D.S.O., p.s.c. [l] s.16Dec
Nicholson, G.H., s. 30Oct.12	R.A.) 4Dec.12	h.p. 2June13	Sutton, H. C., s. 16Dec.
Bickford, E. (late R.A.)	ⓌⒸ Smyth, N. M.,	Makins, E., D.S.O.,	Carter, E. E., C.M.G.,
g., s. 30Oct.12	e.a. [F] 4Dec.12	h.p., p.s.c. [l] 2June13	M.V.O. (late A.S.C.),
Tudor, E. A. T.,	Young, J. R., h.p.		p.s.c., e. (A.S.C.)
h.p. (late R.E.) 30Oct.12	Lee, F, [L] s. 4Dec.12		Record Office) 16Dec.

COLONELS :———ROYAL MARINES.

Aston, Sir G. G.,	Gordon, C. L., R. Mar.	Marchant, A. E., C.B.,	Mercer, D., R. Mar.,
K.C.B., R. Mar.	(temp. Brig.- Gen.)	R. Mar., A.D.C. 7June10	s. 22Jan.
Art.,p.s.c., A.D.C.24May05	[R] 10Oct.09		
Talbot,H.L.,R.Mar.	Roe, E. C. B., R. Mar.	Curtoys, C. E. E.,	
Art. (temp. Brig.	(temp.Brig.-Gen.)28Dec.09	R. Mar. 11Apr.12	
Gen.) [F] 26Jan.08			
Kennedy,C. H., C.B.,	White, H. S. N.,	Trotman, C. N.,	Chown, E. E.,
R. Mar. (temp.	M.V.O., R. Mar.	R. Mar. 12Oct.13	R. Mar. 22Jan.
Brig.-Gen.) [R] 10Dec.08	(temp.Brig.-Gen.)11May10		

COLONELS :———INDIAN ARMY.

Atkinson, F. G., C.B.	Egerton,R. G.,C.B.	Johnstone, A. A. J.	Barratt, W. C.,
10Feb.04	(temp. Brig.-Gen.)	(temp. Brig.-Gen.) s.	C.B.,D.S.O. [F] 25July
Tinley, G, F. N., C.B. [l]	s. 6June07	11June07	Hodson, G. B., C.B.,
30Jan.07	Aitken, A. E., (temp.	Tighe, M. J., C.B.,	D.S.O., s. 13Nov.
Gastrell, E. T. 30Jan.07	Brig.-Gen.) s. 9June07	C.I.E., D.S.O.[F] 8Dec.07	Bingley, A. H., C.I.E.,
Rodwell, E. H., C.B.,	Cox, H, V., C.B., C.S.I.	Delamain, W. S., C.B.,	s. 19Mar.
p.s.c. (temp. Brig.-	(temp.Brig-Gen.)s.9June07	D.S.O., s. 12Jan.08	Harrison, T. A. 1Apr.
Gen.) s. 30Jan.07	Wapshare, R. (temp.	Price, C. H. U., C.B.,	Ewart, R. H., C.I.E.,
Thackwell, C. G. R.,	Brig.-Gen.) s. 10June07	D.S.O. 1Mar.08	D.S.O., A.D.C. 1May
C.B., D.S.O. 1May07	Loch, H. F., p.s.c.	Stewart, J.M., C.B.	ƜⒸWalker, W. G.,
Thomson, W. D. 1May07	(temp.Brig.-Gen.)	A.D.C., s. 20Mar.08	C.B. 8May
Hutchinson, F. P.,	s. 10June07	Dick, A. R., C.B. 16July08	Shore, O. B. S. F., C.B.,
C.B. [L] 1May07	Cowper, M., C.I.E.	Jacob, C. W., s. 1Oct 08	D.S.O.,p.s.c. [L] (temp.
Richardson, F. B. W.	(temp.Brig.-Gen.) s,	Malleson, W., C.I.E.	Brig.-Gen.) s 30July
11May07	Watson, W. A.,C.B.,	[F] 20Oct.08	Buchanan, K. J., C.B.
Steele, St. G. L., C.B.	C.I.E.,p.s.c.(temp.	Marlow, B. W., C.I.E.	27Sept.
[L] 1June07	Brig.-Gen.) s. 10June07	23 Dec. 06	Campbell, A. A. E.,
Yate, F. H. 1June07	Wadeson, F.W. G.	Fane, V. B., C.B. 1Jan.09	s. 29Oct.
	(temp. Brig.-Gen.) s.	Twigg, H. C., C.B. 4Feb.09	Beynon, W. G. L., D.S.O.,
Dobbie, W. H., C.B.	10June07	Lindesay, A. L., s. 18Feb.09	s. 10Nov.
(temp. Brig.-Gen.)	Johnson, C. E. (temp.	Shakespear,L.W.,s.2Apr.09	Brooking, H. T., C.B.,
s. 6June07	Brig.-Gen.) s. 11June07	Palin, G, W., C.B.,	s. 21Nov.
		C.I.E. 1May09	

Officers of the Army on the Active List.

COLONELS:—INDIAN ARMY—contd.

Hudson, H., *C.B.*, *C.I.E.*,(*temp.* Brig.-Gen.), s. 17Feb.11	Mainwaring, C. V. 3Oct.11	Dunsterville, L. C. [L] 1May12	Miles, P. J 31Jan.13
Williams, A. B. C., *C.B.* (*temp.* Brig.- Gen.) s. 3May11	Hoghton, F. A., s. 23Oct.11	Andrews, L. J. 26June12	Lang, E. B. 14Feb.13
	Woodyatt, N. G., s.25Oct.11	Carruthers, R. A., *C.B.* 29June12	Sullivan, R. E. 21Feb.13
	Fowler, C. A., *D.S.O.* 12Nov.11		Cripps, A. W. 13Mar.13
Fowler, F. J., *D.S.O.*, s. 6May11	Eustace, A. H., *D.S.O.* 1Dec.11	Newbold, A. W. 11Aug.12	Colomb, G. H. C. 24Mar.13
	ᴅᴄCobbe, A. S., *D.S.O.*,	Mead, H. R. 19Aug.12	Brown, R. J. R 24Mar.13
Oswald, W. A. 29June11	*p.s.c*., *A.D.C.* 1Dec.11	Betham, R M. 1Sept.12	Walton, W. C. 31Mar.13
Woodward, J. A. H. 30June11	Millar, W. H. 26Dec.11	Savage, W. H. 1Sept.12	Hendley, C. E. 23Apr.13
Grimston, *Sir* R. E., *K.C.V.O., C.I.E.* (*temp.* Brig.-Gen.) Eq. (Inspr.-Gen., Impl. Serv. Troops, *India*) 13Aug.11	Cartwright, C. M. 1Jan.11	Cox, F. W. H. 21Sept.12	Walters, H. F. 1May13
	Holloway, B., *p.s.c.* [L] s. 14Jan.12	Mathewes, J. R. 21Sept.12	Crocker, S. F. 31May13
	Edwards, Fitz J M., *D.S.O., p.s.c.* (*temp.* Brig.-Gen.), s. 14Jan.12	Johnston, H. M. 5Oct.12	Clay, C. H., *p.s.c.* [l] 30Sept.13
		Fasken, W. H. 12Oct.12	Bernard, H. C. 22Oct.13
		Thomas, F. H. S. 23Oct.12	Soady, G. J. FitzM. 22Oct.13
	Thring, R. H. D., *C.B.* 23Feb.12	Blakeney, W. E. A. 23Oct.12	Murray, F., *D.S.O.* 22Oct.13
Fisher, J., *C.B.* [L] 29Aug.11	Muspratt, F. C. 1Apr.12	Kennedy, H. 30Dec.12	Gayer, E. A. 28Nov.13
Hardy, T. H., s. 25Sept.11		Commeline, F.H.B. 31Dec.12	Burton, R. G. [L] 19Dec.13
			Cole, E. H. 2Jan.14

BREVET COLONELS:——CAVALRY, ROYAL ARTILLERY, ROYAL ENGINEERS, INFANTRY AND ARMY SERVICE CORPS.

Thesiger, G. H., *C.B.*, *C.M.G.*, Rif. Brig., *p.s.c.* [l] 29Nov.06	Marshall, W. R., Notts. & Derby. R. 26June08	Hasler, J., E. Kent R. 11Jan.10	Ryder, F. J., h.p. 20Dec.11
	Gale, H. R., R.E., *q.s.* 22Aug.08	Gorges, E. H., *D.S.O.* (Comdt. W. Afr. R.) 10May10	Koe, L. C. (Comdt. Peking Legation Guard, 28 *Jan.* 11) 8Oct.12
Heneker, W. C. G., *D.S.O.*, N. Staff. R., *A.D.C.* 24Oct.07	Dyas, J. R., h.p., *p.s.c.* [l] 22Dec.08	Jackson, S. C. F., *D.S.O.*, Hamps. R. [L] 7Sept.10	
Thompson, W. A. M., R.F.A., *p.s.c.* 26June08	Somerville, T.C.F., *M.V.O.*, s. 26June09	Dowell, G. C., R.G.A. 10Oct.10	ᴅᴄGordon, W. E., Gord. Highrs., *A.D.C.* 9Oct.13

BREVET COLONELS:——ROYAL MARINES.

Paris, A., *C.B.*, h.p., R. Mar. Art., *p.s.c.* [L] 28Sept.06	Campbell, G. M. R. Mar. Art. 12Mar.11	Conway-Gordon, L., R. Mar. Art., *p.s.c.* 10Oct.11

BREVET COLONELS:——INDIAN ARMY.

Blyth, F. A. 13June04	Westlake, A. P., *D.S.O.* 29Nov.06	Justice, C. Le G. 11May07	Balfour, J. H. 23Mar.08
Gott, G. A. 23Feb.05	Whistler, A. E. 30Jan.07	Hancock, F. H. 4June07	Leonard, A W. 2Oct.08
Onslow, R. C. 11Sept.05	Hodgson, G. E. 1May07	Dennys, W. A. B. 6June07	Herbert, L. N. [l] 4Apr.09
	Hunter, J. G., *C.B.* 1May07		Knight, W. C., *D.S.O.*, *p.s.c.* [L] *A.D.C.*, s. 19Mar.12
Maxwell, G. W. 28Oct.05	Aplin, P. J. H., *D.S.O.* [L] 1May07	Unwin, G.B., *D.S.O.* 15Sept.07	Peterson, F. H., *D.S.O.* [l] 6June12
Forbes, A. W. 11Sept.06	Dobbie, H. H. 1May07	Templer, H. 28Oct.07	

E 2

Officers of the Army on the Active List.

COLONELS AND BREVET COLONELS :———ARMY MEDICAL SERVICE, ARMY VETERINARY SERVICE, INDIAN MEDICAL SERVICE, ARMY ORDNANCE DEPARTMENT AND ARMY PAY DEPARTMENT.

Jackson, R. W. M., *C.B.*, *C.M.G.*, A. Ord. Dept. 22Aug.02

Law, R. T. H., A. Ord. Dept. *(temp. Brig.-Gen.) (Inspr. of A. Ord. Services)* 2Nov.04

Butcher, G. J., *C.B.*, *C.M.G.*, A. Ord. Dept. *(temp. Brig.-Gen.) (Dep. Dir. of Ord. Stores)* 19Jan.05

Crawford, R., A. Ord. Dept., *f.* 2June06

Bray, C. A.,*C.B.*, *C.M.G.*, A. P. Dept. 29July06

Gaussen, J. S., A. P. Dept. 11Mar.07

Rutherford, C., *C.B.*, *C.M.G.*, *F.R.C.V.S.* *(late A.V.C.)* 17May07

Hazleton, E. H., *F.R.C.V.S.* *(late A.V.C.)* 15Oct.07

Thackwell, E. L. R., A. P. Dept. 18Oct.07

Seymour, E. H., A. Ord. Dept.,*f.*, *s.* 29Nov.07

Collings, G. D., *D.S.O.*, A. P. Dept. 13Jan.08

Blenkinsop, L. J., *D.S.O.* *(late A.V.C.)* 15Mar.08

Angell, F. J., A. Ord. Dept. 1Apr.08

Perry, H. W., A. Ord. Dept. 21June08

Minchin, W. C., A. P. Dept. 9Nov.08

Lowry, J., A. P. Dept. 17Nov.08

Hill, F. W., A. P. Dept. 1Jan.09

Taylor, R. H. B., A. Ord. Dept. 24Apr.09

Newland, E. W., A. P. Dept. 1May09

Bunny, F. W. Mc.T., A. Ord. Dept. 2Aug.09

Lambert, W., A. Ord. Dept., *p.a.c. (Chf. Inspr. of Equipt. and Stores)* 21Sept.09

Carter, J. T., A. P. Dept. 21Sept.09

Firth, R. H., *F.R.C.S.* *(late R.A.M.C.)* 10Nov.09

Grainger, T., *C.B.*, *M.D.*, Ind. Med. Serv. 3Dec.09

Porter, R., *M.B.*, h.p. *(late R.A.M.C.)* 14Jan.10

Smith, G. B., A. P. Dept. 23Jan.10

Harris,G. F. A.,*C.S.I.*,*M.D.*, *F.R.C.P.*, Ind. Med. Serv. 1Mar.10

Manifold, C. C., *C.B.*, *M.B.*, Ind. Med. Serv. 29Mar.10

O'Keeffe, M. W., *M.D.*, h.p. *(late R.A.M.C.)* 23Apr.10

Nuthall, C. E., *(late A.V.C.)* 4June10

Dennys, G. W. P., Ind. Med. Serv. 16June10

O'Donnell, T. J., *D.S.O.*, h.p. *(late R.A.M.C.)* 7July10

Bamber, C. J., *M.V.O.*, Ind. Med. Serv. 12July10

Parsons, H. D. E., *C.M.G.*, A.Ord. Dept. 1Aug.10

Sawyer, R. H. S., *M.B.*, *F.R.C.S.I.*, *(late R.A.M.C.)* [L] 3Aug.10

Culling, J. C. *(late R.A.M.C.)* 8Aug.10

Henderson, R. S. F., *M.B.*, *K.H.P.* *(late R.A.M.C.)* 22Nov.10

Mathew, C. M., *C.B.*,*D.S.O.*, A.Ord.Dept. 26Nov.10

Grant, D. St. J. D., *M.B.*, Ind. Med. Serv. 1Jan.11

Cleveland, H. F., Ind. Med. Serv. 1Jan.11

Dorling, L., *D.S.O.*, A. P. Dept. 12Jan.11

Butler, E. R. C., *F.R.C.V.S.* *(late A.V.C.)* 18Jan.11

Birrell, W. G.,*M.B.* *(late R.A.M.C.)* 15Mar.11

Hendley, H., *M.D.*, Ind. Med. Serv. 7Apr.11

Jencken, F. J., *M.B.*, *(late R.A.M.C.)* 12May11

Horrocks,W.H.,*M.B.*, R.A.M.C. 20May11

Smyth, J., *M.D.*, Ind. Med. Serv. 7June11

Treherne, F. H., *F.R.C.S. Edin.* *(late R.A.M.C.)* 13June11

Fitton, G. W., A.P. Dept. 5July11

Barratt, H. J. *(late R.A.M.C.)* 20Oct.11

Trevor, H. O, *(late R.A.M.C.)* 26Oct.11

Pike, W. W., *D.S.O.*, *F.R.C.S.I.* *(late R.A.M.C.)* 9Nov.11

Evans, A. O., Ind. Med. Serv. 21Nov.11

Irwin, J. M.,*M.B.*(late R.A.M.C.) 11Dec.11

Melville, C. H., *M.B.*, R.A.M.C. 24Feb.12

Nichol, C. E., *D.S.O.*, *M.B.* *(late R.A.M.C.)* 9Mar.12

Westcott, S., *C.M.G.* *(late R.A.M.C.)* 20Mar.12

Hehir, P., *M.D.*, *F.R.C.S. Edin.*, Ind. Med. Serv. 25Mar.12

Skinner, B. M., *M.V.O.*, *(late R.A.M.C.)* 4May12

Kirkpatrick, R., *C.M.G.*, *M.D.* *(late R.A.M.C.)* 21May12

Grayfoot, B. B., *M.D.*, Ind. Med. Serv. 26Aug.12

Smith, F., *D.S.O.*, R.A.M.C. 4Sept.12

Lynden-Bell,E.H.I., *M.B.*(late *R.A.M.C.*) 19Sept.12

Leishman, *Sir* W. B., *Knt.*, *F.R.S.*, *M.B.*, *F.R.C.P.*, *K.H.P.*, R.A.M.C. 15Oct.12

Tate, A. E. *(late R.A.M.C.)* 31Dec.12

Hickson, S., *M.B.*, *K.H.S.*, *(late R.A.M.C.)* *(Inspr. of Med. Services)* 2Jan.13

Magee, A. H., A. P. Dept. 13Jan.13

Faunce, C. E. *(late R.A.M.C.)* 26Jan.13

Geddes, R. J.,*D.S.O.*, *M.B.* *(late R.A.M.C.)* 5Feb.13

Sloggett, H. M. *(late R.A.M.C.)* 27Mar.13

Anley, H. A., A. Ord. Dept.,*f.*, *s.* 1Apr.13

Hale, T. W., A. Ord. Dept. [F] 1Apr.13

Robertson, R., *M.B.*, Ind. Med. Serv. 30June13

Seton, B. G., Ind. Med. Serv. 30June13

Maher, J. *(late R.A.M.C.)* 13Sept.13

Hunter, G. D., *D.S.O.* *(late R.A.M.C.)* [F] 15Sept.13

McCrimmin, J., *C.B.*, *C.I.E.*, Ind. Med. Serv. 1Oct 13

Moore, J., *F.R.C.V.S.*, *(late A.V.C.)* 15Oct13

Thompson, H. N., *D.S.O.*, *M.B.* *(late R.A.M.C.)* 17Nov.13

Manders, N. *(late R.A.M.C.)* 21Dec.13

Birt, C. *(late R.A.M.C.)* 1Jan.14

Dyson, T. E., *M B.*, Ind. Med. Serv. 11Jan.14

Russell, M. W. *(late R.A.M.C.)* 14Jan.14

Banatvala, H. E., Ind. Med. Serv. 2Apr.14

Reilly, C. C. *(late R.A.M.C.)* 23Apr.14

Strickland, P. C. H., Ind. Med. Serv. 15May14

Holt,M.P.C.,*D.S.O.*, R.A.M.C. 4July14

Jones,F.W.C.,*M.B.* *(late R.A.M.C.* 14July14

Gibbard,T.W.,*M.B.*, *K.H.S.*, R.A.M.C. 14July14

OFFICERS, NOT SHEWN IN ANY REGIMENT OR CORPS, EXTRA REGIMENTALLY EMPLOYED.

LIEUT.-COLONELS.

Dowell, A. J. W. 29Aug.08	Roy, J. W. G. 8Jan.11	Sillem, A. F., *p.s.c., q.s.*, 17Feb.12	Hawker, C. J. [F] 29Nov.13
Fowle, T. E., *p.s.c.* [*l*] 10Oct.08	Marker, R. J., *D.S.O., p.s.c., q.s.* 11Mar.11	Morse, C. J. 20Mar.12	Browne, G. H. S. 2Mar.14
Montagu-Stuart-Wortley, Hon. A.R., *D.S.O., p.s.c.,* [L] 15Oct.10	Cunliffe, F. H. G. 22Sept.11	Turton, R. D. 14Nov.13	Gunn, G. 13Mar.14

MAJORS.

Maude, F. S. de M.	25Feb.03
Atherley, P.C.F.	21Sept.04
Umfreville, P.	13Dec.05
Green, T. H. M., *D.S.O.*	5Aug.07

CAPTAINS.

Bell, L. R. G.	6Jan.01
Whiffen, T. W.	30May04
Harris, *Hon.* A. F. W.	23Nov.05
Kinsman, W. A. C., *D.S.O.*	13Jan.07

LIEUTENANT.

Vaux, H. G.	4Mar.03

RIDING-MASTER.

Sykes, W. (*hon. maj.* 20Feb.10) 20Feb.95

QUARTER-MASTERS.

Dyke, J. S., *M.V.O.* (*hon. maj.* 1Jan.03)	13Nov.86	Steele, J. (*hon. capt.* 18 Dec. 11)	18Dec.01
Dixon, C. J. (*hon. maj.* 1May 06)	1May91	Heath, T.A. (*hon.capt.* 24Jan.13) (*War Office*)	24Jan.03
Bett, J. (*hon. maj.* 26July 08)	6July93	Smyth, R. W. (*hon. capt.* 11 *May* 14)	11May04
Fletcher, C. W. (*hon. maj.* 5Feb.11)	5Feb.96	Skeats, T. G., *hon. lt.* (*War Office*)	16Nov.04
Stretton, A. J., *M.V.O.* (*hon. maj.* 25 *Mar.*11)	25Mar.96	Kellett, J. A., *hon. lt.* (*War Office*)	1Apr.05
Hynes, E. T. (*hon. maj.* 24June11)	24June96	Crook, A., *hon. lt.*	11Oct.05
Duff, J. C. (*hon. maj.* 5Apr.14)	5Apr.99	Betts, J., *hon. lt.*	3Apr.07
Bankes, E. (*hon. capt.* 29Nov.00)	16Aug.99	Oborn, J., *hon. lt.*	18Dec.07
Grimbly, F. J. (*hon. capt.* 20 *June* 10)	20June00		

BANDMASTER.

Ferguson, F., *2nd Lt. in Army* 14Oct.08

UNEMPLOYED OFFICERS ON THE ACTIVE LIST.

COLONELS AND BREVET-COLONELS.

(Arranged according to date of being placed on half-pay.)

Name.	Half-Pay	Colonel.	Name.	Half-Pay	Colonel.	Name.	Half-Pay	Colonel.
Nicholson, J. S., C.B., C.M.G., D.S.O.	21Aug.05	16Feb.05	James, W.R,W., (late R.A.) g.	1Oct.13	6June12	Shute, C. D., p.s.c.	24Mar.14	2June13
Dyas, J. R., p.s.c. [l]	22Dec.09	22Dec.08	Wright, H. B, H. (late R.E.)	1Oct.13	6June12	Jackson, H. K., D.S.O. (late R.A.)	1Apr.14	5Aug.07
Scaife, H. B.	2Feb.11	19July11	Gilpin, F. C. A., C.B.(late A.S.C.)	15Oct.13	2July05			
V.C.Brown-Synge Hutchinson, E. D.	22Feb.11	29Nov.06	McGrigor, C. R., C.B., p.s.c. [l]	28Oct.13	30Dec.04	Everett, H. J., p.s.c. [l]	21Apr.14	16Dec.13
Blackden, L. S.	8July11	26July09						
Montagu, E., p.s.c. [L]	7Jan.12	4Oct.11	DuCane, H. J., C.B., M.V.O. (lateR.A.)p.s.c. [L]	29Nov.13	15Oct.05	O'Keeffe, M. W., M.D., (late R.A. M.C.)	23Apr.14	23Apr.10
Delmé-Radcliffe C., C.V.O., C.B., C.M.G., p.s.c. [L]	26Jan.12	8Mar.09	Daniell, F.F.W.	1Jan.14	2June13	Dawkins, C. T., C.M.G.,	27Apr.14	19Feb.07
Kent, H. V. (late R.E.)	22June12	19July11	Tudor, E. A. T. (late R.E.)	5Jan.14	30Oct.12	Young, J. R. (late R.E.)	4May14	4Dec.12
Thomson, A. G., C.B. (late R.E.)	18Sept.12	8Feb.05	Ryder, F. J.	8Jan.14	20Dec.11			
Du Boulay, N. W. H. (late R. A.) p.s.c.	25Nov.12	30Aug.01	Porter, R., M.B. (late R.A.,M.C.)	14Jan.14	14Jan.10	Pink, F.J., C.B., C.M.G., D.S.O., q.s.	14May14	16Nov.04
Smith, G. R. F., C.V.O., C.B., p.s.c.	1Jan.13	16Oct.05	Makins, E., D.S.O., p.s.c. [l]	2Feb.14	2June13	MacMahon, J.J. (late R.A.)	18May14	4Dec.12
Hobbs, P. E. F., C.M.G. (late A.S.C.)	12Jan.13	2Apr.06	Nugent, O. S.W., D.S.O., p.s.c. [l] A.D.C.	14Feb.14	23June09	Baldwin, A. H.,	1June14	4Oct.11
St.John G,F.W., C.B.(late R.A.)	29Jan.13	29Nov.06	Chichester, A. A., D.S.O., p.s.c.	19Feb.14	2June13	Hill, F. F., C.B., D.S.O.	25June14	14Sept.05
Parker, F. J.	15June13	4Dec.12	VanStraubenzee C.H.C.	24 Feb.14	2June13	Lumley, Hon. O. V. G. A.	27June14	10Feb.04
Fuller, R. W., D.S.O. (late R.A.)	15July13	11Sept.09	Haggard, H.	1Mar.14	2June13	Cooper, E. J., C.B., M.V.O., D.S.O.	30June14	28Nov.04
Boyle, R. C.	23July13	6Mar.13	Cayley, W. de S.	7Mar.14	2June13			
Gibbon, J. A. (late R.E.)	1Aug.13	7Mar.12	St.John, C.W R. (late R.E.)	9Mar.14	10Dec.07	O'Donnell, T.J D.S.O. (late R.A.,M.C.)	7July14	7July10
Reynolds, A. R. (late R.E.)	27Aug.13	7Mar.12	Maxwell, R. P.	11Mar.14	2June13	Armitage, E.B., C.B. (late R.A.) g.	18July14	8July05
Pery, C. C. J. (late R.E.)	1Sept.13	6June12	Peytor, W. E. C.V.O., C.B., D.S.O., p.s.c.	22Mar.14	5May05			
V.C. Phipps-Hornby, E. J., C.B. (late R.A.)	10Oct.13	22Mar.05				Short, A. H., (late R. A.)	—	30Aug.11

Unemployed Officers on the Active List—(*continued*).

(Arranged according to Seniority.)

LIEUTENANT-COLONELS.

Cordue, W. G. R. (*late R.E.*) 1June07
Radclyffe, C. E., *D.S.O.* 1Dec.09

Smith, R. A. 11Feb.10
Young, C. H. 22Mar.10

Dunlop, A. S. (*late R.A.*) *p.s.c.* [L] 19July11
White, E. D. 28Oct.11

Garsia, H.G.A., *D.S.O.*, A.S.C. [F] e.a. 2Feb.14

MAJORS.

Adam, W. A., *p.s.c.* [L] 19Feb.05
Graham, C. L. 13May05
Herbert, E. S. [F], e.a. 24May06
Raymond, H. E., e. [L] 3July07

Whishaw, E. R. [F] 1Jan.09
Smalley, H. D. 4Aug.09
Stanley, Hon. G. F., R.A., m.p. 5Jan.10
Drake, W. H., R.A. [F], e.a. 2Apr.10 bt. lt.-col. 14May12

Hewitt, E. P., R.A.M.C. 27Apr.10
Glossop, B. R. M. 6Aug.10
Wren, E. C. 2Oct.10
McCalmont, R. C. A., m.p. 19Nov.10

Penny, A. T., *M.V.O.* 24Mar.11
Sword, W. D. 4Nov.11
Sladen, C. St. B., R.E. 22July12
Stephens, F. A., R.A.M.C. 14Nov.12

CAPTAINS.

Tullibardine, J. G., *Marq. of*, *M.V.O.*, *D.S.O.*, m.p. 20Nov.99 bt. maj. 29Nov.00
Sharp, A. G. 9June00
O'Neill, *Hon.* A. E. B., m.p. 3Jan.02
Liddon, M. R. 21Jan.02
Knapp, C. A. 6Feb.02
Welsh, F. A. M. 20Apr.02

Lomer, C. J. McI. 4Aug.04
Dumaresq, H. W. 2Feb.05
Symes-Thompson, A. H., R.A. 23Jan.05
Lewin, C. M. 19June05
Hill, A. F. S., R.E. [L] 23Mar.06
Field, A. L. 1Oct.06

Roberts, D. W., R.A. 19Sept.07
Chadwick, R. S. 15Mar.08
Druce, V. P. 21June08
Heyworth, H.P.L. 11Sept.08
Milner, R. E. D. 12Sept.08
Sale-Hill, A. R. S. 6June09
Adams, G. C. 28July09
Bate, T. R. F., R.A. 30Mar.10

Palmer, B. O. 23July10
Lancaster, H. 13Mar.12
Duncan, H. A. 25May12
Sheppard, E. 1June12
Swinton, A. J., R.E. [l] 2June12
Leyland, R. H. 30Oct.13
Skelton, E. G. 12Nov.13

LIEUTENANTS.

Bosanquet, E. M., R.A. 3Apr.01
Lynch, F.J.E., R.A. 21Jan.02
Stevenson, G. E. de St. C. [L] 19Mar.04
Morgan, C. E. 1Oct.04
Tyler, G. M., R.A. 16July05
Hearle, F. J. 23May06
Arkwright, R.A. 8Sept.06

Gwatkin, R. T. 20Aug.07
Sweet-Escott, H. B., R.E. 25June08
Fawcett, E. H. 15Aug.08
Benton, I., R.A. 25July09
Wemyss, M. J., f.o. 30July09
Hervey, G. C. I. 11Dec.09
Dobson, G. W. [l] 23Apr.10

Ferguson, R. H. 9May10
Athill, L. F. I., R.A., c.o. 23July10
Shaw, G. C., R.A., c.o. 18Dec.10
Hudson, H. F. 1Apr.11
Douglas-Pennant, Hon. A. G, S., s. 24May11
Fraser, M. H., c.o. 19Sept.11

Miller, A. E., c.o. 14Feb.12
Acton, E. L. L. 1Mar.12
Blackett Ord, M. 10Apr.12
Snell, E. A. G., c.o. 20Nov.12
Butler, A. C. P. 28Jan.13
Murphy, C. F., c.o. 22Jan.14

2nd LIEUTENANTS.

Field, R. E. 18Sept.09
Kelly, J. C. 27Apr.10
Palmer, L. E. 4Mar.11
Hanbury-Williams, C. F. E. 22May12

RIDING-MASTER.

Thwaite, P., *hon. lt.* 10Oct.03

SURGEON-CAPTAIN.

Lupton, A.C., *M.B.* 28Jan01

ROYAL FLYING CORPS.

" Per Ardua ad Astra."

CENTRAL FLYING SCHOOL.

(Upavon, Salisbury Plain.)

(Rly. Stns., Pewsey, G.W.R. and Ludgershall, Mid. & S.W.R.)

Commandant	Paine, Capt. G. M., C.B., M.V.O., R.N.	15May12
Assistant Commandant (graded as Squadron Commander)	}Trenchard, Bt. Maj. H. M., C.B., D.S.O., R. Sc. Fus. ..{	23Sept.13 1Oct.12
Secretary	Lidderdale, Asst. Paymr. J. H., R.N. (Reserve, R. Naval Air Service)	15May12
Medical Officer	Lithgow, Capt. E. G. R., R.A.M.C.	
Quarter-Master	V⊕Kirby, Hon. Lt. F. H., Qr.-Mr.	20May12 hon. lt. 26Apr.12
Instructor in Meteorology	Dobson, G., Esq., M.A.	10Feb.13
Instructors in Flying	Gerrard, Sqn. Comdr. E. L., R.N. (Bt. Maj. R. Mar.) ..	15May12
	Shepherd, Sqn. Comdr. P. A., R.N.	5Dec.12
	Webb-Bowen, Capt. T. I., Bedf. R.	24June13
	MacLean, Capt. A. C. H., R.·Scots	18Dec.13
	Board, Capt. A. G., S. Wales Bord.	.. .. ..	1May14
Instructor in Theory and Construction ..	Breese, Flight Lt. C. D., R.N.	18Dec.13
Officer in charge of Transport (graded as Flight Commander)	}Wanklyn, Lt. F. A., R.A.	6Oct.13

Under Instruction.

Naval Wing (Royal Naval Air Service).

Borne in 'Pembroke.'

Hooper, Flight Lt. (actg.) G. W. W., R.N.
Bromet, Flight Lt. (actg.) G. R., R.N.
Tomkinson, Flight Lt. (actg.) L., R.N.
Smyth-Pigott, Flight Lt. (actg.) J. R. W., R N.

Barr, Flight Sub-Lt. (prob.) F. M. L., R.N.
Wanklyn, Flight Sub-Lt. (prob.) H. G., R.N.
Cripps, Flight Sub-Lt. (prob.) J. M. R., R.N.

Military Wing.

Pitcher, Capt. D. Le G., Ind. Army.
Wallace, Lt. (on prob.) G. P., S. Afr. Def. Forces.
Creed, Lt. (on prob.) G. S., S. Afr. Def. Forces.
van der Spuy, Lt. (on prob.) K. R., S. Afr. Def. Forces.
Emmett, Lt. (on prob.) E. C., S. Afr. Def. Forces.
Turner, Lt. (on prob.) B. H., S. Afr. Def. Forces.
Williams, Lt. (on prob.) M. S., S. Afr. Def. Forces.
Cockerell, 2nd Lt. (on prob.) S. P., R.F.C., Spec. Res.
Kinsman, Maj. G. R. V., R.F.A., g.
Kane, Capt. J. F. A., Devon R.
Heathcote, Capt. J. R. C., Cam'n Highrs.
Gaye, Capt. A. D., Bedf. R.
Landon, Capt. J. H. A., 4 Bn. Essex R.
Ellis, Capt. A. J., 3 Bn. S. Wales Bord.
Nixson, Capt. H. L., 3 Bn. R. Lanc. R.
Mansergh, Lt. W. G., Manch. R.
Ludlow-Hewitt, Lt. E. R., N. Ir. Rif.
Mayne, Lt. H. G. L., K.O. Sco. Bord.

Sanders, Lt. J. D. G., R.F.A.
Tennant, Lt. J. E., S. Gds.
Mills, Lt. G. D., Notts. & Derby R.
Kinnear, Lt. J. L., L'pool R.
Moore, Lt. B. F., R. War. R.
Rawson-Shaw, Lt. K., R.F.A.
Eberli, Lt. F. H., R.G.A.
Hawker, Lt. L. G., R.E.
McDonald, Lt. C. Y., Sea. Highrs.
Cunningham, Lt. J. A., R.F.A.
Graves, Lt. E. P., R.F.A.
Carpenter, Lt. G. G., Suff R.
Leighton, Lt. J. B. T., S. Gds.
Morgan, Lt. A. E., 6 Bn. R. Fus.
Hanlon, 2nd Lt. D. R., R.G.A.
Lawrence, 2nd Lt. G. A. K., R.F.A.
Smith, 2nd Lt. S. W., R.F.A., Spec. Res.
Skene, 2nd Lt. R. R. R.F.C., Spec Res.

ROYAL FLYING CORPS—contd.

NAVAL WING (ROYAL NAVAL AIR SERVICE).

(Borne on Books of H.M.S. ' Pembroke.')

Central Air Office—
Scarlett, Wing Comdr. F. R., R.N. Inspecting Captain of Air Craft (temp.)		23Dec.13
Owen, Capt. P., R. Mar. (temp.)		23Dec.13
Lenn, Fleet Paymr. F., R.N.		7May 13
Robinson, Asst. Paymr. A. A. E., R.N.		7May 13
McKean, Asst. Paymr. L. D., R.N.		7May 13

For Armament Duties with Aircraft.

Squadron Commander Clark-Hall, R. H., R.N. 22Mar.13

For Wireless Telegraphy Duties with Aircraft.

Flight Commander .. Ireland, de C. W. P., R.N. 14Aug.13

For Navigating Duties with Aircraft.

Flight Commander .. Crocker, W. R., R.N." 30June13

For Torpedo Duties with Aircraft.

Flight Lieutenant .. Hyde-Thomson, D. H., R.N. 13June14

For Meteorological Duties with Aircraft

Dunboyne, Capt. FitzW. G. P., Lord, R.N.(ret.) 3Nov.13

For Overseeing Duties with Airships.

Squadron Commander *Randall, C. R. J. (at Works of Messrs. Vickers, Ltd., Barrow) 18Dec.13
Flight Lieutenant *Cave-Browne-Cave, T. R. (at Works of Sir W.G. Armstrong, Whitworth & Co.,
Newcastle-on-Tyne) 18Dec.13

* Borne in 'President.'

Naval Flying School, Eastchurch—
Staff—
Wing Commander Samson, C. R., R.N.,		Officer Commanding	1Apr.12
Squadron Commanders { Briggs, E. F., R.N. (For Machinery and Overseeing Duties)			21May12
{ Courtney, I. T., R.N., Lt. (temp. Capt.), R. Mar.			5Dec.12
Flight Lieutenants { Osmond, E., R.N.			1Jan.14
{ Dalrymple-Clark, I. H. W. S., R.N.			5May14
Warrant Officers (2nd grade) { Brownridge, J. J., R.N. (For Repair Work)			3Apr.13
{ Floyd,W. F., R.N.			15May13
Staff Surgeon .. Wells, H. V., R.N.			20Feb.12

Attached to Naval Flying School.
	Vernon, H. D., R.N.	17Apr.13
	Bowhill, F. W., R.N.	17Apr.13
Flight Lieutenants	Marix, R. L. G., R.N.	1Nov.12
	Littleton, H. A., R.N.	1Nov.12
	Finch Noyes, C. R., R.N.	13Aug.13
	Beevor, F.H., R.N. (2nd Lt. 18 Hrs , Spec. Res.)	3June14
Warrant Officer (1st grade) Ellison, W. H., R.N.		4June13

Isle of Grain Naval Air Station—
Squadron Commander Seddon, J. W., R.N. (In Command)	31Dec.12
Flight Commander Babington, J. T., R.N.	6May14
Gaskell, A. B., R.N. (Lent Central Flying Sch. as Asst. Instr.)	13Aug.13
Brodribb, F. G., R.N.	13Aug.13
Flight Lieutenants { Williamson, H. A., R.N.	5May14
Fowler, L. G. V., R.N.	17Dec.13
Cave Browne Cave, H. M., R.N.	28Apr.14
Staff Surgeon .. O'Hea, J., R.N.	11Aug.13

Attached to Isle of Grain Air Station.
	Collet, C. H., R.N. (Lt. R. Mar. Art.)	17Dec.13
	Robinson, C. E., R.N. (Lt. R.Mar.)	29Apr.14
	Cull, J. T., R.N.	29Apr.14
	Ash, B. D., R.N.	29Apr.14
Flight Lieutenants	Rainey, T. A., R.N.	1Jan.14
	Young, D. G., R.N.	1Jan.14
	Peirse, R. E. C., R.N. (Lent Central Flying Sch. as Asst. Instr.)	1Oct.13
	Draper, C., R.N.	29Apr.14
	Busk, H. A., R.N.	29Apr.14
	Newton-Clare, E. T., R.N.	29Apr.14
Warrant Officer (2nd grade) Jones, T. D., R.N.		1May13

(381—2)

ROYAL FLYING CORPS—*contd.*

NAVAL WING (ROYAL NAVAL AIR SERVICE)—*contd.*

Calshot Naval Air Station—
Squadron Commander..	Longmore, A. M., R.N. (*In Command*)	15Jan.14
Flight Commanders .. {	Travers, J. L., R.N.	29Mar.13
	Bigsworth, A, W., R.N.	15Aug.13
	Chambers, E. T. R., R.N.	5May14
Flight Lieutenants .. {	Miley, A. J., R.N.	2Oct.13
	Edmonds, C. H. K., R.N.	13Aug.13
	Grosvenor, *Lord* E. A., R.N.	6May14
Warrant Officers, 2nd grade {	Scarff, F. W., R.N.	—
	Hancock, W. A., R.N.	—Dec.13
Staff Surgeon	O'Connell, C. J., R.N.	27May14

Felixstowe Naval Air Station—
Squadron Commander..	Risk, C. E., R.N. (Capt. R. Mar.) (*In Command*)	15Apr.13
Flight Commander ..	Rathborne, C. E. H., R.N. (Capt. R. Mar.) [*l*] ..	15Aug.13
Flight Lieutenant	Nanson, E. R. C., R.N.	5May14
Warrant Officer, 2nd grade ..	Staddon, L. R., R.N.	24Mar.14

Yarmouth Naval Air Station—
Squadron Commanders {	Gregory, R., R.N.(*For Charge of Group*) ..	15Apr.13
	Courtney, C. L., R.N.	15Apr.13
Flight Lieutenants .. {	Fawcett, H., R.N. (Capt. R. Mar.)	18Aug.13
	Sitwell, W. G., R.N.	1Jan.14
	Bone, R. J., R.N.	5May14
Warrant Officer, 2nd grade..	Kershaw, R. H., R.N.	1Jan.14
	Bobbett, H. C., R.N. (*For charge of stores and maintenance duties*)	4Nov.13

Fort George Naval Air Station (Inverness-shire)—
Flight Commander	Oliver, D. A., R.N. (*In Command, temp.*)	15Jan.14
Flight Lieutenant	Ross, R. P., R.N.	15Aug.13

Dundee Naval Air Station—
Squadron Commander.. ..	Gordon, R., R.N., Capt. (*temp. Maj.*) R. Mar. (*In Command*) ..	15Aug.13
Flight Lieutenants .. {	Barnby, A. C., R.N. (Capt. R. Mar.)	28Nov.13
	Kilner, C. F., R.N. (Capt. R. Mar.) ..	5May14

Farnborough Naval Air Station—
Squadron Commander.. {	Woodcock, H. L., R.N. (*In Command, and for Naval Airship No. 4 in Command*)	29May14

Wing Commander ..	Maitland, A. M., R.N., Capt. (*temp. Lt.-Col.*) Essex R.	1July14
Squadron Commander..	Waterlow, C. M., R.N., Lt. (*temp. Capt.*) R.E. ..	1July14
Flight Commanders .. {	Pigot, R., R.N. (Capt. Rif. Brig.)	1July14
	Hetherington, T. G., R.N. (Lt. 18 Hrs.)	1July14
	Fletcher, J. N., R.N (Lt. R.E.)	1July14
	Boyle, *Hon.* J. D., R.N. (Lt. Rif. Brig.)	1July14
	Mackworth, J. D., R.N. (Lt. R. W. Surr, R.)	1July14

Warrant Officers, 2nd grade {	Everett, F., R.N.	30Jan.13
	Dearman, H., R.N.	23Apr.14
	King, C., R.N.	3May13
Paymaster	Michell, H. A., R.N.	22Jan.14

Under Instruction.
Flight Lieutenants .. {	Sparling, E. H., R.N.	11May14
	Lock, R. G., R.N.	11May14
	Cunningham, A. D., R.N.	11May14
	Dalgleish, J. W. O., R.N.	11May14
Flight Sub-Lieutenant	Corbett-Wilson, A., R.N. (*prob.*)	15Mar.14

Kingsnorth Naval Air Station—
Wing Commander .. {	Usborne, N. F., R.N.(*In Command, and for Naval Airship No. 3 in Command*)	1Apr.14
Flight Lieutenant ..	Hicks, W. C., R.N. (*For Naval Airship No. 3*)..	30June13
Warrant Officer, 2nd grade ..	Blundell, G. A. J., R.N.	29May14

For Special Service.
Squadron Commanders {	Boothby, F. L. M., R.N.	29May14
	Davies, Lt. R. B., R.N.	29May14

RESERVE, NAVAL WING.

Williams Freeman, Lt. F. A. P., R.N. ..	10Dec.12	Lidderdale, Asst. Paymr. J. H., R.N. ..	17Apr.13
Busteed, Sub-Lt. H. R., R.N.R.	4Oct.13		

ROYAL FLYING CORPS—contd.

MILITARY WING.

(Head-Quarters—South Farnborough.)

Officer Commanding and Officer in charge of Records	Sykes, Bt. Maj. (temp. Lt.-Col.) F. H., 15 Hrs., p.s.c. [l]	South Farnborough	{ 13May12 25Feb.11
Assistant to Officer in charge of Records	Burch, Maj. W. E. S., ret. pay (Res. of Off.)	.. ..	24June12

Recruit Depôt	.. ..	South Farnborough.	5th Squadron	Gosport.
Kite Section ..	.. ..	South Farnborough.	6th „ „ ..	South Farnborough.
1st Squadron ..	.. ..	South Farnborough.	7th „	South Farnborough.
2nd „ ..	.. ..	Montrose.	8th „	Not yet formed.
3rd „ ..	.. ..	Salisbury Plain.	Aircraft Park	South Farnborough.
4th „ ..	.. ..	Salisbury Plain.		

Squadron Commanders.

3 Brooke-Popham, Bt. Maj. H. R. M., Oxf. & Bucks. L.I., p.s.c.	20May12	5 Higgins, Maj. J. F, A., D.S.O., R A., g. ..	30May13
2 Burke, Bt. Maj. C. J., R. Ir. Regt... ..	20May12	7 Salmond, Bt. Maj. J. M., R. Lanc. R.	{ 31May13 12Nov.12
a.p.Carden, Capt. (temp. Maj.) A. D., R.E. ..	20May12	c.f.s.Webb-Bowen, Capt. T. I., Bedf. R. ..	24June13
4 Raleigh, Bt. Maj. G. H., Essex R. ..	{ 20Nov.12 1July12	6 Becke, Bt. Maj. J. H. W., Notts. & Derby R.	{ 1Feb.14 28Oct.12
Musgrave, Capt. (temp. Maj.) H., R.E., p.s.c. [L] (Hd.-Qrs.)	30Apr.13	1 Longcroft, Bt. Maj. C. A. H., Welsh R.	{ 1May14 20Nov.12

Flight Commanders.

r.d.Beor, Capt. B. R. W., R.A. ..	1July12	7 Cholmondeley, Lt. (temp. Capt.) R., Rif. Brig.	{ 1May14 19Jan.13
5 Conner, Lt. (temp. Capt.) D. G., R.A. ..	1July12		1May14
4 Reynolds, Lt. (temp. Capt.) H. R. P., R.E.	1July12	5 Carmichael, Lt. (temp. Capt.) G. I., R.A.	11Mar.13
3 Fox, Lt. (temp. Capt.) A. G., R.E. ..	{ 20Nov.12 13May12	6 Harvey, Lt. (temp. Capt.) E. G., Wilts. R.	{ 1May14 17Apr.13
k.s.Brabazon, Maj. Hon. C. M. P., I. Gds. ..	30May13	4 Soames, Lt. (temp. Capt.) A. H. L., 3 Hrs.	{ 1May14 17Apr.13
2 Dawes, Capt. G. W. P., R. Berks. R. ..	30May13	1 Holt, Lt. (temp. Capt.)F.V.,Oxf.&Bucks. L. I.	{ 1May14 17Apr.13
3 Herbert, Capt. P. L. W., Notts. & Derby R.	30May13		
c.f.s.Wanklyn, Lt. F. A., R.A.	6Oct.13		
c.f.s.MacLean, Capt. A. C. H., R. Scots	{ 18Dec.13 11Apr.13	7 Picton-Warlow, Capt. W., Welsh R. ..	{ 1May14 14Aug.13
4 Shephard, Capt. G. S., R. Fus. [l]	{ 1Jan.14 28Nov.12	2 Todd, Capt. G. E., Welsh R.	{ 1May14 14Aug.13
2 Waldron, Capt. F. F., 19 Hrs. ..	{ 1Jan.14 27Jan.13	1 Bourke, Capt. U. J. D.,Oxf.&Bucks.L.I.	{ 1May14 17Apr.13
c.f.s.Board, Capt. A. G., S. Wales Bord. ..	{ 1Mar.14 18Apr.13	3 Charlton, Capt. L. E. O., D.S.O.,Lan. Fus. p.s.c.	{ 1May14 28Apr.14

Flying Officers.

k.s.Porter, Lt. G. T., R.A.	13May12	r.d.Read, Lt. A.M., North'n R.	17Apr.13
4 Playfair, Lt. P. H. L., R.A.	28Nov.12	2 Dawes, Lt. L., Midd'x R.	17Apr.13
3 Wadham, 2nd Lt. V. H. N., Hamps. R.	6Dec.12	5 Small, Lt. F. G., Conn. Rang. ..	17Apr.13
6 Lawrence, Lt. W., 7 Bn. Essex R. ..	6Dec.12	5 Glanville, Lt. H. F., W.I.R.	17Apr.13
4 Atkinson, Lt. K. P., R.A...	11Jan.13	3 Conran, Lt. E. L., 2 Co. of Lond. Yeo. ..	17Apr.13
2 Martyn, Lt. R. B., Wilts. R. ..	14Jan.13	6 Roupell, 2nd Lt. N. S., R.F.C. Spec. Res.	17Apr.13
4 Allen, Lt. D. L., R. Ir. Fus. [l] ..	15Jan.13	3 Christie, Lt. A., R.A.	30Apr.13
k.s.Hubbard, 2ndLt. T.O'B.,R.F.C.,Spec.Res.	4Mar.13	4 Chinnery, Lt. E. F., C. Gds.	30Apr.13
3 Joubert de la Ferté, Lt. P. B., R.A. [L] ..	7Mar.13	5 Abercromby, Lt. R. O., R.F.C. Spec. Res.	13May13
4 Gould, Lt. C. G. S., R.A.	3Apr.13	2 Rodwell, Lt. R. M., W. York. R. ..	14Aug.13
k.s.James, Lt. B. T., R.E...	16Apr.13	4 Mulcahy-Morgan, Lt. T. W., R. Ir. Fus. ..	14Aug.13
5 Mellor, Capt. C., R.E. [l]	17Apr.13	5 Gill, Lt. N. J., R.A.	14Aug.13

(384)

ROYAL FLYING CORPS—contd.

MILITARY WING—contd.

Flying Officers—contd.

4 Mills, Lt. R. P., 5 Bn. R. Fus. 14Aug.13	2 Spence, Lt. C. B., R.A... .. .. ..28Apr.14
3 Shekleton, Lt. A., R. Muns. Fus. 14Aug.13	3 Read, Lt. W. R., 1 D.G. 28Apr.14
3 Fuller, 2nd Lt. E. N., R.F.C. Spec. Res. ..14Aug.13	2 Hartree, 2nd Lt. A, R.A. 3May14
5 Wilson, 2nd Lt. C.W., R.F.C. Spec. Res. ..14Aug.13	MacNeece, Lt. W. F., R.W. Kent R. .. —
4 Small, Lt. R. G. D., Leins. R. 9Sept.13	6 Burdett, Capt. A. S., York & Lanc. R.[L]. —
2 Noel, Lt. M. W., L'pool R. 11Sept.13	6 Murphy, Capt. C. F. De S., R. Berks. R. —
3 Birch, Lt. W. C. K., York R. 11Sept.13	2 Ross-Hume, Capt. A., Sco. Rif. .. —
2 Corballis, Lt. E. R. L., R. Dub. Fus. ..13Sept.13	4 Cox, Capt. G. H., 3 Bn. N. Staff. R. —
3 Pretyman, 2nd Lt. G. F., Som. L.I. ..15Sept.13	2 Bonham-Carter, Lt. I. M., North'd Fus. —
2 Harvey-Kelly, Lt. H. D., R. Ir. Regt. ..11Nov.13	2 Crosbie, Lt. D. S. K., Arg. & Suth'd
5 Grey, Capt. (*Hon. Lt. in Army*) R., War.	Highrs. —
R.H.A. 17Dec.13	7 Farie, Lt. C. A. G. L. H., High. L.I. —
Cogan, Lt. F. J. L., R.A. [L] 17Dec.13	3 Lindop, Lt. V. S. E., Leins. R. —
a.p.Lewis, Lt. D. S., R.E. 17Dec.13	6 Wellesley, Lt. Lord G., G. Gds. —
2 Lewis, Lt. R. E., W.I.R. 17Dec.13	a.p.Verney, Lt. R. H., A.S.C. .. —
4 Mitchell, Lt. W. G. S., High. L.I. ..17Dec.13	5 Bayly, Lt. C. G. G., R.E. —
5 Brock, Lt. H. Le M., R.War. R... ..17Dec.13	2 Holbrow, Lt. T. L. S., R.E. —
4 Hosking, Lt. C. G., R.A. 17Dec.13	3 Barratt, Lt. A. S., R.F.A. —
4 Mapplebeck, Lt. G. W., 4 Bn. L'pool R. ..17Dec.13	7 Broder, Lt. P. A., 5 Bn. Worc. R. —
2 Vaughan, Lt. R. M., N. Innis. Fus. ..18Dec.13	3 Cruikshank, Lt. G. L., 3 Bn. Gord. Highrs. —
5 Penn-Gaskell, Lt. L. Da C., 3 Bn. Norf. R. 26Feb.14	2 Malcolm, 2nd Lt. G. J., R.F.A. —
3 Stodart, 2nd Lt. D. E., R.F.C. Spec. Res. 5Feb.14	5 Rabagliati, 2nd Lt. C. E. C., Yorks. L.I... —
6 Humphreys, 2ndLt.G.N., R.F.C. Spec.Res. 26Feb.14	Russell, 2nd Lt. (*on prob.*) A. L., R.F.C.,
6 Marsh, Lt. A. C. E., R.A. 28Apr.14	Spec. Res. —
5 Borton, Lt. A. E., R. Highrs... .. ..28Apr.14	1 Thomson, 2nd Lt. (*on prob.*) A. A. B.,
6 Roche, Lt. H. J. A., R. Muns. Fus. ..28Apr.14	R.F.C., Spec. Res. —
7 Barton, Lt. R. J. F., R. Sc. Fus. 28Apr.14	5 Strange, 2nd Lt. (*on prob.* L. A., R.F.C.,
6 Freeman, Lt. W. R., Manch. R ..28Apr.14	Spec. Res. .. .. .. —
2 Mansfield, Lt. W. H. C., Shrops. L.I. ..28Apr.14	

Adjutant	Barrington-Kennett, Lt. B. H., G. Gds.	20May12
Officer in charge of Stores (graded as Flight Commander)	a.p.Beatty, Capt. W. D., R.E...	{ 8Aug.13 / 1June13 }
Officer in charge of Mechanical Transport (graded as Flight Commander)	a.p.Hynes, Lt. G. B., R.A.	{ 1Oct.13 / 13May12 }
Officer in charge of Workshops (graded as Flying Officer)	Verney, Lt. R. H., A.S.C.	16Mar.14
Quarter-Master	Pryce, Hon. Lt. W. J. D., Qr.-Mr.	20June12
		hon. lt. 20June12

RESERVE.

Flying Officers.

Henderson, Col. (*temp. Brig.-Gen.*) Sir D., K.C.B., D.S.O., p.s.c. (*Dir.-Gen. of Mil. Aeronautics*), ...21Sept.12	Hooper, Lt. A. F. A., N. Staff. R. .. 28Apr.14
	Stopford, Lt. G. B., R.A. .. .. —
	Binney, Lt. F. B., R.F.A. .. —
Cook, Lt.-Col. H. R., R.G.A. [L] 23June13	Worthington-Wilmer, Lt. H. F. M., R. Scots 28Apr.14
Cameron, Bt. Lt.-Col. N. J. G., Cam'n Highrs..	Bewes, Lt. R. C. H., L'pool R. 17Dec.13
p.s.c. 17Dec.13	Marks, Lt. C. H., Res. of Off. [l] 17Apr.13
Boyd-Moss, Bt. Maj. L. B., S. Staff. R. ..1May13	Smith, Lt. S. C. W., 3 Bn. E. Surr. R. ..22Jan.13
Ashmore, Maj. E. B., M.V.O., R.A., p.s.c. ..22Jan.13	Dobie, 2nd Lt. W. F. R., Gord. Highrs. ..28Apr.14
Forman, Maj. A. B., R.H.A. 14Aug.13	Bryan, 2nd Lt. L. A., S. Ir. Horse .. 29May14
Fulton, Maj. J. D. B., C.B., R.A. [L]	Bell, 2nd Lt. C. G., R.F.C. Spec. Res. .. 9Nov.12
(*Aeronautical Inspn. Dept.*) 17Dec.13	Smith-Barry, 2nd Lt. R. R., R.F.C., Spec.
Brancker, Maj. W. S., R.A., p.s.c., s. ..14Aug.13	Res. 2June13
Leighton, Maj. Sir B. B. M., Bt., Tp, West.	de Havilland, 2nd Lt. G., R.F.C. Spec. Res. 24Nov.12
& Cumb. Yeo.	Metford, 2nd Lt. L. S., R.F.C. Spec. Res. ..14Aug.13
Ellington, Capt. E. L., R.F.A., p.s.c. ..17Dec.13	Spratt, 2nd Lt. N. C., R.F.C. Spec. Res. ..25Mar.14
Salmond, Capt. W. G. H., R.A., p.s.c. [l] s. ..17Apr.13	Ware, 2nd Lt. D. C., R.F.C. Spec. Res. .. 28Apr.14
Prankland, Capt. T. H. C., R. Dub. Fus.,	Rickards, 2nd Lt. G.B., R.F.C., Spec. Res.
p.s.c.	(*Hon. Capt. in Army 21 Aug. 01*) ..14Aug.13
MacDonnell, Capt. H. C., R. Ir. Regt. 9Mar.14	Perry, 2nd Lt. E. W. C., R.F.C. Spec. Res. ..14Aug.13
Boger, Capt. R. A., R.E. 28Apr.14	Payze, 2nd Lt. (*on prob.*) A., R.F.C., Spec.
Tucker, Capt. F. St. G., Worc. R. 13Apr.14	Res. —
Griffith, Capt. G. M., R.G.A. 17Dec.13	Adams, 2nd Lt. (*on prob.*) F. P., R.F.C.,
Dowding, Capt. H. C. T., R.G.A., p.s.c. ..28Apr.14	Spec. Res. —
Unwin, Capt. E. P., R.A. 17Apr.13	Barrington-Kennett, 2nd Lt. V. A., R.F.C.,
Darbyshire, Capt. C., 4 Bn. Lan. Fus. (Capt. ret. pay) 4July14	Spec. Res. 14Aug.13

(385)

ROYAL FLYING CORPS—*contd.*

MILITARY WING—*contd.*

SPECIAL RESERVE.

2nd Lieutenants (on probation).

Charteris, R. L.	.. 17July12	Adams, F. P.	.. 13Aug.13
Davies, E. K.	.. 5Oct.12	Baumann, E. B.	.. 20Aug.13
Lerwill, F. W. H.	.. 25Jan.13	Paterson, R. R. O.	.. 20Aug.13
Hammond, J. J.	.. 26Feb.13	Strange, L. A.	.. 8Oct.13
Fuller, H. C.	.. 15Mar.13	Joubert de la Fertè, J. C.	.. 8Nov.13
Russell, A. L.	.. 14June13	Skene, R. R.	.. 15Nov.13
Thomson, A. A. B.	.. 25June13	Blake, M. B.	.. 3Dec.13
Hardman, W. L.	.. 26July13	Cockerell, S. P.	.. 3Jan.14
Payze, A.	.. 26July13	Howell, O. B.	.. 7Jan.14

AERONAUTICAL INSPECTION DEPARTMENT.

(Head-Quarters—South Farnborough.)

Chief Inspector	Fulton, Maj. J. D. B., *C.B.*, R.A. [L] *f.c.r.*	{ 17Dec.13 20May12
Inspector of Engines	Bagnall-Wild, Capt. R. K., Res. of Off.	.. 6Jan.14
Inspector of Aeroplanes	Cockburn, G. B., *Esq.*	{ 1July14 1Apr.14
Assistant Inspectors	{ Ellerton, A. S., *Esq.*	..22Dec.13
	{ Windsor, M., *Esq.*	.. 1May14

INDIAN CENTRAL FLYING SCHOOL.

(Sitapur.)

Commandant	Massy, Capt. S. D., 29 Punjabis	.. 1Dec.13
Instructors	⎧ Newall, Lt. C. L. N., 2 Gúrkha Rif.	.. 17Nov.13
	⎨ Reilly, Lt. H. L., 82 Punjabis	.. 28Dec.13
	⎩ Hoare, Capt. C. G., 39 Horse	.. 14Apr.14

CAVALRY.

1st Life Guards.

[*Hyde Park.*]

The Royal Arms.

"Dettingen,"
"Peninsula," "Waterloo,"
"Tel-el-Kebir," "Egypt, 1882,"
"Relief of Kimberley,"
"Paardeberg,"
"South Africa, 1899-1900."

Uniform, scarlet.
Facings, blue. *Plume*, white.
Agents—Messrs. Cox & Co.

Colonel-in-Chief.
THE KING.

Colonel.
Grenfell, Field-Marshal *Rt. Hon.*
F. W., Lord, *G.C.B., G.C.M.G.,*
Col. Comdt. K. R. Rif. C., *q.s.*
30Apr.07
10Apr.05

Lt.-Colonel. (1)
Cook, E. B., *M.V.O.*   11Nov.10
16Jan.09

Major. (1)
H. H. Adolphus C. A. A. E.
G. P. L. L., *Duke of Teck,*
G.C.B., G.C.V.O., C.M.G.
Personal A.D.C. to the King
(*Hon. Col.* 8 Bn. Lond. R.)
6Dec.06
bt. lt.-col. 11Nov.10

Majors. (2)
Cavendish, Lord J. S., *D.S.O.*
12Apr.11
Brassey, E. H., *M.V.O.* 21Oct.11

Captains. (6)
Darell, L. E. H. M.   16Sept.05
Stanley, *Hon.* A. F. 4Apr.06
Grosvenor, Lord H. W. 13May08
Wyndham, *Hon.* E. S. 10May11
Monckton-Arundell, *Hon.*
G.V.A.   21Oct.11
Mundy, G. E. M., *Adjt.* 10Nov.11
Hardy, L. H.   20Nov.12
Astor, J. J.   11Dec.13
Wyndham, *Hon.* E. H. 11Dec.13

Lieutenants. (8)
Leigh, J. C. G.   19July10
Butler, J. G. A.   15Feb.11
Caledon, E. J. D., *Earl of* 10May11
Foster, P. W. W.   10Nov.11
Smith, A. L. E.   22Oct.12
Sutton, *Sir* R. V., *Bt.* 20Nov.12
Spicer, A. N. F.   17Dec.13
Leyland, C. D.   7Feb.14

2nd Lieutenants. (3)

2nd Lieutenants (on prob.)
Denison, *Hon.* H. W. C. 3Dec.13
St. George, H. A. B.   4Jan.14

Adjt. Mundy, G. E. M., *capt.* 10Nov.11
R.M. Plumb, L. R., *hon. lt.* 6Jan.09
Q.M. Yeatman, C.   14May04
hon. capt. 14May14

Medical Officers.
Cowie, Surg.-Maj. R. M. 27Sept.11
Anderson, Surg.-Lt. E. D.
4Jun.13

Veterinary Officer.
Rees-Mogg, Vety.-Capt.
G. B. C.   3Aug.12
13Feb.12

Special Reserve.

Lieutenant.
Tweeddale, W.G.M., *Marq.*
of, late Lt. 1 L.G. 26Nov.08
16July10

2nd Life Guards.

[*Windsor.*]

The Royal Arms.

"Dettingen,"
"Peninsula," "Waterloo,"
"Tel-el-Kebir," "Egypt, 1882,"
"Relief of Kimberley,"
"Paardeberg,"
"South Africa, 1899-1900."

Uniform, scarlet.
Facings, blue. *Plume*, white.
Agents—Messrs. Cox & Co.

Colonel-in-Chief.
THE KING.

Colonel.
Dundonald, Lt.-Gen. D. M. B. B.
Earl of, K.C.B., K.C.V.O., ret.
pay (*Res. of Off.*) [R] 30Apr.07

Lt.-Colonel. (1)
Ferguson, A. F. H.   12Jan.11
12Jan.07

Major. (1)
Trotter, A. R., *M.V.O., D.S.O.*
12Jan.07
bt. lt.-col. 18Jan.11

Majors. (2)
H.S.H. Prince Alexander A. F.
W. A. G. *of* Teck, *G.C.B.,*
G.C.V.O., D.S.O. 12Jan.11
Dawnay, *Hon.* H., *D.S.O.,*
p.s.c. [F]   18Jan.11

Captains. (6)
Ashton, H. C. S.   19Feb.07

Cavalry.

2nd Life Guards—contd.

Captains—contd.

Gurney, T. C.	6Mar.09
Penn, F.	18Jan.10
Belper, A. H., *Lord*	2May10
Montgomerie, V. R.	4May10
Cuninghame, W. W. S.	24May12

Lieutenants. (8)

Pemberton, F. P. C.	21Feb.09
Hoare, A. S.	15Dec.09
t. Sinclair, *Sir* A.H.M.,*Bt.*	10June10
Montgomerie, *Hon.* F. C.	10June10
Menzies, S. G., *Adjt.*	2Aug.11
Murray-Smith, A.G.	4July12
Wallace, D. E.	4July12
Speed, E. J. L.	24Dec.13
Bethell, W. A. V.	24Dec.13
Beaumont,*Hon.*W. H. C.	3Apr.14

2nd Lieutenants. (3)

Fenwick-Palmer, R. G.	18Jan.13
Carlton, A. R. M.-S.-W., *Visct.*	22Jan.13

Adjt. Menzies, S. G., *lt.*	3Aug.13
R.M. Holderness, W.	4Dec.12
	16Dec.08
hon. capt.	16Dec.13
Q.M. Hidden, H., *hon. lt.*	24Aug.12

Director of Music.

Hall, C. W. H., *M.V.O., hon. lt.*   6June 14

Medical Officers.

Power, Surg.-Maj. J. H.	21Oct.03
Luxmoore, Surg.-Capt. E. J. H.	27Sept.11
	30Jan.08

Veterinary Officer.

Barry, Vety.-Maj. E. P. J., *F.R.C.V.S.*   5Dec.10

Royal Horse Guards.

(*The Blues.*)

[*Regent's Park.*]

The Royal Arms.

"Dettingen," "Warburg,"
"Beaumont," "Willems,"
"Peninsula," "Waterloo,"
"Tel-el-Kebir," "Egypt, 1882,"
"Relief of Kimberley,"
"Paardeberg,"
"South Africa, 1899-1900."

Uniform, blue.
Facings, scarlet. *Plume,* red.
Agents—Messrs. Cox & Co.

Colonel-in-Chief.

THE KING.

Colonel.

𝔙𝔈, 𝔈. 𝔐. Wood, Field-Marshal
Sir H. E., *G.C.B., G.C.M.G.,
p.s.c.* [R] *Constable of the
Tower of London.*   16Nov.07

Lt.-Colonel. (1)

Wilson, G. C., *M.V.O.*   7Oct.11
   7Oct.07

Major. (1)

FitzGerald, G. J., *M.V.O.* 16Jun.06
   bt. lt.-col. 7Oct.11

Majors. (2)

Crichton, H. W., *Visct., M.V.O., D.S.O.,* Eq.	7May10
Tweedmouth, D. C., *Lord, M.V.O., D.S.O.*	7Oct11
	12Aug.08

Captains. (6)

m,p, Castlereagh, *C.S.H., Visct., M.V.O.*	17Jan.10
	6Apr.04
Brassey, H. E.	28Sept.04

Captains—contd.

Pembroke and Montgomery, R., Earl of, *M.V.O.*	18Jan.06
FitzGerald, J. P. G. M.	4Apr.08
s. Howard-Vyse, R. G. H., *p.s.c.*	4Apr.08
Bowlby, G. V. S.	6May08
Innes-Ker, *Lord* A. R.	10May09
Gerard, F. J., *Lord*	12June09
Foster, A. W.	7Oct.11
Harrison, J. F.	10May12
Northampton, W. B., Marq. of, *Adjt.*	25Sept13

Lieutenants. (8)

s. Mackintosh, A. A.	5July08
Worsley, C. S., *Lord*	6Oct.08
Philipps, *Hon.* C. E. A.	30July09
Combe, H. C. S.	7Oct.11
Turnor, A. C.	25Nov.11
Heath, P. V.	13Apr.12
Sutherland-Leveson-Gower, *Lord* A. St. C.	26May12
Naylor-Leyland, G. V.	1Apr.14

2nd Lieutenants. (2)

Titchfield, W. A. H., *Marq. of*	16Mar.14
Fenwick, K. R. G.	25May14

2nd Lieutenant (*on prob.*)

Wilson, A. T. 22Apr.14

Adjt. Northampton, W. B., *Marq. of, capt.*	25Sept.13
R.M. Vaughan, C. G., *hon.lt.*	22Oct.13
Q.M. Harford, C. E., *hon. lt*	13Dec.05

Medical Officers.

Pares, Surg.-Maj. B.	17Feb.06
Bodington, Surg.-Capt. P. J., *M.B.*	1Mar.07
	14Nov.03

Veterinary Officer.

Pallin Vety.-Maj., W. A., *F.R.C.V.S.*   13Aug.13
   6Jan.12

| 392 | 393 | 394 |

Cavalry.

Colonels in charge of Records.

Dragoon Guards, Dragoons and Lancers, (and King Edward's Horse)	.. ..	Crole Wyndham, Col. W. G., *C.B.*, *p.s.c.*	*Canterbury* 1Feb.11
Assistant to Col. i/c Records..	..	Cordeaux, Maj. W. W., ret. pay (*Res of Off.*) (Hon. Lt.-Col. ret. Terr. Force.)	—
Hussars (and Irish Horse) ..	.. ..	Milner, Col. G. F., *D.S.O.*	*York* .. 27June14
Assistant to Col. i/c Records ..	..	Richardson, Hon. Capt. F., Qr.-Mr. ret. pay	.. 1July05

1st (King's) Dragoon Guards.

[*Lucknow.*]

Depôt—*Dunbar.*)

The Royal Cypher within the Garter.

"Blenheim," "Ramillies,"
"Oudenarde," "Malplaquet,"
"Dettingen," "Warburg,"
"Beaumont," "Waterloo,"
"Sevastopol," "Taku Forts,"
"Pekin, 1860," "South Africa,
1879," "South Africa, 1901-02."

Uniform, scarlet.
Facings, blue.   *Plume*, red.
Agents—Messrs. Cox & Co.

Colonel-in-Chief.
Field-Marshal *His Imperial Majesty* Francis Joseph I., *Emperor of* Austria *and King of* Hungary, *K.G.*   25Mar.96

Colonel.
Brownlow, Maj.-Gen. W. V., *C.B.*, ret. pay   13June08

Lt.-Colonel. (1)
Bell-Smyth, J. A., *p.s.c.*   14June14

Majors. (4)
Williams, H. J., (*Comdg. Depôt*)   14June06
Wickham, H. F.   14June10
Hunt, R. S.   31Mar.11
                      14July10
Rasbotham, D. A.   14June14

Captains. (5)
Turner, A. M., *Adjt.*   21Apr.06
*m.a.*Renton, W. G. F.   7Dec.06
Cheape, G. R. H.   1Jan.08

Captains—contd.
s.c. ₩₡Hore-Ruthven, *Hon.* A. G. A. [F]   11Apr.08
i.v. Appleton, H. M.   16May08
Spurrier, R. S.   9Apr.10
t. Cheape, L. St. C.   9Apr.10
Wienholt, E. A.   17Dec.12
Harvey, S. E.   3Dec.13
Cooper, W. R. F.   14June14

Lieutenants. (8)
Fleming, H. M.   6Nov.07
Hawkins, L. H.   18Feb.08
White, L. W.   25Mar.10
Alexander, L. W.   9Apr.10
Fox, R. G.   13May10
Sprot, E. W. H.   10Apr.13
Gladstone, T. H.   23Dec.13
f.c. Read, W. R.   14June14
Hatfeild, H. S.   14June14

2nd Lieutenants. (7)
Ward, B. M.   7Feb.12
Carleton-Smith, D, L. G.   7Feb.12
Card, F. W. F.   3Sept.12
Muir, W. H.   25Feb.14

Adjt. Turner, A. M. *capt.*   17Dec.12
Q.M. Wells, W. T. J.   12Sept.03
            hon. capt. 12Sept.13

Special Reserve.
Captain.
Brown, D. C., Capt. ret. pay   9Feb.10

Lieutenant.
Crossley, A. A.   6May10

2nd Dragoon Guards (Queen's Bays.)

[*Aldershot (for Dublin).*]

(Depôt—*Newport, Mon.*)

The Cypher of Queen Caroline within the Garter.

" *Pro Rege et Patria* "

"Warburg," "Willems,"
"Lucknow,"
"South Africa, 1901-02."

Uniform, scarlet.
Facings, buff.   *Plume*, black.

Agents—Messrs. Cox & Co.

Colonel.
₡. ₤, Seymour, Hon. Gen. *Sir* W. H., *K.C.B.*, ret. pay
            20Jan.94
            2Nov.83

Lt.-Colonel. (1)
Wilberforce, H. W.   1Apr.11

Majors. (4)
Browning, J.A.   5July11
Mathew-Lannowe, B. H.   29July11
Ing, G. H. A.   5Aug.11
Harman, A. E. W.   28Sept.11

Cavalry.

2nd Dragoon Guards—contd.

Captains. (3)

Springfield, G. P. O.	21Sept.04
Pinching, M. C. C.	3Apr.07
Stone, E.	27Nov.12
Chance, E. S., p.s.c. [l], Adjt.	25Dec.12 19Oct.12
Hall, H. W.	21June13

Lieutenants. (8)

Heydeman, C. A.	15Dec.09
Newton, R. G. M.	4June10
Champion de Crespigny, C. N.	12Nov.10
Vern in 1988	1Jan.06
d. Single, F. A.	25Nov.10
Milne, F. D. R.	29July11
Lamb, A. J. R.	13Oct.11
Walker, E.	8June12
McGrath, N. G. S.	9Oct.12
	21Feb.12
Bushell, C. H.	30June13

2nd Lieutenants. (5)

Cardew, H. D. St.G.	7Feb.12
Misa, V. H.	4Sept.12
Kingstone, J. J.	4Sept.12
Barnard, R. T.	5Feb.13

2nd Lieutenant (on prob.)

Paul, G.	4Mar.14

Adjt. Chance, E. S., capt. 4June13

Q.M. Boag, H. 17Jan.06
 27Feb.01
hon. capt. 27Feb.11

Special Reserve.

Captains.

Evans, D. H., *late Lt. 2 D.G.* (*Remount Service*)	8July11
Sloane, A. D., Capt. ret. pay	5Aug.11

Lieutenant.

Tapp, W. H., *late Lt. 2 D.G.*	1Dec.10 3July12

3rd (Prince of Wales's) Dragoon Guards.
[*Cairo*].

(Depôt—*Newport, Mon.*)

The Plume of the Prince of Wales.
The Rising Sun in second corner,
and the Red Dragon in the third corner.

"Blenheim," "Ramillies,"
"Oudenarde," "Malplaquet,"
"Warburg," "Beaumont,"
"Willems,"
"Talavera," "Albuhera,"
"Vittoria," "Peninsula,"
"Abyssinia,"
"South Africa, 1901-02."

Uniform, scarlet. *Facings*, yellow.
Plume, black and red.

Agents—Messrs. Holt & Co.

Colonel.

Talbot, Maj.-Gen. Hon. Sir R. A. J., K.C.B., ret. pay [R]	14June07

Lt.-Colonel, (1)

Smith-Bingham, O. B. B., D.S.O.	2July12

Majors. (4)

Lomer, R. E. McI.	21Dec.07
s. Burt, A.	10May11 22Aug.02
s. Weir, G. A., p.s.c.	2July12 18Oct.13
Mason, P. G.	14June13

Captains. (3)

s. Lascelles, E. ff. W.	10July04
Neville, T. V. T. T.	6Sept.09 3Jan.11 3Dec.04
t. Cliff, G. T.	8Apr.12
c.o. Gibbs, J. T.	3Apr.12

Captains—contd.

Owston, L. V., Adjt.	3Apr.12
Leslie, C. G.	22June12 18Feb.11
Kevill-Davies, G. R.	23June12
Stewart, P. D.	2Oct.12 1Jan.06

Lieutenants (7)

Joseph, U. E. C.	6Sept.09
Coles, E. R.	28Mar.11
More, N. McL.	28Mar.11
Elliott, G. R.	28Mar.11
Holt, H. P.	20Sept.11
Chapman, E. W.	26Nov.11
Talbot, H. R.	26Feb.13
	16Sept.12

2nd Lieutenants. (6)

Benton, G. K.	4Sept.12
Allen, R. B.	4Sept.12
Newton-Deakin, C. H.	22Jan.13

2nd Lieutenant (on prob.)

Grimshaw, H. A.	5June12
Adjt. Owston, L. V., capt.	20Sept.11
Q.M. Donald, J., hon. lt.	8Oct.13

Special Reserve.

Captains.

p.s. Hodgkinson, J. F. (a) (H) (q), p.v.c.	25May10 11Oct.06
Sadler, G. G., Capt. ret. pay	8Feb.11

Lieutenants.

Worthington, N. K., *late Lt. 3 D.G.*	26Jan.10
Kingham, T. S., *late Lt. 3 D.G*	24Sept.10
Wright, E.	5Mar.10

Cavalry.

4th (Royal Irish) Dragoon Guards.
[*Tidworth.*]
(Depôt—*Newport, Mon.*)

The Harp and Crown and the Star of the Order of St. Patrick.
"Peninsula," "Balaklava," "Sevastopol," "Tel-el-Kebir," "Egypt, 1882."

Uniform, scarlet.
Facings, blue. *Plume*, white.
Agents—Messrs. Holt & Co.

Colonel.
Bethune, Lt.-Gen. E. C., *C.V.O., C.B., p.s.c.* (*Dir. Gen. of the Terr. Force*) 24Nov.08

Lt.-Colonel. (1)
Mullens, R. L., *p.s.c.* [*l*] 5Aug.11

Majors. (4)
Solly-Flood, A., *D.S.O., p.s.c.* 19Aug.08
Bridges, G. T. M. *D.S.O., p.s.c.* [*l*] 19Aug.08
   22Aug.02
Hunter, C. F. 19Oct.13
Hutchison, R., *p.s.c.* 25Nov.13

Captains. (3)
Sewell, H. S. 25Sept.07
Gurney, H. E. 25Sept.07
Hornby, C. B. 10Oct.09
c.o. Carton de Wiart, A. 26Feb.10
Oldrey, R. J. B., *Adjt.* 21Jan.11
r. Dorman, E. M. 3Aug.12
t. Oppenheim, R. W. 3Aug.12
McGillycuddy, R. K. 3Aug.12
~~FitzGerald, G. H.~~ 25Nov.13

Lieutenants. (8)
v Gallaher, A. 26Feb.10
Aylmer, J. W. 26Oct.10
d. Hickman, Sir A. E., Bt. 11Mar.11
Sanderson, O. B. 3Aug.12
Darley, D. G. F. 18July13

2nd Lieutenants. (5)
Fetherstonhaugh, R. G. 19Jan.12
Pigeon, F. B. B. 4Sept.12
Holman, J. 17Sept.13
Gordon-Munro, R. 25Feb.14

Adjt. Oldrey, R. J. B., *capt.* 21Jan.14

R.M. Sanders, S. G. 6Dec.12
   hon. capt. 6Dec.12
Q.M. Dunham, F. A., *hon. lt.* 3Jan.14

Special Reserve.
Captain.
Wright, A., Lt. ret. pay 26Feb.13

2nd Lieutenant.
Elmslie, K. W. 12May09

5th (Princess Charlotte of Wales's) Dragoon Guards.
[*Aldershot.*]
(Depôt—*Dunbar.*)

"*Vestigia nulla retrorsum.*"
"Blenheim," "Ramillies," "Oudenarde," "Malplaquet," "Beaumont," "Salamanca," "Vittoria," "Toulouse," "Peninsula," "Balaklava," "Sevastopol," "Defence of Ladysmith," "South Africa, 1899-1902."

Uniform, scarlet.
Facings, dark green.
Plume, red and white.
Agents—Messrs. Cox & Co.

Colonel.
Marsland, Hon. Maj.-Gen. W. E.
ret. pay 12Dec.12

Lt.-Colonel. (1)
Ansell, G. K., *p.s.c., q.s.* 12Aug.11

Majors. (4)
Winwood, W. Q., *D.S.O.* 10Mar.04
Gage, M. F., *p.s.c., Mil. Attaché* 6Feb.09
   8Mar.07
s. Kearsley, R. H., *p.s.c.* 6Mar.12
Head, M. R. 3Aug.12

Captains. (4)
Black, M. A. 12Aug.07
Partridge, R. C. 23Jan.11
Pankhurst, H. E. 18Feb.11
Crawshay, M. 1Apr.11
Balfour, E. W. S., *Adjt.* 6Mar.12
Pleydell-Bouverie, H. 4Oct.13
Holland, J. E. D. 10June14
   4July08

Lieutenants. (8)
Lechmere, R. B. H. 11Mar.08
Williams, V. D. S. 6July10
d. Nettlefold, E. J. 18Feb.11
Winterbottom, A. D. 1Apr.11
Wiley, H. C. 6Mar.12
Martin, E. S. D. 18Nov.13

2nd Lieutenants. (6)
Sassoon, E. 7Feb.12
Mitchell, L. F. 20Sept.13
   18July13
Collier-Johnson, N. S. 24Dec.13
Adjt. Balfour, E. W. S., *capt.* 16July12
Q.M. Howlett, J. F., *hon. lt.* 24Oct.06

Special Reserve.
Lieutenant.
White, F. G. *late Lt.* 5 D.G. 23Jan.11
   12Nov.12

2nd Lieutenants.
Patteson, J. D. 9Apr.10
Nettlefold, J. H. 17July11
Williams, G. G. A. 6Sept.11
Hornsby, J. A. 24Feb.12
Wallace, E. G. (*on prob.*) 24Dec.13
Hill, H. M. (*on prob.*) 18Feb.14

6th Dragoon Guards (Carabiniers).
[*Canterbury.*]
(Depôt—*Newport, Mon.*)

"Blenheim," "Ramillies," "Oudenarde," "Malplaquet," "Warburg," "Willems," "Sevastopol," "Delhi, 1857," "Afghanistan, 1879-80," "Relief of Kimberley," "Paardeberg," "South Africa, 1899-1902."

Uniform, blue.
Facings, white. *Plume*, white.
Agents—Messrs. Cox & Co.

Allied Regiments of Union of South Africa Defence Forces.
1st Mtd. Rif. }
2nd Mtd. Rif. } (Natal Carabineers.)

Colonel.
Fryer, Lt.-Gen. *Sir* J., *K.C.B.*
ret. pay [R] 18Sept.02

Lt.-Colonel. (1)
Annesley, J. H. A., *D.S.O.* 1May13

Majors. (4)
Kirby, S. R., *p.s.c.* 14Oct.05
Home, W. G. 22Nov.05
   22Aug.02
Watson, W. E., *D.S.O.* 23Apr.10
Webster, S. W. 1May13

Captains. (3)
Sadler, H. 25July07
Rasch, F. C. 1May08
s. Knight, C. D. 6July08
Kennard, M. N. 1May13

Lieutenants. (8)
Kidd, J. N. 11Jan.05
Compton, P. H., *Adjt.* 13Aug.06
Kerans, P. M. A. 2July07
d. Blackburn, J. H. J. 6July08
Preston-Whyte, J. N. 28Apr.10
s. Anstruther, J. A. [*l*] 9Jan.12
Barnsley, R. M. 12Oct.13
Chanter, E. R. [*l*] 21Dec.12
Gower, J. R. 11Jan.13
Kirkley, E. St. B. 9May13

2nd Lieutenants. (5)
Gill, W. T. 17Sept.13
Barnard, V. H. 17Sept.13
Hunter, K. S. 2Dec.13

Adjt. Compton, P. H., *lt.* 28Apr.13

R.M. Lloyd, A. E. 27Aug.02
   20Feb.01
   hon. capt. 20Feb.11

Q.M. Haywood, A. N. 19Jan.10
   18Apr.01
   hon. capt. 18Apr.11

Cavalry.

7th (Princess Royal's) Dragoon Guards.
[*Secunderabad.*]
(Depôt—*Newport, Mon.*)
In the centre the Coronet of Her late Majesty the Empress and Queen Frederick of Germany and Prussia as Princess Royal of Great Britain and Ireland.

"Blenheim," "Ramillies," "Oudenarde," "Malplaquet," "Dettingen," "Warburg," "South Africa, 1846-7," "Tel-el-Kebir," "Egypt, 1882," "South Africa, 1900-02."

Uniform, scarlet.
Facings, black.
Plume, black and white.
Agents—Messrs. Cox & Co.

Colonel-in-Chief.

H.R.H. the Princess Royal.

Colonel.

Ewart, Maj.-Gen. *Sir* H. P., *Bt., G.C.V.O., K.C.B.*, ret. pay, Eq.   10Feb.09

Lt.-Colonel. (1)

Lempriere, H. A., *D.S.O., p.s.c., q.s.*   18Mar.11

Majors. (4)

Sparrow, R.   26Aug.03
Dyer, J. E. F.   6June03
             29Nov.00
Clay, B. G.   6Feb.09
        6Mar.07
Campbell, N. D. H. (*Comdg. Depôt*)   18Mar.11

Captains. (5)

Chappell, W. F.   1May03
t. Whetherly, W. S., *p.s.c.,* 15June03
Mansel, J. L.   4Mar.06
t. Lindsay, M. E.   6Apr.07
Greene, J.   9Nov.10
Watson, E. C.   9Nov.10

Captains—contd.

s. McCulloch, A. J., *p.s.c.* 12Mar.11
Cairnes, T. A. E.   22Apr.11
Montgomery, J. [*l*]   16Dec.11
                 18July08
Herapath, D. K, MacK. 10June14
                6Mar.12

Lieutenants. (8)

Wood, R. G. P.   20June08
Scott, F. J., *Adjt.*   4July08
c.o. Lane, C. W. T.   23Apr.09
Friend, A. L. T.   16Dec.11
Noble, R.   17Dec.11
Ansdell, R. C.   4June12
Busk, W. R.   18Sept.13
Roberts, R. G.   12Nov.13
Sanford, S. A.   18Feb.14

2nd Lieutenants. (7)

Mann, R. L.   3Sept.12
Mellor, J. S.   10Dec.13

Adjt. Scott, F. J., *lt.*   23Apr.12

R.M. Huxtable, A. E. V.   17June08
hon. capt.   17Jun.13

Q.M. Hiatt, A., *hon. lt.*   6June06

Special Reserve.

Captain..

p.s. Caillard, W. M. C. Du Q., 4July08
Capt. ret. pay (Q) (*H*)   25Apr.14

1st (Royal) Dragoons.
[*Potchefstroom (for Longmoor.)*]

(Depôt—*Dunbar.*)

The Crest of England within the Garter.

"*Spectemur agendo.*"
An Eagle.

"Tangier, 1662-80," "Dettingen," "Warburg," "Beaumont," "Willems," "Fuentes d'Onor," "Peninsula," "Waterloo," "Balaklava," "Sevastopol," "Relief of Ladysmith," "South Africa, 1899-1902."

Uniform, scarlet.
Facings, blue. *Plume*, black.
Agents—Messrs. Cox & Co.

Colonel-in-Chief.

Field-Marshal His Majesty William II., German Emperor, King of Prussia, K.G., G.C.V.O.   5May94

Colonel.

Lindley, Maj.-Gen. *Hon.* J. E., *p.s.c.*   22Mar.12

Lt.-Colonel. (1)

Steele, G. F.   2Feb.14

Majors. (4)

s. McNeile, H. D.   27Jan.09
m.p. Guest, Hon. C. H. C., *p.s.c.*
                   30June10
                   2Feb.10
Nairne, *Lord* C. M., *M.V.O.* [*l*] Eq.   30June10
Leighton, B. E. P.   4Apr.14

Captains. (3)

Dorington, T. P.   23Jan.05
Hardwick, P. E.   9Aug.05
s. Tomkinson, H. A.   22Dec.08
t. Hodgson, W. T.   27Jan.09
Tidswell, C. R.   1Apr.09

Cavalry.

Captains—contd.

t.	Irwin, T. S.	8Jan.10
d.	Chapman, A. H. D.	5Feb.10
	Charrington, A. C.	12Apr.10
s.	Atkinson, W. H. J. St. L.	17Oct.11
	Miles, E. W. T.	17Oct.11
	Houstoun, R., Adjt.	17Oct.11
e.a.	Cosens, G. P. L.	4Apr.14
t.	Turner, C. W.	4Apr.14
	Jump, H.	4Apr.14

Lieutenants. (7)

Wilson-Fitzgerald, F. W.	12Apr.10
Edwardes, G. D'A.	12June10
Grenfell, Hon. J. H. F.	6Oct.11
Waterhouse, A. W.	18Oct.11
Sclater-Booth, Hon. J. L. R.	13Aug.13
Leckie, J. H.	7Nov.13
Hewett, H. M. P.	4Apr.14

2nd Lieutenants. (6)

Swire, C. G. W.	4Feb.11
Pitt-Rivers, G. H. L. F.	19Jan.12
Williams Wynn, W.	19Jan.12
Browne, W. P.	17Sept.13
de Trafford, H. E. F.	24Jan14
Henderson, R. H. W.	25Feb.14

Adjt.	Houstoun, R., capt.	12Sept.11
Q.M.	Jones, T.	5Jan.09
		11Sept.01
	hon. capt.	11Sept.11

2nd Dragoons.
(Royal Scots Greys).

[York (for Edinburgh).]

(Depôt—Dunbar.)

The Thistle within the Circle and Motto of the Order of the Thistle.

"*Second to None.*"
An Eagle.
"Blenheim," "Ramillies,"
"Oudenarde," "Malplaquet,"
"Dettingen," "Warburg,"
"Willems," "Waterloo,"
"Balaklava," "Sevastopol,"
"Relief of Kimberley,"
"Paardeberg,"
"South Africa, 1899-1902."

Uniform, scarlet. *Facings*, blue. *Plume*, white.

Agents—Messrs. Cox & Co.

Colonel-in-Chief.

His Imperial Majesty Nicholas II. Emperor of Russia, K.G. 8Dec.94

Colonel.

C. Browne, Maj.-Gen. A. S. M., ret. pay	11July05
	2Mar.08

Lt.-Colonel. (1)

Bulkeley-Johnson, C. B. [F] 19Aug.11

Majors. (4)

Collins, W. F.	1Apr.03
Lawson, A., p.s.c., q.s.	9Jan.04
Seymour, A. G.	19Aug.11
Swetenham, F.	9Dec.11

Captains. (4)

Fordyce, R. D.	7Feb.02
Long, W., D.S.O.	23Apr.02
H.R.H. Prince A. F. P. A. of Connaught, K.G., K.T., G.C.V.O., Personal A.D.C. to the King	27Apr.07
	bt maj. 14Oct.13
Duguid-McCombie, W. McC.	23June09
t. Pickering F. A. U.	10Apr.11
Hardy, S. J., Adjt.	1Aug.11

Captains—contd.

Bonham, E. H., M.V.O.	6Oct.11
Laurie, P. R. (Priv. Sec. to Chief of the Impl Gen. Staff)	6Oct.11
t. Winch, A. B.	6Oct.11
Borwick, M.	6Oct.11
Estcourt, T. E.	4Nov.11
t. Readman, J. J.	4Nov.11
Hardy, E. J.	4Nov.11

Lieutenants. (8)

Ebrington, H. W., Visct.	25June10
d. Denison-Pender, H. D.	10Apr.11
Pigot-Moodie, G. F. A.	27June11
Leven and Melville, A. A., Earl of	5July11
Callander, W. H. B.	1Aug.11
St. Germans, J. G. C., Earl of	6Oct.11
Cornwallis, W. S.	19Aug.12
Bowlby, L. H. S.	28May13
Crabbe, J. G.	26Mar.14

2nd Lieutenants. (6)

Rodney, G. B. H. G., Lord	19Jan.12
Scott Robson, H. N.	7Feb.12
Galsford-St. Lawrence, C. H.	4Sept.12
Baillie, Sir G. G. S., Bt.	4Sept.12
Cooper, G. J. R.	28Sept.13
Compton, E. R. F.	28 Jan. 14

Adjt.	Hardy, S. J., capt.	1Aug.11
Q.M.	Ross, T. M., d.	20Feb.01
	hon. capt.	20Feb.11
	Coutts, D., hon. lt.	14June13

Special Reserve.

Captains.

×Sprot, M., late Lt. Res. of Off. (q) ⓢ (H)	26Oct.12
Johnstone, M. J. C. S., late Lt. Res. of Off. (H) ⓢ (Q)	4Jan.13

2nd Lieutenant.

Stevenson-Reece, G. M. [L] (*on prob.*) 13Sept.13

Cavalry.

3rd (King's Own) Hussars.

[Shorncliffe.]

(Depôt—Bristol.)

The White Horse within the Garter

"Nec aspera terrent."

"Dettingen," "Salamanca,"
"Vittoria," "Toulouse,"
"Peninsula," "Cabool, 1842,"
"Moodkee," "Ferozeshah,"
"Sobraon," "Chillianwallah,"
"Goojerat," "Punjaub,"
"South Africa, 1902."

Uniform, blue. Collars, scarlet.
Busby-bag, Garter blue.
Plume, white.
Agents—Messrs. Cox & Co.

Colonel.

s.	Byng, Maj.-Gen. Hon. J. H. G., C.B., M.V.O., p.s.c.	3May12

Lt.-Colonel. (1)

	Kennedy, A. A., p.s.c.	2Apr.13

Majors. (4)

	Willcox, W. T.	12Dec.06
	Clinch, H. W.	31Mar.11
		13July10
s.a.	Kelly, P. J. V. [F]	2Apr.13
	Combe, H.	3Dec.13

Captains. (3)

	Du Pre, F. J.	16Jan.08
c.o.	Burnside, F. R.	18July08
	Doble, J. J.	31Jan.11
t.	Tylden-Wright, W. R.	24Oct.11
	Watson, F. C., Adjt.	16Dec.11
		27Nov.06
	Olive, T. B.	2Mar.12
		20June03
	Grubb, R. R. de C.	12Jan.14

Lieutenants (8)

c.o.	~~Sherlock, G. L. E.~~	~~17Dec.08~~
	Bagnell, R. A.	9Feb.10
	Clarke, C. F.	27Apr.10
f.c.	Soames, A. H. L.	31Jan.11
	Leechman, C. B.	5Sept.11
	Petherick, J. C.	5Sept.11
	Bell, A. H. M.	6Sept.11
d.	MacCaw, G. H. [L]	3Aug.12
		4Aug.06
	Cliff, W. McC.	17Apr.13
	Whiston, L. F. H.	4Feb.14
	Eastwood, N. W.	3Apr.14

2nd Lieutenants. (5)

	Howard, Hon. D. S. P.	19Jan.12
	Eliot, J. H.	3Sept.13
	Taylor, D. P. B.	17Sept.13
	Huggins, C. L.	25Feb.14
Adjt.	Watson, F. C., capt.	12Jan.14
Q.M.	Clark, F. P., hon. lt.	15Nov.05

Special Reserve.

Captain.

	Atkinson, J. E., Lt. ret. pay (H) (Remount Service)	11Feb.14

Lieutenant.

	Turner, G. R., Lt. ret. pay (H) (Remount Service)	19Sept.08
		4Feb.14

2nd Lieutenant.

	Hole, S. J. M. (on prob.)	19July13
		1Mar.12

4th (Queen's Own) Hussars.

[Curragh.]

(Depôt—Dublin.)

"Mente et Manu."

"Dettingen," "Talavera,"
"Albuhera," "Salamanca,"
"Vittoria," "Toulouse,"
"Peninsula," "Ghuznee, 1889,"
"Affghanistan, 1889," "Alma,"
"Balaklava," "Inkerman,"
"Sevastopol."

Uniform, blue. Busby-bag, yellow.
Plume, scarlet.
Agents—Messrs. Cox & Co.

Colonel.

	Montgomery Moore, Gen. Sir A. G., K.C.B., ret. pay [R]	9July04
		4Jan.92

Lt.-Colonel. (1)

	Hogg, I. G., D.S.O., p.s.c.	13May13

Majors. (4)

s.	Watkin, H. G., p.s.c.	13May09
	Howell, P., p.s.c.	14May13
	Darley, J. E. C.	14June13
	Mockett, H. B.	16May14

Captains. (8)

t.	Bell, A. D.	19June08
t.	Neilson, W.	15Sept.09
t.	Steele, A. R.	22Jan.10
	Pragnell, T. W.	24Feb.12
	Stokes, A. V. W.	24Feb.12
t.	Laing, N. O.	1Mar.12
	Blood, B.	2Apr.13
		27July10
	Scott, H. S. L. [l]	1Mar.14
	Evans, H. K. D., Adjt.	19June14

Lieutenants. (8)

	North, K. C.	22Jan.10
	King, F.	28Oct.10
d.	Levita, F. E.	4Mar.11
c.o.	Austin, E.	3May11
	Bibby, J. D.	6June13
	Falkner, R. J. V.	22Jan.14
	Heyman, W. A. C.	6Feb.14

2nd Lieutenants. (5)

	Sword, J. H.	17Sept.13
	Lonsdale, J. R. McC.	17Sept.13
	Falkner, B. B.	27Jan.14
	Heinekey, G. A.	25Feb.14

2nd Lieutenant (on prob.)
Greville, G. G. F. ... 25May12

Adjt. Evans, H. K. D., capt. 19June14
Q.M. Burton, G. R., hon. lt. 22Oct.04

Special Reserve.

Lieutenants.

	Cripps, L. H., late Lt. 4 Hrs.	15Sept.09
		3May11
(p.s.)	Schuster, A. F. (H)	9July10
		11Aug.08
	Tichborne, Sir J. H. B. D., Bt., late Lt. 4 Hrs.	7Dec.10
		4Mar.14

2nd Lieutenant.

	Radclyffe, M. F.	4June13
	Henry, C. C. (on prob.)	7Feb.14

5th (Royal Irish) Lancers.

[*Dublin (for Aldershot*).]
(Depôt—*Woolwich*.)
The Harp and Crown.
" *Quis separabit.*"
"Blenheim," " Ramillies,"
"Oudenarde," " Malplaquet,"
"Suakin, 1885."
"Defence of Ladysmith,"
"South Africa, 1899-1902."

Uniform, blue. Facings, scarlet
Plume, green.
Agents—Messrs. Cox & Co.

Colonel.
Allenby, Maj.-Gen. E. H. H.,
C.B., p.s.c. [L] (*Inspr. of Cav.*) 3Feb.1?

Lt.-Colonel. (1)
Parker, A. 16Jan.1?

Majors. (4)
Jardine, J. B., D.S.O. [F] 2Nov.0?
s. Cape, H. A. 6Nov.0?
McTaggart, M. F. 22May0?
s.c. Chance, O. K. 16Jan.1?

Captains (3)
s. McClintock, A. G. 3July07
Maddick, H. 16Nov.07
Henley, Hon.A. M., p.s.c.
  (*Priv. Sec. to Sec. of State for War*) 16Nov.0?
t. Tyrrell, G. G. M. 16May0?
Cooper, H. A. 22May09
Jenings, H. C. 1Feb.1?
Vallance, V. de V. M. 15Jan.1?

Lieutenants. (8)
Robinson, B. W. 3July0?
Wordsworth, J. L. 16May0?
Juler, G. C. 24Mar.09
Macdougall, A. I., *Adjt.* 22May09
Alexander, Hon. H. C. 1Mar.1?
s. Wall, T. L. 14Sept.1?
Batten Pooll, J. A. 28Jan.1?
Ramsden, E. 1Feb.1?
Gordon-Dill, J. M. 13Mar.1?
Rice, J. A. T. 15Feb.13

2nd Lieutenants. (5)
Robinson, E. W. 9Dec.1?
Stringer, C. H. 7Feb.1?
Coulter, W. H. 7Feb.1?
Fowler, J. D. 3Sept.1?

Adjt. Macdougall, A. I., *lt.* 22May13
Q.M. Burridge,G. J., *hon. lt.* 27Nov.0?

Special Reserve.
Captain.
Sleigh, E. H., Capt. ret.
  pay (*H*) 15Feb.1?
  4Feb.14
2nd Lieutenant
Hay, Hon. I. J. L. 1?June09

6th (Inniskilling) Dragoons.

[*Muttra.*]
(Depôt—*Newport, Mon.*)

The Castle of Inniskilling, with the
St. George's Colours, and
the word "Inniskilling" underneath.
"Dettingen," " Warburg,"
"Willems," "Waterloo "
"Balaklava," " Sevastopol,"
"South Africa, 1899-1902."

Uniform, scarlet. Facings, primrose.
Plume, white.
Agents—Messrs. Cox & Co.

Allied Regiment of Canadian
Militia.
25th Brant Dragoons.
Brantford, Ontario.

Colonel-in-Chief.
Field-Marshal H.R.H. Arthur
W. P. A., *Duke of* Connaught
and Strathearn, K.G., K.T.,
K.P., G.C.B., G.C.S.I., G.C.M.G.,
G.C.I.E., G.C.V.O., Col. G. Gds.
and A.S.C., and Col.-in-
Chief High. L.I., R. Dub. Fus.
and Rif. Brig., *Personal A.D.C.
to the King* 2June97

Colonel.
Rimington, Maj.-Gen.
M.F., C.V.O., C.B., s. 17June12

Lt.-Colonel. (1)
Haig, N. W. 2July12

Majors. (4)
Paterson, E., D.S.O. 14Oct.05
Vincent, B., p.s.c. [F] 14Oct.08
Terrott, C. R. 12Aug 11
FitzGerald, E. A. 2July12

Captains. (5)
t. Nixon, F. B. 5May07
Ritson, R. G. 14Oct.08
  8Jan.07
Bridgewater, C. J. B. 9Aug.10
  22Jan.10
Herringham, G.W., p s.c. 9Mar.10

Captains—contd.
Magawly Cerati de
  Calry, V. A., *Adjt.* 24Mar.10
t. Moncrieff, A. R. 25June10
Fleury Teulon, C. A. 2July12
Bowen, E. C. 15July12
Burnham, G. Le R. 11Feb.13
Sassoon, S. J. 11Feb.13

Lieutenants. (8)
Brooke, J. A. 22Jan.10
Humfrey, J. C. 24Mar.10
Wootten, R. M. 29Mar.12
Barton, N. F. 2July12
Dudgeon, M. F. 31Aug.12
Rimington, R. G. W. 6Nov.12
Freer-Smith, D. F. 26Feb.13
Kemmis, W. D. O. 10May13

2nd Lieutenants. (7)
Dunne, A. S. 22Jan.13
Macintyre, D. I. 13Sept.13
Usher, J. T. 17Jan.14
  10Aug.12
Windham, A. W. G 24Jan.14
Cairnes, F. H. 24Jan.14
Graham, J. M. 10June14

2nd Lieutenant (*on prob.*)
Gascoigne, A. D. F. 10Jan.14

Adjt. Magawly Cerati de
  Calry, V. A., *capt.* 19Mar.12
R.M. Beale, G. H., *hon. lt.* 6May06
Q.M. Siddall, J. R., *d.* 16Aug.99
  hon. capt. 16Aug.09
Macpherson, W., *hon. lt.*
  25Nov.11

Cavalry.

7th (Queen's Own) Hussars.

[Bangalore.]

(Depôt—Bristol.)

The letters "Q.O." interlaced, within the Garter.
"Dettingen," "Warburg," "Beaumont," "Willems," "Orthes," "Peninsula," "Waterloo," "Lucknow," "South Africa, 1901-02."

Uniform, blue.
Busby-bag, scarlet. *Plume*, white.
Agents—Messrs. Cox & Co.

Colonel.

McCalmont, Maj.-Gen. *Sir H., K.C.B., C.V.O.* ret. pay [R]   13May07

Lt.-Colonel. (1)

Poore, R. M., *D.S.O.*   26June11

Majors. (4)

Norton, C. E. G.   8July03
Dalgety, H. B.   26Feb.08
s. Fryer, J.   12Feb.10
Rankin, C. H., *D.S.O.*   26June11

Captains. (5)

d. Leyland, F. B.   10Feb.06
s. Gibbs, W.   20Apr.07
s. Pollok, A. B.   1Nov.07
Paget-Tomlinson, W.   12Apr.10
s.c. Tollemache, Hon. D. P.   9Oct.11
t. Watson, A. C.   11Oct.11
t. Yeatherd, M. L.   14Mar.12
t. Bates, S. G.   11May12
Walker, P. L. E.   10Mar.13
Thornton, T. A.   9Aug.13
r. McCalmont, D. H. B.   9Aug.13
t. McMurrough Kavanagh, A. T.   1Nov.13
Bethell, H. K., *p.s.c.*   14Feb.14 / 24Dec.11
Thompson, *Sir* T. R.L., *Bt., p.s.c.*   18Feb.14 / 22Nov.08
Mason MacFarlane, C. W. [l]   21Mar.14
s. Colmore, H.   15July14 / 31Aug.12

Lieutenants. (8)

Breitmeyer, G. C. A.   22Mar.12
Weatherall, N. E.   11May12
Holland, V. E.   10Mar.13
Hill, G. D.   10Mar.13
Creagh, D. V.   11Mar.13
Hutchison, B. O.   9Aug.13
Evans, R.   1Nov.13
Chandos-Pole, G. R.   25May14

2nd Lieutenants. (7)

Scott, J. B.   3Sept.12
Hallowes, J. C.   17Sept.13
Prothero, R. J.   17Sept.13
Fullerton, R. A. D.   25Feb.14

2nd Lieutenants (on prob.)

Dixson, H. F.   26Oct.12
Fielden, G.   26Mar.13
Adjt.
R.M. Andrews, F. L., *hon.lt.* 18Sept.04
Q.M. Paterson, E. A., *hon.lt.* 30Aug.11

Special Reserve.

Captains.

Kelly, E. D. F., Capt. ret. pay   22Feb.11 / 11May12
Brassey, E. P., Capt. ret. pay (H)   26June11 / 21Mar.14
Cross, E. G. K., Capt. ret. pay   11Mar.13 / 9Aug.13
Meyrick, G. L. T. G., Capt. ret. pay   27Mar.13 / 26Nov.13

8th (King's Royal Irish) Hussars.

[Ambala]

(Depôt—Dublin.)

The Harp and Crown.

"*Pristinæ virtutis memores.*"

"Leswarree," "Hindoostan," "Alma," "Balaklava," "Inkerman," "Sevastopol." "Central India," "Afghanistan, 1879-80." "South Africa, 1900-02."

Uniform, blue.
Busby-bag, scarlet.
Plume, red and white.
Agents—Messrs. Cox & Co.

Colonel.

Mahon, Lt.-Gen. *Sir* B. T., *K.C.V.O., C.B., D.S.O.*   7Mar.10

Lt.-Colonel. (1)

Mussenden, F. W.   19Oct.13

Majors. (4)

McClellan, H. T.   6May05
Wormald, F. W., *D.S.O.* 10Feb.06
Mort, G. M. (*Comdg. Depôt*)   19Oct.09
Van der Byl, J.   19Oct.13

Captains. (5)

Ourell, A.   21July08
Ryder, *Hon.* R. N. D.   19Oct.09
Broadbent, E. R.   2Apr.10
Blakiston Houston, J. E.   2July10
Alexander, P. S.   10June11
Weldon, E. G.   16Oct.12
Cairnes, W. E. P.   3Dec.13
Adlercron, G. R. L., *Adjt.* 4Apr.14

Cavalry.

416

Lieutenants (8)

Regnart, N. S.	25June10
Lawrie, D. C. M.	29Nov.09 / 28Mar.11
Leech, J. C.	22Aug.11
Mulliner, A. R.	21Oct.11
Wathen, L. W. D.	3May12
Pope, D.	16Oct.12
Hornby, R. F.	2Dec.13

2nd Lieutenants. (7)

Atkinson-Willes, G. A.	7Dec.10
King, B. C.	4Feb.11
Baldwin, J. E. A.	9Sept.11
Rowley, G. S.	9Dec.11
Clifford, G. G. J.	5Feb.12
Kennedy, R. L.	5Feb.13
Staniland, E. A.	17Sept.13

Adjt. Adlercron, G.R.L. *capt.* 4Apr14
R.M. Turnbull, J., *hon. lt.* 17Jan.06
Q.M. Hampton, R. C., *d.* 24Jan.03
hon. capt. 24Jan.13
Burns, J., *hon. lt.* 27Jan.12

Special Reserve.

Captain.

Malet, H. C., Capt. ret. pay (Q) (H) 19Apr.10
2May14

417

9th (Queen's Royal Lancers.

[*Tidworth.*]
(Depôt—*Woolwich.*)

The Cypher of Queen Adelaide, reversed and interlaced, within the Garter.
"Peninsula," "Punniar," "Sobraon,"
"Chillianwallah," "Goojerat,"
"Punjaub," "Delhi, 1857,"
"Lucknow," "Charasiah," "Kabul, 1879," "Kandahar, 1880,"
"Afghanistan, 1878-80,"
"Modder River,"
"Relief of Kimberley,"
"Paardeberg,"
"South Africa, 1899-1902."

Uniform, blue.
Facings, scarlet.
Plume, black and white.
Agents—Messrs. Cox & Co.

Colonel.

Bushman, Maj.-Gen. *Sir* H. A., K.C.B., ret. pay [R] 8Aug.00

Lt.-Colonel. (1)

Campbell, D. G. M. 15Mar.12
Majors. (4)
Beale-Browne, D. J. E. 25Apr.06
Brooke, V. R., C.I.E., D.S.O., p.s.c. [L] [F] 6Feb.07
7June05
s. Durand, H. M., *p.s.c.* 15Mar.08
Abadie, E. H. E., D.S.O., p.s.c. 15Mar.12

Captains. (3).

s. Cavendish, F. W. L. S. H., p.s.c. 1May04
s.s. Sadleir-Jackson, L. W. de V., D.S.O. 14Dec.04
Cobden, G. G. 18Sept.05
Lucas-Tooth, D. K. L. 22Jan.10
Brocklebank, R. H. R. 11May10
Grenfell, F. O. [l] 7Sept.12
Edwards, A. N. 7Sept.12
Porter, J. G. 1Nov.12

418

Captains—contd.

Nash-Wortham, B. C. D.	23Apr.13
Court, W. H. R.	20Mar.09 / 23Apr.13
Reynolds, G. F., *Adjt.*	14Jan.14

Lieutenants. (8)

s. Graham, A. C. D.	8Dec.10
d. Bovill, A. C. S.	12Dec.10
s. Benson, R. L.	28Sept.11
Phipps-Hornby, G. H.	8May12
	1Apr.11
Peek, R. G.	7Sept.12
Diggle, L. W.	1Nov.12
Allfrey, F. de V. B.	29Jan.13
Crossley, F. S.	23Apr.13
Straker, J. A.	30Apr.13
Harvey, F. L.	6Oct.13

2nd Lieutenants. (5)

Taylor-Whitehead, H.C.	9Sept.11
Norman, C. W.	19Jan.12
Marden, B. J. N. [l]	4Sept.12
Garstin, C. W. N. [l]	5Feb.13
Taylor-Whitehead, G. E.	3Sept.13
Smith, E. C. E.	17Sept.13
Mather-Jackson, H.	25Feb.14

Adjt. Reynolds, G. F., *capt.* 14Jan.14
R.M. Kemple, J. H. 25Oct.01
20Feb.02
hon. capt. 20Feb.11
Q.M. Letts, W. A., *hon. lt.* 3Aug.12

Special Reserve.

Captain.

Wood, H.F., Capt.ret.pay 18Oct.11

Lieutenants.

Hume, E. K. 24Oct.13

2nd Lieutenants.

Hoffnung-Goldsmid, C. J. (*on prob.*) 23Apr.13
Harvey, D. L. (*on prob.*) 16May14

Cavalry.

10th (Prince of Wales's Own Royal) Hussars.

[Potchefstroom.]

(Depôt—Scarborough.)

The Plume of the Prince of Wales; the Rising Sun; and the Red Dragon.

"Warburg,"
"Peninsula," "Waterloo,"
"Sevastopol," "Ali Masjid,"
"Afghanistan, 1878-79,"
"Egypt, 1884,"
"Relief of Kimberley,"
"Paardeberg,"
"South Africa, 1899-1902."

Uniform, blue.
Busby-bag, scarlet.
Plume, black and white.
Agents—Messrs. Cox & Co.

Colonel-in-Chief.

THE KING.

Colonel.

Downe, Hon. Maj.-Gen. H. R., Visct., K.C.V.O., C.B., C.I.E., ret. pay [R] 22Nov.12

Lt.-Colonel. (1)

Barnes, R. W. R., D.S.O. 4Feb.11

Majors. (4)

Shearman, E. R. A., p.s.c. 12July05
Crichton, C. W. H. (Comdg. Depôt) 4May07
Cadogan, Hon. W. G. S., M.V.O (Equerry to H.R.H. the Prince of Wales, 13 Sept. 12) 14Jan.11
Mitford, Hon. C. B. O. 7Aug.12

Captains (8)

s.c.	Kearsey, A. H. C., D.S.O.	22Feb.05 12Mar.04
s.	Annesley, Hon. A.	9Oct.09 6Apr.07
	Rose, Sir F. S., Bt.	4May07
	Gibbs, W. O.	5Oct.07
t.	Williams, E. H. W.	7May08
	Peto, C. H.	17Sept.10
r.l.	Neilson, J. F.	3May11
	Palmes, E. W. E.	14Mar.12
s.	Palmer, W. L.	17Apr.12
	Fielden, E. A.	7Apr.13
	Stewart, G. C., Adjt.	7Apr.13
	de Tuyll, M. A.	1Jan.14

Lieutenants. (7)

	Gosling, G. E.	18Dec.09
	Turnor, C. R.	17Sept.10
	Brocklehurst, H. C.	3May11
	Gordon Canning, R. C.	14Mar.12
	Greenwood, V. J.	17Apr.12
	Stokes, V. A. P.	7Apr.13
	Armstrong, W. M.	1Jan.14

2nd Lieutenants. (6)

	Brooke, Sir B. S., Bt.	4Jan.11 26Sept.08
	Airlie, D. L. G. W., Earl of	4Sept.12
	Drake, R. F.	4Sept.12
	Murland, W. S.	22Feb.13
	Thomas, R. H. C.	17Sept.13
	Chesham, J. C., Lord	25Feb.14
	Adjt. Stewart, G. C., capt.	10June12
	R.M.Littlewood, W. P.	25Oct.02
	hon. capt.	25Oct.12
	Q.M.Druce, W. hon. lt.	4Jun.13

11th (Prince Albert's Own) Hussars.

[Aldershot.]

(Depôt—Dublin.)

The Crest and Motto of the late Prince Consort.
The Sphinx superscribed "Egypt."
"Warburg," "Beaumont,"
"Willems," "Salamanca,"
"Peninsula," "Waterloo,"
"Bhurtpore," "Alma," "Balaklava,"
"Inkerman," "Sevastopol."

Uniform, blue. Overalls, crimson.
Busby-bag, crimson.
Plume, crimson and white.
Agents—Messrs. Cox & Co.

Colonel-in-Chief.

His Imperial and Royal Highness Frederick William Victor Augustus Ernest, Crown Prince of the German Empire and of Prussia, K.G. 15May11

Colonel.

C. Lyttelton-Annesley, Lt.-Gen. Sir A. L., K.C.V.O., ret.pay[R] 2Apr.02
12Feb.96

Lt.-Colonel. (1)

Pitman, T. T. 29Sept.12

Majors. (4)

	Anderson, R.J.P., D.S.O.	13June08
s.	FitzGerald, P.D., D.S.O., p.s.c. [l]	23Dec.08
	Lockett, W. J., D.S.O.	4Dec.09 8Jan.08
s.	Home, A. F., p.s.c.	3June14

Captains. (8)

s.	Rome, C. S.	18Mar.05
	Halliday, J. A.	18Mar.05
	Rome, C. L.	18Mar.05
s.c.	Paget, A.E.S.L., M.V.O.	22Jan.09
	Lawson, A. B.	22Feb.09
	Sutton, F. H.	16Apr.09
t.	Blakiston-Houston, J.	16Sept.09
	Stewart-Richardson, R. M.	2Nov.12

Cavalry.

12th (Prince of Wales's Royal) Lancers.

[Norwich.]

(Depôt—*Woolwich.*)

The Plume of the Prince of Wales; the Rising Sun; and the Red Dragon.

The Sphinx superscribed "Egypt." "Peninsula," "Waterloo," "South Africa, 1851-2-3," "Sevastopol," "Central India," "Relief of Kimberley," "Paardeberg," "South Africa, 1899-1902."

Uniform, blue.

Facings & Plume, scarlet.

Agents—Messrs. Cox & Co.

Allied Regiment of Canadian Militia.

12th Manitoba Dragoons.
Brandon, Manitoba.

Colonel.

Broadwood, Lt.-Gen. R. G., C.B., ret. pay (*Res. of Off.*) p.s.c. [R]		31Mar.09

Lt.-Colonel. (1)

Wormald, F.		22Aug.12

Majors. (4)

Crawley, E.		29July05
		29Nov.00
Bailey, P. J., *D.S.O.*		22Aug.08
Macnaghten, B.		6Jan.12
Fane, C., *D.S.O.*		28Sept.12

Captains. (3)

	Michell, J. C.		13Sept.05
			5Nov.02
t.	Murray, F. W. S.		27Nov.07
t.	Truman, C. M.		25Mar.08
r.	Reynolds, A. B.		22Aug.08

Lieutenants. (8)

	Arkwright, F. G. A.		27Nov.06
t.	Lowther, J. G.		22Jan.09
s.	Talbot, H. E.		22Feb.09
	Mulholland, Hon. C.H.G., *Adjt.*		16Apr.09
	Bannatyne, J. Fitz G.		14Aug.09
	Marshall, G. G.		16Sept.09
	White, *Hon.* L. H.		28Apr.10
	Spiers, E. L. [L]		2July10
	Peyton, A. T.		16Sept.10
d.	Ainsworth, J. S.		2Nov.12
	Drake, F. V.		31Jan.13
	Hudson, H. C. H.		23Feb.14

2nd Lieutenants. (5)

Bell-Irving, W. O.		7Feb.12
McMurrough Kavanagh, D.		22June12
Pelham, *Hon.* S. G.		19Nov.12
Moke Norrie, C. W.		5Feb.13
Jefferson, L. H.		3Sept.13
Tailby, G. W. A.		24Jan.14
Lumley, R. J.		25Feb.14
Adjt. Mulholland, *Hon.* C.H.G., *lt.*		1Jan.14

R.M. Morton, H. H.		23Nov.92
hon. maj.		23Nov.07
Q.M. Milson, E., *hon. lt.*		21Feb.06

Special Reserve.

Captains.

Lakin, M.L., Capt. ret. pay		23Dec.08
Cayzer, H. S., Capt. ret. pay (*H*)		22Jan.09
		4Mar.14
Bruce, *Hon.* R., Capt. ret. pay		2Mar.11
		3Dec.13
Baggallay, R. R. C., Capt. ret. pay		2Mar.11
		3Jan.14

2nd Lieutenant.

Curtis, A. R. W.		3June11
Parker, W. L. O. (*on prob.*)		25July14

Captains—contd.

	Badger, T. R., *Adjt.*		22Mar.05
e.a.	Maydon, H. C.		4Apr.05
t.	Kirby, W. L. C.		18Sept.09
t.	Wood, R. B.		10Mar.10
	Bell, W. B.		22May11
			29Jan.11

Lieutenants. (7)

	Bryant, C. E.		30May07
	Charrington, H. V. S.		11June07
	Nicholas, B. G.		20Dec.07
	Leatham, E. H.		22Aug.08
	Styles, W. R.		3Jan.09
	Wyndham-Quin, R. S. W. R.		22Mar.09
c.o.	Hornby, J. W.		15May09
	Richardson, D. C. H.		27Aug.10
			18Sept.09
d.	Davidson, P. G.		1Jan.14
	Eden, J.		25May14

2nd Lieutenants. (6)

Moore, R. S. T.		15Sept.09
Wernher, H. A.		25Sept.12
Boden, A. P.		4Jan.14
Spicer, F. F. F.		10June14
Adjt. Badger, T. R., *capt.*		12Feb.13
Q.M. Knop, H. B., *hon. lt.*		22Feb.05

Special Reserve.

2nd Lieutenants.

Leche, J. H., *late 2nd Lt.* 12 Lrs.		9June10
		18Feb.14
Brown, G. M.		28June11
Wroughton, M. C. (*on prob.*)		1Oct.13

Cavalry.

13th Hussars.
[*Meerut.*]
(Depôt—*Dublin.*)
"*Viret in Æternum.*"
"Albuhera," "Vittoria,"
"Orthes," "Toulouse," "Peninsula,"
"Waterloo," "Alma," "Balaklava,"
"Inkerman," "Sevastopol,"
"Relief of Ladysmith,"
"South Africa, 1899-1902."

Uniform, blue.   *Collars*, buff.
Busby-bag, buff.   *Plume*, white.
Agents—Messrs. Cox & Co.

Colonel.
Baden-Powell, Lt.-Gen.
 Sir R. S. S., K.C.B.,
 K.C.V.O., ret. pay(*Res.
 of Off.*) [R]   26Nov.11

Lt.-Colonel. (1)
Symons, A., p.s.c. [*l*]   1July13

Majors. (4)
Cox, R.F. (*Comdg. Depôt*) 6Nov.07
   17July05
Richardson, J. J.   4Dec.09
   28Mar.08
Twist, E. F.   28Sept.12
Marchant, T. H. S.   1July13

Captains. (5)
Eve, W. H.   5Apr.08
Carter, E. J.   3Feb.09
s. Hamilton-Grace, R. S.,
   p.s.c. [*l*]   5May09
   10June05
t. Kennard, W. A.   10Nov.09
   13Dec.06
t. Stocker, E. H.   23June09
s.c. Neill, N. [*l*]   13July10
Steele, C.   13July10
d. Hind, J. H.   25Sept.12
Robinson, S. O.   6Dec.13
Vanneck, W. C. A.   6Dec.13
Lumley, J. N., *Adjt.*   6Dec.13

Lieutenants. (8)
Newton, H. G. T.   13July10
Oakes, J. O.   13Aug.10
Jones, H. L.   8Oct.10
Sassoon, A. M.   25Sept.12
Kennedy, S. V.   1Feb.13
Dawson, J. V.   11Nov.13
Lawson-Smith, T. E.   6Dec.13
Jeffrey, J. A.   6Dec.13

2nd Lieutenants. (7)
Watson-Smyth, G. R.   9Sept.11
Gore, R.   5Feb.13
Kennedy, M C.   24Jan.14
Barrett, J. L. M.   25Feb.14

Adjt, Lumley, J. N., *capt.*   1Jan.13
Q.M. Cooke, A., *hon. lt.*   26Nov.10

14th (King's) Hussars
[*Mhow.*]
(Depôt—*Scarborough.*)
The Royal Crest within the Garter.
The Prussian Eagle.
"Douro," "Talavera," "Fuentes d'Onor," "Salamanca,"
"Vittoria," "Pyrenees,"
"Orthes," "Peninsula,"
"Chillianwallah," "Goojerat,"
"Punjaub,"
"Persia," "Central India,"
"Relief of Ladysmith,"
"South Africa, 1900-02."

Uniform, blue.
Busby-bag, yellow.
Plume, white.
Agents—Messrs. Cox & Co.

Colonel.
Combe, Maj.-Gen. B. A.,
  C.B., ret. pay [R]   9July04

Lt.-Colonel.
Stephen, R. C.   22Feb.13

Majors. (4)
s. Hill-Whitson, T. E. L., p.s.c.   6Aug.10
Applin, R. V. K., D.S.O.   3June11
Campbell, W. R., D.S.O. 21Mar.14
   22Feb.11
s.c. Browne, J. G.   3May12

Captains. (5)
d. Joicey, Hon. H. E.   30Apr.06
Hewitt, R. W.   30Apr.06
Secker, V. H.   14Dec.07
Bridges, E. J.   18Jan.08
t. Woodhouse, J. D. F.   6Apr.08
Astley, A. G. L.   22Aug.09
Mewburn, S. W. R.   6Aug.10
Bruce, T. R., *Adjt.*   1June11
Mocatta, V. E. [l]   17Nov.11
Mason, G. K. M.   3May12
Fotherstonhaugh, A. E. H.   24Dec.12
Hunter-Jones, L.   22Feb.13

Lieutenants. (8)
Darley, C. G.   22Aug.09
Ambler, M. J.   29Sept.09
Miller, J. A. T.   1June11
Pope, A. V.   2Nov.11
Fooks, O. J. F.   17Nov.11
Watson, G. N.   24Dec.12
Cropper, P. G.   22Feb.13
Moule, G. G.   26Nov.13

2nd Lieutenants. (7)
Hamer, G. M.   19Jan.12
Whidborne, C. S. L.   7Feb.13
St. Maur, R. W. M.   7Feb.13
Macintyre, F. P.   4Sept.13
deWend-Fenton, J. D. L. 8Dec.13
Deakin, C. G.   3Sept.13
Woodhouse, R. A. G.   17Sept.13

Adjt. Bruce, T. R., *capt.*   8Sept.13
Q.M. Pridgeon, A. F.,   16Jan.09
   hon. capt.   16Jan.11

15th (The King's) Hussars.
[*Longmoor, East Liss (for York).*]
(Depôt—*Bristol.*)
The Crest of England within the Garter.
"*Merebimur.*"
"Emsdorff."
"Villers-en-Cauchies,"
"Willems,"
"Egmont-op-Zee," "Sahagun,"
"Vittoria," "Peninsula,"
"Waterloo,"
"Afghanistan, 1878-80."

Uniform, blue.
Busby-bag & Plume, scarlet.
Agents—Messrs. Cox & Co.

Allied Regiment of Canadian Militia.

15th Light Horse.

Calgary, Alberta.

Colonel.
Luck, Gen. Sir G., G.C.B.,
 ret. pay [R]   11Dec.04

Lt.-Colonel. (1)
Tagart, H. A. L., D.S.O., p.s.c. [L]   10Oct.13

Majors. (4)
Bramwell, H. D.   17Aug.02
Hambro, P. O., p.s.c.   10Oct.07
Pilkington, F. C.   25Mar.11
s. Knowles, J., p.s.c. [l]   10Oct.11

Captains. (3)
Nugent, Hon. W. A.   19May00
Walker, O. B.   10Oct.08
Courage, A.   10Oct.08
t. Livingstone-Learmonth, N.
 J. C.   2July04
s. Barrett, F. W.   16Sept.05
d. Bingham, Hon. J. D. Y.   1July08
Nelson, C., e.   1Oct.08
f.c. Sykes, F. H., p.s.c. [l]   1Oct.08
   bt. maj. 3June13

Cavalry.

16th (The Queen's) Lancers.

[*Curragh.*]
(Depôt—*Woolwich.*)
The Cypher of Queen Charlotte, within the Garter.
"*Aut cursu, aut cominus armis.*"
"Beaumont," "Willems,"
"Talavera," "Fuentes d'Onor,"
"Salamanca," "Vittoria," "Nive,"
"Peninsula," "Waterloo,"
"Bhurtpore," "Ghuznee, 1839,"
"Affghanistan, 1839,"
"Maharajpore,"
"Aliwal," "Sobraon,"
"Relief of Kimberley,"
"Paardeberg,"
"South Africa, 1900-02."

Uniform, scarlet. *Facings*, blue. *Plume*, black. *Agents*—Messrs. Cox & Co.

Allied Regiment of Canadian Militia.

16th Light Horse.
Regina, Saskatchewan.

Colonel-in-Chief.
Gen. *His Majesty* Alfonso XIII, *King of* Spain, K.G., G.C.V.O.   8June05

Colonel.
Babington, Hon. Maj.-Gen. J. M., C.B., C.M.G., ret. pay,   20Aug.09

Lt.-Colonel. (1)
MacEwen, M. L.   19Dec.10

Majors. (4)
Macalpine-Leny, R. L., p.s.o. [†]   1Apr.08
Eccles, C. J.   9June09
Campbell, C. L. K.   27Nov.09
Harris-St. John, C. E. St. J., D.S.O.   19Dec.10

Captains. (3)
Neave, A.   1Apr.03
Bellville, G. E.   27Feb.04
c.o. Macarthur-Onslow, A.W. 29Sept.04
Adams, F. E.   27Nov.09
Shannon, W. J., *Adjt.*   11May14

Lieutenants. (7)

Wells, R. P.	25Oct.05
Pollok, R. V.	24Nov.06
Nicolson, F. A.	13Apr.07
Godman, J.	1June08
e.a. Whittle, C. H. S. [F]	19Dec.08
	26Apr.06
Osborne, B.	22Jan.09
Brace, H. F.	22Sept.11
Arnott, J., Adjt.	9Oct.11
Wheeler, J. B.	11Jan.12
Tylee, J. M.	22Nov.13
Stanhope, C. J. L.	1Apr.14

2nd Lieutenants. (6)

Hardinge, Hon. E. C.	9Sept.11
Liddell, C. H.	4Nov.11
Straker, G. H.	3Sept.12
Cubitt, A. G.	3Sept.13
Hoare, C. M.	24Dec.13
Rogerson, J. C.	25Feb.14
Adjt. Arnott, J., *lt.*	24Nov.12
R.M. Richer, F. A. (*Remount Service*)	26Oct.95
hon. maj.	26Oct.10
Q.M. Marsh, F. C., *hon. lt.*	4July06

Special Reserve.

Lieutenants.

Muir, M. A., Lt. ret. pay (H) ⓢ   15Feb 06
        22Nov.13
Bruen, H. A., *late Lt.* 15 Hrs.   1July08
        16 Apr.13

2nd Lieutenant.

Rouse-Boughton, E. H.   1Apr.13

Lieutenants. (8)

s. Howard, H.C.L. p.s.o.	3Sept.02
Beddington, E. H. L., p.s.o. [†]	13Aug.03
s. Brooke, G. F. H.	6Sept.06
t. Graham, M.	23May07
t. Copland-Griffiths, E.	15Jan.09
Nash, E. R.	15Jan.09
Cheyne, J. L.	15May09
Horn, T. L.	22Jan.10
d. Evans, H. L.	20Apr.10
	27July08
Beech, R. A. J.	25Jan.11
Tempest-Hicks, C.E.H.	21Feb.12
s.s. Loyd, R. L.	1Mar.13
Cross, D. R.	16Apr.13
Davies, R. G. R.	20May14

2nd Lieutenants. (5)

Clark, J. G. W.	13Sept.11
Allen, J. E. R.	19Jan.12
Ramsbottom Isherwood, L. C.	22May12
Adjt. Shannon, W. J., *capt.*	11May14
Q.M. Arls, C. J., *hon. lt.*	3Sept.08

Special Reserve.

Lieutenant.

Holmpatrick, H. W., *Lord, late* Lt. 16 Lrs. (H)   8Mar.09
        4July14

2nd Lieutenants.

Longridge, R. B.	14Dec.08
Macneill, W. M.	22Dec.09
	7Mar.07
Arbuthnot, M.A.	25July10

Cavalry.

17th (Duke of Cambridge's Own) Lancers

[*Sialkot.*]

(Depôt—*Woolwich.*)

Death's Head " *Or Glory.*"

" Alma," " Balaklava,"
" Inkerman," " Sevastopol,"
" Central India,"
" South Africa, 1879,"
" South Africa, 1900-02."

Uniform, blue.
Facings & Plume, white.
Agents—Messrs. Cox & Co.

Colonel.
s. Haig, Lt.-Gen. Sir D., K.C.B.,
  K.C.I.E., K.C.V.O., p.s.c.[R]
  A.D.C.   14May12

Lt.-Colonel. (1)
Tilney, W. A.   30Oct.11

Majors. (4)
Legard, D'A., p.s.c. [*l*]   11Oct.05
Carden, R. J. W.   30Oct.07
Fletcher, A. F.(*Comdg.Depôt*)
                              15May12
s. Fisher, B. D., p.s.c.   7Jan.14

Captains. (5)
Melvill, T. P.   27Jan.06
Bruce, R. W. V.   9May06
t. Talbot, D. H.   9May06
t. Lockett, V. N.   4Feb.07
Watt, D. Y., p.s.c.   23Dec.11
                              17Oct.08
Nutting, H. S.   14Aug.13
t. Sopper, E.   16Sept.13
Nicholls, M. G.   13Oct.13
Parbury, H. F.   15Apr.14
t. Platt, L. S.   15Apr.14
Boles, D. C., *Adjt.*   2May14
Turnor, H. B.   2May14

Lieutenants. (8)
Dubs, C. E. D.   2June11
Eckstein, H. F.   27June11
Plowden, H. R. H.   9Feb.12
s. Egerton, E. B.   23June13
Clements-Finnerty, H. 16Sept.13
Venn, E. N. L.   13Oct.13
Lacaita, F. C.   15Apr.14
Wynne-Jones, C. L.   2May14

2nd Lieutenants. (7)
Black, G. B.   24Oct.11
Fowler, R. St. L.   25Oct.11
Cornwallis, F. W. M.   19Jan.12
Butler, J. A. N.   4Sept.12
Hay, C. E. E.   5Nov.13
✻ Adjt. Boles, D. C., *capt.* 23Oct.11
R.M.Butler, J. H.   10Oct.03
                              hon. capt. 10Oct.11
Q.M.Callaghan, S.   16Apr.04
                              20Mar.01
                  hon. capt. 20Mar.11

18th (Queen Mary's Own) Hussars.

[*Tidworth (for Hounslow,*)]

(Depôt—*Scarborough.*)

" *Pro Rege, pro Lege, pro Patria conamur.*"

" Peninsula," " Waterloo,"
" Defence of Ladysmith,"
" South Africa, 1899-1902."

Uniform, blue.
Busby-bag, blue.
Plume, scarlet & white.
Agents—Messrs. Cox & Co.

Allied Regiment of Canadian Militia.

18th Mtd. Rif.

Portage la Prairie, Manitoba.

Colonel-in-Chief.

THE QUEEN.

Colonel.

Brabazon, Hon. Maj.-Gen. Sir
  J. P., K.C.B., C.V.O., ret.
  pay, q.s. [R]   10Nov.13

Lt.-Colonel. (1)
Burnett, C. K.   19Feb.14

Majors. (4)
Corbett, C. H.   19Nov.04
Leveson,C.H.,D.S.O.[F] 19Feb.06
s. Haag, E. C., p.s.c. [L]   19Feb.10
                              29Nov.00
Stewart, N. St. V. R.   19Feb.14

Captains. (3)
Thackwell, C. J., D.S.O. 27Aug.04
Bayford, E. H., D.S.O.   20Mar.06
m.c. Lyon, E. L.   20June09
Sopper, F. W.   7Nov.09
Jury, E. C., p.s.c.   7Nov.08
Wood, C. L.   22Dec.09
t. Malet, H. W.   19July11

Lieutenants. (8)
Waudby, C.   22July05
                              30May04
Neame, B., *Adjt.*   11May07
Holdsworth, W.   6June07
f.c. Hetherington, T. G.   20June09
d. Joynson, W.   22Dec.09
Cobb, J. W.   10Aug.10
Haslam, P. L. C.   24Mar.11
Denroche-Smith, A. J.   10Apr.12
Pilter, C.   26May12
Taylor, C. T.   18July13
Stobart, F. E.   20Aug.13

2nd Lieutenants. (5)
Lloyd, L. S.   19Jan.12
Nicholson, A. K.   22Jan.13
Summers, W. A.   25Feb.14
Taylor, E.   10June14
*Adjt.*Neame, B., *lt.*   20June12
R.M.Lawrence,T., *hon.lt.* 15Oct.04
Q.M.Dunkley, F. A., *d.*   2Jan.01
                hon. capt. 2Jan.11
Parsons, W. H., *hon. lt.*   5July11

Special Reserve.

Captains.

Anderson, G. H., Capt.
  ret. pay   8June12
✕Grigg, R. S., *late* Lt. 18
  Hrs. (H)   25Feb.14

Lieutenants.

Gore-Langton, G. W., *late*
  Lt. 18 Hrs.   27July10
                               5Mar.13

Waring, C.H.,*late* Lt.h.p.
  (*Remount Service*)   19July11
                              13Dec.13

2nd Lieutenants.

f.c. Beevor, C. F.   22Mar.11
Firth, G.   12Oct.12
                               1Apr.12

Cavalry.

19th (Queen Alexandra's Own Royal) Hussars.

[*Hounslow (for Tidworth.)*]
(Depôt—*Bristol*.)

The Elephant, superscribed "Assaye."
"Mysore," "Seringapatam,"
"Niagara,"
"Tel-el-Kebir,"
"Egypt, 1882-1884."
"Abu Klea,"
"Nile, 1884-85,"
"Defence of Ladysmith,"
"South Africa, 1899-1902."

Uniform, blue.
Busby-bag & Plume, white.
Agents—Messrs. Cox & Co.

Colonel-in-Chief.

QUEEN ALEXANDRA.

Colonel.

French, Field-Marshal *Sir* J. D. P., *G.C.B., G.C.V O., K.C.M.G.*, Col.-in-Chief R. Ir. Regt. [R] 14Feb.02

Lt.-Colonel. (1)

Greenly, W. H., *D.S.O., p.s.c.*[L] 6Jan.12

Majors. (4)

	Egerton, G. A.	1Apr.08
		22Aug.02
s.	Franks, G. D.	3Jan.08
	Parsons, A. W.	20Jan.12
	McClure, C. R.	14Mar.14

Captains. (3)

t.	Northen, E.	20Feb.07
	Tanner, H. O'S. F.	17Oct.08
	Platt, H. E. A.	1June12
c.o.	Lambart, G. E. O. F.	4Sept.12
t.	Bonham-Carter, G.	4Sept.12
	Macfarlane, H. E., *Adjt.*	17Feb.13
	Lyon, W. E.	14July13
t	Bailward, J.	1Mar.14
f.c	Waldron, F. F.	25June14
	Bullock Marsham, F.W.	25June14

Lieutenants. (8)

	Summers, A. S. M.	16July10
	Osborne, G.	28Mar.11
	Francis, J. C. W.	22Mar.12
	Bigge, H. J.	30Sept.12
	Bowden-Smith, P. E.	7Oct.12
	Settle, R. H. N. [*l*]	27Jan.13
d.	Davidson, E. G.	17Feb.13
	Bannatyne, E. J.	28Mar.14
	Hay, B. McE. A.	25June14

2nd Lieutenants. (5)

	Williams, J. G.	22Jan.13
	Bolitho, W. T. M.	24May13
	Murray, E. D.	17Sept.13
	Tremayne, C. H.	10June14
	Horne, W. G.	10June14
Adjt.	Macfarlane, H. E., *capt.*	14July13
Q.M.	Berrow, J., *d.*	2Aug.02
	hon. capt.	2Aug.12
	Bird, R. E., *hon. lt.*	6Aug.12

Special Reserve.

Captain.

Alexander, F. D., Capt. ret. pay ⓢ (*Remount Service*) 17Aug.10
 14Mar.14

2nd Lieutenant.

Codrington, C.W,G,H. 10Feb.12
 28Jan.14

20th Hussars.

[*Colchester.*]

(Depôt—*Scarborough*.)

"Vimiera,"
"Peninsula,"
"Suakin, 1885,"
"South Africa, 1901-02."

Uniform, blue.
Busby-bag, crimson.
Plume, yellow.
Agents—Messrs. Cox & Co.

Colonel.

Gough, Maj.-Gen. H. S., *C.B., C.M.G.*, ret. pay (*Res. of Off.*) [R] 31May10

Lt.-Colonel. (1)

Edwards, G. T. G. 9Sept.11

Majors. (4)

e.a.	Jennings Bramly, A. W. [F]	9Sept.11
	Cook, G. T. R.	18Oct.13
		6Sept.11
s.d	Cawley, J. S., p.s.c. (t)	14Mar.14
	Richardson, M. E.	20May14

Captains (3)

t.	Love, E. W. P.	5June09
	Little, A. C.	13Mar.11
	Cowlard, J. F.	15July11
t.	Hurndall, F. B.	15July11
	Sanford, G. A., *Adjt.*	9Sept.11
	Mangles, C. S.	16Oct.12
s.	Osborne, R. H.	14Jan.13
	Darling, J. C.	14June13
	Barne, S.	4Apr.14

Lieutenants. (8)

	Micholls, W. H. M.	21Apr.10
.{	Soames, H. M.	15July11
	Beech, D. C. M.	9Sept.11
d.	Silvertop, W. A.	16Oct.12
	Sparrow, R. W.	14Jan.13
	Bairstow, G. W. I.	22Mar.13
	Peploe, D. S.	14June13
	Hall, W. D'A.	20July13
	McConnel, J. K.	2Aug.13

2nd Lieutenants. (5)

	Thompson, R. M.	19Jan.12
	Galbraith, J. W. S.	3Sept.13
	Goodhart, J. H.	17Sept.13
	Upton, J. T.	17Sept.13
	Carew, F. L.	25Feb.14
Adjt.	Sanford, G. A., *capt.*	16Oct.12
Q.M.	Adams, W., *hon. lt.*	2Apr.13

Special Reserve

Lieutenant

Keyser, C. N., *late* Lt. 20 Hrs. 30Sept.10
 19July13

2nd Lieutenants.

Carr, A. W. (*on prob.*)	27Sept.13
Dodgson, H. C.(*on prob.*)	10Oct.13
Heap, G. T. (*on prob.*)	10Oct.13
Taylor, C. de W. (*on prob.*)	21Mar.14

(487)

Cavalry.

21st (Empress of India's) Lancers.

[Rawal Pindi (for Risalpur)]

(Depôt—Woolwich.)

"Khartoum."

Uniform, blue.

Facings, french grey.

Plume, white.

Agents—Messrs. Cox & Co.

Colonel.

Benson, Maj.-Gen. Sir F. W., K.C.B., ret. pay (Res. of Off.), p.s.c. [R]   2July09

Lt.-Colonel (1).

Smyth, R. N., D.S.O.   7Sept.10

Majors. (4)

Scriven, J. B.   7Oct.06
   2Aug.02
s. Fraser, H. F., e.   27Apr.07
Brinton. O. W.   7Sept.10
s. Cecil, R. E.   10Dec.13

Captains. (5)

Pilcher, A. S.   30Oct.01
Anderson, P. H. A.   16May06
Delmege, C. H.   14Sept.07
t. Wheler, G. B. H.   12Oct.07
Horsley, C. D.   1Nov.10
t. Lumley-Smith, T. G. L.   16Jan.12
Reynolds, G. N.   4Apr.12
d. Boyd-Rochfort, H.   4Apr.12
Godfree, D. W.   4Apr.12
Lister, C. C., Adjt.   1Oct.12
t. Gardner, G.   1Oct.12
Cotesworth, C. H.   4May14

Lieutenants. (8)

Learoyd, G. E. D.   20Sept.09
Evans, J. W. D.   1Nov.10
Methven, D. M.   1Oct.11
Howes, S.   16Jan.12
s.s. Blake, St. J. L. O'B. A. ff.   1Oct.12
Hollings, J. H. B.   1Oct.12
Purdey, J. A.   1Oct.12
Brierley, R. W.   4May14
Thompson, N. R.   May14

2nd Lieutenants. (7)

Holland, W. T. F.   4Sept.12
Payne Gallwey, P. F.   4Sept.12
de Pret, J. [L]   14Sept.12
Kekewich, S.   3Sept.13
Maybery, R. A.   17Sept.13
Sebag-Montefiore, G. E.   24Jan.14

2nd Lieutenant (on prob.)

Pigott, Sir B., Bt.   25Apr.14
Adjt.Lister, C. C., capt.   6July13
Q.M.Laughton, J. V., d.   18June04
   hon. capt. 18June14
Ward, R., hon.lt.   24Feb.12

DEPÔTS.

No. 1 (Eastern.)
Woolwich.

Maj. Fletcher, A. F., 17 Lrs.
Capt. Boyd-Rochfort, H., 21 Lrs.
Lt. Evans, H. L., 16 Lrs.
Lt. Bovill, A. C. S., 9 Lrs.
Lt. Davidson, P. G., 12 Lrs.
Qr.-Mr. Laughton, J. V., 21 Lrs., hon. capt.

No. 2 (Irish.)
Dublin.

Maj. Mort, G. M., 8 Hrs.
Capt. Hind, J H., 13 Hrs.
Lt. Levita, F E., 4 Hrs.
Lt. Ainsworth, J. S., 11 Hrs.
Qr.-Mr. Hampton, R. C., 8 Hrs., hon. capt.

No. 3 (Northern.)
Scarborough.

Maj. Crichton, C. W. H., 10 Hrs.
Capt. Joicey, Hon. H. E., 14 Hrs.
Lt. Joynson, W., 18 Hrs.
Lt. Silvertop, W. A., 20 Hrs.
Qr-Mr. Dunkley, F. A., 18 Hrs., hon. capt.

No. 4 (Western.)
Newport, Mon.

Maj. Campbell, N. D. H., 7 D.G.
Capt. Moncrieff, A. R., 6 Dns.
Lt. Single, F. A., 2 D.G.
Lt. Blackburn, J. H. J., 6 D.G.
Lt. Hickman, Sir A. E., Bt., 4 D.G.
Qr.-Mr. Siddall, J. R., 6 Dns., hon. capt.

No. 5 (Southern.)
Bristol.

Maj.
Capt. Leyland, F. B., 7 Hrs.
Capt. Bingham, Hon. J. D. Y. 15 Hrs.
Lt. McCaw, G. H., 3 Hrs.
Lt. Davidson, E. G., 19 Hrs.
Qr.-Mr. Berrow,J., 19 Hrs., hon. capt.

No. 6 (Scottish.)
Dunbar.

Maj. Williams, H. J., 1 D.G.
Capt. Chapman, A. H. D., 1 Dns.
Lt. Nettlefold, E. J., 5 D.G.
Lt. Denison-Pender, H. D., 2 Dns.
Qr.-Mr. Ross, T. M., 2 Dns., hon. capt.

(488)

REMOUNT SERVICE.
Under the control of the Director of Remounts, War Office, Whitehall, S.W.

Depôts.

United Kingdom (5)

No. 1 Depôt	.. .. ..	{ Dublin { Lusk Farm
No. 2 Depôt	.. .. ..	Woolwich
No. 3 Depôt	.. .. ..	Melton Mowbray
No. 4 Depôt	.. .. ..	{ Arborfield Cross, near Reading { (Ry. Stn., Wokingham, S.W.R. & S.E.R.)
No. 5 Depôt	.. .. ..	Pinckard's Farm, Chiddingfold, Godalming

South Africa (1)

Depôt .. .. Roberts' Heights, Pretoria.

Inspectors of Remounts. (3)

Wood, Lt.-Col. D. E., ret. pay	{ 15June05 { 15Aug.03
Bridge, Col. C. H., *C.B., C.M.G.*, ret. pay	{ 15June05 { 14Oct.03
Ferrar, Maj. (*temp. Lt.-Col.*) H. M., ret. pay (*Res. of Off.*)	{ 25Nov.10 { 1Jan.10

Superintendents of Depôts (7)

No. 1 Depôt { Dublin	Wildman, Hon. Capt. S. B., Qr.-Mr. A.S.C.	1Sept.13
{ Lusk	Royston Pigott, Capt. W. M., A.S.C.	7Dec.11
No. 2 Depôt, Woolwich ..	Harlow, Hon. Maj. G., Qr.-Mr. A.S.C.	16Oct.01
No. 3 Depôt, Melton Mowbray ..	Sanders, Hon. Capt. S. G., Ridg.-Mr. 4 D.G.	14Sept.12
No. 4 Depôt, Arborfield Cross	Badcock, Maj. G. H., ret. Ind. Army	28Mar.14
No. 5 Depôt, Pinckard's Farm ..	Lawrie, Capt. A. S., A.V.C.	23May13
Depôt, Roberts' Heights, Pretoria	Findlay, Bt. Maj. H., E. Kent R.	13Mar.11

Deputy Assistant Directors of Remounts (24)

Aldershot Command	McLaughlin, Lt.-Col. H. J., *D.S.O.*, Res. of Off.	{ 1Apr.14 { 27Apr.05
Eastern Command	{ Richardson, Maj. F. J., *D.S.O.*, 4 Bn. Arg. & Suth. Highrs. { Capt. ret. pay (*Res. of Off.*) { Matcham, Capt. W. E., *D.S.O.*, ret. pay (*Res. of Off.*) .. { Adye, Col. W., *C.B.*, ret. pay, *p.s.c.*	31July11 10Apr.12 1Apr.14
Irish Command	{ Gartside-Spaight, Maj. C. W., ret. pay .. { King, Capt. W. H., ret. pay (*Capt. 3 Bn. Conn. Rang.*) .. { Fowle, Col. J., *C.B.*, ret. pay (*Res. of Off.*) (*Hd.-Qrs. and Comdt., No. 1 Depôt*) ..	{ 24July12 { 1May10 14Dec.12 20June14
London District	Elwes, Maj. W. V. J. C., ret. pay (*Res. of Off.*)	28Apr.14
Northern Command ..	{ Hood, Capt. E. T. F., Linc. Yeo. (Lt. ret. pay) { Nevile, Capt. M. M. H., 3 Bn. York R. (Capt. ret. pay) { Dowell, Maj. G. W., ret. pay (*Res. of Off.*) .. { Anderson Pelham, Capt. C. H., Res. of Off. ..	31July11 { 23July12 { 17Apr.13 6Dec.12 10Dec.12
Scottish Command ..	{ Bridge, Capt. W. B. C., ret. pay (*Res. of Off.*) .. { Cadell, Lt.-Col. J. F., ret. pay, (*Res. of Off.*) *p.s.c.*	2Dec.12 1Apr.14
Southern Command ..	{ Fair, Lt.-Col. J. G., *D.S.O.*, ret. pay (*Res. of Off.*) { Norton, Lt. (*temp. Capt.*) J. H. (*Res. of Off.*) { Shaw, Capt. F. S. K., ret. pay (*Res. of Off.*) { Sandars, Maj. E. C., ret. pay (*Res. of Off.*) { Hankey, Capt. S. R. A., S. Irish Horse ..	31July11 18Aug.11 1Dec.11 { 18Dec.12 { 29Dec.11 11Dec.12
Western Command ..	{ Hine-Haycock, Capt. V. R., *D.S.O.*, ret. pay (*Res. of Off.*) { Wilson, Capt. H. S., ret. pay (*Res. of Off.*) { Goring, Maj. A., ret. pay (*Res. of Off.*) { Urquhart, Maj. E. W. L., ret. pay (*Res. of Off.*)	25Nov.10 2Aug.11 3Aug.11 31Dec.12
South Africa	Findlay Bt. Maj. H., E. Kent R. .. .. (*Pretoria*)	13Mar.11

Remount Service.

District Remount Officers (85).

EASTERN COMMAND (15).

No. 1 (W. Norfolk) Dist.	Beauchamp, Bt. Col. *Str* H. G. P., *Bt., C.B.,* ret. pay	1Apr.14
No. 2 E. Norfolk) Dist.	Petre, Lt.-Col. B. J., *late* 5 Bn. Norf. R. (Maj. ret.)	1Apr.14
No. 3 (Northamptonshire) Dist.	Alexander, Capt. F. D., 19 Hrs., Spec. Res. (Capt. ret. pay)	1Apr.14
No. 4 (Huntingdon and Camb.) Dist.	Andrewes, Capt. E. A., North'n Yeo.	1Apr.14
No. 5 (Cambridgeshire) Dist.	Evans, Capt. D. H., 2 D.G., Spec. Res.	1Apr.14
No. 6 (Suffolk) Dist.	Hambro, Capt. H. E., ret. pay (*Res. of Off.*)	17Apr.14
No. 7 (Herts and Bedfordshire) Dist.	Part, Capt. D. C. Res. of Off.	1Apr.14
No. 8 (N. Essex) Dist.	Wood, Lt.-Col. E. FitzG. M., *D.S.O.,* Lond. Brig. R.G.A., Maj. ret. pay (*Res. of Off.*) *p.s.c.* [*l*]	4Apr.14
No. 9 (S. Essex) Dist.	Dawes, Maj. E. S., 1 Co. of Lond. Yeo. (Capt. ret.)	1Apr.14
No. 10 (Middlesex) Dist.	Massy, Bt. Col. W. G., ret. pay, *p.s.c.*	1Apr.14
No. 11 (Surrey) Dist.	Thompson, Maj. H. A., ret. pay, (*Res. of Off.*)	1Apr.14
No. 12 (N. Kent) Dist.	Grepe, Capt. A. W., ret. pay (*Res. of Off.*)	7Apr.14
No. 13 (E. Kent) Dist.	Eyre, Capt. H. E. J., Res. of Off.	1Apr.14
No. 14 (W. Sussex) Dist.	Middleton, Col. H. J. J., u.s.l. Ind. Army	1Apr.14
No. 15 (E. Sussex) Dist.	O'Brien, Hon. Brig.-Gen. E. D. J., *C.B.,* ret. pay	4Apr.14

IRISH COMMAND (3).

No. 1 (Northern) Dist.	Pratt, Capt. A. C., ret. pay (*Res. of Off.*).	1Apr.14
No. 2 (Central) Dist.	Beamish, Capt. H. D., ret. pay (*Res. of Off.*)	1Apr.14
No. 3 (Southern) Dist.	Purvis, Col. J. A. R., ret. pay (*Res. of Off.*)	1Apr.14

LONDON DISTRICT (3).

No. 1 (N.W., W. and S.W.) Dist.	Barry, Hon. Capt. J., Qr.-Mr. ret. pay	1Apr.14
No. 2 (S. and S.E.) Dist.	Phillips, Col. A. L., ret. Ind. Army	1Apr.14
No. 3 (N., N.E. and E.) Dist.	Wood, Hon. Lt.-Col. J. W. M., *M.V.O.,* Qr.-Mr. ret. pay	1Apr.14

NORTHERN COMMAND (20).

No. 1 (Alnwick) Dist.	Allgood, Maj. W. H. L., ret. pay (*Res. of Off.*)	1Apr.14
No. 2 (Newcastle) Dist.	Waring, Lt. C. H., 11 Hrs., Spec. Res.	1Apr.14
No. 3 (Bishop Auckland) Dist.	Atkinson, Capt. J. E., 3 Hrs., Spec. Res. (Lt. ret. pay)	1Apr.14
No. 4 (Durham) Dist.	Going, Maj. G. N., ret. pay (*Res. of Off.*)	4June14
No. 5 (Richmond) Dist.	Shute, Bt. Col. A. B., ret. pay	1Apr.14
No. 6 (Scarborough) Dist.	Foljambe, Capt. *Hon.* G. W. F. S., ret. pay (*Res. of Off.*)	1Apr.14
No. 7 (Hull) Dist.	Cardwell, Capt. C. A., 3 Bn. Oxf. and Bucks. L.I. (Capt. ret.pay)	1Apr.14
No. 8 (Skipton) Dist.	Fife, Maj. R. D'A., ret. pay (*Res. of Off.*).	1Apr.14
No. 9 (York) Dist.	Pearson, Capt. R. S., York. Hrs. Yeo. (*Lt. Res. of Off.*)	1Apr.14
No. 10 (Doncaster) Dist.	Dougall, Maj. W., ret. pay (*Res. of Off.*)	1Apr.14
No. 11 (Wakefield) Dist.	Goater, Hon. Capt. C., Dep. Commy. Ind. Army Dept., ret.	1Apr.14
No. 12 (Leeds) Dist.	Graham, Maj. W., W. Rid. R.G.A. (Capt. (D.O.) ret. pay)	18Apr.14
No. 13 (N. Nottingham) Dist.	Kent, Maj. P. N., Notts. (Sher. Rang.) Yeo., Capt. ret. pay (*Res. of Off.*)	1Apr.14
No. 14 (S. Nottingham) Dist.	Waite, Hon. Maj. A. W., Ridg.-Mr. ret. pay	1Apr.14
No. 15 (Derbyshire) Dist.	Tristram, Capt. U. H., Notts. and Derby Mtd. Brig., T. & S. Col.	1Apr.14
No. 16 (N. Lincolnshire) Dist.		
No. 17 S. Lincolnshire) Dist.	Vigne, Lt.-Col. R. A., ret. pay (*Res. of Off.*)	1Apr.14
No. 18 (Leicestershire and Rutland) Dist.	Fairfax, Capt. B. C., ret. pay (*Res. of Off.*)	28May14
No. 19 (N. Staffordshire) Dist.	Bulkeley, Lt. F. R., Res. of Off.	1Apr.14
No. 20 (S. Staffordshire) Dist.	Arkwright, Lt. E. H., Res. of Off.	1Apr.14

SCOTTISH COMMAND (12).

No. 1 (Caithness) Dist.	Fellows, Capt. B. C., ret. Ind. Army	1Apr.14
No. 2 (Inverness) Dist.	Roney-Dougal, Capt. G. B., ret. pay (*Res. of Off.*)	1Apr.14
No. 3 (Aberdeen) Dist.	King, Hon. Lt.-Col. A. J., *D.S.O.,* Fife and Forfar Yeo., Maj. ret. pay (*Res. of Off.*) *g.s.*	1Apr.14
No. 4 (Fife) Dist.		
No. 5 (Perth) Dist.	Sandys-Lumsdaine, Maj. F. M., ret. pay (*Res. of Off.*)	1Apr.14
No. 6 (Argyll) Dist.	Finlay, Lt. A. C. M., ret. pay (*Res. of Off.*)	1Apr.14
No. 7 (Glasgow) Dist.	Parker, Hon. Maj. G., Ridg.-Mr. ret. pay	1Apr.14
No. 8 (Lothians) Dist.	Stewart-Dick-Cunyngham, Maj. *Str* N., *Bt., late* Sco. Horse Yeo.	1Apr.14
No. 9 (Border) Dist.	Du Plat Taylor, Maj. St. J. L. H., *D.S.O.,* ret. pay (*Res. of Off.*).	1Apr.14
No. 10 (Lanark) Dist.	Gillon, Maj. A., 4 Bn. High. L.I.	1Apr.14
No. 11 (Ayr) Dist.	Croshaw, Ma. O. M., Lanark (Glasgow) Yeo. (*Capt. Res. of Off.*)	1Apr.14
No. 12 (Dumfries) Dist.	Mitchell, Maj. A. J., ret. pay (*Res. of Off.*)	11May14

F

Remount Service.

District Remount Officers—contd.

SOUTHERN COMMAND (20).

No. 1 (Berkshire) Dist.	Eastwood, Maj. H. de C., *D.S.O.*, ret. pay (*Res. of Off.*)	1A...14
No. 2 (Buckinghamshire) Dist.	North, Maj. P. W., 3 Bn. R. Berks. R., Capt. ret. pay (*Res. of Off.*) [L]	1Apr.
No. 3 (Hampshire) Dist.	Tompson, Bt. Maj. H. W., ret. pay (*Res. of Off.*)	1Apr.14
No. 4 (S. Gloucestershire) Dist.	Rycroft, Capt. A. R. H., W. Kent Yeo.	1Apr.14
No. 5 (N. Gloucestershire) Dist.	Yardley, Lt.-Col. J. W., ret. pay	1Apr.14
No. 6 (W. Somersetshire) Dist.	Hill, Maj. R. F. W., 3 Bn. Devon R.	1Apr.14
No. 7 (E. Somersetshire) Dist.	Dickinson, Capt. S. C., 3 Bn. Som. L.I.	1Apr.14
No. 8 (Wiltshire) Dist.	Francis, Maj. O. L, ret. pay (*Res. of Off.*)	20Apr.14
No. 9 (S. Oxfordshire) Dist.	Lawrence, Capt. W. E., ret. pay (*Res. of Off.*)	1Apr.
No. 10 (N. Oxfordshire) Dist.	Hessey, Maj. H. C., ret. pay (*Res. of Off.*)	1Apr.1
No. 11 (S. Warwickshire) Dist.	Stapleton-Bretherton, Maj. (*Hon. Capt. in Army*) F. B. J., TD, *late* Lancs. Hrs. Yeo.	1Apr.14
No. 12 (N. Warwickshire) Dist.	Loftus, Capt. St. J. D. T., Res. of Off.	1Apr.14
No. 13 (Central Warwickshire) Dist.	Hobson, Maj. E. S. C., ret. pay (*Res. of Off.*)	1Apr.14
No. 14 (N. Worcestershire) Dist.	Champion, Capt. J. F., *M.V.O.*, Res. of Off.	1Apr.14
No. 15 (S. Worcestershire) Dist.	Orr-Ewing, Lt. J., Res. of Off.	1Apr.14
No. 16 (E. Cornwall) Dist.	Peel, Lt. W. C., Res. of Off.	1Apr.14
No. 17 (W. Cornwall) Dist.	Williams, Maj. G. T., ret. pay (*Res. of Off.*)	1Apr.14
No. 18 (W. Devonshire) Dist.	Campbell, Capt. A. J., ret. pay (*Res. of Off.*)	1Apr.14
No. 19 (E. Devonshire) Dist.	Cobham, Maj. H. W., ret. Ind. Army	1Apr.14
No. 20 (Dorsetshire) Dist.	Hall, Maj. D. K. E., 3 Bn. Dorset R. (*Maj. Res. of Off.*)	1Apr.14

WESTERN COMMAND (12)

No. 1 (Cumberland, Westmorland and part of Lancashire) Dist.	Moore, Lt.-Col. F. T. T., 3 Bn. Yorks. L.I. (Maj. ret. Ind. Army)	1Apr.14
No. 2 (Lancashire, Blackburn) Dist.	Hood, Capt. C. H., Shrops. R.H.A., Capt. ret. pay (*Res. of Off.*)	1Apr.14
No. 3 (Manchester) Dist.	Richer, Hon. Maj. F. A., Ridg.-Mr. 15 Hrs.	25Apr.14
No. 4 (Liverpool) Dist.	Thomson, Capt. J. W. D., ret. pay (*Res. of Off.*)	1Apr.14
No. 5 (Cheshire, Birkenhead and Chester) Dist.	Underwood, Maj. J. W., ret. pay (*Res. of Off.*)	1Apr.14
No. 6 (Cheshire, Macclesfield) Dist.	Cradock, Capt. H. F. C. A., Res. of Off.	1Apr.14
No. 7 (Flint, Denbigh, Carnarvon and Anglesey) Dist.	Jones, Lt.-Col. (*Hon. Capt. in Army*) A. W., 4 Bn. High. L.I.	6June14
No. 8 (Shropshire, Montgomery and Radnor) Dist.	Hayes, Capt. J. H., Shrops. Yeo. (*Capt. Res. of Off.*)	1Apr.14
No. 9 (Cardigan, and part of Carmarthen) Dist.	Griffiths, Lt.-Col. C., ret. Ind. Army	1Apr.14
No. 10 (Pembroke, and part of Carmarthen) Dist.	Turner, Lt. G. R., 3 Hrs., Spec. Res. (Lt. ret. pay)	1Apr.14
No. 11 (Brecknock and Glamorgan) Dist.	Lister, Maj. W. C., Hamps. Yeo.	1Apr.14
No. 12 (Hereford and Monmouth) Dist.	Stephens, Capt. G. E. B., ret. pay (*Res. of Off.*)	1Apr.14

Veterinary Officers Attached.

No. 2 Depôt	Neale, Capt. W. W. B., A.V.C.	6Sept.11
No. 4 Depôt	O'Rorke, Capt. F. C., *F.R.C.V.S.*, A.V.C.	1Feb.1!
No. 2 Depôt	Burridge, Capt. T. E., A.V.C.	14Feb.1!
No. 5 Depôt	Lawrie, Capt. A. S., A.V.C.	28May1!
No. 3 Depôt	Nimmo, Capt. J. S., A.V.C.	4Aug.1!
No. 1 Depôt	Andrews, Capt. J. O., A.V.C.	17Oct.1!
Depôt, Roberts' Heights, Pretoria	Aitken, Capt. J. J., A.V.C	17Nov.1!

SPECIAL RESERVE.

I. Irish Horse.
II. King Edward's Horse (The King's Oversea Dominions Regiment).

I. IRISH HORSE.

North Irish.
South Irish.

North Irish Horse.
Skegoniel Avenue, Belfast.

Uniform, Green. *Facings*, White. *Plume*, Green.¹

Hon. Colonel.
Shaftesbury, A. A. C., Earl of, K.P., K.C.V.O., (*Brig. Comdr.*, 1 *S. W. Mtd. Brig.*) .. 7June13

Lt.-Colonel.
✗Maude, E. A., Maj. ret pay (*Res. of Off.*) (*H*).. .. .. .. 1Jan.13

Majors. (b)
✗Cole, J. H. M., *Visct.* 17July03
✗Massereene and Ferrard, A.W.J.C., *Visct., D.S.O.*, Maj. ret. pay 18May07
✗Hamilton - Russell, Hon. A., Maj. ret. pay (*Res. of Off.*) 28Jan.08
 .. .. .. 27Jan.09
✗Farnham, A. K., *Lord*, late Lt. 10 Hrs. 20Nov.12

Captains. (4)
✗Waring, H. (*H*)*.. .. 6Feb.09
✗Bramston - Newnan, R. G. O., *M. V. O.*, Capt. ret. pay 17Nov.09
King-King, E., Lt. ret. pay 2Nov.10
Herdman, E. C. (*H*) .. 21Apr 13
Yates, R. L. (*H*) 7June14

Lieutenants (5).
✗Ker, D. A. W., *late Lt.* 6 D.G. 16Sept.00
 .. .. .. 20May05
Ross, R. D. (*H*) 23Apr.12
Combe, S. B. 22Apr.13
Grant, J. 22Apr.13

2nd Lieutenants. (8)
Jocelyn, R. S., *Visct.* .. 23May10
Hughes, T. W. G. J. .. 22June10
Close, M. S. (*on prob.*) 4Dec.12
Nugent, A. C. (*on prob.*) 19Mar.13
Maude, E. A. W. (*on prob.*) .. 23Apr.13

Adjutant.
Dorman, E. M., Capt. 4 D.G. 11Mar.11
(*Capt. in Army* 3Aug.12)

Quarter-Master.
Pittaway, J. E., *hon. lt.* 8Jan.13

Hon. Chaplain.
Stack, Rev. W. A., *M.A.* (*attd.*) 6July04

South Irish Horse.
Beggars Bush Barracks, Dublin.

Uniform, Green. *Facings*, Red and Green.

Hon. Colonel.
✗*Field Marshal* H.R.H. *Arthur W. P. A.*, Duke of Connaught and Strathearn, K.G., K.T. K.P., G.C.B., G.C.S.I. G.C.M.G.,G.C.I.E.,G.C.V.O., Col. G. Gds. and A.S.C., and Col.-in-Chief 6 Dns., High. L.I., R. Dub. Fus. and Rif. Brig., *Personal A.D.C. to the King* .. 7July08

Lt.-Colonel.
✗Decies, J. G. H., *Lord*, *D.S.O.*, Maj. ret. pay (*Res. of Off.*) .. 20Jan.12

Majors. (5)
✗Burns-Lindow, I. W., Capt. ret pay (*H*) ⑤ .. 21Dec.04
✗Browne-Clayton, R. C., Maj.ret.pay (*Res.of Off.*) 2Nov.07
 22May09
✗Wicklow, R. F., *Earl of, late* Capt. Res. of Off. 16June09
✗Stern, H. J. J. .. 15May11
✗Berry, H. E., Lt. ret. pay (*H*) 9Apr.12

Captains. (4)
✗Hamilton Stubber, R., Capt. ret. pay.. .. 6Dec.06
✗Hankey, S. R. A., Capt. ret. pay (*Dep. Asst. Dir. of Remts. S. Comd.*) 26Jan.10
 17Aug.12
Norton, H. E., Capt. ret. pay 3June11
✗Watt,A.H.,Capt. ret. pay 9Apr12

Lieutenants, (5)
(*p.s.*)Furlong, N. C. B. .. 19May09
(*p.s.*)O'Grady, G. (*H*) .. 2July10
Smythe, R. 24Nov.10
Wardell, J. M. (*H*) .. 9Apr 12
✗Blackett, R., Capt. ret. pay (*Res. of Off.*) 8May12
✗Brooke, F. H., *late Lt. K. R. Rif. C.* .. 8May12

2nd Lieutenants. (8)
Bryan, L. A., *f.c.r.* .. 10May09
Roche-Kelly, v. .. 31May09
Dudgeon, J. H. .. 14May12
Trant, L. D. 15May12
Kirk, C. G. P. (*on prob.*) 7Feb.14

Adjutant.
McCalmont, D. H. B., Capt. 7 Hrs. .. 28Nov.12
(*Capt. in Army* 9Aug.13)

Quarter-Master.
Chilcott, W. J., *hon. lt.* 4Sept.12

Medical Officer.
✗MacCabe, F. F., *M.B.*, Surg-Capt |.. .. 5Feb.07

F 2

(443—4)

Special Reserve.

11. KING EDWARD'S HORSE
(THE KING'S OVERSEA DOMINIONS REGIMENT).

King Edward's Horse (The King's Oversea Dominions Regiment).

The Duke of York's Headquarters, Chelsea, S.W.

Uniform, Drab—*Facings*, Scarlet *Plume*, Black.

Allied Regiment of Canadian Militia.
8th Princess Louise's New Brunswick Hussars, Sussex, N. Brunswick.

Allied Regiments of Australian Commonwealth.
1st (Central Queensland) Lt. Horse
2nd Lt. Horse (Queensland Mtd. Inf.)
3rd (Darling Downs) Lt. Horse
4th Lt. Horse (N.S. Wales Northern Rivers Lrs.)
5th Lt. Horse (New England Lt. Horse)
6th Lt. Horse (Hunter River Lrs.)
7th Lt. Horse (N.S. Wales Lrs.)
9th Lt. Horse (N.S. Wales Mtd. Rif.)
11th Lt. Horse (Aust. Horse)
13th (Gippsland) Lt. Horse
15th Lt. Horse (Victorian Mtd. Rif.)
16th (Indi) Lt. Horse
17th (Campaspe Valley) Lt. Horse
19th (Yarrowee) Lt. Horse
20th (Corangamite) Lt. Horse
22nd Lt. Horse (S. Aust. Mtd. Rif.)
23rd (Barossa) Lt. Horse

Allied Regiments of Australian Commonwealth—contd.
24th (Flinders) Lt. Horse
25th Lt. Horse (W. Aust. Mtd. Inf.)
26th Lt Horse (Tasmanian Mtd. Inf.)
27th (N. Queensland) Lt. Horse
28th (Illawarra) Lt. Horse
29th Lt. Horse (Port Phillip Horse)

Allied Regiments of Dominion of New Zealand.
1st Mounted Rifles (Canterbury Yeomanry Cavalry).
Queen Alexandra's 2nd Mounted Rifles.
3rd (Auckland) Mounted Rifles.
4th (Waikato) Mounted Rifles.
5th Mounted Rifles (Otago Hussars).
6th (Manawatu) Mounted Rifles.
7th (Southland) Mounted Rifles.
8th (South Canterbury) Mounted Rifles.
9th (Wellington East Coast) Mounted Rifles.
10th (Nelson) Mounted Rifles.
11th (North Auckland) Mounted Rifles.
12th (Otago) Mounted Rifles.

Allied Regiment of Union of South Africa Defence Forces
5th Mtd. Rif. (Cape Light Horse).

Colonel-in-Chief.
THE KING.

Lt.-Colonel.

Majors. (5)
p.s.✗James, L. 11June06
✗Hermon, E. W., Capt.
    ret. pay 22Feb.11
✗Pearch, W. B. (*Hon.*
    Lt. in Army 19 *Dec.*
    02) (A) (*H*) 15Jan.13
Dick, M. F. (*H*) .. 15Jan.13

Captains. (4)
p.s.Corlette, H. C. (*H*)(Q) 9July06
p.s.*Adams, N. P.* (*H*) ⓢ .. 20Jan.08
Russell, G. G. (Q) .. 5Nov.12
✗Wilkinson, J. F. M. .. 15Feb.13
MacDonald, J. N. .. 1June13

Lieutenants. (5)
Furse, R. D. (q) (*H*) ⓢ.. 26July11
Waddy, R. G. (*Public Health*
    *Dept., Egypt,*6 Jan. 13) 20Sept.
Shaw, C. A. 5Nov.12
Schwann, H. 6Jan.13
Barber, B. H. 1June13
Harvey, W. C. P. (*H*) 11June13

2nd Lieutenants. (8)
Creswick, H.F. 26July07
Cameron, A. G. (*H*) .. 20Feb.08
Ling, F. G. 8June12
Holland, W. D. A. .. 3Aug.12
Cooper, H. M. H. .. 5Apr.13
Feilding, Hon. H. S. 17May13
Mackinnon, D. (*on prob.*)
        25Mar.14

Adjutant.
✗Reynolds, A. B., Capt.
    12 Lrs. 22Jan.14
    (*Capt. in Army* 22 Aug. 08)

Quarter-Master.
✗Kennedy, W., *hon.*
    m. (*Hon. Lt. in*
    Army 5 Sept. 02) .. 25June04

Medical Officer.
Henderson, W. S., *M.D.,*
    Surg.-Capt. .. 1Apr.08

Chaplain.
Hunns, Rev. A., *M.A.,*
    D.C.L., Chapl. 3rd
    Class (T.F.) (*attd.*) .. 21June12
            21June02

This corps is administered by a Committee consisting of:—

Stamfordham, Lt.-Col. *Rt. Hon.* A. J., *Lord, G.C.I.E., G.C.V.O., K.C.B., K.C.S.I., K.C.M.G.,* ret. pay, Eq.
Northcliffe, A. C. W., *Lord.*
Lucas-Tooth, *Sir* R. L., *Bt.*
Reid, *Rt. Hon. Sir* G. H., *G.C.M.G.*
Benson, Maj.-Gen. *Sir* F. W., *K.C.B.,* ret. pay (*Res. of Off.*), *p.s.c.* [R]
French, *Sir* S. R., *K.C.M.G.*
Philipps, *Sir* O. C., *K.C.M.G.*
Collins, Capt. R. H. M., *C.M.G.,* ret. *R.N.*
Lawrence, Col. *Hon.* H. A., *p.s.c., late* King's Colonials Yeo. Lt.-Col. ret. pay (*Maj. Res. of Off.*)
Fortescue, Col. H., *late* King Edward's Horse, Lt.-Col. ret. pay.
Bandeman, Lt.-Col. Y. S., | *late* King Edward's Horse, Maj., ret. pay (*Res. of Off.*)
MacKenzie, *Hon.* T.
James, Maj., L., King Edward's Horse.
Wallington, E. W., *Esq., C.V.O., C.M.G., late* Lt. 3Bn. Oxf. L.I.

Secretary .. .. .. Morrish, A. G., *Esq.*

YEOMANRY.
TERRITORIAL FORCE.
Order of Precedence of the Regiments of Yeomanry.

1. Royal Wiltshire.
2. Warwickshire.
3. Yorkshire Hussars.
4. Nottinghamshire (Sherwood Rangers).
5. Staffordshire.
6. Shropshire.
7. Ayrshire.
8. Cheshire.
9. Yorkshire Dragoons.
10. Leicestershire.
11. North Somerset.
12. Duke of Lancaster's Own.
13. Lanarkshire.
14. Northumberland.
15. Nottinghamshire Hussars, South.
16. Denbighshire.
17. Westmorland and Cumberland.
18. Pembroke.
19. Royal East Kent.
20. Hampshire.
21. Buckinghamshire.
22. Derbyshire.
23. Dorset.
24. Gloucestershire.
25. Herts.
26. Berks.
27. 1st County of London.
28. Royal 1st Devon.
29. Suffolk.
30. Royal North Devon.
31. Worcestershire.
32. West Kent.
33. West Somerset.
34. Oxfordshire.
35. Montgomeryshire.
36. Lothians and Border Horse.
37. Lanarkshire(Glasgow).
38. Lancashire Hussars.
39. Surrey.
40. Fife and Forfar.
41. Norfolk.
42. Sussex.
43. Glamorgan.
44. Lincolnshire.
45. City of London.
46. 2nd County of London.
47. 3rd County of London.
48. Bedfordshire.
49. Essex.
50. Northamptonshire.
51. East Riding of Yorkshire.
52. 1st Lovat's Scouts.
53. 2nd Lovat's Scouts.
54. Scottish Horse.

REGIMENTS OF YEOMANRY.

[Dates shown prior to 1 April, 1908, are those of the Officers' corresponding rank in a late unit of Imperial Yeomanry.]

Ayrshire.

(*Earl of Carrick's Own.*)
"South Africa, 1900-02."
Ayr.

Uniform, Blue.
Facings and Busby-Bag, Scarlet.
Plume, Scarlet and White.

Hon. Colonel.
Hamilton-Campbell, W.K., D.S.O., TD (*Hon. Lt.-Col. in Army*) (*Lt.-Col. ret. T.F.*) 14Jan.14

Lt.-Colonel.
p.s.✗Boswell, J. D. TD(*Hon. Capt. in Army 25 July 02*) 3July13

Majors. (5)
Ralston-Patrick, R. .. 1Mar.09
Houldsworth, W. T. R. 9Nov.09
Kennedy, J. C. ⓖ (*H*) 21June12
Kennedy, N. (*H*) 7June13
Montgomerie, A. S., *Lord, late* Lt. 2 L. G. (q) ⓖ (*H*) 3July13

Captains. (4)
p.s.Thomson, J. G. O.(*H*).. 25Feb.10
p.s.Dunlop, T. C. 21June12

Lieutenants. (5)
Bell, J. 25Feb.10
Murdoch, J. A. D.(*H*).. 25Feb.10
Cooper, W. D. 25Feb.10
MacAndrew, C.G.(*H*)..21June12
Renshaw, C. S. B. .. 14Sept.12

2nd Lieutenants. (8)
Howatson, C. N. 18June08
Dubs, C. I. A. 1July10
Campbell, P. M... .. 20Mar.11
Butler, E. P. 18Mar.13
Arthur, T. A. 8Apr.13
Kennedy, *Lord* H. .. 12Mar.14
Shairp, N... .. .. 28Mar.14
Neilson, J.A., *jun.* .. 14Apr.14
Angus, R. E. 14Apr.14

Adjutant.
Montgomerie, *Hon.* F. C., Lt. 2 L.G., *capt.* 1Feb.14

Quarter-Master.
Hamilton, A., *hon. lt.* 21Feb.14

Medical Officers.
Robertson, Capt. A., R.A.M.C. (T.F.) (*attd.*) 9Dec.11
9June08

Bedfordshire.

Ashburnham Road, Bedford.

Uniform, Blue. Facings, White.
Plume, Black and White.

Lt.-Colonel.
p s.Peel, W. R. W., *Visct.* (*H*)
17Dec.11

Majors. (5)
p.s.✗Peel, *Hon.* S. C. [F](*H*) 27May08
Green, S. J. 1Aug.09
Fordham, W. A. (*H*) ..19Mar.13
✗Selby-Lowndes, W., *jun.* (*Hon. Lt. in Army 15 Sept.* 00) .. 15July13
Peel, *Hon.* A. G. V. .. 15July13

Captains. (4)
✗Dodds, J.H.H.,(*Hon.Lt. in Army,*6 *Feb* 02), *late* Lt.Impl.Yeo.(S.Africa) (*Vice-Consul, Harrar, Abyssinia,* 23 *Nov,* 11) 22Jan.13
✗Walker, J. B., *late* Capt. 14 Hrs. 19Mar.13
✗St. John, *Hon.* M. St. A. T., *late* Lt. K.O. Sco. Bord. (*Lt. Res. of Off.*) 16July13

Lieutenants. (5)
(p.s.)Russell, C. F. W. .. 1Apr.08
(p.s.)Davis, S. P. 38pt.08
Benning, A. C. S. .. 23May10
Headlam, C. M... .. 7June11
Proby, G. 29Jan.14

2nd Lieutenants. (8)
Dugdale, E. T. S. .. 27Mar.12
Holmes, J. 1Apr.12
Gore, J. F. 2Apr.12
Hargreaves, G. De la P. 23July12
Lascelles, A. F. 8Jan.13
Trevor, S. L. 1Mar.13
Jones, L. E. 3May13
(p.s.)Howey, J. E. P. .. 1Mar.14

Adjutant.
✗Tyrrell, G. G. M., Capt. 5 Lrs 13Mar.13

Quarter-Master.
✗Pearce, J., Qr.-Mr. (*hon. capt.*) ret. pay, *hon. capt.* 11Aug.13

Medical Officers.
p. Skelding, H., M.B., Surg. Capt. 12Sept.05
12Mar.02

Chaplain.
Scott, Rev.R. C. F., B.A., Chapl. 4th Class (T.F.) (*attd.*) 1Apr.08
28Mar.03

Berks.

(*Hungerford.*)
"South Africa, 1900-01."
Yeomanry House, Castle Hill, Reading.

Uniform, Blue. Facings, Scarlet.

Hon. Colonel.
Willes, G. S., TD(*Lt.-Col. & Hon. Col., ret. Yeo. Cav.*) 5June95

Lt.-Colonel.
p.s.Karslake, J. B. P., TD .. 6May14

Majors. (5)
✗Henderson, H. G., *late* Capt. 1 L.G. .. 28Apr.06
✗Wigan,J.T., *late* Capt. 13 Hrs. 19Mar.09
✗Gooch, E. S. (*H*) *late* Lt. 7 Hrs. 27Sept10
Nickisson, J. L... .. 7 Nov.10

Captains. (4)
p.s.✗Stone, C.C.(*Hon. Capt. in Army* 3 Sept.02) (*H*)11June02
p.s.Slaughter, E. M. (q) .. 28Sept.05
✗Hughes, R. 1Mar.11
p.s.✗Wilder, G. M. 11Feb.14

Lieutenants. (5)
p.s.West, A. T. 1Feb.09
Walmesley, C. T. J. G., *late* Lt. 17 Lrs... .. 1Mar.10
Niven, W. E. G. 1Mar.11
p.s. Pearson, R. L. (*H*) .. 14May13
(*local capt. O.T.C.* 1May09)
✗Foster,E.B.G., *late* Lt. G. Gds. 15May13
Wroughton, P. M. N. .. 11Feb.14

2nd Lieutenants. (8)
Henderson, E. B. .. 30Mar.08
Portal, G. E. 1Jan.10
Benyon, H. A. 10Jan.10
Krabbé, C. B. 28Feb.12
Crosland, H. P... .. 4Mar.12
Bishop, A. C., *late* Lt. 3 Bn. Essex R. (*H*) .. 2Apr.13
Barry, E. C. T. 2Dec.13
Ainger, T. E. ⓖ 24Jan.14
Hillsborough, E. W. P. W. B. T. S., *Earl of* .. 12Feb.14

Adjutant.
Hurndall, F. B., Capt. 20 Hrs. 16Oct.12

Quarter-Master.
Henson, A. W., *hon. lt.* 28Mar.13

Medical Officers.
Kennard, Lt. D. G., R.A.M.C.(T.F.)(*attd.*) 17May09

Yeomanry. Territorial Force.

Buckinghamshire.
(*Royal Bucks Hussars.*)
"South Africa, 1900-01."
Buckingham.

Uniform, Green—*Facings and Busby-Bag*, Scarlet. *Plume*, White.

Hon. Colonel.
Lawson, Hon. *H. L. W.*,
TD (*Lt.-Col. & Hon. Col.
T. F. Res.*) 18Oct 13

Lt.-Colonel.
✗Grenfell, C. A., TD .. 18Oct.13

Majors. (5)
✗Grenfell, J. P. 21May08
Disraeli, C. R. (*H*) ⊕ (*b*)
(*a*) *p.s.* 15Oct.09
de Rothschild, L. N. (*H*) 8June14

Captains. (4)
Goetz, C. E. G. (*H*) .. 12July10
Swire, G. W. (*H*).. .. 1Apr.13

Lgt Lancers **Lieutenants. (5)**
p.s. Grenfell, R. N. .. 1Sept.08
(*p.s.*) Cripps, F. H. .. 23Nov.08
de Rothschild, E. A. .. 12July10
Ponsonby, *Hon.* B. B. .. 6Sept.13
Pauncefort - Duncombe,
Sir E. P. D., *Bt.* .. 6Sept.13

2nd Lieutenants. (8)
Primrose, *Hon.* N. J. A. 10Feb.09
Smith, T. C. 10Feb.09
Boswell, J. I. C. 2June09
Lawson, E. F. 1July10
de Rothschild, A. G. .. 10Dec.10
Lawson - Johnston, A.
McW. 1Feb.11
Bulteel, J. C. 15May11
Fairbairn. S. G., *late*
2nd Lt. 2 Dns. .. 20Mar.14

Adjutant.
Gardner, G., Capt. 21 Lrs.
13Mar.14

Quarter-Master.
✗Cole, C. W., *hon. lt.* .. 1Mar.11

Medical Officers.
Pearson, Lt. G. B.,
R.A.M.C.(T.F.)(*attd.*) 1Dec.12

Chaplain.
Shaw, *Rt. Rev.* E. D.,
*Bishop Suffragan of
Buckingham, M.A.*,
Chapl. 3rd Class(T.F.)
(*attd.*) 18July13
                       18July03

Cheshire.
(*Earl of Chester's.*)
"South Africa, 1900-01."
Old Bank Buildings, Chester.

Uniform, Blue—*Facings*, Scarlet.
Busby-Bag, White. *Plume*, Red and White.

Hon. Colonel,
p. Harrington, C. A., *Earl
of*, Col., *A.D.C., hon. c.
(Lt.-Col. & Hon. Col.
ret. Impl. Yeo.*) 30Sept.05

Lt.-Colonel.
p. Wilson, H. M. 8June13

Majors. (5)
✗Westminster, H.R.H.,
*Duke of, G.C.V.O., late
2nd Lt.* R.H.G. .. 19May06
✗Phillips Brockelhurst,
R. W. D., TD (*Hon. Lt.
Army* 29May01) *hon.l.c.* 17Jan.08
Verdin, R. N. H., *late
2nd Lt.* 3 Bn. Ches. R.
(*H*).. .. .. 5Jan.11
✗Barbour, R. (*Hon. Lt.
in Army* 9Sept.01) (*H*) 8June13

Captains. (4)
p.s.✗Egerton, *Hon.* M. (*H*) 13Sept.08
p.s. Glazebrook, P. K. (*H*) ⊕ 5Jan.11
p.s. Tomkinson, C. W. (*H*).. 20Mar.12
p.s. Holland, W. W. (*H*) .. 8June13

Lieutenants. (5)
p.s. de Knoop, J. J. J. (*H*) .. 17Jan.08
✗Hermon, J. V., *late* Lt.
6 D.G. 21Dec.08
p. J'armay, I. B. 9May11
Stanley, *Hon.* Sir *A. L.,
K.C.M.G., late* Capt. R.
Ang. R. E. (Mila.)
(*Gov., Victoria.* 21 Jan.
14) 20Mar.12
Egerton-Warburton, G.
(*H*), ... 8June13
Wilbraham. G. H. de V. 17Nov.13
Ashton, S. E. 18Nov.13

2nd Lieutenants. (8)
Soames, W. N. .. 2July12
Sparrow, W. G. K. .. 1Aug.13
Brooks. T. M. 10Sept.13
Egerton, P. de M. W. .. 12May14

Adjutant.
Lockett, V. N., Capt.
17 Lrs. 14Aug.13

Quarter-Master.
p. Cooper, G., *hon. maj.* 4Feb.03

Medical Officers.
Gray, Maj. E., R.A.M.C.
(T.F.) (*attd.*) .. 27Nov.11
                       25Apr.00
Baxter, Lt. A., M.D.,
R.A.M.C. (T.F.)(*attd.*) 7Oct.12

Chaplain.
Armitstead, *Rev.* J. H.,
M.A., Chapl. 4th Class
(T.F.) (*attd.*) 1Mar.14

Denbighshire.
(*Hussars.*)
"South Africa, 1900-01."
1, Erdigg Road, Wrexham.

Uniform, Blue—*Facings and Busby Bag*, Scarlet. *Plume*, White.

Hon. Colonel.
p. Mesham, A., *formerly*
Capt. 1 Dns.(*Lt.-Col.&
Hon.Col. late Yeo. Cav.*) 20Feb.92

Lt.-Colonel.
✗Sykes, H. P., Capt.ret.
pay (*Capt. Res. of Off.*) 21Dec.10

Majors. (5)
✗Ward, T., Maj. ret. pay
(*Res. of Off.*) *hon l.c.* 20Nov.03
                       24Aug.04
Clegg, H. N. M. (*Capt.
Res. of Off.*) .. 1Dec.11
Mayhew, J. D. (*H*) .. 1Apr.13
Fletcher, H. F. (*H*) ⊕ 1Dec.13
Dashwood - Tandy, R.,
late Lt. Lan. Fus. ..19Apr.14

Captains. (4)
(p.s.) Mayhew, G. D. (*H*) .. 11June10
Howell-Evans, H. J. .. 1Dec.11
Fosbery, C. L. 1Dec.11
Mayhew, J. J. 1June12
Turner, J. H. 1Feb.14

2nd Lieutenants (8)
Sandbach, G. R. 12May11
Rooper, J. R. 1May12
Spencer, R. (*H*) 1Oct.12
Springmann, J. B. .. 9Jan.13
Williams, J. J. L. .. 17July13
Mayhew, C. W. .. 9May14

Adjutant.
Platt, L. S., Capt. 17 Lrs.
23June13

Quarter-Master.
Brand, T., *hon. lt.* .. 1Apr.14

Medical Officers.

Chaplain.
St. Asaph, *Rt. Rev.* A. G.,
Lord Bishop of, D.D.,
Chapl. 1st Class(T.F.)
(*attd.*) 1Apr.08
                       2Aug.07

Yeomanry. Territorial Force.

Derbyshire.
The United Red and White Rose ensigned with the Imperial Crown.
"South Africa, 1900-01."
91, Siddall's Road, Derby.

Uniform, Blue—*Facings,* Scarlet.
Plume, Red and White.

Hon. Colonel.
Chandos-Pole, R. W., TD
(*Lt.-Col. & Hon. Col.
ret. Impl. Yeo.*) .. 28July06

Lt.-Colonel.
p.s.✗Cavendish-Bentinck, *Lord* H. C., TD 22Aug.12

Majors. (5)
p.s.Peacock, F. W., TD .. 17Sept.01
p.s.Winterbottom, W. D... 5May06
p.s.Gretton, H. F., TD, *late* Capt. 3 Bn.N. Staff. R. 5Apr.11

Captains. (4)
Clark, J. N. D'A., *late* Lt. 3 Bn. Derby R. .. 5Apr.11
p.s. McCreagh - Thornhill, M. C. (*H*) *p.v.c.* .. 5Apr.11
p.s.Strutt, G. A. (*H*) 11Dec.13
Shuttleworth, A. A.(*H*)*P.c.* ⓖ 4Feb.14

Lieutenants. (5)
(p.s.)Brocklehurst,*Sir* P.L., Bt., ... 11June11
(p.s.)Betterton, A. H. (*H*).. 11June11
Vernon, G. F. A., *Lord* 1June12
Sherrard, J. O., *late* Lt. R. A. 3Feb.13
(p.s.)Allsebrook, G. C. .. 3Jan14

2nd Lieutenants. (8)
(p.s.)Walker, P. A. C. (*b*) 9Mar.07
(p) Wilson, W., jun. .. 23Apr.08
Winterbottom, G. .. 5Nov.08
Johnson, J. G. T. .. 25Feb.10
Worthington, L. J. .. 1Mar.10
Birchenough, R. P. 10Dec.11
Branfill, C. A. 11Dec.11
Hartington, E. W. S., *Marquis of* 17Jan.13
Feilden, W. M. B. .. 3Apr.13

Adjutant.
✗Brocklebank, R. H. R., Capt. 9 Lrs. 1Nov.12

Quarter-Master.
Hodgson, J. B., *hon. lt.* 11Oct.12

Medical Officers.
✗Wilson, Capt. R. M., M.D., R.A.M.C. (T.F.) (attd.) 1Mar.14

Chaplain.
Gore, *Rev.* G. H., *M.A.*, Chapl. 4thClass(T.F.) (a'td.) 27July12

Royal 1st Devon.
"South Africa, 1900-01."
9, Dix's Field, Exeter.

Uniform, Scarlet—*Facings,* Blue.
Plume, Scarlet and White.
Busby-Bag, Scarlet.

Hon. Colonel.
Shelley, Sir J., Bt., TD (*Lt.-Col. & Hon. Col. ret. Impl. Yeo.*) 10Feb.02

Lt.-Colonel.
Acland, A. D., TD, ⓖ (*H*) *P.c.* 7Dec.10

Majors. (5)
Hambleden, W. F. D., *Visct.* (*H*) .. 10Feb.02
p.s.✗Wyatt-Edgell, M. R. A. (*Hon. Lt. in Army* 11 Sept. 02) (*H*) *p.v.c.* ..10Feb.06
✗Lethbridge, J. G. B., Lt. ret. pay(*Capt.Res. of Off.*)ⓖ'4May06
p. ✗St. Maur, R. H. (*H*).. 1Sept.09
p.s.✗Vivian, G. C. B., *Lord, late* Lt. 17 Lrs. (*Lt. Res. of Off.*) 6Sept.13
Hole, W. G. (*H*) ⓖ .. 1June14

Captains. (4)
Peek, *Sir* W., *Bt.* .. 1Dec.13
Johnstone, G. H. .. 18Apr.14

Lieutenants. (5)
Hunter, R. C. 21Nov.10
Hain, E. 8June12
Knight-Bruce, R.E. C.ⓖ 26June12
Shelley, J. F. 1Dec.13
Hawker, R. S. .. 18Apr.14

2nd Lieutenants. (8)
Agar-Robartes, *Hon.* A. V. 31Dec.11
Holley, E. J. H. 13Jan.13
Fox. H. E. 27Mar.13
Petherick, G. G., *l ite* 2nd Lt. 2 L.G. 3Feb.14
Acland, W. H. D., *late* 2nd Lt. 2 Dns , Spec. Res. 11Mar.14

Adjutant.

Quarter-Master.
Collins, H., *hon. lt.* .. 19July11

Medical Officers.
✗Bird, Lt. A. C., R.A.M.C. (T.F.) (*attd.*) 12Aug.06

Chaplain.
Dupuis, *Rev.* E. J. G., *M.A.*, TD. Chapl. 2nd Class (T.F.) (*attd.*) .. 1Apr.08
15Mar.90

Royal North Devon.
(*Hussars.*)
"South Africa, 1900-01."
Barnstaple.

Uniform, Blue—*Facings* and *Busby-Bag,* Scarlet.
Plume, Scarlet and White.

Hon. Colonel.
p.s. Fortescue, H. F., *Earl*, K.C.B.,TD, Col.,*A.D.C.* (*Lt.-Col. & Hon. Col. ret. Impl. Yeo.*) .. 2Apr.04

Lt.-Colonel.
p. Sanders, R. A., TD .. 13May11

Majors. (5)
p.s.Bayly, J., TD 5Mar.04
p.s.✗St. Hill, G. H TD, (*Hon.* (*H*)ⓖ *Lt. in Army* 27 Sept. 00), ... 12July05
p.s.Greig, M. J. 20June08
p.s.✗Thynne, A. C., *D.S.O.* (*Hon. Capt. in Army* 1 *Aug.* 02) 20June12
Mardon, A. C.(*H*) .. 22Apr.14

Captains. (4)
p.s.Wills, *Sir* G. A. H., *Bt.* 6July13

Lieutenants. (5)
Bampfylde, *Hon.* G. W. W., *late* Lt. G. Gds. .. 13Feb.09
Salaman, M. H. .. 29Jan.11
Money-Coutts, *Hon.* H. B. 15Aug.11
✗Ruston, W. 16Feb.13
Clemson, J. O. .. 7July13

2nd Lieutenants. (8)
Dawson, V. J. 21July09
✗Cave, A. L., *late* Capt. 10 Hrs. 15Sept.10
Miers, P. P. .. 1Feb.13
Hope, L. N. 21June13
Williams, G. P. .. 1July12
Kenyon-Slaney, P. P. .. 6Oct.13
Wills, F. N. H. 18Nov.13
Fortescue, *Hon.* D. G. 13Dec.13

Adjutant.
✗Winch, A. B., Capt. 2 Dns. 10ct.13

Quarter-Master.
✗Olden, G. W., *hon. lt.* 25Jan.13

Medical Officers.
Harper, Maj. J. R., TD, R.A.M.C. (T.F.) (*attd.*)19May0
28Mar.9
Gibbs, Lt. S. R., R.A.M.C. (T.F.) (*attd.*) .. 12Oct.06

Chaplain.
Fuller, *Rev.* A. R., *M.A.*, Chapl. 4thClass(T.F.) (*attd.*) 31Aug.12

Yeomanry. Territorial Force.

Dorset.
(*Queen's Own.*)
"South Africa, 1900-01."
Sherborne.

Uniform, Blue—Facings and Busby-Bag, Scarlet—Plume, White.

Hon. Colonel.
Goodden, J. R. P.,
TD, *late Lt.* 4 D.G., *hon. c.* .. 11Apr.00

Lt.-Colonel.
p.s.Troyte-Bullock, E. G.,
late Capt. 1 Dns. .. 10Mar.14

Majors. (5)
✗Batley, R. C. (*Hon. Capt. in Army* 26July01) .. 12Apr.02
p.s.✗Goodden, J. B. H. (*Hon. Lt. in Army* 12Jan.01) 16Oct.08
Wynford, P. G., Lord,
Capt. ret. pay (*Capt. Res. of Off.*) .. 1Nov.08
p. Castleman, E. W. F. (H) 10July12
Baker, Sir R. L., Bt. (H)23Mar.14

Captains. (4)
Reeves, V. C. M. (H) .. 4Oct.13
Alexander, W. A. (H) .. 4Oct.13

Lieutenants. (5)
(p.s.)Gordon, R. G. S. (*Hon. 2nd Lt. in Army* 12 July 01), *late Lt.* 3 Bn. Shrops. L.I. .. 16Oct.08
Digby-Wingfield-Digby, F. J. B. 12May10
Pass, A. D. (H) .. 28Jan.11
Browne, H. V. .. 4Oct.13
Kennard, V. G., *late 2nd Lt.* 5 Bn. Rif. Brig. .. 4Oct.13

2nd Lieutenants. (8)
Carter, G. V., *late 2nd Lt.*, 16 Lrs. .. 8Sept.09
Kennaway, A. L. .. 4June10
Lees, Sir T. E. K., Bt., *late 2nd Lt.* 15 Hrs. .. 1Nov.11
Dammers, G. M.ⓢ 12Mar.12
Busk, P. 1Apr.12
Lees, B. P. T. .. 6Aug.12
.. 27Mar.12
Dawson-Damer, *Hon.* G. S. 20Nov.12

Adjutant.
✗Livingstone-Learmonth, N. J. C., *Capt.* 15 Hrs. 3Sept.11

Quarter-Master.
p. ✗Parsons, W. P. (*Hon. Lt. in Army* 5 Sept. 01), *hon. capt.* 18May03

Medical Officers.
Rickett, Lt. G. R., *M.D.*, R.A.M.C. (T. F.) (*attd.*) *late Lt.*, 3 Midd'x R.G.A. Vols.) 1May11

Chaplain.
Kindersley, Rev. O. E., *M.A.*, Chapl. 3rd Class (T.F.) (*attd.*) .. 21May12
21May02

Essex.
An escutcheon charged with three seaxes.
"*Deous et Tutamen.*"
17, Sir Isaac's Walk, Colchester.

Uniform, Green—Facings, Scarlet—Plume, Scarlet.

Hon. Colonel.
Warwick, F. R. C. G.,
Earl of, TD, (*Lt.-Col. & Hon. Col. ret. T.F.*) .. 16Nov.01

Lt.-Colonel.
p.s.Deacon, E., *late Lt.* 1 D.G. (H) 18Jan.11

Majors. (5)
p.s.Whitmore, F. H. D. C. 28Dec.01
p.s.✗Roddick, A. (*Hon. Lt. in Army* 18 *July* 01) .. 27Jan.09
p.s.✗Gold, G. G. .. 18Jan.11
Buxton, A. (H) 17June12
Hill, E. (H).. .. ..17June12

Captains. (4)
p.s.Ruggles-Brise, E. A.(H) 18Jan.11
Parker, J. O. .. 3Aug.12
Proby, R. G., *late Lt.* R.A. 1June13

Lieutenants. (5)
Edwards, R. 3Sept.12
Wedd, E. P. W. .. 3Sept.12
Hine, V. T. G. .. 1June13
Johnston, G. S. 19Sept.13
Tower, C. C. 19Sept.13

2nd Lieutenants. (8)
Gilbey, C. N. . .. 13July10
Holt, H. P. .. 17Jan.12
Chaplin, J. C. .. 18Jan.12
Tufnell, S. J. .. 18May12
Egerton-Green, J. W. E. 8Mar.13
Swire, J. K. .. 25July13
27Mar.14
Reid, G. P. N. .. 17Oct.13
Buxton, T. F. .. 16Mar.14

Adjutant.
✗Steele, A. R., *Capt.* 4 Hrs. 2Jan.12

Quarter-Master.
✗Sayer, E. J., *hon. lt.* .. 9Mar.11

Medical Officers.
White, Lt. G. F., *M.D.*, R.A.M.C. (T.F.) (attd.) 8Mar.13

Chaplain.
Oliver, Rev. A., *M.A.*, Chapl. 4th Class(T.F.) (*attd.*) 21June12

Fife and Forfar.
The Thane of Fife.
"South Africa, 1900-01."
Kirkcaldy.

Uniform, Scarlet—Facings, Blue.

Hon. Colonel.
p.s. Erskine, T. H., VD (*Lt.-Col. & Hon. Col. ret. T.F.*) 13Mar.12

Lt.-Colonel.
p.s.Mitchell, A., TD (H) .. 12Nov.11

Majors. (5)
p.s.✗Gilmour, J., jun. (*Hon. Capt. in Army* 26Aug.01) 28Sept.01
p.s.✗King, A. J., *D.S.O.*, q.s.,
Maj. ret. pay (*Maj. Res. of Off.*), *hon. l.c.* (H) (Remount Service) .. 8Sept.06
Younger, J., jun. .. 1Aug.09
Russell, G... .. .. 18Apr.12
Nairn, R. S. 28Apr.13

Captains. (4)
p. de Prée, C. G., *late Lt.* 15 Hrs... .. .. 11July03
p.s.Mitchell, S. (H) .. 18Apr.12
Osborne, G. E. B. (H) .. 5Dec.12
p.s.✗Jackson, G. E. (t) .. 28Apr.13

Lieutenants. (5)
(p.s)Hutchison, A. 20Jan.09
Ogilvie, D. D. .. 12Nov.11
Hutchison, R. O. .. 28Apr.13
Stewart, R. W. 28Apr.13
MacLeod, G. R. (*Lt. Res. of Off.*) 25Mar.14

2nd Lieutenants. (8)
Smith-Sligo, R. W. M. G. 28Oct.09
Colville, D., jun... .. 28Oct.09
Cox, F. B. H. 20Nov.09
Don, W. G. 1July12
Nairn, I. C. 7Dec.12
Sharp, H. S. .. 31Jan.13
Robertson, J. R. 26Mar.13

Adjutant.
✗Lindsay, M. E., *Capt.* 7 D.G. 9Apr.13

Quarter-Master.
✗Simonds, H., *hon. capt.*1Nov.07

Medical Officers.
Tuke, *Capt.* A. L. S., *M.B.*, R.A.M.C. (T.F.) (*attd.*) 10Dec.10
27Feb.06

Chaplain.
Thompson, Rev. G. S., *B.D.*, TD [C.S.], Chapl. 2nd Class (T.F.) (*attd.*) 6July13
6July98

Yeomanry. Territorial Force.

Glamorgan.

Bridgend.

Uniform, Blue—*Facings and Plume,*
White.

Hon. Colonel.
Plymouth, Rt. Hon.
E.G.,Earl of,C.B.,hon.c. 3Aug.01

Lt.-Colonel.
p.s.Nicholl, J. I. D. 20June14

Majors. (5)
p.s.Bruce, G. T. 4Oct.02
Vivian, Hon. O. R.,
M.V.O. 21Nov.03
Moore-Gwyn, J. G., *late
Lt.* 5 Bn. Worc. R. .. 11Apr.12

Captains. (4)
p.s.Cope, W. 31Mar.08
Helme, E. (H) 23Dec.08
p.s.✗Prichard, R.G.M.(Hon.
Lt. in Army 19 Aug. 01) 24Feb.12

Lieutenants. (5)
✗Price, Sir F. C. R., Bt,
late Lt. R. W. Fus. .. 23Dec.08
Carne, G. S. N. ⑤ .. 8Mar.10
Bruce, Hon. J. H. .. 9Mar.10
Lewis, R. W. 8Oct.11
✗Miers, R. H. P. .. 24Feb.12

2nd Lieutenants. (8)
Fisher, O. 21Oct.08
Aylett-Branfill, C. L. .. 19Apr.09
David, E. J. C. 1Mar.11
Fisher, P. 1Jan.12
Llewellyn, G. R. P. .. 15Apr.12
Wilson, R. C. 15Sept.13

Adjutant.
Astley, A. G. L., Capt.
14 Hrs. 24Dec.12

Quarter-Master.
Barrett, A. S., hon. lt. 1Nov.13

Medical Officers.
p. Simons, Maj. R. J. R. C.,
R.A.M.C.(T.F.)(attd.)11May12
10June96

Chaplain.
Nicholl, Rev. H. S., Chapl.
th Class (T.F.) (attd.) 5Mar.11

Gloucestershire.
(*Royal Gloucestershire
Hussars.*)
"South Africa, 1900-01."
The Barracks, Gloucester.

Uniform, Blue.—*Facings,* Blue.
Busby Bag, Scarlet. *Plume,* Scarlet
and White.

Hon. Colonel.
Beaufort, H. A. W. F.,
Duke of, TD, Col.,
A.D.C., late Lt.-Col. .. 14May04

Lt.-Colonel.
✗Playne, W. H. (Hon.
Capt. in Army 7 May
02) 16Apr.13

Majors. (5)
✗Elwes, H. C., M.V.O.,
Capt. ret. pay (H) .. 3June09
Yorke, R. M., Capt. ret.
pay (H)⑤ 27May12
Palmer, A. J. (H) .. 27May12
p.s.Forster, R. C. (H) .. 30Mar.13
✗Clifford, H. F.(Hon. Lt.
in Army 18Aug.01)(H) 1Nov.13

Captains (4).
Birchall, J. D. (H) .. 24July12
p.s.Baker, M. G. L. (H) .. 24July12
p.s.Longworth, T. J. (H) .. 1Nov.13
✗Turner, C. E. 1Nov.13

Lieutenants. (5)
Horlick, G. N. 24July12
Elcho, H. F., Lord .. 24July12
Howard, A. H. S., late
Capt. Carmarthen
R.G.A. (Mila.), (Hon.
Lt. in Army 7 Oct. 00) 30Mar.13
✗Hicks-Beach, Hon. M.
H. late Capt. 4 Bn.
Glouc. R., (Hon. Lt. in
Army 18July 01)(H) 1Nov.13
Sands, M. A. 13Dec.13

2nd Lieutenants. (8)
Calvert, H. M. 1Sept.09
Colledge, J. T. 1Mar.10
Gething, H. B. 25Mar.11
Wykeham - Musgrave,
A. G. 12Mar.12
Strickland, A. W. .. 1Oct.12
Guise, A. W. E., late Lt.
3 Bn. Glouc. R. .. 1Dec.12
Herbert, E. J. B. 15Feb.13
Mitchell, F. A. 24Feb.13
Bengough, J. C. 19Nov.13
Apsley, A. A., Lord .. 9Apr.14

Adjutant.

Quarter-Master.
✗Adderley, S. W., Qr.-
Mr. (hon. lt.) ret.
pay (Res. of Off.), hon.
capt. 16Aug.06

Medical Officer.
Bramwell, H., TD, M.D.,
F.R.C.S. (Edin.) Surg.-
Lt.-Col. 20May03
9June86

Chaplain.
Gloucester, Rt. Rev. E.
C. S., Lord Bishop of,
D.D., Chapl. 1st Class
(T.F.) (attd.) 1Apr.08
2May97

Hampshire.
(*Carabiniers.*)
Two carbines in saltire, in the first
and fourth corners a white rose and
in the second and third a red rose.
"South Africa, 1900-01."
Hyde Close, Winchester.

Uniform, Blue.—*Facings and Plume,*
White.

Hon. Colonel.
Crichton, Hon. Sir H.G.L.,
K.C.B., TD, Col. A.D.C.,
Hon. Lt.-Col. ret. pay 10June05

Lt.-Colonel.
p.s.✗Seely, Rt. Hon. J.E.B.,
D.S.O.,TD(Hon.Capt.in
Army 10July01) hon.c.
20June07
p.s.✗Nicholson, A. C., TD
18 July 01) 14June12

Majors. (5)
Nicholson, R. (H) .. 6Dec.02
p.s.✗Greenwell, B. E. (Hon.
Lt. in Army 19June01) 15Apr.07
p.s.Ashburton, F. D. E.,
Lord 19Oct.07
Baxendale, J. F. N.,(Hon.
Lt. in Army 5 Dec. 00)
(late Capt.3Bn.Hamps.
R.) (Q) (H) ⑤ .. 22June13
Lister, W. C. (Remount
Service) 19Sept.13

Captains. (4)
p.s.✗Crawford, H. H. (Hon.
Lt. in Army 7 Feb. 03)
(H) 2nd Cl. Dist. Offr. S.
Provs. Nigeria { 1Jan.14
{ 24Mar.06)
9Oct.07
p.s.Hamond-Graeme, E. H
M. (H) 1Apr.08
Jervoise, F. H. T. (H) 22July10
p.s.Timpson, L. (H).. .. 22June13
p.s.Stocker, A. H. 19Apr.14

Lieutenants. (5)
(p.s.)Good, C. H. B. 22July10
Lucas, Rt. Hon. A. T., Lord
17Aug.10
✗Elwes, L. B., Lt. ret.
pay (H) 22June13

2nd Lieutenants. (8)
(p.s.)Butler, Hon. F. A. .. 12Oct.08
(p.s.)Franklyn, H. A., late
Lt. Durh. L.I. 28Nov.08
White, R. D. 1Mar.09
Gribble, P. Le G. .. 23Feb.10
Montagu-Stuart-Wortley,
R. N. 25Mar.12
Schwerdt, G. F. I. .. 1Aug.13
Long, J. A. E. 30Mar.14

Adjutant.
Readman, J. J., Capt.
2 Dns. 12Oct.11

Quarter-Master.
✗Ross, G J. M., hon. lt. 26Oct.10

Medical Officers.
p.s.Ahrens, H. A., Surg.-
Capt. 28Nov.03
21Mar.06

Chaplain.
Brownlow, Rev. H. A
Chapl. 4thClass(T.F.)
(attd.) 1Nov.11

Yeomanry. Territorial Force.

Herts.
"South Africa, 1900-01."
Hertford.

Uniform, Scarlet—*Facings*, White.
Plume, Black.

Hon. Colonel.
Clarendon, Rt. Hon. *E.*
  H., Earl of, G.C.B.,
  G.C.V.O., TD, Col.,
  A.D.C. 7Feb.03

Lt.-Colonel.
p.s.Smith, A. H., TD 12Apr. 13

Majors. (5)
p.s.✕Sheppard, S. G., *D.S.O.*,
  (*Hon. Lt. in Army*
  28 Sept. 02) 20Dec.05
p.s.✕Kersey, H. M., *D.S.O.*
  (*Hon. Maj. in Army*
  27 July 02) 1Oct.09
Sheppard, E. B. 25Aug.13
Halsey, R. (*H*) .. 25Aug.13
Wyld, H. J. (*H*) .. 25Aug.13

Captains. (4)
p.s.de Falbe, C. F. G. W.(*H*)
    29Jan.11
Clayton, A. C. W. .. 20Oct.13
Drake, J. H. (*H*) .. 9May14

Lieutenants. (5)
Part, A. O. 1Aug.10
Ward, A. S. 1Aug.10
Smith, R. H. M. A. .. 20Oct.13
Leslie, J. 20Oct.13
Barnett, R. F. .. 1Feb.14

2nd Lieutenants. (8)
Ram, L. A. J. G... .. 15Feb.10
Ponsonby, V.C. 1Jan.11
Gibbs, W. D. 15Feb.11
Holland-Hibbert, T. .. 15Nov.11
Cunliffe, G.. .. .. 6May12
Bury, C. O. H. .. 2Oct.12
Charrington, G. N. 22Nov.13
Hol'and-Hibbert, W. 22Nov.13
Leslie, H. W. E. 16June14

Adjutant.
Lumley-Smith, T. G. L.,
  Capt. 21 Lrs. .. 4May14

Quarter-Master.
Nicholls, W. H., TD, *hon. maj.*
    10June10

Medical Officers.
Ward, Capt. G. S., R.A.M.C.
  (T.F.) (*attd.*) .. 30Nov.08
    5May03

Chaplain.

Royal East Kent.
(*The Duke of Connaught's Own.*)
(*Mounted Rifles.*)
"South Africa, 1900-01."
Canterbury.

Uniform, Rifle-Green—*Facings*,
Scarlet. *Plume*, Red and Green.

Hon. Colonel.
✕*Field-Marshal* H.R.H.
  Arthur W. P. A., Duke
  of Connaught and
  Strathearn,K.G., K.T.,
  K.P., G.C.B., G.C.S.I.,
  G.C.M.G., G.C.I.E.,
  G.C.V.O., Col. G. Gds.
  and A.S.C., and
  Col.-in-Chief, 6 Dns.,
  High. L.I. R. Dub.
  Fus. and Rif. Brig.
  Personal A.D.C. to
  the King 7Feb.96

Lt.-Colonel.
Guilford, F. G., Earl of,
  late Lt. 4 Bn. Glouc.R. 30Dec.11

Majors. (5)
Winch, G. B. 31Mar.08
✕Twisleton - Wykeham-
  Fiennes, H. E. (*Capt.
  Res. of Off.*) 1July08
p. Blake, A. O'B. ff. .. 13Jan.10
p. Winch, I. G. (*H*). .. 22May12
✕Filmer, Sir R. M., Bt.
  (*Lt. Res. of Off.*) .. 22May12

Captains. (4)
Lewis, A. F. L. (*H*) .. 22May12
Sebag-Montefiore, R. M.
  (*H*).. .. .. 22May12
✕Prescott-Westcar, C.H.
  B., late Lt. 14 Hrs. .. 23May12

Lieutenants.(5)
Dawes, H. H. (*H*) .. 9Nov.08
(p.s.)Crundall, E. R. (*H*) .. 14Dec.08
(p.e.)Harris, Hon. G. St. V.
  (*H*).. .. .. 18Jan.10
(p.s.)Balston, C. H. (*H*) .. 22May12
Friend, J. I. H. 9June13

2nd Lieutenants. (8)
Sassoon, Sir P.A. G. D., *Bt.*
    7Nov.07
Tylden, J. R. 23Nov.09
Barlow, K. 26Mar.11
Peto, R. H. 24May12
Hatfield, C. E. 26Feb.13
Allfrey, H. L. 1May13
Dawes, E. S. 20May14

Adjutant.
Wheler, G.B.H., Capt. 21Lrs.
    16Jan.12

Quarter-Master.
Carlisle, A., *hon. lt.* .. 6May09

Medical Officers.
Fox, C. T., Surg.-Capt. 26Aug.11
    26Feb.06

Chaplain.
Timins, Rev. F. C., *M.A.*,
  Chapl. 3rd Class (T.F.)
  (*attd.*) 26July09
    26July99

West Kent.
(*Queen's Own.*)

"South Africa, 1900-01."
Drill Hall, Union Street, Maidstone.

Uniform, Blue—*Facings* and Busby.
Bag, Scarlet. *Plume*, Red and White.

Hon. Colonel.
Abergavenny, W., Marq.
  of, K.G., TD, late Cor. &
  Sub.-Lt. 2 L.G... .. 17Feb.75

Lt.-Colonel.
p.s.Whitburn, C. W. S., TD. 3June14

Majors. (5)
p.s.Camden, J.C., Marq., TD 10May05
p.s.Sackville, L. E., Lord. 21Mar.06
p.s.✕Pott, R. B. (*Hon. Capt.
  in Army* 19 Aug. 01) .. 21Mar.06
p.s.✕Scott, Sir S. E., Bt.,
  late Lt. R.H.G. (*Hon.
  Lt. in Army* 11 May 01) 5Mar.10

Captains. (4)
p.s Style, G. M. 17June05
p.s.Marsham, C. G. B. (*H*) 1May08
p.s.✕Rycroft, A. R. H. (*H*)
  (*Remount Service*) 4Apr.09
✕Stewart, B (q)(*H*).. 19Apr.13

Lieutenants. (5)
(p.s.)Smith, O. M. (*H*) .. 4Apr.09
p.s.Marsham, C. H. B. (*H*) 4Aug.09
Mills, Hon. C. T. .. 28July10
Simpson, R. C. 29July10
Ponsonby, C. E... .. 20Apr.14

2nd Lieutenants. (8)
Christie, H. A. H. .. 1Jan.11
Campbell, D. S.(*H*) .. 16Feb.11
Lubbock, Hon. H. F. P.,28Mar.11
Buxton, R. V. 11Nov.11
Drummond, A. V., late Lt.
  3 Bn. Oxf.&Bucks. L.I. 19Feb.13
Mills, Hon. A. R. .. 7May13
Benson, G. H. .. 23July13

Adjutant.
✕Nixon, F. B., Capt. 6 Dns.
    15July12

Quarter-Master.
Knowlden, R., Qr.-Mr.
  (*hon. capt.*) ret. pay,
  hon. capt. 24Nov.09

Medical Officers.
Trouton, G. W., *M.D.*,
  Surg.-Capt. 13Dec.02
    15Nov.99

Chaplain.
Matthews, Rev. C. H.
  S., Chapl. 4th Class
  (T.F.) (*attd.*) .. 20Sept.09

Yeomanry. Territorial Force.

Lanarkshire.
"South Africa, 1900-02."

Lanark.

Uniform, Blue—*Facings,* Scarlet.

Hon. Colonel.

Home, C. A., Earl of,
K.T., TD, Col. (*King's Body Gd. for Scotland*) 16Dec.96

Lt.-Colonel.

Lamington, C. W. A. N.,
Lord, G.C.M.G., G.C.I.E.,
TD (*King's Body Gd. for Scotland*) 23May10

Majors. (5)

p.s.Findlay, R., TD. 15July05
p.s.Dunglass, C. C. A., *Lord*
15July05
Cranstoun, C. J. E. (*H*) 12June11
Johnson-Ferguson, E. A J.
13June12
p.s.Tower, W. M., Capt.
ret. pay (*H*)⊕ 20July13

Captains. (4)

p.s ✗Monteith, H. J. J. L.
(*Hon. Lt. in Army
9 Oct. 02*) 9May11
Scott Mackirdy, E. M. 28Apr.12
Thorburn, W. H. .. 1June14

Lieutenants. (5)

(p.s.)Cranstoun, G. H. H. E.
(*H*).. .. .. .. 1Apr.08
(p.s.)Marshall, A. C. .. 1Apr.08
Lambton, C. 28Apr.12
Wilson, J. 7May13

2nd Lieutenants. (8)

Fawcett, L. G. F, E. .. 1May09
Strang, J. 1Nov.09
Hutchison, J. R. H. .. 15Apr.12
Marshall, H. R. 22Oct.12
Leadbetter, J. G. G. .. 21Jan.14

Adjutant.

✗Pickering, F.A.U., Capt.
2 Dns. 10Apr.11

Quarter-Master.

Medical Officers.

McKenzie, Lt. J. C., *M.B.,*
R.A.M.C. (T.F.) (*attd.*)
20Apr.14

Lanarkshire.
(*Queen's Own Royal Glasgow and Lower Ward of Lanarkshire.*)
"South Africa, 1900-01."

Yorkhill Parade, Yorkhill, Glasgow.

Uniform, Dark Blue—*Facings,*
Scarlet. *Plume,* Black.

Hon. Colonel.

p. Glen-Coats, Sir T.G., Bt.,
C.B., VD (*Hon. Col.
ret. Vols.*) 5Aug.11

Lt.-Colonel.
p.s.✗Connal, K.H.M.,TD (*Hon.
Lt. in Army* 1May01) 25June10

Majors. (5)

Cayzer, H. R. (*H*) .. 21Dec.09
Wardle, J. R. 18July10
Cross, Sir W. C., *Bt.*(*H*) 18July10
✗Croshaw, O. M., late
Capt. 19 Hrs. (*Res. of
Off.*) (*Remount Service*) 29Jan.13

Captains. (4)

p.s.Cross, P. A. M. (*H*) .. 8Sept.08
Salvesen, R. H. (*H*) *I. of M.*
.. 18July10
Macfarlane, W. (*t*) .. 4Apr.13

Lieutenants. (5)

Baird, H. S. M. 14Mar.11
Galloway, T. L 14Mar.11
Glen-Coats, A. H. .. 18May11
Hollis, G. D. 18May11

2nd Lieutenants. (8)

Stewart, C. B. 12Dec.11
Jackson, D. F. 21Feb.12
Gallie, R. A. 20Mar.12
Salvesen, E. T. 27Dec.12
Glen, R. R. 22Jan.13
Gow, L. H. 29Jan.13
Collins, J. R., *late 2nd
Lt.* 16 Lrs., Spec. Res. 24Feb.13
Morrice, W. 11May14

Inst. of Musk.
Salvesen, R. H., *capt.* 1May11

Adjutant.
Laing, N. O., Capt. 4 Hrs.
21Nov.13

Quarter-Master.
Langley, S., *hon. maj.*.. 11Mar.08

Medical Officers.
p.s.Kelly, Maj. H., *M.D.,* TD,
R.A.M.C. (T.F.) (*attd.*) 18Feb.05
10May90
Brownridge, Lt. J. L.
R.A.M.C.(T.F.)(*attd.*) 4May08

Chaplain.
Georgeson, Rev. F. H.,
M.A. [U.F.C.] Chapl.
4th Class (T.F.)(*attd.*) 1Dec.09

Lancashire Hussars.
"South Africa, 1900-02."

Prince Alfred Road, Liverpool.

Uniform, Blue.—*Busby Bag,*Crimson.
Plume, Crimson and White.

Hon. Colonel.

Hopwood, E. R. G., TD
(*Hon. Col. ret. Impl.
Yeo*). 20Sept.07

Lt.-Colonel.

p.s.Earle, T. A., TD 19Oct.12

Majors. (5)

✗Pilkington, E. S., TD
(*Hon. Lt. in Army* 20
*Mar.*01) (*H*) 12Mar.04
Dewhurst, C. 1Sept.10
✗Stanley, *Hon.* F. W.
late Capt.10 Hrs.(*Capt.
Res. of Off.*) .. 23Mar.11
Aspinall, J. R. (*H*) .. 3May14

Captains. (4)

p.s.de Wend Fenton, W. R.
(*H*).. .. .. 1May09
Bromilow, H. A. (*H*) .. 13July10

Lieutenants. (5)

Fermor - Hesketh, T.,
late 2nd Lt. R.H.G. .. 7May10
✗Ridderborg, S. G. O.,
late Lt. 1 D.G. .. 31May10
1Sept11
Pilkington, G. L. .. 1June10
Rawstorne, T. G. .. 1July11
Wood, A. R. (*H*) 10July11

2nd Lieutenants. (8)

Legh, *Hon.* R. W. D. .. 1Mar.10
Rothwell, C. F. U, (*H*) 1Apr.12
Gossage, A. F. W. .. 5Oct.12
Aspinall, G. .. 25Dec.13
Lathom, E. W., *Earl of* 1May14

Adjutant.
✗Talbot, D. H., Capt.
17 Lrs. 18Nov.11

Quarter-Master.
p. Mountford, W., *hon.
capt.* 12Mar.04

Medical Officers.
Dun, Capt. R. C., *M.B.,
F.R.C.S.,* R.A.M.C.
(T.F.) *late* Capt. 1 W.
Gen. Hosp. (*attd.*) .. 7Jan.12
7Oct.11

Chaplain.
Sylvester, *Rev.* Canon
S. A. K., *M.A.,* Chapl.
4th Class(T.F.) (*attd.*) 1Apr 08
3Sept.04

Yeomanry. Territorial Force.

Duke of Lancaster's Own.
The Red Rose of Lancaster.
"South Africa, 1900-02."
Lancaster House, Whalley Road,
Whalley Range, Manchester.

Uniform, Scarlet.—*Facings*, Blue.
Plume, White.

Colonel-in-Chief.
THE KING.

Lt.-Colonel.
p. Tilney, R. H., TD .. 23Mar.12

Majors. (5)
p.s.✗Hardcastle, H. M., TD
(Hon. Lt. in Army
1May01) 13May03
Shepherd-Cross, T. A. S. 12Mar.04
Johnson, E. (H) 22Apr.05
p. Bibby, H. L. @ 7Jan.08
Molloy, L. G. S. 25Oct.11

Captains. (4)
p.s.✗Royds, W. E., *late Lt.*
7 Hrs. 3June05
28Apr.08
*p.s.*Forwood, T. B. (Hon. Lt.
in Army 1 Oct. 02) .. 24Nov.06
*p.s.*Shaw, F., jun. 23Mar.12
Hesketh, W. 4Dec.13

Lieutenants. (5)
Jones, W. P. M. 1July11
Greenall, J. E. 1July11
Bates, D. H. 23Mar.12
Birley, C. F. 21June13
Hornby, H. R. 4Dec.13

2nd Lieutenants. (8)
Fitzherbert-Brockholes,
J. W. 4Oct.11
Sharpe, E. W. 4Dec.11
18Sept.10
Sanderson, H. W. .. 22Feb.12
Greenshields, R. L. .. 9May12
Hartley, C. R. 11May12
11Jan.11
Percival, F. N. 4July12
Boddington, P. 28July13
Crook, P. J. .. 21Jan.14

Adjutant.
✗Love, E. W. P., *Capt.*
20 Hrs. 14Jan.13

Quarter-Master.
✗Hanbidge, R. W., *hon.
maj.* (A) (b) 5May01

Medical Officers.
✗Green, Capt. F. J., *M.D.*,
R.A.M.C. (T.F.) (*attd.*) 11Apr.11
19Jan.07
✗Crane, Lt. J. H., *M.D.*,
R.A.M.C. (*attd.*) 22Jan.13

Chaplain.
✗Powell, *Rev.* F. H., *Chapl.*
4th Class (T.F.) (*attd.*) 1Apr.08
9Mar.05

Leicestershire.
("*Prince Albert's Own.*")
"South Africa, 1900-02."
Leicester.

Uniform, Blue—*Facings*, Scarlet.
Busby-Bag, Red. *Plume*, White.

Hon. Colonel.
✗Blair, F. G., C.B., TD,
hon. c. (Hon. Lt.-Col. *in
Army* 3July00) 28Mar.06

Lt.Colonel.
✗Evans - Freke, *Hon.*
P. C. (*Hon.Lt.in Army*
10July01) 17Dec.13
22Feb.13

Majors. (5)
Robinson, A. H., TD .. 7June05
✗Ricardo, W. F. (*Maj.
Res. of Off.*) 27Mar.08
✗Martin, W. F. (*Hon.
Lt. in Army* 10July01) 6Aug.11
✗Byron, W. (*Hon. Capt.
in Army* 10 July 01) .. 4June13
✗Stewart, G. (*Capt. Res.
of Off.*) 18Feb.14

Captains. (4)
Codrington, G. R. .. 27Apr.12
Newton, C. N., *late Capt.*
2 L.G. 26 May 12

Lieutenants. (5)
Hanbury, E. R. 1Apr.11
Peake, C. 1Apr.11
Greaves, G. M. 19Sept.13
Thomson, S. P. D. .. 6Nov.13
Best, T. W., *late 2nd
Lt.* 16 Lrs. 7May14

2nd Lieutenants. (8)
Bonn, W. B. L. .. 1Aug.12
Johnson, W. S. F. .. 16Mar.13

Adjutant.
Ballward, J., *Capt.* 19 Hrs.
1Mar.14

Quarter-Master.
✗Crowley, J., Rid.-Mr. (*hon.
it.*) *ret. pay* (*Res. of Off.*)
hon. capt. 8Mar.11

Medical Officers.
Burkitt, Maj. J. C. S.,
M.D., R.A.M.C. (T.F.) 8Apr.14
(*attd.*) 15May08

Chaplain.
Bros, *Rev.* H. S., *Chapl.*
4th Class (T.F.) (*attd.*) 1Apr.13

Lincolnshire.
Old Barracks, Lincoln.

Uniform, Green.
Facings, White. *Plume*, Green.

Hon. Colonel.
Brownlow, Rt. Hon.
A. W. B., Earl, VD, Col.,
A.D.C., *late* Ens. &
Lt. G. Gds. 10Aug.01

Lt.-Colonel.
p.s. Ancaster, G., Earl *of*,
TD 18Feb.11

Majors. (5)
p.s. Wilson, T., TD 18July03
Royds, E. 19Aug.10
✗Gibbes, F. D., Capt. ret.
pay (*Res. of Off.*) .. 1Mar.12
✗Sleight, R. (H) 10May13

Captains. (4)
✗Hood, E. T. F., Lt.
ret. pay (q) (*Dep. Asst.
Dir.of Remts.,N.Comd.*) 9Mar.10
p.s. de Paravicini, P. C. F. 23Apr.10
Foster, G. B. 10May13

Lieutenants. (5)
(*p.s.*)Jessop, T. 7May09
Trollope, T. C. 30June10
(*p.,*)Wright, R. 30June10
Thornewill, C. C. .. 24Feb.13
Stanhope, *Hon.* R. P. .. 8Dec.13

2nd Lieutenants. (8)
Pelham, *Hon.* M. H. .. 14Dec.10
Newman, E. D. 14Apr.11
Crookes, A. D. F. .. 12Mar.13
Torr, J. H. T. 17May13
27Apr.09
Wintringham, J. W. .. 10Oct.13
Wilson, C. 9May14

Adjutant.
✗Cliff, G. T., *Capt.* 3 D.G. 1Apr.12

Quarter-Master.
✗Waghorn, A. E., *hon.lt.* 28Sept.10

Medical Officers.
✗Openshaw, Lt. - Col.
T. H., C.M.G., M.B.,
F.R.C.S., TD, R.A.M.C.
(T.F.) (*attd.*) 22Feb.08
14Jan.88
p. Purves, R. B., M.B.,
F.R.C.S.Edin., Surg.-
Capt. 14Nov.10
14May07

Yeomanry. Territorial Force.

City of London.
(*Rough Riders.*)
"South Africa, 1900-02."
39, Finsbury Square, E.C.

Uniform, Blue Grey.
Facings, Purple.
Plume, Light Blue.

Hon. Colonel.
p.s. ✗Maitland, F. C., Visct. (Hon. Capt. in Army 31Aug.00) (Gent.-at-Arms),(*Lt.-Col. & Hon. Col. ret. T.F.*)(*H*) .. 23July08

Lt.-Colonel.
p.s. ✗Boulton, O. E., TD (*Hon. Lt. in Army* 21Nov.00) 5Feb.13

Majors. (5)
p.s. ✗Gore, F. W. G., TD, hon. l.o. 5Apr.02
p.s.✗Villiers, C. H., Capt. ret. pay (Gent.-at-Arms), hon. l.o. .. 12May03
Polson, T. A. (Q) .. 1Jan.10
✗Clarke, G. V., D.S.O., late Capt. 18 Hrs. .. 4July12
✗Weisberg, H.(Q) (*H*).. 11Apr.14

Captains. (4)
p.s. Davson, I. B. (*H*) (q) .. 31July09
Gunston, C. B. (*H*) .. 17Apr.10
Knollys, F. R. A. N. (*H*).. .. .. 1June13
Feilding, R. C. .. 29Nov.13

Lieutenants. (5)
(p.) Lambert, S. (*H*) 13Nov.08
(p.s.)Mitchell, R. M. (*H*) .. 8Apr.09
(p.) Woolf, J.(*H*) 31July09
Pery, Hon. E. C. 1June13
Goldsworthy, E. W. .. 26Oct.13

2nd Lieutenants. (8)
Pixley, E. G. 1Apr.12
Robins, T. E. 15Apr.12
May, E. G. K. S... .. 1Nov.12
Lindsay-Smith, L. .. 20Feb.13
Ridsdale, A. H. 9Oct.13
Williams, G. A. 13Nov.13
Palmer, E. T. L. ..20June14

Adjutant.
✗Malet, H. W., Capt. 18 Hrs, ... 1Jan.13

Quarter-Master.
p. Shawyer, A. C., Rdg.-Mr. (hon. capt.), ret. pay (*Res. of Off.*) hon. maj. 1Nov.07
.. .. .. 5Apr.06

Medical Officers.
p.s. McQueen, R. M., *Surg.-Capt.* 2Jan.09
 3July05

Chaplain.
Sinclair, Ven. Archdeacon W. M., *M.A., D.D.,* Chapl. 3rd Class (T.F.) (*attd*) 31Jan.10
 31Jan.00

1st County of London.
(*Middlesex Duke of Cambridge's Hussars.*)
"South Africa, 1900-01."
Duke of York's Headquarters, Chelsea, S.W.

Uniform, Green. *Facings,* Black.
Busby-Bag, Scarlet.
Plume, Green and Scarlet.

Hon. Colonel.
✗Kitchener of Khartoum, Field Marshal H. H., Earl, K.P., G.C.B., O.M.,G.C.S.I.,G.C.M.G., G.C.I.E., Col. Comdt. R.E., q.s. 5July10

Lt.-Colonel.
Duncan, W., TD, ⓒ 28Apr.10
Majors. (5)
p.s.Brodie, H. C. 14May07
p.s.✗Dawes, E. S., Capt. ret. (*H*) (*Remount Service*) 24July07
p.s.✗Ailesbury, G. W. J. C., Marq. of, *D.S.O.,* Maj. ret. Impl. Yeo. (*H*) .. 16Oct.08
✗Lafone, A. M. (*H*) .. 18May12
p.s.✗Lawrence, A. S. (Capt. Res. of Off.) (Hon. Capt. in Army 23 Apr. 03)(*H*) (Comdt.,Somaliland Camel Corps 30Oct. 13
{ 17Feb.13}
 24July13
p.s.Fletcher, H. P. (*H*) .. 24July13

Captains. (4)
p.s. Higgens, C. R. (*H*) .. 7July10
Pawling, S. H. (*H*) .. 27July12
Marcuse, W. D. [l] (*H*) 24July13
✗Watson, O. C. S., *Lt.* ret. pay (*Res. of Off.*)(*H*)
 12Nov.13

Lieutenants. (5)
Carr Gomm, M. C. (*Asst. Engr. P.W. Dept.,* S. Provs. Nigeria { 1Jan.14
{ 17Apr.12}
McDougall, A. 17Mar.11
Bullivant, R. P... .. 18May12
Dalziel, P. B. 27July12
Devonshire, F. V. .. 24July13
 ..13Nov.13
2nd Lieutenants. (8)
Fletcher, E. T. D. .. 24Apr.11
Brodrick, A. L. .. 1Jan.12
Carus-Wilson, C. D. 8June12
Macaskie, S. S. .. 14Nov.12
Gossell, K. O. T. .. 14June13
Dale, A. B. [L] .. 28June13
Van den Bergh, S. J. .. 11Mar.14
Dalton, A. H. 3Apr.14
Adjutant.
Neilson, W., Capt, 4 Hrs.1Mar.12
Quarter-Master.
✗MacDonald, W. Capt. ret. pay, *hon. capt.* .. 19Feb.14

Medical Officer.
Sargent, Lt. P.W.G., *M.B., F.R.C.S., R.A.M.C.*(T.F.) (*attd.*) 30Mar.12

Chaplain.
Blakeway, Rev. P. J. T., *M.A.,* Chapl.2nd Class (T.F.)(*attd.*) 11July09
 11July94

2nd County of London.
(*Westminster Dragoons.*)
"South Africa, 1902."
Elverton Street, Westminster, S.W.

Uniform, Scarlet—*Facings,* Purple.
Plume, White.

Hon. Colonel.
✗Burn, C.R., Col., Lt.-Col. ret. pay, *A.D.C.* (Gent.-at-Arms) (*Lt.-Col. & Hon. Col. ret. Impl. Yeo.*) 19Nov.10

Lt.-Colonel.
p. Lumb, E. J. M., *late Lt.* 2 L.G. (*H*) 16Dec.13

Majors. (5)
✗Pitt, T. M. S., Capt. ret. pay (*H*) ⓒ .. 2Nov.07
✗Howard de Walden, T. E., Lord, late Lt. 10 Hrs. (*Hon. Col.* 4 Bn. R. Sc. Fus.) .. 4June10
✗Morrison-Bell, E. W., Capt. ret. pay .. 23Nov.10
✗Gillilan, E. G., *late* 2nd Lt. H. Gds. (*H*) .. 1June13
Haig, J. 1Jan.14

Captains. (4)
✗DG Norwood, J. (Capt. Res. of Off.) .. 1Feb.11
Vesey, Hon. O. E., *late Lt.* 9 Lrs. 19Nov.12
Jaffe, A. C... .. .. 1June14

Lieutenants. (5)
Magniac, O. C. 22Nov.01
Conran, E. L., *f.o.* .. 12Aug.12
Lewis, O. (*H*) 18Apr.13
Davson, T. G. (q) .. 1Jan.14

2nd Lieutenants (8)
Hogg, G. J. 11May12
Walford, W. 10June12
Cleland, L. H. F. .. 1July12
✗Moggridge, H. W. .. 28Apr.13
Burdett, H. G. 13June13

Adjutant.
Oppenheim,R.W.,Capt. 4 D.G. 1Oct.11

Quarter-Master.
✗Diggory, C. J., Qr.-Mr. (*hon. capt.*) ret. pay, *hon. capt.* 4July14

Medical Officers.
p. Avery, Capt. L. A., *R.A.M.C.*(T.F.)(*attd.*)15Aug.06
 24Dec.02

Yeomanry. Territorial Force.

3rd County of London.
(*Sharpshooters.*)
"South Africa, 1900-02."
Henry Street, St. John's Wood.
N.W.

Uniform, Green.
Facings and Busby-Bag, Green.
Plume, White.

Hon. Colonel.
✗Dunraven and Mount-earl, Rt. Hon. W. T., Earl of, K.P., C.M.G. (*Hon. Capt. in Army* 6July01) 6Aug.04

Lt.-Colonel.
p.s.✗Jarvis, A. W., C.M.G., M.V.O., TD, Lt. ret. (*Hon. Lt.-Col. in Army* 11Sept.02).. .. 2July09

Majors. (5)
p.s. ✗Curley, H. J.,TD (*Hon. Capt.in Army* 3Aug.01) 11June06
✗Gage, Æ. M, B., *hon. l.c.*
 2Nov.06
 20Jan.03
✗Haig, O... .. .. 15May10
p s.Howell, O. A. 13Oct.12
✗Bell, E. J., *late Capt.* R.F.A. Spec. Res., *formerly Capt. Ind. Army* 16July13

Captains. (4)
p.s.✗Fremantle, J. M. (*Hon. Capt. in Army* 18Aug.02) (*H*) (*a*) (*b*) (*2nd Class Resdt., N. Provs. Nigeria*
 { 1 Jan. 14
 { 2Nov. 04) 2Nov.03
Jarvis, L. K, ... 15Oct.06
p. Eaton, R. W. 15May10
✗Cutbill, C. A.(*Hon. Lt. in Army* 15Dec.01), *late Lt. Impl. Yeo.* (S. Africa) 13Oct.12
✗Albery, I. J. (*H*) .. 26July13

Lieutenants. (5)
✗James, H. 24Feb.12
Francis, D'A. J. (*H*) *l. of M.* 13Oct.12
Tuck, D. A. 22May13
Tuck, W. R. 24Aug.13
FitzGerald, G. M. .. 5Apr.14
Carter, F. W. 5Apr.14

2nd Lieutenants. (8)
Sanderson, E. L. .. 7Sept.11
Weiss, M. A. 3May12
Parish, C. D. W. .. 7Apr.13
Schuster, L. F., *late 2nd Lt., Res. of Off.*. .. 15Oct.13
de Pass. E. A. 4Feb.14
Anson, E. H. 13Mar.14
Thorpe. G. G. 8June14
Puckle, H. 9June14
Miles, F. H. H. 30June14

Inst. of Musk.
Francis, D'A. J.,*lt.* .. 9Mar.12

Adjutant.
✗Truman, C. M., Capt. 12 Lrs. 7Oct.12

Quarter-Master.
p. ✗Parsons, C. W., *hon. maj.* 19Sept.08

Medical Officers.
Moxon, Capt. H. R., R.A.M.C. (T.F.)(*attd.*)18Dec.12
 18June09

Lothians and Border Horse.
A Garb.
"South Africa, 1900-01."
7, Wemyss Place, Edinburgh.

Uniform, Scarlet—*Facings*, Blue.
Plume, White.

Hon. Colonel.
Haddington, G., Earl of, K.T., TD, Col., A.D.C., *late Lt.-Col. (King's Body Gd.for Scotland)* 24Oct.94

Lt.-Colonel.
p.s.✗Binning,G.,Lord,C.B., M.V.O., Bt. Col. ret. pay 28Apr.06

Major (2nd in Command).
p.s.✗Montagu-Douglas-Scott, Lord G. W. (*Capt. Res. of Off.*) 4Sept.06
 24May06

Majors. (4)
p.s.✗Wauchope,D.A.,D.S.O. (*t*) (*Hon. Lt. in Army* 17 July 01) 18Mar.02
Cadell, H. F., TD. .. 18Mar.02
p.s ✗Stewart, W. B. (*Hon. Lt. in Army* 11 Oct. 00) 9Jan.04
✗Waring, W., *late Capt.* 1 L.G. 6July10

Captains. (4)
✗Ramsay, J.R.(*Hon.Lt. in Army* 26 July 01) .. 18Mar.02
Baird, W.A. 6July10
p.s.✗Cowan, A. G. 4Aug.12
Steel, S. S. 19Oct.12

Lieutenants. (5)
Pringle, L. J., *late Capt.* Rox. & Selk. V.R.C. .. 1Apr.08
Stevenson, H. J. .. 6July10

2nd Lieutenants. (8)
Linlithgow, V. A. J., Marq. of 1June08
Younger, C. F. 15Dec.09
Hay, R. A. 6Apr.11
Stewart, H. S. ⊕. .. 14May13
Hepburne-Scott, W. T. 5June13
Marshall, J. R. 8June13
Hay, Lord E. D. J. .. 10Feb.14
Tulloh, T. A. G. .. 11Feb.14
Guest, *Hon.* O. M. .. 20Feb.14
 3Oct.09

Adjutant.
Turner, C. W., Capt. 1 Dns.
 7Nov.11

Quarter-Master.
✗Stubbs,W.,Qr.-Mr.(*hon. capt.*), ret. pay, *hon. maj.* 1Aug.06

Medical Officers.
p.s.Cameron, Maj. J., R.A.M.C., (T.F.) (*attd.*) .. 18Sept.08
 13May96

Chaplain.
Veitch, *Rev.* W.. *M.A.* [C.S.]Chapl. 2ndClass (T.F.) (*attd.* 15Apr.14
 Apr.99

1st Lovat's Scouts.
"South Africa, 1900-02."
Beauly, N.B.

Uniform, Blue—*Facings*, Blue.

Hon. Colonel.
✗Lovat, S. J.,Lord, K.C.V.O., C.B., D.S.O., Col., A.D.C. (*Hon Col. 4 Bn. Gord. Highrs.*) (*Col. ret. T.F.*) 4June13

Lt.-Colonel.
p.s.✗Fraser-Tytler, E. G., *late Lt. Impl. Yeo.* (S. Africa) 12Apr.13

Majors. (5)
p.s.✗Grant, E., *late Lt. Impl. Yeo.* (S. Africa) 30Mar.03
p.s.✗MacDonald, K. L. (*Hon. Res. in Army* 5 Dec. 00) 30Mar.03
p.s ✗Campbell - Orde, A. J., Bt., *late Lt. Impl. Yeo.* (S. Africa) (*H*).. .. .. 30Mar.03
p.s.Cameron, E. C. (*H*) .. 1Mar.09

Captains. (4)
p.s.Dewar, H. R. (*H*) .. 1Mar.09
Jones, W. E. (*H*) .. 15June09
✗Maxwell, A. E., *late Capt. G. Gds.* (*Capt. Res. of Off.*) .. 14Nov.10
p.s.Gray, D., TD (*H*) .. 26Sept.11
p.s.✗St. John Secker, J., *late Lt. Midd'x R.* (*Lt. Res. of Off.*) .. 12Apr.12

Lieutenants. (5)
(p.s.)McLean, W. (*H*) .. 1Mar.09
(p.s.)Fraser-Tytler, J.F. (*H*) 15June09
(p.s.)Hilleary, E. L. 16Mar.10
Cameron, A. 12Apr.12
p.s.Howard, *Hon.* B. E. F... 12Apr.12
Coles, D. (*H*) 12June12

2nd Lieutenants. (8)
Ferguson, A. 23Mar.12
Kennedy, A. J. A. .. 18May12
Bowhill, A. H. 1Feb.13
Calder, G. G. 22May13
Mackay, J. I. MacD. .. 22Apr.14

Adjutant.

Quarter-Master.
p. ✗Pococke, H. (*Hon. Lt. in Army* 15July02) *hon. maj...* 30Mar.03

Medical Officers.
Leach, Capt. J., *M.B.,* R.A.M.C.(T.F.)(*attd.*) 18May11
 30Mar.03

Chaplain.
Bonallo, *Rev.* J., *B.D.* [C.S.] Chapl.4thClass (T.F.) (*attd.*) 1Apr.10

Yeomanry. Territorial Force.

2nd Lovat's Scouts.
"South Africa, 1900-02."
Beauly, N.B.

Uniform, Blue—*Facings,* Blue.

Hon. Colonel.
✗Lovat, S.J., Lord, K.C.V.O., C.B., D.S.O., Col., A.D.C. *(Hon. Col. 4 Bn. Gord. Highrs.)(Col. ret. T.F.)* .. 4June13

Lt.-Colonel.
p.s.✗Stirling, A. (H), Capt. ret.*(Res. of Off.)* .. 18Aug.0⁹

Majors. (5)
p.s.Barclay, J... .. .. 23Apr.04
p.s.✗Baillie, D.G.*(Hon. Lt. in Army* 1Dec.00) .. 1Mar.0⁹
✗McNeill, A.J., Bt.Maj. ret. pay *(Capt. Res. of Off.)* 21July10
Bt. Maj, in Army 29May01
Munro-Ferguson, H.,*late* Lt. 3 Bn.R.Highrs.(H) 21Feb.11
✗Campbell, Hon. R. A., Capt. & Bt. Maj., Res. of Off. 27Apr.14

Captains. (4)
p.s.Burton-Mackenzie, E. N. (H).. .. .. 21Feb.11
p.s.Campbell, Hon. I.M.(H) 1Feb.14

Lieutenants. (5)
p.s.Robertson, J. A... .. 1Mar.09
Grant, J. P., jun. .. 21Feb.11
Henderson, H.K.H. (H) 12June12
Forsyth-Grant, I. .. 8Jan.14
Millar, J. S. L.⑤ .. 8Jan.14

2nd Lieutenants. (8)
Loyd, L. F. I. 1May10
Gilmour, A. 21Jan.11
Fraser-Mackenzie, J. O.A. 29May11
✗Mackintosh, W. .. 7June11
Forbes, J. 7June11
Murray, K. 10June11
Sutherland, W. G. .. 6Mar.12
Melville, Hon. I. L. 15Dec.13
McCorquodale, K. .. 2Jan.14

Adjutant.
✗Wood, R. B., Capt. 12 Lrs. 11Mar.13

Quarter-Master.
Flannery, M. J., *late* Commy. *(hon. capt.)* ret. pay Ind. Army, *hon. lt.* 1Nov.09

Medical Officers.
Lovett-Campbell, Lt. A. G., M.B., R.A.M.C (T.F.)*(attd.)* 28May04

Montgomery-shire.
"South Africa, 1901."
Welshpool.

Uniform, Scarlet—*Facings,* Black.
Plume, White.

Hon. Colonel.
Williams-Wynn, Sir H. L. W., Bt., C.B.,TD (Hon. Col. ret. Impl. Yeo.) .. 1Nov.07

Lt.-Colonel.
p.s.✗Williams-Wynn, R.W. H. W., D.S.O.,TD (Hon. Capt. in Army 13Aug. 01) hon. c. .. 31Oct.06
bt. col. 22Feb.13

Majors. (5)
p.s.✗Walton, F. J. *(Hon. Lt. in Army* 14Aug.01) 18July06
p.s.✗Dugdale, W. M. *(Hon. Capt. in Army* 28Sept.02) 31Oct.06
p.s.Harrison, G. R. D. .. 18Sept.10
Whitaker, W. H. B. (H) 1May14
Sykes, H. R. (H) .. 1May14

Captains. (4)
Lees, J. D. (H), *late* 2nd Lt. 2 D. G. 5Nov.10
✗Parry, D. B., Capt.ret. pay.. .. .. 5Nov.10
Stable, W. N. (H) .. 1May14

Lieutenants. (5)
Bonnor-Maurice, T. I. 1Mar.11
Bardwell, T. B. .. 1Mar.11
Evans, J. D. D., *late* Lt. 3 Bn. S. Wales Bord. (H) 1May1⁷
Frost, J. D. ③ (H) .. 1May14

2nd Lieutenants. (8)
Freeman, A. F., *late* Lt. Unattd. List (T.F.) .. 15Apr.11
Gough, W. H. J., *late* Lt. 1 Dns. 25Jan.12
Wynn, A. R. 26Jan.12
✗Phillips, F. A. .. 27Jan.12
Bankes, R. W. .. 15Oct.12

Adjutant.
Copland-Griffiths, E., Lt. 16 Lrs. *capt,* 1Mar.13

Quarter-Master.
✗Mercer, W., *hon. lt.* 1Apr 13

Medical Officers
Swettenham, Capt. A. W. W., R.A.M.C (T.F.) *(attd.)* .. 24May12
27May0⁹
Elliott, Lt. W. E. L., M.D., R.A.M.C. (T.F.) *(attd.)* 1Feb.13

Chaplain.
Woosnam, Rev. Canon C. M., M.A., Chapl. 4th Class (T.F.) *(attd.)* 1Apr.12

Norfolk.
(The King's Own Royal Regiment.)
The Royal Arms.
In each of the four corners the Royal Cypher ensigned with the Imperial Crown.

Cattle Market Street, Norwich.

Uniform, Blue.
Facings and Plume—Yellow.

Colonel-in-Chief.
THE KING.

Hon. Colonel.
His Majesty Haakon VII., King of Norway, K.G.,G.C.B.,G.C.V.O. 23Dec.05

Lt.-Colonel.
p.s.Seymour, C. D... .. 24May13

Majors. (5)
p.s.Morse, A. F., *late* Lt. 6 Dns. (H) .. 26July01
p.s.✗Buxton, A. R. *(Hon. Capt.in Army* 1Sept.01) 2Nov.07
p.s.✗Gurney, C. F. *(Hon. Capt. in Army* 5 Sept. 02) 20Nov.11
Bullard, G. T. 15Feb.13
Gurney, Q. E. (H) .. 1Feb.14

Captains. (4)
p.s.Barclay, J. F. 24Sept.09
Hastings, A. E. D., Lord (H) 1May10
Buxton, I... .. .. 26Apr.13
p.s.Barclay, M. E. .. 1Feb.14

Lieutenants. (5)
(p.s.)Birkbeck, H. A. .. 1Oct.09
Paul, J. D... .. 16Aug.11
Buxton, R. G. 21Dec.12
Every, Sir E. O., Bt ⑤.. 26Apr.13
Wodehouse, J., *Lord* 1Feb.14

2nd Lieutenants. (8)
Birkbeck, O. .. 6Apr.11
Flower, N. A. C. 1Feb.13
Lawson-Johnston, P. G. 1Feb.13
Birkbeck, G. 13Aug.13
Neumann, G. C. J. .. 7Feb.14

Adjutant.
McMurrough Kavanagh, G. T., Capt. 7 Hrs. 1Nov.13

Quarter-Master
Sayer, J. A., *hon. lt.* .. 22Mar.11

Medical Officers.
p.s.Gordon-Dill, J. F., M.D., Surg.-Maj. 14July07
15May15

Chaplain.
ffolkes, Rev. F. A. S., M.V.O., B.A., Chapl. 3rd Class (T.F.) *(attd.)* 4Jan.12
4Jan.02

Yeomanry. Territorial Force.

Northamptonshire.

Territorial Head Quarters, Clare Street, Northampton.

Uniform, Blue—Facings, Light Blue Plume, Light Blue and White.

Hon. Colonel.

✗Annaly, L., Lord, K.C.V.O. (Hon. Col. ret. Impl. Yeo.) 10Oct.08

Lt.-Colonel.

p.s.✗Wickham, H. (Hon. Maj. in Army 21 Sept. 02) 15Jan.10

Majors. (5)

p, ✗Renton, A. L. (Capt. Res. of Off.) 5Mar.02
Tryon, R. (Lt. Res. of Off.) 3Feb.04
p.s.Cazenove, E. 27Nov.07
Bucknall, L. C. (H) .. 4May11
Campbell, H. B. (H) .. 4May11

Captains. (4)

Andrewes, E. A. (H) (Remount Service) .. 16May08
✗Middleton, G. G., late Capt. 2 Dns. 15Jan.10
✗Lowther, Sir C. B., Bt., late Capt. 8 Hrs. .. 4May11
Manning, T. E. .. 18Apr.12

Lieutenants. (5)

Gilliat, F. L. 25Aug.09
Nickalls, P. W., late Lt. Durh. L.I. 20May11
✗Robarts, G., late Lt. R.H.G. 27Mar.12
Wartnaby, C. R. A. .. 5June12
Cazenove, R. de L. .. 10Oct.13

2nd Lieutenants. (8)

Compton, Lord S. D. .. 10Feb.12
Cross, J. L. 10Feb.12
Murland, J. M. G. .. 20Mar.12
Frederick, Sir C. E. St. J., Bt. 4Mar.12
Horton, G. T. S. .. 31Dec.13

Adjutant.

Lowther, J. G., Lt. 11 Hrs., capt. 23Feb.14

Quarter-Master.

Challen, F., hon. lt. .. 1May11

Medical Officers.

p, Allison, Maj. J., M.D., R.A.M.C.(T.F.) (attd.) 19Dec.09
25May98

Northumberland.

(Hussars.)
"Imperial Service."
"South Africa, 1900-02."
Northumberland Road, Newcastle-on-Tyne.

Uniform, Blue.
Busby-Bag, Scarlet. Plume, Scarlet and White.

Hon. Colonel.

✗Bates, C. L., D.S.O. (Hon. Col. ret. T.F.) .. 24May13

Lt.-Colonel.

Ridley, M. W., Visct. (Hon.Col. 5 Bn.North'd Fus.) 22May13

Majors. (5)

✗Cookson, P. B., Maj. ret. pay (Res. of Off.) .. 25Mar.13
Selby-Bigge, D. L. .. 27May05
✗Burrell, W. M., Capt. ret. pay 7June13
✗Johnston, L. (Hon. Lt. in Army 28Sept.02) (H) 7June13

Captains. (4)

p.s.✗Charlton, W. H. (Lt. Res. of Off.) (H), p.v.c. 15 Oct.10
p.s. Campbell, D. E.(H) .. 17June11
p.s. Sidney, H., late Lt. 5 Bn. R. Fus. (H), p.v.c. (a) (b) P.c. 7June13
p.s. Burrell, S. (H) 7June13

Lieutenants. (5)

(p.) Ridley, Hon. J. N. .. 13Mar.12
Astley, Hon. C. M. .. 8Jan.13
Rea, J. G. G. 8Jan.13

2nd Lieutenants. (8)

Burdon, W. W. 27Mar.09
Bigge, W. E. 11Sept.09
Pease, R. A. 2May10
Drummond, Hamilton, M.B., late Surg.-Lt. North'd Yeo. 16Dec.11
Joicey, E. R. 14Mar.12
Laing, C. H. 15Mar.12
Blake, F. E. C. .. 20Jan.13
Eustace-Smith, P. .. 16Apr.13
Ridley, A. H. 5 Nov.13
Stobart, R. L. 25Feb.14

Adjutant.

✗Kennard, W. A., Capt. 13 Hrs. 9Apr.12

Quarter-Master.

✗Moores, W., hon. lt, 20Apr.12

Medical Officers.

Drummond, Lt. Horsley, M.B., R.A.M.C. (T.F.) (attd.) late Capt. 1 N. Gen. Hosp., R.A.M.C. (T.F.) 8June12

Nottinghamshire.

(Sherwood Rangers.)
"South Africa, 1900-02."
Retford.

Uniform, Green. — Facings, Green.
Busby-Bag, Scarlet. Plume, Green and White.

Hon. Colonel.

Galway, G. E. M., Visct., C.B., TD, Col. A.D.C. 19Dec.03

Lt.-Colonel.

✗Whitaker, A. E., Capt. late Res. of Off. (H) .. 2Jan.10

Majors. (5)

✗Peacock, H. O. (Hon. Lt. in Army 31Oct.00) 14Nov.03
Thorpe, H. 2Jan.10
p.s. ✗Thorpe, J. S., Capt. ret. (H) 14June13
Birkin, P. A. (H) .. 14June13
Kent, P. N., Capt. ret. pay (Res. of Off.) (Remount Service) .. 13May14

Captains. (4)

p.s. Mirrlees, A. J. (H) .. 2Jan.10
p s. Willey, F. V. (H) .. 14June13
p.s. Wade-Palmer, A. N. .. 13May14

Lieutenants. (5)

✗Hall, H. C. (Hon. Lt. in Army24Sept.02)(H)(Station Magistrate, 2nd Grade, Nigeria, {1Jan.14
{21Feb.03) 1May01
p.s. Tallents, H. (H) .. 2Jan.10
(P.) Bainbridge, O. J. .. 14June13
Puxon, E. F. M. .. 14June13
Turner, D. W. .. 13May14

2nd Lieutenants. (8)

MacRae, J. N. 1June11
Pawson, A. C. .. 28Feb.12
Anstey, T. C. R. 28Feb.13

Adjutant.

Woodhouse, J. D, F., Capt. 14 Hrs. .. 1Oct.11

Quarter-Master.

✗Murray, J. hon. lt, .. 1Apr.10

Medical Officers.

p, Thomson, G., M.B., Surg.-Capt. 13Sept.05
16Apr.02

Chaplain.

Scott-Moncrieff, Rev. C. E., M.A., Chapl. 4th Class (T.F.) (attd.) .. 1Apr.08
14May04

481 | 482 | 483

Yeomanry. Territorial Force.

Nottinghamshire.
(South Nottinghamshire Hussars.)
"South Africa, 1900-02."
Derby Road, Nottingham.

Uniform, Blue.—*Busby-Bag*, Scarlet. *Plume*, Red and White.

Lt.-Colonel.
p. Trotter, C. W., TD, hon. c. .. .. .. 31 Mar 08
p. Seely, F. E., TD. .. 29May12

Majors. (5)
p. Bruce, P. R. (t) ⑥ .. 31Mar.08
Bayley - Worthington, A. B. 15Apr.08
p. ✗Barber, T. P. (*Hon. Lt. in Army* 9 Oct. 01) 17Aug,10
Ley, H. G. (H) .. 29 May12
✗Birkin, H. L. (H) (*Hon. Lt. in Army* 23 June 01) 4June13

Captains. (4)
Smith, B. A. (H) .. 1Mar.09
Warwick, P. H. (H) .. 17Aug.10
p.s. Cantrell-Hubbersty, G. A. J. (H) 29May12

Lieutenants. (5)
p.s. Thornton, P. S. .. 1Apr.08
(p.s.) Milward, G. G... .. 1Mar.09
Heymann, W. G. .. 17Aug.10
Chaworth-Musters, J. N. 1Jan.11
Jeffcock, W. P. .. 12July13

2nd Lieutenants. (8)
Fillingham, G. A. .. 16Apr.12
Macmillan, C. D. .. 1 Apr.13
Birkin, T. R. C. (H) .. 21June13
Hanson, R. 1Mar.14
Hoyle, C. F. 1June14

Adjutant.
Sopper, E., Capt. 17 Lrs. 16Sept.13

Quarter-Master.
Roach, H. T., hon. lt. .. 1Jan.11

Medical Officers.
Rowe, W. T., M.D., Surg.-Capt. 27July11
22May00

Chaplain.
✗Baynes, Rt. Rev. Bishop A. H., D.D., Chapl. 1st Class (T.F.) (attd.) 1Apr.08
3Nov.01

G

Oxfordshire.
(Queen's Own Oxfordshire Hussars.)
"South Africa, 1900-01."
Oxford.

Uniform, Dark Blue—Facings and Busby-Bag, Mantua Purple. *Plume*, Mantua Purple and White.

Hon. Colonel.
✗Valentia, A., Visct., C.B., M.V.O., TD, (*Hon. Col. ret. Impl. Yeo.*) (*Hon. Col. in Army* 1 Jan.01) 24Sept.04

Lt.-Colonel.
p.s. Dugdale, A., TD (H) .. 10Mar.14

Majors (5)
✗Twisleton-Wykeham-Fiennes, Hon. E. E. (*Hon. Lt. in Army* 1May01) 27May05
✗Churchill, Rt. Hon. W. L. S., late Lt. S. Afr. Lt. Horse, formerly Lt. 4 Hrs. .. 27May05
Churchill, V. A. F. C., Visct., G.C.V.O. late Lt. C. Gds. .. 12July05
✗Churchill, J. S. S. .. 1Apr.11
Nicholl, C. R. I. (H) ..23 Apr 13

Captains. (4)
Fell, A. H. (H) .. 12July11
✗Scott, J. W., Capt. ret. pay 26July13

Lieutenants. (5)
(p.s.) Fleming, V. (H) .. 24Apr 09
Dillon, A. H. .. 23June10
Scott, L. F. .. 26 Aug.10
Twisleton - Wykeham-Fiennes, Hon. G. R. C. 24Oct.11
Smith, Rt. Hon. F. E... 8Nov.13

2nd Lieutenants. (8)
✗Hermon-Hodge, R E. U., late Lt. Oxf. L.I. 1July09
Child-Villiers, Hon. A. G. 18Sept.09
Fleming, P. 29Dec.10
Hutchinson, G. T. .. 23Oct.11
Fane, H. A. .. 24Oct.11
Pepper, W. 2Nov.11
Palmer, G.H. 5Oct.12
Pearce, J. J. (*late Capt. Unattd. List* (T.F.) .. 3Dec.13
Keith-Falconer, A. W... 26Jan.14

Adjutant.
Bonham-Carter, G., Capt. 19 Hrs. 17Feb.13

Quarter-Master.
✗Lidington, B. W., hon. maj. 20Feb.04

Medical Officers.
Proudfoot, Capt. F. G., M.D., R.A.M.C. (T.F.) (attd.) 3Mar.09
Hogarth, A.H., Surg.-Lt. 30July04

Chaplain.
Minchin, Rev. C. H., M.A., Chapl. 4th Class (T.F.) (attd.) 13Dec.11

Pembroke.
(Castlemartin.)
"Fishguard."
"South Africa, 1901."
Tenby.

Uniform, Blue—*Facings*, White.

Hon. Colonel.
Scourfield, Sir O. H. P., Bt., TD 2Aug.90

Lt.-Colonel.
p.s. Williams, O. H. S., TD 1Oct 12

Majors. (5)
✗Spence-Jones, C. J. H., Capt. ret. (H) .. 8Mar.05
✗Collis, R. H., D.S.O., Capt. ret. pay (H) .. 1Apr.08
✗Stewart, W. E. L., D.S.O., Capt. ret. pay 9Jan.09
Davies-Evans, D. W. C. (H) 1Apr.11

Captains. (4)
Higgon, J. A., Capt. ret. pay (Res. of Off.) .. 8Mar.10
✗Partridge, L., Capt. ret. pay 1Aug.11
p.s. Jones, E. G. (Hon. Lt. in Army 28Jan.03) (H) 22Apr.12

Lieutenants. (5)
(p.s.) Gabbett, W. H. .. 23Aug.05
Woodcock, J. B. H. .. 22Apr.12
Bishop, J. W. 22Apr.12
Yorke, J. H. L. 3Oct.12
Barclay, R. C. E. .. 3Oct.12

2nd Lieutenants. (8)
Lambton, E. (Irrigation Dept., Egypt, 16 Aug. 09) 16Aug.09
Bowen, J. B. ⑥ 15Mar.10
Barnes, C. G. S. .. 1Sept.10
Jones, T. C. 12 Apr.13
Morgan, F. S. 1Mar.14

Adjutant.
Williams, E. H. W., Capt. 10 Hrs. 14Mar.12

Quarter-Master.
Willmott, J., hon. lt. 1Nov12

Medical Officers.
Wilson, J., M.D., Surg. Capt. 2Sept.05
20July98
Mathias, Lt. C. D., R.A.M.C.(T.F.)(attd.) 29May07

Yeomanry. Territorial Force.

Scottish Horse.

St. Andrew's Cross.
In each of the four corners the Thistle ensigned with the Imperial Crown.

"South Africa, 1900-02."

Dunkeld, N.B.

Uniform, Atholl Grey—*Facings*, Yellow.—*Plume*, Black cock Feathers.

Lt.-Colonel Commandant.

✗Tullibardine, J. G., Marq. of, *M.V.O.*, *D.S.O.*, Bt. Maj. h.p., *hon. c.* .. 1Jan.09

Lt.-Colonels. (2)

p.s. Scrymsoure - Steuart-Fothringham, W. T. J., *late Lt.* S. Gds. .. 1Apr.08
p.s.✗Farquhar, M. G., *D.S.O., late Capt.* Thorneycroft's Mtd. Inf. (*H*) 1July14

Majors. (10)

Stirling, J. A., *late Lt.* S. Gds. (q) (*H*).. 1May07
Leslie, A. S. (*H*).. .. 15Oct.10
✗Moir-Byres, P., Maj. ret. pay (*Res. of Off.*) 1Mar.11
Baird, J. L., *C.M.G.* .. 1July12
✗Bruges, W. (Hon. Lt in Army 14 Jan. 03) .. 16May13
Crawford-Leslie, R. W. H. (*H*) 20July13
Wedderburn Ogilvy, J. A. (*H*) 1July14
Aitchison, W. (*H*) .. 1July14

Captains. (8)

p.s.MacGregor, E. M. (*H*).. 15Oct.10
Bullough, J. 31Mar.11
Murray, J. (*H*) .. 1Aug.11
Mackenzie, H. M. *H*).. 16May13
Rundell, W. W. O. .. 16May13
Dawson, S. 16May13
Butchart, H. J. (*H*) .. 20July13
p.s. Lyle, A. M. P. (*H*) .. 1July14
Dewar, J. 1July14

Lieutenants (10)

Murray, E. M... .. 1Oct.11
(p.s.)Proctor, W. F. (*H*) .. 2Oct.11
.. .. .. 11Mar.09
p.s.Campbell, B. A .. 16May13
Robertson, A. F. .. 16May13
Grogan, A. W. .. 16May13
Woodman-Smith, J. .. 16May13
Fergusson, R. A. A. .. 20July13
Cowan, J. R. C. .. 1July14
Mathers, J. A. .. 1July14
Don, F. P. 1July14
Greenlees, W. L. .. 1July14

2nd Lieutenants. (16)

Gordon, C. 1Jan.08
Campbell, J. H. A. |1May12
Ogilvie-Forbes, G. A. D.
.. .. .. 1May12
Gammell, J. A. H. .. 12Dec.12
Stirling, P. D. .. 17Dec.12
Lothian, J. 5Mar.13
Butler, J. R. M. .. 16May13
Couper, J. D. .. 18June13
McIntyre, A. C. .. 1Apr.14
Ramsay, J. D. .. 8Apr.14
Graham, M. W. A. P. 1June14
Doune, F. D., *Lord* .. 25May14

Adjutants. (2)

Erskine, *Sir* T. W.H.J., *Bt.*, Capt. Cam'n Highrs. 15Jan.12
✗McCallum, C. H. M., Capt. High. L.I. .. 11Dec.12

Quarter-Masters. (2)

✗Black, J., *hon. lt.* .. 1Dec.11
✗Haven, C. J., *hon. lt.* 6Mar.13

Medical Officers.

p.s.Sloan, Ma¹. S. M., *M.B.*, *late Capt. R.A.M.C.* Spec. Res. R.A.M.C. (T.F.) (*attd.*) .. 22May14
.. .. .. 25Apr.14
Simpson, Lt, J.A., *M.B.*, R.A.M.C.(T.F.) (*attd.*) 12Oct.10

Chaplain.

✗Robertson, *Rev.* J., *D.S.O., D.D.,* [C.S.] Chapl. 2nd Class, ret. pay, Chapl. 1st Class (T.F.) (*attd.*) .. 7July09
Lamont, *Rev.* D., *M.A.*, [C.S.] Chapl.4th Class (T.F.) (*attd.*) .. 1Apr.08

Shropshire.

The Arms of the Shropshire County Council.
"South Africa, 1900-02."
Shrewsbury.

Uniform, Blue—*Facings*, Scarlet. *Plume*, Red and White.

Hon. Colonel.

Harlech, G. R. C., *Lord*, TD (*Hon. Col. ret. Impl. Yeo.*) 1Apr.08

Lt.-Colonel.

✗Lloyd, A. H. O., *M.V.O., late Capt. G.* Gds. 22Jan.13

Majors. (5)

Heywood-Lonsdale, H. H., *late Capt. G.* Gds. 16Apr.02
Heywood- Lonsdale, J. P. H... .. .. 11Apr.06
Kynaston, W. R. O. (*H*) 8Feb.10
Corbett, C. U., Lt. ret. pay.. .. .. .. 22Jan.13

Captains. (4)

Lloyd, J. D. S. (*H*)
I. of M. 20Dec.10
p.s. Meredith, H. C. (*H*) .. 28Feb.11
✗Hayes, J. H., *late Capt. 3 D.G. (Cant. Res. of Off.) (Remount Service)* .. 6May11
p.s. Southwell, A. R. P. J. M., *Visct.* (Hon. Capt in Army 1 Nov. 00) (*H* 13Mar.12

Lieutenants. (5)

(p.s.)Croft, O. G. S. (*H*) ..29June11
(p.) Ormsby-Gore, *Hon.* W. G. A.
.. .. .. 29June11
Swire, D. W. (*H*) .. 29June11
✗Jenkins, C. E. (*Lt. Res. of Off.*) (*H*) .. 1Apr.12
Wolryche-Whitmore, G. C., *late Lt. 3 Bn.* Shrops. L.I. (*H*) .. 17Nov.13

2nd Lieutenants. (8)

Hopton, E. M. 1Apr.10
Mostyn Owen, G. C. .. 1Feb.11
Frank, P. E. ⑤ .. 16Jan.12
Tillard, P. A., *late Lt.* R. Fus. 13Feb.13
Lovett, T. M., *late 2nd Lt. G. Gds. Spec. Res.* 19Feb.13
Pettit, H. R. 12Apr.13
Rogers, G. C. 14Apr.13
Hanmer, G. W. E. .. 15Jan.14
Cawley, O. 1June14

Inst. of Musk.

Lloyd, J. D. S., *capt.* .. 1Apr.11

Adjutant.

✗Kirby, W. L. C.,Capt. 12 Lrs. 10Nov.13

Quarter-Master.

Felton, W., TD, *hon. maj.* 1June07

Medical Officers.

Downes, Lt. T. W. H., R.A.M.C.(T.F.) (*attd.*) 13Apr.12
Scott, Lt. W., *M.B.*, R.A.M.C. (T.F.) (*attd.*) .. 15Apr.12

Chaplain.

✗Lambart, *Rev.Hon.* H. E. S. S., *M.A.*, Chapl. 4th Class (T.F.) (*attd.*) 19May09

Yeomanry. Territorial Force.

North Somerset.

"South Africa, 1900-01."

Bath.

Uniform, Blue—*Facings and Plume*, White.

Hon. Colonel.

ⒽⒸ, ⒨. Roberts, *Field Marshal* Rt.Hon.F. S., Earl, K.G., K.P., G.C.B., O.M., G.C.S.I. G.C.I.E.,VD,*Col.Comdt. R. A., Col, I. Gds.* [R.] 15Oct.04

Lt.-Colonel.

✗Glyn, G. C., *D.S.O.* .. 10Mar.14

Majors. (5)

p.s. Benthall, J. L., TD .. 24Aug.01
✗Langman,A.L.,C.M.G., (H) 23Apr.07
Gibbs, A. H. 26June12

Captains. (4)

p.s. Spencer, H. G. .. 5Nov.04
Matthews, H. B. (H) 28Mar.12
✗Lubbock,G.(*Hon.Capt. in Army* 10July01) .. 26June12

Lieutenants. (5)

(p.s.)Gibbs, E. L. 1Apr.09
Batten-Pooll, W. S. .. 9Nov.09
Pitt, B. 2Dec.09
p. Tyssen, J. H. S. (H) .. 24Aug.12
English, R E. 24Aug.12

2nd Lieutenants.(8)

Davey, J. S. 12Apr.09
Mitchell, A. B. .. 12Apr.09
Longrigg, G. E. 14July09
Gibbs, G. M. 1Jan.10
Wills, W. D. M. 1Nov.10
Gibbs, R. C.-B. 1Oct.12
Gibbs, L. C. 1Nov.12
Christie, R. A. B. .. 4Jan.13
Fry, L. H. 1Nov.13
Garton, J. A. 14Mar.14
  .. .. .. 1Jan.10
O'Callaghan, C. T. .. 3Apr.14

Adjutant.

Bates, S. G., Capt. 7 Hrs. Nov.13

Quarter-Master.

Holwell, F. A. B., *hon. lt.* 28Nov.09

Medical Officers.

Chaplain.

West Somerset.

"South Africa, 1900-01."

County Territorial Hall, Taunton.

Uniform, Blue—*Facings*, Scarlet. *Busby-Bag*, Red. *Plume*, White.

Hon. Colonel.

Barrett, W., TD (*Hon. Col. ret. T.F.*) 5Dec.11

Lt.-Colonel.

p.s. Marriott-Dodington, R. (*Hon. Capt. in Army* 5 Dec. 00) (H).. .. 8Nov.1₁

Majors. (5)

p.s. Shuldham, F. N. Q. Ⓢ (H) 11Apr.07
Stenhouse, V. D. (H) ..25Mar.09
Kennedy, F. M. E., Bt. Maj. ret. pay (*Capt. Res. of Off.*) *t.a.* 23Feb.11
✗Channer, O. R. M.(H) 10July11
Hamilton, J. A. C., *late Capt.* A.S.C. 1Jan.12
✗Barry, A. P., Capt. ret. pay (*Res. of Off.*) (Q) 7Apr.13

Captains. (4)

Goodford, J. W. (H) .. 15July11
Mackenzie-Ashton, P.A. (H) 15July11
Cely-Trevilian,M.F.(H) 1Jan.12

Lieutenants. (5)

Poole, G. S. 3May09
Rodd, E. F. S. 15July11
Hayward, C. R. .. 15July11
Tritton, L. J. 7Apr.13
Benson, P. G. R. .. 29June13
Lee, C. F., *late Lt.* K. R. Rif. C. .. .. 3 Apr. 14

2nd Lieutenants. (8

Hill, A. B. (*Hon. 2nd Lt. in Army* 27 July 02) *late 2nd Lt. 3 Bn.* E. Surr. R. 18June 12
Wicksteed, F. 19Dec.12
Wilson, R. W. 8Jan.13
Sugden-Wilson, W. H. 3Apr.13
Whitehead, J. 26 Mar.14
Wakefield, J. H. .. 26 May14
Rattray, T. A. 28May14

Adjutant.

Bell, A. D., Capt. 4 Hrs. 1Mar.14

Quarter-Master.

Cousins, G., *hon. lt.* .. 16June12

Medical Officers.

Farrant, C. *Surg.-Capt*, 3Mar.06
  16July02
Bain, Capt. W., *M.B.*, R.A.M.C.(T.F.) (*attd.*) 30July12
  7Mar.07

Chaplain.

Milne, *Rev.* E. A. Chapl. 4th Class (T.F.) (*attd.*) .. 12Feb.12

Staffordshire.

(*Queen's Own Royal Regt.*)

"South Africa, 1900-01."

Bailey Street, Stafford.

Uniform, Blue—*Facings and Busby Bag*, Scarlet. *Plume*, White.

Lt.-Colonel.

p.s.✗Bromley Davenport, W., *D.S.O.*, TD (*Hon. Lt.- Col. in Army* 10July01) 7Apr.1₀

Majors. (5)

Clowes, H. A., *late* Capt. 1 L.G. *hon. l.c.* .. 15Aug.06
p.s.✗Wight-Boycott, T. A., *D.S.O.* (*Hon. Lt.-Col. in Army* 18 Nov. 02) 19Dec.06
Heywood, G. P. (H) ..12Sept.11
Hardy, B. (H) 7June13

Captains. (4)

p.s.✗Webb, W. H. .. 26Apr.10
Lewisham W., *Visct.* (*Hon. Col.* 7 Bn. W. *Rid. R.*) 23Apr.12
Wiggin, C. R. H. (H) 24Apr.12
Ratcliff, R. A. .. 7June13

Lieutenants. (5)

(p.s.)Mander, C. A. .. 21Oct.09
Vaughan Wil iams, R.Ⓢ 26Apr.10
(p.)Anson, G. H. 23Apr.12
Trench, S. J. le P. *late Capt.* 6 Bn. S. Staff R.21 Aug 12

2nd Lieutenants. (8)

Loveridge, S. G. .. 13Dec.10
Sidebottom, R. .. 28Jan.11
Borough, J. G. B. 25Apr.11
Cameron, E. 30Dec.11
Paul, G, D 4Mar.12
Negus, A.V. 19Feb.13
Manley, R. S. 24July13
Wolseley, E. C. J. .. 19Aug.13

Adjutant.

Watson, A. C., Capt. 7 Hrs. 27Mar.13

Quarter-Master.

p. Cartwright, Z., TD, *hon. maj.* .. .. .. 5Apr.0₴

Medical Officers.

Palmer, A. H., *Surg.- Capt.* 24June08
  24Dec.04

Chaplain.

Smith, *Rev.* H., *M.A.*, Chapl.4th Class(T.F.) (*attd.*) 1Apr.08
  14Aug.06

G 2

Yeomanry. Territorial Force.

Suffolk.

(*The Duke of York's Own Loyal Suffolk Hussars.*)
"South Africa, 1900-01."
Bury St. Edmunds.

Uniform, Green—*Facings and Busby-Bag*, Scarlet. *Plume*, White.

Colonel-in-Chief.
THE KING

Lt.-Colonel.
p.s.✕Jarvis, F. W... .. 7May13

Majors. (5)
p.s.✕Guinness, Hon. W. E,
(*Hon. Capt. in Army*
16 *July* 01) .. 21Feb.03
Tomkin, J. W. R. (*Capt.*
Res. of Off.) 23Apr.04
p.s.✕Barne, M., Capt. ret.
pay 21Dec.06
✕Courage, H. F. (*H*) .. 11Oct.13
Goldsmith, F. (*H*) .. 21May14

Captains. (4)
✕Pym, C. E., *late Capt.*
5 Lrs. 20July12
p.s.Agnew, J. S. 22May14
p.s.Greene, E. A. (*H*) .. 4June14
p.s.Grissell, T. De la G.(*H*) 4June14

Lieutenants. (5)
Cadogan, Hon. E. C. G.,
(*H*) 13Apr.10
Lygon, Hon. H. .. 12Apr.13
Paterson, E. W. .. 23May14
Barker, G. P. 5June14

2nd Lieutenants. (8)
Hodgson, P. K. .. 1Feb.13
Agnew, V. C. W. .. 8Feb.13
Pemberton, R. O. W. .. 9May13
Musker, H. 30Mar.14
Parker, W. S. H. .. 31Mar.14
17July13

Adjutant.
✕Northen, Capt. E., 19 Hrs.
1June12

Quarter-Master.
Earle, T., *hon. capt.* .. 1Mar.09

Medical Officers.
Stork, Lt. E S., *M.R.,*
R.A.M.C.(T.F.)(*attd.*) 22Apr.13

Chaplain.
Powles,Rev.E.,M.A.,Chapl.
4th Class (T. F.)(*attd.*) 1Apr.08
18July09

Surrey.

(*Queen Mary's Regiment.*)
Melbourne House, King's Avenue,
Clapham Park, S.W.

Uniform, Blue—*Facings*, Blue.

Hon. Colonel.
Midleton,Rt. Hon. St. J.,
Visct. 26June01

Lt.-Colonel.
Humphery, *Sir* J.,*Knt.* 15May12

Majors. (5)
p.s.✕Thesiger, Hon. E. R.
(*Hon. Capt. in Army*
3Sept.02) 25June04
✕Calvert, C. A., Capt.
ret. pay 1Apr.08
4Dec.07
Borwick, G. O. (*H*) .. 23Mar.12
Barclay, R. W. 15May12

Captains. (4)
p.s.Bonsor, R. 22July11
p.s.Bray, J. 28Feb.12
Barclay, T. H. 23Mar.12
Mirrielees, F. D. (*H*) .. 15May12

Lieutenants. (5)
Everidge, J. 8Aug.12
Bell, H. J. 8Aug.12
Horne, A. E. 8Aug.12
Bell, E. 8Aug.12

2nd Lieutenants. (8)
Brodrick, Hon. G. St. J. 16Mar.09
Chichester. A. O'N. C. 22Mar.11
Brass, W. 20Jan.12
Heath, L. C. 5June12
Powell, M. 22Jan.13
Shepherd, F. McA. .. 11Aug.13
Rickards, E. 29Apr.14
Phillips, F. R. 17June14

Adjutant.
✕Hodgson, W. T., Capt.
1 Dns. 1Nov.11

Quarter-Master.
p. West, A. J., *hon. m.* 3June01

Medical Officers.
r. Gayer,R. C., *Surg.-Capt.* 17Sept.06
17Mar.03

Chaplain.

Cadet Unit affiliated
"E" Cadet Squadron, Surrey
(Queen Mary's Regt.) Yeo.

Sussex.

Drill Hall, Church Street,
Brighton.

Uniform, Blue—*Facings*, Yellow.

Hon. Colonel.
Abergavenny, W., Marq.
of, K.G., TD, *late* Cor.
& Sub.-Lt. 2 L.G. .. 28Sept.01

Lt.-Colonel.
✕March, C. H., *Earl of*,
M.V.O., D.S.O., (*Maj.*
Res. of Off.) 3July14

Majors. (5)
Whitfeld, G. S. (*H*) .. 3July08
✕Innes, J. A., D.S.O.,
late Capt. Rif. Brig... 17Jan.09
McKergow, R. W. .. 6Aug.12

Captains. (4)
p.s.Pearson, Hon. W. H. .. 4Jan.11
p.s.Lyon, A. W. W., *late* Lt.
Suss.R.G.A.(Mila.)(*H*) 27July12
Nevill, G. T. M. 6Aug.12
✕Weller-Poley, E. H.,
M.V.O. (Lt.Res.of Off.) 5Nov.13
p.s.Edwards, H. I. P. (*H*) .. 6May14

Lieutenants. (5)
Pearson, Hon. B.C. (*H*) 17Mar.11
28July10
Hornung, C. B R, (*Lt. Res.*
of Off.) 5Apr.11
Sayer, A. C. Ⓢ 27July12
Kekewich, H. L. .. 6Aug.12
Scott, A. J. L. 6May14

2nd Lieutenants. (8)
Mair, R. P. 24Jan.10
Brown, C. C. 14Mar.10
Cardwell, R. McK. .. 2Dec.10
Godman, G. W. Ⓢ .. 18July11
Powell-Edwards, W. G. H.
26Oct.11
Sayer, H. 1Nov.12
Penfold-Wyatt, H. G. 1Nov.12
✕Woodman, L. C. .. 7Feb.13
Burn, R. C. W .. 6May14

Adjutant.
✕Blakiston-Houston,J.,
Capt. 11 Hrs. 19Sept.11

Quarter-Master.
✕Spedding, C. G., Commy.
of Ord. (*hon. Maj.*) ret.
pay, *hon. maj.* 19Feb.12

Medical Officers.
p.s.Dauber, Capt. J. H.,
M.B., F.R.C.S.(I.), R.A.M.C.
(T.F.)(*attd.*) 15Aug.06
7Jan.03
Steinhaeuser, R.,
M.B., *Surg.-Lt.*. 27Mar.07

Chaplain
Campion, Rev. F. H., Chapl.,
4th Class (T.F.)(*attd.*) 22Feb.09

Yeomanry. Territorial Force.

Warwickshire.
"South Africa, 1900-01."
St. John's, Warwick.

Uniform, Dark Blue—*Facings, Busby-bag and Plume*, White.

Hon. Colonel.
Warwick, F.R.C.G. Earl of, TD, (*Lt.-Col. & Hon. Col. ret. T. F.*) .. 24Mar.12

Lt.-Colonel.
p.s.Dugdale, F., *C.V.O.*, TD, Eq. 16Dec.11
(*Equerry to the Queen 21 June* 10)

Majors. (5)
p.s.✗Charteris, R. B., TD, (*Hon. Lt. in Army* 19Jan.01), *hon. l.c.* .. 14Feb.08
Richardson, R. A. (*H*) 16Apr.10
Mills, J. D. (*H*) .. 23Feb.11
✗Granville B., Capt. ret. pay (*H*) ⑤ 23Feb.11
✗Pepys, W., *late* Capt. 13 Hrs. (*Maj. Res. of Off.*) (*H*) ⑤ 16Dec.11

Captains. (4)
p.s.Chamberlayne, E. T. .. 16Apr.10
✗Guernsey, H.G., *Lord*, *late* Lt. I. Gds. (*H*) (*Lt. Res. of Off.*) .. 17Aug.10
✗Hodgkinson, G. H., *late* Capt. 13 Hrs. 9Feb.12

Lieutenants. (5)
Napier, R. G. C., *late* 2nd Lt. G. Gds. .. 23Feb.11
✗Gillespie, J. G.,*late* Lt. Durh. L.I. .. 2June11
Smith-Ryland, H. D. .. 2June11
Joynson, L. B. ⑤ .. 10Feb.11
Wheatley, C.J.H. .. 20Jan.13

2nd Lieutenants. (8)
Pemberton, E. G. .. 1Jan.11
Coulston, H. C. 11Mar.11
Shirley, E.C. 30Mar.11
Leather, R. T... .. 15Dec.11
Lloyd, G. A. .. 8June12
p.s. Tate, H.B., *late* 2nd Lt. 4 Bn. Durh. L.I. .. 15Feb.13
Jackson, G. C. .. 25Mar.14
Motion, A. K... .. 25Mar.14

Adjutant.
Stocker, E. H., Capt. 13 Hrs. 1Sept.13

Quarter-Master.
✗Valintine, R., *hon. capt.* 30June06

Medical Officers.
p. Bullock, R., TD, *Surg.-Maj.* (*hon. Surg.-Lt.-Col,*) 30Aug.02 26Apr.90

Chaplain.
Goodenough, *Rev.* L.W.V., *M.A.*, Chapl. 4th Class (T.F.) (*attd.*) .. 1Apr.08 28Mar.08

Westmorland & Cumberland.
"South Africa, 1900-01."
Penrith.

Uniform, Scarlet—*Facings*, White. *Busby-Bag*, Scarlet—*Plume*, Red and White.

Hon. Colonel.
p. Lonsdale, H. C., Earl of (*Hon. Col. ret. T.F.*) .. 16Nov.08

Lt.-Colonel.
p.s.Fothergill, S. R. .. 9Feb.11

Majors. (5)
p.s.✗Leighton, *Sir* B. B. M., *Bt.* TD, *f.c.r.* 27May05
p.s.✗Beddington, C. (*Hon. Lt. in Army* 11Sept.01) *bt. lt. col.* 25Apr.06
✗Dunne, F. P. N. (*H*).. 27May11
✗Salkeld, C., Capt. ret. pay.. .. .. 24May12
Little, W. O. (*H*) *p.v.c.* .. 14Apr.13

Captains. (4)
p.s.Senhouse, G. J. P. (*H*) 7Dec.11
Lees, E. B. 20Jan.12
Cropper, J. W. .. 24May12
p. Lawson, G. 14Apr.13

Lieutenants. (5)
Paget-Tomlinson, T. R., *late* Capt. W. of Scot. R. F. Res. A. (*Hon. Lt. in Army* 4Oct.04).. 9Dec.11
Sandys, G. O., *late* Lt. R. Scots 16Mar.12
Cowper, G. T. M. C. .. 24Apr.12
Fothergill, G. S. .. 24May12
Hazlehurst, C. A. C. .. 20Mar.13
Vane, *Hon.* C. W. .. 14Apr.13

2nd Lieutenants (8)
Leighton, R. T. .. 15Dec.11
Parker, F. C. F. .. 20Feb.12
Prince, C. E. 16Apr.12
Hasell, E. W. 3Oct.12
Gaddum, W. F. (*late* 2nd Lt. Res. of Off.*).. 4Mar.14

Adjutant.
✗Irwin,T.S., Capt.1 Dns. 17Oct.11

Quarter-Master.
Jones, J. H., Qr.-Mr (*hon. capt.*) ret. pay, *hon. maj.* 16Apr.09

Medical Officers.
Livingstone, J., *M.B.*, *Surg.-Capt.* 10Feb.11
23Aug.02
Paul. Lt. E. C. B., *M.B.*, F. R. C. S, (*Edin.*), R.A.M.C.(T.F.)(*attd.*) 4Feb.13

Chaplain.
Hasell, *Rev.* G. E., *M.A.*, Chapl. 1st Class (T.F.) (*attd.*) 1Apr.08 7Apr.74

Royal Wiltshire.
(*Prince of Wales's Own Royal Regiment.*)

"South Africa, 1900-01."
The Butts, London Road, Chippenham.

Uniform, Blue—*Facings*, Scarlet.

Hon. Colonel.
Lansdowne, Rt. Hon. H.,C.K.,Marq. of, K.G., G.C.S.I., G.C.M.G., G.C.I.E. 24Feb.97

Lt.-Colonel.
p. Palmer, G. L., TD .. 25May11

Majors (5)
p. Fuller, *Sir* J. *M. F.*, Bt., K.C.M.G., TD.. .. 17Aug.01
p. ✗Thynne, U. O., *D.S.O.*, *late* Lt. K. R. Rif. C. 22Apr.03
p. ✗Thynne, *Lord* A. G. (*Hon. Lt. in Army* 28 July02) 1Nov.08
p.s.✗Awdry, C. S. (*Hon. Lt. in Army* 20Aug.01) .. 30Nov 08
p.s.✗Poore, R. A., *D.S O.* .. 14Apr.11
p.s Fuller, W. F. (*H*) .. 14Apr.11

Captains. (4)
p.s.Fuller, R. F. 30Nov.06
p.s.Richardson-Cox, E. (*H*) 30Nov.06
✗Palmer, A. L., Capt. ret. pay 14Apr.11
p.s.Lamb, B. (*H*) 14Apr.11

Lieutenants. (5)
p.s.Awdry, R. W. (*H*) .. 29June01
p.s.Mann, W. H. 3Dec.01
(p.s.)Henderson, A... .. 14Apr.11
Buxton, G. J. 14Apr.11

2nd Lieutenants. (8)
Rooke, J. W. 4Oct.09
Long, R. E. O. 15Sept.10
✗Ward,H.R.,.(*Hon.Capt. in Army* 11 Oct.02) 25Apr.11
Rooke, W. M .. 7Sept 11
Awdry, E. P. .. 20Dec,11
Edmunds, P. M. L. .. 3Feb.12
Sumner, M. G. 15Nov.12
Davy, D. H. 31May13
28Feb.11
Herbert, S... .. .. 11May13

Adjutant.
Edwards, A.N., Capt. 9 Lrs., *capt.* 13Apr.12

Quarter-Master.
p ✗Lawrence, A.. *hon. lt.* 29Mar.69

Medical Officers.
Maurice, Lt. G. K., R.A.M.C.(T.F.)(*attd.*) 23June12
Briscoe, Lt. W. T., R.A.M.C.(T.F.)(*attd.*) 8July12

Chaplain.
Waugh, *Rev.* W. L., *M.A.*, Chapl.4th Class (T.F.) (*attd.*) .. . 1Apr.08 27May05

Yeomanry. Territorial Force.

Worcestershire.
(The Queen's Own Worcestershire Hussars.)
"South Africa, 1900-02."
Worcester.

Uniform, Blue—*Facings,* Busby-Bag *and Plume,* Scarlet.

Hon. Colonel.
Cobham, C. G., Visct.
(*Hon. Col. ret. Impl.*
Yeo.) 29Mar.05

Lt.-Colonel.
✗Dudley,*Rt.Hon.,*W.H.,
Earl of, G.C.B.,G.C.M.G.,
G.C.V.O., TD (*Hon.*
Maj. in Army 29
Oct. 00) 10Nov.13

Majors. (5)
Wiggin, W. W. 27Feb.04
p.s.✗Selwyn, H. J. (*Hon.*
Lt. in Army 31 *Jan.*
01) (*H*) 10Nov.06
Coventry, *Hon.* C. J.,
late Capt. 5 *Bn. Worc.*
R. 16June09
✗Knight, E. A. 10Aug.10
✗Gray-Cheape, H. A.(*Hon.*
Capt. in Army, 9 *Oct.* 02)
(*Hon. Maj. ret. Spec. Res.*)
(*Capt. Res. of Off.*) .. 10Nov.13

Captains. (4)
✗Lyttelton,*Hon.*,J.C., *late*
Lt. Rif. Brig. .. 9Apr.09
p.s.Tomkinson, H. (*H*) .. 28Oct.11
Williams-Thomas, F. S. (*H*)
(q) ⓢ (*asst. Dist.*
Offr. S., Provs.,Nigeria
{ 1 an.14 24July12
{ 29May11)
Hampton, H. S., *Lord,*
late Lt. Rif. Brig. (*H*) 22July13
Wiggin, M. W. (*H*) .. 19May14

Lieutenants. (5)
Wiggin, G. R. 7June11
Todd, A. M, (*H*) 7June11
Colville, R. A., *late* 2nd
Lt. C *Gds.* 23Mar13
Wilson, H. N. S. .. 13Nov.13

2nd Lieutenants. (8)
Holland, E. 27June10
Albright, M. C. .. 29June10
Hunter, G. J. 17Dec.10
Windsor, I. M., *Visct.,..* 6Feb.11
Ednam, W. H. E., *Visct.* 6Jan.12
Watts, R. J., *late Lt.*
5 *Bn. Worc. R.* (*H*) P.c. 4 May 12

Adjutant.
Cheape, L. St. C., Capt.
1 D.G. 3July12

Quarter-Master.
✗Bell, W., *hon. lt.* .. 11May09

Medical Officers.
Teichmann, Lt. O.,
R.A.M.C.(T. F.) (*attd.*)
.. 16Sept.11

Chaplain.
Deane, *Rev. Canon* A. C.,
M.A., Chapl.,4th Class
(T.F.) (*attd.*) 6Sept.10

Yorkshire Dragoons.
(Queen's Own.)
"South Africa, 1900-02."
Doncaster.

Uniform, Blue—*Facings and Plume,*
White.

Hon. Colonel.
✗Scarbrough, A. F. G. B.,
Earl of, K.C.B., TD,
Col., *A.D.C.* (*Col. ret.T.F.*)
.. .. 1Apr.08

Lt.-Colonel.
p.s Smith, W. McK., TD .. 3June14

Majors. (5)
p.s.✗Smith, S. A. (*Hon. Lt.*
in Army 16*Jan.*01) (*H*) 3June06
p.s.Milnes-Gaskell, E. (*H*) 12Sept.06
Ingham, J. L. (*H*) .. 6Nov.11
Smith, P. G. ⓢ (*H*) .. 21May12

Captains. (4)
p.s.Wright, M. N. (*H*) .. 9May08
Wood, *Hon.* E. F. L. .. 6Apr.14

Lieutenants. (5)
(p.s.)Lipscomb, W. T. (*H*).. 9May08
(p.s.)Thompson, R. (*H*) .. 9May08
Foster, J. B. 6Nov.11
Cooper, H. 29May13
(p.s.)Brooke, R. W. (*H*) .. 6Apr.14

2nd Lieutenants. (8)
Hirst, C. J. 24Feb.09
Childe, H. N. 25June09
Green, E. A. L., *late Lt.*
2 L.G. 1May10
Leng, D. C. 15May10
Deltus, S. S.-M. 20Feb.12
Tinker, B. 26Sept.12
Shaw, J. E. D. 27June13

Adjutant.
Yeatherd, M. L., Capt.
7 Hrs. 11Mar.13

Quarter-Master.
Leach, W. R., *hon. lt.* .. 1June09

Medical Officers.
Mackay, P.B., TD, *Surg.-*
Maj. 27May05
.. .. 18Mar.93

Chaplain.
Sandford,*Rev.Canon* F.G.,
M.A., Chapl., 4th Class
(T.F.)(*attd.*) 10June11

Yorkshire Hussars.
(Alexandra, Princess of Wales's Own.)
"South Africa, 1900-02."
York.

Uniform, Blue—*Busby-Bag,* Scarlet.
Plume, Black and Scarlet.

Hon. Colonel.
Bolton, W. T., Lord,TD (*Hon.*
Col. ret. Impl. Yeo.) .. 1Apr.13

Lt.-Colonel.
p.s.Stanyforth, E. W., TD 3Feb.12

Majors. (5)
p.s.Deramore, R. W., *Lord,*
TD 18June04
p.s.Helmsley, C. W. R.,
Visct. 1Nov.06
✗Watt, A. F. (*H*) .. 1May09
Hawkes, F. H.(*H*) .. 1May09
Collins, A. E. 30Sept.09
Herbert,E.A. F. W.,TD,
late Capt. York. Art 13Apr.12

Captains (4)
✗Pearson, R. S. (*Lt. Res.*
of Off.) (*Remount Ser-*
vice) 29Aug.06
p.s.Collins, E. A. D.(*H*) .. 1Nov.06
3 *Bn. York. R.* .. 1Aug.08
✗York, E., *late Capt.* 1 Dns.
(*Capt. Res. of Off.*) .. 19Mar.09
p.s.✗Gutch, W. (*H*) (*Hon.*
(*Capt.in Army* 24Sept.02)13Apr.12

Lieutenants. (5)
p.s.Lawson, D. 27Apr.09
p.s.Foster, G. R. 1May09
(p.) Walker, R. B. 3June11
p.s. ✗Charlesworth, W. G. 17Feb.12
(*H*) 3June06
(p.)Turton, E. S. 13Apr.12

2nd Lieutenants. (8)
Samuelson, F. H. B. .. 15June09
Riley-Smith, W. .. 1Oct.09
Preston, T. 21Dec.10
Wailes-Fairbairn,N.W.F.6Apr.11
Foster, C. G. 9Oct.11
Hunter J.C. 2Mar.12
Lascelles. H. G. C., *Visct.,*
late 2nd *Lt.* G. *Gds.* (2nd
Lt. Res. of Off.) .. 2Jan.13
Beckett, *Hon.* R. W. E. ..13Feb.13
Ryder, C. F. 11Feb.14

Adjutant.
Graham. M., Lt. 16 Lrs.
capt. 26Jan.12

Quarter-Master.
✗Collins,W.H.,Qr.-Mr.
(*hon. capt.*) *ret. pay,*
hon. m 1Dec.08

Medical Officers.
p.s.Cheetham, W. H., *M.D.*,
Surg.-Capt. 6Oct.06
5Apr.02
Bullen, Capt. C. H.,
R.A.M.C.(T.F.)(*attd.*) 24Jan.12
24July08

Chaplain.
Pennyman, *Rev.* W. G.,
M.A., Chapl. 4th Class
(T.F.) (*attd.*).. .. 1Apr.09

Cadet Unit Affiliated.
Yorkshire Squadron, Imperial
Cadet Yeomanry.

Yeomanry. Territorial Force.

East Riding of Yorkshire.

Railway Street, Beverley.

Uniform, Maroon—*Facings*, Light Blue—*Plume*, Light Blue and White

Hon. Colonel.

⚔Stracey - Clitherow, J.B.,(*Lt.-Col. ret. T.F.*), (*Maj. ret. pay*) .. 6June12

Lt.-Colonel.
Langdale, P., Capt. ret. pay (*H*) 15May12

Majors. (5)

⚔Garnock, R.B.,*Visct.*, Maj. ret. pay (*Res. of Off.*) 1May12
⚔Wilson, *Hon.* G. G., D.S.O.,*late Lt.* 11 Hrs. 20Dec.12
p.s.⚔Buxton, G. C. (*Hon. Capt. in Army* 19*Aug*.01) 15Feb.13
22Mar.06
⚔Reynard, C. E., *formerly* Capt. 12 Lrs. 3May13

Captains. (4)

p.s.Cadman, P. S. C. (*H*) .. 1Apr.12
Walker, J. (*H*).. .. 5Oct.12
Bardwell, T. G. N. .. 22Jan.14

Lieutenants. (5)

Hodgson, R. V. (*H*) .. 18Feb.12
Menzles, K. G. (*H*) .. 29Feb.12
Lyon, C. G. 3Apr.12
Lloyd, C. G. 18Feb.13
Scott, R. W. R. 23Jan.14
14Feb.13

2nd Lieutenants. (8)

Woodhouse, G. H. .. 13Aug.11
Rice, H. T. 14Aug.12
Pearson, H. W. .. 1Aug.13
Sykes, N. C. M. 12Jan.14

Adjutant.

⚔Tylden-Wright, W. R., Capt. 3 Hrs... .. 24Oct.11

Quarter-Master.

⚔Burch, F., Qr.-Mr. (*hon. capt.*) ret. pay, (*Res. of Off.*) *hon. m.* 6June09

Medical Officers.

⚔Draper, R. A., *Surg.-Capt.*
14Sept.06
14Mar.03

SIGNAL SERVICE.

Eastern Mounted Brigade Signal Troop.
Commander.
Every, Lt. *Sir* E. O.,*Bt.*, Norf. Yeo. Ⓢ 1Nov.13

Highland Mounted Brigade Signal Troop.
Commander.
Millar, Lt. J. S. L., 2 Lovat's Scouts Yeo. Ⓢ 1Feb.14

London Mounted Brigade Signal Troop.
Commander.

Lowland Mounted Brigade Signal Troop.
Commander.
Stewart, 2nd Lt. H. S., Lothians & Bord.Hse. Yeo. Ⓢ 1Dec.13

North Midland Mounted Brigade Signal Troop.
Commander.
Vaughan-Williams, Lt. R. Staff. Yeo.Ⓢ .. 27Jan.14

Notts & Derby Mounted Brigade Signal Troop.
Commander.

South-Eastern Mounted Brigade Signal Troop.
Commander.
⚔Weller-Poley, Capt. E. H., *M.V.O.*, Suss. Yeo. (*Lt. Res. of Off.*) 5Nov.13

1st South Midland Mounted Brigade Signal Troop.
Commander.
Joynson, Lt. L. B., War. Yeo. Ⓢ 23May11

2nd South Midland Mounted Brigade Signal Troop.
Commander.
Ainger, 2nd Lt. T. E., Berks. Yeo. Ⓢ.. .. 1Mar.14

South Wales Mounted Brigade Signal Troop.
Commander.
Bowen, 2nd Lt. J. B. Pemb. Yeo. Ⓢ 21Jan.14

1st South-Western Mounted Brigade Signal Troop.
Commander.

2nd South-Western Mounted Brigade Signal Troop.
Commander.

Welsh Border Mounted Brigade Signal Troop.
Commander.
Fletcher, Maj. H. F.(*H*) Denbigh Yeo. Ⓢ 1May13

Yorkshire Mounted Brigade Signal Troop.
Commander.

ROYAL REGIMENT OF ARTILLERY.

The Royal Arms and Supporters, with a Gun.
"*Ubique*" (above). "*Quo Fas et Gloria ducunt*" (below the Gun).
Uniform—Blue. Facings—Scarlet. Busby-bag—Scarlet. Plume—White.
Agents—Messrs. Cox & Co.

Allied Regiment of Canadian Permanent Force.
The Royal Canadian Artillery.
Quebec, Province of Quebec.

Colonel-in-Chief.

THE KING.

Master-Gunner, St James's Park.. ᚖℭ, ᚒ. Roberts, Field-Marshal *Rt. Hon. F. S., Earl, K.G., K.P., G.C.B., O.M., G.C.S.I., G.C.I.E.,* VD., Col. Comdt. R.A., Col. I. Gds. [R] 29Nov.04

Colonels. Commandant.	Colonels Commandant—contd.	Removed from the Regiment and still on the Active List.	General Officers—contd.
ℭ. Hastings, Hon. Gen. F. W., *C.B.,* ret. pay [R] 16Sept 93	Nicholson, Maj.-Gen. S. J., *C.B.,* ret. pay 7May06		Hadden, Maj.-Gen. Sir C. F., *K.C.B., p.a.c. (President, Ord. Board)* 6Apr.10
ℭ. ᚑ. Biddulph, Gen. *Sir R., G.C.B., G.C.M.G.,* ret. pay [R] 6Mar.95	Richardson, Maj.-Gen. J. B., ret. pay 19Sept.06	General Officers. Wingate, Gen. *Sir F. R., G.C.B., G.C.V.O., K.C.M.G., D.S.O., q.s.* [L] [R] [F] e.a. 5Nov.13	
ᚖℭ. ᚑ. Roberts, Field-Marshal *Rt. Hon. F. S., Earl, K.G., K.P., G C.B., O.M., G.C.S.I., G.C.I.E.,* VD. (late Ben.) [R] 7Oct.96	Rundle, Gen. *Sir* H. M. L., *G.C.B., G.C.M.G., G.C.V.O., D.S.O., q.s.,* 2Aug.07		Brunker, Maj.-Gen J. M. S., *s.* 22June10
	Pretyman, Maj.-Gen. *Sir* G. T., *K.C.M.G., C.B.,* ret. pay, *g.* [R] 22Sept.08	Murray, Lt.-Gen. *Sir* J. W., *K.C.B., p.s.c.,* [L] *s.* 1Apr.09	May, Maj.-Gen. E. S., *C.B., C.M.G.,* [*l*] *s.* 7Jan.11
ᚑ. Griffin, Lt.-Gen. E.C., u.s.l. (*late Ben.*) 23Feb.00	Stewart, Gen. *Sir* R. MacG., *G.C.B., q.s., g.,* ret. pay [R] 18June09		Adye, Maj.-Gen. J., *C.B., p.s.c.,* [F] *s.* 19June11
Elliott, Maj.-Gen. E. D., u.s.l. (*late Ben.*) 4Sept.01	Hutchinson, Maj.-Gen. W. F. M., ret. pay, *p.s.c.* 11Sept.09	Grierson, Lt.-Gen. *Sir* J. M., *K.C.B., C.V.O., C.M.G., p.s.c.* [L] [R] [F] ᚑ. ᚒ. ℭ., *s.* 7May10	Blewitt, Maj.-Gen. W. E., *C.B., C.M.G., g., s,* 24July11
ᚑ. Ward, Maj.-Gen. F. W., *C.B.,* u.s.l. (late Ben.) r.h.a. 1May02	Holley, Maj.-Gen. E.H., ret. pay 26Nov.10	Sclater, Lt.-Gen. *Sir* H. C., *K.C.B.* [R] Adjt.-Gen. to the Forces (2nd Mil. Member), Army Council) 23June11	
Chapman, Gen. *Sir* E. F., *K.C.B.,* u.s.l. (late Ben.) *p.s.c.* [R] 14Jan.03	Turner, Maj.-Gen. *Sir* A. E., *K.C.B., q.s.,* ret. pay [R] 28Jan.11		Burton, Maj.-Gen. B., *C.B., s.* 17Dec.11
ℭ. ᚑ. Williams, Maj.-Gen. *Sir* A. H. W., *K.C.V.O.,* ret. pay, r.h.a. 23Apr.03	Hunter, Maj.-Gen. W., ret. pay, *p.a.c.* 16Feb.11	Anderson, Lt.-Gen. C. A., *C.B., s.* 12May14	Lindsay, Maj.-Gen. W. F. L., *C.B., D.S.O., g., s,* 7Feb.12
Forster, Lt.-Gen. B. L., ret. pay [R] 24July04	Wodehouse, Gen. *Sir* J. H., *G.C.B., C.M.G.* ret. pay [R] [F] 12Jan.12	Rochfort, Maj.-Gen. *Sir* A. N., *K.C.B., C.M.G.* (*Lt.-Gov. Jersey*) 10June07	Hamilton Gordon, Maj.-Gen. A., *C.B., p.s.c., s.* 22Jan.13
ℭ. ᚑ. Markham, Lt.-Gen. *Sir* E., *K.C.B.,* ret. pay [R] r.h.a. 25Aug.04	Tyler, Maj.-Gen. T. B., *C.S.I.,* ret. pay [R] 17Oct.12 Elles, Lt.-Gen. *Sir* E. R., *G.C.I.E., K.C.B.,* ret. pay, *p.s.c.* [R] [F] 22Oct.12	Bannatine-Allason, Maj.-Gen. R., *C.B.* [F] 1Jan.09	Johnston, Maj.-Gen. J. T., *C.B., p.s.c., g.* [L] *s.* 19May13
ℭ. Nicolls, Maj.-Gen. O. H. A., ret. pay, *p.s.c.* 29Nov.04	French, Maj.-Gen. *Sir* G. A., *K.C.M.G.,* ret. pay 5Nov.12	Barker, Maj.-Gen. J. S. S., *C.B., p.s.c., s.* 8May09	
ℭ. ᚑ. Geary, Lt.-Gen. *Sir* H. Le G., *K.C.B.,* ret. pay [R] 24Dec.04	Creagh, Maj.-Gen. A. G., *C.B.,* ret. pay, *p.s.c.* [R] [F] 19Nov.12		Hickman, Maj.-Gen. H. P., *g.* 3June13
Saward, Maj.-Gen. M. H., u.s.l. (*late Ben.*) 22Feb.05	Wace, Maj.-Gen. R., *C.B.,* ret. pay 5Sept.13	Keir, Maj.-Gen. J. L., *C.B., p.s.c., g., s.* 7July09	
Owen, Gen. *Sir* J. F., *K.C.B.,* ret. pay, *p.a.c.* [R] 26Feb.06	O'Callaghan, Maj.-Gen. *Sir* D. D. T., *K.C.V.O.,* ret. pay, *g.* [R] 27Sept.13	Penton, Maj.-Gen. A. P., *C.V O., C.B., p.a.c., s.* 7Dec.09	Kemball, Maj.-Gen. G.V., *C.B., D.S.O., p.s.c., g., s.* 8Apr.14
Harness, Maj.-Gen. A., *C.B.,* ret. pay 12Apr.06	Scott, Maj.-Gen. *Sir* C. H., *K.C.B.,* ret. pay, *g.* [R] 21Apr.14	Baldock, Maj.-Gen. T. S., *C.B., p.s.c., s,* 1Jan.10	Hunter-Blair, Maj.-Gen. W. C. 22Apr.14

Royal Regiment of Artillery.

Removed from the Regiment and still on the Active List—contd.

Colonels.

Granet, E. J., *C.B., p.s.c.*
[L] *Mil. Attaché* 31July04

VℓPhipps-Hornby,
E. J., *C.B.* 22Mar.05

Armitage, E. H.,
C.B., g. 8July05

Montgomery, R. A. K.,
*C.B., D.S.O., p.s.c.,
g. (temp. Brig.-Gen.),
s.* 22Aug.05

Headlam, J. E. W.,
*C.B. D.S.O., g., (temp.
Brig.-Gen.) s,* 22Aug.05

Money, A. W., *C.B.,
p.s.c. (temp. Brig.-
Gen.), s.* 10Sept.05

Mercer, H. F., *C.B.,
A.D.C. (temp. Brig.-
Gen.)* 1Oct.05

Du Cane, H. J., *C.B.,
M.V.O., p.s.c.* [L]
15Oct.05

Findlay, N. D., *C.B.,
p.s.c.,* [l] *(temp. Brig.-
Gen.), s.* 15Oct.05

Paget, W. L. H., *C.B.,
M.V.O. (temp. Brig.-
Gen.), s.* 3Nov.05

Nicolls,E.G., *C.B.,g.
(temp. Brig.-Gen.)
(Inspr. of R.G.A.)* 3Nov.05

Milne,G.F., *C.B., D.S.O.,
p.s.c.* [l] *(temp. Brig.-
Gen.) s.* 8Nov.05

Scott, A. B., *C.B.,D.S.O.
(temp. Brig.-Gen.), s.*
22Jan.06

Kelly, R. M. B. F.,
*C.B., D.S.O., g. (temp.
Brig.-Gen.) s.* 1May06

vonDonop, Sir S. B.,
*K.C.B., g. (local &
temp. Maj.-Gen.)
Mast.-Gen. of Ord.
(4th Mil. Member,
Army Council)* 13May06

Horne, H.S., *C.B.(temp.
Brig.-Gen.)(Inspr.of
R.H. & R.F.A.)* 23May06

Colonels—contd.

Wing, F. D. V., *C.B.,
(temp. Brig.-Gen.) s.*
23May06

Triscott, C. P., *C.B.,
D.S.O., q.s. (temp.
Brig.-Gen.) s,* 15July06

Smith, H.G., *C.B., g.
(temp. Brig.-Gen.)
(Dir. of Art.)* 20July06

Fanshawe, E. A. s.
29July06

Du Cane, J. P., *C.B.
(temp. Brig.-Gen.), s.*
27Nov.06

St. John, G. F. W.,*C.B.*
29Nov.06

Biddulph, G. W.,
g., s. 29Nov.06

Stanton, R. E., *C.B.,
D.S.O., p.s.c., A.D.C.
(temp. Brig.-Gen.), s.*
1Dec.06

Fairholme, W. E.,*C.M.G.,
M.V.O., p.s.c.* [L]
Mil. Attaché 19Jan.07

Forestier-Walker,
G. T., *p.s.c.* [L]
*A.D.C. (temp. Brig.
Gen.) s.* 18Feb.07

Stuart, R. C. O., *f.
(temp. Maj.-Gen.)* 3June07

Minchin, F. F.,*p.a.c.
(Ind. Ord. Dept.)* 13July07

Jackson, H K., *D.S.O.*
5Aug.07

Bushe, T. F., *C.M.G.,
p.a.c.,* 10Oct.07

Smith, S. C. U., *g.* [l]
*(temp. Brig.-Gen.)
s,* 14Oct.07

Smith, G. B., *(temp.
Brig.-Gen.) s.* 7Nov.07

Nelson, E. F., *g., f. (temp.
Brig.-Gen.) s.* 22Nov.07

Colonels—contd.

Prinsep, D. G., *g.,
(R.H. & R.F.A.
Records)* 23Apr.08

Gardiner, H. L., *g.,
s.* 13June08

Stokes, A., *D.S.O., g.
(temp Brig.-Gen.)s.*
14Nov.08

Perceval, E. M.,
*D.S.O., p.s.c. (temp,
Brig.-Gen.), s.* 14Nov.08

Barlow, Sir H. W. W.,
*Bt., C.B., p.a.c. (Ord.
Fact.)* 14Nov.08

Holland, A. E. A., *M.V.O.,
D.S.O., q.s., g. (temp.
Brig.-Gen.), m.a.* 14Nov.08

Johnson, F. E., *D.S.O.
(temp.Brig.-Gen.) s.*
20Dec.08

Strange, R. G., s. 15Jan.09

Campbell, H.M.,s. 8June09

Goold-Adams,H.E.F.,
*C. M. G., g. (Member
Ord. Board)* 17July09

Fuller, R. W., *D.S.O.*
11Sept.09

Cockburn, W. F., *g.
(temp. Brig.-Gen.)
s,* 19July11

Chamier, G. D., *C.M.G.,g.
(R.G.A. Records)* 19July11

Drake, B. F., s. 19July11

Du Boulay, N. W. H.,
p.s.c. 30Aug.11

Carte, T. E., s. 30Aug.11

Crowe, J. H. V., *p.s.c.
[L] s.* 30Aug.11

Short, A. H. 30Aug.11

Purse, W. T., *D.S.O.,
p.s.c.* [L] *s.* 4Oct.11

McLeod, W. K., s. 4Oct.11

Johnstone, F. B.,
D.S.O., s. 4Oct.11

Colonels—contd.

Crampton, F. H., s. 4Oct.11

Browne, S. D., s. 6Dec.11

Martel, C. P., *p.a.c.,
s.* 6Dec.11

Meeres,C.S.,*p.a.c.,s.*6Dec.11

Wynne, J. G. E., *g., s.*
7Mar.12

Jendwine,H.S.,*g.,s.* 7Mar.12

Duffus, G. S., s. 7Mar.12

Caulfeild, C. T., s. 7Mar.12

Hussey, A. H., s. 6June12

James, W. R. W., *g.*
6June12

Lecky, R. St. C., s. 6June12

Renny, S.M., *C.I.E.* 6June12

Duhan, W. W. T.,
g., s. 6June12

Bickford, E., *g., s.* 30Oct.12

Mullins, A. J.,*g.,s.* 30Oct.12

Gay, A. W., *D.S.O.,
p.s.c.* [l] *s.* 30Oct.12

Crawford, A., *p.s.c.,
[l], e.a.* 4Dec.12

Heffernan, N. B.,*p.a.c.,
g. (Member, Ord.Board)*
4Dec.12

Rich, H. H., s. 4Dec.12

MacMahon, J. J. 4Dec.12

Butler, H. H., s. 4Dec.12

Scott, C. D., s. 6Mar.13

Bingham, Hon.F. R.,
s. 2June13

Fisher, F. T., *p.a.c., s.*
16Dec.13

Lieutenant-Colonel.

Dunlop,A.S., *p.s.c.* [L]
19July11

Royal Regiment of Artillery.

ROYAL HORSE AND ROYAL FIELD ARTILLERY.

The Royal Arms and Supporters, with a Gun.

"*Ubique*" (above) "*Quo Fas et Gloria ducunt*" (below the Gun).

Colonel in charge of Records .. Prinsep, Col. D. G., *g*... .. Woolwich Dockyard .. 18July14
Asst. to Col. in charge of Records Williams, Hon. Capt. R.C.W., Qr.-Mr. ret. pay (*Res. of Off.*)

Lt.-Colonels.	Lt.-Colonels—contd.	Majors.	Majors—contd.
Radcliffe, W. C. A., *t*. 5Mar.09	Peake, M., C.M.G.[F]*s*. 17Nov.11	Broadrick, F. B. D, 20Jan.02 VanStraubenzee, C. C. 27Feb.02	Hoare Nairne, E. S., *p.s.c.* [*l*], *m.a.* 13Apr.04 23June02
Fox, R. F., *D.S.O.* 5Aug.09	White-Thomson, H. D., *D.S.O., r.h.a.* 29Nov.11	Lake, H. A. 22Mar.02	Strong, W. 13Apr.04
Cloeté, E. R. H. J., *r.h.a.* 23Sept.09	Staveley, W. C., *g.* 1Dec.11	Thwaites, W., *p.s.c.* [*l*] *s.* 20Aug.02	Brock, H. J. 19Aug.04
Macbean, W. A., *p.s.c.* [L] 1Oct.09	Birch, J. F. N., *r.h.a.* 30Jan.12	*bt. lt.-col.* 26Nov.13 Sandys, W. B. R., *r.h.a.* 1Nov.02	Budworth, C. E. D., *M.V.O.* [L], *r.h.a.*1Sept.04 29Nov.00
Cunliffe Owen, C. 10Oct.09	Thompson, W. A. M., *p.s.c.* 15Feb.12	Spedding, E. W. 19Jan.03	Coates, R.C.,*D.S.O.* 1Nov.04
Breeks,R.W.,*r.h.a.*15Oct.09	*bt. col.* 26June08	Kirby, A. D. 26Jan.03	Simpson Balkie, H.A.D.
Goff, A. H. S. 7Dec.09	Prescott-Decie, C. 1Apr.12	29Nov.00	*p.s.c.* [*l*] [F]*r.h.a.* 1Nov.04 22Aug.02
Gray, P. E., *g.* 17Dec.09	de Rougemont, C. H., *M.V.O., D.S.O.,p.s.c.*	Sclater-Booth, Hon. W. D., *r.h.a.* 4Apr.03	Hardman, R S. 13Feb.05
Smith, E. P., *g.* [*l*] 18Dec.09	[F]*r.h.a.* 18May12	Cunliffe Owen F., *p.s.c.* [L], *Mil. Attaché*12Sept.03	Vallentin, H. E. 13Feb.05
Onslow, W. H.,*g.* 23Dec.09	Cardew, G. A. 18May12	Wellesley, R. A. C. 19Oct.03	Hinton, G. B. 13Feb.05
Geddes, J. G. 23Jan.10	Tennant, H. I.,*p.s.c., e.* 21July12	Lyon, F., *D.S.O., p.s.c.* [L] 21Oct.03	Le Mottée, R.E.A., *t.* 15Feb.05
Walker, A. L. 13Feb.10	Heath, F. W. 29July12	Rotton, J. G., *r h.a.* 21Oct.03	Thomas, H. M.,*g.* 5Apr 05 29Nov.00
Gordon, L. A. C. 13Feb.10	Elton, F. A. G. Y. 12Aug.12	Sanders, G. H. 14Nov.03	Nevinson,T. St. A. B.,*r.h.a.* 23Apr.05
Gordon, L. G. F., *D.S.O., g.* 13Feb.10	Duffus, E. J. 26Aug.12	Ward, M. C. P., *p.s.c.* [*l*], *s.* 15Nov.03	Emery, W. B., *t.* 3May05
Sandilands, H. G., *g.* 14Feb.10	Potts, F., *g.* 20Nov.12	Rugge-Price, C. F. 21Nov.03	Gillman,W., *D.S.O.,p.s.c., s.* 12May05
Robinson, W. A., *r.h.a.* 15Mar.10	Quinton, F. W. D. 28Dec.12	Christie, H. A. 9Dec.03 22Aug.02	Grove. E.W.,*D.S.O* 14Nov.05
Lushington, S., *C.M.G.* [*l*] 23Apr.10	Uniacke, H. C. C., *s.* 1Jan.13	Cartwright, G. N. 9Dec.03	Stockley, A. C., *t.* 14Nov.05
Lawrie, C. E., *D.S.O.* [F] 23Apr.10	Ravenhill, F. T. 4Jan.13	Molony, T. S. C. *D S.O., p.s.c.* 3Feb.04	Marsden, R. T. 14Nov.05
Graham, L. 12May10	Ouseley, R. G., *D.S.O., g.,f.* 5May13	Buckle, A. S., *p.s.c., g.* [*l*] 2Mar.04	Bowring, A. H. 21Nov.05
Maxwell, J. McC. 20July10	England, F. P., 19May13	Anderson, A. T., *g.* 2Mar.04 22Aug.02	Bright, R. A., *p.s.c., q.s., e., r.h.a.* 2Dec.05
Fasson, D. J. M., *p.s.c.* [L] 24Sept.10	Carey, G. G. S. 1July13	Eardley-Russell, E, S. E. W., *M.V.O.* *p.s.c.* [L] 2Mar.04	Peel, E. J. R. 11Feb.06 Alexander, C. H. W. 25Apr.06
Geddes, G. H. 24Sept.10	Stockdale, H. E. 17Aug.13	Ballard, C. N. B. 2Mar.04	Sykes, C. A., *r.h.a.* 16May05 Metcalfe, S. F., *g.* 1Aug.06
Rouse, H., *D.S.O., r.h.a.* 14Nov.10	Ford, C. H. 12Sept.13	Saunders, W. P., *t.* 5Mar.04 29Nov.00	Shepperd, M. C., *t.* 20Sept.06 Cape, G. A. S., *p.s.c.* 17Nov.06
Humphreys, G., *D.S.O.,* 14Nov.10	Elkington, R. J. G., *g.* 12Sept.13	Rettie, W. J. K. 16Mar.04	Gilbson,G.[F]*r.h.a.*22Nov.06 Hext, L., *g.* 22Nov.06
Askwith, H. F., *r.h.a.* 20Dec.10	Butler, A. T. 1Oct.13	*s.* 26Mar.04 *bt. lt.-col.* 21Feb.14	Kelly, H. E. T.,*g.,s.* 23Mar.07 Wylde, R. D. 1Apr.07
White, G. F. 15Jan.11	Sharp, F. L. 1Oct.13	Massy, E. C., *t.* 26Mar.04	Willis, E. H. 3Apr.07
Cooper, P. T., *g.,i.* 11Feb.11	Arbuthnot, D. 19Oct.13	Nicholson, G. H. W. [F] 1Apr.04 29Nov.00	Ashworth, L. T. 5Apr.07 Greathed, R. N.,*p.s.o.* [L] *s.* 18May07
Lambert, E. P. 11Feb.11	Biddulph, H. 12Dec.13	Barker, F. E. L. 1Apr.04	Stirling, C., *p.s.c., e., g.s., s.* 9June07
Battiscombe, C. 13Feb.11	Stevens, C. F. 5Mar.14	Stewart, C. G., *D.S.O., p.s.c.* [*l*] [F] 1Apr.04	29Nov.00
Cleeve, E. S. 1Aug.11	Fitzmaurice, R., 5Mar 14	Tighe, F. A. 1Apr.04	Browell, W. B.,*g.* 1July07
Cameron, E. C. 12Oct.11	Tyler, J. A. 16May14	MacMunn, G. F., *D.S.O., p.s.c., q.s., s.* 1Apr.04	Phillpotts, L.M.,*D.S.O.,g.* 3July07
Hall, E. F. 1Nov.11	MacCarthy, M. J. 8June14	*bt. lt.-col.* 10May13	Manley, W. G. H. 10July07
	Ross-Johnson, C. M., *D.S.O.* [L] 13June14	Coates, B. R., *g.* 13Apr.04 Johnstone, H.,*g.,f.,s.* 13Apr.04	Bayly, A. R. 14Oct.07 Drake, H. M. 21Oct.07

Royal Regiment of Artillery.

Royal Horse and Royal Field Artillery—contd.

Majors—contd.

Mallock, A.M.R., t. 20Nov.07
Smith, L.A., r.h.a. 11Dec.07
Parry, C. F. P. 13June14
    20July07
Wilson, C. H., g.,t. 25Dec.07
Delaforce, E. F. 19Jan.08
De Prée, H. D., p.s.c., s.
    19Jan.08
Madocks, W. R. N., p.s.c.,
q.s. 19Jan.08
    29Nov.00
Tudor, H. H., [L]
    19Jan.08
Falmer, C.E., D.S.O., e.a.
    4Mar.08
Kirwan, B. R., g.,s. 6Mar.08
Boyce, H. A., p.s.c. [L] s.
    6Mar.08
Lane, F. C. 6Mar.08
Perreau, A. M. 6Mar.08
Washington, C. F. G.
    14Mar.08
White, G. H. A., r.h.a.
    1Apr.08
Packard, H. N. 1Apr.08
Henning, P. W. B. 1Apr.08
Stewart, D. B 1Apr.08
Ravenhill, C. 1Apr.08
Baillie, G. 15Apr.08
Henry, J., t. 15May08
Short, W. A. 1June08
Smyth, G. A. 20June08
England, R. 27June08
Montgomery, H. M. de F.,
p.s.c., e. [L], s. 3July08
Plummer, E.W.,e. 16Aug.08
Kay, W. H., r.h.a. 17Aug.08
Cubitt, T.A., D.S.O., p.s.c.,
g. 12Sept.08
    21Mar.01
Stapylton, G. J. C. 12Sept.08
Bruce, T. 12Sept.08
Wheatley, P., r.h.a. 21Jan.09
    29Nov.00
Evans, G., c., p.s.c. 15Feb.09
Ward, H. D. O. 18Feb.09
Monkhouse, W. P.,
M.V.O., r.h.a. 27Feb.09
Charlton, C. E. C. G.
[F] r.h.a. 19Apr.09
Ashmore, E. B., M.V.O.,
p.s.c., f.c.r. 19Apr.09
Dennistoun, J. G.,
r.h.a. 19Apr.09
Evans, W., D.S.O.,
r.h.a. 19Apr.09
Montgomery, A. A.,
p.s.c. [l] s. 5June09
Kincaid-Smith, K. J.,
D.S.O., s. 5June09
Atkinson, B., p.s.c.,o.r.
[L] s. 5June09
Lloyd, H. G. 8June09
Liveing, C. H., p.a.c.
    8June09

Majors—contd.

Davson, H. M., r.h.a.
    13June09
Maule, H. N. St. J.,
e. 19June09
    29Nov.00
Wardrop, A. E., r.h.a.
    5Aug.09
Forman, D.E., r.h.a.48Sept.09
Johnstone, J. H. W. 28Sept.09
Tilney, N.E., r.h.a.28Sept.09
    22Aug.02
Ellershaw, W., 1Oct.09
Byron, J., e., s. 1Oct.09
Swann, C. J. H., e.g.1Oct.09
Garstin, H. E., o.c. 2Oct.09
Oldfield, L. C. L. 2Oct.09
Mackenzie, F. W. 2Oct.09
Houstoun, A. 9Oct.09
Walshe, F.W.H., p.s.c. s.
    10Oct.09
Bond, H. H., g., s. 10Oct.09
de Berry, P. P. E., e.
    15Oct.09
Ollivant, J. S., D.S.O., e.,
r.h.a. 20Oct.09
Keyworth, R. G.,
    20Oct.09
Seligman, H.S.,
r.h.a. 13Dec.09
Macnaghten, E. B., g., s.
    18Dec.09
Lamont, J. W. F.,
r.h.a. 20Dec.09
Stevenson, E. H., D.S.O.,
    29Nov.09
    16Jan.10
Harpur, E. B. 13Feb.10
Wynter, H. T. 13Feb.10
Harding Newman, E.,
g., s. 13Feb.10
Davies, W.P.L., p.s.c.,
s. 13Feb.10
Thompson, W. G.,
r.h.a. 13Feb.10
Johnson, R. M., p.s.c., s.
    14Feb.10
Eden, W. R., D.S.O.,
r.h.a. 26Feb.10
Nutt, A. C. R. 15Mar.10
Hamilton, C. L. C.,
p.s.c. 30Mar.10
Doyle, J. F. I. R.,
p.s.c. [l] t. 30Mar.10
Carey, H. E. 1Apr.10
Stanton, F.H.G., p.s.c. [l]
s. 2Apr.10
    29Nov.00
Wilson, L. M., g., s. 23Apr.10
Clarke, H. C. S. 23Apr.10
Ritchie, C. MacI. [l]
    23Apr.10
Atlay, H. W. 12May10
Mair, G. T., D.S.O., c.o.
    13May10
Edwards, A. C. 13May10
Brooke, E.W.S. [l] 28May10
Seagram, T. O. 2July10
Stallard, S. F. 3July10
Hawkes, S. St. L. G.
    20July10
Cotton, A. S. 24Sept.10

Majors—contd.

Radcliffe, P.P. de B., p.s.c.
[L] s. 17Oct.10
Musgrave, A. D. 14Nov.10
Phipps, H. R. 14Nov.10
Arbuthnot, A. G. 14Nov.10
Koebel, H. A., e.[L]3Dec.10
Forman, A. B., f.c.r.,
r.h.a. 24Dec.10
Birley, R. A. 1Feb.11
Lewin, H. F. E. [F]
    8Feb.11
Edwards, W. E., p.a.c., s.
    11Feb.11
Walthall, E. C. W. D.,
D.S.O. 11Feb.11
FitzGerald, M. J. F.
    11Feb.11
Barnes, C. C., g. 1Apr.11
Wheeler, E. L. 1Apr.11
Ingham, C. St.M. 12Apr.11
Peck, H.R., s. 20Apr.11
    22Aug.02
Wainewright, A. R.
    20Apr.11
Smith, H. B. 22Apr.11
Miller, H. de B., D.S.O.,
p.a.c., [l] s. 9May11
Weber, W. H. F., p.s.c.
[l] s. 21July11
Scott, C. W., p.a.c.,
    21July11
Barton, P., g. 21July11
Winter, O. de l'E. 24July11
Wilson, F. A., D.S.O.,
    1Aug.11
Gray, H. McN. 1Aug.11
Archdale, T. M., D.S.O.
    15Aug.11
Newcome, H. W., g.,
s. 21Aug.11
Newman, E. C., p.s.c., s.
    21Aug.11
Higgins, J. F. A., D.S.O.,
g., f.c. 30Aug.11
Birch, E. M., D.S.O.,
p.s.c. [l] s. 30Sept.11
Kirke, K. St. G., o. 30Sept.11
Griffith, R. H. 12Oct.11
Bethell, A. B. [F] 1Nov.11
Kemble, F. A., t. 10Nov.11
Bayley, G. H. W. 10Nov.11
Blois, D. G. 17Nov.11
Rudkin, W. C. E., D.S.O.
    29Nov.11
Madocks, C. 15Feb.12
Belcher, H. T., D.S.O., g.
    15Feb.12
Game, P. W., p.s.c., s.
    15Feb.12
Buzzard, F. A., p.s.c., g., s.
    15Feb.12
Street, H. E., p.s.c.,
    15Feb.12
Hinde, A., p.s.c., s. 15Feb.12
Gosset, F. W., p.s.c.,
    15Feb.12
Bolster, G. E., s.c. 17Feb.12
Calthrop, E. F., p.s.c.
[L] Mil. Attaché 17Feb.12

Majors—contd.

Smith, H. R. W. M.17Feb.12
Gordon, G. H., g. 23Apr.12
Pattisson, J. H. 26Apr.12
Thackeray, C. B., e.9May12
Goldie, M. L.,
D.S.O., M.V.O., 10May12
Holland, C. S., 12May12
Ramsden, R. E., g. 15May12
Logan, F.D., p.s.c. 19June12
Jones, E. H. 19June12
Lewis, P. E., p.s.c.,
s. 27July12
Furnivall, W. 27July12
Allcard, H., D.S.O. 29July12
Lough, A. T. 12Aug.12
Hope, J. W., p.s.c., s. 13Aug.12
Farquhar, J., p.s.c., s.
    16Aug.12
Stirling, W., g. 26Aug.12
Mackey, H. J. A.,
M.V.O. 5Oct.12
Henvey, R., p.s.c. [l]
s. 5Oct.12
    6Nov.03
Pringle, H.G., p.s.c.[l],
s. 5Oct.12
Kinsman, G. R. V.,
g.f.c. 28Dec.12
Tovey, G. S., s. 1Jan.13
Head, A. E. M. 4Jan.13
Deshon, F. G. T., g. 6Jan.13
Fulton, J. D. B., C.B.
[L], f.c.r. (Aeronautical Inspn. Dept.)16Jan.13
Paterson, P. J. [l] 16Jan.13
Brancker, W. S., p.s.c.,
f.c.r., s. 27Jan.13
Livingstone-Learmonth,
J. E. C. 8Mar.13
Hudson, A. R. [l] 13Sept.13
Wynne, H. E. S., s.12Sept.13
Burne, E. R. 12Sept.13
Tailyour, G. H. F., s.
    30Sept.13
Downer, J.G., p.s.c., s.
    30Sept.13
Hill, H. W., g., s. 1Oct.13
Buchanan-Dunlop,
    26Nov.13
    28Feb.02
Elliot, E. H. H. 26Nov.13
Clark, W. E. 17Mar.14
Phillips, E. H., D.S.O.
    28Mar.14
Gethin, R. W. St. L.,
o., s.c. 1Apr.14
Stopford, H. F.,
m.a. 1Apr.14
Smith-Rewse, H. B. W.,
p.s.c. [L] 1Apr.14
Bartholomew, W. H.,
p.s.c., s. 16May14
Rainsford-Hannay, F.,
s.c. 16May14
Gill, D. H. 6June1

Royal Regiment of Artillery.

Royal Horse and Royal Field Artillery—contd.

Captains.

Captains.	Captains—contd.	Captains—contd.	Captains—contd.
Warburton, W. M. 1Apr.02	Wickham, T. E. P., D.S.O., Adjt. 6Jan.06	Ballingall, H. M. 21Oct.07	Popham, G. L., t. 10Aug.08
Hartland-Mahon, M. C. J. 9Apr.02	Sheppard, P., D.S.O. 11Feb.06	Thellusson, Hon. H. E. 9Nov.07	Atchison, H. W. 11Aug.08
Campbell, N. St. C. 3Feb.04	Browning, C. H.[t]13Mar06	Cooke, E. D. M. H., t. 12Nov 07	Jervis. N. G. M., Adjt. 11Aug.08
Willis, S. G. R. [l] 3Feb.04	Hackworth, F. J. A., p.s.c., s. 16Apr.06	Naper, L. A. D., t. 20Nov.07	Lewer, L. W., g., s. 17Aug.08
Wyatt, G. N. [l] m.a.4Feb 04	Davidson, N.R., s.c. 15Apr.06	Williams, R. C. 1Nov.07	Shaw, R. A., t. 19Aug.08
Rochfort-Boyd, H. C., [L] 2Mar.04	Colville, J. R., g. 17Apr.06	Lascelles, R. H., r.h.a. 21Nov.07	Salt, H. F., s.c. 1Sept.08
Stanley, F. [l], co. 2Mar.04	Maturin, R. G., D.S.O. 21Apr.06	Leggett, E. H. G., g., s. 1Dec.07	Scarlett, J. A., Adjt., r.h.a. 1Sept.08
Furse, E. W., s.c. 2Mar.04	Sherbrooke, N. H., s.c. 20June06	Warren, L. E. 1Dec.07	Robinson, F. W. 12Sept.08
Forsyth, J. A. C. 5Mar.04	Woollcombe-Adams, C. E. G. [F] 27June06	Goschen, A. A., D.S.O., r.h.a. 4Dec.07	McLean, C. W. W. r.h.a. 12Sept.08
Ellington, E. L., p.s.c., f.o.r. 27Apr.04	Woodroffe, C.R. [l], s. 27June06	Crofton, M., r.h.a.19Dec.07	Sherlock, D.J.C.E 25Sept.08
Goff, L. T., Adjt. 2May04	Harris, O.M., r.h.a.27June06	Cavendish, H. C..s. 4Jan.08	Hay, E. S., t. 26Sept.08
Nevill, H. L., D.S.O., p.s.c., g. 10May04	West, F. G. 11July06	Hamilton, H. A., o.c. 19Oct.07	Thornton, G. St. L. 5Oct.08
Twidale, W. C. E., o., e., o.d. 14July04	Blathwayt, G. W. 18July06	Murray, F. M., t. 19Jan.08	Bower, C. E. S. 16Oct.08
Shewell, E. F. 14July04	Simpson, H. C. 25Aug.06	Ironside, W. E. [L] s.c. 18Feb.08	Finlayson, R. G., r.h.a., Adjt. 20Oct.08
Hawksley, J. P. V. [F] 14July04	Cossart, A. R. B., s 21Sept.06	Higgon, A. B. 3Mar.08	Dunbar, J.C., r.h.a. 21Oct.08
Meyricke, R. J. C. 18Sept.04	Buckle, H. 19Nov.06	Stewart, D. 3Mar.08	Younger, A. A. S. 21Oct.08
Bedwell, E. P.[l] 30Oct.04	Hezlet, R. K., p.a.c., o.d. 1Apr.09	Balston, G. R., r.h.a., Adjt. 25May14	Forbes, Hon. D.A., M.V.O., s. 21Oct.08
Paxton, H. W., o.[L] t. 10Oct.04	Mellor, A., r.h.a. 5Dec.06	Vernon, L. D. 21Nov.07	Fergusson, V. M., T., s. 29Oct.08
Spiller, D. W. L., t. 10Oct.04	Craven, W. S. D., g., r.h.a. 5Dec.06	Ballard, J. A. 3Mar.08	Cockcraft, L. W. La 2Dec.08
Browne, E. W. 23Jan.05	Cornes, H., g., Adjt. 5Apr.07	Clark, C. H., t. 4Mar.08	Henderson, J.A., t. 4Dec.08
Jameson, W. K.E. [l], s. 23Jan.05	Harris, A. G. R. C. [L] 12Apr.07	Lloyd, O. S. 6Mar.08	Spinks, C. W., e.a. 23Jan.09
Butler, B. A. B. 23Jan.05	Thomson, A. F., s. 13Apr.07	Laurie, E. C., p.a.c., s. 14Mar.08	Meldon, P. A., c.o. 4Feb.09
Shaw-Stewart, B. H. 24Jan.05	Furse, G. A. 29Apr.07	Queripel, L. H., t. 17Mar.08	Skinner, E. J., r.h.a.4Feb.09
Turner, A.J., p.s.c, s 30Jan.05 bt. maj. 31Jan.05	Chenevix-Trench, F. M., p.s.c. [L] s. 15May07	Hare, G. A., o, t. 1Apr.08	Brousson, F., Adjt.15Feb.09
Allardyce, J. G. B., r.h.a. 7Feb.05	Bryant, F. C., c. o. 24May07	Addison, A. M, 1Apr.08	Spencer-Smith, D. C. [l] r.h.a., Adjt. 18Feb.09
Norton, W. H., e. 13Feb.05	White, R. W. [L], Adjt. 27May07	Savile, L. W., s. 1Apr.08	Bowles, J. de V. 22Feb.09
Martelli, H. de C., s.c. 31Mar.05	Riddell, J. B., o., Adjt. 27May07	Godman, L. 1Apr.08	Willis, A., o. 22Feb.09
Cuninghame, E. W. M. [L] 1May05	Bourchier, R. W. H., t. 8June07	Jelf, W. W., r.h.a. 1Apr.08	Boyd, H. A., Adjt 26Feb.09
West, A.H.D., r.h.a. 27Oct.05	Bridges, A. H., r.h.a. 9June07	Marryat, R., t. 1Apr.08	Bartram H. B., r.h.a. 27Feb.09
Dobson, M. C., s.c. 28Oct.05	Asser, V., D.S.O., m.a. 3July07	Anderson, T.G., e.a. 1Apr.08	Hawkins, C. F. 20Mar.09
St. John, E. F., s.c. 14Nov.05	Taylor, G.J.S., r.h.a. 5July07	Preeston, N. P. R. 1Apr.08	Nixon, Sir C. W., Bt., s. 25Mar.09
Reichwald W. F. [L] s. 14Nov.05	Drought, G. T. A. 22Aug.07	Duthie, A. M., r.h.a.1Apr.08	Masters, G. 30Mar.09
Thomson, R.G.[L] s.14Nov.05	Crozier, B. B. 18Sept.07	Curling, J., r.h.a. 4Apr.08	Muirhead, M. [l] 19Apr.09
Littledale, A. C. 21Nov.05	Cowell, H. P. J., r.h.a. 27Sept.05	Saunders, C. H., p.a.c., o.d. 4Apr.08	Sarson, E. V., Adjt.19Apr.09
Anstruther, R. A. 24Nov.05	Lynch-Staunton, R. K., Adjt., r.h.a. 14Oct.07	Steel, E. A., e.,o.,f.o. 4Apr.08	Young, C.S., p.a.c., s. 1June09
Salmond, W. G. H., p.s.c. [l] f.o.r., s. 2Dec.05		Stillwell, W.D., Adjt.11Apr.08	Gibbon, J.H., t. 2June09
Schrottky, C. E. G., o., t. 6Dec.05		Cox, C. H. F. [L] e.a. 11Apr.08	Phillips, J.L., r.h.a. 2June09
Karslake, H., D.S.O., p.s.c. 20Dec.05		Potter, C. F., p.s.c 5May08	Rogers, W. L. Y., Adjt. 6June09
Parsons, W. F., r.h.a. 1Jan.06		Roberts, I.D'E., e.a. 18May08	Sinclair, T. C. 5Aug.09
		Belgrave, J. D., p.s.c. 28May08	Vickery, C.E., D.S.O. [L] [F] e.a. 23Sept.09
		Reynolds, D. 1June08	Jackson, H. S. 23Sept.09
		Gray, W. K. 4June08	Murray, W. A., t. 24Sept.09
		Armitage, C. C., s.c.14July08	Bayley, R. 25Sept.09
		Erskine, A. E., r.h.a., Adjt. 14July08	Fisher, H. G. 9Oct.09
		Hebert, C., t. 27July08	Boone, B.G., Adjt.[l] 12Oct.09 6May08
		Burnyeat, H. P., r.h.a. 4Aug.08	Johnson, R. H., s.c. 15Oct.09
		Ingram, J. M. 5Aug.08	Jones, E. A. 19Oct.09

Royal Regiment of Artillery.

Royal Horse and Royal Field Artillery—contd.

Captains—contd.		Captains—contd.		Captains—contd.		Captains—contd.	
Eden, A. G.	23Jan.10	Parbury, F. N.	1Jan.11	Wilmer, E.R.G., Adjt.		Allsup, E. S.	6July13
Napier, V. M. C., s.c.	1Feb.10	Sykes, F. B., c.o.	1Jan.11		1Nov.11		26May13
Johnston, R. G. M.		Wilson, P. H., t.	10Jan.11	Young, H. G., Adjt. 1Nov.11		Mascall, F. E.	31July13
	1Feb.10	Miller, G. R.	15Jan.11	Hill, C. R.	1Nov.11		29Jan.13
Pulley, C.	1Feb.10	Waycott, E. W. J. 22Jan.11		Gardner-Waterman, A.		Ayton, H. R., c.o.	27Aug.13
Grice-Hutchinson, C.B., t.	1Feb 10	Hamilton, G. T., c.o. 22Jan.11			3Nov.11	Blumenthal, A. Z., i.v.	27Aug.13
Bradbury E. K., r.h.a.		Kirkland, T.	23Jan.11	Heneage, A. P.	22Jan.12	Dundas, J. C., g., Adjt.	
	4Feb.10	Greaves, H. M., e., t. 1Feb.11		Wynter, H. W.	22Jan.12		27Aug.13
Renny-Tailyour, J. W. r.h.a.	8Feb.10	McClymont, R. A. 7Feb.11		Blair, W. K. P.	31Jan.12	Denniss, C. E. B., t.12Sept.13	
Raikes, L. T.	13Feb.10	Lyster, P. G.	9Feb.11	Cooper, C. G. A., t.	5Feb.12	Joll, H. H.	12Sept.13
Paul, W. R., g., s.	13Feb.10	Turner, G.F.B., p.a.c., s.		McGowan, T.	15Feb.12	Batchelor, V. A. [L]	13Nov.13
Prance, R. C.	13Feb.10		11Feb.11	Gethin, F. D. S., p.a.c., s.		Harvey, A. F. B., p.a.c.	
Powell, J. H. S.	13Feb.10	Oldham, P. H. L., s. 11Feb.11		Carlyon, T.	17Feb.12		21Dec.13
Bucknill, L. M.	13Feb.10	Sanderson, R. H., r.h.a.	11Feb.11	Staveley, A. G.	26Feb.12	Hayley, W. B., t.	21Dec.13
Farran, G. F.	16Feb.10	Woodside, A. McB.11Feb.11		Wallinger, E. A. (l)	27Feb.12	Yorke, P. G., Adjt.	21Dec.13
Marshall, F. H., o. 20Feb.10		Mecredy, H., o.c.	23Feb.11	Sadler, H. K., Adjt. 1Mar.12		Body, K. M., o., o.d.	21Dec.13
Stevens, C. M. H., Adjt.		Leech, A. G.	23Feb.11	Lyon, C. D. G., t.	1Mar.12	Denison, H.	21Dec.13
	24Feb.10	Blathwayt, H.W., t		Colley, C. C.	13Mar.12	Bolitho, E. H. W., Adjt.	21Dec.13
Boyd, A. O., e.	24Feb.10		23Feb.11	Roe, J. W.	13Mar.12	French, T. N.	14Feb.14
Warren, W. R.	24Feb.10	Butchart, J. A., s.	23Feb.11	Neville, G. C., Adjt.	1Apr.12	Rose, H. A. L.	17Mar.14
Cowan, J. De B.	15Mar.10	Reeves, R. C., Adjt.24Feb.11		Powell, R. ff.	1Apr.12	Milford, K. E., t.	17Mar.14
Harvey, C. G. S., t. 30Mar.10		Bartholomew, A. W.		Twisleton-Wykeham-Fiennes, N. I. E. 23Apr.12		Eddis, L. A., g., Adjt.	17Mar.11
Harrison, J. M. R., r.h.a.	31Mar.10		1Mar.11	Lawrence, C. T., t.	26Apr.12	Povah, J. W.	17Mar.14
Taylor, B. W., Adjt. 1Apr.10		Joyce, L. W., t.	1Mar.11	Hale, D. B., t.	26Apr.12	Dodgson, R.C., Adjt. 18Mar.14	
Rawlins, S. W. H., s.c.	1Apr.10	Mann, G. D., c.o.	22Mar.11	Phillips, C. C.	26Apr.12	Ward, B. S.	24Mar.14
Adams, R. J.	1Apr.10	Scarlett, Hon, R. F., r.h.a. Adjt.	1Apr.11	Theobald, A. C. L. 26Apr.12		Mansfield, H.M.L.	1Apr.14
Webber, H. A. W., t.	1Apr.10	Wray, H. C.	1Apr.11	Hovil, R.	26Apr.12	Fullerton, C. D., Adjt.	1Apr.14
Carrington, C. R. B.		Tompson, R. H. D., D.S.O., g., (l) s.c.	1Apr.11	Parbury, E., t.	9May12	King, G. H.	18Apr.14
	1Apr.10	Lewin, E. O., r.h.a.	3Apr.11	Barber-Starkey, W. H. J.	9May12	Heygate, C., c.o.	23July14
Poston, W.J.L., e.a. [F]	23Apr.10	Burden, W. MacC., o., s.	12Apr.11	McLay, W. J., s.	10May12	Gillman, A. G.	23July14
Stebbing, N. A.	5May10	Waddell-Dudley, A. N. t.	12Apr.11	Vaughan, H. H. S., Adjt.	10May12	Robertson, N. B.	23July14
Sinclair, J. N., t.	13May10	Grieve, F.C.L., Adjt. 20Apr.11		Gregory, G.M.A., Adjt.		Cripps, C. W.	23July14
Langford, E. G.	11June10	Cousens, R. B., t.	25Apr.11	Milman, L. C. F., o., m.a.	2May12	Leech, C. J. F., Adjt.	23July14
Curling, W. G.	11June10	Reid, W. R., Adjt.	9May11		12May12	Haining, R. H., e.	23July14
Ramsden, J. V., Adjt.13July10		Howell, H. G., c.o.	15May11	Coldwell-Horsfall, J. H.	15May11	Thorburn, J. F. P.	23July14
Longstaff, R.	27July10	Burton, F. C. D., s. 15May11		Millar, J. H. B.	26July12	Boyce, C. E., t.	23July14
Hunter, D. H. K.	3Aug.10	Hunt, C. O. C.	15May11	Oliver, G.B. [l]	27July12	Bridgeman, Hon. H. G. O.	23July14
Cooper, C. F., t.	3Aug.10	Jones, W. A. F.	15May11	Hulton, H. H., Adjt. 29July12		Walford, J. C.	23July14
McGrath, A. T., Adjt.	18Sept.10	Salmond, F.W., t.	29May11	Corbould-Warren, E.	3Aug.12	Cree, W. C. H.	23July14
	21Aug.07	Heather, V. J.	28June11	Robinson, L. J. W., o.	10Aug.12	Baylay, E. J. L.	23July14
Paynter, W. P., r.h.a.	17Oct.10	Tweedie, D. K.	28June11	Harrisson, R. D.	12Aug.12	Ivens, C. W. M., t.	23July14
Carruthers, J., M.V.O., s.	14Nov.10	Macdona, B. V.	24July11	Paul, C. T. S., g	16Aug.12	Potter, K. M., Adjt.	23July14
Parrington, J. W., g.	14Nov.10	Mortimore, C. A.	24July11	Heelas, P. J. B.	16Aug.12		
Nornabell, H. M., Adjt.	14Nov.10	Bailey, F. G. G.	15Aug.11	Budge, P. P., s.	26Aug.12	**Lieutenants.**	
Bower, H. G. L.	14Nov.10	Maclaverty, C. F. S., c.o.	21Aug.11	White, A. K. G.	26Aug.12	Blake, C. B., t.	16Nov.04
Newland, A. E.	15Nov.10	Mowbray, J. L., p.s.c.	21Aug.11	Beor, B. R. W., f.c.	4Jan.13	Clayton, W. A., t.	16Nov.04
Cullerne, C. P.	16Nov.10	Arthur, H. B. C. [L] Adjt.	21Aug.11	Gover, C. R.	4Jan.13	Carrington, R. H., r.h.a.	16Nov.04
Anderson, S. M., c.o.3Dec.10		Crofton, M. R. H. 23Aug.11		Congreve, F. L.	6Jan.13	Cooper, G. S., Adjt.	4Dec.04
Gregory, K. H.	16Dec.10	Burdon, C. W., m.a.	30Aug.11	Benson, R., s.	6Jan.13	Maitland, R. C. F., s.	4Dec.04
Elam, H. W. T.	16Dec.10	Rich, C. S., Adjt.	12Sept.11	Spencer-Smith, G. M.	16Jan 13	Walker, C. E., t.	4Dec.04
Gidley, C. de B., t.	20Dec.10	Boase, G. O., p.a.c., s.	2Oct.11	Walter, B.	22Jan.13	Waller, R.C.F., c.o.	4Dec.04
Gregson, H. O.	24Dec.10	Chambers, W. T.	2Oct.11	Turnbull, P.	1Dec.12	Halliday, W. J. F.	4Dec.04
Walch, J. C.	24Dec.10	Main, A. K., Adjt.	9Oct.11	Geary, J. A.	27Jan.13	Duke, B. L., m.	21Dec.04
Anderson, E. O.	31Dec.10	Marshall, E. T.	10Oct.11	Robinson, P. G.	13Feb.13	Campbell, J. D.	21Dec.04
Unlacke, C. D. W., r.h.a.	31Dec.10	Blount, G. H. N., Adjt.	1Nov.11	Shaw, W. M., t.	17Aug.12	Carlisle, T. R. M. [l]	21Dec.04
Kelly, R. H. V., o., e., o.d.	1Jan.11	Jervis-Smith, E.J., t. 1Nov.11		D'Arcy, J. I., t.	2Apr.13	Longmore, J. C.	21Dec.04
				Anstey, E. C., p.s.c. 10May13		Graham, Lord D. M., (l) s.	21Dec.04
				Lanyon, O. M.	10May13	Clutterbuck, L. St. J. R., p.a.c., s.	21Dec.04
						Meade, G. W., r.h.a.	21Dec.04

Royal Regiment of Artillery.

Royal Horse and Royal Field Artillery—contd.

Lieutenants—contd.

- T.H., r.h.a 21Dec.04
- A. F. 21Dec.04
- K., r.h.a. 21Dec.04
- N., t. 21Dec.04
- W.A., r.h.a. 21Dec.04
- H. 21Dec.04
- R. T., s. 21Dec.04
- L., r.h.a. 21Dec.04
- C.E., m.a. 21Dec.04
- M. J. K., t. 21Dec.04
- A. S. 21Dec.04
- J. L. [L] 21Dec.04
- E. [l] t. 21Dec.04
- J. L. [L], f.c. 21Dec.04
- W. L., c.o. 4Jan.05
- 5Oct.04
- wne, S. [l], 18Apr.05
- 21Dec.04
- L. E. O. 24May05
- M. J. 24May05
- y-Osborne,
- J. H., t. 24May05
- E. U. 24May05
- J. F. K., r.h.a. 24May05
- V.H., Adjt. 24May05
- H., t. 27Nov.06
- 7May05
- K. 24May05
- e, W., c.o. 19June05
- r.h.a. 31July05
- L., r.h.a. 31July05
- A., Adjt. 31July05
- F. J. 31July05
- C., t. 31July05
- A.J.R., t. 31July05
- A., t. 31July05
- c.o. 31July05
- Sir T. P., a. 31July05
- B., Adjt. 31July05
- D. A. 31July05
- ubenzee, 31July05
- h.a. 31July05
- her, H. 31July05
- A. 31July05
- J. C. M. 31July05
- C. J. H., r.h.a. 31July05
- lson, H. G., r.h.a. 31July05
- H. W., r.h.a. 31July05
- W., c.o. 31July05
- E., t. 31July05
- C. L. T., 24Dec.05
- 24Dec.05
- vynne, A. H., 24Dec.05
- C., r.h.a. 24Dec.05
- G. N. [l], 24Dec.05
- a, A. G., r.h.a. 24Dec.05
- A.F., r.h.a. [L] 24Dec.05
- E. F., r.h.a. 24Dec.05
- W. A., t. 24Dec.05
- F., e.a. 24Dec.05
- I. 24Dec.05
- G. F. R. 24Dec.05

Lieutenants—contd.

- Massy, H. R. S., t. 24Dec.05
- Selby, C. W., [l] r.h.a, 24Dec.05
- FitzGibbon, F. 24Dec.05
- Grosvenor, Hon. R. E. 24Dec.05
- Palmer, R. L., r.h.a. 24Dec.05
- Lucas, C. C., r.h.a. 24Dec.05
- Fairbank, H. N. 24Dec.05
- Rose, D. D. 24June06
- Temple, T., o. 24June06
- Findlay, C. B., r.h.a. 24June06
- Plummer, M.V., c.o.24June06
- Clayton, E., p.s.c.[L]15July06
- Ramsay, J. R., r.h.a, 15July06
- Purser, A. W., t. 15July06
- Fleming, E.C. r.h.a.15July06
- Tenison, W. P. C. 15July06
- Macdonald, D. R. 15July06
- Soames, M. A. 15July06
- Pease-Watkin, E. H. P. 15July06
- Hutchison, H. O., r.h.a. 15July06
- Mackenzie, E. J. B. 15July06
- Galloway. R. L., t. 15July06
- Hermon Hodge, G. G., r.h.a. 15July06
- O'Brien, A. U. M. 12Dec.06
- Hutchinson, E. M. [L] e.a. 28Dec.06
- Symons, H. 2Dec.07
- Butler, Hon. T. P. P., e.a. 28Dec.06
- Burkhardt, V.R., c.l.23Dec.06
- Thuburn, J. O., e.a. 23Dec.06
- Peebles, R. E. 23Dec.06
- Newton, T. C. [L], r.h.a. 28Dec.06
- Holland, R. T., r.h.a. 28Dec.06
- Fraser, A.H.[l]o.c. 28Dec.06
- Pierson, C.E., r.h.a.23Dec.06
- Marsh. A. C.E., f.c, 23Dec.06
- Giffard, R., s. 23Dec.06
- Gillum, W. W. [l] m.a,
- Harrison, P. F., r.h.a. - 23Dec.06
- Boddam-Whetham, S. A., Adjt. 24Dec.06
- Giffard, J., r.h.a. 24Dec.06
- Wallace, J. T., r.h.a. 24Dec.06
- Ommanney, C.H., t. 28Dec.06
- Ward, C. F., r.h.a. 28Dec.06
- Radcliffe, S.R., [l] t.28Dec.06
- Block, A., t. 11Apr.07
- Montgomery, R. N. V., t. 4June07
- Ellis, R. S., r.h.a. 29July07
- McConnel, M. H., r.h.a. 29July07
- Rutherfoord, D. G. C.,

Lieutenants—contd.

- Grant Suttie, H.F., r.h.a. 29July07
- Murray, G. 29July07
- Pile, F. A., r.h.a. 29July07
- Lawson, C.G., r.h.a.29July07
- Davies, H. L., r.h.a.29July07
- Ball, K. M., r.h.a. 29July07
- Gardiner, R. H. 29July07
- Conner, D. G., f.c. 29July07
- Durie, T. E. 29July07
- Richardson, G. C. r.h.a. 29July07
- Hill, L. R. [L] 29July07
- Moore, J. H., Adjt. 29July07
- Curle, W. S. N., t. 29July07
- Geldard, C. 29July07
- Elliott, V., t. 29July07
- Grant, H. De B., t. 29July07
- St. Clair, G. J. P., r.h.a, 29July07
- Kerans, H. J. D. [l]18Oct.07
- Imbert-Terry, H.B., r.h.a. 24Dec.07
- Burton, A. R., t. 3Dec.07
- Ryan, R. S. [L], r.h.a. 3Dec.07
- Dendy, M. H. r.h.a. 21Dec.07
- Cowan, W.McC.C. 21Dec.07
- Mann, W. r.h.a.21Dec.07
- Burns, S. F. 21Dec.07
- Crocker, J. C. 21Dec.07
- Bridge, C. E. D. [L], r.h.a. 21Dec.07
- Weldon, G. 21Dec.07
- Vaux, F.B., p.a.c. 21Dec.07
- Merriman, G. H. [L] r.h.a. 21Dec.07
- Daubuz, C., r.h.a. 21Dec.07
- Walsh, R. H. 21Dec.07
- Parbury, K., r.h.a.21Dec.07
- Baxter, H. H. 17May08
- Broad, C.N. F., s.o.17May08
- Leach, G. P., r.h.a.27July08
- Gregory, M. 27July08
- Knyvett, C. L. 27July08
- Nunn, J. H. r.h.a. 27July08
- Adam, R. F., r.h.a, 27July08
- Eeles, C. A. 27July08
- White, J. L. C., r.h.a. 27July08
- Wilson, D. L. C., r.h.a. 27July08
- ArcherHoublon, R., r.h.a. 22Nov.08
- Dawson, A. 20Dec.08
- Phillips, M. A. 20Dec.08
- Bell, S. P. [l] 20Dec.08
- Maxwell, E. B., r.h.a. 20Dec.08
- Barstow, W. A. T., r.h.a. 20Dec.08
- Allen, E.H. [l] m.a. 20Dec.08
- Holland, C. [l] 20Dec.08
- Sandeman, T. F., r.h.a. 20Dec.08
- Greenshields, D. J., r.h.a. 20Dec.08
- Dunbar, A. J. 20Dec.08
- Dresser, P. B. 4May09

Lieutenants—contd.

- Budden, E.F. r.h.a.29June09
- Sebag-Montefiore, T. H., r.h.a. 25July09
- Agnew, K. M. 25July09
- Martin, H.G., r.h.a.25July09
- Burne, A.H., r.h.a. 25July09
- Wallace, C. H. 25July09
- McLeod, N. M., r.h.a. 25July09
- Hall, E. C. 25July09
- Sanders, J.D G., f.c.25July09
- Ling, R. W., m.a. 25July09
- Mullings, J. R. 25July09
- Fitze, G. G., r.h.a. 25July09
- Park, A. St. J. L. 25July09
- Rickards, G. A., r.h.a. 25July09
- Worsley, H. G., r.h.a. 25July09
- Cherry, R. G. 25July09
- Dolphin, V. O. 25July09
- Watson, G. E. B., r.h.a. 25July09
- Carfrae, C. T. 12Dec.09
- Pownall, H.R., r.h.a. 2Dec.09
- Lemmon, C. H., t. 20Dec.09
- Preston, C. O'D. [l] 20Dec.09
- Stopford, G.B., f.c.r.20Dec.09
- Collins, H. G., c.o. 20Dec.09
- Archdale, A. Q., r.h.a. 20Dec.09
- Allen, R. A. [l], Adjt. 20Dec.09
- Lowry-Corry, H. C. r.h.a. 20Dec.09
- Simpson. W.A.J., c.o. 20Dec.09
- Twisleton-Wykeham-Fiennes, Hon. I. M., r.h.a. 20Dec.09
- Farrant. H. 20Dec.09
- Cunningham, A. G. 20Dec.09
- Mundy, L. F. H., r.h.a. 20Dec.09
- Simpson, H. D. 20Dec.09
- Benham, F. B. 20Dec.09
- Gough, J.B., r.h.a.20Dec.09
- Custance, S. N., c.o.20Dec.09
- Gale, H. D., c.o. 20Dec.09
- Deprez, A.E., r.h.a.20Dec.09
- Henderson, C. E. P. [l] 20Dec.09
- Lee, K. W. 20Dec.09
- Heath, E. G. 20Dec.09
- Taylor, V. A. H. 20Dec.09
- Strickland, G. T. 20Dec.09
- Osmaston, U. E. 19Jan.10
- Allen, R. W. 19Jan.10
- Parker, B.F., r.h.a. 25May10
- Edwards, F. G. de B., r.h.a. 25May10
- Farren, R. H., r.h.a.23July10
- Rait Kerr, W. C. 23July10
- Almack, E.P., r.h.a.23July10
- Marriner, B. L. 23July10
- Roney-Dougall, A. R. 23July10
- Joubert, de la Ferte, P. B. [L], f.c. 23July10
- Noakes, S. M. 23July10
- Price, J. T., r.h.a. 23July10

Royal Regiment of Artillery.

Royal Horse and Royal Field Artillery—contd.

Lieutenants—contd.

Marston, J. E., r.h.a.	23July10
McMaster, H.	23July10
Fairtlough, E. V. H., s.s.	23July10
Cornwall, J. H. M. (L), m.a.	23July10
Allen, R. F. C.	23July10
Rashleigh, R. N.	23July10
Welsh, W. M. M. O'D.	23July10
Woodhouse, A. J.	23July10
Brooke, A.C., r.h.a.	23July10
Lambert, A. F.	23July10
Montanaro, C. A. H., o.c.	23July10
Dudding, H. N. N.	2Mar.12
	23July10
Granet, G. E. A. (l)	23July10
Peel, D. R.	23July10
Wason, S. R.	23July10
Paige, D.	23July10
Patterson, A.	23July10
Robertson, H.M.M.	23July10
Robinson, A.	7Dec.10
Pyne, F. S.	18Dec.10
Ferguson, P. H.	18Dec.10
Lucas, J. de B. T.	18Dec.10
Townsend, M. D.	18Dec.10
Massy, C. W., Adjt.	18Dec.10
Butler-Stoney, R. B.	18Dec.10
Harford, H. H.	18Dec.10
Purey Cust, R. B.	18Dec.10
Crossman, F. L. M., Adjt.	18Dec.10
Pery-Knox-Gore, I. C.	18Dec.10
Shilstone, W.R., o.c.	18Dec.10
Rendel, A. J.	18Dec.10
Smithson, R.	18Dec.10
Harding, F. E. B.	18Dec.10
Green, W. W.	18Dec.10
Gibbs, A. J.	18Dec.10
Rait Kerr, S. C.	18Dec.10
Cory, G. N.	18Dec.10
Orde, J. B.	18Dec.10
Studd, M. A.	18Dec.10
Beresford-Peirse, N. M. de la P., t.	18Dec.10
Stephenson, D. C.	18Dec.10
Boscawen, Hon. G. E., s.	18Dec.10
McMaster, W.	18Dec.10
Chetwynd-Stapylton, H. M.	18Dec.10
Huleatt, F. H.	18Dec.10
Williamson, H. N. H.	18Dec.10
Gordon, C. C. (l)	23May11
Scott, J.	29July11
Penrose, J., s.s.	29July11
Benson, G. R.	29July11
Hill, D. (l)	29July11
Atkinson, S.	29July11
Rome, R. C. (L)	29July11
Pollard, G. E. (L)	29July11
Cadell, C. A. E.	29July11
Macpherson, A. D.	29July11
Akerman, W.P.J.	29July11
Bowen, G. E. S. (L)	29July11
Colfox, W. P.	29July11
Morgan, F. H. L	29July11
Tristram, G. H.	29July11

Lieutenants—contd.

Barkworth, J. S.	29July11
Rhodes, B. F.	29July11
Binney, F. B., f.c.r.	29July11
Field, L.	29July11
Scott, D.	12Dec.11
Butler, W. V. H.	12Dec.11
Langford, C. C.	12Dec.11
Miller, R. B.	18Dec.11
Carmichael, G. I., f.c.	18Dec.11
MacDonald, H. S.	18Dec.11
Playfair, Hon. L. G. H. L.	18Dec.11
Chaytor, F. C.	18Dec.11
Wilson, E. W. G.	18Dec.11
Charles, A. A. M.	18Dec.11
Pinney, G. A.	18Dec.11
Cochrane, D. J., s.s.	18Dec.11
Love, R. H. A. D.	18Dec.11
Leach, R. S.	18Dec.11
Green, G. A. L.	18Dec.11
Martin, E. T.	18Dec.11
Forsyth, A. F. J.	18Dec.11
Magrath, M. H.	18Dec.11
Crewdson, W. T. O.	18Dec.11
Wye, F. P.	10Feb.12
Wanklyn, F. A., f.c.	24June12
Wurtele, H. A. S.	24June12
Brownlow, C. A. L.	23July12
O'Brien, L. B.	23July12
Bayne-Jardine, C. W.	23July12
Burrard, G.	23July12
Fleet, A. L. E.	23July12
Russell, J.	23July12
Thomson, J. N.	23July12
Fayle, D. B. W.	23July12
Buist, C. N.	23July12
Stanford, J. (l)	23July12
Anne, H. O. D.	23July12
Younger, J. E. T.	23July12
Dennis, J. O. C.	23July12
Spencer, S. A.	23July12
Freer, R. C.	23July12
Christie, A., f.c.	23July12
Eden, H. C. H.	23July12
Anderson, E. L.	23July12
Barry, J. R.	23July12
Mason MacFarlane, F. N. (L)	23July12
Clarke, J. E. L.	23July12
Moorhead, E. J.	23July12
Stewart-Cox, A.	23July12
Ardagh, R. W.	23July12
Kempe, H. F. E.	23July12
Atkinson, K P., f.c.	23July12
Cotter, K.	23July12
King-Harman, L. H.	23July12
Dorling, L. R. G.	23July12
Browne, H. S.	26July12
Marshall, C. F. K.	11Dec.12
Griffith, A. L. P.	23Dec.12
Hutton, T. J.	23Dec.12
Ellis, H. S.	23Dec.12
Fisher, D. R. D.	23Dec.12
Bolton, C. D.	23Dec.12
Elles, P. G. M.	23Dec.12
Schreiber, E. C. A.	23Dec.12
Glendinning, H. J.	23Dec.12
Tuke, C. W. R.	23Dec.12
Jones-Bateman, L.	23Dec.12
Smyth, G. O. S.	23Dec.12
Chisholm-Batten, J. de H.	23Dec.12

Lieutenants—contd.

Crippin, H. W. (l)	23Dec.12
Brereton, C. L	23Dec.12
Franklyn, G. E. W.	23Dec.12
Cammell, G. A.	23Dec.12
Campbell, C. W.	23Dec.12
Palmer, E. A.	16Feb.13
Mackie, W. B.	23June13
Caldwell, K F. T.	23July13
Trenchard, F. A.	23July13
Bather, E. J.	23July13
Morrison, R. F.	23July13
Ireland, K. G.	23July13
Darley, C. C.	23July13
Graham, S. D.	23July13
Lister, C. M.	23July13
Playfair, P.H.L., f.c.	23July13
Buchan, D. A.	23July13
Studdert, R. H.	23July13
Frith, O. T., c o	23July13
Hosking, C. G., f.c.	23July13
Hayes, A. T. H	23July13
Rawson-Shaw, K. f.c.	23July13
Kaye, G. L.	23July13
Welsh, W. G. F. d	23July13
Crookshank, A. C.	23July13
Wilson, F. W. B.	23July13
Blewitt, E.	23July13
Shaw, R. de V.	23July13
Battersby, J. W.	23July13
Ferguson, S. F. M.	23July13
Harvey, H. le F F.	23July13
Smith, W. H.	23July13
Hayter, J. G.	23July13
Gordon, H. G.	23July13
Holden, H. C. L.	23July13
Maitland-Dougall, W. E.	23July13
Gardner, E.	23July13
Russell, C. C.	23July13
Reid, R. D. S.	23July13
Temple, C.	23July13
Burkinshaw F.W.	23July13
Giffard, S.	23July13
Armytage, H. W. H.	23July13
Lee, S. S. (L)	23July13
Leventhorpe, G. S.	24July13
Harbord, K. B.	7Dec.13
Thornton, W. H. J.	23Dec.13
Housden, E.J.T. (l)	23Dec.13
Spence, C. B., f.c.	23Dec.13
Riecke, A. F. M.	23Dec.13
Gilpin, R.	23Dec.13
Richards, F. H.	23Dec.13
Pellereau, J. C. E.	23Dec.13
Ryan, C. E.	23Dec.13
Beall, R. D.	23Dec.13
Harvey, K. W.	23Dec.13
Cunningham, J. A., f.c.	23Dec.13
Pritchard, W.D. (l)	23Dec.13
Graves, E. P., f.c.	23Dec.13
Delahaye, J. V.	23Dec.13
Willcocks, H. F.	23Dec.13
Bateman, B. M. B.	23Dec.13
Barratt, A. S., f.c.	23Dec.13
Morton A. H.	23Dec.13
Loch, K. M. (l)	23Dec.13
Mansfield, G. E.	23Dec.13
Maples, J. C.	23Dec.13
Fisher, C.L.	23Dec.13
Perceval, C. P. W.	23Dec.13
Tayleur, C. L. O.	23Dec.13

Lieutenants—contd.

Watson, V. C.	23Dec.13
Adam, N. M.	23Dec.13
Archibald, S. C. M.	23Dec.13
Williams, R. S. A.	23Dec.13
O'Brien, H. R. H.	23Dec.13
Le Breton, F. H.	23Dec.13
Kemp, G. C.	23Dec.13
Nixon, G. F.	23Dec.13
Robertson, E. J. M.	23Dec.13
Duncan, W. E.	23Dec.13
Lloyd, C. H.	23Dec.13
Body, O. G., c.o.	23Dec.13
Wissman, J. R. (l)	23Dec.13
Woods, E. A.	23Dec.13
Napier, A. F. S.	23Dec.13
Peppe, F. H.	23Dec.13
Vining, P. L.	23Dec.13
Knight, J. P.	23Dec.13
Armitage, E. L.	8Jan.14
	23Dec.13
Handford, D. J. (l)	27May14
Van Straubenzee, A. B.	21June14
Thiele, N. W.	16July14
Baynham, C. T.	20July14
Rainy, A. R.	20July14
Hart, S.	20July14
Beresford, G. A.	20July14
Morton, D. J. F. (l)	20July14
Inchbald, P. E.	20July14
Browning, L.	20July14
Harrison, W. R. E.	20July14
Danby, W. A.	20July14
Lodge, H. R.	20July14
Landon, G. de L. (L)	20July14
Latham, E.	20July14
Bates, A. G.	20July14
Roney-Dougal, C. N.	20July14
Campbell, J. O.	20July14
Sumpter, G. (L)	20July14
Mostyn, J. C.	20July14
MacNeece, J. D.G.	20July14
Cottrell, A. F. B.	20July14
Lund, O. M.	20July14
Beatson, C. E. S.	20July11
Huttenbach, N. H.	20July14
Murray, P. H.	20July14
Hulsh, M. W.	20July14
Hewson, A. C.	20July14
Lindsay, G. W. T.	20July14
Simson, R. F.	20July14
Beckett, C. T.	20July14
Jackson, E. H. P.	20July14
Lutyens, L. G.	20July14

2nd Lieutenants.

Neville, A. G.	9Dec.11
Walrond, V.	9Dec.11
Malcolm, J. G., f.c.	22Dec.11
Turner, W. A. S.	22Dec.11
Tidmarsh, G. D.	22Dec.11
Straker, H. G.	22Dec.11
Fletcher, W. G.	22Dec.11
Cleland, J. R.	22Dec.11
Broadhurst, G. H.	23Dec.11
Thomson, D.	23Dec.11
Fraser-Tytler, P.S.	23Dec.11
Barry, F.	23Dec.11
Macnair, J. L. P.	23Dec.11
Harriott, W. G.	23Dec.11

Royal Regiment of Artillery.

Royal Horse and Royal Field Artillery—contd.

2nd Lieuts.—contd.		2nd Lieuts.—contd.		2nd Lieuts.—contd.		Adjutants—contd.	
Bryans, H. M.	23Dec.11	Maxwell, P.MacM.	19July12	Deacon, W. H.	19Dec.13	Cooper, G. S., *lt.*	3Sept.13
Du Buisson, T. G.	23Dec.11	Freer, N. W. W.	19July12	Fardell. F. H.	19Dec.13	Vaughan, H. H. S., *capt.*	
Macleod, P.	23Dec.11	Cross, T. E. K.	19July12	Marsh, S. G. B.	19Dec.13		15Sept 13
Foljambe, R. F. T.	23Dec.11	Earle, E. G. (*l*)	19July12	Heath-Caldwell, M. F.		Cornes, H., *g., capt.*	1Oct.13
Maxwell, A.	23Dec.11	Temple, E.	19July12		11Dec.13	Allen, R. A. (*l*) *lt.*	1Oct 13
Wells-Cole, N. W.	23Dec.11	Sassoon, F.	19July12	Waller, E. G.	19Dec.13	Roddam-Whetham.	
Macleod, A. R.	23Dec.11	Messervy, G.	4Dec.12	Trevenen, S. V.	19Dec.13	S.A. *lt.*	10Oct.13
McKay, C. I.	23Dec.11	Pilliner R. C. L.	4Dec.12	Lyne, C. E. L.	19Dec.13	Rendel, R.M., *lt.*	1Nov.13
Mann, E. H.	23Dec.11	Loewe, L.	14Apr.13	Skipwith, G. A.	19Dec.13	Reid, W. R., *capt.*	8Nov.13
Chaworth-Musters, A.			4Dec.12	Gatehouse, R. P.	19Dec.13	Eddis, L. A., *g.*,	
	23Dec.11	Mills, F. L. V.	20Dec.12	Rusher, A. E.	19Dec.13	*capt.*	29Nov.13
Swinton, W.	23Dec.11	Morgan, W. D.	20Dec.12	Hawker, T. M.	19Dec.13	Lynch-Staunton, R. K.	
Johnstone, G, H.	23Dec.11	Hog, R. T. A.	20Dec.12	Groome, R. E. C.	19Dec.13	*capt., r.h.a.*	16Dec.13
Stillman, R. C. B.	23Dec.11	Batten, J. F.	20Dec.12	Boylan, E. T. A. G.	19Dec.13	Nornabell, H. M.,	
Anderson, T. R.	23Dec.11	Thomas, G. I.	20Dec.12	Thomson, V. H.	19Dec.13	*capt.*	27Dec.13
Davidson, F. H. N.		Johnson, P. E.	20Dec.12	Evans. M. P.	19Dec.13	Longmore,C.M., *lt.* 19Jan.14	
(*l*)	23Dec.11	McConnel, D. F.	20Dec.12	Rogers, C. H.	10June14	Spencer-Smith, D.	
Hancocks, A. C.	23Dec.11	Hutchison,C.R.M.	20Dec.12			C. (*l*) *capt., r.h.a.*	
Richardson, J. H. K.		Gordon, R. E.	20Dec.12				22Jan.14
	23Dec.11	Johnstone, J. A.	20Dec.12	**Adjutants.**		Boyd, H. A., *capt.*	22Jan14
Staveley, R.	23Dec.11	Kane, R. E.	20Dec.12			Scarlett, Hon. H.	
Towell, R. H.	23Dec.11	Ritchie, H. G.	20Dec.12	Sarson, E. V., *capt.* 1Mar.11		R., *capt., r.h.a.* 22Jan.14	
Lawrence, G. A. K.,		Barkworth, H. E.	20Dec.12	White, R. W. (L) *capt.*		Dundas, J. C., *g., capt.*	
f.c.	23Dec.11	Schreiber, O. R.	20Dec.12		6Aug.11		15Mar.14
Nottidge, E.	26Nov.12	Hayes, H. G.	20Dec.12	Ramsden, J.V., *capt.*		Hornsby, F. H., *lt.* 17Mar.14	
	23Dec.11	Reynolds, B. T.	20Dec.12		11Aug.11	Hulton, H. H., *capt.*29Mar.14	
Hollwey, J. B.	23Dec.11	Paul, L. I. C.	20Dec.12	Riddell, J. B., *o., capt.*,		Grieve, F.C.L..*capt.*3June14	
Dunn, K. F. W.	23Dec.11	Herbert, O. W. E.	20Dec.12		1Sept.11	Arthur, H. B. C. (L)	
Harrison, H. T.	23Dec.11	Archer, R. A.	20Dec.12	Young, H. G., *capt.*9Sept.11		*capt.*	4June14
Orr-Ewing, M. R.	22May12	Gosset, W. B.	20Dec.12	Stillwell, W.D., *capt.*1Oct.11		Yorke, P. G., *capt.* 6July14	
MacIlwaine, A.H.	22May12	Bulteel, S. D.	20Dec.12	Fullerton, J.C.,*capt.*1Oct.11		Dodgson, N. C., *capt.*	
Wingfield Digby, K,E.,		Carne, E. F.	20Dec.12	Balston, G. R., *capt.*,			6July14
	22May12	Lutyens, E. G.	20Dec.12	*r.h.a.*	9Oct.11		
English, M. W.	19June12	Tyler, H. A.	20Dec.12	Crossman, F. L. M.			
Gossage, E. L.	19July12	Mirrlees, W. H. B.	20Dec.12	*lt.*	12Oct.11	**Riding-Masters.**	
Rogers, W. F.	19July12	Bligh, J. F.	20Dec.12	Goff, L. T., *capt.*	12Nov.11		
Bevir, C. E. F.	19July12	Peppé, W. T. H.	20Dec.12	Warton, E. B., *lt.*	26Dec.11	Brogan, T. H., *r.h.a.*	
Wingate Gray, W. S.		Burrows, E. W. M.	20Dec.12	Rogers, W. L. Y.			14Sept.89
	28Mar.18	Duff, G. L. A.	20Dec.12	*capt.*	29Dec.11	*hon. maj.* 14Sept.04	
	19July12	Neve, R. B.	20Dec.12	Gregory, G. M. A., *capt.*		McCombie, A. W.,	
Bishop, C. B. J.	19July12	Antrobus, R. H.	15Feb.13		1Mar.12	*r.h.a.*	5Apr.93
Hess, A. G.	19July12	Porter, G.A.	24May13	Moore, J.,H., *lt.*	20June12	*hon. maj.* 5Apr.08	
Huggins, H. W.	19July12	Clery, N. C.	24May13	Finlayson, R. G., *capt.*,		Fleming, P.	3Feb.94
Oldfield, R. W.	19July12	Chapman, H. E.	18July13	*r.h.a.*	22July12	*hon. maj.* 3Feb.09	
Dale, E. C. B.	19July12	Tucker, J. A.	18July13	Forsyth, J. C., *lt.* 13Aug.12		Clarke, T.	6Mar.05
Morrison, D. St. G.	19July12	MacLeod, R. W.	18July13	Erskine, A. E., *capt.*,		*hon. maj.* 6Mar.10	
Price-Williams, H.	19July12	Wright, N. J. R.	18July13	*r.h.a.*	1Sept.12	Aherne, D., *r.h.a.* 10Apr.97	
Doake, S. H.	16July13	Perceval, R. R. M.	18July13	Reeves, R. C., *capt.* 9Oct.12		*hon. maj.* 10Apr.12	
	19July12	Peskett, A. H.	18July13	Main, A. K., *capt.* 11Oct.12		Connell, T., *r.h.a.* 23Feb.98	
Steevens, D. J.	19July12	Watson, W. D.	18July13	Potter, K. M., *capt.* 22Oct.12		*hon. maj.* 28Feb.13	
Empson, A.	19July12	McNair, J. K.	18July13	Wickham, T. E, P.,		Caddington, T. G. A.	
Middleton, A. A.	19July12	Devenish, G. W.	18July13	D.S.O., *capt.*	24Oct.12	*r.h.a.*	15Feb.99
Spencer, E. A.	19July12	Farmer, J. D. H.	18July13	Bolitho, E. H. W.,		*hon. maj.* 15Feb.14	
Hadden, N. C. C.	19July12	Hay-Webb, C.R.F.	18July13	*capt.*	29Oct.12	Naylor, H. W.	28Mar.00
Martin, G. N. C.	19July12	Morgan, F. E.	18July13	Jervis, N. G. M., *capt.*		*hon capt.* 28Mar.10	
Fluke, A. C.	19July12	Graham, F.	18July13		10Nov.12	Hagan, J.	4Apr.00
Glynn, R. T. W.	19July12	Dennis, M. E.	18July13	Massy, C. W., *lt.*	18Nov.12	*hon. capt.* 4Apr.10	
Purchas, E. C.	19July12	Owen, N. M.	18July13	Nevile, G. C., *capt.*		Taylor, A.	2May00
Peck, C. H.	19July12	Morse, G. S.	18July13		23Nov.12	*hon. capt.* 2May10	
Cameron, C. H.	19July12	Connal, A. W. C.	18July13	McGrath, A. T., *capt.*		Sims, T. A.	15May01
Harman, J. B.	19July12	Nugee, G. T.	18July13		6Dec.12	*hon. capt.* 15May11	
McNaughton, F.L.	19July12	Durand, A. A. M.	18July13	Scarlett, J. A., *capt.*		Caddington, C. E. 15May01	
				r.h.a.	1Feb.13	*hon. capt.* 15May11	
Booth, L. E.	19July12	Benett-Stanford, V.		Bowles, J. A., *lt.*	1Feb.13	Bastyan, S. J., *r.h.a.*	
Harbord, G. M.	19July12		18July13	Boone, H. G., *capt.* 7Feb.13			16Oct.01
Edge, J. D.	19July12	Nicoll, D. A.	18July13	Wilmer, E. R. G.,		*hon. capt.* 16Oct.11	
Drennan, J. S.	19July12	Marriott, A. P.	18July13	*capt.*	14Mar.13	Lynch, J., *hon. lt.* 18June10	
Tuite-Dalton, G.	19July12	Boothby, J. H.	18July13	Leech, C.J.F., *capt.* 13Apr.13		Wark, R. G., *hon. lt.*	
Walsh, A. C. M.	19July12	Scott-Watson, W.	18July13	Brousson, F., *capt.*11Apr.13			27July10
Jardine, C. A.	19July12	Harman, A. L.	18July13	Stevens, C. M. H.,		Dann, B., *hon lt.*,	
Simpson, G. P.	19July12	Copeland, R. R.	18July13	*capt.*	22May13	*r.h.a.*	22Mar.11
Latham, H. B.	19July12	Forman, A. T.	10Dec 13	Sadler, H. K. *capt.* 1June13		Wright, A.E., *hon. lt.*	
Crowe, W. H. F.	19July12	Lee, P. W.	10Dec.13	Rich, C. S., *capt.* 28July13			23Nov.12
Myburgh, P. S.	19July12	Coghlan, W. H.	10Dec.13	Blount, G. H. R., *capt.*		Wark, J., *hon. lt.*, 24Sept.13	
Taylor, A. G.	19July12				29July13	*r.h.a.*	
Lindsay, C. F. T.	19July12	Harvey, G. F.	14Feb.14	Taylor, B. W., *capt.*		Burchell, F., *hon. lt.*,	
			10Dec.13		4Aug.13	*r.h.a.*	22July14

ROYAL GARRISON ARTILLERY.

The Royal Arms and Supporters, with a Gun.

"*Ubique*" (above), "*Quo Fas et Gloria ducunt*" (below the Gun).

Colonel in charge of Records .. Chamier, Col. G. D., *C.M.G.. g.* .. .. *Dover* 21Mar.13
Asst. to Col. in charge of Records, Tremaine, Maj. R., ret. 1July05

Lt.-Colonels.		Lt.-Colonels—contd.		Majors.		Majors—contd.	
Muspratt-Williams, C.A.	25May09	Stanton, F. W. S., *D.S.O.*	22Nov.11	Cuming, A. T., *g.*[*l*]24Apr.08 6Dec.03		Macdonald, R. J., *g., f.*	12May06
Walker, M.	10ct.09	Cook, H. R. [L] *f.c.r.*4Dec.11		Tancock, O. K., *i.*	15July04	Bland, W. St. C., *g.*	17July06
Phillips, H. de T., *i.*	10ct.09	Logan, D. F. H.	16Dec.11	Alexander, W. P., *g.*	20July04	*bt. lt.-col.*	10May13
Jackson, L. D., *g.*	2Nov.09	Perceval, C. J., *D.S.O.*, *p.s.c.* [L]	21Dec.11	Crowe, M. A. C., *p.a.c.,*	10Aug.04	Molesworth, R. P.	17July06
Carleton, M. L.	7Nov.09	Napier, W. J., *g.*	21Dec.11	Palmer, H. R.	7Sept.04	Chapman, L. J., *i.*	17July06
Hoblyn, E. F.	1Feb.10	Maunsell, F. G. [L] 11Jan.12		Phipps, C.E., *p.a.c., s.*	27Sept.04	Leahy, H. G., *p.a.c., g., s.*	22Sept.06
Dowell, G. C.	1July10	Bertie-Clay, N. S., *i.* 18May12		Gorton, R. St. G., *p.s.c.* [*l*]	9Oct.04	Fraser, L. D., *g.* [L]	22Sept.06
	bt. col. 100ct.10	Eyre, M. S. (*local col.*) 18May12		Head, H. F.	9Oct.04	Patch, F. R., *i.*	22Sept 06
Lane, H. E. B.	7Sept.10	Dennis, M. J. C., *s.* 20May12		Phillips, T. R.	9Oct.04	Franks, G. McK.,*p.s.c.* [*l*] [F]	29Nov.00 29Sept.06
Grier, H. D., *i.*	11Sept.10 120ct.10	Lyle, G. S. B., *g.* 20May12		Brewster, R. F., *g.*	2Nov.04	*bt. lt.-col.*	21Feb.12
Jennings, H. A. K., *f.* (*temp. Col.*), *s.* 12Oct.10		Kirke, H. L.	13July12	Knapp, K. K.	16Nov.04	Roberts, H. B., *p.s.c.* [L]	29Sept.06
		Eteson, H. C. W.,*g.*9Aug.12		Kelsall, H. J., *g.*	22Nov.04	Young, H. A., *f.*	29Sept.06
Adair, H. R., *p.a.c., s.*	120ct.10	Norris, A. G., *g., f.* 2Sept.12		Harvest, H. H.	1Jan.05	*bt. lt.-col.*	21Feb.14
Stevenson, R. C.	16Oct.10	Warren, W. L. Nov.12		Nichol, W. D., *g.*	4Jan.05	Peile, A. J., *g., s*	29Sept.06
Cooper, E. S., *p.a.c., g.*	29Dec.10	Roberts, M. B., *g.* [L] 25Nov.12		Brake, H. E. J., *C.B.*, *D.S.O.*	6Jan.05	Pitman, A. C.	21Dec.06
Babington, D. M.,*C.I.E., i.*	5Jan.11	Bateman, B. M. 25Nov.12		Hare, R. H., M.V.O., D.S.O., *p.s.c., g.* [L] *m.o.*	29Nov.00 6Jan.05	Seddon, E. McM.	10Feb.07
Parker, J. L., *i.*	5Jan.11	Merriman, R. G., *D.S.O.*	29Jan.13			Hutchinson, F. P., *g.*	7May07
Foote, H. B., *g. t.*	1Apr.11	Hardy, W. K.	29Jan.13	Forestier-Walker, C. E. [L], *i.*	6Jan.05	Scott, A. F. S.	9Aug.07
Bell, C. T., *i.*	1Apr.11	Wood, T. B., *p.s.c.* [*l*]	15Feb.13	Church, G. R. M.	1Feb.05	Carter, E. P.	1Sept.07
Smeaton, C. O.	11Apr.11	Ogg, G. S., *i.*	15Feb.13	Courtenay, M. H., *g.*1Feb.05		Jennings, W.	1Sept.07
Currie, A. C., *g.* (*local Col.*)	25Apr.11	Saltren-Willett, A. J.	15Feb.13	Hamilton, P. D., *g.*	5July05	Moore, St. L. M., *g.*	1Sept.07
		Marsh, H. E., *g.*	14Mar.13	Smallwood, F. G., *C.V.O., f.*	12Oct.05	Arthy, W.	1Sept.07
Vincent, H. O., *g.*	25Apr.11	Iles, H. W., *g.*	31Mar.13	Curme, W. C., *g.*	12Oct.05	Thrupp, F. M., *g., f.* 3Apr.08	
Brownlow, C. W.	26Apr.11	Hudson, T. R. C., *p.s.c.* [L]	1Apr.13 29July11	Jones, W. H.	14Feb.06	Brett, H. G., *i.*	8May08
Campbell, M.S.C., C.I.E., *f.*, (*Ord. Consulting Offr. for India*)	27Apr.11	Stansfeld, J. R., *p.a.c., s.*	1May13	Phillipps, C., *g.*	20Feb.06	Elliot, H. M., *g., c.o.* 9June08 McHardy, A. A., *D.S.O., p.s.c., s.* 9June08	
		Marshall, T. E.	31May13	Kenyon, L. R., *p.a.c., t.* *bt. lt.-col.*	2Mar.06 10May13	Corrie, W. F. T., *p.a.c., g.*	20June08
Robinson, W. H.	27Apr.11	Clark, C. W., *g.*	15July13	Beynon, H. L. N., *p.s.c.* [*l*]	2Mar.06	Pennethorne, H. E., *g.*	24June08
Williamson Oswald, O. C., *i.*	17July1	Tyler, A. M., *p.a.c., g.*	6Aug.13	Taylor, C. S.	15Mar.06	Tyler, R. E.	4July08
Kaye, R. A., *g.*	1Aug.11	Perkins, A. E. J.,*g.* 10ct.13		Comyn, E. W.	11Apr.06	Walles, W. E., *f.*	14Nov.08
Pullen, A. F., *g.* [*l*] [F]	29Sept.11	Davidson, F. M., *g.*28Jan.14		Cadell, H. E.	28Apr.06	Kirkpatrick, A. R. Y	28Nov.08
Buckle, C. R., *D.S.O.* (*local Col.*)	11Oct.11	East, L. W. P., *D.S.O., p.s.c.* [*l*]	15Apr.14	Douglas, A. P., *s.*	2May06	Moultrie, H.C., *g., s.* 12Dec.08 Edlmann, E. E., D.S.O., *t.*	15Dec.08
Benson, R. P. (*temp. Col.*) *s.*	16Oct.11	Jenour, A. S., *g.*	18May14	Barron, N. G., *g., s.* 2May06		Tomkins, E. L., *g., f.* 15Dec.08 Home, R. E., D.S.O., *p.a.c., s.*	4Jan 09
		Tancred, T. A.	25May14	Stiffe, A. F. E.	12May06	Johnston, G.N., *g., c.o.* 4Jan 09 Galloway, F. L., *p.a.c., g.*	14Jan.09
						Bellairs, N. E. B., *p.a.c.*	28Jan.09
						Lethbridge, S.	31Jan.09

Royal Regiment of Artillery.

Royal Garrison Artillery—contd.

Majors—contd.

Butcher, F. S., *g*.	31Jan.09
Mackintosh, J. B., *g*.,1Mar.09	
McCulloch, R. H. F., *D.S.O.* [L]	8Mar.09
Dent, F. W.	17Apr.09
Metcalfe, F. H., *g*.	19Apr.09
Massie, R. H., *t*.	21Apr.09 29Nov.00
Thorp, A. H., *g*.	5May09
Ellershaw, A.	8May09
Farmar, W. C. R.	18May09
Williams, A. C., *g*., *s*,	25May09
Holdsworth Hunt, W. H.,*g*.	25May09
Bishop, C. F., *g*.	28May09
Woods, G. G., *s*.	13July09 1Jan.03
Noott. C. C.. *g*.. (see Ord. Board)	13July09
Blanford, W. G.	13July09
Craig, R. A., *p.a.c.*, *f*., *s*.	7Aug.09
Bruce, J. E. L., *t*.	7Aug.09
Craster, E. H. B.	7Aug.09
Sherer, J. D., *g*.	8Sept.09
de Brett, H. S., *D.S.O.*, *p.s.c.* [L], *s*.	15Sept.09
Jacob, W. H. B., *g*., *f*. [l] *s*.	7Oct.09
Kane, A. H., *g*.	23Jan.10
De Sausmarez, C., *D.S.O.*,	21July10
	16July08
Howorth, H. G., *p.a.c.*, *g*., *s*.	21July10
Smith, A. G.	1Aug.10
Burton, H.C.H., *g*.	7Sept.10
Fife, R. B.	11Sept.10
Hepper, L. L., *t*.	20Sept.10
Tulloch, D. F.	12Oct.10
de Winton, R. S.	16Oct.10 29Nov.00
Gray, C. L. R.	2Nov.10
Owen, C. R. B.,*p.a.c.*,*s*,	3Dec.10
Wynter, F. A., *D.S.O.*	3Dec.10
Lewes, P. K., *g*., *s*.	7Dec.10
Bushe, C. K.	31Dec.10
Paine, J. H., *D.S.O.*, *t*.	31Dec.10
Waring, R., *p.a.c.*, *f*., *s*.	2Jan.11
Bullen, S. D.	17Mar.11
Donovan, C. C., *i*.	18Mar.11

Majors—contd.

Eady, C. E.	18Mar.11
Morris, R. C., *g*.	1Apr.11
Cotter, H. J., *i*.	1Apr.11
Haynes, K. E., *g*., *s*.	12Apr.11
Easton, F. A.	12Apr.11
Robinson, S. W.	25Apr.11
le Pelley, E. C., *g*.	25Apr.11
Lyddon, W. G., *p.a.c.*, *g*., *s*.	26Apr.11
Lawrence-Archer, J. H., *t*.	26Apr.11
Walker, E. W. M., *g*.,26Apr.11	
Whitehead, E. L'E. [l]	27Apr.11
Wilkinson, A. C.	7May11
Reade, P. N. G., *g*.	10May11
Hope, W. H. W., *p.a.c.*, *s*.	15May11
Lowis, P. S.	15May11
Bowen, H. W., *t*.	20May11
Muspratt-Williams, R. L.	20May11
Parker, R. H., *g*.	21May11
Bland-Hunt, E. S. de V., *g*.	27May11
Rumbold, W. E., *g*., 3Aug.11	
Mayne, M. H., *g*.	21Aug.11
Twiss, F. A., *M.V.O., g*.	27Sept.11
Fergusson, A. C., *g*., *i*.	28Sept.11
Palmer, C. C., *p a.c.,s.*	29Sept.11
Halse, S.C., *p.a.c.*, *f* ,*s*.	29Sept.11
Haymes, R. L.,*g.*, *o*. 7Oct.11	
Anley, W. B., *g*.	7Oct.11
Chrystie, J., *g*.	7Oct.11
Kennedy, A. C., *i*.	16Oct.11
Ollivant, A. H., *p.s.c.* [L] (G.S.O., 2nd grade, *Admiralty*)16Oct.11	
Corbett, E. F.	16Oct.11
Pritchard, C. G.	16Dec.11
Molesworth, H. E. 18May12	
Hall, H. C., *g*.	21May12
Marton, R. O., *D.S.O., g*.	29May12
Phipps, C. F.	29May12
Wyatt, F. O., *M.V.O*.	24July12
Nicholl, D. FitzR., *D.S.O., g*.	9Aug.12
Mackenzie,G.B.,*g*.17Aug.12	
Freeth, C. J. D., *g*.,*t*.2Sept.12

Majors—contd.

Tyrrell, G. E. [L]	2Sept.12
Owen, C. H. W.	2Sept.12
Rowan-Robinson, H., *p.s.c.* [L] *m.a.*	14Sept.12
Sturrock, G. C., *g*.	14Sept.12
Fowler, W. J., *g*.	14Sept.12
Lockhart, R. N., *g*.	4Oct.12
Corrie, G. G. W.	4Oct.12
Stülpnagel, C. W.	9Nov.12
Riddell, R. B.	22Nov.12
Wilkinson, M. L.,*p.a.c .*, *g*., *s*.	29Nov.00 25Nov.12
Currie, I. B. F., *g*.	25Nov.12
Hanna, J. C., *g*.	6Dec.12
Scott, E. B., *g*.	1Jan.13
Nuttall. C.M., *g*.	29Jan.13
Boyd, S. O.	29Jan.13
Massie, J. H., *D.S.O., g*., *s*.	15Feb.13
Luke,T.M.,*D.S.O.*,*s*.15Feb.13	
Kelly, C. R.	15July13
Holbrooke, P. L., *g*., *s*.	6Aug.13
Collingwood, C. W. *g*. (Sec.,*R.A.Commee*) 1Jan.14	
Rickard, F. M., *p.a.c.*, *s*.	1Jan.14
Webb, A. H., *g*.	1Jan.14
Buzzard, C. N., *e*.	6Jan.14
Carey, W.L.J. *o*.[l] *i*.28Jan.14	
Loring, W.	28Jan.14
Ewart, C. N.	18Feb.14
Howard-Vyse,C.,*g*.21Feb.14	
Galwey, R. H., *g*.	13Mar.14
Thorp, A., *g*.,	15Mar.14
Tyrrell, J. F., *t*.	1Apr.14
Luck, B. J. M., *g*.	1Apr.14
Brierley, S. T., *D.S.O., g*.	1Apr.14
Sargeaunt, H. G., *g*., *s*.	1Apr.14
Hart, H. T., *g*.	1Apr.14 10May13
Armitage,W.T., *g*.	1Apr.14
Nugent, G. R. H.,*p.s.c.* [L] *s*.	1Apr.14
Keogh, T. M.	1Apr.14
Keogh, J. H.	1Apr.14
Riddell, E. V. D., *p.s.c*., *s*.	15Apr.14
	22Aug.02
Suther, P., *g*.	15Apr.14
Ogg, W, M., [L]	23Apr.14

Captains.

Wilkins, G. H. C., *g*. 1Apr.00	
Hollinshead, H. N. B., *f*.	1Apr.00
Chevallier, F. E. de C., *g*.	1Apr.00
Swettenham, W. A. W.	1Apr.00
Ward-Simpson,*A.C S., p.a.c., s*.	1Apr.00
Keyes, A. J. H., *g*.	1Apr.00
Hardcastle,E.L.,*g*.,*s*.1Apr.00	
Rolland, C. E. T., *p.a.c.*, *s*.	2Apr.00
Castens, W. E., *p.a.c.*, *g*.	2Apr.00
Dwyer, G. T. C., *s*.	9Apr.00
Blanford, C. F., *i*.	9Apr.00
Thompson, A. J.	7May00
Moore, W. H., *D.S.O., p.s.c.* [l]	9May00
Jacob, A. L. B., *g*.	28May00
Crutckshank, P.H., *g*., *Adjt*.	1June00
Kemble, W. E., *o*., *g*.	15June00
Blount, G. P. C., *g*., *s*.	1July00
Finch, G. F. C.	1July00
Grose, J.	26July00
Beer, V. L., *g*.	29Sept.00
Vander Kiste, F. W.	10Oct.00
Normand, S. R.	10Oct.00
Walker, W. B.	10Oct.00
Stanbrough,L. K.	10Oct.00
Castle, R.W., *Adjt*.	26Nov.00
Barton, R. L., *g*.	2Nov.00
Gardiner, H.W.,	17Dec.00
Disney-Roebuck, A. W., *g*.	18Dec.00
Bayley, L. S. [L]	23Jan.01
Richey, F. W., *i*.	12Feb.01
Robinson, J.A. P.	15Feb.01
Alexander, W. D	1Mar.01
Ker, C. A., *D.S.O.*, *p.s.c.*	1Mar.01
Wilkes, G. S., *o*., *i*.	1Mar.01
Bird, M. H. C. *p.* , *c*., *g* [L] *s*.	4Mar.01
MacFarlan, J. B., *i*.	1Apr.01
Hearn, H. S., *e.a.*	1Apr.01
Greene, A. C. R., *p.s.c.*	1Apr.01
Clapham, D., *g*., *s*.	1Apr.01
Climo, P. R.	14May01
Riach, G. H.	1June01
Vandeleur, H. M., *p.a.c.*, *g*., *s*.	12June01

Royal Regiment of Artillery.

Royal Garrison Artillery—contd.

Captains—contd.

Hutchison, K. D., Adjt. 12June01
Wighton, E. 9July01
Thomas, C. S. W. 6July01
Colvile, A. M. [l] i. 24Aug.01
Cock, H. C. L., p.s.c., i. 2Sept.01
McGhee, A.S. P., o. 2Sept.01
Beasley, J.H. M., g., Adjt. 4Sept.01
Creswell, E. F., g., s. 11Sept.01
Evans, C. L. 10Oct.01
Cobbe, I. S., o.,i. 8Nov.01
Greig, H. I., g., s. 18Nov.01
Jones, J. H. H., g. 18Nov.01
Spalding, W. B. 30Nov.01
Kirke, W. M. St. G., p.s.c., s. 4Dec.01
 bt. maj. 21Feb.14
Sanders, W. O. S., g., s. 21Dec.01
Haig, A. G., Adjt. 23Dec.01
Carr, H. G. 24Dec.01
Campbell, K. G., g.,i. 4Jan.02
Hill, R. R., p.s.c., g. [l] i. 22Jan.02
Mitchell, A., i.v. 22Jan.02
Sitwell, N. S. H. 22Jan.02
Riccard, J. S. 22Jan.02
Hardinge, T. S. N., g., s. 24Jan.02
Price,O.L., [l] Adjt. 31Jan.02
Niven, O. C., g., s. 1Feb.02
Crozier, C. D., p.a.c., s. 1Feb.02
Harvey, W. K., o., g. 5Feb.02
Dreyer, J. T., g , s. 6Feb.02
Cruickshank, H. St J., p.a.c. 7Feb.02
Hayes-Sadler, J., i. 8Feb.02
Ogilvie, G., p.a.c., o. 19Feb.02
Cowie, D. G. 20Mar.02
Wakefield, T. M. [l] 9Mar.02
Courtney, F. H. 29Mar.02
Green, A. F. U., p.s.c., s. 9Mar.02
Johnston,H.B.H.,m.6Jan.11
 4Jan.02
Alexander, R. C. J. 1Apr.02
Leggett, W. N., g., s. 2Apr.02
Inglis, C. E. 2Apr.02
Brind, J. E. S., s.c. 11Apr.02
Haywood, A. H.W. [L] c.o. 19Apr.02
Spicer, P. L., g., Adjt. 1Sept.03
Bennett, F. L [l] 5Sept.03
Peiniger, R. F. 8Sept.03

Captains—contd.

Badham-Thornhill, G. [L], c.o. 19Sept.03
Stenhouse, J. L. 26Sept.03
Cotter, E. B., o. 26Sept.03
Maitland-Addison, J. F. R. N., p.a.c.o., s. 26Sept.03
Moberly, A.H., g.,s 18Nov.03
Browne W. L., p.a.c., s. 7Jan.04
Tandy, E. N., p.s.c. 7Jan.04
Ramsay, H. A., p.s.c., g., s. 15Jan.04
Dean, A. C H.,g., s. 16Jan 04
Ensor, F. C. C., p.a.c., g., o.d. 18Jan.04
Mathews,W.V.D.,g. 23Jan.04
Brancker, H. R., g., s. 30Jan.04
Pollard, C. J. K. [l] 1Feb.04
Lock, K. F., g., s. 1Feb.04
Langhorne, J. A. D., g., i. 1Feb.04
Snowdon, H. S. K., o. 10Feb.04
Langton, A.V., e. [l] 10Feb.04
Andrewes, F. F., g., Adjt. 15Feb.04
Disney, J. W.K., o.17Feb.04
Hamersley, H. St. G., g. 20Feb.04
Colbeck, B. B., Adjt. 25Feb.04
Campbell, R.W. P. 21Apr.14
 18Sept.03
Clarke, H., o.c. 3Mar.04
Murray,A.D.,g..s.o. 3Mar.04
Lockhart, H. W., o., m.a. 4Mar.04
Hall, B. A. M. 9Mar.04
Loveday. F. W., p.s.c., s. 9Mar.04
Watson, R. H. M. 26Mar.04
Reeves, H. C. 8Apr.04
Smith, S. 9Apr.04
Russell, W. C. P. 12Apr.0
Sutton, F. Apr. 0
Grant, H. F. L.,p.s.c. [l], s. 16Apr.04
Tanner, C. J.,p.a.c., o.d. 16Apr.04
Cunningham, H. T., p.a.c., o.d., g. 22Apr.04
Hasselis-Yates, G.A. 2May04
Brown,B.H.,p.a.c.,i. 5May04
Macalpine-Leny, W. H. 13May04
Benson, R. H. R. [L] o.c. 17May04
Daubuz, R. F., g. 19June04
Wadlow,H., g., c.o. 30June04
Rynd, F. F. D.S.O. I. 30June04
Saward, P. S., g., t. 30June04
Budgen,W.N.,Adjt. 5July04
Lewis, H. A., g., s. 11July04

Captains—contd.

Holme, H. L. [L] 10July05
Hickling, C. I. 22July05
Campbell, C. A. H., o.o., 27July05
Wahl, C. E. J. [L] 5Aug.05
Marindin, C. C., p.s.c. 16Sept.05
Fishe, A. F. B. 9Oct.05
King, A. E., p.a.c. 5Dec.05
Tuke, G. F. S., Adjt. 5Dec.05
Smyth, F. J. N. 24Jan.06
Bond, E. L. g., s. 1Feb.06
Murrow, H. L., i.v. 4Mar.06
Swayne, O. R., D.S.O. 15Mar.06
Poole, H. R., g. 29Mar.06
Ridout, J. Y.H.,g.,s.29Mar.06
Beamish,W.S.,o.,t. 29Mar.06
Thomas, R. A.,p.a.c. 1Apr.06
Beattie,M.A.,g.[l] s. 1Apr.06
Warrington-Morris, W.D., o.c. 1Apr.06
Fowler, E. G. 1Apr.06
Preston, P. H. H., g. 1Apr.06
Croudy, C. R., g., i. 1Apr.06
Crawford, R. D., g. 1Apr.06
Barne, W. B. G., p.s.c., s. 28Apr.06
Lyon, C. A. 28Apr.06
Dobbyn, G. H. W. 4May06
Reed, O., i. 12May06
Edmeades, W. A., g., s. 14May06
Connolly, L. J. R., g., t. 19May06
Henderson, H. E. 23May06
Field, K. D., g., i. 24May06
Meares, M., o., o.d. 1June06
Eliot, N., p.a.c. 1June06
Goff, T. C. [L] 2June06
Watson, F. S., o., g. 6June06
Ford, G. T. 14Mar.07
Barron F.W.,g., s c.1Apr.07
Hoskyn, R., g. 16Apr.07
Barrington, J. F., i. 27Apr.07
Roche, L. V. 3May07
Smythe, R. C. 8May07
Ingham, R. J. FitzG., p.a.c. 18Sept.07
Barker, C. H. 18Sept.07
Galloway, L., D.S.O. 7Oct.07
MacClellan, G. P. 19Oct.07
MacEwen, K. G., g., s. 4Dec.07
Leah, T. C. 1Dec.07
Everard, C. J., g. 22Jan.08
Graham, C.A.L., Adjt. 1Apr.08
Turner, W. M. FitzH., g., Adjt. 6May08
Powell, R. M., s. 6May08
Whitfield, R. L. D., o., o.d. 12Oct.09
 9Nov.08

Captains—contd.

Browne, B. S. [L] 7Sept.10
Traill, H. E. O'B. 13Sept.10
Standbridge, W. J 28May10
 Adjt. 30Nov.10
Hope, J. U., g. 30Nov.10
Nugent, W. V., s. 3Dec.10
Gillett, C. R., g., s. 7Dec.10
Robinson,T.A. F.,g. 7Dec.10
Clark, R. H. B.,t. 16Dec.10
Cudlip, E. P. 2Jan.11
Walker, J. B. [L] 2Jan.11
Burke, H. F. 2Jan.11
Bunbury, R. S. 2Jan.11
Smythe, A. G. C., g. 2Jan.11
Hill, G. N., i. 2Jan.11
Hattersley-Smith,W.P.A. 2Jan.11
Lister, F. H. [l] s.o.11Jan.11
Perrott, H. S. 18Jan.11
Bennett, W. P. 22Jan.11
Byrne, J. D. 23Jan.11
Reeves, S. R., i. 28Jan.11
Grinlinton, J.L.,g. 28Jan.11
Warwick, H. B., o., o.d. 10Feb.11
Marshall, H. S. 10Feb.11
Foll, H. H., Adjt. 10Feb.11
Miles, E. 14Mar.11
Page, C. F. G. 15Mar.11
Matthews,A.M.,Adjt. 18Mar.11
Morrison, J., i. 30Mar.11
Lucy, R. S. 30Mar.11
Fitzgerald, N. D'A. 6Apr.11
Redfern, G. H. 11Apr.11
Adams, H. R., g., Adjt. 26Apr.11
Gardner, J. A. 7May11
Drysdale, A. I., s. 10May11
Bromley, C. R. S. 25May11
Carey, F., t. 27May11
Hunt, W. M. 27May11
Heaslop, A. C. 27May11
Erskine-Murray, A., Adjt. 28May11
Fraser, T. C 9June11
Kemble, H. M., Adjt. 16Oct.11
Adams, L C., p.a.c. 26Oct.11
Toppin, S. M., e.a. 26Oct.11
Perry, S. 15Nov.11
Knowles, G. L. 24Nov.11
Nanson, M. R. C. 24Nov.11
Lumsden, W.F..c.o.24Nov.11
Bateson, J. H, t. 16Nov.11
Bassett, J. C. 21Aug.12
Routh, A. L. 22Aug. 12
Moore, W. A. [l] 28Sept.12
Hutton-Squire, R. H. E. 1Nov.12
Finnis, F. A., c.o. 7Nov.12

Royal Regiment of Artillery.

Royal Garrison Artillery—contd.

Captains—contd.

Ford, C. W., g., t.	7Nov.12
Gunter, A. C., Adjt.	9Nov.12
Jackson, M. A., g.	12Nov.12
Taylor, L. R. E. W., p.s.c., f.c.r.	22Nov.12
Spencer, F. E.	22Nov.12
Smart, G. E., i.	22Nov.12
Robertson-Glasgow, N., i.	22Nov.12
Daubeny, G. B.	22Nov.12
Arnott, R., t.	26Nov.12
Douglas, R.V., p.s.c., g., s.	23Jan.13
Hume Spry, C.A.N.	23Jan.13
Waring, J.	20Feb.12
Graham, R. C. D., i.v.	20Jan.13
Lamb, B.	1Feb.13
	18Feb.13
	20Feb.12
Hay, H.G. FitzG., g., Adjt.	4Apr.13
Gatt, C. A.	24Apr.13
Mompalao DePiro, G.	1May13
Gee, E. D. F., e.a.	5May13
Coe, J.	5May13
Christian, W. F.	5May13
Griffith, G. M., Adjt., f.c.r.	5May13
Dunne, T. F. K.	5May13
Baker, F. N., o., g.	9May13
Drought, T. A. W.	9May13
Caldecott, E. L.	9May13
Phillips, F. R., i.	12May13
Jenkin, F. C. [F]	12May13
Brierley, G. W.	12May13
Macleay, D.	12May13
Matthews, E. D., g.	16May13
Phillips, E. S.	16May13
d'Aptce, J.E.F., g., t.	23May13
Carwithen, S	23May13
Way, J., Adjt.	23May13
O'Connor, F. H. P., o., o.d.	23May13
Orton, C. A., t.	23May13
Morgan, F. A. S.	23May13
Lawes, T. C.	23May13
Peck, S. C. p.a.c., s.	26May13
Fanshawe, L. A., o.	26May13
Smith, H.W.T., Adjt.	26May13
Nicholson, W. S.	26May13
Urquhart, A. M.	26May13
Sewell, H. E., g.	26May13
Parker, W.	26May13
de Watteville, H. E., p.s.c.	26May13
{L] s.	26May13
Lenfestey, L. d'E.	26May13
Whyte, T. A.	26May13
Rowley, C. P.	26May13
Shaw, J. F. de F.	26May13
Maunde-Thompson, F. G. o., s.	26May13
Cunningham-Cunningham, T., o., d., Adjt.	26May13
Holme, H. C. [L]	26May13
Begg, R. H., t.	26May13
Vines, C. E., p.a.c.	26May13
Carson, R.	26May13
Cummins, E. J., g., Adjt.	26May13
Cardell, W. B., m.	26May13
Dickins, F., i.	26May13
Chamier, H. A. G.	6July13
	1Apr.08
Waller, R. S. DeW.	18July13

Captains—contd.

Nicolls, O. C. C., g.	28July13
Strover, M. R.	18Aug.13
Dowding, H. C. T., p.s.c., f c.r.	18Aug.13
Sandford, D. A., g., e.a.	18Aug.13
Whiting, E. LeG., i.	18Aug.13
Holdich, G. W. V., p.s.c. [l]	18Aug.13
Bagshawe, W. F. M., p.a.c. [l] e.a.	18Aug.13
Cameron, A. H.[L]18Aug.13	
Bryant, J. M., i.	18Aug.13
Mascall, M. E.	18Aug.13
Carter, E. G. W.	18Aug.13
Ferguson, K.B. [L]	18Aug.13
Lindsay, W. D., i.	18Aug.13
Dunsterville, H.E., g., s.	18Aug.13
Milman, O. R. E., p.a.c., o.d.	18Aug.13
Allen, H., Adjt.	18Aug.13
Garwood, H. P., Adjt.	18Aug.13
Clarke, J. S. S., g.	18Aug.13
Dreyer, G. V., i.	18Aug.13
Brancker, J. D. D., [L] s.c.	29Aug.13
Thompson, W. R.	8Sept.13
McGowan, W. H., t.	28Nov.13
Thomas, A. G.	19Dec.13
Rothwell, R. S., t.	19Dec.13
Duncan, W. B.	19Dec.13
Downing, W. C.	19Dec.13
Davies, L. M., i.	19Dec.13
Rashleigh, P., Adjt.	19Dec.13
Douglas-Jones, E. D	19Dec.13
Barker, W. H., t.	19Dec.13
Johnston, C. E. L. [L] i.	19Dec.13
Farfan, A. J. T., i.	21Dec.13
Reid, F. H.	21Dec.13
Stevens, H. R. G. [L] t.	21Dec.13
Edmond, J. H., i.	21Dec.13
Little, E. M., i.	21Dec.13
White, G. F. C., t.	21Dec.13
Gregory, A. J. R., g [L] t.	21Dec.13
King, J. F., o.	21Dec.13
Salvin, H. C. J.	21Dec.13
Routh, G. M., i.	21Dec.13
Biggs-Davison, J. N., t.	21Dec.13
Hibbert, S. E.	21Dec.13
Edwards, B., o.o.	21Dec.13
Mitchell, P. R.	21Dec.13
Maxwell, W. W., g.	4May14
Erskine, W.A.	4May14
Humphreys, H. J., g., t.	4May14
Gunn, H. B. L. G., g., Adjt.	4May14
Simson, N. C.S., o.o.	4May14
D'Esterre, J. C. E.	4May14
Edwards, I. A. E.	4May14
Matterson, A. G.	4May14
Robertson, W.C., g.	15May14
Cole, A. F.	15May14
Stephens, L N.	15May14
Yates, C. McG., e., t.	15May14
Hare, E.F.	15May14
Webber, H. H.	29May14

Captains—contd.

Leefe, J. B.	23July14
Strachan, D. A.	23July14
Ratton, J. H., o.o.	23July14
Allen, A. H., o.	23July14
Patterson, J., i.	23July14
Crosse, R. M. g. [l] s.	23July14
Tresidder, G.W. W.	23July14
Charles, E. E.	23July14
deCetto, V. B. A.	23July14
Pratt, E. R. [L]	23July14
Carey, J. L. R., g.	23July14
Elphinstone-Dalrymple, Sir F. N.. Bt.	23July14
Medill, P. M.	23July14
Kirby, H. A.,	23July14
Cotter, G. E' S.	23July14
Burney, A. E C., t.	23July14
Kenyon, H. E., i.	23July14

Lieutenants.

Izard, F. V.	17May04
Thackwell, N. E. O., g., r.	9June04
Pask, I. A. J.	6June04
Forbes, R.M N., t.a.	6June04
Watson, E. V.	30June04
Thom, J. H., i.	30June04
Renshaw, R. A.	4July04
Alford, A. C. R., [L] t.	23July04
Lane, H. E., o.	23July04
Hetherington, C. G.	10Aug.04
Donnelly, T.	16Aug.04
Mead, S., g., s.	27Aug.04
Lecky, M. D., g., o.o.	3Sept.04
Nicholson, St. J.R., g., Adjt.	15Sept.04
Wehner, A. F. P., g. [L]	5Oct.04
Russell, G. A.	11Oct.04
Barron, A. F. N., t.	17Oct.04
Hearle, A. B., g., t.	1Nov.04
Percival, D.	16Nov.04
Tute, C. S., o., o.o.	28Nov.04
Lovell, E. H.	21Dec.04
Willis, F. W.	21Dec.04
Campbell, D. D. H., t.	21Dec.04
Corbett, G. R. de la C.	21Dec.04
Wingate-Saul, N.W., o., o.d.	4Jan.05
	4Dec.05
Skrimshire, C.V.S., o.o.	30Jan.05
Montague, S. F., p.a.c	4Apr.05
Langhorne, A. P. Y., D.S.O.	4Apr.05
Smithers, H.	17Apr.05
Ford, J. P. W.	24May05
Wilson, E. R. C., t.	24May05
Apletre, R. C.	24May05
Furnell, C. H. M.	24May05
Matthews, G. W.	24May05
Wiltshire, P. S.	2Aug.06
	17Apr.04
Pepper, W. B.	24May05
Pellew, V. H. L.	24May05

Lieutenants—contd.

Pepper, J. W., t.	24May05
Beckett, W. H. F.	16July05
Smyth, R. A. N.	31July05
Dunsterville, K. F., g., s.	31July05
Garrett, R. C., i.	31July05
Brown, H. D. L.	31July05
O'Reilly-Blackwood, E.H.	31July05
Rowe, R. H., o.o.	31July05
Burrowes, A., Adjt.	31July05
Healing, N. C.	31July05
Maclean, M.F.A., o.	31July05
Rowe, W. B.	31July05
Dutton, R. M. L., t.	31July05
Farmer, C., t.	31July05
Gilbert, D. P., o.o.	31July05
Down, C. B., i.	31July05
Sneyd, D. G. T., i.	31July05
Edwardes, L.C., o., t.	31July05
Larmour, L.C., o.	31July05
Savory, R. H.	3Sept.05
Fitz Roy, R. H.	3Sept.05
Loughborough, A.H., t.	24Dec.05
Bovill, C.	24Dec.05
Gordon, W.	24Dec.05
Seys, R. C. [L]	24Dec.05
Pierson, C. F. L.	24Dec.05
Dobbin, A. W., o.o.	24Dec.05
Kyngdon, W. F. R.,	24Dec.05
Martin, W. M. J., o,	24Dec.05
Greig, A. D., t.	24Dec.05
Smyth, H. E., p.a.c., o.d.	24Dec.05
Hebert, A., t.	24Dec.05
Bake, S. R G., t.	24Dec.05
Somerville, J. A. H. B., i.	24Dec.05
Aitken, N.W., Adjt.	24Dec.05
Hippisley, A.	24Dec.05
Johnston, J. H., t.	24Dec.05
Simon, P. S.	24Dec.05
Rawson, C. D., t.	24Dec.05
Payne, D. W.	24Dec.05
Sunderland, B. G. E.	24Dec.05
Saulez, A. T.	24Dec.05
Scovil, F. H.	24Dec.05
McDiarmid, J.I.A.	24Dec.05
Sturges, C. H. M.	24Dec.05
Bell, M. D., t.	24Dec.05
Campion, D.J.M., t.	24Dec.05
Forbes, J. L.	24Dec.05
Gale, H. J. G., t.	24Dec.05
Justice, P. W.	24Dec.05
Daly, D.	24Dec.05
Tod, C. D.	12Feb.06
Cream, R. T. C., Adjt.	24June06
Halford, E. S., g.	24June06
Chapman, P. C., t.	15July05
Hare, J. W.	15July05
Drake-Brockman, V., [L] i.	15July05
Cruickshank, A. L.	15July05
Lewis, W. H.	15July05
Trenchard, G. B B., i.	15July05
Donnelly, G. H.	15July05
Bagnall, H. G.	15July05
Langley, A. W., o.o.	15July05

Royal Regiment of Artillery.

Royal Garrison Artillery—contd.

Lieutenants—contd.

Wilson, R. E., t.	15July06
Shaw, H. P. J., t.	15July06
Wordsworth, R. G.	15July06
Ventris, E. F. V.	15July06
Simonds, J. de L.	15July06
Nixon, E. J., s.	15July06
Grylls, G., p.a.c. o.d.	15July06
Davidson, C. G. F.	15July06
Kirkpatrick, C. D.	15July06
Jarrett, A. F. V.	15July06
Heath, C. J., Adjt.	15July06
Marsden, J. W.[l].f.l.	15July06
Reynolds, C. H., t.	15July06
MacMahon, G.P.R.	15July06
Hudson, P.	12Dec.06
Clarke, R. H.	12Dec.06
Moore, H. G., t.	12Dec.06
Disney. B. T.	22Dec.06
Rees, L. W. B., c.o.	23Dec.06
Chadwick, E. W.	23Dec.06
Buckland, G. N., t.	23Dec.06
Ross, C., p.a.c., s.	23Dec.06
Leslie, W. [L], t.	23Dec.06
Goldney, H. W.	23Dec.06
Low, G. S.	23Dec.06
Wade-Gery, R. H., m.a.	23Dec.06
Campbell, W. H.	
McN.,p.a.c.,e.,o.d.	23Dec.06
Gibson. A. C. V., p.a.c.,o.d.	
Haskard, D. D., t.	23Dec.06
Sansom, H. A., o.c.	23Dec.06
Lindsell, W. G., s.	23Dec.06
Long, W. E. L., o., t.	23Dec.06
Garnett, C. L.	23Dec.06
Mackintosh, W. A. O. C.	23Dec.06
Birch, P.Y. [l], t.	23Dec.06
Higgon, L.H., t.	23Dec.06
Bill, J. G.	23Dec.06
Sayers, R. C.	23Dec.06
Hickes, L. D., c.o.	23Dec.06
Evans, P. H., o., s.	11Apr.07
	29Jan.07
Atkinson, W. H. B., m.	4June07
Hughes-Gibb, C. P.	4June07
Ryan, F.T., Adjt.	4June07
Knight. J., t.	4June07
Landon, R. P., t.	29July07
Edwards, W. M.	29July07
Dobson, A. E. A., p.a.c. [L] s.	29July07
Rideout, F. M.	29July07
Dickson, J. McA., m.a.	29July07
Crawford, A.E., t.	29July07
Wilmot, S. D.	29July07
Sykes, M.	29July07
Fry, W. H., o.	29July07
Sidebottom, A. L., Adjt.	29July07
Price, J.	29July07
Pfeil, F. W.	29July07
Brooke,F.R.R.,m.a.	29July07
Jones, C. G. P.	29July07
Newton, P. 1.	29July07
Leslie-Smith, G. L.	29July07
Layard, C. P. J.	29July07
Begbie, P. F. G.	29July07
Hopkins, G. R., p.a.c., o.d.	29July07
Davies, O. H.	29July07
Freeland, K. F., t., t.v.	29July07
Walker, M. G. E.	29July07

Lieutenants—contd.

Gattskell, H. W., p.a.o., s.	29July07
Woollcombe, F. R.	29July07
Creery, A.	29July07
Kinloch, R. I. H., p.a.c. [l]	17Sept.07
Gardiner, D. A.	18Oct.07
Tuohy, R D.	21Dec.04
Guise, V. R.	3Dec.07
Douglas-Jones, S. D.	3Dec.07
Ollivier, G. L.	17Dec.07
Armstrong, W. F.	21Dec.07
McIver K. I., m.a.	21Dec.07
Ellis, J. V. J., t.	21Dec.07
Shedden. G. P.	21Dec.07
Cummins, A.A..c.o.	21Dec.07
Veitch, A.	21Dec.07
Bignell, R. G., t.	21Dec.07
Thompson, H. S.	21Dec.07
Dodgson, D. S.	21Dec.07
Hogan, E. O., t.	17May08
Gay, C. H., Adjt.	17May08
Yorke, F. A.	28June08
Campbell, T. [L] t.	27July08
Dimmock, H.L.F. [l] m.a.	27July08
Roome,G.McC.,p.a.c.	27July08
Clarke,E.M.C.,p.a.o.	27July08
Cameron, C. P. G.	27July08
Cherry, A. H. M.	27July08
Scott, W. F. F.	27July08
Bussell, S. F. B.	27July08
Leeson, L. K.	27July08
Curling, E. R.	28Sept.08
Hunter, J. C. G. [l], p.a.c.	
Heywood, T. G. G. [L]	22Nov.08
Hitchcock, F. B.	22Nov.08
Ryan, C. J.	16Dec.08
Richardson, G. P.	20Dec.08
Day, C. L. t.	20Dec.08
Elliott, B. H., g.	20Dec.08
Pearce, P. M.	20Dec.08
Hynes, G. B., f.c.	20Dec.08
Colson, C.	20Dec.08
Smith, J. C. J.	17Apr.09
Macrae,A.E.,p.a.c.	29June09
Moore, H. T.	25July09
Fryer, F. E.	25July09
Russell, O.A.	25July09
Stebbing, H. T., t.	25July09
Porter, G. T, f.c	25July09
Holmes, H.	9Apr.14
	22June08
Fishe, N. H. [l]	25July09
Clayton, I. N.	25July09
Wyllie, R.	25July09
Thomas, H. R.	12Dec.09
Mills, H. P. F.	12Dec.09
Drake-Brockman, W. H. G. [l]	12Dec.09
Thicknesse, F. W.	20Dec.09
Fane, O. E., o., c.o.	20Dec.09
Halliday, F. S.	20Dec.09
MacLeod, M.	20Dec.09
Keene, G.	20Dec.09
Chapman, A. C.	20Dec.09
Bingham, C. H.	20Dec.09
Perram, G. T. C., s.	20Dec.09
Greenwood, T. C.	27June10
Hogg, O. F, G., o.c.	23July10
Bewley, B. J.	23July10

Lieutenants—contd.

Paris, H. G.	23July10
Becher L. B. A.	23July10
Roberts, H. W. [l] s.	
Keene, H. N. J.	23July10
	7Dec.10
Ashby, H. D., r.l.	23July10
Crofton, R., s.	18Dec.10
Cox, H. A.	18Dec.10
Curtis, A, D	18Dec.10
Sargeaunt, P. R.	18Dec.10
Purcell, L. G.	18Dec.10
Duke, V. G.	18Dec.10
Fooks, H. E.	18Dec.10
Caldecott. J. L., s.	12Feb.11
Meredith, J. C.	23May11
Neate, A. C. B. [L]	23May11
Montague, J. E. F.	29July11
Prichard, F. H. [l]	
Godfery. M. V. S.	29July11
Butterworth, B. M. G.	18Dec.11
de Kantzow, J. E.	18Dec.11
Rossiter, F. N. C.	17May08
Lowndes, R. C.	23July12
Prickett, L.	23July12
Francis, H. F.	23July12
Fargiter, B. B.	23July12
Chambers,C.C.,o.l.	23July12
Wright, S. N.	23July12
Firebrace, R. C. W, G. [L]	23July12
	26July12
Smith, I. P.	23July12
Phillips, A. H. D.	23Dec.12
Cardew, J. W	23Dec.12
Nevill, P.	23Dec.12
Bristow, L. C.	23Dec.12
Ritter, J. A.	23Dec.12
Floyd, B. E.	23July13
O'Leary, B. J. [L]	23July13
Tennent, C. B.	23July13
Campbell, G. F.	23July13
Heaton-Ellis, J. S., t.	
	23July13
Harker, A. W. A.	23July13
Banks, C. D'A. S.	23July13
Bois, D. G.	23July13
Eberlt, F. H., f.c.	23July13
Hughes-Hallett, W. E.	
Jenkins, W. M.	23July13
Gould, C. G. S., f.c.	23 July13
Withers, R. E.	23July13
Milner, R. J. N.	24July13
	19Jan.12
Shaw, H. A.	7Dec.13
Bingham, W.	28Dec.13
Troup, F. C. A., t.	23Dec.13
Rouquette, H. R.	
	23Dec.13
Treatt, B. D. C.	18Dec.13
Richards, D. J. R.	23Dec.13
Stevenson, J. H. M.	
	18Dec.13
Pym, J. A.	28Dec.13
Wildey, A. W. G.	28Dec.13
Collins, P. R. M.	28Dec.13
Gill, N. J., f.c.	28Dec.13
Montague, P. J. A.	28Dec.13
Leslie, A. S. W.	8Jan.14
Turbutt, R. B.	14Apr.14
Thomas, A. C.	27May14
Underhill, N.	27May14
Gage, B. A. H.	16July14
	23Dec.12

Lieutenants—contd.

Pollock, A. J. C.	20July14
Simpson, F. W. H	20July14
Curry, W. L.	20July14
Olliver, C. O.	20July14
Gilpin, W. J.	20July14
Taylor, C. C.	20July14
Gaussen, B.	20July14
Kellie, R. H. A.	20July14
Freeth, F. J. R.	20July14
Mucklow, C.	20July14
Richard, L. F.	20July14
Hall, A. C. S.	20July14
Wilson, I. C.	20July14
Hay, A. [l]	20July14
Kennedy, A. S. C.	20July14
Luard, E. A. P.	20July14

2nd Lieutenants.

Skinner, R. O.	9Dec.11
Parker, G. L.	9Dec.11
Heywood, H. F.	1July12
Hartree, A., f.c.	26Nov.12
	9Dec.11
Williams, F. P. J.	9Dec.11
Hawes, L. A.	23Dec.11
Johnston, M. A. B.	23Dec.11
Steel, J. V.	23Dec.11
Carew, R. L, O.	23Dec.11
Smyth, V. G.	23Dec.11
Stansfeld, L. R.	23Dec.11
Sanders, B. J. M.	23Dec.11
Campbell, D. A.	23Dec.11
Scott, E. C.	23Dec.11
Gubbins, M. N. T.	23Dec.11
Joll, L. D.	23Dec.11
Tomlinson, S. C.	23Dec.11
Hanlon, D. R., f.c.	23Dec.11
Goldney, L. P.	23Dec.11
Milligan, E. D.	23Dec.11
Smith, G. L. S.	23Dec.11
Hawkins, J. C. B.	23Dec.11
Cooke, J. G, M. B.	23Dec.11
Brown, L. N. F.	23Dec.11
Williams, E. J.	23Dec.11
Roupell, F. L. L. F.	23Dec.11
Hamilton, H. de C.	23Dec.11
Buckland. A. W.T.	22May12
Fardell, D. O.	19July12
Mackenzie, D.M.S.	19July12
Murphy, J. M.	19July12
Philpot, G.	19July12
Chidson, M. R.	19July12
Aston, E. N.	19July12
Collingwood, S.	19July12
Parkes, N. C.	19July12
Garry, R. V. M.	19July12
Field, D. J.	19July12
Greenwell Lax, A. W.	
	19July12
Sandys, M.¦T.	19July12
Collins, S. St. B.	19July12
Deane, J. A. L.	19July12
Wilson, R. B.	19July12
English, J. V.	19July12
Cumming, O. S.	28Mar.13
Caudle, H. C. R.	19July12
Mackenzie, H. N.	19July12
Kilner, H. R.	14Apr.13
	23Dec.11
Dymott, K. G.	16July13
	20Dec.12
Macgregor, A.	20Dec.12
Greene, H.	20Dec.12
Tanner, C. C. P.	20Dec.12

Royal Regiment of Artillery.

Royal Garrison Artillery—contd.

2nd Lieuts.—contd.

Pratt, F. W. H.	20 Dec. 12
Upson, H. C.	20 Dec. 12
Brian, H. C.	20 Dec. 12
Hebbert, G. K. P.	20 Dec. 12
Allpress, H. V.	20 Dec. 12
Armstrong, R. A.	20 Dec. 12
Fuge, W. V. G.	20 Dec. 12
Campbell, E. G.	20 Dec. 12
McIntyre, H. M. J.	20 Dec. 12
Moriarty, J. H.	20 Dec. 12
Shaw, S.	20 Dec. 12
Pemberton, A. L.	18 July 13
Hare, C. E.	18 July 13
Evans, D. S. C.	18 July 13
Heath, C. P.	18 July 13
Morgan, D. N.	18 July 13
Chambers, F. G.	18 July 13
Dobbin, R. A. S.	18 July 13
Goodman, E. W.	18 July 13
Borradaile, C. H. A.	18 July 13
Gill, R. C.	18 July 13
Peters, R. B.	18 July 13
Cottrell, G. F.	18 July 13
Brittan, C. H.	18 July 13
Noel, J. A. V.	18 July 13
Romanis, D. G.	18 July 13
Garratt, L. F	18 July 13
Gurney, L.	18 July 12
Hire, D. A. H.	18 July 13
Hallifax, F. P.	18 July 13
Teesdale, P. H.	18 July 13
Penrose, C. Q. L.	18 July 13
Carter, A. R.	18 July 13
Benfield, K. V. B.	18 July 13
Crosse, T. G.	18 July 13
Holden, W. C.	10 Dec. 13
Moncxton, M. H.	20 Dec. 13
	23 Dec. 19
Formilli, G. C.	14 Feb. 14
	19 July 12
Gulland, A. H.	10 Dec. 13
Ashby, G. S. M.	10 Dec. 13
Hordern, H. M.	19 Dec. 13
Bensley, C. J. F.	19 Dec. 13
Mullaly, D. J. St. C.	19 Dec. 13
Fasken, D. E.	19 Dec. 13
Lee, E. A.	19 Dec. 13
Harrison, E. G. W. W.	19 Dec. 13
Culverwell, E. R.	19 Dec. 13
Michaelis, C. D. A.	19 Dec. 13
Leigh, J. A.	19 Dec. 13
Lang, N. C.	19 Dec. 13
Caristie, C. M.	19 Dec. 13
Goldney, R. M.	19 Dec. 13
Somerscales, F. J.	19 Dec. 13
Bowen, E. G. A.	19 Dec. 13
Hilton, R.	19 Dec. 13
Moores, B. S. K. G.	19 Dec. 13
Painter, G. W. A.	19 Dec. 13
Pickthall, P. J. T.	19 Dec. 13
Warren, P. J. K.	19 Dec. 13
Cawson, L.	19 Dec. 13
Vale, H. C. S. [l]	19 Dec. 13
Gould, L. T. N.	19 Dec. 13
Shipster, F. F.	19 Dec. 13
Howett, R. B.	19 Dec. 13
Bell, L. G. R. F. H.	19 Dec. 13
Chadwick, R. M.	19 Dec. 13
Laurie, J. R.	19 Dec. 13
Towers, L. C.	19 Dec. 13
Eastwick-Field, W. L.	19 Dec. 13
Spong, C. A. T.	19 Dec. 13
Churcher, G. M.	19 Dec. 13
Morris, E. B.	19 Dec. 13

2nd Lieuts.—contd.

Prohert, G. O. C.	10 June 14
Lushington, F.	10 June 14
Cameron, P. G. [l]	10 July 14
Illiot, F. E.	10 June 14
Leslie W. A. A.	1 June 14
Stannard, A. J.	10 June 14
W lliamson, R. H.	10 June 14
Birbeck, J. H. B.	10 June 14

Adjutants.

Haig, A. G., capt.	25 May 11
Turner, W. M. Fitz H., g., capt.	27 July 11
Gunn, H. B. L. G., g., capt.	12 Oct. 11
Erskine-Murray, A.,	1 Dec. 11
Nicholson, St. J. R., g., lt.	5 Dec. 11
Spicer, P. L., g., capt.	13 Feb. 12
Heath, C. J., lt.	21 Feb. 12
Price, O. L. [l] capt.	13 Mar. 12
Beasley, J. H. M., g., capt.	29 Mar. 12
Cruickshank, P. B., g., capt.	4 Apr. 12
Ryan, F. T., lt.	4 June 12
Rashleigh, P., capt.	5 June 12
Budgeon, W. N., capt.	20 Aug. 12
Castle, R. W., capt.	22 Aug. 12
Cream, R. T. C., lt.	1 Sept. 12
Colbeck, B. B., capt.	4 Nov. 12
Garwood, H. P., capt.	19 Nov. 12
Graham, C. A. L., capt.	5 Feb. 13
Matthews, A. M., capt.	4 Mar. 13
Rycroft, F.	14 May 04
Kemble, H. M., capt.	8 Apr. 13
Hutchison, K. D., capt.	24 Apr. 13
Tuke, G. F. S., capt.	20 May 13
Standbridge, W. J., capt.	28 June 13
Cummins, E. J., g., capt.	10 Oct. 13
Andrewes, F. E., g.	14 Nov. 13
Adams, H. R., g., capt.	1 Jan. 14
Cunningham-Cunningham, T., o., e., capt.	21 Jan. 14
Aitken. N. W., lt.,	12 Feb. 14
Griffith, G. M., capt., f. or	14 Mar. 14
Gunter, A. C., capt.	23 Mar. 14
Allen, H., capt.	1 Apr. 14
Gay, C. H., lt.	1 Apr. 14
Hay, H. G. FitzG., g., capt.	6 Apr. 14
Foll, H. H., capt.	9 Apr. 14
Way, J., capt.	22 Apr. 14
Sidebottom. A. C., lt.	26 Apr. 14
Smith, H. W. T., capt.	1 June 14

Royal Artillery.

DISTRICT OFFICERS.

Majors.

Clarke, R.	14 Jan. 07
Williams, J. A.	13 Nov. 08
Cole, R.	30 Dec. 10
Munro, T.	31 Jan. 11
Chapman, J. T.	2 July 12
Smith, D., m.a.	10 Aug. 12
Rowley, W. H.	10 Aug. 12
Newton, J. T.	14 Oct. 12
Latham, C. R.	8 July 13

Captains.

Wells, J.	3 Sept. 04
Turner, C. H.	6 Jan. 06
Windrum, F.	7 Jan. 06
Dale, R. W.	24 June 08
O'Sullivan, P.	10 Aug. 12
Lee, G., s.	14 Oct. 12
Hunter, J.	24 Mar. 13
Austin, T.	8 July 13
Anderson, F. C.	27 Sept. 13
Fellows, C. G., m.	27 Sept. 13
Dameral, C. J.	10 Oct. 13
Langston, D.	10 Dec. 13
McKenzie, D. A.	5 Apr. 14
Allen, R. H.	25 May 14

Lieutenants

Williams, W. G.	21 Dec. 01
Follett, J. E. G.	11 Jan. 02
Borrett, W. J.	7 May 02
Prewer, W. H. R.	23 Aug. 02
Dovey, F. W.	17 Jan. 03
Harris. J.	25 Apr. 03
Rycroft, F.	14 May 04
Towers, W. H.	14 May 04
Cope, E. R.	14 May 04
Coyne, R.	14 May 04
Ellison, W. R.	28 May 04
Bailey, W. E.	3 Dec. 04
Leach, J.	25 Jan. 05
Brewster, R. E. B.	
Amey, F., s.	29 Mar. 05
Redgate, J.	29 Mar. 05
Silcott, W.	6 May 05
Spinks, G. C.	17 May 05
Reid, D.	17 May 05
Aggett, W. R.	18 Oct. 05
Moore, W. J.	17 Feb. 06
Stevens, E. J.	21 Feb. 06
Pawson, W.	8 Aug. 06
Everton, W. T. A.	7 Sept. 07
Broadhurst, O.	12 July 11
Lyle, J., s.	23 Aug. 11
Bolton, F.	28 Oct. 11
Cockaday, W. G. C.	3 Feb. 12
Davies, T. W. E.	3 Feb. 12
Kershaw, C. H.	3 Feb. 12
Martin, R.	3 Feb. 12
Bailey, H.	3 Feb. 12
Slade, R.	3 Feb. 12
Farrow, A. E.	27 Mar 12
Allen, J. T.	10 Aug. 12
Westell, C. E.	16 Oct. 12
Harris, C.	23 Nov. 12

Lieutenants—contd.

Syrett, F. G.	23 Nov. 12
Bell, W. J.	25 Dec. 12
Walker, T. H.	25 Dec. 12
Owen, E.	8 Jan. 13
Warton, H. C.	7 May 13
Fulcher, G. E. T.	22 Oct. 13
Tompkins, J. W.	10 Dec. 13
Faston, W. T. J.	4 Mar. 14
Wales, A. H.	20 June 14

QUARTER-MASTERS.

Spence, R. G. I., r.g.a. (Ord. Bd.)	24 May 99
hon. maj.	24 May 14
Fulcher, G. A., r.g.a. l Apr. 01 (War Office)	
hon. capt.	1 Apr. 11
Brown, R. P., r.g.a.	29 July 08
hon. capt.	29 July 13
Rowland, F., r.g.a.	25 May 02
hon. capt.	25 May 14
McDonald, J. P., r.f.a.	15 June 04
hon. capt.	15 June 14
Ramsay, W. J., hon. lt., r.g.a.	16 Nov. 04
O'Brien, J., hon. lt., r.g.a.	25 Jan. 05
Adamson, G. R., hon. lt., r.f.a.	29 Apr. 05
Mitchell, A., hon. lt., r.f.a.	3 Oct. 06
Webb, W. T., hon. lt., r.f.a.	22 Dec. 06
Shean, W., hon. lt., r.g.a. (War Office)	1 Nov. 07
Drayson, T., hon. lt., r.g.a.	8 Jan. 08
Stammas, T. H., hon. lt., r.h.a.	6 June 08
Keough, F., hon. lt., r.f.a.	18 July 08
Graham, D., hon. lt., r.g.a.	5 Sept. 08
Taylor, R., hon. lt., r.g.a.	22 Dec. 09
Robinson, W. C., hon. lt., r.g.a.	13 May 11
Smith, D. W., hon. lt., r.g.a.	4 Oct. 11
Donahoe, P., hon. lt., r.g.a.	16 Dec. 11
Skinner, J. H., hon. lt., r.g.a.	6 Jan. 12
Armstrong, T., hon. lt., r.g.a.	10 Apr. 12
Ashweek, F., hon. lt., r.g.a., r.	27 Apr. 12
Griffin, A. J., hon. lt., r.f.a.	27 Apr. 12
Phillips, W. J., hon. lt., r.h.a.	18 May 12
Williams, E. E., hon. lt., r.f.a.	11 Sept. 12
Bates, F. J., hon. lt., r.g.a.	14 Sept. 12
Yates, J. C., hon. lt., r.f.a.	14 Sept. 12
Doyle, J. C., hon. lt., r.g.a.	9 Oct. 12
Nightingale, T. G. H., hon. lt., r.f.a.	18 Jan. 13
Kerrison, T. W., hon. lt., r.g.a., r.	23 Apr. 13

ROYAL FIELD ARTILLERY.

SPECIAL RESERVE.

Captains.

p.s.Wall, W. T. J. L. *(Hon. Lt. in Army 7 Nov. 00)*	*Irish Comd.*	13Feb.00
p.s.✗Haslewood, B. T. ⑤	*Newcastle-on-Tyne*	8June04
p.s.✗Devenish, A. H. N., Capt. ret. pay ⑤	*Hilsea*	4Mar.05
p.s.✗Knolles, R. M. (H) ⑩ *(Hon. Lt. in Army 11 Oct. 00)*	*Irish Comd.*	6May05
p.s.Tritton, O., Capt. ret.(I)	*Hilsea*	22May05
p.s.Hill, R. B. (I)	*Uganda*	27May05
p.s.Thompson, W. *(Hon. 2nd Lt. in Army 13 Oct. 00)*	*Newcastle-on-Tyne*	5June05
p.s.Hallowes, B. H. C. *(Asst. Land Surveyor, Hong Kong, 10 Jan. 14)Athlone*		12June05
p.s.Cushen, E. W. (a) p.v.c.	*E. Comd.*	25Oct.05
p.s.Ostler, H. B.	*Newcastle-on-Tyne*	1Feb.06
p.s.Sherlock, E. (I)	*Irish Comd.*	3May06
p.s ✗Despard, W. H. C., Capt. ret. pay	*Hilsea*	16May06
Pratt, P. G.	*Irish Comd.*	6June06
p.s.Cullum, E. G. L. (I)	*S. Comd.*	23June06
p.s.Esmonde-White, J. *(Hon. 2nd Lt. in Army 14 Oct. 00) g.*	*Athlone*	4Oct.06
p.s.Stanham, H. S. (A)	*S. Comd.*	6Oct.06
p.s.Hay, B. H. L.	*S. Comd.*	1Nov.06
p.s.Dresser, H. B.	*S. Comd.*	30Aug.07
✗Mayall, C. G., Lt. ret. pay, *t. Reading*		4Sept.07
✗Harrison, A. H., Capt. ret. pay	*Woolwich*	18Sept.07
p.s.✗Mallock, C. H., Capt. ret. pay *Hilsea*		4Dec.07
Barnwell, A. S.	*Glasgow*	8Feb.08
✗Marten, A.J., Capt. ret. pay	*Woolwich*	16May08
p.s.Jameson, J. C. E.	*Preston*	26May08
p.s.Robson, J. S.	*E. Comd.*	18June08
p.s.Frazer, E. F.	*Athlone*	13July08
p.s.✗O'Callaghan, R. G. D., *late Lt. 6 Dns. Irish Comd.*		4June10
Evans, H. J. A., Capt. ret. pay		20Apr.11
Corbett-Smith, A., *formerly 2nd Lt. R.A.*	*E. Comd.*	30Sept.11
Dane, J. A., Lt. ret. pay ⑤	*E. Comd.*	24Dec.12
Burnett-Stuart, G. R., Lt. ret. pay	*Woolwich*	23Dec.12
Wall, M. D., Capt. ret. pay *(Res. of Off.)*	*Athlone*	15July14

Lieutenants.

Ditmas, H. E. C., Lt. ret. pay	*Woolwich*	3Apr.01 25Dec.09
✗Jackson, F. W. F., Lt. ret. pay *(Asst. Col. Sec., Gold Coast,* { 10Mar.11 30July04)	*Gold Coast*	3Apr.01 20Nov.09
O'Malley, C. A. G., Lt. ret. pay	*Woolwich*	21Dec.03 4Dec.09
p.s.Lloyd-Barrow, R. A.	*Hilsea*	31Mar.06 15Nov.08
Adcock, G. H. J.	*Athlone*	7Apr.06
Bittleston, K.G., Lt. ret. pay *Woolwich*		19June06 4Nov.11
Bellingham, R. C. N., Lt. ret. pay, *s.*	*Athlone*	23Dec.06 26Oct.12
Ziegler, C. L., Lt. ret. pay	*Preston*	23Dec.06 16Mar.12
p.s.von Roemer, C. W.	*Hilsea*	4Mar.07
p.s.Blackiston, H. (A)	*Nigeria*	7Jan.08
Baxendale, G. V.	*Hilsea*	31Jan.08
p.s.Browne, M. G.	*Athlone*	5Aug.08
de Caen, H. F. B.	*Athlone*	13Oct.08
p.s.Creasy, E. C.	*Shanghai*	30Dec.08
Voysey, R. A. E. (q)	*Hilsea*	5Nov.10
p.s.Douglas, S. T.	*E. Comd.*	9Oct.12
Radford, R. H.	*Preston*	1Jan.13
Odlum, W. J., *late* 2nd Lt. R.F.A.	*Irish Comd.*	5Feb.13
✗Dixon-Spain, J. E. *(Hon. Lt. in Army 27Mar.01)*	*Woolwich*	27Apr.13
Redfern, W. A. K. *(Hon. Attaché, Madrid, 16 Oct. 13)*	*Woolwich*	9May13
Hawkins, J. D. C.	*Hilsea*	1Oct.13
Duff, W. L. C.	*Glasgow*	1Feb.14
Stomm, P. W. J. A.	*Newcastle-on-Tyne*	18Mar.14
Davies, V. C.	*Hilsea*	2June14

2nd Lieutenants.

Hussey, T. *(Asst. Dist. Commr. S. Leone 12Jan.14) Newcastle-on-Tyne*		2June09
Feilden, R. H.	*Preston*	25Aug.09
Cumming, C. E.	*Glasgow*	22Sept.09
Pease, G. B. R.	*Bulford*	17Nov.09
Mitchell, C. C.	*Athlone*	5Feb.10
Naismith, J. O.	*Glasgow*	30Mar.10

Royal Field Artillery.

Special Reserve—*contd.*

2nd Lieuts.—contd.

Robinson, W. H.	*Glasgow*	16Apr.10
Wilson, H. J. M.	*Preston*	16Apr.10
Marson, A. A.	*Woolwich*	20July10
Furlong, G. O.	*Athlone*	27Aug.10
Tait, J. W.	*Glasgow*	1Oct.10
McDavid, J. W.	*Glasgow*	8Oct.10
O'Brien, T. J. A.	*Athlone*	11Jan.11
McGee, W. R. A.	*Athlone*	13May11
Buckley, E. S.	*Athlone*	17June11
Arbuthnot, R. W. M.	*Sheffield*	21June11
Russell-Wood, L.	*Newcastle-on-Tyne*	26July11
Gottwaltz, R. L.	*Woolwich*	6Sept.11
Coren, E. W.	*Bulford*	16Dec.11
Poer, H. P. B.	*Newbridge*	16Dec.11
Driscoll, E. J. (*on prob.*)	*St. John's Wood*	6Jan.12
Austin, V. J.	*Preston*	6Jan.12
Phillipson, J. T.	*Aldershot*	20Mar.12
Power, K. W.	*Kildare*	27Mar.12
Thomas, L. B.	*Bulford*	1Apr.12
Goodwin, W. E.	*W. Comd.*	8May12
Barclay, C. E.	*Woolwich*	11May12
Hickey, J.	*Kildare*	3July12
Whattou, S. M. de H.	*Exeter*	3Aug.12
deBurgh, H. G.	*Newbridge*	25Sept.12
Harbord, S. G.	*Brighton*	1Oct.12

2nd Lieuts.—contd.

Hollwey, J. B.	*Newbridge*	1Oct.12
Abraham, M. H.	*Aldershot*	30Oct.12
Dyson, W. G.	*Sheffield*	14Dec.12
Selby, J. G.	*Ewshott*	4Jan.13
Anderson, A.	*Woolwich*	15Feb.13
Gaunt, O.	*Deepcut*	1Mar.13
Montagu, J. G. E.	*Hilsea*	1Apr.13
Browning-Paterson, N. A.		1Apr.13
Smith, S. W., *f.c.*		19Apr.13
Thompson, R. L.	*Glasgow*	23Apr.13
Hoult, J. M.	*Cahir*	24May13
Quiller-Couch, B. B.	*Bulford*	7June13
Hannam, S. P.	*Shorncliffe*	18June13
Pullen, J. W.	*Newcastle-on-Tyne*	21June13
Lawton, P. N. A. C. (*on prob.*)	*Shorncliffe*	3Sept.13
Motion, M. D. (*on prob.*)	*Woolwich*	24Sept 13
Voysey, J. C. (*on prob.*)	*Aldershot*	21Jan 14
Harris, H. P. H. (*on prob.*)[l]	*Brighton*	14Feb.14
Godsal, H. (*on prob.*)	*Aldershot*	7Mar.14
Lyons, R. C. (*on prob.*)	*Woolwich*	21Mar.14
Gerrard, E. (*on prob.*)	*Newbridge*	27May14
Russell, G. B. (*on prob.*)		3June14
Wood, A. (*on prob.*)	*Woolwich*	17June14
McEwen, W. G. (*on prob.*)	*Aldershot*	4July14
Trouton, D. G. (*on prob.*)	*Newbridge*	4July14

ROYAL HORSE ARTILLERY.

Head Quarters, Woolwich.

28 Batteries.

Depôt (Woolwich). Riding Establishment (Woolwich).

Key to Allotment of Batteries to Brigades.

Battery	R.H.A. Brigade	Battery	R.H.A. Brigade	Battery	R.H.A. Brigade	Battery	R.H.A. Brigade	Battery	R.H.A. Brigade	Battery	R.H.A. Brigade	Battery	R.H.A. Brigade
A	I.	E	III.	I	VII.	M	VIII.	Q	VIII.	U	XI.	Y	XIII.
B	I.	F	IV.	J	IV.	N	IX.	R	X.	V	XII.		
C	II.	G	V.	K	VI.	O	V.	S	IX.	W	XII.		
D	III.	H	VI.	L	VII.	P	X.	T	XI.	X	XIII.		

ROYAL HORSE ARTILLERY BRIGADES.

I.—Ambala.

Lt.-Colonel.
Rouse, H., *D.S.O.*

Adjutant.
Erskine, A. E., *capt.*

A. Batt. *(The Chestnut Troop).*
Ambala.

Maj.	Simpson-Balkie, H. A. D. *p.s.c.* [*l*]
Capt.	Duthie, A. M.
Lt.	Walker, H. W.
Lt.	Richardson, G. C.
Lt.	Twistleton-Wykeham-Fiennes, *Hon.* I. M.

B. Battery
Ambala.

Maj.	Forman, D. E.
Capt.	McLean, C. W. W.
Lt.	Brooke, A. C.
Lt.	Daubuz, C.
Lt.	Deprez, A. E.

II.—

C. Battery
Canterbury.

Maj.	Lamont, J. W. F.
Capt.	Philips, J. L.
Lt.	Bridge, C. E. D. [L]
Lt.	Fitze, G. G.

III.—Newbridge.

Lt.-Colonel.
Breeks, R. W.
Adjutant.
Scarlett, J. A., *capt.*

D. Battery.

Maj.	Gillson, G.
Capt.	Sanderson, R. H.
Lt.	Watson, G. E. B.
Lt.	Gough, J. B.
Lt.	Parker, R. E.

E. Battery.

Maj.	Forman, A. B.
Capt.	Bartram, H. B.
Lt.	Palmer, R. L.
Lt.	Walwyn, C. L. T.
Lt.	Maxwell, E. B.

IV.—

F. Battery.
St. John's Wood
(for Aldershot).

Maj.	Ollivant, J. S., *D.S.O., e.*
Capt.	Parsons, W. F.
Lt.	Meade, G. W.
Lt.	Davies, H. L.
Lt.	Sebag-Montefiore, T. H.

J. Battery.
Aldershot (for St. John's Wood).

Maj.	Seligman, H. S.
Capt.	Curling, J.
Lt.	Merriman, G. H.
Lt.	Dendy, M. H.
Lt.	Burne, A. H.

V.—Ipswich.

Lt.-Colonel.
White-Thomson, H. D., *D.S.O.*
Adjutant.
Finlayson, R. G., *capt.*

G. Battery.

Maj.	Davson, H. M.
Capt.	Unlacke, C. D. W.
Lt.	Carrington, R. H.
Lt.	Fitzwilliams, J. K. L., [L]
Lt.	Sandeman, T. F. (*attd.*)

O. Battery.

Maj.	Tilney, N. E.
Capt.	Cowell, H. P. J.
Lt.	Selby, C. W. [*i*]
Lt.	Wallace, J. T.
Lt.	Barstow, W. A. T. (*attd.*)

VI.—Trowbridge.

Lt.-Colonel.
Cloeté, E. R. H. J.
Adjutant.
Spencer-Smith, D. C. [*l*] *capt.*

H. Battery.
Trowbridge.

Maj.	Budworth, C.E.D., *M.V.O.* [L]
Capt.	Skinner, E. J.
Lt.	Imbert-Terry, H. B.
Lt.	Hermon-Hodge, G.
Lt.	Mundy, L. F. H. (*attd.*)

K. Battery.
Christchurch.

Maj.	White, G. H. A.
Capt.	Bridges, A. H.
Lt.	Pierson, C. E.
Lt.	Fleming, E. O.
Lt.	Parbury, K. (*attd.*)

VII.—Aldershot.

Lt.-Colonel.
Birch, J. F. N.
Adjutant.
Scarlett, *Hon.* H. R., *capt.*

I. Battery.

Maj.	Thompson, W. G.
Capt.	Burnyeat, H. P.
Lt.	St. Clair, G. J. P.
Lt.	Worsley, H. G.
Lt.	Edwards, F. G. de B.

L. Battery.

Maj.	Sclater-Booth, *Hon.* W. D.
Capt.	Bradbury, E. K.
Lt.	Campbell, J. D.
Lt.	Giffard, J.
Lt.	Marston, J. E.

VIII.—

M. Battery.
Risalpur.

Maj.	Bright, R. A., *p.s.c., q.s., e.*
Capt.	Taylor, G. J. S.
Lt.	Price, J. T.
Lt.	Archdale, A. Q.
Lt.	Lowry-Corry, H. C.

Q. Battery.
Sialkot.

Maj.	Eden, W. R., *D.S.O.*
Capt.	Lascelles, R. H.
Lt.	Don, J. A.
Lt.	Ward, C. F.
Lt.	Budden, E. F.

| 586 | 587 | 588 | 589 |

Royal Horse Artillery.

IX.—
Secunderabad
(for Mhow).

N. Battery.
Secunderabad
(for Mhow).

Maj. Rotton, J. G.
Capt. Harris, O. M.
Lt. Carlisle, T. H.
Lt. Hutchison, H.O.
Lt. Adam, R. F.

S. Battery.
Bangalore
(for Mhow).

Maj. Sykes, C. A.
Capt. Renny-Tailyour, J. W.
Lt. West, H. C.
Lt. Newton, T.C. [L]
Lt. Greenshields, D. J.

X.—Woolwich.

Lt.-Colonel.
de Rougemont, C. H., *M.V.O., D.S.O., p.s.c.*
Adjutant.
Lewin, E. O., *capt.*

P. Battery.

Maj. Kay, W. H.
Capt. Allardyce, J.G. B.
Lt. Day, N. A. L.
~~Lt. Talbot, E. L.~~
Lt. Ellis, R. S. (attd.)

R. Battery.

Maj. Wardrop, A E.
Capt. Mellor, E.
Lt. Norton, E. F.
Lt. Clibborn, C. J. H.
Lt. Holland, R. T. (attd.)

XI.—

T. Battery.
Abbassia.

Maj. Tudor, H. H. [L]
Capt. Goschen, A. A., *D.S.O.*
Lt. Ryan, R. S. [L]
Lt. Archer Houblon, R.
Lt. Rickards, G. A.

U. Battery.
Lucknow.

Maj. Dennistoun, J. G.
Capt. Paynter, W. P.
Lt. Rolleston, A. G.
Lt. Findlay, C. B.
Lt. Pownall, H. R.

XII.—Meerut.

Lt.-Colonel.
Askwith, H. F.
Adjutant.
Lynch-Staunton, R. K., *capt.*

V. Battery.

Maj. Sandys, W. B. R.
Capt. Harrison, J. M. R.
Lt. Nicholls, W. A.
Lt. Grant-Suttie, H. F.
Lt. Nunn, J. H.

W. Battery.

Maj. Smith, L. A.
Capt. West, A. H. D.
Lt. Farren, R. H.
Lt. Gordon, J. K.
Lt. Soames, M. G.

XIII.—Mhow
(for Secunderabad).
Lt.-Colonel.
Robinson, W. A.
Adjutant.
Balston, G. R., *Ca*

X. Battery
(Mhow, for Bangalore).

Maj. Keyworth, R.G.
Capt. Dunbar, J. C.
Lt. Lockhart, J. F. K.
Lt. Larcom, *Sir* T. P. Bt.
Lt. McLeod, N. M.

Y. Battery
(Mhow, for Secunderabad).

Maj. Wheatley, P.
Capt. Crofton, M.
Lt. Lush-Wilson, H.G.
Lt. Ball, K. M.
Lt. Leach, G. P.

AMMUNITION COLUMNS, ROYAL HORSE ARTILLERY, INDIA.

"*A*" Campbellpore.
Lt. Van Straubenzee, A.W.

"*B*" Sialkot.
Lt. Wilson, D. C.

"*C*" Ambala.
Lt. White, J. L. C.

"*D*" Ahmednagar. (temp.)
Lt. Ramsay, J. R.

"*E*" Mhow.
Lt. Mann, W. E.

"*F*" Meerut.
Lt. Martin, H. G.

"*G*" Lucknow.
Lt. McConnel. M. H.

"*H*" Secunderabad.
Lt. Brooke, A. F.

"*I*" Lahore Cantonment.
Lt. Harrison, P. F.

DEPOT, WOOLWICH.
Depôt.

Maj. Charlton, C. E. C. G.
Capt. Craven, W. S. D., *g.*
Lt. Almack, E. P.

Lt. Lawson, C. G.
Qr.-Mr. Taylor, R., *hon. lt.*

RIDING ESTABLISHMENT, WOOLWICH.

Maj. Monkhouse, W. P., *M.V.O.*
Capt. Jelf, W. W.

Lt. Lucas, C. C.
Lt. Pile, F. A.

Rid.-Mr. Aherne, D., *hon. maj.*
Rid.-Mr. Dann, B., *hon. lt.*

Rid.-Mr. Wark, F., *hon. lt.*

Riding-Masters, India and S. Africa.
Connell, T., *hon. maj.* — Ambala.
Bastyan, S. J., *hon. capt.* — Meerut.

Riding-Masters, Home.
Caddington, T. G. A., *hon. maj* — Aldershot.
McCombie, A. W., *hon. maj.* — Woolwich.
Brogan, T. H., *hon. maj.* — Newbridge.

Phillips, W. J., *hon. lt.* — Aldershot.

Quarter-Masters.
Stammas, T. H., *hon.* — Woolwich.

Royal Field Artillery.

ROYAL FIELD ARTILLERY.
(Head Quarters, Woolwich.)

147 Batteries.   6 Depôts.

Key to Allotment of Batteries of Royal Field Artillery.

Battery	R.F.A. Brigade	Battery	R.F.A. Brigade	Battery	R.F.A. Brigade	Battery	R.F.A. Brigade	Battery	R.F.A. Brigade	Battery	R.F.A. Brigade	Battery	R.F.A. Brigade	Battery	R.F.A. Brigade
1	XLV.	20	IX.	39	XIV.	58	XXXV.	77	VI.	96	XIX.	115	XXV.	134	XXXII.
2	XIII.	21	II.	40	XLIII.	59	XVIII.	78	VII.	97	XIX.	116	XXVI.	135	I.
3	XLV.	22	XXXIV.	41	XLII.	60	XLIV.	79	VI.	98	XX.	117	XXVI.	136	Reserve
4	VII.	23	XL.	42	II.	61	VIII.	80	XV.	99	XX.	118	XXVI.	137	Reserve
5	XLV.	24	XXXVIII.	43	XII.	62	III.	81	X.	100	XX.	119	XXVII.	138	II.
6	XL.	25	XXXV.	44	XIII.	63	V.	82	X.	101	XXI.	120	XXVII.	139	Reserve
7	IV.	26	XVII.	45	XLII.	64	V.	83	XI.	102	XXI.	121	XXVII.	140	III.
8	XIII.	27	XXXII.	46	XXXIX.	65	VIII	84	XI.	103	XXI.	122	XXVIII.	141	Reserve
9	XLI.	28	IX.	47	XLIV.	66	IV.	85	XI.	104	XXI.	123	XXVIII.	142	IV.
10	XVII.	29	XLII.	48	XXXVI.	67	I.	86	XII.	105	XXII.	124	XXVIII.	143	Reserve
11	XV.	30	XLIII.	49	XL.	68	XIV.	87	XII.	106	XXII.	125	XXIX.	144	V.
12	XXXV.	31	XXXVII.	50	XXXIV.	69	I.	88	XIV.	107	XXII.	126	XXIX.	145	Reserve
13	I.	32	XXXIII.	51	XXXIX.	70	XXXIV.	89	I.	108	XXIII.	127	XXIX.	146	VI.
14	IV.	33	XXXIII.	52	XV.	71	XXXVI.	90	XVI.	109	XXIII.	128	XXIX.	147	Reserve
15	XXXVI.	34	XXXVIII.	53	II.	72	XXXVIII.	91	XVI.	110	XXIII.	129	XXX.		
16	XLI.	35	XXXVII.	54	XXXIX.	73	V.	92	XVII.	111	XXIV.	130	XXX.		
17	XLI.	36	XXXIII.	55	XXXVII.	74	VI.	93	XVIII.	112	XXIV.	131	XXX.		
18	III.	37	VIII.	56	XLIV.	75	III.	94	XVIII.	113	XXV.	132	XXXI.		
19	IX.	38	VII.	57	XLIII.	76	X.	95	XIX.	114	XXV.	133	XXXI.		

ROYAL FIELD ARTILLERY BRIGADES.

I.—Edinburgh.

Lt.-Colonel.
Elton, F. A. G. Y.

Adjutant.
Goff, L. T., *capt.*

13th Battery.

Maj. Smith, H. R. W. M.
Capt. King, G. H.
Lt. Archer, H.
Lt. Bowen, G. E. S. [L]

67th Battery.

Maj. Blois, D. G.
Capt. Ballingall, H. M.
Lt. Binney, F. B., *f.c.r.*
2nd Lt. Johnstone, J. A.
2nd Lt. Taylor, A. G.

69th Battery.

Maj. Coates, D. R., *g.*
Capt. Higgon, A. B.
Lt. Davidson, L. E. O.
2nd Lt. Booth, L. E.

II.—Cahir.

Lt.-Colonel.
Thompson, W. A. M., *p.s.c., bt. col.*

Adjutant.
Massy, C. W., *lt.*

21st Battery.

Maj. Phillpotts, L. M., *D.S.O., g.*
Capt. Bowles, J. de V.
Lt. MacDonald, H. S.
2nd Lt. Harbord, G. M.

42nd Battery.

Maj. Brock, H. J.
Capt. Robertson, N. B.
Lt. Harding, F. E. B.
Lt. Barry, J. R.
2nd Lt. Burrows, E. W. M.
2nd Lt. Marsh, S. G. B.
(attd.)

53rd Battery.

Maj. Rugge-Price, C. F.
Capt. Heather, V. J.
Lt. Battersby, J. W.
2nd Lt. Bevir, C. E. F.
2nd Lt. Connal, A. W. C.

III.—Jullundur

(for Woolwich)

Lt.-Colonel.
Walker, A. L.

Adjutant.
Jervis, N. G. M., *capt.*

18th Battery.
Jullundur
(for Woolwich).

Maj. Manley, W. G. H.
Capt. Wray, H. C.
Lt. Waller, H. W. L.
Lt. Graham, S. D.

62nd Battery.
Multan
(for Woolwich).

Maj. Drake, H. M.
Capt. Younger, A. A. S.
Lt. Smyth, G. O. S.
Lt. Beckett, C. T.
2nd Lt. Hay-Webb, C. R. F.

75th Battery.
Peshawar
(for Woolwich).

Maj. Rudkin, W. C. E., *D.S.O.*
Capt. Macdona, B. V.
Lt. Grosvenor, Hon. R. E.
2nd Lt. Tulte-Dalton, G.

IV.—Secunderabad.

Lt.-Colonel.
Gordon, L. A. C.

Adjutant.
Warton, R. B., *lt.*

7th Battery.

Maj. Rettie, W. J. K.
Capt. Marshall, F. H., *o.*
Lt. Beall, R. D.
2nd Lt. Anderson, T. R.

14th Battery.

Maj. Kirby, A. D.
Capt. Turnbull, P.
Lt. Rutherfoord, D. G. C.
Lt. Colfox, W. P.
Lt. Pritchard, W. D. [l

66th Battery.

Maj. Delaforce, E. F.
Capt. Theobald, A. C. L.
Lt. Halliday, W. J. F.
Lt. Elles, P. G. M.
2nd Lt. Martin, G. N. C.

Royal Field Artillery.

V.—Lucknow.
Lt.-Colonel.
Gordon, L. G. F., D.S.O., g.
Adjutant.
Arthur, H.B.C. [L] capt.

63rd Battery.
Cawnpore.
Maj. Smith, H. B.
Capt. Raikes, L.T.
Lt. Carlisle, T. R. M. [l]
Lt. Gilpin, R.

64th Battery.
Fyzabad.
Maj. Perreau, A. M.
Capt. Millar, J. H. B.
Lt. Preston, C. O'D. [l]
Lt. Burrard, G.
Lt. Kemp, G. C.

73rd Battery.
Lucknow.
Maj. Marsden, R. T.
Capt. Warren, W. R.
Lt. Glendinning, H. J.
Lt. Murray, P. H.
2nd Lt. Orr-Ewing, M. R.

VI. (Howr.)—
Jhansi.
Lt.-Colonel.
White, G. F.
Adjutant.
Bolitho, E. H. W., capt.

74th (Howr.) Battery.
Jhansi.
Maj. Lough, A. T.
Capt.
Lt. Temple, T., o.
Lt. King-Harman, L. H.
2nd Lt. Temple, E.

77th (Howr.) Battery.
Meerut.
Maj. Swann, C.J.H., e., g.
Capt. Ward, B. S.
Lt. Spencer, R. A.
Lt. O'Brien, L. B.
Lt. Adam, N. M.

79th (Howr.) Battery.
Jhansi.
Maj. Grove, E.W., D.S.O.
Capt. Robinson, P. G.
Lt. Wilson, F. W. B.
2nd Lt. Hayes, H. G.

VII.—Rawal Pindi.
(for Kirkee).
Lt.-Colonel.
Prescott Decie, C.
Adjutant
Hornsby, F. H., lt.

4th Battery.
Maj. Mackenzie, F. W.
Capt. Hovil, R.
Lt. Allen, R. F. C.
Lt. Moorhead, E. J.
Lt. Peppe, F. H.

38th Battery.
Maj. Atlay, H. W.
Capt. Twisleton - Wykeham - Fiennes, N.I.E.
Lt. Burne, S. F.
Lt. Bolton, C. L.

78th Battery.
Maj. Ritchie, C. MacI. [l]
Capt. Hunter, D. H. K.
Lt. Tristram, G. H.
Lt. Latham, E.

VIII. (Howr.)—
Kildare.
Lt.-Colonel.
Duffus, E. J.
Adjutant.
Yorke, P. G., capt.

37th (Howr.) Battery.
Maj. Jones, E. H.
Capt. Reynolds, D.
Lt. Rawson-Shaw, K.
f.c.
2nd Lt. Morgan, W. D.
2nd Lt. Earle, E. G. [l]

61st (Howr.) Battery.
Maj. Wilson, F. A., D.S.O.
Capt. McClymont, R. A.
Lt. Housden, E. J. T. [l]
2nd Lt. Edge, J. D.
2nd Lt. Tyler, H. A.

65th (Howr.) Battery.
Maj. Livingstone-Learmonth, J. E. C.
Capt. French, T. N.
Lt. Palmer, E. A.
Lt. Cunningham, J. A.,
2nd Lt. Richardson, J.H.K.
2nd Lt. Groome, R. E. C. (attd.)

IX.—Meerut.
Lt.-Colonel.
Potts, F., g.
Adjutant.
Wilmer, E. R. G., capt.

19th Battery.
Meerut.
Maj. Buckle, A. S., p.s.c., g. [l]
Capt. Cripps, C. W.
Lt. Gregory, M.
Lt. Durie, T. E.
Lt. Townsend, M. D.

20th Battery.
Bareilly.
Maj. Anderson, A. T., g.
Capt. Parbury, F. N.
Lt. Bell, S. P. [l];
Lt.

28th Battery.
Meerut.
Maj. Phillips, E. H., D.S.O.
Capt. Potter, C. F., p.s.c.
Lt. Marriner, B. L.
Lt. Burkinshaw, F.W.
Lt. Hart, S.

X.—Kirkee
(for Jullundur).
Lt.-Colonel.
Cleeve, E. S.
Adjutant.
Sarson, E. V., capt.

76th Battery.
(for Multan).
Maj. Nevinson, T. St. A. B. L.
Capt. Lloyd, O. S.
Lt. Love, R. H. A. D.
2nd Lt. Latham, H. B.
2nd Lt. Reynolds, B. T.

81st Battery
(for Peshawar).
Maj. Barton, P., g.
Capt. Batchelor, V.A. [L]
Lt. Rendel, A. J.
Lt. Bayne - Jardine, C. W.
Lt. Harvey, K. W.

82nd Battery
(for Jullundur).
Maj. Maule, H. N. St. J.,
e.
Capt. Bayley, E. J. L.
Lt. Dorling, L. H. G.
Lt. Wingate, G. F. R.
2nd Lt. Gordon, R. E.

XI.—Jubbulpore.
Lt.-Colonel.
Maxwell, J. McC.
Adjutant
Vaughan, H. H. S., capt.

83rd Battery.
Maj. Plummer, E. W., e.
Capt. Cowan, J. De B.
Lt. FitzGibbon, F.
Lt. Macpherson, A. D.
2nd Lt. Thomson, D.

84th Battery.
Maj. Thomas, H. M., g.
Capt. Langford, E. G.
Lt. Russell, H.
2nd Lt. Hollwey, J. S.
2nd Lt. Morgan, F. E.

85th Battery.
Capt. Blair, W. K. P.
Lt. Pease-Watkin, E. H. P.
2nd Lt. Carne, E. F.
2nd Lt. Marriott, A. F.

XII. (Howr.)—
Clonmel.
Lt.-Colonel.
Humphreys, G., D.S.O.
Adjutant.
McGrath, A. T., capt.

43rd (Howr.) Battery.
Fethard.
Maj. Burne, E. R.
Capt. Woodside, A. McB.
2nd Lt. MacIlwaine, A. H.
2nd Lt. Hadden. N.C.C.
2nd Lt. Hog, R. T. A.

86th (Howr.) Battery.
Clonmel.
Maj. Hardman, R.
Capt. Jones, W. A. F.
Lt. Chetwynd-Stapylton, H. M.
Lt. Trenchard, F. A.
Lt. Mansfield, G. E.

87th (Howr.) Battery.
Kilkenny.
Maj. Belcher, H. T., D.S.O., g.
Capt. Powell, J. H. S.,
f.c.
Lt. Sanders, J. D. G.,
Lt. Crippin, H. W. [l]
Lt. Russell, C. C.

XIII.—Bangalore
(for St. Thomas' Mount).
Lt.-Colonel.
Tyler, J. A.
Adjutant.
Taylor, B. W., capt.

2nd Battery.
Bangalore.
(for St. Thomas' Mount).
Maj. Paterson, P. J. [l]
Capt. Coldwell-Horsfall, J. H.
Lt. Lucas, J. de B. T.
Lt. Buchan, D.
2nd Lt. Thomas, G. I.

8th Battery.
Bellary.
(for Kamptee).
Maj. Kirke, K. St. G., o.
Capt. Littledale, A.C.
Lt. Magrath, M. M.
Lt. Pellereau, J. C. E.
2nd Lt. Harrison, H. T.

44th Battery.
Bangalore.
(for Belgaum).
Maj. Houstoun, A.
Capt. Povah, H. M. J.
Lt. Alves, H. M. J.
Lt. Beckley, T. H.
Lt. Cammell, G.A.

Royal Field Artillery.

XIV.—Colchester.

Lt.-Colonel.
Ross-Johnson, C. M.,
D.S.O. [L]
Adjutant.
Fullerton, J. C., *capt.*

39th Battery.

Maj. Eardley-Russell,
E.S.E.W., M.V.O., p.s.c. [L]
Capt. Boyd, A. O., e.
Lt. Jones-Bateman, L.
Lt. Riecke, A. F. M.
Lt. Jackson, E. H. P.
2nd Lt. Porter. G. A. (attd.)

68th Battery.

Maj. Short, W. A.
Capt.
Lt. Brereton, C. L.
Lt. Loch, K. M. [l]
2nd Lt. Fraser-Tytler, P.S.
2nd Lt. Nugee, G. T. (attd.)

88th Battery.

Maj. England, R.
Capt. Walch, J. C.
Lt. Dawson, A.
Lt. Hayter, J. G.
2nd Lt. McNaughton, F. L.

XV.—Kildare (for Fermoy & Waterford).

Lt.-Colonel.
Stevens, C. F.
Adjutant.
Leech, C. J. F., *capt.*

41th Battery.

Maj. Henning, P. W. B.
Capt. Buckle, H.
Lt. Younger, J. E. T.
2nd Lt. Maxwell, P, MacM.
2nd Lt. Coghlan, W. H.
2nd Lt. Lyne, C. E. L. (attd.)

52nd Battery.

Maj. Nutt, A. C. R.
Capt. Barber-Starkey, W H. J.
Lt. Rome, R. C. [L]
2nd Lt. Broadhurst, G. H.
2nd Lt. Neve, R. B.

80th Battery.

Maj. Birley, R. A.
Capt. Bartholomew, A. W.
Lt. Hewson, A. G.
2nd Lt. Macleod, R.
2nd Lt. Mirrlees, W. H. B.
2nd Lt Scott - Watson, W. (*Attd.*)

XVI.—Nowshera.

Lt.-Colonel.
Quinton, F. W. D.
Adjutant.
Potter, K. M., *capt.*

89th Battery.

Maj. Furnivall, W.
Capt. Bayley. A. F.
Lt. Roney-Dougal, C. N.
Lt. Crewdson, W. T. O.
2nd Lt. Crowe, W. H. F.

90th Battery.

Maj. Stockley, A. U.
Capt. Eden, A. G.
Lt. Dolphin, V. O.
Lt. Fleet, A. L. E.
Lt. Fayle, D. B. W.

91st Battery.

Maj. Bowring, A. H.
Capt. Ingram, J. M.
Lt.
Lt. Armytage, H. W. H.
Lt. Beatson, C. E. S.

XVII.—Allahabad.

Lt.-Colonel.
Smith, E. P., g. [l]
Adjutant.
Moore, J. H., *lt.*

10th Battery, Barrackpore.

Maj. Winter, O. de L'E.
Capt. Ballard, J. A.
Lt. Darley, C. C.
Lt. Lodge, H. R.
2nd Lt. Hancocks, A. C.

26th Battery, Allahabad.

Maj. Pattisson, J. H.
Capt. Harvey, A. F. B., p.a.c.
Lt. Chance, A. F.
Lt. Crocker, J. C.
Lt. Woodhouse, A. J.

92nd Battery, Dinapore.

Maj. Stallard, S. F.
Capt. Williams, R. C.
Lt. Giffard, S.
2nd Lt. Peppé, W. T. H.
2nd Lt. Nicoll, D. A.

XVIII.—Lahore Cantonment.

Lt.-Colonel.
Ouseley, R. G., D.S.O., g., f.
Adjutant.
Cooper, G. S., *lt.*

59th Battery. Lahore Cantonment.

Maj. Ravenhill, C.
Capt. Hunt, C. O. C.
Lt. Heath, E. G.
Lt. Welsh, W. M. M. O'D.
Lt. Beresford, G. A.

93rd Battery. Ferozepore.

Maj. de Berry, P. P. E., e.
Capt. McGowan, T.
Lt. MacKenzie, F. J. B.
Lt. Eden, H. C. H.
2nd Lt. Harriott, W. G.

94th Battery. Lahore Cantonment.

Maj. Willis, E. H.
Capt. Bower, H. G. L.
Lt. Harford, H. H.
Lt. Park, A. St. J. L.
2nd Lt. Maxwell, A.

XIX.—St. Thomas' Mount (For Rawal Pindi).

Lt.-Colonel.
Macbean, W. A., p.s.c. [L]
Adjutant.
Rogers, W. L. Y., *capt.*

95th Battery. Kamptee (for Rawal Pindi).

Maj. Broadrick, F.B.D.
Capt. Bedwell, E. P. [l]
Lt. Manley, J. C. M.
Lt. Pyne, F. S.
Lt. Barkworth, J. S.

96th Battery. Belgaum (for Rawal Pindi).

Maj. Smyth, G. A.
Capt. Elam, H. W. T.
Lt.
Lt. Temple, G.
2nd Lt. Lutyens, E. G.

97th Battery. St. Thomas' Mount (for Rawal Pindi).

Maj. Archdale, T. M., D.S.O.
Capt. Denison, H.
Lt. Charles, A. A. M.
2nd Lt. Middleton, A. A.

XX.—Neemuch.

Lt.-Colonel.
Gray, P. E., g.
Adjutant.
White, R. W. [L] *capt.*

98th Battery. Nasirabad.

Maj. Stevenson, F. H., D.S.O.
Capt. Heelas, P. J. B.
Lt. Orde, J. R.
Lt. Crookshank, A. C.
2nd Lt. Drennan, J. S.

99th Battery. Neemuch.

Maj. Musgrave, A. D.
Capt. Anderson, E. O.
Lt.
Lt. Wilson, E. W. G.
Lt. Martin, E. T.

100th Battery. Neemuch.

Maj. Ramsden, R.E., g.
Capt. Fergusson, V. M.
Lt. Hall, E. C.
Lt. Rait Kerr, S. C.
Lt. Mason MacFarlane, F. N. [L]

XXI.—Hyderabad.

Lt.-Colonel.
Tennant, H. L., p.s.c., e.
Adjutant.
Stillwell, W, D., *capt.*

101st Battery. Hyderabad

Maj. Rainsford-Hannay, F.
Capt. Roe, J W.
Lt. Murray, G.
Lt. Scott, J.
Lt. Lee, S. S. [L]

102nd Battery. Hyderabad.

Maj. Allcard, H., D.S.O.
Capt. Wynter, H. W.
Lt. Scott, D.
Lt. Mullings, J. R.
Lt. Browning, L.

103rd Battery. Karachi.

Maj. Goldie, M. L., D.S.O., M.V.O.
Capt. Paul, C. T. S., g.
Lt. Ireland, K. G.
Lt. Van Straubenzee, A. B.
2nd Lt. Johnson, P.E.

XXII.—Roberts' Heights, Transvaal.

Lt.-Colonel.
Fasson, D, J. M., p.s.c. [L]
Adjutant.
Boddam-Whetham, S. A., *lt.*

104th Battery. Roberts' Heights.

Maj. Lake, H. A.
Capt. Willis, A., o.
Lt. Pinney, G. A.
Lt. Sumpter, G. [L]
Lt. MacNeece, J. D. G.

105th Battery. Potchefstroom.

Maj. Harpur, E. H.
Capt. Bucknill, L. M.
Lt. Williams, R. S. A.
2nd Lt. Barry, F.
2nd Lt. Bishop, C. B. J.

106th Battery. Roberts' Heights.

Maj. Bolster, G. p.s.c.
Capt. Phillips, C. C.
Lt. Chaytor, F. C.
Lt. Delahaye, J. V
2nd Lt. Dennis, M. E.

Royal Field Artillery.

XXIII.—Bulford
(for Bangalore).
Lt.-Colonel.
Butler, A. T.
Adjutant.
Forsyth, J. C., *lt.*

107th Battery.
Bulford
(for Bellary).
Maj. Hext, L. J.
Capt. Fisher, H. G.
Lt. Rhodes, B. F.
Lt. Ferguson, S. F. M.
2nd Lt. Wingate - Gray, W. S.
2nd Lt. Fardell, F.H.(attd.)

108th Battery.
Bulford
(for Bangalore).
Maj. Carey, H. E.
Capt. Allsup, E. S.
Lt. Anderson, E. L. B.
Lt. Smith, W. H. W.
Lt. Campbell, J. O.

109th Battery.
Bulford
(for Bangalore).
Maj. Metcalfe, S. F. *g.*
Capt. Harris A.G.R.C.[*l*]
Lt. Hill, D. [*l*].
2nd Lt. Loewe, L.
2nd Lt. Herbert, O. W. E.

XXIV.—Ballincollig.
Lt.-Colonel.
Lawrie, C. E., *D.S.O.*
Adjutant.
Boyd, H. A., *capt.*

110th Battery.
Maj. Griffith, R. H.
Capt. Johnston, R.G.M.
Lt. Purey Cust, F. B.
Lt. Harbord, K. B.
2nd Lt. Peskett, A. H.

111th Battery.
Maj. Walthall, E.C.W. D., *D.S.O.*
Capt. Jackson, H. S.
Lt. Studd, M. A.
Lt. Leach, R. S.
2nd Lt. Dunn, K. F. W.

112th Battery.
Maj. Browell, W. B., *g*
Capt. Mansfield H. M. L.
Lt. O'Brien, H. R. H.
2nd Lt. Lawrence, G. A. K., *f.c.*
2nd Lt. Dale, E. C. B.

XXV.—Deepcut,
Farnborough.
Lt.-Colonel.
Geddes, J. G.
Adjutant.
Blount, G. H. R., *capt.*

113th Battery.
Maj. Ellershaw, W.
Capt. Norton, W. H. *e.*
Lt. Fairbank H. N.
Lt. Hill, L. R.[L](attd.)
Lt. Battersby, C. F. P.
2nd Lt. McConnel, D. F.

114th Battery.
Maj.
Capt. Marshall, E. T.
2nd Lt. Du Buisson, T. G.
2nd Lt. Steevens, D. J.
2nd Lt. Gossage, E. L.

115th Battery.
Maj. Johnstone, J. H. W.
Capt. Sheppard, P., *D.S.O.*
Lt. Schreiber, E, C. A.
Lt. Franklyn, G. E. W.
2nd Lt. Gosset, W. B.
2nd Lt. Tucker, J. A. (attd.)
2nd Lt. Waller,E.G.(attd.)

XXVI.—Aldershot
(North Camp)
(for Shorncliffe.)
Lt.-Colonel.
Cunliffe-Owen, C.
Adjutant.
Allen, R. A. [*l*] *lt*,

116th Battery.
Maj. Nicholson, G. H. W.
Capt. Oliver, G. B. [*l*]
Lt. Gibbs, A. J.
Lt. Simson, R. F.
2nd Lt. Fluke, H.

117th Battery.
Maj. Packard, H. N.
Capt. Hawkins, C. F.
Lt. Hayes, A. T. H.
2nd Lt. Balfour, J. M.
2nd Lt. Heath-Caldwell, M. F.

118th Battery.
Maj. Bayly, A. R.
Capt. Sinclair, T. C.
Lt. Gardner, H.
Lt. Thornton, W.H.J.
2nd Lt. Malcolm, G. J., *f.c.*

XXVII.—Newbridge.
Lt.-Colonel.
Onslow, W. H.
Adjutant.
Ramsden, J. V., *capt.*

119th Battery.
Maj. Alexander, E. W.
Capt. Walford, J. C.
Lt. Pollard, G. B.[L]
Lt. Kaye, G. L.
2nd Lt. Davidson, F. H. N.
2nd Lt. Boothby, J. H. (Attd.)

120th Battery.
Maj. Holland, C. S.
Capt. Congreve, F. L.
2nd Lt. Foljambe, R. F. T.
2nd Lt. Lindsay, C. F. T.
2nd Lt. Bulteel, S. D.

121st Battery.
Maj. Ballard, C. N. B.
Capt. Masters, G.
Lt. Paige, T.
2nd Lt. Staveley, R.
2nd Lt. Chapman, H. E.

XXVIII.—Dundalk
(for Bordon).
Lt.-Colonel.
Cameron, E. C.
Adjutant.
Bowles, J. A., *lt.*

122nd Battery.
Maj. Sanders, G. H.
Capt. Jones, R. A.
Lt. Peel, D. R.
Lt. Lutyens, L. G.
2nd Lt. MacLeod, R. W.

123rd Battery.
Maj. Bayley, G. H. W.
Capt. Gillman, A. G.
Lt. Miller, R. B.
2nd Lt. Spencer, E. A.
2nd Lt. Antrobus, R. H.

124th Battery.
Maj. Kinsman, G. R. V., *g., f.c.*
Capt. Browning, C. H.
Lt. Studdert, R. H.
Lt. Rainy, A. R.
2nd Lt. Duff, G. L. A.
2nd Lt. Evans, M.P. (attd.)

XXIX.—Shorncliffe.
(for Dundalk).
Lt.-Colonel.
Stockdale, H. E.
Adjutant.
Stevens, C. M. H., *capt.*

125th Battery.
Maj. Lloyd, H. G.
Capt. Gray, W. K.
Lt. Smithson, R.
Lt. Reid, R. D. S.
2nd Lt. Devenish, G. H. (attd.)

126th Battery.
Maj. Wellesley, R. A. C.
Capt. Lanyon, O. M.
Lt. Granet, G. E. A. [*l*]
Lt. Playfair, Hon. L. G. H. L.
Lt. Ellis, H. S.

127th Battery.
Maj. Spedding, E. W.
Capt. Mascall, F. E.
2nd Lt. Wells-Cole, N. W.
2nd Lt. Pilliner, R. C. L.
2nd Lt. Jardine, C. A.

XXX. (Howr.)—
Bulford
(for Woolwich).
Lt.-Colonel.
Staveley, W. C., *g.*
Adjutant.
Sadler, H. K., *capt.*

128th (Howr.) Battery.
Maj. Strong, W.
Lt. Leech, A. G.
Lt. Perceval, C. P. W.
Lt. Mann, E. H.
Lt. Archer, R. A.
2nd Lt. McNair, J.K.(attd.)

129th (Howr.) Battery.
Maj. Ashworth, L. T.
Capt. Karslake, H., *D.S.O., p.s.c.*
Lt. Morrison, R. F.
Lt. Nixon, G. F.
2nd Lt. Cross, T. E. K.
2nd Lt. Boylan, E. T. A. G. (attd.)

130th (Howr.) Battery.
Maj. Stapylton, C. J. G.
Capt. Newland, A. E.
Lt. Wason, S. R.
2nd Lt. Johnstone, G. H.
2nd Lt. Hutchison, C. R. M.

XXXI.—
Sheffield.
Lt.-Colonel.
Fitzmaurice, R.
Adjutant.
Wickham, T. E. P., *D.S.O., capt.*

131st Battery.
Maj. Washington, C.F.G.
Capt. Miller, G.R.
Lt. Carfrae, C. T.
Lt. Bather, E. J.
2nd Lt. Mills, F. L. V.

132nd Battery.
Maj. Ward, H. D. O.
Capt. Geary, J. A.
Lt. Archdale, A. S.
Lt. Symons, H.
Lt. Taylor, V. A. H.

133rd Battery.
Maj.
Capt. Muirhead, R. [*l*]
Lt. Baxter, H. H.
Lt. Bateman, B. M. B.
Lt. Morton, D. J. F. [*l*]

XXXII.—Woolwich.
(for Bulford).
Lt.-Colonel.
MacCarthy, M. J.
Adjutant.
Crossman, F. L. M., *lt.*

27th Battery.
Maj. Vallentin, H. E.
Capt. Mortimore, C. A.
Lt. Armitage, E. L.
Lt. Lloyd, C. H.
2nd Lt. Turner, W. A. S.

134th Battery.
Maj. Ward, H., *g.*
Capt. Pulley, C.
Lt. Hutton, T. J.
2nd Lt. Straker, H. G.
2nd Lt. Rogers, W. F.

Royal Field Artillery.

135th Battery.
- Maj. Liveing, C. H., p.a.c.
- Capt. Hawksley, J. P. V
- 2nd Lt. Macleod, A. R.
- 2nd Lt. McKay, C. I.
- 2nd Lt. Rogers, C. H. (attd.)
- 3 Lond. Brig. R.F.A.

XXXIII.—Exeter
(for Bordon).

Lt.-Colonel.
Graham, L.
Adjutant.
Reeves, R. C., *capt.*

32nd Battery.
- Maj. Hinton, G. B.
- Capt. Woollcombe-Adams, C. E. G.
- Lt. Gardiner, R. H.
- Lt. Stewart-Cox, A.
- 2nd Lt. Purchas, E. C.

33rd Battery.
- Maj. Oldfield, L. C. L.
- Capt. Drought, G. T. A.
- Lt. Walshe, E. U.
- Lt. Holden, H. C. L.
- 2nd Lt. Neville, A. G.
- 2nd Lt. Rusher, A. E.

36th Battery.
- Maj. Cotton, A. S.
- Capt. Joll, H. H.
- Lt. Knyvett, C. L.
- Lt. Maitland-Dougall, W. E.
- Lt. Griffith, A. L. P.

XXXIV.—Aldershot.

Lt.-Colonel.
Sandilands, H. G., *g.*

Adjutant.
Boone, H. G., *capt.* [l]

22nd Battery.
- Maj. Wynter, H. T., f. [l]
- Capt. Bailey, F. G. G.
- Lt. Wissman, J. R. [l]
- 2nd Lt. Cameron, C. H.
- 2nd Lt. Copeland, R. R. (attd.)

50th Battery.
- Maj. Seagram, T. O.
- Capt. Sherlock, D. J. C. E.
- Lt. Clarke, J. E. L.
- Lt. Maples, J. C.
- Lt. Le Breton, F. H.
- 2nd Lt. Durand, A. A. M. (attd.)

70th Battery.
- Maj. Clarke, H. C. S.
- Capt. Heneage, A. P.
- Lt. Simpson, H. D.
- Lt. Robertson, E. J. M.
- 2nd Lt. Batten, J. F.

XXXV.—Woolwich.

Lt.-Colonel.
Lambert, E. P.

Adjutant.
Young, H. G., *capt.*

12th Battery.
- Maj. Christie, H. W. A.
- Capt. Colley, C. C.
- Lt. Lee, K. W.
- Lt. Williamson, H. N.
- Lt. Dennis, J. C. C.

25th Battery.
- Maj. Evans, W., D.S.O.
- Capt. Gover, C. R.
- Lt. Dresser, P. B.
- Lt. Graves, E. P., f.c.
- 2nd Lt. Kane, R. E.

58th Battery.
- Maj. Phipps, H. R.
- Capt. Warren, L. E.
- Lt. Clayton, E., p.s.c. [L]
- Lt. Noakes, S. M.
- Lt. Chisholm-Batten, J. de H.

XXXVI.—Ewshott, Farnham.

Lt.-Colonel.
Hail, E. F.
Adjutant.
Hulton, H. H. *capt.*

15th Battery.
- Maj. Barnes, C. C., g.
- Capt. Anstey, E. C., p.s.c.
- Lt. Inchbald, P. E.
- 2nd Lt. Walrond, V.
- 2nd Lt. Wright, N. J. R.

48th Battery.
- Maj. Stewart, C. G., D.S.O., p.s.c. [l]
- Capt. Powell, R. H.
- Lt. Macdonald, D. R.
- Lt. Pery-Knox-Gore, I. C.
- Lt. Campbell, C. W.

71st Battery.
- Maj. Scott, C. W., p.a.c.
- Capt. Cree, W. C. H.
- Lt. Farrant, M.
- 2nd Lt. Chaworth-Musters, A.
- 2nd Lt. Walsh, A. C. M.
- 2nd Lt. Hawker, T. M. (attd.)

XXXVII. (Howr.)—Woolwich (for Bulford).

Lt.-Colonel.
Battiscombe, C.
Adjutant.
Dodgson, R. C., *capt.*

31st (Howr.) Battery.
- Maj. Van Straubenzee, C. C.
- Capt. Hartland-Mahon, M. C. J.
- Lt. Butler-Stoney, R. B.
- Lt. Bates, H.
- 2nd Lt. Simpson, G. P.

35th (Howr.) Battery.
- Maj. Koebel, H. A., e. [L]
- Capt. Wallinger, E. A. [l]
- Lt. Phillips, M. A.
- Lt. Agnew, K. M.

55th (Howr.) Battery.
- Maj. Cartwright, G. N.
- Capt. Coiville, J. R., g
- Lt. Ferguson, P. H.
- 2nd Lt. Hess, A. G.
- 2nd Lt. Doske, S. H.
- 2nd Lt. Oldfield, E. W. (attd.)

XXXVIII.—Fermoy
(for Kildare).

Lt.-Colonel.
Fox, R. F., D.S.O.
Adjutant.
Rich, C. S., *capt.*

24th Battery. Fermoy.
- Maj. Arbuthnot, A. G.
- Capt. Walter, B.
- Lt. Thomson, J. N.
- 2nd Lt. Wingfield-Digby, K. E.
- 2nd Lt. Benett-Stanford, V.

34th Battery. Fermoy.
- Maj. Wainewright, A. R.
- Capt. Carlyon, T.
- Lt. Napier, A. F. S.
- 2nd Lt. Swinton, W.
- 2nd Lt. Empson, A.
- 2nd Lt. Morse, G. S. (Attd.)

72nd Battery. Waterford.
- Maj. Tighe, F. A.
- Capt. Staveley, A. G.
- Lt. Henderson, C. E. P.
- Lt. Cory, C. N.
- 2nd Lt. Peck, C. H.

XXXIX.—Bordon
(for Aldershot).

Lt.-Colonel.
Carey, G. G. S.
Adjutant.
Nornabell, H. M., *capt.*

46th Battery.
- Maj. Baillie, G.
- Capt. Addison, A. M.
- Lt. Fisher, C. L.
- Lt. Smeed, C. W.
- 2nd Lt. Paul, I. I. C.
- 2nd Lt. Skipwith, G. A.

51st Battery.
- Maj. Coates, R. C., D.S.O.
- Capt. West, F. G.
- Lt. Shaw, G. D. A.
- Lt. O'Brien, A. U. M.
- 2nd Lt. Graham, F.

54th Battery.
- Maj. Peel, E. J. R.
- Capt. Robinson, L. J. W., o.
- Lt. Mitchell, J. L. [L] (attd.)
- Lt. Osmaston, U. E.
- Lt. Blewitt, R.
- Lt. Cottrell, A. F. B.

XL.—Bulford.

Lt.-Colonel.
Elkington, R. J. G., g.
Adjutant.
Reid, W. R., *capt.*

6th Battery.
- Maj. Brooke, E. W. S. [l]
- Capt. Anstruther, R. A.
- Lt. Archibald, S. C. M.
- 2nd Lt. Bryans, H. M.
- 2nd Lt. Bligh, J. F.

23rd Battery.
- Maj. Ingham, C. St. M.
- Capt. Lyster, P. G.
- 2nd Lt. Macnair, J. L. P.
- 2nd Lt. Sassoon, F.
- 2nd Lt. Harman, L. A.
- 2nd Lt. Thomson, V. H. (attd.)

49th Battery.
- Maj. Lyon, F., D.S.O., p.s.c. [L]
- Capt. Ellington, E. L., p.s.c.
- Lt. Morton, A. H.
- Lt. Browne, H. S.
- 2nd Lt. Owen, N. M.

XLI.—Bordon
(for Exeter).

Lt.-Colonel.
Lushington, S., C.M.G. [l]
Adjutant.
Brousson, F., *capt.*

9th Battery.
- Maj. Wylde, R. D.
- Capt. Rochfort-Boyd, H. C. [L]
- Lt. Rose, D. D.
- Lt. Huttenbach, N. H.
- 2nd Lt. Price Williams, H.

16th Battery.
- Maj. Lewin, H. F. E.
- Capt. Carrington, C. R. B.
- Lt. Anne, H. O. C.
- Lt. Atkinson, S.
- 2nd Lt. Messervy, G.

17th Battery.
- Maj. Evans, C., p.s.c.
- Capt. Mowbray, J. L., p.s.c.
- Lt. Stephenson, D. C.
- Lt. Lund, O. M.
- 2nd Lt. Glynn, R. T. W.
- 2nd Lt. Farmer, J. D. (attd.)

| 610 | 611 | 612 | 613 |

Royal Field Artillery.

XLII.—Bulford.
Lt.-Colonel.
— Geddes, G. H.

Adjutant.
Riddell, J. B., capt., o.

29th Battery.
Maj. Bethell, A. B.
Capt. Preeston, N. P. R.
Lt. Allen, R. W.
Lt. Huish, M. W.
2nd Lt. Harman, J. B.
2nd Lt. Perceval, R. R. M. (attd.)

41st Battery.
Maj. Bruce, T.
Capt. Belgrave, J. D., p.s.c.
Lt. McMaster, H.
2nd Lt. Towell, R. H.
2nd Lt. Schreiber, O. R.
2nd Lt. Trevenen, S. V.

45th Battery.
Maj. Gray, N. McN.
Maj. Belcher, H. T., D.S.O., g. (attd.)
Capt Nevill, H. L., D.S.O., p.s.c., g.
Lt. Eliott, R H.
2nd Lt. English, M. W.
2nd Lt. Myburgu, P. S.

XLIII. (Howr.)—
Deepcut, Farnborough.
Lt.-Colonel.
Sharp, F. L.

Adjutant.
Eddis, L. A., capt., g.

30th (Howr.) Battery.
Maj. Wheeler, F L.
Capt. Longstaff, K.
Lt. Woods, E. A.
Lt. Cowan, W. McC.C.
Lt. Lindsay, G. W. T
2nd Lt. Watson, W. D. (attd.)

40th (Howr.) Battery.
Maj.
Capt. Chambers, W. T.
Lt. Marshall. C. F. K.
Lt. Handford, D. J. [l]
2nd Lt. Freer, N. W.

57th (Howr.) Battery.
Maj. Deshon, F G. T., g.
Capt. Robinson, F. W
Lt. Rait Kerr, W. C.
Lt. Leventhorpe, G. S.
Lt. Duncan, W. E.

XLIV.—(Howr.) Brighton.
Lt.-Colonel.
Arbuthnot, D.

Adjutant.
Nevile, G. C., capt.

47th (Howr.) Battery.
Maj. Edwards, A. C.
Capt. Crozier, B. B
Lt. Cherry, R. G.
Lt. Robertson, H. M. M.
Lt. Caldwell, K. F. T.

56th (Howr.) Battery.
Maj. Barker, F. E. L.
Capt. Blathwayt, G. W.
Lt. Harvey, H. le F. F.
2nd Lt. Tidmarsh, G. D.
2nd Lt. Barkworth, H. E.
2nd Lt. Gatehouse, R. P. (attd.)

60th (Howr.) Battery.
Maj. Mackey, H. J. A., M.V.O.
Capt. Gregson, G. K., o.
Lt. Willcocks, H. F.
Lt. Knight, J. P.
2nd Lt. Stillman, R. C. B.

XLV.—Leeds.
Lt.-Colonel.
Goff, A. H. S

Adjutant.
Main, A. K., capt.

1st Battery.
Maj. Head, A. E. M.
Capt. Vernon, L. D.
Lt. Stopford, G. B., f.c.r.
Lt. Ardagh, R. W.
Lt. Stanford, J. [l]

3rd Battery.
Maj. Cape, G.A.S., p.s.c.
Capt. Forsyth, J. A. C.
Lt. Wye, F. P.
2nd Lt. Harvey, G. F.

5th Battery.
Maj. Thackeray, C.B., e.
Capt. Meyricke, R. J. C.
Lt. Weldon, C.
Lt. Dudding, H. N. N.
2nd Lt. Ritchie, H. G.

I. Reserve.— Newcastle-on-Tyne.
Lt.-Colonel.
Heath, F. W.

Adjutant.
Longmore, C. M., lt.

136th Battery.
Maj. Parry, C. F. P.
Capt. Adams, R. J.
Lt. Dunbar, A. J.
Lt. Roney Dougal, A. R.

137th Battery.
Maj. Hudson, A. R. [l]
Capt. Harrisson, R. D.
Lt. Wurtele, H. A. S.
Lt. Landon, G. de L. [L]

II. Reserve.—Preston.
Lt.-Colonel.
Ravenhill, F. T.

Adjutant.
Cornes, H. capt., g.

138th Battery.
Maj. Clark, W. E
Capt. Haining, R. H., e.
Lt. Geldard, C.
Lt. Vining, P. L.
2nd Lt. Cleland, J. R.

139th Battery.
Maj.
Capt. Thornton, G. St. L.
Lt. Lee-Warner, H. G.
Lt. Welch, W. G. F.
Lt. Fisher, D. R. D.

III. Reserve—Hilsea.
Lt.-Colonel.
Ford, C. H.

Adjutant.
Rendel, R. M. lt.

140th Battery.
Maj. Gordon, G. H., g.
Capt. Atchison, H. W.
Lt. Walsh, R. H.
Lt. Eeles, C. A.
Lt. Benham, F. B.

141st Battery.
Maj. Logan, F. D., p.s.c.
Capt. Trench, D. le P.
Lt. Wallace, C. H.
Lt. Brownlow, C.A.L.
Lt. Mackie, W. B.

IV. Reserve.— Woolwich.
Lt.-Colonel.
Biddulph, H.

Adjutant.
Grieve, F. C. L., capt.

142nd Battery.
Maj. FitzGerald, M. J. F.
Capt. Browne, E. W.
Lt. Rashleigh, R. N.
Lt. Cadell, C. A. E.
Lt. Danby, W. A.

143rd Battery.
Maj.
Capt. Maturin, R. G., D.S.O.
Lt. Duggan, F. J.
Lt. Butler, W. V. H.
Lt. Richards, F. H.

V. Reserve.—Athlone.
Lt.-Colonel.
England, E. P.

Adjutant.
Gregory, G. M. A., capt.

144th Battery.
Maj. Elliot, E. H. H.
Capt. Tweedie, D. K.
Lt. Tenison, W. P. C.
2nd Lt. Nottidge, C.

145th Battery.
Maj. Molony, T. C. W., D.S.O., p.s.c.
Capt. Thorburn, J. F. P.
Lt. Coker, L. A.
Lt. Lister, C. M.
2nd Lt. Fletcher, W. G.

VI. Reserve.— Glasgow.
Lt.-Colonel.
Cardew, G. A.

Adjutant.
Dundas, J. C., g., capt.

146th Battery.
Maj. Stewart, D. B.
Capt. Bower, C. E. S.
Lt. Shaw, R. de V.
Lt. Green, G. A. L.
Lt. Tayleur, C. L. O.

147th Battery.
Maj. Smith-Rewse, H. B., p.s.c. [L]
Capt. Shaw-Stewart, B.H.
Lt. Tuke, C. W. R.
Lt. Barratt, A. S., f.c.
Lt. Mostyn, J. C. M.

Royal Field Artillery.

AMMUNITION COLUMNS, ROYAL FIELD ARTILLERY, INDIA.

No. 1, Nowshera.

Capt. Gardner-Waterman, A.
Lt. Kempe, H. F. C.
Lt. Watson, V. C.
Lt.(D.O.)Bell, W. J.

No. 2, Rawal Pindi.

Capt. Farran, G. F.
Lt. Langford, C. C.
Lt. Forsyth, A. F. J.
Lt.(D.O.)Bailey, H.

No. 3, Lahore. Cantonment.

Capt. Willis, S. G. R. [l]
Lt. Digby, A. K.
Lt. Field, L.
Lt.(D.O.)Walker, T. H.

No. 4, Hyderabad.

Capt. Shewell, E. F.
Lt. Huleatt, F. H.
Lt. Gordon, C. C. [l]
Lt.(D.O.)Slade, R.

No. 5, Deesa.

Capt. Stebbing, N. A.
Lt. Morgan, F. H. L.
Lt. Ryan, C. E.
Lt.(D.O.)Syrett, F. G.

No. 6, Kirkee.

Capt. Corbould-Warren, E.
Lt. Peebles, R. E.
Lt. Robinson, A.
Lt.(D.O.)Bolton, F.

No. 7, Meerut.

Capt. Cullerne, C. P.
Lt. Benson, G. R.
Lt. Freer, R. C.
Lt.(D.O.)Martin, R.

No. 8, Fyzabad.

Capt. Campbell, N. St. C.
Lt. Cotter, R. K.
Lt.
Lt.(D.O.)Kershaw, C. H.

No. 9, Secunderabad.

Capt. Crofton, M. R H.
Lt. Holland, C. [l]
Lt. Lambert, A. F.
Lt.(D.O.)Cockaday,W.G.C.

No. 10, Bangalore.

Capt. Parrington, J. W., g.
Lt. Akerman, W. P. J.
Lt. Gordon, H. G.
Lt.(D.O.)Davies, T. W. E.

No. 11, Jubbulpore.

Capt. Waycott, E. W.
Lt. Green, W. W.
Lt. McMaster, W.
Lt.(D.O.)Farrow, A. E.

No. 12, Jhansi (Howr.)

Capt. Kirkland, T.
Lt. Strickland, G. T.
Lt.
Lt.(D.O.)Harris, C.

DEPÔTS.

No. 1 Depôt,
(Commanded by O.C. I. Reserve Brig.)

Newcastle-on-Tyne.

Capt. White, A. K. G.
Qr.-Mr.Webb, W. T., *hon. lt.*

No. 2 Depôt,
(Commanded by O.C. II. Reserve Brig.)

Preston.

Capt. Stewart, D.
Qr.-Mr. Williams, E. E., *hon. lt.*

No. 3 Depôt,
(Commanded by O.C. III. Reserve Brig.)

Hilsea (Cosham Railway Station).

Capt. Thellusson, Hon. H. E.
Qr.-Mr.Mitchell, A., *hon. lt.*

No. 4 Depôt,
(Commanded by O.C. IV. Reserve Brig.)

Woolwich.

Capt. Gregory, K. H.
Capt. Bridgeman, Hon. H. G. O. (attd.)
Lt.(D.O.)Owen, E.
Qr.-Mr.Keough, F., *hon.*

No. 5 Depôt,
(Commanded by O.C. V. Reserve Brig.)
Athlone,
Capt. Curling, W. G.
Lt.(D.O.)Allen, J. T.
Qr.-Mr.Nightingale, T. G. H. *hon. lt.*

No. 6 Depôt,
(Commanded by O.C. VI. Reserve Brig.)
Glasgow.
Capt. Hill, C. R.
Lt.(D.O.) Follett, J. E. G.
Qr.-Mr. McDonald, J. P., *hon. capt.*

RIDING-MASTERS—INDIA & S. AFRICA.

Naylor, H. W., *hon. capt.* — Lucknow.
Lynch, J., *hon. lt.* — Bangalore.
Fleming, F., *hon. maj.* — Jhansi.
Wark, R. G., *hon. lt.* — Rawal Pindi.
Wright, A. E., *hon. lt.* — Kirkee.

RIDING MASTERS—HOME.

Taylor, A., *hon. capt.* — Newcastle.
Clarke, T., *hon. maj.* — Aldershot.
Sims, T. A., *hon. capt.* — Bulford.
Caddington, C. E., *hon. capt.* — Ipswich.
Hagan, J., *hon. capt.* — Kildare.

QUARTER MASTERS.

Robinson, W. C., *hon. lt.* — Aldershot.
Griffin, A. J., *hon. lt.* — Bulford.

H

ROYAL GARRISON ARTILLERY.

MOUNTAIN DIVISION

Batteries.

Lt.-Colonels.		Adjutants.	
Dowell, G. C., *bt. col.*	*Jutogh.*	Castle, R. W., *capt.*	*Quetta.*
Cook, H. R. [L] *f.c.r.*	*Quetta.*	Colbeck, B. B., *capt.*	*Jutogh.*
Stanton, F. W. S., *D.S.O.*	*Murree Hills.*	Haig, A. G., *capt.*	*Murree Hills.*

No. 1 Batt.,

Khaira Gali.

Maj.	Wyatt, F. O., *M.V.O.*
Capt.	Carr, H. G.
Lt.	Hippisley, A.
Lt.	Newton, P. I.
Lt.	Colson, C.

No. 2 Batt.,

Jutogh.

Maj.	Molesworth, H. E.
Capt.	Leah, T. C.
Capt.	Mascall, M. E.
Lt.	Kirkpatrick, C. D.
Lt.	Price, J.

No. 3 Batt.,
Quetta.

Maj.	Easton, F. A.
Capt.	Hassells-Yates, G. A.
Lt.	Wright, S. H.
Lt.	Scovil, F. H.
Lt.	Fooks, H. E.

No. 4 Batt.,
Quetta.

Maj.	Bullen, S. D.
Capt.	Reeves, H. C., *g.*
Lt.	Daly, D.
Lt.	Jarrett, A. F. V.
Lt.	Low, G. S.

No. 5 Batt.,
Jutogh.
(for Rawal Pindi).

Maj.	Lowis, P. S.
Capt.	Preston, P. H. H., *g.*
Lt.	Seys, R. C. [L]
Lt.	Healing, N. C.
Lt.	Lewis, W. H.

No. 6 Batt.,

Rawal Pindi.

Maj.	Corrie, G. G. W.
Capt.	Barker, C. H.
Lt.	Clarke, R. H.
Lt.	Wordsworth, R. G.
Lt.	Layard, C. P. J.

No. 7 Batt.,

Cairo.

Maj.	Knapp, K. K.
Capt.	Hall, B. A. M.
Lt.	Armstrong, W. F.
Lt.	Rouquette, H.R.H.

No. 8 Batt.,

Quetta.

(for Rawal Pindi).

Maj.	Gray, C. L. R.
Capt.	MacClellan, G. P.
Lt.	Montague, J. E. F.
Lt.	Veitch, A.
Lt.	Pargiter, R. B.

No. 9 Batt.,

Kalabagh

(for Quetta).

Maj.	Mackintosh, J.B., *g.*
Capt.	Fowler, E. G.
Capt.	Carter, E. G. W.
Capt.	Salvin, H. C. J.
Capt.	Medill, P. M.

Extra Captain.

Bennett, W. P.—*Murree Hills.*

ROYAL GARRISON ARTILLERY.

HOME.

Lt.-Col.	Tancred, T. A.	} 1st Heavy Brig., Fareham (26, 35 & 108 Batts.)
Adjt.	Matthews, A. M., *capt.*	
Lt.-Col.	Hudson, T. R. C., *p.s.c.* [L]	} 2nd Heavy Brig., Woolwich (24, 31 & 48 Batts.)
Adjt.	Graham, C. A. L., *capt.*	
Lt.-Col.	Smeaton, C. O.	} Siege Art. Brig., Plymouth (39 & 107 Cos.)
Adjt.	Allen, H., *o., capt.*	
Lt.-Col.	Lane, H. E. B.	} Sheerness (2,18,19&22Cos.)
Adjt.	Cream, R. T. C., *lt.*	
Dist. Offr.	Rowley, W. H., *maj.*	
Qr.-Mr.	Graham, D., *hon. lt.*	
Dist. Offr.	Cope, E. R., *lt.*	Tilbury
Lt.-Col.	Perkins, A. E. J.	} Shoeburyness (14 Co.)
Armt. Major	Phillipps, C., *g., maj.*	
Qr.-Mr.	Skinner, J. H., *hon. lt.*	
Lt.-Col.	Buckle, C. R., *D.S.O., local Col.*	} Harwich (13 Co.)
Dist. Offr.	Tompkins, J. W., *lt.*	
Lt.-Col.	Roberts, M.B., *g.* [L]	
Armt.Major	Fife, R.B., *maj.*	
Armt. Offr.		} Dover (40 & 46 Cos.)
Adjt.	Cunningham, T., *o., e., capt.*	
Dist. Offr.	Newton, J. T., *maj.*	
Dist. Offr.	Chapman, J. T., *maj.*	Newhaven
Dist. Offr.	Windrum, F., *capt.*	Woolwich
Dist. Offr.	Cole, R., *maj.*	Tower, London
Lt.-Col.	Eyre, M. S., *local col.*	} Londonderry (15 Co.)
Dist. Offr.	Towers, W. H., *lt.*	
Lt.-Col.	Perceval, C. J., *D.S.O., p.s.c.* [L]	} Queenstown Harbour (10,43 & 49 Cos.)
Adjt.	Smith, H.W. T., *capt.*	
Qr.-Mr.	Brown, R. P., *hon. capt.*	
Dist. Offr.	Wales, A. H., *lt.*	Berehaven
Lt.-Col.	Marsh, H. E., *g.*	} Tynemouth (12 & 47 Cos.)
Dist.-Offr.	Dovey, F. W., *lt*	
Armt. Offrs.	Bland-Hunt, E. S. deV., *g., maj.*	
	Suther, P., *g., maj.*	
	Drake-Brockman, W. H. G., *lt.* [l]	
Dist. Offr.	Fulcher, G. E. T., *lt.*	Redcar
Lt.-Col.		} Leith Fort (21 Co.)
Adjt.	Nicholson, St. J. R., *g., lt*	
Dist. Offr.	Dale, R. W., *capt.*	
Dist. Offr.	Anderson, F.C., *capt.*	Aberdeen
Lt.-Col.	Robinson, W. H.	} Gourock
Dist. Offr.	Austin. T., *capt.*	
Lt.-Col.	Logan, D. F. H.	} Outer Defences, Portsmouth (29 & 67 Cos.)
Adjt.	Sidebottom, A. L., *lt.*	
Lt.-Col.	Kaye, R. A.	} Inner Defences, Portsmouth (37 & 42 Cos.)
Adjt.	Griffith, G. M., *capt., r.o.r.*	
Armt. Offr.	Inglis, C. E., *capt.*	} Portsmouth
Dist. Offr.	Pawson, W., *lt.*	
Dist. Offr.	Rycroft, F., *lt.*	
Qr.-Mr.	Ramsay, W. J., *hon. lt.*	
Lt.-Col.	Currie, A. C., *g.* (*local col.*)	} Weymouth (16,28 & 30 Cos.)
Adjt.	Erskine-Murray, A. *capt.*	
Dist. Offr.	Munro, T., *maj.*	
Lt.-Col.	Clark, C. W., *g.*	} Sandown (32 & 34 Cos.)
Adjt.	Gay, C. H., *lt.*	
Lt.-Col.	Hoblyn, E. F.	} Golden Hill (11 & 33 Cos.)
Adjt.	Price, O. L., *capt.* [l]	
Lt.-Col.	Wood, T. B., *p.s.c.* [l]	} Eastern Section, Plymouth (33 & 45 Cos.)
Adjt.	Rashleigh, P., *capt.*	
Lt.-Col.	Lyle, G. S. B., *g.*	} Western Section, Plymouth (38 & 41 Cos.)
Adjt.	Budgen, W. N., *capt.*	
Armt. Offr.	Drought, T. A. W., *capt.*	} Plymouth
Armt. Offr.	Smythe, A. G. C., *g., capt.*	
Dist. Offr.	McKenzie, D. A., *capt.*	
Dist. Offr.	Coyne, R., *lt.*	
Dist. Offr.	Silcott, H. W., *lt.*	
Lt.-Col.	Marshall, T. E.	} Falmouth
Dist. Offr.	O'Sullivan, P., *capt.*	
Lt.-Col.	Carleton, M. L.	} Pembroke Dock & 57 Cos.)
Adjt.	Aitken, N. W., *lt.*	
Dist. Offr.	Moore, W. J., *lt.*	
Lt.-Col.	East, L. W. P., *D.S.O., p.s.c.* [l]	} Cardiff
Dist. Offr.	Clarke, R., *maj.*	
Armt. Offr.		} Seaforth
Dist. Offr.	Allen, R. H., *capt.*	
Armt. Major	Hamilton, P. D., *g., maj.*	Guernsey
Dist. Offr.	Borrett, W. J., *lt.*	Alderney

H 2

Royal Garrison Artillery.

ABROAD.

Lt.-Col.	Iles, H. W., *g*.	
Adjt.	Garwood, H. P., *capt*.	Hong Kong
Armt.Offr.	Brewster, R. E. B. (*D.O.*), *lt*.	(83,87 & 88 Cos.)

Lt.-Col.	Stevenson, R. C.	
Adjt.	Kemble, H. M., *capt*.	Ceylon
Armt. Offr.		(93 Co.)

Lt.-Col.	Saltren-Willett, A. J.	
Adjt.	Gunn, H. B. L. G., *g*., *capt*.	Bermuda
Armt.Offrs	Nicolls, O. C. C., *capt*. Matterson, L. G.,*capt*. de Cetto, V.B.A.,*capt*, Bingham, W., *lt*.	(3 & 95 Cos.)

Lt.-Col.	Cooper, E. S.,*p.a.c*., *g*.	
Adjt.	Tuke, G. F. S., *capt*.	South Africa
Dist. Offr.	Hunter, J., *capt*.	(84 & 97 Cos.)
Armt. Offr.	Gatt, C. A., *capt*.	

Lt.-Col.	Jenour, A. S., *g*.	Mauritius
Adjt.	Cruickshank, P. H., *g*., *capt*.	(56 Co.)

Lt.-Col.	Brownlow, C. W.	
Adjt.	Heath, C. J., *lt*.	Singapore
Armt. Offr.	Scott, E, B., *g*., *maj*.	(78 & 80 Cos.)
Armt. Offr.	Izard, F. V., *lt*.	

Lt.-Col.	Merriman, R. G.,*D.S.O.*	
Adjt.	Hutchison, K. D., *capt*.	Sierra Leone
Dist. Offr.	Bailey, W. E., *lt*.	(50 Co.)

Armt.Offrs	Smyth, F. J. N., *capt*. Moore, W. H., *D.S.O.*, *p.s.c.* [*l*] *capt*. Phillips,A.H.D., *lt*.	Jamaica (66 Co.)

Lt.-Col.	Eteson, H. C. W., *g*.	N. Section, Gibraltar
Adjt.	Ryan, F. T., *lt*.	(6,9,54& 55 Cos.)

Lt.-Col.	Tyler, A. M., *p.a.c*., *g*.	S. Section, Gibraltar
Adjt.	Cummins, E. J., *g*., *capt*.	(4, 7 & 8 Cos.)

Armt.Offrs	Thrupp, F. M., *g*., *f*., *maj*. Nicholl, D. Fitz R., *D.S.O.*, *g*., *maj*. Turner, C. H., *capt*., *D.O.* Redgate, J., *lt*., *D.O.* Harris, J., *lt*., *D.O.* Broadhurst, O., *lt*., *D.O.* Everton, W. T. A., *lt*., *D.O.* Firebrace, R. C. W. G., *lt*. [L] Easton,W.T.J.,*lt. D.O*	Gibraltar
Qr.-Mr.	Smith, D. W., *hon lt*.	
Armt. Off.	Daubuz, R.F.,*g*.,*capt*.	

Lt.-Col.	Jackson, L. D., .	Eastern Dist., Malta
Adjt.	Foll, H. H., *capt*.	(1 & 102 Cos.)

Lt.-Col.	Bateman, B. M.	Western Dist., Malta
Adjt.	Andrewes,F.E.,*capt*., *g*.	(5, 96, 99 & 100 Cos.)

Lt.-Col.	Norris, A. G., *g*., *f*.	Central Dist., Malta
Adjt.	Hay,H,G,Fitz G.,*g*., *apt*.	(63 & 85 Cos.)

Armt.Offrs.	Latham, C. R., *maj*. (*D.O.*) Wells, J. *capt.* (*D.O.*) Adams, L. C., *p.a.c.*, *capt*. Leach, J., *lt* (*D.O.*) Stevens,E J.,*lt*.(*D.O.*) Warton, H. C., *lt*. (*D.O.*) Swayne,O.R., *D.S.O.*, *capt*. Poole, H. R., *g*.,*capt*. Robertson, W. C., *g*., *capt*. Disney, B, T., *lt*. Hughes-Hallett, W. E., *lt*. Pratt, T.W.R.,*2nd lt*. Fuge, W. G.,*2nd lt*. Shaw, S., *2nd lt*.	Malta
Qr.-Mr.	Yates, J. C., *hon. lt*.	
Dist. Offr.	Langston, D., *capt*.	

Lt.-Col.	Warren, W. L.	
Adjt.	Gunter, A. C., *capt*.	Aden
I.G.	Hope, J., U., *g*. *capt*.	(61, 70 & 76 Cos.)
A.-I. G.	Elliott, B. H., *g*., *lt*.	

Lt.-Col.	Napier, W. J., *g*.	Rurki
Adjt	Way, J., *capt*.	(59 Co.)

Lt.-Col.	Vincent, H. O., *g*.	Bombay
Adjt.	Standbridge, W. J., *capt*.	(52, 77, 79 & 85 Cos.)
I.G.	Grinlinton, J. L., *g*., *cupt*.	

Lt.-Col.	Pullen, A. F, [L], *g*.	Rangoon
Adjt. & I.G.	Beasley, J. H. M., *g*., *capt*.	(64 & 75 Cos.)

Lt.-Col.	Hardy, W. K.	Heavy Arty. Peshawar

Lt.-Col.	Davidson, F. M., *g*.	Karachi
Adjt. & I.G.	Turner, W. M. Fitz H., *g*., *capt*	(69 Co.)

Lt.-Col.	Maunsell, F. G. [L]	Nowgong

ROYAL GARRISON ARTILLERY.

87 Companies.
12 Heavy Batteries.
4 Depôts.

Order of Precedence of Companies and Batteries.

1.	46 Co.	21.	14 Co.	41.	23 Co.	61.	64 Co.	81.	55 Co.
2.	41 ,,	22.	99 ,,	42.	34 ,,	62.	88 ,,	82.	56 ,,
3.	32 ,,	23.	28 ,,	43.	29 ,,	63.	22 ,,	83.	69 ,,
4.	86 Batt.	24.	42 ,,	44.	79 ,,	64.	4 ,,	84.	75 ,,
5.	84 Co.	25.	93 ,,	45.	44 ,,	65.	5 ,,	85.	61 ,,
6.	62 ,,	26.	40 ,,	46.	1 ,,	66.	12 ,,	86.	52 ,,
7.	7 ,,	27.	35 Batt.	47.	8 ,,	67.	13 ,,	87.	50 ,,
8.	100 ,,	28.	39 Co.	48.	21 ,,	68.	20 ,,	88.	60 ,,
9.	37 ,,	29.	45 ,,	49.	11 ,,	69.	15 ,,	89.	9 ,,
10.	70 ,,	30.	2 ,,	50.	63 ,,	70.	6 ,,	90.	10 ,,
11.	54 ,,	31.	48 Batt.	51.	59 ,,	71.	82 ,,	91.	16 ,,
12.	101 ,,	32.	102 Co.	52.	74 ,,	72.	87 ,,	92.	17 ,,
13.	66 ,,	33.	3 ,,	53.	67 ,,	73.	96 ,,	93.	18 ,,
14.	95 ,,	34.	94 ,,	54.	80 ,,	74.	47 ,,	94.	19 ,,
15.	65 ,,	35.	97 ,,	55.	43 ,,	75.	38 ,,	95.	24 Batt.
16.	71 Batt.	36.	91 Batt.	56.	73 ,,	76.	36 ,,	96.	26 ,,
17.	85 Co.	37.	57 Co.	57.	49 ,,	77.	83 ,,	97.	104 ,,
18.	90 Batt.	38.	68 ,,	58.	76 ,,	78.	107 ,,	98.	108 ,,
19.	72 ,,	39.	78 ,,	59.	81 ,,	79.	30 ,,		
20.	51 Co.	40.	77 ,,	60.	33 ,,	80.	31 Batt.		

| 627 | 628 | 629 | 630 |

Royal Garrison Artillery.

No. 1 Company.
(Formed in 1846.)

Malta.

Maj. Curme, W. C., *g.*
Capt. Jacob, A. L. B., *g.*
Lt. Bristow, L. G.
Lt. O'Leary, B. J. [L]
Lt. Eberli, F. H., *f.c.*

No. 2 Company.
(Formed in 1795.)

Sheerness.

Maj. Owen, C. H. W.
Capt. Chamier, H. A. G.
Capt. Douglas-Jones, E. D.
Lt. Curry, W. L.
2nd Lt. Borradaile, C. H. A.

No. 3 Company.
(Formed in 1800.)

Bermuda.

Maj. Moore, St. L. M., *g.*
Capt. Redfern, G. H.
Capt. Duncan, W. B.
Lt. Rowe, W. B.
Lt. Ritter, J. A.

No. 4 Company.
(Formed in 1859.)

Gibraltar.

Maj. Parker, R. H., *g.*
Capt. Eliot, N., *p.a.c.*
Lt. Curling, R. R.
Lt.
2nd Lt. Upson, H. C.

No. 5 Company.
(Formed in 1859.)

Malta.

Maj. de Winton, R. S.
Capt. Daubeny, G. B.
Lt. Brown, H. D. L.
Lt. Banks, C. D'A. S.
Lt. Wildey, A. W. G.

No. 6 Company.
(Formed in 1861.)

Gibraltar.

Maj. Armitage, W. T., *g.*
Capt. Harvey. W. K., *o.,g.*
  bt. lt.-col.
Lt. Montague, S. F., *p.a.c.*
Lt. Fishe, N. H. [l]
Lt. Thomas, A. C.

No. 7 Company.
(Formed in 1757.)

Gibraltar.

Maj. Bland, W. St.C., *g.*,
  bt. lt.-col.
Capt. Robinson, J. A. P.
Lt. Richard, L. F.
2nd Lt. Murphy, J. M.

No. 8 Company.
(Formed in 1846)

Gibraltar.

Maj. Ellershaw, A.
Capt. Sewell, H. E., *g.*
Lt. Pfeil, F. W.
2nd Lt. Cumming, O.S.

No. 9 Company.
(Formed in 1897.)

Gibraltar.

Maj. Cuming, A. T., *g.* [L]
Capt. Browne, B. S. [L]
Lt. Richardson, G. P.

No. 10 Company.
(Formed in 1897.)

Queenstown Harbour.

Maj. Cadell, H. E.
Capt. Disney-Roebuck, A. W., *g.*
Lt. Ryan, C. J.
2nd Lt. Chadwick, R. M.
2nd Lt. Spong, C. A. T.

No. 11 Company.
(Formed in 1846.)

Golden Hill.

Maj. Arthy, W.
Capt. McGhee, A. S. P., *o.*
2nd Lt. Pemberton, A. L.
2nd Lt. Formilli, G. C.
2nd Lt. Hilton, R.
2nd Lt. Leslie, W. A. A.
  (attd.)

No. 12 Company.
(Formed in 1860.)

Tynemouth

Maj. Webb, A. H., *g.*
Capt. Rowley, C. P.
Lt. Leslie A. J., R.M.
2nd Lt. Cawson, L. D. (attd.)

No. 13 Company.
(Formed in 1860.)

Landguard Fort.

Maj. Jones, W. H.
Capt. Carson, R.
2nd Lt. Goodman, E. W.
2nd Lt. Morris, E. B.
2nd Lt. Probert, G. O. C.
  (attd.)

No. 14 Company.
(Formed in 1771.)

Shoeburyness.

Maj. Fowler, W. J., *g.*
Capt. Taylor, L. R. E. W.
Capt. Downing, W. C.
2nd Lt. Kilner, H. R.
Lt. Harrison, E. G. W. W.

No. 15 Company.
(Formed in 1860.)

Londonderry.

Maj. Tyrrell, G. E. [L]
Capt. Hare, E. F.
Lt. Savory, R. H.
2nd Lt. Michaells, C. D. A.

No. 16 Company.
(Formed in 1898.)

Weymouth.

Maj. Rumbold, W. E., *g.*
Capt. Waring, J.
Capt. King, J. F., *o.*
Lt. Bill, J. G.
Lt. Dodgson, D. S.

No. 17 Company.
(Formed in 1898.)

Alderney.

Maj. Morris, R. C., *g.*
Capt. Beer, V. L., *g.*
Capt. Cameron, A. H. [L]
Capt. Thompson, W. R.
Lt. Justice, P. W.
Lt. Fry, W. H., *o.*
Lt. Cox, H. A.

No. 18 Company.
(Formed in 1898.)

Sheerness.

Maj. Keogh, T. M.
Capt. Thompson, A. J.
Capt. Hibbert, S. E.
2nd Lt. Lee, E. A.
2nd Lt.
2nd Lt. Somerscales, F. J.

No. 19 Company.
(Formed in 1898.)

Sheerness.

Maj. Smith, A. G.
Capt.
Lt. Wehner, A. F. P., *g.* [L]
2nd Lt. Chambers, F. G.
2nd Lt. Benfield, K. V. B.

No. 20 Company.
(Formed in 1860.)

Jersey.

Maj. Roberts, H. B., *p.s.c.* [L]
Capt. Hollinshead, H. N. B.
Lt. Renshaw, R. A.

Royal Garrison Artillery.

No. 21 Company.
(Formed in 1846.)

Leith.

Maj. Kelsall, H. J., *g.*
Capt. Hutton-Squire, R. H. E.
Lt. Holmes, H.
2nd Lt. Romauis, D. G.
2nd Lt. Fasken, D. E.
2nd Lt. Cameron, P. G. [*l*] (attd.)

No. 22 Company.
(Formed in 1859.)

Sheerness.

Maj. Thorp, A. H., *g.*
Capt. Finch, G. F. C.
Lt. Willis, F. W.
2nd Lt. Monckton. M. H.
2nd Lt. Laurie, J. R.

No. 23 (Siege) Company.
(Formed in 1811.)

Fort Grange (Gosport).

Maj. Chrystie, J., *g.*
Capt. Heaslop, A. C.
Lt. Russell, A. G.
Lt. Davidson, C. G. F.
Lt. Rideout, F. M.
Lt. Leeson, L. K.

No. 24 (Heavy) Battery.
(Formed in 1900.)

Woolwich.

Maj. Brake, H. E. J., *C.B., D.S.O.*
Capt. Miles, E.
Lt. Mackintosh, W. A. O. C.
Lt. Walker, M. G. E.
Lt. Douglas-Jones, S. D.

No. 26 (Heavy) Battery.
(Formed in 1900.)

Fort Wallington.

Maj. Brierley, G. T., *D.S.O., g.*
Capt. Macleay, D.
Lt. Ford, J. P. W.
Lt. Smith, J. C. J.
2nd Lt. Hanlon, D. R., *f.c.*

No. 28 Company.
(Formed in 1778.)

Weymouth.

Maj. Stülpnagel, C.W.
Capt. Alexander, W. D.
2nd Lt. Scott, E. C.
2nd Lt. Crosse, T. G.
2nd Lt. Painter, G. W. A.

No. 29 Company.
(Formed in 1819.)

Portsmouth.

Maj.
Capt. Stanbrough, L. K.
2nd Lt. Hire, D. A. H.
2nd Lt. Gurney, L.
2nd Lt. Birbeck, J. H. B. (attd.)

No. 30 Company.
(Formed in 1879.)

Weymouth.

Maj. Wynter, F. A., *D.S.O.*
Capt. Hickling, C. L.
Lt. Becher, L. B. A.
2nd Lt. Culverwell, E. R.
2nd Lt. Goldney, R. M.

No. 31 (Heavy) Battery.
(Formed in 1879.)

Woolwich.

Maj. Franks, G. McK., *p.s.c.* [*l*] *bt. lt.-col.*
Capt. Galloway, L., *D.S.O.*
Lt. Goldney, H. W.
Lt. Neate, A. C. B. [L]
2nd Lt. Stansfeld, L. R.

No. 32 Company
(Formed in 1743.)

Sandown.

Maj. Scott, A. F. S.
Capt. Henderson, H. E.
Capt. Watson, R. H. M. (attd.)
Lt. Prichard, F. H. [*l*]
2nd Lt. Christie, C. M.

No. 33 Company.
(Formed in 1855.)

Golden Hill.

Maj. Wailes, W. E., *f.*
Capt. Kemble, W. E., *o., g.*
Capt Allen, A. H., *o*
Lt. Yorke, F. A.
2nd Lt. Cottrell, G. F.
2nd Lt. Warren, P. J. K.

No. 34 Company.
(Formed in 1812.)

Sandown.

Maj. Head, H. F.
Capt. Dowding, H. C. T., *p.s.o., f.c.r*
Lt. Ollivier, G. L.
2nd Lt. Dobbin, R. A. S.
2nd Lt. Bell, L. G. R. F. H.

No. 35 (Heavy) Battery.
(Formed in 1794.)

Fort Fareham.

Maj. Wilkinson, A. C.
Capt. Caldecott, E. L.
Lt. Cruickshank, A. L.
Lt. Shedden, G. P.
Lt. Paris, H. G.

No. 36 Company.
(Formed in 1863.)

Plymouth.

Maj. Reade, P. N. G., *g.*
Capt. Nanson, M. R. C.
Lt. Pellew, V. H. L.
2nd Lt. Lang, N. C.
2nd Lt. Pickthall, P. J. T.

No. 37 Company
(Formed in 1757.)

Portsmouth.

Maj. Dent, F. W.
Capt. Jones, J. H. H., *g*
2nd Lt. Evans, D. S. C.
2nd Lt. Carter, A. R.
2nd Lt. Leigh, J. A

No. 38 Company.
(Formed in 1863.)

Plymouth.

Maj. Loring, W.
Capt. Routh, A. L.
Capt. Pratt, E. R. [L]
2nd Lt. Bensley, C. J. F.
2nd Lt. Moores, B. S. K. G.

No. 39 (Siege) Company.
(Formed in 1794.)

Plymouth.

Maj. Ewart, C. N.
Capt. Burke, H. F.
Lt. Sturges, C. H. M.
Lt. Creery, A.
2nd Lt. Hawes, L. A.
2nd Lt. Moriarty, J. H.

No. 40 Company.
(Formed in 1791.)

Dover.

Maj. McCulloch, R.H.F, *D.S.O.* [L]
Capt. Parker, W.
2nd Lt. Hare, C. E.
2nd Lt. Hallifax, F. P.
2nd Lt. Eastwick-Field, W. L.

No. 41 Company.
(Formed in 1718.)

Plymouth.

Maj. Craster, E. H. B.
Capt. Courtney. F. H.
Capt. Thomas, A. G.
2nd Lt. Heath, C. P.
2nd Lt. Teesdale, P. H.

No. 42 Company.
(Formed in 1781.)

Portsmouth.

Maj. Tyler, R. E.
Capt. Grose, J.
Lt. Smyth, R. A. N.
Lt. Pierson, C. F. L.
Lt. Hudson, N.
2nd Lt. Williamson, R. H. (attd.)

Royal Garrison Artillery.

No. 43 Company.
(Formed in 1854.)
Queenstown Harbour.

Maj. Pennethorne, H. E., g.
Capt. Langton, A. V., e. [l]
Lt. Stephens, L. N.
2nd Lt. Noel, J. A. V.
2nd Lt. Gulland, A. H.
2nd Lt. Churcher, G. M.
(attd.)

No. 44 Company.
(Formed in 1845.)
Pembroke Dock.

Maj. le Pelley, E. C., g.
Capt. Smythe, R. C.
Lt. Bovill, C.
2nd Lt. Holden, W. C.
2nd Lt. Hordern, H. M.

No. 45 Company.
(Formed in 1794.)
Plymouth.

Maj. Hanna, J. C., g.
Capt.
2nd Lt. Gill, R. C.
2nd Lt. Penrose, C. Q. L.
2nd Lt. Rowett, R. B. (attd.)
2nd Lt. Elliot, F. E, (attd.)

No. 46 Company.
(Formed in 1705.)
Dover.

Maj. Bellairs, N. E. B., p.a.c.
Capt. Swettenham, W. A. W.
Lt. Wyllie, R. [L]
2nd Lt. Ashby, G. S. M.
2nd Lt. Brittan, C. H.
2nd Lt. Stannard, A. J.
(attd)

No. 47 Company.
(Formed in 1862.)
Tynemouth.

Maj. Hart, H. T., g.
Capt Bassett, J. C.
Lt. Butterworth, B. M. G.
2nd Lt. Garry, R. V. M.
2nd Lt. Vale, H. C. S. [l]
2nd Lt. Lushington, F.
(attd)

No. 48 (Heavy) Battery.
(Formed in 1795.)
Woolwich.

Maj. Phipps, C. F.
Capt. Walker, J. B. [L].
Lt. Furnell, C. H. M.
Lt. Greenwood, T. C.
2nd Lt. Gubbins, M. N. T.

No. 49 Company.
(Formed in 1854.)
Queenstown Harbour.

Maj. Jennings, W.
Capt.
2nd Lt. Garratt, L. F.
2nd Lt.
2nd Lt. Bowen, E. G. A.

No. 50 Company.
(Formed in 1895.)
Sierra Leone.

Maj. Burton, H. C. H., g.
Capt. Chevallier, F. E. de C., g.
Capt.
Lt. Meredith, J. C.
Lt. Scott, W. F. F.
2nd Lt. Brown, L. N. F.

No. 51 Company.
(Formed in 1771.)
Allahabad.

Maj. Sherer, J. D. g.
Capt. Rynd, F. F., D S.O. [L]
Lt. Wilmot, S. D.
Lt. Bussell, S. F. B.
2nd Lt. Collins, S. St. B.

No. 52 Company.
(Formed in 1895.)
Bombay (for Karachi).

Maj. Alexander, W. P., g.
Capt. Roche, L. V.
Lt. Underhill, N.
2nd Lt. Johnston, M. A. B.
2nd Lt. Smith, G. L. S.

No. 54 Company.
(Formed in 1759.)
Gibraltar.

Maj. Buzzard, C. N., e.
Capt. Disney, J. W. K., o.
Lt. Matthews, G. W.
Lt. Milner, R. J. N.
2nd Lt. Philpot, G.

No. 55 Company.
(Formed in 1886.)
Gibraltar.

Maj. Galloway, F. L., p.a.c., g.
Capt. Goff, T. C. [L]
Lt. Cherry, A. H. M.
Lt. Withers, R. B.
2nd Lt. Mackenzie, D. M. S.

No. 56 Company.
(Formed in 1885.)
Mauritius.

Capt. Walker, E. W. M., g.
Capt. Phillips, E. S.
Lt. Keene, H. N. J.
2nd Lt. Buckland, A. W. T.
2nd Lt. Parkes, N. C.

No. 57 Company.
(Formed in 1808.)
Pembroke Dock.

Maj. Seddon, E. McM.
Capt. Campbell, R. W. P.
Capt. Marindin, C. C., p.s.c
Lt. Donnelly, T.
2nd Lt. Peters, R. B.
2nd Lt. Mullaly, D. J. St. C.
2nd Lt. Shipster, F. F.

No. 59 (Siege) Company.
(Formed in 1846.)
Rurki.

Maj. Kirkpatrick, A. R. Y.
Capt. Hunt, W. M.
Lt. Leslie-Smith, G. L.
Lt. Brian, H. C.
Lt. Campbell, G. F.

No. 60 Company.
(Formed in 1895.)
Quetta.

Maj. Mayne, H. B., g.
Capt. Gardner, J. A.
2nd Lt. Williams, F. P. J.
2nd Lt. Caudle. H. C. R.

No. 61 Company.
(Formed in 1891.)
Aden.

Maj. Whitehead, E. L' E. [l]
Capt. Murray, A. D., g.
2nd Lt. Williams, E. J.
2nd Lt. Collingwood, S.
2nd Lt. Macgregor, A.

No. 62 Company.
(Formed in 1757.)
Calcutta (for Aden).

Maj. Corbett, E. F.
Capt. Lyon, C. A.
Lt. Lovell, E. H.
Lt. Kingscote, A. R. F.
2nd Lt. Tanner, C. C. P.

No. 63 Company.
(Formed in 1846.)
Malta.

Maj. Eady, C. E.
Capt. Keyes, A. J. H., g.
Lt. Godfery, M. V. S.
Simpson, F. W. H.
(attd.)

No. 64 Company.
(Formed in 1855.)
Rangoon.

Maj. Pitman, A. C.
Capt. Pollard, C. J. K. [l]
Lt. Stevenson, J. H. M.
2nd Lt. Deane, J. A. L.

Royal Garrison Artillery.

No. 65 Company.
(Formed in 1760.)

Malta.

Maj.	Macdonald, R. J., g., f.
Capt.	Hoskyn, R., g.
Lt.	Gaussen, B.
Lt.	Mucklow, C.
Lt.	Freeth, R. J. R.

No. 66 Company.
(Formed in 1759.)

Jamaica.

Maj.	Butcher, F. S., g.
Capt.	Lucy, R. S.
Capt.	Knowles, G. L.
Lt.	Turbutt, R. B.
2nd Lt.	Field, F. D. [l]
2nd Lt.	Greenwell-Lax, A. W.
2nd Lt.	Sandys, M. T.

No. 67 Company.
(Formed in 1848.)

Portsmouth.

Maj.	Twiss. F. A. M.V.O., g.
Capt.	Holme, H. L. [L]
Capt.	Leefe, J. B.
Lt.	O'Reilly-Blackwood, E. H.
2nd Lt.	Chidson, M. R.
2nd Lt.	Morgan, D. N.

No. 68 Company.
(Formed in 1803.)

Barian.

Maj.	Riddell, R. B.
Capt.	Bennett, F. L. [l]
Lt.	Prickett, L.
2nd Lt.	Allpress, H. V.

No. 69 Company.
(Formed in 1887.)

Manora (for Aden).

Maj.	Brewster, R. F., g.
Capt.	Dobbyn, G. H. W.
Capt.	D'Esterre, J. C. E.
Lt.	Kennedy, A. S. C.
2nd Lt.	Fardell, D. O.

No. 70 Company.
(Formed in 1758.)

Aden (for Bombay).

Maj.	Corrie, W. F. T., p.a.c., g.
Capt.	Everard, C. J., g.
Lt.	Rossiter, F. N. C.
2nd Lt.	Wilson, R. R.
2nd Lt.	Greene, H.

No. 71 (Heavy) Battery.
(Formed in 1765.)

Nowgong.

Maj.	Hutchinson, F. P., g.
Capt.	Fishe, A. F. B.
Lt.	Pask, I. A. J.
Lt.	Chapman, A. C.
Lt.	

No. 72 (Heavy) Battery.
(Formed in 1771.)

Peshawar.

Maj.	Courtenay, M. H.
Capt.	Fraser, T. C.
Lt.	Larmour, L. C., o.
Lt.	Halford, E. S., g.
Lt.	Simonds, J. de L.

No. 73 Company.
(Formed in 1854.)

Delhi.

Maj.	Robinson, S. W.
Capt.	Arnott, R.
Lt.	Donnelly, G. H.
Lt.	Gardiner, D. A.
Lt.	Russell, C. A.

No. 74 Company.
(Formed in 1848.)

Fort Agra.

Maj.	Blanford, W. G.
Capt.	Snowdon, H.S.K., o.
Lt.	Jenkins, W. M.
2nd Lt.	English, J. W.
2nd Lt.	Hebbert, G. K. P.

No. 75 Company.
(Formed in 1887.)

Rangoon.

Maj.	Nichol, W. D., g.
Capt.	Sutton, F.
Lt.	Percival, D.
Lt.	Tennent, C. B.
2nd Lt.	Carew, R. L. O.

No. 76 Company.
(Formed in 1855.)

Aden (for Bombay).

Maj.	Harvest, H. H.
Capt.	Mathews, W. V. D., g. [l]
Lt.	Jones, C. G. P.
Lt.	Lowndes, R. C.
Lt.	Hall, A. C. S.

No. 77 Company.
(Formed in 1806.)

Bombay.

Maj.	Kelly, C. R.
Capt.	Perry, S.
Capt.	Maxwell, W. W., g.
Lt.	Lane, H. E., o.
Lt.	Guise, V. R.

No. 78 Company.
(Formed in 1803.)

Singapore.

Maj.	Holdsworth-Hunt, W. H., g.
Capt.	Watson, F. S., o.
Capt.	Shaw, J. F. de F.
Lt.	Pollock, A. J. C.
Lt.	Olliver, C. O.
2nd Lt.	Cooke, J. G. M. B.

No. 79 Company.
(Formed in 1845.)

Bombay.

Maj.	Bishop, C. F., g.
Capt.	Lamb, B.
Lt.	Corbett, G, R. de la C.
Lt.	Watson, E. V.
Lt.	Hay, A. [l]

No. 80 Company.
(Formed in 1848.)

Singapore.

Maj.	Galwey, R. H., g.
Capt.	Jackson, M. A., g.
Lt.	McDiarmid, J. I. A.
Lt.	Treatt, D. B. C.
2nd Lt.	Hawkins, J. C. B.

No. 81 (Siege) Company.
(Formed in 1855.)

Rurki.

Maj.	Metcalfe, F. H., g.
Capt.	Byrne, J.D.
Lt.	Duke, V. G.
2nd Lt.	Aston, E. N.
2nd Lt.	Dymott, K. G.

No. 82 Company.
(Formed in 1862.)

Ferozepore.

Maj.	Kane, A. H., g.
Capt.	Wilkins, G. H. C., g. W. P. A.
Lt.	Bingham, C. H.
Lt.	Francis, H. F.
Lt.	Harker, A. W. A.

No. 83 Company.
(Formed in 1863.)

Hong Kong.

Maj.	Hall, H. C., g.
Capt.	Hattersley-Smith, W.
Capt.	Coe, J.
Lt.	FitzRoy, R. H.
Lt.	Chambers, C. C.
Lt.	Nevill, P.
Lt.	Gilpin, W. J.

No. 84 Company.
(Formed in 1757)

Capetown.

Maj.	Boyd, S. O.
Capt.	Holme, R. C. [L]
Lt.	à Beckett, W. H. F.
Lt.	Begbie, R. P. G.
Lt.	Montague, P. J. A.

| 643 | 644 | 645 | 646 |

Royal Garrison Artillery.

No. 85 Company.
(Formed in 1765.)

Bombay (for Calcutta)

Maj.	Keogh, J. H.
Capt.	Cudlip, E. P.
Lt.	Curtis, A. D.
Lt.	Wilson, I. C.

No. 86 (Heavy) Battery.
(Formed in 1748.)

Multan.

Maj.	Molesworth, R. P.
Capt.	Van der Kiste, E. W.
Lt.	Saulez, A. T.
Lt.	Garnett, C. L.
Lt.	Hughes-Gibb, C. P.

No. 87 Company.
(Formed in 1862.)

Hong Kong.

Maj.	Currie, I.B.F., g.
Capt.	Hume-Spry, C.A.N.
Lt.	Collins, P. R. M.
Lt.	Taylor, O. C.
2nd Lt.	Sanders, B. J. M.
2nd Lt.	Goldney, L. P.

No. 88 Company.
(Formed in 1857.)

Hong Kong.

Maj.	Pritchard, C. G.
Capt.	Barton, R. L., g.
Capt.	Mompalao de Piro, G.
Lt.	Pym, J. A.
2nd Lt.	Joll, L. D.
2nd Lt.	Campbell, D. A.
2nd Lt.	Roupell, F. L. L. F.

No. 90 (Heavy) Battery.
(Formed in 1768.)

Nowgong.

Maj.	Palmer, H. R.
Capt.	Marshall, H. S.
Lt.	Gordon, W.
Lt.	Moore, H. T.
Lt.	Heywood, T. G. G. [L]

No. 91 (Heavy) Battery.
(Formed in 1802.)

Rurki.

Maj.	Phillips, T. R.
Capt.	Russell, W. C. P.
Capt.	Edwards, I. A. E.
Capt.	Charles, E. E.
Lt.	Keene, G. G.

No. 93 Company.
(Formed in 1786.)

Ceylon.

Maj.	Muspratt-Williams, R. L.
Capt.	Smith, S.
Capt.	Wahl, C. E. J. [L]
Capt.	Mitchell, P. R.
Lt.	Mills, H. P. F.
Lt.	Purcell, R. G.
2nd Lt.	Steel, J. V.
2nd Lt.	Tomlinson, S. C.

No. 94 Company.
(Formed in 1802.)

Rawal Pindi.

Maj.	Stiffe, A. F. E.
Capt.	Dunne, T. F. K.
Lt.	
2nd Lt.	Skinner, R. O.
2nd Lt.	Campbell, E. G.

No. 95 Company.
(Formed in 1760.)

Bermuda.

Maj.	Lockhart, R. N., g.
Capt.	Robinson, T. A. F., g.
Lt.	Smith, I. P.
Lt.	Cardew, J. W.
2nd Lt.	Parker, G. L.

No. 96 Company.
(Formed in 1862.)

Malta.

Maj.	Taylor, C. S.
Capt.	Castens, W. E., p.a.c., g.
Lt.	Sargeaunt, P. R.
Lt.	Gage, B. A. H.
Lt.	Shaw, H. A.

No. 97 Company.
(Formed in 1802.)

Simonstown.

Maj.	Nuttall, C. M., g.
Capt.	King, A. E., p.a.c.
Capt.	Webber, H. H.
Lt.	MacLeod, M.
2nd Lt.	Hamilton C. de C.

No. 99 Company.
(Formed in 1778.)

Malta.

Maj.	Howard-Vyse, C., g.
Capt.	Brierley, G. W.
Lt.	Hetherington, C. G.
Lt.	Sayers, R. C.
Lt.	Richards, D. J. R.

No. 100 Company.
(Formed in 1757.)

Malta.

Maj.	Marton, R. O., D.S.O., g.
Capt.	Macalpine Leny, W. H.
Lt.	Woollcombe, F. R.
Lt.	Luard, E. A. P.
2nd Lt.	Milligan, E. D.

No. 101 Company.
(Formed in 1759.)

Quetta.

Maj.	Bushe, C. K.
Capt.	Ford, G. T.
Lt.	Edwards, W. M.
2nd Lt.	Mackenzie, H. H.
2nd Lt.	McIntyre, H. M. J.

No. 102 Company.
(Formed in 1799.)

Malta.

Maj.	Fraser, L. D., g. [L]
Capt.	Carwithen, S.
Lt.	de Kantzow, J E
Lt.	Floyd, B. E.
Lt.	Bois, D. G.

No. 104 (Heavy) Battery.
(Formed in 1901.)

Campbellpore.

Maj.	Farmar, W. C. R.
Capt.	Alexander, R. C. J.
Lt.	Payne, D. W.
Lt.	Bewley, B. J.
Lt.	Hare, J. W.

No. 107 (Siege) Company.
(Formed in 1863.)

Plymouth.

Maj.	Mackenzie, G. B., g.
Capt.	Evans, C. L.
Capt.	Tresidder, G. W. W.
Lt.	Tod, C. D.
Lt.	Sunderland, B. G. E.
Lt.	Simon, P. B.

No. 108 (Heavy) Battery.
(Formed in 1904.)

Fort Nelson.

Maj.	De Sausmarez, C., D.S.O.
Capt.	Tandy, E. N., p.s.c.
Capt.	Erskine, W. A.
Capt.	Elphinstone-Dalrymple, Sir F. N., Bt.
Lt.	Hitchcock, F. B.

Legation Guard.

Peking.

Capt.	Christian, W. F.
Lt.	Kellie, R. H. A.

Detachment.

Khartoum.

Capt.	Stenhouse, J. L.
Lt.	Tuohy, R. D.

| 647 | 648 | 649 | 650 |

Royal Garrison Artillery.

DEPÔTS.

No. 1 Depôt. *Newhaven.*	*No. 2 Depôt.* *Fort Rowner, Gosport.*	*No. 3 Depôt.* *Citadel, Plymouth.*	*No. 4 Depôt.* *Great Yarmouth.*
Maj. Church, G. R. M.		Maj. Thorp, A., *g.*	Maj. Anley, W. B., *g.*
Capt. Whyte, T. A.	Maj. Tulloch, D. F.	Capt. Holdich, G. W. V., *p.s.c.* [*l*]	Capt. Morgan, F. A. S.
Capt. Clarke, J. S. S., *g.*	Capt. Bromley, C. R. S.	Lt. Smithers, H.	Lt. Fryer, F. E.
Lt. Reid, D. (D.O.)	Capt. Strachan, D. A.	Lt. Westell, C. E.(D.O.)	Lt. Spinks, G. C. (D.O.)
Qr.-Mr.Drayson, T., *hon. lt.*	Lt. Ellison, W.R.(D.O.)	Qr.-Mr.Bates, F. J., *hon. lt.*	Qr.-Mr.Armstrong, T., *hon. lt.*
	Qr.-Mr.O'Brien, J., *hon. lt.*		

GUNNERY STAFF COURSE, 1913-14.

Royal Horse and Field Artillery.	*Royal Horse and Field Artillery*—contd.	*Royal Garrison Artillery*	*Royal Garrison Artillery.*—contd.
Capt. Butler, B. A. B.	Capt. Thornton, G. St. L.	Capt. Thompson, A. J.	Capt. Stephens, L. N.
Capt. Simpson, H. C.	Capt. Prance, R. C.	Capt. Normand, S. R.	Lt. Davies, O. H.
Capt. Furse, G. A.	Capt. Godman, L.	Capt. Riach, G. H.	*Royal Australian Garrison Artillery*
Capt. Warburton, W. M.		Capt. Wighton, E.	Capt. Watts, B. A. G.
		Capt. Bunbury, R. S.	
		Capt. Page, C. F. G.	
		Capt. Phillips, F. R.	

LOCAL BATTALION OF ROYAL GARRISON ARTILLERY.
HONG KONG—SINGAPORE BATTALION.

Major .. .. .. Comyn, E W. .. .. .. Hong Kong.
Adjt. .. .. .. Spicer, P. L., *capt., g.* .. .. Hong Kong.

No. 1 Co., Hong Kong.	*No. 2 Co., Hong Kong.*	*No. 3 Co., Hong Kong.*	*No. 4 Co., Mauritius.*
Capt. Wakefield, T. M. (*l*)	Capt. Reid, F. H.	Capt. Moore, W. A. [*l*]	Capt. Lawes, T. C.
Lt. Bagnall, H. G.	Lt. Halliday, F. S.	Lt. Sykes, M.	Lt. Wiltshire, P. S.
Lt. Cameron, C. P. G.	Lt. Thomas, H. R.	2nd Lt. Smyth, V. G.	Lt. Clayton, I. N.
Lt			
Subadar, Hakam Singh	Subadar, Sundar Singh	Subadar, Mohamad Din	Subadar, Ramzan Khan
Jemadar, Bhan Singh	Jemadar, Natha Singh	Jemadar,	Jemadar, Bagh Ali

No. 5 Co., Singapore.

Capt. Matthews, E. D., *g.*
Lt. Thompson, H. S.
Lt. Thicknesse, F. W.

Subadar, Roshan Khan
Jemadar, Iman Din Khan

Subadar Major.			*Jemadars.*		
Muhammed Ali	.. Hong Kong ..	6Oct.10	Jewa Singh ..	.. .. Hong Kong ..	26Oct.04
Subadars.			Iman Din Khan	.. Hong Kong ..	16July10
Hakam Singh	.. Hong Kong ..	13Oct.09	Bagh Ali ..	.. Hong Kong ..	12Oct.10
Roshan Khan	.. Hong Kong ..	16July10	Bhan Singh	.. Hong Kong ..	25Aug.11
Ramzan Khan	.. Hong Kong ..	6Oct.10	Natha Singh	.. Mauritius ..	25Aug.11
Mohamad Din	.. Singapore ..	12Oct.10	(*To take precedence from 25 Feb. 12*)		
Sundar Singh	.. Mauritius ..	25Aug.11	Mehdi Shah	.. .. ..	12June13

LOCAL COMPANY OF ROYAL GARRISON ARTILLERY.
Sierra Leone Co.

Maj. Crowe, M. A. C., *p.a.c.*	Lt. MacMahon, G. P. R.
Capt. Perrott, H. S.	Lt. Forbes, J. L.
Capt. Traill, H. E. O'B.	Lt. Pearce, P. M.
Capt. Fitzgerald, N. D'A.	

ROYAL GARRISON ARTILLERY.
SPECIAL RESERVE.
Precedence by Counties.

1. The Antrim.   2. The Cork.

The Antrim.

Carrickfergus.

(*Officers serving on 6 Nov. 00 in the corresponding Militia unit hold honorary Army rank equivalent to the Militia regimental rank they then held. Other officers entitled to honorary Army rank have it shown against their names.*)

Hon. Colonel.
Shaftesbury, A. A. C., Earl of, K.P., K.C.V.O. (*Brig. Comdr.*, 1 S.W. Mtd. Brig.) 7June13

Lt.-Colonel.

Majors. (2)
p.s. Hill, R. M. (I) 25June08
p.s. Baird, W. 11Aug.09

Captains. (4)
p.s. Hill, F. G. (I) 25Jan.02
p.s. ✗Blackwood, C. H. 2Apr.06
p.s. Cowan, F. E. P. 14May07
p.s. Dobbs, A. F. 22July08
p.s. Brenan, G. (H) 1May09
p.s. Moriarty, O. N. 11Aug.09
p.s. Thomas, A. L. (A) 6July10
p.s. Brett, R. G., *late Lt.* Leic. R. (q) ⑧ (*Resdt. Magistrate, Ireland,* 10 Dec 12) 8Feb,12

Lieutenants. (10)
p.s. Glasson, B. 1June07
p.s. Lees, L. W. W. (A) 2Dec.08
  1Apr.08
p.s. Glasson, C. J. H. 17Jan.09
Barras, H. W. 8Dec.10
✗Wood, M., *late 2nd Lt.* R. Ir. Regt. 4Mar.11
Smyth, R. A. E. 5July11
Hezlet, C. O. 8Feb.12
Gilliland, W. H. (*Asst. Dist. Commr., Gold Coast,* 27Apr.14) 16Oct.12
2nd Lieutenants (6)
McClay, J. S. C. 7Dec.10
Brewster, H. 13May11
Brooks, O. H. (*Asst. Commr. of Police, N. Provs., Nigeria,* 2Jan. 14) 8May12
Scott-Deakin, R. 6May11
  3May13
  5Feb.13
Crawford-Clarke, R. W. B. 10May13
Swain, C. D. D., 25June13
Rogers, C. V. (*on prob.*) 8Nov.13
  4Dec.12

Instructor of Artillery.
Moriarty, O. N., *capt.* 1May09

Adjutant.

Quarter-Master.
Kerrison, T. W., Qr.-Mr. R.A., *hon. lt.*

The Cork.

Fort Westmoreland, Spike Island, Queenstown Harbour.

(*Officers serving on 6 Nov. 00 in the corresponding Militia unit hold honorary Army rank equivalent to the Militia regimental rank they then held. Other officers entitled to honorary Army rank have it shown against their names.*)

Hon. Colonel.
Bandon, J. F., Earl of, K.P. 19July08
  31July78

Lt.-Colonel.
p.s. ✗Kirkwood, S. F. (A) (*Maj. Mtla.*) (*Hon. Capt. in Army* 14 Oct. 00) 18Sept.12

Major.
p.s. ✗Jobson, M. B., (H) (A) (I) 1Aug.08

Captains (6)
p.s. Beamish, R. de B. 31Jan.03
p.s. Scantlebury, V. J. (I) (*Hon. 2nd Lt. in Army* 4Oct00).15July05
  28June02
p.s. ✗Fenner, H. H. (*Hon. Lt. in Army* 3 Sept. 02) 18June06

Supplementary Officers.

Captains.
p.s. Greer, H. F. V. 1May08

Lieutenants.
p.s. Walker, F. V. 1May00
Leigh, P. L. (*local Capt. O.T.C.* 3 June 11) 1Aug.09
Whitefoord, P. G. (*on prob.*) 17June14
  2June06
  9Oct.09

2nd Lieutenants.
Rice, F. J. 13Nov.09
Sharp, R. F. H. (*on prob.*) 30Mar.10
Cassels, J. W. W. (*on prob.*) 7Dec.10
Mackenzie, K. S. (*on prob.*) 4Jan.11
Holbrook, F. G. (*on prob.*) 6Jan.12
Dyer, W. W. (*on prob.*) 6Jan.12
O'Connor H. A. (*on prob.*) 1Mar.12
Pratt, J. E. (*on prob.*) 4Apr.12
  19June12
  21Sept.12
  14June11
Young, C. H. N. (*on prob.*) 10Ct.12
Griffin, R. M. J. (*on prob.*) 26Oct.12
Clarke, R. A. O. (*on prob.*) 26Feb.13
Munro, A. J. R. (*on prob.*) 15Mar.13
Bishop, A. G. (*on prob.*)
Leslie, H. F. (*on prob.*)
Strachan, S. C. (*on prob.*)

Captains—contd.
p.s. Graham, G. W., I. of A. 2Jan.08
p.s. Morgan, J. R. T. 1Jan.09
✗Bartley, S. C., Capt. ret. pay 13July10
Bull, H., Capt. ret. pay (Q) 22Mar.11
Stephens, B. T., Lt. ret. pay, o. 31July12

Lieutenants. (8)
p.s. Tivy, G. L. W. 9June07
Hogan, A. J. 1July12
Chearnley, C. L. 1Jan.14
Linley-Howlden, R. C. 1Jan.14

2nd Lieutenants. (4)
Chads, W. J. 1Oct.13
Forsayeth, F. N. (*on prob.*) 8Oct.13
Manly, E. C. J. (*on prob.*) 8Nov.13

Instructor of Artillery.
Graham, G. W., *capt.* 28Apr.14

Adjutant.
Thackwell, H. E. O., Lt. R.A., g. 18Apr.14
(*Lt. in Army* 3June 04)

Quarter-Master.
Ashweek, F., Qr.-Mr. R.A., *hon. lt.*

Weymouth 2May03
Plymouth 1May00
  20Aug.00
  1Aug.09
  17June14
Plymouth 9Oct.09
  2June06

Dover 13Nov.09
Fareham 30Mar.10
Portsmouth 7Dec.10
Portsmouth 4Jan.11
Malay States 6Jan.12
Plymouth 6Jan.12
Sheerness 6Jan.12
Sandown 1Mar.12
Sandown 1Apr.12
Sandown 19June12
Ceylon 21Sept.12
  14June11

Sheerness 1Oct.12
Portsmouth 26Oct.12
Plymouth 26Feb.13
Dover 15Mar.13

p.s. ✗Brooke-Hitching, P. M., *late Lt.* R.War. R. ⑧ (H)
p.s. Lucy, E. S. (*Hon. Lt. in Army* 18 Oct. 00)
Congreve, W. M., *late Lt.* Res. of Off.
p.s. Hodges, N. J.

Duncan, M. W.
Hyde-Clarke, S. H.
Ford, C. C.
Parrington, L.
Nelson-Cookes, H.
Pepper, J. G. W.
Vyner, R. G. J. C.
Marriott, F. C.
Gonne, V. C. M.
O'Farrell, G. H. M.
O'Brien, T. E. S.

Springfield, C.H.D.O.
Sharp, D. C. G.
Blowey, H. F. T.
Mills, V. H. (*on prob.*)

Ceylon 23Mar.10
  10July05
Japan 16Oct.12
Portsmouth 14Dec.12
  27Feb.13
  4Apr.14

Harwich 7May13
Fareham 6Aug.13
  3Sept.13
Dover 27Sept.13
Dover 10Oct.13
Plymouth 10Oct.13
Plymouth 29Oct.13
Londonderry 5Nov.13
  1Apr.13
Fareham 3Dec.13
Plymouth 6Dec.13
Dover 28Jan.14
Leith 21Mar.14
Portsmouth 1Apr.14
  1Apr.14
Portsmouth 4July14

TERRITORIAL FORCE.
HONOURABLE ARTILLERY COMPANY.

Dates shewn prior to 1 April, 1908, are those of the Officers' corresponding rank in the Hon. Art. Co. before transfer to the Territorial Force.

"South Africa, 1900-02."

Captain-General and Colonel.
THE KING.

Lieut.-Colonel.
p. ✗Denbigh and Desmond, R. R. B. A. A., *Earl of*, C.V.O., TD, Col.,*A.D.C., late* Capt. R.A. (*t*) (A) 4Mar.93

Quarter-Master.
Mayhew, G. H., hon. lt. 13May11

Chaplain.
Shaw, *Rev.* G. W. H., *M.A.*, Chapl. 4th Class (T. F.) (*attd.*) 17May13

A Battery, Honourable Artillery Co. (1st City of London Horse Artillery).

Armoury House, Finsbury, E.C.

Battery.

Major.
Eugster, O. L [L] (Q) 1May13

Captain.
Dyer, C. N. (q) 1Jan.14

Lieutenants. (2)

2nd Lieutenant. (1)
Huggins, B. F. 15Mar.13
Von Treuenfels, C. O. 12Apr.13
Catley, J. T. 25Mar.14

Adjutant.
Sinclair, J. N., Capt. R.A. 1Apr.12

Medical Officer.
p.s. Reece, R. J., *M.D.*, Surg. - Lt. - Col.) (*Hon. Surg.-Col.*) 14May06
28Apr.86

Ammunition Column (London Mtd. Brig.)

Captain.
Lucas-Tooth, A. L. 14Feb.14

Lieutenant.

‡ *2nd Lieutenant.*
Durston, C. C. 25Mar.14

[Uniform—*Blue*. Facings—*Scarlet*. Plume—*Red and White.*]

B Battery, Honourable Artillery Co. (2nd City of London Horse Artillery).

Armoury House, Finsbury, E.C.

Battery.

Major.
Preston, *Hon.* R. M. P., *late* Lt. R.A. 22July13

Captain.
p.s. Pettit, C. E. (A) (Q) 13May11

Lieutenants. (2)
Ward, K. O. 1Mar.14
Smith, J. B. 16Mar.14

2nd Lieutenant. (1)

Adjutant.
Sinclair, J. N., Capt. R.A. 1Apr.12

Medical Officer.
p. Taylor, J. F., *Surg.-Capt.* 10Mar.08
10Sept.04

Ammunition Column (South-Eastern Mtd. Brig.)

Captain.
Harris, H. 16Mar.14

Lieutenant.
Landsberg, H. V. 16Mar.14

[Uniform—*Blue*. Facings—*Scarlet*. Plume—*Red and White.*]

Honourable Artillery Co., Infantry.

Armoury House, Finsbury E.C.

Major.
p. ✗Treffry, E. (*Hon. Capt. in Army* 8 *Feb.* 08) (*Lt. Res. of Off.*) 20Feb.04

Captains. (4)
p. ✗Hanson, H. T. (*Hon. Lt. in Army* 9 *Oct.* 02) 20Feb.04
p.s. ✗Cooper, P. C. (Q) (*H*) 22Jan.06
p.s. Whyte, C. A. J. 18Sept.12
p.s. Ward, A. L. 15Jan.13

Lieutenants. (5)
p.s. Cole, R. C. (*H*)(*t*)4Dec.05
p.s. Garnsey, E. (Q) 4Dec.05

Lieuts.—contd.
p.s. Wright, L. (*H*) (q) 7Mar.07
Newton, W. S. (*H*) 18Sept.12
Douglas, M. G. 19Aug.13

2nd Lieutenants. (4)
Dobson, E. L. 20Apr.12
Goddard, J. ⊕11Sept.12
Gosnell, R. P. 14May13

‡ *Quarter-Master.*
p. Elam, W., hon. m. 21Feb.00

Medical Officers.
p.s. James, W. C., *M.D.*, Surg.-Lt.-Col. (*Hon. Surg.-Col.*) 5Feb.06
9Jan.86

Carnwath, Lt. T., M. B., R. A. M. C. (T.F.) (*attd.*) *late* Lt. R.A.M.C., Spec. Res. 10Apr.12

[Uniform—*Scarlet*. Facings—*Blue*.]

‡ This rank is not provided for in the Territorial Force Tables of Establishments.

659 | 660 | 661 | 662

Royal Horse Artillery. Territorial Force.

ROYAL ARTILLERY.
TERRITORIAL FORCE.

Dates shewn prior to 1 April, 1908 are those of the Officers' corresponding rank in a late unit of the Volunteer Force.

Order of Precedence of the Several Counties (except for Defended Ports).

1. Northumberland.	12. Lancashire.	23. Lincolnshire.	34. Suffolk.	44 City of Dundee.
2. Hampshire.	13. Renfrewshire.	24. Kircudbright.	35. Monmouthshire	45. City of Glasgow.
3. Devonshire.	14. Dorsetshire.	25. Inverness-shire.	36. Staffordshire.	46. Derbyshire.
4. Sussex.	15. Fifeshire.	26. Cumberland.	37. Carnarvon.	47. Hertfordshire.
5. Edinburgh (City).	16. Glamorgan.	27 Durham.	38. Bute.	48. Northamptonshire
6. Midlothian.	17. Yorkshire (E.Rid.)	28. Cromarty.	39. { City of London.	49. Wiltshire.
7. Norfolk.	18. Ayrshire.	29. Ross-shire.	{ CountyofLondon	50. Berkshire.
8. Banff.	19. Argyll.	30. Nairn.	40. Worcester.	51. Leicestershire.
9. Kent.	20. Gloucestershire.	31. Shropshire.	41. Warwick.	52. Nottinghamshire.
10. Forfarshire.	21. Yorkshire (N.Rid.)	32. Yorkshire(W.Rid.)	42. Cardigan.	
11. Essex.	22. Cheshire.	33. Somersetshire.	43. City of Aberdeen.	

I. Royal Horse Artillery.
II. Royal Field Artillery.
III. Royal Garrison Artillery (Mountain and Heavy).
Iv. Royal Garrison Artillery (for Defended Ports).

I. ROYAL HORSE ARTILLERY.

[The order of precedence of batteries is denoted by numerals in brackets.]

Ayrshire.
[4]
Ayr.
Battery.
Major.
✕Meikle, J. H. 17May13
Captain.

Lieutenants. (2)
2nd Lieutenant. (1)
Smith, A. 14 Jan. 12
Morris, G. T. 7Mar.13
Adjutant.
Walker, C. E., Lt.
R.A., *capt.* 19June14
Medical Officers.
Douglas, Lt. C.,
M.B., R.A.M.C.
(T.F.) *(attd.)* 19May10
Chaplain.
Milligan, Rev. O. B.,
B.D. [O.S.] Chapl.
4th Class (T.F.)
(attd.) 1Jan.10

Ammunition Column
(Lowland Mtd. Brig.)
Captain.

Lieutenant.

2nd Lieutenant.
Dunlop, W. G. 7 Jan. 12

Berkshire.
[10]
Yeomanry House,
Castle Hill, Reading.
Battery.
Major.
✕Mayall, C. G.,
Lt. ret. pay, Capt.
R. F. A. Spec.Res.
26May08
✕Wilson, L. O., D.S.O.,
Capt. ret. 22July11

Lieutenants. (2)
✕Mayall, G., late Lt.
Notts and Derby R.
21July08
Brooke, B. W. D.
12May09
2nd Lieutenant. (1)
Craig, J. W. A..
late Lt. Ches.
R. 6June14
Adjutant.
Thorneycroft, G.E.M.,
Lt.R.A., *capt.*14Nov.13
Medical Officers.
Roberts, Maj. A.,
F.R.C.S.,R.A.M.C.
(T.F.) *(attd.)* 8Aug.13
8Feb.05

Ammunition Column
(2nd S. Midland
Mtd. Brig.)
Captain.
Dubourg, S. J. 1Jan.09
Lieutenant.
Hartnoll, J. 3June14

Essex.
[2]
Market Road,
Chelmsford.
Battery.
Major
Hamilton, Hon.
R. G. A. (*Master*
of Belhaven), late
Lt. 3 Hrs. 20May14
Captain.
O'Hagan, M. F.
T., Lord(H) 20May14
Lieutenants. (2)
Kirk, A. H. 18June09
Dickson, A. G. 20May14
2nd Lieutenant (1)
Petersen, W. S. 1May14
Adjutant.
Evans-Gwynne,A.H.,
Lt. R.A., *capt.* 1Oct13

Medical Officers.
Ransford, Lt. A. C.,
R.A.M.C. (T.F.)
(attd.) 22Feb.09
Chaplain.
Naters,Rev.C.C.,Chapl.
4th Class (T.F.)
(attd.) 1July12

Ammunition Column
(Eastern Mtd. Brig.)
Captain.
✕Daniell, W.A.B.9July1
Lieutenant.
Flannery,H.F. 20May14

Glamorgan.
[3]
Port Talbot.
Battery.
Major.
p.s.David, L, (H) 5July13
Captain.
p.s.David, T, J. (H) 4July03
Lieutenants. (2)
Jones, R. N. 26May13
2nd Lieutenant (1).
Milford, K. E.,
Capt. R A. 22Sept.13
Medical Officer.
p. Taylor, Maj. H. N. A.,
M D., R.A.M.C.
(T.F.)*(attd.)* 6May12
30Dec.99
Thomas, Capt.G.M.A.,
R.A.M.C. (T.F.)
(attd.) 23Oct.11
Chaplain.
Williamson, Rev.
Z. P., Chapl. 3rd
Class(T.F.)*(attd.)*
1Apr.08
28July97

Ammunition Column
(South Wales
Mtd. Brig.)
Captain.
p.s.Jones, R. T. P. (H)
13Oct.06
Lieutenant
p.s.Jenkins, M. G. 24Sept.04

Hampshire.
[1]
Southampton.
Battery.
Major.
✕Arderne, D. D.,
Maj. ret. pay (*Res.*
of Off.) 10Oct.13
Captain.
Gillson, F. 16 Feb. 12
Lieutenants. (2)
Elliott, N. M. 2Jan.14
2nd Lieutenant. (1)
Joyce, L. W.,Capt.
R.A. 1Oct.12
Medical Officers.
Henry, Capt. R.,
R.A.M.C. (T.F.)
attd.) 9July14
9Jan.11
Chaplain.
Keymer, Rev. B. W.,
Chapl.4th Class (T.F.)
(attd.) 22Apr.12

Ammunition Column
(1st South Western
Mtd. Brig.)
Basingstoke.
Captain.
✕Baillie, J. A.,
D.S.O., late Lt.
Steinsaecker's
Horse 19Nov.09
Lieutenant.

Royal Horse Artillery. Territorial Force.

Inverness-shire.
[5]
Margaret Street, Inverness.
Battery.
Major.
p, Baillie, J. E. B.,
M.V.O., VD, late
Capt.3Bn.North'd
Fus., *hon. c.* 1Apr.03
Captain.
Lieutenants. (2)
Fraser-Tytler, N. [¹]
17Nov.10
Fraser-Mackenzie,
E. R. L. 2Mar.14
Baillie,G.E.M.,2Mar.14
2nd Lieutenant. (1)
Adjutant.
Cooke,E.D.M.H.,
Capt. R.A. 18July12
Medical Officers.
p, Moir, Lt.-Col. J. M.,
M.D.,VD,R.A.M.C.
(T.F.) (*attd.*) 10Feb.08
13Jan.94
p, Wilson, Maj. G.,
M.B., R.A.M.C.
(T.F.)(*attd.*) 1May11
28Dec.98

*Ammunition Column
(Highland
Mtd. Brig.)*
Drill Hall, King Street,
Nairn.
Captain.
p.s. Fraser, D. (A) 22Dec.08
Lieutenant.

Leicestershire.
[11]
1, Magazine Square,
Leicester.
Battery.
Major.
✗Du Pre, W. B. (Hon.
Lt. *in Army* 24
Oct.00) (Q) 21Aug.08
Captain.
p.s. Crawshay-Williams,
E., *late* Lt. R.F.A.
1May09
Lieutenants. (2)
Noel, H. E. 1Dec.11
2nd Lieutenant. (1)
Griffith, H. L. W.
1July12
Adjutant.
Waddell-Dudley, A. N.,
Capt. R.A. 11Aug.11
Medical Officer.
Thomas, Capt. T.
N., R.A.M.C.
(T.F.) (*attd.*) 17Dec.12
17June09

*Ammunition Column
(North Midland
Mtd. Brig.)*
Captain.
Lieutenant.
Bennion, C. F. 1Nov.10

Nottinghamshire.
[12]
Derby Road,
Nottingham.
Battery.
Major.
p.s.✗Laycock, J. F.,
D.S.O., (Hon. Capt.
in Army, 4July00)
hon. l.c. 26July08
Captain.
Myddelton,R.E. 29July08
Lieutenants. (2)
✗Corbet, B. D'A.
(*Capt. Res. of Off.*)
15July09
✗Harrison, C. P. (Hon.
Capt.inArmy 24Sept.02)
17July09
2nd Lieutenant. (1)
Cholmondeley,
Lord G. H. 27Mar.09
Armstrong,O.A.11May12
Adjutant.
Hayley,W.B.,Capt.
R.A. 20Jan.12
Medical Officers.
Robinson, Capt. G. E.
J. A., M.D.,R.A.M.C.
(T.F.), (*attd.*) 8Apr.12
Allen, Capt.C.H.,M.B.,
F.R.C.S. (Edin.),
R.A.M.C. (T.F.)
(*attd.*) 17May12
17Nov.08
Chaplain.
Bruce, Rev. F. R. C.,
D.D., Chapl. 4th Class
(T.F.)(*attd.*) 2Feb.10

*Ammunition Column
(Notts. & Derby Mtd.
Brig.)*
Captain.
p.s. White, Sir A.W., Bt.,
late Capt. Yorks.
R. F. Res. A. (Hon.
Lt. *in Army* 13 Oct.
00) 20Sept.08
Lieutenant.
Drummond, G. H.
27Apr.09
15Apr.08

West Riding.
[7]
Wentworth Woodhouse,
Rotherham.
Battery.
Major.
✗Fitzwilliam, W. C.
deM.,Earl,K.C.V.O.,
D.S.O.,Capt. & Hon.
Maj. 3 Bn. Oxf. &
Bucks. L. I., (Hon.
Capt. in Army 4July
01) 21July08
bt. lt.-col. 22Feb.13
Captain.
✗Walker, H. M.,
Capt. ret. pay
(*Res. of Off.*) 14June08

Lieutenants. (2)
Foster, P. B. 4May08
Whitworth, H. 17May12
2nd Lieutenant. (1)
Adams, J. B., *late*
Lt. R.N. Res. 4Mar.13
Bingley, H. J. 19Mar.14
Adjutant.
Diggle, J. N., Lt.
R.A. 4Feb.12
Medical Officer.
p. Barber, P. E.,
Surg.-Maj. 25Apr.12
25Apr.00
White, Lt. E.,
R.A M.C.(T.F.)
(*attd.*) 14Oct 13

*Ammunition Column
(Yorkshire
Mtd. Brig.)*
Captain.
✗Conolly, E. M.,
Capt. ret. pay
(*Res. of Off.*) 17Apr.10
Lieutenant.
Elwis, J. S. 18Apr.13

Shropshire.
[6]
Shrewsbury.
Battery.
Major.
p, Newill, R.A., TD (A)
7Mar.03
Captain.
✗Hood, C.H., Capt.
ret pay (*Res. of Off.*)
(Remount Service)
1Jan.13
Lieutenants. (2)
Jones. G. W. @ 23June10
Newill, R. D. 1Apr.14
2nd Lieutenant. (1)
Morgan, H. P. 1Dec.11
Adjutant.
✗Rich, E.E., Lt.R.A.,
capt. 9Oct.12
Medical Officer.
p, Mackie, G., M.B.,
Surg.-Capt. 22June06
22May01
Chaplain.
✗Roach, Rev. F. H.,
Chapl. 4th Class
(T.F.)(*attd.*) 1Aug.12

*Ammunition Column
(Welsh Border
Mtd. Brig.)*
Church Stretton.
Captain.
p.s.Bulstrode, C. V.
(A) 19Apr.09
29Nov.07
Lieutenant.
Leake, H. J. 1Apr.14

Somerset.
[8]
County Territorial Hall.
Taunton.
Battery.
Major.
Aikenhead, F.,
Maj. ret. pay.
(*Res. of Off.*)g.10Dec.13
Captain.

Lieutenants. (2)
p, Bath, R., *late* Capt.
3V.B.Som.L.I.30Sept.11
Bailey, W. H., *late*
Lt.5 Bn. Notts. &
Derby R. 19Apr.13
2nd Lieutenant. (1)
Clowes, M. 8Oct.13
Adjutant.
Lyon, C. D. G.,Capt.
R.A. 4Oct.12
Medical Officer.
Dewdney,Capt.E.L.D.,
R. A. M. C. (T.F.)
(*attd.*) 17Sept.12
17Mar.09
Chaplain.
Day, Ven. *Archdeacon*
C.V.P., M.A., Chapl.
4th Class (T.F.)
(*attd.*) 21Mar.12

*Ammunition Column
(2nd South Western
Mtd. Brig.)*
Captain.

Lieutenant.

Warwickshire.
[9]
9, Clarendon Place,
Leamington.
Battery.
Major.
✗Gemmell,W.A.S., Maj.
ret. pay (*Res. of Off.*)
4June14
Captain.
Lieutenants. (2)
2nd Lieutenant. (1)
Woodhouse, R. C.
16Dec.11
Adjutant.
Murray, W.A., Capt.
R.A. 29May11
Medical Officer.
Clayton, Lt. F.,
M.D.,R.A.M.C.
(T.F.) (*attd.*) 18Nov.12
Chaplain.
Melville, Rev. W. G.,
M.A., Chapl. 3rd Class
(T.F.)(*attd.*) 30May11
30May06

*Ammunition Column
(1st South Midland
Mtd. Brig.)*
Captain.
✗Grey, R, (Hon. Lt.
in Army 28Nov.00)
f.c. 15Mar.14
Lieutenant.
Clonmell, R. C.,
Earl of 29July11
2nd Lieutenant.
Poulett, W. J. L.,
Earl,*late* 2nd Lt.
4 Bn. High L.I.
26Feb.13

---

‡ This rank is not provided for in the Territorial Force Tables of Establishments.

Royal Field Artillery. Territorial Force.

II. ROYAL FIELD ARTILLERY.

[The order of precedence of brigades is denoted by numerals in brackets.]

1st East Anglian Brigade.

[9]

The Barracks, Surrey Street, Norwich.

Hon. Colonel.
p.s. Stradbroke, G.E.,J.M.,
Earl of, C.V.O.,C.B.,
VD. Col., A.D.C.
1Apr.08

In command.
✕Le Mottée, R. E. A.,
Maj. R.A. (*Temp. Lt.-
Col. Terr. Force*)
14Dec.11

Orderly Officer.
Martin, H. S., *lt.*
19Sept.12

Adjutant.
Harvey, C. G. S. Capt.
R.A. 18Apr.14
Medical Officer.

1st Norfolk Battery.

Nelson Road, Great Yarmouth.

Major.
p.s. Wiltshire, P. 14May10

Captain.
Ruddock, H.G.19Sept.12

Lieutenants (2)
Miles, O. 19Sept.12

2nd Lieutenant (1)

2nd Norfolk Battery.

The Barracks,
Surrey Street, Norwich.

Major.

Captain.
Hodges, C. E. 26Apr.13

Lieutenants.
Scott, G. J. 22June14
Kempson, W. R.,
late 2nd Lt. Res.
of Off. 22June14

2nd Lieutenant (1)

3rd Norfolk Battery.

The Barracks,
Surrey Street, Norwich.

Major.
p. Allen, S. G., TD 1Apr.08

Lieutenants (2)
Lane, R.H. 1July13
Claridge, J. W. L.
22 June14

2nd Lieutenant (1)

1st East Anglian Ammunition Column.

The Barracks,
Surrey Street, Norwich.
Captain.

Lieutenants. (2).
Hawksley, J. 1July13
2nd Lieutenants (2).

Cadet Unit affiliated to the Brigade.
Cadet Norfolk Artillery.

2nd East Anglian Brigade.

[14]

Artillery House, The Green, Stratford, E.
Lt.-Colonel.
Duff, W. S., TD 15July11

Orderly Officer.
Duff, A. R. (*t*) 16Mar.09
lt. 3Sept.10
Hough, A. D., *2nd lt.*
21Jan.14

Adjutant.
Lawrence, C. T.,
Capt. R.A. 9June13
Medical Officers.
p. Troup, Maj. G. A.,
M.D., R.A.M.C.
(T.F.) (*attd.*) 1Apr.08
8July96
Watson, Capt. W.
D., R. A. M. C.
(T.F.) (*attd.*) 8Aug.08
8Feb.05

Chaplains.
Seally, *Rev.* A. H. W.,
Chapl. 4th Class
(T.F.) (*attd.*) 1 Apr.08
28May07
Spilsbury, *Rev.* J.
H.G., Chapl. 4th
Class (T.F.)(*attd.*)
11May11

1st Essex Battery.

Artillery House, The Green,
Stratford, E.

Major.
Castellan,V.E. 15July11

Captain.
Wilson, H. R. 3Sept.13

Lieutenants (2)

2nd Lieutenant (1)
Duff, C. G. 15July11
Radford, J. W. 20Feb.12
Mortimer, P. E. N.
1Dec.12
Conoley, D. J. 8Feb.13

2nd Essex Battery.

17, Victoria Road, Romford.

Major.
Castellan, C. E.1Apr.08

Captain.

Lieutenants (2)
Capon, H. V. 24Apr.11
Matcham, A. W.
16Mar.12
2nd Lieutenant (1)
Pryce, E. C. 13May14

3rd Essex Battery.

Artillery Drill Hall,
Grays.

Major.

Captain.
Kemsley, M. H.
1Sept.12

Lieutenants. (2)
✕Cunliffe, E. H. 1Apr.09
Pendlebury, W. J.
von M. 1June12

2nd Lieutenant. (1)
Dudding, L. E. G.
28June12
Brooks, H. R. G.2Nov.12

2nd East Anglian Ammunition Column.

Artillery House, The Green,
Stratford, E.

Captain.
p.s. Hatton, R. A. (Q).
1July10

Lieutenants (2)
Tibbs, H. G. 3Sept.10

2nd Lieutenants (2)
Conoley, O. F. 8Feb.13
Harris, W. J. 14May13
Hibbert, J. P. M.
19June13
Challis, J. H. T.7Feb.14
Trower, W. G. 22Apr.14

3rd East Anglian (Howitzer) Brigade.

[37]

The Drill Hall, Gt. Gipping
Street, Ipswich.

Lt.-Colonel.
p.s.Stradbroke, G. E.
J. M., Earl of,
C.V.O., C.B.,
VD, Col. A.D.C.24Nov.88

Orderly Officer.
Kenyon, J. R., Lt.
30June12

Adjutant.
Montgomery, R.
N. V., Lt. R.A.,
capt. 23July12

Medical Officer.

Chaplain.
Thompson, *Rev.* G. H.,
Chapl. 4th Class,
(T.F.) (*attd.*) 1Apr.08
26Mar.05

Royal Field Artillery. Territorial Force.

1st Suffolk (Howr.) Battery.

The Drill Hall, Beccles Road, Lowestoft.

Major.

Captain.
Smith, S.   11Feb.13

Lieutenants (2).

2nd Lieutenant (1)
Brooks, R. W., 25May12
Cooper, S. G.   7Mar.13

2nd Suffolk (Howr.) Battery.

Drill Hall, Gt. Gipping Street, Ipswich.

Major.
Miller, H. W.   31May13

Captain.
p. Ward, F. S.   1Mar.13

Lieutenants (2)
Fraser, D. C.   20Mar.14

2nd Lieutenant (1)
Wolton, R. N.   24July13

3rd East Anglian (Howr.) Ammunition Column.

The Drill Hall, Arnold Road, Lowestoft.

Captain.
Everett, N.   14Feb.14

Lieutenant.

2nd Lieutenant.

Cadet Unit affiliated to the Brigade.
Beccles Cadet Corps, R.F.A.

4th East Anglian Brigade.

[55]

28, St. Andrew's Street, Hertford.

Hon. Colonel.
⚔Salisbury, Rt. Hon., J. E. H., Marq. of, G.C.V.O., C.B., TD, R., Col., A.D.C. (H)   17Feb.09

Lt.-Colonel.
Exeter, W. T. B., Marq. of, late Capt. 3Bn. North'n R.   21Jan.14

Orderly Officer.

Adjutant.
⚔Bourchier, R. W. H., Capt., R.A.   1Sept.11

Medical Officer.
Walker, Lt. J., M.B., R.A.M.C. (T.F.) (attd.) 18Mar.13

Chaplain.
Chaplin, Rev. A., Chapl. 4th Class (T.F.) (attd.) 1July12

1st Hertfordshire Battery.

Artillery Buildings, Harpenden Road, St. Albans.

Major.

Captain.
Bailey, E. A. H.,1June12
Smith, J. U.   1July12

Lieutenants. (2)
Newton, A. D. 15June12
Luxmoore, L. A. 1Feb.14
               26July13

2nd Lieutenant. (1)

2nd Hertfordshire Battery.

Clarendon Hall, Watford.

Major.
Holland, G. R. 1June12

Captain.

Lieutenants. (2)
Agnew, A. G. 15June12
Foot, R. C.   1Feb.14

2nd Lieutenant. (1)

Northamptonshire Battery.

Drill Hall, Queen's Street, Peterborough.

Major.

Captain.
p. ⚔Walker, T. H. (Hon.Lt.in Army 18 July 02)   1May11

Lieutenants. (2)
p.s. Stanley, F.E.C. (H)   13Aug.04
Phillips, C. J. H.   15June12

2nd Lieutenant. (1)

4th East Anglian Ammunition Column.

28, St. Andrew's Street, Hertford.
Captain.

Lieutenants (2).

2nd Lieutenants (2).

The Cheshire Brigade.

See page 739.

1st Highland Brigade.

[10]

North Silver Street, Aberdeen.

Hon. Colonel
Aberdeen, Rt. Hon. J. C., Earl of, K.T., G.C.M.G., G.C.V.O. (King's Body Gd. for Scotland) 14Jan.88

Lt.-Colonel.
p. Duncan, M. M., vD (Q)   23Aug.13

Orderly Officer.
Cooper, J. R., lt.   10June12

Adjutant.
⚔Devitt, K. H., Lt. R.A., capt. 27Sept.12

Medical Officers.
p. Stephen, Capt. J.H., R.A.M.C. (T.F.) (attd.) 13Mar.09
               30Apr.04
Agassiz, Capt. C.D.S., M.B., R.A.M.C. (T.F.) (attd.) 30Oct.13
               30Apr.10

Chaplain.
Donald, Rev. G. H., M.A., [C.S.] Chapl. 4th Class (T.F.) (attd.)   1Apr.08

1st City of Aberdeen Battery.

North Silver Street, Aberdeen.

Major.
p.s. Rae, J. E. (A)   9Jan.13

Captain.
p.s. Edwards, J. H. (A)   23Aug.13

Lieutenants (2)
Macdonell, J. F.   10June12
Duffus, J. C.   21May13

2nd Lieutenant. (1)
Jameson, A. S. 24Mar.14

2nd City of Aberdeen Battery.

North Silver Street, Aberdeen.

Major.
p.s. Garden, J. W. (A) (Q)   23Aug.13

Captain.
p.s. Davidson, L. J. (A) (t)   31Mar.13

Lieutenants (2)
Innes, A.   10June12
Collie, J. S. G. 5May14

2nd Lieutenant. (1)
Stobie, J.F.R. ⓢ4Oct.13

3rd City of Aberdeen Battery.

Major.
p.s. Fleming, F.(Q)17May11

Captain.
p.s. Kay, F. W. (q) 13June03

Lieutenants (2)
Ledingham, R. M.   5May14

2nd Lieutenant (1).
Davidson, L.M. 19Feb.14

Royal Field Artillery. Territorial Force.

1st Highland Ammunition Column.
North Silver Street, Aberdeen.
Captain.
p.s. Davidson, T.(A) 8June06
Lieutenants (2)
p.s. Barclay-Milne, J. (A) 8June06
Mellis, G. D. 10June12
2nd Lieutenants (2)
Mackie, J. C. D. 18Feb.14

2nd Highland Brigade.
[13]
Dudhope, Drill Hall, Brown Street, Dundee. Dundee.
Hon. Colonel.
Playfair, G. J., Lord, C.V.O., Hon.Brig.-Gen. ret. pay 12Dec.03
Lt.-Colonel.
p. Laing, D., TD 6Jan.12
Orderly Officer.
Adjutant.
Ivens, C. W. M., Capt. R.A. 1Dec.12
Medical Officer.
Price, L. T., M.B., Surg.-Lt. 22May07
Chaplains.
Davidson, Rev. H. M., M.A., VD, [C.S.] Chapl. 2nd Class(T.F.)(attd.) 1Apr.08
8Dec.88
Sutherland, Rev. A. N., M.A. [U.F.C.] Chapl. 3rd Class(T.F.)(attd.) 1Apr.10
24Apr.96
Durward, Rev. C., D.D.[C.S.]Chapl. 4th Class (T.F.) (attd.) 16July09

Forfarshire Battery.
Arbroath.
Major.
Captain.
Fraser, H. 1Apr.13
Wilson, S. C. 17May13
Lieutenants. (2)
Gibb, A. R. 13Aug12
2nd Lieutenant. (1)
Meikle, J. B. 7Jan.13

Fifeshire Battery.
Leven.
Major.
Shepherd, W., TD. 5Dec.07
Captain.
Shepherd, W. K.O. 1July10
Lieutenants. (2)
Shepherd, J.O. 1Apr.10
Shepherd, S.O. 12May12
2nd Lieutenant. (1)
Sandeman, B S. 5July12

City of Dundee Battery.
Dudhope, Drill Hall, Brown Street, Dundee.
Major.
p.s. Mudie R. A., TD, Hon. l.c. (Q) 26May06
Captain.
p. Malcolm, K. S. 12May06
Lieutenants. (2)
Tawse, J. G. 12May12
2nd Lieutenant. (1)
Wighton, A. A. 1May13
Medical Officer.
p. Greig, Maj. D. M., M.B., TD., R.A. M.C. (T.F.) (attd.), late Surg. Med. Staff 3Dec.04
15Apr.93

2nd Highland Ammunition Column.
Dudhope, Drill Hall, Brown Street, Dundee.
Captain.
p.s. Jenkins, J. H.(A)(q) 15May13
Lieutenants. (2)
2nd Lieutenants. (2)
Duffus, J. M. C. 1May13

3rd Highland (Howr.) Brigade.
[22]
8, South Street, Greenock.
Hon. Colonel.
p.s.Scott, C. C., VD (Hon. Col. ret, T.F.) 20Sept.13
Lt.-Colonel.
p.s. Macfarlane, P. C. 17May13
Orderly Officer.
Adjutant.
Medical Officer.
Squair, Capt. F. W., M.B., R.A.M.C. (T.F.)(attd.) 17Nov.10
17May07
Chaplain.
Macpherson, Rev. J. F., B.D., VD,[C.S.]Chapl. 1st Class(T.F.) (attd.) 1Apr.08
9Jan.78

1st Renfrewshire (Howr.) Battery.
8, South Street, Greenock.
Major.
p. Robertson, G. R. G. 22Apr.09
Scott, C. C. S. 19Nov.10
Lieutenants (2).
2nd Lieutenant (1).

2nd Renfrewshire (Howr.) Battery.
8, South Street, Greenock.
Major.
p.s. Hamilton, J. W. (A) 1Apr.08
Captain.
Paterson, D. 6Apr.10
Lieutenants (2)
Fulton, C.G. 19Nov.10
Walker, H. C. 19Nov.10
2nd Lieutenant (1)
Kennedy, J. Y. M. 15Feb.13

3rd Highland (Howr.) Ammunition Column.
Cathcart.
Captain.
Weir, J. G. 1June09
Lieutenant.
McCusker, C. H. 19Nov.10
2nd Lieutenant.
Manuel, G. W. 11June12

Renfrewshire Small Arm Section Ammunition Column.
Cathcart.
Lieutenant.
‡ *2nd Lieutenant.*
Willock, D. C. 21Oct.11

1st Home Counties Brigade.
[6]
Drill Hall, Church Street, Brighton.
Lt.-Colonel.
p.s.Cusack-Smith, Sir T. B., K.C.M.G., ⓟ (A) 21Jan.11
Orderly Officer.
Fowler, G. H. M., capt. 6May13
Adjutant.
✕Hale, D.B., Capt. R.A. 3Jan.12
Medical Officer.
p. Preston, Capt. J. A., R.A.M.C. (T.F.) (attd.) 8June10
8Dec.06
Chaplains.
Sheffield, Rt. Rev. L. H., Lord Bishop of, D.D., Chapl. 1st Class(T.F.)(attd.) 11July09
15Jan.96
Hoskyns, Rev. Canon B. G., M.A., Chapl. 4th Class (T.F.) (attd.) 1Apr.08
30Apr.07

1st Sussex Battery.
Drill Hall, Church Street, Brighton.
Major.
p.s. Boxall, A. P.(A) 6May13
Captain.
p. Darke, H. C. (A) 6May13
Lieutenants (2)
Baines, J. H. 6May13
2nd Lieutenant (1)
Flynn, T. H. 3Apr.12
Wyley, D. H. Fitz T. 12June13

‡ This rank is not provided for in the Territorial Force Tables of Establishments.

Royal Field Artillery. Territorial Force.

1st Home Counties—contd.

2nd Sussex Battery.
Drill Hall, Church Street, Brighton.

Major.
*Rigden, W. P. 1Apr.08

Captain.
Havers, H. L. 28Mar.12

Lieutenants (2)
Wade, H. R. 6May13
Davison, H. B. B. 19Nov.13

2nd Lieutenant (1)
Cole, C. H. T. 20Nov.13

3rd Sussex Battery.
Drill Hall, Marmion Road, Hove.

Major.
Barton, P. H. 8Aug.11

Captain.
Cawood, W. B. C. 6May13

Lieutenants (2)
Gribble, H. C. 19Feb.10
Clayton, C. L. 28Mar.12

2nd Lieutenant (1)
Gribble, D. S. 29May12
Collins, G. R. G. 13Mar.14

1st Home Counties Ammunition Column.
Worthing.

Captain.
p.s. Holman, H. F. (A) 10Oct.06

Lieutenants (2)
Moore, E. S. 8June12
   6May11

2nd Lieutenants (2)
Bowles, H.C.B. 1Nov.13
Barker, J. W. 6Nov.13
Colman, L. M. 1Mar.14
Kempthorne, H. S. 28Apr.14

Cadet Units affiliated to the Brigade.
1st Cadet Battalion, 1st Home Counties Brigade R.F.A. (Imperial Service Cadet Corps), Brighton.
Steyne School Cadet Corps.
The Brighton Brigade, Sussex Cadets.

2nd Home Counties Brigade.
[7]

The Goffs, Eastbourne.

Hon. Colonel.
Brassey, T., Earl, G.C.B., TD [F] 2Dec.91

Lt.-Colonel.
p. Roberts, A. C., TD, hon. c. (A) 19Oct.10
   4July03

Orderly Officer.
Hulbert, H. R., Capt., hon. m. (Q) 7Jan.14

Adjutant.
Blathwayt, Capt.
H. W., R.A. 14Feb.14

Medical Officers.
p. Coigate, Lt.-Col. H., M.D., VD, (hon. Surg.-Col.) R.A.M.C. (T.F.) (attd.) 4Mar.99
   8Feb.79
p. Boyd, S. McC., Surg.-Capt. 27Sept.99
   14Sept.98
Heiser, Lt. A. L., R.A.M.C. (T.F.) (attd.) 4Sept.08

Chaplain.
White, Rev. H. R., Chapl. 4th Class (T.F.) (attd.) 26June12

4th Sussex Battery.
The Goffs, Eastbourne.

Major.
p.s. Moss, B. W. H. (A) 15Aug.08

Captain.
Sutton, T., jun (q) 1Feb.14

Lieute (2)
Stevens, L. 27Mar.12

2nd Lieutenant (1)
Muir Smith, E. H. 5June12

5th Sussex Battery.
Hatherly Road, St. Leonard's-on-Sea.

Major.
✗Beardsley, W.J., Capt. ret. pay 27Mar.12

Captain.

Lieutenants (2)
Hepworth, G.P. 25Mar.13
Schneider, L. W. 26Mar.13

2nd Lieutenant (1)
Crewdson, R. B. 10Aug.13
Simmons, R. D. H. 1Oct.13

6th Sussex Battery.
The Downs, Bexhill-on-Sea.

Captain.
p.s. Bradford, S. H. (A) 1Mar.07

Lieutenants (2)
Lloyd, R. H. 22July13

2nd Lieutenant (1)
Rogers C. E. 27May14
   24Mar.10

2nd Home Counties Ammunition Column.
Hailsham.

Captain.
p.s. Plomley, N. H. (A) 1May09
   20Nov.07
p.s. Strickland, G. F. 31Mar.11

Lieutenants (2)
Strickland, W. E. 27Mar.12
Fry, J. L. 14Apr.13
   1Jan.12

2nd Lieutenants (2)

Cadet Units affiliated to the Brigade.
Imperial Service Cadet Corps, Eastbourne.
St. Leonard's Collegiate School Cadet Co.

3rd Home Counties (Cinque Ports) Brigade.
[11]

Dover.

Hon. Colonel.
Northbourne, W.H., Lord 10Aug.98

Lt.-Colonel.
p. Hayward, F. G., TD (A) 8June12

Orderly Officer.

Adjutant.
Beresford-Peirse, N. M. de la P., Lt. R. A., Capt. 1Aug13

Medical Officers.
p. Gilbert, Lt.-Col. J. W. T., VD, R.A.M.C. (T. F.) (attd.) 23June06
   22May86
p. Berry, Maj. J. B., TD, R.A.M.C. (T.F.) (attd.) 12Dec.03
   28Nov.91
p. Sutcliffe, Capt. W. G., R. A. M. C. (T.F.) (attd.) 1Apr.08
   23Aug.05

1st Kent Battery.
DrillHall, Liverpool Street, Dover.

Major.
p.s Carder, C. D. (A) 1July13

Captain.
✗Gilmore, A. E. 14June13

Lieutenants (2)
Hoare, F. C. 1May13

2nd Lieutenant (1)

2nd Kent Battery.
Drill Hall, Shellon Street, Folkestone.

Major.
p.s. Kennett, W. B. (A) 21Jan.11

Captain.
p.s. Weston, S.L. (A) 7Dec.07

Lieutenants (2)
Wise, S. A. 25Apr.11

2nd Lieutenant (1)
Loyd, V. G. 1May13

3rd Kent Battery.
Drill Hall, High Street, Ramsgate.

Major.
p.s. Page, S. H. (A)ⓈⓈ 3Feb.12

Captain.
p.s. Searles, P. A. (A) 6July07

Lieutenants (2)
Heslop, W. T. B. 25Apr.11

2nd Lieutenant (1)
Chard, R. H. 23July13
Clarke, E. A. 10Dec.13

3rd Home Counties (Cinque Ports) Ammunition Column.
Drill Hall, Deal.

Captain.
p.s. Denne, R. T. (A) 1July13

Lieutenants (2)
Denne, L. G. L. 1Feb.13

2nd Lieutenants.
Edgar, L. A. 11May13

Royal Field Artillery. Territorial Force.

4th Home Counties (Howitzer) Brigade.
[12]

"Trevethan," Bexley Road, Erith, Kent.

Hon. Colonel.
Camden, J.C., Marq., TD.,
Maj. W. Kent Yeo. 23Aug.09

Lt.-Colonel.
Pleydell-Bouverie,
Hon. S. (H) 14June09

Orderly Officer.

Adjutant
Denniss, C. E. B.,
Capt. R.A. 1Jan.13

Medical Officers.
Mayston, Lt. R. W ,
R.A.M.C. (T.F.)
(attd.) 27Oct.08
Murison, Lt. W, R.,
R.A.M.C. (T.F.)
(attd.) 17Nov.08

Chaplain.
Milton, Rev. T. B.,
Chapl. 4th Class
(T.F.) (attd.) 11May10

4th Kent (Howr.) Battery.
Erith.

Major.
Smith, D. K. 1July12

Lieutenants (2)
Wheeler, J. F. 16Feb.12
Pelham, D. V. 27Mar.12

2nd Lieutenant (1)
Mitchell, E. H. 29July13
Cooper, E. J. 10June14

5th Kent (Howr.) Battery.
Erith.

Major.
✗Thomas, S. E. (Hon.
Lt. in Army 1May02) 27Oct.08

Captain.
✗Thompson, J. C. G. 30May12

Lieutenants (2)
Coombs, R. L. 27Mar.12
Taverner, G. B. R. 2Aug.12

2nd Lieutenant (1)
Gascoyne-Cecil,
J, A. 27July13

4th Home Counties (Howr.) Ammunition Column.
Erith.

Captain.

Lieutenant.
Collyer, T. W. 25June13

2nd Lieutenant.
Grune, G. D, J.
12Nov.13
May, J. S. 14Mar.14

1st East Lancashire Brigade.
[16]

50, King Street, Blackburn.

Hon. Colonel.
Shuttleworth, Rt.
Hon. U. J., Lord
12Aug.10

Lt.-Colonel.
Frankish, T. (A) 23Sept.13

Orderly Officer.
Wilson, J., 7Apr.09
lt. 22June10

Adjutant
✗Clark, C. H.,
Capt. R.A. 18Sept.13

Medical Officers.
Gunn, Capt. A.A., M.B.,
R.A.M.C. (T.F.)
(attd.) 16Dec.12
16June09
Kirkness, Capt.
J. M., M.B.,
R.A.M.C.(T.F.)
(attd.) 1Aug.13
1Feb.10

Chaplain.
Morris, Rev. A. J.,
M.A., Chapl. 4th
Class (T.F.) (attd.)
1Apr.08
3Feb.04

4th Lancashire Battery.
50, King Street, Blackburn.

Major.

Captain.
Bickerdike, R. B. 12May12

Lieutenants (2)
Yates, R. 29June11

2nd Lieutenant (1)
Nuttall, E. 13Dec.12
Eccles, H. B. 16Dec.12

5th Lancashire Battery.
Church.

Major.

Captain.
Browning, J. C. 12Aug.12

Lieutenants (2)

2nd Lieutenant (1)
Higham, A. E. 7Oct.12
Higham, T. A. 24Nov.12
Bury, J. 14May13

6th Lancashire Battery.
Burnley.

Major.
Birtwistle, A. (A) 3Jan.12

Captain.
Birtwistle, W. 6Dec.11

Lieutenants (2)
Jobling, G. A. 28Mar.14
Ridehalgh, G. 28Mar.14

2nd Lieutenant (1)
Woodward, F. C. 18Oct.13

1st East Lancashire Ammunition Column.
Blackburn.

Captain.
Blythe, A. L. 15Mar.13

Lieutenants (2)

2nd Lieutenants (2)
Hemmons, B. 2Nov.13
Howson T. A. 5Nov.13
Hartley, G. P. 10Feb.14
Hartley, R. 10Feb.14

2nd East Lancashire Brigade.
(The Manchester Artillery).
[20]

Hyde Road, Manchester.

Hon. Colonel.
p.s. Birley, R. K., C.B.,
VD (A) ⊕ 25Mar.09

Lt.-Colonel.
p. Bowler, H., TD 23Mar.13

Orderly Officer.

Adjutant.
✗Paxton, H. W.,
o. [L] Capt. R.A. 4Nov.13

Medical Officer.
Corbin, Capt. H. E.,
R.A.M.C. (T.F.)
(attd.) 20May12
24Sept.08

Chaplain,
Smith, Rev. H. J., M.A.
Chapl. 4th Class
(T.F.) (attd.) 28June09

15th Lancashire Battery.
Hyde Road, Manchester.

Major.
Walker, L. E. 24Mar.13

Captain.
Keymer, S. A. (A) 1June12

Lieutenants (2)
Stott, S. R. 26Mar.11

2nd Lieutenant (1)
Adamson, J. 2Oct.13

16th Lancashire Battery.
Hyde Road, Manchester.

Major
Leigh, T. H. (A) 28June09

Captain.

Lieutenants (2)
Isherwood, G. A. M. 18Feb.10
Rumney, T. 19June13

2nd Lieutenant (1)
Claus, F. H. 10Mar.14

17th Lancashire Battery.
Hyde Road, Manchester.

Major.
p.s. Hall, J., TD. 25Mar.09

Captain.
p. Dempster, C. 28June09

Lieutenants (2)
Kilvert. V. 28Nov.09

2nd Lieutenant (1)

2nd East Lancashire Ammunition Column.
Hyde Road, Manchester.

Captain.

Lieutenants (2)
Moreland, C. 19June13

2nd Lieutenants (2)
Kessler, C. E. 4Sept.11
Jackson, F. J. G. ?Apr.14

Royal Field Artillery. Territorial Force.

3rd East Lancashire Brigade (The Bolton Artillery). [21]

Drill Hall, Bolton.

Hon. Colonel.
p. Musgrave, H. E., VD. (t) (A) (Hon. Col. ret. Vols.) 27Apr.12

Lt.-Colonel.
Walker, C. E., TD (A) 25Feb.14

Orderly Officer.
(p.) Wingfield, F. (A) capt. 30May08

Adjutant.
Block, A., Lt. R.A., capt. 26Aug.12

Medical Officer.
p. Cosgrave, A., TD Surg.-Maj. 2Aug.02
13July89

Chaplain.
Chapman, Rev. Canon T. A., Chapl. 4th Class (T.F.) (attd.) 15May09

18th Lancashire Battery.

Drill Hall, Bolton.

Major.
Brown, D. 24May12

Lieutenants (2)
Lomax, J. A, B. 27Aug.10
Thwaites, J. M. 1May12

2nd Lieutenants (1).
Scowcroft, H. D. 1Mar.14

19th Lancashire Battery.

Drill Hall, Bolton.

Major.
p.s. Dobson, B. P. (A) 1Sept.11

Captain.
p.s. Higgin, R. G. (A) 8Dec.11

Lieutenants (2)
Smith, N. B. 1May12
Clapham, P. K. 24May12

2nd Lieutenant (1)

20th Lancashire Battery.

Drill Hall, Bolton.

Major.
Ryder, T., TD, ⓟ (A) 1Apr.08

Captain.
Rothwell-Jackson, H. L. (A) 26May09

Lieutenants (2)
Brown, C. R. 27Aug.10

2nd Lieutenant (1)
Scowcroft, C. I. 25Feb.11
Knowles, F. 1Mar.14

3rd East Lancashire Ammunition Column.

Drill Hall, Bolton.

Captain.
p. Nall, J., jun. (A) 20Mar.12

Lieutenants (2)
Thompson, J. 1May12

2nd Lieutenants (2)
Stewart, H.L.G. 1Mar.13
Lewis, J. 1Mar.14

4th East Lancashire (Howitzer) Brigade (The Cumberland Artillery). [30]

Workington.

Hon. Colonel.
Lonsdale, H. C., Earl of (Hon. Col. ret. T. F.) 20Dec.84

Lt.-Colonel.
p. Dudgeon, J. H., VD (A) 9Mar.10

Orderly Officer.
Thompson, M. F., 2nd lt. 3Jan.12

Adjutant.
Massy, H.R.S., Lt.R.A., capt. 15Jan.13

Medical Officer.
Rigg, A. H., Lt. R.A.M.C. (T.F.) (attd.) 1Apr.07

Chaplain.

1st Cumberland (Howr.) Battery.

Carlisle.

Major.

Captain.
p.s. Valentine, C. A. (A) 2July07

Lieutenants (2)
Bowman, A. H. 29June12
Marks, H. N. 11July12

2nd Lieutenant (1)
Marks, G. W. 16Mar.12

2nd Cumberland (Howr.) Battery.

Workington.

Major.

Captain.
p.s. Mason, D. J. (A) 3June05
Highet, W. T. (A) 1Apr.14

Lieutenants (2)
Highton, L. 30June12

2nd Lieutenant (1)
Smith, R. A. 15Mar.13
Ellison, J. M 25Aug.13

4th East Lancashire (Howr.) Ammunition Column

Workington

Captain.
p.s. Burnyeat, R. W. (A) 9Apr.13

Lieutenant.

2nd Lieutenant.
Richards, A. S. E. 16May13

1st West Lancashire Brigade. [15]

Windsor Barracks, Spekeland Street, Liverpool.

Hon. Colonel.
p. Wilson, T., C.B., VD (Hon. Col. ret. Vols.) 2Jan.98

Lt.-Colonel.
p Osborn, L. J., VD (A) 9Sept.11

Orderly Officer.

Adjutant.
Kennedy, A. J. R., Lt. R.A., capt. 8Sept.13

Medical Officers.
Richards, Capt. H.E.S., M.D., R.A.M.C. (T.F.) (attd.) 15Dec.13
Davis, Lt. W. J. H., R.A.M.C. (T. F.) (attd.) 2May13

Chaplain.
Adams, Rev. W. J., VD, Chapl. 1st Class (T.F.) (attd.) 22Oct.87

1st Lancashire Battery.

Windsor Barracks, Spekeland Street, Liverpool.

Major.
Walker, A. N. (A) 9Sept.11

Captain.
p. Johnson, E. P. (A) 9Sept.11

Lieutenants (2)
p.s. Aikman, W. W. (A) 21May12

2nd Lieutenant (1)
Ronald, B. K. 28Sept.10

2nd Lancashire Battery.

Windsor Barracks, Spekeland Street, Liverpool.

Major.
p. Walker, G. L. (A) 16Aug.09

Captain.
Nesbitt, J. T. 1Oct.10

2nd Lieutenant (1)

3rd Lancashire Battery.

Windsor Barracks, Spekeland Street, Liverpool.

Major.
p. Heap, R. R. (q) (A) 1Jan09

Captain.
p.s. Thomson, A.F. (A) 15Feb.13

Lieutenants (2)
p.s. Adams, T. D. (A) 1Jan.09

2nd Lieutenant (1)
Cohan, E. M. 9May11

1st West Lancashire Ammunition Column.

Windsor Barracks, Spekeland Street, Liverpool.

Captain.
Johnson, G. B. (A) 1May07

Lieutenants (2)
Miller, W. R. (A) 1Jan.09

2nd Lieutenants (2)
Stephenson, S. S. 15Oct.10
Eills, W. 23Feb.14

| 691 | 692 | 693 | 694 |

Royal Field Artillery. Territorial Force.

2nd West Lancashire Brigade.
[17]

Drill Hall,
Stanley Street, Preston.
Hon. Colonel.
Trimble, C. J.,
C.M.G., VD (A)
(Hon. Col. ret.
T.F.) (Lt.-Col. &
Hon.Col.T.F.Res.)
14 Mar. 14
Lt.-Colonel.
Ryland, A. W., VD,
✪(A) 20 Dec. 13
Orderly Officer.
Sharples, S., *2nd lt.*
29 May 12
Adjutant.
Greaves, H. M. *e.*,
Capt. R.A. 13 Nov. 13
Medical Officers.
p. Lamport, Maj.
H. C., *M.B.*, TD,
R.A.M.C.(T.F.)
(*attd.*) 27 Sept. 02
13 July 89
Crawford, Lt. A. N.,
F.R.C.S.I., R.A.M.C.
(T.F.) (*attd.*) 12 July 12
Chaplain.
Collinson. Rev. S. E.,
Chapl. 4th Class
(T.F.) (*attd.*) 1 Apr. 08
6 Feb. 04

9th Lancashire Battery.
Drill Hall,
Stanley Street, Preston.
Major.
Simpson, S., TD
(A)(Q) 1 Apr. 08
Captain.
p.s. Miller, T.H.(Q) 28 May 02
5 July 99
Lieutenants. (2)
p.s. Foster, J. H. (A)
(q) 28 Apr. 06
Smith, S. (A) 23 Nov. 10
Lieutenant. (1)
Bowdler, W.A. 12 Aug. 12

10th Lancashire Battery.
Drill Hall, Dallas Road,
Lancaster.
Major.
Captain.
p.s. Wilson, H. D. (A)
(t) 7 Feb. 03
Lieutenants. (2)
Smith, B. J. 15 July 11
Helme, R. E. 12 Apr. 12
2nd Lieutenant. (1)
Wilson, G. F. E.
1 Sept. 13
Downton, A.M. 18 Dec. 13

11th Lancashire Battery.
Drill Hall, Yorkshire Street,
Blackpool.
Major.
✪Topping, T. E., D.S.O.,
TD (Hon. Capt. in
Army 19 Dec, 01) (Q)
1 Apr. 08
Captain.
p.s. Furness, C. C. (q) ✪
28 May 09
Lieutenants. (2)
Plant, E. F. 16 July 10
2nd Lieutenant. (1)
Bowdler, A. R. H.
1 Mar. 13
Lawrence, H. M.
1 May 13

2nd West Lancashire Ammunition Column.
Drill Hall, Stanley Street,
Preston.
Captain.
p. Leigh, E, (A) 7 Feb. 08
Lieutenants. (2)
Hudson, J. 28 Nov. 10
2nd Lieutenants. (2)
Swindells, A.C. 14 Feb. 13
Hall, R. W. P. 19 Dec. 13
Wünsch, A. E. 7 May 14

3rd West Lancashire Brigade.
[18]

65, Admiral Street,
Liverpool.
Hon. Colonel.
Gossage, W. W., VD,
(Hon. Col. ret.
T.F.) 1 Feb. 10
Lt.-Colonel.
Reynolds, J. P. (A)
6 Jan. 09
Orderly Officer.
Bragg, W. H., *2nd lt.*
10 Nov. 13
Adjutant.
Hallett, A. M.,
Lt. R.A., *capt.*1Feb.14
Medical Officers.
p. Bailey, F. W.,
Surg.-Capt. 12 June 07
12 Dec. 03
Wills, H. R. G., *M.B.*,
R.A.M.C.,(T.F.)(*attd.*)
27 July 12

Chaplain.
Elcum, Rev. C. C.,
M.A., TD, Chapl.
1st Class (T.F.)
(*attd.*) 25 Mar. 13
25 Mar. 93

12th Lancashire Battery.
65, Admiral Street,
Liverpool.
Major.
p.s. Stead, R. (A) 3 Aug. 11
Captain.
p.s. Kirby, E. B. (A)
23 Mar. 10
Lieutenants. (2)
Castle, G. E. 30 Apr. 12
Beazley, H. G. 29 Jan. 13
2nd Lieutenant. (1)
Bicket, T. B. 5 July 12

13th Lancashire Battery.
1, Earp Street,
Garston.
Major.
Decker, H. J., TD
17 June 08
Captain.
p.s. Williams, J. C. M.
(A) 2 Feb. 10
Lieutenants. (2)
Archer, R. S. 30 Apr. 12
Rimmer, E. 30 Apr. 12
2nd Lieutenant. (1)
Jacob, A. M. 1 Apr. 12

14th Lancashire Battery.
Widnes.
Major.
p.s. Rimmer, S.(A) 21 June 09
Captain.
Bibby, A. H. 21 July 13
Lieutenants. (2)
Maclaran, M. S. 2 Mar. 11
2nd Lieutenant. (1)
Tipton, R. J. 16 Mar. 11
Shelmerdine, H.N.
23 Feb. 12

3rd West Lancashire Ammunition Column.
65, Admiral Street,
Liverpool.
Captain.
Archer, R. S., VD,
hon. m. (A) 18 June 02
Lieutenants. (2)
Gossage, A. W. 6 Nov. 13
2nd Lieutenants. (2)
Chambers, W. J. B.,
4 Jan. 11
Rimmer, A. E. 8 Nov. 13

4th West Lancashire (Howitzer) Brigade.
[19]

Edge Lane, Liverpool.
Hon. Colonel.
✪Bethune, Lt.-Gen
E. C., C.V.O.,
C.B., Col.4 D.G.,
p.s.c. (Dir.-Gen.
of the Terr.
Force) 14 Feb. 14
Lt.-Colonel.
p. Melly, S. H., TD 24 Jan. 14
Orderly Officer.
Tod, A. C, (A)
lt. 30 Mar. 09
Adjutant.
Burton, A. R., Lt.
R.A., *capt.* 25 July 11
Medical Officers.
Young, Capt.F.W.B.,
M.B., R.A.M.C.
(T.F.) (*attd.*) 7 May 12
7 Nov. 08
Smith, Lt. G. F. R.,
M.B., R.A.M.C.
(T.F.) (*attd.*) 12 Feb. 13
Chaplain.
Coop, Rev. J. O.,
M.A., TD, Chapl.
1st Class (T.F.)
(*attd.*) 16 Dec. 13
16 Dec. 93

7th Lancashire (Howr.) Battery.
Edge Lane, Liverpool.
Major.
Wolff, J. A. (A) 24 Jan. 14
Captain.
p. Moore, W. A. M. (A)
(t) 30 May 09
Lieutenants. (2)
Darbishire, H. D.
30 Apr. 10
Sing, L. M. 24 Jan. 14
2nd Lieutenant. (1)
Rae, G. K. L. 1 Nov. 12

Royal Field Artillery. Territorial Force.

4th West Lancashire—contd.

8th Lancashire (How.) Battery.
Edge Lane, Liverpool.

Major.
p. Morter, S. P., TD, ⊕ (A) 30May09

Captain.
p. Hemelryk, E. V. 24Jan.14

Lieutenants. (2)
Brocklebank, T. G. 3May13
                    1Apr.10
Cotton, V. E. 18Apr.14

2nd Lieutenant. (1)
Barstow, J. N. 21Mar.14

4th West Lancashire (How.) Ammunition Column.
Edge Lane, Liverpool.

Captain.
p. Moss, W. E. (A) 19Mar.04

Lieutenant.
Overton, P. J. S. 6Aug.10

2nd Lieutenant.

1st London (City of London) Brigade.
[41]
Handel Street, Bloomsbury, W.C.

Hon. Colonel.
The Rt. Hon. the Lord Mayor of London for the time being.

Lt.-Colonel.
p. Stollery, J., VD, hon. c. 4Jan.99

Orderly Officer.

Adjutant.
✗Salmond, F. W., Capt., R.A. 20Oct.11

Medical Officers.
p. Stedman, Maj. H., M.D., R.A.M.C. (T.F.) (attd.) 23Nov.08
                    3Apr.97
Donald, Lt. R., R.A.M.C. (T.F.) (attd.) 28July11

1st City of London Battery.
Handel Street, Bloomsbury, W.C.

p. Janes, T. H. 30July04

Captain.
Jones, H. P. 10May12

Lieutenants. (2)
Hurst, S. H. 10May12

2nd Lieutenant. (1)
Watson, W. E. 4Oct.13

2nd City of London Battery.
Handel Street, Bloomsbury, W.C.

Major.
p. Batt, W. E. (A) 3Aug.10

Captain.
June14

Lieutenants. (2)

2nd Lieutenant. (1)
✗Reid, A. V. 18Dec.12
Hummel, H. V. 12July13

3rd City of London Battery.
Handel Street, Bloomsbury, W.C.

Major.
p.s. Thomas, F. D. B. 9Aug.10

Captain.
Inglis, T. S. 8July13

Lieutenants. (2)
Thomas, F. D. 12Dec.12

2nd Lieutenant. (1)
Oakley, H. J. P. 14Feb.14

1st London (City of London) Ammunition Column.
Handel Street, Bloomsbury, W.C.

Captain.
p.s. Liddle, G. J. (A) 9Feb.12

Lieutenants. (2)

2nd Lieutenants. (2)

2nd London Brigade.
[42]
Royal Arsenal, Woolwich.

Hon. Colonel.
✗Grierson, Lt.-Gen. Sir J. M., K.C.B., C. V. O., C. M. G. (late R.A.), p.s.c [L] [R] [F] 𝔄.𝔙.ℭ.
s. 28Oct.12

Lt.-Colonel.
p.s. Tasker, R.B., VD (Q) (A) 27Nov.12

Orderly Officer.
Rickards, T.M. 10Feb.11

Adjutant.
Henderson, J. A.,' Capt. R.A. 1Nov11

Medical Officer.
Fergusson, Lt. N. M., M.B., R.A.M.C. (T.F.) (attd.) 15Jan,11
Wotherspoon, Lt. J., M.B., R A.M.C. (T.F.) (attd.) 17June13

Chaplain.
Hall, Rev. H. A., M.A., Chapl. 4th Class (T.F.) (attd.) 1Feb.11

4th County of London Battery.
Beresford Street, Woolwich.

Major.
p.s. Odam, W. T. (Lt. Res. of Off.) (A) (t) 17Nov.08
p. Aschwanden, S.W.L.(A) 26May12

Captain.
Holmes, G.T. 1June09
                    17Nov.08

Lieutenants (2)
Martell, R. W. 24Feb.12

2nd Lieutenant. (1)
Thornton, J. C. 1Mar.12
Smail, J. D. 16Sept.12

5th County of London Battery.
Beresford Street, Woolwich.

Major.
p. Grandage, W.B. 3Oct.12

Lieutenants. (2)
Hamilton, G. M. 21May07
Lee, R. T. 24Feb.12
Godman, J. F. 3Oct.12

2nd Lieutenant. (1)
Hanbury, C. E. R. 21Oct.12
Booth, J. C. 20Dec.13

6th County of London Battery.
Eltham.

Major.

Captain.
p. Jackson, A. C. S. 3Oct 12

Lieutenants. (2)
Parish, J. B. A. 20June12
Griffiths, G. J. 8June13
Marsden, W. A. J. 20Feb.14

2nd London Ammunition Column.
Beresford Street, Woolwich.

Captain.
Gaitskell, C. E. F. 5Dec.12

Lieutenants. (2)
p. Holthouse, C. S. 21May07
Fox, E. J. 18Nov.10
Wolfe, G. B. 20Apr.13

2nd Lieutenants. (2)
Prentice, A. A. 27Sept.12
Beattie, R. J. 26Nov.12

Cadet Unit affiliated to the Brigade.
1 Woolwich Cadet Corps.

3rd London Brigade.
[43]
Artillery Barracks, Leonard Street, City Road, E.C.

Hon. Colonel.
Thompson, A. C. 1Oct.07

Lt.-Colonel.
Prechtel, A. F., TD, (A) 3Dec.13

Orderly Officer.

Adjutant.
Elliott, V., Lt. R.A., capt. 1Nov.12

Medical Officers.
✗Sutherland, Capt. D. S., M.D., R.A.M.C. (T.F.) (attd.) 30Sept.12
                    30Mar.08

Chaplain.

Royal Field Artillery. Territorial Force.

7th County of London Battery.
Artillery Barracks, Leonard Street, City Road, E.C.

Major.
p.s.Hind, J. W. (A) 1July13

Captain.

Lieutenants. (2)
Goodyear, E. T. P. 9June11

2nd Lieutenant. (1)

8th County of London Battery.
Artillery Barracks, Leonard Street, City Road, E.C.

Major.

Captain.
Geard, W. L. 21Dec10
p.s.Fitch, V. F. (A)18Apr14
5July05

Lieutenants. (2)
Young, E. C. 10Apr12

2nd Lieutenant. (1)

9th County of London Battery.
Artillery Barracks, Leonard Street, City Road, E.C.

Major.

Captain.
Harris, A. 23June13

Lieutenants. (2)
Clack, T. S. 1Feb11
11Dec09
Malcomson, T. S. 1Feb14
27July11

2nd Lieutenant. (1)

3rd London Ammunition Column.
Artillery Barracks, Leonard Street, City Road, E.C.

Captain.
Reynolds-Major, E. H. 16Jan13

Lieutenants. (2)

2nd Lieutenants. (2)
Waylen, A. F. 16Apr13
Talbot, R. C. 16Apr13
Squire, J. H. 8Apr14

4th London (Howitzer) Brigade.
[44]
Ennersdale Road, Lewisham, S.E.

Hon. Colonel.
Dewey, T. C. 25Mar05
Lt.-Colonel.
p.s. Lea, E. T., TD 22Feb 11
Orderly Officer
Rutherford, P.T., late Lt. R.A.M.C. (T.F.) 2nd lt. 4Dec12
Adjutant.
Grant, H. De B., Lt. R.A., capt. 1Apr12

Medical Officers.
✗Thomson, Maj. C., R.A.M.C.(T.F.)(attd.) (Maj. ret. Ind. Med. Serv.) 1Nov13
p. Moore, Capt. Y. T. G., R.A.M.C. (T.F.) (attd.) 1Apr11
1Oct07

Chaplain.
Hough, Rev. W. W., Chapl. 4th Class (T.F.) (attd.) 1Apr08
10Jan06

10th County of London (Howr.) Battery.
Ennersdale Road, Lewisham, S.E.

Major.
p.s.✗Finch, E. W. (A) 30Dec12

Captain.
p.s.Dymott, G. L. (q) 22Feb11

Lieutenants. (2)
Gray, J. V. 25Apr12
Moreing, A. H., late Lt. A. Motor Res.26Apr.13

2nd Lieutenant. (1)
Bowater, N. V. 27Oct13

11th County of London (Howr.) Battery.
Ennersdale Road, Lewisham, S.E.

Major.
p.s.Bowater, F. H. 1Apr08

Captain.
p.s.Warrens, E. R. C. (A) 22June10

Lieutenants. (2)
Wright, K. V., 31Mar13
Warrens, B. C. St. G. 1July14
Johnsen, O. C. W. 1July14

2nd Lieutenant. (1)

4th London (Howr.) Ammunition Column.
Ennersdale Road, Lewisham, S.E.

Captain.
Macmin, B. 21June13

Lieutenant.
Beck, W. C. 6Oct09

2nd Lieutenant.
Bowater, F. V. 17Nov13
Mallett, G. 8Apr14

5th London Brigade.
[45]
76, Lower Kennington Lane, S.E.

In Command.
✗Massy, E. C., Maj.R,A.(Temp. Lt.-Col. Terr. Force) 27June13

Orderly Officer

Adjutant.
Purser, A. W. Lt. R.A. capt. 28July13

Medical Officers.
p. Faulder, Capt. T. J., R.A.M.C. (T.F.) (attd.) 9Jan11
9July07

Chaplain.
Steer, Rev. W. H. H., M.A., Chapl. 3rd Class (T.F.) (attd.) 2Aug12
2Aug02

12th County of London Battery.
76, Lower Kennington Lane, S.E.

Major.
✗Mylrea, W. P. G.,Maj. ret. pay (Res. of Off.) 1Mar14

Captain.
Williams, F. A. 1Feb14

Lieutenants. (2)

2nd Lieutenant. (1)
Pollock, H. H. 19Jan14
Winch, G. B. 2Apr14
16Apr13

13th County of London Battery.
76, Lower Kennington Lane, S.E.

Major.
Scammell,A. G.20Dec12

Captain.
Hanworth, H. H. 1Feb14

Lieutenants. (2)
(p.) MacMahon, N. C. M. 4June09

2nd Lieutenant. (1)
Christian, E. 25Mar14

14th County of London Battery.
Porteous Road, Paddington, W.

Major.

Captain
York, R. L. 20May11

Lieutenants. (2)

2nd Lieutenant (1)
Williams, W. W. 2July13
Shuter, A. E. 25Feb14

5th London Ammunition Column.

Captain.
Hatfield, E. R. 1Feb14

Lieutenants. (2)
Barry, L. C. 28Dec12
11Aug11
Marriott, E. C. 12June13

2nd Lieutenants. (2)
Stapley, F. G. 1Apr14
Lindo, G. M. 8May14

Royal Field Artillery. Territorial Force.

6th London Brigade.
[46]
105, Holland Road, Brixton, S.W.

Hon. Colonel.
Esher, R.B., Visct., G.C.B., G.C.V.O. 1June10

Lt.-Colonel.
p.s. ✕MacHugh, R. J. (Q) 27Apr.12

Orderly Officer.

Adjutant.
O'Malley, M. J. K., Lt. R.A. capt. 16Aug.13

Medical Officer.
Welch, Capt. C. H., R.A.M.C. (T.F.) (attd.) 22May13
 9Mar.09

Chaplain.
Gough, Rev. A. W., M.A., Chapl. 4th Class (T.F.) (attd.) 5May10

15th County of London Battery.
105, Holland Road, Brixton, S.W.

Major.
p. ✕ Bayley, H. (A) (t) (Hon. Lt. in Army 1 Dec. 00) 28Oct.12

Captain.
Austin, W. D. 15June12

Lieutenants. (2)
Love, P.A. 1Apr.10
2nd Lieutenant.
Corsan, R. A. 27Apr.12
Barnard, W. J. 25June14

16th County of London Battery.
105, Holland Road, Brixton, S.W.

Major.

Captain.
Gordon, A. C. 1Jan.13
Lieutenants. (2)
Bertie, C. P. 1Jan.13
Cooper, W. 1Jan.13
2nd Lieutenant. (1)
Brasnett, N. V. 4Feb.14

17th County of London Battery.
105, Holland Road, Brixton, S.W.
Major

Captain.
Clifton, P. J. 1Jan.13
p.s. Ensor, F. G. (A) 1Apr.13
 19Nov.07
Lieutenants. (2)
2nd Lieutenant. (1)
Bruce, R. 14Apr.14
Moore, L.W.B. 15Apr.14
Greer, S. T. L. 27Apr.14

6th London Ammunition Column.
105, Holland Road, Brixton, S.W.
Captain.

Lieutenants. (2)

2nd Lieutenants. (2)

7th London Brigade.
[47]
High Street, Fulham, S.W.

Lt.-Colonel.
p.s. Chambers, C.E., vD, (Q) (a) (b) 9June94
 bt. col. 24Dec.13
Orderly Officer.
Ogilvie, A. G., 2nd Lt. 21 Aug.11

Adjutant.
✕Marryat, R., Capt. R.A. 18May11
 20Mar.11
Medical Officer.
Spurgin, Capt. P.B., R.A.M.C. (T.F.) (attd.) 16May13
 16Nov.09

Chaplain.

18th County of London Battery.
High Street, Fulham, S.W.

Major.
p.s. Mead, H. G. (A) 20Jan.10
Captain.
Callaghan, E. F. 1July10

Lieutenants. (2)
Lloyd, L. S. 22June13
2nd Lieutenant. (1)
Coates, W. G. 6Dec.11
Moncrieff, D.C. 2Aug.13

19th County of London Battery.
Drill Hall, Wood Lane, Shepherd's Bush, W.

Major.

Captain.
Gorell, H. G., Lord 19Apr.12

Lieutenants. (2)
Marshall, E. H. 10Dec.09
Wood, N. E. 1Apr.10
2nd Lieutenant. (1)
Saunders, R. A. 4July14

20th County of London Battery.
High Street, Fulham, S.W.

Major.
p.s. Peal-W, E. (A) 20Jan.10
Captain.
Daniels, G. P. 17May11
Lieutenants (2).
(p.) Cooper, P. A. 8Apr.13
 1Apr.08
2nd Lieutenant. (1)
Clegg, M. T. G. 8July11
Burgess, R. E. 19July13

7th London Ammunition Column.
High Street, Fulham, S.W.
Captain.
Egerton-Warburton, C. W. 1Oct.13

Lieutenants. (2)
Allhusen, O. 1Apr.13
Oliver, G. Y. 22June13
2nd Lieutenants. (2)
Simonds, J. 1Sept.13
 1Oct.12

8th London (Howitzer) Brigade.
[48]
"Oaklands," St. Margarets Road, Woolwich, S.E.

Hon. Colonel.
Griffith, F. (Hon. Col. ret. T.F.) 12July11
In Command.
✕Emery, W. B., Maj. R.A. (Temp. Lt.-Col. Terr. Force) 12April.11

Orderly Officer.
Largen, W. G. lt. 20July10
Adjutant.
Popham, G. L., Capt. R.A. 1Sept.13
Medical Officer.

Chaplain.
Christopherson, Rev. D., Chapl. 4th Class (T.F.) (attd.) 9Mar.11

21st County of London (Howr.) Battery.
"Oaklands," St. Margarets Rd., Woolwich, S.E.

Major.
p.s. Eton, E. (A) 2Aug.12
Captain.
p.s. Gaskain, W. D. (A) 3Aug.12

Lieutenants. (2)
McVeagh, H.J. 4Feb.12
White, E. C. 10Aug.12
2nd Lieutenant. (1)
Tomlinson, R. G. 5July13

22nd County of London (Howr.) Battery.
"Oaklands," St. Margarets Rd., Woolwich, S.E.

Major.
p.s. Eley, E. H. (A) 1Apr.08
Captain.
Osborne, F.B. 25Feb.11

Lieutenants. (2)
de Witt, F. 28Mar.14
Mohr, G. A. G. 25Apr.14

2nd Lieutenant. (1)
Hamlett, H.W.10Dec.13
Kindell, F. P. 2Mar.14

8th London (Howr.) Ammunition Column.
"Oaklands," St. Margarets Rd., Woolwich, S.E.

Captain.
Pollard, C.A. Ⓢ 20July10
Lieutenant.

2nd Lieutenant.
Bevan, W. H. 28Mar.14
Taylor, S. 11May14

Royal Field Artillery. Territorial Force.

1st Lowland Brigade.
[8]

Edinburgh.
Hon. Colonel.
Rosebery, Rt. Hon.
A. P., Earl of,
K.G., K.T., VD,
(*King's Body Gd.*
for Scotland) 7Jan.03
Lt.-Colonel.
Findlay, J. L.,
VD (A) 7June09
Orderly Officer.
Combe, A. C., *lt.*
17Aug.12
Adjutant.
Cousens, R.B., Capt.
R.A. 1Nov.11
Medical Officers.
✗Taylor, W. M., *M.D.*,
Surg.-Maj. (Hon.
Lt. in Army 29Nov.
01) 18Sept.13
4Feb.99
Gardiner, Lt.W.T.,
M.B., R.A.M.C.
(T.F.) (*attd.*) 24Oct.12
Chaplains.
Williamson *Very Rev.*
A. W., D.D. [C.S.]
Chapl. 1st Class
(T.F.) (*attd.*) 2Aug.13
1Jan.10
Welch, Rev. A. C., *Th. D.*
[U.F.C.] Chapl. 4th
Class (T.F.) (*attd.*)
1Dec.09

1st City of Edinburgh Battery.
30, Grindlay Street, Edinburgh.
Major.
p.s.Inches, E. J. (A)
1Apr.08
Captain.
p.s.Sime, W. (A) 1Apr.08
Lieutenants (2)
(p.)Blair, H. A. 27Jan.09
(p.)Simpson, A, G. ⑬
lt. 20June10
2nd Lieutenant (1)
Gardiner, R. W.
20Nov.11

2nd City of Edinburgh Battery.
30, Grindlay Street, Edinburgh.
Major.
Mackinlay, C., TD (A)
1Apr.08
Captain.
Porter, W. G. 16Feb.13
Lieutenants (2)
(p.)Reid, R. E. S. 20June10
Cheyne, H. 11Feb.11
2nd Lieutenant (1)
Galletly, I. 5Jan14
Veresmith, D. J. C.
29Apr.14

Midlothian Battery.
30, Grindlay Street, Edinburgh.
Major.
Anderson, W.
H., TD, (A) 17Aug.12
Captain.
Mackinlay, F. B.
11Feb.11
Lieutenants (2)
(p.)Scott, J. M. B. 27Jan.09
Johnstone, C. H. C.
16Feb.13
2nd Lieutenant (1)
Buchan, H. F. W. W.
8June12

1st Lowland Ammunition Column.
30, Grindlay Street, Edinburgh.
Captain.
p. Mitchell-Innes, N.
F. W. (A) 8Dec.09
8Aug.08
Lieutenants (2)
Maxwell, W. 31Oct.12
Paulin, N. G. 5Jan.14
2nd Lieutenants (2)
Kermack, S. G. 8Apr.11
Matheson, A. 6Jan.14
11Nov.12

2nd Lowland Brigade.
[26]

Irvine.
Hon. Colonel.
p.s.MacTaggart Stewart, Sir
M. J., Bt., VD. 22Dec.88
In command.
✗Wilson, C. H., Maj.
R.A. (Temp.
Lt.-Col. Terr.
Force) 9May11
Orderly Officer.

Adjutant.
Elverson, J. H.,
Lt.R.A., *capt.* 27Jan.14
Medical Officers.
Thomson, Lt.-Col. J.,
M.D., VD, R.A.M.C.
(T.F.) (*attd.*) 19Feb.02
7Sept.81
p.✗Aitken, Capt. J., M.D.,
R.A.M.C. (T.F.)
(*attd.*) 15Sept.10
15Mar.07
Chaplains.
Ross, *Rev. W., M.A.*
[U.F.C.], Chapl.
4th Class (T.F.)
(*attd.*) 1Dec.c9
Adamson, Rev. R.
[U.F.C.], Chapl.
4th Class (T.F.)
(*attd.*) 30Oct.11

1st Ayrshire Battery.
Irvine.
Major.
Walker, J. W., TD,
1Apr.08
Captain.
Breckenridge, W.
1Apr.13
Lieutenants (2)
Breckenridge, M. W.
1Aug.11
Reid, R. 10Apr.14
2nd Lieutenant (1)

2nd Ayrshire Battery.
Kilmarnock.
Major.
Milligan, J. 6Apr.11
Captain.
Watson, J. B. 1Feb.14
Lieutenants (2)
Huddleston, R.M.C.
1Mar.13
Findlay, J. 1Apr.14

2nd Lieutenant (1)

Kirkcudbrightshire Battery.
Kirkcudbright.
Major.
Brown, A., TD 1Apr.08
Captain
p.s.Paterson, E. W.20Feb.11
Lieutenants (2)
Corrie, A. 1June11
McDowall, A. 1June11
2nd Lieutenant (1)

2nd Lowland Ammunition Column.
Ardrossan.
Captain.
p.s.Allan, J. M. (A) 1May10
Lieutenants (2)
Crawford, A.R. 1June11
2nd Lieutenants (2)
Hogarth, B. 30Mar.12
Gibb, R. P. F. C. R.
16May13

3rd Lowland Brigade.
[52]

8, Newton Terrace,
Charing Cross,
Glasgow.
Hon. Colonel.
Cayzer, Sir C. W., Bt.
23Mar.96
Lt.-Colonel.
Grant, P., TD 27May11
Orderly Officer.
Higgins, J. W., *lt.*
15Sept.10

Adjutant.
Hay, E. S., Capt.
R.A. 1Mar.12
Medical Officers.
p. ✗Kay, Maj. T., M.B.,
R.A.M.C. (T.F.)
(*attd.*) 3May12
29Nov.99
Bruce, Capt. R., M.B.
R.A.M.C. (T.F.)
(*attd.*) 17Sept.12
17Mar.09
Chaplains.
Campbell, Rev. A. J.,
B.A. [C.S.] Chapl. 4th
Class (T.F.) (*attd.*)
6Mar.14
Hutton, Rev. J. A.,
M.A. [U.F.C.] Chapl.
4th Class (T.F.) (*attd.*)
6Mar.14

1st City of Glasgow Battery.
Berkeley Street,
Charing Cross, Glasgow.
Major.
Lightbody, J. 27May11
Captain.
Gray, T. 27Mar.13
Lieutenants (2)
Harrison, I. R.15Sept.10
Coats, J. W. 15Sept.10
2nd Lieutenant (1)
Turner, A. L. 2Feb.13

2nd City of Glasgow Battery.
Percy Street, Maryhill, Glasgow.
Major.
Kinnear, W. 1Feb.13
Captain.
p.s.Galloway, J. M.6June07
Lieutenants (2)
Laird, W. W. 6 Jan.11
Morrice, J. A., jun.
18Mar.13
2nd Lieutenant (1)
Jones, E. 11Oct.12

3rd City of Glasgow Battery.
Keppochhill,
Springburn, Glasgow.
Major.
Easton, D. T., TD,
1Apr.08
Captain.
p.s. Miller, D, C. (A)
(q) 1Feb.13
2nd Lieutenant (1)
Moffat, G. K. 6Sept.12
Kirsop, C. R. J. 8Jan.13
Macgregor, J. 9Feb.13

Royal Field Artillery. Territorial Force.

3rd Lowland Ammunition Column.
Percy Street, Maryhill, Glasgow.
Captain.
p. Costigane, S. C. E. 28Apr.06
Lieutenants (2)
Brown, J. 15Sept.10
2nd Lieutenants (2)
Finlay, W.G.K. 3Feb.13
Hughes, T. V. 23Jan.14
Dixon, A. M. 23Feb.14

4th Lowland (Howitzer Brigade. [53]
8, Newton Terrace, Charing Cross, Glasgow.
Hon. Colonel.
p. Grant, A. B., M.V.O., vD (Hon. Col. ret. T.F.) 23Nov.12
In command.
✗Sheppard, H. C., Maj. R.A. (temp. Lt.-Col. Terr. Force) 26Apr.12
Orderly Officer.
Watson, W., lt. 6Apr.10
Adjutant.
Cooper, C. F., Capt. R.A. 9Oct.11
Medical Officers.
p.s. Forrest, Maj. R. W., M.B., R.A.M.C. (T.F.) (attd.) 24June13
21Feb.00
Chaplain.
Swanson, Rev. W. S., M.A. [U.F.C.]
Chapl. 4th Class (T.F.) (attd.) 1Dec.09

4th City of Glasgow (Howr.) Battery.
Butterbiggins Road, Govanhill, Glasgow.
Major.
Simpson, G. S. 18July13
Captain.
p.s. Walker, T. M. (A) 9Mar.13
Lieutenants (2)
(p.)Peden, A. 6Apr.10
Dunlop, H. R. 2Mar.14
2nd Lieutenant (1)
Chalmers, H. S. 8Dec.13

5th City of Glasgow (Howr.) Battery.
Elder Street, Govan, Glasgow.
Major.
Stewart, R. R. 23June12

Captain.
p.s.Harrison, J. (A) (Q) 18Sept.07
Lieutenants (2)
Orr, F. G. 6Jan.11
Young K. M. 14Apr.14
2nd Lieutenant (1)
Whitson, R. A. 8Apr.13

4th Lowland (Howr.) Ammunition Column.
Butterbiggins Road, Govanhill, Glasgow.
Captain.
p. Maxwell, D.A. 18June13
Lieutenant.
Speirs, G. C. T. 9Mar.13
2nd Lieutenant
Baird, A. G. M. 9May14
Buchanan, J. Mc A. 9May14

1st North Midland Brigade. [29]
Artillery Drill Hall Grimsby.
Hon. Colonel.
p. Grange, E. L., TD, ⓟ (A) (Lt.-Col. & Hon. Col. ret. T.F.) 8July10
Lt.-Colonel.
p. Tonge, J., VD, (t) (A) 2July10
Orderly Officer.
Adjutant.
✗Spiller, D. W. L., Capt. R. A. 7Nov.11
Medical Officers.

1st Lincolnshire Battery.
Artillery Drill Hall, Boston
Major.
✗Lamb, J. E. (hon. Capt.in Army 19 Oct.00) 15July13
Captain.
Read, J. J. 16July13
Lieutenants (2).
Giles, O. B. 9Dec.13
2nd Lieutenants (1).
Wright, S. C. 1Dec.11

2nd Lincolnshire Battery.
Artillery Drill Hall, Grimsby.
Major.
Mountain, H. 3July10
Captain.
Lewis, H. 1July12
Lieutenants.
McAulay, F. W. 15July13
2nd Lieutenant (1)
Morris, C. 1Nov.12

3rd Lincolnshire Battery.
Louth.
Major
Smethurst, W. W. 15Feb.11
Captain.
Jackson, S. H. 1Feb.13
Lieutenants (2)
Fuller, E. B. 15May11
2nd Lieutenant (1)

1st North Midland Ammunition Column.
Artillery Drill Hall Grimsby.
Captain.
Hinton, J. H. 15July13
Lieutenants
David, R. F. 2Dec.11
✗Cliff, R. B. T., late 2nd Lt. 6 Dns. 3Dec.11
2nd Lieutenants (2)

2nd North Midland Brigade. [39]
Drill Hall, Victoria Square, Shelton, Stoke-on-Trent.
Hon. Colonel.
Favell, T. M., VD (Hon. Col. ret. T.F.) 1Mar.09
Lt.-Colonel.
✗Child, StrS.H., Bt., M.V.O., late Lt. I. Gds. (Lt. Res. of Off.) 8Feb.10
Orderly Officer.

Adjutant.
Grice-Hutchinson, C. B., Capt. R. A. 30 Mar.12
Medical Officer.
✗Richmond, Capt. T. H., M.B., R.A.M.C. (T.F.) (attd.) 2Feb.12
2Aug.08
Chaplain.

1st Staffordshire Battery.
Drill Hall, Victoria Square, Shelton, Stoke-on-Trent.
Major.
p.s. Kent, J. (A) 1Apr.09
Captain
p. Walmsley, J. H. (A) 1May09
16Aug.05
Lieutenants (2)
(p.)Goddard, J. V. 1Apr.09
Morris Eyton, C. R. 1Sept.13
2nd Lieutenant (1)
Frain, R. C. 9June14

2nd Staffordshire Battery.
Drill Hall, Victoria Square, Shelton, Stoke-on-Trent.
Major.
p.s. Kent, W. J. (A) (Q) 1Apr.08
Captain.
Stringer, G. E. 3Aug.13
Lieutenants (2)
2nd Lieutenant (1)
Parkin, B. 15Dec.11
Johnson, J. L. 13June14

3rd Staffordshire Battery.
Leek.
Major.
Challinor, W. F.1Apr.08
Captain.
p Ward, B. T. 2Apr.09
Lieutenants (2)
p. Nicholson, A. F. 1Apr.09
p. Nicholson, B. L. 1Nov.09
2nd Lieutenant (1)

2nd North Midland Ammunition Column.
Drill Hall, Victoria Square, Shelton, Stoke-on-Trent.
Captain.
Collis, F. R. 2Mar.12
2nd Lieutenants (2)
Brunt, F. G. 19June11

Royal Field Artillery. Territorial Force.

3rd North Midland Brigade.
[40]
West Park, Wolverhampton.

Lt.-Colonel.
p.s. Leveson-Gower, C. C.
Maj. ret. Ind. Army
1Apr.09

Orderly Officer.

Adjutant.
Stirling, W. A., Lt.
R.A., capt. 1Apr.12

Medical Officer.

Chaplain.
Gordon, Rev. W.,
M.A., Chapl. 4th
Class (T.F.)(attd.)
1Apr.12

4th Staffordshire Battery.
West Park, Wolverhampton.

Major.
Mathews, J. R. T.
29Nov.11

Captain.
Ford, B. J. T. 10July12

Lieutenants (2)
Rambaut, G. M.
26Sept.13
Bamford, H.J. 27Sept.13

2nd Lieutenant (1)
Beddows, W. J. 6Feb.13

5th Staffordshire Battery.
Drill Hall, West Bromwich.
Major.
✕Caddick, C. J. (t)
22May13
Captain.
p.s.Lee, C. B. 25June13

Lieutenants (2)
Smith, W. S. 6Nov.11

2nd Lieutenant (1)
Cave, T. W 1July14

6th Staffordshire Battery.
Bailey Street, Stafford.

Major.
de Satgé, H. V. B.,
late Maj. 4 Bn. E.
Surr. R. (Hon.
Capt. in Army 13
July 01) (H) 15July11

Captain.
Meynell, F. H. L.
15Feb.12
Lieutenants (2)
Wrottesley, F. J.
14Aug.09
Wight-Boycott,
A. C. H. B, 1Nov.11

2nd Lieutenant (1)

3rd North Midland Ammunition Column.
West Park, Wolverhampton.
Captain.
✕Brazier-Creagh, K.C.,
late Capt. Impl.
Light Horse 1Apr.09
Lieutenants (2)
Salt, C. J. 27Mar.13

2nd Lieutenants (2)
Thursfield, J. H. 1Mar.13

4th North Midland (Howitzer) Brigade.
[54]
91, Siddal's Road, Derby.

Hon. Colonel.
Chandos-Pole-Gell,
H. A. (Lt.-Col.
ret. T F.) (Capt.
Res. of Off.) 1May13

Lt.-Colonel.
✕Gisborne, L. G. (Hon.
Capt. in Army 10
July01) 8June12

Orderly Officer.
Eddowes, N. R. B.,
2nd lt. 16Apr.13

Adjutant.
Webber, H. A. W.,
Capt. R.A. 14Apr.13

Medical Officers.
St. John, Capt. W.St. A.,
R.A.M.C. (T.F.)
(attd.) 1Oct.11
1Apr.08
Greaves, Capt. F.L.A.,
F.R.C.S., R.A.M.C.
(T.F.) (attd.) 17Aug.12
17Feb.09
Chaplain.
Sharp, Rev. W. C. G.,
M.A., Chapl. 4th
Class (T.F.)(attd.)
1Dec.12

1st Derbyshire (Howr.) Battery.
91, Siddal's Road, Derby.

Major.
✕Crompton, F. G.,
late Lt. 2 D.G. (q)
1Aug.13
Captain.

Lieutenants (2)
(p.)Walkden, G. G. 1May09
Newton, H. L., 30June13

2nd Lieutenant (1)
Haslam, E. S. 7Feb.13

2nd Derbyshire (Howr.) Battery.
91, Siddal's Road, Derby.

Major.
p. ✕Drury-Lowe, W. D.,
late Capt. G. Gds.
(Capt. Res. of Off.) 6Aug.08
Captain.

Lieutenants, (2)
(p.)MacMichael, E.C.M.
1Apr.12
Haslam, W. K. S.
1Apr.14

2nd Lieutenant (1)

4th North Midland (Howr.) Ammunition Column.
91, Siddal's Road, Derby.
Captain.

Lieutenant.

2nd Lieutenant.
Smith, R. J. E. 27Dec 12
Cattle, J. H. N. 2May14

1st South Midland (Gloucestershire) Brigade.
[27]
Artillery Grounds, Clifton, Bristol.

Hon. Colonel.
Ord, F.C., C.B., VD,
late Capt. R.A.,
g. (A) (Hon. Col,
ret. T.F.) 8Dec.09

Lt.-Colonel.
✕Balfour, A. M., Maj.
ret. pay (Res. of
Off.) 7Dec.09

Orderly Officer.
✕Stone, A. E., lt.
1Mar.14

Adjutant.

Boyce, C. E., Capt.
R.A. 17Dec.11

Medical Officers.
Corfield, Capt. C.,
R.A.M.C. (T.F.)
(attd.) 22May13
18Mar.09
Finlay, Lt. D. E.,
M.B., R.A.M.C.,
(T.F.) (attd.) 18ept.13
Chaplain.

1st Gloucestershire Battery.
Clifton, Bristol.
Major.
p.s.Austin, R. L. (A)
22Jan.14
Captain.
Dunscombe, E.J.
22Jan.14

Lieutenants (2)

2nd Lieutenant (1)
Lane, H. P. 4Jan.13
Fullerton, J. B. 4Jan.13

2nd Gloucestershire Battery.
Clifton, Bristol.
Major.
p. Wise, W. H., VD, hon.
l.c. (A) 13Dec.07
Captain.
Burbidge, E. D. 5Dec.13

Lieutenants (2)
Kellar, J. B. 1Jan.12
2nd Lieutenant (1)
James, G. S. 11Jan.13

3rd Gloucestershire Battery.
Barracks, Gloucester.
Major.
p. Metford, F. K. S,
VD, hon. l.c. (t) (A)
8Aug.08
Captain.
Browne, G. D., 1May14

Lieutenants (2)
(p.) Priday, C.F. H.15Mar.09
Ryan, W. O. 1Aug.13
2nd Lieutenant (1)
Metford, C. K. S.
24Dec.13

1st South Midland Ammunition Column.
Clifton, Bristol.
Captain.
p.s.Hillman, V. A. (A)
13Dec.07

Lieutenants (2)

2nd Lieutenants (2)
Estcourt, M. R. 1Aug.13
Gedye, E. L. 4Feb.14

Royal Field Artillery. Territorial Force.

2nd South Midland Brigade.
[49]
24, Southfield Street, Worcester.

Hon. Colonel.
Beauchamp, Rt. Hon. W., Earl, K.G., K.C.M.G., 5Nov.02

Lt.-Colonel
p.s. Bullock, E. C.TD. (A) 27July12

Orderly Officer.

Adjutant.
Galloway, R. L., Lt. R.A., *capt.* 1June14

Medical Officers.
p. Oldham, A. C., Surg.-Maj. 19July12
21Dec.98
p. Mackie, G., Surg.-Capt. 24Aug.06
24Feb.06

Chaplains.
James, Rev. S. R., M.A., vD, Chapl. 3rd Class (T.F.) (*attd.*) 1Apr.08
17Nov.97
Hough, Rev. G. F., M.A., Chapl. 3rd Class (T.F.) (*attd.*) 30May10
30May00

Unposted.

Captain.
r. Tassell, D. S. M. (A) 15Sept.06
13Feb.04

1st Worcestershire Battery.
24, Southfield Street, Worcester.

Major.
✗Lattey, J. C. (*Capt.Res. of Off.*) 26Sept.12

Captain.
p.s. Penny, A.F.(A) 16July10

Lieutenants (2)
Cavenagh, T. F. 30Aug.11
Ludlow, P. H. 20May13
5June11

2nd Lieutenant (1)

2nd Worcestershire Battery.
George Street, Kidderminster.

Major.
p.s. Taylor, G. H.(A)8May11

Captain.
Thompson, S.J.(A) 1May13

Lieutenants (2)
Meacher, E. 30June10
Adshead, B. T. 30Aug.11

2nd Lieutenant. (1)
Woodward, G. R. 21Feb.14

3rd Worcestershire Battery.
Easemore Road, Redditch.

Major.
p.s.Tunbridge,W. S. (A) 15Oct.09

Captain.
Smith,F,W,(A)28Sept.12

Lieutenants (2)
Tunbridge, W, S. 30Aug.11
Rice, G. V. 28Aug.13

2nd Lieutenant (1)
Hobson, A. C. W. 16Dec.12

2nd South Midland Ammunition Column.
Clarence Road, Malvern.

Captain.
p.s.Smith-Carington, M. C. H. (A) 28Aug.13

Lieutenants (2)
Dixey, J. C. 1Apr.11
Lyon, R. C. G, 1Nov.12

2nd Lieutenants (2)

3rd South Midland Brigade.
[50]
Stoney Lane, Birmingham.

Hon. Colonel.
Rogers, Sir H., Knt.

In Command.
✗Saunders, W. P., Maj. R. A. (*temp. Lt.-Col.Terr.Force*) 26July12

Orderly Officer.

Adjutant.
Curle, W. S. N., Lt. R.A., *Capt.* 7Feb.12

Medical Officer.
Murray, Lt. W., *M.D.*, R.A.M.C (T.F.) (*attd.*) 15Sept.10

Chaplain.
Smith, Rev. Canon J. R., M.A., Chapl. 3rd Class (T.F.) (*attd.*) 14Nov.10
14Nov.00

1st Warwickshire Battery.
Stoney Lane, Birmingham

Major
Cox, W. T. (A) 1Apr.08

Captain.
p.s. Sutherland, J. M. (A) 15Oct.10

Lieutenants (2)
Haynes, H. P. 26Feb.11

2nd Lieutenant (1)
McDowell,C. T. J. 29Jan.13
Newman, A. W, 1July13

2nd Warwickshire Battery.
Stoney Lane, Birmingham.

Major.
Daniel, T. J., late Lt. Lanc. R.F.A. (Mila.), ⓈB, (Q) 1Apr.08

Captain
p.s. Walduck, H. J.(A) 26June11

Lieutenants (2)
Patterson, B. W. . 23Aug.10
Pritchett, T. B., 23Aug.10

2nd Lieutenant (1)
Hewitt, J. R. 1Nov.12

3rd Warwickshire Battery.
Stoney Lane, Birmingham.

Major
Rowse, A. (A) 26June11

Captain.
p.s.Constantine, A. (A) 1Apr.08

Lieutenants (2)
Lenke, E. 23Aug.10

2nd Lieutenant (1)
Robinson,S.H. 13Mar.13
Whitehorse, H. 1July13

3rd South Midland Ammunition Column.
Stoney Lane, Birmingham.

Captain.
Ward, W, (A) 7Jan.14

Lieutenants (2)

2nd Lieutenants (2)

4th South Midland (Howitzer) Brigade.
[51]
Quinton Road, Coventry.

Hon. Colonel.
Mulliner, H. H. 1May08

In command.
✗Mallock, A. M. R., Maj. R.A. (*temp. Lt.-Col,Terr.Force*) 15June11

Orderly Officer.
Vallancey, H. H. d'E., *lt.* 18Apr.14

Adjutant.
Kidd, G. E., Lt. R.A. (*l*) *capt.* 6Jan.13

Medical Officer.
✗Davidson,Lt. D.,*M.B.* R.A.M.C (T.F.) (*attd.*) 10July13

Chaplain.
McNulty, Rev. C.T.B., Chapl. 4th Class (T.F.) (*attd.*) 11Mar.10

4th Warwickshire (Howr.) Battery.
Quinton Road, Coventry.

Major.
West, F. C. B. 30Dec 10

Captain.
p. Fowler, C. 1Feb.12
16Aug.09

Lieutenants (2)
Field, S. R. 10Nov.09
Field, M. G. 1July12

2nd Lieutenant (1)
Wyley, W. R. F. 23Dec.13

5th Warwickshire (Howr.) Battery.
Rugby (*temp.*).

Major.
Nickalls, C.P. 3June14

Lieutenants (2)
Saunders, E.K. 1June08
Anderson, R. R. W. 3June14

2nd Lieutenant (1)
Leather, J. H. 1Apr.14

4th South Midland (Howr.) Ammunition Column.
Quinton Road, Coventry.

Captain.
✗Browne, G. B., *late Lt.Lan.Fus.* 20Aug.11

Lieutenant.
Lucas, G. B. L. 18Apr.14

2nd Lieutenant.
Hayes, M. S. 17Dec.12
Brodribb, F. B.10July14

723 | **724** | **725** | **726**

Royal Field Artillery. Territorial Force.

1st Northumbrian Brigade.

[1]

Drill Hall, Barrack Road, Newcastle-on-Tyne.

Hon. Colonel.
p. Northumberland, Rt. Hon. H. G., Duke of, K.G., VD (Col. late Mila.) A.D.C. 29Mar.99

Lt.-Colonel.
p. Fenwick, G. (A) ⊕ 28Mar.14

Orderly Officer.
Graham, J., Lt., TD, hon. m. 1Apr.08

Adjutant.
Ommanney, C. H., Lt. R.A., capt. 1Nov.12

Medical Officers.
✕Wreford, J. (Hon. Capt. in Army 18 Aug.01), Surg.-Maj. 21Jan.08
7Nov.94
p. Nesham, R.A., Surg.-Capt. 8Aug.03
7Feb.00

Chaplain.
Parkinson, Rev. C., M.A., Chapl. 4th Class (T.F.)(attd.) 1Apr.08
18Feb.05

1st Northumberland Battery.

Drill Hall, Barrack Road, Newcastle-on-Tyne.

Major.
✕Bell, H. S., D.S.O. (Hon. Lt. in Army 18 Aug.01) (A) 28Mar.10

Captain.
Meagher, H. L., (q) 21Mar.10

Lieutenants (2)
p.s. Wilkinson, C. L. (A) 1Feb.09
Shiel, F. R. A. 5Aug.10

2nd Lieutenants (1)

2nd Northumberland Battery.

Drill Hall, Barrack Road, Newcastle-on-Tyne.

Major.

Captain.
p.s. Harrison, F. E. H. (q) 28Mar.10

Lieutenants (2)
Law, A. H. 2Aug.10
Pybus, H. 6May14

2nd Lieutenant (1)
Dyer, A. O. 1Oct.13

3rd Northumberland Battery.

Drill Hall, Barrack Road, Newcastle-on-Tyne.

Major.

Captain.
p. ✕Johnston, F. G. D. (Hon. Lt. in Army 18 Aug.01) (A) (t) 12Dec.03

Lieutenants (2)
Chaldecott, H.R. 1Aug.10
Southern, N. 4Aug.10

2nd Lieutenant (1)

1st Northumbrian Ammunition Column.

Drill Hall, Barrack Road, Newcastle-on-Tyne.

Captain.
p. Parmeter, N. L. (A) 13Feb.09

Lieutenants (2)
Walker, W. E. 27May14

2nd Lieutenants (2)
Miley, M. 1Apr.13
Dryden, R. H. 27May14

2nd Northumbrian Brigade.

[25]

Wenlock Barracks, Anlaby Road, Hull.

Lt.-Colonel.
Moss-Blundell, F. B. 17Dec.13

Orderly Officer.

Adjutant.
Lemmon, C. H., Lt. R.A., capt. 13Feb.13

Medical Officers.
p. Foley, T. McC., VD, Surg.-Lt.-Col. (hon. Surg.-Col.) 20July07
20July87
p. Tinley, Capt. W. E. F., M.D., R.A.M.C. (T.F.) (attd.) 1Oct.10
1Apr.07

Chaplain.
Ram, Rev. S. A. S., M.A., Chapl. 4th Class (T.F.)(attd.) 1Apr.08
4Aug.06

1st East Riding Battery.

Park Street, Hull.

Major.

Captain.
p. Murray, W. (A)10Dec.06
p.s.Wellsted, C. G. (A) 21June14

Lieutenants (2)

2nd Lieutenant (1)
Wade, H. F. 16July12

2nd East Riding Battery.

Park Street, Hull.

Major.
p.s. Allen, H.B. (A) 16May13

Captain.
p.s. Dossor, J.M. (A)19Aug.07

Lieutenants (2)
Robinson, H. F. N. 7Aug.12

2nd Lieutenant (1),
Hutchinson, W.
H. H. 28Nov.12

North Riding Battery.
Scarborough.

Major.
p.s. Wright, A. G. W. (Hon. 2nd Lt. in Army 13Oct.00) 28June13

Captain.

Lieutenants (2)
Ness-Walker, W. P. 14Sept.13

2nd Lieutenant (1)
Abbott, C. 29Sept.13
Cooper, A. P. 20Feb.14
Cooper, W. H. 20Feb.14

2nd Northumbrian Ammunition Column.
Park Street, Hull.

Captain.

Lieutenants (2)
Watson, J. 13Apr.11
p.s. Hillerns, H. W. O., (A) 7July12

2nd Lieutenants (2)
Robinson, T. 24Nov.13
Macnamara, H. C. 9May14

3rd Northumbrian (County of Durham) Brigade.

[31]

Drill Hall, Seaham Harbour.

Hon. Colonel.
Londonderry, Rt. Hon. C.S., Marq. of, K.G.,G.C.V.O., C.B., VD., Col. A.D.C.(Lt.-Col. & Hon Col ret. T.F.) 7Dec.10

Lt.-Colonel.
✕Doyle, J, F. I. H., Maj. R.A., p.s.c.(l) (temp.Lt.-Col.Terr. Force) 6June14

Orderly Officer.
Abbott, T. J. lt. 1Feb.12

Adjutant.
Radcliffe, S. R., Lt. R.A., (l) capt. 2Jan.12

Medical Officers.
p. Todd, Maj. D. F., TD, R.A.M.C. (T.F.) (attd.) 30Apr.04
13Apr.92

Chaplain.

| 727 | 728 | 729 | 730 |

Royal Field Artillery. Territorial Force.

1st Durham Battery.

Drill Hall, Seaham Harbour.

Major.
Guthe, T. P. (A) 3July12

Captain.
Warham, J. 20July13

Lieutenants (2)
Yeaman, K. S. 2Feb.12
MacDonald, J. 20June13

2nd Lieutenant (1)
Milburn, W. 3May13

2nd Durham Battery.

Durham.

Major.
p.s.Cluff, F. W. 2Dec.10

Captain.
p.s.Pickersgill, F. L. (A) ⑧ 1Jan.13

Lieutenants (2)
Common, L. A. 19June13
Hay, D. 28Feb.14

2nd Lieutenant (1)
Linklater, V. M. 17Feb.14

3rd Durham Battery.

Armoury, West Hartlepool.

Major.
p.s. Pearson, G. T. (A) 10Dec.10

Captain.
Cooper, C. B. 2Jan.13

Lieutenants (2)

2nd Lieutenant (1)

3rd Northumbrian (County of Durham) Ammunition Column.

Drill Hall, Seaham Harbour.

Captain.
Merryweather, J. W. 9July13

Lieutenants (2)
Common, C. R. 4June11

2nd Lieutenants (2)
Squance, E. L. 7May13
Adamson, J. 14Mar.14
Johnson, G. F. 30Apr.14

4th Northumbrian (County of Durham) (Howitzer) Brigade.

[32]

Bolingbroke Street, South Shields.

Hon. Colonel.
p. Dawson, W. J., VD. (Hon. Col. ret. Vols.) 8Oct.04

In command.

Orderly Officer.
p.s.Todd, H. L., *lt*. 25July11
19May06

Adjutant.
D'Arcy, J. I., Capt. R.A. 26July13

Medical Officers.
Scott, Lt. S., M.B., R.A.M.C. (T.F.) (attd.) 11Oct.13

Chaplain.
Wilkinson, Rev. G. K., Chapl. 4th Class (T.F.) (attd.) 1Apr.08
23Aug.02

4th Durham (Howr.) Battery.

Bolingbroke Street, South Shields.

Major.
p.s. Chapman, R. (A) 1Apr.08

Captain.
p.s.Armstrong, F. M. (A) 24Feb.06

Lieutenants (2)
Rennoldson, H. F. 24Sept.11
Chapman,C.L. 29July13

2nd Lieutenant (1)
Brigham, K.B. 27Nov.11

5th Durham (Howr.) Battery.

Artillery Drill Hall, Hebburn-on-Tyne.

Major.
p.s.Higginbottom, T. A. (A) 13Feb.08

Captain.
p.s.Paynter, F. P. (A) 27Nov.07

Lieutenants (2)
Angus, E. G. 23Apr.10
Anderson, K. 26Sept.11

2nd Lieutenant (1)

4th Northumbrian (County of Durham) (Howr.) Ammunition Column.

Bolingbroke Street, South Shields.

Captain.
p. Grunhut, V. P. J. 2Jan.04

Lieutenant.

2nd Lieutenants.

1st West Riding Brigade.

[33]

Fenton Street, Leeds.

Hon. Colonel.
Coghlan, C., C.B., VD (Lt.-Col. & Hon. Col. ret. T.F.) 1May14

Lt.-Colonel.
Hirst, E. A. 21Dec.13

Orderly Officer.
Day, R., *lt*. 1May13

Adjutant.
Abbott, T. A., Lt. R.A. capt. 7June12

Medical Officer.

p. Nightingale, J., M.D., TD, Surg.-Maj. 13Aug.10
Anning, Lt. G. P., R.A.M.C. (T.F.) (attd.) 12Aug.93
22Nov.13

Chaplain.

Dykes, Rev. E. H., M.A., Chapl. 4th Class (T.F. (attd.) 1Apr.08
2May04

1st West Riding Battery.

Fenton Street, Leeds.

Major.
Barran, P. A. (A) 6June14

Captain.
p.s. Peake, G. C. (A) (t) 6June14

Lieutenants (2)
Gordon, C. F. 20Mar.12

2nd Lieutenants (1)
Lupton, L. M. 28Mar.12
Briggs, D. C. 29Mar.12

2nd West Riding Battery.

Bramley.

Major.
p.s. Lucey, W. F. (A) 7Aug.13

Captain.
Nickols, H., jun. (A) 19June12

Lieutenants (2).
Lupton, A.M. 19Sept.11
Briggs, R. M. C. 1Apr.14

2nd Lieutenant (1).

| 731 | 732 | 733 | 734 |

Royal Field Artillery. Territorial Force.

3rd West Riding Battery.

Fenton Street, Leeds.

Major.
Middleton, F. (q)
  19June12
Captain.
p.s. Butler, B. H. (A)
  7Aug.13

Lieutenants (2)
Emsley, C. H. 20Sept.11
Hudson, E. C. 1June14

2nd Lieutenant (1)
Gordon,A.McD.20Feb.11

1st West Riding Ammunition Column.

Fenton Street, Leeds.

Captain.
p. Horsfield, R. M.(A)
  20Mar.12

Lieutenants (2)

2nd Lieutenants (2)
Middleton, A. L.
  1Dec.11
Nickols, N. F. 10June13
Lawson, E. A. C.
  1June13
Barran, H. B. 11Dec.13

2nd West Riding Brigade.

[34]

Valley Parade, Bradford.

Hon. Colonel.
Foster,H.A., TD 24Feb.97

Lt.-Colonel.
p.s.Foster, E. H., TD
  15Feb.08

Orderly Officer.

Adjutant.
✘Cooper, C.G.A.,
 Capt. R.A. 14May14

Medical Officers.
Peck, E. G., Surg.-Maj.
  1Apr.08,
  4July96
West-Watson, Lt. W.
 N.W.,M.D.,R.A.M.C.
 (T.F.) (attd.) 18Apr.12

Chaplain.
Briggs, Rev. Canon R.,
 M.A., VD, Chapl. 1st
 Class (T.F.) (attd.)
  1Apr.08
  30Aug.87

4th West Riding Battery.

Valley Parade, Bradford.

Major.

Captain.
p.s. Edelstein, A. J. (A)
  21Mar.12

Lieutenants (2)
Northrop,G.W.13July13

2nd Lieutenant (1)
de St. Paër,L. E.8Apr.14
  27Apr.12
Mossop, G. N. 1July14

5th West Riding Battery.

Halifax.

Major.
p.s. Whitley, E. N. (A)
  1Apr.08

Captain.

Lieutenants (2)
Shaw, R. M. 13July13
Hobson, C. T. 13July13

2nd Lieutenant (1)
Crossley, C. 2Dec.12

6th West Riding Battery.

Heckmondwike.

Major.
Priestley, F. N.
  27May11

Captain.

Lieutenants (2)
Pickering, E.W.
  13July13

2nd Lieutenants (1)
Critchley, L. C. 26May13
Blackburn, G. 16Apr.14

2nd West Riding Ammunition Column.

Valley Parade, Bradford.

Captain.
Gadie, A. 15Dec.07

Lieutenants (2)
Thornton,W.H.13July13

2nd Lieutenants (2)

3rd West Riding Brigade.

[35]

NorfolkBarracks,Sheffield.

Hon. Colonel.
✘Norfolk, Rt. Hon.
 H., Duke of, K.G.,
 G.C.V.O., VD (Hon.
 Capt. in Army
 16Jan.01) (Hon. Col.
 ret. T.F.) 22Aug.64

Lt.-Colonel.

p. Clifford, C., VD,
 (A) 15Aug.09

Orderly Officer.
Lovegrove, J., Qr.-Mr.
 (Hon. Capt.),ret. pay
  5Oct.12

Adjutant.
✘Wilson, P. H., Capt.
 R.A. 1Sept.11

Medical Officers.
p. Cuff, A. W., M.B.,
 Surg.-Capt. 9May03
  9May00
Favell, Lt. R. V.,
 R.A.M.C. (T.F.)
 (attd.) 15Apr.10

7th West Riding Battery.

NorfolkBarracks,Sheffield.

Major.
Clench, G. McD.,
 TD (H) 16Aug.09
Captain.
p. Jendwine, J. H. W.,
  12Apr.02

Lieutenants (2)
Oakes, G. 2Nov.10
Clifford, E. C. 6Nov.10

2nd Lieutenant (1)

8th West Riding Battery.

NorfolkBarracks,Sheffield.

Major.
p. Stephenson, H. K.,
 VD, hon. l.c. 7Sept.98

Captain.

Lieutenants (2)
Howson, W. 3Nov.10
Caporn, A. C. 29May13

2nd Lieutenant (1)
Hunter, M. J. 2May10
Howson, H. G. 7Oct.11

9th West Riding Battery.

NorfolkBarracks,Sheffield.

Major.
p. Gainsford, A. J., TD (A)
  1Apr.08

Captain.
Sales, W. 21Jan.11

Lieutenants (2)
Dust, F. W. 4Nov.10
Fowler, G. N. 10Oct.13

2nd Lieutenant (1)
Willey, J. 1July10
Benson, R. C. 29Mar.12

3rd West Riding Ammunition Column.

NorfolkBarracks,Sheffield.

Captain.
p. Allen, C. 7Sept.10
Craven, A. 1Feb.12

Lieutenants (2)

2nd Lieutenants (2)
Haynes, A. H. 12Mar.11
Blake, S. J. 19Mar.11

735 | 736 | 737 | 738

Royal Field Artillery. Territorial Force.

4th West Riding (Howitzer) Brigade.
[36]
Otley.

Hon. Colonel.
p. Dawson, W. S., TD
(Lt.-Col. ret. T.F.)
)May14

Lt.-Colonel.

Orderly Officer.
White, F. W., 2nd Lt.
16Sept.12

Adjutant.
✗Shaw, R. A., Capt.
R.A. 26Feb.12

Medical Officers.
p. Galloway, Capt.
W. H., R.A.M.C.
(T.F.) (attd.) 27Sept.05
11June02
Sproat, Capt. H. B.,
M.D., R.A.M.C.
(T.F.) (attd.) 27July12
27Jan.09

Chaplain.
Pattinson, Rev. R.,
M.A., Chapl. 4th
Class (T.F.) (attd.)
27Jan.09

10th West Riding (Howr.) Battery.
Otley.

Major.

Captain.
Duncan, K. 11June11

Lieutenants (2)
Kitchin, M. 15Oct11
Dawson, W. V. 2Feb.14

2nd Lieutenant (1)
Jackson, H. H. 19Feb.10
Duncan, H. S. 1Mar.10

11th West Riding (Howr.) Battery.
Ilkley.

Major.
Aykroyd, H. E. 1Apr.08

Captain.
Steinthal, P. C. 1Feb.14

Lieutenants (2)
Paton, R. H. 14Oct.11
p. Dixon, S. C.(Col.)
22Mar.13
14Feb.08

2nd Lieutenant (1)
Scott, J. C. 7May14
Maufe, F. W. B. 25May14

4th West Riding (Howr.) Ammunition Column.
Burley.

Captain.
Arnold-Forster,
F. A. 1July13

Lieutenant.
Benn, J. R. T. 10Apr.12

2nd Lieutenant.
Eddison, J. H. 1May12

1st Welsh (Howitzer) Brigade.
[23]

Drill Hall, Swansea.

Hon. Colonel.
Jersey, J., Lt. Hon.
V. A. G., Earl of,
G.C.B., G.C.M.G.
18June79

In Command.
✗Henry, J., Maj. R.A.
(temp. Lt.-Col. Terr.
Force) 31July12

Orderly Officer.
Davies, J., Lt. late Qr.-
Mr. (hon. capt.) 1
Glam. R.G.A.
(Vols.) 1Apr.09

Adjutant.
Faber, S. C., Lt. R.A.,
capt. 10Feb.13

Medical Officers.
p. Davies, D. A., M.B.,
Surg.-Maj. 1July09
26June97

Chaplain.
Williams, Rev. D.,
M.A., Chapl. 4th
Class(T.F.)(attd.)
17July12

Unposted.
Captain.
p. Thomas, C. J. H.
25Oct.05

1st Glamorgan (Howr.) Battery.
Drill Hall, Swansea.

Major.
p.s. Gregor, G. T. (A) (t)
1July09
Captain.

Lieutenants (2)
Simpson, C. S. ⓖ
23Nov.09
Portsmouth, O.S.
23Nov.09

2nd Lieutenant (1)
Watkins, W. B. 27June13

2nd Glamorgan (Howr.) Battery.
Briton Ferry.

Major.

Captain.
p.s.Gardner, G. B. S.
(A) 25Aug.06

Lieutenants (2)
Davies, J. S. 23Nov.09
Benyon-Winsor, B. R.
21Apr.11

2nd Lieutenant (1)
Gardner, C. H. 4Sept.12

1st Welsh (Howr.) Ammunition Column.
Morriston.

Captain.
p.s. Harris T. R. (A)
10July12

Lieutenant.

2nd Lieutenant.
Thomas, G. E. 24May13
Hooper, S. 4June13

2nd Welsh Brigade
[24]

Drill Hall, Cardiff.

Hon. Colonel.
Gaskell, J., vD (Hon.
Col. ret. T.F.) 18Dec.09
Lt.-Colonel.
p. Gilling, H. T., TD.
(Q) 29Nov.13

Orderly Officer.
Treasure, R. W. C.,
lt. 24Feb.10

Adjutant.
✗Blake, C. B.,
Lt. R.A., capt.1May13

Medical Officers.
p. Downing, Lt.-Col. C.,
vD, (hon. Surg.-Col.)
R.A.M.C. (T.F.)
(attd.) 2Mar.08
3Mar.88
p. Thomas, A., M.B.,
Surg.-Capt. 12Nov.04
26Sept.01

Chaplain.
Llandaff, Rt. Rev. J.P.,
Lord Bishop of, M.A.,
D.D., Chapl. 1st Class
(T.F.) (attd.) 1Apr 08
16Dec.76

3rd Glamorgan Battery.
Drill Hall, Cardiff.

Major.
Jones, W. E.(H)29Nov.13

Captain.
Gaskell, G.W.(H)
20Jan.11

Lieutenants (2)
(p.) Jones, R. J. 23Jan.08
Prichard, J. 25Mar.11

2nd Lieutenant (1)

4th Glamorgan Battery.
Drill Hall, Cardiff.

Major.
p. ✗Gaskell, J. C.,TD (Hon.
lt. in Army 30May
01) (Q) (H)[L] 1Apr.08
Captain.
Gaskell, J. G. 29Nov.13

Lieutenants (2)
Jenkins, D. R. 20Jan.11
Treharne, D. E. 24May11

2nd Lieutenant (1)

Cardiganshire Battery.
Aberystwyth.

Major
p.s. Rea, J. C. (A) 20May12

Captain.

Lieutenants (2)
Evans, D. 10Jan.13
p. Cookson, G. H.,
late 2nd Lt.
R.F.A. (A) 10Jan.13

2nd Lieutenant.
Morgan, J. G. 10Jan.13
Evans, H. J. 19Mar.15
Jones, E. T. ⓢ 25Oct.13

2nd Welsh Ammunition Column.
Drill Hall, Cardiff.

Captain.
p. Jones, C. T. (H) 13Oct.06

Lieutenants (2)

2nd Lieutenants (2)

| 739 | 740 | 741 | 742 |

Royal Field Artillery. Territorial Force.

The Cheshire Brigade.
[28]

County Buildings, Old Prison Yard, Shipgate Street, Chester.

Hon. Colonel.
p. ⚔LLoyd, W. N., M.V.O., Maj. ret. pay (Gent. at Arms) *hon. c.* (A) 18July06

Lt.-Colonel.
p. Bonnalie, F. J., TD (A) 12May06

Orderly Officer.

Adjutant.
Shaw, W. M., Capt. R.A. 13Nov.12

Medical Officer.
Hollies, Lt.-Col. G., M.D.,VD,R.A.M.C. (T.F.) (*attd.*) 1Aug.07 16Apr.87

Chaplains.
Bidlake, Rev. W., M.A., Chapl. 4thClass (T.F.) (*attd.*) 15Mar.09
Toogood, Rev. J. H., M.A., Chapl. 4th Class (T.F.)(*attd.*) 8May09

1st Cheshire Battery.
Shipgate Street, Chester.

Major.
Dickson, V. H. (A) 1Apr.08

Captain.
Jackson, F. V. M. 16July12

Lieutenants (2)
p.s.Frost, H. K. 23Nov,09
Meredith, D. W. 20Apr.10
p.s.Parry,H.M.(A) 30June11 6Oct.06

2nd Lieutenant (1)
Cullimore, C. 24Oct.13

2nd Cheshire Battery.
Shipgate Street, Chester.

Major.

Captain.
p.s.Frost, J. M. (A) 16July11

Lieutenants (2)
Carver, G.A. 23Nov.09
Armitage,P.M.18Mar.12

2nd Lieutenant (1)
Armitage, R. 4Jan.10
Hinds, W. G 22Apr.14

3rd Cheshire Battery.
Major.
Powell, A. T. 28May10

Captain.

Lieutenants (2).

2nd Lieutenant (1)
Dickson, F. L. 31July10 29Apr.07
Phillips,J.O.R. 21May13
Welch, W. 2June13

The Cheshire Ammunition Column.
Shipgate Street, Chester.

Captain.

Lieutenants (2)
Gardner, R. W. 1Apr.11
2nd Lieutenants (2)
Mason, H. B. 16Nov.12

4th Welsh Brigade.
[38]

Drill Hall, Lime Street, Newport, Mon.

Hon. Colonel.
p. Wallis, C. T., VD, (*Lt.- Col. & Hon. Col. ret. Vols.*) 13June14

Lt.-Colonel.
p.s. Williams, D. E., VD, (A) 7Nov.11

Orderly Officer.
Mullock, C. G., 2nd lt. 5Apr.14

Adjutant.
Kerans, H. J. D., Lt. R.A.[l]*capt.* 10Apr.12

Medical Officer.
Howard-Jones, Maj. J., M.B., R.A.M.C. (T.F.) (*attd.*) 17Nov.08 24Apr.97

Chaplain.
Mathews, Rev. A. A., Chapl. 4th Class (T.F.) (*attd.*) 18May09

1st Monmouthshire Battery.
Drill Hall, Lime Street, Newport, Mon.

Major.
p.s. Linton, E. M. 24May14

Captain.

Lieutenants (2)
(p.s.)Charlton, P. 23Apr.09

2nd Lieutenant (1)
Duckham,T. H. 4Apr.12
Jones, P. E. R. 9May13

2nd Monmouthshire Battery.
Risca, Mon.

Major.

Captain.
p. Pearson,T.W.(A)1Apr.08

Lieutenants (2)
(p.s.)Savours, D. S. 15Jan.10
Orders, W. M. 19Apr.14

2nd Lieutenant (1)
Budd, C. F. N. 1Apr.13

3rd Monmouthshire Battery.
Griffithstown, Mon.

Major.

Captain.
Davies, A. H. 9Feb.13

Lieutenants (2)
(p.s.)Phillips, F, B, 23Apr.09
Davy, J K, 19Apr.14
Moore, I. C. L, 19Apr.14

2nd Lieutenant (1

4th Welsh Ammunition Column.
Drill Hall, Lime Street, Newport, Mon.

Captain.
p. Wyman, R. (A) 4June13

Lieutenants (2)
Moore, T. E. L. 19Apr.14

2nd Lieutenants (2)
Huggett, J. I. 5Nov.13

Cadet Unit affiliated to the Brigade.
The Newport Cadet Corps, R.F.A.

1st Wessex Brigade.
[2]

St. Paul's Road, Portsmouth.

Hon. Colonel.
⚔ⒷⒸ, 🎖 Roberts, Field-Marshal Rt.Hon.F.S., Earl, K.G., K.P., G.C.B.,O.M.,G.C.S.I., G.C.I.E., VD, Col. Comdt. R. A., Col. I. Gds. [R] 15Aug.01

Lt.-Colonel.
Cheke, E. G., Maj. ret. pay (*Res. of Off.*) [L] 2Oct.11

Orderly Officer.

Adjutant.
Jervis-Smith, E. J., Capt. R.A. 1Apr.13

Medical Officer.

Chaplain.

1st Hampshire Battery.
St. Paul's Road, Portsmouth.

Major.
p.s.Flowers, E. (A) 1Jan,12

Captain
James, H. 4Dec.13

Lieutenants (2)
Flowers, C. 1May13

2nd Lieutenant. (1)
Adams, L. H. 16Dec.12

| 743 | 744 | 745 | 746 |

Royal Field Artillery. Territorial Force.

2nd Hampshire Battery.

St. Paul's Road, Portsmouth.

Major.
p.s. Cogswell, A. E. (Q)   1Apr.08

Captain.
p.s. Tyler, N. (A)   23Jan.08
House, M. H. N. (A)   21Oct.13

Lieutenants (2)
Day, A. B. H.   2May13

2nd Lieutenant (1)
Linington, G. F.   23Sept.13
Burbidge, F. C.   7Oct.13

3rd Hampshire Battery.

Walpole Road, Gosport, Hants.

Major.
Terry, P. McK.   1Apr.08

Captain.
House, P. J. (A)   27Apr.13

Lieutenants (2)

2nd Lieutenant (1)
Foster, D. S.   1Apr.14
Giles, J. H. R.   7Apr.14

1st Wessex Ammunition Column.

St. Paul's Road, Portsmouth.

Captain.
✗Collins, A., Rtd.-Mr. (hon. lt.) ret. pay (Res. of Off.)   13Apr.08

Lieutenants. (2)
✗Patterson, A. S., Qr.-Mr. (hon. capt.) ret. pay 11Nov.09

2nd Lieutenants (2)

2nd Wessex (Howitzer) Brigade.

[3]

Ryde, Isle of Wight.

Lt.-Colonel.
✗Powell, H. L., Maj. ret. (Res. of Off.)   15Jan.13

Orderly Officer.

Adjutant.
✗Clayton, W. A., Lt.R.A.,capt.21Nov.13

Medical Officers.

Chaplain.

4th Hampshire (Howr.) Battery.

Ventnor, Isle of Wight.

Major.
✗Malcolmson, J. J.   26July13

Captain.

Lieutenants (2)
Tozer, W.   20Apr.11

2nd Lieutenant (1)
Raeburn, W. R.   9July13
Winslow, L. C. 10Nov.13
Watkins, E. L. C.
   5Mar.14
   21Sept.11

5th Hampshire (Howr.) Battery.

Freshwater, Isle of Wight.

Major.

Captain.

Lieutenants (2)
Thomson, H. G.31May10
Flux, R. L.   1May14

2nd Lieutenant (1)

2nd Wessex (Howr.) Ammunition Column.

Ryde, Isle of Wight.
Captain.

Lieutenant.
Hartnall, A. J. 11Aug.10
Sparrow, R. P., late 2nd Lt. R. Ang.
R.E. (Mila) 24Feb.13

2nd Lieutenant.
Swain, C. de P. D.
   15June13
   5Feb.12

3rd Wessex Brigade.

[4]

The Armoury, Prospect Place, Swindon.

Lt.-Colonel.
Bedford-Pim, E. H., Maj. ret. pay (Res. of Off.)   27July13

Orderly Officer.
Rolph, C. T., Capt. (Dist. Off.) ret. pay capt.   15Dec.13

Adjutant.
Gidley, C. de B., Capt. R. A.   3Apr.11

Medical Officers.
Woodstock,Capt.C.P., R.A.M.C. T.F.)
(attd.)   1July13
   1Jan.10

Chaplain.

6th Hampshire Battery.

Victoria Drill Hall, Bournemouth.

Major.
✗ Wade, H. A. L. H., Maj. ret. pay (Res. of Off.) p.s.c., e. [L]   14Jan.14

Captain.
p.s. Fogerty, J. F. (A)   13Feb.04

Lieutenants (2)
Langley-Taylor,W.L.
   12Nov.10
Carrell,F.B.H. 16Nov.11

2nd Lieutenant (1)
Frazer, D. V.   14Jan.14
Jensen, E. C. H.15Jan.14
   16May13

Chaplain.
Lacey, Rev. F. G., Chapl.4th Class (T.F.) (attd.) 1Mar.09

Dorsetshire Battery.

Barrack Street, Bridport.

Major.
Livingstone-Learmonth, F. L. C., Capt.ret. pay (Res. of Off.)   1Jan.14

Captain.

Lieutenants (2)
(p.) Nantes, G. D, 1Mar.09
Sanctuary, C. T.
   6Aug.11

2nd Lieutenant (1)
Duke, A. B. C. 9Nov.12
Dyer, G. S.   1June13

Wiltshire Battery.

The Armoury, Prospect Place, Swindon.

Major
Suffolk, H. M. P., Earl of (Hon. Capt. in Army 28 July01)   3June08

Captain.
Gouldsmith, C. C.   24July08

Lieutenants (2)
Robinson, T. H.
   7June10
✗Glynn, E. F. 7June10

2nd Lieutenant (1)

3rd Wessex Ammunition Column.

Malmesbury.

Captain.
p. Forrester, A.L.10Aug.08

Lieutenants (2)
Cooper, J. C. 7June10

2nd Lieutenants (2)

↓ 2

Royal Artillery. Territorial Force.

R.F.A.—contd.
4th Wessex Brigade.
[5]
Exeter.

Lt.-Colonel.
✗Talbot, G. R. Fitz R.,
Capt. ret. pay (*Res.
of Off.*) (Hon. Maj.
ret. Mila.) *g.* 1Apr.08

Orderly Officer.

Adjutant.
✗Naper, L. A. D.,
Capt. R.A. 16Oct.12

Medical Officers.
Harris, Maj. J.H., *M.D.*,
TD. *late* Maj. 1 Devon
R.G.A. (Vols.),
R.A.M.C. (T.F.)
(*attd.*) 1Apr.08
Coleridge, Capt. A.
✶ *M.B.,* R.A.M.C.
(T.F.)(*attd.*) 28Sept.12
23Mar.09

Chaplain.
Courtenay, *Rev. Hon.*
H. H., Chapl. 4th
Class (T.F.)(*attd.*)
13Jan.10

1st Devonshire Battery
Exeter.

Major.
p.s. Perowne, J. T. W.
VD, *hon. l.c.* (Q) (*H*)
1May11
3Dec.04
Captain.
Timms, T. H. 28Feb.13

Lieutenants (2)
Michelmore, H. T.
5May10

2nd Lieutenant (1)
Rickeard, C. R.
30Nov.10
Symes, A. L. 1Feb.13

2nd Devonshire Battery.
Paignton.

Major.

Captain.
Vickers, S. 22Apr.13

Lieutenants (2)
2nd Lieutenant (1)
Manley, R.T. 8Nov.12

3rd Devonshire Battery.
Tavistock.

Major.
Arden, T.A.(A) 14July12

Captain.
p.s. Bailey, T. P. 14July12

Lieutenants
Spear, J. W. C. 5May10

2nd Lieutenant (1)
Allhusen, R. 1Nov.13
19July13

4th Wessex Ammunition Column.
Crediton.

Captain.
Harbottle, E. J., ✪,
(*H*) 11July03

Lieutenants (2)
2nd Lieutenants (2)
McLeod, A. A. 8Jan.12
Napier, M. 19July13

III. ROYAL GARRISON ARTILLERY.
(a) Mountain, (b) Heavy.
(a) MOUNTAIN.

4th Highland (Mountain) Brigade.
Russell Street, Rothesay.

Lt.-Colonel.
p. Robertson, C. McL.,
TD (A) 23Nov.12
Orderly Officer.
Macdonald, A. H.
10Oct.11
lt. 8Sept.13
Adjutant
Bateson, J. H.,
Capt. R.A. 14Nov.13
Chaplains.
Oswald, *Rev.* R, *M.A.*,
B.D. [C.S.], Chapl.
3rd Class (T.F.)
(*attd.*) 28June09
28June99
McCallum, *Rev.* J.
S. [C.S.] Chapl.
4th Class (T.F.)
(*attd.*) 1Apr.08
12Oct.06
Hewison, *Rev.*J.K,
D.D.[C.S.],Chapl.
4th Class (T.F.)
(*attd.*) 21Dec.10
McNaughton, *Rev.*
J. MacK., Chapl.
4th Class (T.F.)
(*attd.*) 24June14

Argyllshire (Mtn.) Battery.
Campbeltown.

Major.

Captain.
p. MacKelvie, T. 8Feb.05
p.s. Allan, B. (A 29Aug.06

Lieutenant (2)
Duncan Wallace, T.
8Sept.13

2nd Lieutenant (1)
Sutherland, D.
R. G. 11Feb.13

Medical Officer.

Ross and Cromarty (Mtn.) Battery.
Lochcarron, Ross-shire

Major.
p.s. Campbell, A., VD
(A) 28June13
Captain.
p.s. Nicolson, T. (A)
11Aug.13
Lieutenants (2)
p.s. Ross, W. A. (A) 8Sept 13
2nd Lieutenant (1)
Morrison, A. 15Feb.13
Smith A. E. D. 1Apr.13
Adjutant.
Burney, A. E. C.,
Capt. R.A. 14Dec.11
Medical Officers.
p. Mackenzie, Lt.-Col. M.,
VD, R.A.M.C. (T.F.)
(*attd.*) 23Oct.06
23Oct.06

Buteshire (Mtn.) Battery.
Rothesay.

Major.
McKinlay, A. M., TD,
(A) 11Aug.13

Captain.
p.s. Stewart, W. A. (A)
11Aug.13

Lieutenants (2)
Alexander, T. W.
21Sept.11
Murray, J.C.M, 8Sept.13

2nd Lieutenant (1)
Hill, A. H. 30July12

Medical Officer.
p. Penney, Maj. D. J.,
M.B., R.A.M.C.
(T F.) (*attd.*)20Sept.11
4May95

4th Highland (Mtn.) Ammunition Column.
Tarbert, Lochfyne, N.B.

Captain.
p.s. Hicks, G. (A) 8Sept.13

Lieutenants (2)
p.s. Todd. W. (A) 29Aug.06
Mundell, G. 8Sept.13

2nd Lieutenant.
Smith, J. S. 17May13

Royal Garrison Artillery. Territorial Force.

(b) HEAVY.

[*The order of precedence of Batteries is denoted by numerals in brackets.*]

(*For Heavy Artillery in Defended Ports, see p.* 759.)

East Anglian (Essex.)

[4]

Artillery House, Stratford Green, E.

Battery.

Major.
p.s. Wood, S. E.　　1Apr.10

Captain.
p.s. Jolly, E.　　1June10
　　　　　　　18Nov.07

Lieutenants (2)
Roberts, F.　　22Feb.12
Cousin, A. J.　　7Apr.14

2nd Lieutenant (1)
Fox, C. W. N.　6June12

Adjutant.
Moore, H.G., Lt.R.A.,
　capt.　　18Feb.13

Chaplain.
Edwards, Rev.
C. P., Chapl.
4thClass(T.F.)
(attd.)　　22Dec.13

Ammunition Column.

Lieutenant.
Knightley, P. D. J.
　　　　　　22Feb.12

Highland (Fifeshire.)

[7]

Drill Hall, Elgin Street, Dunfermline.

Battery.

Major.
p.s. Bruce, E. J., Lord
(Hon. 2nd Lt. in
Army 7Oct.00)
　　　　　　14Sept.08
Captain.
p.s. Morton, J., *late* Capt,
1 Fife R.G.A.(Vols.)
　(A)　　4Mar.13

Lieutenants (2)
Sutherland, J. F.
　　　　　　7June12

2nd Lieutenant (1)
Robertson, A.　3Mar.13
Robertson, W.　9Mar.13

Adjutant.
Humphreys, H. J.,
Capt. R.A.　21Oct.12

Medical Officer.
Mallace, Lt. A. C.,
M.B., R.A.M.C.
(T.F.) (attd.) 29Apr.13

Ammunition Column.

¿2nd Lieutenant.
Ashton, J. H.　24Dec.13

Home Counties. (Kent.)

[3]

Faversham.

Battery.

Major.
Gowlland, E. L.4Mar.11

Captain.
p.s. Berry, S. C. (A)
　　　　　　17June11

Lieutenants (2)
p.s. Cheetham, C. E. (A)
　　　　　　1July07
Aveling, T.　20Mar.13

2nd Lieutenant (1)
Hedley, H. J. 25Sept.12

Adjutant.
Higgon, L. H., Lt.
R.A., capt.　24Oct.13

Ammunition Column.

Lieutenant.

¿ 2nd Lieutenant.
Walker, C. E.　29Apr.14

Lancashire Brigade.

Sefton Barracks, Upper Warwick Street, Toxteth Park, Liverpool.
Lt.-Colonel.
p. Pugh, D.C., VD,
(Maj. ret. T.F.)15Feb.13
Adjutant.
Apletre, R. C., Lt. R.
A., capt.　10Dec.11

Medical Officer.
Brown, Capt. T., M.B.,
R.A.M.C. (T.F.)(attd.)
　　　　　　3Oct.12
　　　　　　3Apr.09

1st Lancashire.

[5]

Sefton Barracks, Upper Warwick Street, Toxteth Park, Liverpool.

Battery.

Major.
p. Stitt, J. C. (A)　5May12
Captain.

Lieutenants (2)
McFarlane, L. R.
　　　　　　13Mar.14
2nd Lieutenant (1)
Thompson, P. 15Dec.13
　　　　　　3Sept.13
Royston, C. F. 19Feb.14

Ammunition Column.
Upper Warwick Street, Liverpool.
Lieutenant.

2nd Lancashire.

[6]

Sefton Barracks, Upper Warwick Street, Toxteth Park, Liverpool.

Battery.

Major.
Winter, H. S. (A)
　　　　　　9May11
Captain.
Eaton-Hall, R. 1Apr.13
Lieutenants
Marsh, J. R. 13Mar.14
2nd Lieutenant (1)
Hargrave, R. N.
　　　　　　13May14

Ammunition Column.
Upper Warwick Street, Liverpool.
Lieutenant.
¿ 2nd Lieutenant.
Thomas, E. A.　4Apr.13

London Brigade.

Head-Quarters, Offord Road, Islington, N.
Hon. Colonel.
Wakefield, Sir C. C.,
Knt.　　7May14
Lt.-Colonel.
✕Wood, E. Fitz G.
M., D.S.O., Maj.
ret. pay (Res. of
Off.) D.S.O.,d] (Remount Service)
　　　　　　29Apr.14
Adjutant.
d'Apice, J. E. F.,
Capt. R.A., g. 26Mar.14
Medical Officer.
p Hobbs, Capt. J.,
F.R.C.S.I., R.A.M.C.
(T.F.) (attd.) 7Nov.06
　　　　　　7May09

1st London.

[12]

Offord Road, Islington, N.

Battery.

Major.

Captain.
Grice, T. H.　23July13
　　　　　　21Mar.05
Lieutenants (2)
Mattey, A. G. (A)
　　　　　　21Apr.10
2nd Lieutenant (1)

Ammunition Column.

Lieutenant.
Smith, A. M. (q) 1Apr.08

2nd London.

[13]

Offord Road, Islington, N.

Battery.

Major.

Captain.
Brown, H. B.　23July13

Lieutenants (2)
Dance, H. B. 25Aug.10
Harrison, E. C. 23July13
2nd Lieutenant (1)
Hodgson, A. G. O.,
(Asst. Resdt.,
Nyasaland Prote.,
18 Jan. 13)　27Sept.12

Ammunition Column.

Lieutenant.
Low, S.　　26Apr.13

¿ This rank is not provided for in the Territorial Force Tables of Establishments.

Royal Garrison Artillery. Territorial Force.

R.G.A. (Heavy)—contd.

Lowland (City of Edinburgh).
[2]
McDonald Rd, Edinburgh.

Battery.

Major.
p.s. Cameron, J. B. (A)   10Dec.13

Captain.
p.s. Grant, R. W. L. (A) (*Attorney Gen., Nyasaland Prote.,* 23Apr.09)   24Dec.04
Somerville, J.L. 17June14

Lieutenants (2)
Inglis, J. E.   2Dec.11
McCrae, W. B.   2Mar.14

2nd Lieutenant (1)
Thomson, E. G.   1Jan.14

Adjutant.
Birch, P. Y. [t] Lt. R.A., *capt.*   6Nov.13

Ammunition Column.
Lieutenant.

North Midland (Staffordshire).
[10]
R.G.A. Drill Hall, Wilfred Place, Hartshill, Stoke-on-Trent.

Battery.

Major.
Hind, W. (Q)   1Apr.08
  bt. lt.-col. 6Jan.12

Captain.
Chapple, F.J.(q)   22Mar.11

Lieutenants (2)
p.s. Lovatt, W.M.(q) 1Apr.09
(p.) Stringer, G. F. (t)(A)   15June10
Roscoe, H.   1Feb.13

2nd Lieutenant (1)
Sproston, T.E. 22Mar.11
Urquhart, J. A. B.   1July13

Adjutant.
Ellis, J. V. J., Lt. R.A., *capt.* 13Feb.12

Ammunition Column.

Lieutenant.
Wain, P. H.   1Mar.12

South Midland (Warwickshire.)
[14]
The Metropolitan Works, Saltley, Birmingham.

Battery.
Birmingham.

Major.
Greg, J. R.   1Apr.08

Captain.
Leney, C.   1Jan.12
Chandler, A.L. 22May13

Lieutenants (2)
Gold, E. L.   12Mar.14
Royle, G. T. F. 12Mar.14

2nd Lieutenant (1)
Cooper, D. F.   7Mar.14

Adjutant.
Hearle, A. B., *o.*, Lt. R.A., *capt.* 3Oct.13

Ammunition Column.
Wednesbury.

Lieutenant.
(p.s.)Squires, T. L. 30Oct.09

Northumbrian (North Riding).
[8]
Middlesbrough.

Battery.

Major.
p. Hennah, C. T., Capt. ret. pay, *hon. l.c.*   11June04

Captain.
p.s. Hedley, W. (A) 24Dec.02
p. Lennard, J. F. W.   1Jan.08
p. Stubbs, T. D. H. (A)   1Jan.08
(t)   1Jan.08

Lieutenants (2)
p.s. Barnley, G. W. W. (A)   2Dec.05
Douglas, N.   19Aug.11
Ingham, D.P. 28Sept.13

2nd Lieutenant (1)
Harris, E.   24June12

Adjutant.
Greig, A. D.
Lt. R.A., *capt.* 10July13

Chaplain.
Pennington, *Rev.* C. G. T. S., *M.A.,* Chapl. 4th Class (T.F.) (*attd.*) 1Apr.08

Ammunition Column.

Lieutenant.
p.s. Hill, J. N. (A) 12May09
'Treasury Asst.
3rd Grade Nigeria
{1Jan14
{22Sept.13} 21May02

West Riding.
[9]
York.

Battery.

Major.
Graham, W., Capt. (D.O.) ret. pay (*Remount Service*)   17Apr.13

Captain.

Lieutenants (2)
Bentley, W. W. (*Survey Probr., Ceylon,* 8Feb.13)   20Sept.11
Cooper, C. H. S. 1Jan.14

2nd Lieutenant (1)
Wyatt, L. S.   13Apr.14
Ware, I. N.   1May14

Adjutant.
Edwards, L. C., Lt. R.A., *o, capt.* 8May13

Chaplain.
Campbell, *Rev.* W. O. F., Chapl. 3rd Class (T.F.) (*attd.*)   2Aug.12
  2Aug.02

Ammunition Column.
Lieutenant.
Scott, J. P.(A) 1Apr.10

Welsh (Carnarvonshire).
[11]
Bangor.

Battery.
Bangor.

Major.
Hughes, W. H. 20Dec.13

Captain.
Savage, W. H. 20Dec.13

Lieutenants (2)
Brymer, G.   12Mar.14
Dargie, A.   12Mar.14

2nd Lieutenant (1)
Dew, N. A.   23May11
Brymer, W. W. 5Aug.13

Adjutant.
White, G. F. C.,
Capt. R.A.   9Apr.13

Ammunition Column.
Llandudno.

Lieutenant.
Owen, C. W. 23Nov.09

Wessex (Hampshire).
[1]
Cosham.

Battery.

Major.
p.s. Hoare, G. S.   5July1:

Captain.
p.s. Warner, G. H. 5Dec.1:

Lieutenants (2)
p.s. Reynolds, C.H. 20July0

2nd Lieutenant (1)
King, E. T.   26Apr.1
Napier-Martin, J. G. F. N. 28Apr.1·

Adjutant.
Stevens, H. R. G., Capt. R.A. [L]   17Jan.1

Ammunition Column
Lieutenant.

Royal Garrison Artillery. Territorial Force.

iv. ROYAL GARRISON ARTILLERY.
(for Defended Ports).
Order of Precedence of the Several Groups.

1. Tynemouth.
2. Hants.
3. Devon.
4. Sussex.
5. Forth.
6. Cornwall.
7. Kent.
8. Clyde.
9. North Scottish.
10. Essex and Suffolk.
11. Lancashire and Cheshire.
12. Dorset.
13. Glamorgan.
14. East Riding.
15. Pembroke.
16. Durham.
17. Orkney.

Clyde.
(3 *Companies.*)
2, King Street, Port Glasgow.
Hon. Colonel.
Inverclyde, J. C., Lord 27Mar.09
Major.
Rogerson, J., TD (A) 13July12
Adjutant.
Loughborough, A. H., Lt. R.A., *capt.* 27Dec.12
Medical Officers.
p.s. Butler, Maj. A., M.B., R.A.M.C. (T.F.), (*Hon. Capt. in Army* 18July01)(*attd.*)5Nov.07
7Aug.95
Chaplains.
Burns, Rev. J. G., B.D. [U.F.C.] Chapl. 3rd Class (T.F.) (*attd.*) 27Apr.11
27Apr.01
Porteous, Rev. D. J. M., E.D., (C.S.) Chapl. 4th Class (T.F.) (*attd.*)
1Apr.08
13Dec.07

No. 1 Co.
Port Glasgow.
Captain.
p.s. Lithgow, J. (A) 1Apr.08
Lieutenants (2)
Campbell, H. 22June10
2nd Lieutenants (3)
Gray, D. D. 27Nov.12
Glen, M. A. B. 27Feb.13
Bremner, R. H. 15May13

No. 2 Co.
Helensburgh.
Captain.
p. Buchanan, J. G. (A) 17May10
Lieutenant.
Anderson, J. G. 17Jan.11
Anderson, W. K. 27Nov.13
2nd Lieutenant.

No. 3 Co.
Dumbarton.
Captain.
p.s. Doig, P. (A) 1Apr.08
Lieutenant.
Paul, A. J. R. 5May13
2nd Lieutenant.
Denny, J. R. 28Apr.13

Unposted.
2nd Lieutenants.
Moubray, A. R. St. J. 27Nov.12
Stevens, C. V. 3Nov13

Cornwall (Duke of Cornwall's).
(2 *Heavy Batteries and* 5 *Companies.*)
Falmouth.
Hon. Colonel.
⚔St. Levan, J. T., Lord, C.V.O., C.B., Col. ret. pay 5July13
Lt.-Colonel.
p. Shapcott, H., VD, (A) 19Aug.10
Adjutant.
Farmer, C., Lt. R. A., *capt.* 1Nov.11
Medical Officers.
p. Andrew, E. G., Surg.-Capt. 5Oct.09
30July04
Harris, Lt. D.R., M.D., R.A.M.C. (T.F.) (*attd.*) 7Jan.11
Chaplain.
Maddrell, Rev. T. F., M.A., Chapl. 4th Class (T.F.) (*attd.*) 10May09

No. 1 Heavy Batt.
Padstow.
Major.
Cumberledge, J. A. 4Dec.08
Captain.
p.s. Bowley, T. K. (A) 23July04
Lieutenants. (2)
Mills, T. G. 1Apr.11
Williams, W. B. 1Apr.11
2nd Lieutenant.
Treffry, R. C. 2Feb.14

No. 2 Heavy Batt.
Penzance.
Major.
p.s.⚔Oats, F. F. 19Aug.10
Captain.
p.s. Oats, G. (A) 29June12
Lieutenant.
Caldwell, O. R. 28Aug.12
2nd Lieutenant.

Companies.
Major.
Chellew, T. J. (A) 3June11

No. 3 Co.
Looe.
Captain.
Peter. R. A. 10May13
Lieutenant.
2nd Lieutenant.

No. 4 Co.
Marazion.
Captain.
Lieutenant.
2nd Lieutenant.
Read, R. H. 15June09
Barbary, J. E. T. 8Apr.13

No. 5 Co.
St. Ives.
Captain.
p. Best, P. (A) 29June12
Lieutenant.
2nd Lieutenant.

No. 6 Co.
Falmouth.
Captain.
Goldman. C. S. 30Dec.10
Lieutenant.
p.s. Rogers, E. A. G. (A) 24Mar.06
2nd Lieutenant.

No. 7 Co.
Truro.
Captain.
Gill, A. W. 18Mar.10
Lieutenant.
p.s. Douglas, J.G.③ [l] 1Oct.08
Hancock, W. V. G. 1Apr.11
2nd Lieutenant.

Devonshire.
(2 *Heavy Batteries and* 4 *Companies.*)
Artillery Drill Hall, Lambhay Hill, Plymouth.
Hon. Colonel.
Jeune, E. B. (Lt.-Col. ret. T.F.) 1Apr.13
Lt.-Colonel.
Adjutant.
Reynolds, C. H., Lt. R.A., *capt.* 15Feb.13

Medical Officers.
p.s. Ward, J. P. S., Surg.-Maj. 6Apr.08
21Nov.94
Kettlewell, G. D. Surg.-Lt. (No. 1 Heavy Batt.) 1Jan.08
Chaplains.
Ponsonby, Rev. S. G., M.A., VD, Chapl. 1st Class (T.F.) (*attd.*) 1Apr.08
29May86
Sidgwick, Rev. J. A., M.A., Chapl. 4th Class (T.F.) (*attd.*) (No 2 Heavy Batt.) 1Apr.08
4Oct.02
Ault, Rev. F. E., Chapl. 4th Class (T.F.) (*attd.*) 29Oct.12

No. 1 Heavy Batt.
Ilfracombe.
Major.
p.s. Thomas, F. H. 1Aug.13
Captain.
Lieutenants (2)
Day, T. F. 7May12
Gould, G. S. 4Sept.13
2nd Lieutenant.

No. 2 Heavy Batt.
Devonport.
Major.
p.s. Blundell, C. W. (A) 9Nov.07
Captain.
Andrew, A. J. 20Mar.12
Lieutenants. (2)
2nd Lieutenant.
Thompson, G. 7May13
Companies.
Major.
p.s. Moon, H. E. P., TD (A) 14Nov.11

No. 3 Co.
Plymouth.
Captain.
p.s. Vosper, T. (A) 1Feb.08
p.s. Scaife, A. J. P. (A) 1Feb.08
Lieutenant.
Hart, W. J. 7July09
2nd Lieutenant.

No. 4 Co.
Plymouth.
Captain.
Rogers, E. S. 31Dec.11
Lieutenant.
Dawe, C. P. Y. 14May13

No. 5 Co.
Devonport.
Captain.
Davy, R. H. 1Apr.12
Lieutenant.
2nd Lieutenant.

| 763 | 764 | 765 | 766 |

Royal Garrison Artillery. Territorial Force.

R.G.A. (for Defended Ports)—*contd.*

Devonshire—*contd.*

No. 6 Co.
Devonport.
Captain.
p.s.Ellis, A. O, 1Feb.08
Lieutenant.
2nd Lieutenant.
Walling, R. V. 17May13

Dorsetshire.
(3 *Companies.*)
Lower St. Alban's Street, Weymouth.
Hon. Colonel.
✗Digby, Col. E. H. T., Lord, late C. Gds.
28Nov.00
Major.
Raymond, M. J. (A) 16May14
Adjutant.
Yates, C. McG., Lt. R. A., a capt. 27Sept.13
Medical Officer.
p. Laurie, Maj. C. R., TD, R.A.M.C. (T.F.) (attd.) 26July05
25Mar.93

No. 1 Co.
Swanage.
Captain.
Gill, W. R. 13May14
Lieutenant.
2nd Lieutenant.
Aglionby, H. 26Mar.12
Symes, G.G.H. 15Nov.13

No. 2 Co.
Poole.
Captain.
Budge, W. H. 1June07
Lieutenant.
2nd Lieutenant.
Bee, F. B. W 4May12
Spain, P. C. 17Oct.13

No. 3 Co.
Portland.
Captain.
Lieutenant.
Jenkins, L. 6Nov.12
2nd Lieutenants.
Saunders, J. J. 8May14
Clark, A. D. McK. 11June14

Durham
(1 *Heavy Battery and 4 Companies.*)
Armoury, West Hartlepool.
Hon. Colonel.
Lauder, R., VD, (Hon. Col. ret. Vols.) 24June05

Adjutant.
Gregory, A. J. R., Capt. R.A. 22May12
Medical Officers.
p. Ayre-Smith, Capt. A., M.D., R.A.M.C. (T.F.) (attd.) 22May09
22Nov.05
Burn, Capt. F. W., M.B., R.A.M.C. (T.F.) (attd.) 3July11
3Jan.08
Chaplains.
Hunter, Rev. C. B. R., Chapl. 4th Class (T.F.) (attd.) 20Feb.10

Heavy Batt.
Sunderland.
Major.
Marr, J. L. (A) 11Sept.12
Captain.
p.s. Speeding, J. H. (A) 14Oct.06
Barker, H. F. 11Sept.12
Lieutenants. (2)
Hedley, G. H. 18Sept.11
Boulton, S. W. 1Jan.12
Cameron, P. B. 6Jan.12
2nd Lieutenant.

Companies.
‡ *Lt.-Colonel.*
p. Robson, L., VD, (A) (‡) 6Aug.10
Major.

No. 1 Co.
West Hartlepool.
Captain.
Horsley, S. 5Mar.11
Lieutenant.
✗Walsh, J. M. 2Jan.11
2nd Lieutenant.
Cory, S. M. 18Feb.13

No. 2 Co.
West Hartlepool.
Captain.
Bennett, A. C. 12Feb.14
Lieutenant.
Clarkson, A. D. 4Feb.14

No. 3 Co.
West Hartlepool.
Captain.
Barraclough, E. 4July12
Lieutenant.
Young, C.R.M. 12Feb.14
2nd Lieutenant.

No. 4 Co.
Hartlepool.
Captain.
Trechmann, O. L. 1Nov.11
Lieutenant.
Trechmann, R. W. 8Mar.13
2nd Lieutenant.
Farmer, J. H. 1Apr.14

East Riding.
(4 *Companies.*)
Park Street, Hull.
Hon. Colonel.
p. Downs, A.J., TD (A) (Maj. ret. T.F.) 13Nov.09
Major.
Hall, R. (A) 12Nov.09
✗Orton, C. A., Capt. R.A. 1Nov.11
Adjutant.
Medical Officers.
p. Scott, A. W., Surg.-Capt. 7Jan.05
14Dec.01
Watson, Lt. G. H., R.A.M.C. (T.F.) (attd.) 6Jan.13
Chaplain.
Allderidge, Rev. S. C., Chapl. 4th Class (T.F.) (attd.) 15May09

No. 1 Co.
Captain.
p. Pawley, F. L. (A) 5May11
Lieutenant.
Allderidge, C. D. 8May11
Robson, E. L. 3May14
2nd Lieutenant.
Soady, J. H. 30June13

No. 2 Co.
Captain.
p.s. Hamilton, F. M. (A) 20Feb.04
Lieutenant.
Watson, W. B. 9July11
Brown, A. 5Dec.12
2nd Lieutenant.
Keighley, R.E.C. 7Jan.14

No. 3 Co.
Captain.
Holman, F. 3Dec.13
Lieutenant.
Fenner, J. H. 3May14
2nd Lieutenant.
Bean, N. B. 3Jan.14

No. 4 Co
Captain
p. Denham, H. A. (A) 5Dec.12
Lieutenant.
2nd Lieutenant.
Ward, J. G. 10June13
Downs, W. S. 3Jan.14
Costello, W. H. 12May14

Essex and Suffolk.
(4 *Companies.*)
Main Road, Dovercourt.
Hon. Colonel.
Pretyman, E. G., late Capt. R.A. 3May99
Adjutant.
Clark, R. H. B., Capt. R.A. 4Feb.13
Medical Officers.
Chaplains.
Pierce, Rev. F. D., Chapl. 4th Class (T.F.) (attd.) 22Dec.09
Telford, Rev. J. A., M.A., Chapl. 4th Class (T.F.) (attd.) 29June10

No. 1 Co.
Harwich.
Major.
p. Nalborough, F. G., TD, (A) [‡] 1July05
Captain.
p.s. McLearon, W. 6July05
p. Ward, H.M.A. 29Sept.10
Lieutenants. (2)
p. Hepworth, W.C.P. 21Aug.07
p. Hepworth, D. 15Dec.08
(p.) Peake, A. R. H., TD 15Dec.08
2nd Lieutenants. (2)

No. 2 Co.
Stratford.
Major.
p.s. Dieck, F. R. 25June13
Captain.
Biddell, A. 15June14
Lieutenant.
Simmons, E. G. 15June14
2nd Lieutenant.
Moore, R. H. 21Mar.14

No. 3 Co.
Southend.
Major.
Lloyd, C., TD 1Apr.08
Captain.
Lieutenants. (3)
Robertson, A. W., jun. 1Apr.11
2nd Lieutenants (2)
Robertson, W. H. 2Mar.09
Newby, N. C. 20May14

No. 4 Co.
Ipswich.
Major.
Miller, H. 23July13
Captain.
Cobbold, F. A. W. 23July13
Lieutenants (2)
Ripley, O. H. 23July13
2nd Lieutenants (2).

‡ This rank is not provided for in the Territorial Force Tables of Establishments.

Royal Garrison Artillery. Territorial Force.

R.G.A. (for Defended Ports)—contd.

Forth.

(6 Companies.)
Easter Road Barracks, Edinburgh.
Hon. Colonel.
McIver, Sir L., Bt.
    2Dec.96
Lt.-Colonel.
p. O'Connor, H., VD (A)
    27Mar.12
Majors. (2)
p.s. Macmillan, A. (A)
  (*Nos. 5 & 6 Cos.*)
    1Apr.12
p.s.Horne, R. J. M.
  (A) ⓖ /(Q)(*Nos.* 1, 2, 3, ⓖ *& 4 Cos.*) 7June13
    2Apr.12
Adjutant.
Alford, A. C. R.,
  Lt. R.A. [L] *capt.*
    6Jan.13
Medical Officers.
Beesly, Capt. L.,
  R.A.M.C. (T.F.)
  (*attd.*) 1June13
    17June09
Chaplain.
Watt, Rev. L. MacL.,
  B.D., Chapl. 3rd
  Class (T.F.) (*attd.*)
    1Apr.13

No. 1 Co.
Edinburgh.
Captain.
.s.Lindsay,J.H.(A)1June13
Lieutenant.
Milne, J. R. 1Apr.12
2nd Lieutenant.
Fownes, H. H. 16Dec.13

No. 2 Co.
Edinburgh.
Captain.
Lieutenant.
Cameron, J. D.12Aug.10
Anderson, S.T.S.
    29Apr.14
2nd Lieutenant.
Melrose, J. D.L. 4Apr.13
Thomson, E.J. 17Dec.13

No. 3 Co.
Edinburgh.
Captain.
Miller, A.C.,(s.)(q)
    1Apr.12
Lieutenant.
2nd Lieutenant.
Saidler, J. R. 16Aug.11

No. 4 Co.
Edinburgh.
Captain.
s.Scott, A., TD, *hon. m.*
  (A) ⓖ 4July03
    14July97
Lieutenant.
2nd Lieutenant.
Payn, J. R. 21May13
Innes, L. W. 20June14

No. 5 Co.
Kirkcaldy.
Captain.
Lieutenant.
Wyllie, W. B. 12Aug.10
Hogarth, J. 1June13
McLaren, T. 15June13
2nd Lieutenant.

No. 6 Co.
Burntisland.
Captain.
p.s. Saidler, T. W. (A)
    30Dec.09
Lieutenant.
2nd Lieutenant.
Flemington, R.R., jun.
    14June13
Boyd, W. D. 23Jan.14

Unposted.
Captains.
p. Young, J. M. 29Mar.05
  Swanston, J. D. 21Jan.08
p. Grant, L. C. 21Jan.08
p.s. Macmillan. R. J. A.
  (A) (*Med. Offr. (temp.*),
  Uganda 19 June 13)
    1Apr.08

Glamorgan.

(5 Companies.)
Drill Hall, Cardiff.
Hon. Colonel.
Plymouth, Rt. Hon.
  R. G., Earl of, C.B.
    1Nov.90
Lt.-Colonel.
p. Handcock, J. J., TD
    24Aug.09
Major.
p. Lewis, W., TD, (A)
    10Dec.07
Adjutant.
Biggs-Davison, J. N.,
  Capt. R.A. 1Jan.13
Medical Officers.
p. Parsons, C. O.,
  Surg.-*Maj.* 25Mar.12
    8Feb.00
Chaplain.
Henderson, Rev.
  A., B.A., Chapl.
  3rd Class (T.F.)
  (*attd.*) 21Dec.11
    21Dec.01

No. 1 Co.
Cardiff.
Captain.
Brown, W. R. (A)
    3June13
Lieutenant.
Ferrier, W. L. (A)
    31Jan.11
2nd Lieutenant.
England, J. H. 8Feb.11

No. 2 Co.
Cardiff.
Captain.
p.s. Thomas, A. P. (A)
    7Apr.06
Lieutenant.
Bell, J. 27May10
2nd Lieutenant.
Greenway, G. 1June10

No. 3 Co.
Cardiff.
Captain.
p. Tweedy, A. C., TD,
  hon. m. (A) 13Apr.01
Lieutenant.
Carr, A. G. 29July11
2nd Lieutenant.
Haig, R. W. A. de H.
    1Mar.12

No. 4 Co.
Penarth.
Captain.
p. Vyvyan-Robinson, H.
    15Apr.06
Lieutenant.
Payne, T. M. 3June13
2nd Lieutenant.
Hort, C. R. 27Apr.14

No. 5 Co.
Barry.
Captain.
p. Vyvyan-Robinson, C.
  (A) 11May09
Lieutenant.
James, P. M. 3June11
2nd Lieutenant.

Unposted.
Captain.
p. Bradley, W. B., TD,
  hon. m. (A) 13Apr.01

Hampshire.

(1 Heavy Battery and 7 Companies.)
St. Mary's Road, Southampton.
Hon. Colonel.
p. Harrison Hogge, J. H.,
  TD, (Hon. Col. T.F.
  Res.) 25July14
Lt.-Colonel.
p. Dawe, J. E., TD, (A)
    5Dec.13
Adjutant.
⋈Connolly, L. J. R.,
  Capt. R.A. 16May14
Medical Officers.
p. Morley, Capt. G. F.,
  R.A.M.C. (T.F.)
  (*attd.*) 12Apr.12
Chaplain.
Stevens, Rev. S.W.,
  M.A., LL.M., TD,
  Chapl. 1st Class
  (T.F.)(*attd.*) 9Jan.09
    9Jan.98

No. 1 Heavy Battery.
Southampton.
Major.
p.s. Chapiin, F. H. (Hon.
  03) (*Lt. Res. of Off.*)
  (Q) 1Apr.08
Captain.
Lieutenants (2).
Storry, H. A. B.
  (H)(t) 25May.14
    4Jan.05
2nd Lieutenant.
Smith, G. 19Nov.13
    10June11
Beadle, C. R. G.
    20Jan.14

Companies.
Majors (2).

No. 2 Co.
Southampton.
Captain.
p.s. Grove-Blackwell,
  G. (A) [l] 5July05
Knight, J. 4Dec.13
Lieutenant.
2nd Lieutenant

No. 3 Co.
Eastleigh.
Captain.
Fear, E. J. E. 15Sept.07
Lieutenant.
Carter, S. T. 13Dec.11
Solomon, E.E. 27Sept.13
2nd Lieutenant.

No. 4 Co.
Portsmouth.
Captain.
p.s.Barrell, W. H.,
  jun. (A) 28Sept.09
Lieutenant.
Dittman, W. E.14Mar.13
2nd Lieutenant.
Jones, S. B. 20Mar.12

No. 5 Co.
Southampton.
Captain.
Lieutenant.
2nd Lieutenant.
Field, A. D. 9Mar.14

No. 6 Co.
Woolston.
Captain.
Arnold, B. M. 4Dec.13
Lieutenant.
2nd Lieutenant.
Levien, M.D.W.E B.
    9July12
Hamilton, F.C. 24Je...13
Gudgeon, S. E. 20Apr.14

| 771 | 772 | 773 | 774 |

Royal Garrison Artillery. Territorial Force.

R.G.A. (for Defended Ports –contd.

Hampshire—contd.

No. 7 Co.
Southampton.
Captain.
Jacob, E. D. E. 6Aug.13
Lieutenant.
2nd Lieutenant.
Thornback, A. H. 27Feb.14

No. 8 Co.
Eastleigh.
Captain.
p.s. Bagshaw, F. V. (A) 27Jan.09
Lieutenant.
King, C. S. 27Sept.13
2nd Lieutenant.
Bate, A. C. L. 9Dec.13

Kent.
(3 *Companies.*)
Sheerness.
Hon. Colonel.
Parker, Sir H.G.G., Knt. 14June11
Adjutant.
Ford, C. W., Capt. R.A., *g.* 12Dec.12
Medical Officers.
Wall, Lt. D. L., *M.B.*, R.A.M.C. (T.F.)(*attd.*) 21Feb.12
Chaplain.

No. 1 Co.
Fort Clarence (Rochester).
Major.
Captain.
Passby, W. H. 31Oct.11
Lieutenants 2).
Sawbridge. C. G. 7Mar.14
1Jan.11
2nd Lieutenants (2).
Buckle, C. 5June12
Godfrey, R. 20May13
Box, S. T. 24Jan.14

No. 2 Co.
Gravesend.
Major.
Gadd, W.L., VD, Hon. Lt.-Col. ret, Vols. *hon.l.c.* ⑬ 10May05
Captain.
Lieutenants. (2)
Gadd, W. E. B. 4Feb.14
Cadic, B. F. 4Feb.14
2nd Lieutenant.
Porter, H. A. 1Nov.11
Warlters, E. P. 10Dec 13
Seel, L. 25June14

No. 3 Co.
Dover.
Major.
p.s. Welch. J. G.(Q) 9Nov.12
Captain.
✕Morrison, A., Lt. ret. pay, *g.*
⑬ 17Aug.12
Lieutenant.
Laker, S. J. 10July12
2nd Lieutenant.
Pearce, F. D. 13July12
Welch, H. C. 3May13

Lancashire and Cheshire.
(8 *Companies.*)
19, Low Hill, Liverpool.
Hon. Colonel.
p. Brown, Sir A. H., Bt., VD., *late Cornet* 5 D.G., *hon. c.* 15Feb.88
Lt.-Colonel.
Arden, T. H., TD(A) 8Jan.13
Majors (3)
Darbyshire, F. N. J. (A) (Nos.3 & 4 Cos.) 11July10
p. Luya, C. J. (A) (Nos. 5 & 6 Cos.) 8Jan.13
Adjutant.
Barker, W. H., Capt. R.A. 16Dec.11
Medical Officers.
Donnell, Capt. J. H., *M.B.*, R.A.M.C. (T.F.) (*attd.*) (Nos. 5 & 6 Cos) 5May13
5Nov.09
Reed, Lt. E. W., *M.B.*, R.A.M.C. (T.F.) (*attd.*) (Nos.7&8 Cos.)19Mar.10
McCune, Lt. W. S., *M.B.*, R.A.M.C. (T.F.) (*attd.*) 3Jan.14
Chaplains.
Postlethwaite, Rev. W.C., *M.A.*, Chapl. 4th Class (T.F.) (*attd.*) (Nos. 7 & 8 Cos.) 1June10
Bridge Rev.D., *M.A.*, Chapl. 4th Class (T.F.) (*attd.*) (Nos. 1, 2, 3 & 4 Cos.) 1June11

No. 1 Co.
Drill Hall, Low Hill, Liverpool.
Captain.
Lieutenant.
2nd Lieutenant.
Carr, B. A. 7Oct.12
Travis, N. B. 7Oct 12

No. 2 Co.
Drill Hall, Low Hill, Liverpool.
Captain.
Lieutenant.
Cattley, W. A. 1June10
2nd Lieutenant.
Withers, G. E. 11Mar.13

No. 3 Co.
Drill Hall, Low Hill, Liverpool.
Captain.
Lieutenant.
Wheeler,J.E.(q)11Oct.11
2nd Lieutenant.
Gittins, H. N. 13Nov13

No. 4 Co.
Drill Hall, Low Hill, Liverpool.
Captain.
p.s. Liardet, C. F. (A) 8Mar.05
Lieutenant.
Thomson, C. 13June11
Mallinson, G. G. 13June11
2nd Lieutenant.
Benjamin, L. A. 6Dec.13

No. 5 Co.
Drill Hall, Riverview Road, Seacombe.
Captain.
Lieutenant.
Allen, J. S., jun. 13June11
2nd Lieutenant.
Paterson,T. S. 15Sept.13

No. 6 Co.
Drill Hall, Riverview Road, Seacombe.
Captain.
Lieutenant.
Brothers, C. S. 23Apr.13
2nd Lieutenant.

No. 7 Co.
Barrow.
Captain.
p.s.Oughterson, G. H. (Hon. Lt. in Army 6 Oct. 00), late Lt. Cardigan R.G.A. Mila. (H)(I)(A) 15Mar.10
Lieutenant.
Thompson, R. P. 27May14
2nd Lieutenant.
Holmes, A. A. 21Jan.13

No. 8 Co.
Barrow.
Captain.
Maas, N. N. 11Sept.13
Lieutenant.
2nd Lieutenant.
Mossop, H. 1Sept.12
Balfour, R.W. 3Dec.13

Orkney.
(7 *Companies.*)
Kirkwall, Orkney.
Lt.-Colonel.
Slater, J., VD. 29July1
Majors. (2)
Hepburn, D., TD (A) ⑬ 1Apr.
Davidson, W. H. B. TD 29Aug.
Adjutant.
Johnston, J. H., Lt. R.A., *capt.* 5June
Chaplains.
Dickey, Rev. W. J. S., *D.D.* [C.S.] Chapl. 2nd Class (T.F.)(*attd.*) 1Feb
Millar, Rev. G. [U.F.C.] Chapl. 4th Class (T.F.) (*attd.*) 21July

No. 1 Co.
Kirkwall.
Captain.
p.s. Peace. D. B.(A) 2Aug
Lieutenant.
Cormack, J. S. 3Ma
2nd Lieutenant.

No. 2 Co.
Sanday.
Captain.
p.s. Brims, W. M. (A) 1Ap

No. 3 Co.
Shapensay.
Lieutenant.
Dennison, J. R. 1Ja
Barclay, G. 1Ja
2nd Lieutenant.

No. 4 Co.
Stromness.
Captain.
p.s. Draver, D. L. (A) 1A
Lieutenant.
Marwick, J. G. 1Ja
2nd Lieutenant.

No. 5 Co.
Evie.
Captain.
p.s. Mackay, J. (A) 1A
Lieutenant.
Mowat, T. R. 1M
2nd Lieutenant.

No. 6 Co.
Holm.
Captain.
p.s. White, J. (A) 29A
Lieutenant.
Swanney, C. E. 3N
2nd Lieutenant.

No. 7 Co.
Kirkwall.
Captain.
p.s. Peace, T. S, (A) 1A
Buchanan, F. 19J
Lieutenant.
Shearer, J. D. M. 3N
2nd Lieutenant.

Royal Garrison Artillery. Territorial Force.

R. G. A. (for Defended Ports)—contd.

Pembroke.
(*3 Companies.*)
Drill Hall, Milford Haven.

Hon. Colonel.
✗Kensington, H., Lord, D.S.O., *late Lt.*
15 Hrs. 12Feb.09
Major.
Price, T. W. (*No. 1 Co.*) 23Sept.12
Adjutant.
Pepper, J. W.,
Lt.R.A.,*capt* 29Dec.13
Medical Officers.
Griffith, Capt. W. S.,
M.B., R.A.M.C.,
(T.F.) (*attd.*) 2Jan.09
19June01
Tolputt, Capt. P. T.,
R.A.M.C. (T. F.)
(*attd.*) 18Dec.12
26Nov.08

No. 1 Co
Milford Haven.
Captain.
✗Wilson, H. S. K. 27Nov.12
Lieutenant.
2nd Lieutenant.
Birt, R. D. T. 27Feb.12
Thomas,H.J.P.31May13

No. 2 Co.
Saundersfoot.
Captain.
Forbes, E. A. 11Aug.08
Lieutenant.
Mathias-Thomas, F.
E. L. 21Jan.11
2nd Lieutenant.

No. 3 Co.
Fishguard.
Captain.
Dunsdon, G. E. 7Dec.08
Lieutenant.
2nd Lieutenant.
Rumsey, V. de M. O.
26Nov.08
Johns, H. D. 23Apr.14

Unposted.
Captain.
Scannell, J. B. 26Nov.08

North Scottish.
(*4 Companies.*)
Broughty Ferry.

Hon. Colonel.
✗Davidson, J., Col.
ret. pay 8Dec.13

Lt.-Colonel.
p.s.Adamson, R. H., TD,
hon. c. (A) 28May06
Major.
Low, R. W.(H)(q)
ⓔ 28Apr.12
Adjutant.
Campbell, T. Lt. R.A.
capt. [L] 31Jan. 14
Medical Officers
p. Colman, Capt. H. C.,
M.B., R.A.M.C.
(T.F.) (*attd.*) (*No. 3 Co.*) 3Apr.07
24Jan.00
p. Fergusson, Capt. W.
M.,R.A.M.C.(T.F.)
(*attd.*) (*No. 1 Co.*) 15Oct.10
15Apr.07
Chaplains.
Campbell, Rev. A.
J., M.A., VD,
[U.F.C.] Chapl.
1st Class (T.F.)
(*attd.*)(*No. 3 Co.*)
1Apr.06
19Mar.87
Taylor, Rev. W.,
M.A. [C.S.]
Chapl. 3rd Class
(T.F.)(*attd.*)(*No. 4 Co.*) 7May12
7May01

No. 1 Co.
Territorial Barracks,
Fonthill Road, Aberdeen.
Major.
p.s. Minto, W. B. G. (A)
1Apr.06
Captain.
Lieutenants. (2)
Shepherd,L. L. 27Apr.13
Savege, J. M. 27Apr.13
2nd Lieutenants. (2)
Macbeth, I. L. F.
1May12
Lumsden,C.G. 22June12
Wilson, A. 27May14

No. 2 Co.
Cromarty.
Captain.

Lieutenant.
2nd Lieutenant.
Neill, W. V. 4July14

No. 3 Co.
Broughty Ferry.
Captain.
p.s. Couper, T. S. (A) 28Apr.12
Lieutenant.
Longden, A. A.20June11
2nd Lieutenant.
Macdonald, W. R.
30Dec.13

No. 4 Co.
Drill Hall, Montrose.
Captain.
Lieutenant.
Hills, F. B. 22Apr.11
2nd Lieutenant.
Wood, W. M. 20Apr.14

Unposted.
Major.
p. Robertson, O., VD,
hon. l.c. (t) 22Mar.03
Captains.
p.s.*Reid*, D. J., hon. m.
(A) 17Jan.03
p. Bain, A., VD, hon. m.
25Jan.03

Sussex.
(2 *Companies*).
117, Gloucester Road,
Brighton.
Adjutant.
✗Saward, P, S., g.,
Capt. R.A. 1Nov.13
Medical Officers.
Shaw, Lt R. H.,
M.D., R.A.M.C.
(T.F.) (*attd.*) 20May11
Chaplain.
Marona, Rev. C. A.,
Chapl. 3rd Class
(T.F.) (*attd.*) 30Apr.12
30Apr.02

No. 1 Co.
Brighton.
Major.

Captain.
p. Martineau, A. J.(A)(Q)
11Mar,11
Lieutenants (2)
Grinsted, W. F. H.
1Apr.11
Dow, W, A. 1Oct.13
2nd Lieutenants (2)
Beaumont, M. 18May12
Roberts, K. S. 16Sept.13

No. 2 Co.
Lewes.
Captain.
p. Loud, F. 10Oct.08
Lieutenant.
p. Beard, G. R. 10Oct.06
Thomas, H. A. 1Jan.12
2nd Lieutenant.

Tynemouth.
(*4 Companies.*)
Military Road, North
Shields.
Hon. Colonel.
p. Pilter, W. F., C.B.,
VD, hon. c. 16Feb.01
Major.
p. Nicholson,J.H.1Apr.08
p. Wait, J. A. 27May08
Adjutant.
Bake,S.R.G.,Lt.R.A.,
capt. 13Jan.14
Medical Officers.
p. Cromie, J., *Surg.-Maj.*
17July05
23Dec.96
Blandy, Capt.
F. D., M.D.,
R.A.M.C. (T.F.)
(*attd.*) 3Nov.15
3May10
Chaplain.
Greene, Rev. R. D. R.,
Chapl. 4th Class
T.F (*attd.*) 26Feb.14

No. 1 Co.
North Shields.
Captain.
Todd, S.M.(A) 23Dec.11
Lieutenant.
Todd, C. E. 22Dec.11
2nd Lieutenant.
✗Robson, L. 15Nov.11

No. 2 Co.
North Shields.
Captain.
Stansfield, G. H., jun.,
(A) 17Sept.09
Lieutenant.
Angus, K. F. 12Feb.12
2nd Lieutenant.
✗l'Anson-Robson,
W. L. 15Nov,11

No. 3 Co.
Seaton Delaval.
Captain.
p. Allen,J.P.(A) 18June02
Lieutenant.
Pyne, A.P., *late Lt.A.
Motor Res.* 21Nov.11
5Apr.11
2nd Lieutenant.
Fawcett, L. N. 15Nov.11

No. 4 Co.
Blyth.
Captain.
p.s. Alderson, A. S. (A)
1Apr.08
Lieutenant.
Reader, H. C. 12Feb.12
2nd Lieutenant.
Stewart, R. S. 10Oct.13
Unposted.
Captain.
Green, C. F. 23Dec.11

ROYAL MALTA ARTILLERY.

[Malta.]

The Royal Cypher and a Maltese Cross,
"Egypt, 1882."

Uniform—*Blue.* Facings—*Scarlet.*

Honorary Colonel .. .. THE KING.

Lieut.-Colonel (1)	*Captains—contd.*	*Lieutenants—contd.*	*Instructor in Gunnery.*
Trapani, A., *M.V.O., g.* 25Nov.09	Carbonaro, O. M., *g.* 4Apr.00	Falzon Sant Manduca, A. V. 16Aug.99	Savona, P., *lt., g.* 1May11
	Micallef, V. C., *g.* 26May00	Ganado, W. L. 5Sept.00	
	De Domenico, J. M. *o., g.* 5Sept.00	Mizzi, R., *g.* 5Sept.00	
	Salomone, J. 5Sept.00	Gatt, W. R. [*l*] 15Sept.03	
		Gouder Carbone, S. A. 8Dec.03	
Majors. (3)		Bonavita, J. 8Dec.03	*Medical Officer* (1)
		Gatt, A. J. 22Mar.05	
Vella, A., *g.* 17Feb.97		Semini, A. J. [L] 22Mar.05	Mifsud, A. E., *surg.-maj.* 1Apr.09
Savona, W. [*l*] 21July97		Micallef-Eynaud, A. 22Mar.05	Vella, R., *M.D., surg.-maj.* 2Jan.13
Savona, E., *g.* 1Apr.99			Randon, R., *M.D., surg.-capt.* [F] 5Oct.07
	Lieutenants and 2nd Lieutenants. (11)	*2nd Lieutenants.*	
Captains. (3)		*Adjutant.*	
Vella, W. D. 11Aug.97	*Lieutenants.*	Burrowes, A., Lt. R.A., *capt.* 26Aug.12	*Hon. Chaplain.*
Ganado, A. W. 11Aug.97	Reynaud, E. H. [*l*]16Mar.98	*Quarter-Master.*	Muscat, *Very Rev. Monsignor Canon* P. 19Aug.96
Denaro, C. A., *g* [L]1Apr.99	Savona, P., *g., i.g.* 16Aug.99	Caruana, C., *hon. lt.* 24Dec.13	

Head-quarters. (*Attd. to No.* 2 *Co.*)	*No.* 1 *Co.*	*No.* 2 *Co.*	*No.* 3 *Co.*
Lt.-Col. Trapani,A.,*M.V.O., g.*	Maj. Savona, W. [*l*]	Maj. Savona, E., *g.*	Maj. Vella, A., *g.*
Capt. & Adjt. } Burrowes, A.	Capt. Carbonaro, O. M., *g.*	Capt. Ganado, A. W.	Capt. Micallef, V. C., *g.*
Lt. Savona, P., *g.*	Lt. Mizzi, R., *g.*	Lt. Reynaud, E. H. [*l*]	Lt. Bonavita, J.
Lt. & Qr.-Mr. } Caruana, C.	Lt. Gouder Carbone, S. A.	Lt. Falzon Sant Manduca, A. V.	
Surg.-Maj. } Mifsud, A. E.	Lt. Semini, A. J. [L]	Lt. Ganado, W. L.	
	Lt. Micallef-Eynaud, A.	Lt. Gatt, W. R.	
Attached.		Lt. Gatt, A. J.	
Capt. Vella, W. D.			
Surg.-Maj. } Vella, R., *M.D.*		*Attached.*	*Attached.*
Surg.-Capt. } Randon, R.,*M.D.*		Capt. Denaro, C. A., *g.*[L]	Capt. De Domenico, J. M. O., *g.*
		Capt. Salomone, J.	

BERMUDA MILITIA ARTILLERY.

Commandant and Adjutant.	*Captains.* (2)	*Lieutenants.* (2)	*2nd Lieutenants.* (2)
Caddell, W. B., Capt. R.A. 15June14	Tucker, C. H. 30Dec 95	Outerbridge, F. S. H. 28Sept.01	Hamilton, S. 30June11
	Dill, T. M. 18Oct.07	Smith, F. E. 10Aug.12	Smith, H. C. 4Mar.13

CORPS OF ROYAL ENGINEERS.

The Royal Arms and Supporters—" *Ubique*," and " *Quo Fas et Gloria ducunt.*"

Uniform—Scarlet. Facings—Blue.

Agents—Messrs. Cox & Co.

Colonel in charge of Records	.. ..	Ward, Col. B. R. [L]	.. .. Chatham 17Oct.12
Assistant to Colonel in charge of Records	..	Shute, Hon. Capt. W. J., Qr.-Mr., ret. pay	.. 28Sept.06

Stations of the Head Quarters of Units.

1st Co.	Gibraltar (Fortress)	32nd Co.	Gibraltar (Fortress)	A Co.	Chatham (Depôt)
2nd Co.	Cairo (Field)	33rd Co.	Fort Camden, Crosshaven	B Co.	Chatham (Depôt)
3rd Co.	Dover (Fortress)		Co. Cork (Fortress)	C Co.	Chatham (Depôt)
4th Co.	Gosport (Fortress)		Det. C. Bn., Berehaven	D Co.	Chatham (Depôt)
5th Co.	Aldershot (Field)		Det. C. Bn. Lough Swilly	E Co.	Chatham (Depôt)
6th Co.	Weymouth (Fortress)	34th Co.	Channel Isles (Fortress)	F Co.	Chatham (Depôt)
7th Co.	Shorncliffe (Field)	35th Co.	Pembroke Dock (Fortress)	G Co.	Chatham (Depôt)
8th Co.	Longmoor Camp, East Liss (Railway)		Det. C. Bn., Cardiff	H Co.	Army Head Quarters, India
9th Co.	Woolwich (Field)		Det. C. Bn., Liverpool	L Co.	Chatham (Depôt)
10th Co.	Longmoor Camp, East Liss (Railway)	36th Co.	Sierra Leone (Fortress)	M Co.	Chatham (Depôt)
11th Co.	Aldershot (Field)	38th Co.	Cork (Field)	Signal Units:—	
12th Co.	Moore Park, Kilworth (Field)	39th Co.	Sheerness (Fortress) Det. C. Bn. (Gravesend)	1st Signal Squadron, Longmoor East Liss	
13th Co.	York (Survey)	40th Co.	Hong Kong (Fortress)	1st Signal Troop, Aldershot	
14th Co.	Dublin (Survey)	41st Co.	Singapore (Fortress)	2nd Signal Troop, Tidworth	
15th Co.	Gibraltar (Fortress)			3rd Signal Troop, Curragh	
16th Co.	North Shields (Coast Bn.) Sect., Paull-on-Humber Sect., Middlesbrough	42nd Co.	Gosport (Fortress)	4th Signal Troop, Canterbury	
		43rd Co.	Mauritius (Fortress)	5th Signal Troop, York	
17th Co.	Curragh (Field)	44th Co.	Jamaica (Fortress)	" A " Signal Co., Aldershot	
18th Co.	Falmouth (Fortress)	45th Co.	Gibraltar (Fortress)	" B " Signal Co., Limerick	
19th Co.	Southampton (Survey)	47th Co.	Simonstown (Fortress)	1st Signal Co., Aldershot	
20th Co.	Devonport (Fortress)		North Queensferry (Coast Bn.)	2nd Signal Co., Aldershot	
21st Co.	Harwich (Fortress)	49th Co.	Sect., Greenock	3rd Signal Co., Bulford, Salisbury Plain	
22nd Co.	Yarmouth, Isle of Wight (Fortress)		Sect., Broughty Ferry	4th Signal Co., Woolwich (temp.)	
23rd Co.	Aldershot (Field)	54th Co.	Chatham (Field)	5th Signal Co., Carlow (temp.)	
24th Co.	Malta (Fortress)	55th Co.	Pretoria (Field)	6th Signal Co., Limerick (temp.)	
25th Co.	Hong Kong (Fortress)	56th Co.	Bulford, Salisbury Plain (Field)	7th Signal Co., S. Africa	
26th Co.	Bordon (Field)			" K " Signal Co., Aldborough House, Dublin	
27th Co.	Bermuda (Fortress)	57th Co.	Bulford, Salisbury Plain (Field)	1st Bridging Train, Aldershot	
28th Co.	Malta (Fortress)	59th Co.	Curragh (Field)	2nd Bridging Train, Chatham	
29th Co.	Chatham (Works, Line of Communication)			1st Field Squadron, Aldershot	
30th Co.	Plymouth (Fortress)			4th Field Troop, Curragh	
31st Co.	Ceylon (Fortress)			Training Depôt for Field units Aldershot	
				Railway Depôt, Longmoor	
				Colonial Survey Section, Federated Malay States, Penang	
				1st Printing Co., Chatham	

Colonel-In-Chief.

THE KING.

Colonels Commandant.

Maunsell, Gen. *Sir* F. R., *K.C.B.*, u.s.l. (*late Ben.*) [R]	9Nov.86
Montagu, Hon. Gen. *Sir* H. W., *K.C.B.*, ret. pay	5June87
Goodfellow, Lt.-Gen. C. A., u.s.l. (*late Bo.*)	2Feb.98
Tomkins, Gen. W. P., *C.I.E.*, u.s.l. (*late Ben.*)	12June98
Walker, Gen. G. W., u.s.l. (*late Mad.*)	5July99

Colonels Commandant—contd.

Strahan, Lt.-Gen. C., u.s.l. (*late Ben.*)	23Dec.01
Edwards, Lt.-Gen. *Sir* J. B., *K.C.B., K.C.M.G.*, ret. pay 15Feb.03	
Harrison, Gen. *Sir* R., *G.C.B., C.M.G.*, ret. pay, p.s.c. [R]	23Mar.03
Dawson-Scott, Gen. R. N., ret. pay	13Mar.05
Warren, Gen. *Sir* C., *G.C.M.G., K.C.B.*, ret. pay [R]	7Apr.06

Colonels Commandant—contd.

Kitchener of Khartoum, Field-Marshal H. H., *Earl, K.P., G.C.B., O.M., G.C.S.I., G.C.M.G., G.C.I.E.*, q.s.	13Apr.06
Moysey, Maj.-Gen. C. J., *C.M.G.*, ret. pay [R]	24Jan 12
Fraser, Maj.-Gen. *Sir* T., *K.C.B., C.M.G.*, ret. pay, p.s.c. [R]	25July12
Blood, Gen. *Sir* B., *G.C.B.*, ret. pay [R]	9July14

Royal Engineers.

Removed from the Corps and still on the Active List.

Field-Marshal.

Nicholson, W. G., Lord, G.C.B., q.s. [R] [F] 19Junell

General Officers.

Hart, Gen. Sir R. C., K.C.B., K.C.V.O., p.s.c. [R] [F] 16May14
Lawson, Maj.-Gen. H. M., C.B., p.s.c. [R] [F] (Lt.-Gov., Guernsey) 12Feb.07
Aylmer, Maj.-Gen. F. J., C.B., s. 19Feb.09
Maxwell, Maj.-Gen. R. C., C.B., s. 28July09
Kelly, Maj.-Gen. F. H., C.B., s. 4Dec.09
Ferrier, Maj.-Gen. J. A., C.B., D.S.O. [l] 15June10
Mullaly, Maj.-Gen. H., C.B., C.S.I. 9Oct.10
Gorringe, Maj.-Gen. G. F., C.B., C.M.G., D.S.O., q.s. [F] s. 6Sept.11
Friend, Maj.-Gen. L. B., C.B., s. [F] 3June12
Scott-Moncrieff, Maj.-Gen. G. K., C.B., C.I.E., Dir. of Fortns. and Works 1Oct.12
Heath-Caldwell, Maj.-Gen. F. C., C.B., p.s.c. s. 11July14

Colonels.

Sandbach, A. E., C.B., D.S.O., p.s.c. (temp. Brig.-Gen.) 10Feb.04
Thomson, A. G., C.B. 8Feb.05
Capper, J. E., C.B., s. 28Jan.06
Rice, S. R., C.B. (temp. Brig.-Gen.) 12Feb.06
Gubb, F. M., C.B., D.S.O. (temp. Brig.-Gen.) 16Apr.06
Roper, A. W., C.B. 31July06
Elliot, G. S., McD. [L] [F] s. 13Aug.06
Kirkpatrick, G. M., C.B., p.s.c. temp. Brig.-Gen.), s. (India) 12Oct.06
Hunter-Weston, A. G., C.B., D.S.O., p.s.c. [L] [F] (temp. Brig.-Gen.), s. 29Nov.06
Cowie, C. H. (India) 29Nov.06
Stewart, W. R., s. 29Nov.06
Renny-Tailyour, T. F B., C.S.I. (India) 29Nov.06
Browne, C. A. R. (India) 8Jan.07
Nanton, H. C., s. (India) 1Feb.07
Curtis, R. S., C.M.G., D.S.O. [F] s. 20Feb.07
Williams, G. (temp. Maj.-Gen.) (India) 14Mar.07
Huskisson, W. 4Apr.07
Anderson, F. J. (temp. Brig. Gen.) 21June07
Heath, G. M., D.S.O., p.s.c., s. (temp. Brig.-Gen.), s. 20Aug.07
Horniblow, F. H. 20Sept.07
Burrard, S. G., K.C.S.I. (India) 15Nov.07
St. John, C. W. R 10Dec.07

Removed from the Corps and still on the Active List—contd.

Colonels—contd.

Russell, W., s. 29Mar.08
Dallas, J. (India) 22Apr.08
Stuart, A. M., s. 6May08
Dundee, W. J. D., C.I.E. (India) 16July08
Grant, A. 12Aug.08
Huleatt, H. [L] [F] 12Aug.08
Maclagan, R. S., C.B., C.S.I. (India) 12Aug.08
Fowke, G. H. [F] (temp. Brig.-Gen.) (Inspr. of R.E.) 22Aug.08
Thackwell, O. M. R. (India) 4Oct.08
Baddeley, C. E. (India) 22Oct.08
Hill, C., (temp. Brig.-Gen.) s. 22Nov.08
Petrie, R. D. 5Dec.08
Edmonds, J, E., C.B., p.s.c. [L] s. 13Feb.09
Boileau, F. R. F., p.s.c., [l] s.31Mar.09
Glanville, F., D.S.O. (India) 1Apr.09
Ellis, W. M. (India) 1Apr.09
Hemming, E. H., s. 18July09
Walton, E. W. (India) 25July09
Jones, L., s. 5Aug.09
Craster, S. L. (India) 13Aug.09
Hythell, W. J. (India) 28Sept.09
Ward, B. R. [L] (R.E. Record Office) 1Oct.09
Buckland, R.U.H., A.D.C. [F] s. 28Oct.09
Harper, G. M., D.S.O., p.s.c. [l] s. 19July11
Godby, C. [F] s. 19July11
Davidson, S., s. 19July11
Kent, H. V. 19July11
Houston, E. (India) 19July11
Brown, W. B. 30Aug.11
Painter, A. C., s. 30Aug.11
Rose, C. S. (India) 6Dec.11
Williams, H. B., D.S.O., p.s.c. [L] s. 7Mar.12
Morton, W. R. [L] (India) 7Mar.12
Gibbon, J. A. 7Mar.12
Reynolds, A. R. 7Mar.12
Pery, C. C. J. 6June12
Wright, H. B. H. 6June12
Elmington, J. C. (India) 6June12
Roe, C. H. (India) 6June12
Close, C. F., C.M.G. (Dir.-Gen. Ord. Survey) 6June12
Tudor, E. A.T. 30Oct.12
Macdonogh, G. M. W., p.s.c [L] s. 30Oct.12
Brewin, J. P. (India) 3)Oct.12
Young, J. R. 4Dec.12
MacAdam, W., s. 4Dec.12
Powell, S. H., [l] s. (India) 2June13
Hedley, W. C., s. 16Dec.13

Lieutenant-Colonel.

Cordue, W. G. R. India 1June07

Lt.-Colonels.

Baylay, F. Newcastle-on-Tyne (local col.) 9June09
Speranza, W. S. 20Sept.09
Harrison, G. H. Chatham 1Oct.09
Dealy, J. A. Abbottabad 27Oct.09
Ewbank, W., p.s.c. Lucknow 15Nov.09
Livingstone, Edinburgh 15Dec.09
H. A. A., C.M.G.
Laurence, Secunderabad 22Jan.10
R. T. R.
Le Breton-Simmons, G. F. H, Malta 26Jan.10
Liddell, W. A. Dover 30Jan.10
Schreiber, A. L., Aldershot 29Mar.10
D.S.O.
Tulloch, J. A. S., Curragh 9Apr.10
p.s.c. [l]
Evans, U. W. 22Apr.10
Bland, E. H. York 6May10
Stokes-Roberts, Rawal E. R. B. Pindi 23May10
Gale, H. R., q.s. Weymouth 22June10
bt. col. 22Aug.08
Close, G. D. Exeter 12Aug.10
Sorsbie, R. F. 12Aug.10
Jones, H. B. Woolwich 12Aug.10
Lee, R. P. Gibraltar 12Aug.10
Edwards, R. F, Liverpool 12Aug.10
(local Col.)
Ridout, D. H. Singapore 1Oct.10
Von Hugel, N. G. Plymouth 4Oct.10
Cartwright, G. S. Gosport 7Oct.10
Lenox-Conyngham, G. P. Dehra Dun 22Oct.10
Dunsterville, E. L. Jhansi 15Nov.10
Bigge, T. A. H. Chatham 22Nov.10
Atkinson, E. H. Rurki 5Dec.10
de V., C.I.E.
Skinner, T. C. Pembroke 31Dec.10
Dock
Colnaghi, D. H. S. Africa 1Apr.11
Twiss, J. H. Longmoor 1Apr.11
Camp
Moore, A. T. Aldershot 1Apr.11
Prentice, H. Mauritius 1Apr.11
Johnson, E. P. Bangalore 1Apr.11
Scudamore, W. V. Bombay 4July11
Swiney, A.J.H. 18July11
Duff, G. M. Nowshera 25July11
Twining, P.G., M.V.O. Rurki 6Aug.11
Joly de Lotbiniere, Calcutta 6Aug.11
A. C. de L., C.S.I., C.I.E.
Picton, R. E. Quetta 13Aug.11
Kirby, N. Bareilly 18Aug.11
Wilson, H. F. A. 28Sept11
Paul, E. M. [L] Ceylon 1Oct.11
Perceval, C. C. Sheerness 31Dec.11
Fowler, J. S. Aldershot 31Dec.11
D.S.O., p.s.c. [L] s. 18Jan.11
Radcliffe, P.J.J. Hong Kong 31Dec.11
Heycock, C. H. Barrackpore 18Jan.12
Seaman, E. C. Malta 1June12
Murray, V. Calcutta 12June12
Blair, E. McL. Capetown 22June12
Weedon, F. F. India 1July12
Murray, J. H. S. Quetta 26Aug.12

Royal Engineers.

Lt.-Colonels—contd.

Blakeway, J. P.   *Nagpur* 1Oct.12
Coffin, Campbell,   *Ambala* 1Oct.12
   p.s.c.
Babington. S. C. *Potchefstroom*
   2Nov.12
Digby, W. T.   *Portsea* 23Nov.12
Fraser, T., p.s.c.   *Wellington*,
   [L]   *Madras* 19Dec.12
Pilcher, A. J.   *Allahabad* 25Dec.12
Brooker, E. P.   *Ord. Survey, Southampton* 15Jan.13
Vanrenen, J. E. (l)   *Cork* 13Mar.13
Williams, S. F.   *Colchester* 15Mar.13
Fair, F. K., p.s.c. [L]   *Dublin* 1Apr.13
Fraser, H. A. D.   *Srinagar* 16Apr.13
Collins C B.   *Dehra Dun* 19Apr.13
Campbell, G. P.   *Peshawar* 4July13
Ainslie, C.   *Calcutta* 10July13
Ryder, C. H. D., *Basra*,
   D.S.O. (l)   *Persian Gulf* 14July13
Boys, R. H. H., D.S.O.
   Aldershot 1Aug.13
Wilson, C. S.   *Bulford* 27Aug.13
   Camp
Burn, E. M. J. [L]
   Ferozepore 1Sept.13
Robertson, C. L.,   *Shillong* 25Sept.13
   C.M.G.
Clayton, H. E. G.   *Bermuda* 1Oct.13
Burnaby, C. G.,   *Jamaica* 22Oct.13
Kemp, G. C. (l)   *Fermoy* 14Nov.13
Barton, H. J. (l)   *Karachi* 5Dec.13
Ogilvie, E. C.   21Dec.13
Marshall, H. J. M.   *Bannu* 5Jan.14
Rotheram, W. H.   *Perth* 8Mar.14
Waghorn, W. D.   21Mar.14
Mair R. J. B.   *Mauritius* 5Apr.14
Austin, H. H.,   *Quetta* 4May14
   C.M.G., D.S.O.,   1sJan.11
   p.s.c. (l) [F] s.
Lathbury, H. O. *Jubbulpore* 16May14
Dobbs, C. R.   *Belfast* 9June14
Haig, E. H.   *Shoeburyness* 17June14

Majors.

Nathan, Sir M.,   *London* 18Sept.98
   G.C.M.G. (*Res. list*)
   bt. lt.-col. 9Jan.07
Leslie, G. A, J.   *Jullundur* 22Oct.05
Franklyn, C. de M. *London* 26Dec.05
   16July04
Bond, R. F. G.   *Kohat* 15Nov.05
Rivett-Carnac, S. G.*Raipur* 29Nov.05
Scholfield, G. P.   *London* 5Dec.05
   22Aug.02
Bigge, G. O.   *Guernsey* 13Feb.06
Hingston, G. B., s.   *Simla* 19Feb.06
Thuillier, H. F.   24Mar.06
Davy, C. W.   *Hong Kong* 1Apr.06
Des Vœux, H. B. *Devonport* 1Apr.06
Rushton, H. W.   *Jorhat* 1Apr.06
Whitlock, G. F. A.   *Ord.*
   Survey, Dublin 1Apr.06
Pike, C. F. B.   *Curragh* 1Apr.06
Versturme-Bunbury, C. H.
   Bermuda 2June06
Palmer, W. L.   *Queenstown* 4July06
Stockley, H. R., C.I.E., s. 24July06
Caulfeild, St. G. R. S.
   Harwick 25July06
Godfrey-Faussett, E. G. 5Aug.06
   Aldershot 29Nov.00

Majors—contd.

Cochrane, T. H., *Tientsin* 6Aug.06
   M.V.O.
Winsloe, A. R., D.S.O.
   Lucknow 13Aug.06
F C Watson, T. C.   *Bombay* 18Aug.06
Smyth, W. C. *Secunderabad* 23Sept.06
Harvey, R. N., D.S.O.   S.M.E.25Sept.06
   bt. lt.-col. 26Nov.13
Brady, D.   *Bulford Camp* 28Sept.06
Hume, A. H. B. (l)   *Allahabad* 27Oct.06
Matheson, J. C., *Valparaiso*, 3Nov.06
   f.o.   *Chile*
Grant, P. G. [L]   e.a. 17Nov.06
Swinton, E. D.,   *London* 31Dec.06
   D.S.O. (l)
Laurence, G. C. R. *Sheerness* 31Dec.06
Fuller, F. G., p.s.c., (l) s. 31Dec.06
   Plymouth 22Aug.02
Coffin, Clifford,   *Chatham* 18Jan.07
   p.s.c. [L]
Smith, G. E.,   C.M.G.
   Chester 25Jan.07
Shelley, B. A. G. *Devonport* 16Feb.07
Watling, F. W., p.s.c. [L]
   Chester 8Apr.07
Greer, R. E.   *Bareilly* 1June07
Riach, A. H. D.   *Loralai* 22June07
Close, L. H.   22June07
Galloway, J. J.   *Dublin* 1July07
Nugent, C. H. H., s.   *Simla* 3Aug.07
Joly de Lotbinière,
   H. G., D.S.O. *Netheravon* 26Aug.07
   29 Nov.07
Coldstream, W. M.   *Calcutta* 1Oct.07
Weekes, H. W., s.   S.M.E. 1Oct.07
Saunders, F. W.   *Aden* 2Nov.07
Scott, G. T.   *Malta* 23Nov.07
Griffith, G H.   *Delhi* 19Dec.07
Hemming, N. M., s. *Woolwich* 25Dec.07
Wilkinson, C. N.   *Lahore* 8Feb.08
McCormick, A. I. C. *Bombay* 13Mar.08
Walker, G.   *Curragh* 26Mar.08
Sanders, G. A. F.,   *Poona* 16Apr.08
   p.s.c., s.
Kelsall, F. W.   19Apr.08
Roberts, G. B. [F] *Gibraltar* 22May08
Lesslie, W. B., s.   *Simla* 27June08
   7Sept.04
Panet, A. E.   4July08
Bremner, A. G.   *Kirkee* 10July08
Henniker, A. M., s. *Aldershot* 14July08
Pyne, W. M.   *Hong Kong* 26July08
Muter, R. S.   *Bombay* 1Aug.08
Falcon, C. G.   *York* 1Aug.08
   29Nov.06
Westropp, F. M.   *Karachi* 27Aug.08
Cameron, H. A.   *Lahore* 18Sept.08
Gwynn, C. W.,   *Australia* 1Oct.08
   C.M.G., D.S.O.,   16Feb.09
   p.s.c., e., co.
Gugisberg,   S. *Nigeria* 4Oct.08
   F. G., C.M.G., c.o.
Dumaresq, A. H., s.
   War Office 29Oct.08
Thompson, W. M. *Gibraltar* 14Nov.08
F C Colvin, J. M. C.   *Quetta* 21Nov.08
   p.s.c., q.s., s.   22Aug.02
Dickson, W. E. R. *Karachi* 5Jan.09
   (l) s.
Denis de Vitré,   *Aldershot* 27Jan.09
   P. T.
Griffith, D. M.   *Aldershot* 20Feb.09
Cunningham, A. H.   *Burki* 8Mar.09
Lubbock, G.   *Risalpur* 5Apr.09
Wait, H. G. K., s.   S.M.E. 6June09

Majors—contd.

Lees, W. E.   *Shorncliffe* 21June09
Close, F. M.   *Ord. Survey,*
   Southampton 27July09
Oldham, L. W. S.   *Nagpur* 27July09
Crookshank, S.   *Delhi* 27July09
D'A., C.I.E., M.V.O.
Beach, W. H., s. *Ootacamund* 27July09
Cumberlege, A. F.   *Mhow* 27July09
Meyer, J. L.   *Poona* 1Oct.09
Knox, R. F.   *Chatham* 27Oct.09
Craven, A. J.   *Singapore* 15Nov.09
   26June02
Turner, H. H.   *Simla* 23Nov.09
Macdonald, R. H. *Chatham* 11Dec.09
Christie, H. R. S.   *Belfast* 22Jan.10
Beazeley, G. A. *Dehra Dun* 26Jan.10
West, R. H.   *Ryde* 30Jan.10
Hildebrand,   *Limerick* 14Feb.10
Sheppard, S. H.   *Quetta* 14Feb.10
   D.S.O., p.s.c., s.   bt. lt.-col. 10May13
Sargeaunt, A. F.   *Kilworth* 14Feb.10
Singer, C. W.   *Curragh* 14Feb.10
Boileau, G. H.   *Karachi* 14Feb.10
Gordon, H. W., f.o. *Rhodesia* 14Feb.10
Hingston. E.   *Chatham* 14Feb.10
Walker, H. J.   *Hilsea* 14Feb.10
Lewis, R. H., s. *War Office* 14Feb.10
Hopkins, N. J.   *Bulford* 14Feb.10
Rundle, F. P. *Secunderabad* 14Feb.10
Rolland, A.   14Feb.10
Traill, W. S.   *Dublin* 29Mar.10
Crosthwait, H. L.   29Mar.10
Campbell,   *Rawal Pindi* 4July10
   H.B.D.
Carpenter, C. M. *I. of Wight* 25July10
Elliott, C. A.   25July10
Chancellor, Sir   *Mauritius* 25July10
   J. R., K.C.M.G.,
   D.S.O., p.s.c. [L]
Hunter, C. G. W.   *Quetta* 25July10
Brunner, F. W.,   m.a. 25July10
   p.s.c
MacGeorge, J. B. *Rajputana* 25July10
Manser, W. E., c.o. *Australia* 25July10
Jelley, R. F.   *Malta* 25July10
Walker, R. S. [L] *Edinburgh* 25July10
Hawksley, R. P. T.
   Pietermaritzburg 25July10
Hearn, G. R.   25July10
Tyler, A. H.   *Salisbury* 25July10
Faber, S. G. [L] *Shorncliffe* 31Dec.10
Stevenson, A. G., D.S.O. [F]
   Plymouth 31Dec.10
Woodroffe, A. J. F. *Peru* 12Jan.11
Bowman-Manifold, M. G. E.,
   D.S.O., p.s.c. [L] [F]
   Aldershot 13Feb.11
Rundall, C. F. (l) s. *Plymouth* 13Feb.11
Greenstreet, C. *Dera Ismail*
   B. L.   *Khan* 13Feb.11
Bonham, C. B. (l) *Sierra* 13Feb.11
   Leone
Tandy, E. A.   *Dehra Dun* 13Feb.11
Gillam, R. A.   *Cork* 13Feb.11
Barnardiston, E.   *Simla* 13Feb.11
Freeland, H. F. E., M.V.O. 13Feb.11
Owen, S. L.   *Malta* 13Feb.11
Scott, A. C. [L]   *Falmouth* 13Feb.11

Royal Engineers.

Majors—contd.

Cusins, A. G. T. *Pretoria* 13Feb.11
Pritchard, H. *Bordon* 13Feb.11
 L., D.S.O. [F]
MacInnes, D. S., *Staff Coll.* 16July11
 D.S.O., p.s.c., q.s., s.
Mackesy, J. P. *Pretoria* 24July11
 p.s.c.
Gardiner, A. *Lahore* 24July11
Sewell, J. W. S. *Gibraltar* 24July11
Stockley, E. N. *Edinburgh* 24July11
Johnston, W. J., s., *S.M E.* 24July11
Barstow, J. B. *Woolwich* 24July11
Knox, G. S., c.o. *Kuala* 24July11
 Lumpur
Carey, A. B. c.o. *Canada* 24July11
Mildred, S. *Bordon* 13Nov.11
Vesey, C. E. G. *Cairo* 6Dec.11
Grubb, A. H. W., *Aldershot* 12Feb.12
 D.S.O.
Moir, J. P., D.S.O., e.a. 12Feb.12
Howard, F.G., *M.V.O.*
 Bulford Camp 12Feb.12
Tylden-Pattenson, E. C. 12Feb.12
 bt. lt.-col. 6June12
Sandys, E. S. *Aldershot* 12Feb.12
Jones, W. H. *London* 12Feb.12
Garwood, F. S. *Glasgow* 12Feb.12
Wood, H. *Dehra Dun* 12Feb.12
Pridham, G. R. *Egypt* 12Feb.12
Gillespie, R. St. J.
 Secunderabad 12Feb.12
Biddulph, H., s. *S.M.E.* 22July12
Harvey, C. B. *Ceylon* 22July12
Winsloe,H.E. *Ahmednagar* 22July12
Bowdler, B. W. S., p.s.c. [L] s.
 War Office 22July12
Elliott,G.C.E.,c.o.*Australia* 22July12
Pearson, H. D. [F] e.a. 22July12
Broughton, T. D.,*Darjeeling* 22July12
Hopkins, L. E. *Lahore* 22July12
Robertson, W., *Chatham* 22July12
 p.s.c.
Turner, E.V. [F] *Dublin* 22July12
 23July03
Anderson,C.F. [L] *Simla* 22July12
Browne, F. M. *Cork* 22July12
Russell-Brown, C.*Aldershot* 22July12
Crozier, J. *Dover* 22July12
Le Mesurier,H.G.*Bangalore* 22July12
King, R. G. 22July12
Wolff, A. J. *Canada* 10Feb.13
Garwood, J. R., *Gosport* 10Feb.13
Loch, S.G., *Bannu* 10Feb.13
 D.S.O.,p.s.c., s. 31Feb.12
Wilson, S. H., *London* 10Feb.13
 p.s.c. [?]
Kelsall, T. E. *Gosport* 10Feb.13
Ogilvie, C. 10Feb.13
Cowie,H.McC.*Basra Persia* 10Feb.13
Thompson, R. L. B., s. 10Feb.13
 War Office
Gervers, F.R.S. *Dagshai* 10Feb.13
Russell, W. K. *Bombay* 10Feb.13
Gunter, C. P. 10Feb.13
Cowie,H.E.C.,D.S.O.*Lahore* 10Feb.13
Henderson, E. G., p.s.c., s.
 [L] *Portsmouth* 10Feb.13
Rich, E. T. *Maymyo,Burma* 25July13
 16July13
Hodgson, P. E. *Quetta* 25July13
McClintock, *Bangalore* 25July13
 R.L., D.S.O. 2Apr.14
rookshank, A. A. [L]
 Gravesend 25July13
Jack, E. M., s. *War Office* 25July13

Majors—contd.

Craster, J. E. E. *Hong Kong* 25July13
Savage, A. J., s. *Woolwich* 25July13
Bovet, W. *Kirkee* 25July13
White, F.A.K. *Gibraltar* 25July13
Borradaile, B. *Tientsin* 25July13
McHarg, A.A. [l] *Mussoorie* 25July13
Fuller, C. G., *War Office* 25July13
 s., [L] s.
Chaldecott, W.H. 25July13
Tandy, M. O'C. 25July13
Iles, F. A.[L] *I. of Wight* 25July13
Armstrong, B. H. O., s.
 War Office 25July13
North, C. N. *Aldershot* 25July13
Macfie. W. C. *Aldershot* 27Feb.14
Corry, H. F., D.S.O. *India* 27Feb.14
Mainprise,B.W.,p.s.c.*Rurki* 27Feb.14
Kensington,G.B.,*Longmoor* 27Feb.14
 Camp
Clarke, C. J. 27Feb.14
Smyth, G. J. W. 27Feb.14
Mahon. E.W.S. *Chatham* 27Feb.14
Done, R. J. [F] *Liverpool* 27Feb.14
Hoysted, D. M. F. *Lond n* 27Feb.14
Foulkes, C. H. *Chatham* 27Feb.14
Thomson, O.B., *War Office* 28Mar.14
 p.s.c. [L] s. 2Apr.14
Macrory, R.M. *Jamaica* 1Apr.14
Osborne, G. F. F. *Lucknow* 27June14

Captains.

Manley, E. N. *Maymyo* 1Apr.04
Bell, H. L. G. *Portsea* 1Apr.04
Garrett, A. ff *Nagpur* 1Apr.04
Monro, J. D. *Sierra Leone* 1Apr.04
Charles, J. R. E. *Simla* 1Apr.04
 D.S.O., p.s.c., s. bt. maj. 16July06
Turner, F. G. *Lahore* 1Apr.04
Danford, B. W. Y. *Fermoy* 1Apr.04
Holme, A. S. [L] *Lahore* 1Apr.04
Hogg, C. C. H. *Rajputana* 1Apr.04
Moore, H. T. G. *Chatham* 1Apr.04
Mozley, E. N. *Ord. Survey,* 1Apr.04
 York
King,W. A. de C. *Plymouth* 1Apr.04
Connor, I. J. *York* 1Apr.04
Symons, C. B. O. *Chatham* 1Apr.04
Earle, E.G. *Bangalore* 1Apr.04
Rooke, E. H. *Chatham* 1Apr.04
Waller, R. L.,c.o. *Australia* 1Apr.04
Magniac. C. L. *Madras* 1Apr.04
Carden, A. D.,f.c. *South* 1Apr.04
 Farnborough
Stevens, A. C. J. *Shoebury-* 1Apr.04
 ness
Mance, H. O.,D.S.O., s.
 War Office 1Apr.04
Irvine,F.D.,p.s.c., *Australia* 1Apr.04
 c.o.
Brough, A. *Calcutta* 1Apr.04
Rose, L. St. V. *Pretoria* 1Apr.04
White, J. R. *Curragh* 1Apr.04
Robinson, A. C. *Ord. Survey,*
 Edinburgh 1Apr.04
Blandy, L. F. *Aldershot* 1Apr.04
Haslam, B. J., p.s.c. [L]
 Agra 1Apr.04
Phillpotts, B. S. *Queenstown* 1Apr.04
Painter, G. B. *Malta* 1Apr.04
Nation,J.J.H., s,*War Office* 1Apr.04
Moore, E. O'H. *Dover* 10Aug.04
 1Apr.04
Frith, G. R., *War Office* 26June04
 p.s.c., bt. maj. 26Nov.13
Willis,G.H.,*M.V.O.* 3Aug.04
Jackson, L. C. *Aldershot* 3Aug.04
 C.M.G., p.s.c.

Captains—contd.

McClintock, R. *Woolwich* 3Aug.04
 S.,p.s.c.,q.s., bt. maj. 4Aug.04
Barron, W. E. 3Aug.04
Durnford, G. E. J., *Pembroke* 3Aug.04
 Dock
Simon, M. St. L. s. *War Office* 3Aug.04
Butterworth,R.F.A. *Malta* 6Aug.04
Place, C. O., D.S.O.,
 p.s.c. [L] s. *Chester* 7Aug.04
Eustace, F. R. H. *Bannu* 8Aug.04
Skipwith, J.W. *Aldershot* 24Sept.04
Betty, P. K. *Gibraltar* 24Sept.04
Addison, G. H. *Aldershot* 1Oct.04
Douglas, W. S., *Edinburgh* 22Oct.04
 p.s.c. [L] s.
Pollard-Lowsley. *Simla* 21Dec.04
 H. de L., *C.I.E.*
Wace, E. G., *War Office* 11Jan.05
 p.s.c. [L] s.
Ommanney, R., 14Jan.05
 p.s.c.
Walker, R. *Portsmouth* 25Jan.05
McKechnie, D. *Egypt* 7Feb.05
Musgrave, H., *South* 1Mar.05
 p.s.c. [L], f.c. *Farnborough*
Mathews,W.F. *Moradabad* 11Mar.05
Greig, R. H., D.S.O., *Adjt.*
 Longmoor 14Mar.05
Charteris, J., *Aldershot* 21Mar.05
 p.s.c.
Mellor, C. [l], f.c. *Gosport* 21Mar.05
Taylor, L. R. J. *Plymouth* 21Mar.05
 W.
Oakes, R., s. *War Office* 21Mar.05
Brandon, O. G. *Bristol* 21Mar.05
Thomas, R. H. *Dehra Dun* 21June05
Gracey, T. *York* 21July05
Cunnington, *Cape Town* 25July05
 R. H.
Johnson, *Chatham* 29July05
 C.R.,D.S.O.
Walker, A. R. *Mauritius* 13Aug.05
Jones, D. C. *Dublin* 21Sept.05
Akerman,C.S.A.,*R.E.Depôt* 21Sept.05
Goodwin, *Waltham Abbey* 21Sept.05
 G. J. P., [l] s.
Langman, J. A. *Gravesend* 21Sept.05
Evans, W. H., s. *Chatham* 21Sept.05
Moore, J. O'H. *Potchef-* 21Sept.05
 stroom
Evans, A. S. *Ferozepore* 25Sept.05
Robertson,F.W.,s.,*Woolwich* 15Nov.05
Henrici, E. O. *Ord. Survey,* 23Dec.05
 Southampton
Forster, D., p.s.c. *Dera* 23Dec.05
 Ismail Khan
Sankey, C. E. P., s. *S.M.E.* 26Dec.05
Izat,W.R.*Domohani, India* 31Dec.05
Malan, L. N. *Quetta* 31Dec.05
Hammond,R.C.,c.o.*Canada* 31Dec.05
Evans, G. F. *Ord. Survey,* 31Dec.05
 Carlisle
McEnery, J. A. *Netheravon* 31Dec.05
Campbell, P.H. *Malta* 1Jan.06
Sanders, A. R. C., p.s.c.
 Peshawar 18Jan.06
Oldham, G. M. *Abbottabad* 3Feb.06
Giles, V. [L] *Naina Tal* 22Feb.06
Skinner, R. *Bannu* 8Mar.06
Biggs, C. W., s. *War Office* 23June06
Wagstaff, C. M., *Simla* 23June06
 p.s.c., [L]
Behrens, T. T. *Woolwich* 3June06

Royal Engineers.

Captains—contd.

Cowan, S. H.	m.a.	1July06
Walton, C.	Paksey	25July06
Kealy, P. H.	Delhi	27July06
Sherrard, L. A.	Brighton	27July06
Watkins, F S.	Capetown	29July06
Hogg, P. G. H.	Mount Abu, India	27Aug.06
Hepper, A, W.		31Aug.06
Neville, L. J. N.	Chatham	23Sept.06
Maxwell, W. F.	Ambala	28Sept.06
Doucet, L. C.	Sierra Leone	24Sept.06
A. de B., c.o.		
Browne, C. M., D.S.O.	Travancore	23Dec.06
Lewis, H. L.	Chatham	23Dec.06
Winterbotham.	Ord. Survey,	23Dec.06
H. St. J. L.	Southampton	
O'Connor, P. B. [L]	s.c.	29Dec.06
Charles,E.M.S.,Ord. Survey, Dublin		1Jan.07
Hobbs, R. F. A., D.S.O., p.s.c.	Chatham	9Jan.07
Ponsonby, R. G.	Malta	9Mar.07
Cunningham,A.B.	Aldershot	16Mar.07
Molesworth, E.K.		23Mar.07
Mackworth, H. L.. D.S.O. [L] [F] c.o.	Australia	23Mar.07
Cooke,G.S.C.	Ord. Survey. Southampton	28Mar.07
Bell, A. H. [L]	Quetta	23Mar.07
Evans, L.	Calcutta	23June07
Smith, H. C., s.	Aldershot	23June07
Newcombe, S. F.	War Office	23June07
[F]		
Goldney, F.G.B.	Aldershot	23June07
Birney, C. F.	Lahore	23June07
Goldingham, R. E. D., Aldershot		4Mar.05
		1Apr.04
Noble, W. J. W.	Murree	23June07
Russell, R. E. M. [F]	s.a.	23June07
Rathbone, H. E. F.	Ord. Survey, Shrewsbury	23June07
Stack, G. H.	Jullundur	23June07
Grove, T. T. [L]	s.c.	23June07
Brown, G.A.P.	Londonderry	23June07
Phillimore, R. H.	Ranchi, E. Indies	23June07
Barker, J. S., M.V.O.	Indore State	23June07
Loch, G. C. B.	Staff Coll. 23June07 Quetta	
Denison, G.W.,t.Manchester		18Sept.07
Baylay, A. C.. r.	Monmouth	23Dec.07
Paris, A. L.	Kirkee	23Dec.07
Kitto, W. A.	Colchester	23Dec.07
Hill, E. F. J.	Rurki	23Dec.07
Walker, A. D. [L]	Saharanpur	23Dec.07
Fleming, J. G.	Jersey	23Dec.07
King,L.N.F.I.,c.o.	E. Africa	1Jan.08
Henderson,H.M.	Chatham	12Jan.08
Edgeworth, K. E.	Dublin	26Jan.08
Cargill, S. T.	Chatham	13Feb.08
Kelly, H. H. [F]	Aldershot	8Mar.08
Thomson, D. A.	Rurki	9Mar.08
Gandy, H. G. [F]	Limerick	14Mar.08
Giles,F.L.N.,c.o. N.Nigeria		23Mar.08
Dobson, A. C.	Singapore	23Mar.08
Thompson, F. V.	Hythe	23Mar.08
Burgess, B.		23Mar.08

Captains—contd.

French, P. H., Ord. Survey, Bristol		23Mar.08
Johnston, W. H.	s.c.	23Mar.08
Carr-Harris, E. D.	Quetta	19June08
Bingay, H. L., s.	Chatham	19June08
Hordern, C.	Gosport	25June08
Spalght, T. H. L., t.	Leeds	25June08
Webber, N. W.	s.c.	25June08
Elles, H. J.	s.c.	25June08
Haswell, C. H.	Abbottabad	25June08
Francis, W. E. F.	Dublin	25June08
Mackintosh,E.E.B.[F] e.a.		28June08
Reid, C. S.	Ord. Survey, Southampton	7July08
Noble, N. D.	Edinburgh	28July08
Dobbie, W. G. S., p.s.c., [l]		
Macrae, W.	Woolwich	6Aug.08
	Gorakhpur	9Aug.08
Millard, E. D.	Quetta	20Aug.08
Hill, R. C. R.	Rurki	25Sept.08
Cusins, A. F.	Jubbulpore	25Sept.08
Galbraith, J. P.,Ord.Survey, Belfast		22Nov.08
Carey, W. L.de M.	Dublin	22Nov.08
Ooningham, A. E.,s. [F] S.M.E.		22Nov.08
Stokes A. W. [F], t.Bedford		22Nov.08
Sandes, E. W. C.	Rurki	22Nov.08
Davidson, A. E.	MoorePark	22Nov.08
Wilbraham,	Chatham	22Nov.08
B. H., s.		
Collins, D. S.	Plymouth	22Nov.08
Lefroy, H. P. T.	Aldershot	22Nov.08
Du Boulay, A. H.,t. London		22Nov.08
Walcot, B., p.s.c., s. E.Comd.		6Jan.09
Turner, J. F.	Gilgit	6Jan.09
Thorp, G., s.	Plymouth	6Jan.09
Molesworth, F. C.	Bombay	6Jan.09
Reid, A. W.	Salisbury	6Jan.09
Campbell, A. [l]		6Jan.09
Ogilvy, D.	Ahmednagar	6Jan.09
Turner, A. G., f.o.	Rhodesia	6Jan.09
Day, H. E.	Aldershot	6Jan.09
Hood, Hon. F. G.	Malta	6Jan.09
Cooper, W. C., t.	London	6Jan.09
Jones, O. G. D., t.	Sheffield	6Jan.09
MacLeod, M. N.		2May10
Prickett,C.H. Bulford Camp		2May10
Conran, W. D. B. Bangalore		2May10
Hammond, F. D.	London	2May10
Arbuthnot, A. D. S.	Kirkee	2May10
Watson, C. S. M. C.	Calcutta	2May10
Smith, V. P., s.	S.M.E.	2May10
Taylor, M. G.	s.c.	2May10
Twiss, A. M.	Kirkee	2May10
Mainguy, R. F. [L]	Sierra Leone	2May10
Burn, R. N.	Abbottabad	2May10
Clarke, H. B.	Chatham	14May12
		22Nov.08
Clogstoun, H. O., c.o. Australia		2May10
Cardew, A. M. [L]		2May10
Trew, R. J. F., s.	Woolwich	2May10
Ross, A. J.	e.a.	2May10
Williams, G. C., c.o. Nairobi, E. Africa		2May10
Pears, G. B. [L]	Egypt	2May10
Jordan, P. O. L.	Aldershot	2May10
Renton, N. W.,t. Eastbourne		2May10
Baker, E. C.	Bangalore	25June10
Archbold,F.H.W.Nowshera		25June10

Captains—contd.

Battye, B. C.		18Aug.10
Couchman,H.J.	Calcutta	18Aug.10
Day, J.	Limerick	18Aug.10
Legh, F. B.	Ceylon	18Aug.10
Young, E. deL.		18Aug.10
Broke-Smith, P. W. L.		
Gaskell, H. S.	Peshawar Dehra Dun	18Aug.10 18Aug.10
Boyd, S.		18Aug.10
Yule. G. U.	Gambila	18Aug.10
Prince, P. E.	Bangalore	18Aug.10
Bremner, A. D.	Gosport	18Aug.10
St.G.		
Trevelyan, H.	Wynberg	18Aug.10
Holt-White, F. R.,t. London		18Aug.10
Lynch, C. St. J.		18Aug.10
Stace, R. E., s.	Bombay	18Aug.10
Haig, D. de H.	Rangoon	18Aug.10
Hawtrey, H. C.	Bombay	18Aug.10
Bald, P. R.	Aldershot	18Aug.10
Kelly, W. H.	Ord. Survey, Southampton	18Aug.10
Mansfield, J. R. W.	Malta	18Aug.10
Lees, E. F. W.	Chatham	10Dec.10
Cox, E. W. [L] s.	War Office	21Dec.10
Bird, A. J. G.		21Dec.10
North, H.N. Fort Sandeman		21Dec.10
Kent, L. M,	Calcutta	21Dec.10
Powell, A. E.		21Dec.10
Festing, J. E. G.	Neemuch	1Jan.11
Anderson, E. P.	Lahore	18Jan.11
Bisset, J. S., t.	Glasgow	4Feb.11
Piggott, F. S. G. [L], s.	War Office	4Feb.11
Evans, C. E., [l]	Hong Kong	4Feb.11
Porter, M. T.		4Feb.11
Wood, J. C. I. [l]	Weymouth	4Feb.11
Boger, R.A., f.c.r.	Chatham	4Feb.11
Loring, E. J	Quetta	4Feb.11
Trenchard, O. H. B.		4Feb.11
Wyatt, F. J. C	Chatham	4Feb.11
Master, G., Adjt. Aldershot		4Feb.11
Doherty Holwell, R. V. Carlow		4Feb.11
Pratt, R. E. B.	Inverness	31Oct.11
Garforth, W.		23Jan.12
Wells, G. F.	Chatham	23Jan.12
Purcell, V. E.	Woolwich	23Jan.12
Maurice, L, C., t.	Bath	23Jan.12
Roberts, W. H.	Punjab	23Jan.12
Yates, A. St. J.	Cork	23Jan.12
Fox, B. H.	Kohat	23Jan.12
Hamilton,S.W.S.	Calcutta	23Jan.12
Herring, H.W.R. E, Depôt		23Jan.12
Borton, W. N.	Tank	23Jan.12
Palmer, C. H.	Peshawar	23Jan.12
Heron, J. B., s.	S.M.E.	23Jan.12
Carden, E. D.	Aldershot	23Jan.12
Le Breton, E. P.		23Jan.12
Darlington, A. J. Aldershot		23Jan.12
Scovell, R. H.	S.M.E.	23Jan.12
Redman, A. S., s.	War Office	28Feb.12
Agnew, H. C.		23Feb.12
Bushell, C. W.		21Dec.12
Sopwith, G. E.		21Dec.12
Campbell, J. D.	Bangalore	21Dec.12
Chesney, C. H. R.	Ambala	21Dec.12
Edwards, C. O'R.	Chatham	21Dec.12
Pye, K. W.	Bangalore	21Dec.12
Owen, A. L.	Waterford	21Dec.12
Tomlinson,H.W.	Chakrata	21Dec.12
Rogers, E. [L]	Ord. Survey, Norwich	21Dec.12
Hall, G. L., s.	War Office	21Dec.12
Rainsford-Hannay, A. G.	e.a.	21Dec.12

Royal Engineers.

Captains—contd.

Fenton, G.C.V. *Wellington*, 21Dec.12
   Madras
Ouchterlony, *Coomassie* 21Dec.12
   J. P. H., *c.o.*
Ogle, A. E., *s. Gosport* 21Dec.12
Cardew, E. B. 21Dec.12
Græme, J. A. *Delhi* 21Dec.12
Morshead, H. T. 21Dec.12
Pakenham- *Fort William* 21Dec.12
   Walsh, W. P.
Beatty, W. D., *f.c.* 21Dec.12
   S. Farnborough
Ferguson, F. A. *e.a.* 21Dec.12
Fisher, J. T. *Queenstown* 21Dec.12
Paxton, A. N. [L] *Limerick* 21Dec.12
Coke, B. E. [*l*] *t. Birmingham* 21Dec.12
Coode, A. M., *c.o. Nairobi* 21Dec.12
Chenevix-Trench, *Curragh* 21Dec.12
   L. [*l*]
Oakes, G. F. T. *Shillong* 21Dec.12
McQueen, J. A., *t.*
   Newcastle-on-Tyne 21Dec.12
Prichard, W. C. H., *s.*
   Gosport 21Dec.12
James, E. A. H., *Student,* 21Mar.13
   Japanese Language
   Tokyo
Edgar, D. K. *Secunderabad* 19June13
Thwaites, *Portsmouth* 26June13
   H. F. O. [F] *t.*
Kirke, E. St. G. *Lucknow* 31July13
Kelly, E. H. 31July13
Hall, H. A. L., *c.o. Gold Coast* 31July13
Dawson-Scott, J. K., *s. S.M.E.* 31July13
Bocquet, R. N. *Lucknow* 31July13
Bassett, T. P. *Bangalore* 31July13
Walker, E. C. [*l*] 31July13
Barnes, L. E., *p.s.c.* 31July13
Hearson, J. G. *Ord. Survey,* 31July13
   Southampton
Pemberton, S. *Secunderabad* 31July13
Pollock, H. C. *Jhansi* 31July13
Wright, H. L., *t. London* 2Aug.13
Neame, A. L. C., *s. War Office* 16Aug.13
Benskin, J. *m.a.* 17Aug.13
Norton, W. R. *Malta* 23Aug.13
Mackesy, P. J., *c.o. Gold* 23Aug.13
   Coast
Wyncoll, C. E. F., *t. Cannock* 10Sept.13
Wright, T. *Bulford Camp* 10ct.13
Moore, H. F. B. S., *r. Beaumaris* 10ct.13
Mount, A. H. L. *Delhi* 10ct.13
Ling, C. G. *m.a.* 10ct.13
Bowen, J. A. B. P. *Lahore* 15Oct.13
Satterthwaite, C. R. *Chatham* 24Dec.13
Edgeworth, J. A. *Dublin* 24Dec.13
Richardson, J. S. *Kirkee* 24Dec.13
Kidner, W. E. 24Dec.13
Micklem, R. *e.a.* 24Dec.13
Macaulay, R. K. A. *Chatham* 17Jan.14
Squires, R. E. *Poona* 18Jan.14
Eddis, B. L., *s. S.M.E.* 31Jan.14
Owen, R. A. *m.a.* 14Mar.14
Trench, A. H. C. *Simla* 24Mar.14
Bamberger, C. D. W. *Jhansi* 24Mar.14
Morris, H. H. J. G. *Madras* 24Mar.14
Tyrrell, W. G. *Chatham* 24June14
Binney, E. V. *Kirkee* 15July14
Bond, L. V. 15July14
Westland. F. C. *Woolwich* 15July14
Haig, W, de H *Allahabad* 15July14
Field, J. A. *Calcutta* 15July14
Nottidge, G. *Poona* 15July14
Aston, C. J. *Longmoor* 15July14
   Camp
Woodhouse, E. *Longmoor* 15July14
   Camp
Day, W. E. *e.a.* 15July14
McNeill, A. G. *e.a.* 15July14

Lieutenants.

King, F. J. M. *Maymyo,* 21Sept.05
   Burma.
Cree, D., *c.o. E. Africa* 23June06
Mansel, R. A. S. *Chatham* 23June06
Edwards, H. M. *New Zealand* 21July06
   c.o.
Colbeck, C. E. 25July06
Pringle, J. C. 27July06
Stallard, R. H. *Calcutta* 27July06
Hunter, R. G. P. *Quetta* 29July06
Egerton, C. H. [*l*] [F] *e.a.* 27Aug.06
Shakespear, A. T. *m.a.* 31Aug.06
Harris, T. B. *Bangalore* 28Sept.06
Iremonger, A. R. A *Bermuda* 28Sept.06
Deed, L. C. B. *Malakand* 28Sept.06
Townend, F. W. *Rawal Pindi* 24Sept.06
Bulkeley, H. I., *c.o. S. Nigeria* 9Oct.06
Bartlett, L. A. *Tochi* 1Nov.06
Marryat, J. R. *Paksey* 23Dec.06
Dobbs, G. E. B. *Limerick* 23Dec.06
Rhodes, J. P. *Gosport* 23Dec.06
Sharpe, P. H. *S.M.E.* 29Dec.06
Wedd, A. P. W., *t. Aberdeen* 1Jan.07
Dawson, E. F. S., *s. S.M.E.* 3Jan.07
Maxwell, G. A. P. 16Mar.07
Stoehr, C. F. *Aden* 23Mar.07
Wickham, J. C. *Bangalore* 23Mar.07
Morgan, M. E. *Ord. survey* 23Mar.07
   Southampton
Chase, A. A. *Dehra Dun* 23Mar.07
Hobart, P. C. S. 15Apr.07
Fuller, C. A., *t. Liverpool* 29May07
Shannon, C. E. *Plymouth* 23May07
Morrell, M. [*l*] *Pembroke* 23June07
   Dock
Jackson, R. D. *Harwich* 23June07
Pitman, C. E. *Rutherglen* 23June07
Osborne, E. A. *Pretoria* 23June07
Blunt, W. S. *e.a.* 23June07
Gray, J. F. [*l*] 23June07
Becher, L. E., *s. R. Arsenal,* 23June07
   Woolwich
Heymann, F. A., *Canada* 23June07
   c.o.
Lewis, C. G. *Calcutta* 23June07
Rawlence, N. *Quetta* 23June07
Bird, C. A. 23June07
Collins, A. E. J. *Aldershot* 23June07
Lewis, D. S., *f.c.* 23June07
   S. Farnborough
Rivers-Moore, C. N., *t.* 10Aug.07
   Plymouth
Chenevix-Trench, *e.a.* 1Sept.07
   R. [*l*]
Scott, M. A. H. *Bangalore* 23Dec.07
Perry, W. E. 23Dec.07
Waterlow, C. M., *f.c. South* 23Dec.07
   Farnborough
Vasey, C. J. W. *Isle of Wight* 23Dec.07
Watson, J. *Dublin* 23Dec.07
deFonblanque, P. *Hong Kong* 23Dec.07
Sinauer, E. M. [F] *Longmoor* 11Jan.08
   Camp
Stagg, M. *Aden* 26Jan.08
Richard, J. H. *Dover* 2Feb.08
Smyth, G. B. F. [L] *Curragh* 3Feb.08
Smythies, B. E. [*l*] *s. Plymouth* 11Feb.08
Wilson, B. T. *e.a.* 8Mar.08
Hunt, W. H. A. *Sheerness* 14Mar.08
Martin, A. D. De K. *Rawal* 23Mar.08
   Pindi
Palmer, H. W. T. [*l*]
Collin, F. S. *Gibraltar* 23Mar.08
Cave-Browne, W. *Peshawar* 23Mar.08
Lord, R. C. *Barrackpore* 23Mar.08
Hamilton, R. *Chitral* 23Mar.08

Lieutenants—contd.

Waterhouse, G. G. [*l*] *m.a.* 23Mar.08
Wynne, O. E., *s. War Office* 10Apr.08
Bliss, P. W. *Gosport* 19June08
Taylor, G. B. O., *Chatham* 19June08
   [*l*] *t.*
Simon, V. H. *S. Africa* 25June08
Gowlland, G. C., *s. S.M.E.* 25June08
Toogood, H. de C. [L] *Malta* 25June08
Swinburne, T. A. S. *Curragh* 25June08
Huddleston, P. G. 28June08
Jesson, E. P. *Aldershot* 4Dec.09
   7July08
Sim, G. E. H. *Aldershot* 31July08
Shepherd, G. J. V. *Dover* 28July08
Gemmill, J. D. *Gibraltar* 6Aug.08
Woodhouse, H. L. *Sialkote* 9Aug.08
Marsden, R. M. W. *Lydd* 20Aug.08
Jackson, C. V. S. *Sierra* 25Sept.08
   Leone
Jones, C. La T. T.. *c.o.* 25Sept.08
   Bloemfontein
Heath, J. T. *Potchefstroom* 22Nov.08
Brown, A. H. *Cairo* 22Nov.08
Kentish, H. E., *s. S. Nigeria* 22Nov.08
   c.o.
Sayer, A. P. *Weymouth* 22Nov.08
Buchanan, A. G. B. *Pem-* 22Nov.08
   broke Dock
Townshend, F. H. E. 22Nov.08
Doule, F. McC. 22Nov.08
Johnston, D. S. *Bombay* 22Nov.08
Tomlin, J. L. *Longmoor* 22Nov.08
   Camp
Izat, A. *Kathiawar* 22Nov.08
Moores, C. G. *Bulford Camp* 22Nov.08
Day, A. F. *Bulford Camp* 22Nov.08
Robinson, A. V. T. *Gibraltar* 22Nov.08
Everett, M. 22Nov.08
Fraustadt, L. [*l*] *Calcutta* 30Nov.08
Mason, K. *Dehra Dun* 6Jan.09
Nation, C. F. *m.a.* 6Jan.09
Hughes, H. B. W. *Peshawar* 6Jan.09
Price, F. *Aldershot* 6Jan.09
Gibson, A. W. S. *Gosport* 6Jan.09
Campbell, C. S. *S. Africa* 6Jan.09
Hogg, D. McA. [*l*] *Bangalore* 6Jan.09
Glenday, A. G. [*l*] *Quetta* 6Jan.09
Alabaster, E. O., *c.o. Canada* 6Jan.09
Hayes-Sadler, *Cawnpore* 6Jan.09
   E. J. B.
Rhodes, G. D. 6Jan.09
Witts, F. V. B. *Rurki* 6Jan.09
Kisch, F. H. *Quetta* 6Jan.09
Brown, F. L. *Weymouth* 6Jan.09
Worledge, *Pekin* 6Jan.09
   J. P. G.
Sneathman, J. M. *Pretoria* 1Apr.10
Clarke, E. H. *Mandalay* 2May10
Owen, L. C. *Longmoor* 2May10
Preedy, C. *East Ranyoon,* 2May10
   Burma
Chater, A. F. *Rurki* 2May10
Gill, A. G. *Mauritius* 2May10
McNelie, H. C. *Malta* 2May10
Budden, F. H. *Fyzabad* 2May10
Fox, E. B. *Rangalore* 2May10
Almond, R. L. *Banga'ore* 2May10
Cash, J. N. *Jamaica* 2May10
Foster, T. H. *Aldershot* 2May10
Momber, E. M. F. [L] *Hong* 2May10
   Kong
Buckingham, W. E. *Hong* 2May10
   Kong
White, M. FitzG. G. *Sheerness* 2May10
Nosworthy, F. P. *Dehra Dun* 2May10
Tottenham, C. G. L. [*l*] *Calcutta* 2May10
Michelli, P. F. M. *Malta* 2May10
Roome, H. E. *Maymyo* 2May10
Walton, C. *Lahore* 2May10
Spackman, P. G. *Egypt* 16May10

Royal Engineers.

Lieutenants—contd.

MacGeorge, H. **C.**
    I. of Wight 25June10
Reynolds, H. R. P., *f.c.*
    Salisbury Plain 25June10
Fox, A. G., *f.c.*   *Salisbury* 30July10
    Plain
Carson, C. F.   *Lahore* 18Aug.10
Greig, J. P. S. *War Office* 18Aug.10
Scott, A. H. [L]   *Malta* 18Aug.10
Cracroft-Amcotts, W. [l]
    Gibraltar 18Aug.10
Pain, W. E.   *Limerick* 18Aug.10
McKay, H. M.   *Mussoorie* 18Aug.10
Neame, P.   *Gibraltar* 18Aug.10
Bateman, H, H., *s. S.M.E.* 18Aug.10
Rawson, G. G. *Aldershot* 18Aug.10
Napier-Clavering, N, W.
    Malta 18Aug.10
Gompertz, A. V. [l] *Loralai* 18Aug.10
Campbell, M.G.G. *Kirkee* 18Aug.10
Bowles, J. C. *Mauritius* 18Aug.10
Chippindall, J.E. *Singapore* 18Aug.10
Kitchin, E. G.   *Risalpur* 18Aug.10
Pressey, H. A. S. *Hong Kong* 18Aug.10
Anderson, M. A. *Gibraltar* 18Aug.10
Pakenham-Walsh,
  R. P., *c.o.*   *Australia* 18Aug.10
Wellesley, E. V. C. W.
    Malta 18Aug.10
Finnimore, A. C. *Singapore* 18Aug.10
Pyne, H. G.   *Cork* 8Sept.10
Sealy, E.M.W., *f.o. Rhodesia*21Dec.10
Robson, R. G. G.   *Delhi* 21Dec.10
Wright, R. G. *Shorncliffe* 21Dec.10
Heath, F. P. *Hong Kong* 21Dec.10
Fitzpatrick, N. T.
   Fort Sandeman 21Dec10
Dunhill, C. M. G.
   Ahmednagar 21Dec.10
Whiteley, E. C.   *Kirkee* 1Jan.11
Rohde, J. H.   *Kirkee* 13Jan.11
Geary, H. N, G. *Karachi* 4Feb.11
Smith, A. G.   *Bordon* 4Feb.11
Egerton, R. R. *Aldershot* 4Feb.11
Grasett, A. E.   *Limerick* 4Feb.11
Matheson, C. L. T.,   4Feb.11
  c.o.   *Gold Coast*
Raikes, J. W. J. *Longmoor* 4Feb.11
               Camp
Boulnois, P.K. *Bulford Camp*4Feb.11

Gosset, H. H. E.   *Lahore* 4Feb.11
Clough, A. B., *c.o.* *Nigeria* 4Feb.11
Hyland, F. G. [l] *Plymouth* 4Feb.11
Webb, M. W. T. *Longmoor* 18 Mar.11
              Camp
Morris, E. L.   *Chatham* 1Apr.11
Dewing, R. E.   *Gosport* 5Apr.11
Fowle, W. M. *Rawal Pindi* 6Aug.11
Hutchison, J. A.   (*Survey*
  Duty, Malay States,
  17 *May* 12) *Seremban Negri*
    Sembilan 11Sept.11
Fordham, H.M. *Hong Kong*18Sept.11
Buller, F. E. *Secunderabad* 31Oct.11
Martel, G.Le Q. *Woolwich* 20Dec.11
Roberts, J. R.   *Sialkote* 23Jan.12
Pusent, J. R. *Aldershot* 23Jan.12
Turner, R. A. *Moore Park* 23Jan.12
Bradney, E. *Rawal Pindi* 23Jan.12
Vale, J. S.   *Aldershot* 23Jan.12
Trevor, H. S.   *Lahore* 23Jan.12
Greswell, H. G. *Kirkee* 23Jan.12
Carr, W. B. H. *Hong Kong* 23Jan.12
James, D. A. *Montrose* 23Jan.12
Stone, R.G.W.H. *Aldershot* 23Jan.12
Britten, W. E.   *Hangu* 23Jan.12
Farley, E. L.   *Ranikel* 23Jan.12
Tillard, J. A. S. *Aldershot* 23Jan.12
Gordon, R. E. *Rawal Pindi* 23Jan.12

Lieutenants—contd.

Fletcher, J. N., *f.c.*   *South*
    Farnborough 23Jan.12
Hanna, W. F. *Moore Park* 23Jan.12
Morse, A. H.   *Lucknow* 28Feb.12
Findlay,G.deC.E.*Chatham* 28Feb.12
Phipps, C. C.   *Bangalore* 10Mar12
Miller,   *Jamaica* 25July12
  T. W, D. [l]
Wheeler, E. O.   *Meerut* 21Dec.12
King, C. J. S.   *Lahore* 21Dec.12
Carnduff,K.MacL *Curragh* 21Dec.12
Deane, G. R. H. *Jamaica* 21Dec.12
Oates, R. W.   *Singapore* 21Dec.12
Bond, R. L.   *Aldershot* 21Dec.12
Sandford, H. R. *Bombay* 21Dec.12
Slater, O.   *Calcutta* 21Dec.12
Stafford, J. H. *Aldershot* 21Dec.12
Martin, K. J, [L] *Aldershot* 21Dec.12
Glennie, E. A.   *Karachi* 21Dec.12
Kerrich,   *S. Africa* 21Dec.12
  W. A. FitzG.
Streeten, G.   *Malta* 21Dec.12
Hounsell, R H. S. *Ambala* 21Dec.12
Pennycuick,M.A.C.*Curragh* 21Dec.12
Simson, I. *Longmoor Camp* 21Dec.12
Pottinger, C.E.R. *Curragh* 21Dec.12
Winter, W. O. *Rly. Course,* 21Dec.12
         G.W. Rly.
Wemyss, H. C. B. [l]   21Dec.12
      Aldershot
Adams, C. C.   *Aldershot* 21Dec.12
Hutton, G. A. *Bulford Camp* 21Dec.12
Yearsley, K. D. *Risalpur* 21Dec.12
Sykes, A. C. *Wellington,* 21Dec.12
        Madras
Macready, G. N. [l]   21Dec.12
      Aldershot
Briggs, H. S. *Queenstown* 21Dec.12
Douglas, J. K.   *Bombay* 12Dec.12
Ealt Kerr, R. S. *Kirkee* 21Dec.12
Cruickshank, A. J. *Jhansi* 21Dec.12
Wagstaff, H. W.   *Hangu* 4Jan.13
Guinness, V.E.G. *Karachi* 31Mar.13
Carter, J. J.   *Ceylon* 19June13
Lewis, A. P. A. *Bermuda* 26June13
Peache, W. W.*Isle of Wight* 31July13
Evelegh. E. N *Aldershot* 31July13
Joly de Lotbinière, H. A.
    Rly. Course, L. & S.W.
    Rly., Easileigh 31July13
Cheetham, G. [L] *Aldershot* 31July13
McMullen. D. J. *Mech. Eng.*31July13
    Course, G.N. R'y.,
      Doncaster
Mason, A.   *Delhi* 31July13
Clery, V.A.C.   *Woolwich* 31July13
Calthrop, E. E.   *Bordon* 31July13
Dewing, R. H.   *Madras* 31July13
Bayly, C G.G., *f.c. Upavon* 31July13
Flint, R. H.   *Curragh* 2Aug.13
Drake-Brockman, A. T.
  R.A.
Oxley, W. H. *Gibraltar* 17Aug.13
Gouriay, K. I. *Shorncliffe* 28Aug.13
Holbrow, T. L. S., *f.c. Up-* 23Aug.13
        avon
Watson, G. D.   *Rurki* 20Sept.13
Urquhart, H.A. *Gibraltar* 27Sept.13
Hawker, L. G.,*f.c. Queens-* 10Oct.13
    town Harbour
Johnston, E. F. *Mech. Eng.* 1Oct.13
  Course, L. & S.W. Rly.,
        Eastleigh
Euler, W. E. [l]   *Cork* 1Oct.13
Reid, L. C. *Longmoor Camp* 1Oct.13
Mallins, J. W. D.   15Dec.13
      Darlington
Lewin, R. A. H. *Plymouth* 24Dec.13
Drew, F.   *Bangalore* 24Dec.13
Hamilton, H. W. R. *Rurki* 24Dec.13
Papillon, A.H.B. *Bangalore* 24Dec.13

Lieutenants—contd.

Elsdale, R.   *Limerick* 24Dec.13
Cadell, H. M.   *Carlow* 17Jan.14
Greenwood,   *India* 17Jan.14
Fitzmaurice,   *Kirkee* 31Jan.14
  M. A. R. G.
Harman E. *Queenstown* 4Mar.14
Matthews, A. B. *Bangalore* 24Mar.14
Kermack, H. N. *Plymouth* 24Mar.14
Perkins, Æ. F. Q. *Aldershot* 24Mar.14
Buchanan, E. J. B. *Kirkee* 6June14
ffrench-Mullen,*Queenstown* 24June14
  D. R St. J. J.
Crawford, K. B S. *Kirkee* 15July14
Martin, C.G. *Bulford Camp* 15July14
Sweeny, S. F. C. *Aldershot* 15July14
Aitken, A. B.   *S.M.E.* 15July14
Mansergh, G. E. *Aldershot* 15July14
Tyler, A.   *Aldershot* 15July14
Cardew, R. W.   *S.M.E.* 15July14
Wellesley, G. J. *Aldershot* 15July14
Penney, T. M. M. *S.M.E.* 15July14
Young, E. K. *Aldershot* 15July14

2nd Lieutenants.

Leventhorpe, J. A. *Gosport* 19July12
Luby, M.   *S.M.E.* 19July12
Bourdillon, J. I. F. *S.M.E.* 19July12
West, C. A.   *Aldershot* 19July12
Mulvany, C. F.   *Gosport* 19July12
Parker, C. L. Y. *Gosport* 19July12
Broadway, H. A. *Gosport* 25July12
Fenwick, C. D. A. *S.M.E.* 26Aug.12
Miller, G. L.   *S.M.E.* 20Dec.12
Carr, A. C. H.   *S.M.E.* 20Dec.12
Fowle, F. E.   *S.M.E.* 20Dec.12
Joseph, S. H.   *S.M.E.* 20Dec.12
Odling, E. R. M. *S.M.E.* 20Dec.12
Renny-Tailyour, H. F. T.
        S.M.E. 20Dec.12
Godsell, K. B.   *S.M.E.* 20Dec.12
Latham, G. H.   *S.M.E.* 20Dec.12
Jackson, A. M.   *S.M.E.* 20Dec.12
Wingate, M. R.   *S.M.E.* 20Dec.12
Woolner, C. G.   *S.M.E.* 21Dec.12
Bebb, B., J. M. *S.M.E.* 25Dec.12
Semple, H. S.   *S.M.E.* 4Jan.13
Matthews, M.   *S.M.E.* 15Jan.13
Doyle, J. B. H. *S.M.E.* 20Feb.13
Greenwood, E. H. de L.
        S.M.E. 27June13
Tickell, E. F.   *S.M.E.* 18July13
Eave, K. McC.   *S.M.E.* 18July13
Batho, J.   *S.M.E.* 18July13
Josh, J. C. P.   *S.M.E.* 18July13
Grimsdale, G. E. *S.M.E.* 18July13
Playfair, I. S. O. *S.M.E.* 18July13
Norman, W. J.   *S.M.E.* 18July13
Vullinmy, C. H. H. *S.M.E.* 18July13
Ruse, E. W.   *S.M.E.* 1Aug.13
De'Ath, G. D.   *S.M.E.* 10Aug.13
Orange-Bromehead,
  F. E.   *S.M.E.* 27Aug.13
Mcintosh, A. C. *S.M.E.* 1Oct.13
Eady, H. G.   *S.M.E.* 1Oct.13
Pank, R. D.   *S.M.E.* 1Oct.13
Sleigh, C.   *S.M.E.* 1Oct.13
Hutson, H. P. W. *S.M.E.* 19Dec.13
Pattinson, W. F. *S.M.E.* 19Dec.13
Christie, R. C.   *S M E.* 19Dec.13
Kiggell, J.   *S M E.* 19Dec.13
Dening, B. C. [l] *S.M.E.* 18Feb.14
Scobie, F. MacK. *S.M.E.* 21Feb.14
Hamblin, W. E. *S.M.E* 21Mar.14
Osborn, G. C.   *S.M.E.* 1Apr.14
MacLean, L. J.   *S.M.E.* 1Apr.14
Vibart, N. M.   *S.M.E.* 1Apr.14
Haycraft, T. W. R. *S.M.E.* 1Apr.14
Kellie, G. H. S.   *S.M.E.* 1Apr.14
Inglis, J. A. P.   *S.M.E.* 1Apr.14
Withington, R. L. *S.M.E.* 1Apr.14
Atkinson, O. D.   *S.M.E.* 1Apr.14

Royal Engineers.

Adjutants.		Quarter-Masters—contd.		Quarter-Masters—contd.	
Master, G., capt.	R.E. 10Oct.12	Baker, W. E.	Londonderry 4June04 hon. capt. 4June14	Smith, T., hon lt, Waterford 7Nov.08 hon. lt.	
	Troops.	Collier, E. A.	Chatham 3July04 hon. capt. 3July14	Sneesby, W.N., Singapore 4Sept.09 hon. lt.	
Greig, R. H., D.S.O., capt.	Aly. Cos. & Depot 31Oct.13	Stevens,A.C.,hon.lt.Sheffield 8Nov.06		Walker, A., War Office 21Sept.10 hon. lt.	
Macaulay, R. K. A., capt.	Training Bn., Chatham 1June14	Westbrook, R.	War Office 13Oct.06 hon. lt.	Evans, W. R., War Office 17Nov.10 hon. lt.	
Riding Master.		Leak, C. H.,	War Office 17Oct.06 hon. lt.	Gill, H.,hon. lt.,r.Beaumaris 26Dec.10	
Griss, J. E.	Aldershot 12Sept.94 hon. maj. 12Sept.09	Stoyle, W., hon.lt. Tidworth 24Oct.06		Jones, W., hon. lt. Gibraltar 2Jan.11	
		Reid, W., hon. lt. Chatham 16Feb.07		Brewin, A. J. M., Dover 4Jan.11 hon. lt.	
		Quinlan, J. T., Jamaica 16Mar.07		Hilton, M., hon. lt. Curragh 13May11	
Quarter-Masters		Parslow, A. J., Dublin 17Apr.07 hon. lt.		Plowright, Portsmouth 7June11 E. H. J., hon. lt.	
Friar, R.	Edinburgh 21June00 hon. capt. 21June10	Barber, R., hon. lt. London 13July07		Johnson, T., Ord. Survey hon. lt., Southampton 2Aug.11	
Mitchell, H.	R. Arsenal, 6July01 Woolwich hon. capt. 6July11	Knowles,V.,hon.lt. Warwick 7Aug.07 hon. lt.		New, E. J., hon. lt. Malta 30Aug.11	
		Pickles, G. A., Weymouth 31Aug.07 hon. lt.		Chudleigh, W. G., Cardiff 24Aug.12 hon. lt.	
Dale, W. H. [F]	Chester 2Nov.00 hon. capt. 2Nov.11	Parslow, W. T.,hon. lt.Malta 6Apr.08		Shaw, W. J., Chatham 19Oct.12 hon. lt.	
Nicklen, J. R.	War Office 18Dec.01 hon. capt. 18Dec.11	Burrington, G., Dublin 27May08 hon. lt.		Cutting, F., Woolwich 27Oct.12 hon. lt.	
Shearburn, A. D.	War Office 1Jan.02 hon. capt. 1Jan.12	Rolls, E. J., S. Africa 27May08 hon. lt.		Hodgson, F. C., Limerick 30Dec.12 hon. lt.	
Butler, G. J.	Plymouth 16Apr.02 hon. capt. 16Apr.12	James, R. J., Gibraltar 27May08 hon. lt.		Dormor, R. D., Fermoy 3Jan.13 hon. lt.	
Gahagan, J. J.	S.M.E. 23Apr.02 hon. capt. 23Apr.12	Crombie, G. W., Hong 3June08 hon. lt. Kong		Lemon, G., Monmouth 4Mar.14 hon. lt.	
Tennent, T. H.	Aldershot 20Sept.02 hon. capt. 20Sept.12	Littlefield, A. O., Aldershot 3June08 hon. lt.		Harkness, J. P., Armagh 4Apr.14 hon. lt.	
McElwee, J. T.	Glasgow 8Oct.02 hon. capt. 8Oct.12	Morgan, W., hon. lt. York 3June08		White, F. J., Athlone 2May14 hon. lt.	
Downs, E. R.,	Egypt 28Mar.04 hon. capt. 28Mar.14	Baker, W. C., Colchester 3June08 hon. lt.		McDonald, E., Cork 27June14 hon. lt.	
		Dean, W. G., Capetown 3June08 hon. lt.			

COAST BATTALION.

–	Company or Section.	Station.	–	–	Company or Section.	Station.	–
Majors.				*Lieuts.,—contd.*			
Brown, W. G. C.	Staff Officer	War Office	1Apr.03	Tucker, J. E.	Sect. 49 Co.	North Queensferry	7Aug.07
Bailey, J. H.	–	War Office	1July05	Pocock, J. C.	Det. 35 Co.	Cardiff	21Sept.07
Captains.				Barr, W.	Sect. 16 Co.	Paull on Humber	18Nov.08
Flitcroft, E. A.	6 Co.	Weymouth	20Apr.10	Wright, A. T.	Sect. 16 Co.	Middlesbrough	23Jan.09
Shearburn, R.	49 Co.	Greenock	20Apr.10	Johns, F. N.	Det. 35 Co.	Liverpool	12June09
Burton, H. E.	16 Co.	North Shields	4June11	Spanner, H. T.	Det. 33 Co.	Berehaven	18Apr.10
Collins, J.	16 Co.	Jarrow-on-Tyne	21Dec.12	Reid, I. W.	Det. 35 Co.	Liverpool	26Apr.11
Lieutenants.				Sanford, A. J.	18 Co.	Falmouth	28Sept.12
Craig, W. P.	Det. 33 Co.	Buncrana.	29May07	McSweeney. J.	Det. 34 Co.	Alderney	25Mar.14

ATTACHED—FOR ARMY SIGNAL SERVICE.

Captain.				*Lieutenants—contd.*			
Sadleir-Jackson, L. W. de V., D.S.O., 9 Lrs.	1 Sig. Sqdn.		2Sept.12	Hargreaves, C. F., E. Lan. R.	1 Sig. Co.		10ct.12
Lieutenants.				Dickinson, D. P., Welsh R.	6 Sig. Co.		10ct.12
Hitchins, E.N.F.,W.Rid.R.	5 Sig. Co.		8Aug.12	Naylor, H. B., S. Staff.R.	5 Sig. Co.		10ct.12
Wright, G.M. H., R. Ir.Fus.	4 Sig. Co.		8Aug.12	Fairtlough, E. V. H. R. A.	2 Sig. Troop		10ct.12
How, W. F., R. Ir. Rif. ..	4 Sig. Co.		8Aug.12	Mair, J. A. E., York. R.	4 Sig. Co.		22Dec.13
Johnston, A. C., Worc. R. ..	3 Sig. Co.		10Aug.12	Allan, A. C., Cam'n Highrs.	6 Sig. Co.		14Jan.14
Orange-Bromehead, J. W., Yorks. L.I.	6 Sig. Co.		10Aug.12	Swayne, J. G. des R., Som. L.I.	5 Sig. Co.		28Feb.14
Dammers, R. W., Notts. & Derby R.	3 Sig. Co.		10Aug.12	Lyod, R. W., 16 Lrs.	1 Sig. Troop		16Mar.14
Firth, C. W. M., Dorset R.	1 Sig. Co.		11Aug.12	Deakin, C., Worc. R.	3 Sig. Co		13Apr.14
Penrose, J. P., R.A.	3 Sig. Troop		26Aug.12	Blake, St. J. L., O. B. A. ff., 21 Lrs.	5 Sig. Troop		11May14
Sampson, G. E., R. Innis. Fus.	2 Sig. Co.		2Sept.12	Pearce Edgcumbe, Lt. O., D. of Corn. L.I.	2 Sig. Co.		27May14
Willan, R. H., K. R. Rif. C	1 Sig. Co.		21Sept.12				
Cochrane, D. J., R.A. ..	4 Sig. Troop		26Sept.12				

Royal Engineers. Special Reserve.

ROYAL ENGINEERS.
SPECIAL RESERVE.
Order of Precedence.
Monmouth.
Anglesey.

Royal Anglesey.
Beaumaris.

(*Officers serving on 13 Oct. 00 in the corresponding Militia unit hold honorary Army rank equivalent to the Militia regimental rank they then held. Other officers entitled to honorary Army rank have it shown against their names.*)

Hon. Colonel.
Williams-Bulkeley, Sir R. H.,
 Bt. (Hon. Col. ret. Mila.) 11Mar.12

Lt.-Colonel.
p.s. Matthews-Donaldson, C. G.,
 Maj. ret. pay, hon. c. (*H*)
 ⓜ, p.v.o. (b) (g) 18Oct.05

Major.
p.s. Harvey, G. C. (*H*) 12Nov.07

Captains (3).
p.s. Springfield, D. O., hon. m.
 (Hon. Lt. in Army 10 Oct. 00)
 (*H*)(*P*) 27May03
p.s. McClymont, R. K. (*H*) 6Oct.06
p.s. Wilson, C. E. (*H*) 30Jan.08
p.s. Williams, R. (*H*) 17Mar.12
p.s. Parrington, M. (Hon. 2nd
 Lt. in Army 11 Oct. 02)
 (*H*) (b), P.c. (a) 21May12
p.s. Darby-Dowman, H. D'E. (*H*)
  1Feb.13
p.s. (P) Gyll-Murray, B. M. B. II.,
  6Feb.14

Lieutenants (6).
(p.s.) Towneley-Bertie, Hon.
 M. H. E. C. (*H*) 29Aug.07
Bolsover, G. 8Aug.12

2nd Lieutenants (5).
Doran, C. C. H. 9Apr.10
Coates, C. P. (on prob.) 24Sept.13
Pechell, H. C. (on prob.) 1Oct.13
Barker, J. M. (on prob.) 16May14
Adjt. Moore, H. F. B. S.,
 Capt. R.E. 23Aug.12
 (Capt. in Army 1Oct.13)
Qr.-Mr. ✗Gill, H., Qr-Mr. R.E., hon. li.
 [Scarlet—Facings, Blue.]

Royal Monmouthshire.
Monmouth.

(*Officers serving on 31 Oct. 00 in the corresponding Militia unit hold honorary Army rank equivalent to the Militia regimental rank they then held. Other officers entitled to honorary Army rank have it shown against their names.*)

Hon. Colonel.
p.s. ✗Raglan, G. Fitz R. H.,
 Lord C. B., late Capt.
 G. Gds. (Hon. Col. ret.
 Mila.) (*H*) 12Mar.13

Lt.-Colonel.
p.s. ✗Lindsay, H. E. M., C.B.
 Maj. ret. pay (*H*) 19Mar.08

Major.
p.s. ✗Forestier-Walker, R. S.
 (Hon. Capt. in Army
 14 Oct. 01) 19Mar.08

Captains (4).
p.s. ✗Vaughan, C. J., hon. m.
 (*H*) 6May03
p.s. ✗Digby, K. E. [L] (*H*) 28May04

Captains.—contd.
p.s. ✗Evans, C. G. (Hon. Lt. in
 Army 5 Oct. 02)(*H*)(Surveyor, Survey Dept.,
 Nigeria, 29Apr.14) 1June07
p.s. David, M. (*H*) 8June12
p.s. (P) Studdert, T. G. H.
 (*H*), P.c. 20Sept.12
p.s. Vyvyan, C. A. 5May13
p.s. Moreton, P. C. R. (*H*) 19Mar.14
p.s. Harris, F. C. (*H*) 9May14

Lieutenants. (8)
(p.s.) ✗Wauton, E. B., P.c.
 (Asst. Dist. Offr., S.
 Prov., Nigeria { 1Jan.14
  { 17May09)
p.s. Forster, T. G. B. (*H*) 1Oct.10
p.s. Cowie, H. C. 28Oct.11
 Budge, C. S. G. (Surveyor
 Probr., Malay States,
 30May13) 9Dec.11
Kettle, W. J. 26Sept.12

2nd Lieutenants. (7)
Rogers, T. D. D. 26Apr.13
Moore, H. E. 1May13
Hodgkinson, L. P. (on
 prob.) 7Jan.14
Low, G. (on prob.) 7Jan.14
Chandler, H. M. 28Jan.14
 (on prob.) 10Apr.12
Crawford-Clarke, W. H.
 (on prob.) 7Feb.14
Beck, P. L. (on prob.) 5Sept.13
Adjt. Baylay, A. C., Capt. R.E. 7Nov.12
 (Capt. in Army, 23Dec.07)
Qr.-Mr. Lemon, G., Qr. Mr. R.E.,
 hon. lt.
 [Scarlet—Facings, Blue.]

Postal Section.
General Post Office, London.

Lt.-Colonel.
✗Price, W., C.M.G., vD (Hon. Maj. in
 Army 20 June 03) (Dir. of Army
 Postal Services) 31Mar.13

Majors (2).
✗Warren, P. (Hon. Lt. in Army
 6 Aug. 03) (*H*) 31Mar.13

Captains (2).
Powney, J. T. (*H*) 31Mar.13

Lieuts. and 2nd Lieuts. (5).
Lieutenant.
Lidbury, D. J. 11June13
Hoobins, T. P. (on prob.) 4Mar.14
Braund, T. B. (on prob.) 4Mar.14

2nd Lieutenants.
Henderson, J. G. (on prob.) 18Apr.14
Newsome, R. H. A. (on prob.) 18Apr.14

Motor Cyclist Section.
Subalterns. (8)
2nd Lieutenants.
✗Howard, S. A. 15Aug.13
   3Dec.10
Selwyn, A. H. 3Sept.13
Jones, S. B. 3Oct.13
   7Jan.11

Supplementary Officers.

Majors.
(P) ✗Baskerville, C. H. L. Lt.-Col. ret. pay
 (Res. of Off.) hon. l.c. (*H*) ⓜ ⓟ S. Comd. 7Feb.97
Bartley, E. B., hon. l.c. (Maj. Res. of Off.)
 (*H*) E. Comd. 5June01
Somerset-Leeke, A. Fitz R. W. H. hon. l.c.
 (*H*) Hon. Capt in Army14Oct.00)
  S. Comd. 26Sept.03
(P) Holland, C. G., hon. l.c. (*H*) Hon. Capt.
 in Army7Nov.00.) E. Comd. 19Mar.04

Captains.
p.s. Blackwell, L. N., hon. m. (*H*) (Hon. Capt
 in Army 7Nov.00) 15June98
(P) Prior, J. H., D.S.O' (*H*) (Hon. Lt. in
 Army 7Nov.00) Plymouth 8May01
(P) Sebastian-Smith, C. A. (t) (*H*) (a) (*H*)
 Lt. in Army 1Nov.00) S. Comd. 14Apr.02

Royal Engineers.

Special Reserve—*contd.*

Supplementary Officers—*contd.*

Captains—contd.

(P) Buckley, P. N. (H) (*Hon. Lt. in Army 7Nov.*00) (*Mil. Offr. attd. to Staff of High-Commr., C'wealth of Australia* { 2*Apr.*10 / 3*Mar.*04) 27June08
P) Spottiswood, T. W. F. (H) (*Hon. Lt. in Army 7Nov.*00) *Sheerness* 19Mar.04
(P) de Salis, H. J. N. (*Hon. 2nd Lt. in Army 7Nov.*00) 9Oct.04
(P) Rudge, J. F. (H) (*Hon. Lt. in Army 7Nov.*00) *Plymouth* 10Oct.08
p.s.✗Rye, R. B. T. (*Hon. Lt. in Army* 14*Oct.*00) *Cork* 1Jan.09
(P) Muntz, R. H. (*Hon. 2nd Lt. in Army 7Nov.*00) *S.E. Coast Def.* 11Apr.10
(P)✗Anson, J. A. (H) (*Hon. 2nd Lt. in Army* 14*Oct.*00) *Plymouth* 11June10
(P) Watson, I. N. H. (*Hon. 2nd Lt. in Army 7Nov.*00) *Falmouth* 18July10
p.s.Guinness, O. H. (*t*) (H) (*Hon. 2nd Lt. in Army* 14*Oct.*00) *S. Coast Def.* 21Sept.10
(P) Tucker, W. G. (H) *Gosport* 28Nov.11
(P) Allen, H. C. G. *Cork* 19Feb.12
(P) Hime, F. R. *Gosport* 19Mar.14

Lieutenants.

p.s.Heathcote, G. N. (*Asst. Dist. Offr., S. Prov., Nigeria* { 1*Jan.*14 / 5*Sept.*13) *E. Comd.* 30July04 / 30Jan.04
Pickard, J. A. A., 23June07
late Lt. R.E. *Longmoor Camp* 20Dec.11
Fishbourne, C.E.,Lt. ret. pay *Woolwich* 23June07 / 4Jan.13
p.s.Bullmore. E. C. *Plymouth* 3Feb.09
Gurney, C. R. (*Empld. under Sudan Govt.* 8*Oct.*10) *Aldershot Comd.* 27Jan.14
Hill, F. G. (*Tempy. empld.*) *Aldershot* 27Jan.14
Stavert, W. D. *Shorncliffe* 27Jan.14
Lundie. R. C. *Chatham* 27Jan.14
Howorth, B. *Woolwich* 27Jan.14
Pearson, S. *S. Comd.* 27Jan.14
Haseldine, J.F. *Aldershot* 27Jan.14
Kaye-Parry. E. *Limerick* 27Jan.14
Porter, H. W. *Curragh* 27Jan.14

2nd Lieutenants.

Wells, R. C. *Bulford* 27Jan.09
Platts, M. G. 27Jan.09
Richardson, T. C. *Curragh* 26June09
Clifford, F. A. *Woolwich* 26June09
Bates, F. (*Tempy. empld.*) *N. Comd.* 26June09
McAlister, A. *Aldershot* 26June09
McLaughlin, W. R. *Curragh* 26June09
Cole, T. S. *Aldershot* 26June09
Ireland, F. W. 26June09
Marshall, A.R. *Bulford* 26June09
Foot, S. H. (q) *Aldershot* 26June09
Wadsworth, G. W. *Limerick* 26June09
Smith, R. A. B. *Cork* 8Jan.10
Cran, P. McL. (*Asst.Eng.,P.W.D., Gold Coast*, { 3*July*12 / 15*Feb.*11) 8Jan.10
Morris, J. H. 8Jan.10
Linnell, T. F. (*Asst. Eng., Uganda Rly. Staff*, { 1*Apr.*14 / 14 *ept.*11) *Irish Comd.* 8Jan.10
Gurney, M. W. E. R. *Aldershot* 8Jan.10
Schneider, R. H (*Surveyor, Nigeria* { 27*May*14 / 24*May*11) *Irish Comd.* 8Jan.10
Hall, G. F. 8Jan.10
Griffin, A. C. 8Jan.10
Burford, W. B. *S. Comd.* 8Jan.10

2nd Lieuts.—contd.

Hammonds, D. H. 8Jan.10
Evans, E. A. *Cork* 25June10
Bradley, C. H. (*P.W.D.,Ceylon,*5*Aug.*11) 25June10
✗Irving, A. G. *Aldershot* 25June10
Ferguson, J. (*Survey Probr., Ceylon,* 3*May*12) 25June10
Goodwin, J. A. *Limerick* 25June10
Smith, H. A. T. (*Asst. Eng., P.W.D., E. Afr. Prote.* 17*Aug.*11) *Aldershot* 25June10
Portway, D. (q) *Carlow* 25June10
Bellamy, C. G. H. 25June10
Weston, G. E. (*Survey Probr., E. Afr. Prote.* 12*Oct.*11) *Aldershot* 25June10
Hulbert, C. G. K. *Aldershot* 25June10
Sheldon, C. D. *Bordon* 25June10
Roche, R. T. H. 25June10
Evans, G. F. *E. Comd.* 25June10
Holt, H. W. *Bulford* 25June10
Dewar, A. (*P.W.D., Egypt,* 12*Dec.*13) *Irish Comd.* 21Jan.11
Stevenson, C. Y. *Irish Comd.* 21Jan.11
Higgs, H. J. (*P.W.D. Egypt*) *E. Comd.* 21Jan.11
Bailey, E. E. (*Irrigation Dept., Egypt,* 14*Feb.*12) 21Jan.11
Rawlings, P. T. (*Empld. under Sudan Govt.* 19*Dec.*12) *E. Comd.* 21Jan.11
Hitchcock, G. E. W. (*P.W.D., Egypt,* 22*Feb.*12) 21Jan.11
Moore, E. (*P.W.D., Egypt,* 23*Feb.*12) 21Jan.11
Grundy, F. *Aldershot* 21Jan.11
Rhodes, G.E. 11Mar.11 / 7May10
Broade, G. E. W. *Woolwich* 17June11
Morris, R. D. *Aldershot* 5July11
Masters, H. J. *Aldershot* 5July11
Whitfield, J. B. *Chatham* 5July11
Temperley. E. E. V. 5July11
Hawes, C. G. 5July11
Green, D. H. 5July11
Pennell, K. E. L. 5July11
Wynne-Jones, M. *Aldershot* 26June12
Wylie, A. F *Shorncliffe* 26June12
Adams, E. S. R. (*on prob.*) 26June12
Pound, G. T. *Shorncliffe* 26June12
MacFeat, P. D. (H (*Asst. Eng., P.W.D., E. Afr. Prote.*, 19*Nov.*13) 17July12
Macnamara, H. J. *Kilworth* 17Aug.12
Warde, R. H. *Chatham* 8Sept.12
Rean, W. F. (*on prob.*) 21June13
Crofton, E. V. M. (*on prob.*) 21June13
Farmer, N. J. C. (*on prob.*) 21June13
McCreary, R. (*on prob.*) 21June13
Mariette, E. E. (*on prob.*) 21June13
Parkes, A. J. (*on prob.*) 21June13
Collier, A. E. (*on prob.*) 21June13
Stanley, E. S. (*on prob.*) 21June13
Manley, J. D. (*on prob.*) 21June13
Paddison, R. H. (*on prob.*) 9July13
Gill, G. E (*on prob.*) 16July13
Napier-Clavering, F. D. (*on prob.*) 28July13
Heron, J. J. (*on prob.*) 11July14
Richmond, G. W. (*on prob.*) 11July14
Ash, S. H. o n *prob.*) 11July14
Holmes, A. P. H. (*on prob.*) 11July14
Bell, W. I. *on pr.b.*) 11July14
Barnes, E. E. *on prob.*) 11July14
Ure, C. McG. (*on prob.*) 11July14
Lowson, N. C. (*on prob.*) 11July14
Monckton, F. H. (*on prob.*) 11July14
Seabrooke, F. H. (*on prob.*) 11July14
Key, D. P. (*on prob.*) 11July14

ROYAL ENGINEERS (MILITIA).
Malta Division.

ROYAL ENGINEERS.
TERRITORIAL FORCE.
ORDER OF PRECEDENCE OF THE SEVERAL COUNTIES.

1. County of London.
2. City of Glasgow.
3. Lanarkshire.
4. Lancashire.
5. Northumberland.
6. W. Riding of Yorkshire.
7. N. Riding of Yorkshire.
8. Gloucestershire.
9. Cheshire.
10. Hampshire.
11. Devonshire.
12. Somersetshire.
13. Durham.
14. City of Aberdeen.
15. Sussex.
16. Bedfordshire.
17. Glamorgan.
18. Renfrewshire.
19. City of Edinburgh.
20. Staffordshire.
21. Wiltshire.
22. Kent.
23. Warwickshire.
24. E. Riding of Yorkshire.
25. Carmarthenshire.
26. City of Dundee.
27. Essex.
28. Cornwall.
29. Dorsetshire.

Dates shewn prior to 1 April, 1908, are those of the Officers' corresponding rank in a late unit of the Volunteer Force.

i. Divisional Engineers.
ii. Signal Service—
   a. Divisional Signal Companies and Infantry Brigade Signal Sections.
   b. Signal Companies (Army Troops).
iii. Fortress Engineers.
iv. Electrical Engineers.
v. Engineer and Railway Staff Corps.

1. DIVISIONAL ENGINEERS.

[The order of precedence of groups is denoted by numerals in brackets.]

East Anglian
[13]

Ashburnham Road,
Bedford.

Hon. Colonel.
×*Kitchener of Khartoum, Fd. Marshal H. H.,* Earl,
K.P., G.C.B., G.C.S.I., O.M., G.C.M.G., G.C.I.E., q.s., Col. Comdt. R.E.
        8May01

Lt.-Colonel.
p. Wells, G. H. (*H*)
C.R.E.E.Ang.Div.)
        22July11

Adjutant.
×Stokes, A. W.,
Capt R.E. 29June11

Medical Officers.
Hartley, Maj.
A. C., *M.D.,*
R.A.M.C. (T.F.)
(*attd.*)   31Jan.12
        4July00
Cruickshank, Lt.
W. J., *M.B.*
R.A.M.C. (T.F.)
(*attd.*)   30May13

1st East Anglian Field Co.
Ashburnham Road,
Bedford.

Major.
Wilson, F. 22July11

Captain.

Lieutenants. (2)
(p.) Walker, G. G. 25Jan.10

2nd Lieutenants (2).
Berry, A. J. 25July12
        26June12
Story, T. H. 21Dec.12
Langley, A. G. 11July13
Wilson, M. M. 22Apr.14

2nd East Anglian Field Co.
Ashburnham Road,
Bedford.

Major.
Steinmetz, A. B. S.
(*Lt. Res. of Off.*)
        1Apr.08

Captain.
Mowat, M. 16Apr.12
        26Aug.07

Lieutenants. (2)
(p.) Preston, B. W.10Jan.06
Michaelis, G.M.31Mar.14

2nd Lieutenants. (2)
Smith, T. H. 18Dec.12
Kent, L. B. 11July13
Rogers, G. A. 13June14
        8Apr.14

Highland
[3]

80, Hardgate, Aberdeen.

Hon. Colonel.
p. *Anstice,*Sir K.H.,K.C.B.,
Maj. ret. pay *(Hon.*
Col. ret. Vols. 29Apr.14

Lt.-Colonel.
p. Cornwall, G. A.,
vD, (*t*) (*C. R. E.*
High. Div.) 9July10

Adjutant.
Wedd, A. P. W., Lt.
R.E., capt. 16Feb.14

Chaplain.
Walker, Rev. G., B.D.
(C.S.), Chapl. 3rd
Class (T.F.) (*attd.*)
        3Apr.11
        8Apr.01

1st Highland Field Co.
21, Jardine Street,
Glasgow.

Major.
p.s.Spencer, O. L., TD
(Q)   1Apr.08

Captain.
p.s.Jackson, C.M. 19Mar.14

Lieutenants. (2)
(p.) Mayor, J. B. 15Dec.10
Barr, A. D. S. 19Mar.14

Highland—contd.

2nd Lieutenants (2).
Cleghorn, A. 23Mar.10
Niven, R. O. 5June12

2nd Highland Field Co.

80, Hardgate, Aberdeen.

Major.
Kinghorn, H. J.,
TD   9July10

Captain.
p. Mitchell, R. 9July10

Lieutenants. (2)
(p.s.)Barron, W.P.,
A. *al.Inst. C.E.* 4Oct.11
(p.s.)Ledingham, G. A.
        23June12

2nd Lieutenants. (2)
Glegg, R. 25June12

Medical Officer.
p. Philip, Capt. F., *M.B.,*
R.A.M.C. (T.F.)
(*attd.*)   2Dec.09
        2June06

Home Counties
[12]

Ordnance Yard,
Eastbourne.

Lt.-Colonel.
Cheesewright, W. F.
(*C R.E., Home Cos.*
Div.)   12July13

Adjutant.
Benton, N. W.,
Capt. R. E. 18Aug.12

Medical Officer.
Martin, Capt. A. A.,
M.D., R.A.M.C.
(T.F.)(*attd.*) 10Oct.09
        10Apr.06

Home Counties—contd.

Chaplain.
Eliot, *Rev.* E. F. W.,
M.A., Chapl. 4th
Class. (T.F.)(*attd.,*)
        19Oct.06

1st Home Counties Field Co.
Ordnance Yard,
Eastbourne.

Lt.-Colonel.
p.s.*Hales,* E. G. 20Jan.06
Major.

Captain
Sparrow, W. A.
        1Oct.12

Lieutenants. (2)
(p.) Wormald, W. J.
        23Oct.07

2nd Lieutenants. (2)
Garrett, S. C. 29Mar.10
Herbert, D. L. 10Mar.11
Thomas, H D. 8July13

2nd Home Counties Field Co.
Tower Road West,
St. Leonards-on-Sea.

Major.
p. Sanders, H. W. (q)
        1Apr.12

Captain.
(p.) Bryan, C.C. 12Oct.10

2nd Lieutenants (2)
Challoner, W. H. C.
        3Apr.11
Chester, C. C. 10July11

Cadet Unit affiliated.
University School, Cadet
Company, Hastings.

---

‡ This rank is not provided for in the Territorial Force Tables of Establishment.

Royal Engineers. Territorial Force.

Divisional Engineers—contd.

East Lancashire.
[6]
73, Seymour Grove,
Old Trafford, Manchester.
Hon. Colonel.
Galloway, W. J.
25June02
Lt.-Colonel.
p. Newton, C. E.,
M. Inst. C.E.
(C.R.E., E. Lan. Div.) 12Mar.13
Adjutant.
✗Denison, G. W.,
Capt. R.E. 31Aug.12
Medical Officer.
English, Capt. S.,
M.B., R.A.M.C.
(T.F.) attd.) 30Mar.07 30Mar.07
Chaplain.
Perry, Rev. S. N.,
M.A., Chapl 2nd Class (T.F.), (attd.)
9Jan.11
15May01

1st East Lancashire Field Co.
73, Seymour Grove,
Old Trafford, Manchester.
Major.
Tennant, S. L. (Q) 12Mar.13
Captain.
p.s. Mousley, J. H. 12Mar.13
Lieutenants. (2)
Riddick, J. G. 19June11
2nd Lieutenants. (2)
Mackenzie, L. A. 13 Feb.12
Fruhe-Sutcliffe, R.
22Apr.13
Taunton, O. 9June13
Gough. D. E. 2Mar.14
Woods, B. H., late
2nd Lt. Res. of Off. 16Apr.14

2nd East Lancashire Field Co.
73, Seymour Grove,
Old Trafford, Manchester.
Major.
p. Fielding, H. A. (Q)
1Apr.08
Captain.
p. Carlyle, R. 12Mar.13
1June12
Lieutenants. (2)
Carver, O. A. 1June12
p. Wray, E. H., hon. capt. (b) 18May13
2nd Lieutenants. (2)
Woolley, T. G 18Sept.12
Bull, G. J. O. 10June13
Gracey, R. L. 2Mar.14

West Lancashire.
[5]
Engineer Hall,
Croppers Hill, St. Helens.
Hon. Colonel.
Sefton, Rt. Hon.
O. C., Earl of 4Feb.14

West Lancashire—contd.
Lt.-Colonel.
p. Sayce, G. E., TD,
Ⓟ(C.R.E.,W. Lan. Div.) 1Apr.13
Adjutant.
p.s. ✗Cunningham.
Capt. H.H.B.,
M.D., F.R.C.S.I.,
R.A.M.C. (T.F.)
(attd.)/ Lt. Res. of Off.) Ⓟ (H) 3Aug.12
Chaplain.
Rich, Rev. L. J.,
M.A., Chapl. 4th Class (T.F.)(attd.)
1Apr.08
21June99

1st (The St. Helens) West Lancashire Field Co.
Engineer Hall,
Croppers Hill, St. Helens.
Major.
p. Taberner, W., TD,
(l) 4July06
Captain.
p. Fox, J. H. (q) 7Dec.10
27Apr.07
Lieutenants. (2)
p.s. Lomax, L. 24Feb.08
Dixon-Nuttall, J. F.
14Dec.12
2nd Lieutenants. (2)

2nd (The St. Helens) West Lancashire Field Co.
Engineer Hall,
Croppers Hill, St. Helens.
Major.
Captain.
p.s. Brown,C.T.(H)25July00
p. ✗Campbell, H. La T.
(Hon. Lt. in Army
6 July 02) 5May10
4Nov.05
Lieutenants. (2)
Broom, T. C.,
A.M.Inst.C.E. 8May01
p.s. Dixon-Nuttall, W. F.
13Sept.05
Meston-Reid, J.
2July14
2nd Lieutenants. (2)
Carr, W. M. 18Sept.13

1st London.
[2]
10 Victoria Park Square
Bethnal Green, E.
Lt.-Colonel.
p. Walters, G. W., TD,
Ⓟ(C.R.E.,1 Lond. Div.) 29Jan.13
Adjutant.
✗Du Boulay, A. H.,
Capt. R.E. 1Mar.10

Medical Officers.
p. Dingle, Maj. W. A.,
M.D.,TD,R.A.M.C.
(T. F.) (attd.) 9Aug.02
5Mar.90
Chaplain.
Perry, Rev. Preb.
G. H., M.A., Chapl.
3rd Class (T.F.) (attd.) 9Aug.09
9Aug.99

1st London Field Co.
10, Victoria Park Square, E.
Major.
Denniss, E. W. 8Aug.13
Captain.
p.s. Joseph,R.H.(H)9Dec.07
Lieutenants. (2)
p. Mackenzie, R. H.
21Aug.07
Schwarz,W.H. 2Aug.13
2nd Lieutenants. (2)
Gamage, C. M. 7May13
Capell, G. O. 27May14

2nd London Field Co.
10, Victoria Park Square,E.
Major.
Johnstone, O. R. B.
15Aug.11
Captain.
Priday, F. G. 2Aug.13
Lieutenants. (2)
Ryan, B. J.(H)20Aug.11
Higgins, C. 3Aug.13
2nd Lieutenants. (2)
Narracott,R.W.1June11
Davenport, E. J. C.
12Feb.13

2nd London.
[1]
Duke of York's Headquarters, Chelsea, S.W.
Hon. Colonel.
Clifford, E. T.,
VD (Hon. Col.
ret. T.F.) 23May10
Lt.-Colonel.
p. Taylor, H. H., TD,
Capt. Res.of Off.)
Ⓟ(C.R.E. 2 Lond.
Div.) 15Apr.10
Adjutant.
Cooper, W. C.,
Capt. R.E. 18Sept.11
Medical Officer.
Davis, Capt. H.
D., R.A.M.C. (T.F.)
(attd.) 16Oct.12
16Apr.09
Chaplain.
Bevan, Ven. H. E. J.,
M.A., Archdeacon
of Middlesex,Chapl.
3rd Class (T.F.) (attd.) 21Apr.13
21Apr.03

3rd London Field Co.
Duke of York's Headquarters, Chelsea, S.W.
Major.
Sewell,S.D.,TD 16Apr.14
Captain.
p.s. Page, B. C. 16Apr.10
10Oct.06
p.s. ✗Marsh. H. H. S.
(Hon.Lt.in Army
27 Aug. 03) 3Aug.13
9Dec.02
Lieutenants. (2)
p.s. Sherwood,J.D. 10July07
p.s. Cullingford, F. R.
11Dec.12
21Mar.08
2nd Lieutenants. (2)
Davis, H. N. 18Dec.12
Stone, H. B. 7Jan.14

4th London Field Co.
Duke of York's Headquarters, Chelsea,S.W.
Major.
✗Henriques, R. Q.
(Hon. Lt. in Army
30May01) 13Mar.12
Captain.
p.s. Stephens, H. W.
15Mar.12
Lieutenants. (2)
Blogg, E. B.(H) 3July11
Birch, A. G. 28Feb.14
2nd Lieutenants. (2)
Steers, D. H. 6Jan.13
10July12
Booth, J. L. 20Dec.13

Cadet Unit affiliated to the Group.
Royal Engineer Cadets (2nd London Div.)

Lowland.
[4]
Drill Hall,
Rutherglen, N.B.
Hon. Colonel.
Newlands, J. H. C.,
Lord (King's Body
Gd. for Scotland)
11Mar.14
Lt.-Colonel.
o. Symington, T. (C.R.E.
Low. Div.) 28Feb.11
Adjutant.
✗Garwood, F.S., Maj.
R.E. 23Jan.09
Medical Officers.
p. Laird, Capt. T. D.,
R.A.M.C. (T.F.)
(attd.) 1Feb.07
1Aug.08
p. Lithgow, Capt. J.,
M.D., R.A.M.C.,
(T.F.)(attd.) 1Feb.07
1Aug.08
p. Martyn, Capt. S.,
M.B., R.A.M.C.
(T.F.)(attd.) 1Apr.08
1Aug.08

Royal Engineers. Territorial Force.

Divisional Engineers—contd.
Lowland—contd.

Chaplains.
Yuille, Rev. G. S.,
 M.A., B.D. [C S.]
 Chapl. 4th Class
 (T.F.)(attd.) 1Dec.09
Ferguson, Rev. F.,
 M.A.,B.D.,[U.F.C.]
 Chapl. 4th Class
 T.F.)(attd.) 5Feb.13

1st Lowland Field Co.
"Imperial Service."
Drill Hall, Coatdyke, Coatbridge, N.B.
Major.
p.s. Arthur, J. M. 4May12
Captain.
p.s. Spence, M. S. 1Apr.08
Lieutenants. (2)
p. Symington, H. 1Apr.08
2nd Lieutenants. (2)
Shanks, W. 22June12
Clark, G. W. 28Apr.13
Gardner, D. 25Apr 14
Alexander,J.A. 9June14
 1July09

2nd Lowland Field Co.
"Imperial Service."
Drill Hall, Rutherglen, N.B.
Major.
p.s.Motherwell, G. B.
 1Apr.12
 1Aug.03
Captain.
p.s. Reis, P. H. 24June11
 1Aug. 03
p. Downs, W. 5Jan.14
Lieutenants. (2)
(P.) Rolling, B. I. 3Aug.09
(P.) Kidd, T. M. 4May12
p.s.Archibald, W. 18Sept.12
 1Apr.08
2nd Lieutenants. (2)
Pearson, W.G. 22June12
Burns, W. S. 9June14
 18June13

North Midland.
|14|
Norton Hall, Norton Canes, Cannock.
Lt.-Colonel.
Harrison, W. E.
 (C. R. E., N.
 Mid. Div.) 25May12

Adjutant.
Wyncoll, C. E. F.,
 Capt. R.E. 13Mar.09

1st North Midland Field Co.
Drill Hall, Smethwick.
Major.
Tonks, S. W. ⊕ 1June12
Captain.
Beech, E. W. 1June12
Lieutenants. (2)
Gosling, D. E. 1Aug.13
2nd Lieutenants. (2)
Patterson, G. 17Jan.13

2nd North Midland Field Co.
Norton, Cannock.
Major.
Captain.
Hatton, C. 8May08
(p.)Coussmaker, L. J.
 15Mar.13
 26Apr.10
2nd Lieutenants. (2)
Brawn, J. A. 12July12
Welchman, P. E.
 12Mar.13

South Midland.
[9]
32, Park Row, Bristol.
Hon. Colonel.
✠M. Harrison, Gen. Sir
 R., G.C.B.,C.M.G.,
 Col. Comdt. R.E.
 [R] 7Nov.95
Lt.-Colonel.
p. ✠Sinnott, E. S.
 M.Inst. C.E., vD.
 (Hon. Lt. in Army 28 Dec.00)
 (t) (E) (C.R.E.
 S. Mid. Div.)
 11May12
Adjutant.
Brandon, O.G., Capt.
 R.E. 25Mar.11
Chaplain.
Wood, Rev. G. R.,
 M.A., Chapl. 3rd
 Class (T.F.)(attd.)
 1Apr.08
 13Jan.97

1st South Midland Field Co.
32, Park Row, Bristol.
Major.
Williams, J. L. V.S.,TD.
 14May12
Captain.
p. Gardiner, E. 1 Aug.08
 3Feb.04
Lieutenants. (3)
Hosegood, C. B. 1Feb.13
2nd Lieutenants. (2)
Davies, O. S. 1June10
Carey,J.MacL. 30Jan,13

2nd South Midland Field Co.
32, Park Row, Bristol.
Major.
p.s.✠Lambert, B. R.
 (H) (Hon. Lt. in
 Army 13Aug.02)
 15May12
Captain.
p. Eberle, G. S. J. F.
 3Feb.04
Lieutenants. (2)
Briggs, E. 18Sept.10
Wills, B. B. 28June13
2nd Lieutenants. (2)
Wright, A. J. M.,
 late Lt. 2 Glouc.
 R. E. (Vols.) 6July10
Whitwill, M. 28June13
 14Feb.12

Northumbrian.
[7]
Barras Bridge,
Newcastle-on-Tyne.
Lt.-Colonel.
p. Crawford, F. S.,
 vD, hon. o. (C.R.E..
 North'b'n.Div.) 23May07
Adjutant.
✠Mc Queen,J.A., Capt.
 R.E. 1Nov.13
Medical Officer.
Simpson,Lt.R.W.,
 M.B., R.A.M.C.
 (T.F.) (attd.) 28Mar.11
Chaplain.
East, Rev. W. R.,
 Chapl. 2nd Class
 (T.F.)(attd.)1Dec.13
 9Mar.98

1st (The Newcastle) Northumbrian Field Co.
Barras Bridge,
Newcastle-on-Tyne.
Major.
✠Pollard, G. C.
 Hon. Lt. in Army
 3Jun.01) 1Feb.13
Captain.
Lieutenants.
p. Burnup, E. C. 18Mar.07
 Stowell, W. R. 23Mar.13
2nd Lieutenants (2)
Travers, D. G.
 Le. M. G. 21Sept.11
 Stroud, H. C. 12June12
 McKelvie, J. 23Mar.13

2nd (The Newcastle) Northumbrian Field Co.
Barras Bridge,
Newcastle-on-Tyne.
Major.
McPherson, J. E., TD
 (t)(H) 1Jan.08
Captain.
p. Taylor, H. W. 1Oct.11
 24Jan.06
Lieutenants. (2)
Douglas, J. W. 1Oct.11

2nd Lieutenants. (2)
Dudley, B. 20Mar.12
Gibson, R. 24Mar.13
Forster, T. 6Feb.14

West Riding.
[8]
Glossop Road, Sheffield.
Hon. Colonel.
p. Bingham, Sir J. E.,
 Bt., vD 3Nov.00
Lt.-Colonel.
p. Bingham, A. E., vD
 (C.R.E. W. Rid.
 Div.) 8Dec.12
Adjutant.
Jones, O.G.D., Capt.
 R.E 23Feb.12
Medical Officers.
p. Turner, A C., Surg.-
 Capt. 7Nov.03
p. Benson, J.M., M.B.,
 Surg.-Capt. (Med.
 Offr., N. Provs.,
 Nigeria } 1Jan.14
 (16Apr.13)
 26Sept.10
 26Mar.07
Lee, Lt. W. E., M.D.,
 R.A.M.C. (T.F.)
 (attd.) 18June13

1st West Riding Field Co.
Sheffield.
Major.
Haywood, R. B. ⊕
 6Aug.13
Captain.
p. Flockton, C. B. 8Dec.13
Lieutenants (2).
Langley, J. K. B.
 8Dec.12
Price, F. L. 5July13
 9Sept.11
2nd Lieutenants. (3)
Seaman, W. A. (H)
 29Oct.09
Scott, E. I. 4Aug.11
✠Long, H. 1Feb.14

2nd West Riding Field Co.
Sheffield.
Major.
p. Colley, L. E., TD 1Apr.08
Captain.
p. Dodworth, G. N.
 5July13
Lieutenants (2)
Middleton, W. 11May10
Collier, P. P. 5July13
2nd Lieutenants. (2)
Price, C. L. 30Oct.09
Colver, E. W. 28Feb.13
Neill, F. A. 18Apr.13

Royal Engineers. Territorial Force.

831	832	833	834
Divisional Engineers—contd. **Welsh.** [10] 59, Charles Street, Cardiff. *Lt.-Colonel.* p. ✕Hutchison, R. L. (*Hon. Lt. in Army* 17June01) (*H*) (q) (*C.R.E. Welsh Div.*) 16Nov.10 *Adjutant.* *Medical Officers.* Dawson, H. G. F., *Surg.-Lt.* 4Dec.04 **Cheshire Field Co.** 79a, Harrowby Road, Birkenhead. *Major.* *Captain.* p. Marquis, M. C.16May11	*Lieutenants.* (2) (p.)Hanmer, M. S. 20Jan.06 Ward, J. P. 21July12 *2nd Lieutenants.* (2) Richardson, D. B. 23Dec.11 Halsall, L. A. 23Oct.12 Duncan, B. A. 1Dec.13 **Welsh Field Co.** Llanelly. *Major.* p. Nevill, R. A. 1Apr.08 *Captain* Francis, J. (*H*) 1Apr.08 *Lieutenants.* (2) Trubshaw, H. E. 20Apr.10 Burn, H. S. 20Apr.10 *2nd Lieutenants.* (2) Falcon, W. 11Mar.10 John J. H. 5July12 Phillips, W.N. 30Oct.13	**Wessex.** [11] The Drill Hall, Upper Bristol Road, Bath. *Hon. Colonel.* Savile, H. B. O., C.B., *vD. Capt. ret. pay* 9Aug.7‡ *Lt.-Colonel.* p.s. Keen. S., TD (Q), (*C.R.E. Wessex Div.*) 1Apr.08 *Adjutant.* Maurice, L. C., Capt. R.E. 26Mar.13 *Medical Officer.* p.s. Stocker, E. G., *Surg.-Maj.* 12Jan.14 21May02 **1st Wessex Field Co.** The Drill Hall, Upper Bristol Road, Bath *Major.* Dutton, R. B. 16Jan.13 *Captain.* Harvey,S.L.(*t*) 1June13	*Lieutenants.* (2) Harbutt, N. C. 18Sept.12 Pitt, R. B. 1June13 *2nd Lieutenants.* (2) **2nd Wessex Field Co.** Churchill Road, Weston-super-Mare. *Major.* ✕Keen, J. F. (*Hon. Lt. in Army* 5Sept.02) (*Q*)(*H*) 11Dec.08 p.s. Fry, P. G. 18Mar.13 *Captain.* Lockett, R. F. (q) 14Sept.13 *Lieutenants.* (2) Wills, R. B. M. 14Sept.13 Wills, M.C.M. 19June14 *2nd Lieutenants.* (2) Cary, A. L. F. 26Nov.13 Brandling,J.B. 5June14

II. SIGNAL SERVICE.

Director of Army Signals } Ogilvie, Lt.-Col. (*temp. Col.*) A. M. J., C.B. .. General Post Office, London, 14July13
(Home Defence) (*Lt.-Col. & temp. Col.* 1July14)
Asst. Directors of Army { Booth, Maj. A. C. 1July14
Signals (Home Defence) { Brown, Capt. H. 1July14

    a. Divisional Signal Companies and Infantry Brigade Signal Sections.
    b. Signal Companies (Army Troops).

a. DIVISIONAL SIGNAL COMPANIES AND INFANTRY BRIGADE SIGNAL SECTIONS.

East Anglian Divisional Signal Co.	Highland Divisional Signal Co.	Home Counties Divisional Signal Co.	East Lancashire Divisional Signal Co.
Hd.-Qrs. & No. 1 Sect. Ashburnham Road, Bedford. *Captain.* *Lieutenant.* Randall, H. J. 31Mar.14 Pemberton, R. F. 31Mar.14 No.2.(*Norfolk and Suffolk*) Section. *Commander.* No. 3. (*East Midland*) Section. *Commander.* p.s. Wightman, Lt. C. F., 1 Bn. Herts R. Ⓢ 1May13 No. 4. (*Essex*) Section. *Commander.*	Hd.-Qrs. & No. 1 Sect. 80, Hardgate, Aberdeen. *Captain.* p.s. Robertson, A. 4Oct.11 *Lieutenant.* p.s. Bruce, R. 4Oct.11 8Sept.06 No. 2. (*Seaforth and Cameron*) Section. *Commander.* No. 3. (*Gordon*) Section. *Commander.* Johnston, Lt A. McK., 4 Bn. Gord. Highrs. 7July13 No. 4. (*Argyll and Sutherland*) Section. *Commander.*	Hd.-Qrs. & No. 1 Sect. 23, Gloucester Place, Brighton. *Captain.* Saunders, H. C.23Jan.08 *Lieutenant.* Bartlett, E. C. 27Nov.11 ‡*2nd Lieutenant.* Parsons, R. H. 7Dec.10 No. 2. (*Surrey*) Section. *Commander.* Perkins, Lt. W. J., jun., 5 Bn. W. Surr. R. Ⓢ (q) 1May13 No. 3. (*Kent*) Section. *Commander.* Emery, Lt. T. S., 4 Bn. E. Kent R.Ⓢ 9Sept.13 No.4.(*Middlesex*) Section. *Commander.* Fisher,Capt.C.J., 10 Bn. Midd'x R. Ⓢ (q) 1May13	Hd.-Qrs. & No. 1 Sect. 73, Seymour Grove, Old Trafford, Manchester. *Captain.* p. Lawford,A.N.(*H*)4May12 19June11 *Lieutenant.* Broad, G. L. 11Dec.13 No. 2. (*Lancashire Fusiliers*) Section. *Commander.* No. 3. (*East Lancashire*) Section. *Commander.* Robinson, 2nd Lt. G. N., 4 Bn. E. Lan. R. 1May13 No. 4. (*Manchester*) Section. *Commander.* Pilkington,Capt.E. F., 6 Bn. Manch. R. 1May13

‡ This rank is not provided for in the Territorial Force Tables of Establishment.

Royal Engineers. Territorial Force.

Signal Service—contd.

West Lancashire (The St. Helens) Divisional Signal Co.
Hd.-Qrs. & No. 1 Sect.
Engineer Hall, Croppers Hill, St. Helens.

Captain.
p. Oppenheim, W., TD, hon.m. 15Mar.99

Lieutenant.
Lamb, L. 28May14
1Jan.13

No. 2. (South Lancashire) Section.

Commander.
Crooks, Lt. F., 5 Bn. S. Lan. R. ⑤ 1May13

No. 3. (Liverpool) Section.

Commander.
Edwards, 2nd Lt. G.B., 5 Bn. L'pool R. ⑤ 1Oct.13

No. 4. (North Lancashire) Section.

Commander.

1st London Divisional Signal Co.
Hd.-Qrs. & No. 1 Sect.
10. Victoria Park Square, E.

Captain.
p.s. Kennard, G. C. 8July13

Lieutenant.

‡ *2nd Lieutenant.*
Barnett, E. J. 7May13

No. 2. (1st London) Section
Commander.

No. 3. (2nd London) Section
Commander.
King, Lt. H.H., 8 Bn. Lond. R. ⑤ 1May13

No. 4. (3rd London) Section
Commander.
Freeman, Capt. R. C., 12 Bn. Lond. R. ⑤ 1May13

2nd London Divisional Signal Co.
Hd.-Qrs. & No. 1 Sect.
Duke of York's Headquarters, Chelsea, S.W.

Captain.
Alexander, Capt. *Sir* L.C.W., *Bt.*, 23 Bn. Lond. R., *late* Lt. G. Gds. ⑤ 3Aug.13

Lieutenant.
Bruce, W. F. 3July13

‡ *2nd Lieutenant.*
Deedes, J. G. 25Mar.14

No. 2. (4th London) Section.
Commander.
Herbert, Lt. R. B., 13 Bn. Lond. R. ⑤ 1May13

No. 3. (5th London) Section
Commander.
De Meza, Lt. J., 19 Lond. R. ⑤ 14Feb.14

No. 4. (6th London) Section.
Commander.

Lowland Divisional Signal Co.
Hd.-Qrs. & No. 1 Sect.
Drill Hall, Rutherglen, N.B.

Captain.
Angwin, A. S. 1Apr 08

Lieutenant.
Turner, F. G. 10Aug.11
Mallett, E. 14June13

No. 2. (Scottish Rifle) Section.
Commander.

No. 3. (Highland Light Infantry) Section.
Commander.
McMichael, 2nd Lt. J. jun., 9 Bn. High.L.I. ⑤ 3June14

No. 4. (South Scottish) Section.
Commander.

North Midland Divisional Signal Co.
Hd.-Qrs. & No. 1 Sect.
Drill Hall, Booth Street. Stoke-on-Trent.

Captain.
Lewis, E. A. 3Nov.13

Lieutenant.
Hear', N. 3May14

‡ *2nd Lieutenant.*
Lewis, L. H. 19Mar.14

No. 2. (Staffordshire) Section.
Commander.

No. 3. (Notts and Derby) Section.
Commander.
Forman, Lt. D. P., 7 Bn. Notts & Derby R. ⑤ 15Aug.13

No. 4. (Lincoln and Leicester) Section.
Commander.

South Midland Divisional Signal Co.
Hd.-Qrs. & No. 1 Sect.
32, Park Row, Bristol.

Captain.
p. Burbey, J. L. 3Feb.04
p. Arrowsmith-Brown, J. A. 5May06
28Mar.06

Lieutenant.
p.s. Heaven, J. G. 5Nov.04

No. 2. (Warwickshire) Section.
Commander.
Edwards, 2nd Lt. H. W., 5 Bn. R. War. R. ⑤ 3Aug.13

No. 3. (Gloucester and Worcester) Section.
Commander.
Bennett, Lt. J. S., 4 Bn. Glouc. R. ⑤ 3Aug.13

No. 4. (South Midland) Section.
Commander.

Northumbrian (The Newcastle) Divisional Signal Co.
Hd.-Qrs. & No. 1 Sect.
Barras Bridge. Newcastle-on-Tyne.

Captain.
p. Dodds, W. H. 23Apr.02

Lieutenant.

‡ *2nd Lieutenant.*
⚥Lincoln, J.W. 21May13

No. 2. (Northumberland) Section.
Commander.
Bainbridge Lt. T. L., 5 Bn. North'd Fus. ⑤ 4June13

No. 3. (York and Durham) Section.
Commander.

No. 4. (Durham Light Infantry) Section.
Commander.
Bagnall, Capt. C. L., 9 Bn. Durh. L.I. 1May13

West Riding Divisional Signal Co.
Hd.-Qrs. & No. 1 Sect.
Sheffield.

Captain.
p. Barker, C., TD 5July99

Lieutenant.
Emmerson, H. H. 11May10

No 2. (1st West Riding) Section.
Commander.

No.3. (2nd West Riding) Section.
Commander.

No.4. (3rd West Riding) Section.
Commander.
Monier-Williams, Lt. C. V., 5 Bn. York & Lanc. R. ⑤ 1July13

---

‡ This rank is not provided for in the Territorial Force Tables of Establishment.

| 839 | 840 | 841 | 842 |

Royal Engineers. Territorial Force.

Signal Service—contd.

Welsh Divisional Signal Co.

Hd.-Qrs. & No. 1 Sect.
The Drill Hall,
Park Street Cardiff.

Captain.
p.s. Isaac, T. A.   1May08

Lieutenant.
Arnold W.   1Aug.10

‡ *2nd Lieutenant.*
Jones. W.   5Dec.10
No. 2. (*Cheshire*) *Section.*

Commander.

No. 3. (*North Wales*) *Section.*

Commander.
Hampson, Lt. W.,
7 Bn. R. W. Fus. ⓢ
    4Mar.14

No. 4. (*Welsh Border*) *Section.*

Commander.
Watkins, Lt. I. E.
M. (H) ⓢ 2 Bn.
Mon. R.   1May13

Wessex Divisional Signal Co.

Hd.-Qrs. & No. 1 Sect.
The Priory,
Colleton Crescent, Exeter.

Captain.
p.s Varwell, E. H.
(q) (H) [l]   18Dec.06

Lieutenant.
Collins, S. M. ⓢ29May12
    3Apr.07
‡ *2nd Lieutenant.*
Michelmore, W. G.
    3Feb.13

No. 2. (*Devon and Cornwall*) *Section.*

Commander.
Vicary, 2nd Lt. J.
ⓢ 5 Bn. Devon
R.   16July13

No. 3. (*South - Western*) *Section.*

Commander.
(p.) Wilson, Lt. C.M.
ⓢ 4 Bn. Wilts. R.
    23June13

No.4. (*Hampshire*) *Section Commander.*

Lothian Infantry Brigade Signal Section.
Commander
Liddle, W., Lt. 9 Bn R Scots
ⓢ   12Nov.13

Black Watch Infantry Brigade Signal Section.
Commander.

South Wales Infantry Brigade Signal Section.
Commander.

---

b. SIGNAL COMPANIES (ARMY TROOPS.)

[*The order of precedence of groups is denoted by numerals in brackets*].

London District
[1]
Palmer Street,
Westminster, S.W.

Hon. Colonel.
p.s. ✕Bain, A., TD, M.
Inst. C. E.   (I).,
M. I. E. E.   (Hon.
Maj. in Army
2 Nov. 02)   (Hon.
Col. ret. Terr.
Force)   14July12

Lt.-Colonel.
✕Leaf, E. H.,
A.M.Inst.C.E.
Hon. Capt. in
Army 2Nov.02)
    13July12

Adjutant.
Wright, H. L., Capt.
R.E.   15Oct.10

Medical Officers.
p. Masters, Maj. J. A.,
M.D., R.A.M.C.
(T.F.) (attd.)   1Apr.08
    30May00

London Wireless Signal Co.
Palmer Street,
Westminster, S.W.

Captain.
(P)✕Fulton, H.(Q)(Hon.
Maj. ret. Spec.
Res.) (Hon. Lt. in
Army 28Dec.00) [l]
    1Nov.13
    18Sept.12

Lieutenant.
Kingston, J. R. 1Feb.13
2nd Lieutenant.
Chittick,H. S. 1May12

London Cable Signal Co.
Palmer Street,
Westminster, S.W.

Major.
G. F.S. ✕O'Shaughnessy,
J. J. F., M.I.E.E.
(Hon. Capt. in
Army 29 Sept. 02)
(Telegraph Engr.,
Gold Coast,
{ 8June14
{ 14Oct.05)‡   1Apr.08

p. ✕Williams, G. B.,
M. Inst. C.E.,
A. M. I. E. E.
(Hon. Lt. in
Army 30May01).
    5July11

p. Humphery, S. W.,
A.M.I.E.E.   1Feb.13
Captain.

Lieutenants (2)
Pelly, D. G.   1June11
2nd Lieutenants. (2)
Pedlar, M. K. 17June11
Vigers, T. W. 14June13
Ward, W. A. B. K.
    1June14

London Airline Signal Co.
Palmer Street,
Westminster, S.W.

Major.
Bidder. M. McC.,
A.M. Inst. C. E.
    1Feb.13
Captains. (2)
Thomas, H. C. 1Feb.13
p.s. Emley, M. W. (H) ⓣ
    15Feb.13

Lieutenants. (2)
Ranson,G.H.(t)27Oct.11
    8Jan.10
Baker Cresswell,
H. G.   1Feb.13

2nd Lieutenant. (1)
Jones, B. M.   1Dec.10

Northern Command.
[4]
Leeds.
Lt.-Colonel.
p. Brown, J. W. H.,
TD.   6Mar12
Adjutant.
Spaight, T. H. L.,
Capt. R.E.   26Feb.10
Medical Officers.
p Waite, H., Surg.-
Maj.   4Feb.09
    3July97
Chaplain.
Green, Rev. W. H.,
B.A., LL.D., Chapl.
4th Class (T.F.)
(attd)   1Apr.08
    11Aug.06

Northern Wireless Signal Co.
Leeds.
Captain.
p. Bray, A.   20Sept.13
    1Apr.12
Lieutenant.
Barker, N. L. 27May14
    1Apr.08
2nd Lieutenant.
Beaumont, J.B.1Sept.13

Northern Cable Signal Co.
Leeds.
Major.
p. Hordern, J. B., TD
    1Apr.12
Captain.
p. Hey, D.   1Apr.12
    31Mar.08
Lieutenants. (2)
(p.) Bray, G.   12Dec.10
McLaren, H.   1Apr.12
2nd Lieutenants. (2)
Jackson, W. F.   1Mar.12
Raworth, R. G, 1Feb.13

Northern Airline Signal Co.
Leeds.
Major.
p. Stott, W. A.   3Aug.12

Captains. (2)
p.s. Boyle, W.   3Aug.12
p. Johnson, F. A.20Sept.13
    14Nov.03
p. Denham, R. I. 20Sept.13
    6Oct.06
Lieutenants. (2)

2nd Lieutenant. (1)
Tasker, R. B.   18Jan.13

Cadet Unit affiliated.
Leeds Postal Telegraph
Messengers' Cadet
Company.

---

‡ This rank is not provided for in the Territorial Force Tables of Establishment.

Royal Engineers. Territorial Force.

Signal Service—contd.

Scottish Command.
[2]

21, Jardine Street, Glasgow.

Hon. Colonel.
✕Kitchener of Khartoum, Fd. Marshal H. H., Earl, K.P., G. C. B., G. C. S. I., O. M., G. C. M. G., G. C. I. E., q.s., Col. Comdt. R.E. 21Dec.98

Lt.-Colonel.
p. Gourlay, J., TD (Q) 5July13

Adjutant.
Bisset, J. S., Capt. R.E. 22Mar.12

Medical Officers.
p. Walker, Capt. J., M.B., R.A.M.C. (T.F.)(attd.) 1Dec.06 13May03

Chaplain.
Gardner, Rev. M. [C.S.] Chapl. 3rd Class (T.F.) (attd.) 1Apr.08 9Oct.94
McLaren, Rev. K. D. [C.S.] Chapl. 4th Class (T.F.) (attd.) 1July09

Scottish Wireless Signal Co.

21, Jardine Street, Glasgow.

Captain
p.s. Easton W. C. (t) 9Oct.13 25Apr.00

Lieutenant.

2nd Lieutenant.
Fulton, D. F. 1Jan.12

Scottish Cable Signal Co.

21, Jardine Street, Glasgow.

Major.

Captain.
p.s. Kerr, J. C. M. 26May06

Lieutenants (2)
p. Stevenson, J. (t) 1Dec.06 6Sept.05

2nd Lieutenants. (2)
Gilchrist, H. G. 2Jan.12
Muirhead, J.S. 25Feb.13
Blair, R. 4Nov.13

Scottish Airline Signal Co.

21, Jardine Street, Glasgow.

Major.
Rose, J. A., TD (q) 9Oct.13

Captains. (2)
p.s. Murdoch, J. D. ⊕ 1Dec.06 6Jan.04
Grange, G. R.(t) 9Oct.13

Lieutenants (2)
p. Barrie, J. H. 1Dec.06 6Sept.05

2nd Lieutenant. (1)
Russell, J. 2Feb.10
Mackinlay, R. W. 12Jan.12
Macmillan, C.H. 17Dec.13
Snodgrass, E I. 4May14

Southern Command.
[5]

The Barracks, Great Brook Street, Birmingham.

Hon. Colonel.
Lodge, Sir O. J., Knt. 28Jan.09

Lt.-Colonel.
Lister, J. F., M.I.E.E. 1Apr.08

Adjutant.
Coke, B. E., Capt. R.E. [l] 30Nov.12

Chaplain.
Henry, Rev. J., Chapl. 4th Class (T.F.) (attd.) 18Mar.09

Southern Wireless Signal Co.

The Barracks, Great Brook Street, Birmingham.

Captain.
Handley, A., M.I.E.E. 10May12

Lieutenant.
Mowat, J. B. 10May12

2nd Lieutenant.
Bailey, J. W. 19May14

Southern Cable Signal Co.

The Barracks, Great Brook Street, Birmingham.

Major.

Captain.
Bowker, R. B., A.M.I.E.E. 1Apr.08

Lieutenants (2)
Tebbitt, C. E. 16Feb.09
Mitton, E. J. 1July12

2nd Lieutenants. (2)
Cosens, C.R.G. 15Mar.11

Southern Airline Signal Co.

The Barracks, Great Brook Street, Birmingham.

Major

Captains. (2)
Dickinson. A. J., A.M.I.E.E. (Q) 14Apr.10
Danielson, J. W. 10Feb.12

Lieutenants. (2)

2nd Lieutenant. (1)
Martin, G.P.W. 12Feb.12
Heckford, C. A. J. 10June13
Clayton, J.H.R. 1Feb.14

Western Command.
[3]

38, Mason Street, Edge Hill, Liverpool.

Hon. Colonel.
p. Robinson, J. F., VD, hon. c. 10Jan.08

Lt.-Colonel.
Leigh, F. A. C., M. Inst. C. E., M. I. Mech. E., M.I.E.E. (H) 6Mar.12

Adjutant.
Fuller, A. C., Lt. R. E., capt. 31Aug.12

Medical Officer
Halton, Capt. H., M.D., R.A.M.C. (T.F.)(attd.) 1Feb.13

Chaplain
Potter, Rev. J. P. N., Chapl. 4th Class (T.F.) (attd.) 9May12

Western Wireless Signal Co.

38, Mason Street, Edge Hill, Liverpool.

Captain.
p.s. Robinson, A. H. (q) A.M.I.E.E. 24Nov.13 3Feb.04

Lieutenant.

2nd Lieutenant
Serjeant, H. L. 8Apr.13
Saunderson, D. B. 6Sept.13

Western Cable Signal Co.

38, Mason Street, Edge Hill, Liverpool.

Major.
Whitney, G. P. 1June10

Captain.
Dodd, W. T. 23Mar.12

Lieutenants. (2)

2nd Lieutenants. (2)
Laurie, A.O. 21Sept.11
Grierson, J. B. 11Feb.13
Murphy, M. 2Sept.13

Western Airline Signal Co.

38, Mason Street, Edge Hill, Liverpool.

Major.
Newell, S. M. Q) 11Aug.09

Captains. (2)
p.s.Rollo, W. S. 26Nov.13

Lieutenants. (2)
Brierley, L. B. 4Oct.11

2nd Lieutenant. (1)
Carter, W. R. 13June13

Royal Engineers. Territorial Force.

III. FORTRESS ENGINEERS
[*The order of precedence of groups is denoted by numerals in brackets.*]

City of Aberdeen.
[6]
80, Hardgate, Aberdeen.
Works Co.
Captain.
p. Reid, J. (t) 25June04
Lieutenant.
Harper, C. 18Feb.14
2nd Lieutenant.
Wilson, J. R. 18Aug.13
Medical Officer.
p. Sinclair, Maj. W., TD,
M.B., R.A.M.C.
(T.F.) (*attd.*) 30Apr.04
2Apr.92

Cinque Ports.
[13]
Electric Lights Co.
16, Bench Street, Dover.
Captain.
Hawke, W. C. 20Oct.08
Lieutenant.
Mowll, J. H. 25Apr.11
2nd Lieutenant.
Hooper, H. U. 15July09

Cornwall.
[17]
Falmouth.
Major.
Medical Officer.
p.s. Browne, Maj. C. R.,
M.D., R.A.M.C.
(T.F.) (*attd.*) 5Jan.14
28May02
Electric Lights Co.
No. 1 Co.
Falmouth.
Captain.

Lieutenant.
Hainsworth, W. H.
12Apr.11
2nd Lieutenant.
Annear, J. C. 4June14

Works Cos. (2)
No. 2 Co.
Fowey.
Captain.
Hawkins, W. B. S.
9Dec.09
Lieutenant.
2nd Lieutenant.
No. 3 Co.
Penryn.
Captain.
✗Ford, J. A. 15Feb.09
Lieutenant.
Granam, H. S. 11Apr.13
2nd Lieutenant.
Dawe, H. 12Dec.13

Devonshire.
[4]
Mutley Barracks,
Plymouth.
Hon. Colonel.
✗Lt. Harrison, Gen.
Sir R., G.C.B.,
C.M.G., Col.
Comdt. R.E. [R]
20Jan.09
Major.
Bastard, W. E. P.
23Nov.08
bt. lt.-col. 24Dec.13
Adjutant.
Rivers-Moore, C.N.,,
Lt. R.E., *capt.*
3Sept.13
Medical Officers.
Bolus, Lt. P. R.,
M.B., R A M C.
(T.F.) (*attd.*) 1June11
Chaplain.
Chaytor, Rev. H. J.,
M.A., Chapl. 4th
Class (T.F.) (*attd.*)
1May12
Quarter-Master.

Works Cos. (3).
No. 1 Co.
Torquay.
Captain.
Garrett, H. A. (A)
1Apr.08
18July03
Lieutenant.
Ganderton, H.
S. 17June13
2nd Lieutenant.
Appleton, G. L. 1Dec 13
No. 2 Co.
Exeter.
Captain.
p. Goodman, W.H.7Feb.06
Lieutenant.
2nd Lieutenant.
Cocks, W. R. 1Mar.14
Woollcombe, H. W.
1May14
No. 3 Co.
Exeter.
Captain.
p.s. Commin, J. H. 29Mar.07
Lieutenant.
2nd Lieutenant.
Sweet, A. H. 21Feb.14

Electric Lights Cos. (2)
No. 4 Co.
Mutley Barracks, Plymouth
Captain.
Stone, H., A.M.I.E.E.
(q) (H) 26Nov.13
Lieutenant.
2nd Lieutenant.
Haslehust, E.T. 4Dec.09
Bone, J. 1Apr.14

No. 5 Co.
MutleyBarracks.Plymouth
Captain.
P.S. Hooper, G. 1Apr.08
Lieutenant.
Bulteel, F. T. 26Nov.13
2nd Lieutenant.
Bone, G. F. 1Apr.14

Cadet Units affiliated to
the Group.
No. 1 (Yealmpton) Cadet
Company, Devon (Fortress)
R.E.
No. 2 (Plymouth) Cadet
Company, Devon (Fortress)
R.E.

Dorsetshire and Wiltshire.
Major.
Wright. F. G.,
M.I. Mech. E. 16Oct.12

Dorsetshire.
[18]
"Imperial Service."
Sidney Hall,
Weymouth.
Electric Lights Co.
Captain.
✗Colson, D. F. 1Apr.08
Lieutenants. (2)
Graves, A. [I] 31Jan.10
Graves, E. C. 3May13
2nd Lieutenant. (1)
Marshall, W. H. U.,
M.I.E.E.,
A.M.I.Mech.E.1Dec.12
Medical Officer.

Wiltshire.
[11]
Drill Hall, Church Rd.,
Swindon, Wilts.
Works Co.
Captain.
Wilson, C. S. 16Oct.10
Lieutenant.
Dawson, J. 30June14
2nd Lieutenant
Knapp, G. E. C. 9July13

City of Dundee.
[15]
52, Taylor's Lane, Dundee.
Works Co.
Captain.
Lieutenant.
Luis, I. M. 24May14
2nd Lieutenant.
Black, A. 29July14

Durham.
[5]
Western Road,
Jarrow-on-Tyne.
Major.
Terry, A. M. 27Nov.12
Quarter-Master
Hall, S. T., *hon. lt.*
22Sept.11
Medical Officers.
p. Weir, Capt. D. H.,
M.D., R.A.M.C.
(T.F.) (*attd.*)10Aug.09
10Feb.06
Chaplain.
Duncan, Rev. A. L,
B.A., Chapl. 4th Class
(T.F.) (*attd.*) 1May14
Works Cos. (3)
No. 1 Co.
Jarrow-on-Tyne.
Captain.
p. Woodeson, W. A.
1June13
30Jan08
Lieutenant.
Hall, J. 8. 28May14
2nd Lieutenant.
O'Hagan, C. S. 3Oct.12
No. 2 Co.
Jarrow-on-Tyne.
Captain.
p. Williams, T. R. 22Apr.05
2nd Lieutenant.
Paterson, H. 18Feb.13
No. 3 Co.
Gateshead.
Captain.
p.s. Tate, G. 27Nov.12
2nd Lieutenant.
Shanley, H. J. 4Oct.12
Paterson, H. 12Oct.12

City of Edinburgh.
[10]
28, York Place,
Edinburgh
Major.
p.s. Ogilvie, A., TD.20Apr.12
Medical Officer.
p. Wilson, Maj. J.,
M.B., R.A.M.C.
(T.F.) (*attd.*) 10July10
19Oct.98
Chaplain.
Christie, Rev. G., B.D.
[C,S.] Chapl. 3rd
Class (T.F.) (*attd.*)
23Aug.09
23Mar.98
Works Co.
No. 1 Co.
28, York Place, Edinburgh.
Captain.
p.s. Park, J, D. 1Dec.09
Lieutenant.
Leslie, J. 1Dec.09
2nd Lieutenant.
Cooper, C. G. T.
25Nov.13

Royal Engineers. Territorial Force.

Fortress Engineers—
contd.

Electric Lights Co.
No. 2 Co.
28, York Place, Edinburgh.
p.s Peebles, A. C. 20Apr.12
Lieutenant.
Primrose, A. F. 20Apr.12
2nd Lieutenant.
Mackenzie, A. D.
22June12

Essex.
[16]
Market Road,
Chelmsford.

Electric Lights Co.
Captain.
Neville, H. A. D. 21June11
Lieutenant.
2nd Lieutenant.
Dees, B. 23Feb.11
Powley, F. W. M.
13July12

Glamorgan.
[8]
The Drill Hall, Park Street
Cardiff.
Major.
P.S. Evans, A. O. (q)
4May12
Medical Officers.
Rees, Maj. A., TD.
(hon. Surg.-Lt.-Col.)
R.A.M.C.(T.F.)
(attd.) 16Aug.02
24Oct. 88
Kent, Lt. P. W.,
R.A.M.C.(T.F.)
(attd.) 12Mar.13
11June12
Chaplain.
Longdon, Rev. J. S.,
M.A., Chapl. 4th
Class (T.F.)(attd.)
13Aug 12

Works Cos. (2)
No. 2 Co.
Drill Hall, Park Street,
Cardiff.
Captain.
Biggs, G. T. 4May12
Lieutenant.

2nd Lieutenant.

No. 2 Co.
Drill Hall,
Gladstone Road, Barry.
Captain
P.S. Jones, E. W. 9Apr.09
1May08
Lieutenant.
Hybart, F.R. 4May12
Graham, W.H. 8July14
2nd Lieutenant.

Electric Lights Co.
No. 3 Co.
Drill Hall, Park Street,
Cardiff.
Captain.
P.S. Edwards, T. O.,
TD 9Apr.09
11July00
Lieutenants. (2
Stanfield, J. R. M.
3June10
Second Lieutenant.
Rees, E. S. 1Mar.13
Klombies, G. R.,
late 2nd Lt. 2 D.G.
13Apr.13

Hampshire.
[3]
Commercial Road,
Portsmouth.
Lt.-Colonel
Fry, W. H., TD,⊕
22May12
Adjutant.
Thwaites, H. F. O,
Capt. R.E. 20Nov.13
Quarter-Master.
p. Pearce, W., hon.
m. (H) 27Sept.05
Medical Officers.
p. Emmett, Maj. R.
R.A.M.C.(T.F.),
(attd.) (Works
Cos.) 28Oct.08
24Apr.97
Cambell, Jas. C.,
M.B., R.A.M.C.,
(T.F.) (attd.)
(E.L. Cos.) 7Feb.12
Chaplains.
Hawksley, Rev. W.
C., M.A., TD, Chapl.
1st Class (T.F.)
(attd.) 25July11
25July11
Sedgwick, Rev. S.
N., Chapl. 4th
class(T.F.)(attd.)
9Apr.12

Works Cos. (3)
No. 1 Co.
Hampshire Terrace,
Portsmouth.
Captain.
p.s. Flowers, S. (q) 28Aug.12
Lieutenant.
Webber, F. H. E.
28Aug.12
2nd Lieutenant.
Maunsell, R. G. F.
1July12

No. 2 Co.
Hampshire Terrace,
Portsmouth.
Captain.
Davies, H. 13May14
Lieutenant.
2nd Lieutenant.
Sherwin, C. E. 10Mar.13

No. 3 Co.
Eastleigh.
⸱ *Major.*
Mead, T. W. 22May12
Captain.
p.s. Bevis. C. T (t) 22May12
Lieutenant.
Szlumper, G. S.,
A.M. Inst. C.E.
. 17Dec.10
1Apr.10
2nd Lieutenant.
Williams, E.O. 1July12

Electric Lights Cos.(3)
No. 4 Co.
Hampshire Terrace,
Portsmouth.
⸱ *Major.*
p, North, E., TD ⊕25Apr.06
Captain.
p.s.Gilbert, H. D. ⊕5Feb.04
Lieutenant.
p.s.Brown, W. B. 2Nov.08
p. Couzens, G. E.13June14
2nd Lieutenant.
Bevis, H. V. 26June14

No. 5 Co.
Freshwater.
Captain.
p.s.White, A. V. (Q)6Aug.04
Lieutenant.
(p.) King, P. G. 23Dec.08
2nd Lieutenants (2)
Hill, S. 4Oct.13

No. 6 Co.
Gosport.
Captain.
p. ✗Lambert, A. P.
(Hon. Lt. in
Army 3 Sept. 02)
19June01
p.s.Bevis, R. H. P. (t)
27July12
Lieutenant.

Kent.
[12]
Submarine Mining School,
Gillingham.
Hon. Colonel.
Salomons, Sir
D.L.G.S., Bt. 6Nov.08
Major.
p. Stephens, H. F.,
TD, M. Inst.
C.E. 1Apr.12
Adjutant.
Taylor, G. B. O., Lt.
R.E. [l] capt.16Dec.11
Quarter-Master.
✗Clark, T. J., Qr.-
Mr. (hon. capt.)
ret. pay,hon. capt.
17June11
Medical Officer.
Chaplain.
Hickin, Rev. H. A.,
Chapl. 4th Class
(T.F.) (attd.) 1May12

Works Cos. (3)
No. 1 Co.
Drill Hall, Tonbridge.
Captain.
p.s.Langridge, W. F. (H)
30Aug.03
Lieutenant.
Higginson, J. S. F.
1Mar.12
2nd Lieutenant.
Wellington, A. M.
27Jan.12
Cooksey, R. A. 1July14

No. 2 Co.
Drill Hall, Ashford.
Captain.
Lieutenant.
2nd Lieutenant.
Tyler, H. W.,
A.M.I.E.E. 13July12
Punter, J. W., late
Lt. Madras Rly.
Vols. 21Dec.12

Igglesden, C. H., late
Lt. Kent (Fort.)
Engrs. 11June13

No. 3 Co.
Southborough.
Captain.
Ruston, A. F. G.
18Mar.12
Lieutenant.
Stranders, V.[l] 15Aug.13
Salomons, D.R.H.P.
15Aug.12
2nd Lieutenant.

Electric Lights Cos.(2)

No. 4 Co.
Submarine Mini⸱g School,
Gillingham.
Captain.
Lieutenant.
✗Devey, H. W.,
A.M.I.E.E. 15Aug.13
2nd Lieutenant.
Bowen, J. P.,
A.M.Inst.C.E.25Oct.13

No. 5 Co., Gravesend.
Captain.
Grace. C.B.,A.M.I.E.E.
1Nov.09
2nd Lieutenant.
Lefeaux, E.,
A.M.I.E.E. 4Mar.11

Cadet Unit affiliated to
the group.
Cadet Battalion Kent
(Fortress) R.E.

⸱ One major only is provided for in the Territorial Force Tables of Establishments.

| 855 | 856 | 857 | 858 |

Royal Engineers. Territorial Force.

Fortress Engineers— contd.

Lancashire.
[1]
Tramway Road, Aigburth, Liverpool.

Hon. Colonel.
p.s. Montgomery, R., VD, late Maj. 11June04
Major.
p.s. Jones, J. H. 26Feb.13 22Apr.05
Medical Officers.
p.p.s. Lloyd, J. W., TD, Surg.-Maj. 1Apr.08 4July03
p.s. Owen, J., Surg.-Capt. 5Oct.08 5Apr.05
Chaplain.
Baynes, Rev. J. P. M.A., VD, Chapl. 1st Class (T.F.)
(attd.) 1Apr.08 19July76

Electric Lights Cos.(2)
No. 1 Co.
Liverpool.
Captain.
p.s. Jones, A. H. 4July02
Lieutenant.
Williams, H. C., A.M. Inst. C.E. 24Nov.09
Jemmett, F. R., A.M. Inst. C.E. 11Dec.10

No. 2 Co.
Captain.
p.s. Mitchell, A. C., A.M.Inst.C.E. 8Apr.13
Lieutenants. (2)
Walker, A. G., A.M. Inst. C.E. 24Nov.09
2nd Lieutenant.
Rimmer, E. J., A.M. Inst. C.E. 3June09
Russell, J. D. 10Mar.14

Works Co.
No. 3 Co.
Liverpool.
Captain.

Lieutenant.
Bell, G. K., A.M. Inst., C.E. 24Nov.09
2nd Lieutenant.
Biggs, J. R. 16July09
Newell, J. A. 3Dec.13
10June11

Renfrewshire.
[9]
Fort Matilda, Greenock.
Major.
p.s. ✗Anderson, A. H., TD, (Capt. Res. of Off.) 18Dec.12
Medical Officer.
p. Whiteford, Maj. J.H.G., M.B., TD, R.A.M.C. (T.F.) (attd.) (E.L. Co.) 18June04 4May02
Chaplains.
Maclean, Rev. A. M., B.D., [C.S.] Chapl. 3rd Class (T.F.) (attd.) (Works Co.) 1Apr.08 5Sept.97
Reid, Rev. H., M.A. [U.F.C.] Chapl. 4th Class (T.F.) (attd.) (E.L. Co.) 1May09

Works Co.
No. 1 Co.,
Paisley.
Captain.
Hodgart, H. M. 21Jan.14
Lieutenant.
McWilliam, J. 21Jan.14
2nd Lieutenant.
Brown, O. McN. H. 14Nov.12

Electric Lights Co.
No. 2 Co.
Greenock.
Captain.
p.s. Rowan, R. H. 18Dec.12
Lieutenants (2).
Thorne, W. C. 1Apr.12
Bell, F. A. 7June13
2nd Lieutenants (2)
Reid, A. 18Sept.13

East Riding.
[4]
Colonial Street, Hull.
Major.
✗Newell, E. M. (Hon. Lt. in Army 12Aug. 02) (H) 1Apr.08
bt. lt.-col. 24Dec.13

Works Co.
No. 1 Co.
Colonial Street, Hull.
Captain.
Bell, H. 11May 08
Lieutenant.
Fontaine, H. J. 20May08
2nd Lieutenant.
Alexander, H. S. 29June09
Hall, P. de H. 18May10
Huntley, A. G. 16Mar.14

Electric Lights Co.
No. 2 Co.
Colonial Street, Hull.
Captain.

Lieutenant.
Wightman, O. N. 12May08
Hide, J. S. 22July11

North Riding.
[2]
Bright Street, Middlesbrough.

Electric Lights Co.
Captain.
p.s. Winterschladen, H, TD 16June98
p.s. Hedley, G. 13Feb.04
Lieutenant.
p.s. Kirby, F. W. 26Mar.02

Sussex.
[7]
Works Co.
Drill Hall, Seaford.
Captain.
Sanders, P. R. 18June13
Lieutenant.

2nd Lieutenant.
Whelon, C. E. 3June13
Medical Officer.
McGlashan, Lt. J., M.D., R.A.M.C. (T.F.) (attd.) 31Mar.09

Wiltshire.
(See Dorsetshire & Wiltshire).

v. ELECTRICAL ENGINEERS.

[*The order of precedence of groups is denoted by numerals in brackets.*]

London.
[1]
(6 *Companies*).
Drill Hall, 46, Regency Street, Westminster, S.W.
Hon. Colonel.
✗Crompton, R.E.B., C.B., M.I.E.E., M.I.Mech.E., late Lt.57Ft.(Hon.Maj. in Army)(Hon.Col. ret. T. F.) 24June11

Lt.-Colonel.
p. LeRossignol, A. E., M.I.E.E. 9July14
Adjutant.
Holt-White, F. R., Capt.R.E. 20Nov.13
Quarter-Master.
No. 1 Co.
Major.
Edgcumbe, K.W.E., M.I.E.E. 9July14

Captains. (2)
Merrett, W. H., A.M.I.E.E. 1Apr.08
p. ✗Thorn, C. H. R., A.M.I.E.E. 28Jan.10

Lieutenants. (2)
Outram, H. W. S., A.M.I.E.E. 1Dec.10
Edmunds, H. M. 12Mar.12
Tufnell, H. C. C., A.M.I.E.E. 12Mar.12

2nd Lieutenants. (2)
Haworth, H. F., A.M.I.E.E. 9Nov.10
Morse, L. G. E., A.M.I.E.E. 15Feb.11

No. 2 Co.
Captain.
p. ✗Rich, T., A.M.I.E.E. (Hon. Lt. in Army 3 Sept. 02) 1Apr.08
Hammerton, W. E. 9July14
Lieutenant.

Royal Engineers. Territorial Force.

iv. ELECTRICAL ENGINEERS—continued.

London—contd.

No. 3 Co.

Captain.
p.s.✕Webb-Bowen, H. E.,
A.M.I.E.E.,
A.M.I.Mech.E. 3Mar.09

Lieutenant
Vitty, T. H., A.M.I.E.E.
4Feb.10
Cope, H. A., A.M.I.E.E.,
9July14

‡*2nd Lieutenant.*
Digby, W. P.,
A.M.I.E.E.,
A M I.Mech.E. 9May10
20Jan.09

No. 4 Co.

Lieutenant.
Clarke, F. C.,
A.M.I.E.E. 4Feb.10

2nd Lieutenant.
Busk, E. T., A. M. I.
Mech. E. 15Feb.11

No. 5 Co.

Captain.
Bunn, W., A.M.I.E.E.,
TD, hon.maj. 27Jan.10

Lieutenant.
Masters, F. H.,
A.M.I.E.E. 4Feb.10

2nd Lieutenant.
Hunter, E. B.,
A.M.I.E.E. 17Nov.10

No. 6 Co.

Major.
p. ✕Phillips, J. H. S.,
A.M.I.E.E. (Q)
9July10

Captains.
p. ✕Levin, A. E.
A.M.I.E.E. 1Apr.08
p. Kaye, G. W. C.,
A.M.I.E.E. 9July10

2nd Lieutenant

Tyne.
[2]

(4 *Companies*).
North Shields.

Hon. Colonel.
✕Percy, A. I., Earl,
Capt. ret. pay, Capt.
G. Gds., Spec. Res.
20 Mar.12

Lt.-Colonel.
p.s. Scott, F. G., VD,
14Nov.11

Medical Officers.
p. Gibbon, Lt.-Col. F. W.,
VD, R.A.M.C. (T.F.)
(t) (attd.) 31Mar.08
7May87

Chaplain.
Lloyd, Rev. H. L., B.A.
Chapl.4th Class(T.F.)
(attd.) 15Mar.17

No. 1 Co.

Captain.
p.s.Tasker, A. K. 14Nov.11

Lieutenant.
Campbell, C. M.,
A.M.I.E.E. 2Dec.13

2nd Lieutenant.
Mountain, K. A.,
A.M.I.E.E. 1Mar.13
Sharp, R. 11Mar.14

No. 2 Co.

Captain.
p.s.Short, O. M. 18Feb.12

Lieutenant.
Firmin, N. H. 1Sept.11

2nd Lieutenant.
Pyne, F. D.,
A.M.I.E.E., A.M.I.
Mech. E. 1Mar.13
Monkhouse, S. E.,
A.M.I.E.E. 2Dec.13

No. 3 Co.

Major.
p.s.Robinson, E. 14Nov.11
Captain.
p.s.Swift, E. 2Dec.13

Lieutenants (2)
Forster, C. M.
A.M.I.E.E. 17May13
Fairbairn-Crawford,
I. F., A.M.I.Mech.E.
2Dec.13

2nd Lieutenant
Ward, W. G.,
A.M.I.E.E. 30Aug.11
Bowers, F. H. 17May13

No. 4 Co.

Major.
p.s.Toomer, C. R.,
VD. 4June04

Captain.
p.s.Arnison, C. 1Sept.11

2nd Lieutenants.
Russell, G. L. L.,
A.M.I.E.E. 4Mar.12
Young, J. 11Mar.14

Unposted.

Captain.
p.s.Bruce, G. A.,
M.I.E.E. 13June03

Lieutenant.
p.s.Buck, M. W. 3May12

v. ENGINEER AND RAILWAY STAFF CORPS.

15, Dean's Yard, Westminster, S.W.

Hon. Colonel.
✕Scott, Maj.-Gen. D.A.,
C.V.O., C.B., D.S.O.,
ret. pay (Res. of Off.)
1Apr.08

Lt-Colonels. (30)

Lt.-Col. Commandant.
Forbes, W. 21Mar.14
lt.-col. 4Nov.99

Lt.-Colonels.
Barry, A. J., M. Inst.
C.E. 11Aug.97
Aspinall, J. A. F.,
M. Inst. C.E., M. I.
Mech. E. 11Aug.00
Williams, H. W.
15Sept.00
Baggallay, H. C.,
VD, M. Inst. C.E.,
hon. c. 28Nov.00
Blyth, B. H., M.Inst.
C.E. 23Apr.02
Eyles, Sir G.L., K.C.M.G.
M.Inst.C.E. 28May02
Fay, Sir B., Knt. 4June02
Lyster, A. G., M.Inst.
C.E. 15July02
Ross, A., TD, M. Inst.
C.E. 25July03

Lt.-Colonels—contd.
Cooper, D. 23Jan.04
Dent C. B. D. H.
14May04
✕Hawkshaw, O.,
late Capt. 4 Bn.
N. Staff. R. (Hon.
Capt. in Army
12June02) 1May05
Granet, Sir W. G.
Knt. 29Oct.06
Denniss, C. S. 9Jan.07
Worthington, W.
B., M.Inst.C.E., M.
I. Mech. E. 30May07
Fitzmaurice, Sir M.,
Knt., C.M.G., M.
Inst. C.E., M. I.
Mech. E. 1Apr.08
Matheson, D. A.,
M.Inst.C.E. 10Oct.10
Wilson, M. FitzG.,
M. Inst. C.E. 27Oct.10
Dent, F. H. 5July11
Bagwell, J. P., late
Capt. 4 Bn. R. Ir.
Regt. (Hon. Capt.
in Army 6 July 01)
3Feb.12

Lt.-Colonels—contd.
Walker, H. A. 28Feb.12
Potter, F. 6Mar.12
Morgan, C. D.,
M.Inst.C.E. 5Nov.12
Geddes, E. C. 29Jan.13
Neale, E. A. 6Mar.13
Harrison, C. A., M.
Inst. C.E. 10Dec.13
Turnbull, Sir R.,
Knt. M.V.O. 6Mar.14
Palmer, F., C.I.E.,
M. Inst. C.E. 11May14
Williamson, S. 19May14

Majors. (25)
✕Lucas, C. J., VD,
hon. l.c. 23Oct.78
Cowdray, W. D.,
Lord 1July90
Tempest, P. T.,
M.Inst.C.E. 26Mar.02
Lucas, Sir A. C., Bt.
25June02
Aird, Sir J., Bt. [F]
18Sept.02
Rattray, D. C.,
M.Inst.C.E. 21Aug.05
Jones, E. D., M.Inst.
C.E. 16Oct.07

Majors—contd.
Holmes, H., M.V.O.
1Feb.09
Scott, F. F. 10July09
Grinling, W. J. 10July09
Trench, E. F. C.,
M.Inst.C.E. 1Jan.10
Watson, H. A. 15Mar.10
Jones, H., M. Inst.
C.E. 16Mar.10
Wainwright, H. S.,
M.Inst.C.E. 7May10
Clow, W. 17Sept.10
Paterson, W. A.,
M. Inst. C.E. 13Oct.10
Nott, L. P. 26Oct.10
Randall, F. G. 17Jan.11
Aldington, C. 12May11
Cox, E. C. 25Oct.11
Ball, J. B., M.Inst.C.E.
24Feb.12
Grierson, W. W.,
M. Inst. C.E. 9Oct.12
Brown, C. J.,
M. Inst. C.E. 10Dec.13
Szlumper, A. W.,
M. Inst. C.E. 2Apr.14

Unallotted. (5)
[Uniform—Blue. Facings—Scarlet].

‡ This rank is not provided for in the Territorial Force Tables of Establishments.

K

| 863 | 864 | 865 | 866 |

FOOT GUARDS.

GRENADIER GUARDS.

Regtl. Hd.-Qrs. - - Buckingham Gate, S.W.

| 1st Bn. .. Warley (for Chelsea Barracks). | 2nd Bn. .. Chelsea Barracks (for Aldershot) | 3rd Bn. .. Wellington Barracks. |

The King's Colours:—
    1st Battalion.—Gules (crimson): In the centre the Imperial Crown; in base a Grenade fired proper.
    2nd Battalion.—Gules (crimson): In the centre the Royal Cipher reversed and interlaced or, ensigned with the Imperial Crown; in base a Grenade fired proper; in the dexter canton the Union.
    3rd Battalion.—As for 2nd Battalion, and for distinction, issuing from the Union in bend dexter a pile wavy or.

The Regimental Colours:—
    The Union: In the centre a Company Badge ensigned with the Imperial Crown; in base a Grenade fired proper.
    The 30 Company Badges are borne in rotation, 3 at a time, one on the Regimental Colour of each of the Battalions.
    The following honorary distinctions are borne upon each of the King's and Regimental Colours:—
"Tangier, 1680," "Namur, 1695," "Gibraltar, 1704-5," "Blenheim," "Ramillies," "Oudenarde," "Malplaquet," "Dettingen," "Lincelles," "Egmont-op-Zee," "Corunna," "Barrosa," "Nive," "Peninsula," "Waterloo," "Alma," "Inkerman," "Sevastopol," "Tel-el-Kebir," "Egypt, 1882," "Suakin, 1885," "Khartoum," "Modder River," "South Africa, 1899-1902."

Uniform—Scarlet. Facings—Blue. *Agents*—Messrs. Cox & Co.

Colonel-in-Chief .. .. THE KING.

Colonel - Field-Marshal H.R.H. Arthur W. P. A., *Duke of* Connaught and Strathearn, K.G., K.T., K.P., G.C.B., G.C.S.I., G.C.M.G., G.C.I.E., G.C.V.O., Col. A. S. C., and Col.-in-Chief 6 Dns., High. L.I., R. Dub. Fus. and Rif. Brig., *Personal A.D.C. to the King* 1May04

Officer Commanding the Regt. and Regtl. Dist. .. Scott-Kerr, Col. R., *C.B., M.V.O., D.S.O.* 30July10
                                                                col. 14Feb.07

Lt.-Colonels. (3)	Majors—contd.	Captains—contd.	Captains—contd.
2Corry, N. A. L., *D.S.O.* 28Oct.10	2Russell, Hon. A. V. F., *M.V.O.*, p.s.c. [L] (*Mil. Attaché*) 24Jan.10	s.c. Brooke, B. N. 10Nov.07	Gregson, L. M. *Regtl. Adjt.* 9July10
3Fisher-Rowe, L. R. 20July11	29Nov.00	3Montagu Douglas Scott, Lord F. G. 22Jan.08	1Symes-Thompson, C. 9July10
1Ardee, R. Le N., Lord 14Feb.12	*Jeffreys*, G. D. (*Comdg. Depôt*) 28Oct.10	3Champion de Crespigny, C. R. 14Feb.08	3Gosselin, A. B. R. R. 31Aug.10
		2Colston, E. M., *M.V.O.* 6May08	3Pike, E. J. L. 31Aug.10
Majors. (12)	3Stucley, H. St. L. 14Feb.12	c{ 3Stephen, D. C. L. 3June08	3Thorne, A. F. A. N. 22Mar.13
3Smith, W. R. A. [F] 12Dec.06	1Weld Forester, Hon. A. O. W. C., *M.V.O.* 3Sept.12	3Wellesley, Lord R. 3June08	d. Leatham, R.E.K. 22Mar.13
1Earle, M., *D.S.O.,p.s.c.* 20July07	2Gordon-Lennox, Lord B. C. 13Aug.13	2Ponsonby, Hon. C. M. B., *M.V.O.* 3June08	*Lieutenants.* (30)
s.Corkran, C. E., *p.s.c.* 14Sept.07		1Nicol, W. E. [l] [F] 11July08	e.a.Somerset, Hon. FitzR. R. 1July06
26June02			3Moss, G. C. G. 4Jan.07
2Loch, E. D., Lord, *M.V.O., D.S.O.,* p.s.c. 15Aug.08	2Hamilton, G. C., *e.* 23Jan.05	3Payne-Gallwey, W. T., *M.V.O.* 11July08	1Stewart, E. O. 27Mar.07
bt. lt.-col. 10May13		2Powell, E. G. H. 16Sept.08	s. Gort, J. S. S. P. V., Visct., M.V.O. 1Apr.07
1Trotter, E. H., *D.S.O.* 26Sept.08	1Colby, L. R. V. 30Sept.05	s. Dennistoun, I. O., *M.V.O.* 8June10	1Rennie, G. 24July07
3Clive, G. S., *p.s.c.* [L] 17July09	c.o.Seymour, Lord H. C. 27Apr.07	1Makgill-Crichton-Maitland, M.E. 9July10	s. Cavendish, R. H.V., *M.V.O.* 27July07
s. Gathorne-Hardy, Hon. J. F., p.s.c. [l] 9Oct.09 *bt. lt.-col.* 26Nov.13	s.c. Vivian, V., M.V.O. 14Sept.07		f.c.Barrington-Kennett, B. H. 10Aug.07
			2MacDougall, I., *Adjt.* 10Nov.07

GRENADIER GUARDS—contd.

Lieutenants—contd.

e.a. *Diggle, W. H.* 10Mar.08

2 Ridley, E. D. 14Mar.08

1 *Rasch, G. E. C., Adjt.* 16May08

3 Forbes, Hon. *A. L. C.,* *Master of Forbes) Adjt.* 3June09

2 Cecil, *Hon.* W. A. 11July08

3 Rose, I. S. C. 15Aug.08

3 Hughes, J. S. 16Sept.08

3 Murray, W. R. C. 21Oct.08

1 Antrobus, E. 21Nov.08

2 Needham, *Hon.* F. E. 13Feb.09

3 Vivian, G. N. 18Dec.09

2 Walker, C. F. A. [L] 5Jan.10

s. Pilcher, W.S. 1Apr.10

1 Perry, G. E. 9July10

Thorne, T. F., J. N., Adjt., Depôt 29Sept.10

1 Tudway, H. R. C. 29Sept.10

2 Mackenzie, A. K. 19Nov.10

2 Welby, R. W.G. 24May11

2 Des Vœux, F.W. 25Oct.11

1 Aubrey-Fletcher, H.L., *M.V.O.* 8Nov.11

3 Van Neck, P. 14June12

s. *Greville,* C. H. 27July12

Lieutenants—contd.

3 Symons, T. E. R. 24Aug.12

1 Hamilton, *Lord* C. N. 24Aug.12

f.c. 1 Wellesley, *Lord* G. 15Sept.12

1 Bailey, *Hon.* W. R. 28Sept.12

2 Wolrige-Gordon, R. 1Oct.12

3 Congleton, H. B. F., *Lord* 22Mar.13

d. Dowling, C. M. C. 22Mar.13

2 *H.H. Prince* A. A. *of Battenberg, G.C.V.O.* 15Aug.13

2 Manners, *Hon.* J. N. 3Sept.13

3 Stewart, W. A. L. 3Sept.13

1 Stocks, M. G. 18Oct.13

2nd Lieutenants. (24)

1 Miller, F. W. J. M. 7Feb.12

1 Harcourt-Vernon, G. C. Fitz H. 1Aug.12

2 Legh, *Hon.* P. W. 1Aug.12

3 Beaumont-Nesbitt, F. G. 4Sept.12

3 Marshall, F. G. 4Sept.12

1 Tufnell, C. W. 4Sept.12

1 Mackenzie, H. W. R. 4Sept.12

2 Nugent, G. G. B. 4Sept.12

2nd Lieuts.—contd.

3 Kenyon-Slaney, R.O.R. 1Feb.13

3 Walter, S. 5Feb.13

3 Gerard, C. R. 3Sept.13

2 Pickersgill-Cunliffe, J. R. 17Sept.13

1 Somerset, N. A. H. 17Sept.12

2 Vereker, R. H. M. 17Sept.13

1 Lambert, R. S. 19Nov.13

2 Cuninghame, A. K, S. 10Dec.13

1 Darby, M. A. A. 24Jan.14

2 Cecil, G. E. [l] 25Feb.14

3 Steere, J. H. G. L. 25Feb.14

Regimental Adjutant.

Gregson, L. M., *capt.* 1Jan.14

Battalion Adjutants.

1 Rasch, G. E. C., *lt.* 15Aug.12

3 Forbes, Hon. A. L. C. *(Master of Forbes) lt.* 1Jan.13

2 MacDougall, L., *lt.* 10Mar.14

Quarter-Masters.

2 Skidmore, J. H., *hon. lt.* 11May16

3 Acraman, W. E., *hon. lt.* 24Apr.12

1 Teece, J., *hon. lt.* 4May12

Director of Music.

Williams, A., *M.V.O., Mus. Doc., hon. lt.* 6June14

Special Reserve.

Captain.

Percy A, I., *Earl, (Hon. Col. Tyne Elec. Eng., R.E.)* Capt. ret. pay [F] 14Feb.12

Lieutenant.

Sykes, C. A. V., *late Lt. G. Gds.* 14Sept.07 24Aug.12

2nd Lieutenants.

Fisher-Rowe, C.V., *late 2nd Lt. G. Gds.* 31July10 2Aug.13

Brabourne, W. W., *Lord, late 2nd Lt. G. Gds.* 14Feb.11 16Dec.11

Lloyd, M. K. A., *late 2nd Lt. G. Gds.* 1Aug.11 16Apr.13

Rhodes, A. T. G. *(A.D.C. to G.O.C. Mil. Forces, Domn. of New Zealand"* 1Jan.13) 16Dec.11

Rowley, C. S. 26June12 Duckworth-King, *Sir* G. H. J., *Bt.* 10Aug.12

Sitwell, F. O. S. 7Dec.12

Percy, *Lord* W. R. 19Feb.13 26Feb.12

871 | 872 | 873 | 874

COLDSTREAM GUARDS.

Regtl. Hd.-Qrs. ... ... Buckingham Gate, S.W.

1st Bn. *Aldershot (for Tower of London).* | 2nd Bn. *Windsor.* | 3rd Bn. *Chelsea Barracks (for Wellington Barracks).*

The King's Colours :—

1st Battalion.—Gules (crimson): In the centre the Star of the Order of the Garter proper, ensigned with the Imperial Crown; in base the Sphinx superscribed "Egypt."

2nd Battalion.—Gules (crimson): In the centre a Star of eight points argent within the Garter, ensigned with the Imperial Crown; in base the Sphinx superscribed "Egypt"; in the dexter Canton the Union.

3rd Battalion.—As for the 1st Battalion, and for difference in the dexter Canton, the Union, and issuing therefrom in bend dexter, a pile wavy or.

The Regimental Colours :—

The Union: In the centre a Company Badge ensigned with the Imperial Crown; in base the Sphinx superscribed "Egypt."

The 24 Company Badges are borne in rotation, 8 at a time, one on the Regimental Colour of each of the 3 Battalions.

The following honorary distinctions are borne upon each of the King's and Regimental Colours :—

"Tangier, 1680," "Namur, 1695," "Gibraltar, 1704-5," "Oudenarde," "Malplaquet," "Dettingen," "Lincelles," "Talavera," "Barrosa," "Fuentes d'Onor," "Nive," "Peninsula," "Waterloo," "Alma," "Inkerman," "Sevastopol," "Tel-el-Kebir," "Egypt, 1882," "Suakin, 1885," "Modder River," "South Africa, 1899-1902."

Uniform—Scarlet. *Facings*—Blue. *Agents*—Messrs. Cox & Co.

Colonel-in-Chief .. .. THE KING.

Colonel .. .. ℭ. Seymour, Gen. *Lord* W. F. E., *K.C.V.O.*, ret. pay [R] 11Mar.11

Officer Commanding the Regt. and Regtl. Dist. Monck, Col. C. S. O., *p.s.c.* 1Jan.13
col. 6June12

Lt.-Colonels. (3)	Majors—contd.	Captains—contd.	Captains—contd.
3Feilding, G. P. T., *D.S.O.* 3Sept.12	3Campbell, J. V., *D.S.O.* 21June13	3Heywood, C. P., *p.s.c.* 27Mar.09	s. 3*Darell, G. M.* 1Nov.10
1Ponsonby, J., *D.S.O.* 28Oct.13	c.o. Jenkins, F. 15Oct.13	*Crawford, R. B. J., Regtl. Adjt.* 27Mar.09	2Gregge-Hopwood, E. B. G. 1Nov.10
2Pereira, C. E. [F] 29Nov.13	1Grant, C. J. C., *p.s.c.* 28Oct.13	1Christie-Miller, E. G. 1June09	1Fuller-Maitland. W. A. 27June11
	s.c.Darell, W. H. V. 29Nov.13	1Gibbs, J. E. 29Jan.10	3Brocklehurst, J. H. 7Aug.11
	2Macgregor, P. A., *D.S.O.* 29Nov.13	d. Brown, G. H.,e.29Jan.10	e.a.*Bentinck, H. D.* 1Apr.12
Majors. (12)	s. Windsor Clive, G., *p.s.c.* 8Apr.14	1*Paget, G. M.* 16May10	3Brabazon, *Hon.* E. W. M. M. 4Apr.11
s. Steele, J. McC. 28Oct.06 29Nov.00	*Captains.* (13)	3Tritton, A. G. 16May10	1Warde-Aldam, W. St. A. 15Oct.13
2Markham, R. A. [F] 26June07	3Monck, *Hon.* C. H. S. 21Nov.03	2Phillips, J. H. J. 18May10	1Edwards, G. J 24Jan.14
s. Studd, H. W.,*D.S.O.*, *p.s.c.* [l] 24June08	2Hardy, F. 8Sept.06	3*Whitbread, R.* [F] 18May10	
1Hamilton, *Hon.* L. d'H., *M.V.O.* 29Jan.10	s. Longueville, E. 22Jan.07	2*Barttelot*, Sir *W. B., Bt.* 18May10	*Lieutenants.* (30)
3Matheson,T.G.18May10	1Egerton, A. G. E. 23Mar.07	3*Vaughan, G. E.* 18May10	2Leigh-Bennett, A. 22Jan.07
s. Farquhar, F. D., *D.S.O.*, *p.s.c.* [l] 8Oct.10	2Follett, G. B. S., *M.V.O.* 3Sept.08	3Burton, S. J. 1Nov.10	2Gordon, C. L. 28Mar.07
	2Pryce Jones, H. M. 16Feb.09	2Egerton, J. S. 1Nov.10	1*Pollock, F. R.* 15June07
	s. Banbury, C. W. 27Mar.09		

COLDSTREAM GUARDS—contd.

Lieutenants—contd.

1 Gore-Langton, F. W. 6Sept.07
1 Soames, A. G. 21Sept.07
1 Tollemache, E. D. H. 21Dec.07
e.a. *Brand*, J. C. 3Sept.08
c.o. *Mackinnon*, L.N.A. 23Jan.09
3 Bingham, D.C. 14Mar.09
3 Keppel, Hon. R. O. D. 27Mar.09
s. *Lawrence*, P. R. B. 28Apr.09
1 *Campbell*, G. A., *Adjt.* 1June09
2 Towers-Clark, W. T. 20July09
1 Smith, G. K. F. 29Dec.09
3 Horlick, J. N. 8Jan.10
1 Clutterbuck, T. B. 30Apr.10
2 Graves-Sawle, R. C. 12May10
3 Daniell, N. A. 16May10
3 *Wyndham*, P. L. 18May10
2 *Lambton*, G. 18May10
2 *Dawnay*, A. G. C., *Adjt.* 18May10
2 Legge-Bourke, N. W. H. 6June10
c.o. *Bentinck*, A. W. D. 1Nov.10
3 *Alexander*, J. U. F. C., *Adjt.* 3Dec.10
1 Cocks, J. C. S. 7Jan.11
1 Bourne-May, J. B. S. 27June11

Lieutenants—contd.

f.c. *Chinnery*, E. F. 1July11
3 Rowley, G. R. F. 7 Aug.11
1 Curtis, T. L. C. 22 Jan.12
2 Loyd, H. C. 1Apr.12
3 Smith, A. F. 4Apr.12
2 Verelst, H. W. 19Feb.13
2 Petre, L. G. C., *Lord* 1Mar.13
2 Bewicke-Copley, R. L. C. 30Apr13
3 Gordon-Ives, V. M. G. 13June13
2 Gibbs, L. M. 19July13
3 Hawarden, R. C. *Visct.* 10Sept.13
1 Wynne Finch, J. C. 15Oct.13
1 Younger, J. M. 15Oct.13
3 Windsor Clive, *Hon.* A. 8Nov.13
d. Hall, D. M. B. 24Jan.14

2nd Lieutenants. (24)

3 Trotter, A. 9Sept.11
2 Taylor, S.G. F. 9Sept.11
2 de Trafford, H. E. 9Sept.11
1 Sturt, *Hon.* G. P. M. N. 7Feb.12
3 Jackson, C. S. 24Feb.12
2 Marsham, C., *Visct.* 2Mar.12
1 Smith, M. B. 1Aug.12
3 Longueville, F. 4Sept.12
3 Corbet, *Sir* R. J., *Bt.* 22Jan.13
3 Cublitt, H. A. 1Feb.13

2nd Lieuts.—contd.

2 Lockwood, R. W. M. 1Feb.13
1 Lane, G. R. 5Feb.13
3 de Winton, W. 5Feb.13
1 Freeman-Thomas, *Hon.* G. F. 17Sept.13
2 Ramsay, A. H. M. 17Sept.13
1 Hardy, A. E. 17Sept.13
1 Britten, F. C. R. 17Sept.13
2 Shaw-Stewart, W, G. 18Sept.13
2 Winn, *Hon.* R. G. 24Jan.14
1 Browne, *Hon.* M. H. D. 24Jan.14
1 Tufnell, C. E. 2 Feb.14
2 Darwin, C. J. W. 25Feb.14
3 Cottrell Dormer, C. M. 10June14

Regimental Adjutant.

Crawfurd, R. B. J., *capt.* 1May14

Battalion Adjutants.

1 Campbell, G. A., *lt.* 15Jan.12
2 Dawnay, A. G. C., *lt.* 6June13
3 Alexander, J. W. F. C., *lt.* 1June14

Quarter-Masters.

2 Wright, S. 11Oct.05 *hon. capt.* 18Dec.13
3 Prichard, F. T., *hon. lt.* 25Jan.08
1 Boyd, J., *hon. lt.* 1Apr.11

Director of Music.

Mackenzie Rogan, J., *M.V.O., Mus. Doc., hon. capt.* 6June14

Special Reserve.

Lieutenants.

Fane, H. N. 13Jan.09 22June10
Wavell-Paxton, R G., *late Lt. Res. of Off. (Hon. Attaché, Vienna, 6 Feb.* 12) 25Dec.09
Feilding, R. E. A., *Visct., late Lt. C. Gds.* 16Feb.09 3Dec.10
Campbell, A. W. G., *late Lt. C. Gds.* 1Oct.10 2Aug.13
Watkins, H. G., *late 2nd Lt. Res. of Off.* 31Aug.12
Walker, *Sir* R, J. M., *Bt., late Lt. C. Gds.* 15Sept.13 8Nov.13

2nd Lieutenants.

Brougham, *Hon.* H. 26July11
Wallis, H. D. 9Mar.12
Boscawen, *Hon.* E. H. J. 27July12
Ibbetson, C. C. 23Oct.12
Whidborne, G. F. 1Feb.13
Beauchamp, E. A. (*on prob.*) 4Feb.14
Boscawen, *Hon.* V.D., (*on prob.*) 14Mar.14

| 879 | 880 | 881 | 882 |

SCOTS GUARDS.

Regtl. Hd.-Qrs. ... ... Buckingham Gate, S.W.

1st Bn. .. .. *Aldershot (for Warley)*. | 2nd Bn. *Tower of London (for Chelsea Barracks)*.

The King's Colours :—
  1st Battalion.—Gules (crimson): In the centre the Royal Arms of Scotland, ensigned with the Imperial Crown. Motto, "*En ! Ferus Hostis ;*" in base the Sphinx superscribed "Egypt."
  2nd Battalion.—Gules (crimson): In the centre the Thistle, and the Red and White Roses conjoined, issuant from the same stalk all proper, ensigned with the Imperial Crown; Motto, "*Unita Fortior ;*" in base the Sphinx superscribed "Egypt;" in the dexter canton the Union.

The Regimental Colours :—
  The Union: In the centre a Company Badge ensigned with the Imperial Crown; in base the Sphinx superscribed "Egypt."
  The 24 Company Badges are borne in rotation, 2 at a time, one on the Regimental Colour of each of the two Battalions.

  The following honorary distinctions are borne upon each of the King's and Regimental Colours :—
  "Namur, 1695," "Dettingen," "Lincelles," "Talavera," "Barrosa," "Fuentes d'Onor," "Nive," "Peninsula," "Waterloo," "Alma," "Inkerman," "Sevastopol," "Tel-el-Kebir," "Egypt, 1882," "Suakin, 1885," "Modder River," "South Africa, 1899-1902."

Uniform—Scarlet.   *Facings*—Blue.   *Agents*—Messrs. Cox & Co.

Colonel-in-Chief .. .. THE KING.

Colonel .. Methuen, Field-Marshal P. S., Lord, *G.C.B., G.C.V.O., C.M.G.* [R 1May04

Officer Commanding the Regt. and Regtl. Dist. .. Heyworth, Col. F. J., *D.S.O.* 9Oct.13
col. 6Dec.11

Lt.-Colonels. (2)	Majors—contd.	Captains—contd.	Lieutenants. (21)
2Bolton, R. G. I., 1Jan.12	1Van De Weyer, B. G., 1Jan.12	1Stracey, R. G. 25Feb.05	1Jolliffe, B. G. 13Dec.04
1Lowther, H. C., *C.V.O.,C.M.G., D.S.O., q.s.* [L] 9Oct.13	2Cator, A. B. E. 9Oct.13 s. m.p.Dalrymple, J. J., *Visct.* 24Jan.14	s. Alston, F. G. 30May05	2Hamilton-Wedderburn, H. K., *Adjt.* 4Jan.04
		Fox, C. V.[F] 28Apr.06	12Nov.04
		1Wickham,W.J. 6June06	2Loder, G. H. 11Jan.05
		2Orr-Ewing, N. A. 5June07	1Campbell, C. F. F. 29Mar.05
	Captains. (9)	1de la Pasture, C. E. 5June07	3Aug.05
Majors. (8)		1Romer, M. 5June07	2Taylor, H. 30May05
	e.a.*Romilly, B. H. S., D.S.O.* [F] 7Mar.04		s. Orr, A. R. 3June05
s. Hore Ruthven, *Hon.* W. P. (*Master of Ruthven*), *D.S.O., p.s.c., e.* 25Apr.06	*Tempest, R. S., Regtl. Adjt.* 12Mar.04	1Hamilton, C. F. P. 2Jan.12	s. Egerton Warburton, J. 6June06
	1*Stephen, A. A. L., D.S.O.*[F] *Adjt.* 10Apr.04	2Kinnaird, *Hon.* D. A. (*Master of Kinnaird*) 3Feb.12	2Steuart-Menzies, R. 2Feb.07
2Fraser, *Hon.* H. J., *M.V.O.* 12June07			2Fitz-Wygram, *Sir* F. L. F., *Bt.* 6Mar.09
1Maclean, H. F. 4July08	*Bulkeley*, T. H. R., *C.M.G., M.V.O.* 1July04	2Mackenzie, *Sir* V. A. F., *Bt., M.V.O.* 3July12	s. Warner, E. C. T. 7Aug.09
1Carpenter-Garnier, J. T. 10Oct.08	1Royds, A. H. 1Nov.04		1Ross, H. C. E. 20Feb.10
		Balfour, R. F. 18Jan.13	c.o.Trafford, E. B. 6Apr.10
2Gordon-Lennox, Lord E. C., *M.V.O.* 25Apr.10	2Paynter, G. C. B. 14Dec.04	d. Astley-Corbett, J. D. P. 8Mar.13	s. Smith, B. W. 14May10
			2Cochrane, T. H. D. B., *Lord* 22Aug.10

SCOTS GUARDS—contd.

Lieutenants—contd.

Fletcher, B. L. 11Nov,11

2Douglas-Dick,A.W.
J. J.   11Nov,11

1de Teissier, G. F.
          28Dec.11

1Macindoe, J.D. 1Jan.12

1Balfour, C. J. 8Mar.12

1Colquhoun, *Sir* I.,
Bt.   1Apr.12

2Dyer, *Sir* J. S., *Bt.*
          3July12

*f.c.*1Tennant, J. E. 7Aug.12

1Gipps, R. N. 19Jan.13

2Hulse, *Sir* E. H. W.,
Bt.   8Mar.13

d. Monckton,F.A.16Apr.13

2Jones, H. R. I. 3May13

*f.c.*1Leighton, J. B. T.
          11Mar,14

2Gordon-Ives, C. M. G.
          25Mar.14

2nd Lieutenants. (16)

1Lawson, W. B. W.
          4Sept.12

1Compton-Thornhill,
R. A.   4Sept.12

1Ogilvy, *Sir* G. N.,
Bt.   22Jan.13

2Loyd, G. A. 1Feb.13

2Cottrell Dormer, C.
          1Feb.13

2Carnegie, C. A.,
Lord   5Feb.13

2Garlies, R.A.R.,
Lord   3Sept.13

2Clive, P.R.,*Visct,*
          3Sept.13

1Monckton, G.V.F.
          17Sept.13
2Wynne Finch, W. H.
          1Feb.14

2nd Lieutenants (on prob.)

1Minto, V. G.
L. G., *Earl of* 26Feb.13

1Menzies, A. G. 20Aug.13

1Mackenzie, E. D.
          11Feb.14

Regimental Adjutant.

Tempest, R. S.,
capt.   3Feb.14

Battalion Adjutants.

Hamilton-Wedderburn, H. K.,
lt.   9Oct.13

1Stephen,A.A.L.,
D.S.O., capt. 1Apr.14

Quarter-Masters.

1Kinlay, D., *hon. lt.*
          3May09

2Ross, T., *hon. lt.*
          3May13

Special Reserve.

Captains.

⚔Coke, *Hon.* J. S.,
late Capt. S. Gds.
ret. pay 6Mar.09
          27Apr.12

Kemble, H. L.,
M.V.O., Capt.,
ret. pay 1Jan.12
          3July12

Bury, W. E. G. L.,
Visct., Capt. ret.
pay   8June12

Captains—contd.

⚔Gordon, G. C. D.,
Capt. ret. pay 8June12
          18Jan.13

Jervoise, A. F. C.,
Capt. ret. pay
          19Jan.13
          8Mar.13

Lieutenants.

⚔Harford, F. R.,
late Lt. S.
Gds.   12Mar.04
          4June13

Dalrymple-Hamilton,
N.V.C., *late* Lt.
Res. of Off. 10Apr.04
          25Nov.11

Wickham, J. L., *late*
Lt. S. Gds. 6Mar.09
          20Dec.11

Drummond, D. R.,
late Lt. Res. of
Off.   20Apr.11
          8July11

Brooke, R. C. 8June12
          21May13

Saumarez, *Hon.* J. St.
V. B., *late* Lt. S. Gds.
          9Oct.13
          4Apr.14

2nd Lieutenant.

Gibbs, R. C. M.
          27Sept.13

IRISH GUARDS.

Regtl. Hd.-Qrs. .. .. .. Buckingham Gate, S.W.
1st Bn. .. .. Wellington Barracks (for Aldershot).

The King's Colours:—1st Battalion.—Gules (crimson): In the centre the Royal Cypher or, within the Collar of the Order of St. Patrick with badge appendant proper, ensigned with the Imperial Crown.

The Regimental Colours:—The Union, in the centre a Company Badge ensigned with the Imperial Crown. The 8 Company Badges are borne in rotation.

Uniform—Scarlet. *Facings*—Blue.

Agents—Messrs. Cox & Co.

Colonel-in-Chief .. .. THE KING.

Colonel .. ҦҴ.ӍӅ. Roberts, Field-Marshal *Rt. Hon. F. S., Earl, K.G., K.P., G.C.B., O.M., G.C.S.I., G.C.I.E.*, VD, Col. Comdt. R.A. [R] 17Oct.00

Officer Commanding the Regt. and Regtl. Dist., ҦҴFitzClarence, Col. C., .. p.s.c. 14July13
col. 6Mar.13

Lt.-Colonel.	Captains—contd.	Lieutenants—contd.	Battalion Adjutant.
1Morris, *Hon.* G. H., p.s.c. [l] 14July13	d. Berners, H. H. 5Dec.12	1Blacker Douglass, R. St. J. 27Jan.13	1FitzGerald, *Lord* D., *capt.* 2June13
	1Perceval, A. A. C. P. S. 27Jan.13	1Walker, C.A.S. 19Feb.13	
Majors. (4)	1Mulholland, *Hon.* A. E. S. 14July13	1Fitzgerald, J.S.N. 2May14	*Quarter-Master.*
1Crichton, H. F.25Mar.08			1Hickie, H., *hon. lt.* 12Feb.14
1Herbert-Stepney, H. A. 7Feb.12	1Guthrie, J. N. 18Sept.13	*2nd Lieutenants.* (8)	
f.c. Brabazon, *Hon.* C. M.P. 19Feb.13	1Vesey, *Hon.* T. E. 18Oct.13	Pigott, St. J. R. 25Mar.14 10Dec.13	
s. Butler, *Hon.* L. J. P., p.s.c. 14July13	1FitzGerald, Lord D., *Adjt.* 18Oct.13		*Special Reserve.* Captain.
	Lieutenants. (11)	*2nd Lieutenants (on prob.)*	Hamilton, *Lord* A. J., Capt. ret. pay 2Dec.09
Captains. (5)	d. Bailie, T. M. D.29Mar.11	1Woodroffe, N. L. 12Feb.13	5Mar.13
1Tisdall, C. A. Sept.09	1Gough, E. J. F.25Nov.11		
	1Greer, E. B. 17Apr.12	1Roberts, J. T. P. 20Sept.13	*Lieutenants.*
m.c.Hepburn-Stuart-Forbes-Trefusis, *Hon.* J. F. 26Oct.09	1Stafford-King-Harman, E. C. 11June12	1Hughes-Onslow, O. 11Feb.14	Innes-Ker, *Lord* R. E. late Lt. I.G. 8Sept.09
	1Alexander, *Hon.* H. R. L. G. 5Dec.12	1Livingstone-Learmonth M. J. 11Feb.14	3June14
s. Reid, P. L. 19Nov.10	1Reynolds, W. C. N. 27Jan.13		s. Hope, W. E., *late* Lt. I. Gds. 22Jan.10
1Broughton, *Sir* H. J. D., *Bt.* 29 Mar.11	1Gough, *Hon.* H. W. 27Jan.13	1Miller, A.G.L.J. 9May14	18Sept.11

GUARDS DEPÔT.
Caterham.

Officer Commanding .. .. .. Jeffreys, Maj. G. D., G Gds. 1June11
Adjutant .. .. Thorne Lt. T. F. J N., G Gds 1June13
Quarter-Master .. .. .. Walker, F. 13Jan.97
			hon. maj. 13Jan.12

INFANTRY RECORD OFFICES.

Record Office.	Colonel and Assistant to Colonel.	Regiments.
Cork	Col. in charge of Records— Scrase-Dickins, Col. S. W. .. .. 29July12 Asst. to Col. in Charge of Records— Warner, Capt. E. H. L., ret. pay (Res. of Off.) 10Oct.08	R. Ir. Regt., Conn. Rang., Leins. R., R. Muns. Fus.
Dublin	Col. in charge of Records— Napier, Col. H. E. .. .. .. 25June14 Asst. to Col. in charge of Records— Crump, Hon. Capt. J. C., Qr.-Mr. ret. pay 20July05	R. Innis. Fus., R. Ir. Rif., R. Ir. Fus., R. Dub. Fus.
Exeter	Col. in charge of Records— Western, Col. W. G. B., C.B., p.s.c. [L] .. 7Feb.11 Asst. to Col. in charge of Records— Goodwyn, Maj. J. H., ret. pay (Res. of Off.) .. 21Aug.11	Devon. R., Som. L.I., D. of Corn. L.I., Hamps. R., Dorset. R., Wilts. R.
Hamilton	Col. in Charge of Records— Paterson, Col. S. .. .. .. 27July12 Asst. to Col. in charge of Records— Caird, Maj. L. H., ret. 1July05	R. Scots, R. Sc. Fus., K.O. Sco. Bord., Sco. Rif., High. L.I.
Hounslow	Col. in charge of Records— O'Donnell, Col. H., p.s.c. .. .. 14May14 Asst. to Col. in charge of Records— Martin-Leake, Capt. W., ret. pay (Res. of Off.) 15Apr.10	R. W. Surr. R., E. Kent R., R. Fus., E. Surr. R., R. Suss. R., R. W. Kent R., Midd'x R.
Lichfield	Col. in charge of Records— Churchward, Col. P. R. S., C.B. .. .. 26Dec.12 Asst. to Col. in charge of Records— Howe, Bt. Maj., F. H., ret. pay (Res. of Off.) 1Mar.14	Linc. R., Leic. R., S. Staff. R. Notts. & Derby. R., N. Staff. R.
Kinnoull St., Perth	Col. in charge of Records— Mackintosh, Col. G., C.B. [l] .. .. 1Apr.12 Asst. to Col. in charge of Records— Cavaye, Maj. G. E., ret. pay (Res. of Off.) .. 20July05 (Hon. Lt.-Col. Mila.)	R. Highrs., Sea. Highrs., Gord. Highrs., Cam'n Highrs., Arg. & Suth'd Highrs.
Preston	Col. in charge of Records— Tudway, Col. R. J., C.B., D.S O. .. .. 5Sept.11 Asst. to Col. in charge of Records— Daniel, Maj. C. J., D.S.O., ret. pay (Res. of Off.) 1July05	R. Lanc. R., L'pool R., Lan. Fus., E. Lan. R., Bord. R., N. Lan. R., Manch. R.
Shrewsbury	Col. in charge of Records— Evans, Col. H. J., p.s.c. [l] .. .. 18Feb.13 Asst. to Col. in charge of Records— { 14Oct 08 Parr, Maj. C., ret. pay (Res. of Off.) .. { 19Dec.06	Ches. R., R. W. Fus., S. Wales Bord., S. Lan. R., Welsh R. Shrops. L.I.
Warley	Col. in charge of Records— Travers, Col. J. H. du B. .. .. .. 16May14 Asst. to Col. in charge of Records— FitzGerald, Capt. G. E. F., ret. pay (Res. of Off.) 1July05	Norf. R., Suff. R., Bedf. R. Essex R., North'n R.
Old Barracks, Warwick	Col. in charge of Records— Hacket-Thompson, Col. F., C.B. .. .. 21Apr.11 Asst. to Col. in charge of Records— Southey Maj. J. H. W., ret. pay (Res. of Off.) 1July05	R. War. R., Glouc. R., Worc. R., Oxf. and Bucks. L.I., R. Berks R.
Winchester	Col. in charge of Records— Fortescue, Col. F. A., C.B., p.s.c. .. .. 1July12 Asst. to Col. in charge of Records— Russell, Maj. L. G., ret. 1July05	K. R. Rif. C., Rif. Brig.
York	Col. in charge of Records— Watson, Col. J. E., C.B. .. .. .. 24June11 Asst. to Col. in charge of Records— Ottley, Lt.-Col. G. F., D.S.O., ret. pay (Res. of Off.) 9July05	North'd Fus., W. York. R., E. York. R., York. R., W. Rid. R., Yorks. L.I., York & Lanc. R., Durh. L.I.

In the case of Territorial Infantry Officers dates shewn prior to 1 April, 1908, are those of the Officers' corresponding rank in a late unit of the Volunteer Force.

Order of Precedence of the Several Counties in the Infantry of the Territorial Force.

1. Devonshire.
2. Middlesex.
3. Lancashire.
4. Surrey.
5. Pembrokeshire.
6. Derbyshire.
7. Oxfordshire.
8. Cheshire.
9. Wiltshire.
10. Sussex.
11. Edinburgh (City).
12. Essex.
13. Northumberland.
14. Renfrewshire.
15. Northamptonshire.
16. Dorsetshire.
17. Norfolk.
18. Staffordshire.
19. Berkshire.
20. Gloucestershire.
21. Brecknockshire.
22. Suffolk.
23. Stirlingshire.
24. Bucks.
25. Lanarkshire.
26. Kent.
27. Glamorgan.
28. Nottinghamshire.
29. Merionethshire.
30. Yorkshire (W. Rid.).
31. Leicestershire.
32. Midlothian.
33. Aberdeenshire.
34. Roxburgh.
35. Monmouthshire.
36. Cornwall.
37. Ross-shire and Cromarty.
38. Worcestershire.
39. Inverness-shire.
40. Warwickshire.
41. Lincolnshire.
42. Denbighshire.
43. Hampshire.
44. Somersetshire.
45. Forfar.
46. Cambridgeshire.
47. Shropshire.
48. { City of London. County of London.
49. Yorkshire (E. Rid.).
50. Hertfordshire.
51. Perthshire.
52. Berwickshire.
53. Sutherland.
54. Kincardineshire.
55. Haddington.
56. Ayrshire.
57. Dumfries.
58. Elgin.
59. Argyll.
60. Cardigan.
61. Durham.
62. Wigtown.
63. Yorkshire (N. Rid.).
64. Cumberland.
65. Herefordshire.
66. Dumbartonshire
67. Huntingdon.
68. Carnarvonshire.
69. Montgomeryshire.
70. Carmarthen.
71. Caithness.
72. Kirkcudbright.
73. Westmorland.
74. Fifeshire.
75. Bedfordshire.
76. Linlithgowshire.
77. Selkirkshire.
78. Banffshire.
79. Radnorshire.
80. Flintshire.
81. Clackmannan.
82. Peeblesshire.
83. Kinross-shire.
84. Anglesey.
85. Shetland.
86. City of Dundee.
87. City of Glasgow.
88. City of Aberdeen.
89. Rutland.

INFANTRY.

THE ROYAL SCOTS (LOTHIAN REGIMENT).
Regimental District No. 1 [No. 2 District].

The Royal Cypher within the Collar of the Order of the Thistle with the Badge appendant. In each of the four corners the Thistle within the Circle and motto of the Order, ensigned with the Imperial Crown. The Sphinx, superscribed "Egypt."

"Tangier, 1680," "Namur, 1695," "Blenheim," "Ramillies," "Oudenarde," "Malplaquet," "Louisburg," "Havannah," "Egmont-op-Zee," "St. Lucia, 1803," "Corunna," "Busaco," "Salamanca," "Vittoria," "St. Sebastian," "Nive," "Niagara," "Peninsula," "Waterloo," "Nagpore," "Maheidpoor," "Ava," "Alma," "Inkerman," "Sevastopol," "Taku Forts," "Pekin, 1860," "South Africa, 1899-1902."

Regular and Special Reserve Battalions.

Uniform—Scarlet.   *Facings*—Blue.   *Agents*—Messrs. Cox & Co.

1st Bn. } (1st Foot)	{ *Allahabad (for Rawal Pindi.)*	3rd Bn. (Edinburgh Light Inf. Mil.) .. *Glencors*
2nd "	{ †*Plymouth.*	
Depôt ..	*Glencorse, Milton Bridge, N.B.*	Record Office .. .. *Hamilton.*

Territorial Force Battalions.

4th Bn.	..	*Forrest Hill, Edinburgh.*	8th Bn.	*Haddington.*
5th "	..	*Forrest Hill, Edinburgh.*	9th "	*89, East Claremont Street. Edinburgh.*
6th "	..	*33, Gilmore Place, Edinburgh.*		
7th "	..	*Dalmeny Street, Leith.*	10th "	*Linlithgow.*

Colonel .. .. .. ₡. Moncrieff, Lt.-Gen. G. H., VD, ret. pay [R] .. 20Aug.08

1st and 2nd Battalions.

Lt.-Colonels. (2)
1 Callender, D. A. 7 Aug.12
2 McMicking, H., D.S.O., p.s.c., q.s. 14 Aug.12

Majors. (5)
2 Dundas, R. C. 22Nov.05
2 Duncan, F. J., D.S.O. [L] 22Nov.05
22 Aug.02
(3) 2 Dyson, H. B. [l]
(*Comdg. Depôt*) 27 Mar.07
1 Loch, G. G. 14 Aug.08
1 Nash, H. E. P. 8 Oct.10
1 Wingate, G. H. F. 5 Apr.11
s. Moir, A. J. G., p.s.c. 29Nov.00
7 Aug.12
2 Tweedie, G. S. 14 Aug.12

Captains. (14)
1 Drysdale, W., p.s.c. 19Nov.02
s. Mackenzie, J. H., p.s.c. 22 Apr.03
e.a. Smith, L. K., D.S.O. 9 May03
2 Price, C. L., D.S.O., *Adjt.* 3Nov.03
2 Leggatt, A.F.S. 4Nov.03
(3) 1 Croker, A. E. 24Nov.03
~~2 Duncombe~~-Shafto, A., D.S.O. 20 May 06
2 Dec.03
(3)1 Tanner, F. C. [l] 20 May08
15 Feb.04
r. Budge, H. L. 29 Nov.04
s. Mudie,T.C.,p.s.c. 16 May05
2 Baillie Hamilton, G. D. 22 Jul05
30 May 04
s. Charteris, N. K. 25 Sept.06
1 Fargus, N. R. S. 9 Sept.08

Captains—contd.
t. Stanton, H. A. S. 9 Mar.09
1 Lumsden, A. F. 5 Oct.09
(3) 2 Dryburgh, N. M. 5 Oct.09
Carlton, H. D. (*Comdt. Detention Barracks*) 18 Oct.09
1 Johnston, E. J. F. 18 Oct.09
1 Colchester-Wemyss, J. M. 10 Sept.10
9 Aug.08
c.o. *Anderson, F.* 5 Apr.13
2 Hill-Whitson, E.C. 5 Apr 13
t. Gillatt, J. M. 18 Apr.13
e.a.*Scott, J. M.* 18 Apr.13
1 Stanley-Murray, H. E. 26 June 13
t. Romanes, J.G.P. 26 June 13
t. Elphyn, G.D.P. 26 June 13
d. Hewat, A.M.C. 15 July18
f.c. MacLean, A.C.H. 20 Aug.13
2 Morrison, P. 20 Aug.13

Lieutenants. (19)
c.o. *Mackenzie, J. M.* 16 May 05
1 Robertson, K.S. 6 Jan.06
1 *Farquharson, L. S.*, *Adjt.* 5 Apr.06
t. McCallum, R.E. 4 May07
2 Saward, H. D. 17 Aug.07
2 Henderson, M. 28 Sept.07
t. Hamilton, J. K. 9 Sept.08
1 Stewart, N. S. 24 Sept.08
(3)1 Perry, B. H. H. 11 Apr.09
1 Povah, F. [l] 17 Oct.09
1 Bell, T. 18 Oct.09
1 Clark, G.W.B. 22 Mar.11
1 Burke. J. A 1 Apr.11
c.o. *Scott-Moncrieff, R.* 3 Feb.12
1 Worthington-Wilmer, H.F.M., f.c.r. 14 Feb.12
2 Laidlay, J. W. 16 Mar.12
(3) 1 Errington, L. 3 July12
c.o. *Thompson, G. M.*
2 Strange, G. C. C. 13 Feb.13
19 Feb.13
c.o. *Acheson, C. D.* 11 Apr.13
2 Hall, G. E. 11 Apr.13

Lieutenants—contd.
1 Buchanan, K. G. 18 Apr.13
2 Graves, C. G. [l] 26 June 13
2 Godfrey, E. A. 15 July 13
1 St. John, F. O. 15 July 13
1 Playfair, L. 12 Nov.13

2nd Lieutenants. (12)
2 Combe, E. P. 3 Sept.12
2 Hay, G. H. 26 July 13
1 Currie, D. R. 3 Sept 13
1 Chree, W. J. 3 Sept.13
1 Renny, A. H. 3 Sept.13
1 Bidie, G. M. V. 3 Sept.13
2 Crockatt, N.R. 17 Sept.13
1 Young, N. M. 10 Dec.13
1 Cole-Hamilton, C, W. E. 24 Jan.14
1 Robson-Scott, T. S. 25 Feb.14
2 McDougall, D. J. 25 Feb.14
2 Donaldson, A. J. L. 25 Feb.14
(2) Ross, R. C. 25 Feb.14

Adjutants.
1 Farquharson, L. S., *lt.* 28 Aug.11
2 Price, C. L., D.S.O. *capt.* 20 Feb.14

Quarter-Masters.
r. Harris, W. H. 13 Sept.99
hon. capt. 13 Sept.09
2 Everingham, A. E., 2 Nov.01
hon. capt. 2 Nov.11
1 Fairall, W. G. H., *hon. lt.* 4 Mar.14

3rd Battalion.

(*Officers serving on 28 May 02 in the corresponding Militia unit hold honorary Army rank equivalent to the Militia regimental rank they then held. Other officers entitled to honorary Army rank have it shown against their names.*)

Hon. Colonel.
p.s. ✕ Montagu-Douglas-Scott, Lord H.F. (*Hon. Col. ret. Spec. Res.*) 21 Dec.91

Lt.-Colonel.
p.s. ✕ Ellesmere, J. F. G. S. *Earl of, M.V.O.* 11 Nov.12

Major.
r.e. Dyson, H. B. [l] 27 Mar.07

Captains (5).
p.s. ✕ Newport, O., *Visct. hon. m.* 29 Apr.99
p.s. ✕ Strutt, E. L. 20 Feb.00
p.s. ✕ Northey, C.B. 11 Jul03
✕ Grant, J.C.H. 11 July 03
r.e. Tanner, F.C. [l] 20 May08
15 Feb.04
✕ Bussell, T. A. 15 Feb.04
Capt. ret. pay 6 May05
p.s. Bruce, Hon. H. L. 5 Apr.13
(H) 19 May06
p.s. Heathcote, R. E. M. (H) 24 Apr.08
✕ Hutchison, C. K.,
Capt. ret. pay 4 Feb.09
r.e. ✕ Dryburgh, N. M.
5 Oct.09
r.e. Perry, B. H. H. 1 Apr.09

Montagu-Douglas-
Scott, D. J. 1 May 09
Scarisbrick, C. E. 11 Aug.10
Cazenove, B. de L. 11 Aug.10
r.e. Errington, L. 3 July 12

Special Reserve.
2nd Lieutenant.
Robertson, A. (*on prob.*) 2 May14
r.e. Errington, L. 3 July12

† *Postal Address—Crownhill, S.O., Devon.*

THE ROYAL SCOTS (LOTHIAN REGIMENT)—(Regtl. Dist. No. **1**)—*contd.*

3rd Bn.—*contd.*

2nd Lieutenants. (8)
Graham Watson,
A.F. 28Oct.11
Trotter, A. N. 21Dec.12
Menzies, V. M. G.
(on prob.) 4Apr.14
Bulteel, M. C. (on
prob.) 16May14

Adjutant.
✠Budge, H. L.
Capt. R. Scots.1Feb.14
(*Capt.in Army*29Nov.04)
Quarter-Master.
✠Harris, W. H.,
hon. capt.

4th Battalion (Queen's Edinburgh Rifles).

"South Africa, 1900-02."

Forrest Hill, Edinburgh.

Hon. Colonel.
The Lord Provost of
Edinburgh for the time
being.

Lt.-Colonel.
p.s. Younger, W. J. (Q)
(H) ⑤ 1May13

Majors. (2)
p.s. ✠Dunn, S. R., TD.
(*Hon. Capt. in
Army* 9Oct.02) (H)
⑤(Q) t.a., *hon.l.c.*
25June06
p.s. Gray, J. (H) 1May13
p.s. Simpson, J. G., TD,
(t) (H) 18Sept.13

Captains. (8)
p.s. Jones, A. E. L. (H)
(Q) 23July04
10Sept.06
p.s. Henderson, J. N.
⑤ (H) 16Mar.07
p.s. Rutherford, R. W. G.
⑤ (H)(Q) 13Dec.07
p.s. Sinclair, W. C. C. (t)
7Jan.11
Pollock, J.D.(t) 17Apr12
Skae, E. T. (q) 1May13
p.s. Tait, T. R. (q) 8July13
Robertson, J. 18Sept.13

Lieutenants. (8)
Mackie, R,E.(q)10Mar.10
Low, J. W. 17Apr.12
Morham, J. 10July12
Mathers, J. A. 1 Mar.13
Allan, G. F. 18May13
Gray, J. 18May13
Young, J. 8July13
Considine, P. F.
18Sept.13

2nd Lieutenants. (8)
Allan, G. G. 5June12
Barker, T. L. 21Dec.12
Stewart, D. M. 21Dec.12
Logan, J. 26Apr.13
Macrorie, R. D. 10May13
Kemp, A. J. O. 11Oct.13
Paterson, C. 12Nov.13
Riddell, J. 15Nov.13
Grant, L. R. 16Dec.13
Byres, G.M. 21Mar.14

Adjutant.
Hamilton, J. K. M.,
Lt. R. Scots, *capt.*
6Mar.14

Quarter-Master.
✠Smith, A., Qr.-Mr.
(*hon. capt.*) *ret.
pay, hon. capt.* 7Mar.14

Medical Officers.
Paterson, Lt. H.,
M.B., R.A.M.C.
(T.F.) (*attd.*) 17Nov.10
Watson, Lt. A. P.,
M.B., F.R.C.S.,
R.A.M.C. (T.F.)
(*attd.*) *late* Lt.
6 Bn. R. Scots.
4May12

Chaplains.
Ewing, Rev. W., *M.A.*
[U.F.C.] Chapl. 4th
Class (T.F.) (*attd.*)
1Jan.10
Lumsden, Rev. J.,
B.D., [C.S.]Chapl.
4th Class (T.F.)
(*attd.*) 24July13

[*Uniform—Dark Grey.
Facings—Black.*]

5th Battalion (Queen's Edinburgh Rifles).

"South Africa, 1900-02."

Forrest Hill, Edinburgh.

Hon. Colonel.
Macdonald, Col. Rt.
Hon. Sir J. H. A.,
K.C.B., VD, (*Hon.
Col. ret. Army
Motor Res.*) (*King's
Body Gd. for
Scotland*) 5June01

Lt.-Colonel.
p.s. Wilson, J. T. R. ⑤
17Apr.12

Majors. (2)
p.s. McDonald, J.
(t)(H) 9Dec.09
p.s. Rhind, T.D.⑤ 17Apr.12

Captains. (8)
p.s. MacIntosh, J. D. (t)
26Mar.04
p.s. McLagan, D. C. (q) ⑤
13Nov.06
p.s. Oliver, W. G. M. (Q)
15Mar.07
p.s. Lindsay, D.A.(t)18Feb 11
White, A. (q) ⑤ (H) ⑤
25Feb.,12
p.s. Mure, A. H. (t) 17Apr.12
Macrae, A. W. U.
22Aug.12
p.s. Ross, J. P. (H)(Asst.
Dist. Commr. (on
prob.), Gold Coast,
28 Apr. 13) 7Feb.14
Blair, E.J. (q) (H)
7Feb.14

Lieutenants (8).
(p.s.) Wilson, J. W, S.
15Aug.07
Russell, W. 25Feb.12
Gunn, J. P. 21June12
Robertson, F. W.
22Aug.12
Rex, E. R. 22Dec.12
Smith, J. M. 22Dec.12
Darling, T. 16Sept.13
Kerr, A. 5Feb.14
Turnbull, W. E. 7Feb.14

2nd Lieutenants. (8)
Sillars, D. 8Jan.12
Maule, E. 24Nov.12
Kerr, W. S. 24Nov.12
Paterson, A. H. S.
6Dec.12
Watt, A. S. (*Asst.
Dist. Commr., Gold
Coast, 12 Jan.* 14)
27Feb.13
Kemp, C, J. ⑤ 14June13
Gibson, G. 8Oct.13
Gunn, J. L. 24Jan.14
Hislop, W. B. 21Mar.14
Aitchison, J. B.
21Mar.14
Sutherland, G. O.
6May14

Adjutant.
✠Hepburn, W. D.,
Capt. Sea. Highrs.
28Aug.11

Quarter-Master.
Wilson, J., *hon. lt.*
6July10

Medical Officers.
p.s. Clark, Maj, J. A,
M.B., R.A.M.C.
(T.F.) (*attd.*) 31Mar.06
3Mar.94
p.s. Scott, Maj. J.,
M.D., R.A.M.C.,
(T.F.) (*attd.*) 21Jan.13
27Feb.01

Chaplains.
Fergusson, Rev. J.
[C.S.] Chapl. 4th
Class (T.F.) (*attd.*)
1Apr.06
2June06
Miller, Rev. J. H., *M.A.*
[U.F.C.] Chapl. 4th
Class (T.F.) (*attd.*)
4June09

[*Uniform—Dark Grey.
Facings—Black.*]

6th Battalion.

"South Africa, 1901-02."

33, Gilmore Place,
Edinburgh.

Hon. Colonel.
✠Kitchener of Khartoum, Fd. Marshal
H.H., Earl., K.P.,
G, C.B., O.M.,
G.C.S.I., G.C.M.G.,
G.C.I.E., Col.Comdt.
R.E., q.s. 19Aug.(
Lt.-Colonel.
p.s. Turnbull, T. E., VD
8Feb.

Majors. (2)
p.s. Edgar, F., TD (Capt.
Res. of Off.) (Q) (H)
⑤ (2nd Class Dist.
Offr., N. Provs.
Nigeria { 1Jan.14
{ 30Dec.05)
28Oct.
p.s. Whitton, K.,TD 28Oct.
p.s. Watson, W. E. (t)
25Feb.

Captains. (8)
p.s. Adams, J,W,(Q)26Oct.
p.s. Milligan, J. M. (t) (H)
26Feb.
p.s. Ross, G. A. S, 22Mar.
p.s. MacLeod, R, C,TD,(H)
⑤ (a) (q) (b) 28Oct.
p.s. McCrae, G. (t) 28Oct.
Aitken, J, E,(t) 20Jan.
p.s. Brown, H. 2Apr.
p.s. Todd, J. A. 25Feb.

Lieutenants (8)
p.s. Turner, J. A. L. (q)
(H) 16May
(p.s.)McIntosh, R. S.
28Oct.
p.s. Livingstone, A. R. W.
(q) (H) ⑤ (Asst.
Dist. Offr., S. Provs.,
Nigeria, { 1Jan.14
{ 20 Mar.,12
(p.,) Slater, J. M. 7Apr
(p.,) Mowat, J. H. 20Jan.
Douglas, W. A. 2Apr
Atkinson, J. J. 20Apr.
Johnston, J. 4May
Thorburn, J. L. (Supervisor of Customs, 2n
grade, Nigeria,
13May14)
9Mar.
Mustard, A. L. 13May

2nd Lieutenants. (8)
Gray, W. B. 14Feb
Mackenzie, F. B.
14Feb
Simpson, J. C. 21Feb
Burns, W. 19Oct
Brydone, T. 19Oct
Brown, R. J. 19Oct
Aitchison, T. D.
30Ma;
Nicol, J. L. 12Jun
Lornie, F.R.T. 23Jun

Adjutant.
✠Gillatt, J. M.,Capt.
R. Scots. 26Jun

Quarter-Master.
Johnston, R., *hon. lt.*
7Oc

THE ROYAL SCOTS (LOTHIAN REGIMENT)—(Regtl. Dist. No. **1**)—*contd.*

6th Bn.—*contd.*

Medical Officers.
p.s. Martin, Capt. W. L.,
 M.B., R.A.M.C.,
 (T.F.) (*attd.*) 6Apr.08
 18Mar.96
Wallace, Lt. R.N.,
 M.B., R.A.M.C.
 (T.F.) (*attd.*) 19Mar.10

Chaplains.
Burns, *Rev.* T., *D.D.*
 [C.S.] Chapl., 4th
 Class (T.F.) (*attd.*)
 1Apr.08
 12July05
Black, *Rev.* J. M.,
 M.A. [U.F.C.]
 Chapl. 4th Class
 (T.F.) (*attd.*) 12May09

[Uniform—*Scarlet*
 Facings—*Blue*].

7th Battalion.

"South Africa, 1900-02."

Dalmeny Street, Leith.

Hon. Colonel.
Rosebery, Rt. Hon.
 A. P., Earl of,
 K.G., K.T., VD,
 (King's Body Gd.
 for Scotland) 12Feb.10

Lt.-Colonel,
p.s. Peebles, W. C.,
 TD ⊕ (*H*) 22Feb.10

Majors. (2)
p.s. Sanderson, A. W.
 (*t*) (*H*) 21Dec.08
p.s. Hamilton, J. D.
 L. (*t*) 22Feb.10

Captains. (8)
p.s. Smith, J. MacD.
 (*H*) (Q) 20Mar.01
p.s. Dawson, J. D. 14Jan.05
p.s. Watson, G. L. (*t*)
 ⊕ 14Mar.06
p.s. Mitchell, A. M. ⊕
 2Nov.07
p.s. Wightman, A. J.
 24May11
p.s. Peebles, J.R.(*t*) 1June11
p.s. Mitchell, M. (*t*)
 17Apr.12
Ewing, W. T. 24Nov.13

Lieutenants. (8)
Clark, T. (*H*) 15Feb.10
Bertram, J. N. 1May10
Kermack, W. R.
 (q) 1June11
Mackenzie, L. do A.
 11Dec.11
Cushny, A. O. 17Apr.12
Salvesen, C. R. 24Nov.13
Riddell, N.C.⊕ 5May14

2nd Lieutenants. (8)
Bell, J. C. 24Sept.13
Young, J. A. 9Jan.14
Thomson, E. J. 1Apr.14

Adjutant.
Romanes, J. G. P.,
 Capt. R. Scots,
 3Feb.12

Quarter-Master.
Archibald, A., TD.,
 hon. m. 7Apr.06

Medical Officer.
Mill, Lt.-Col. J., *M.B.,*
 VD, R.A.M.C (T.F.)
 (*attd.*) 20Feb.07
 9Feb.87

Chaplains.
Harvey, *Rev.* J.,
 M.A. [U.F.C.]
 Chapl.4thClass
 (T.F.) (*attd.*) 12May09
Swan, *Rev.* W.,
 B.D., Chapl. 4th
 Class(T.F.)(*attd*)
 22Apr.12
[Uniform—*Scarlet*,
 Facings—*Blue*.]

8th Battalion.

"South Africa, 1901."
Haddington.

Hon. Colonel.
p. Hepburne-Scott, Hon.
 W. G. VD (Master
 of Polwarth (*Lt.-
 Col. T. F. Res.*)
 20Feb.14

Lt.-Colonel.
p. Cowan, C. M.,TD
 20Feb.14

Majors. (2)
p.s. Brook, A., VD
 (Q)(*H*) 1Mar.08
 Tweedie, R. W.,
 TD 20Feb.14

Captains. (8)
p.s. Stirling, J., *t.a.* 7Apr.06
p. Jardine, W. 2June06
p. Ballantyne, C.,
 jun. 2June06
p. Thorburn, W., jun.
 2June06
p.s. Glover,T.S. 8Jan.09
p. ✗Gemmill, W. 23Apr.10
p.s. Tait, J. 11May13
p.s. Todrick, T. 24June14
 1Apr.06

Lieutenants. (8)
(p.s.) Ballantyne, G. H.
 1Apr.07
(p.) Mitchell, T. B.,
 jun. 23Apr.10
p.s. *Inch,* W. H. (*H*)
 I. of M. 1May10
Stewart, T. 20Sept.11
Watson, T. W. 23Oct.12
Burt, A. 11May13
Kerr, R. B. 9Oct.13
Burnet, W. 8Mar.14

2nd Lieutenants. (8)
Nicholson, D. 20Feb.13
Plew, F. G., jun.
 20Feb.13
Stewart, D. M. 12July13
Dawson, W. R.13Aug.13
Young, J. 1Nov.13
Pringle, J. S. 3Nov.13
Kemp, J. C. 20Nov.13
Christie, D. 9May14
Roughead, F. A.
 10May14

Inst. of Musk.
Inch, W. H., *lt.*
 12June09

Adjutant.
✗Grant-Suttle, G. D.,
 Capt. R. Highrs.
 25Sept.11

Quarter-Master.
p. Thorburn, W. E.,
 TD, *hon. m.* 7June05

Medical Officers.
p.,p.s.Crombie, Maj. J.
 F., R.A.M.C.
 (T.F.) (*attd.*)
 ⊕ 26May10
 24Mar.06
Anderson, Lt. M.C.,
 R.A.M.C. (T.F.)
 (*attd.*) 11June14

Chaplains.
Stewart, *Rev.* A. [C.S.]
 Chapl. 2nd Class
 (T.F.) (*attd.*) 24Oct.09
 24Oct.94
Kerr, *Rev.* J., *M.A.*
 [C.S.] Chapl. 2nd
 Class (T.F.)(*attd.*)
 3Apr.12
 3Apr.97
Pryde, *Rev.* R. H.
 [C.S.] Chapl. 3rd
 Class (T.F.)(*attd.*)
 17Aug.11
 17Aug.01
Scott, *Rev.* R. B., *B.A.*
 [C.S.] Chapl. 4th
 Class (T.F.)(*attd.*)
 1Apr.08
 7Mar.03
Williamson, *Rev.*
 H. M. [U.F.C.]
 Chapl. 4th Class
 (T.F.) (*attd.*) 1June09

[Uniform—*Scarlet,*
 Facings—*Blue.*]

Cadet Units affiliated.
North Berwick Cadet Corps.
Haddington Cadet Corps.
Tranent Industrial School Cadet Corps.
Prestonpans Cadet Corps.

9th (Highlanders) Battalion.

"South Africa, 1901-02."
89, East Claremont Street, Edinburgh.

Hon. Colonel.
✗Hamilton, Gen. Sir
 I. S. M., G.C.B.,
 D.S.O., q.s., 𝔄.𝔇.ℭ.,
 Col. Cam'n Highrs.
 31Aug.01

Lt.-Colonel.
p. Blair, A. S. (*H*) ⊕ Dec.11

Majors. (2),
Hule, D. H. (*t*) 21Oct.09
Cameron, J. S. T.
 (*H*) 17Dec.12

Captains. (8)
p.s. Collow-Campbell,
 J., TD, *hon. m.* (*t*)
 (*H*) 24June05
p. Moncreiff, R. H.
 FitzH. (q) 14Mar.08
Ferguson, J. 15Dec.08
Cowan, G. D. 15Dec.08
p.s. Lucas, F. R.(*H*)21Oct.08
Aitken, A. C. 12June12
Blair, P. A. 1Dec.12
Wallace, R. J. 17Dec.12

Lieutenants. (8)
Robertson, J. L.
 26Nov.09
Strachan, G. S. 2Apr.11
Bell, D. 12June12
Lyon, W. S. S. 17Dec.12
Lindsay W. C. S.
 3Apr.13
Liddle, W. ⊕ 13July13
Bennet Clark, T, W.,
 14Nov.13
p.s. Green, G. H., *late
 Capt. 4 Bn. R.
 Scots* (*t*) 10Dec.13
Macdonald, N. 22Jan.14

2nd Lieutenants. (8)
Urquhart, W. M.
 26July11
Haddon, D. A. R.
 4May12
Maxwell, A.D. 18Sept.12
Blair, P. J. 12Feb.13
Smith-Grant, J. G. S. C.
 12Feb.13
Lindsay, R. S. 18Apr.13
Yeats, B. E. 15Jan.14
Fraser, S. 28Mar.14

Adjutant.
✗Dudgeon, R. M., Lt.,
 Cam'n Highrs.,
 capt. 1Mar.12

Quarter-Master
p. Gordon, A., *hon.
 capt.* 6Aug.00

Medical Officers.
p. Cumming, Maj. J.,
 R.A.M.C. (T.F.)
 (*attd.*) 29Mar.12
 31Aug.00
p. Bowie, Capt. J. M.,
 M.D., R.A.M.C.
 (T.F.) (*attd.*) 1May10
 1Nov.06

Chaplains.
Stevenson,*Rev.* W.R.,
 h.A. [C.S.], Chapl,
 4th Class (T.F.)
 (*attd.*) 1Apr.08
 31Oct.0
Sclater, *Rev.* J. M. P.
 M.A. [U.F.C.],
 Chapl 4th Class
 (T.F.) (*attd.*) 1May09

[Uniform—*Scarlet,*
 Facings—*Blue*

THE ROYAL SCOTS (LOTHIAN REGIMENT)—(Regt). Dist. No. **1**)—*contd.*

10th (Cyclist) Battalion.

"South Africa, 1901-02."
Linlithgow.

Hon. Colonel.

Rosebery, Rt. Hon. *A.P.*, Earl of, K.G., K.T., VD, (*King's Body Gd. for Scotland*) 18Apr.74

Lt.-Colonel.
p.s.×Henderson, M. W., TD (*t*) (*Hon. Lt. in Army* 9*Aug*.01) 11July08

Major,
Simpson, A. P. 1Nov.12

Captains. (8)

p.s.Ogilvy, S. G. 10Dec.04
Sutherland, D. M. 1Apr.08
Hutchison, T. W. 29May09
Wolfe, G., jun. (*H*) 8Oct.10
Gray, A. J. 17Feb.11
Mason, J. 1Nov.12
Bartle, T 1Dec.12

Lieutenants. (5)

Forsyth, T. 8Oct.10
Anderson, J. M. M. 28Feb.12
Johnston, J. T. 28Feb.12
Wright, J. 1Nov.12
Mungle, J. 1Dec.12

2nd Lieutenants. (4)

Milne, W. Ⓢ 5Apr.11
Richard, A. M. 28Feb.12
Wakelin, H. 5Nov.13
Stuart, A. A. 25Nov.13
Brown, R. A. 9Jan.14
Henderson, J.R. 9Feb.14
Robertson, A. 18June14

Adjutant.
Jackson, E. D., Capt. K.O. Sco. Bord., 1Nov.13

Quarter-Master.
×Grassick, G. L., *hon. lt.* 26June12

Medical Officers.

p. Kirk, Lt.-Col. R., *M.D.*, VD, R.A.M.C. (T.F.) (*attd.*) 4Nov.05 9July82
p. Young, Maj. W., *M.B.*, VD, R.A.M.C. (T.F.) (*attd.*) 25Sept.08 10Mar.88
p. Cross, Capt. R., R.A.M.C. (T.F.) (*attd.*) 25Sept.08 2Apr.04

Chaplain.

Lindsay, *Rev.* J., *M.A.* [U.F.C.] Chapl. 2nd Class T. F.) (*attd.*) 3June11 3June96
[Uniform—*Scarlet.* Facings—*Blue.*]

THE QUEEN'S (ROYAL WEST SURREY REGIMENT).
Regimental District No. **2** [No. **10** District.

The Cypher of Queen Catherine, within the Garter. In each of the four corners the Paschal Lamb with motto
"*Pristinæ virtutis memor.*"
"*Vel exuviæ triumphant.*" A Naval Crown, superscribed "1st June, 1794."
The Sphinx, superscribed "Egypt."
"Tangier, 1662-80," "Namur, 1695," "Vimiera," "Corunna," "Salamanca," "Vittoria," "Pyrenees,"
"Nivelle," "Toulouse," "Peninsula," "Ghuznee,1839," "Khelat," "Afghanistan,1839," "South Africa, 1851-2-3,"
"Taku Forts," "Pekin, 1860," "Burma, 1885-87," "Tirah," "Relief of Ladysmith," "South Africa, 1899-1902."

Regular and Special Reserve Battalions.
Uniform—Scarlet. Facings—Blue. Agents—Messrs. Cox & Co.

1st Bn. } (2nd Foot) { *Bordon, Hants. (for Woking).* | 3rd Bn. (2nd R. Surrey Mil.) .. *Guildford.*
2nd „ } { *Roberts' Heights, Transvaal.* |

Depôt .. .. .. *Guildford.* Record Office .. *Hounslow.*

Territorial Force Battalions.
th Bn. .. .. .. *Croydon.* | 5th Bn. .. .. *Guildford.*

Colonel .. .. Kelly-Kenny, Gen. *Sir* T., *G.C.B., G.C.V.O.,* ret. pay, *p.s.c.* [R] 16Apr.02

1st and 2nd Battalions.
Lt.-Colonels. (2)
2Coles, M. C. 2Oct.12
1Warren, P. 2Mar.13

Majors. (8)
⚔ 1Pilleau, H. C., *D.S.O.* 16Sept.05
s. Pell, B. T., *D.S.O.* 29Sept.06
s. Wilkins, H. St. C., *p.s.c.* [*l*] 2Mar.09
2Crofts, L. M. 17Feb.12
2Bottomley, H. R. 2Oct.12
4Aug.02

(3) 1Warden, H. F. (Comdg. Depôt) 2Mar.13
s. Mudge, A. 24Sept.13
s. Kenrick, G. E. R. *D.S.O., p.s.c.* 4Feb.14

Captains. (14)
s. Tufnell, A. W., *p.s.c.* [*l*] 7May00
2Whinfield, H. C. 3July00
1*Wilson, C. E., Adjt.* 24Aug.01
c.o Smith, H. W., *D.S.O.* 24Aug.01
r. Tringham, A. M., *D.S.O., p.s.c.* 22Jan.02
s. Mangles, R. H., *D.S.O., p.s.c.* 20Feb.02
E. B., *p.s.c.* 11Nov.02
bt. maj. 10May13
1Heath, M. G. 3Jan.03
c.o. ⚔ *Wright, W. D., p.s.c.* [*l*] 22Jan.03
(3) 1McNamara, A. E., *p.s.c.* 22Jan.03
s. *Vesey, I. L.B., p.s.c.* 22Jan.03
1Watson, C. F., *D.S.O., p.s.c.* 7July03
e.a. *Koebel, C.E.* 8Nov.03
s.c. Stenhouse, H. W. 20May06
26Mar.04
s. Rainsford-Hannay, J. 5Oct.04
4Alleyne, W. H. 2Jan.07
e.a. *Bacon, C.R.K.* 2Aug.10
—1Stanley-Creek, ⚔ 50
R.F.S. 2Aug.10
2Weed*ug,* T. 29Sept.10

Captains—contd.
(8) 2Fearon, P. J. 15Oct.10
1Clarke, R. G. 22Jan.11
1Watson, S. T. 22Jan.11
1Hunter, H. N. A. 22Jan.11
2Lewis, H. F. 23Jan.11
1Dyer, G. N. 29Aug.11
c.o. Adams, G. S. C. 28Mar.12
(3) 2Roberts, F. J. 28Mar.12
e.a. *Maude, E. W.* 18Apr.12
c.o. Feneran, E. C. 18Apr.12
2Master, H.F.H. 19Apr.12
s.c. Lee, R. T. 2Mar.13
(1) *Longbourne, F. C.* 2Mar.13
t. Parnell, G, 2Mar.13
2Esdaile, P. C. 2Mar.13
2Fuller, W. B. 8Mar.13

Lieutenants. (20)
s. *Haddon-Smith, W. B.* 22Jan.07
v. Henriques, R. L. Q. 4Dec.07
2Roberts, A. N. S. 15Feb.08
3Dec.04
1Foy, M. V. 8May09
2Heath. R. L. G. 1Jan.10
t. Hamilton, A. P. 29Sept.10
(3) 1Denton, F. W. H. 15Oct.10
1Kenny, B. M. 15Oct.10
c.o. Giffard, G. J. 22Jan.11
(3) 2Kemp-Welch, M. 22Jan.11
1Pringle, R. S. 23Jan.11
1Boyd, J. D. 10Feb.11
c.o. Oldfield, G.C.O. 1Apr.11
c.o. Beattie, A. E. 29Aug.11
f.c. Mackworth, J. D. 6Dec.11
2Browne, J. A. L. 28Mar.12
2Haigh, C. R., *Adjt.* 18Apr.12
1Pain, M. W. H. 19Apr.12
1Hayes, W. 4Oct.12
1Basset, R. A. M. 1Nov.12
2Thomas, A. C. 1Feb.13
1Hull, H. C. E. 2Mar.13
1Iremonger, H. E. 8Mar.13
2Wilson, D. R. 8Mar.13
2Bethell, E. W. 8Mar.13
2 Williams H.C. 11Jan.14
2Olliver, G. K. 25Apr.14

2nd Lieutenants. (12)
2Furze, E.K.B. 22May12
1Drew, E. D. 22May12
2Ingram, G. S. 3Sept.12
1Eastwood, F. M. 4Sept.12
1Strong, R. H. B. 4Dec.12
2Ross, R. K. 5Feb.13
1Buchan, T.O.M. 24May13
2Bird, J. G. H. 24May13
2Philpot, R. H. 3Sept.13
2Gabb, G. M. 3Sept.13
2Blount, C. H. B. 17Sept.13
2Collis, J. G. 25Feb.14

Adjutants.
1Wilson, C. E., *capt.* 8Oct.11
2Haigh, C. R., *lt.* 11Jan.14

Quarter-Masters.
r. Nicholson, W.H. 16Feb.01
hon. capt. 8Sept.09
2Wort, C. H. J. 11May04
1Wallis, M. S. 28June11
hon. lt. 29Mar.11

Special Reserve.

2nd Lieutenants.
Thompson, H. J. P. (*local Capt., O.T.C.,* 4 *Oct.* 13) 25May10
Cooper, C. 28June11
Ashcroft, A. A. 30Sept.11
Rose-Troup, J. M. 10Apr.12
Bushell, C. 17Apr.12
Tanqueray, T. (*attd. O.T.C.*) 8May12
Pound, M. S. 5June12
Hayes, J. B. 29Jan.13
Green, W. R. C. 15Mar.13
Burkitt, F. T. 15Mar.13
(on prob.) 4June13
Hunt, F. R. W. *(attd, O.T.C.)* 14June13
Heinekey, R. S. 14June13
Davies, R. E. 2Aug.13
Holmes, T. S. *(on prob.* 4July14

3rd Battalion.
Officers serving on 1 *Apr.* 02 *in the corresponding Militia unit hold honorary Army rank equivalent to the Militia regimental rank they then held. Other officers entitled to honorary Army rank have it shown against their names.)*

Hon. Colonel.
p.s. ⚔ *Fairlough, F. H. C.M.G. (Hon. Col. ret. Mtla.) (Hon Lt.-Col. in Army* 2Apr.02) (*H*) 6Sept.08 13Dec.08

Lt.-Colonel.
p.s. ⚔ *Shaw, A. G.* 23Oct.11

Major.
r.e. ⚔ *Warden, H. F.* 2Mar.13
⚔ *Porter, A.S.M.,*
Capt. ret. pay [*l*]
(*a*) (*b*) (*H*) *p.v.c.* 1Oct.13

Captains. (5)
r.e. ⚔ *McNamara, A.E., p.s.c.* 22Jan.03
p.s. Barton, E. DeL. *(H)* 10June07
p.s. Thornycroft, J. R. M. (*H*) 1Apr.c8
⚔ *Lambert, A. F.,*
Capt. ret. pay 19Aug.08
⚔ *Storey, F. B., Capt. ret. pay* 1Nov.09
11Jan.13
r.e. ⚔ *Fearon, P. J.* 15Oct.10
r.e. ⚔ *Roberts, F. J.* 28Mar.12
Hodgson, C. B. M. *(t)* (*H*) 1Oct. 13

Lieutenants, (11)
r.e. *Den*ton, F. W. H. 15Oct.10
22Jan.11
Hodgson, H. E. A. 1Dec.11
Phillips, W. A. 1Dec.11
White, G. A. 18Sept.12
Rawson, F. P. S. 1June13

| 913 | 914 | 915 | 916 |

THE QUEEN'S (ROYAL WEST SURREY REGIMENT)—(Regtl. Dist. No. 2)—contd.

3rd Bn.—contd.

2nd Lieutenants. (8)
Seaton, J. A. M. 10Feb.12
Connor, F. G. (on prob.) 1Apr.13
Trench, P.R.O. 10Oct.13
Ive, D. 10Oct.13
Hopkinson, J. A. L. (on prob.) 10Oct.13
Schunck, R. H. (on rrob.) 5Nov.13
Brown, D. A. (on prob.) 14Mar.14
Le Bas, O. V. (on prob.) 1Apr.14

Adjutant.
✗Tringham, A. M., D.S.O., Capt. R. W. Surr. R. 4Dec.11
(*Capt. in Army* 22Jan.02)

Quarter-Master.
✗Nicholson, W. H., *hon. capt.*

4th Battalion.

"South Africa, 1900-02."

Croydon.

Hon. Colonel.
Edridge, Sir F. T., Knt. 7Apr.06

Lt.-Colonel.
✗Cutler, N. E. (*Hon. Lt. in Army* 9 Oct. 02) 15Aug.09

Majors (2)
Roper, S. D. 19Mar.08
Hooke, U. L. (H) 6July10

Captains. (8)
p.s. Wise, C. W., (a) (Q) (H), I. of M. 27Mar.07
p.s. Atkins, H. R. ⓢ 17Oct.08
Potter, R. W., (H) 14May09
Gosney, H. J. (H) 15Aug.09
p.s. Oswald, K. A. 15Aug.09
Bennett, G. R. 28Nov.11
Dibdin, L. G. (H) 17Feb.12
Hooker, W. S. (q) (H) 8Mar.14

Lieutenants, (8)
Crowley, J. C. 18Sept.08
Keith, S. 15Aug.09
Helps, M. D. 17Dec.10
Turner, W. 17Dec.10
Evans, B. L. 28Nov.11
Jefferis, A. R. 28Sept.12
Featherstone, O. 17May13
Williams, J. C. 28Mar.14

2nd Lieutenants. (8)
Fearon, J. G. 17June10
Turner, E. L. 24June10
Potter, A. G. 2Dec.10
Pryce, W. H. 12June12
Falcon, R.R.B. ⓢ 28Nov.12
Brown, E. J. 12Mar.13
Moss, R. L. 18June13
Kingzett, E.P. 25Sept.13
Potter, D. R. 9May14
Birley, G. H. 20May14

Inst. of Musk.
Wise, C. W., *capt.* 1Dec.09

Adjutant.
✗Orpen-Palmer, H.B.H., Capt. R. Ir. Fus. [l] 1Nov.12

Quarter-Master.
✗Greer, J., Qr.-Mr. (*hon. maj.*) ret. pay, *hon. maj.* 16Dec.11

Medical Officers.
p. Paget, Capt W. G., R.A.M.C. (T F.) (attd.) 25Feb.10
Morris, Lt. E. M., R.A.M.C. (T.F.) late Capt. Unatt. List (T.F.) (attd.) 20Mar.14

Chaplain.
Dodds, *Rev.* M.T., M.A., Chapl. 4th Class (T.F.) (attd.) 22June12

[Uniform—Scarlet,
Facings—Blue.]

Cadet Unit affiliated.
West Croydon Cadets.

5th Battalion.

"South Africa 1900-02."
Guildford.

Hon. Colonel.
Ashcombe, Rt. Hon. G., Lord 23June94

Lt.-Colonel.
p. Brodrick, Hon. A. G., TD 1July12

Majors. (2)
p. ✗Waterlow, J. F., D.S.O., TD (*Hon. Capt. in Army* 1Dec.00) 27May08
Sladen, St. B. R., TD (*t*) (H) 20May11
Smallpeice, F. W. 1July12

Captains. (8)
p.e. ✗Few, R. J. (*Hon. Capt. in Army* 30 June01) (Q) (H) 14May02
p. Thompson, G. M. ⓣ 24Oct.03
p. Tredgold, A.F. 25Jan.07
p.s. Hodges, W.L. 3May07
✗Harris, H. H. M., late Capt. High L.I. (*Capt. Res. of Off.*) 25Feb.09
p. Stacey, M. B. 7Jan.11
Master, C. E. H. 1July12
Bray, F. E. 28Nov.12

Lieutenants. (8)
(p.s.)Dodson, C. W. (*local Capt. O.T.C.* 15Jan.10) (q) 28June09
Gabb, H. P. 17Aug.10
Whittington, P. R. 8 Jan.11
Whittington, L. 26Jan.11
Yetts, L. M. 30June10
Atkinson, R. L. 20May11
Perkins, W. J., *jun.* ⓢ (q) 1Nov.11
Shilcock, J. W. 1July12
Jardine, J.E.B. 23Nov.12

2nd Lieutenants. (8)
Spens, W. P. 20Jan.12
Mountford, E. W. 17Feb.12
Cleverly, O. S. 11Sept.12
Jardine, L. W. 16Nov.12
Ardagh, F. D. 25Jan.13
Braithwaite, G. G. 12July13
Longbourne, W. L. J. 9May14

Adjutant.
✗Parnell, G., Capt. R. W.Surr.R. 1Nov.12

Quarter-Master.
p. Harris, W. R., *hon. m.* 6May04 22July10

Medical Officers.
Bailey, Capt. L. D., R.A.M.C. (T.F.) (attd.) 4Aug.13 19June09
Caldicott, Capt. C. H., M.B., R.A.M.C. (T.F.) (attd., 22Jan.14 22July10

Chaplains.
Kirwan, *Rev.* E. C., Chapl. 3rd Class (T.F.) (attd.) 8May11 8May01
Burkitt, *Rev.* H. J., M.A., Chapl. 3rd Class (T.F.) (attd.) 4Jan.12 4Jan.02

[Uniform—Green,
Facings—Scarlet.]

Cadet Units affiliated.
The Frimley and Camberley Cadet Corps.
G. and H. (Surrey) Cos., 1st C. B. Hamps. R.

THE BUFFS (EAST KENT REGIMENT).

Regimental District No. **3** No. **10** District.

The Dragon. In each of the four corners the united Red and White Rose ensigned with the Imperial Crown.
"*Veteri Frondescit Honore.*"

"Blenheim," "Ramillies" "Oudenarde," "Malplaquet," "Dettingen," "Guadaloupe, 1759," "Douro," "Talavera," "Albuhera," "Vittoria," "Pyrenees," "Nivelle," "Nive," "Orthes," "Toulouse," "Peninsula," "Punniar," "Sevastopol," "Taku Forts," "South Africa, 1879," "Chitral," "Relief of Kimberley," "Paardeberg," "South Africa, 1900-02."

Regular and Special Reserve Battalions.

Uniform—Scarlet. Facings—Buff. Agents—Messrs. Cox & Co.

1st Bn. } (3rd Foot) { *Fermoy.*	3rd Bn. (East Kent Mila.)	.. *Canterbury*
2nd " } { *Wellington, Madras.*		
Depôt .. .. *Canterbury.*	Record Office	.. .. *Hounslow.*

Territorial Force Battalions.

4th Bn. .. ..*Canterbury.* | 5th Bn. .. .. .. *Drill Hall, Ashford.*

Allied Regiment of Canadian Militia.

2nd Regiment "Queen's Own Rifles of Canada" .. .. *Toronto, Ontario.*

Colonel-in-Chief .. .. *His Majesty,* Christian X., *King of* Denmark, K.G., G.C.B., G.C.V.O. .. 12May14
Colonel .. .. .. Kekewich, Maj.-Gen. R. G., C.B., ret. pay (*Res. of Off.*) q.s. 5Oct.09

1st and 2nd Battalions.

Lt.-Colonels. (2)

1Hill, H. C. de la M.
  4Aug.10
2Geddes, A. D., *p.s.c.* [L]
  7Feb.11

Majors. (8)

1Hulke, L. I. B. 23June06
1Hasler, J. 7Feb.07
  bt. col. 11Jan.10
(3)1Eaton, W. A. (*Comdg. Depôt*) 28Aug.07
1Finch Hatton, E.
  H., *D.S.O.* 4July08
1McDouall, R., *D.S.O.*
  4Aug.10
s.Trevor, W. H. [L]
  7Feb.11
2Porter, C. L. 16Mar.12
2Reeves, F. S. 12Nov.13

Captains. (14)

2Power, R. E. 24Feb.00
1Bright, R. 11Mar.00
2Worthington, C. A.
  20June00
s Findlay, H. 23Oct.00
  bt. maj. 22Aug.02
1Groves-Raines R.
  G. D. 14Feb.03
r. Cresswell, A. S. 20Feb.04
s. James, G. M., *p.s.c.*
  20May08
  30May04
2Tomlinson, F. W.1July04
1Lucas, L. W.,
  Adjt. 7Feb.07
(3)2Norman, E. C. 8Feb.11
t. Collison-Morley,
  H. D., 13Mar.11
1Beovor, H. 10June11
*c.o.*Green, M. W. 21Oct.11
*c.o.*Soames, L. H. 21Oct.11
1Studd, F. C. R. 21Oct.11
2Fort, L. 21Oct.11
*m.c.*Trueman, A. P. H.
  2Mar.12

Captains.—contd.

2Smith, L. H. 19June12
c.o.Crookenden, J. 24July12
c.o.Potter, H. B. 24July12
(3)2Gould,E.G.F.L.24July12
(3)1Friend, R. S. I. 7Sept.12
1Lee, G. 26Feb.13
2Jackson,J.V.R.25Mar.14
t. Hardy, H. 25Mar.14
i.v. Thewles, H. A. 9May14
1Furley, B.E.[L] 5July14

Lieutenants (19).

(8) 2Davidson, C. E. G.
  27Mar.09
1Hall, P. S. B. 15Sept.09
2Hart, N S. 6Apr.10
2Sill, J. S. 25June10
c.o Philips, J. D. 18Sept.10
2Scarlett, Hon. P. G.,
  Adjt. 18Sept.11
c.o.Thomson, A. B. 13Mar.11
1Wheler, T. 18Mar.11
2Anderson,D.K. 1Apr.11
1Cattley, C. F. 10June11
c.o.Allen, J. F. W. 16Sept.11
1Hamilton, G. F.
  21Oct.11
(3) 1Terry, C. E. A.
  30Nov.11
2Morgan, H. de R.
  2Mar.12
2Archer, J. W. B.9Mar.12
c.o.Stronge, H. C. T. [l]
  8May12
2Peareth, A. J. 19June12
2Brice, M.M. [l] 21Mar.14
  1Apr.11
1McDougall, R. 26Aug.12
2Sharp, J. B. 7Sept.12
2Buttanshaw, E. H. U.
  1Oct.12
2Wilkins, D. A. 7Jan.13
1Homan, R. W. 26Feb.13

2nd Lieutenants. (12)

1Thornhill,G.R. 19Jan.12
2 Earle, N. V. 14Feb.12
1Vertue, N. G. 13Mar.12
1Morley, H. C. C.
  22May12
2Howe, G. R. 4Sept.12

2nd Lieuts.—contd.

2Thomas, D. V. 4Sept.12
2Causton, L. P. 25Dec.12
1Jackson, H. W. 22Jan.13
1Bayard,R.A.R. 22Jan.13
2Davis, W. R. 22Jan.13
2Strettell,E.F.D.5Feb.13
1Noott, M. 24May13
(1) Allen, E. H. 24Jan.14
  Adjutants.
2 Scarlett, Hon. P. G.,
  lt. 4 Aug. 11
1Lucas, L. W.,
  capt. 10Oct.12

Quarter-Masters.
r. Stainforth, W. R.
  14Dec.01
  hon. capt. 14Dec 11
2Foster, F. W.,
  hon. lt. 21June13
1Cook, T., *hon. lt.*4Oct.12

Special Reserve.

2nd Lieutenants
Raikes, H. R. 4May12
Silverwood-Cope, A. L.
  (on prob.) 5July13

3rd Battalion.

(*Officers serving on* 17July92 *in the corresponding Militia unit hold honorary Army rank equivalent to the Militia regimental rank they then held. Other officers entitled to honorary Army rank have it shown against their names.*)

Hon. Colonel,
XBrinckman, Sir T.
  F., Bt., C.B. (*Hon. Col, ret. Mila.*)
  (*Hon. Lt.-Col. in Army* 18 July 02)
  28June08
  15July07

Lt.-Colonel.
p.s.XHirst, H. D, (*H*)
  30June12

Major.
*r.e.*XEaton, W. A. 28Aug.07

Captains. (5)
XWells, W. N. (*H*)
  4Mar.06
p.s.XSlacke, R. C.,
  late 2nd Lt. E.
  Kent R.(*H*) 23Dec.07
XChapman, G. A. E.,
  Lt. ret. pay 25June10
XChichester, E. B.,
  Lt. ret. pay 11Aug.10
*r.e.*XNorman, F. C. 8Feb.11
  24July12
*r.e.*XFriend, R. S. I.7Sept.12
p.s.XWard, H. E. (*H*)
  (*Hon. 2nd Lt. in*
  Army 26Sept.92)
  11Jan.13
  15Jan.13

Lieutenants. (11)
Child, R, D. de Q.,
  Lt. ret. pay 23Jan.02
  22Jan.10
r.e. Davidson, C. E. G.
  27Mar.09
Baker, R. H.W.
  26Nov.11
Stanfield,C.C. 26Nov.11
r.e. Terry, C. E. A. 30Nov.11
O'Neal, G. 1June12
Glyn, R. S. 20Jan.13
2nd Lieutenants. (8)
Sargent, L. O. 20Mar.12
Asprey, M. 1Apr.12
Chapman, C. M. B.
  21Dec.12
Wilson, C. T. N.
  W. 5Feb.13
Keeble, W. R. 19Feb.13
Jackson, A. R. 2Aug.13
  12June12
Cronk, W. G. (*on*
  prob.) 14Mar.14
Barham, W. S. (*on*
  prob.) 22July14
Adjutant.
XCresswell, A. S.,
  Capt. E. Kent R.
  1Jan.13
  (*Capt. in Army* 20Feb.04)
Quarter-Master.
XStainforth, W. R.,
  hon. capt.

THE BUFFS (EAST KENT REGIMENT)—(Regtl. Dist. No. 3)—contd.

4th Battalion.

"South Africa, 1900-02."

Canterbury.

Hon. Colonel.
✘Harris, G. R. C., Lord, G.C.S.I., G.C.I.E., TD, Col. A.D.C. 16Mar.89

Lt.-Colonel.
✘Gosling, G. (*Hon. Capt. in Army 10 July* 01) 8Feb.13

Majors. (2)
Skey, E. O. 1Mar.09
Matthews, G. L. 8Feb.13

Captains. (8)
Atkinson, A. 18June04
p.s. Dunstan, F. M. 21May07
p.s. Kingsford, G. M. (*H*)(Q)*I.of M.* 1Aug.09
Heggs, T. B. 1June10
Sherren, A. O. 1June10
Collard, B. S. 26Apr.12
Lomer, H. G. E. 15Nov.13
Grant, L. B. 6May14

Lieutenants. (8)
G gg, A. C. 26Apr.12
Arnold, V. 8Feb.13
Williamson, C. G. 11Oct.13
Harbord, R.E. 15Mar.14
Lowe, A. S. 23Apr.14
Witts, C. S. F. 23Apr.14
Emery, T. S. @ 23Apr.14
Cremer, H. L. H. 23Apr.14

2nd Lieutenants. (8)
Howell, C. J. 13Nov.13
Taunton, R. G. 7Feb.14
Taunton, H. L. 7Feb.14
Dixon, H. O. 13May14
Harrison, W. A. 20May14
Harrison, E. G. 27May14

Inst. of Musk.
Kingsford, G. M., *capt.* 1Oct.10

Adjutant.
Wade, C., Capt. K. O. Sco. Bord. 9Apr.13

Quarter-Master.
Keeler, F. H., *hon. lt.* 25Jan.13

Medical Officer.
Oliver, Maj. H. S., R.A.M.C. (T.F.) (*attd.*) 24Feb.10 2July98

Chaplain.
Sargent, *Rev.* S. H. G., *M.A.*, Chapl. 3rd Class (T.F.) (*attd.*) 21Feb.10 21Feb.00

[Uniform—*Scarlet.*
Facings—*Buff.*]

Cadet Units Affiliated.
New College (Herne Bay) Cadet Corps.

Chatham House (Ramsgate) Cadet Corps.

Herne Bay College, Cadet Corps.

Depôt, Royal Marine Cadet Corps.

5th (The Weald of Kent) Battalion.

"South Africa, 1900-02."

Drill Hall, Ashford.

Hon. Colonel.
p. Hussey, E. W., VD, (*Hon. Col., ret. Vols.*)(*T*) 21Oct.11

Lt.-Colonel.
p. Mace, J. M., TD, (*t*) 1June09

Majors. (2)
Murton, C. D., TD 3June09
✘Knight, L. C. E., Capt. ret. pay (*Res. of Off.*) 8Mar.13

Captains. (8)
p.s. Kingsland, C. P. 24May07
p.s. Clarke, E. 13July07
Fraser, J. S. 1Apr.08
p. Body, J. 13Dec.10
p. Muckley, A. F. 9Feb.12
Cheney, H J. (*H*) 7Jan.05
21Nov.13
Cheesman, A. E. (*H*) 4June14

Lieutenants. (8)
Collings, T. H. O. 25Feb.10
Marchant, F. O. 13Dec.10

Lieuts—contd.
Buss, B., jun. 25Mar.11
Adam, A. G. A. 22Jan.14

2nd Lieutenants. (8)
Wikinson, D. S. 11May12
Blomfield, H. M. 25Dec.12
Waite, J. T. 26Apr.13
Burns, E. B. 14Jan.14

Adjutant.
✘Hardy, H. S., Capt. E. Kent R. 23Jan.13

Quarter-Master.
p. Varty, G. F., TD, *hon. maj.* 22Apr.03

Medical Officers.
p. Paget, Maj. P., R.A.M.C. (T.F.) (*attd.*) 28Dec.07
Collingridge, Lt. 26Feb.96
W. R., R.A.M.C. (T.F.) (*attd.*) 3Dec.13

Chaplain.
Carmichael, *Rev.* D.W.W., *M.A.*, Chapl. 4th Class (T.F.) (*attd.*) 20May14

[Uniform—*Scarlet.*
Facings—*Buff.*]

THE KING'S OWN (ROYAL LANCASTER REGIMENT).

Regimental District No. **4** [No. 3 District].

The Royal Cypher within the Garter. In each of the four corners the Lion of England.
"Namur, 1695," "Gibraltar, 1704-5," "Guadaloupe, 1759," "St. Lucia, 1778," "Corunna," "Badajoz," "Salamanca," "Vittoria," "St. Sebastian," "Nive," "Peninsula," "Bladensburg," "Waterloo," "Alma," "Inkerman," "Sevastopol," "Abyssinia," "South Africa, 1879," "Relief of Ladysmith," "South Africa, 1899-1902".

Regular and Special Reserve Battalions.

Uniform—Scarlet. *Facings*—Blue. *Agents*—Messrs. Cox & Co.

1st Bn. } (4th Foot)	{ Dover.	3rd Bn. (1st R. Lancashire Mil.) .. Lancaster.
2nd "	{ Lebong.	
Depôt ..	Lancaster.	Record Office .. .. Preston.

Territorial Force Battalions.

4th Bn. .. .. *Ulverston.* | 5th Bn. .. .. *Lancaster.*

Colonel-in-Chief .. .. .. THE KING.

Colonel .. .. .. Hunter, Gen. Sir A., G.C.B., G.C.V.O., D.S.O. 26Mar.13.

1st and 2nd Battalions.

Lt.-Colonels. (2)
2Martin, A. R. S., p.s.c. 13Dec.12
1Dykes, A, McN., p.s.c. 1Aug.13

Majors. (8)
f.o, Samson, L. L. R., C.M.G. [L] 10July07
2Anderson, F. W. A. 7Apr.10
1Parker, R. G., 1June06
(3)1Creagh-Osborne, H. P. 26June10
(Comdg. Depôt) 24Oct.11
1Wilson, H. H. [F] 25July12
1Morrah, J. H. 13Dec.12
2Dobson, R. N. 23Apr.13
2Lysons, N. L. S. 1Aug.13

Captains. (14)
s. Jackson, T. D., M.V.O. D.S.O. 7Oct.01
r. Clough, H.K. 22Jan.02
(2) Borrett, O. C. 22Jan.02
1Nixon, J. A. 19Apr.02
s. Browne, A. D. M. 14Sept.04
1Grover, C. W. 15Mar.05
2Joiner, A. G. 14Nov.06
(3) 1Foster, A.H.B. 15Nov.07
s.c. Luckock, R. M 22Jan.07
1Higgins, T.C.R. 10July07
e.a. Conran, O. M. 10July07
1Theobald, F. G. 10July07
2Weatherhead, G. E., Adjt. 8Sept.07
2Kaulbach, H. A. 6Nov.07 18May07
s.c. Gribbon W.H.[I]6Nov.07
1Clutterbuck, H. 20Nov.07
2Bois, J. 20Nov.07
1Cowper, L. I. 20Nov.07
t. Young, J. M. 28Nov.07
2Phillips. C. G. 18Dec.07
2Money, R. 22Aug.09
Sparenborg, H. R. [L] 22Jan.10

Captains—contd.
f.o. Salmond, J. M. 26June10
bt. maj. 22June14
(3)2Hodgson, O. L. 1Jan.11
1Somerville, W. A. e.a. Marshall, C. C. 26Mar.13
(3)2Scott, T. R. 26Mar.13
c.o. FitzGerald, T. O. 29July13

Lieutenants. (19)
2Ray, R. A. 9May06
e.a. 1Pott, A. J. 15Nov.06
i. Booth, F. 6Feb.08
1Uzielli, T. J., Adjt. 22Jan.07
1Keith, G. T. E. 4May07
(3) 1Phelps, R. M. 10July07
2Forwood, T. B. 7Sept.07
c.o. Thornycroft, E. G. M. 2Nov.07
1Robinson, D.C. Bowe 6Feb.08
2Bromiley, J.N. 23Nov.07
2Todd, V. O. 6Feb.08
1Birley, B. L. 15Feb.08
c.o. Finch, H. S. 9Nov.08
1Carter, C. R. 30Dec.09
2Stokes, H. D., M.V.O. 26June10
2Morrell, J. F. B., M.V.O. 1Apr.11
(3) 2Morris, A. G. A. 12Apr.11
p.d. Greenwood, J. F. [l] 24May11
2Rawlinson, L. H. 1Sept.11
1Steele-Perkins, C. S. 12Sept.11
1Woodgate, L. S. 7Oct.11
1Blackburn, G. A. 26Mar.13
c.o. Barclay, G. E. 17Apr.13
2Jebb, H. C. E. 17Apr.13
2Hibbert, L. R. 29July13

2nd Lieutenants. (12)
2Shelley, J. P. 4Oct.10
2Packard, J. E. E. 5Oct.10
2Harford, G.L. 20Sept.11
2Peake, M. C. 20Sept.11
1Irvine, C.G.S. 11Oct.11
2Thorne, W.A.L. 11Oct.11
1Statter, W.E. G. 9Dec.11
2de Cordova, V.L. 14Feb.12
1Matthews, R. C. [l] 4Sept.12
1Burke, E. B. 5Feb.13

2nd Lieuts.—contd.
2Seddon, A. D. 24May13
1Bevan, J. A. 17Sept.13
(1) Aitchison, R. A. C. 17Sept.13

Adjutants.
1Uzielli, T.J., lt. 11Aug.11
2Weatherhead, G. E., capt. 28Oct.12

Quarter-Masters.
r. Jepson, C. W. 1July96
hon. maj. 1July11
1Wilson, G. 24Feb.00
hon. capt. 24Feb.10
2Johnson, T. H., hon. lt. 20Apr.04

Special Reserve.

Captain.
de Carteret, H. J. T., Lt. ret. pay 29Dec.13

2nd Lieutenant.
Broadhurst, A. G. W. (on prob.) 21Mar.14

3rd Battalion.

(Officers serving on 5Feb.02 in the corresponding Militia unit hold honorary Army rank equivalent to the Militia regimental rank they then held. Other officers entitled to honorary Army rank have it shown against their names.)

Hon. Colonel.
✗North, B. N., C.B., M.V.O. (Hon. Col. late Mila.) (Hon. Lt.- Col. in Army 6 Feb. 02) 19July06

Lt.-Colonel.
✗Graham. J. M. A., D.S.O., Capt. ret. pay (H) 11May13

Major.
r.e. ✗Creagh-Osborne, H. P. 24Oct.11
p.s. ✗Worsley-Taylor, J. (Hon. Capt. in Army 4 Aug. 01) 11May13

Captains. (5)
p.s. ✗Harper, A. G. M. N. (Hon. Capt. in Army 4 Aug. 01) (Asst. Dist. Offr., S. Provs., Nigeria, { 1 Jan. 14 { 2 May 08) 24Dec.00
p.s. Nornabelle, J. S. (H) (b) 28May02
✗Hibbert, W. C. T., Capt. ret. pay 21June05
r.e. ✗Foster, A. H. B. 15Nov.06
r.e. Hodgson,C.L. 1Jan.11
r.e. Scott, T. R. 26Mar.13
c.o. ✗Wright, H. S., late Lt. R. Lanc. R. (Asst. Dist. Commr., E. Afr. Prote. { 15 July 14 { 26 July 11) 11May13
p.s. Nixson, H. L. (H) f.c. 11May13
Berkeley, J, J. F. (H) 18June13
r.e. Phelps, R.M. 13July07
p.s. Coulston, J. H. C. 1Apr.09
r.e. Morris, A.G.A. 12Apr.11
Jamieson, J. P. 1Apr.12
Bridson, C. E. R. 1Aug.12
Stevens,C.E.B. 1Aug.12
Douglas, A. S. D. B. 27Sept.13
Hardy, J. H. 28Nov.13

2nd Lieutenants. (6)
Beaumont, G. R. R. (on prob.) 2Aug.13
Aston, K. (on prob.) 9Aug.13
Brammall, L.H. 8Aug.13
Goodwin, J, C. 3Dec.13
Barnes, F. G. L. 21Feb.14
Brockelbank, L. S. (on prob.) 20May14
Baker, C. F, T., (on prob.) 4July14

Adjutant.
✗Clough, H. K., Capt. R. Lanc. (Capt. in Army 22Jan.02) 1Jan.13

Quarter-Master.
✗Jepson, C. W., hon. maj.

THE KING'S OWN (ROYAL LANCASTER REGIMENT) (Regtl. Dist. No. 4)—contd.

4th Battalion.

"South Africa, 1900-02."

Ulverston.

Hon. Colonel.
Cavendish, Rt. Hon.
Lord R. F., Lt.-Col.
5 Bn.   4Mar.11

Lt.-Colonel.
p. Wadham, W.F.A., VD.
(*Capt. Res. of Off.*)
ⓟ (*H*)   6Oct.12

Majors. (2)
p. Pooley, E. B. (*t*)3June11
p. Thompson, R. (*t*)
(*H*)   6Oct.12

Captains (8)
Barnes, N. E. (*H*)(Q)
26Oct.04
p. ✗Wadham, G. D. (*Hon.
Capt. in Army*
26July02)   10Oct.06
p.s. Little, R. P. (*H*)
20Aug.07
p. ✗Caddy J., *late Lt.
R. Lanc. R.,
(H*)   20Aug.07
p. Barratt, W. D, 3June11
p. Pearson, W. G. ⓟ (*H*)
3June11
Barrow, J. V.   1July14

Lieutenants. (8)
McNaughtan, D L.
4Nov.09
Balfour, G. B. (*H*)
4May10
Fothergill, J. S.
(*Empld. under
Federated Malay
States Rlys.*)
18 Oct. 13)   4May10
Morrell, R. D'A.6Sept.12
Mawson, J. M. (*H*)
6Sept.12
Kennedy, W. H.
B. R.   1May14

2nd Lieutenants. (8)
Huthwaite, H. Y.
10Feb.13
Beardsley, A.   13Feb.13
Fisher, J.   12Mar.13
Walker, G. H. 12May13

Adjutant.
Jackson, V. A., Capt.
York & Lanc. R.
1Jan.14

Quarter-Master.

Medical Officer.
Rutherford, Maj. A. F.,
M.B., R.A.M.C. (T.F.)
(*attd.*)   1Feb.14
12Nov.10

Livingston, Lt. J.,
F.R.C.S. (*Edin.*),
R.A.M.C. (T.F.)
(*attd.*)   23May14

Chaplains.
Leonard, Rev. J. G.,
M.A., Chapl. 4th
Class (T.F.) (*attd.*)
1Apr.06
28Apr.06

[Uniform—*Scarlet*,
Facings—*Blue*.]

5th Battalion.

"South Africa, 1900-02."

Lancaster.

Hon. Colonel.
✗Hunter, *Gen.* Sir A.,
G.C.B., G.C.V.O.,
D.S.O., Col. R.
Lanc. R.[R] 27Feb.01

Lt.-Colonel.
Cavendish, Rt. Hon.
Lord R. F, (*Hon.
Col. 4 Bn.*)   28Aug.08

Majors. (2)
p. Bates, J. H. (*H*)
14June08
Cadman, E. C.,
*late 2nd Lt.
W.I.R.* (*H*)   1May14

Captains. (8)
p. Kean, J. H.   8Nov.02
Sharpe, G. W. 1Sept 10
p. Wright, W. O. 28Sept.10
p. Atkinson, E. 15Jan.13
p. Seward, F. W. 27Feb.13
p. Fawcett, W.   1May14
Eaves, F.   1May14
Bingham, F.M. 2May14

Lieutenants. (8)
Carter, W. A. R.
20July11
Parsons, W. J. 20June12
Jeffrey, N. S., *late
Capt.* R.A.M.C.
(T.F.)   17Aug.12
Simpson, C. V. M.
16Jan.13
Deed, W. R. W.
(*attd. O.T.C.*) 11Mar.13
Preston, R. J. H.
1May14
Mather, R.   26May14
Evans, E. M. L. 26May14

2nd Lieutenants. (8)
Dochard, A. A. 19Dec.12
Milnes, G. C.   1May13
Seward, A. S. 12June13
Coupland, H.   1Jan.14

Adjutant.
Young, J. M., Capt.
R. Lanc. R.   1Jan.13

Quarter-Master.
Hodgkinson, A.,
hon. lt.   9July09

Medical Officers.
Falkner, Lt. A. H.
R.A.M.C. (T.F.)
(*attd.*)   26Nov.10
George, Lt. W.,
M.B., R.A.M.C.
(T.F.) (*attd.*) 13Dec.13

Chaplain.
Bonsey, Rev. W. H.
B.A., Chapl. 4th
Class (T. F.) (*attd.*)
17May06

[Uniform—*Scarlet*,
Facings—*Blue*.]

THE NORTHUMBERLAND FUSILIERS.
Regimental District No. 5 [No. 5 District.]

St. George and the Dragon. In each of the four corners the united Red and White Rose slipped ensigned with The Royal Crest.
"*Quo fata vocant.*"

"Wilhelmstahl," "St. Lucia, 1778," "Roliça," "Vimiera," "Corunna," "Busaco," "Ciudad Rodrigo," "Badajoz," "Salamanca," "Vittoria," "Nivelle," "Orthes," "Toulouse," "Peninsula," "Lucknow," "Afghanistan, 1878-80," "Khartoum," "Modder River," "South Africa, 1899-1902."

Regular and Special Reserve Battalions.
Uniform—Scarlet. Facings—Gosling Green. Agents—Messrs. Cox & Co.

1st Bn.	(5th Foot)	Portsmouth.	3rd Bn. (Northumberland Mil.) Newcastle-on-Tyne.
2nd "		Sabathu.	
Depôt	.. ..	Newcastle-on-Tyne.	Record Office .. .. .. York.

Territorial Force Battalions.

| 4th Bn. | .. .. | Hexham. | 6th Bn. .. | St. George's Drill Hall, Northumberland Road, Newcastle-on-Tyne. |
| 5th " | .. .. | Walker, Newcastle-on-Tyne. | 7th " | .. .. .. Alnwick. |

Colonel.. .. .. ₰. Milman, Hon. Lt.-Gen. Sir G. B., K.C.B., ret. pay .. 2May99

1st and 2nd Battalions.

Lt.-Colonels (2)
2Enderby, S. H. 23Nov.09
   14Oct.10
1Ainslie, H. S. 17Feb.12
   23Nov.13

Majors, (8)
2 Turner, F. C., p.s.c.
  [L] 2Dec,08
   29Nov.00
atman, C., D.S.O.
   17Feb.04
s. Percival, A. J.-B.,
  D.S.O., p.s.c., q.s.
  [F] 15Aug.08
(3) 1Fishbourne, C. E.
  (Comdg. Depôt) 1Sept.09
   29Nov.00
2Moulton-Barrett,
  E. M. 23Nov.09
s. Wood, C.M.A., p.s.c.
  [F] 14Oct.10
2Crispin, H. T. 8Feb.11
   29Nov.00
s. Wright, W.C. 23 Nov.13
Captains, (14)
s. Shoubridge, T. H.,
  D.S.O., p.s.c. 9May00
  bt. lt.-col. 21Feb.14
s. Armstrong, C. A.
   12May00
  bt. maj. 26June02
s. Buckley, B. T., p.s.c.
  [L] 12May00
  bt.maj. 20Feb.01
1Toppin, H.S.[l] 12May00
r. Wild, W. H. 19May00
(3) 2Williams, E. E.,
  D.S.O. 1July00
2Girdwood, A C.
  D.S.O., p.s.c. 1July00
s. Festing, F. L. 28Feb.01
m.c.Wreford Brown, C.
  W., D.S.O. 15Apr.01
1Sandilands, H. R.
   18June01
t.v. Clifford, W., D.S.O.
   12Oct.01
1Gatehouse R. F.
   12Oct.01
(3)(2)Jones,A.C.L.H, 12May00
1Matthews, J. H.
  [l] 12Oct.01
t. Archer, H. W. 26June07
(3)1Gordon, E. B. 22Aug.07
1St. John, B. T. 19June09
s.c, Kershaw, S. H. 1Sept.09

Captains—contd.
t. Cruddas, B. 12Sept.09
1Herbert, W. N.,
  Adjt. 4Jan.11
2Auld, R. T. K., Adjt.
   4Jan.11
2Hart, A. C. 4Mar.11
1Fletcher, R. S. [L]
   4Sept.12
1Forster,E.L.D. 10ct.12
1Selby, B. H. 10ct.12
2Foster, O. B. 11Oct.13
2Gibson, W. 15Oct.13
t. Athill, F. R. I. 15Oct.13
2Gething, B. W. E.
   23Nov.13
2Lamb, R. M. R.27Nov.13
r. Thornton, C. E. 27Nov.13
Lieutenants. (19)
1Booth, R. M. St. J.
   28Aug.04
f.c.1Bonham-Carter, I. M.
   21Sept.04
1Ovans, H. L. 5Nov.04
1Stephen, H. C. 5Mar.05
c.o. Milne-Home, A. C.
   24Sept.08
1Sloper, G. O. 19Feb.09
(3) 1Platt, W., D.S.O.
   19June09
✠Cogan, C. T. S. 1Sept.09
1Watkin, F. E. 4Sept.09
2Sidney, P. 4Jan.11
2Leverson, G. R. F.
   18Feb.11
(1) Garnier, A. P. [l]
   18Feb.11
t. Nicholls, H. L. F.
   18Feb.11
(3)2Chenevix-Trench,
  J. F. 4Mar.11
2Baxter, E. H. 10ct 11
2Rushbrooke, W P.H.
   23Dec.11
c.o. Salier, E. L. 10Apr.12
2Brownlow, W. H. C.
  [l] 4Sept.12
2Sutherland, H. O.
   1Oct. 12
2Molineux, G. K.
   1Nov.13
2Heyder, H. M. 20Nov.13
2Mahon, B. E. S.23Nov.13
1Vachell, R. T. 27Nov.13
2nd Lieutenants. (12)
2Barkworth, H. R.
   4Mar.11
1Barrett, L. A. 15Mar.11
2Williams, K.G.14Feb.12
1Swaine, E. S. 14Feb.12

2nd Lieuts.—contd.
1Boyd, E. F. 3Sept.12
1Gunner, B. G. 4Sept.12
2Legard, G. P. 23Jan.13
2Powell, H. I. 23Jan.13
2Cramsie, A. B. 5Feb.13
2Corbet-Singleton,
  F. B. 24Jan.14
1Buckley, E. G. M.
   24Jan.14
2Markham,C.H.24Jan.14
(1)Dorman-Smith,
  E. E. 25Feb.14
Adjutants.
1Herbert, W. N.,
  capt. 10ct.12
2Auld, R. T. K., capt.
   27June13
Quarter-Masters.
r. Wallace, J. 28Mar.00
  hon. capt. 28Mar.10
1Landen, R. A. 16Mar.01
2Allan. W, M. 14May04
  hon. capt. 16May.11

Special Reserve.
Lieutenant.
✠Hervey-Bathurst,
  B. E., late Lt. Bord.
  R. 19Apr.13
2nd Lieutenants.
Edwards, C. J., (on
  prob.) 2Apr.13
Kingdon. L.
  (on prob.) 12Nov.13
Thompson, C. J.
McK. 18Apr.14
Lawson, J. O.
  (on prob.) 6May14

3rd Battalion.

(Officers serving on 8July01 in the corresponding Militia unit hold honorary Army rank equivalent to the Militia regimental rank they then held. Other officers entitled to honorary Army rank have it shown against their names.)

Hon. Colonel.
Northumberland, Rt.
  Hon. H., Duke
  of, K.G., VD, (Col.
  late Mila.), A.D.C.
   2Aug.08
   8Feb.99

Lt.-Colonel,
✠Roundell, R. F.
   6Mar 14
Major.
r.e.✠Fishbourne, C.E.'
   1Sept.09
   29Nov.00
p.s.✠Burdon, E. G. G.,
  (H) 6Mar,14
Captains, (5)
r.e.✠Williams, E. E.,
  D.S.O. 1July00
✠Rickman, A. W.,
  (Q) (H) ⓔ 22Apr.01
r.e.✠Jones, A.C.L.H.
   20Jan09
   12Oct 11
(3)✠Lloyd, M. 8Nov.05
Hawkes, O. P. 1Nov.06
r.e.✠Gordon, E.B. 22Aug.07
Lieutenars. (11)
Holderness, G. C.,
  Lt. ret. pay 21May02
   9Aug.13
Lambert, J. M. 1Nov.06
r.e.✠Platt, W., D.S.O.
   19June09
Lamb, E. J. 6June10
r.e.Chenevix-Trench,
  J.F. 4Mar 11
Hobbs, B. G. C.
   2Dec.12
Roddam, R. C, (H)
   2Dec.12
Hodgson, C.L. C.
   2Dec.12
2nd Lieutenants. (8)
Surtees, A. B. 23Jan.13
Geddes, F. 1Apr.13
Coles, D. M.
  (on prob.) 25June13
Hoffman, R. H.
  (on prob.) 10ct.13
Van Neck, C. H.
  (on prob.) 10ct.13
Mortished, L. E.
  (on prob.) 14Mar.14
Adjutant.
✠Thornton, C. E.,
  Capt. North'd Fus.
   6June11
(Capt. in Army 27Nov.13)
Quarter-Master.
✠Wallace, J., hon. capt.

THE NORTHUMBERLAND FUSILIERS.—(Regtl. Dist. No. 5)—contd.

4th Battalion.
"South Africa, 1900-02."
Hexham.

Hon. Colonel.
Joicey, E. (Hon. Capt. in Army) Maj. ret.
Mila. 19July13

Lt.-Colonel.
Foster, A. J., (Hon. Capt. in Army, 2 Oct. 00) (Maj. Res. of Off.) Hon. Lt.-Col. late North'd R.F. Res. A.)(T) 19July13

Majors. (2)
Dixon, E., TD 15Sept.10
⊗Stephenson, W. E. (Hon. Lt. in Army 21 June 01)(H) 9Apr.12

Captains. (8)
p. Gibson, B. D. (H) 1Apr.08
⊗Hankin, S., late Lt. 3 Bn.Norf. R. (Q), (H) 29Sept.10
p. Robinson, F. (H) 27Mar.12
Robb, W. (H) 5Dec.12
Robb, J. R. 5Dec.12
Chipper, C. 19Dec.13
Dixon, E. C. 16Feb.14

Lieutenants. (8)
Plummer,L, D.14June10
Logan, R.S.M. 16Nov.12
Webster, R. B. 12Jan.14
Bell, H. .t.l. 1Mar.14

2nd Lieutenants. (8)
Carrick, H. M. 4Oct.13
Goodall, H. 24Nov.13
Joicey, C.M. 17Mar.14
Ayton, M. 25Apr.14
Hunting, G. L. 16May14

Adjutant.
Cruddas, B., Capt.
North'd Fus.
11Dec.13

Quarter-Master.
⊗Wynnsford, W. H., hon. lt. 16Apr.12

Medical Officers.
Routledge, Lt. R.L., M.B., R.A.M.C. (T.F.) (attd.) 26Nov.11

Chaplain.
Wilkinson, Rev. L. J., M.A., Chapl. 3rd Class T.F. (attd.) 28May12
28May02

[Uniform—Scarlet.
Facings—Gosling Green.]

Cadet Unit affiliated.
The Haltwhistle Cadets.

5th Battalion.
"South Africa, 1900-02."
Walker, Newcastle-on-Tyne.

Hon. Colonel.
Ridley, M.W., Visct., Lt.-Col. North'd Yeo. 30Mar.10

Lt.-Colonel.
MacDonald, D. R. 5Oct.10

Majors. (2)
Myles, D. (t) 13Oct.11
Carlile, T. J. 1July12

Captains. (8)
p.s.Harle, W. E. 19July10
p. Luhrs, H. 8Dec.10
p.s.Nash, F. O. C. (Q) (H) 3Apr.11
Irwin, A. 10Jan.12
⊗Armstrong, G. 10Apr.13
Phillips, P. P. 11Apr.13
Forrett, P. D. 12Apr.13
Stobart, W. C. S. 25Oct.13

Lieutenants. (8)
Tweedy, I. M. 8June12
Hill, D. 5Dec.12
Stafford, H. L. 20Jan.13
Toovey, A. N. 10Oct.13
Bainbridge, T. L.
Ⓢ 2Oct.13
Kinsella, F. J. 3Oct.13
Dodds, G. W. 4Oct.13
Leask, J. C. 1Jan.14
Fairweather, C. W. 2Mar.14

2nd Lieutenants. (8)
North, N. M. 5Sept.12
Gibson, H. N. 22Feb.13
Graham, W. G. 8Mar.13
Babst, E. 1July13
Syms, F. N. 6Sept.13
Redman, G. S. 20Oct.13
Middleton, G. H. 21Oct.13
Leete, W. H. 2Nov.13
Sinclair, J. G. 1June14

Adjutant.
⊗Soltau-Symons,L.C. Capt. Durh. L.I. 24Sept.11

Quarter-Master.
Holloway, R. J., hon. lt. 17May10

Medical Officer.
p. Grinling, Capt. F. N., R.A.M.C. (T.F.) (attd.) 31Mar.06
6Sept.02
Phillips, Lt. W. J., M.B., R.A.M.C. (T. F.) (attd.) (late Capt. 1 N. Gen. Hosp.) 7Feb.14

Chaplain.
Wardroper, Rev. A. S., Chapl. 2nd Class (T.F.)(attd.) 1May10
1May95

[Uniform—Scarlet.
Facings—Gosling Green.]

6th Battalion.
"South Africa, 1900-02."
St. George's Drill Hall, Northumberland Road, Newcastle-on-Tyne.

Hon. Colonel.
Grey, Rt. Hon. A. H. G., Earl G.C.B., G.C.M.G., G.C.V.O. 5Feb.10

Lt.-Colonel.
p.s.⊗Spain, G. R. B. (Hon. Capt. in Army 22 July 02) (H)19Sept.12

Majors. (2)
Lovibond, J. L.16Mar.12
Hedley, J. R. (H) 19Sept.12

Captains. (8)
p. Sowerby, W.H.14Mar.06
p.s. Hunter, G. E. (Q) 4June08
(q) Ⓠ Ⓢ 4June08
p.s.Dryden, N, McL. (q)® ® 4June08
p.s.Temperley, E. 25May11
p.s.Hunter, H. T. 28Jan.12
p.s.Gracie,A.B.(q)15May12
7Feb.07
Rogers, A. D, S.1June12
Parkinson, G. T. 19Sept.12

Lieutenants. (8)
p.s.Balfour, F. C. C, 1July07
Blayney, O. G. 25May11
Ryott, H. A. 25Nov.11
Burnand, R.F. (H) 19Sept 12
Thompson, A. B. 19Sept.12
Bowden, E. R. 25Dec.12
Noble, W. B. 4Mar.14
Richardson, M. G, F. 4Mar.14
Garton, A. R. 28May14
15July13

2nd Lieutenants. (8)
Judges, F. C. 4Dec.12
Tweedy, T. C. 1Sept.13
Proctor, E. J. 17Oct.13
Harrison, R. F. 26Jan.14
Fawcus, E. A. 26Jan.14
Ramsay, N. B. 27Jan.14
Mather, E. N. 9Feb.14
McLaren, F. M. 9Feb.14

Adjutant.
⊗Athill, F.R.I., Capt. North'd Fus. 1Nov.11

Quarter-Master.
Megoran, W. M., hon. lt. 12June12

Medical Officers.
Harrison, Capt. W. J.,M.B.,R.A.M.C. (T.F.) (attd.) 29Oct.13
29Apr.10
Hunter, Lt. T. C., M.D., R.A.M.C. (T.F.) (attd.) 8Sept.11

Chaplain.
Crawhall,Rev.Canon T. E.,M.A., Chapl. 3rd Class (T.F.) (attd.) 11Sept.09
11Sept.99

[Uniform—Scarlet
Facings—Gosling Green.]

Cadet Unit Affiliated.
Allan's School Cadet Unit.

7th Battalion.
Alnwick.

Hon. Colonel.
p. Northumberland.
Rt. Hon. H. G.,
Duke of, K.G.,
VD (Col, late Mila.)
A.D.C. 30July08

Lt.-Colonel.
⊗Scott, R. (Hon. Capt. in Army 9 July 01) 2Aug.08

Majors. (2)
p. Reavell, G., TD (Q) 4Feb.08
Gillespie, J. J., TD (H) 29June12

Captains. (8)
p.s. Weddell, A. H. M, (H) 1Apr.08
Mitchell, C. (Lt. Res. of Off.) 1Aug.08
p.s. Reynolds, P, G. 25Apr.12
22Aug.09
Liddell, Hon. G. W. (H) 19Oct.12
Milburn, E. W. (H) 1Nov.13
Small, H. R. 1Nov.13

Lieutenants. (8)
Thompson, J. E. N.,late Qr.-Mr. (hon.capt.) 14June11
Merivale, V. 1Nov.13

2nd Lieutenants. (8)
Jobling, G. MacK. 25Jan.13
Watson-Armstrong, Hon.W.J.M. 26Feb.13
Swan, P. C. 18Mar.13
Craigs, W. N. 21June13
Flint, J. A. 4Feb.14
Ridley, F. 1May14
Small, F. W. 27May14
Cowen, F. B. 27May14

Adjutant.
Archer, H. W. Capt.
North'd Fus. 1Jan.12

Quarter-Master.
⊗Neville, R. P.,
hon. lt. 14June11

Medical Officers.
p. Mackay, Maj. W. B., M.D., TD, R.A.M.C. (T. F.) (attd.) 1Aug.03
9Mar.89

Chaplain.
Smith, Rev. C. M.,
Chapl. 4th Class
(T.F.) (attd.) 26June13

[Uniform—Scarlet.
Facings—Gosling Green.]

Cadet Unit Affiliated.
The Morpeth Grammar
School Cadet Company

THE ROYAL WARWICKSHIRE REGIMENT.

Regimental District No **6** [No. **7** District.]

The Antelope. In each of the four corners the united Red and White Rose slipped ensigned with the Imperial Crown.

"Namur, 1695," "Martinique, 1794," "Rolica," "Vimiera," "Corunna," "Vittoria," "Pyrenees," "Nivelle," "Orthes," "Peninsula," "Niagara," "South Africa, 1846-7, 1851-2-3," "Atbara," "Khartoum," "South Africa, 1899-1902."

Regular and Special Reserve Battalions.

Uniform—Scarlet. Facings—Blue. Agents—Messrs. Cox & Co.

1st Bn.	(6th Foot)	Shorncliffe.	3rd Bn. (1st Warwick Mil.)	Warwick.
2nd „		Malta.	4th „ (2nd Warwick Mil.)	Warwick.
Depôt		Warwick	Record Office..	Warwick.

Territorial Force Battalions.

5th & 6th Bns.	Thorp Street, Birmingham.	7th Bn.	Coventry.
		8th „	Aston Manor, Birmingham.

Colonel .. .. .. Feilden, Maj.-Gen. H. B., C.B., ret. pay .. 19June04

1st and 2nd Battalions.

Lt.-Colonels. (2)
1 Elkington, J. F. 6Apr.10
2 Loring, W. L. 24Feb.14
3Feb.12
6Apr.14

Majors. (8)
2 Pigott, V. R. 11Jan.05
(3)1 Toogood, A. S.
(Comdg. Depôt)14Feb.10
1 Poole, A. J. 6Apr.10
2 Forster, G. N. B.
21Oct.11
s. Christie, W. C. [F]
6Nov.12
22Aug.02
s. Brewis, R. H. W.
4Dec.12
1 Day, D. A. L. 24Feb.14
1 Meiklejohn, R. F.,
D.S.O., p.s.c.,
e. [t] 6Apr.14

Captains. (14)
2 Foster, P. J. 19Dec.00
Hart, H.C.
1 Besant, P. E. 22Jan.01
2 Taylour, G. R. 17Feb.01
2 Methuen, C. O'B. H.
19Feb.01
Hassall, O.(Comdt. Detention Barracks)
16Nov.01
r. Blomfield, C.G.M. [t]
15Nov.01
s. Moore, C. D. H.,
p.s.c. 16Nov.01
c.o. Macdonald, C. E.,
p.s.c. 22Mar.02
s. Thomson, H. G. A.
p.s.c. [t] 22Mar.02
s. Lefroy, B. P., D.S.O.,
p.s.c. 2Aug.02
Costeker, J. H. D.,
D.S.O., p.s.c. 3June03
i.v. Marriott, G. B. 1July03
r. Hore, C. B. 10July08
(3) Nevill, C.C. R.18Nov.08
2 Sydenham, E.G.,
Adjt. 22Jan.09

Captains—contd.
1 Sinnott, H. C. 22Jan.09
(3) Haddon, J. B. 24Feb.10
1 Burnard, C. F. 23Mar.10
(3)1 Wood, R. 1Apr.10
c.o. Fox, R.W. 1Apr.10
i.v. Waterworth, G. F.,
D.S.O. 15July10
1 Bannerman, J.A.M.,
Adjt. 14Dec.12
1 Tomes, C. T. 14Dec.12
2 Schooling, E. C.
8Jan.13
2 Whaley, T. 2July13
1 Shelley, E. V. M
24Feb.14
2 Follett, F. B. 14Apr.14
t. Davies, C. E. 14Apr.14
1 Bentley, C. A. C.
17Apr.14
c.o. Fitsell, R. 13May14
2 Peck, A. J. 13May14

Lieutenants. (20)
1 Gilliat, C. G. P.
1Apr.09
t. Davidson, P. V.
19June09
w.a.Dakeyne, H. W.
17Sept.09
(3)1 Knight-Bruce,
J. H. W. 27Oct.09
o.c. Marwood, C. P. L.
24Feb.10
p.d.Thompson, H. H.
1Apr.10
1 Montgomery, B. L.
1Apr.10
(3) 2 Macky, J. B. B. 2Sept.10
p.d.Dible, J. K. V. 28Sept.10
1 Bamber, C.C.[t] 14Dec.10
f.c. Brock, H. L.M. 16Nov.12
2 Duke, J. P. 22Nov.12
1 Onslow, E. M. 14Dec.12
2 Ozanne, W. 25Dec.12
2 Collins, N.B.F. 26Dec.12
2 Brown, I. A. 1Jan.13
1 Walker, H.J.I. 4Jan.13
2 Swinhoe, L. R. 8Jan.13
f.c.2 Moore, B. P. 29Apr.13
2 Ratcliff, J. E. 13Aug.13
2 Knyvett, J. S. 20Aug.13

Lieuts.—contd.
1 Knapton, O. A. 17Oct.13
1 Maunsell, C. F.17Dec.13
1 Wasey, C.W.C.14Apr.14
2 Somerville, G. H. R. B.
13May14
1 Jackson, A. H. K.
25June14

2nd Lieutenants. (12)
1 Chichester-Constable, C. H.J.5Feb.13
2 Matear, N. H. L.
24May13
1 Bretherton, I. T.
17Sept.13
1 Briscoe, E. V. 17Sept.13
1 Dalton, C. E. 10Dec.13
2 Richardson, R. F.
24Jan.14
2 Stainforth, R. T.
24Jan.14
2 Harrison, M.C. 25Feb.14
1 Tillyer, R. B. B.
10June14

Adjutants.
2 Sydenham, E. G.,
capt. 2July13
1 Bannerman, J.A.M.,
Capt. 27Sept.13

Quarter-Masters.
r. Wood, W. 8Dec.97
hon. maj. 8Dec.12
r. Coyne, T. 24Feb.00
hon. capt. 24Feb.10
1 Harwood, T.H. 7Jan.03
hon. capt. 7Jan.13
1 Hyde, W. N., hon lt.
29Dec.09

———

Special Reserve.

Captain.
p.s. Clyne, C. (H)(Q)
(a)(b) 6Oct.06
11Mar.14

2nd Lieutenants.
Surgey, H. N. 1Oct.13
Brindley, P. S. (on prob.) 3June14
Martineau, C. (on prob.) 22July14

3rd Battalion.

(Officers serving on 29Sept.02 in the corresponding Militia unit hold honorary Army rank equivalent to the Militia regimental rank they then held. Other officers entitled to honorary Army rank have it shown against their names.)

Hon. Colonel.
Leigh, F. D., Lord
8June08
16Sept.07

Lt.-Colonel.
p.s. ✕Clyne, J. F. (Q)
(H) p.v.c. (a) ⑧
1June11

Major.
p.s. ✕Hacket, J. L.(H)
20June07
r.e. ✕Toogood, A. S.24Feb.10

Captains. (5)
p.s. ✕Hodgson, C. A. R.
(H)(b) 16Mar.01
p.s. ✕Anstey, H. C. 12Mar.04
p.s. Mulgrue, E. C.
(H) 7May04
✕Mitchell, A. S.,
Capt. ret. pay
(H)⑧ 19Dec.06
p.s. Vaughan, A. D., late
2nd Lt. Welsh R.
(H) 18Sept.07
r.e. ✕Nevill, C.C.R.18Nov.08
r.e. ✕Haddon, J. B.
24Feb 10
r.e. Wood, R. 1Apr'10

THE ROYAL WARWICKSHIRE REGIMENT—(Regtl. Dist. No. 6)—contd.

3rd Bn.—contd.

Lieutenants. (11)
✘Hamilton, R. C.,
  Lt. ret. pay 8Dec.03
    15Sept.09
r.e. Knight-Bruce,
  J. H. W. 27Oct.09
r.e. Macky, J. B. B. Sept.10
Pilkington, L. G.
    27Nov.12
Cowper, C. P. 27Nov.12

2nd Lieutenants. (8)
Boocock, W. N.
    20Jan.12
Bullock, T. M. 9Apr.13

Adjutant.
✘Hore, C. B., Capt.
  R. War. R. 11May12
  (Capt. in Army 10July08)

Quarter-Master.
✘Coyne, T., hon. capt.

4th Battalion.

(Officers serving on 3June01 in the corresponding Militia unit hold honorary Army rank equivalent to the Militia regimental rank they then held. Other officers entitled to honorary Army rank have it shown against their names.)

Hon. Colonel.
Gildea, Sir J., K.C.V.O.,
  C.B. (Hon. Col.
  ret. Mila.) 9Aug.08

Lt.-Colonel.
✘Williams, A. E.
    25Feb.11

Majors. (3)
Maunsell, A. J.S., Maj.
  ret. pay (Res. of Off.)
    8Jan.09
    4Nov.11
p.s.✘Lancaster, J. C.
  (H) 9Jan.09
p.s. Hammack, S. G.,
  late Lt. Hon. Art.
  Co. (H) 7Nov.11

Captains. (6)
Dale, C. H., late
  Lt. R. W. Fus.
    15June09
p.s.✘Longden, W. M.,
  late Lt. A.S.C.
  (H) 22Dec.09
    1Aug.05
✘Browne, G. W.,
  Capt.ret.pay,21Jan.11
✘Lacon, Sir G. H.
  U., Bt., late Lt.
  R. War. R. 16Dec.11
✘Walmisley-Dresser,
  H. J., Lt. ret. pay
    26Oct.12
Brownfield, R. J.,
  Lt. ret. pay 20Aug.13

Lieutenants. (11)
p.s. Miller, G.S. (H)
    1May06
McCormick, J. H. G
  (H) 18Feb.09
Walker, H. E.. late
  2nd Lt. R. War.
  R. 7Feb.12
Lucas, J. M. 13July13

2nd Lieutenants. (8)
Isham, V. A. R. 10Oct.12
Irvine, G. F.
  (on prob.) 25Apr.14

Adjutant.
✘Blomfield, C.G.M.,
  Capt. R. War. R.
  [l] 31Jan.12
  (Capt. in Army 16Nov.01)

Quarter-Master.
✘Wood, W., hon. maj.

5th and 6th Battalions.

"South Africa, 1900-02."

Thorp Street, Birmingham.

Hon. Colonel.
5Hart, C. J., C.B.,
  VD., hon. c. (Q)
  (Hon. Col. ret. T.F.)
    8Oct.09

Lt.-Colonels. (2)
p. 6Martineau, E., VD,
  ⓒ 15Aug.09
p.s.5Parkes, A. I., TD
  (q) (H) 1Apr.14

Majors. (4)
p. Dixon, J. E. TD, (t)
  (H) 1Apr.08
5Pauli, A. W. F.,
  T.D. 22June12
6Danielsen, F. G. (Q)
  [L] 27Aug.13
5Sydenham, E. V.
  (Q) 1Apr.14

Captains. (16)
p. 5Carter, P. H. (Q)
    18July00
p.s.6✘Chatterley, F. M.
  (Hon. Lt. in Army
  9July01) 11June01
p. 6Fyshe, J. A. (t) 7Jan.03
p. 6Parkes, H. H. (t)
    30Oct.03
p. 5Marriott, G. M. (t)
    7May04
p. 6Pitman, H. E. 21May04
p.s.5Lea, E. I. (H) 16June07
p. 6Shannessy, J. J. (q)
    2Jan.08
p. 5Clayton, F. T. (H)
    1Apr.08
p. 5✘Bindloss, E. A. M.
  (Hon. Lt. in Army
  5July02) 1Jan.12
p.s.6Bowater, J. (H)
    20Apr.12
p.s.5Jennens, K.(t) 22June12
5Nuthall, A. W.
  (H) 19Feb.13
6Tombs, W. L. P.
    27Aug.13
6Deakin, F. H. 1Apr.14
5Rabone, J. K. 15July14

Lieutenants. (16)
5Seymour, J. A.
  (local Capt.
  O.T.C. 9June13)
    6Sept.09
(p.)6Forbes, S. W. 6Sept.09
6Turner, A. 30Oct.09
6Davis, K. R. 30Oct.09
5Francis, J. 30Oct.09
5Jeavons, E. V. 30Oct.09
p.s.5Kirkby, W. H. ⓒ
  (H) (local Capt.,
  O.T.C. 1 May09)
    30Oct.09
5Retallack, W. C.
    30Oct.09
5Alabaster, A. S.
    5Apr.10
(p.)Mellor, J. L. 1Jan.12
6Rabone, A. B. 20Apr.12
(p.)5Partridge, C. E.
    4May12
6Crockford, L. C.
    22June12
6Martineau, W.ⓒ
    19Feb.13
6Astbury R. H. 22Mar.13
5Lunt, D. G. 27Aug.13
5Riddell, C. E. 1Apr.14

2nd Lieutenants. (16)
5Suckling, C. V. 1June09
6Elkington, A.D. 7July09
5Edwards, H. W. ⓒ
    3Dec.00
5Bennett, P. D. 10June19
5Gell, W. C. C. 21Jan.13
    12May11
5Keay, E. D. 30Mar.12
5Robinson, P.E. 1Nov.12
6Greener, L. L. 22Mar.13
6Simms, W. 28June13
    1June11
5Showell, J. 28Nov.13
5Edginton, R. W. L.
    28Nov.13
5Powell, J. L. 2May14
    8May11
5Saundby, R.H.M.S.
    15June14
5Forbes, E.W. 29June14

Adjutants. (2)
6Davidson, P. V.
  Lt. R. War. R. capt.
    21Feb.12
5✘Davies, C. E.,
  Capt. R. War. R.
    17Oct.13

Quarter-Masters. (2)
p. 6Yorke, B., TD, hon. m.
    19May05
5Taylor, D., Qr.-Mr.
  (hon. capt.) ret.
  pay, hon. m. 2Dec.11

Medical Officers.
5Hingston, Capt.
  A. A., M.B.,
  R.A.M.C. (T,F.)
  (attd.) 1Oct.11
    1Apr.08
6Wilkinson, Lt.
  K.D., M.B.,
  R.A.M.C.(T.F.)
  (attd.) 23Jan.14

Chaplains.
6Birmingham, Rt.
  Rev. H. R.,Lord
  Bishopof, D.D.,
  Chapl.1st Class
  (T.F.) (attd.) 20Feb.12
5Blofeld, Rev. S.,
  B.A., Chapl. 4th
  Class (T.F.)(attd.)
    14Apr.10
5Fenn, Rev. J. G.,
  B.A., Chapl.
  4thClass(T.F.)
  (attd.) 12June11

[Uniform—Scarlet,
Facings—Blue.]

7th Battalion.

"South Africa, 1900-02."
Coventry.

Hon. Colonel.
Leigh, F. D., Lord
    13June03

Lt.-Colonel.
p.s. Ash, T. F., TD 5Mar.13

THE ROYAL WARWICKSHIRE REGIMENT—(Regtl. Dist. No. 6)—contd.

7th Bn.—contd.

Majors. (2)
⚔Smith, A. P. (Hon. Lt. in Army 30May 01) (t)　18Oct.11

Captains. (8)
p,s.Seabroke, C.　23Aug.05
p. ⚔Knox, J. M. (Hon. Lt. in Army28June02)　23Aug.05
p,s.Hake, H.E., I. of M., H.　20Apr.09
Fayerman, A. G. F. (H)　22June10
Overell, L.D.(H)3Aug.12
Caldicott, J. R.　6July13

Lieutenants. (8)
Hanson, F. S.　13Apr.10
Greg, O. M.　1Jun.11
Sutton, C. G.　18Aug.12
Bushill, W. N.　1Dec.13
Godfrey-Payton, A.　14Dec.13
Thomas, E. H.　25May14

2nd Lieutenants. (8)
Johnson, P. W.16Feb.12
Mason, H. B.　18Mar.12
Hammerton, R. L.　1Oct.12
Johnson, W. G. 28Jan.13
Hoskins, H. R. 18June13
Dumas, A. B.　6Nov.13
Kibler, P. G.　1Mar.14
Bedworth, A.C. 1Apr.14
　　　　　　　20June13

Inst. of Musk.

Hake, H. E., capt.　21Apr.09

Adjutant.
⚔Johnstone, B., Capt. R. W. Kent R.　26Mar.13

Quarter-Master.
p. Jones, B. F., hon. capt.　7May04

Medical Officers.
Krumbholz, Capt. C. J. I., M.B., R.A.M.C. (T.F.) (attd.)　21Apr.11
　　　　　　　13Oct.07
Morris, Lt. A., R.A.M.C.(T.F.) (attd.)　10Nov.12

Chaplain.
Rudgard, Rev. W. D., M.A., Chapl. 4th Class (T;F.) (attd.)
　　　　　　　1Apr.08
　　　　　　　15Mar.07

[Uniform—Scarlet, Facings—Blue.]

Cadet Units affiliated

2 C.B.R. War. R.
Bablake School (Coventry) Cadet Company

8th Battalion.

Aston Manor, Birmingham.

Hon. Colonel.
du Cros, A. P. (H)　22July08

Lt.-Colonel.
Innes, E. A. (t) [L]　17May13

Majors. (2)
Douglas, W. J. (H)　10Oct.09
⚔Tuke, G. H.　1Aug.13

Captains. (8)
p,s.Caddick, A. A. (q) ⓉⒶ　1Apr.08
⚔Townsend, J. N.　10Apr.08
p. Whitehouse, W. E.　11Apr.08
p,s.Whitehouse, P. H.　11Apr.08
　　　　　　　1Apr.08
Laing, W. G.　9Dec.08
p,s.Trowell,A.A.(H)1Oct.09
Simcox, J. R. R. (q)　29Oct.11
Green, H. M. (q) 1Aug.13

Lieutenants. (8)
Temple, H.E. [l] 1Nov.10
Taylor, R. V.　1June11

Lieuts.—contd.

Venables, C. R. 1June12
Haigh, D. H.　1June13
Green, L. H.　1June13
Westwood, W. T.　5July13
Ludlow, S. W. 1Aug.13
Boundy, A. E. ⓑ　21Nov.13
Crisp,C.H. (H) 29Nov.13

2nd Lieutenants. (8)
Bloch, R. A.　21Jan.14
Adams, D. A.　21Jan.14
Whitehill,, R. D.　21Jan.14
Richardson, S. O. B.　4Feb.14
Hoskins, C.　25Apr.14

Adjutant.
⚔Sladen, G. C., Capt. Rif. Brig.　22July13

Quarter-Master.
⚔Taylor, E. D., hon. lt.　10Apr.08

Chaplain.
McKelvie, Rev. R. F. S., Chapl. 4th Class (T.F.) (attd.)　29Apr.12

[Uniform—Scarlet Facings—Blue.]

Cadet Unit affiliated.

1 C.B. R. War. R.

THE ROYAL FUSILIERS (CITY OF LONDON REGIMENT).

Regimental District No. **7**. [No. **10** District.]

The United Red and White Rose within the Garter and the Crown over it.
In each of the four Corners the White Horse.

"Namur, 1695," "Martinique, 1809," "Talavera," "Busaco," "Albuhera," "Badajoz," "Salamanca,"
"Vittoria," "Pyrenees," "Orthes," "Toulouse," "Peninsula," "Alma," "Inkerman," "Sevastopol,"
"Kandahar, 1880," "Afghanistan, 1879-80," "Relief of Ladysmith," "South Africa, 1899-1902."

Regular and Special Reserve Battalions.

Uniform—Scarlet.   Facings—Blue.   Agents—Messrs. Cox & Co.

1st Bn. } (7th Foot) {	*Kinsale* (for Pembroke	5th Bn.(Royal Westminster Mil.) .. *Hounslow.*
2nd „	*Calcutta.* Dock).	6th „ (Royal South Middlesex Mil.) .. *Hounslow.*
3rd „	*Lucknow.*	7th „ (Royal London Mil.)*Artillery Place,Finsbury.*
4th „	*Parkhurst.*	
Depôt	*Hounslow.*	Record Office .. .. *Hounslow.*

Colonel-in-Chief .. .. THE KING.

Colonel .. .. Barton, Maj.-Gen. *Sir* G., *K.C.V.O., C.B., C.M.G.,* ret. pay, *p.s.c.* [R.]   1May00

1st, 2nd, 3rd and 4th Battalions.

Lt.-Colonels. (4)
3duMaurier, G. L. B., *D.S.O.* 29Apr.11
4McMahon, N. R., *D.S.O., p.s.c.* 3May11
1Fowler-Butler, R. 12Mar.12
2Newenham, H. E. B. 18June12

Majors. (16)
2Lyon-Campbell, C, H. D. 22Nov.05
4Mallock, T. R., *D.S.O.* 28Nov.05
3Johnson, A. V. 19Dec.06
1Hely-Hutchinson, R. G. 5May07
1Roberts, A. C. 16Nov.07
s. North, E. B. [*l*] [F] 1Apr.09
2Hancock, M, P.28Nov.09
1Price, B. G., *D.S.O.* 5Mar.10
*c.o.*Sweny, W. F. 25May10
s. Walker, H. A., *p.s.c.* 3Sept.10
26Mar.06
(5) 1Annesley, A,C. (*Comdg. Depôt*)21Dec.10
2Brandreth, L. 3May11
(6) 4Robertson, J. C. [*l*] 4Oct.11
s. Hickie, C. J. 12Mar.12
2Guyon, G. S. 18June12
3Baker, E. M. 12Feb.13

Captains. (28)
4Cole, M. L. S. O.12Jan.01
4Byng, A. M. 16Mar.01
27June00
4Ashburner, L. F., *M.V.O., D.S.O., p.s.c.* 13July01
r. Fisher, J. L., D.S.O. 13July01
4Carey, L.W.Le M.[*i*][F] 13July01
s.c.Jeffcoat, A. C., D.S.O., e. 14Dec.01

Captains—contd.
1Palairet, C. A. H. 2July03
s. May,R.S.,*p.s.c.* [*l*] 3Nov.03
bt. maj. 4Nov.08
*s.c.*2Clarke, M. O. 12Feb.04
r. Villiers-Stuart,P., e. 10Sept.04
t. Stevens, G. A. 10Sept.04
*e.a. Gardner, N.W.*10Sept.04
*w.a.*Brand, E. S. 19Oct.04
2Moore, F. 19Oct.04
*s.c.*3Meinertzhagen, R. 22Oct.04
r. Burnett Hitchcock, H. W. G. 22Oct.04
*m.c.*Frederick, E. B. 22Oct.04
s.c. Lowe, S. J.[L] 9June05
4Forster, H. C. 28Nov.05
(5)2Hodgson, M. R. K. 4May07
*m.c.*Hill, W. P. H. 4May07
t. Rayner, W. B. F. 5May07
(6)3Packe, E. C. 5May07
2Daniell, W. A. B. 28June08
2Wickham, C.H. 28June08
c.o. Elliott-Cooper, G. D'A. 28June08
t. Docker, G. A.M.19Sept.08
*c.o.*Birchall, A. P. 1Oct.08
s. Forster, F. A. 10Apr.09
3Nicholson, E. H. 26Apr.09
4Whinney,H.F. 16Nov.09
1Puzey, A, K. 22Nov.09
(5)1FitzClarence,A. C. 22Nov.09
4Bowden-Smith, W. A. C. 28Nov.09
1Howlett, R., *Adjt.* 16Dec.09
3Williams, I. H. J. 29Jan.10
t. Hawes, G. E. 21Feb.10
c.o. Savile, *C.R.U.* 21Feb.10
(5)2 de Trafford, T. C. 5Mar.10

Captains—contd.
(6)4Pipon, R. H. 3June10
4Attwood, A. F. 1Mar.12
3Ozanne, E, G. 28Apr.12
e.a.Hewitt, A.C. 24Apr.12
1Gubbins, S. 24Apr.12
(6) 3Pope, A. N. 24Apr.12
s.c. 2Hudson, A. C. 26Apr.12
1Chard, W. W. 11May12
3Ford, R. N. 18June12
3Dunnington-Jefferson, *J. A., Adjt.* 4Sept.12
1Alexander, P. R. M. 19Sept.12
2Shafto, *T. D., Adjt.* 1Oct.12
t. Maude, C. G. 1Oct.12
f.c. Shephard, G. S. [*l*] 16Jan.13
t. Needham, D. A. F. 16Jan.13
3Nation, R. F. 25Oct.13
9Jan.13
2Leslie, F. K. 25Mar.14
1Tyndall, W.H. 15Apr.14

Lieutenants. (38)
2Laverton, *R. M.* 7Dec.07
3Smith, E. C. 20Aug.08
3Fenn, A. A. 20Aug.08
3Crankshaw, E. N. S. 19Sept.12
(5)2Cope, T. G. 28Sept.08
c.o.Critchley-Salmonson, R. E. 1Oct.08
1Wilson, P. N.W. 1Oct.08
4Thomas- *O' Donel, G. O'D. F., Adjt.* 6Jan.09
10Apr.09
3Dawes, H. F. 26Apr.09
3Anderson, W.F.20Aug.09
(5)1Routley, R. H. C. 5June12
20 Aug.08
1Goodliffe,G V.22Nov.09
3Lathom-Browne, H. 28Nov.09
2Cripps, H. H. 29Jan.10
4Harding, C. E. H. 16Oct.10
16Dec.09

Lieuts.—contd.
1Charles, A. A. H. 5Mar.10
4Steele, F. W. A. 15Apr.10
4Harter, J. F. 3June10
c.o.Hebden, R. H. 9Nov.10
c.o.Galbraith, J. E. E. 9Nov.10
(6)3Asslin, G. H. 20Jan.11
1Tower, B. C. B. 25May11
1Stapleton-Bretherton, W. S. 18Oct.11
2Hope-Johnstone, H. 1Jan.12
3Beresford-Ash, D.[*l*] 20Jan.12
3Elliott-Cooper, N. B. 7Feb.12
3Pattinson, H. L. 14Feb.12
1Pinching, P. K.19Feb.12
4Cooper, O. S. 1Mar.12
2Tottenham, R, G. 23Apr.12
4Tower, K. F. B. 24Apr.12
4Dease, M. J. 24Apr.12
1Marshall, H. M. 26Apr.12
(6)4Estill, D. E. 4Sept.12
1Parry-Jones, M. M. 19Sept.12
3Waddell-Dudley, R. R. 28Nov.12
2Whitaker, N.R. 6Dec.12
6Jan.09
4Barton, P. G. 15Jan.13
3Legge, H. M. 16Jan.13
3Gostling, B. W. W. 25Mar.14
2Stephen, C. G. 25Mar.14
3Harter, C. J. 15Apr.14

2nd Lieutenants. (24)
2Astley, A G. 30Aug.11
11Mar.11
4Beazley, J. R. 7Feb.12
4Longman, F. 13Feb.12

THE ROYAL FUSILIERS (CITY OF LONDON REGIMENT)—(Regtl. Dist No. 7)—contd.

1st, 2nd, 3rd & 4th Bns.—contd.

2nd Lieutenants—contd.
1Coxhead, M.E. 13Feb.12
4Sampson, F.A. 13Feb.12
3Trasenster, W.A. 13Feb.12
4Mead, J. F. 14Feb.12
1Bell, M. C. 14Feb.12
2Scudamore, J. V. 13Mar.12
2de Trafford, E. E. G. A.
 [l] 13Mar.12
3Griffith, R. V. de B. 13Mar.12
1Cooper, R. F. 13Mar.12
3North, E. S. 4Sept.12
2Mundey, L. C. 4Sept.12
1Groube, L. F. B. 4Sept.12
2Collings, E. P. 19Oct.12
1Sutton, C.L.M. 4Dec.12
2Jebens, F. J. 4Dec.12
2O'Connell, M. J. A. 4Dec.12
2Huggett, H. E. V. 5Feb.13
1Fisher, W.L.T. 24May13
4Jackson, R. R. W. 3Sept.13
2Anstice, J. S. R. 17Sept.13

Adjutants.
3Dunnington-Jefferson, J. A., capt. 1Oct.11
2Shafto, T. D., capt. 1Oct.12
Thomas-O'Donel, G. O'D. F., lt. 15Jan.13
1Howlett, R.,capt.1Oct.13

Quarter-Masters.
r. Nagle, W. J. H. 6Apr.98
 hon. maj. 6Apr.13
1Carter, W. 4Aug.00
 hon. capt. 4Aug.10
r. Metcalfe, H. F.
 hon. lt. 25Mar.08
3Clarke, E., hon. lt. 10Nov.09
4Cross, F. C.,
 hon. lt. 10Sept.10
r. Moss, W., hon. lt. 24Feb.12
2Harding, E., hon. lt. 28Jan.14

Special Reserve.
Captain.
p.s.✠Lembcke, C. E.,
 late Lt. Res. of
 Off. (Hon. 2nd Lt.
 in Army 28 July
 01) [L] [H] 3June11

2nd Lieutenants.
Hardman, F. McM. 22July12
Bunker, S. W.
 (2nd Asst.Govt.
 Analyst,Straits
 Settlements, 17
 May 13) 25Jan.13
Hobbs, F. M. (on prob.) 17Dec.13
Russell, C. H. (on prob.) 4Mar.14

5th Battalion.

(Officers serving on 26July02 in the corresponding Militia until hold honorary Army rank equivalent to the Militia regimental rank they then held. Other officers entitled to honorary Army rank have it shown against their names.)

Hon. Colonel.
Esher, R. B., Visct.,
 G.C.B., G.C.V.O. 16Aug.08

Lt.-Colonel.
✠Henry, V., Maj. ret,
 pay (Res. of Off.) 4May08

Major.
✠Legge, S. F., Maj.
 ret. pay (Res. of
 Off.) 7Mar.06 25May10
r.e. ✠Annesley, A. C., 21Dec.10

Captains. (5)
p.s.✠Penny, A. F. (H) ⓐ 4Apr.98
p.s.✠Cowell, E. J. E. (H) 18June04
p.s.✠Cosens, F. W. U.,
 late Lt.13 Hrs. (H) 28May06
r.e.✠Hodgson, M. R. K. 4May07
r.e.✠FitzClarence,
 A. A. C. 22Nov.09
r.e. de Trafford, T. C. 5Mar.10
Batten, J. B., Capt.
 ret. pay 24Aug.12
✠Lynch-Staunton,
 H. G., Capt. ret.
 pay (Res. of Off.) 11Feb.14

Lieutenants. (11)
r.e. Cope, T. G. 28Sept.08
r.e.Routley, R.H.C.5June12 20Aug.08
Shaw, H. J. (H) 10Ct.10
f.c. Mills, R. P. (H) 10Ct.10
Magnay, P. M. 11Aug.12
Scholefield, R. S. [l]
 late 2nd Lt. Conn.
 Rang. 3Dec.13

2nd Lieutenants. (8)
Malone, H. A. P. 26Mar.13
Foulger, H. C. (Admin.
 Offr. in E. Africa
 27Apr.14) 8Oct.13

Adjutant.
✠Burnett Hitchcock, H. W. G.,
 Capt. R. Fus. 1Jan.12
 (Capt. in Army 22Oct.04)

Quarter-Master.
Nagle, W. J. H., hon. maj.

6th Battalion.

(Officers serving on 15Oct.00 in the corresponding Militia unit hold honorary Army rank equivalent to the Militia regimental rank they then held. Other officers entitled to honorary Army rank have it shown against their names.)

Hon. Colonel.
Edgcumbe, Hon. C. E.,
 late Capt. and Lt.-
 Col. G. Gds. 28June06 11Feb.88

Lt.-Colonel.
Batt, R. C., M.V.O.,
 Capt.ret.pay(Res.
 of Off.) 15Aug.13

Major.
r.e. ✠Robertson, J. C.
 [l] 4Oct.11

Captains. (5)
✠Lucas, W. G., late
 Lt. R. Fus. 10Oct.05
p.s. Turney, L. W. (H) 31Aug.06
Jennings, E. C.,
 Capt.ret.pay[l]6Mar.07
r.e. ✠Packe, E. C. 5May07
✠Waller, Sir F. E.,
 Bt., Capt. ret. pay 22Jan.08
r.e.✠Pipon, R. H., 3June10
r.e.Pope, A. N. 24Apr.12
✠Frewen, T., late
 Capt. Leic. R.
 (H) 3July12

Lieutenants. (11)
Orred, R. G. 4Aug.10
r.e.Asslin, G. H. 20Jan.11
Noel, Hon. R.E.T.M.
 (Asst. Commr. of
 Police, S. Provs.,
 Nigeria, {1 Jan, 14
  {1Sept. 13}) 15July12
r,e, Estill, D. E. 48ept.12
f.c. Morgan, A. E. 29June13
Lucas, G. C. 29June13
Combe, B. A. 29June13
Sandars, S.E. 29June13

2nd Lieutenants. (8)
Westby, H. W T.
 (on prob.) 10July12
Mostyn, W. R. S. 27Nov.12

Adjutant.
✠Fisher, J. L., D.S.O.,
 Capt. R. Fus. 20May12
 (Capt.in Army13July01

Quarter-Master.
✠Metcalfe, H. F.,
 hon. lt.

7th Battalion.

(Officers serving on 18Oct.00 in the corresponding Militia unit hold honorary Army rank equivalent to the Militia regimental rank they then held. Other officers entitled to honorary Army rank have it shown against their names.)

Hon. Colonel.
✠Rudyerd-Helpman,
 R.H.R., Col. (Hon.
 Capt. in Army
 19 Oct. 00) 31July09

Lt.-Colonel.
✠Cockerill, G. K.,
 Maj. ret. pay (Res.
 of Off.) p.s.c. [l] 30 Mar,14

Majors. (3)
✠Hesketh, R. J. I.
 (H) 22Aug.13
7Wells, C. E. (H) 22Aug.13
✠Chichester, Hon.
 A. C. S., Capt. ret.
 pay 30Mar.14

Captains. (6)
p.s. Cartwright, J. C.,
 late 2nd Lt. R.
 Fus. (H) 17June07
p.s. Cartwright, W. R.
 (H) (g) 17June07
p.s. de la Perrelle, J. N.
 (H) 17June07
✠L'Estrange Malone,
 E. G. S., Capt. ret.
 pay 19Sept.08
 21Feb.12
p.s.✠Stead, F. J. (q)
 (H) 20Aug.10
North-Bomford, J.G.,
 Capt. ret. pay 23Oct.12
 18Jan.13

Lieutenants.
p.s. Hayes, C. J. (H)1June08
Dupree, V. 0Aug.10
Walker, H. J. 1Nov.11
Ginman, T. 1Feb.13
Morris, A. (H)
 (l, of M.) 1Feb.13
Carr. F. (Asst. Commr.
 of Police, N. Provs.,
 Nigeria, 1 May 14) 1Feb.13
Hilton, B.G.S. 1Feb.13
Goddard,A.W. 15Feb.14

2nd Lieutenants. (8)
Gorst, E. W. 25Jan.13
Moxon, G. J. M. 1Oct.13
Dennis, A. I. M.
 (on prob.) 1Apr.14
dams, R. N.
 (on prob.) 18Apr.14

Inst. of Musk.
Morris, A., lt. 5May14

Adjutant,
Villiers-Stuart, P.,
 Capt. R. Fus., e. 18Dec.12
 (Capt.in Army10Sept.04)

Quarter-Master.
Moss, W., hon. lt.

THE ROYAL FUSILIERS (CITY OF LONDON REGIMENT)—(Regtl. Dist. No. 7)—contd.

The following Territorial Battalions are affiliated to the Regiment—
for details, see pages 1569 to 1576:—

1st (City of London) Battalion, The London Regiment (Royal Fusiliers)
2nd (City of London) Battalion, The London Regiment (Royal Fusiliers).
3rd City of London) Battalion, The London Regiment (Royal Fusiliers).
4th (City of London) Battalion, The London Regiment (Royal Fusiliers).

The following Cadet Unit is affiliated to the Regiment :—

1st Ca   Battalion, The Royal Fusiliers (City of London Regiment

THE KING'S (LIVERPOOL REGIMENT).
Regimental District No. 8. [No. 3 District.]

The White Horse within the Garter. "*Nec aspera terrent.*" In each of the four corners the Royal Cypher, ensigned with the Imperial Crown. The Sphinx, superscribed "Egypt."

"Blenheim," "Ramillies," "Oudenarde," "Malplaquet," "Dettingen," "Martinique, 1809," "Niagara," "Delhi,1857," "Lucknow," "Peiwar Kotal," "Afghanistan,1878-80," "Burma, 1885-87," "Defence of Ladysmith," "South Africa, 1899-1902."

Regular and Special Reserve Battalions.

Uniform—Scarlet. *Facings*—Blue. *Agents*—Messrs. Cox & Co.

1st Bn. } (8th Foot) { Aldershot.	3rd Bn. .. (2nd R. Lancashire Mil.)	.. Seaforth.
2nd „ Peshawar.	4th „ .. (2nd R. Lancashire Mil.)	.. Seaforth.
Depôt .. .. Seaforth.	Record Office	Preston.

Territorial Force Battalions.

5th Bn. 65, St. Anne Street, Liverpool.	8th Bn. .. 75, Shaw Street, Liverpool.
6th „ Prince's Park Barracks, Upper Warwick Street, Liverpool.	9th „ .. 57, 59 and 61, Everton Road, Liverpool.
7th „ 99, Park Street, Bootle.	10th „ .. 7, Fraser Street, Liverpool.

Volunteer Rifle Corps.
Isle of Man .. .. Douglas.

Allied Regiment of the Australian Commonwealth.
8th Australian Infantry Regiment.

Colonel .. .. C. Clive, Gen. E. H., ret. pay, p.s.c. 30Dec.06

1st and 2nd Battalions.

Lt.-Colonels. (2)
1 Bannatyne, W. S., p.s.c. [L] 17Feb.12
2 Crocker, G. D. 17Feb.12

Majors. (8)
s. Stewart, R. S., p.s.c. [L] 17Feb.04
2 Carter, B. C. M. [F] 8July08
1 Steavenson, C. J. 24Aug.08
17Feb.08
22Aug.02
2 Hyslop, F. 12Dec.08
s. Jones, L. M., D.S.O. 18Sept.09
(3)1 Bailey, V. T. (*Comdg. Depôt*) 17Feb.12
2 Leader, L. F. 30Oct.12
1 Harington. C. H., D.S.O., p.s.c. 15Apr.14
21Feb.12

Captains. (14)
1 Sheppard, T. W. 21Mar.00
c.o. Pinwill, W. R., p.s.c.,e. 21Mar.00
2 Fox, R. P. 21Mar.00
c.o. Hawthorn, G. M. P. 1Sept.00
1 Howard-Vyse, G. A. 7Dec.06
1 Potter, H. C. [F] 1Dec.09
r. Jones, R. C. R. 11Jan.01
2 Gauntlett, V. C. 20May08
s.o. Schuster. L. R. 14Aug.09
(1) Feneran, F. E., 18Sept.12
1 Batten, J. H. S. 1Dec.09
(3) 1 Wheen, J. 1Apr.10
1 Hall, E. R. A. 4July10
1 Grounds, N. B, C.B. 4July10
(1) Kyrke-Smith, A. K. 4July10
1 Hudson, P., Adjt. 4July10
w.a. Dinnen, C. H. [l] 4July10

Captains—contd.
(3) 2 Norris, S. E. 4July10
2 Haseldine, R. H. 4July10
24Sept.10
(1) Yates, C. M. 6Aug.10
14Dec.10
1 Marshall, F. 11Nov.10
2 Beeman, S.W. 29Feb.12
19Oct.10
2 Wright, H. L. 24Apr.12
w.a. O'Flynn, D. R. C. D. 8June12
t. Brook, T. F. 8June12
2 Uniacke, J. B. 14Aug.12
f. 1 Tanner, R. E. 16 Sept.12

Lieutenants. (19)
2 Bulkley, E. B. M. 17Oct.08
c.o. King, D. M. 4Nov.08
2 Skinner, G.E.M. 1Apr.09
2 Harden, F. G. 22May09
r. Browne, J.H.L. 14Aug.09
2 Scott-Tucker, D. G. H. H. 14Sept.09
2 Goff, C. E. 21Oct.09
t. Gilbert, H. H. 1Dec.09
2 Charsley, R. B. 1Apr.10
f.c. Noel, M. W. 1Apr.10
1 Furneaux, P. T. 6May10
2 Briggs, F. C.C. 29June10
1 Doll, P. W. K. 10Apr.12
(3) 2 Howard, W. J. H. 24Apr.12
1 Baily, R. H. 8June12
a s. Fleming, N. [l] 2Nov.12
2 Alban, C. E. R. G., *Adjt.* 26Feb.13
f.c.1 Kinnear, J. L. 8Mar.13
2 Trevor, C. P. 16May13
(3) 1 Bewes, R. C. H., f.c.r. 1Sept.13
1 Snatt, P. C. 17Nov.13
2 Levick, A. U. 1Jan.14
1 Horton, L.E,L. 4Feb.14
1 Synge, W. A. T. 4Feb.14

2nd Lieutenants. (12)
1 Ryan, J. H. A. 14Feb.12
1 Tudor, R. G. 3Sept.12
2 Hannay, W. A. 4Sept.12
2 Towers, G. M. 4Dec.12

2nd Lieuts.—contd.
2 Tate, A. R. W. 21Dec.12
2 Cross, E. C. 25Dec.12
1 Phipps, C. J. 17Sept.13

Adjutants.
1 Hudson, P., *capt.* 16Sept.12
2 Alban, C. E. R. G. *lt.* 4July13
r. Bailey, J. 28Dec.98
hon. maj. 28Dec.13
2 Woodham, L. 27June00
hon. capt. 27June10
1 Ball, E., *hon. lt.* 17Aug.07
r. Jones, A. R., *hon. lt.* 14Oct.11

Special Reserve.
2nd Lieutenants.
Rosling D. W. Sept.13
Bargh, G. (*on prob.*) 18Feb.14
Nichols, A. R. (*on prob.*) 14Mar.14
Denny, B, M. R. (*on prob.*) 23May14
4Apr.14

3rd Battalion.

(*Officers serving on 15 Sept.02 in the corresponding Militia unit hold honorary Army rank equivalent to the Militia regimental rank they then held. Other officers entitled to honorary Army rank have it shown against their names.*)

Hon. Colonel.
Hesketh, Sir T. G. F., Bt., *late Maj. Mila.* 2Aug.08
12Sept.94

Lt.-Colonel.
Hobson, H. H. (*H*) (*Hon. Capt. in Army* 3July01) 30Oct.10

Major.
p.s. Clifford, F. (*Hon. Capt. in Army 12 Jan* 01) (*H*) (*Q*) 10June11
r.e. Bailey, V. T. 17Feb,12

Captains. (5)
p.s. Byrne, A. J. H. (*H*) 27June03
p.s. Lawrence, A. G., *Lord* (*Hon. Lt. in Army* 5Dec.00) 18Feb.05
Whitaker, C. W. (*H*) 1Oct.13
p.s. Jones, W. E. (*H*) 1June07
Grey, G., Lt. ret. pay (*Q*) 9Nov.08
r.e. Wheen, J. 2June09
r.e. Norris, S.E. 1Apr.10
r.e. Beeman, S.W. 4July10
29Feb.12
19Oct.14

Lieutenants. (11)
(p.s.) Mitchell, G. S. (*H*) 10Oct.07
Savage, A. M. 10Jan.11
Sweet-Escott, M. R. 24Feb.11
Colman, C. J. 24Feb.11
r.e. Howard, W.J.H. 24Apr.12
Shepherd, W. M. 13May11
r.e. Bland, P. R. (*Hon. 2nd Lt. in Army* 16Sept.02) 24Apr.12
r.e. Bewes, R. C. H., f.c.r. 11Sept.13

2nd Lieutenants. (8)
Young, P, M. 20Jan.12
Baker, E. B. 17Apr.12
Webb, H. M. T. 1May13
Wallace, H. B. (*on prob.*) 18Dec.13
Coode-Adams, R.W. H. (*on prob.*) 11Mar.14
Moore, O. H. (*on prob.*) 1Apr.14

Adjutant.
Browne, J. H. L., Lt. l'pool R. 7Feb.14 (*Lt. in Arm* 14Aug.09)

Quarter-Master.
Jones, A. R., *hon. lt.*

THE KING'S (LIVERPOOL REGIMENT)—(Regtl. Dist. No. 8)—contd.

4th Battalion.

(Officers serving on 15 Sept. .02 in the corresponding Militia unit hold honorary Army rank equivalent to the Militia regimental rank they then held. Other officers entitled to honorary Army rank have it shown against their names.)

Hon. Colonel.
Hesketh, Sir T. G. F., Bt., late Maj. Mila. 19July08
12Sept.94

Lt.-Colonel.
p.s. ✗Allen, J. W. 15July13

Majors. (3)
p.s. ✗Beall, E. M. (H) 25Aug.09
p.s. ✗Sims, J. H. L. (H) 14Oct.11
Stomm, W. J. [L] (Hon. Lt. in Army 13July 01) (H) (Q) 15July13

Captains. (6)
p.s. ✗Jenkins, G. H. (H) 1. of M. 1June02
✗Harford, C. L., Capt. ret. pay (Res. of Off.) 11Nov.03
28Aug.12
✗Simpson, E. H. Lt. ret. pay 9Apr.10
Earle, A. T. (H) (b) 27Oct.11
Coltart, A. H. (H) 15July13
Macpherson, B. W., (H)(Asst.Dist. Off., S. Provs., Nigeria, 12Jan.14) 15July13

Lieutenants. (11)
✗Stanford-Samuel, W. ⓢ (H) (b) 4Feb.11
f.c. Mapplebeck, G. W. 6Dec.12
Lumsden, D.A. 20May14
Sleigh, J. H. 20May14

2nd Lieutenants. (8)
Kilpatrick, N.B. (on prob.) 8Nov.13

Inst. of Musk.
p.s. ✗Jenkins, G. H. (H) capt. 31Jan.14

Adjutant.
✗Jones, R. C. R., Capt. L'pool, R. 28Sept.12
(Capt. in Army 11Jan. 1)

Quarter-Master.
✗Bailey, J., hon. m.

5th Battalion.

"South Africa, 1900-02."
65, St. Anne Street, Liverpool.

Hon. Colonel,
✗Derby, Rt. Hon. E. G. V., Earl of, G.C.V.O., C.B. 15June08
p. McMaster, J.M., VD, hon. c. (Q) 28Apr.06

Majors. (2)
p.s. Shute, J. J., jun. 15Jan.12
p.s. ✗Cohen, S. S. G. (Hon. Lt. in Army 7Aug.02) 24Apr 14

Captains. (8)
p.s. Fairclough, R. J. 4Apr.03
p.s. Woodhouse, H. K. S. (Q) 8May07
✗Grindley, J. H. (Hon. Lt. in Army 27 Dec. 00) 2Apr.08
p. ✗Buckley, A.(Hon. Lt. in Army 7 Aug. 02) 25Apr.10
p.s. Greig, W. E.ⓢ (Q) 6June14
28Apr.06
p.s. Quack, H. H. K. 20Sept.11
p. ✗Grindley, D. R. (H) I. of M. 16Jan.12

Lieutenants. (8)
Longbottom, W. 28Nov.09
Hawkes, P. W. (H) 28Nov.09
Evans, W. L. 18Nov.10
Duncan, H. J. 13May11
Eills, C. (H) 16Jan.12
Ockleston, W. H. (H) 29May12
Palmer, E. B. 19June13
Kynaston, N. E. V. 17June14

2nd Lieutenants. (8
Edwards, G. B. ⓢ 20May11
Owen, W. L. 6Mar.12
Bower, R. 9June13
Keet, H. G. 17June14
Furber, E. L. 26June14
Ambler, P. 26June14
Inst. of Musk.
✗Grindley, D. R., capt. 6Feb.14

Adjutant.
✗Briscoe, G. S., Lt. Worc. R., capt. 23Nov.13

Quarter-Master.
✗Burnett, W., hon. lt. 1July13

Medical Officers.
Anderson, Capt., E.L., M.B., R.A.M.C. (T.F.) (attd.) (Med. Offr., S. Provs., Nigeria, {1 Jan. 14 {6Jan. 12) 7Apr.10
Robinson, Capt. G. H., M.D., R.A.M.C (T.F.) (attd.) 23May12
Bernstein, Lt. I. B., R.A.M.C. (T.F.) (attd.) 14May12

Chaplains.
Liverpool Rt. Rev. F. J., Lord Bishop of, D.D., Chapl. 1st Class (T.F.) (attd.) 1Apr.08
Ainslie, Rev. Canon R. M., M.A., TD, Chapl. 1st Class (T.F.) (attd.) 19Sept.00
13Dec.90
Gregson, Rev. W. J. [R.C.], Chapl. 4th Class (T.F.) (attd.) 21May10
[Uniform—Green. Facings—Black.]

6th (Rifle) Battalion.

"South Africa, 1900-01."
Prince's Park Barracks, Upper Warwick Street, Liverpool.

Hon. Colonel.
✗Burnett, Gen. Sir C. J., K.C.B., K.C.V.O., ret. pay, Col. R. Ir. Rif. 22Apr.10

Lt.-Colonel.
p. Spenceely, H. D., TD, (t) 18May12

Majors. (2)
p. Davison, H., TD 1Feb.07
p. Harrison, E. J. 19May12

Captains. (8)
p.s. Wainwright, R. 26Mar.02
p.s. ✗Wedgwood, B. R. 25Mar.08
p. Brocklehurst, L. H. (Q) (H) 22June10
p.s. Bennet, R. E. W. K. 22June10
p.s. Turner, W. A. 29July11
Beazley, J. G. B. 19May12
p.s. Westby, G. H. A. ⓢ 1Nov.12
p.s. McKaig, J. B. 14May13

Lieutenants. (8)
p.s. Montgomery, W. S. 14May09
(p.s.)Buckley, E. C. G. 1Nov.09
Broad, W. H. 22June10
Trench, J. R. 22June10
Wilson, T. W. 25Mar.11
Gordon, E. 19May12
Stewart, H. 13July12
Higgin, W. W. ⓢ 14May13

2nd Lieutenants. (8)
Dobell, R. L. 2Mar.10
Barrett, H. S. 30July10
Stenhouse, A. H. 1Nov.11
Oliver, E. L. 1Nov.12

Adjutant.
Teall, G. H., Capt. Linc. R. 9Jan.14

Quarter-Master.
Goulding, E. S., hon. capt. 23Jan.08

Medical Officers.
p. ✗Martin, Maj. J. G., M.B., R.A.M.C. (T.F.) (attd.) 26Oct.13
26Oct.01
Seddon, Lt. H., M.B., R.A.M.C. (T.F.) (attd.) 1Feb.14

Chaplains.
Lichfield, Rt. Rev. J. A., Lord Bishop of, D.D., Chapl. 1st Class (T.F.) (attd.) 16May10
31May07
Wakeford, Rev. J., M.A., B.D., Chapl. 4th Class (T.F.) (attd.) 10May09
Horan, Rev. F. S., M.A., Chapl. 4th Class (T.F.) (attd.) 1June11
[Uniform—Green. Facings—Scarlet.]

7th Battalion.

"South Africa, 1900-02."
99, Park Street, Bootle.

Lt.-Colonel.
p. Stott, W. H., TD 1Jan.09

Majors. (2)
Hemelryk, P. H. 12May12
Hughes, A. (t) 4July14

Captains. (8)
p. Bean, C. A. 9May03
p.s. Marriott, S. C. (H) (t) 10Feb.06
p.s. Petit Jean, H. 1Nov.06
p.s. Eckes, J. A. 14Apr.07
Harvey, J. 13May12
p. Chandler, R. A. (H) 25Mar.13

Lieutenants. (8)
Dean, J. S. 1Dec.10
Meyer, C. D. 1Dec.10
Thompson, J.G. 1Dec.10
Adams, W. G. 1Dec.10
Tweedale, M. 1Jan.12
Alexander, H. G. 27Feb.13
Adams, L. K. 25Mar.13

2nd Lieutenants. (8)
Paterson, J.C. 1Nov.11
Allan, W. S. 2Nov.11
Pittendrigh, W. L. 1Sept.12
Dawson, T. W. 7Feb.13
Roper, L. W. 9June13
Shaw, R. 22Dec.13

THE KING'S (LIVERPOOL REGIMENT)—(Regtl. Dist. No. 8)—contd.

7th Bn.—contd.

Adjutant.
Shute, J. V., Capt.
 Dorset R. 7Sept.12

Quarter-Master.
⚹Johnson, W.,
 hon. lt. 7Apr.14

Medical Officers.
p. Price, Maj. A.,
 R.A.M.C. (T.F.)
 (attd.) 28Apr.12
 3Aug.04
p. Blumberg, Maj. H.
 D'A., R.A.M.C.
 (T.F.) (attd.) 29July12
 11July00

Chaplain.
Collier, Rev. H. F. S.,
 B.A., Chapl. 4th
 Class (T.F.) (attd.)
 1Aug.09

[Uniform—*Scarlet.*
Facings—*Blue.*]

Cadet Unit affiliated.
Southport Cadet Corps.

8th (Irish) Battalion.

"South Africa, 1900-02."

75, Shaw Street, Liverpool.

Hon. Colonel.
Kenmare, V. C., Earl
 of, C.V.O. 8Sept.06

Lt.-Colonel.
Cooney, J. A., TD 8June09

Majors. (2)
McCullagh, J. R.,
 1Jan.10
Dranfield, A. 4May13

Captains. (8)
p.s.Davies, E. A. 8Nov.06
p.s.Carbines, J. H. 30Jan.08
p. Benson, A. R. 8June09
 Meadows,A.H.16May11
 Murphy, F. P. S.
 1July12
Bailes, T. L. ⓢ 4May13
Smith, J. J. 20May14

Lieutenants. (8)
Harris, S. 1June10
Roche, J. A. 1June10
Murphy, L. A. M.
 1July12
Williams, G. 1July12
Finegan, H. M. 1July12
⚹Sheath, W. A. S.
 17May13
Smitham, J. E.15Nov.13

2nd Lieutenants. (8)
Keating, R. P. 18Jan.11
Mateer,A.J.P.18Sept.11
Manley, H. C. 17Oct.12
Brown, G. 22Nov.12
Pickles, E. S. 13Jan.13
Downes, H. L. 24Feb.13
Traynor, P. J. 15May13
Murphy,E.M. ⓢ18Sept.13
Riley, J. 8Sept.13
Bell, J. 18Dec.13
Wylie, W. R. 30Jan.14
Willson,C.H.M.28Mar.14

Adjutant.
Dene, A. P., Capt.
 D. of Corn. L.I.
 24Feb.13

Quarter-Master.
⚹Clarke, H. G.,
 hon. lt. Oct.13

Medical Officers.
⚹Bayer, Capt. H. M.,
 R.A.M.C. (T.F.)
 (attd.) 1May09
Gardiner, Lt. D.
 P. H., M.B.,
 R.A.M.C. (T.F.)
 (attd.) 1Nov.11

Chaplain.
⚹Brindle, Rt. Rev.
 R., Bishop, D.S.O.,
 Chapl. 1st Class
 ret. pay, hon.
 Chapl. (T.F.)
 (attd.)[R.][R C.]
 5Mar.10

[Uniform—*Green.*
Facings—*Black.*]

9th Battalion.

"South Africa, 1900-01."

57, 59 and 61, Everton Road, Liverpool.

Hon. Colonel.
Walker, W. H. 17Mar.97

Lt.-Colonel.
p. Watts, L., VD, 4Feb.11

Majors. (2)
p. Lloyd, J. E., VD (H)
 6Nov.09
Clarke, R. J.,TD 4Feb.11

Captains. (8)
p. Warde, A. 17Aug.01
p. Finch, F. G. (q)16July04
p.s. Wells, F. 22Apr.05
p.s. Radford, A. L. 17Dec.07
p.s. McLoughlin, G. M.
 (H), I. of M. Nov.09
p. Paris, J. G. (H) 4Feb.11
p. McMillin,W.J. 6Apr.11

Lieutenants. (8)
(p.)Watts, N. L. 6Nov.09
p. Owens, F. G. 6Apr.10
(p.)Williams, R. M. (H)
 4Feb.11
Van Gruisen, N. A. R.
 19Mar.11
Evans, F. S. 21May11
Buckley, F. 27July12
Mostyn, W. J. 8Feb.13

2nd Lieutenants. (8)
Pilkington, C.G.9May11
Orford, T. 16June11
Hunt, J. W. B. 21Feb.12
Fulton, A.W. 17Feb.12
Lederer, P.G.A.1Mar.12
Nairn, G. A, S. 1June13
Hill, C. G. R. 7Aug.13
McCann, A. C. 28Apr.14
Fawcett, A. H. 28Apr.14

Inst. of Musk.
McLoughlin, G. M.,
 capt. 16Mar.09

Adjutant.
Nicholls, H. L. F.,
 Lt.North'd Fus.,
 capt. 1Nov.13

Quarter-Master.
⚹Burnett, R., hon.lt.
 8June10

Medical Officers.
p. Barnes, Maj. E. W.,
 TD. (hon. Surg.-
 Lt.-Col.) R.A.M.C.
 (T.F.)(attd.) 18Sept.02
 14Dec.89
p. ⚹Mahoney, Capt.
 M. J., M.D.,
 R.A.M.C. (T.F.)
 (attd.) (hon.
 Lt. in Army 18
 June01) (H) 10Apr.07
 7May04

Chaplain.
Jones, Rev. W. S.,
 Chapl.4th Class
 (T.F.) (attd.) 8July09

[Uniform—*Scarlet.*
Facings—*Blue.*]

10th (Scottish) Battalion.

"South Africa, 1902."

7, Fraser Street, Liverpool.

Hon. Colonel.
⚹Tullibardine, J. G.,
 Marq. of, M.V.O.,
 D.S.O., Bt. Maj.,
 h.p. 13June14

Lt.-Colonel.
Nicholl, W. (Q) 3Oct.11

Majors. (2)
Blair, G. A. 1Apr.10
Davidson, J. R. (t)
 19July12

Captains. (8)
p.s. Fairrie, A. 23Apr.02
p. Maxwell, W. H.16Feb.07
p.s. Thin, E. G. 21Dec.10
Twentyman,A.17Sept.12
Anderson,A.S.17Sept.12

Captains—contd.
p.s. Lockhart, R. H. D.
 18Sept.12
Dickinson, R. F. B.
 18Sept.12

Lieutenants (8)
Campbell, D. A.
 (H)ⓢ 30Apr.10
(p.) McKinnell, B. 30Apr.10
p.s. Mitchell, E.H.21June11
Macleod, D. 3Aug;12
Dickinson, G. F.
 17Sept.12
Rae, G B. L. 17Sept.12
Gatehouse, L. R. A.
 18Sept.12
Renison, W. J. H.
 5Feb.13

2nd Lieutenants. (8).
Turner, F. H. 18May12
Cunningham, R.D.
 5June12
Whitson, H. T. 28Dec.12
Gemmell, K. A.28Dec.12
Cookson, A. 9May14
McGilchrist,A.M.
 9May14

Adjutant.
James, C. P., Capt.
 Arg. & Suth'd
 Highrs. 22Oct.13

Quarter-Master.
McDougall, C., hon.
 maj. 10Oct.07

Medical Officers.
Kidston, Capt. N. W.,
 M.B., R.A.M.C
 (T.F.)(attd.) 1Nov.13
 1May10
Chavasse, Lt. N. G.
 M.B., R.A.M.C.
 (T.F.)(attd.) 2June13

Chaplains.
Bodel, Rev. J., B.A.,
 [E.P.] Chapl. 3rd
 Class(T.F.) (attd.)
 27Feb.11
 27Feb.01
Connell, Rev. J.,
 M.A., B.D. [E.P.],
 Chapl. 4th Class
 (T.F.) (attd.) 1Apr.08
 1Jan.08
Hamilton, Rev. J.,
 M.A. [C. S.] Chapl.
 4th Class (T. F.)
 (attd.) 3Jan.13

[Uniform—*Drab.*
Facings—*Scarlet.*]

THE KING'S (LIVERPOOL REGIMENT)—(Regtl. Dist. No. **8**)—*contd.*

7th (Isle of Man) Volunteer Battalion. (*late* 1st Isle of Man.) Douglas.	*Captain* (1) p. Mackenzie, T., *hon. m.* 8Aug.00 *Lieut. and 2nd Lieut.* (2) *Lieutenant.* p. Cowle, J. H. 1Sept.10	*2nd Lieutenant.* Mylchreest, J. S. 1Sept.10 *Medical Officer.* p. Richardson, W., *M.D., Surg.-Maj.* 13Feb.08 / 13Feb.96	*Acting Chaplain.* Jolly, *Rev.* R.B., *M.A.* 4July14 [Uniform—*Scarlet.* Facings—*Blue.*]

THE NORFOLK REGIMENT.
Regimental District No. 9. [No. 9 District.]

The Figure of Britannia.
"Havannah," "Martinique, 1794," "Rolica," "Vimiera," "Corunna," "Busaco," "Salamanca," "Vittoria," "St. Sebastian," "Nive," "Peninsula," "Cabool, 1842," "Moodkee," "Ferozeshah," "Sobraon," "Sevastopol," "Kabul, 1879," "Afghanistan, 1879-80," "Paardeberg," "South Africa, 1900-02."

Regular and Special Reserve Battalions.

Uniform—Scarlet. Facings—Yellow. Agents—Messrs. Holt & Co.

1st Bn.	(9th Foot)..	{ Holywood	3rd Bn. (1st Norfolk Mil.) .. Norwich.
2nd „		Belgaum (for Jubbulpore)	
Depôt	.. ..	.. Norwich.	Record Office .. .. Warley.

Territorial Force Battalions.

4th Bn...	..	Drill Hall, St. Giles, Norwich.	6th Bn... .. Cattle Market Street, Norwich.
5th „	.. ..	East Dereham.	

Allied Regiment of the Australian Commonwealth.
9th Australian Infantry Regiment (Moreton Regiment).

Colonel-in-Chief .. .. THE KING.

Colonel .. C. Browne, Hon. Gen. H. R., C.B., ret. pay [R] 8Oct.03
24Oct.94

1st and 2nd Battalions.

Lt.-Colonels. (2)
2Peebles, E. C., D.S.O. 1Sept.12
1Ballard, C. R., p.s.c. [l] 12Jan.13

Majors. (8)
2Bell, F. de B 12Jan.09
(3) 1Carroll, J. W. V. [F]
(Comdg. Depôt) 28Sept.11
2Lodge, F. C. 19Sept.00
s. Hare, R. W., D.S.O., 15Nov.11
  p.s.c., q.s. 13Mar.12
s. Gordon, W. F. L. 1Sept.12
1Orr, J. B., D.S O. 12Jan.13
2Cramer-Roberts, W. E. 11Mar.14
1Done, H. R. 1June14

Captains. (14)
1Luard, C. E., D.S.O., p.s.c. 4Feb.05
s. Jones-Bateman, L.N. 25Feb.05
2Oldman, R. D. F., D.S.O. 25Feb.05
(3)1Atkinson, J. C. 22Mar.05
t. Day, F. R. 29Mar.05
e.a. Hadow, A. L. 7June05
e.a. Mostyn, J. P. 16Jan.06
r. Grissell, B. S. 16Jan.06
s. Wickham, C. G., D.S.O. 16Jan.06
s.c. Scobell, S. J, F. 24Jan.06
2 Lanyon, C. V. 8Feb.06
t. Ward, A. E. M 12May06
c.o.Temperley, A.C. 20May08
18Dec.07

Captains—contd.
e.a.Harman, F. de W. [F] 10Oct.08
1Brudenell-Bruce,R.H. 7Jan.09
c.o.Archer, F. J. E. 12Jan.09
2Willett, H. L. 13Feb.09
(3)2Otter, R. J. C. 20Feb.09
1Snepp, E. N. 11Mar.09
t. Stone, P. V. P. 11Mar.09
1Cresswell, F. J., Adjt. 18Mar.12
2Daunt, W. J.O'B., 13Mar.12
t. Higson, F. 13Mar.12
2Marshall, R.D. 16July12
2de Grey, G., Adjt. 1Sept.12
1Clark, R. 12Mar.13
1Megaw, W. C. K. 26Mar.13
(3) 2Montgomerie, E. W. 26Mar.13
2Northcote, G. B. 9Apr.13
c.o Balders, A. W. 1June14
2Horner. E. T. 1June14
c.o.Shand, N.P. 20June14
1Otter, R. 20June14

Lieutenants. (19)
1Lyle, G. C. 24Apr.09
2Downs, R. A. 12Jun.09
2Shakeshaft, A. J. [l] 5Aug.09
2Floyd, A. B. 11Sept.09
2Blakiston, L. W. 18Sept.09
1Briard, E.F.V. 24Nov.09
1Nixon, E. C. 28Sept.11
1Foley T.A.F. 14Oct.11
2Hall, H. E. 16Mar.12
2Frere, R. T 10July12
1Openshaw, H. M. 16July12
(3) 1Reynolds, R. T. H. 25Jan.13
1Broadwood, E. H. T. 26Mar.13
2Orton, J. O. C. 26Mar.13
2Hudson, F. W. 9Apr.13
2Hayter, A. C. T. 16July13
2Farebrother, H. S. 16July13
2Holland, J. R. 1June14
1Jephson, M. 2 20June14

2nd Lieutenants. (12)
1O'Connor, A.C. 19Jan12
w.a.McBride, S. G. 24Aug.12
1Wills, O. S. D. 4Sept.12
1Boosey, F. C. 4Dec.12
1Oakes, J. E. 5Feb.13
1Paget, G. N. 24May13
2Read, J. F. W. 3Sept.13
2Peacocke, H.L. 3Sept.13
2Brownrigg,J.H.3Sept.13
2Bullock, H. J. 17Sept.13
1Patteson,R.W. 25Feb.14
2Berney-Ficklin, H. P. M. 10June14

Adjutants.
1Cresswell, F. J., capt. 5Aug.13
2de Grey, G., capt. 28Nov.13

Quarter-Masters.
r. Colgan, P. 25Apr.10
  hon. capt. 25Apr.10
1Armstrong, W. J., hon. lt. 16Aug.05
17Dec.06
2Richardson, J. T., hon. lt. 22Dec.06

Special Reserve.
2nd Lieutenants.
Lywood, O. G. W. G., 9Nov.12
Reeve, A. E. 21Mar.14
3May13

3rd Battalion.

(Officers serving on 11Apr.02 in the corresponding Militia unit hold honorary Army rank equivalent to the Militia regimental rank they then held. Other officers entitled to honorary Army rank have it shown against their names)

Hon. Colonel.
✕Custance, F. H., C.B. (Hon. Col. ret. Mila.) (Hon. Lt.-Col. in Army 12Apr.02)
31May08
8Feb.05

Lt.-Colonel.
✕Tonge, W. C., D.S.O., Maj. ret. pay (Res. of Off.) 27Aug.10

Major.
p.s.✕Baillie, A. H.(Hon. Capt. in Army 12Apr.02)(H) 7Feb.06
r.e.✕Carroll, J. W. V. 2Sept.11
19Sept.09

Captains. (5)
✕Margesson, E. W., Bt. Maj. ret. pay (Capt. Res. of Off.) hon. m., q.s. 20Aug.95
12May06
✕Levinge, H. G., Bt. Maj. ret. pay (Capt. Res. of Off.) hon. m. 15Sept.97
24Jan.06
✕Blair, A. H. (H) (Hon. Capt. in Army 18July01) 13July98
p.s.✕Jickling,C.M.28May02
p.s.Fowler,E.G. (H)6Feb.04
r.e. ✕Atkinson, J. C. 22Mar.05
p.s.✕Johnson, W. F., Lt. ret. pay (H) 17Jan.06
r.e.✕Otter, R. J. C. 20Feb.09
✕Reddie, R. A., Lt. ret. pay [l] 17June12
✕Bagwell, J., M.V.O., Capt. ret.pay(H) 16July12
Bowlby, T. R., Capt. ret. pay 20June14
25Jan.13
r.e. Montgomerie, E. W. 26Mar.13
Longfield, J. P., M.V.O., Lt.ret. pay 26Mar.13
9Apr.14

THE NORFOLK REGIMENT—(Regtl. Dist. No. 9)—contd.

3rd Bn.—contd.

Lieutenants. (11)

p.s. Penn-Gaskell, L. Da
C. (H) (a) ⓖ f.c.
    27Apr.06
    28May04
(p.s.)Lightfoot, M. F. R.
  (H)   28Apr.06
✗Filgate, R. J.,
  Lt. ret. pay 27Feb.08
    12July11
Wodehouse, C. J.
D'E. B. (H) 19June10
Teeling, A.M.A.I.
de L. 19July12
r.e.Reynolds, R. T. H.,
    25Jan.13

2nd Lieutenants. (8)

Balders,C. M. (on prob.)
    22July14

Adjutant.

✗Grissell, B. S.,
  Capt. Norf. R.
    30Dec.13
  (Capt. in Army1tJan.06)

Quarter-Master.

✗Colgan, P., hon. capt.

4th Battalion.

"South Africa, 1900-02."

Drill Hall, St. Giles, Norwich.

Hon. Colonel.

✗Leicester, T. W.,
  Earl of,G.C.V.O.,
  C.M.G., Col. ret.
  pay A,D,C, 23Feb.02

Lt.-Colonel.

✗Harvey, J. R. D.S.O.
  (Hon.Lt.-Col.in' Army
  1Oct.03) 1Jan.07
  bt. col. 24 Dec.13

Majors. (2)

Mornement,E.,
  TD 19May06
Wood, F. G. W. 17May10

Captains. (8)

p. Long, H. C. 29Aug.00
p.s.Fletcher,H.R.26Sept.00
p. Burrell, C. W. W.
    12July05
p.s. ✗Chamberlin, F. G.
  (Hon. Capt. in
  Army 1Oct.02)
    28Apr.06
p.s. Rudd, H. R. 3Nov.06
Andrews, W. H. M.
  (Lt. Res. of Off.)
  (H) l. of M. 5June12
Hines, C.P.(H)24June12
    1Feb.10

Lieutenants. (8)

Back, H. K. 21Apr.10
Fisher,G. K. T. 21Apr.10
Coxon,S.H.N.17June10
Youngs, J. B. 9Nov.10
Giles, H. L. 5June12
Bacon, A. E. W.2July13
Hazard, W.N. 16Apr.14
Flatt, T. N. 17Apr.14

2nd Lieutenants. (8)

Boswell, C. ⓖ 11May12
Corke, V. C. C. 14Aug.12
Harvey, R. P. 14June13
Morgan, W. V. 17Sept.13
Taylor, H. M. 17Sept.13
Walsh, L. W. 29Oct.13
Hampton,G.K.28Mar.14

Inst. of Musk.

Andrews,W. H. M.,
  capt. 1Apr.09

Adjutant.

✗Day, F. R., Capt.
  Norf. R. 10Dec.11

Quarter-Master.

Moore, R. W.,
  hon.lt. 16May11

Medical Officer.

Owens, Lt. J. H.,
  R.A.M.C. (T.F.)
  (attd.) 4May12

Chaplain.

Hardy,Rev. E. W.,
  Chapl.3rd Class
  (T.F.) (attd.) 1Apr.08
    23Oct.95
Westcott, Ven. Arch-
  deacon, F. B., M.A.,
  B.D., Chapl. 4th
  Class (T.F.) (attd.)
    10May13

[Uniform—Scarlet.
Facings—Yellow.]

5th Battalion.

"South Africa, 1900-02."

East Dereham.

Hon. Colonel.

p. ✗Albemarle, A. A. C.,
  Earl of,K.C.V.O.,C.B.
  VD Col. A.D.C.
  (Hon. Lt.-Col. in
  Army 1Dec.00), hon.
  c. 22Sept.06

Lt.-Colonel.

Thomas, A. W., TD,
    26Nov.13

Majors. (2)

Morgan, H. R., VD,
    26Nov.13
p.s.Rowell, H. E. (Q)
    1June14

Captains. (8)

p. ✗Barton, W. J.
  (Hon.Lt.in Army
  28June02) 24Jan.03
p.s.Purdy, T. W. (H)
    11Feb.05
p.s.Gledhill, W. G. 11Apr.06
p.s.Beck, F. R., M.V.O.
    19May06
p. Hall, T. B. 14July06
p. Bridgwater, H. N.
  (H) (Q) 30Jan.07
p.s.Holmes, H. E. (H)
    30Jan.07
p.s.Pattrick, A. D. 7Mar.14

Lieutenants. (8)

(p.s.)Coxon,S.A. T.14Dec.06
p.s.Blake, W. L. 15June07
p.s.Knight, A., M,V.O.,
  (H, I. of M. 2Oct.08
(p.s.)Smith, H. G. 1Apr.09
(p.)Coxon, A. C. M. 1May12
Mason, A. 4Feb.14
Wenn, W. 7Mar.14
Durrant, H. A. 1May14

2nd Lieutenants. (8)

Oliphant, T. 22Jan.13
Pearce, R. J. F.23Jan.13
Coles, S. 4April14

Inst. of Musk.

Knight, A., M.V.O.,
  lt. 18Feb14

Adjutant.

Ward, A. E. M.,
  Capt.Norf.R. 14Oct.11

Quarter Master.

Parker, S., hon.
  lt. 16Apr.13

Chaplain.

Grant, Rev. A.
  R. H., M.A.,
  Chapl.4thClass
  (T.F.) (attd.) 28May12

[Uniform—Scarlet.
Facings—Yellow.]

6th (Cyclist) Battalion.

Cattle Market Street, Norwich.

Hon. Colonel.

p. Patteson, H. T. S.,
  VD (Hon. Col. ret.
  Vols.) (t) 25July03

Lt.-Colonel.

p.s. ✗Prior, B. H. L.
  (Hon.Lt.in Army
  17June01) 1Apr.08

Major.

Ayre, F. S. 15May08

Captains. (8)

p.s.Salter, W.E.(H)12July05
p.s.Dewing, S. H. 15May08
p.s.Tunbridge, S. T. 1Feb.09
p.s.Cockrill, O. H. 14Feb.12
Barnham, G. W.
    20May13
Coulton, A. E. 29July13

Lieutenants. (5)

Philpott, C. P. 1Apr.09
Trotter, M. A. 6Dec.11
Miles, J.G. 5Apr.13
Lee, R. H. D. 8Jan.14

2nd Lieutenants. (4)

Bolingbroke, C. B.
    3Mar.13
Fison, F. H. 12Mar.13
Applewhaite,
  G. R. 3 Dec.13
Dixon, A. H. 22Apr.14

Adjutant.

Higson, F., Capt.
  Norf.R. 14Oct.11

Quarter-Master.

Spurling, T. W.,
  hon. lt. 13June13

Medical Officer.

Rose, Lt. E. F.,
  R.A.M.C. (T.F.)
  (attd.) 4Mar.1

Chaplain.

Packer, Rev.G.F.,
  Chapl. 4th Class
  (T.F.) (attd.) 17May09

[Uniform—Scarlet.
Facings—Yellow.]

THE LINCOLNSHIRE REGIMENT.
Regimental District No. **10**. [No. **6** District.]

The Sphinx, superscribed "Egypt."
"Blenheim," "Ramillies," "Oudenarde," "Malplaquet," "Peninsula," "Sobraon," "Mooltan,"
"Goojerat," "Punjaub," "Lucknow," "Atbara," "Khartoum," "Paardeberg," "South Africa, 1900-02."

Regular and Special Reserve Battalions.

Uniform—Scarlet. Facings—White. Agents—Messrs. Cox & Co.

1st Bn. } (10th Foot) { *Portsmouth.*
2nd „ }   { *Bermuda.*
Depôt .. .. *Lincoln.*

3rd Bn. (R. North Lincoln Mil.) .. *Lincoln.*

Record Office .. .. .. *Lichfield.*

Territorial Force Battalions.

4th Bn. .. .. .. *Drill Hall, Lincoln.* | 5th Bn. .. .. *Infantry Drill Hall, Grimsby.*

Allied Regiment of Canadian Militia.

19th "Lincoln" Regiment .. .. *St. Catharines, Ontario.*

Colonel .. .. .. Simpson, Maj.-Gen. C. R., *C.B., p.s.c.* [L] s. 10May14

1st and 2nd Battalions.

Lt.-Colonels (2)
2 McAndrew, G. B. [l] 26July12
1 Smith, W.E.B. 11Mar.14

Majors. (8)
2 Howley, J. J., *D.S.O.* 11Mar.06
1 Barlow, C. C. L. 30Oct.07
2 Cox, S. FitzG. 6Oct.08
(3)1 Edwards, L. (*Comdg. Depôt*) 11Mar.10
      22Aug.02
2 Boxer, H.E.R. 25Mar.11
s. Toogood, C., *D.S.O.* 15May12
Plunkett, E. A., *p.s.c.* [L] [F] *Mil. Attaché* 26July12
1 Grant, D.H.F. 3Aug.12

Captains. (14)
1 Orr, H. M. C. 2Jan.03
t. Wilson, R. H. G. 25Oct.04
1 Greatwood, F. W. 19Nov.04
s. Hollins, C. E. 19Nov.04
2 Elkington, W. E. W. 20May05
      28Jan.05
s.c. Spring, F. G. 5Nov.05
t. Johnson, A. B. 5Nov.05
(3)2 Johnston, R.H. 5Nov.05
1 Hoskyns, H. C. W. 22Dec.05
o.d. Lewis, L.C., o. 22Dec.05
(3)2 Dawson, H.E. 12Feb.06
1 Rose, F. C. 25July06
2 Wellesley, C. G. V. 13Jan.08
2 French, E. N. 17Jan.11
2 Bastard, E. 6Jan.12
1 Drake, R. E., *Adjt.* 3Aug.12
t. de Hoghton, V. 15Jan.13
(3)1 Tollemache, L. de O. 15Jan.13
1 Butt, G. K. 11June13
2 Hopwood, A. H. 15Aug.13
2 Browne, P. L. 4Oct.13
1 Ellison, G. M. [l]4Nov.13
r. Barker, M.G.H. 18Dec.13
t. Teall, G. H. 9Jan.14

L 2

Captains—contd.
c.o. Wickham, J.D.D. 23May14
s. 1Boys, E.J. deC. 23May14

Lieutenants. (20)
(3)2 Magrath, J. R. G. 7Sept.07
m.c. Priestman, J. H. T. [l] 8Oct.10
t. Toynbee, R. L. 19Oct.10
  2 Lloyd, E.P., *Adjt.* 28Dec.10
1 Peddle, A. W. P. 3Feb.11
(3)1 Blackwood, F. H. 10May11
1 Buller, L. M. 21June11
1 Holmes, C. C. 2Nov.11
2 Whinney, F. S. 25Nov.11
a. Thruston, B. 28Nov.11
2 Griffin, J.A.A. 11May12
2 Hansen, P. H. 3Aug.12
2 Richards, E. F. O. 5Aug.12
2 Impey, E. H. 10Oct.12
2 von Poellnitz, H. W. 31Oct.12
2 Wiseman, W. F. G. 6Nov.12
2 Eagar, H. St. G. 15Jan.13
2 Lindsell, E. H. 28May13
2 Leslie, E. B. 18July13
2 Swann, H. N. 15Aug.13
2 Welchman, E. L. 9Jan.14
2 Billiat, J. J. 22Jan.14

2nd Lieutenants. (12)
2 Peake, C. G. W. 19Jan.12
2 Huntington, N.J.S. 4Dec.12
2 Wylie, A. W. 22Jan.13
1 Baines, A. E. C. 22Jan.13
1 Wales, E. W. 22May13
2 Montague, F.D. 3Sept.13
1 Hutchinson, C. 3Sept.13
1 Herapath, R. FitzK. B. 8Sept.13
1 Snell, A. P. 8Sept.13
1 Robertson, W. M. 10Dec13
1 Cave-Orme, R. W. 25Feb.14
1 Barnes, E. 25Feb.14
1 Marshall, H. 10June14

Adjutants.
1 Drake, R. E., *capt.* 4Nov.13
2 Lloyd, E. P., *lt.* 16Nov13

Quarter-Masters.
1 Fitzpatrick, T. 12Dec.94
  hon. maj. 12Dec.09
2 Skinner, E.W. 3Mar.01
  hon. capt. 13Mar.11
r. Hammond, T., 25Dec.01
  hon. capt. 25Dec.11

Special Reserve.

2nd Lieutenants.
Trist, L. H. (q) (H) (*local Maj., O.T.C.* 17Apr.12) 17Feb.12
Ingoldby, H. (*on prob.*) 23Apr.13
McConkey, A.I.G. (*on prob.*) 14Mar.14

3rd Battalion.

(*Officers serving on 6 Oct. 02 in the corresponding Militia unit hold honorary Army rank equivalent to the Militia regimental rank they then held. Other officers entitled to honorary Army rank have it shown against their names.*)

Hon. Colonel.
Swan, C. A., C.M.G. *hon. c.* (H) 17Feb.09

Lt.-Colonel.
p.s. Fane, W. V. R. 16Feb.14

Major.
r.e. Edwards, L. 11Mar.10
    22Aug.02
Cole, J.A. (H)(*Hon. Capt. in Army,* 12Oct.00) 16Feb.14

Captains. (5)
p.s. Massingberd, S., *hon. m.* 9May00
Milnes, H. R. (H) 9Apr.04
r.e. Johnston, R. H. 5Nov.05
r.e. Dawson, H.E. 12Feb.06
Jarvis, C. F. C., *Capt. ret. pay* 6June06
    22Jan.10
Pitt, W. N., *Lt. ret. pay* 8Oct.10
Richardson, J. F., *Capt. ret. pay* 3Aug.12
    4Oct.13
r.e. Tollemache, L. de O. 15Jan.13

Lieutenants. (11)
p.s. Wyatt, A. T. E. (F) 22May08
r.e. Magrath, J. R. G. 7Sept.07
r.e. Blackwood, F. H. 10May11
Farebrother, C. B. 24Feb.12
Peskett, R. F. 24Feb.12
Bransbury, V. D. B. 13Mar.14
Torr, J. H. G. 14May14
Fenwick, W. L. 29June14

2nd Lieutenants. (8)

Adjutant.
Barker, M. G. H. *Capt. Linc. R.* 18Dec.13
(*Capt. in Army* 18Dec.13)

Quarter-Master.
Hammond, T., *hon. capt.*

THE LINCOLNSHIRE REGIMENT—(Regtl. Dist. No. 10)—contd.

4th Battalion.

"South Africa, 1900-02."

Drill Hall, Lincoln.

Hon. Colonel.

Hutchinson, A., VD,
(Hon. Col. ret. Vols.)
31Mar.08

Lt.-Colonel.

Jessop, J. W. 14Sept.10

Majors. (2)

Barrell, G. J., (H) (Q) 17Jan.11
✗Cooper, O. 27Apr.12

Captains. (8)

p.s. Earl, R. M. 12Feb.02
p. Sills, G. R., TD (t) (H) 6Jan.04
Howes, H. A. 6Aug.04
Thompson, B. C. 29Mar.05
Tetley, F. E. (H) 30Dec.07
Hart, L. H. P. (H) 14Feb.11
Dean, H. G. (H) 21Mar.11
p. ✗Staniland, M.(H) 27Apr.12

Lieutenants. (8)

Ellwood, A. A. (H)
I. of M. 14July10
(p.s.)Bellamy, H. M.
8Nov.10
Jessop, J. C. 11Nov.10

Lieutenants—contd.

Phillips, W.M. 14Feb.11
Ellwood, C.H. 17June11
Myers, W. R. 22Feb.12
Lloyd, C. F. A 27Apr.12
p.s. Salaman, G. H. 1July13

2nd Lieutenants. (8)

Gray, C. S. 25Mar.10
Burrows, E. 14May10
Grinling, E. J. 18Dec.10
Marris, H. C. 11Dec.11
Newton, R. W. 10Feb.13
Beaulah, E. A. 27Feb.13
Clark, A. H. 14May13
Wood, M. H. 13Aug13
Reed, L. A. 9May14
Pennell, L. R. 8July14

Inst. of Musk.

Ellwood, A. A., lt. 10Feb.09

Adjutant.

✗Johnson, A. B.,
Capt. Linc. R.
28Nov.11

Quarter-Master.

p. Simpson, W. S., TD, hon. maj. 21Mar.00

Medical Officers.

Berry, Maj. H. P.,
M.B., TD, R.A.M.C.
(T.F.) (attd.) 13Sept.02
22June89
p. Green, A. S., M.B.,
Surg.-Capt. 18July06
25Dec.01

Chaplain.

Ashby, Rev P. O.,
M.A., Chapl. 4th
Class (T.F.) (attd.) 1July12

[Uniform—Scarlet
Facings—White.]

5th Battalion.

"South Africa, 1900-02."

Infantry Drill Hall,
Grimsby.

Hon. Colonel.

p.s. Walker, G. B., VD,
(Hon. Col. ret.
Terr. Force) 30Aug.12

Lt.-Colonel.

Sandall, T. E., TD, ⊕ 11May12

Majors. (2)

p. ✗Stephenson, H., TD
(Hon. Lt. in Army
24Sept.01) ⊕ 4Mar.03
Marshall, H. D.,
TD 1Sept.12

Captains. (8)

p. Sleight, E. 19Dec.00
p.s. ✗Robinson, H. I.
(Hon. Lt. in Army
12Sept.02) 14Jan.05
p.s. Wilson, H. G. (H) 10Oct.09
p.s. Scorer, H. S (H) 29Jan.10
Hadfield, J. H. (H) 3Aug.12
Falkner, H. F. N. 18Sept.12
p.s. Bell, H. A.(H) 13Feb.13
Hitzen, E. J. 26July13

Lieutenants. (8)

(p.s.) Nicholson, H. W, 26Apr.10
Dixon, O (H) 4Nov.11
Sowter, G. H. J. 4Nov.11
Crosby, R. D. 4Nov.11
Ingoldby, F. J. M. ⊕ 1Sept.12
Fieldsend, R. S. 1Sept.12

2nd Lieutenants. (8)

Finnie, B. K. 3Mar.13
Ellis, W. A. 17May13
Dyson, E. 6May13
Sheel, H. 15Dec.13

Adjutant.

de Hoghton, V.,
Capt. Linc. R. 15Jan.13

Quarter-Master.

✗Plumtree, W. H.,
hon. lt. 27Apr.12

Medical Officers.

p. Nicholson, Maj.
J. W., TD, R.A.M.C.
(T.F.) (attd.) 28Jan.09
28July97
p. Duncan, Maj. J. M.,
M.B., R.A.M.C.,
(T.F.) (attd.) 4July12
4July00

Chaplains.

Standen, Rev. Canon
J. E., M.A., Chapl.
4th Class (T.F.)
(attd.) 3Apr.10
18July06
Lenton, C. H., M.A.,
Chapl. 4th Class
(T.F.) (attd.) 1Apr.13

[Uniform—Scarlet.
Facings—White.]

THE DEVONSHIRE REGIMENT.
Regimental District No. **11**. [No. **8** District.]

The Castle of Exeter. "*Semper fidelis.*"
"Dettingen," "Salamanca," "Pyrenees," "Nivelle," "Nive," "Orthes," "Toulouse," "Peninsula,"
"Afghanistan, 1879-80," "Tirah," "Defence of Ladysmith," "Relief of Ladysmith," "South Africa, 1899-1902."

Regular and Special Reserve Battalions.
Uniform—Scarlet. Facings—Lincoln Green. Agents—Messrs. Cox & Co.

1st Bn. } (11th Foot) { *Jersey* (for Aldershot).	3rd Bn. (1st Devon Mil.).. .. .. Exeter.	
2nd " *Cairo*.		
Depôt .. .. Exeter.	Record Office .. .. ..Exeter.	

Territorial Force Battalions.
4th Bn. .. .. Exeter.	6th Bn... .. .. Barnstaple.	
5th " .. .. .. *Millbay*, Plymouth.	7th " .. .. Exeter.	

Colonel.. .. .. .. Bullock, Lt.-Gen. *Sir* G. M., K.C.B., *p.s.c,* s. .. 9Dec.10

1st and 2nd Battalions.

Lt.-Colonels. (2)
1Gloster, G. M. 2Oct.10
2Travers, J. O., *D.S.O.*
22Nov.12

Majors. (8)
1Williams, E. G.
7May06
2Radcliffe, J. F.,
D.S.O. 7May07
1Warwick, C. S. 10Oct.07
*w.a.*Law, J. P. [*l*] 22Nov.08
(1) Maynard, C. C. M.
D.S.O., p.s.c. [*l*] 2Nov.10
23July10
s. Morris, E. M. 22Nov.12
s. Young, E. D. [L] [F]
19Feb.14
2Goodwyn, W. M.
16July14

Captains. (14)
2Ingles, J. D., *Adjt.*
12Nov.10
1Luxmoore, N. 15Feb.11
18Apr.10
(3) 1Holland, T. C. B., *e.*
(*Comdg.Depôt*)12Apr.01
2Sunderland, A. J. E.
11May04
r. Vaughan, E.J.F.[F]
8Jan.08
13July01
2Lafone, C. A. 20Dec.01
1Harris, T. B. 30Dec.01
(1) Smyth-Osbourne,G.N.T.,
p.s.c. [*l*] 8Mar.02
(1) Hewlett,E.,*p.s.c* 20May08
13Dec.02
2Watts, G. I. 1Apr.03
2Blunt. D. H. 27Apr.03
*o.d.*Hawley, S. T., *p.a.c., e.*
1Jan.04
(1) Storey, H. I. 19May04
1Besly, B. H. 8Feb.06
1Green, G. F 13Mar.06
s.c. Soafe, W. E. 22Jan.07
*f.c.2*Lake, J. F. A. 3Apr.07
(3) 2Milne, R. J. 7May07
2Spencer, C, J. 14July08
(3) 2Street, H. 18Feb.11
17Jan.09

*Captains—*contd.
1Whipple, H. C. 4Nov.11
1Elliot, H. G. 4Nov.11
t. Woolcombe, J. M.
4Nov.11
e.a. Lewis, R. P. 16Dec.11
(3) 1Imbert-Terry, C. H. M.
16Dec.11
2Jenkins, M.I.G. 3Jan.13
t. Wrey, R. C. 3Jan.13
1Jeffreys, D. R. 15Jan.13

Lieutenants. (20)
2Featherstone, R.B.
7Dec.04
1Worrall, P. R. 14Dec.04
t. Woolcombe, L. D.
19Apr.05
2Eardley-Wilmot, H.
20May08
9July05
2Legge, R. G. 13Mar.06
(1) *Northcote, A. F.* 14Jan.07
2Cartwright, J. R.
22Jan.07
o.o. Llewellyn, J. M. 8Feb.08
1Maton, L .E. L.,
Adjt. 19Sept.08
2Park, J. A 19Sept.08
1Prior, G. E. R. 18Nov.09
o.o. Ditmas, T. O, B. 3Jan.10
2Belfield, A. G. N.
23Mar.10
2Anderson-Morshead,
R. H. 30Apr.10
1Dunsterville, G. E.
9July10
4Sept.06
2Parker, O. M. 8Sept.10
2Cobb, F. R. 9Nov.10
(3)2Hancock, R.E. 1Feb.11
2Holdsworth, F. J. C.
1Apr.11
(1) Yeo, B. H. 1Apr.11
2Bristowe, R. O. 4May11
1Anstey, G. A. 7June11
(3)1Kekewich, A. St. J. M.
16Aug.11
2Andrews, J.A. 12Oct.11
(1) Nation, S.C. 16Dec.11
1Fleming, W. A. 1Mar.12
1Lang, C.F.W. 20July12

2nd Lieutenants. (12)
2Vaughan, G. C.
14Sept.10
2Bates, R. P. 7Dec.10
1Joy, T. C. B, 24Mar.11
1Alexander, W. J.
25Mar.11

*2nd Lieuts.—*contd.
1Gotto, C. H 27May11
1Haynes, O. C. 20Sept.11
2Mac Mullen, A. G.
20Sept.11
2Cope, A. H. 20Sept.11
2Cox, H. J. H. 7Oct.11
1Beaufort, V.A. 6Jan.12
1Bolitho, J. B. 7Feb.12
1Clegg, W. L. 10Apr.12
(1)Tillett, A. 4Dec.12
(1) Copner, A. B. 5Feb.13

Adjutants.
2Ingles, J. D., *capt.*
11Feb.12
1Maton, L.E.L., *lt.*
20Aug.12

Quarter-Masters.
1Mumford, E. 18Nov.99
hon. *capt.* 18Nov.09
r. Mitchell. G. E.20Sept.02
hon. *capt.* 20Sept.12
2Palmer, G., *hon.*
lt. 14June11

Special Reserve.

2nd Lieutenants.
Mulock, E. E. 5Mar.13
Wedderspoon,
W. G. F. (on
prob.) 24June14

3rd Battalion.

(*Officers serving on 16 July 01
in the corresponding Militia unit hold honorary
Army rank equivalent to
the Militia regimental
rank they then held. Other
officers entitled to honorary Army rank have it
shown against their
names.*)

Hon. Colonel.
✕Mountsteven, F. H.,
C,M.G. (*Hon.Col.ret.
Mila.*) (*Hon. Lt.-Col.
in Army* 21Oct.00)
28June08
18June04

Lt.-Colonel.
p.s. Boles, D. F. (*H*)
2Apr.10

Major.
Hill, R. F. W. (*H*)
(*Remount Service*)
5Apr.13

Captains (5).
Mitford, B. V. (*Hon.
Capt. in Army*
21Oct.00) ⑬ (*H*)
11May96
r.e. ✕Holland, T.C.B., *e.*
12Apr.01
p.s. Granville, G.
20DeS.02
p.s. ✕Bramwell, A. B.
8Feb.98
p.s. ✕Chichester, H. A.
(*H*) 15Aug.06
p.s. Sprye, H. de L, (*H*)
5Dec.06
r.e. ✕Milne, R. J. 7May07
r.e. ✕Street, H. 11Feb.11
r.e. ✕Imbert-Terry, C.H.M.
11Jan.09
16Dec.11

Lieutenants. (11)
p.s. Quicke, E. O. St.
C. G. (*H*) 28Sept.08
St. B.S. (q)(*H*)5Nov.10
r.e. Hancock, R. E. 1Feb.11
r.e. Kekewich, A. St.
J. M. 16Aug.11
Sherwell, W. V. (*H*)
23Mar.12
Ainslie, D. A. L.
25Apr.13
Toms, A. W. 14Feb.14

2nd Lieutenants. (8)
Larder, G. S. M.
6Nov.12
Hall, E. C. H.
(on *prob.*) 16July13
Hibbert, P. A.
(on *prob.*) 25Feb.14
Austin, P. H.
(on *prob.*) 25Feb.14
Burke, V. B. (on
prob.) 16May14
Bond, B. F. (on
prob.) 22July14

Adjutant.
✕Vaughan, E. J. F.,
Capt. Devon. to.
25Feb.14
(*Capt. in Army*13July01)

Quarter- Master.
✕Mitchell,(G.E.,*hon.capt.*

THE DEVONSHIRE REGIMENT.—(Regtl. Dist. No. **11**)—*contd.*

4th Battalion.

"South Africa, 1900-01."
Exeter.

Hon. Colonel.
Kennaway, Rt. Hon. Sir
J. H., Bt., C.B., VD.,
hon. c.   31Dec.02

Lt.-Colonel.
p. Acland Troyte, H. L.,
(H)   5Mar.13

Majors (2).
p.s.Anstey, A.   1Apr.08
Cosens, F. R. S.
(H)   6Mar.13
Tremlett, C. P.ⓒ (H)
           7Mar.13

Captains (8).
p. Townsend, H.ⓒ 11July03
p. Pollard, L.   11July03
p. Harvey, F. J. ⓒ
(H)   2Jan.04
p. Forward, W.G. 21June05
p.s.Percy-Hardman,
W. H. (H) I. of M.
           21June05
p.s.Anderson-Morshead,
R. Y. (H)   1Aug.09
p.s.Carter, F.   7Mar.13

Lieutenants. (8)
(p.)Cardew, G.E.,o.c. 1July08
Lart, C.E.(A)(H)7Apr.10
           7Nov.00
Thoday, F.A. 17July12
Wippell, A. G. 22Aug.12
Logan, W.   5Feb.13
Orchard, J. W.
           25Oct.13

2nd Lieutenants (8).
Roberts, W. T. 19Dec.12
Carpenter, E.
           12Feb.13
Vodden, A.C.ⓢ 21Apr.13
Edwards, C. G. 4June13
Snell, W.   22May13
Sparkes, W. L. 20June13
Gregory, S. B. 3Sept.13
Jervis, W. W. 17Jan.14

Inst. of Musk.
Percy-Hardman,
W. H., capt. 1Apr.09

Adjutant.
✗Woollcombe, J. M.,
Capt. Devon R.,
           3Jan.13

Quarter-Master.
Deeks, C. H., hon.
m.   1Feb.03

Medical Officer.
Fisher, Lt. T. A.,
R.A.M.C. (T.F.)
(attd.)   20Jan.13

Chaplains.
Couchman, Rev. R. H.,
Chapl. 4th Class
(T.F.)(attd.) 1Apr.08
           1Nov.06
Botwood, Rev. E. K.,
B.A., Chapl. 4th
Class (T.F.)(attd.)
           25Oct.12

[Uniform—Green.
Facings—Black.]

Cadet Unit affiliated.

The Exeter Cathedral
School Cadet Company.

5th (Prince of Wales's) Battalion.

"South Africa, 1900-01."
Millbay, Plymouth.

Hon. Colonel.
p. Mount Edgcumbe, Col.Rt.
Hon. W. H., Earl of,
G.C.V.O., VD, late
Capt. Cornwall
Rangers, Mila.
(t)   29May89

Lt.-Colonel.
p. ✗Hawker, E. B.
(Maj. ret.) 12Apr.13

Majors (2).
p.s.✗Windeatt, F.K. (Hon.
Lt. in Army 9July01)
(§)   25Mar.05
Clark, F. A. 12Apr.13

Captains (8).
p. Carder, W.J.T. 20Sept.02
p. Corbett, W. E. M.
           4Mar.03
p. Davis, F. J. 13May08
p. Phillips, H. S. 13May08
p. Windeatt,J.(H)12Nov.04
p.s.Vicary, G. D.,(H)
           13July06
p.s.✗Sparrow, J. D.(H)
           13July06
Roseveare, E. (H)(q)
           4Aug.06
p. Leest, E. M. 4Aug.06
Spooner, C.N. 12Apr.13
Loveys, W. G. 19Apr.14

Lieutenants. (8)
p. Windeatt,G. E. 2Apr.04
p.s.Pridham, H. 25Feb.07
(p.) Hacker, N. 22Dec.10
Goldsmith, H. M.
           22Dec.10
Brown, J. A. 22Dec.10
Piper, F. E.   3June11
Winnicott, V. R.
           19Apr.14
Abraham, A. C. 29July14

2nd Lieutenants. (8)
Vicary, J. ⓢ 6Feb.12
Donaldson, A. L.
           15June12
Hosking, W. 10Dec.12
Snell, W. J. B. 10Mar.13
Bewes, C.T.A. 28Apr.13
Church, A. G. W.
           10Nov.13
Clapperton, R. H.
           11Mar.14
Beer, W. R.   19Apr.14

Adjutant.
✗Carroll, Capt. H. A.,
R. Muns. Fus.
           18Nov.12

Quarter-Master.
p. Greenslade, E. W.,
hon. m.   16Aug.02

Medical Officers.
Gladstone, Lt. A.E.,
R.A.M.C.(T.F.)(attd.)
           16May11

Chaplain.
Cocks, Rev. E. G.,
Chapl. 3rd Class
(T.F.)(attd.) 28Mar.13
           28Mar.03

[Uniform—Scarlet.
Facings—Lincoln Green.]

Cadet Units affiliated.
The Plymouth Lads' Brigade Cadet Corps.
The Haytor (Newton Abbot) Cadet Corps.

6th Battalion.

"South Africa, 1900-01."
Barnstaple.

Lt.-Colonel.
✗Radcliffe, N. R.
D.S.O., Capt. ret.
pay (Res. of Off.)
           22Mar.13

Majors. (2)
Manning, N.S. 12Dec.10
Newcombe, B. B., TD,
           23May12

Captains. (8)
p. Brown, G.W.F. 4July03
p. Macindoe, J. G. (H)
           19Mar.05
p. Bazeley, W. N. 12July11

Lieutenants. (8)
Seldon, A. A.
(Admin. Offr. E. Africa
Prote. 26 Dec. 13)1July09
(p.s.)Pearce, J. 1July09
(p.s.)Oerton, G. B. ⓒ
           3July09
Stranger, J. S. 1June10
Trevenen, W.B.12July11
Smyth-Richards,
F. G.   27Feb.12
German, W. H. 18Oct.12
Watson, G. C. 18Dec.12
Bryant, W. J. 26Dec.13
Bowhay, E. G. 27Dec.13
           28Aug.09
Mason, A. S. 9Mar.14
           7Feb.11

2nd Lieutenants. (8)
Verney, F. E. 12July11
Reavell, H. S. 15Apr.12
Waldram, R. L.
           14Sept.12
Jewell, H. A. 10Feb.14
Crew, F. A. E. 22Mar.14
Wicksteed, H. 30Mar.14

Adjutant.
Woollcombe, L.D.
Lt. Devon R.,
capt.   10Apr.12

Quarter-Master.
p. Lock, C., hon. m.
           20May04

Medical Officers.
p. Kendle, Maj. F. W.,
R.A.M.C. (T.F.)
(attd.)   21Feb.13
           14Nov.00
Valentine, Capt. W.A.,
M.D.,   R.A.M.C.
(T.F.) (attd.), 24May12
           14May08

Chaplain.
Atherton, Rev. E. C.,
M.A., Chapl. 2nd
Class (T.F.)(attd.)
           4July11
           4July96

[Uniform—Scarlet.
Facings—Lincoln Green.]

THE DEVONSHIRE REGIMENT—(Regtl Dist. No. 11)—contd.

7th (Cyclist) Battalion.

Exeter.

Hon. Colonel.

Ellicombe, G. J., Lt.-Col. ret. pay (Lt.-Col. ret. Terr. Force)   31 May 12

Lt.-Colonel.

p. Sanders, G. W. G., Maj. ret. pay (*Res. of Off.*) (Q) (H) 29 May 12

Major.
Hibberd, H. S. 12 Aug. 12

Captains. (8)

p.s. Martin, G. H. (*t*)   1 Dec. 07
Ball, W. F.   1 July 10
Whitemore, S. T.   6 July 11
Goodridge, A.   1 Nov. 12
Hems, H. T.   1 Nov. 12
Gorwyn, A. J.   22 Nov. 13

Lieutenants. (5)

Wilton, T.   5 June 11
Veitch, J. L.   1 May 13

2nd Lieutenants. (4)

Endle, T. O.   18 Aug. 13
Best, J. P   20 Aug. 13
Jones, C. E. T.   18 Oct. 13
Jones, F.   20 Dec. 13
Puckridge, G. M.   11 Dec. 13
Clarke, E. G.   13 Dec. 13
Brearley, A. J.   1 April 14

Adjutant.

✗ Wrey, R. C., Capt. Devon. R.   1 Mar. 12

Quarter-Master.

Horswell, J., *hon. lt.*   21 Mar. 14

Medical Officers.

Ryan, Lt. R. P., R.A.M.C. (T. F.) (*attd.*)   1 Feb. 11
Brydon, Lt. J. E., *M.B.*, R.A.M.C. (T.F.) (*attd.*) 3 Jan. 14

Chaplain.

[Uniform—*Scarlet*, Facings—*Lincoln Green*.]

Cadet Unit affiliated.
Dartmouth Cadet Company.

THE SUFFOLK REGIMENT.

Regimental District No. **12**. [No. **9** District.]

The Castle and Key, superscribed "Gibraltar, 1779-83," and with the motto,
"*Montis Insignia Calpe,*" underneath.
"Dettingen," "Minden," "Seringapatam," "India," "South Africa, 1851-2-3," "New Zealand,"
"Afghanistan, 1878-80," "South Africa, 1899-1902."

Regular and Special Reserve Battalions.

Uniform—Scarlet.   *Facings*—Yellow.   *Agents*—Messrs. Cox & Co.

1st Bn. } (12th Foot) {	Khartoum (*for Ranikhet*).	3rd Bn. (West Suffolk Mil.)	Bury St. Edmunds.
2nd ,,	Curragh.		
Depôt ..	.. Bury St. Edmunds.	Record Office	Warley.

Territorial Force Battalions.

4th Bn.	.. Portman Road, Ipswich.	6th Bn.	Ipswich.
5th ,, ...	.. Bury St. Edmunds.		

Allied Regiment of Dominion of New Zealand.
3rd (Auckland) Regiment ("Countess of Ranfurly's Own").

Colonel .. .. **C.** Ward, Hon. Lt.-Gen. *Hon.* B. M., *C.B.*, ret. pay 10Jan.04

1st and 2nd Battalions.

Lt.-Colonels. (2)
1 Wallace, W. B., *p.a.c.* 7Jan.12
cl 2Brett, C. A. H., *D.S.O.* 24Feb.14

Majors. (8)
1 Clifford, H. F. H. 7June10
(3)2 Crooke, C. D. P. (Comdg. Depôt) 25June10
2 Doughty E. C. 8July11
1 Smith, H. d'A. 11Oct.11
2 Peebles, A. S., *D.S.O.* 7Jan.12
1 White, F. A., *D.S.O.*
2 Wilson, F. T. D. 24Feb.14
2 Barnardiston, S.J.B., *D.S.O.* 2Mar.14

Captains. (14)
r. Sinclair Thomson, G. A. L. 21Feb.05
c.o.Newstead, G. P. 15Mar.05
s. Walford, G. H., *p.s.c.* 8Apr.05
1 Cooper, F. S. 21Oct.05
c.o.Coles, E. G. 20May08
2 Wood-Martin, F. W. 23Dec.05
m.c.Maycock, F. W. C., *D.S.O.* 11Feb.06
1 Jourdain, E. N. 17Sept.08
s. Nicholson, W. N., *p.s.c.* 7May10
(3)1 Taylor, A. G. 7May10
2 Orford, E. E. 7June10
t. Cockburn, R. 25June10
(3)1 Currey, V. F. 17Aug.10
e.a. Smith, H. C. 4Jan.11
1 Brander, G. E. 18Jan.11
2 Reid, E. H. 9Mar.11
1 Thomas, H. E. 9Mar.11
2 Pearson, E. E. 9Mar.11
1 Walker, P. S. 8July11
c.o.Terry, W. J. 7Jan.12

Captains—contd.
(3)2 Robinson, J. H., *o.* 7Jan.12
2 Campbell, W. M. 24Feb.14
t. Needham, R. M. B. 24Feb.14
1 Balders, D. V. M., *Adjt.* 24Feb.14
c.o. Willis, M. H. S. 2Mar.14
m.c.Stubbs, G. C. 2Mar.14
2 Cutbill, A. M., *Adjt.* 2Mar.14
2 Hepworth, L. F. 2Mar.14

Lieutenants. (20)
e.a.Bond, I. R. B. 27Feb.08
c.o.Silver, S. W. H. 17Sept.08
2 Bittleston, N. A. 2Jan.09
1 Arnold, K. F. F. W. 6Ma.,.09
1 Campbell, J. A. 2Aug.09
c.o.Carew, P. F. 7Dec.09
1 Leach, R. W. 8Feb.10
(3)1 Harris, P. C. 17Aug.10
c.o. Metssner, C. W. 11Jan.14
(3)2 Attree, F. W. W. T. 28Sept.10
1 Leith-Hay-Clark, N. 22Oct.10
c.o.Smith, E. C. 1Jan.11
2 Gadd, H. R. 4Jan.11
2 Reynolds, T. W. 1Apr.11
1 Williams, E. C. T. B. 1May11
1 Moysey, E. 1May11
s. Chalmers, R. 8July11
1 Bolton, D. St 29Nov.11
2 Oakes, N. B. 1Nov.12
1 May, E. C. 12Sept.13
c.o.Macpherson, A. l. 11Jan.14
1 Forbes, D. K. 1Feb.14
1 Bradley, B. 1Feb.14
f.c.1 Carpenter, G. G. 24Feb.14
1 Wood, O. I. 2Mar.14

2nd Lieutenants. (12)
1 Smith, C.F.B. 23Sept.11
2 Morgan, J. B. 11Oct.11
1 Hunt, E. D. C. 19Jan.12
2 Péreira, F. V. C.
1 Selby, H. P. 13Mar.12
2 Backhouse, E. H. W. 24May13
?Harvey, R.G.C. 25Feb.14

Adjutants.
2 Cutbill, A. M., *capt.* 1Nov.12
1 Balders, D. V. M., *capt.* 31Dec.13

Quarter-Masters.
r. Potter, J. T. 7Feb.94
hon. maj. 7Feb.09
2 Blackwell, W., 17Jan.03
hon. capt. 17Jan.13
1 Godbolt, B., *hon. lt.* 26Mar.13

Special Reserve.

2nd Lieutenant.
s. Payne, L. G. S. 16Nov.12

3rd Battalion.

(*Officers serving on 27 Sept. 02 in the corresponding Militia unit hold honorary Army rank equivalent to rank they then held. Other officers entitled to honorary Army rank have it shown against their names.*)

Hon. Colonel.
Greene, Sir E. W., *Bt.* 7June06

Lt.-Colonel.
✗ Lloyd, S. E. M., Maj. ret. pay (*Res. of Off.*) (Q) (g) (H)
⌧ (a) 25June10

Major.
r.e.Crooke, C. D. P. 25June10
Allfrey, F. E., *Capt.* ret. (H) 21Dec.11

Captains. (5)
Cautley, W. O., *late* 2nd Lt. 3 Hrs., *hon. me.* 18Nov.99
p.s.✗ Jackson, E. A. (*Hon. Capt in. Army* 30May01)
hon. me. (H) 19Nov.04
 13Feb.04

Captains—contd.
✗ Hausburg, E. F., *Capt. ret. pay* (Q) (H) 22Jan.10
r.e.✗ Taylor, A. G. 7May10
r.e.✗ Robinson, J. H., *o.* 7Jan.12
p.s.Cautley, H. L., *late Lt.* 4 D. G. 8May12
p.s.Winn, A. (H) 23Aug.13

Lieutenants. (11)
Pollock-Hodsoll, G. B. (H) 8Aug.03
p.s.Shapter, L. H. (H) 18Mar.05
r.e.Harris, P. C. 17Aug.10
r.e.Attree, F.W.W.T. 22Oct.10
Rushbrooke, B, D. (*Empld.with British N. Borneo Co.,* —Aug.13) 25Mar.12
George, T. L. 23Apr.13
Hamilton Jackson, E. E. H., *late* 2nd Lt. Suff. R. 23Aug.13

2nd Lieutenants. (8)
Dowse, R. J. O. 7Feb.12
Phillips, V. M. G.
Nicholls, P. C. 11Sept.12
Berrill, F. C. 4Dec.12
Carthew, P. R. W. 12Mar.13
Payne, G. H. (*on prob.*) 4June13
Myddelton, E. G. (*on prob.*) 4June13
James, H. P. 24Sept.13
Roe, C. C. 8Nov.13
Wilder, R. E. P. (*on prob.*) 7Jan.14
Ainsley, C. (*on prob.*) 14Mar.14

Adjutant.
✗ Sinclair Thomson, G. A. L., *Capt.* Suff. R. 25June12
(*Capt. in Army* 21Feb.05)

Quarter-Master.
✗ Potter, J. T., *hon. maj.*

THE SUFFOLK REGIMENT—(Regtl. Dist. No. **12**)—contd.

4th Battalion.

A Castle.

"South Africa, 1900-02."

Portman Road, Ipswich.

Hon. Colonel.

Gwydyr, W. M. C., Lord   5Apr.05

Lt.-Colonel.

p. Garrett, F., TD 11May12

Majors. (2)

p. Turner, F. W., TD (*t*)   19May06
Pretty, F. (*H*)   21May12

Captains. (8)

p. Mason, M. F.   26Nov.04
p. Garrett, S.   23Dec.05
p.s. Clarke, E. P.   9Oct.06
p.s. Money, F., TD, hon. m.   21Sept.07
Brown, E. L.   16Dec.11
Cubitt, F. S.   16May12
Rodwell, F. J.   22July12
   10July12
Mitchell, H. D. 25Feb.13

Lieutenants. (8)

p. Glanfield, B. St. J.   19Oct.08
Catchpole, C.   20July10
Pretty, H.   16Dec.11
Ling, H. F.   16May12
Turner, H. K.   22Feb.13
Turner, M. A.   25Feb.13
Brunger, R.   7June13

2nd Lieutenants. (8)

Pain, J. W.   20Jan12
Henley, H. C.   16Mar.12
Ffrench, D. M. 5Mar.13
Stebbings, G. W.   12Mar 13
Row, H. A.   29May13
Richards, L. J. 30May13
Frere, J. G.   17June14

Adjutant.

Cockburn, R., Capt. Suff. R.   11Aug.12

Quarter-Master.

Dooley, W., Qr.-Mr. (hon. capt.) ret. pay (*Res. of Off.*) hon. capt.   22Apr.11

Medical Officers.

Wells, Capt. J.D., M.B., R.A.M.C. (T.F.)(*attd.*) 11Feb.13
   11Aug.09
Jeaffreson, Lt. G.C., R.A.M.C. (T.F.) (*attd.*)   7Nov.10

Chaplains.

Carter, Rev. H., M.A., Chapl. 4th Class (T.F.)(*attd.*) 16Aug.09

Barber, Rev. R. W., Chapl. 4th Class (T. F.)(*attd.*) 2Oct.09

[Uniform—*Scarlet.* Facings—*Yellow.*]

5th Battalion.

A Castle.

"South Africa, 1900-02."

Bury St. Edmunds.

Hon. Colonel.

Rowley, Sir J. T., Bt., VD (*Hon.Col.ret.Vols.*)   9Aug.02

Lt.-Colonel.

p.s. Armes, W. M., TD (*H*)   21June11

Majors. (2)

p. Wright, C. F. 20May08
Hargrave, H. J.   20May14

Captains. (8)

p. Johnson, H. H. (*H*) *I. of M.* 15Jan.09
p. ✗Kendle, R. H. (*Hon. Capt. in Army* 30May01) (*H*)   5Oct 13
   16July02

Captains—contd.

p.s. Lacy-Scott, G. (*H*)   15June11
Ennion, S. J.   3Apr.12
Oliver, C. M. 1Aug.12
p. Oliver, B. E. 17Sept.12
Ledward, G. W.   1Nov.12

Lieutenants. (8)

Jackson, R. M. 19Apr.10
Mahomed, F. 28Apr.11
Rowley, J. R. 1Aug.12
Tait, W. I.   1Aug.12
Gross, R.M.W. 1Aug.12
Dennis, A.   1Nov.12
Wolton, H. C. 1Nov.12
Ledward, R. B. ⑧   10Feb.14
Rooke, N.   27May14

2nd Lieutenants. (8)

Warnes, G. L. 1Feb.12
Kilner, H. G. 8Mar.12
Hargrave, W. B.4Dec.12
Catchpole, T. J.   31Dec.12
Parker, A. S. 15Jan.13
✗Long, G. H. 3May13
Wilson, P. G. 19Sept.13
Wolton, E. D. 15Dec.13
Ashton, E. M. 21Mar.14

Inst. of Musk.

Johnson, H. H., capt.   19Dec.11

Adjutant.

✗Lawrence, H. M., Capt. Sco. Rif.   6May11

Quarter-Master.

Wills, J. J, L. L., hon. lt.   7July12

Medical Officers.

p. Cale, Capt. W. J., R.A.M.C. (T.F.) (*attd.*) 15June10
   15Dec.06
Everett, Lt. H. F., R.A.M.C. (T.F.) (*attd.*)   17Sept.12

Chaplains.

Spencer, Rev. Canon A. J, M.A., TD, Chapl. 1st Class (T.F.)(*attd.*) 5May14
   5May99
Colville-Wallis, Rev. W., M.A., Chapl. 2nd Class (T.F.) (*attd.*) 15Mar.14
   15Mar 99

[Uniform—*Scarlet.* Facings—*Yellow.*]

6th (Cyclist) Battalion.

Ipswich.

Lt.-Colonel.

Pretty, W.T.,TD 9Aug.11

Major.

Beevor, C. P.   5Aug.12

Captains. (8)

Josselyn, J., *late Maj.* Madras Art. Vols.   1June10
Bevan, E. B., *late Lt.* 3 Bn. Suff. R. 12Oct.10
p.s. Elliston, W.R. 10Sept.13
Peacock, M. R. 1May14

Lieutenants. (5)

Wilson, T.   12Oct.10
Cobbold, C. J. F. (*H*)   21May13
Rands, E. C. ⑧ (*H*)   21May13
Thirtle, A. J.   6May14

2nd Lieutenants. (4)

Beney, E. R. 24July12
Hammond, E. F. E.   18Nov.12
Symns, J. L. 28Sept.13

Adjutant.

Sharland, A. A., Capt. E. Lan. R.   14Nov.11

Quarter-Master.

Campbell, J., hon. lt.   9Aug.11

Medical Officer.

Gibb, Maj., W. A., M.D., R.A.M.C. (T.F.) (*attd.*) 3Dec.13
   3June05

Chaplain.

Key, Rev. S.W., M.A., Chapl. 4th Class (T.F.) (*attd.*) 6June14

[Uniform—*Scarlet.* Facings—*Yellow.*]

PRINCE ALBERT'S (SOMERSET LIGHT INFANTRY).
Regimental District No. **13**. [No. **8** District.]

The Sphinx superscribed "Egypt." A Mural Crown, superscribed "Jellalabad."
"Gibraltar, 1704-5," "Dettingen," "Martinique, 1809," "Ava," "Ghuznee, 1839," "Affghanistan, 1839," "Cabool, 1842." "Sevastopol," "South Africa. 1878-9," "Burma, 1885-87," "Relief of Ladysmith," "South Africa, 1899-1902."

Regular and Special Reserve Battalions.

Uniform—Scarlet.   *Facings*—Blue.   *Agents*—Messrs. Cox & Co.

1st Bn. } (13th Foot) {	Colchester.	3rd Bn. (1st Somerset Mil.)	Taunton
2nd ,, }	Quetta.		
Depôt	Taunton.	Record Office	Exeter.

Territorial Force Battalions.

4th Bn. .. .. .. Lower Bristol Road, Bath. | 5th Bn. .. ..County Territorial Hall, Taunton.

Allied Regiment of Canadian Militia.

13th "Royal Regiment" .. .. Hamilton, Ontario.

Colonel .. Payne, Maj.-Gen. R, I., C.B., D.S.O., s. 5Apr.14

1st and 2nd Battalions.

Lt.-Colonels. (2)
1Swayne, E. H.
    27Nov.13
Platt, E. H. R. C. R.
    21Apr14

Majors. (8)
1Compton, C.W.19Mar.09
2Bowker, W. J., D.S.O.
  [*l*] 26June09
2Hardman, H.Fitz*W.*
    27Nov.09
1Thoyts, F. G. G. 2Apr.10
s. Thicknesse, J. A.
    3Mar.11
2Troyte-Bullock, C. J.
    26Aug.13
(2)1Rawling, C. G.,
  C.I.E. (*Comdg.*
  Depôt) 27Nov.13
1Prowse, C. B. 21Apr14

Captains. (14)
2Wardlaw, P.M. 23May03
1Yatman, A. H. 16July03
s. Currie, R.A. M.,
  p.s.c. 1Jan.04
(2) 1Maud, C. C., D.S.O.
  [F] 3Feb.04
*m.c.*Paterson, A. W. S.
    26Feb.04
2Harrison, J. S. N.
    1Apr.04
s. Allfrey, H. I. R.
    15Apr.04
e.a.Little, C. H. 30May04
2Wilson, A. E. J.
  [F] 20May04
    30May04
1Jones-Mortimer, L.A.
    23Aug.06
2Burges-Short, H. G. R.
    13June06
1Hargreaves, A. J. G. [*l*]
    26Feb.07
(2)2Ritchie, T. F.
    20May08
    18Sept.08
1Freestun, W. H. M.
    1Mar.09
2Worrall, E. W. [L]
    6June09
1Worthington-Wilmer,
  L. E. C., e, 23July09

Captains—contd.
1Watson, W. 17Aug.09
e.a.Bally, E. D. 27Nov.09
(3)2Samuda, C. M. A.
    22Dec.09
*m.c.*Mordaunt, O. C.
    22Jan.10
s.c. Thurlow, E. G. L.
    18Sept.11
2Stone, N. H. 21Apr.14
t. Walsh, T. A. 21Apr14
r. Fleming, J. 21Apr.14

Lieutenants. (20)
(3) 2Campbell, N. A. H.
    2July04
f o. Smith, I. M. [L]
    20May05
1Bradshaw, F.S.12June06
t. Miles, C. W. 10Nov.06
2Lawson, G. W. 20May08
    1Dec.08
2Wasbrough, S. V.
    31Dec.07
o.o. Dickinson, H.C. 16Jan.08
2Atkinson, G. N. 15Feb.08
1Sutton, W. M., *Adjt.*
    19Sept.08
2Majendie, V. H. B.
    21Dec.08
2Waddy, R. H. 21Dec.08
2Mills, F. S. 6June09
1Whittuck, G. E. M.
    23July09
r.l. Watts. R.A, B.P.
    17Aug.09
(3) 1Bellew, F. D. 27Nov.09
2Steer, G. P. 4Jan.11
1Bennett, R. H. E.
    3Mar.11
1Montgomery, R. V.
    1Apr.11
2Williams, C.A., 18Sept.11
2Kenworthy, D. 16Sept.11
1Taylor, J. B. 12Dec.12
2Roche, V. W., *Adjt.*
    5Feb.13
o.l. Denny, R. B. 5Nov.13
1Philby, O. G. B. 5Nov.13
2Molesworth, G. N.
    10Jan.14
o.l. Moore, R. L. 21Apr.14
s.s. Swayne, J. G. des R.
    21Apr.14
1Prideaux, G.A. 21Apr.14

2nd Lieutenants, (12)
f.c. Pretyman, G. F.
    25Mar.11
2Howe, W. T. 4Oct.11
1Parr, G. R. [L] 14Feb.12
1Lane, H. 22Jan.13
2Willis, N. O. 8Sept.13
1Pretyman, E. R.
    17Sept.13
2Ludlow, C. W. P.
    10Dec.13
1Read, A. B. 10Dec.13
1Rowley, H. A. 24Jan.14
1Ford, C C. 25Feb.14
1Caillard, F.C.V.D.
    25Feb.14
2Kennedy, J. H. 10June14

Adjutants.
1Sutton, W. M., *lt.*
    1Jan.13
2Roche, V. W., *lt.*
    16Nov.13

Quarter-Master
2Owens, D. J., *hon lt.*
    3May05
r. French, H., *hon.lt.*
    15Jan.10
1Neate, A., *hon. lt.*
    9May14

Special Reserve.
2nd Lieutenants.
Filleul, L. A. 20Jan.12
Pereira, W. T. 12June12
Henson, S. R.
  (*on prob.*) 17Sept.13
Shannon, R. W.
  (*on prob*) 21Jan.14

3rd Battalion.

(*Officers serving on 4 Dec. 00 in the corresponding Militia unit hold honorary Army rank equivalent to the Militia regimental rank they then held. Other officers entitled to honorary Army rank have it shown against their names.*)

Hon. Colonel.
Henley, H. C. (Hon. Col. ret. *Mila.*) 28Aug.08
    17Nov.97

Lt.-Colonel.
p.s.✕Llewellyn, A.,(*Hon.*
  Capt. in Army 15
  May 02)(*H*) 28Jan.11

Major.
✕Jerrard, A. G. A.,
  Capt. ret. 10Feb.12
r.e. ✕Rawling, C. G.,
  C.I.E. 27Nov.13

Captains. (5)
r.e.✕Maud, C. C.,
  D.S.O. 3Feb.04
r.s.✕Ritchie, T. F.
    20May08
    18Sept.07
r.e.✕Samuda, C.M.A.
    22Dec.09
✕Maud, W. H.,
  C.M.G., *Capt.*
  ret. pay (*Res.*
  of Off.) 1Feb.10
✕Llewellyn, W. W.,
  Lt. ret. pay 10Feb.12
*p.s.*Broderip, J. Y. M.
  (*H*) 23Mar.12
Dickinson, S. C.
  (*t*) (*H*) (*Remount*
  Service) 31May13

Lieutenants. (11)
r.e.✕Campbell, N. A. H.
    2July04
*r.e.*Bellew, F. D. 27Nov.09
Holt, C. T. 13June10
Orr, R. C. 16Dec.11
Milln, K. J. 25Mar.13
Leacroft, R. J. R.
    25Mar.13
Vincent, J. W. M.
    25Mar.13
Gallwey, W. V. D.
    25Mar.13
MacBryan, J.C.W.,
  late 2nd Lt. Som.
  L. I. 25Oct.13
*p.s.*Hussey,H.(*H*) 21Feb.14
Newton, A. V. 21Mar.14

PRINCE ALBERT'S (SOMERSET LIGHT INFANTRY)—(Regtl. Dist. No. 13)—contd.

3rd Bn.—contd.

2nd Lieutenants. (8)
Bush, J. S. 2July12
Edwards, D. C. H. 1Oct.13
Corballis, B.J. (on prob.) 29Oct.13
Snape, F, W. (on prob.) 4Feb.14
Swabey, A. M. E. (on prob.) 7Feb.14

Adjutant.
Fleming, G., Capt. Som. L.I. 1Mar.12
(Capt.inArmy,21Apr.14)

Quarter-Master.
✗French, H., hon. lt.

4th Battalion.

"South Africa, 1900-01."

Lower Bristol Road, Bath.

Hon. Colonel.
p. Langworthy, V. U., vD, late Maj. 4 Bn. Som. L.I. (Hon. Col. ret. Vols.) 11Aug.00

Lt.-Colonel.
✗Cox, W. C., Maj. ret. pay(Res.ofOff.) 7Jan.12

Majors. (2)
p. Openshaw, E. H. (Q) hon. l.c. 27May05
p. Bishop, C.R. (t) 28Jan.07

Captains. (8)
p. Graves-Knytton, R. B. (H) 27July01
p. Baily, E. M. 7June05
p. Bunting, L. K., TD 2Apr.07
Strachey, Hon. E. 14Oct.11
p Timmins, T. B. 27Apr.12
✗Bealey, A. C. 22Aug.12
p.s. Allen, H. C. 25Sept.12
p. Moger, R. 18Sept.13

Lieutenants. (8)
Worger, W. 5July11
Lewis, E. 7Sept.11
Baker, A. H. 25June12
Phillips, W. E. 15Mar.13
Bishop, G. W. R. (H) 26Feb.14
McLaren, D. J. 3May14

2nd Lieutenants. (8)
Moger, W. 5Sept.13
Cary, R. T. O. 15Sept.13
Tanner, H. R. 2Oct.13
Coombs, A. P. 26May14
Wilson, S. 9June14
Lewis, W. 29June14

Adjutant.
Miles, C. W., Lt. Som. L. I., capt. 12Dec.12

Quarter-Master.
May, A., hon. lt. 1June12

Medical Officers.
Lace, Maj. F., TD, R.A.M.C. (T.F.) (attd.) 1Mar.09
3Feb.94

Chaplain.
Jackson, Rev. K. C., M.A., Chapl. 4th Class (T.F.)(attd.) 21Nov.12
Stancomb, Rev. J.M.D., B.A., Chapl. 4th Class (T.F.) (attd.)11June13

[Uniform—Scarlet.
Facings—Blue.]

5th Battalion.

"South Africa, 1900-01."

County Territorial Hall, Taunton.

Hon. Colonel.
p.✗ftt. Patton, H. B., C.B. (Col. ret. Vols.) 21Aug.12

Lt.-Colonel.
✗Cooke-Hurle, E.F., Maj. ret. pay (Res. of Off.) 4Jan.13

Majors. (2)
Paull, J. R., TD, (t) 21Nov.10
Brutton, R. H. (H) 21Nov.10

Captains. (8)
p. Kite, E. B. (H.)30Aug.02
p. ✗Watson, D. S.(Hon. Lt. in Army 4June 01) 1Aug.03
p. Urwick, F. D. (H)(t) 21Jan.05
p.s.Burridge, W. T. (H) 28July06
p.s.Gifford, R. E. (H), I. of M. 1July11
Goodland, C.H. 7May12
p.s.Bradford, W. H.(H) 1Nov.13
Major, A. O. 1Nov.13

Lieutenants. (8)
(p.) Arnold, G. F. ⓐ 1Jan.09
Harris, F. J. 1July11
Timms, A. S. 28Feb.12
Duke, J. 1Oct 12
Calway, F. H. F. 15Nov.13
Hawken, C. C. H. 1Apr.14

2nd Lieutenants. (8)
Ruck, C. F. L. 29Jan.12
Staley, F. C. 3Jan.13
18Sept.06
Blake, J. H. 16Jan.13
Rawlings, G. N. 22May13

Inst. of Musk.
Gifford, R. E., capt. 16June09

Adjutant.
✗Walsh, T. A., Capt. Som. L. I. 1Jan.14

Quarter-Master.
Bond, T., hon. lt. 14Aug.13

Medical Officers.
Murphy, Lt. C. F., R.A.M.C. (T.F.) (attd.) 29Nov.10
Brimblecombe, Lt, S. L., R.A.M.C. (T.F.)(attd.) 11May11

Chaplains.
Newton, Rev. W. L., Chapl. 4th Class (T.F.) (attd.) 13Jan.11

[Uniform—Scarlet.
Facings—Blue.]

THE PRINCE OF WALES'S OWN (WEST YORKSHIRE REGIMENT).

Regimental District No. **14**. [No **5** District.]

The Prince of Wales's Plume. The White Horse. "*Nec aspera terrent.*"
The Royal Tiger, superscribed "India."
"Namur, 1695," "Tournay," "Corunna," "Java," "Waterloo," "Bhurtpore," "Sevastopol,"
"New Zealand," "Afghanistan, 1879-80," "Relief of Ladysmith," "South Africa, 1899-1902."

Regular and Special Reserve Battalions.

Uniform—Scarlet. *Facings*—Buff. *Agents*—Messrs. Cox. & Co.

1st Bn. } (14th Foot)	{ *Lichfield (for Aldershot).*	3rd Bn. (2nd West York Mil.)	.. York.
2nd "	{ *Malta (for Dagshai).*	4th " (4th West York Mil.)	.. York.
Depôt ..	York.	Record Office ..	.. York.

Territorial Force Battalions.

5th Bn.	York.	7th and 8th Bns.	.. Carlton Barracks, Leeds.
6th "	Belle Vue Barracks, Bradford.		

Allied Regiment of Dominion of New Zealand.
16th (Waikato) Regiment.

Colonel .. .. .. Fry, Maj.-Gen. W., *C.V.O., C.B., s.* .. .. .. 28 Feb. 14

1st and 2nd Battalions.

Lt.-Colonels. (2)
2 Phillips, G. F. (*local and temp. Col.*) 23 Feb. 12
1 Towsey, F. W. 7 Mar. 14

Majors. (8)
(8) 1 Barrington, T. P.
(*Comdg. Depôt*) 7 Mar. 06
1 Lang, G. G. 8 Dec. 07
2 Drew, G. B. 23 Feb. 08
s. Price, G. 3 Oct. 09
m.c. Daly, A. C., *p.s.c.* [1]
1 Mar. 10
26 June 02
s. Hume-Spry, L., *D.S.O.*, *p.s.c.* 23 Feb. 12
1 Ingles, A. W. 7 Mar. 14
s. Howard, T. N. S. M.
14 Mar. 14

Captains. (14)
2 Cooper-King, R. G., *e.*
24 Nov. 00
Wood, M. D. 24 Nov. 00
s. Lowe, P. E. H. 24 Nov. 00
2 Ingpen, P. L. 1 Mar. 01
e.a. Logan, M. H. 1 Mar. 01
2 Spencer, A. A. W. 12 Dec. 01
s. Deverell, C. J., *p.s.c.*
23 Feb. 04
2 Francis, S. G., *D.S.O.*
18 Apr. 04
2 Crossman, G. L.,
D.S.O. 26 May 04
e.c. Nicholson, O. H. L.,
D.S.O. 17 Aug. 04
1 Boyall, A. M., *D.S.O.*
19 Jan. 05
(3) 2 Cuthell, A. H. 1 Mar. 05
t. Soames, G. H. 20 May 08
20 May 05
(3) 2 Lemon, F. J. 7 Nov. 08
c.o. Ross, A. M. 11 June 09
1 Grant-Dalton, E. F.
9 Apr. 13
p.s.c. 8 Oct. 09
e.a. Barlow, C. L. 8 Feb. 10
1 Fryer, P. S. 8 Feb. 10
t. Wilkinson, S. J. 5 Mar. 10
1 Lupton, A. W. 5 Mar. 10
1 Harington, H. 5 Mar. 10
s.c. Welchman, E. T.,
D.S.O. 7 Mar. 10
1 De la Pryme, W. H. A.,
Adjt. 16 Apr. 10
1 Fisher, M. 9 July 10
r. Grant-Dalton, D.,
11 Aug. 10

*Captains—*contd.
c.o. Clothier, J. K. 23 Jan. 11
r. Marten, C. P. 23 Jan. 11
e.a. Grigg, S. T. 4 Feb. 11
(3) 1 Armitage, F. A. W.
4 Feb. 11
c.o. Hawley, F. H. 22 Jan. 14
e.a. Davenport, W. A.
22 Jan. 14
t. Cradock-Hartopp,
L. M. 22 Jan. 14
m.c. Green, S. H. 22 Jan. 14
e a. Hobbs, H. F. C. 7 Mar. 14
2 Harington, H. D.
14 Mar. 14
2 Ind, R. J. W. 28 Mar. 14
1 Long-Price, C. E.
8 Apr. 14

Lieutenants. (20)
c.o. Geary-Smith, A. 3 Oct. 09
c.o. Berkley, J. H. 9 Oct. 09
c.o. Hawkins, E.B.B. 7 Mar. 10
1 Costin, B. D. 1 Apr. 10
c.o. Phillips, C. G. 18 Apr. 10
2 Colvin, R. A., *Adjt.*
2 July 10
c.o. Gordon-Alexander,
L.D. 5 July 10
1 Meautys, T. G. 9 July 10
(3) 2 Maufe, S. B. 10 Nov. 10
1 Pickering, H. E.
10 Nov. 10
c.o. Tilly, J. C. 23 Jan. 11
(3) 1 Loveband, A. R.
3 Jan. 12
s. Torr, W. W. T. 10 Jan. 12
2 Daly, V. A. H. 5 Feb. 12
1 Henderson, K. S. S.
3 Apr. 12
f.c. Rodwell, R. M. 17 Apr. 12
1 Eliot, W. L. 18 Sept. 12
c.o. Blackburn, J. C. 10 Oct. 12
2 Foljambe, Hon.
B. M. O. S. 20 Oct. 12
1 Thompson, O. C. W.
19 Dec. 12
p.d. Bilderbeck, W. J. H.
9 Apr. 13
2 Newell, J. G. 12 May 13
2 Arnold, A. H. 12 May 13
2 Ramsbotham, W. H.
2 July 13
2 Perry, G. H. G. 14 Aug. 13
1 Stewart, K.E.S. 29 Oct. 13
2 Harington, F.J. 1 Nov. 13
2 Pickthall, W. E. C.
22 Jan. 14
2 Lowry, A. E. E. [1]
7 Mar. 14
1 Davies, L. A. 25 Mar. 14
2 Shaw, B. H. G. 6 May 14

2nd Lieutenants. (12)
1 Lawson-Smith, J.
3 Sept. 13
1 Langran, W.H. 17 Sept. 13
1 Ratcliffe, B. L. 17 Sept. 13
1 Wright, F. L. 17 Sept. 13
1 Carew, J. 24 Jan. 14
2 Horsford, T. R. O'B.
24 Jan. 14
2 Ruttledge, J. F. 25 Feb. 14
2 Kerr, L. M. 10 June 14

Adjutants.
1 De la Pryme, W. H. A.,
capt. 27 June 12
2 Colvin, R. A., *lt.* 1 Aug. 13

Quarter-Masters.
r. Roberts, W. A., 1 May 02
hon. capt. 1 May 12
2 Andon, W. 23 July 10
28 Nov. 08
hon. capt. 22 May 14
1 Butler, E.G., *hon. lt.*,
3 Aug. 12
r. Hinchcliffe, C.,
hon. lt. 14 Dec. 12

Special Reserve.
2nd Lieutenants.
Milner, G. 25 June 13
Wilson, E. W. 25 June 13
Perkins, J. C. 25 June 13
Whitley, H. C. (*on prob.*) 1 Oct. 13
Stockdale, G. N.
(*on prob.*) 14 Mar. 14
Gill, J. (*on prob.*)
14 Mar. 14
Mocatta, W. E. (*on prob.*) 18 July 14

3rd Battalion.
(*Officers serving on 1 Oct. 02 in the corresponding Militia unit hold honorary Army rank equivalent to the Militia regimental rank they then held. Other officers entitled to honorary Army rank have it shown against their names.*)
Hon. Colonel.
THE KING.

Lt.-Colonel.
XMinogue, J. O'B.,
Maj. ret. pay (*Res. of Off.*) 13 Dec. 12
Major.
r.e. XBarrington, T. P.
7 Mar. 06
XCliff, H.T.(*H*) 19 May 13

Captains. (5).
Isacke, R., Capt.
ret. pay (*Res. of Off.*) (*H*) 7 Mar. 02
p.s.c. XSalmon, T. G. (*H*) ⓑ
28 Mar. 14
21 Nov. 03
r.e. XCuthell, A. H. 1 Mar. 05
p.s.l. X Anson, J. F. J. (*H*) 22 Jan. 07
p.s. Dawson, W. S. (*H*)
30 Sept. 07
r.e. XLemon, F. J. 7 Nov. 08
r.e. XArmitage, F. A. W.
4 Feb. 11
XSpence, H. B., Lt.
ret. pay 17 Feb. 12

Lieutenants. (11)
r.e. Maufe, S. B. 10 Nov. 10
r.e. Loveband, A.R. 3 Jan. 12
Wilson, L. 12 May 14
Geddes, A. A. 12 May 14

2nd Lieutenants. (8)
Tennent, O. M.
(*on prob.*) 4 Mar. 14

Adjutant.
XMarten, C. P.,
Capt. W. York R.
10 Mar. 12
(*Capt. in Army* 23 Jan. 11)
Quarter-Master.
XHinchcliffe, C., *hon. lt.*

4th Battalion.
(*Officers serving on 25 Mar. 02 in the corresponding Militia unit hold honorary Army rank equivalent to the Militia regimental rank they then held. Other officers entitled to honorary Army rank have it shown against their names.*)
Lt.-Colonel.
XTottie, J. B. G.
(*H*) 27 Nov. 08

THE PRINCE OF WALES'S OWN (WEST YORKSHIRE REGIMENT)—Regtl. Dist No. 14)—contd.

4th Bn.—contd.

Majors. (3).
p.s.Birt, A. W. (H) (b) 27Nov.11
✘McLaren, R. J., Capt. ret. pay 28June13
✘Bedingfeld, E.G. 11Oct.13

Captains. (6)
p.s.✘Frankish, W. E. (H) 16Jan.04
p.s.Stevens, F. J. (H) 11Apr.07
✘Slade, C. G. M., Lt. ret. pay 24Apr.07
p.s.Harkness, P. Y. (H) 1May08
✘Smart, G. H., Lt. ret. pay 19May09

Lieutenants. (11).
Bennett, M. G. B. 4Aug.12
(p.s.)Spencer, R. F., late Lt. Durh.L.I. (H) I. of M. 3Sept.13
Leach, R. B. 3Dec.12
Morkill, R. F. 3Dec.12
Bastow, F. S. ⓢ (H) 3Dec.12

2nd Lieutenants. (8)
Singleton, J. H. P.A. (on prob.) 1Oct.13
Kinnell, G. R. (on prob.) 28Jan.14
Robson, A. R. P. (on prob.) 22July14
Inst of Musk.
Spencer, R. F., capt. 3June14

Adjutant.
✘Grant-Dalton, D., Capt. W. York. R. 16Jan.12
(Capt. in Army 11Aug.10)
Quarter-Master.
✘Roberts, W, A., hon. capt.

5th Battalion.
"South Africa, 1900-02."
York.

Lt.-Colonel.
p. ✘Wood, C.E., vᴅ (Hon. Capt. in Army 24June01) (t) 13Mar.14

Majors. (2)
Oddie, W., ᴛᴅ 13Mar.14
p. ✘Cattley, R.(Hon.Capt. in Army 24Sept.02) (H) 29Apr.14

Captains. (8)
p. Thompson, F. C. (t) 6Jan.04
p. McConnell, J. W. (H) 30Dec.05
p. Cross, E. P. 28Mar.06
p. ✘Dale, A.P.(H)13Aug.11
Mackay, D. P. 24July12
Scott, H. C. 24July12
✘Lansdale, R.R. (a) 13Mar.14

Lieutenants. (8)
p.s. Williamson, P. G. 6Oct.06
(p.s.)Bulmer, C 15Aug.09
(p.s.)Sowerby, G. 18Aug.10
Foxton, J.A. 18Aug.10
Peters, J. C. 1Sept.11
(p.) Bland, B. S. 24July12
Mandeville, P. (H) 24July12
Grace, J. E. 18Sept.13
Tucker, F. 13Mar.14

2nd Lieutenants. (8)
Radcliffe, J. F. E. 14Sept.11
Oldfield, F. W. F. 18Aug.10
Freeman, W. H. 24May12
Gaunt, A. 25May12
Green, D. 22Aug.12
Foulds, C. E. 17June13
Wood, R. M. 30Apr.14

Adjutant.
✘Wilkinson, S. J., Capt, W. York R. Feb.13

Quarter-Master.
p. Hill, J.R., hon.m. 1Mar.07

Medical Officers.
p. Stoddart, A. R., M.B., Surg.-Maj. 31Jan.08 22Jan.96
Ray, Capt. M. B., M.D., R.A.M.C. (T.F.) (attd.) 9May14
Shadwell, Lt. H. W., R.A.M.C. (T.F.) (attd.) 11Mar.13

Chaplain.
Macpherson, Rev. R., Chapl. 4th Class (T.F.) (attd.) 1Apr.08 4Aug.06

[Uniform—Scarlet
Facings—Buff.]

6th Battalion.

"South Africa, 1900-02."
Belle Vue Barracks, Bradford.

Hon. Colonel.
✘Helme, Sir G. C., K.C.B., C.M.G., Lt.-Col. ret. pay, Hon. Col. Mila. 1Oct.07

Lt.-Colonel.
Wade, H. O. (H) ⓢ 18Oct.13
Scott, C. E. (t) 11Aug.10
Johnson, H. A., TD, (Q) 4Dec.13

Captains. (8)
p. Clough, R., jun. (Q) 5Nov.04
p. Anderton, H.L. 24Dec.04
Fawcett, E. (H) (a) 4Jan.05
Walker, A. C. C. 18Sept.10
p. Barker, H. W. (t) 28Feb.11
p. Middleton, L. S. (b) 3Jan.14

Lieutenants. (8)
Emsley, J. A. (H) I of M. 1May10
Appleyard, W. 15July11
Miller, N. 1Nov.11
Fell, R. G. 25July13
Heselton, J. L. 1Apr.14
Oddy, J. L. 1Apr.14

2nd Lieutenants. (8)
Tetley, W. G. 1Nov.13
Hamlyn, H. J. 1Feb.14
von Halle, J.J. 20Mar.14
Bernhard, F.H. 25Apr.14
Inst. of Musk.
Emsley, J.A., lt. 29July14

Adjutant.
✘Sandeman, G. R., Lt. Bord. R., capt. 1Jan.14

Quarter-Master.
✘Hill, W. H., Qr.-Mr. (hon. capt.) ret. pay hon. capt. 14Mar.13

Medical Officers.
p. Lodge, Maj. S., M.D., TD, R.A.M.C. (T.F.) (attd.) 14Sept.06 10Mar.94
Hughes, Lt. B , M.R., F.R.C.S., R.A.M.C., T.F. (attd.) 1Mar.14

Chaplains.
Ryan, Rev. V. J. M.A., VD, Chapl. 1st Class (T.F.) (attd.) 1Apr.08 26Nov.87
Whincup, Rev. R., M.A., Chapl. 4th Class (T.F.) (attd.) 21June12

[Uniform—Scarlet
Facings—Buff.]

Cadet Unit affiliated. The Bradford Postal Telegraph Messengers' Cadet Corps.

7th and 8th Battalions (Leeds Rifles).

"South Africa, 1900-02."
Carlton Barracks, eeds.

Hon. Colonel.
✘Mends, H. R. Hon. Brig.-Gen. ret. pay. 1Jan.13

Lt.-Colonels.
p. 7Kirk, A. E., VD, (t) (H) 17Oct.12
8Clark, E. K., TD (t) 7Apr.13

Majors. (4)
8Alexander, J. W., TD ⓢ 9Mar.10
7Tetley, C.H.(H)8Sept.11
7✘Bousfield, H. D. (Hon. Lt. in Army 24June01) 9Sept.11
8Hudson, R. A. (t) 7Apr.13

Captains. (8)
p. 7Redmayne, J.B.20Apr.07
p.s.8Hess, A. F. 6June08
o.s.8Sykes, S. S. 8June08
8Braithwaite, E. W. (H) 9Feb.09
8Berry, W. 9Feb.09
p. 7Stockwell, G. E. (C.(H) I, of M. 9Feb.09
o.s.8Lupton, F. A. (H) 23Feb.09
o.s.8Longbottom, T. 20Sept.11
7Watson, F. L. 1Mar.13
7Lupton, M. 1May13
7Glover, W. E. 1May13

Lieutenants. (16)
8Salter, R. 1Dec.10
8Wilson, A. 1Dec.10
7Clarke, E. J. 1Dec.10
8Brooke, W. H. 24Jan.11
7Watson, G. L. 24Jan.11
7Wilcockson, L. M. 20Sept.11
8Waddington, R. M. (H) 6Oct.11
8ap Ellis, A. ⓢ 1Mar.12
28June10
8Greenwood, W.H. 1July13
7Braithwaite, W.H. 1July13
8Adams, H.A. 1July13
8Hartnell, C. 1July13
8Gawthorpe, J.B. 1July13
7Roberts, E. 23Aug.13

2nd Lieutenants. (16)
8Kitson, Hon. R. D., late Lt. A. Motor Res. 25Apr.12
7May, J. M. 1May12
7Tarr, W. 15July12
7Calvert, R. C. 28Nov.12
7Walling, E. 18Mar.13
8Hossell, L. C. 18Mar.13
8Elkington, S. H. 1June13
7Briggs, R. S. 29July13
7Glazebrook, A. B. 1Jan.14
8Reay, T. P. 1Jan.14
7Bickersteth, R. M. 1Feb.14
8Powys, D. A. 1Feb.14

Inst. of Musk.
8Lupton, F A., capt. 1Nov.09
7Stockwell, G. E. St. C., capt. 17Oct.12

Adjutants. (2)
7Cradock-Hartopp, L.M., Capt. W. York R. 1Nov.13
8Dundas, A. C., Lt. Middx. R., capt. [t] 29Jan.14

Quarter-Masters. (2)
p. 7Booth, E., TD, hon. m. 5Apr.02
8Boult, F., hon. lt. 15Feb.09

Medical Officers.
p. 7Holmes, J., Surg.- Capt. 5Feb.13 16Aug.02

Chaplains.
7Bickersteth, Rev. S., D.D., Chapl. 2nd Class (T.F.) (attd.) 1Apr.08
6Feb.92
8Woollcombe, Rev. H. St. J.S., Chapl. 4th Class (T.F.) (attd.) 1Jan.14

[Uniform—Green.
Facings—Black.]

THE EAST YORKSHIRE REGIMENT.

Regimental District No. **15**. [No. **5** District.]

The White Rose.
"Blenheim," "Ramillies," "Oudenarde," "Malplaquet," "Louisburg," "Quebec, 1759,"
"Martinique, 1762," "Havannah," "St. Lucia, 1778," "Martinique, 1794, 1809," "Guadaloupe, 1810,"
"Afghanistan, 1879-80," "South Africa, 1900-02."

Regular and Special Reserve Battalions.

Uniform—Scarlet. Facings—White. Agents—Messrs. Cox & Co.

1st Bn. } (15th Foot) { York.
2nd „ }   { Kamptee.

3rd Bn. (East York. Mil.) .. .. Beverley.

Depôt .. .. Beverley. Record Office .. .. .. York.

Territorial Force Battalions.

4th Bn. .. Londesborough Barracks, Hull. | 5th Bn. .. Park Street, Hull.

Colonel .. .. .. Grove, Maj.-Gen. Sir C., K.C.B., ret. pay, p.s.c. [R] .. 23Sept.01

1st and 2nd Battalions.

Lt.-Colonels. (2)
1Benson, R. E. 15Aug.11
2Sweetman, M. J. 1Mar.14

Majors. (8)
2Armstrong, W. H. 13June06
s. Clarke, J. L. J., p.s.c. [l] 15Aug.07 29Nov.00
1Young, W. H. 29Apr.08 22Aug.02
2Powell, H. H. 28Aug.10
(3)1Moore, H.G.A. 28 Aug.11 (Comdg. Depôt) 21Feb.05
Warren-Swettenham, T. R. E. W. 3Sept.10
1Campion, W. E. 16Apr.13 22Aug.02
2Pike, W. N. 1Mar.14

Captains. (14)
1Bogle, B. W. 28Aug.01
1Wilson, A. H. 29Jan.03
—1Edwards, E. L. P. 15May03
s. Headlam, T. A. 2June03
r. Berthon, C. P. 20June04
(3)2Twiss, E. F. 30Dec.05
1Lawrence, B.,c. 16Sept.07
2Wilkinson, O. C. 28Sept.07
s.c. Harvey, F. H. 4Apr.08 3Aug.07

Captains—contd.
2Riall, C. P. B. 3Oct.08
(3)1Kino, A. R. 6July10
of 1Anderson, D.F., Adjt. 28Aug.10
1Hind, F. 3Sept.10
(3)2Wrangham, D. G. 26Apr.11
1Cowper, M. G. 28Feb.12
1Maxwell, P. B., p.s.c. [L] 29Oct.12
2Hill, L. G. 29Oct.12
Trimble, J. B. O. 18Dec.12
2Hopkins, R. S. [l] 18Dec.12
2Woodmass, K. T. 18Dec.12

Lieutenants. (19)
2Bray, E. A. 20Apr.05
w.a.Browne, W.S. 8July05
Douglas, G.S.A. 30May04 20May08 20Dec.05
i.v. Stow, M. B. 10Feb.06
2Plimpton, K.A. 20Apr.07
1Leadley-Brown, C. L. 7Sept.07
2Wailes, H. F., Adjt. 28Sept.07
Inglefield, V. E. 8Oct.07
(3)2Coles, J. H. 20May08 27Nov.07
2Saunders, H. C. R. 24Apr.09
s. Wallace, E. 26May09
1Sasse, F. H. 20Oct.09
s.s.Mair, J. A. F. 6July10
w.a.Porter, J. S. 3Sept.10
1Markham, J.A. 3Sept.10
2Ottley, A. G. 11Jan.11
(3)1Grant, A. 1Apr.11
2Hutchinson, B.S.C. 24June14 26Apr.11
1Broadley, W. W. B. 6Oct.11
2Noel, J. B. L. 17Jan.12
1Cosens, H.S.F. 28Feb.12
2Eccles, M. 29Oct.12
2Cart de Lafontaine, A. E. C. 16Apr.13
1Blacker, N.V. 12Dec.13
2Hardiman,H.J. 22Dec13

2nd Lieutenants. (12)
2Prichard, F. G. 4Mar.11
2Addyman, O. J. 25Mar.11
2Wilson, E. S. 14Feb.12
1Smallwood, G. R. 4Dec.12
2Kennard, P. N. 22Jan.13
1Clutterbuck, P. 3Sept.13
1Robson, T. M. 17Sept.13
1Scott, R. T. F. 17Sept.13
1Carruthers, F. 10Dec.13
1Willats, H. L. 25Feb.14
1 Hartcup, J. A. 10June14

Adjutants.
1Anderson, D. F., capt. 30July12
2Wailes, H. F., lt. 31Mar.13

Quarter-Masters.
2Cunningham, F. G. 1May97
hon. maj. 1May12
r. Springhall, J. W., hon. lt. 19Oct.07
1Horrocks, J., hon. lt. 25Nov.11

Special Reserve.
2nd Lieutenants.
Pease, M.R., late 2nd Lt. E. York R. 10July12 4July14
Mellor, A. W. (on prob.) 4Apr.14
Bottomley, T. R. (on prob.) 18Apr.14

3rd Battalion.

(Officers serving on 10 Oct. 02 in the corresponding Militia unit hold honorary Army rank equivalent to the Militia regimental rank they then held. Other officers entitled to honorary Army rank have it shown against their names.)

Hon. Colonel.
Duncombe, G. A. 19July06 21Feb.03

Lt.-Colonel.
p.s. Strickland-Constable, F. C. (H) 3Mar.13

Major.
r.e. Moore, H. G. A. 28Aug.11 21Feb.06
Wrangham, D. F. 3Mar.13

Captains. (5)
Walker, E. W. (H) 19June05
r.e. Twiss, E. F. 30Dec.05
r.e. Kino, A. R. 6 July10
r.e. Wrangham, D.G. 26Apr.11
p.s. Head, W. G. H. (H) 21Feb.13

Lieutenants. (11)
r.e. Coles, J. H. 20May08
r.e. Grant, A. 27Nov.07 1Apr.11
Staveley, F. S. 3Aug.12

2nd Lieutenants. (8)
Waterfall, V. 27Jan.12
Elrington, G. G. C. 10Oct.12
Nightingale, P. R. (on prob.) 4Apr.14
Huntriss, C.J.(on prob.) 25July14

Adjutant.
Berthon, C. P., Capt. E. York. R. 10Oct.11
(Capt. in Army 20June04)

Quarter-Master.
Springhall, J. W., hon. lt.

THE EAST YORKSHIRE REGIMENT—(Regtl. Dist. No. **15**)—*contd.*

4th Battalion.

"South Africa, 1900-01."

Londesborough Barracks,
Hull.

Hon. Colonel.

⚔Sykes Sir M., Bt.,
Lt.-Col. 5 Bn.
York R. (*Hon.*
Capt. in Army) 1Apr.13

Lt.-Colonel.

p.s.Shaw, G. H., VD,
(t)   6Jan.12

Majors. (2)

Holdich, T. W., TD,
(t)   24Nov.07
Easton, A.(t) 21July12

Captains. (8)

r. Earle, C. ⊕ 11July00
p.s.Gosschalk, H.J.(H)(t)
   18June04
p. Theilmann, C. E.
[L]   1Jan.07
p.s.Farrell, B. 24Nov.07
p.s.Sissons, A. (H) 20Feb.08
p. Robson, P. 17June11
Morrill, T. J. 18May12
Quibell, S. B. 25Apr.13

Lieutenants. (9)

Sharp, B. M. R. (H)
   27Nov.10
Shaw, A. G. ⑱ 18Nov.11
Ingleby, C. J. 18Nov.11
Lawrence, G. E.
   18May12
Easton, C. 26Dec.12
Dales, H. 14June13
Judge, C. H. 14June13
Holtby, E. 14June13

2nd Lieutenants. (8)

Rishworth, J. 4Apr.12
Parker, T. S. 26Apr.13
Seed, H. N. 20Feb.14

Adjutant.

⚔Wilkinson, W. T.,
D.S.O., Capt. K. O.
Sco. Bord. 10Mar.13

Quarter-Master.

Cook, F. W. hon. lt.
   21 Jan. 12

Medical Officers.

p. Falkner, Lt.-Col.
H. G., R.A.M.C.
(T.F.) (*attd.*) 1Apr.08
   23June94
Harland, Capt. W.C.F.,
M.B., R.A.M.C.
(T.F.) (*attd.*) 6Oct.13
   6Apr.10

Chaplain.

Lillingston, *Rev.* A.
B.G., *M.A.*, Chapl.
4th Class (T.F.)
(*attd.*) 1Apr.08
   June05

[Uniform—*Scarlet*.
Facings—*White*.]

5th (Cyclist) Battalion.

Park Street, Hull.

Hon. Colonel.

Londesborough, W. F.
H., Earl of, K.C.V.O.,
late Hon. Col. 2 V.B.
E. York R. 1Oct.09

Lt.-Colonel.

Aske, *Sir* R. W.,
Knt., (H) 20Aug.10

Major.

Blackburn, W. H., VD,
   20Aug.10

Captains. (5)

p. Green, W. 1Apr.09
⚔Turton, E. (H)
I. of M. 1Oct.10
Groves, W. R. (H)
   1Oct.10
Sinton, C. McD. 1Oct.10
Butterfield, A. E.
   1Oct.10
Woodger, S. R. (H)
   12Aug.12
   15May08

Lieutenants. (5)

Schottlander, A.
   2Oct.10
Gibson, C. E. 2Oct.10
Woods, A. 17Oct.11

Lieutenants—*contd.*

Jeff, R. H. 17Oct.11
Bickersteth, E. H.
   17Oct.11

2nd Lieutenants. (4)

Philip, K. 15May11
Audas, F. E. 20Apr.13
Jefferson, G. W. 17Feb.14

Inst. of Musk.

Turton, E., *capt.* 2Oct.10

Adjutant.

Groom, G. B., Lt.
W.I.R., *capt.* 1Nov.11

Quarter-Master.

⚔Evans, A., hon lt.
   20Mar.14

Medical Officer.

Munro, Lt. H. L., *M.D.*,
R.A.M.C. (T.F.)(*attd.*)
   1Mar.11

Chaplain.

[Uniform—*Green*.
Facings—*Scarlet*.]

THE BEDFORDSHIRE REGIMENT.
Regimental District, No. 16. [No. 9 District.]
The United Red and White Rose.
"Namur, 1695," "Blenheim," "Ramillies," "Oudenarde," "Malplaquet," "Surinam," "Chitral." "South Africa, 1900-02."

Regular and Special Reserve Battalions.
Uniform—Scarlet. *Facings*—White. *Agents*—Messrs. Holt & Co.

1st Bn. } (16th Foot) {	Mullingar.	3rd Bn. (Bedford Mil.) .. .. Bedford.
2nd ,,	Roberts' Heights, Transvaal.	4th ,, (Hertford Mil.) .. .. Hertford.
Depôt	Bedford.	Record Office. .. .. Warley.

Territorial Force Battalion.
5th Bn. .. ..Gwyn Street, Bedford.

Colonel .. .. Pilcher, Maj.-Gen. T.D., C.B., p.s.c. [L] [R] s, ... 22Apr.14

1st and 2nd Battalions.

Lt.-Colonels. (2)
2Coates, H.W.U., D.S.O. 1Sept.13
1Griffith, C. R. J., D.S.O. 16Oct.13

Majors. (8)
(3)1Roche, B. R. (Comdg.Depôt)22July06
2Traill, J. M. 6Dec.06
2Stares, R. P. 10Oct.08
(1)Onslow, C. C. 8June10
1Thorpe, E. I. de S. [l] 21Sept.12
s, Jebb, G. D., D S.O., p.s.o. 15Feb.13
29 July11
1Allason, W. [L] 16Oct 13
ⓒ ℭ 1Mackenzie, J. 4Apr.14

Captains. (14)
2Lemon, A. B. 22July06
f. Denne, W. H. 22July06
s c. Jackson, H. C. 2Nov.06
f.c. Webb-Bowen, T. I., 6Dec.06
2Hall, A. G. 6Dec.06
r. Poyntz, H. S. 13Jan.07
(3) 2Liddell, J. S. 21May08
t. Younghusband, H. 10Oct.08
2Bassett, F. M. 16Dec.08
(3) 1Saner, A. E. 18Apr.09
t. Dann, W. R. H. 5Jan.10
s. Monteith, J. C. 5Jan.10
2Tottenham, W. E. W. 5Mar.10
t. Smithers, H. O. H. 1Apr.10
8June10
m. Cumberlege, C. E. 1Apr.10
e.a.Northcote, C. S. 1Apr.10
1Milling, J. McM. 29Sept.10

Captains—contd.
1Ker, C. H. 20Nov.12
2Foss, C. C., Adjt. 20Nov.12
s. Gale, F. H. 5Dec.12
1McCloughin, R. J. 22Jan.13
c.o. Lawder, N. W. 22Jan.13
(3) 2Gaye, A.D., f.c. 22Jan.13
1Macready, J., Adjt. 22Jan.13
2Patron, A. J. 19Apr.13
w.a. Robertson, J. R. 7May13
1Edwards, F. H. 7May13
s. Richardson, A. W. C. 9Aug.13
2Lyddon, E. H. 16Oct.13
1Newington, C. 19Dec.13
2June11
1Le Huquet, R. 20Jan.14
2Moyse, J. J. 12Feb.14

Lieutenants. (20)
2Garnett-Botfield, C. S. 5Mar.10
1Mayne, J. H. 1Apr.10
1Courtenay, H. 1Apr.10
1Wagstaff, W. W.8June10
1Shearman, C. E. G. 1Mar.11
(8) 1Huntriss, H.E. 3May11
c.o. Dawes, H. B. 2Jan.12
1Corah, A. G. 10Feb.12
1Davenport, J.S.13Mar.12
1Gledstanes, S. A. 20Mar.12
(3) 2Bignell, G. 1Apr.12
2Punchard, E. E. 11June12
1Pope, C. 30Oct.12
2Thom. R. R. L. 30Oct.12
2Mills, B. D. 22Jan.13
2Gott, G. E. 1Apr.13
2Anderson, W. C. 1Apr.13
2Thomson, D. G. C. 19Jan.14
1Hatch, R.B.L. 20Jan.14
1Coventry, W.St. J. 21Jan 14
2Fanning, E.G. 12Feb.14

2nd Lieutenants. (12)
2Bastard, W. 19Jan.12
1Rendell, L. W. 23Nov.12
1Birch, J. C. A. 5Feb.13
2Kuhn, A. E. 17Sept.13
2Paterson, J.A.17Sept.13
2Fernandes, D. L. de T. 17Sept.13
2Wright, G. D. C. 24Dec.13
2Bell, C. O. 20May14

Adjutants.
2Foss, C. C., capt. 11Feb.12
1Macready, J., capt. 18Apr.12

Quarter-Masters.
r. Thorpe, A. 22Jan.96
hon. maj. 22Jan.13
2Cressingham, H. 14Feb.08
hon. capt. 14Feb.13
r. Barry, R. J., hon. lt. 2Oct.09
1Peirce, A. E., hon. lt. 5Apr.11

Special Reserve.

2nd Lieutenant.
Litchfield, J. 4May12

3rd Battalion.
(*Officers serving on 4 Dec. 0(in the corresponding Militia unit hold honorary Army rank equivalent to the Militia regimental rank they then held. Other officers entitled to honorary Army rank have it shown against their names.*)

Lt.-Colonel.
Amphill, O. A. V., Lord, G.C.S.I., G.C.I.E. 11June0

Major.
r.e.✗Roche, B. R. 22July06
p.s.✗Windham, H. S. (H) 10June12

Captains. (5)
r.e. Liddell, J. S. 21May08
p.s. Green, H. P. (H) 4Dec.08
✗Balfour, P., Capt. ret. pay 24Mar.09
r.e.✗Saner, A. E. 18Apr.09
Orlebar, B. J. (H) 10June12
r.e. Gaye, A. D., f.c. 22Jan.13

Lieutenants. (11)
Duke, W. A. C.
Lt. ret. pay 21Mar.08
27Nov.09
r.e. Huntriss, H. E. 3May11
r.e. Bignell, G. 1Apr.12
Downes, V.C. 10July13
Walker, W. A. B. 15July13
Edwards, E. A. J. 13May14
Horsford, T. G. M. 13May14

2nd Lieutenants. (8)
Paine, D. M. 20Aug.13
Wingfield, A. E. F. 18Oct.13
Richardson, A. J. (on prob.) 24Jan.14

Adjutant.
✗Poyntz, H. S., Capt. Bedf. R. 1Dec.13
(Capt. in Army 13Jan.07)

Quarter-Master.
✗Thorpe, A., hon. maj.

THE BEDFORDSHIRE REGIMENT (Regtl. Dist. No. **16**)—*contd.*

4th Battalion.

(*Officers serving on 11June02 in the corresponding Militia unit hold honorary Army rank equivalent to the Militia regimental rank they then held. Other officers entitled to honorary Army rank have it shown against their names.*)

Hon. Colonel.

Fellows, R. B., C.B. (*Hon. Col. ret. Mila.*) 14June06

Lt.-Colonel.

✗Salisbury, *Rt. Hon.* J. E. H., *Marq. of*, G.C.V.O., C.B., TD, Col., A.D.C. (*H*) 29Oct.92

Majors. (3)

✗Heaton-Ellis, C.H.B., *hon. l.c.* (*H*) 6July98
✗Boulton, C. P., D.S.O. (*H*) 11July12
✗Croft, R. P. (*H*) 23Sept.13

Captains. (6)

p.s.✗Greenwell, A. E. 6Feb.03
p.s.✗Wolff, C. H. (*H*) (q) (*Chief of Police and Supt. of Prisons, Egba Govt., Nigeria* {27Nov.12 {1Sept.09) 17Sept.04
p.s.Halsey, W. J. (*H*) 22Jan.06
p.s.Collings-Wells, J. S. (*H*) 3Jan.07

Captains—contd.

✗Carthew, T. W. C., Lt. ret. pay 9Apr.10
p.s.Hanbury, R. F. (*H*) 11July12

Lieutenants. (11)

Stonor, Hon. E. M., late 2nd Lt. North'd Fus. 26Dec.06
 27Dec.07
Andrews, L. H. G. (*Empld. with Trinidad Police 16 June 12*) 1May11
Tollemache, H. W. M. (*H*) I. of M. 2Dec.11
Charlton, St. J. A. 2Dec.11
Rough, W. A. S. 27Jan.12
Harding, R. D. S. 17Mar.13
Cavan, P. C. 22May13

2nd Lieutenants. (8)

Inst. of Musk.
Tollemache, H. W. M., *lt.* 18Apr.14

Adjutant.
Wild, W. H., Capt North'd Fus. 1Oct.11
(*Capt. in Army 19May00*)

Quarter-Master.
Barry, R. J., *hon. lt.*

5th Battalion.

"South Africa, 1900–02."

Gwyn Street, Bedford.

Hon. Colonel.

✗Jackson, S., Maj, ret. pay (*Hon. Col. ret., T.F.*) 7Feb.12

Lt.-Colonel.

p. Butler, F. N. 20Jan.12

Majors. (2)

✗Brighten, E. W. 20Jan.12
Clutton, J. (*H*) 3Apr.14

Captains. (3)

p.s.Metcalfe, C. H. F. (*H*) 25Jan.09
Taylor, J. W. (*H*) 24Sept.10
Hill, J. E. 2May13
p.s.Meakin, W. K. 16May14
 10May13

Lieutenants. (8)

Norris, G. J. (*H*) 1Apr.11
Webb, R. L. 1Apr.11
Batten, J. K. 2May13
Smythe, R. M. 2May13
Cumberland, B. C. 2May13
Forrest, R. 3Apr.14

2nd Lieutenants. (8)

Dunstan, R. A. 4Aug.10
Baker, C. T. 25Oct.12
Andreini, E. V. 26Apr.13
James, C. R. 25May13
Miskin, C. H. 4Feb.14
Lydekker, C. R. 14Mar.14
Chirnside, W. S. 28Mar.14
Shoosmith, F. S. 27May14
Franklin, T. A. 3June14
Ballance, F. W. 17June14
Clark, R. O. 1July14
Hobbs, F. B. 1July14
Hobbs, G. N. 1July14

Adjutant.

Younghusband, H., Capt. Bedf. R. 12Feb.14

Quarter-Master.

Kiddle, E., *hon. lt.* 14Jan.14

Medical Officer.

McBride, Capt. J. B., R.A.M.C. (T.F.) (*attd.*) 25Mar.05
 26Feb.02

Chaplain.

Baker, *Rev.* W. W. C., M.A., Chapl. 3rd Class (T.F.) (*attd.*) 23Apr.12
 23Apr.02

[Uniform—*Scarlet*.
Facings—*White*.]

THE LEICESTERSHIRE REGIMENT.
Regimental District No. **17**. [No. **6** District.]

The Royal Tiger, superscribed "Hindoostan."

"Namur, 1695," "Louisburg," "Martinique, 1762," "Havannah," "Ghuznee, 1839," "Khelat,"
"Affghanistan, 1839," "Sevastopol," "Ali Masjid,"
"Afghanistan, 1878-79," "Defence of Ladysmith," "South Africa, 1899-1902."

Regular and Special Reserve Battalions.
Uniform—Scarlet. Facings—White. *Agents*—Messrs. Cox & Co.

1st Bn. ⎫ (17th Foot) ⎰ *Fermoy.*
2nd ,, ⎭ ⎱ *Ranikhet (for Dinapore).*   3rd Bn. (Leicestershire Mil.) .. ..*Leicester.*

Depôt .. *Leicester.*   Record Office .. .. .. *Lichfield.*

Territorial Force Battalions.
4th Bn. .. .. *Oxford Street, Leicester.* | 5th Bn. .. .. .. *Drill Hall, Loughborough.*

Colonel .. .. ℭ. Tompson, Hon. Maj.-Gen. W. D., *C.B., r.f.p.*   29July12

1st and 2nd Battalions.

Lt.-Colonels. (2)
1 Croker, H. L. 11Nov.10
2 Blackader, C. G., D.S.O. [l] 10Sept.12

Majors. (8)
2 Drew, T. M. 11Nov.06
2 Gordon, H. [F] 26June07
1 Smith, H. S. 4Sept.08
2 Knatchbull, R. N., D.S.O. 10Sept.08
1 Dent, B. C. 11Dec.09
1 Dwyer, B. C., p.s.c. [l] 11Nov.10
(3)1 Challenor,E.L.,(Comdg. Depôt) 20July12
2 Paul, J. R. A. H., D.S.O. 10Sept.12

Captains. (14)
s. Haig, C. H. 1Apr.02
(3) 2Lewis, F. 26Apr.02
s. Young, W. H. W., p.a.c. 18Dec.07
c.o. Puckle, T. N. 11Dec.01
1 Gruchy, F. Le M N., 1Feb.08
3Mar.08
2 Grant, H. A. 20Sept.05
s.c. Hare, C. T. M. 9Oct.05
Bromfield, W. T. 29Dec.06
11Dec.05
c.o. Henderson, R. F. S. 29Apr.07
(3) 1Brock, A. W. S. 29Apr.07
(3) 2Colquhoun, A. F. R. 4Sept.08
c.o. Davies, C. S. 4Sept.08
c.a. Ross, E. H. 4Sept.08
s. Liddell, C. G. 17Oct.08
o.d. Dixon, W. C., *c., o.* 17Oct.08
t. Creagh, P. H. 13Nov.08
s. Bacchus, J. 11Dec.09
2 Romilly, F. H. 9Feb.10
1Apr.06

Captains—contd.
1 Hawes, R. F. 16May10
2 Tristram, L. B. C. 9Oct.12
1 Tollemache-Tollemache, L. S. D. O. F.-f. T.-T de O. P. 9Oct.12
1 Tidswell, E. S. W., *Adjt.* 14Oct.12
2 Latham, F., *Adjt.* 8Mar.13
t. Stevenson, H. D. M. 8Mar.13
2 Clarke, B. F. 8Mar.13
r. Gillespie, R. H. 8Mar.13
1 Utterson, A. T. Le M. 18May13
t. Dyer Bennet, R. S. 1Sept.13
1 Wilson, W. C. 1Nov.13
1 Yalland, R. R. 1Nov.13
2 Weir, D. L. 2May14

Lieutenants. (19)
(1) Copeman, M. G. B. 8Sept.09
c.o. Viney, P. E. 16May10
(3) 2Tanqueray-Willaume, H. C. 28Mar.11
1 Rolph, C. C. 27Mar.11
(3) 1Morgan, N. A. 1Apr.11
c.p. Pinder, H. S. 1June11
2 Le Fanu, R. [l] 14Sept.11
1 Brown, H. B. 18Sept.11
2 Wardle, M. K. 25Oct.11
1 Waller, J. T. 3July12
1 Frain, T. [L] 9Oct.12
2 Chudleigh, C. A. E. 14Oct.12
1 Mosse, J. W. E. 1Dec.12
i. Williams, S. C. 19Feb.13
2 Ames, R. H. 8Mar.13
1 Weyman, A. 8Mar.13
1 Smeathman, C. 8Mar.13
15May13
1 Dods, W. H. G. 18May13
2 Dickinson, G. C. 18Sept.13
1 Herring-Cooper, J. G. 1Nov.13
2 Tunks, G. P. D'A. G. 28Mar.14
1 Bayfield, H. L. 16May14

2nd Lieutenants. (12)
2 Lowther, R. A. N. 4Sept.12
2 Quayle, G. A. 4Sept 12
1 Grimble, H. N. H. 4Dec.12
2 Grylls, T. R. 22Jan.13
2 Wateridge, E. L. 24May13
2 Seton-Browne, M. W. 8Sept.13
2 Pakenham, E. H. 8Sept.13
2 Raleigh, H. M. 17Sept.13
1 Wykes, G. N. 10Dec.13
2 Deane, W. P. 24Jan.14
1 Cox, C. H. V. 25Feb.14

Adjutants.
1 Tidswell, E. S. W., *capt.* 14Oct.12
2 Latham, F., *capt.* 28Mar.14

Quarter-Masters.
1 Greasley, J. H. 28May03
hon. capt. 28May13
r. Clover, W. C., *hon. lt.* 10Sept.04
2 Wood, A., *hon. lt.* 25Oct.11

3rd Battalion.

(Officers serving on 4 Oct. 02 in the corresponding Militia unit hold honorary Army rank equivalent to the Militia regimental rank they then held. Other officers entitled to honorary Army rank have it shown against their names.)

Hon. Colonel.
p.s. Rutland, H. J. *s.*, Duke of 21June06
6Oct.06

Lt.-Colonel.
P.s. Palmer, C. H. D. 28Feb.14

Major.
p.s. ✕Turner, C. (H) (b) 21May04
r.e. ✕Challenor, E. L. 20July12

Captains. (5)
p.s. ✕Fuller, P. R., *hon. m.* (H) 28May92
p.s. ✕Radford, R. H. (H) 8Apr.02
r.e. ✕Lewis, F. 26Apr.02
p.s. ✕Harrison, F. D., *p.v.c.* (H) (a) (t) (g) 21May04
p.s. ✕Evans, W. R. (H) *p.v.c.* (Asst. Inspr. Bd. of Agricultured Fisheries, 23 June 09) 26June05
r.e. ✕Brock, A. W. S. 29Apr.07
r.e. ✕Colquhoun, A. F. R. 4Sept.08
Ford, F. I., *Capt. ret. pay* 26Nov.10
✕Bamford, C. A., *Lt. ret. pay* 28Aug.12
Bellwood, C. P., *Lt. ret. pay* 2Apr.13

Lieutenants. (11)
r.e. Tanqueray-Willaume, H. C. 28Mar.11
r.e. Morgan, N. A. 1Apr.11
Herbison, C. W. 16Feb.12
Vandeleur, B. T., late 2nd Lt. Durh. L.I. 1Oct.13

2nd Lieutenants. (8)

Adjutant.
Gillespie, R. H., *Capt.Leic.R.* 27Mar.14
(*Capt. in Army* 8Mar13)

Quarter-Master.
✕Clover, W. C., *hon. lt.*

THE LEICESTERSHIRE REGIMENT—(Regtl. Dist No. 17)—contd.

4th Battalion.

"South Africa, 1900-02."

Oxford Street, Leicester.

Hon. Colonel.
p.s.Rutland, H. J. B.,
Duke of 13Oct.97

Lt.-Colonel.
p. ✗Harrison, W. A., TD,
(Hon. Capt. in
Army 24 June 01)
ⓒ 10May13

Major.
Wykes, L. V. (H)(t)
18Sept.09
Potter, J. A. ⓒ 1May13

Captains. (8)
p.s.Cooper, A. C. 17Jan.07
p.s.Fielding-Johnson,
T. P. 9Aug.07
p.s.Viccars, J.E.(H)(q)
11July08
p.s.✗Baines, J. C. (q)
(H) I. of M. 14May09
p.s.Newill, B. F.(q)26Apr.10
Haylock, H.(H)1May13

Lieutenants. (8)
Faire, R. A. 26Feb.10
Jarvis, W. B. 26Feb.10
Pearce, S. M. 28Feb.11
Harvey, G. J. 1Apr.13
Tarr, F. N. 11May13

2nd Lieutenants. (8)
Parsons, J.S.ⓒ 22Jan.12
Abell, J. G. 23Jan.12
Parr, F. S 27Apr.12
Bradlaw, H. J. 29May12
Whittingham, T.
10May13
Brice, H. C. 10May13
Green, R. S. 1Dec.13

Inst. of Musk.
✗Baines, J. C., capt.
18Sept.09

Adjutant.
Dyer Bennet, R. S.,
Capt. Leic. R. 1Nov.13

Quarter-Master.
✗Ball, E.A., hon.lt.
4July12

Chaplain.
Sanders, Rev. Canon
S. J. W., M.A.,
LL.D., Chapl. 2nd
Class (T.F.),(attd.)
3Mar.09
3Mar.94

[Uniform—Scarlet.
Facings—White.]

5th Battalion.

Drill Hall, Loughborough.

"South Africa, 1900-02."

Hon. Colonel.
✗Ranksborough, Hon.
Maj-Gen. J. F., Lord
C.V.O., C.B., ret.
pay (Extra Equerry
to Queen Alexandra
{ 7 May 10
{ 8 Mar. 01) 1Apr.08

Lt.-Colonel.
p.s.✗Jones, C.H.(Hon.
Lt. in Army 24
June 01) (Q) (H)
19Mar.13

Majors. (2)
Martin, R. E. (t)(H)
19Mar.13
Toller, W.S.N. 17June13

Captains. (8)
p.s.Goward, R. S. 24Jan.06
p.s.Shea,R. P. (q) (local
Maj., O.T.C. 4July10)
16July09
p.s.Jeffries, H. J. F.
(H) I, of M. 20May11
p. Bland, C. (Q) 2Apr.11
p.s.Griffiths, J. L. 19Mar.13
Fowler, S. J. 26Apr.14

Lieutenants. (8)
(p.s.)Hassall, H.S. 26Nov.08
Marsh, A. P. 10Aug.10
Sharp, A. T. 20May11
Jones, R. T. 25Oct.11
Chapman, J. 20Jan.12
Burder, H. G. 11July12
Rawdon-Hastings,
P. C. J. R. 19Mar.13
Burnett, J. 26Apr.14

2nd Lieutenants (8)
Feilden, O. H. 15Jan.12
Vincent, J. D. A.
13June12
Aked, G. 26Oct.12
Shields, C. F. 10Feb.13
Farmer, R. D. 6June13
Moore, A. G. de A.
1Dec.13
Barrowcliff, A. M.
10Jan.14
Lawton, R. C. 16Mar.14

Inst. of Musk.
Jeffries, H. J. F.,
capt. 20Dec.13

Adjutant.
✗Bromfield, W. T.,
Capt. Leic. R.
23July12

Quarter-Master.
Worley, A. A.,
hon. lt. 20May13

Medical Officer.
Haynes, Lt. H. G. L.,
R.A.M.C. (T.F.)
(attd.) 13June11

Chaplains.
Blakeney, Rev.Canon
R., M.A., TD, Chapl.
2nd Class [T.F.]
(attd.) 1Apr.08
15Aug.91
Luxmoore, Rev. W.C.,
M.A., Chapl., 4th
Class(T.F.) (attd.)
10Dec.10

[Uniform—Scarlet.
Facings—White.]

THE ROYAL IRISH REGIMENT.
Regimental District No. **18**. [No. **12** District.]

The Harp and Crown. In each of the four corners Escocheon of the Arms of Nassau.
"*Virtutis Namurcensis Proemium.*" The Sphinx, superscribed "Egypt." The Dragon, superscribed "China."
"Namur, 1695," "Blenheim," "Ramillies," "Oudenarde," "Malplaquet," "Pegu," "Sevastopol,"
"New Zealand," "Afghanistan, 1879-80," "Tel-el-Kebir," "Egypt, 1882," "Nile,1884-85,"
"South Africa, 1900-02,"

Regular and Special Reserve Battalions.
Uniform—Scarlet. Facings—Blue. Agents—Messrs. Cox & Co.
1st Bn. } (18th Foot) { .. Nasirabad. 3rd Bn. (North Tipperary Mil.) .. Clonmel.
2nd „ } { .. Devonport. 4th „ (Kilkenny Mil.) .. .. Kilkenny.
Depôt .. .. Clonmel. Record Office .. .. .. Cork.

Allied Regiment of Dominion of New Zealand.
7th (Wellington West Coast) Regiment.

Colonel-in-Chief .. French, Field-Marshal Sir J. D. P., G.C.B.,G.C.V.O. K,C.M.G., Col. 19 Hrs. [R] 26Mar.13
Colonel .. .. ffl. Gregorie, Maj.-Gen. C. F., C.B., ret. pay [R] 31Dec.97

1st and 2nd Battalions.

Lt.-Colonels. (2)
1Forbes, G. F. R.
  12Mar.12
2Cox, St. J. A. 19Feb.13

Majors. (8)
1Moriarty, R. G. S.
  10Mar.08
2St. Leger, S. E.
  12Mar.08
1Milner, F. E. 19Feb.09
(2) Daniell, E. H. E.,
  D.S.O., p.s.o., q.s.
  28Aug.09
1White, W. H. 18Aug.10
(3) 2Welch, M. H. E.,
  p s.o [l] (Comdg.
  Depot) 12Mar.12
1Lillie, F. S. 19Feb.13
c.o. Lipsett, L. J., p.s.c.,
  e, [l] 17Dec.13

Captains. (14)
c.o.Panter-Downes, E. M.
  6Sept.01
  bt. maj. 22Aug.02
r. Haslam, G. W. P.
  21Feb.03
2Elliot, G.A., e. 14Aug.08
2Martin,R.[l] 28Sept 03
  10July01
e.a.Rees-Mogg, R. J. [F]
  26Aug.04
1Lloyd, E. C. 29Nov.04
2Meller, W. 20May05
  10June05
t. Acton, W. M. 11Aug.06
(2) O'Callaghan, G. A.
  6Apr.07
(2) Furnell, G.O.M. 3Mar.08
2FitzGerald, J. S.,
  p.s.c. 3Mar.08
r. Gregorie, H. G. 8Oct.08
1Knox, A. W. C. 19Oct.08
2George, J. B. 12Oct.08
1Roche-Kelly, E.
  1°u16o9
m. Rudkin, H.E. 20July09
  20Jan.06
i.v. Call, F. 3Aug.09
2Gordon, A. R G., e.
  3Aug.09

Captains—contd.
e.a. Vandeleur, T. B.
  28Aug.09
(3) 1Butler, P. R. 18Sept.09
t. Gledhill, M. R. P. W.
  22Dec.09
(3) 1French, C. A. 22Dec.09
f.c. Burke,C. J. 22Dec.09
  bt. maj. 3June13
1Bowen, F.O. 26Jan.10
m. Biss, H. C. J. 23Feb.10
2MacDonnell, H. C.,
  f.c.r. 25Mar.10
(2) 2Fulda, J. I. 1Apr.10
  s. Childs,B.E.W.10Sept.10
  bt. maj. 21Feb.12
2Forbes, Hon. F.G.A.
  22Jan.12
1Caldecott, A. H.,
  Adjt. 1June12
1Blockley,H.J. 2Nov.13

Lieutenants. (19)
c.o. Ferguson, F. C. 31July07
2Harrison, M. C. C.
  18July08
w.a.Redway, E.G. 17Feb.09
2Frazer, A. D. 3Aug.09
2Phillips, R. E. G.,
  Adjt. 28Aug.09
1Lyons, W. B. 11Oct.09
1Homan, A. S. 6Nov.09
  22Dec.09
1Taylor, T. E. H.
  22Dec.09
2Whitty, P. J. 1Jan.10
1Brown, L. K. V.
  9Mar.10
1Scott, J. D. 29Apr.10
(3) 1Crofton, J.H. 7May10
(3) 1Penrose-Weisted,
  S. R. 23Aug.11
c.o. Brown, H. W. 8Sept.11
2Rushton, F. H. L
  4Oct.11
1Mockler, F. G. R.
  22Jan.12
1Bennett,J. E. 28Mar.12
f.c. Harvey-Kelly, H. D.
  28Oct.12
1Gordon-Ralph, P. J. G.
  24Sept.12
(3)2Foulkes, K. 2Nov.13
2Laing, D. P. 11Nov.13
2Tandy, A. M. S. 4Feb.14
2Anderson, A. E. B.
  27Feb.14
1Pratt, D. H. 15Apr.14

2nd Lieutenants. (12)
1Stacpoole, G. E. G.
  4Nov.11
1Pargiter, A. P. 14Feb.12
1Holmes, N. G. 22May12
2Francis, T. A. 4Sept.12
c. Tibbens, C. B. 22Jan.13
1Pigott,E. J. K. P.
  24Jan.14
1Shine, J. D. 24Jan.14
2Newton-King, A. R.
  24Jan.14
2 Magrath, C. G.
  10June14

Adjutants.
1Caldecott, A. H.
  capt. 1June12
2Phillips, R. E. G.,
  lt. 1Oct.12

Quarter-Masters.
1Fox, J. J. 3Feb.97
  hon. maj. 3Feb.12
2Richings, J., 17June03
  hon., capt. 17June13
r. Mahony, T., hon. lt.
  6Nov.09
r. Harris, S. W.,
  hon. lt. 19Mar.10

Special Reserve.
2nd Lieutenants.
McLoughlin, J. H.
  B.D.(on prob.) 7Jan.14
Nicholson, T. (on
  prob.) 17June14

3rd Battalion.

(*Officers serving on 5July01
in the corresponding
Militia unit hold honor-
ary Army rank equivalent
to the Militia regimental
rank they then held.
Other officers entitled to
honorary Army rank have
it shown against their
names.*)

Hon. Colonel.
Dunalley,H.O'C.,Lord,
  late Lt. Rif. Brig.
  26July08
  10June05

Lt.-Colonel.
Owens, R. L.,
  Maj. ret. pay 3Apr.13

Major.
r.e.×Welch. M. H. E.,
  p.s.c. (l) 12Mar.12
×Farmer, L. L.,
  Capt. ret. pay (Res.
  of Off.) 7May13

Captains. (5)
Dawson, G. S. T. (H)
  4Dec.07
r.e.×Butler, P. R. 18Sept.09
r.e.×French, C.A. 22Dec.09
×Fulda, J. I. 1Apr.10
×Parnis England,
  W. J., Lt.ret. pay
  10Oct.12
Morrogh, J. D.,
  late Lt. R.Ir.Fus.
  S 4July14

Lieutenants. (11)
r.e. Penrose-Weisted,
  S. R. 23Aug.11
Butler, M. H. W.
  1Mar.12
Foulkes, D. 10Apr.13
Guinness, E. C. 10Apr.13
ffrench, C. F. T. O'B.
  18Sept.13
Phillips, E. G. D.
  M. 1Nov.13
r.e. Foulkes, K. 2Nov.13

2nd Lieutenants. (8)
Smyth, J. R. (on
  prob.) 21Mar.14

Adjutant.
×Gregorie, H. G.,
  Capt. R. Ir. Regt.
  21Oct.11
(Capt. in Army 3Oct.08)

Quarter-Master.
×Mahony, T., hon. lt.

THE ROYAL IRISH REGIMENT—(Regtl, Dist, No. **18**)—*contd.*

4th Battalion.

(*Officers serving on 6 July 01 in the corresponding Militia unit hold honorary Army rank equivalent to the Militia regimental rank they then held. Other officers entitled to honorary Army rank have it shown against their names.*)

Hon. Colonel.

Ormonde, Rt. Hon. J. E. W. T., Marq. of, K.P., *late* Capt. 1 L.G. 26July08
7Jan.80

Lt.-Colonel.

✗de Montmorency, M., Maj. ret. pay (*Res. of Off.*) (*H.*) 19Apr.11

Majors. (3)

p.s. Knox, L. 8Aug.09

p.s. Newbery, C.G. 16Dec.11

Poe, J. J. E. (*H*) 19Sept.12

Captains. (6)

p.s. ✗Smithwick, J. A. (*H*) 25Apr.03

Loftus, J. E. B. 27Nov.06

Captains—contd.

✗Christie, J. H., Capt. ret. pay (*H*) 4Dec.09

p.s. O'Brien-Butler, C. D. (*H*) 16Dec.11

Lieutenants. (11)

Cahill, J. N. 15Dec.10

2nd Lieutenants (8)

Bredin, W. E. (on prob.) 24May13
Magner, J. (on prob.) 17Jan.14

2nd Lieuts.—contd.

Stoker, D. H. (on prob.) 24Jan.14
Reardon. W. J. R. (on prob.) 18Feb.14
O'Brien, J. (on prob.) 25Feb.14

Adjutant.

✗Haslam, G. W. P., Capt. R. Ir. Regt. 1June12
(*Capt. in Army* 21Feb.03)

Quarter-Master.

✗Harris, S. W., *hon. lt.*

ALEXANDRA, PRINCESS OF WALES'S OWN (YORKSHIRE REGIMENT).

Regimental District No. **19**. [No. **5** District.]

The Cypher of H.R.H. Alexandra, Princess of Wales, in gold (thereon "Alexandra"), interlaced with the Dannebrog enscribed with the date 1875, and the whole surmounted by the Coronet of the Princess.
"Malplaquet," "Alma," "Inkerman," "Sevastopol," "Tirah," "Relief of Kimberley," "Paardeberg," "South Africa, 1899-1902."

Regular and Special Reserve Battalions.

Uniform—Scarlet.   *Facings*—Grass Green.   *Agents*—Messrs. Holt & Co.

1st Bn. } (19th Foot) { *Barian.*   3rd Bn. (5th West York Mil.) .. .. *Richmond.*
2nd ,,   { *Guernsey.*
Depôt   ..   .. *Richmond.*   Record Office   ..   ..   .. *York.*

Territorial Force Battalions.

4th Bn. .. .. *Northallerton* | 5th Bn. .. .. *Scarborough.*

Colonel-in-Chief .. .. QUEEN ALEXANDRA.

Colonel .. Franklyn, Lt.-Gen. *Sir* W. E., K.C.B., p.s.o., Mil, Sec. to Sec. of State for War .. 2Oct.06

1st and 2nd Battalions.

Lt.-Colonels.
2King, C. A. O. 29Sept.10
1Christian, G., *D.S.O.* [l]
28Mar.11

Majors. (8)
2Caffin, E. G. 23Dec.07
1Alexander, W. L., e.
5Feb.08
c.o. Sinclair-MacLagan,
E. G., *D.S.O.* 28Oct.08
(3) 2Chapman, E. H.
(*Comdg. Depôt*) 11Feb.11
1Edwards, C. V. 28Mar.11
1Mairis, G. B. de M.,
D.S.O., e. 4Nov.11
2Walker, W. B. 3Dec.13
1Carey, M. D. 12Feb.14

Captains. (14)
2Stansfeld, T. W.,
D.S.O. 8Jan.08
19Feb.02
s. Swan, N. E., p.s.o.
18Feb.05
1Bunbury, C. H.
de St. P. 25Dec.05
s. Godman, A. L. 16Jan.06
(2) Brown, E. S. 5Apr.06
2McCall, H. W. 29June06
(3) 1Leatham, B. H.
21July06
2Moss-Blundell, B.
29July06
1Bastow, H. V. 14Feb.08
s. Marsden, C. H. 10Oct.08
1Simonet, K. W. L.
1Apr.09
(3) 2Rollo, W. K. 12May09
2Jeffery, C. G. 25Aug.09
(3) 1Maddison, B. L.
29Sept.10
r. Whatford, S.L. 9Oct.10
t. Westley, J. H. S.
20Jan.11
2Peel, L. 11Feb.11
e.s. *Godwin*, C. C. 11Feb.11
1Ledgard, R. S., *Adjt.*
28Mar.11
m.c. Cumberbatch, H. C.
19July11
c.o. Oakes, O. 29Jan.13
1Lanyon, L. F. 29Jan.13

Captains—contd.
2Levin, H. 23Apr.13
t. Burbury, B. T. 29Sept.13
1Jervelund, C. N.
22Jan.14
2Corser, R. B. 12Feb.14

Lieutenants. (19)
c.o. Ramsden, B. V. 16Jan.08
s.c. *Franklyn*, H. E.
16Jan.08
t. Grant-Dalton, S.
14Feb.08
2Forsyth, C. G., *Adjt.*
12May09
1Mintoft,T.C.[l] 23July09
1Hooton.A.C. 25Aug.09
1Worsdell, G. B.
25Sept.09
1Smith, G. N. N.17Nov.09
c.o. Magee, D. H. 29Sept.10
c.o. Lilley, H. A. 9Oct.10
c.o. Bradford, C. A. 9Nov.10
2Palmer, A. E. G.,
29Nov.10
(3) 2Nevile, G. L. 11Jan.11
1Blackwood, H. F.
16Jan.11
(3)1Richardson, E. J.
20Jan.11
1Atkinson,R.G. 11Feb.11
1Cuff, B. 28Mar.11
2Phayre, R. H. 1Apr.11
1Manly, M. U. 25May11
1Compton-Smith,G.L.
19July11
2Crawley-Boevey, L.
16Nov.12
14Jan.11
1Bagnall, H. S. 23Apr.13
1Bennedik, S. R. W.
29Sept.13
f.o. *Birch*, W.C.K. 27Oct.13
2Ledgard, F. C. 27Oct.13
2Kreyer, H. S. 22Jan.14
1Maude,G.W.E. 12Feb.14

2nd Lieutenants. (12)
2Marriage, L.H.20Sept.11
1Le Sueur, E. G. C.
20Sept.11
2Chauncy, M. A.,
20Sept.11
2Kidd, P. C. 11Oct.11
2Barmby,A.J.W.14Feb.12
2Worsley,W.A. 4Dec.12
2Brooksbank, H. G.
5Feb.13

2nd Lieutenants—contd.
1Errington, J. R. F.
16Sept.13
1Beatson-Bell, A.
24Jan.14
1Middleditch, R. H.
25Feb.14

Adjutants.
2Forsyth, C. G., *lt.*
12Apr.12
1Ledgard, R. S.,
capt. 29Jan.13

Quarter-Masters.
r. Walker, J. 1Oct.08
hon. capt. 1Oct 13
2Pickard, E., *hon.*
28July09
1Howes, W. T.,
hon. lt. 19Mar.13

Special Reserve.

2nd Lieutenants.
Heatly, H. F. 1Apr.13
Lee, N. E. 7Apr.13
Benke, L. L. (on
prob.) 17May13
Brooksbank, S.
(on prob.) 16May14

3rd Battalion.

(*Officers serving on 14 May 02 in the corresponding Militia unit hold honorary Army rank equivalent to the Militia regimental rank they then held. Other officers entitled to honorary Army rank have it shown against their names.*)

Hon. Colonel.
Zetland, Rt. Hon.
L., Marq. of,
K.T., late Lt.
R.H.G. 26May09
17Feb.06

Lt.-Colonel.
p.s.XGunter, *Sir* R. B. N.,
Bt. (H) 8Aug.12

Major.
p.s.XAspinall, R. L.,
D.S.O., hon. l.c.,
Capt. ret. (Q)
(H,@p.v.c.,P.c.
14May06
r.e.XChapman, E. H.
11Feb.11

Captains. (5)
p.s.Hill, R. 21Feb.03
p.s.XWhite, C. R. H)
22Oct.04
r.e.XLeatham, B. H.
21July05
p.s.Gladstone, R. M.
(H) 15May08
r.e. XRollo, W. K. 12May09
XNevile, M. M. H.,
Capt. ret. pay (H) ⑤
29Jan.10
r.e.XMaddison, B. L.
29Sept.10
Raley, W. H. G. (H)
8May13

Lieutenants. (11)
Bell, W. F. I. (H)
1Feb.09
Hanbury, P. (H)
16June09
Gladstone, S. P. (H)
10June10
Wilkie, D. (H)
10June10
r.e. Nevile, G. L. 11Jan.11
r.e. Richardson, E. J.
20Jan.11
Thorne, A. T. 1May12
Walmesley, R. 1May12
Colley, W. H. 28May14
Maude, M. D. W.
28May14

2nd Lieutenants. (8)

Adjutant.
XWhatford, S. L.,
Capt. York, R.9Oct.13
(*Capt. in Army 9Oct.10*)

Quarter-Master.
XWalker, J., *hon. capt.*

ALEXANDRA, PRINCESS OF WALES'S OWN (YORKSHIRE REGIMENT)—(Regtl. Dist. No. **19**)—contd.

4th Battalion.

"South Africa, 1900-02."

Northallerton.

Hon. Colonel.

p. Godman, A. F., C.B.,
VD, (Hon. Col. ret.
Vols.) (t) 30Dec.05

Lt.-Colonel.

✗Bell, M. H. L., TD
(Hon. Capt. in
Army 10July01)
(t) 22Oct.13

Majors. (2)

Scott, H. G. 5Oct.13

Captains. (8).

p. ✗Matthews, H. C.
(Hon. Lt. in Army
26July 02) 30Apr.04
p. Jackson, B. 29Aug.06
p. Graham, A. 4Oct.06
p. Constantine, R. A.
1Mar.11
Bowes-Wilson,
G. H. 1Mar.13
p.s. Constantine, W. W.
(H) 5Oct.13
p.s. Nancarrow, J. V.
17Dec.13
p.s. Charlton, B. H.
(H) I. of M. 1May14

Lieutenants. (8)

p. Mott, W. F. (H) 1Oct.93
Maughan, J. 1Mar.11
Stead, N. W. 1Mar.11
Hutchinson, T. H. (H)
1Mar.13
I'Anson, L. P. 5Oct.13
Chaloner, T. W. P. L.
17Dec.13
Samuelson, G. W.
1May14
Beresford-Peirse,
A.C.P. de la P.
1May 14

2nd Lieutenants. (8)

Scate, C. R. 1Sept.12
Williams, E. 7Mar.13
Jervelund, C.C. 26Apr.13
Richardson, A. J. B.
30Apr.13
Fawcett, H. T. 8Apr.14

Inst. of Musk.

Charlton, B. H.,
capt. 1Jan.13

Adjutant.

✗Eykyn, G. D. P.,
Capt. R. Scots
13Feb.13

Quarter-Master.

Colton, W. H., hon. lt.
5Feb.13

Medical Officers.

de Legh, Maj. H. L.,
M.D., R.A.M.C.
(T.F.) (attd.) 11Nov.08
11Nov.96
Whitehead, C. B.,
M.B., Surg.-Capt.
24Sept.09
24Mar.06

Chaplains.

Holmes, Rev. H. C.,
M.A., VD, Chapl.
1st Class (T.F.)
(attd.) 1Apr.08
31May82
Perkins, Rev. F. L.,
M.A., Chapl. 4th
Class (T.F.) (attd.)
1Apr.08
19May05

[Uniform—Scarlet.
Facings—Grass Green.]

5th Battalion.

"South Africa, 1900-02."

Scarborough.

Hon. Colonel.

Feversham, W. E.,
Earl of, VD. 8May80

Lt.-Colonel.

✗Sykes, Sir M., Bt.
(Hon. Col 4 Bn. E.
York. R.) (Hon.
Capt. in Army 15
May 02) 4Jan.11

Majors. (2)

p. ✗Mortimer, J.,
(Hon. Capt. in
Army 12July01)
(t) (H) 1Apr.08
Wetwan, W. A., TD
(H) 4Jan.11

Captains. (8)

p.s. Pearce, C. H. 1Apr.08
p.s. Purvis, J. B. (H)
4Jan.11
p. Scott, G. J. 21Feb.12
Barber, G. C. 24Apr.13
Robson, F. W. 20Apr.14

Lieutenants. (8).

p.s. Walker, D. H. (H)
1Apr.08
Dufty, T. E. 14June13
Pickles, C. C. 16Sept.13
Wadsworth, J. S.
18Mar.14
Maxwell, G. A. 18Mar.14
Woodcook, F. 8Apr.14
Spofforth, E. R. 8Apr.14
p.s. Brown, H., late Capt.
4 V.B. Suff. R.
18June14

2nd Lieutenants. (8)

Green, R. 12Mar.13
Bentley, R. C. 28Apr.13
1Dec.12
Clarke, A. F. 20Mar.14
Vause, W. 9Apr.14
Purvis, G. B. 22May14
Cranswick, H. S.
22May14

Adjutant.

Grant-Dalton, S.,
Lt. York. R.,
capt. 27Oct.13

Quarter-Master.

✗Rennison, R.,
hon. lt. 14June09

Medical Officer.

Libbey, Capt. E.O.,
R.A.M.C. (T.F.)
(attd.) 16Feb.14
23Mar.10

Chaplains.

Keymer, Rev. B.N.,
M.A., Chapl. 3rd
Class (T.F.) attd.
7Nov.13
7Nov.08
Coates, Rev. C. H.
M.A., Chapl. 4th
Class (T.F.) (attd.)
2Jan.13

[Uniform—Scarlet.
Facings—Grass Green.]

THE LANCASHIRE FUSILIERS.
Regimental District No. **20**. [No **3** District.]

The Sphinx superscribed "Egypt," The Red Rose. "*Omnia Audax.*"
"Dettingen," "Minden," "Egmont-op-Zee," "Maida," "Vimiera," "Corunna," "Vittoria," "Pyrenees,"
"Orthes," "Toulouse," "Peninsula," "Alma," "Inkerman," "Sevastopol," "Lucknow," "Khartoum,"
"Relief of Ladysmith," "South Africa, 1899-1902."

Regular and Special Reserve Battalions.

Uniform—Scarlet.   Facings—White.   Agents—Messrs. Cox & Co.

1st Bn. }(20th Foot){ *Karachi.*	3rd Bn. (7th R. Lancashire Mil.)	.. Bury.
2nd ,, Dover.	4th ,, (7th R. Lancashire Mil.)	.. Bury.
Depôt .. .. .. **Bury.**	Record Office	Preston.

Territorial Force Battalions.

5th Bn.	.. .. *Castle Armoury, Bury.*	7th Bn.	*Drill Hall, Cross Lane, Salford.*
6th ,,	.. .. *Rochdale.*	8th ,, ...	*Drill Hall, Cross Lane, Salford.*

Colonel .. .. .. Blomfield, Maj.-Gen. C. J., *C.B., D.S.O., s.* .. 30June14

1st and 2nd Battalions.

Lt.-Colonels. (2)
1Ormond, H. V. S.
  21Nov.11
2Butler, R. H. K.,
  p.s.c. [*l*]   24June14
  10May13

Majors. (8).
2Adair, A. C. 22Aug.08
1Bishop, H. O. 3Nov.08
1Wade, T. S. H.
  [*L*]   3Nov.08
1Pearson, W. B. 6Feb.10
s. Freeth, G. H. B.,
  D.S.O., p.s.c. 24June10
  bt.lt.-col. 21Feb.12
1Adams, G. S. 30Apr.13
(3) 2Thorne, J. F. V.
  (*Comdg. Depôt*)3May13
2Griffin, C. J. 1Sept.13

Captains. (14)
2Roffey, H. B. 25Jan.00
1Shaw, H. 25Jan.00
s. Allardyce, A. J. 9Feb.00
  bt. maj. 25Mar.02
2Woodman, J. E. S.
  [*l*]   19May00
  22Jan.98
1Willis, R. R. 31July00
1Moody, R.H.M. 20Oct.00
s. de Putron, C.[*l*] 15June01
1Bromley, C., *Adjt.*
  15June01
1Farmar, H.M.,e, 5Oct.01
s. Humphreys, E. T.
  p.s.c.[*l*] 5Oct.01
c. Charlton, L. E. O.,
  D.S.O., p.s.c. 5Oct.01
(3)1Purnell, E. K. 11Jan.02
*s.c.*1Magniac, M. 15Feb.04
21bbetson, C. O. 9Sept.08
Spafford, A. L. 6Feb.10
2Wood, A. C., *D.S.O.*
  15Mar.10
2Spooner, A. H.,
  Adjt. 1Apr.10
t. Kirkby, H. A. 14June10
(3)2Brierley, C. L. 14June10
2North, O. H. 24June10
(3)1Patterson, C. 24June10
*s.c.*Luker, R. 2July10
1Davenport, J. A.
  9Dec.10
t. Wood, G. B. G. 15Jan.12

Lieutenants. (19)
e.a.Beaumont, H. 4May02
1Sidebottom, R. Y.
  15Feb.04
r. Curell, W. B. 15July04
*c.o.*Sargent, J. 14Oct.04
(3)1Ferrers-Guy, M. C.
  18Sept.04
  26Oct.04
1Clayton, R. R. 4Nov.04
1Maunsell, T. B.-L. [*l*]
  11Jan.05
1Haworth, R. 23Jan.05
1Tallents, G. E. 11Mar.05
1Blencowe, A. J. W.
  20May05
r. Madeley, G. H. 8July05
  30May04
2Corbett-Winder, F. F.
  29May09
1Thomas, A. J. N.
  29May09
1Conran, P. W. D.
  23Dec.09
1Cunliffe, T. H. W.
  6Feb.10
2Slingsby, T. 23Feb.10
1Heard, R. J. B. 1Apr.10
1Talbot, A. D. 22June10
1Keenlyside, C. H.
  22Jan.11
2Boyle, D. E. 22Jan.11
1Dawson, E. M. 22Jan.12
1Sayres, H. W. 4May12
2Fulton, J. S. 13June14

2nd Lieutenants (12)
*c.o.*Blakeney, L. St. L.
  20Apr.10
(2) Stuart, C. E. 4May10
(3) 1Lowth, F. R. L. 7May10
2Cross, J. K. C. 13July10
1Rowley, W. J. 5Oct.10
2Humfrey, W. K. 5Oct.10
2Helps, E. P. A.19Nov.10
2Evatt, J. W. 3Dec.10
2Seckham, L. B. L.
  4Mar.11
1Porter, A. M. F. W.
  18July11
1Marshall, D. C. 4Sept.12
2Matthey, E. G. 22Jan.13
2Page, G. F. 5Feb.13
(2) Travers, H. E. F.
  25Feb.14

Adjutant.
2Spooner, A. H.,
  capt. 13July12
1Bromley, C., *capt.*
  4May14

Quarter-Masters.
r. Smith, A. W. 23Feb.96
  hon. maj. 23Feb.13
2Ganly, W. W. 16Aug.99
  hon. capt. 16Aug.09
r. Bowes, W. 17Jan.00
  hon. capt. 17Jan.10
1Featherstone, H. E.
  2Nov.13
  28Nov.13
  hon. capt. 28Nov.13

Special Reserve.
2nd Lieutenants.
Paulson, J. S.1July11
Charleston, F.1July11
Harris, R. C. (on prob.)
  25June13
Greaves, J. (on
  prob.) 22July14

3rd Battalion.

(*Officers serving on 25July 02 in the corresponding Militia unit hold honorary Army rank equivalent to the Militia regimental rank they then held. Other officers entitled to honorary Army rank have it shown against their names.*)

Hon. Colonel.
✗Kitchener of Khartoum, Field Marshal H. H., Earl,
K.P.,G.C.B.,O.M.,
G.C.S.I.,G.C.M.G.
G.C.I.E., *Col.
Comdt. R.E.,g,s.*
  2Aug.08
  11June05

Lt.-Colonel.
✗Cobbett, H. R.
  (*H*) 6Aug.11

Major.
r.e.✗Thorne, J. F. V.
  3May13
✗Woodcock, W. J.,
  *Capt. ret. pay
(Res. of Off.)* 7May13

Captains. (5)
r.e.✗Purnell, E. K.
  11Jan.02
p.s.✗Higgin-Birket, W.
  (*H*) 5Sept.03
✗Braithwaite. A.,
  late Lt. Lan. Fus.
p.s. Tooth, S. L. (*H*)17May07
*p.s.*Heaton Armstrong,
  W. D. F. (*Empld.
under Albanian
Govt.* 5Jan 14) 6May08
*r.e.*Brierley, C. L. 14June10
✗Lyle, W.,*Capt.*
  ret. pay (*H*) 14June10
  13June14
r.e.✗Patterson, C. 24June10

Lieutenants. (11)
r.e.✗Ferrers-Guy, M. C.
  26Oct.04
Smyth, J. 1Aug.11
Bass, C. H. 1Aug.11

2nd Lieutenants. (8)
Lowth, F. R. L. 7May10
Wilkinson, J. R.
  24Aug.10
Keigwin, L. A.24Aug.12
Thacker, G. W.
  (*on prob.*) 1Oct.13

Adjutant.
Curell, W. B.,
  Lt. Lan. Fus. 23Dec.12
  (*Lt. in Army* 15July04)

Quarter-Master.
✗Bowes, W., *hon. capt.*

4th Battalion.

(*Officers serving on 14Oct. 01 in the corresponding Militia unit hold honorary Army rank equivalent to the Militia regimental rank they then held. Other officers entitled to honorary Army rank have it shown against their names.*)

Hon. Colonel.
p.s.✗Romer, F. C., *C.B.,
C.M.G., Capt. ret.
(Hon. Col. ret.
Mila.) (Hon. Lt.-Col.
in Army,* 15Oct. 01)
  (*Q*)(*H*) ⓖ *g.* 30Jan.09

THE LANCASHIRE FUSILIERS—(Regtl Dist No. 20)—contd.

4th Bn.—contd.

Lt.-Colonel.
p.s.✗Turner, J. A., 6Sept.11

Majors. (3)
p.s.✗Watson, H.F.,*D.S.O.*,
  late Capt. Lan. Fus.
  (Q)   8May10
✗Bradbridge, E. U.,
  Capt. ret. pay (Res.
  of Off.) e.   15Mar.13
✗Becke, J. (*Hon. Lt.*
  in Army 16 Dec. 02)
  (H) ⑧ (Q)   1Dec.13

Captains. (6)
p.s.✗Barnsley, A.(*Hon.*
  Lt. in Army 16Dec.
  02) (Q) (H) (b) ⑧
  I. of M.   25May06
p.s.✗Pakenham, H. J. H.
  (H) *late* 2nd Lt. C.
  Gds.   29Nov.07
p.s.Collis-Browne, J. (H)
                  1May10
✗Darbyshire, C.
  *Capt. ret. pay,*6Sept.11
  f.c.r.   22Apr.11
Sneyd, T. H., *late*
  Lt., 2 D.G., 30Oct.12
p.s.Everard, W. J.
  J. E. M. (H) 15May14
  p,v,c. ⑧   12Apr.08

Lieutenants. (11)
✗Ballantine, J. A.,
  Lt. ret. pay(*Asst.*
  Dist. Commr.,
  Gold Coast, 30
  Mar. 10)   27Dec.04
                22June10
Best-Dunkley, B. (H)
                14June09
Wilcox, F. H. C.
                14June09
✗Garratt, F. S., *late*
  Lt. Res.of Off.24July11
                23Oct.12
Nightingale, R. K. T.
                1Dec.13

2nd Lieutenants. (8)
Lowther, T. B. 4Feb.11
Northover, R. 24July11
Blain, T. R. 21Dec.12
Fryer, H. N. (*on*
  prob.)   9May14

Inst. of Musk.
Barnsley, A., *capt.*
                12Mar.14

Adjutant.
✗Madeley, G. H.,
  Lt. Lan. Fus, 12Dec.13
  (Lt. *in Army* 30May04)

Quarter-Master.
✗Smith, A. W., *hon.*
  maj.

5th Battalion.

"South Africa, 1900-02."
Castle Armoury, Bury.

Lt.-Colonel.
p. Isherwood, J., VD,
  ⑫   20Jan.12

Majors. (2)
✗Woodcock, F. A., TD
  (*Hon. Lt. in Army*
  24 June 01) ⑫ 21Jan.12
Whitehead, J. (H)
                5Mar.13

Captains. (8)
p. ✗Webb, W. (*Hon. Lt.*
  in Army 14 June 02)
                10Feb.06
p. ✗Wrigley, E. F. (*Hon.*
  Lt. in Army 14
  June 02)   1Jan.08
p. Ashworth, E. 30Mar.08
p. Kenyon, J. (t) ⑧
                17Dec11
p. ✗Wike, W.   17Dec.11
p. Milnes, S. H. 21Jan.12
p. Hartley, C. E. 28Mar.14
  Horridge, W. (H)
  I. of M.   22Apr.14

Lieutenants. (8)
p. Stonestreet, G. (H)
                1Nov.09
✗Peacock A. H.
                31Dec.09
(p.) Renshaw, J. T.24Jan.12
(p.) Butcher, R. W. 1July12
(p.) Bentley, H. M. 25Apr.13
(p.) Renshaw, A. 18Sept.13
  Hartley, T. F. 28Mar.14
  Kay, G. C.   23Apr.14

2nd Lieutenants. (8)
Bridge, J. K. 1Dec.10
Isherwood, J, V. E.
                28Feb12
Hunt. C. H. C. 1Mar.12
Horridge, G. B. 1Dec.13
Hoyle, H. K. 24Dec.13
Hall, R.   1Jan.14
Lowe, B.   2Jan.14
Yapp, W. C.   23Apr.14

Inst. of Musk.
Horridge, W.,
  capt.   18May14

Adjutant.
✗Wood, G. B. G.,
  Capt. Lan. Fus.
                15Jan.12

Quarter-Master.
✗Cremen, J., Qr.-Mr.
  (*hon. capt.*) ret. pay,
  hon. m.   5Mar.10

Medical Officers.
Nuttall, A. P., *M.D.,*
  Surg.-Maj. 29Nov.07
                13Nov.95
p. Cook, J, W.,*M.B.,Surg.-*
  Capt.   29Nov.99
                1Nov.96

Chaplain.
Hill, *Rev.* J. C., *M.A.,*
  Chapl. 4th Class
  (T.F.) (*attd.,*) 28June09

[*Uniform—Scarlet,*
  Facings— White.]

6th Battalion.

"South Africa, 1900-02."
Rochdale.

Hon. Colonel.
Royds, Sir C. M., Knt.,
  C.B., TD   6Jan.94

Lt.-Colonel.
✗Rochdale, G., Lord
  (*Hon. Lt.-Col. in*
  Army 12 *Oct.* 02)
                13Dec.09

Majors. (2)
p. Heap, H., VD, *hon. l.c.*
                7Feb.06
  Lees, R. L., VD,13Dec.09

Captains. (8)
p.s.Heywood, W. D. 6May03
p.s.Gledhill, J. J. 1Apr.08
  Barker, R. H. 15Apr.10
  Clegg, A. V. 14Feb.12
  Scott, G. ⑧ (H) 26Apr.13
  Woolmer, E. (H),
  I. of M.   29Apr.13
  Crossley, W. B. 5Dec.13

Lieutenants. (9)
Laski, N. J. 1Aug.12
Brierley, R. 1Sept.12
Fry. J.W. L. *late* 2nd
  Lt. W. York, R. 18Sept.12
Leach, R. W. 8Sept.13
O'Neill, S.   6Jan.14
Holden, N. V. 7Jan.14

2nd Lieutenants. (8)
Smith, J. H.   1Apr.13
Holden, G. G. 8Apr.13
Robinson, L.M. 10Jan.14
Lord, J. S.   12Jan.14

Inst. of Musk.
Woolmer, E., *capt.*
                19Dec.13

Adjutant.
✗Spafford, A. L., *Capt.*
  Lan. Fus.   22May

Quarter-Master.
✗Griffiths, W. H.,
  late Capt. D. of
  Lanc. Impl.Yeo.
  (*Hon. Capt. in*
  Army, 1 *Oct.* 02)
  hon. lt.   1Nov.11

Medical Officers.
p. Holt,Maj.T.,*M.B.,*
  TD, *R.A.M.C.*
  (T.F.) (*attd.,*) 12May06
                7Apr.94

Chaplain.
Clarke,Ven.*Archdeacon*
  A. F., *M.A.,* Chapl.
  4th Class (T.F.)
  (*attd.*)   1Feb.10

[*Uniform—Scarlet,*
  Facings—White.]

7th Battalion.

"South Africa, 1900-02."
Drill Hall, Cross Lane,
Salford.

Hon. Colonel.
p.s.Haworth F., VD
  (*Hon. Col. ret. Vols.*)
  (t)   10Feb.06

Lt.-Colonel.
p.s. Maclure, A. F., TD
                17Sept.13

Majors. (2
Bailey, A. J. 8Dec.12
Alexander, C. T.
  (Q)   13Oct.13

Captains (8)
p.s.Cartwright, W. ⑧
                30Nov.07
Law, W. J.(Q) 24Aug.10
Bramall, H.   3Aug.12
Humphreys, A. C.
                26Apr.13
Edge, D.   26Apr.13
p. ✗Marshall, J. (H)
                11Mar.14

Lieutenants. (8)
Alderson, D. 18July12
Waterhouse,R. 26Apr.13
Golland, J.   1June13
Norton, D. G. 24Feb.14
              11Oct.09
Cade, R. H.   31Mar.14

2nd Lieutenants. (8)
p.s.Heywood, W. D. 6May03
Gillies, F. A. 10Mar.14
Saunders, C. E. E. H.
                4Apr.14
Burleigh, B. 21Apr.14

Adjutant.
✗Gledhill, M. R.
  P. W., *Capt. R.*
  Ir. Regt. 15Dec.13

Quarter-Master.
p. Carus, J. M., VD,
  hon. m. (t) 22Apr.99
  maj. 23Dec.91

Medical Officer.
Fitzgerald,Lt. C.C.,
  R.A.M.C. (T. F.)
  (*attd.*)   28Mar.12

Chaplain.
Noott, *Rev.* W. L. O.,
  M.A., Chapl. 4th
  Class (T.F.) (*attd.*)
                1Apr.08
                10Jan.06

[*Uniform—Scarlet,*
  Facings—White.]

8th Battalion.

"South Africa, 1900-02."
Drill Hall, Cross Lane,
Salford.

Lt.-Colonel.
Fallows J. A.,
  TD, (q)   24Jan.14

Majors (2)
p.s.✗Hardy, H. S., VD,*hon.*
  l.c. (*Hon. Capt. in*
  Army 14 *June* 02) (t)
  (H) (b)   26Oct.01
p.s.Baddeley, E. L. (b)
                24Jan.14

Captains (8)
Waterhouse, R. D.
                26Apr.11
Goodfellow, A. J.
                10Oct.11
Ramsbottom, S. 28May13
Humphrey,E.S. 28May13
Bird, M. G.   28May13

Lieutenants (8)
Potter, A. B. 26May14
Biddolph, T.J. 14Dec.11
Bedson, E. H. 14Dec.11
✗Wilde, R.   2May14
McNicol, R. J. 2May14

2nd Lieutenants (8)
Littler, J. T. 6May13
Crook, E. F. 17June13
Frost, R. A. 30Mar.14
Clarke, A.   2Apr.14
Brewis, R. H. 1May14
Lecomber, W.E.17June14

Adjutant.
✗Kirkby, H. A.,
  Capt. Lan. Fus.
                6July14

Quarter-Master.
p. Gollop, C., *hon.m.* (b)
                20Feb.06

Medical Officer.
Dyson, *Capt.* W., *M.D.,*
  R.A.M.C. (T.F.)
  (*attd.*)   10July09
                10Jan.06

[*Uniform—Scarlet,*
  Facings—White.]

Cadet Unit Affiliated.
1st Cadet Company, 8 Bn.
Lan. Fus.

THE ROYAL SCOTS FUSILIERS.

Regimental District No. **21.** [No. **2** District.]

The Thistle within the Circle, and motto of the Order of the Thistle.
In each of the four corners the Royal Cypher ensigned with the Imperial Crown.
"Blenheim," "Ramillies," "Oudenarde," "Malplaquet," "Dettingen," "Martinique, 1794," "Bladensburg," "Alma," "Inkerman," "Sevastopol," "South Africa, 1879," "Burma, 1885-87," "Tirah," "Relief of Ladysmith," "South Africa, 1899-1902."

Regular and Special Reserve Battalions.

Uniform—Scarlet.   Facings—Blue.   Agents—Messrs. Cox & Co.

1st Bn. } 21st Foot {	Gosport.	3rd Bn. (R. Ayr and Wigtown Mil.)	.. Ayr.
2nd „	Gibraltar.		
Depôt	Ayr.	Record Office	Hamilton.

Territorial Force Battalions.

4th Bn. .. .. Kilmarnock. | The Ardeer Co. .. .. .. Ardeer.
5th Bn. .. .. Ayr. |

Colonel .. .. .. **C.** Dalyell, Hon. Lt.-Gen. J. T., ret. pay 12June09
                                                                                                                          1Feb.03

1st and 2nd Battalions.

Lt.-Colonels (2)
2Stuart, D. M. 25Aug.10
1Smith, W. D. 1July11

Majors. (8)
2Smith, A. G. B. 1July03
(1) De la Bère, H. P. 6May05
s. Pollard, J. H.-W.,
  p.s.c. [l] 13June06
2MacGregor, A. C. H. 25Aug.06
(1) Duncan, J., D.S.O.,
  p.s.c., e. [L] 25Aug.10
1Forbes, A. M. H. 1July11
(3) 1Northey, H. H.
  (*Comdg. Depôt*) 24Feb.12
d. Buchanan, F. E. 10Apr.12
                 22Aug.02

Captains. (14)
f.c. Trenchard, H. M.,
  C.B., D.S.O. 28Feb.00
  bt. maj. 22Aug.02
m.c. Barrett, C. J. C. 2May00
m.c. Walsh, R. K. 9Dec.00
1Rose, T. A., D.S.O.
                 16Feb.01
2Burgoyne, R.M. 6May01
s. Gordon, E. I. D.,
  p.s.c. 26Sept.01
Robertson, D. S,
  p.s.c. [L] [F] Mil.
  Attaché 10Jan.02
t. McConaghey, M.E.
             22Jan.02
s. Jackson, C. H. I. 31Jan.02
Teacher, N.McD.
  [F] 12Dec.04
(1) Delano-Osborne,
  O. H., p.s.c. 25Dec.04
2 Whigham,J.C.16Jan05
1 Briggs, G. C. 18Apr.05
s.c. Craufurd,E.Q. 14June05
2Le Gallais, A. G. L'E.
                 20May06
                 8Jan.07
(1) Maitland Makgill
  Crichton, H. C.,
  p.s.c. 6June09
(3)2Beck, E. A. 10Oct.10
  Farquhar, W. A.10Oct.10
(3) 1Hurt, S.F.A.A.21Jan.11
  Browne,G.W. 1Feb.11
1Young, J.E. 23Sept.11

Captains— contd.
2Bruce, A. G. 25Oct.11
r. Connell, A. H. 17Nov.11
1Tullis, J. D. 25Nov.11
1Miller, H. G. B.,
  Adjt. 22Jan.12
2Fairlie, F. 23Jan.12
t. Thompson, H. 23Jan.12
c.o. Gibb, C. 10Apr.12
(1) Boyle, Hon. J. 10Apr.12
s. Bell, A. M. MaoG.
                28Apr.12
2Adair, A. C., e. 18Jan.13
1Goodeve, L. 23Feb.13
c.o.Stewart, J. A. 1Apr.13
(3) 2Brodie, J. 1Apr.13
1Innes,G.V.d'A. 26Apr.13
2Fleetwood, G. C.
                2July13
1Traill, T. B. 18July14
                28July09

Lieutenants. (20)
e.a. Wyllie, J. 6Feb.09
2Horn, R. V. G., Adjt.
               28Sept.10
(3)1Tullis, W. 10Oct.10
2Stewart, H. W. Y.
               21Jan.11
1Stuart, Hon. R. S.
  [L] 11Nov.11
               7Jan.11
(3) 2Dunne, F. T. V. [l]
              1Feb.11
1Stiven, R.W.S.1Apr.11
c.o.Sandilands, E. A.
             14May11
2Kennedy, N. 1Sept.11
1Badham, B.H.23Sept.11
1Lyon, C. J. 25Oct.11
f.c. Barton, J. F.
              25Nov.11
1Pollock,A.J. A.3Jan.12
2Ross Thomson, A.
             22Jan.12
1Stirling-Cookson,
  S.B. 23Jan.12
2Mackenzie, C. G. G.
             17Feb.12
2Bolton, A. C. 10Apr.12
1Critchley-Salmonson,
  D. G. C. 8June12
1Davidson.D.S.10Aug.12
2Thomson,K.C.23Feb 13
2Kennedy, G.R.T.
             1Apr.13
1Henderson, N, W. A.
           12June13
2Tod, W. 28Apr.14
2Thomson, A. A. E, L.
             6May14

2nd Lieutenants. (12)
1Grahame,C.E.13Mar.12
2Utterson-Kelso, J.E.
             4Sept.12
2Alston, C. McC.
             4Sept.12
1Nichol, J. 4Sept.12
2Bowen, J. L. 4Sept.12
1Anderson. E. L. L.
             5Feb.13
2MacGregor-Whitton,
  A. E. H, 2Apr.13
2Buchanan, M. B.
             3Sept.13
2Boyle, E. P. O. 3Sept.13
2Clutterbuck, W. E.
            17Sept.13
2Kennedy, C. N. J.
            17Sept.13
1MacGregor-Whitton,
  P. W. T. 25Feb.14

Adjutants.
1Miller, H. G. B.,
  capt. 1Sept.11
2Horn, R. V. G., lt.
             22Jan.12

Quarter-Masters.
1Finch, W. W.,
  hon. capt. 23July02
r. Paterson, T., hon. lt.
             19Mar.13
             20Apr.10
2Spence, A., hon. lt.
             13Aug.13

Special Reserve.

2nd Lieutenant.
Patterson, W. R. L. 24Apr.12

3rd Battalion.

(*Officers serving on 4 Dec. 00 in the corresponding Militia unit hold honorary Army rank equivalent to the Militia regimental rank they then held. Other Officers entitled to honorary Army rank have it shown against their names.*)

Hon. Colonel.
×Saye and Sele, G. C.,
  Lord, Capt. ret. pay
  (Hon. Col. Mil.,)
  (Hon. Maj. in Army
  5Dec.00) 2Aug.08
             29Sept.07

Lt.-Colonel.
×Agnew, Q. G. K.,
  M.V.O., D.S.O., Maj.
  ret. pay (Res.of Off.)
  (Gent.-at-Arms)
             8Oct.10

Major.
r.e. ×Northey, H.H.
             24Feb.12
×Dick, D. H.A.,
  Maj. ret. pay
  (Res.of Off.) 25Oct.13

Captains. (5)
p.s.×Brook, W. B.(H) c.o.
             1Aug.05
×Forbes, I. R.-I. F.,
  Capt. ret. pay 11Jan.08
×Cox, A. F. J., Lt.
  ret. pay 27June08
r.e. ×Beck, E. A. 1Oct.10
r.e. ×Hurt, S. F.A.A.21Jan.11
×Boyd-Carpenter, J.P.
  late Lt. R. Sc. Fus.
             5Apr.11
Craven, Hon. R. C.
  (Hon. Capt. in
  Army 3 Sept. 02)
             29June12
r.e. Brodie, J. 1Apr.13

Lieutenants. (11)
Ness, G. S. 9Dec.09
r.e. Tullis, W. 10Oct.10
r.e. Dunne, F. T. V. [l]
             1Feb.11
Alexander, A. C. E.
             9Mar.14

2nd Lieutenants. (8)
Law, M. J. N. 6May11
Roche, A. L. 7June11
Bethell, C. A. 27Mar.12
Cozens-Brooke, J.G.S.
             1Apr.12
Chrystie, J. A.
  (on prob.) 19Nov.13
Blatherwick, R.
  (on prob.) 3Dec13

Adjutant.
×Connell, A. H.,
  Capt. R. Sc.
  Fus. 17Nov.11
  (*Capt. in Army17Nov.11*)

Quarter-Master.
×Paterson, T., hon. lt.

THE ROYAL SCOTS FUSILIERS—(Regtl. Dist. No. **21**)—contd.

4th Battalion.

"South Africa, 1900-02."
Kilmarnock.

Hon. Colonel.

✗Howard de Walden,
T.E., Lord, late Lt.
10 Hrs., Maj. 2
Co. of Lond. Yeo.
18Oct.18

Lt.-Colonel.

p.s. Barnett, H., VD,
(Q) 11Feb.10

Majors. (2)

p.s. Balfour, J.R., (H) 10Oct.08
p.s. ✗Alexander, J. 29Apr.10

Captains. (8)

p.s. Stewart, W. (Q) ⊕
24Dec.02
p. Young, H. R. ⊕ 13May03
p.s. Turner, J. R. (H)
6Aug.04
p.s. Willison, J. W. G. (H)
25Nov.09
p.s. Dunn, G. L. (H)
25Nov.09
Kenneth. A. 8Mar.10
p.s. Jamieson, N. 25Oct.12
p.s. Logan, A. 7June13

Lieutenants (9).

Wallace, D. J. 6July11
Dunn, W. L. 6July11
Bruce, J. 6July11
Longmuir, R. G.
1May13
Lewis, M. H. 8June13

2nd Lieutenants. (8)

Mackay, G. D. 26Apr.12
Henry, J. 26Apr.12
McConnell, J. B.
26Apr.12
Robb, J. 11June12
Sturrock, G. 1Apr.13
Pollock, M. K. 1Apr.13
Hamilton, J. G. 1Apr.13
Robertson. D. Y. McL.
16Apr.13
Morton, A. J. 16Apr.13
Barnett, J. 14Aug.13
Kyle, H. G. 9Mar.14
Johnstone, J. H. 9Mar.14

Adjutant.

✗Thompson, H.,
Capt. R. Sc.
Fus. 22Jan.14

Quarter-Master.

p.s., p. Yuille, D. 5Nov.02
capt. 4Oct.02

Medical Officers.

p. ✗Taylor, Capt. J. C.,
M.B., R. A. M. C.
(T.F.) (attd.) (Hon.
Lt. in Army 21Dec.
01) 17Feb.06
Frew, Lt. W.D., R.A.M.C.
(T.F.) (attd.) 1Dec.13

Chaplains.

Ranken, Rev. H., B.D.,
TD [C.S.] Chapl. 1st
Class (T.F.) (attd.)
9Jan.12
9Jan.92
Brown, Rev. H., M.A.,
[U.F.C.] Chapl. 4th
Class (T.F.) (attd.)
17Oct.13

[Uniform—Scarlet.
Facings—Blue.]

———

Cadet Unit Affiliated.
1st C.B. R. Sc. Fus.
(2 companies).

5th Battalion.

"South Africa, 1900-01."

Ayr.

Lt.-Colonel.

✗Pollok-McCall,
J.B., Maj. ret.
pay (Res. of Off.)
[l] 27Apr.12

Majors. (2)

Russell, J. 26July12

Captains. (8)

✗Wilkie, D. M.
(H) 27May12
Cook, J. B. 27May12
p.s. Murdoch, H. C 27May12
Cunningham. S. A.
(H) I. of M. 13Feb.13

Lieutenants. (8)

Haddow, H.R. 20Dec.13
Pollock, H. A. 20Dec.13
Gudgeon, D. N.
20Dec.13
McHarrie, R. 20Dec.13
Joyner, R. A. 9Apr.14
3Aug.11
Bain, E. W. 10Apr.14
Howatson, W. H.
1July14
Brotherston, G.
1July14

2nd Lieutenants. (8)

Crawford, F. A. F.
6Mar.14
Jones, O. P. 22Apr.14
✗Campbell, R. W.
26May14
Rodger, A. J. 17June14
Vivers, J. 17June14
Seymour, C. 18June14

Inst. of Musk.

Cunningham, S. A.,
capt. 27Dec.11

Adjutant.

Farquhar, W. A.,
Capt. R. Sc. Fus.
5Nov.12

Quarter-Master.

✗Taylor, R., hon. lt.
1May12

Medical Officers.

Gairdner, Lt. E. D.,
R.A.M.C. (T.F.)
(attd.) 15July06

Chaplains

Brownlie, Rev. J.,
D.D., VD [U.F.C.]
Chapl. 1st Class
(T.F.) (attd.) 1Apr.10
14Oct.85
Rainie, Rev. W., M.A.,
TD, [C.S.] Chapl. 1st
Class (T.F.) (attd.)
9Nov.12
19Nov.92

[Uniform—Scarlet
Facings—Blue.]

———

Cadet Unit Affiliated.
1st C.B. R. Sc. Fus.
(2 companies).

The Ardeer Company.

Ardeer.

Captain.

Weir, J. M. 1Nov.12

Lieutenant.

Taylor, N. 1Nov.12

2nd Lieutenant.

Thomas, J. 4Dec.12

———

Cadet Unit Affiliated.
1st C.B. R. Sc. Fus.
(2 companies).

THE CHESHIRE REGIMENT.

Regimental District No. 22. [No. 4 District.]

The United Red and White Rose.
"Louisburg," "Martinique, 1762," "Havannah," "Meeanee," "Hyderabad," "Scinde,"
"South Africa, 1900-02."

Regular and Special Reserve Battalions.

Uniform—Scarlet. *Facings*—Buff. *Agents*—Messrs. Cox & Co.

| 1st Bn. | (22nd Foot) | Londonderry. | 3rd Bn. (1st R. Cheshire Mila.) | .. | Chester. |
| 2nd „ | | Jubbulpore (for Allahabad). | | | |

Depôt .. .. .. Chester. | Record Office .. .. Shrewsbury.

Territorial Force Battalions.

| 4th Bn. | .. | Grange Road West, Birkenhead. | 6th Bn. | .. | .. | The Armoury, Stockport. |
| 5th „ | .. | The Drill Hall, Volunteer Street, Chester. | 7th „ | .. | .. | The Drill Hall, Macclesfield. |

Colonel .. .. Graham, Maj.-Gen. E. R. C., C.B., p.s.c., s. .. 18Apr.14

1st and 2nd Battalions.

Lt.-Colonels. (2)
2Pearse, T. H. F.
  18Sept.12
1Boger, D. C. 26June14

Majors. (8)
2Scott, A. de C. 2Nov.07
2Stone, A. 21Apr.08
2Smyth, H. 16Sept.08
  26June10
s. Gosset, A. B. 16Sept.08
  29Nov.00
s. Anderson, W. H.,
  p.s.c. 7Mar.11
  23July10
s. Grove, P. L., e. 16Sept.12
1Chetwynd-Stapylton,
  B. H., p.s.c. 2Aug.13
  10May13
c.o.Hayter, R. J. F., p.s.c.
  [t] 26June14

Captains. (14)
1Dyer, A. J. L. 15Nov.01
t.v. Hughes, C. G. E. [L]
  1Feb.02
2Roddy, E. L. 19Feb.02
s. Crookenden, A., p.s.c.
  [L] 19Feb.02
2Gover, W. W. B. 7Dec.04
2Turner, H. G. 29Mar.05
(3)1Clarke, M. F.,
  (Comdg. Depôt)15Apr.05
(3)2Mahony, F. H. 10Feb.06
1Jones, E. R. 10Feb.06
t.v. Adair, H. S. 26June06
1Dugmore, W. L. E. R.
  22Nov.06
1Shore, J. L. 19Dec.06
1Jackson, E. A. 18Sept.07
w.a.Rich, W. S. 2Nov.07
2Morton, E. 27Nov.07

Captains—contd.
Nye, V. A. [L] [F] 12Feb.08
  30May04
1Tahourdin, V. R.,
  Adjt. 13Feb.08
t. Hodgkin, H. S. 21Apr.08
t. Gosset, C. B. 22July10
  4Apr.09
(3)2Walker, H. S. 27May13
(3)1Loder-Symonds,
  R. F. 2Aug.13
2Savage, F. R. 24Sept.13
2Mallinson, R. 28Jan.14
1Massy, B. E. 4Mar.14
t. Adshead, G. 4Mar.14
1Jolliffe, C. E. 11Apr.14

Lieutenants. (19)
1Hartford, H. I. St. J.
  9Jan.06
2Maxwell, E. C.10Feb.06
c.o. Routh, J. C. 14Apr.06
r. Bengough, L. 27Oct.06
(3)2Thorp, H. O. C.19Dec.06
1Matterson, C. A. K.
  9Aug.07
t. Frost, F. D. 18Jan.08
t. Bently, H. R. 13Feb.08
1Houstoun, G. L. F.
  24Sept.08
c.o.Pring, F. J. H. 12Nov.08
c.o.Forestier-Walker,
  E. A. 20Jan.09
2Will, N. G. H. 20Mar.09
c.o.Freeman, H. G. V. M.
  4Jan.11
2Napier, M. A. 17Jan.11
c.o.Gunn, D. G. 1Apr.11
1Randall, H. C. 1Sept.11
t. Duke, V. W. H. 8Sept.11
2Hodgson, H. J. 24Apr.12
w.a.Scott, R. M. L. 27May13
1Frost, T. L. 20Aug.13
2Nason, E. R. 20Aug.13
2Woodyer, C. de W.
  24Dec.13
2Nares, E. P. 28Jan.14
2Villiers Stuart, P.G.
  4Mar.14
1Elliot, W. G. R.
  14Mar.14
1Campbell, C. A.
  4Apr.14
2Andrews, C. R. 11Apr.14

2nd Lieutenants. (12)
1Sparling, W. H.
  19Jan.12
2Hayes-Newington,
  C. W. 4Sept.12
2Watson, G. T. C.
  5Feb.13
2Clark, E. D. 24Jan.14
2Law, C. H. 24Jan.14
1Milner, A. D. 21Feb.14
2Fairweather, I.
  10June14

Adjutants.
2Hill, A. R., capt.
  22Mar.13
1Tahourdin, V. R.,
  capt. 1Oct.13

Quarter-Masters.
r. Ryan, J., hon. lt.
  14May10
1Sproule, J. C.,
  hon. lt. 9Apr.13
2Cowan, H. G.,
  hon. lt. 8Nov.13

Special Reserve.

2nd Lieutenant.
Jacobs, G. S. 10Feb.14

3rd Battalion.

(*Officers serving on 4Oct.02 in the corresponding Militia unit hold honorary Army rank equivalent to the Militia regimental rank they then held. Other officers entitled to honorary Army rank have it shown against their names.*)

Lt.-Colonel.
p.s. Logan, E. T.,
  D.S.O. 6Apr.12

Major.
p.s.May, G. W. G. (H)
  24May13

Captains. (5)
r.e.Clarke, M. F. 15Apr.05
r.e.Mahony, F. H. 10Feb.06
p.s.Hall, R. (b) (H)26May06
p.lc.Butterworth, S. (H)
  24May13
r.e.Walker, H. S. 27May13
r.e.Loder-Symonds,
  R. F. 2Aug.13

Lieutenants. (11)
r.e.Thorp, H. O. C.
  19Dec.06
r.e.Nicholson, H. W.
  6Oct.12
Harrington, H. N.
  29June13
Newson, N. A. 29June13
Frost, K. T. (H)
  29June13
(q) Watkin, H. G.
  29June13

2nd Lieutenants. (8)
Groves, E. J. 1Oct.12
Stewart, W. L. 5Mar.13
Atkinson, H. N.
  12Mar.13
Bolton, R. H. 1Apr.13
Adshead, M. S. 6Aug.13
Hassall, A. B. (on
  prob.) 10Dec.13

Adjutant.
Bengough, L.,
  Lt. Ches. R. 8Nov.13
  (Lt. in Army 27 Oct. 06)

Quarter-Master.
Ryan, J., hon. lt.

THE CHESHIRE REGIMENT—(Regtl. Dist. No. 22)—contd.

4th Battalion.
"South Africa, 1901-02."
Grange Road West,
Birkenhead.

Hon. Colonel.
p.s. Blood, F. W., VD
(H)(t) Hon. Col.
ret. Vols.) 16Apr.13

Lt.-Colonel.
Hopps, A. B., TD 2Nov.11

Majors. (2)
Pemberton, J. A. 24June12
Prentice, T. A. (Q) (H) 14Dec.12

Captains. (8).
p.s. Newton, W. J. (H) 16Jan.04
p.s. Marquis, W.H. 26Nov.04
p.s. Gregory, F. C. 25Feb.11
Wright, N. G. 11May12
Wilson, G. R. 24June12
Taylor, A. McM. 12Apr.13

Lieutenants (8)
Bazett, A. H. 21Sept.11
Hampson, T.D. 24June12
Leete, W. W.⊛12Mar.1⁸
Preston, A. M. 13Apr.13
Perrin, E. C. 22May13
Paterson, A. B. 9Aug.13
Pegram, J. 20Sept.13
Prince, E. A. 27May14

2nd Lieutenants. (8)
Van Gruisen, H. 30Jan.12
Edgar, B. J. 21Feb.12
Pullon, P. G. 4Dec.12
Oulton, A. N. 24Sept.13
Corden, B. W. 24Sept.13
Sutcliffe, A. J. 24Sept.13
Nicholson, A. G. 7Oct.13
Danson, F. R. 24Nov.13

Inst. of Musk.
Bently, H. R., Lt. Ches. R., capt. 6Oct.12

Quarter-Master.
Medical Officer.
p. Wilson, Maj. A. F., M.D., TD, R.A.M.C. (T.F.) (attd.) 4July10
21Dec.98

Chaplain.
Oakley, Rev. G.D., M.A., Chapl. 4th Class (T.F.) (attd.) 22Apr.12

[Uniform—*Grey*.
Facings—*Scarlet*.]

Cadet Units Affiliated.
1st New Brighton Cadet Corps.
1st Birkenhead Cadet Corps
1st Poulton Cadet Company

5th (Earl of Chester's) Battalion.
"South Africa, 1900-02."
The Drill Hall, Volunteer Street, Chester.

Hon. Colonel.
p.s. Marshall, Sir T. H., Knt., C.B. VD. Hon. Lt.-Col. late 8 Bn. Ches. R. (Hon. Col. ret. Vols.) 2Mar.98

Lt.-Colonel.
p.s. Groves, J. E. G., TD 7June12

Majors (2).
Bromley, C. E., TD (Q) ⊛ 8Aug.12
Fennell, T. L. Q) (H) ⊛ 14Oct.12

Captains (8).
p.s. Watts, H. (H) 16Jan.04
p. Churton, W. A. V. (Q) 26Mar.04
p. ✗Dickson, E. D. (Hon. Lt. in Army 13 Aug. 02 14May10
p. Weissmüller, R. E. (H) 20July10
p. Musgrave, A. J. (t) 17July12
p.s. Hatt-Cook, G. (H) 8Aug12

Lieutenants (8).
p. Davies, J. H. 15July08
(p.) Bourne, E. S. 1June09
Ellington, N. B. (H) 20July10
Brunner, G. H. 1Nov.10
Price, C. A. (H), I. of M. 24Dec.10
Hartley, G. W. C. 8Aug.12
Lake, A.B.M. 11Sept.12
Hodgkin, A. E. 8Apr.14
1 Jan.13

2nd Lieutenants (8).
Burnett, A. 28Nov.11
Vernon, W. 3Jan.12
Freeth, F. A. 10Jan.12
Gamon, S. P. 22Jan.13
Bairstow, E. J. 8Jan.14
Evans, L. 16Jan.14

Inst. of Musk.
Price, C. A., lt. 1 Apr. 10

Adjutant.
✗Adshead, G., Capt. Ches. R. 17Jan.14

Quarter-Master.
✗Dutton, T., Qr.-Mr. (hon. capt.) ret. pay (Res. of Off.) hon. capt. 5Apr.13

Chaplains.
Edwards, Rev. F., M.A., Chapl. 3rd Class (T.F.) (attd.) 12Feb12
12Feb.02
Nowell, Rev. H. N., M.A., Chapl. 4th Class (T.F.) (attd.) 10Dec.12

[Uniform—*Scarlet*.
Facings—*Buff*.]

6th Battalion.
"South Africa, 1900-02."
The Armoury, Stockport.

Hon. Colonel.
✗Ommanney, A.E., C.B., Hon. Brig.-Gen. ret. pay [R] 22July11

Lt.-Colonel.
p.s. Sykes, A. J. 8Mar.11

Majors. (2)
Leah, G.H., TD 21Feb.10
Chaloner, W.(H)(Q) 9Dec.11

Captains. (8)
p. Hesse, H. (t) 26July02
p. Leah, F. A.(Q) 14Feb.03
p. Rivett, F. 5Aug.04
p.s. Rostron, R. (H)(Q) I. of M. 4Dec.10
p. Dodge, W.D.(q) 9Dec.11
p. Stott, H. 20Dec.11
p. Kirk, R. (t) 5Dec.12
p. Heywood, G. B. 4July13

Lieutenants (8)
Diggles, J,M,(H)1Jan.11
Cooke, H. (t) 13Mar.11
Underwood, J. W. 17June11
Gibbons, T. 20Dec.11
Smith, A. W. 29Oct.12
White, C. F. 5Dec12
Hoyle, J. C. 4July13
Christie, A. J. 1Mar.14
10June11

2nd Lieutenants, (8)
Haworth, G.E. 22Mar.12
White, F. 19Nov.12
Innes, W. R. 24Jan.13
Johnston, J.E. 26Feb.13
Norman, R. 1Apr.13
Spence, E. E. 4Feb.14
Norman, C. 4Feb.14

Inst. of Musk.
Rostron, R., capt. 1Sept.09

Adjutant.
Gosset, C. B., Capt. Ches. R. 1Nov.11

Quarter-Master.
Rawlinson, J., hon. m. 24Jan.06

Medical Officer.
p. Sidebottom, Maj. R. B., R.A.M.C., (T. F.) (attd.) 4Oct.08
3Feb.97
Morris. Lt. J., M.B. F.R.C.S., R.A.M.C. (T.F.) (attd.) 8Mar.12

Chaplains.
Bird, Rev. J. G., TD, Chapl. 2nd Class (T.F.) (attd.) 1Apr.08
2Mar.90
Canton, Rev. W. J., TD, Chapl. 2nd Class (T.F.) (attd.) 17Dec.92
Thorpe, Rev. J.H., M.A., B.D., Chapl. 3rd Class (T. F.) (attd.) 28May12
28May02

[Uniform—*Scarlet*.
Facings—*Buff*.]

Cadet Unit Affiliated.
1 C.B. Ches. R.

THE CHESHIRE REGIMENT.—(Regtl. Dist. No. **22**)—contd.

7th Battalion.

The Drill Hall,
Macclesfield.

Hon. Colonel.

Shakerley, Sir W. G., Bt.
TD, late Lt. K. R. Rif.
C. (Hon. Col. ret. T.F.)
7Jan.10

Lt.-Colonel.

Greg, E. W., VD,
(Maj.ret.Mila.)
21Apr.10

Majors

Backhouse, H., TD,
(H)(t) 5Mar.08
Swindells, G. H. (Q)
1Aug.10

Captains (8)

p, Thistlethwaite, T.V.C.,
    TD   15Apr.99
p.s. ✗Cooke, J.K.⊕ 25July03
p. Reade, W.P.(t) 28May04
p. ✗Moir, H. L. (Hon.
    Lt. in Army 2 Sept. 02)
                   7Feb.06
p.s. Heath, G. N. 5Mar.08
p. Turner, R. T. 1Aug.10
p.s. Taylor, F. J. 13July12
p.s. Rigby, H.P.   26Apr.13

Lieutenants. (8)

p.s. Cooke, C.T.   13Dec.05
(p.s.)Finlow, F. J. 14July08

Lieuts.—contd.

Heath, G.   1Aug.10
Cameron, C.N. 13July12
Turner, W. T.   4Feb.14
Irwin, C.   19Feb.14

2nd Lieutenants. (8)

Kenyon, W. D. 12Feb.13
Hinnell, H. G. 26Feb.13
Rippon, C.   7June13
Warrilow, J.W. 8Jan.14
Haddon, T.   9Feb.14
Humphrey, D.   21Feb.14
Cobbold, F. W.
               25Mar.14
Sheldon, P.   4May14

Adjutant.

✗Hodgkin, H. S.,
Capt.Ches.R,11Apr.14

Quarter-Master.

✗Loakman, P. B.,
hon. lt.   21Jan.14

Medical Officers.

Proudfoot, Lt. R., M.B.,
R.A.M.C (T.F.)(attd.)
              20May11

Chaplains.

Broughton, Rev. R.E.,
M.A., Chapl. 4th
Class (T.F.)(attd.)
              26Mar.12
Child, Rev. A. G.,
Chapl. 4th Class
(T. F.) (attd.) 4Apr.12

[Uniform—*Scarlet*.
Facings—*Buff*.]

Cadet Units affiliated.

Macclesfield Industrial
School Cadet Corps.
Macclesfield Grammar
School Cadet Corps.

THE ROYAL WELSH FUSILIERS.
Regimental District No. **23**. [No. **4** District.]

The Plume of the Prince of Wales. In the first and fourth corners the Rising Sun; in the second corner the Red Dragon; in the third corner the White Horse with motto, "Nec aspera terrent."
The Sphinx, superscribed "Egypt."

"Namur, 1695," "Blenheim," "Ramillies," "Oudenarde," "Malplaquet," "Dettingen," "Minden," "Corunna," "Martinique, 1809," "Albuhera," "Badajoz," "Salamanca," "Vittoria," "Pyrenees," "Nivelle," "Orthes," "Toulouse," "Peninsula," "Waterloo," "Alma," "Inkerman," "Sevastopol," "Lucknow," "Ashantee, 1873-4," "Burma, 1885-87," "Relief of Ladysmith," "South Africa, 1899-1902," "Pekin, 1900."

Regular and Special Reserve Battalions.

Uniform—Scarlet. Facings—Blue. Agents—Messrs. Cox & Co.

1st Bn. } (23rd Foot) { .. Malta. 3rd Bn. (R. Denbigh & Flint Mil.) Wrexham.
2nd " } { .. Portland.
Depôt .. .. .. Wrexham. Record Office .. .. .. Shrewsbury.

Territorial Force Battalions.

4th Bn. .. .. Wrexham. | 6th Bn. .. .. .. Carnarvon.
5th " .. .. .. Drill Hall, Flint. | 7th " .. .. .. Newtown, Montgomery.

Colonel-in-Chief, THE KING.

Colonel .. V.C., C.M. O'Connor, Hon. Maj.-Gen. Sir L., K.C.B., ret. pay [R] .. 3June14

1st and 2nd Battalions.

Lt.-Colonels. (2)
2 Delmé-Radcliffe, H.
   [L]   21Aug'11
1 Cadogan, H. O. S.
            12May12

Majors. (8)
f.o. Doughty-Wylie,
   C. H. M., C.B.,
   C.M.G. [F] 21Aug.07
s. Berners, R.A. 4July08
c.o. Braithwaite, W. G.,
   D.S.O., p.s.c. 4May10
1 Gabbett, R. E. P.
            26July11
            12Sept.03
(3) 2Hay, A. [L] (Comdg.
   Depôt)   21Aug.11
c.o. Cockburn, J. B.12May12
2 Williams, O. De L.
            19Apr.13
s. Hill, H., M.V.O.,
   p.s.c.   18June13

Captains. (14)
2 Walwyn, F. J., D.S.O.
            12May04
2 Geiger, G. J. P. [L]
             8Feb.06
Powell, D. [L] 8Feb.06
Kington, W. M., D.S.O.
            20Apr.06
1 Harris-St. John, W.
             5May06
t. Norman, C. C. 17Nov.06
2 Owen, C. S., Adjt.
            17Nov.06
(3) 1Stockwell, C. 12Jan.07
e.a. Bayly, E. A. T. 21Aug.07
t. de Penthény-
   O'Kelly, E. J. 15Feb.08
            28Aug.07
1 Vyvyan, W. G. 1Apr.09
r.a. Kyrke, H.V.V. [F]
             4Dec.09
2 Phillips, R. N. 26April
(3) 2Gwyther, G. H. 6Apr.11
t. Garnett, W. B. 11Apr.11
(3) 1Lloyd, M. E. 11Apr.11
t. Minshull Ford,
   J.R.M. [l] 25May11

Captains—contd.
e.a. Webb-Bowen, H. I.
             1June11
t. Lloyd, R. L. 21Aug.11
1 Barker, R. V. 9Sept.11
i.v. Venables, J. D. 9Sept.11
r. Crawshay, C. H. R.
            23Nov.11
c.o. Fox, L, D'A. 1Oct.12
2 Pery-Knox-Gore,
   W. H. C.   10Oct.12
s. Hutton, G. P. 19Oct.12
e.a. Kearsley, E. R. 18Dec.12
1 Skaife, E. O. [l]
            18Dec.12
2 Samson, A. L. 27Dec.12
t. Wood, C. E. 11Apr.13
2 Jones-Vaughan, E. N.
            19Apr.13
1 Edwards,C. H.18Jan13
1 Smyth-Osbourne,
   J.G.   28Nov.13
2 Lloyd-Mostyn, M. L.
            17Feb.14

Lieutenants. (19)
2 Thomas, G. O. 1Apr.11
(3) 2Stable, L. L. 11Apr.11
c.o. de Miremont, G. E. R.
             3May11
1 Alston, L. A. A.
            10Mar.14
2 Ormrod, L. 9Sept.11
1 Anwyl, M. I. H. 25May11
c.o. Bruzner-Randall,
   J. G.   1June11
2 Childe-Freeman,
   J. A. C. 14Aug.11
(3) 1 Parry, M. P. D. G. 28Aug.11
c.o. Davis, H. H. 14Nov.11
2 Wynne-Edwards,
   J. C.   16May12
1 Dooner, A. E. C. T.
   [L] Adjt. 28Apr.13
2 Maltby, P. C. 19Oct.12
1 Hindson,R. E. 18Dec.12
2 FitzRoy,C.A.E.
            27Dec.12
1 Hoskyns, E. C. L.
            11Apr.13
1 Chance, G. O. de P.
            19Apr.13
2 Holmes, W. G. 15Feb.14

Lieutenants—contd.
1 Barchard,D. M.17Feb.14
1 Courage, J. H. 23Feb.14
1 Poole, B. C. H.26Feb.14

2 Mostyn, P.G.J. 3June14

2nd Lieutenants. (12)
1 Hardie, H. R. 19Jan.12
1 Evans, J. M. J. 5Feb.13
1 Peppé, C. G. H. 3Sept.13
1 Ackland-Allen, H.T.
             3Sept.13
1 Snead-Cox, G. P. J.
            17Sept.13
1 Wodehouse, E.17Sept.13
2 Owen, C.S., capt.
            19Oct.13
1 Dooner, A. E. C. T.,
   [L] lt.   26July14
1 Edwards,C. H.18Jan13
1 Parker, E. A. 20Apr.04
   hon. capt. 20Apr.11
r. Hickman, E. A. hon. lt.
            11Nov.05
2 Yates, H., hon. lt.
            27Jan.12

Special Reserve
Captain.
p.s.Clarke, H. H., late
2nd Lt.   Ches.
R. (H)   16June07
          22Apr.14

3rd Battalion.

(Officers serving on 5 July 01 in the corresponding Militia unit hold honorary Army rank equivalent to the Militia regimental rank they then held. Other officers entitled to honorary Army rank have it shown against their names.)

Hon. Colonel.
Mostyn, L. N. V.,
   Lord   2June08
            4Oct.05

Lt.-Colonel.
Jones-Williams, H. R.
   (Hon. Capt. in Army
   18Oct.00) (H) 15July13

Major.
t. Philips, B. E., hon.
   l.c. (H)   19Aug.05
r.e.⚔Hay, A. [L] 21Aug.11

Captains. (5)
Macartney-Filgate,
   A. R. P. (Hon.
   Capt. in Army 18
   Oct.00)hon.m. 2Jan.95
p.s.⚔Lane, A. P. (Hon.
   Lt. in Army 24
   June 01) hon. m,
   (H)   5Apr.02
p.s.⚔Jones, E. B. (Hon.
   Lt.inArmy 18Oct.
   00) (H)   20May03
France-Hayhurst,F. C.,
   Capt. ret. pay 28May03
            19Feb.13
p.s.Brennan, J. H. (H)
             4June03
p.s.⚔Fairclough, R. (Hon.
   Capt.in Army 7Feb.03)
   (H)(b)   5Mar.04
r.e. Stockwell, C.I. 12Jan.07
   Tringham, L.W.H.,
   Lt.ret. pay (H)8Dec.09
⚔Jones, M. G., late Lt.
   R.W.Fus.,ret.pay[R]
             3Aug.10
r.e. Gwyther, G. H. 6Apr.11
r.e. Lloyd, M. E. 11Apr.11

Lieutenants (11)
p.s.⚔Prichard, T. L.
   (Hon. Lt. in Army
   18Oct.00) (H) 23Feb.01
   Ormrod, J. [F] 4Oct.02
(p.s.⚔Lloyd, L.S. (H) 24May05
   Hadley, F. C. T., (H)
            13Sept,05

THE ROYAL WELSH FUSILIERS—(Regtl. Dist. No. 23)—contd.

3rd Bn.—contd.

Lieuts.—contd.
p s. Blosse, R. C. L. 12July10
×Jones, E. T. 7Nov.10
r.e. Stable, L. L. 11Apr.11
r.e. Parry, M. D. G.
    28Aug.11
p.s. Cuthbert, J.(H)10Nov.11
    21May13
Raffles, R. L. S.(H)
    20Jan.12
Richardson, A. K.
    2June13
Stamper, E. P. F.
    2June13
French, R. M. J.
    2June13

2nd Lieutenants. (8)
Thompson, E. J. V. C.
   (on prob.) 18Sept.10
Gore, G. R. (on prob.)
    14Mar.14

Adjutant.
×Crawshay, F. D. R.,
Capt. R. W. Fus.
    14Sept.12
(Capt. in Army 23Nov.11)

Quarter-Master.
×Hickman, E. A.,
hon. lt.

4th (Denbighshire) Battalion.

"South Africa, 1900-02."

Wrexham.

Hon. Colonel.
Cornwallis-West, W. C.,
VD,(Hon.Col.ret.
Vols.) 19Apr.90

Lt-Colonel.
France-Hayhurst, F.C.,
Capt. ret. pay (Capt.
3 Bn. R. Welsh Fus.)
    4Oct.13

Majors. (2)
p. Johnson, A. E., TD
    21Feb.00
Wilson, W. R. (Q) ⓡ
    7Jan.4

Captains. (2)
p. Davies, J.C. 16May00
p. Mayes, G.R. 14July00
p.s. Bury, T.O. 13Dec.06
Withers, W. N., late
Lt. 6 Bn. R. Ir. Rif.
    5Apr.11
p.s. Roberts, R. 12Oct.12
Davies, A. S.(H) (q)
    5Dec.13
Williams, W. C. B.
    2)May14

Lieutenants. (8)
Evans, J. E. 14May10
Griffith, J. V. 20Mar.12
Davies, A. L. 12Oct.12
Foulkes-Roberts,
P. R. 1Oct.13
Rouffignac, F. D.
    1Oct.13
Davies, C. O. 5Dec.13
Griffith, G. R. 20May14
Hugh-Jones, N. 4June14

2nd Lieutenants. (8)
Bury, C. L. 3May13
Croom-Johnson, B.
    3May13
Harrop, N. M. 21May13
Owen, R. 13Feb.14
Minshall, T. C. W.
    6June14

Adjutant.
Minshull Ford, J.R.M.,
Capt. R. W. Fus. [l]
    21Nov.12

Quarter-Master.
Manfield, T., hon. lt.
    1July12

Medical Officers.
p. Anderson, J. W.,
M.B., Surg.-Capt.
    1June10
    24Mar.06
Drinkwater, Lt. F.
A. W., R.A.M.C.
(T.F.) (attd.) 1Dec.10

Chaplains.
Roberts, Rev. G. I.,
Chapl. 3rd Class
(T.F.) (attd.) 28May10
    11June04
Morris, Rev. R. E.
[W. C. M.], Chapl.
4th Class (T.F.)
(attd.) 7Aug.09
[Uniform—Scarlet.
Facings—Blue.]

5th (Flintshire) Battalion.

"South Africa, 1900-02."
Drill Hall, Flint.

Hon. Colonel.
Roberts, J. S., VD
(Hon. Col. ret.
Vols.) 15July05

Lt-Colonel.
Philips, B. E. (Maj.
& Hon. Lt.-Col.
3 Bn.) (Hon.Capt.
in Army 6 July01)
(H) 15May12

Majors. (2)
p.s. ×Keene, T. M. (Hon.
Capt. in Army 10
June01) (Q) (H),
t.a. 3June03
p. ×Head, B. (Hon. Capt.
in Army 17 June 01)
(Q) (H) 3June13
Williams, E. J. H. ⓡ
    7Aug.13

Captains. (8)
p. Williams, J. L.
    30June06
    3July08
Borthwick, F. H.
(H) 2July12
Beswick, W. 31Mar.13
Trickett, W. E. (H)
    23July13

Lieutenants. (8)
Parry, T. H. 11Oct.10
Marston, J. B. (H)
    29Jan.12
Kingsbury, A. 29Jan.12
Jefferson, H. A.,
    20Sept.13

2nd Lieutenants. (8)
Roberts, E. H.,14June12
Parry, J. E. 15Oct.12
Taylor, K. B, 16Oct.12
Armstrong, T. H.
    16Oct.12
Hughes, J. 1Apr.13
Owens, R. J. 29Apr.13
Astbury, A. N. 29Apr.13
×King, F. J. 29May13
Alexander, G. A.
    29May13
Horner, G. A. 19June13
Williams, H. O.12July13
    23July13
Davies, H.M. 12July13
Corbett, F. 5Aug.13
Bate, T. 8Sept.13
Mocatta, R. M. 16May14
Roberts, D. R. K.
    27June14

Adjutant.
Wood, C. E., Capt,
R. W. Fus. 20Oct.13

Quarter-Master.
Claridge, G., hon. lt.
    13July08

Medical Officers.
p. Swanson, Maj. A. P.,
R.A.M.C. (T. F.)
(attd.) 28Nov.08
    5May97

Chaplains.
Nicholas, Rev. W.
L.,M.A., TD,Chapl.
1st Class (T. F.)
(attd.) 20July09
    20July89
Hook, Rev. P. E. [R.C.]
Chapl. 4th Class
(T.F.) (attd.) 20July09
Griffiths, Rev. J.,
M.A., Chapl.
4th Class (T.F.)
(attd.) 4Apr.13
[Uniform—Scarlet.
Facings—Blue.]

6th (Carnarvonshire & Anglesey) Battalion.

"South Africa, 1900-02."
Carnarvon.

Hon. Colonel.
Greaves, J. E. 16Nov.98

Lt-Colonel.
p.s. Roberts, H. J., TD(H)
    7June12

Majors. (2)
p.s. ×Roberts, R. H. M.,
C.M.G. (H) 27Aug.04
p.s.Tuxford, W. A. (H)
    27June12

Captains. (8)
p.s. Wheeler, A. H. 19Mar.04
p. Jenkins, H. T. 28May04
p. Evans, J. ⓡ 23Dec.05
p.s. Griffith, R. (H) 10Jan.06
p. Battersby, G. L.
    3June13
p. Hughes-Hunter, Sir
W. B. H., Bt, (late
Lt. Denb. Yeo.)
    15Dec.13

Lieutenants. (8)
p.s. Darbishire, C. W. (t)
    8Sept.08
Cemlyn-Jones, T.
    6June10
Roberts, J. H. S.
    6June10
Miller, J. (H) 6June10
Evans, E. H. 20Apr.11
Jones, J. R. M. 2June13
Bracken, R. J. [l] (H)
    2June13
I. of M.
Anthony, J. R., ⓡ
    11June14

2nd Lieutenants. (8)
Stonor, C. H. J.
    1Aug.13
Russell, J. F. 5Dec.13
Evans, J. H. 1July14

Inst. of Musk.
Bracker, R. J., lt.
    11Oct.13

Adjutant.
×Lloyd, R. L., Capt.
R.W. Fus. 30May13

Quarter-Master.
p. Armstrong, T.,
hon. capt. 2May00

Medical Officers.
p. Williams, Capt. J. R.,
M.B., R.A.M.C.
(T.F.) (attd.) 3Aug.04
    20July01

Chaplains.
Richards, Rev. T. H.,
M.A.,Chapl.4thClass
(T.F.) (attd.) 5June12
[Uniform—Scarlet.
Facings—Blue.]

THE ROYAL WELSH FUSILIERS—(Regtl. Dist. No. 23)—contd.

7th (Merioneth & Montgomery) Battalion.

"South Africa, 1900-01."

Newtown, Montgomery.

Hon. Colonel.
Pryce-Jones, E. (Hon. Col. ret. Vols.) 15Sept.08

Lt.-Colonel.
p.s. Jelf-Reveley, A. E. R. (H)(Q) 18May14

Majors. (2)

Captains. (8)

Davies, D. 15July05
Corbett-Winder, W. J., *late* Capt. 4 Bn. S. Wales Bord. (*Hon. Capt. in Army* 6Dec.00) 2Apr.08
✗Arbuthnot-Brisco, R. J. W., *late* Capt. 3 Bn. York R. (*Hon. Lt. in Army* 15May02) (H) I. of M. 8Aug.08
p.s. Pryce-Jones, P. V. (H) 1July09
Owen, O. 1June12
Lloyd-Jones, E. W. (H) 5Dec.12

Lieutenants. (8)

Davies, D. O. 11June10
Williams, I. O. W. 11June10
Davies, J. A. 1June12
Jones, O. C. 1Mar.13
 1Jan.10
Jones, A. M. 18July13

Lieutenants.—contd.

Beadon, B.H.E. 18July13
Johnston, T. C. S. 14Aug.13
Hampson, W.@ 28Feb.14

2nd Lieutenants (8).

Price, E. P. 19Mar.13
Harries, E. G. 1Apr.13
Parkes, G. K. 3July13
Swift, C. B. 20May14

Inst. of Musk.

Arbuthnot Brisco, R. J. W., *capt.* 13Apr.11

Adjutant.

✗Garnett, W. B., Capt. R. W. Fus, 5Apr.13

Quarter-Master.

p.: Richards, W. F., *hon. m.* 2May97

Medical Officers.

p. Humphreys, Maj. C. E., R.A.M.C. (T.F.) (*attd.*) 7June13
 21July97
Greer, Lt. M., R A.M.C.(T.F.) (*attd.*) 21July13

Chaplain.

Hoskins, *Rev.* D., *M.A.* [W. C. M.], Chapl. 4th Class (T.F) (*attd.*) 2Mar 03

[Uniform—Scarlet. Facings—Blue.]

THE SOUTH WALES BORDERERS.
Regimental District No. **24.** [No. **4** District.]

The Sphinx, superscribed "Egypt."
"Blenheim," "Ramillies," "Oudenarde," "Malplaquet,"
"Cape of Good Hope, 1806," "Talavera," "Busaco," "Fuentes d'Onor," "Salamanca," "Vittoria,"
"Pyrenees," "Nivelle," "Orthes," "Peninsula," "Chillianwallah," "Goojerat," "Punjaub," "South
Africa, 1877-8-9," "Burma, 1885-87," "South Africa, 1900-02."

Regular and Special Reserve Battalion.
Uniform—Scarlet. *Facings*—Grass Green. *Agents*—Messrs. Holt & Co.

| 1st Bn. } (24th Foot) { *Bordon.* | 3rd Bn. (R. S. Wales Borderers Mil.) .. *Brecon.* |
| 2nd ,, } | *Tientsin (for Singapore).* | |

Depôt .. .. *Brecon.* Record Office .. .. .. *Shrewsbury.*

Territorial Force Battalion.
Brecknockshire Bn. .. .. *Brecon.*

Colonel .. .. .. Paton, Maj.-Gen. G., *C.M.G.*, ret. pay 26Nov.02

1st and 2nd Battalions.

Lt.-Colonels. (2)
2Casson, H. G. 29Nov.11
1Leach, H. E. B. 9June13

Majors. (8)
2Going, J. 11Dec 05
2Jones, E. W. 7July09
(3)1Gillespie, F. M., *e.*
  (*Comdg. Depôt*) 26Sept.09
2Margesson, E.C. 4Feb.11
s. Pearless,C.W.,*p.s.c.*[L]
  26Mar.12
1Reddie, A. J. 9June13
1Lawrence, W. L.
  4Mar.14
1Welby, G. E. E.11Mar.14

Captains. (14)
*m.a.*Bradley, R. W., D.S.O.
  11Dec.05
*m.c.*Taylor, C. L. 21Feb.06
1Lawrence, F. G.,
  D.S.O. 3Mar.06
r. Collier, B. W. 26Apr.06
1Ward, G.B.C.,*e.* 2Mar.07
(3)1Yates, H. P. 19June07
1Palmer, R. G. 18Dec.07
  7May02
s. Tudor, L. H. 19June07
1Curgenven, W. C.
  19June07
2Greenway, T. C.
  19June07
s.c. Gross, R.F. 29Nov.07
2Prichard, W. O. 1Dec.07
*e.a.*Elgee, H. F. 4Jan.08
*o.o.*Bill, J. F. 5July08
1Gwynn, R. S. 5July08
s.c. Morgan-Owen, L.
  I. G 9June09
f.c. Board, A. G. 9June09
2Ellis, A. H. J. 26Sept.09
t. Lloyd, A. M. O. J.
  1Feb.13
(3)2Fowler, H. G. C.
  [L] 1Feb.13
(3)2Barry, G. T. J. 18Apr.13
1Evans, R. H. 9June13
2Bradstock, J. 9June13
2Birkett, G. H., *Adjt.*
  9June13
2Johnson, D. G. 11Mar.14

Lieutenants (20).
*e.a.*Raikes, G. T. 25May07
1Yeatman, M. E.
  [L] 19June07
2Tippetts, C. M. 7Sept.07
c.o. Webb, S. N. C. 3Oct.07
c.o. Peel, A. R. 1Dec.07
2Habershon, C. B.
  4Jan.08
c.o. Edwards, J.F. 5July08
2Johnson, M.T. 15May09
2Williams, A. E. 9June09
c.o. Hughes, A. A. 18Sept.09
1Paterson, C. J., *Adjt.*
  26Sept.09
2Walker, R. K. B.
  23June10
2Petre, R. L. 22Dec.10
1Ramsden, V. B.
  18Mar.11
(3)2Salmon, F. H.
  1Apr.11
2Coker, J. C. 22June11
2Somerville, D. H. S.
  1Jan.12
c.o. Dickinson, W. V. D.
  2Jan.12
2Godwin-Austen,
  A. R. 5Jan.12
2Cahusac, A. N. 10Apr.12
c.o. Masters, A. C. 21July12
2Rawle, W. 1Feb.13
1Lochner. R. G. 5Mar.13
(3)1Mundy, P. R. M.
  18Apr.13
1Anstey, C. W. 9June13
w.a. Matthews, W. F.
  10Sept.13
2Travers, H. H. 9Oct.13
1Steward, C. K. 11Mar.14
1Hadley, R. B. 21Mar.14

2nd Lieutenants (12)
1Copner, C.J.P. 19Jan.12
1Richards, M.G. 27July12
1Homfray, J. R. 4Sept.12
2Behrens, R. P. 5Feb.13
2MacGregor, C. R.
  5Feb.13
2Morgan, M. C. 24May13
1Dawes, H. D. 3Sept.13
1Baker, C. A. 17Sept.13
1Sills, C. C. 17Sept.13
2Silk, N. G. 25Feb.14

Adjutants.
2Birkett, G. H., *capt.*
  5Feb.12
1Paterson, C. J., *lt.*
  2Sept.13

Quarter-Masters.
1Wilson, W. R.,
  hon. lt. 20Nov.12
2Laman, E. K.,
  hon. lt. 3Jan.14
r. Thomas, G. C. 17Jan.14
  23Feb.01
hon. capt. 23Feb.11

Special Reserve.
2nd Lieutenant.
Graham, E. M.
  27Nov.12

3rd Battalion.

(*Officers serving on 25Mar.02
in the corresponding Militia unit hold honorary Army rank equivalent to the Militia regimental rank they then held. Other officers entitled to honorary Army rank have it shown against their names.*)

Hon. Colonel.
Ormathwaite, A.,
Lord, late Capt.
  1 L.G. 5July08
  30Dec.76

Lt.-Colonel.
p.s.✕Morgan, S. W.
  30June13

Major.
r.e.✕Gillespie, F. M.,
  e. 26Sept.09
p.s.✕Maxwell-Heron, G.
  (H) 9July13

Captains. (5)
p.s.✕Gibson-Watt, J, M.(H)
  8Oct.98
p.s.✕Lake, J. S. R. 24Feb.06
r.e.✕Yates, H. P. 19June07
p.s.✕Ellis, A. J. (H), *f.c.*
  11June11
r.e.✕Fowler, H. G. C.
  [L] 1Feb.13
r.e.✕Barry, G.T.J. 18Apr.13
p.s.✕Crewe-Read, R. O.
  (H) 31Mar.14

Lieutenants. (11)
Dickinson, F. G. (H)
  4July08
(*p.s.*)Lloyd, J. C. (H)
  19Feb.08
*p.s.*James, A. E. L. (H)
  1May09
*r.e.*Salmon, H. M. B.
  1Apr.11
*r.e.*Mundy, P. R. M.
  18Apr.13

2nd Lieutenants (8)
Allaway, T. R. 6Jan.12
Vernon, J. M. L. 1Apr.12
Kelly, B. J. F.
  (on prob.) 1Oct.13
Gilbert, H. A.
  (on prob.) 7Jan.14

Adjutant.
✕Collier, B. W.
  Capt. S. Wales
  Bord. 26Sept.12
  (*Capt. in Army* 26Apr.06)

Quarter-Master.
✕Thomas. G. C.,
  hon. capt.

THE SOUTH WALES BORDERERS—(Regtl. Dist. No. 24)—contd.

Brecknockshire Battalion.

On a mount the Red Dragon passant.

"South Africa, 1900-01."

Brecon.

Hon. Colonel.
✗Glanusk, J. H. R., Lord, C.B., D.S.O., Maj., *late* G. Gds. (*Maj. Res. of Off.*)
    1June07

Lt.-Colonel.
✗Glanusk, J.H.R., Lord, C.B., D.S.O., Maj., *late* G.Gds. (*Maj.Res.of Off.*)
    20Mar.12

Majors. (2)
Thomas, D.W.E., VD (*H*)
    7Apr.11

Captains. (8)
p. Careless, A. L. 5July99
p. Woodliffe, H. D. 23Aug.02
Pugh-Morgan, R.B. 6Oct.12
p.s. Thomas, J. I. P. 23May14

Lieutenants. (8)
(p.) Jones, D. 24June09
Evans, H. W. 24June09
(p.) Cockcroft, E. F. 1June09
Musgrove, E. H. 18Mar.10
Morgan, H. A. (*H*) 7Apr.11
(p.) Prichard, W. J. 7July11
Thomas, G. D. E. 6Oct.12
p. Lewis, W. R. 23May14

2nd Lieutenants. (8)
Harris, D. G. 29July08
Woosnam, R. W. 23Jan.09
Glynne-Jones, R. 23Mar.09
Vigars, F. H. 17Apr.12
Canton, W. J. 15May12
Townley, J. S. 26June12
Adams, R. P. 12Nov.13
Butcher, A. C. S. 26Nov.13
Phillips, A. G. 16Apr.14

Adjutant.
✗Lloyd, A. M. O. J., Capt. S. Wales Bord. 17Mar.13

Quarter-Master.
p. Isaac, W. T., *hon. m.* 18Feb.05

Medical Officers.
p.s. Thomas, Capt. T. P., *late* R.A.M.C.(Mila.) R.A.M.C. (T.F.)
(*attd.*) 16Feb.11
    18June07
Bridge, Lt. J. C., F.R.C.S. (*Edin.*) R.A.M.C. (T.F.)
(*attd.*) 14Oct.11

Chaplains.
Bevan, *Ven. Archdeacon* E. L., *M.A.*, Chapl. 2nd Class (T.F.) (*attd.*) 4Sept.12
    4Sept.97
Rowland, *Rev.* E. [W. C. M.] Chapl. 4th Class (T.F.) (*attd.*) 20May08

[Uniform—*Scarlet*. Facings—*Grass Green*.]

THE KING'S OWN SCOTTISH BORDERERS.
Regimental District No. 25. [No. 2 District.]

The Castle of Edinburgh, with the motto "*Nisi Dominus frustra.*"
In the first and fourth corners the Royal Crest, with the motto, "*In Veritate Religionis confido.*"
In the second and third corners the White Horse, with "*Nec aspera terrent.*"
The Sphinx, superscribed "Egypt."

"Namur, 1695," "Minden," "Egmont-op-Zee," "Martinique, 1809," "Afghanistan, 1878-80," "Chitral," "Tirah," "Paardeberg," "South Africa, 1900-02."

Regular and Special Reserve Battalions.

Uniform—Scarlet.   Facings—Blue.   Agents—Messrs. Cox & Co.

1st Bn. } (25th Foot) { Lucknow.
2nd „ }   { Dublin. | 3rd Bn. (Scottish Borderers Mil.) .. Dumfries.

Depôt .. ..   Berwick-on-Tweed. | Record Office .. .. Hamilton.

Territorial Force Battalions.

4th Bn. .. .. Galashiels. | 5th Bn. .. .. .. Dumfries.

Colonel .. .. .. Woollcombe, Lt.-Gen. C. L., C.B. 31Aug.10

1st and 2nd Battalions.

Lt.-Colonels. (2)
2 Stephenson, C. M.
          3Dec.10
1 Koe, A. S.   10Nov.13

Majors. (8)
2 Haig, A. E., *p.s.c.* [*l*]
          29Nov.05
          20May98
1 Sladen, D. R., *D.S.O.*
          16Oct.07
s. Blair, A., *D.S.O.*,
   p.s.c.   4July08
1 McAlester, W. H. S.
          20July06
(3) 2 Maclean, H. D. N.,
   D.S.O. (Comdg.
   Depôt)   10Nov.09
1 Welch, A. J.   3Dec.10
2 Coke, E. S. D'E.
          10Nov.04
2 Leigh, C., *D.S.O*
   [F]   17June14

Captains. (14)
s. Broadbent, E. N.
   [F]   18May01
m.c. Stewart, P. A. V.,
   p.s.c.   24June01
s. Connell, J. C. W. 9Oct.01
2 Spencer, L. D, [F]
          12Oct.01
1 Hosley, W. J. S. 20May06
          11Jan.02
t. Wilkinson, W. T.,
   D.S.O.   4Dec.03
e.a. Stoney, G. B. 21Sept.04
t. Youngson, T. W.
          19Oct.05
r. Wingate, T. P. 14Jan.06
e.a. Turnbull, H. V. C.
          7June06
2 Macdonald, E. W.
          8Dec.06
s. Todhunter, H.W., *o.*
          3July07
2 Kennedy, C. F. 3July07
2 Cobden, R.   16Oct.07
1 Whigham, R.D. 21May08
2 Smith, G. W. 13May08
1 Antrobus, C. A. 2Aug.08
1 Cooper, A. S. 15Oct.08
i.v. Crake, R. H. 10Nov.08

Captains—contd.
(3) 2 Burnett, A. E.17Dec.08
(3) 1 Hilton, G.   17Apr.09
2 Dering, R. C. Y.,
   Adjt.   17Apr.09
1 Marrow, E. A., *Adjt.*
          1Apr.10
(3) 1 Hopkins, I. B. 6Apr.10
t. Lang, J. C.   26Oct10
t. Wade C.   9Apr.13
e.a. Wylie, P. E. 19Feb14
t. Jackson, E. D. 19Feb14
1 Hartley, J. B. 19Feb14
i.v. Furber, C. T. 19Feb.14
1 Becher, M. A. N.
          15May14

Lieutenants. (19)
e.a. Worsley, R. H. W.
          16Oct.07
2 Pennyman, J. B. W.
          11Dec.07
1 Sanderson, A. J.
          9Mar.08
1 Ogilvy, G. M. H.
          16Oct.08
s. Kirkpatrick, H. C. B.
          10Nov.08
(3) 1 Mayne, H.G.L., *f.c.*
          17Dec.08
1 Sanderson, P. N.
          24Mar.09
1 Murray, C. A. G. O.
          17Apr.09
(3) 2 Maxwell, R. E. W.
          17Apr.09
1 Paterson, A. G.
          15Sept.09
2 Campbell, A. C.
          23Dec.09
1 Cruickshank, H. T.
          1Apr.10
c.o. Campbell, J. K. B.
          26Oct.10
1 Stirling-Cookson, C. S.
          1Apr.11
2 Lindsay, G. H. M.
          1Oct.11
1 Lake, B. C. 2June12
t. Cheatle, W. J. N.
          26Aug.12
1 Grogan, J. C. 9Apr.13
1 Hamilton-Dalrymple,
   J. R.   8May13
2 Joynson, R. 8May13
1 Ainslie, J. A 1June13
1 Renny, S. C. 1Nov.13
2 Holme, R. H P.
          19Feb.14

2nd Lieutenants. (12)
c.o. Taylor, R. R. 4Mar.11
2 Miles, E. G. 3June11
2 Harvey, H. J. 4Nov.11
1 Deighton, F.H. 4Sept.12
2 Hammond, G.P.
          4Dec.12
1 Shorter, R. M. 22Jan.13
2 Oliver-Rutherfurd,
   W. A.   22Jan.13
2 Bell, R. P. M. 24May13
2 Shewen. W. G.
          3Sept.13
1 Agar, E. W. T. 3Sept.13
1 Miller, T.A.G. 24Jan.14
2 Bayley, G. B. 24Jan.14
2 Amos, G. S. 25Feb.14

Adjutants. (2)
2 Dering, R. C. Y.,
   capt.   8Aug.12
1 Marrow, E. A., *capt.*
          15May14

Quarter-Masters.
r. Parkinson, B. E.,
          11Oct.99
   hon. capt. 11Oct.09
2 Murray, A. 9Sept.03
   hon. capt. 9Sept.13
1 Simpson, W., *hon. lt.*
          25Jan.06

Special Reserve.

2nd Lieutenants
Crawshaw, H.
   (on prob.)   14June13
Scott, N. S. (on
   prob.)   14June13
Dering, A. L. Y.
          21June13
Robertson, E.
   (on prob.)   9July13
Teeling, T.F.P.B.J.
   (on prob.)   14Mar.14

3rd Battalion.

(*Officers serving on 18June02 in the corresponding Militia unit hold honorary Army rank equivalent to the Militia regimental rank they then held. Other officers entitled to honorary Army rank have it shown against their names.*)

Hon. Colonel.
p.s. Hume, A. (Hon.
   Col. late Mila.)
   (H) ⊕   2Aug.08
          19Oct.98

Lt.-Colonel.
p.s. ✠Crichton-Browne,
   H. W. A. F., 10June11

Major.
r.e. ✠Maclean, H. D. N.,
   D.S.O.   10Nov.09
Young-Herries, W. D.
   (T) (H)   10June11

Captains. (5)
p.s. Wilkie Dalyell,
   Sir J. B., Bt. (*t*)
   hon. m.   1May95
p.s. ✠Allan, W. L. C., *hon.
   m.* (*t*) (*H*)   3June99
p.s. Henryson-Caird, A. J.
   (H)   11June07
r.e. Burnett, A. E.
          17Dec.08
r.e. Hilton, G. 17Apr 09
r.e. Hopkins, I. B. 6Apr.10
✠Bland, C.E.W.,Capt.
   ret. pay   26Oct.10

Lieutenants. (11)
(*p.s.*) Dudgeon, C. R. (H)
          8July07
r.e. Mayne, H.G.L., *f.c.*
          17Dec.08
r.e. Maxwell, R. E. W.
          17Apr.09
Cox, G. H. 14July13
Sandison, L. M.
          14July13

2nd Lieutenants. (8)
Young-Herries, A. D.
   (on prob.)   6Dec.13
MacRae, I. A.
   (on prob.)   10Jan.14

Adjutant.
✠Wingate, T. P., *Capt.*
   K.O. Sco.Bord.9Mar.12
   (*Capt. in Army*24Jan.06)

Quarter-Master.
✠Parkinson, B. E.,
   hon. capt.

1137	1138	1139	1140

THE KING'S OWN SCOTTISH BORDERERS—(Regtl. Dist. No. 25)—contd.

4th (The Border) Battalion.

South Africa, 1900-02."

Galashiels.

Hon. Colonel.

p. Waldie-Griffith, Sir R. J., Bt., TD (Hon. Col. ret. Vols.) 22Sept.06

Lt.-Colonel.

✗McNeile, J., Maj. ret. pay (Res. of Off.) 3Apr.12

Majors. (2)

Stevenson, A., VD, 16Apr.12

Captains. (8)

p.s. Cochrane, W. E. A. 13May08
p. McCreath, H. G. C. 28Nov.03
p. McDougal, J. 23Jan.04
p.s. Wallace, A. 11Apr.06
p. Mabbott, W. J. (H) 25Mar.07
(Q) 9Dec.07
p.s. Jobson, M. 5June11
p.s. Sanderson, H. (H) 20Jan.12
Macdonald, C. E. 28Feb.12
29Mar.09
p. Locke, H. W., (H) 28Feb.12
Forrest, W. T. 2Apr.12
Roberts, A. T. (H)
I. of M. 10Oct.13

Lieutenants. (8)

(p.s.) Elder, D. L. 15Aug.09
(p.s.) Sharpe, R. W. 10Jan.11
25Mar.07
p.s. Laing, P. L. P. (H) 1Jan.12
Somervail, A. 5Apr.12
Dun, J. M. 18Dec.12
Alexander, T. M. 25Jan.13
Harrison, J. ⓢ 10Oct.13
Muir, T. T., jun. 18Apr.14

2nd Lieutenants. (8)

Bulman, A. 18Dec.12
Lumgair, R. R. M. 19Dec.12
Innes, J. B. 2Apr.13
Henderson, A. H. M. 15May13
Woodhead, P. 17Sept.13

Inst. of Musk.

Roberts, A. T., capt. 26July12

Adjutant.

✗Lang, J. C., Capt.
K. O. Sco. Bord. 26Aug.12

Quarter-Master.

Follis, E. H., hon. lt. 7Apr.10

Medical Officers.

p. Doig, Maj. W.,
M.D., TD, R.A.M.C.
(T.F.) (attd.) 25Aug.12
9Dec.93
p. Barrie, Capt. W. T.,
M.B., TD, R.A.M.C.
(T.F.) (attd.) 30Oct.94
28Feb.91
p. Young, Capt. J.,
M.B., R.A.M.C.
(T.F.) (attd.) 15May01
26Feb.96
p. Taylor, Capt. D. R.,
R.A.M.C. (T.F.)
(attd.) 1Apr.08
8Aug.06

Chaplains.

✗Wilson, Rev. J. R.,
M.A., [C.S.] TD,
Chapl. 1st Class
(T.F.) (attd.) 4May12
4May92
Napier, Rev. J. G. S.,
M.A., [C.S.] Chapl.
2nd Class (T.F.) 11Apr.11
11Apr.96
Wallace, Rev. A. E.,
M.A. [C.S.] Chapl.
4th Class (T.F.)
(attd.) 1Apr.10
15Apr.07
Matheson, Rev. W. S.
[U.F.C.] Chapl.
4th Class (T.F.)
(attd.) 1Nov.09

[Uniform—Scarlet.
Facings—Blue.]

5th (Dumfries & Galloway) Battalion.

"South Africa, 1900-02."

Dumfries.

Hon. Colonel.

p.s. Kennedy, J. M., M.V.O.,
VD. (Hon. Col. ret.
Vols.) 18Oct.06

Lt.-Colonel.

p. Kerr, P. M., TD 10June11

Majors. (2)

p. Millar, W. J., TD 10June11
Bell, E. J. 1Nov.12

Captains. (8)

p. Thorburn, W., TD, hon.
m., (H) 18Oct.02
p. ✗Forde, E. S. 19Sept.03
p. Anderson, A. W. 28Sept.
p. Glover, R. S. 29Nov.05
p.s. ✗Cunningham, R. J. 26May06
Crombie, W. F. 1Nov.12
Dykes, J. J. 2June13
p. Welsh, T. 6June13
26May06

Lieutenants. (8)

(p.) Glover, J. McN. 7Dec.06
(p.s.) Moffat, W. M. (H) 1May07
(p.) Clark-Kennedy, A. K. 20Aug.07
Coventon, E. 7June12
McNeill, A. H. ⓢ 7June12
Maxwell, W. F. J. 1Nov.12
Douglas, R. 22Nov.13
Smith, E. 3June14

2nd Lieutenants. (8)

Watson, W. G. D. 29Mar.05
Gibson, E. N. 7Apr.11
Penman, J. B. 10July12
McGeorge, J. 3Dec.12
Macrae, D. 6Dec.12
Salmond, G. 22July14

Adjutant.

✗Youngson, T. W. Capt.
K. O. Sco. Bord. 17Mar.11

Quarter-Master.

Axson, G. H.,
hon. lt. 20Jan.12

Medical Officers.

p. Livingston, Maj. G. R.,
M.D., R.A.M.C. (T.F.)
(attd.) 26May13
5June01
Saffley, Lt. J., M.B.,
R.A.M.C. (T.F.)
(attd.) 7Jan.14

Chaplains.

Inglis, Rev. J. McD.,
M.A., TD, [C.S.]
Chapl. 2nd Class
(T.F.) (attd.) 1Apr.08
30May91
Campbell, Rev. J. M.
[C.S.] Chapl. 4th
Class (T.F.) (attd.) 1Apr.08
2June06
McGlashan, Rev. L.,
M.A. [C.S.] Chapl.
4th Class (T.F.)
(attd.) 1Aug.10

[Uniform—Scarlet.
Facings—Blue.]

THE CAMERONIANS (SCOTTISH RIFLES).
Regimental District No. 26. [No. 2 District.]

The Sphinx, superscribed "Egypt."   The Dragon, superscribed "China."
"Blenheim," "Ramillies," "Oudenarde," "Malplaquet," "Mandora," "Corunna," "Martinique, 1809,"
"Guadaloupe, 1810," "South Africa, 1846-7," "Sevastopol," "Lucknow," "Abyssinia,"
"South Africa, 1877-8-9," "Relief of Ladysmith," "South Africa, 1899-1902."

Regular and Special Reserve Battalions.

Uniform—Green.	Facings—Dark Green.	Agents—Messrs. Cox & Co.
1st Bn. (26th Foot) ..	Glasgow (for Fort George.)	3rd Bn. (2nd R. Lanark Mil.) .. Hamilton.
2nd „ (90th „) ..	Malta (for Alexandria).	4th „ (2nd R. Lanark Mil.) .. Hamilton.
Depôt	Hamilton.	Record Office .. .. Hamilton.

Territorial Force Battalions.

5th Bn. ..	261, W. Princes Street, Glasgow.	7th Bn.	Victoria Road, Glasgow.
6th „ ..	.. Muirhall, Hamilton.	8th „	149, Cathedral Street, Glasgow.

Colonel .. Laye, Maj.-Gen. J. H., C.V.O., C.B., ret. pay (Res. of Off.) [R.]   .. 31July10

1st and 2nd Battalions.

Lt.-Colonels. (2)
2Bliss, W. M.   10Oct.13
1Robertson, P.R.24Oct.13

Majors. (8)
1Vandeleur, D.B.10Oct.05
   22Aug.02
2Carter-Campbell,
G. T. C.   3Apr.07
   29Nov.00
2Hayes, E. de L.24June08
   22Aug.02
2Ellis, G. A.   24Feb.12
2Lloyd, H.D.W. [F]
   19Feb.13
(3)1Northey, A. C.
   (Oomdg.Depot) 1July13
1Oakley, R.   10Oct.13
1Chaplin, J. G.   24Oct13

Captains. (14)
s. Stewart, I., p.s.c. [l]
   10Apr.00
s. Maxwell-Scott,
W. J., p.s.c. . 22June01
w.a.Caulfeild-Stoker,
M. C. L.   20May08
   29Sept.01
(3)2Mackinnon, A.L.1Apr.03
1Hamilton, F. A. C.
   9May03
r. Sandilands, V. C.
   20May03
1Lee, H. H.   4Nov.03
s. Gilkison, D. S., p.s.c.
   14Jan.05
1Rose, R. H. W. ..   20May08
   4May05
i.v. Ritchie, A. G   15Oct.06
s. Girdwood, E. S.
   22Jan.08
r. Torkington, O. M.
   8Mar.08
m.c. Ewing, D. R.   9Apr.08
2Ferrers, E. B.   14Apr 90
Draffen, F. G.W, 1Apr.10
1MacAllan, A. R.
   17Apr.10
s.c. Turner, J. E.   17Apr.10
t. Bramwell, C. 6June10
c.o. Gordon, J, F. S. [F]
   10Sept.10
   9Apr.10

Captains—contd.
2Smith,H. C. H.12Mar.12
t. Croft, W. D.   12Mar.12
e.a. Worthington-Wilmer,
G. R.   12Mar.12
1Stormonth-Darling,
J. C., Adjt.   12Mar.12
w.a.Taylor, A. C.   1Apr.12
e.a.Thorburn, D. H.
   29Apr.12
(3)1Dodd, P. R.   29Apr.12
   1Feb.13
(3)2Sword, D. C.   1Feb.13
t. Lawrence, H. M.
   1Feb.13
2Maunsell, W. I. [L]
   1Feb.13
(1) McLellan, T. R.   1Feb.13
2Ross-Hume, A., f.c,
   19Feb.13
t. Clerk, R. V.   19Feb.13
1Jack, J. L.   5Mar.13
w.a.Corrie, J.S.M. 14May13
2Kennedy, J. P.14May13
1Orailshelm,H.R.1July13
1Riddell-Webster, T. S.
   24Oct.13

Lieutenants. (20)
2Gray-Buchanan
   W. B.   13Oct.09
2Foster, T.B. G. 26Nov.09
(3)1Hewitt, J. F. 12Mar.10
c.o Baynes, R.M.S. 1Apr.10
2Hunter, R. D.   1Apr.10
2Money, s. C.   17Apr.10
Stanley Clarke,
   A. C. L.   6June10
1Newman, E. W. P.
   10Dec.10
2O'Connor, R. N.6May11
2Kerr, W. J.   29Apr.12
(3)2Wanless-O'Gowan, L.
   23July12
2deBlaquiere, Hon. J.
   23Jan, 13
1Hobkirk, E. W. J.
   1Feb.13
2Dunn, T. E. D. 6Feb.13
1Becher H. O. D.
   15Feb.13
1Drew, C. F.   19Feb.13
2Sim, H. H. C. 10Mar.13
1Foster, D. C. 14May13
2Evetts, J. F. 1July13
2Hopkins, C. R. 1
   24Oct.13
2Loder-Symonds,
   T. L.   13May14

2nd Lieutenants. (12)
2Stirling, C.R.H. 5Feb.13
w.a,Fergusson, V. H.
   15Mar.13
1Ferry, E. L.   8Sept.13
1Graham, D. A. H.
   17Sept.13
1Critchely-Salmonson,
H. S. R.   17Sept.13
1Moncrieff Wright,
D. G.   17Sept.13
1Rooke, C.D.W. 17Sept.13
2Bibby, J. C.   17Sept.13
2Kennedy, M.D.24Jan.14
1Minchin, J. H. C.
   24Jan.14
2Graham, R.   25Feb.14
1Briggs, A. D.   25Feb.14

Adjutants.
2Maunsell, W. I. [L]
   capt.   22July12
1Stormonth-Darling,
   J. C., capt.   24Oct.13

Quarter-Masters.
r. Finn, T.   6July98
hon. maj. 6July13
1Graham, J., hon. lt.
   11May10
r. Haddon, J. T., hon. lt.
   24Dec.13
1Wood, G., hon. lt.
   7Jan.14

Special Reserve.
2nd Lieutenant.
Barley, L. J. (on
   prob.)   14June13

3rd Battalion.
(*Officers serving on 15July02 in the corresponding Militia unit hold honorary Army rank equivalent to the Militia regimental rank they then held. Other officers entitled to honorary Army rank have it shown against their names.*)

Hon. Colonel.
Home, C. A., Earl of,
K.T., TD (Col. late
Yeo. Cav.) (King's
Body Gd. for Scotland)   9Aug.08
   26Nov.04

Lt.-Colonel.
XAnderson, W. C.,
D.S.O., Hon. Lt.-
Col. ret., hon. c.
   17Oct.08
   8Aug.03

Major.
XLuard, G. D., Maj.
ret. pay,(Res. of Off.)
   9May03
r.e.XNorthey, A. C.
   10July12
   1July13

Captains. (5)
r e. XMackinnon, A. L.
   1Apr.12
p.s. XYoung, C. H, [l]
   p.v.c. (H) 20Aug.04
p.s.XClarson, J. H. P,
   (H)   6Jan.11
r.e.XDodd, P. R. 29Apr.12
Stirling, J., Lt.
ret. pay (q) 18June12
r.e.XSword, D. C. 1Feb.13
XFullarton,R.W.F.,
Lt., ret. pay 15Feb.13

Lieutenants. (11)
r.e. Hewitt, J. F. 12Mar.10
Dew, J. F.   10June12
r.e.XWanless-O'Gowan,
J,.   23July12

2nd Lieutenants. (8)
Hill, J. D. (on prob.)
   15Apr.14

Adjutant.
XTorkington, O. M.,
   Capt.Sco.Rif.21Apr.12
   (Capt. in Army 9 Mar.08)

Quarter-Master.
XFinn, T., hon. maj.

THE CAMERONIANS (SCOTTISH RIFLES)—(Regtl. Dist. No. 26)—contd.

4th Battalion.

(*Officers serving on 27June01 in the corresponding Militia unit hold honorary Army rank equivalent to the Militia regimental rank they then held. Other officers entitled to honorary Army rank have it shown against their names.*)

Hon. Colonel.
Home, C. A., **Earl of**, K.T., TD (*Col. late Yeo. Cav.*) (*King's Body Gd. for Scotland*) 9Aug.08
6Nov.02

Lt.-Colonel.
p.s. ✗Lynch, C. J. 29Oct.12

Majors. (3)
p.s. ✗Mellish, R. W. (*H*) 3June11
p.s. ✗Murphy, R. R. W. B., (*H*) 14Dec.11
✗Douglas, A. F., **Capt.** ret. pay (*H*) 10Oct.13

Captains. (6)
p.s. ✗Anderson, J. D. 14Mar.06
Edden, H. W., **Capt.** ret. pay 14Apr.09
Houston, S. C. (*Hon. 2nd Lt. in Army 6Oct.00*) (*I*) (*H*) 10ct.11
6May03
p.s.✗Scott, C. C. (*Hon. Capt. in Army 5 Dec. 00*)(*H*)(*a*) *I. of M.* 10July12
16Mar.00

Lieutenants. (11)
(p.s.)Miller, C. R. E. 30May08
(p.s.)Auchinleck, A. L. (*q*) (*H*) (*Asst. Dist. Offr., N. Provs., Nigeria,* {1 Jan. 14 {31 July 11) 30May08
Bourke, J. F. 1June09
✗Macdonald,A.MacG., *late Lt. Res. of Off.* (*Hon. Lt. in Army 14 Jan. 03*) 1May11
15May12
Mallace, M. ⓢ 2Aug.13
de Merindol, R. F. J. 2Aug.13

2nd Lieutenants. (8)
Robertson, D. H. H. 10Sept.13
White, R. E. (*on prob.*) 28Jan.14

Inst. of Musk.
Scott, C. C., *capt.* 29Dec.13

Adjutant.
Sandilands, V. C., **Capt. Sco.Rif.**23Mar.12 (*Capt. in Army 20May03*)

Quarter-Master.
✗Haddon, J. T., *hon. lt.*

5th Battalion.

"South Africa, 1900-02."

261, W. Princes Street, Glasgow.

Lt.-Colonel.
p.s. ✗Douglas, R. J., TD (*Hon. Capt. in Army 23 June 02*) (*Q*) 25Mar.11

Majors. (2)
Benzie, R. M. (*t*) 25Mar.11
p.s. Paterson, J. C., TD, ⓢ (*H*)(*Q*) 5May12

Captains. (8)
p.s. ✗Kennedy, A. A., TD (*Hon. Lt. in Army 24 June 01*) *hon. m.* (*Q*) 7Jan05
p.s. Rodger, H. T. (*Q*) 31Mar.06
p. Campbell, J. C. (*q*) 14Mar.07
p.s Macalister, W. G. (*Q*) (*H*) 1Jan.09
p.s. Macfarlane, R. (*Q*) 1Apr.09
p.s. Ker, D. E. (*Q*) 25Mar.11
p.s. Aitken, R. C. S. (*q*) 3Apr.12
p.s. Gray, A. M. (*H*) (*t*) *I. of M.* 3Apr.12

Lieutenants (8)
(p.s.)Alexander, A. M. (*q*) 12Feb.07
(p.) Spens, H. B. (*q*) 14Mar.07
(p.) Macgeorge, A. M. 27Jan.10
(p.s.)Crombie, A. G. (*H*) 3Apr.12
(p.s.)Ashby-Brown, K. 3Apr.12
Spens, J. I. 12Apr.13
Loudon, J. 21June13
Smith, G. S. 21Mar.14

2nd Lieutenants.—(8)

Reith, J. C. W. 18Feb.11
Russell, T. 3Apr.12
Grierson, J. M. 26June12
Alexander, W. S. 11Sept.12
Begg, R. W. 24Apr.13
Forrest, J. W. 12Nov13
White, M. M. K. 2Feb.14

Inst. of Musk.
Gray, A. M., **Capt.** 17Mar.10

Adjutant.
Croft, W. D., **Capt. Sco. Rif.** 1Jan.13

Quarter-Master.
✗Brown, J., *hon.lt.* 17Apr.12

Medical Officers.
p Adams, Maj. F. V., TD (*hon.Surg.-Lt.-Col.*) R.A.M.C. (T.F.) (*attd.*) 4Feb.03
3Jan.91
p. Innes, **Capt.** J., R.A.M.C. (T.F.) (*attd.*) 10Apr.10
10Oct.06

Chaplains.
White, Rev. J., M.A.[C.S.]Chapl. 4th Class (T.F.) (*attd.*) 1May09
Simpson, Rev. H. L., M.A.[U.F.C.] Chapl. 4th Class (T.F.) (*attd.*) 27Mar.13

[Uniform—Grey. Facings—Blue.]

6th Battalion.

"South Africa, 1900-02."

Muirhall, Hamilton.

Hon. Colonel.
Hamilton and Brandon, A. D., Duke of 6Nov.95

Lt.-Colonel.
Kay, W. M., TD (*Q*) (*H*) 30Oct.12

Majors. (2)
Dykes, J. 30July10
Shaw, D. P. 23Oct.13

Captains. (8)

p.s. Sharp, R. W., TD, *hon. m.* 15Oct.04
p.s. McKenzie, W. S. 8Nov.05
p.s. Boyd, J., (*t*) 26Mar.07
p.s. Murray, C. J. C. 30July07
p.s. Brown, J. (*q*) (*H*) (*a*) ⓢ 1May09
p.s. McLean, J. C. 31July10
Graham, A. G. (*H*) *I. of M.* 24Oct.12
Anderson, J. ⓢ 23Oct.13

Lieutenants. (8)
(p.s.)Lawrie, A. J. 1May09
(p.s.)Keith, J. H. 1May09
Lusk, J. 31July10
Keith, P. H. 31July10
Bow, W. (*H*) 31July10
Johnston, G. 4May12

2nd Lieutenants. (8)
Hay, J. C. E. 11Mar.13
Wilson, F. J. C. 25Apr.13
Campbell, T. H., *jun.* 10Sept.13
Gray, D. L. 1 Oct.13
Logan, J. G. 28Mar 14

Inst. of Musk.
Graham, A. G. *capt.* 1Feb.13

Adjutant.
✗Draffen, F. G. W., **Capt. Sco. Rif.** 1Apr.12

Quarter-Master.
Hamilton, J., *hon. lt.* 4May12

Medical Officers.
p. Loudon, Maj. J. L., M.B., R.A.M.C. (T.F.) (*attd.*) 9June08
18Apr.96
Mackie, Lt., T. J. (*M.B.*), R.A.M.C. (T.F.) (*attd.*) 13Jan.14

Chaplains.
MacGibbon, Rev. J., B.D., [C.S.] Chapl. 3rd Class (T.F.) (*attd.*) 30Apr.12
Turnbull, Rev. C. S. M.A. [C.S.] Chapl. 3rd Class (T.F.) (*attd.*) 16July12
16July02
Scott, Rev. A. S. D., M.A. [C.S.] Chapl. 4th Class (T.F.) (*attd.*) 28Feb.12
Ferrier, Rev. D., M.A., [U.F.C.] Chapl. 4th Class (T.F.) (*attd.*) 5 Feb.13

[Uniform—Green. Facings - Dark Green.]

THE CAMERONIANS (SCOTTISH RIFLES)—(Regtl. Dist. No. 26)—contd.

7th Battalion.

"South Africa, 1900-02."

Victoria Road, Glasgow.

Hon. Colonel.
Stirling-Maxwell,
Sir J. M., Bt. 13Jan.94

Lt.-Colonel.
×Wilson, J. B. (Hon.
Lt. in Army 23
June02) ⓟ   8Nov.13

Majors. (2)
Templeton, A. I.
(t)   10May09
Wilkie, J. A., TD,
(q)   8Nov.13

Captains. (8)
p.s. Bird, W. T. (Q) (H)
I. of M.   1Feb.07
p.s. Macfarlane, J. G.
ⓠ   1Apr.09
p.s Howatt, J. (Q) 10May09
p.s. Hutchison, R. (H)
              25June10
p.s. Smith, E. 10July11
p.s. Smith, J. A. (q) 20Jan.12
Whitton, P. I. (q)
ⓠ (H)   25Dec.12
p.s. Kirkhope, W. G.
(q)   8Nov.13

Lieutenants. (9)
(p.s.) Blair, R.   1Feb.06
(p.s.) Jarvie, A. 1June11
(p.s.) Johnstone, R. (q)(H)
              15June11
(p.s.) Hodge, H. F. (t)
              10Aug.11
Goodall-Copestake,
H. ⓠ   16Dec.12

Lieutenants—contd.

Nicol, A. S.   16Dec.12
Mather, W.   16Dec.12
Brown, W. W.   16Dec.12
Duff, W.   25Dec.12

2nd Lieutenants. (8)
Anderson, J.K. 30Nov.11
McMillan, J. A.
              26June12
Will, C. P.   1July12
Law, W. R.   1Dec.12
Taylor, D. M. 4Dec.12
Nelson, J. E. 26Mar.13
Nelson, D. R. 13Apr.13
Kirkwood, J.   21Mar.14
Leggat, W.   21Mar.14
Ramsey, J. B. 29Apr.14

Inst. of Musk.
Bird, W. T., capt.
              31Mar.09

Adjutant.
Clerk, R. V., Capt.
Sco. Rif.   1Apr.14

Quarter-Master.
Phillips, J., hon. lt.
              13July11

Medical Officers.
p. Forrest, Maj. T.,
M.B., TD, R.A.M.C.
(T.F.) (attd.) 30Dec.05
              16Dec.93
Graham, Capt. J., M.B.,
R.A.M.C. (T.F.)(attd.)
              7Nov.13
              7May10

Chaplains.
Rankine, Rev. W. H.,
B.D. [C.S.] Chapl.
3rd Class (T.F.)
(attd.)   12June11
              12June01
Maclauchlan, Rev. F.
J., M.A. [U.F.C.]
Chapl. 4th Class
(T.F.)(attd.) 1Dec.09

[Uniform—Green.
Facings—Dark Green.]

Cadet Unit Affiliated.
Hutchesons' Grammar
School Cadet Corps.

8th Battalion.

"South Africa, 1900-02."

149, Cathedral Street,
Glasgow.

Hon. Colonel.
p. Maxwell, W. R., VD
(Hon. Col. ret.
Vols.) ⓟ   27Feb.04

Lt.-Colonel.
p.s. ×Hannan, H.M., TD,
(Hon. Lt. in Army
23June02) (Q) (H)
              12Feb.13

Majors. (2)
p.s. Ker, A. D. TD ⓠ, (H)
              14Dec.09
Findlay, J. M. (Q)
(H)   12Feb.13

Captains. (8)
p.s. Coulson, R. N. (Q)
              13Nov.06
p.s. Boyd, J. M. (t) 9Dec.07
p.s. Macindoe, C. A. D.
              29Dec.09
Pattison, J. W. H.
              1May13
MacLehose, J. A.
              20May13

Lieutenants. (8)

Young, A. S. L
              29Dec.09
McNeill, H. L. 24Jan.10
Young, E.T.   10Mar.12
Macindoe, R.C.B.
              17Jan.13
Church, W. C. 23Dec.13

2nd Lieutenants. (8)
Moore, G. A. C. 26Jan.12
McCowan, H.   2Oct.12
Sloan, W. N.   15Jan.13
Maclay, E.   17Feb.13
Crichton, G. H. 23May13

Adjutant.
×Bramwell, C. G.,
Capt. Sco. Rif.
              18Sept.11

Quarter-Master.
×Bowen H., hon. lt.
              22Nov.13

Medical Officers.
Sloan, Capt. A. B.,
M.D., R.A.M.C.
(T.F.) (attd.) 28Oct.09
              28Apr.06
Kilpatrick, Lt. D.R.,
M.D., R.A.M.C.
(T.F.) (attd.) 5May11

Chaplains.
Muir, Rt. Rev. P.
McA., D.D., [C.S.]
Chapl. 1st Class
(T.F.)(attd.) 24May10
              24June96
Gray, Rev. A. H.,
M.A. [U.F.C.]
Chapl. 4th Class
(T. F.) (attd.) 2Apr.12

[Uniform—Green.
Facings—Dark Green.]

THE ROYAL INNISKILLING FUSILIERS.

Regimental District No. **27**. [No. **11** District.]

The Castle of Inniskilling with three turrets, and St George's colours flying. In each of the four corners the White Horse, with the motto "*Neo aspera terrent*," The Sphinx, superscribed "Egypt."

"Martinique, 1762," "Havannah," "St. Lucia, 1778, 1796" "Maida," "Badajoz," "Salamanca." "Vittoria," "Pyrenees," "Nivelle," "Orthes." "Toulouse," "Peninsula," "Waterloo," "South Africa, 1835, 1846-7," "Central India," "Relief of Ladysmith," "South Africa, 1899-1902."

Regular and Special Reserve Battalions.

Uniform—Scarlet.	Facings—Blue.	Agents—Messrs. Cox & Co.
1st Bn. (27th Foot) .. .. Trimulgherry.	3rd Bn. (R. Tyrone Mil.) .. Omagh.
2nd „ (108th „) .. .. Dover.	4th „ (Fermanagh Mil.) .. Enniskillen.
Depôt .. .. Omagh.	Record Office .. .. Dublin.

Colonel .. Murray, Maj-Gen. *Sir* A. J., K.C.B., C.V.O., D.S.O., p.s.c. (*l*) *s*. 3Aug.11

1st and 2nd Battalions.

Lt.-Colonels. (2)
2Hancox, H. P., p.s.c.
[*l*] 8Nov.10
1 Jones, F. G. 19Feb.14

Majors. (8)
2Wilding, C. A. 7Dec.05
s. Beale, E. J., p.s.c.
8Jan.06
2Pierce, R. C. 8Nov.06
s. Clarke, T. E. 19Feb.10
1Somerville, S.J. 8Nov.10
s. Uniacke, R. F., p.s.c.
[*l*] 17May13
1Kenny, G. W. 29June13
2Byrne, J. A. 19Feb.14

Captains. (14)
Evans, J. 16Nov.00
(3)2Grazebrook, G. C., *e*.
(Comdg. Depôt)
20July01
1Crawford, J. N. 1Aug.01
1Atkinson, E.W. 22Jan.02
2Ponsonby, G. M. p.s.c.
[*l*] 18Jan.08
 19Feb.06
2Auchinleck, D, G. H.
 18Jan.04
1Best. T. A. D. 27Jan.04
1Ridings, C. 27Jan.04
2Roe, S. G. 10July04
2Steward, G. R. V.
[*L*] 29Apr.05
Mathers, D. 6 Jan.06
m. Gordon, A. J. M.5Aug.06
(3) 1Smythe, R. C. 13Jan.07
r. Manders, E. I. 18Sept.08
1Pike, W. 13Jan.10
(3)2Ray, D.DelaC.19Feb.10
e.a. Kenny, W. D. 1Apr.10
2Young, H. N. 1Apr.10
(3)1Armstrong,J.A.21May10
2Lloyd, E. R., *Adjt*.
 21Feb.12
s. Rothwell, W. E. 21Feb.12
1Willock, G. W. 22Mar.12
1Meredith, W. F.
 19Feb.14
s. Hewitt, C. C. 19Feb.14
2Kirkpatrick, J. J.
 19Feb.14

Lieutenants. (19)
2Thompson, H. C.
 30May04
2Ball, R. G. 5Aug.06
1 Crofton, H. L. 9Oct.06
e.a.*Irwin, G. V. C.* 16Feb.07
1Dent, J. R.C. 4May07
s.c.Henderson-Scott,
 A. M. [L] 4May07
r. Frazer, W.P.B. 24Oct.07
1Hammond-Smith,
 M. F., *Adjt.* 24Oct.07
(3) 2Duffin, S. B. 28July09
(3) 1Hartigan, D. McK.
[*l*] 13Jan.10
(2) Geoghegan, J. R.
 19Feb.10
1Edden, H. S. 19Feb.10
1Cockburn-Mercer,
 T. H. 1Apr.10
2Hester, E. H. 1Apr.10
1Wise, T. A. 1Apr.10
s.s. Sampson, G. F. 21May10
1O'Sullivan, G. R.
 7Mar.12
1Reilly, M. J.T. 22Mar.12
1Humphreys, R. H. B.
 3Apr.12
1Shubrick, R. B. 9Oct.12
2Alexander, C. A. M.
 7May13
f.c. Vaughan, R. M.
 29June13
2Mudge, A. E. P. 18Dec.13
2Hinds, R.W.G. 22Jan.14
1MacManus, D.A.M.
 19Feb.14
1Penrose, A.F.K.
 19Feb.14

2nd Lieutenants (12)
1Raymond, E. W. H.
 20Apr.10
2Allen, H. A. 4Sept.12
2Dunlop, C. 22Jan.13
1Tillie, C. G. 5Feb.13
2Braddell, L. A. R.
 3Sept.13
2Henderson, D. F.
 3Sept.13
1Verschoyle, F.H.H.S.
 17Sept.13
2Cox, R. G. S. 24Jan.14
2Stacke, O.G.N. 25Feb.14
2Gilliland, W. M. M.
 25 Feb.14
1McNeill, R. F. R.
 21Mar.14

Adjutants.
2Lloyd, E. R., *capt*.
 29Aug.11
1Hammond-Smith,
 M. F., *lt*. 13Jan.13

Quarter-Masters.
1Morris, W. A., *hon. lt.*
 22Feb.05
2Lumsden, R., *hon.lt*.
 29Dec.09
r. Porter, R.J., *hon.lt*.
 4Dec.12
r. Rattenberry, J. E. S.,
 hon. lt. 4Jan.13

Special Reserve.
Captain.
p.s. ✗Yardley, J. H. R.,
 late Lt. R. Innis. Fus.
 (*H*) 5July11
Lieutenants.
Clarke, F. W. 26July12
 4Feb.14
Allnatt, A. E.
 (*attd. O.T.C.*) 18Sept.13
 9Jan.13
2nd Lieutenants
Thomas, J. G. B.
 19Mar.13
Boyd, H. A. 12Apr.13
Roberts, A. G. M.
 7May13
Moore, E. E. J. 27May14
 6Aug.13
Aplin, K. S. 27June14
 6Aug.13

3rd Battalion.
(*Officers serving on 18 Oct. 00 in the corresponding Militia unit hold honorary Army rank equivalent to the Militia regimental rank they then held. Other officers entitled to honorary Army rank have it shown against their names*).

Hon. Colonel.
Irvine, H., C.B. (*Hon. Col. ret. Spec, Res*.)
 11July14
Lt.-Colonel.
McClintock, J. K.
 (*H*) 29Sept.09

Major.
✗Brush, J. E. R.,
 Capt. ret. pay (*Res. of Off*.) ⓒ (*H*) 5May10

Captains. (5)
r.e.✗Grazebrook, G. C.,
 e. 20July01
p.s. ✗Chaloner, C. W.
 (*H*) (*Jun. Asst. Col. Sec. Gold Coast*) { 1Jan.14
   { 19Sept.10)
 28May04
p.s. ✗Smythe, R.C. 13Jan.07
 (*H*)
r.e ✗Ray, D.DelaC.19Feb.10
✗Thompson, W. P.,
 Capt. ret. pay18May10
 14Aug.09
r.e. ✗Armstrong, J. A.
 21May10
Irwin, Fitz J. M., *late*
 Capt. Res. of Off.
 12Nov.10
Irvine, A. G., *late*
 Lt. R. Naval Res.
 16Sept.11
Lieutenants. (11)
(p.s.)Crawford, E. 14July08
(p.s.)Crawford, F. 14July08
r.e. Duffin, S. B. 28July09
r.e. Hartigan, D. McK.
[*l*] 13Jan.10
Miller, I. F. R. 26July12

2nd Lieutenants.
Lyons, A. C. 26June12
MacDowel, B. G.
 26June12

Williams, F.J. 9Apr.13
Young, H.W. 29June13
 21June11

Adjutant.
✗Manders, E. I., Capt.
 R. Innis. Fus.
 26Oct.11
(*Capt. inArmy* 18Sept.08)

Quarter-Master.
✗Rattenberry, J. E. S.,
 hon. lt.

THE ROYAL INNISKILLING FUSILIERS—(Regtl. Dist. No. **27**)—contd.

4th Battalion.

(*Officers serving on 16 Oct. 00 in the corresponding Militia unit hold honorary Army rank equivalent to the Militia regimental rank they then held. Other officers entitled to honorary Army rank have it shown against their names.*)

Hon. Colonel.

Enniskillen, L. E., Earl of, K.P. 12July08
    8Jan.87

Lt.-Colonel.

✗Kinsman, H. J., Capt. ret. pay
(*Res. of Off.*) 12Sept.13

Majors. (3)

p.s. ✗Beales, W. L. (*H*)
(*Hon. Capt. in Army* 1 *Oct.*02) 4Dec.12
    18June06
✗Mathew, W. M.
⊕ (*H*) 20Feb.13
✗Jarvis, E. H.
(*Hon. Lt. in Army* 16*July*01) (*H*) 12Sept13

Captains (6)

Bayly, C. J. 16July04
p.s. Knaggs, G., ⊛
  p.v.c. (*H*) 14Apr.05
p.s. Crawford, K. H.
  (*H*) 1June06
Hamilton, A. H. B.
  Lt. ret. pay 1May12
p.s. Nixon, W. G.
  (*H*) 20Feb.13
p.s. Browne, J. P.
  (*H*) (g) 12Sept.13

Lieutenants. (11)

(p.s.) Davies, P. J. L.
  (a)(b) (*H*) 26Feb.08
Abbott, E. J. W.
  (*H*) 16May10
Moutray, F. C.
    15May12
Crean, G. J. 15May12
Berry, W. H. S.
    15May12
Daniels, C. H. 20Dec13
Silver, B. J. 20Dec13
Thompson, C. C.
    20Dec13
Huskinson, F. J.
    20Dec13

2nd Lieutenants (8).

Whittington, W. J.
    3Aug.12
Moxsy, A. R.
  (*on prob.*) 24Dec.13

Adjutant.

✗Frazer, W. P. B.,
Lt. R. Innis. Fus.
    7Mar.12
(*Lt. in Army* 24 *Oct.*07)

Quarter-Master.

✗Porter, R. J., *hon. lt.*

THE GLOUCESTERSHIRE REGIMENT.
Regimental District No. **28**. [No. **7** District.]

The Sphinx, superscribed "Egypt."
"Ramillies," "Louisburg," "Guadaloupe, 1759," "Quebec, 1759," "Martinique, 1762," "Havannah,"
"St. Lucia, 1778," "Maida," "Corunna," "Talavera," "Busaco," "Barrosa," "Albuhera," "Salamanca,"
"Vittoria," "Pyrenees," "Nivelle," "Nive," "Orthes," "Toulouse," "Peninsula," "Waterloo,"
"Chillianwallah," "Goojerat," "Punjaub," "Alma," "Inkerman," "Sevastopol," "Delhi, 1857,"
"Defence of Ladysmith," "Relief of Kimberley," "Paardeberg," "South Africa, 1899-1902."

Regular and Special Reserve Battalions.

Uniform—Scarlet.   *Facings*—White.   *Agents*—Messrs. Cox & Co.

1st Bn. (28th Foot) .. Bordon.	3rd Bn. (R. South Gloucester Mil.) .. Bristol.	
2nd ,, (61st ,,) .. Tientsin.		
Depôt .. .. .. Bristol.	Record Office .. .. .. Warwick.

Territorial Force Battalions.

4th Bn. .. .. Queen's Rd., Clifton, Bristol.	6th Bn. .. .. St. Michael's Hill, Bristol.
5th Bn. .. .. The Barracks, Gloucester.	

Colonel .. .. C. Emerson, Hon. Maj.-Gen. A. L., ret. pay, p.s.c. 19July13

1st and 2nd Battalions.

Lt.-Colonels. (2)
1 Lovett, A. C.   25Oct.11
2 Tulloh, G. S.   25July14

Majors. (8)
s. Davie, K. M., p.s.c. [l]
                        22Oct.06
2 Conner, R   25Oct.07
(3) 2 Gardiner, G. F.   8July08
(3) 1 Jordan, R.P., D.S.O.
(Comdg. Depôt)
                        25July10
c.o. Bryant, A., p.s.c. [l]
                        26Oct.11
2 Nisbet, F. C.   26Nov13
1 Ingram, J. O'D.   6May14
1 Gardner, R. M. S.
                        25July14

Captains. (14)
1 Rising, R. E.   24Feb.00
s. 1 Le Mottée, E. D'A.,
D.S.O., p.s.c.
[l]   21Jan.02
s. Wethered, J. R.,
p.s.c.   12July02
1 Temple, W. A. M.
                        27May03
1 Radice, A. H. [L]
Adjt.   2June03
2 Burges, D.   25Oct.03
(3) 1 Ruck, J. E.   25Oct.03
t. Rawson, R. I. [F]
                        11Jan.08
                        12Feb.02
m.c. Wilkinson, R.   13Oct.05
1 Shipway, G. M., p.s.c.
                        13Oct.05
1 McLeod, A. A.   13Oct.05
c.o. Fane, J.   25July06
r. Pagan, A. W.   29Sept.06
2 Isaac, T. W. T.   20May08
                        7Nov.07
1 Pritchett, W.P. 23Oct.08
m.c. Needham, H., p.s.c.
                        17July09
s.o. Richmond, H. C.
                        17July09
e.a. Tweedie, J. L. F.
                        14Jan.11
e.a. Blyth, R. C. P.   14Jan.11
2 McMahon, D. J. B.
                        14Jan.11

Captains—con
e.a. Stephenson, E. S.,
D.S.O.   9June11
(3) 2 Scott, R. D.   9June11
1 Chapman, A. F.
                        12July11
t. Johnson, V.N.   15July11
(3) 2 Brodigan, F.J.   10Jan.12
c.o. Bockett-Pugh, H.A.D.
                        22Jan.12
2 Spear, H. B.   22Jan.12
2 Foord, W P. S.   22Jan.12
c.o. Vinen, H. N.   6May14
2 Finch, F. C.   6May14

Lieutenants. (20)
c.o. Giles, A. H.   22Jan.08
c.o. Inglis, A. McC.   7Apr.08
(3) 2 Capel, A.   15May08
2 Hilton-Green, H. F. L.
                        7Oct.08
t. Bosanquet, G. B.
                        21Nov.08
1 Horsford, H.T.[L]
                        5Mar.09
c.o. Stewart, A. H.   25Dec.09
(3) 1 Scott-Tucker, R. L.H.
                        22May10
2 Vicary, A. C.,
Adjt.   14Jan.11
2 Power, E. G. H. 15Mar.11
c.o. Bowyer-Smith, C.G.
                        1Apr.11
1 Young, F. H. McL.
                        5Apr.11
2 Guild, J. R.   12July11
c.o. Holme, A. C.   15July11
1 Wetherall, H. E. de R.
                        1Nov.11
1 Caunter, J. A. L.
                        6Dec.11
1 Halford, M.W.   6Mar.12
2 Gardner, C. E.   20Apr.12
1 Duncan, D.   29May12
3 Garnier, D. K.   18June13
2 Lachlan, L. A. W. B.
                        6July12
2 Parkinson, W. H.
                        10July12
2 Smalley, J.S.   15Oct.13
2 Greenland, C. S. W.
                        8Mar.14
2 Cox, L. H.   11Mar.14
2 Cure, B. A. C.   6May14

2nd Lieutenants. (12)
1 Davis, B. F. R. 22May12
2 Lyne, L. W. D. 4Sept.12
1 Harding, A. D. 4Sept.12
1 Yalland, W. S. 4Dec.12
1 Baxter, D.   22Jan.13
1 Grazebrook, R. M.
                        5Feb.13
2 Aplin, E. D'O. 5Feb.13
1 Somerset, Hon. N. F.
                        3Sept.13
2 Chapman, W. G.
                        10 Dec 13
Adjutants.
1 Radice, A. H. [L]
capt.   7Oct.11
2 Vicary, A. C., lt.
                        12July14
Quarter-Masters.
r. Wilkins, W.   24June03
hon. capt. June13
1 Hewitt, W. J., hon. lt.
                        25July06
2 Dinham, A. H., hon.lt.
                        29Oct10

Special Reserve.

2nd Lieutenants.
Watkins, W. F. 4Aug.11
Kershaw, M.
(attd. O.T.C.) 3Aug.12
Hippisley, H. E.
                        3Aug.12
Cox, H.   1Mar.13
Cordes, J. L. B. H.
                        26Mar.13
Waddy, B. H. (on
prob.)   18Aug.13
Russell, H. R. (on
prob.)   29June14
Vere, A. A. (on
prob.)   17July14

3rd Battalion.

(Officers serving on 18 July 01
in the corresponding Militia unit hold honorary Army rank equivalent to the Militia regimental rank they then held. Other officers entitled to honorary Army rank have it shown against their names).

Hon. Colonel.
p.s. Guise, Sir W. F. G.,
Bt.   7June06
                        10Feb.97

Lt.-Colonel.
p.s. Burges, G. H. (H)
                        9Oct.13
Major.
r.e. ✕Jordan, R.P.,
D.S.O.   25July13
p.s. ✕Wingfield,M.E.G.R.,
late Lt. 2 L.G. (Hon.
Capt. in Army 28July
01) (H)   9Oct.13
Captains. (5)
p.s ✕Marling, W. J. P.
(Hon. Capt. in Army
28July01)   2Mar.06
r.e.✕Ruck, J. E. 25 Oct 03
✕Baynes, N. W. F.,
late Capt. Res. of
Off.   21Sept.07
                        8Nov.13
Kingscote, E. T.
(H)   9Feb.10
p.s. George, W. K. (H)
                        12May10
r.e. ✕Scott, R. D. 9June11
r.e. Brodigan, F.J. 10Jan.12

Lieutenants. (11)
r.e. Capel, A.   15May08
r.e. Scott-Tucker, J.R.
L. H.   13Aug10
Smith. K. A. R. 6May11
Churchill-Longman,
W. V.   16May12
Morris, T. R. A. 19Mar.13
Swanwick, R. K.
                        2 Aug.13
Greenslade, D. A.
                        11Oct.13
Bush, C. D'A. S.
                        11Oct.13

2nd Lieutenants. (8)
Hartmann, J. F. L,
                        20Jan.12
Roberts, E. G. 15Mar.13
Kearns, A. C. R.
                        1Apr.13
Griffith, R. G.,
(on prob.)   1Oct.13
Hickling, E. R. E.
                        8Oct.12
Brown, L. C. 13Dec.13

Adjutant.
✕Pagan, A. W., Capt.
Glouc. R.15July11
(Capt.inArmy29Sept.06)

Quarter-Master.
✕Wilkins, W., hon. capt.

THE GLOUCESTERSHIRE REGIMENT—(Regtl. Dist. No. 28)—contd.

4th (City of Bristol) Battalion.

"South Africa, 1900-02."

Queen's Road, Clifton, Bristol.

Hon. Colonel.
The Lord Mayor of Bristol.

Lt.-Colonel.
p. ✗Butler, J. B., TD ⓖ 1Apr. 11

Majors. (2)
p. Stotesbury, R., TD (t) (H) 28Apr.06
p. Thompson, J. C., TD 1Apr.11

Captains. (8)
p.s. Baker, H. L., hon. m. (t) 30May00
p. Butler, J. H. 20Dec.02
p. Clarke, W. S. 20Dec.02
p.s. Tilly, C. C. S. (H) (a)(b) I. of M.25Oct.07
Slade, E. C. (H) 14Sept.11
Dennehy, C. J. 27Apr.12
Güterbock, P. G. J. 22May13
p.s. Lewis, W.,(H)(local Capt. O.T.C., 15 Nov. 13) 14Mar.14

Lieutenants. (8)
Taylor, E. (H) 31Mar11
Bennett, J. S. 31Mar.11
Veale, D. 31Mar.11
Holloway, F. A. 14Sept.11
Castle, G. S. 19Dec.12
Young, J. C. L. 10Jan.13
Parkinson, L. G. ⓖ 8June13
Whitwill, T. N. 3Aug.13

2nd Lieutenants. (8)
Wade, H. 3May13
Newth, A. L. W. 12Mar.14
Mansell, R B. 15May14

Inst. of Musk.
Tilly, C C S. capt. 31Mar.09

Adjutant.
✗Rawson, R. I., Capt. Glouc. R. 16Sept.11

Quarter-Master.
✗Wilson, T., Qr.-Mr. (hon. m.) ret. pay hon. m. 30Dec.10

Medical Officer.
Clarke. Capt. R. C., M.B., R.A.M.C. (T.F.) (attd.) 22May13 28Jan.12

Chaplains.
Holt, Rev. V., M.A., Chapl.2nd Class (T.F.) (attd.) 18Dec.10 18Dec.95
Welchman, Rev. W., M.A., Chapl. 4th Class (T.F.) (attd.) 21June14

[Uniform—Scarlet. Facings—White.]

5th Battalion.

"South Africa, 1900-02."

The Barracks, Gloucester.

Hon. Colonel.
✗Bathurst, S. H., Earl, C.M.G. (Col. ret. Mila.) (Hon. Lt.-Col. in Army 28July01) 22Sept.08

Lt.-Colonel.
p.s.Marling, S. S. 10May13

Majors. (2)
p.s. Collett, J. H. 3Mar.09
Tarrant, J. F., TD (Q) 1Sept.13

Captains. (8)
p.s. Champion, S. S. 24Jan.06
p.s. Waller, N. H. 25Apr.10
p.s. Hague, H. (H) I. of M. 14Sept.11
p.s. Moore, E. G., TD, hon. m. (H) (q) 13Oct.11 25July00

Lieutenants. (8)
(p.) Campden, A. E. J. N., Visct. 6Oct.06
Caruthers-Little, R. J. 10Jan.11
Cole, F. W. 10Jan.11
Stuart, R. S. D. 8Apr.13
Sessions, H.C. B. ⓖ 1Sept.13
Cooke, R. McD. F. 1Sept.13
Sumner,L.R.C. 1Sept.13

2nd Lieutenants. (8)

Francillon, F. E. 20Feb.12
Lister, G. A. 20Feb.12
Lister, R. B. 20Feb.12
Fream, W. 21Aug.12
Noel, Hon. C. H. F. 1May13
Snowden, H. P., late 2nd Lt. Res. of Off. 16June13

Inst. of Musk.
Hague, H.,capt.19May09

Adjutant.
Johnson, V. N. Capt. Glouc. R. 18Apr.12

Quarter-Master.
Foote, C. F., hon. lt. 9Apr.12

Medical Officer.
McLannahan, Lt. J.G., R.A.M.C. (T.F.) (attd.) 15July12

Chaplains.
Selby, Rev. W. J., M.A., TD, Chapl. 1st Class (T.F.) (attd.) 4June12 4June92
Helm, Rev. G.F., Chapl. 4th Class (T.F.)(attd.) 4Mar.11

[Uniform—Green. Facings—Scarlet.]

6th Battalion.

St. Michael's Hill, Bristol.

Hon. Colonel.
✗ⓑⓒ Rt. Roberts, Field-Marshal Rt. Hon. F. S., Earl, K.G., K.P., G.C.B.,O.M., G.C.S.I., G.C.I.E., VD, Col. Commdt.R. A., Col. I. Gds. [R] 5Sept.00

Lt.-Colonel.
p.s. Woodcock H. C. (H) 5Apr.11

Majors. (2)

p.s.Carter, T. M. (H) 1Aug.09

Captains. (8)
p.s. Coates, P. L. (H) (q), ⓖ I. of M. 7June05
p.s. Rogers, D. L. 15Aug.06
Protheroe, L. R. 16Aug.07
Coates, C. E. 30June09
Marshall, L.W. 19May11
Hek, F. W. (H) 19May11
Langford, F. J. 24July12
Tame,E.W.(H) 25July12

Lieutenants. (8)
(p.) Cook, D. S. ⓖ (Asst. Dist. Offr., S. Provs., Nigeria, 12Jan.14) 29Oct.09
Twiggs, H. C. 19May11
Young, J. A 20May11
Parker, G. H. N. 20May11
Riseley, G. H. 24July12
Elliott, G. E. 25July12
Laxton, M, H. (H) 22Sept.12
Lennard, E.W. 13July13

2nd Lieutenants. (8)
Nott, T. W. 5Feb.11
Wilkins, M. S. 19May11
Greenall, C. E 1Nov.11
Cherry, H. C. E. ⓖ (H) 28Sept.12
Lowick, W. M. 22Jan.13
Bird, E. W. 14Feb.13
Jowett, C. J. P. C. 12July13

Inst. of Musk.
Coates, P. L., capt. 1Mar.09

Adjutant.
✗Wilson, R. H. G. Capt.Linc.R.18Sept.11

Quarter-Master.

Medical Officers.

Chaplain.
Webster, Rev. J., Chapl. 4th Class (T.F.) (attd.) 1Apr.08 25Aug.06

[Uniform—Scarlet. Facings—White.]

Cadet Unit affiliated.
1st and 2nd Cadet Companies 6 Bn. Glouc. R.

THE WORCESTERSHIRE REGIMENT.
Regimental District No. **29**. [No. **7** District.]

The United Red and White Rose. "*Firm.*" A Naval Crown, superscribed "1st June 1794."

"Ramillies," "Mysore," "Hindoostan," "Rolica," "Vimiera," "Corunna," "Talavera," "Albuhera," "Salamanca," "Pyrenees," "Nivelle," "Nive," "Orthes," "Toulouse," "Peninsula," "Ferozeshah," "Sobraon," "Chillianwallah," "Goojerat," "Punjaub," "South Africa, 1900-02."

Regular and Special Reserve Battalions.

Uniform—Scarlet.   *Facings*—White.   *Agents*—Messrs. Cox & Co.

1st Bn. (29th Foot) .. .. *Cairo.*	5th Bn. (Worcester Mil.)	.. .. Worcester.
2nd „ (36th „) .. .. *Aldershot.*	6th „ (Worcester Mil.)	.. .. Worcester.
3rd „ .. .. .. *Tidworth (for Lichfield).*		
4th „ .. .. *Meiktila.*		
Depôt .. .. *Worcester.*	Record Office ..	.. .. Warwick.

Territorial Force Battalions.

7th Bn. .. .. *Kidderminster.* | 8th Bn. .. .. *Silver Street, Worcester.*

Colonel .. .. ℂ. Higginson, Gen. *Sir* G. W. A., *G.C.B.*, ret. pay [R] .. 29Aug.98

1st, 2nd, 3rd and 4th Battalions.	*Captains*—contd. 1Richardson, C. 20May08	*Lieuts.*—contd. *s.s.* Johnston, A. C. 28June07	2nd *Lieuts.*—contd. 4Chesney, D. 20Sept.11
	8Aug.08	2Gillum-Webb, H. A.	1Tristram,J.H, 20Sept.11
Lt.-Colonels. (4)	e.a.*Gibbs*, W. B. 14Apr.04	23Nov.07	1Conybeare, E. B.
2Westmacott, C. B.	*c.o.* Rose,R.A.DeB. 14Apr.04	3Underhill, W. A.	20Sept.11
2Mar.11	2Dugan, W. J. 16Nov.04	27Nov.07	1Phillips, L. G. 20Sept.11
3Stuart, B.F.B. 14Feb.12	3Eliott, H. R. 17Nov.04	*c.o.* Ripley, H. I. E. 27Nov.07	1Hamilton Cox, M. A.
1Lascelles, A. E.,	(5) 1Nesbitt, A. S. 17Nov.04	1Crawford, O. F. G.	20Sept.11
p.s.c., [*i*] 13Mar.12	*s.* Dunlop, F. P., *p s.c.*	7Dec.07	3Goldsmid, S. A. 4Sept.12
19Feb.10	[L] 17Nov.04	2Stoney, G. J. L. 5Feb.08	2Watson, T. H. 4Sept.12
4Cayley, D. E. 20Mar.14	1Tyrwhitt,F.St.J. [*i*]	2Amphlett, E. P. C.[*i*]	2Smythe, F. F. 4Sept.12
	17Nov.04	5Sept.08	3Harding, P. D. 4Dec.12
Majors. (16)	4Ray, A. D. H. 29Nov.04	1Underhill,E.O.19Sept.08	3Lee, R. H. M. 5Feb.13
3Chichester, W. R.	4Nelson, J. O. 6Jan.05	(6)4Northey, A. [*l*] 24Oct.08	3Harvey, F. B. 3Sept.13
3Aug.04	3Messervy, C. C. 27Apr.06	1Leman, J. F. 22Jan.09	3Bell, P. W. 3Sept.13
s. Farmar, G. J.,*p.s.c.*	1Fitzjohn, T. 25Aug.06	*c.o.*Hudson, E. C. R. 3Feb.09	1Hartnoll, H. P. 3Sept.13
8July06	4Myburgh, C. de F.	*c.o.*Pelly, J. H. 7Aug.09	4Mervyn,J. F.A. 10Dec.13
28Sept.05	15May07	4Crawley,T.H.O.16Oct.09	2Guinness O.C. 25Feb.14
4Seton, C. H. 11Apr.06	3Beresford, C. V.	*c.o.* Davies, F. K. 22Jan.10	*Adjutants.*
4Bartholomew, H. J.,	*Adjt.* 15May07	3Gabb, S. A. 26Mar.10	2Clarke, B. C. S.,
D.S.O. 2Mar.07	(6)4Jefferies, H. St. J.	2Haskett-Smith, E. A.	*lt.* 1Apr.12
1Wodehouse, E.C.F.,	23Aug.08	1Apr.10	1Winnington, J. F. S.,
D.S.O. 27Nov.07	1Pardoe, T. K. 5Sept.08	(6)3Graham, J. M. 2Apr.10	*capt.* 23Nov.12
3Milward, H. D. 8July08	(6) 4Barker, W. 5Sept.08	2Godfray, J. V. 6July10	3Beresford, C.V.,
s. 2Gogarty, H. E., *p.s.c.*	2Bowring, E. L. 1Oct.08	3Clarke, M. E. L. H.	*capt.* 17Nov.13
24Oct.08	(5)1Watson, L. T. 22Jan.09	20Oct.10	4Kerans, E. T. J.,
bt. lt.-col. 21Feb 12	*t.* Whalley, P. R. 17Mar.05	*c.o.*Collins, J. G. 21Dec.10	*lt.* 24Nov.11
1Bacon, B. K. W. 1Apr.09	3Rolph, G. W. 26Mar.10	*s.s.* Deakin, C. 8Jan.11	*Quarter-Masters.*
4Carr, H. A. 11June10	2Stoney, J. P. L. 2Apr.10	4Bridges, J. V. 23Jan.11	3Whitty, A. 17Mar.00
s. Fulton, H. A. 2Mar.11	*s.c.* Simpson, E. M. 23Jan.11	4Wythes, C. A. 27Mar.11	*hon. capt.* 17Mar.00
(6) 3Palmer, C. H.	2Phelips, E. 21Apr.11	4Bush, W. D. 13Mar.11	*r.* Ryder, J. J. 28Mar.00
(*Comdg. Depôt*) 27Jan.12	*c.o.* Brett, K. 28June11	4Gordon, H. 1Apr.11	*hon. capt.* 28Mar.10
s. Green, A. D.,*D.S.O.*,	3Hughes, T. H. 28June11	(5) 1Heymann, E. 5April	*r.* Parker, H.J.,*hon. lt.*
p.s.c. 14Feb.12	*r. Newcombe, W. L.*	(5)2Horsfield, R. B.2Apr.11	8Dec.04
(5) 2Sykes, W. E. 17Feb.13	28June11	4Townsend,G.J.13May.12	1Henson, C., *hon. lt.*
1Lambton, G. C., *D.S.O*	4Linton, C. S. 28June11	1Veasey, J. S. 22June12	25Apr.08
4May12	2Ford, R. J. 1Apr.12	*c.o.* Field, C. S. 17July12	2Batchelor, J., *hon lt.*
4Lang, H. A. 24May13	3Brownell, R. L. D.	1Lilley, C. C. 17July12	6Nov.09
2Hankey, E. B. 20Mar.14	13May12	1Wilkins, K.W. 10Aug.12	4Butler, W.,*hon. lt.*
	4Pollock, D.W. 22June12	2Myddelton-Gavey,	24May13
Captains. (28)	3Tucker,F. St. G.,*j.c.r.*	F. E. 9Feb.13	
1Grogan, G. W. St. G.[L]	22June12	19Dec.10	Special Reserve.
18Jan.08	2Pepys, R. W. 24May13	4Masters, G. E. 26Feb.13	*Captain.*
5Nov.00	*Lieutenants.* (39)	4Stokes-Roberts, A. E.	Kitching, C. H., *late*
2Lea,G.E., *p.s.c.* 29Dec.00	e.a. Davies, G. L. St. A.	24May13	*Capt.* Worc. F.S., ret.
1 *Winnington*, J. F. S.,	3Aug.04	1Ruck, L. H. 4Oct.13	pay 19July12
Adjt. 3Jan.01	4Deans, G. C. 17Nov.04	1Monk, J. M. 23Nov.11	Fitzjohn, G. N., Lt.
4Boyd-Moss, E. W.	*c.o.*Badham, J. F. 17Nov.04	2Vyvyan, R. E. 28Nov.13	ret. pay 11July14
6Feb.01	*t.v. Favicll*,W.F,O.10Dec.04	1Stacke, H. FitzM.	2nd *Lieutenants.*
s. Walsh, M. R., *p.s.c.*	3Traill, R. F. 18Jan.05	13Apr.14	Samut, F. O, 1Apr.12
18Dec.01	2Clarke, B. C. S., *Adjt.*	2nd *Lieutenants.* (24)	Urwick, L. F. 12June12
t. Davidge, G. M. C.	21Apr.06	1Lawrence, E. L. G.	Pritchard. I. T.
21Dec.01	3Goff, J. T. 27Apr.06	5Oct.10	(*on prob.*) 15Mar.13
2Carr, M. R. 21Dec.01	4Gilmour, H. J. G.	2Slaughter, G.A. 8Feb.11	Fyson, C. 4June13
2Porter, C. E. L. 16Jan.07	15June06	3Harrison, C. C. 4Mar.11	Moore, C. F. (*on prob.*)
15Feb.02	4Kerans, E. T. J.	1Roberts, F. C. 4Mar.11	2May14
3de Salis, E. A. A.,	*Adjt.* 28July06	1Slater, R. M. 4Mar.11	Parker, C. W. H.
D.S.O. 2Aug.00	*t.* Briscoe, G. S. 22Sept.06	4Mostyn,T.L.N. 27May11	(*on prob.*) 13May14
r. Stevens, L. M. 17Mar.08	3Henry, C. 12Dec.06	1Giffey, C.K.O.B.	Walpole-Simmons,
3Dorman, L. C. 23Mar.08	*t.v.Dobson*, H.P. 6May07	19Sept.11	(*on prob.*) 25July14
	c.o. Wrenford, A. L. 11May07		

THE WORCESTERSHIRE REGIMENT—(Regtl. Dist. No. 29)—contd.

5th Battalion.

(*Officers serving on 15 Oct. 00 in the corresponding Militia unit hold honorary Army rank equivalent to the Militia regimental rank they then held. Other officers entitled to honorary Army rank have it shown against their names.*)

Hon. Colonel.
Coventry, Rt.Hon.G.W., Earl of 2Aug.08
17Jan.00

Lt.-Colonel.
Brindle, W. S. (*H*) 2Sept.13

Major.
r.e.✗Sykes, W. E. 17Feb.12
✗Custance,A.F., Capt. ret. pay (*Empld. under Foreign Office, 6 Dec. 09*) 2Sept.13

Captains. (5)
*r.e.*Nesbitt, A. S. 17Nov.04
✗Brock, E. N. L., Capt. ret. pay (*Res. of Off.*) 6Sept.07
✗Grimley, H. C. Lt. ret. pay 16May08
r.e.✗Watson, L.T. 22Jan.09
✗Temple, R. D., Lt. ret. pay 11Aug.10
r.e.✗Phelips, E. 21Apr.11

Lieutenants. (11)
*p.s.*McClellan, G. E. G. (*H*) 28Jan.08
Hudson, A. W. 21Aug.09
*f.e.*Broder, P. A. 27Oct.10
*r.e.*Heymann, R. 5Apr.11
*r.e.*Horsfield, R. B.21Apr.11
Curtler, F. G. O. 2Dec.13
Pope, C. M. 2Dec.13

2nd Lieutenants (8).
Field, H. 25June13
Preedy, E. V. C. 1Oct.13

Adjutant.
✗Stevens, L. M., Capt. Worc.R. 21Feb.14
(*Capt. in Army 17Mar.08*)

Quarter-Master.
✗Ryder, J. J., *hon.capt.*

6th Battalion.

(*Officers serving on 10 Oct. 02 in the corresponding Militia unit hold honorary Army rank equivalent to the Militia regimental rank they then held. Other officers entitled to honorary Army rank have it shown against their names.*)

Hon. Colonel.
Coventry, Rt. Hon. G. W., Earl of 23Aug.08
17Jan.00

Lt.-Colonel.
p.s.✗Lea-Smith, F. D. W. 29Mar.11

Major.
✗Gordon, W. A., *C.M.G.* (*H*) 29Mar.11
r.e.✗Palmer, C. H. 27Jan.12

Captains. (5)
✗Vaughan, P. E., Capt. ret. pay 18Dec.01
3May11
✗Wainman, P.S. G., Capt. ret. pay26Apr.02
28Apr.09
*r.e.*Messervy, C. C. 27Apr.06
r.e.✗Jefferies, H. St J. 23Aug.08
r.e. Barker, W. 5Sept.08
Freeman, M., *late* 2nd Lt. Worc. R. (*H*) 13Jan.14

Lieutenants (11).
✗Pickersgill-Cunliffe, J. C., Lt. ret. pay 4Apr.07
4Oct.13
*r.e.*Northey, A. [I] 24Oct.08
*r.e.*Graham, J. M. 2Apr.10
Scott, A. W. H. 21Jan.13
Wynter, R. C. 1Dec.13

2nd Lieutenants. (8)
Morice, C. S. 1Oct.12
Carpendale,M.K.St.J. (*on pr b.*) 14Mar.14
Hale, R. G. S. (*on prob.*) 4Apr.14

Adjutant.
✗Newcombe, W. L., Capt. Worc. R. 28Mar.14
(*Capt. in Army 28June11*)

Quarter-Master.
Parker, H. J., *hon. lt.*

7th Battalion.
"South Africa, 1900-01."
Kidderminster.

Hon. Colonel.
Cobham, C.G., Visct. 2Mar.98

Lt.-Colonel.
p. Garratt, J. W., VD 26Feb.10

Majors. (2)
p. Thomas, C. W., TD (*Q*) 30June09

Captains. (8)
p. Thompson,W.J.23Oct.06
*p.s.*Dore, A. S. W. 1July08
*p.s.*Dusautoy, E. F.(*H*) 30June09
Adam, W. (*H, I.of M.* 31May10
p. Homfray, R. P. (*H*) 14Mar.11
*p.s.*Grosvenor, J.E. (*H*) 28Aug.12
(*p.*) Godson, G. E. (*H*) 9Oct.12
Simpson, F. D. 18June13

Lieutenants. (8)
Tomkinson, F. M. 15Oct.09
Butcher, A. H. 26Feb.10
Somers, F. 14Mar.11
Gough, J. 4Apr.11
Rollason, A. G. 20Jan.12
Adshead. H. 28Aug.12
Harris, T. C. F. 9Oct.12
Cookson, H. E.18June13

2nd Lieutenants.
Homfray, R. 16Sept.11
Addenbrooke, R. G. 25Nov.11
Smellie, W. F. 27Mar.12
Reay, G. H. N. 8Oct.12
Thomas, E. M. 26Oct.12
Hoare, R. W. 4Jan.13
Wood,H.G.W. 11Apr.14
26Aug11

Inst. of Musk.
Adam, W., *capt.* 24Mar.09

Adjutant.
✗Davidge, Capt. G. M. C., Worc. R. 18Nov.12

Quarter-Master.
✗Nield, R. W., *hon. lt.* 5Aug.11

Medical Officers.
p. Addenbrooke, B.,*M.D.*, Surg.-Maj. 9Sept.12
5Dec.00

Chaplains.
✗Thomas, Rev. P. C., *B.A.*, Chapl. 3rd Class (T.F.)(*attd.*) 14Feb.11
14Feb.00

[Uniform—Scarlet Facings—White.]

8th Battalion.
"South Africa, 1900-02."
Silver Street, Worcester.

Hon. Colonel.
Plymouth,Rt.Hon.R.G. Earl of, C.B 6June91

Lt.-Colonel.
✗Peake, W. K., Capt. ret. pay (*Res. of Off.*) 13Mar.11

Majors. (2)
Creak, R. H. H. (*Q*) 6Nov.11
How, F. A. W. 15Aug.13

Captains. (8)
p. Clark, S. H. 30Dec.05
*p.s.*Harry, N. G. 30Dec.05
Kerwood, L. 18July09
p. Clarke, H. T. 6Nov.11
Hunt, W. J. 12Mar.13
Mitchell, H. R. 5July13
p. Creak, A. S. 15Aug.13
Griffiths, H. M. 7June14

Lieutenants. (8)
Cotton,W.E.L. 22June10
Cotton, M. J. (*Asst. Land Ranger,E. Africa Prote.. 10 Sept. 13*) 20May11
Burlingham, R. H. 20May11
Jones, E. S. 1Dec.12
Kerwood, P.M. 12Mar.13
Hemming, F.W. 5July13
Curtler, W.L. 15Aug 13
Bate, J. P. 1Sept.13
Neville, M. M. 7June14

2nd Lieutenants. (8)
Maschwitz, H.C. 7June12
Lousada, C. S. 27July12
Bendyshe, J. N. 21Feb.13
Needham, A. O. 23June13
Newman. H. G.22Nov.13

Adjutant.
✗Whalley, P. R. Capt. Worc.R. 6Apr.14

Quarter-Master.
p. Sallis, D., *hon. maj.* 13May08

Medical Officers.
p. Fowler,H.E.B., *M.D.*, Surg.-Capt. 14July08
14Jan.05

Chaplains.
Wilding, Rev. H. St. J., *M.A.*,Chapl. 4th Class (T.F.) (*attd.*) 1Apr.06
9Apr.04
✗Berry, Rev. B. A., *M.A.*, Chapl. 4th Class(T.F.)(*attd.*) 27Apr.12

[Uniform—Scarlet. Facings—White.]

THE EAST LANCASHIRE REGIMENT.
Regimental District No. **30**. [No. **3** District.]

The Sphinx, superscribed "Egypt."
"*Spectamur Agendo.*"
"Gibraltar, 1704-5," Cape of Good Hope, 1806," "Corunna," "Java," "Badajoz," "Salamanca,"
"Vittoria," "St. Sebastian," "Nive," "Peninsula," "Waterloo," "Bhurtpore," "Alma," "Inkerman,"
"Sevastopol," "Canton," "Ahmad Khel," "Afghanistan, 1878-80," "Chitral," "South Africa, 1900-02."

Regular and Special Reserve Battalions.
Uniform—Scarlet. *Facings*—White. *Agents*—Messrs. Cox & Co.

1st Bn. (30th Foot) ..	*Colchester (for Gibraltar).*	3rd Bn. (5th R. Lancashire Mil.) .. .. *Preston.*
2nd ,, (59th ,,) ..	*Wynberg (for Colchester).*	

Depôt .. .. *Preston.*   Record Office . .. *Preston.*

Territorial Force Battalions.
4th Bn. .. .. *Blackburn.* | 5th Bn. .. .. *Burnley.*

Colonel .. Lake, Lt.-Gen. Sir P. H. N., K.C.M.G., C.B., p.s.c. [R] *Chief of the Gen. Staff, India.* 21Feb.13

1st and 2nd Battalions.

Lt.-Colonels. (2)

2Nicholson, C. L.,
   p.s.c. 17Feb.12
✓ 1Le Marchant, L.
   St.G., D.S.O. 23Sept.13

Majors. (8)
(3)1Lawrence, G.H.
   (Comdg. Depôt)18Mar.08
   22Aug.02
2Maclear, H. 9Mar.10
1Lambert, T S.,p.s.c. [*l*]
   13Sept.11
2Sanders, A. A. 18Sept.12
m.c.Baumgartner, J S.L.,
   p.s.c. 12Feb.13
   29Nov.00
1Da Costa, E.C. 12Mar.13
1Collins, E. R., D.S.O.
   14May13
1Green, J. E. 23Sept.13

Captains. (14)
. Traill, W. H., p.s.c.
   11Sept.01
(3) 1Rutter, E. F. 23Sept.01
2Russell, L. 17Nov.01
2Richardson, R.
   21Nov.01
2Seabroke, G.T. 25Feb.05
s. Hill, G. E. M. 10Mar.06
1Coventry, E. E. 9July06
s.c. Baker, R.D., o. 8Feb.08
1Clayhills, G., D.S.O.
   8Feb.08
1Goodwyn, P. C. W.,
   D.S.O. 8Feb.08
(3) 2Kempson, G. C. D.,
   o. 14Feb.08
2Leake, G. D. 18Feb.08
1Goldie, A. St. L.
   18Mar.08
1D'Esterre, P. O. E.
   1Apr.08
1 Wolseley, E. J., Adjt.
   23June08
c.o. Aubin, A. C. 12Feb.13
r. Paterson, W.O. 12Feb.13

Captains—contd.
c.o. Hornby, C. G. 12Feb.13
2Fletcher, C. 12Feb.13
(3) 2Cane, L. A. F. 14May13
t. Sharland, A. A. 14May13
t. Livingston-James,
   F. M. 14May13
2Skewes-Cox, T. E.
   23Sept.13
2Smith, G. M. 22Jan.14
2Arnott, K. H.L.,
   Adjt. 22Jan14

Lieutenants. (20)
2Newcomen, G. B.
   22Jan.08
s.s. Hargreaves, C. F.
   23Aug.08
c.o. Lenke, O. F. R. 29Aug.08
   24May05
2Gallagher, W. A.
   26Sept.08
2Western, B. C. M.
   7Jan.11
2Molony, B. W. 11Jan.11
1Dyer, J. F. 1Apr.11
c.o. Hughes, F. D. 2Aug.11
   14Feb.11
(3) 2Lutyens, C. G. 21Sept.11
2Deane, L. A 2Nov.11
c.o. Orton, R. E. 14Nov.11
c.o. Gayer, A. E. 17Nov.11
(3) 1Warner, H. M. 9Dec.11
2Thompson, A. B.
   26Dec.11
1Hopkinson, E. C.
   26Dec.11
1Belcher, F. E. 27Dec.11
1Dowling, W.E. 26Apr.12
1Leeson, N. A. 8Aug.12
2Beckham, G.A. 18Nov.12
1MacMullen, M. T.
   12Feb.13
1Canton, H. W. 17Apr.13
2Hoskyn, G. W. V.
   14May13
2Daw, T. H. 11June13
1 Chisholm, W. M.
   23Dec.13
2Boothby, R. S. 22Jan.14

2nd Lieutenants. (12)
1Delmege, E. B. M.
   19Jan.12
1Chadwick, G. E. [*l*]
   19Oct.12
   4Sept.12

2nd Lieuts.—contd.
2Penny, A. H. 5Feb.13
1Tosswill, W. E. 3Sept.13
1Mathews, T. H.
   17Sept.13
2Townsend, I. V.
   17Sept.13
2Martin, C. H. 17Sept.13
2Larkins, E. A. M.
   24Jan.14
1Parker, R. Y. 25Feb.14

Adjutants.
2Arnott, K. H. L., capt.
   23Dec.13
1Wolsely, E. J., capt.
   22Jan.14

Quarter Masters.
2Shaw, J., hon. lt.
   3Sept.10
1Longstaff, R., hon.
   lt. 21Oct.11
r. Naylor, H., hon.
   lt. 12Apr.13

Special Reserve.
Captain.
p.s.Harding, C. R. (Q)
   23Sept.11
   16May06
2nd Lieutenants.
Palmer, R. W. 14Feb.12
Pendlebury, J. W.
   16Mar.12
Salt, W. A. 26June12

3rd Battalion.
(*Officers serving on 25 Mar. 02 in the corresponding Militia unit hold honorary Army rank equivalent to the Militia regimental rank they then held. Other officers entitled to honorary Army rank have it shown against their names*).
Hon. *Colonel.*
Butler-Bowdon, J. E.
   (Hon. Col. ret. Mila.)
   28June08

Lt.-Colonel
✗Lloyd-Carson, C. J.
   (H) 9June14
Major.
r.e.✗Lawrence, G. H.
   18Mar.08
   22Aug.02
Captains (5)
r.e ✗Rutter, E. F. 23Sept.01
Cairns, J. (Q)(H)⑤
   1Apr.06
r.e.✗ Kempson, G. C. D., o.
   14Feb.08
✗Preston, T.H., late
   Lt. Res. of Off.
   12Nov.11
Frampton, W.J.G.S.,
   late Lt. E. Lan. R.
   31July12
r.e. Cane, L. A. F. 14May13

Lieutenants. (11)
Richards, P. E. M.
   (H) (Jun. Asst.
   Sec., Nigeria, 28
   Apr. 13) 18Sept.08
   4June10
Young, A. C. E.23June10
Gerahty, C. C.(Asst.
   Dist. Offr., N.
   Provs., Nigeria,
   { Jan 14
   {22Nov.11) 18Sept.11
r.e Warner, H.M. 9Dec.11
Bellamy, F. H. 1Apr.13
Richards, C. E. M.
   1May13

2nd Lieutenants. (8)
Wade, G. H. T. 10Oct.12
Benham, J. E.
   (Asst. Dist.
   Commr., S. Leone,
   12 Jan. 14) 15Jan.13
Hooper, K. 5July13

Adjutant.
✗Paterson, W. O.,
   Capt. E. Lan. R.
   17Nov.11
(*Capt. in Army* 12 Feb.13)

Quarter-Master.
Naylor, H., hon. lt.

THE EAST LANCASHIRE REGIMENT—(Regtl. Dist. No. **30**)—contd.

4th Battalion.

"South Africa; 1900-02."

Blackburn.

Lt.-Colonel.

p.s. Robinson, F. D., VD,
3Feb.12

Majors. (2)

p.s. Wesley, T. B., hon. l.c.,
VD 12May06
Smith, W. A. 22Mar.14

Captains. (8)

p. Robinson, T. C.
13June00
Elliott, B. G. 16Mar.01
p.s. Polding, J. B. 16Mar.01
p. Wilson, G. R. 31Oct.01
p. Broadbent, C. St. J.
(Q) 28June06
p.s. Wynne, J. C. 20Feb.13
p.s. Dixon, P. 23Mar.14

Lieutenants. (8)

(p.s.) Birtwistle, F. 28May08
p.s. Duckworth, J. B
28May08
Smith, J. T. 20Feb.13
Wolf, P. 20Feb.13
Robinson, A. J. D
13Mar.13
Green, L. 14Aug 13
Sames, W. F. 1Mar 14
Howson, J. A. 24Mar.14

2nd Lieutenants. (8)

Robinson, G. N ⓖ
12Feb.13
Whalley, H. W. 21Feb.13
Thwaites, R. 27Mar.13
Simpson, I. L. 24July13
Dixey, A. C. N.
30Mar.14
Robinson, M. D.
16May14

Adjutant.

✗Livingston-James,
F. M., Capt. E. Lan.
R. 9Dec.13

Quarter-Master.

Bennett, G., hon. lt.
11Jan.09

Medical Officers.

p. Henry, Capt. H.,
M.D., R.A.M.C.
(T.F.) (attd.) 21July10
21Jan.07
✗Linton, Capt. S. F.,
M.B., R.A.M.C.
(T.F.) (attd.), 9Aug.18
9Feb.10

Chaplains.

Corfield, Rev. A. T.,
Chapl. 2nd Class
(T.F.) (attd.) 17Mar.12
17Mar.97
Parkyn, Rev. F. L. C.,
Chapl. 4th Class
(T.F.) (attd.) 1Apr.08
2Apr.04

[Uniform—*Scarlet*, Facings
—*White*.]

5th Battalion.

"South Africa, 1900-02."

Burnley.

Hon. Colonel.

Mitchell, T., C.B.,
VD (Hon. Col.
ret. Vols.) 1Apr.08

Lt.-Colonel.

p. Hoyle, J.C., TD 26July05

Majors. (2)

p. Sharples, W. E., TD
14Sept.07
p. Halstead, D., TD 1June08

Captains. (8)

p. Rodgers, R. C. ⓖ
2Nov.98
p.s. Roberts, A. H. 13Sept.05
p. Welch, C. E. 1Jan.06
p.s. Edwards, D. G. (Q)
26Feb.08
p. Townsend, G. (H)
27Oct.10
p.s. Bolton, H. F. 25July11
p. Jobling, H. ⓖ (t)
19Oct.13

Lieutenants. (8)

Rushton, F.V. (q)(H)
20July1
Walmsley, S. H.20July1
Button, F. J. (H)
(I. of M.) 21Junel1
Robinson, J. C., C. H.
(H) 25July11
Lancaster, C.W. (H)
17June11
Jamieson, P. J.10Dec.12
Sprake, G. E. 4Feb.13

2nd Lieutenants. (8)

Cockshutt, E. M. 2Jan12
Britcliffe, F. 13May13
Hargreaves, R. P.
28May13
Thornber, J. 29May13
Bolton, J. 19June13
Walmsley, W.N. 20Oct.13
Rawcliffe, J. M. 6Jan.14
Whittaker, J. 16May14

Inst. of Musk.

Button, F.J., lt. 1Nov.13

Adjutant.

✗Acton, W. M.,
Capt. E. Ir. Regt.
17Nov.13

Quarter-Master.

Horan, W. E.,
hon. lt. 22June11

Medical Officers.

✗Watson, Lt.-Col.
A. A., VD, R.A.M.C.
(T.F.) (Hon. Maj.
in Army 25Sept.02)
(attd.) 1Nov.07
28Feb.85
p.s. Fitz-Gerald, R. L.,
Surg.-Capt. 18Sept.07
16Jan.04

[Uniform—*Scarlet*. Facings
—*Black*.]

THE EAST SURREY REGIMENT.
Regimental District No. 31. [No. 10 District.]

The United Red and White Rose.
"Gibraltar 1704-5," "Dettingen," "Martinique, 1794," "Talavera," "Guadaloupe, 1810," "Albuhera," "Vittoria," "Pyrenees," "Nivelle," "Nive," "Orthes," "Peninsula," "Cabool, 1842," "Moodkee," "Ferozeshah," "Aliwal," "Sobraon," "Sevastopol," "Taku Forts," "New Zealand," "Afghanistan, 1878-79," "Suakin, 1885," "Relief of Ladysmith," "South Africa, 1899-1902."

Regular and Special Reserve Battalions.
Uniform—Scarlet. *Facings*—White. *Agents*—Messrs. Cox & Co.

1st Bn. (31st Foot)	Dublin.	3rd Bn. (1st R. Surrey Mil.)	Kingston.
2nd „ (70th Foot)	Chaubattia.	4th „ (3rd R. Surrey Mil.)	Kingston.
Depôt	Kingston.	Record Office	Hounslow.

Territorial Force Battalions.
5th Bn. .. 17, St. George's Road, Wimbledon. | 6th Bn. .. Drill Hall, Orchard Road, Kingston-on-Thames.

Allied Regiment of Dominion of New Zealand.
4th (Otago) Regiment.

Colonel .. .. Greaves, Gen. Sir G. R., G.C.B., K.C.M.G., ret. pay [R].. .. .. 1Nov.98

THE EAST SURREY REGIMENT—(Regtl. Dist No. 31.)—contd.

3rd Bn.— contd.

2nd Lieuts.—contd.
Champion, R. S.
   22Feb.13
Dingwall, C. F. 22Apr.13
Luffman, B. L.
   (on prob.) 1Oct.13
Lavender, D.
   (on prob.) 1Oct.13
Emmett, C. P. 1Oct.13
Bridgland, C. A. 1Oct.13
Bryant, J. D. R.
   (on prob.) 14Feb.14
Green, L. J. P.
   on prob.) 28Mar.14
Booth, V.
   (on prob.) 9May14

Adjutant.
✗Appleyard, W.
Capt. E. Surr.
R. 1Oct.13
   (Capt. in Army
   23July09)

Quarter-Master.
✗Clay, H., hon. capt.

4th Battalion,

(*Officers serving on 25 Sept.02 in the corresponding Militia unit hold honorary Army rank equivalent to the Militia regimental rank they then held. Other officers entitled to honorary Army rank have it shown against their names.*)

Hon. Colonel.
Daniell, J, Le G.(*Hon. Col. late Mila.*) 68ept.08
   8Oct.92

Lt.-Colonel.
✗Peel, R. F., Capt.
ret. pay 2Mar.13

Majors. (3)
✗Jackson, F. G.
(*Hon. Capt. in Army*
21Oct.00) [F] 15Jan.10
✗Huth, M. E., Lt.
ret. pay 21June13

Captains. (6)
✗Rumbold, C. F. H.,
   Capt. ret.hon. m.
   (H)(Q) 2Mar.04
Bancroft, P. H. (H)
   15Oct.04
Brodie, F. C., hon.
   m. 2June06
p.s.✗White, A. (Hon.
   Lt. in Army 11
   May02)(H) 30Nov.09
p.s.✗Thompson, G. W.
   (Hon. Lt. in Army
   15May02)(H)
   I. of M. 17Feb.13

Lieutenants (11)
✗Bennett, C. B. F.,
   Lt. ret. pay 18Feb.07
   24Apr.12
Ford, W. S. 15May11
Webber, H. (Asst.
   Dist. Offr., S.
   Provs., Nigeria,
   {1Jan.14
   {13May12 1Jan.13
Ford, E. T. P
   (Asst. Commr. of
   Police, S. Provs,
   Nigeria,1May14)
   20Jan.13

2nd Lieutenants. (8)
Sanders, G. J. T.
   21May13
Inst. of Musk.
Thompson, G.W.,
   capt. 16Apr.13

Adjutant.
Jourdier, M.J.A.,
   Capt. E. Surr.R.
   14Feb.14
   (Capt. in Army 19Feb.13)

Quarter-Master.
✗Pope, J. J., hon. lt.

5th Battalion,

"South Africa, 1900-02."

17, St. George's Road,
Wimbledon.

Hon. Colonel.
Bailey, E. H., vD,
   (Hon. Col. ret. Vols.)
   26Mar.09

Lt.-Colonel.
p.s.Harvey, R. K. TD
   27Sept.09

Majors. (2)
p.s.Bagshaw, W. H.,
   TD, ⊕ 5Oct.06
Gillett, W. A. 2Dec.11

Captains. (8)
p.s.Franks, J. M. (Q)
   23Aug.99
p.s.Roe, G. A. M. 22Oct.06
p.s.Longstaff, F. V. (H)
   Embdd. with Forces,
   Domn. of Canada,
   15 Feb, 12) 28Mar.07
p.s.Whiffen, G. G. 28Mar.07
p.s.Chetwynd-Stapylton,
   G. B. 15June09
Wheatley, A. R.
   1Oct.09
p.s.Hinson, W.⊕(Asst.
   Dist. Commr.,
   Gold Coast, 26
   July 11) 2Oct.09
Eggar, J. N. 6Dec.11
Murray, C. H. 24Oct.12
p.s.Gray, R. (H)(a)(b)
   25May14
   24Jan08

Lieutenants. (8)
Garrett, J. E. 11Mar.10
Smith, G. Le B.11Mar.10
p.s.Hone, E. J. 25Jan.11
   22Dec.06
Hardman, R.C. 3Feb.12
Ingram, C. D. 10July12
Little, C. B. 18Dec.12

2nd Lieutenants. (8)
Crawford, S.C.R.
   17June11
Hodges, R. A. 11May12
Harrison, G. K.
   17July12
Warren, M. C. 27Jan.13
Poston, G. 12Mar.13
Paterson, C. R. S.
   14May13
Statham, N. H. 27July13
Maynard, C. I. F.
   26Sept.13
Grant, J. F. 11Oct.13

Adjutant.
Hughman, G. S.,
   Lt, Middx. R.,
   capt. 11July14

Quarter-Master.
p. Tarran, W., TD, hon. m.
   19Mar.02

Medical Officers.
p. Bates, J. E., M.B.,
   Surg.-Capt. 13Mar.01
   2Feb.98

Chaplain.
Gale, Rev. J. R. C.,
   M.A., Chapl. 4th
   Class (T.F.) (attd.)
   1Apr.08
   18Aug.04

[Uniform—Scarlet,
Facings— White.]

6th Battalion.

"Imperial Service."

"South Africa, 1900-02."

Drill Hall,
Orchard Road,
Kingston-on-Thames.

Hon. Colonel.
Powell, J. L. G., VD,
(Hon. Col. ret. T.F.)
   12Feb.09

Lt.-Colonel.
p.s.Drayson, A. P. (q)
   4June13

Majors. (2)
Merrick, W. TD (q)
   17Apr.09
p.s.✗Hallett, P. (Hon.
   Lt. in Army 26
   July02) (H) 9Aug.13

Captains. (8)
p.s.Whitehouse, A. L. W.
   (H) 9Nov.06
p.s.Watts, H. W. (H)
   1July09
Sandov r, W. L. (Q)
   15Sept.10
Buckingham, F.
   8Oct.10
p.s.Lester, F. (H) 24Nov.10
Armstrong, H. W.
   R. (Asst. Commr.
   of Police, Nigeria
   1May14) 1June13
Marston, A. C.
   21Mar.14

Lieutenants. (8)
Pullman, G. C. 8Oct.10
Edsell, A.R.K. 23June12
Chapple, G. t. 23June12
Plincke, J. F. 23June12
Baker, T. MacD.
   22June12
Eales-White, J, C.
   1June13
Elmslie,G. F. 21Mar.14
Edsell, E. V. 22Apr.14

2nd Lieutenants. (8)
Rowland, J. 21Feb.12
Horner, B. 11May12
Suther, W. C. S.,
   22June12
Price, W. G. 12July13
Rickell, G. C. 12July13
Woodfall, H. A. J.
   12July13
Martindale, H. B.
   12July13
Jefferson, G. K,12July13
Burgan, N. 19July13
Johnson, S. W. 19July13
Onyon, R. R. 23Apr.14
Field, C. D. 29Apr.14
Daniels, C. J. F. W.
   1May14

Adjutant.
✗Montague-Bates,
F. S., Capt. E.
Surr. R. 14Apr.14

Quarter-Master.
✗Osborne, G. H.,
Qr.-Mr. (hon.maj.)
ret. pay, hon. m
   27Jan.12
   22June12

Medical Officers.
p. Brimacombe, Capt.
   R. W., R.A.M.C.
   (T.F.) (attd.) 1Feb.09
   1Aug.05
Webb - Johnson,
   Capt. C., M.B.,
   R.A.M.C. (T.F
   (attd.) 4Dec.12
   23Mar.09

Chaplain.
Wilson, Rev. H. A.,
M.A., Chapl. 4th
Class (T.F.)(attd.)
   23May10

[Uniform—Green.
Facings—Scarlet.]

Cadet Unit affiliated.
Richmond County School
Cadet Corps.

THE DUKE OF CORNWALL'S LIGHT INFANTRY.
Regimental District No. 32. [No. 8 District.]

The United Red and White Rose.

"Gibraltar, 1704-05," "Dettingen," "St. Lucia, 1778," "Dominica," "Roliça," "Vimiera," "Corunna," "Salamanca," "Pyrenees," "Nivelle," "Nive," "Orthes," "Peninsula," "Waterloo," "Mooltan," "Goojerat," "Punjaub," "Sevastopol," "Lucknow," "Tel-el-Kebir," "Egypt, 1882," "Nile, 1884-85," "Paardeberg." "South Africa, 1899-1902,"

Regular and Special Reserve Battalions.

Uniform—Scarlet. *Facings*—White. *Agents*—Messrs. Cox & Co.

1st Bn. (32nd Foot)	Curragh.	3rd Bn. (R. Cornwall Rangers Mil.) Bodmin.
2nd „ (46th „)	Hong Kong.	
Depôt	Bodmin.	Record Office ... Exeter.

Territorial Force Battalions.

4th Bn. ... Truro. | 5th Bn. ... Bodmin.

Colonel ... Stapylton, Hon. Lt.-Gen. G. G. C., ret. pay, m.o.c. ... 16Apr.02 / 28Sept.96

1st and 2nd Battalions.

Lt.-Colonels. (2)
- 2Tuson, H. D., p.s.c. [l] 19Feb.12
- 1Turner, M. N. 1Mar.12

Majors. (8)
- 2Norris, P. B. 12Dec.06
- 1Cornish-Bowden, J. H. T. 19Feb.08
- (1) Cantan, H. T. 1Mar.08
- (3) 1Stokoe, T. R. (Comdg.Depôt) 19Feb.12
- s. Fargus, H., D.S.O. 1Mar.12
- 2Simon, H. S. P. [L] 4Sept.12
- 1Price, T. H. F. 18Sept.12
- 2Dickinson, F. A. [F] 4Jan.13

Captains. (14)
- s. Wetherell, R. M. 12Oct.01
- 1Woodham, C.B. 12Oct.01
- 1Romilly, A.H., e. 1Jan.04
- e.a. Collard, A. M. 19Feb.04
- (3) 2Williams Freeman, A. P., o. 11Apr.04
- s. Goldsmith, H. D., p.s.c. [l] 30Apr.04
- 2Dobbin, H. T. 6July04
- t. Rendall, F. H. S. 6Aug.04
- 2Swainson, J. L. 20May08 14Oct.04
- t. Dene, A. P. 4Nov.04
- 2Stericker, A. W. 16Dec.04
- t. Butler Bowdon, W. E. I. 12Jan.05
- m.c.Kirk, J. W. C. 4May07
- 2Tracy, G. C. 31Dec.08
- r. Mitford, P. L. 13Feb.09
- (3 2Span, F.H. 20Mar.09
- 1Olivier, R. H. 20Mar.09
- 1Trelawny, J. E. S. 20Mar.09
- 2Ward, E. B. 17Mar.10
- 1Phillips, G. F. 20Sept.10
- 2Harrison, H. N. B., M.V.O., Adjt. 20Sept.10

Captains—contd.
- t. Mander, R. 23Jan.11
- e.a. V&Smith, C. L. 26Oct.11
- c.o. Saunders, A. C. 26Oct.11
- t. Venning, W. K. 26Oct.11
- (3) 1Elbrow, G. L. 1Jan.12
- 2Rogers, F. C. C., M.V.O. 20Jan.12
- t. Collins, C. H. G. 11Mar.12
- t. Hodge, R. T. K. 18Sept.12
- e.a. 1Colville, T. R. 26Mar.13

Lieutenants. (20)
- 2Marshall, J. E. 17Oct.06
- 1Crawley-Boevey. M. 4Feb.07
- c.o. Griffiths, A. H. 18Jan.08
- 1Dennis, J. E. W. 20May08
- (1) Brooks, W. T. 24June08
- 1Garcia, C. D. M. 10Nov.08
- Edye, C. V. DeG 28Jan.09
- 2Barker, W. R. 28Jan.09
- c.o. Porcelli, E. G. M. 13Feb.09
- 1Acland, A. N., Adjt. 20Mar.09
- w.a. Richardson, W. M. 5May09 3Aug.07
- 1Buckley, W. P. 20June09
- (3) 2Mathews, S. 1Jan.10
- 2Batson, A. W. 17Mar.10
- 1Benn, I. B. H. 23Jan.11
- 1Bissett, F. W. 1Apr.11
- 2Bisdee, T. E. 1Apr.11
- 1Bradney, J. H. 26Oct.11
- 2Paske, E. L. 8Dec.11
- (3) 1Quicke, N. A. G. 3Jan.12
- 2Brunt, J. C. H. 20Jan.12
- 1Daniell, N. R. 9Mar.12
- 2Rawlinson, W. G. 11Mar.12
- 2Willyams, E. N. 13June12
- 1Hammans, A.J.S. 18Sept.12
- 2Blagrove, R. C. 18Sept.13
- s.s. Pearce Edgcumbe, O. 4Feb.14

2nd Lieutenants. (12)
- 1Mooney, W. McC. J. 19Sept.11
- 1Wingate, R. R. 9Dec.11
- 1LLoyd, H. C. C. 14Feb.12
- 2Webber, S. L. 13Mar.12
- 2Jenkins, E. K. 29May12 4Feb.11
- 2Heygate, L. C. 4Sept.12
- Elliott, T.G.L. 4Sept.12
- 2CarkeetJames, E.H. 4Sept.12
- 1Crane, C. E. 4Sept.12
- 2Harvey, H. L. 3Sept.13
- 2Aston, R. M. 17Sept.13
- 2Hammans, A. W. 24Jan.14

Adjutants.
- 1Acland, A. N., lt. 11Apr.13
- 2Harrison, H. N. B., M.V.O., capt. 4May13

Quarter-Masters.
- 2Church, W. 24Feb.09 8Mar.99
- hon. maj. 8Mar.14
- r. Williams, J., hon. lt. 20Oct.09
- 1Price, W. T. hon. lt. 2Nov.10

Special Reserve.

Lieutenant.
- Mills, A. F. H., late Lt. D. of Corn.L.I. 20Sept.10 4Feb.14

3rd Battalion.

(Officers serving on 4 Dec. 00 in the corresponding Militia unit hold honorary Army rank equivalent to the Militia regimental rank they then held. Other officers entitled to honorary Army rank have it shown against their names.)

Lt.-Colonel.
- p.s. ✕Williams, L. (H) 10Aug.11

Major.
- ✕Pike, C. J. (H) 18Nov.11
- r.e. ✕Stokoe, T. R. 19Feb.12

Captains. (5)
- ✕Barrow, E. E. [l] (H) 16Jan.04
- r.e. ✕Williams Freeman, A. P., o. 11Apr.04
- p.s. Holman, A. F. (H) 21May06
- r.e. Span, F. H. 20Mar.09
- ✕Gepp, E. C., Lt. ret. pay 4Nov.11
- p.s. Burke, D. J. G. (H) 18Nov.11
- r.e. Elbrow, G. L. 1Jan.12

Lieutenants. (11)
- r.e. Mathews, S. 1Jan.10
- Kendall, T. A. 25Nov.11
- r.e. Quicke, N. A. G. 3Jan.12
- Murphy, L. W. 8Apr.14
- Fox. V. 8Apr.14
- Leverton, H. S. 8Apr.14
- Savile, F. C. B. 8Apr.14

2nd Lieutenants. (8)
- Bosanquet, A.P. (on prob.) 4Sept.12
- Byfield, A.T.S. 10Sept.13
- Prynn, N. (on prob.) 13May14
- Wilcox, J. J. (on prob.) 8July14

Adjutant.
- ✕Hingston, F. L., Capt.D. of Corn. L.I. 18Dec.11 (Capt. in Army 18Feb.09)

Quarter-Master.
- Williams, J., hon. lt.

THE DUKE OF CORNWALL'S LIGHT INFANTRY—(Regtl. Dist. No. 32)—contd.

4th Battalion.

"South Africa, 1900-01."

Truro.

Hon. Colonel.

p. Smith, Sir G. J., Knt.,
 VD (Hon. Col. ret. Vols.)
 10Feb.97

Lt.-Colonel.

Hepburn-Stuart-
Forbes-Trefusis
Hon.H.W., Maj.
ret. pay (Res. of
Off.) 1Jan.09

Majors. (2)

p.s.Gray, N., VD, hon.l.c.
 13Dec.05
✗Smith, G. E. S., TD
 (Hon. Lt. in Army
 30 May 01) 25Nov.10

Captains. (8)

p. Ellis, J. 3Apr.01
✗Carus-Wilson,T.(Hon.
 Lt. in Army13Aug.
 02) 16July04
p. Read, G. 15Oct.04
p.s.Lawry, W. D. 25Oct.05
p. Paige, G. P. 19Sept.06
p. Walters, A. 7Feb.07
  Kendall, C. H. 19Apr.14
  Stewart, M. J. (q)
  (H) 25June14

Lieutenants. (8)

Williams, F. 24May10
Rosewarne, E. W.
 1July11
Thomas, C. C. 1July11
Ellis, F. R. 2Feb.13
Francis, E. M. S.
 2Feb.13
Bunt, A. P 21May13

2nd Lieutenants. (8)

Hodge, B. S. 27Jan.13
Breakell, T. K. 27May14
Thomas, J. A. 18May14

Adjutant.

Hodge, R. T. K.,
 Capt. D. of Corn.
 L.I. 15Sept.13

Quarter-Master.

Pool, J. R., hon. lt.
 1June09

Medical Officers.

p. Thomas, Maj. J. T., TD,
  R.A.M.C. (T.F.)
  (attd.) 15Nov.02
  28July88

Chaplains.

Gunning, Rev. J. O.,
 Chapl. 4th Class
 (T.F.) (attd.) 15May12
Hay, Rev. G. H. B.
 [W] Chapl. 4th
 Class (T.F.) (attd.)
 17June12

[Uniform—Scarlet. Facings
 —White.]

Cadet Unit affiliated.

"A" Company, 1st C.B. of
 Cornwall.

5th Battalion.

"South Africa, 1900-01."

Bodmin.

Hon. Colonel.

✗Pole-Carew, Hon.
 Lt.-Gen. Sir R.,
 K.C.B.,C.V.O. [R]
 ret. pay (Maj.-
 Gen. Res. of Off.)
 13Jan.09

Lt.-Colonel.

p. Jerome, E. J., TD
 16July12

Majors. (2)

p. Bawden, W. A.,
  TD 19May09
  Hood, H. J. 18Sept.12

Captains. (8)

p. Whitford,C. E.13June00
p. Meadows, G. S. 7Nov.00
p. Coode, A. P. (t)
 23Aug.02
p. Sturge, F. W. 23July04
p. Edyvean, M. F. 19May09
  Connole, J. S. 12Feb.14

Lieutenants. (8)

Edyvean, R. C. F.
 28Aug.09
Blamey, C. 5June12
Trood, F. T. 18Sept.12
Gilchrist, W. 3Dec.12
Rogers, J. L. 15Feb.14
Nias, A. W. 1Mar.14
Grenfell, E. O. 1Mar.14

2nd Lieutenants. (8)

Haughton, A. L 4July13
Sherwood, E. M, A.
 21Apr.14
Martin, H. S. 21Apr.14
Nicholas, F. L. 27May14

Adjutant.

Mander, R., Capt.
 D. of Corn. L.I.
 1Jan.13

Quarter-Master.

Jago, A. E., hon. lt.
 29June08

Medical Officer.

Salmon Lt. N.G. H.,
 R.A.M.C. (T.F.)
 (attd.) 19Feb.12

Chaplains.

Gush, Rev. R. H.,[W]
 Chapl. 4th Class
 (T.F.) (attd.) 24Mar.10
Browne, Rev. L.,
 M.A., Chapl. 4th
 Class (T.F.) (attd.)
 29May13

[Uniform—Scarlet. Facings
 —White.]

THE DUKE OF WELLINGTON'S (WEST RIDING REGIMENT).
Regimental District No. 33. [No. 5 District.]

The late Duke of Wellington's Crest, with the motto in an escroll above, "*Virtutis fortuna comes.*"
The Elephant, superscribed "Hindoostan."

"Dettingen," "Mysore," "Seringapatam," "Ally Ghur," "Delhi, 1803," "Leswarree," "Deig,"
"Corunna," "Nive," "Peninsula," "Waterloo," "Alma," "Inkerman," "Sevastopol,"
"Abyssinia," "Relief of Kimberley," "Paardeberg," "South Africa, 1900-02."

Regular and Special Reserve Battalions.

Uniform—Scarlet.   Facings—Scarlet.   Agents—Messrs. Cox & Co.

1st Bn. (33rd Foot)	.. .. *Lahore Cantonment.*	3rd Bn. (6th West York Mil.)	.. *Halifax.*
2nd ,, (76th ,,)	.. .. *Dublin (for Limerick)*		
Depôt	.. .. *Halifax.*	Record Office	*York.*

Territorial Force Battalions.

4th Bn.	.. .. .. *Halifax.*	6th Bn.	*Skipton-in-Craven.*
5th ,,	.. .. .. *Huddersfield.*	7th ,, ...	*Milnsbridge.*

Colonel	Belfield, Lt.-Gen. Sir H. E., K.C.B., D.S.O., ret. pay (*Res. of Off.*) p.s.c. [R] 2Aug.09		

1st and 2nd Battalions.

Lt.-Colonels. (2)
1 Watson, W. M. 3Feb.12
2 Gibbs, J. A. C. 6Mar.12

Majors. (8)
(8) 2Parsons, E. M. K.
— (*Comdg. Depôt*) 17Nov.06
1Turner, P. A. 3Feb.08
2Macleod, K. A. 12June09
2Strafford, P. B. 24Nov.09
1Maffett, R. E. 24Feb.11
f.o. Bray, R. N. 6Apr.11
s. Tyndall, W. E. M.,
 D.S.O., p.s.c. 3Feb.12
2Townsend, E. N. 6Mar.12

Captains. (14)
2Healing, R. K. 2Oct.01
 14June00
1St. Hill, *A. A., Adjt.*
 1Feb.02
1Horsfall, A. G. 7Feb.02
(3)1Travers, H. P. 28Feb.02
 28Mar.02
— 2Carter, R. C. 24Feb.04
2Jenkins, E. V., *D.S.O.*
 15Apr.04
1Maples, W. E. 15Apr.04
1Trench, M. V. Le P.
 5June04
1Wilson, J. H. B.
 17Oct.05
1Tidmarsh, R. M.
2Denman-Jubb, C. O.,
 Adjt. 12June06
 26Sept.06
(3) 2 Carlyon, A. S. 29Dec.06
 Liddell, E. M. 18Feb.07
Taylor, E. R. 14June08
(3)2Herapath, L. 16Oct.09
s. Pickering, C. J., e. 16Oct.09
1Keates, W. E. 24Nov.09
1Wellesley, F. H. B.
 24Nov.09

Captains—contd.
— 2Gardiner H. 23Dec.09
— 2Burnett, J. C. 23Dec.09
e.a. *Fairbairn, D. A.*
 23Dec.09
(2) *Ellis, T. M.* 1Jan.11

Lieutenants. (19)
c.o. Clifton, R. B. 10May05
c.o. Bate, W. T. McG.
 10May05
t. Marriner, S. F. 9Aug.05
2Thompson, J. H. L.
 17Oct.05
1Firth, D. 9Mar.06
1Glenn, H. W. 8Sept.06
s.s. Hitchins, E. N. F.
 26Sept.06
1Boutflower, E. C.
 16Feb.07
2Egerton, C. C. 1Jan.08
1Officer, W. G. 25Apr.08
c.o. Hetley, C. R. 18Sept.08
e.a. Peake, F. G. 26Sept.08
c.o. Cholmley, R. S. 10Apr.09
r. *Gillam, T. H. J.*
 14June09
(8) 1Kidd, V. N. 16Oct.09
c.o. Rusbridger, G. S. W.
 24Nov.09
1Cox, M. N. 1Jan.11
1Scott, R. A. 1Apr.11
2Henniker, R. J. A.
 5Apr.11
1Owen, R. H. W. 26Oct.11
1Bald, E. A. 23June12
1Gatacre, E. G. 8Aug.12
1Russell, R. W. 26Apr.13
a.s. Walker, H. N. B.
 16July13
2Ince, C. W. G. 15Nov.13
(3)2de Wend, D. F. 25Jan.14
2Ozanne, W. M. 20Mar.14
2Russell, L. E. 8Apr.14
2Carey, R. O'D. 27Apr.14

2nd Lieutenants. (12)
2Thackeray, F. R.
 13Mar.12
2Oliphant, G. W. 4Sept.12
2Bathurst, C. 4Sept.12

2nd Lieuts.—contd.
1Davis, A. O. L. 5Feb.13
1Fleming, G. T. 26July13
2Grevelink, E. J. Y.
 8Sept.13
1Faulkner, St. J. T.
 8Sept.13
1Tidmarsh, J. M.
 17Sept.13
2Fraser, F. H. 25Feb.14

Adjutants.
1St. Hill, A. A., *capt.*
 9Mar.12
1Denman-Jubb, C. O.,
 capt. 1Jan.14

Quarter-Masters.
2 Ellam, A. 18Sept.99
— *hon. capt.* 18Sept.09
r. Yeoman, W. H., *hon.
 lt.* 20Oct.06
1Oliver, C., *hon. lt.*
 4Mar.14

Special Reserve.

2nd Lieutenant.
O'Kelly, H. K.
 (*on prob.*) 24June14

3rd Battalion.

(*Officers serving on* 10May02
*in the corresponding Militia unit hold honorary
Army rank equivalent to
the Militia regimental
rank they then held. Other
officers entitled to honorary Army rank have it
shown against their
names*).

Hon. Colonel.
Wyllie, A. K., C.B.,
 hon. c. (*Hon. Lt.-Col.
 in Army* 11May02)
 12July08
 1Nov.06

Lt.-Colonel.
p.s. Wayman, H. H.
 5Sept.10

Major.
r.e. Parsons, E. M. H.
 17Nov.06
Kennard, E. C. H.,
 *late Lt. Res. of
 Off.* 7Mar.14

Captains. (5)
r.e. Travers, H. P.
 9Sept.02
 23Mar.02
r.e. Carlyon, A. S. 29Dec.06
p.s. Crawshay, O. T. E.
 (H) (b) 1Dec.08
 23Apr.04
p.s. Moore, N. H. (H)
 1Dec.06
 18July06
p.s. Milbank, R. P. C.
 A. E. (H) (a) (b)
 1Aug.09
 5June05
r.e. Herapath, L. 16Oct.09
Langdale, C. A J.S.,
 Capt. ret. pay [l]
 8Oct.10

Lieutenants. (11)
Williamson, G. 7Sept.07
r.e. Kidd, V. N. 16Oct.09
Owen, H. E. 2Dec.12
r.e. de Wend, D. F. 25Jan.14

2nd Lieutenants. (8)
Young, M. C. B. K.
 1Oct.12
Yates, H. W.
 (*on prob.*) 25Feb.14
Scully, F. W. (*on
 prob.*) 7Mar.14

Adjutant.
Gillam, T. H. J.,
 Lt. W. Rid. Rd.
 25Mar.14
(*Lt. in Army* 14 June 09)

Quarter-Master.
Yeoman, W. H.,
 hon. lt.

THE DUKE OF WELLINGTON'S (WEST RIDING REGIMENT)—(Regtl. Dist. No. 33)—contd.

4th Battalion.
"South Africa, 1900-02."

Halifax.

Hon. Colonel.
Savile, J. S., Lord,
K.C.V.O. 29Aug.00

Lt.-Colonel.
✗Atkinson, H. S., TD.
(*Hon. Lt.in Army*
18 *June* 01) (*H*)
27Nov.12

Majors. (2)
Chambers,E.P. 21Dec.10
Laxton, W. A. 1June14

Captains. (8)
p. ✗Sugden, R. E.
(*Hon.Lt.in Army*
24 *Sept.* 02) (Q)
(*H*) 2Apr.04
Walker, J. 1Apr.08
p.s.Fleming, D. V. ®
1June08
Milligan, V. A. (*H*)
I. of M. 13Sept.10
Winter, D. B. 5Apr.11
Goldthorp, R. H.
15May13
Learoyd, E. P.
(*H*) 7Jan.14
Richardson, A. H.
(*H*) 1June14

Lieutenants. (8)
Andrews, M. P. 1Oct.11
Helliwell, H.D.20July12
Waller, H. N. 1Dec.12
Sutcliffe, D. A. 6May14
Mowat, A. L. 6May14

2nd Lieutenants. (8)
Balme, S. 1Nov.12
Riley, J. T. 20Nov.12
Hirst, C. 1Apr.13

Inst. of Musk.
Milligan, V. A.,
Capt. 13Sept.10

Adjutant.
✗Stanton, H. A. S.,
Capt. R. Scots 1Nov.12

Quarter-Master.
Fielding, T., *hon. lt.*
24Mar.11

Medical Officer.
p. Griffiths, Capt., A. T.,
R.A.M.C. (T.F.) (*attd.*)
5July13

Chaplain.
Burn, *Rev. Preb.*
A. E., D.D., Chapl.
4th Class (T.F.)(*attd.*)
1Apr.08
10July04
Dixon, *Rev.* C. E.,
Chapl. 4th Class
(T.F.) (*attd.*) 11May13

[Uniform—*Scarlet.*
Facings—*Scarlet.*]

5th Battalion.
"South Africa, 1900-02."

Huddersfield.

Hon. Colonel.
p.s.Carlile, Sir E. H.,
Knt., TD, *hon. c.*
23June06

Lt.-Colonel.
Cooper, W., VD. 12Apr.11

Majors. (2)
✗Wilson, H.(*Hon.
Lt. in Army* 18
June 01)℗ 27June13
Holliday, L. B. 6Aug.13

Captains. (8)
p. ✗Crosland, G. W. K.
10Dec.04
p. Norton, G. P. 22Apr.07
p. Eastwood, J.E. 7Dec.11
Wheatley, A. N.
25Apr.13
Senior, E. 24May13
Brierly, S. C. 24May13
Sykes, J. F. 1June14
Stewart, I. 1June14

Lieutenants. (8)
Stott, A. B. 1Nov.09
Bedforth, G. E. 25Apr.13
Rippon, R. 24May13
p. Watson, J. L. (*H*)
I. of M. 24May13
Ellis, G. R. 30June13
Senior, N. 1July14
Sproulle, W. J. M.
1July14

2nd Lieutenants. (8)
Middlemost, D. P.
23Apr.13
Kaye, C. W. D. 15Dec.13
Sykes, K. 2Feb.14
Nesbitt, T. T. 21Mar.14
1Apr.11
Sykes, F. A. 21Mar.14
Haigh, J. M. 25Mar.14
Clapham, J. W. 1Apr 14
Sutcliffe, C. E. 1July14

Inst. of Musk.
Watson, J. L.,
Lt. 30Nov.10

Adjutant.
✗Rendall,F.H.S.,
Capt. D. of Corn.
L.I. 30Sept.11

Quarter-Master.
✗Black, A., Qr.-Mr.
(*hon. capt.*) ret.
pay *hon.capt.*19Feb.11

Medical Officers.
p. Demetriadi, Maj.
L.P., *M.D.,*R.A.M.C.
(T.F.)(*attd.*) 19June09
1Dec.97

Chaplain.
Rolt, *Rev.* C. H.,
M.A., Chapl. 4th
Class (T.F.) (*attd.*)
9Mar.11

[Uniform—*Scarlet.*
Facings—*Scarlet*]

6th Battalion.
"South Africa, 1900-02."
Skipton-in-Craven.

Hon. Colonel.
Arnold-Forster, E. P.,
TD, (*Lt.-Col. ret.
Vols.*) 1Jan.09

Lt.-Colonel.
p.s.✗Birkbeck, J.,*late
Capt.* 4 Bn. Sco.
Rif. (*H*) (*Hon.
Capt. in Army* 28
June 01) 15July11

Majors. (2)
p.s. Ormrod,P.,*late* Capt.
3 Bn. N. Lan. R. (*H*)
1Apr.11
Cass, C. P. 15July11

Captains. (8)
p.s.Bateman, C. M. 2Dec.05
p.s.Wright, M. 2Dec.05
p.s.Marriner, R. V. 1Dec.06
Carson, W. B. 15July11
Wright, T. K. 25 Apr.13
Clarkson, A. B.
25 Apr.13
Chaffers, N. B.26Mar.14
Whittaker, E. G.
9May14

Lieutenants. (8)
Mackenzie, W. A.
1July10
(p) Nicholson, K. 14June11
Sarsby, C. H. 15July11
Horsfall, J. D. 15July11
Dixon, H. 4July12
Ashley, S. P. 25Apr.13
Law, M. C. M. 17June14
1Apr.14

2nd Lieutenants. (8)
Clough, S. H. 21Aug.12
Petty, C. H. 28Aug.12
Slingsby, A. E. K.,
14Jan.13
Knowles, H. 30June13
Supple, E.J.C. 28Sept.13

Adjutant.
✗Marriner. S.F., Lt.
W. Rid. R. *capt.*
26Apr.13

Quarter-Master.
✗Churchman, J.,
hon. lt., 1June11

Medical Officers.
p.s.Gabriel, Maj. W. M.,
TD., R. A. M. C.
(T.F.) (*attd.*) 15Sept.06
16June94
p. Walker, Maj. D.,
R.A.M.C. (T.F.)
(*attd.*) 27July11
10May99

Chaplain.
Hall, *Rev.* S. H.,
M.A., TD, Chapl.
1st Class (T.F.)
(*attd.*) 3Apr.09
3Apr.89

[Uniform—*Scarlet.*
Facings—*Scarlet.*]

Cadet Unit affiliated.
Settle C.B.

7th Battalion.
"South Africa, 1900-02."
Milnsbridge.

Hon. Colonel.
Lewisham, W., Visct.,
Capt. Staff. Yeo.
27Apr.10

Lt.-Colonel.
✗Treble, G. W., C.M.G.
(*Lt.-Col. and Hon. Col.
ret. Vols.*) (*Hon. Lt.-
Col. in Army,*10Oct.02)
(*Capt. Res. of Off.*)
hon. c. 13Feb.10
5Dec.08

Majors. (2)
Tanner, G. 1June10
Charlesworth, M.
1July13

Captains. (8)
p. Wilkinson, S. W.
(*H*) *I. of M.* 2July09
p. Rothery, W. U. 2July09
Crossley, J. H. 16May10
Taylor, R. 16May10
Bagnall, W. G. 28May10
Clark, J. W. 28June14

Lieutenants. (8)
✗Brook, W. 28May10
Chambley, R. 16June10
Haigh, G. 20July10
Lockwood, C. H.
4July10
Pearson, J. S. 4July10
Radcliffe, E.E. 24Jan.12
Whitwam, H. E. (*H*)
20Nov13

2nd Lieutenant (8).
Beaumont, G. 20July10
Ramsden, J. W. A.
22Aug.10
Harris, L. G. R.
25Nov.10
Rigby, C. V. 1Oct.11
Phillips, F. E. 25Oct.11
Greaves, R. T. 21Jan.14
Wood, J. E. 6Mar.14
Tetlow, L. M. 9May14

Inst. of Musk.
Wilkinson, S. W.,
capt. 11Oct.09

Adjutant.
Burbury, B. T.,
Capt. York F.
29Sept.13

Quarter-Master.

Medical Officers.
Bruzaud,Capt.A.S.,
R.A.M.C. (T.F.)
(*attd.*) 4Dec.13
4June10

Chaplains.
Hunt, *Rev.* T. W.,
M.A., Chapl. 4th
Class (T.F.)(*attd.*)
1May09
Leech, *Rev.* J., B.A.,
Chapl. 4th Class
(T.F.)(*attd.*) 15June10

[Uniform—*Scarlet.*
Facings—*Scarlet.*]

THE BORDER REGIMENT.
Regimental District No. **34.** [No. 3 District.]

A Laurel Wreath. The Dragon, superscribed "China."
"Havannah," "St. Lucia, 1778," "Albuhera," "Arroyo dos Molinos," "Vittoria," "Pyrenees,"
"Nivelle," "Nive," "Orthes," "Peninsula," "Alma," "Inkerman," "Sevastopol," "Lucknow,"
"Relief of Ladysmith," "South Africa, 1899-1902."

Regular and Special Reserve Battalions.

Uniform—Scarlet.	Facings—Yellow.	Agents—Messrs. Cox & Co.
1st Bn. (34th Foot) .. Maymyo (for Secunderabad).	3rd Bn. (R. Cumberland Mil.) .. .. Carlisle.
2nd ,, (55th ,,) Pembroke Dock (for Dublin).	
Depôt .. .. Carlisle.	Record Office .. .. Preston.

Territorial Force Battalions.

4th Bn. .. .. Drill Hall, Strand Road, Carlisle | 5th Bn. .. .. Workington.

1st and 2nd Battalions.

Colonel .. .. Chads, Maj.-Gen. W. J., C.B., ret. pay [R] 6Feb.09

Captains—contd
1Muriel, S. H.F.18Apr.09
2Andrews, C. G. W.,
  Adjt. 18Apr.09
1Harrison, G. H.7Mar.10
2Cholmondeley, C. A. J.
  27Apr.10
(3) 1Pershouse, S. 5Apr.11
(3) 1Worrall, S. H. 22Jan.12
1Ellis, A. J., Adjt.
  24Feb.12
t. Blackwood, A. P. [L]
  20Oct.12

Lt.-Colonels. (2)
1Hume, R. O. C. 4Nov.12
2Wood, L. I. 20Oct.13

Majors. (8)
1Moffat, A. S. W.
  20Oct.09
2Bosanquet, J. T. I.
  6Mar.10
1Vaughan, C. D.,
  D.S.O. 15Aug.10
  29Nov.00
1Brooke, G. C. 21Mar.11
(3) 2Broadrick,G.F.
  (Comdg. Depôt) 5Apr.11
1Pollard, A. E. St. V.
  1Apr.12
2Morris,F. G. G. 4Nov.12
2Allen, W. L., D.S.O.
  20Oct.13

Captains. (14)
2Warren, G. E. 21June02
2Molyneux-Seel,
  L. H. [L] 27Aug.02
1Nelson, H. 19Dec.03
(3) 2Gordon, R. N. 1Apr.04
2Pakenham, G. de la
  P. B., p.s.c.
  16Jan.04
2Gillam, W. A.,
  D.S.O. 20May05
  16Aug.02
1Morton, G. A. 20Oct.05
2Lees, E. H. H. 24June06
s. Grubb, H. W., p.s.c.,
  4Feb.07
1Jackson, G. H. N.,
  D.S.O., p.s.c. 15Mar.07
r. Beaty-Pownall, G. E.
  1July08

Lieutenants. (19)
c.o. Chamley, J. W. 27July03
t. Meiklejon, J. R. C.
  A. 5Sept.03
1LeMesurier, F. H. S.
  19Dec.03
  1Apr.04
t.v. Graham, C. E. 9May04
(3) 2Clayton, A. B. 6Oct.04
2Lamb, C. 18Oct.04
t. Sandeman, G. R.
  14Jan.05
1Egerton, P. J. 7June05
2Gerrard, H. V. 3July05
  21Mar.03
1Moore, R.H.H. 16Nov.05
2Radcliffe, M. 31Aug.06
1Forbes-Robertson, J.
  31Aug.06
2Darwell, S. 7Feb.07
t. MacDonald, T. W.
  15Mar.07
1Festing, H. E. 5Dec.08
1Head, R. 13Apr.09
2Watson, W. 7Mar.10
(3) 1Diggle, P. G. W.
  27Apr.10
1Taylor, R. B. 3July10
t.a. Drayson, FitzA.
  18Apr.12
c.o. Pawle, D. W. 22May12
1May, G. E. 22May12
1Heyder, J. G. 17July12
1James, D. A. 4Sept.12
1Warren, J. B. B.
  20Oct.12

2nd Lieutenants. (12).
2Chads, H. F. 9Mar.10
1Cuningham, C. A.
  20Apr.10
2Beves, T. H. 5Oct 10
1Rutherford, A. F. C.
  5Oct.10
c.o. Leslie-Smith, J. L.
  4Mar.11
2Hodgson,G.W.H.
  19Sept.11
1Lay, W. O. 20Sept.11
2Evans, C. H. 19Jan.12
2Chatfield, H. L.
  22May12
1Perry, F. I. L. 7Aug.12
2Surtees, C. G. V.
  22Jan.13
2Clancey. T. J. 5Feb.13

Adjutants.
2Andrews, C. G. W.,
  capt. 2Dec.11
1Ellis, A. J., capt.
  10Oct.13

Quarter-Masters.
r. Austin, F. W. 22Dec.10
  hon. capt. 22Dec.10
1Ennis, W., hon. lt.
  26June09
2Mitchell, F. W., hon.
  lt. 23Aug.10

Special Reserve.
Lieutenant.
Mason, W. E. 3May12
  29 July14

3rd Battalion.

(Officers serving on 1 Nov. 00
in the corresponding Militia unit hold honorary
Army rank equivalent to
the Militia regimental
rank they then held. Other
officers entitled to honorary rank have it shown
against their names.)

Hon. Colonel.
Lonsdale, H. C.,
  Earl of (Hon. Col.
  ret. T.F.) 12July06
  4Feb.91

Lt.-Colonel.
p.s.✕Woodburne, R.W.H.
  (H) 8Aug.08

Major.
✕Ravenscroft, H. V.,
  Maj. ret. pay, hon.
  l.c. (Empld. under
  Sudan Govt., —)
  17Dec.04 ,
r.e.✕Broadrick, G. F.
  5Apr.11

Captains. (5)
p.s. Adam, H. W. D.
  (H) 30May02
r.e. Gordon, R. N. 1Apr.04
p.s.✕Lake-Geere, E. (H)
  28Apr.06
Pyman, J.(H) 19May06
Royle, H. G. F.
  (H) (b) 19May06
p.s.✕Horn, G. M. (A)(H)
  18June06
Sewell, H. W. (H)
  (q) 2Nov.06
r.e. Pershouse, S. 5Apr.11
r.e.✕Worrall,S.H. 22Jan.12

Lieutenants. (11)
r.e.✕Clayton, A. B. 6Oct.04
p.s. Sleigh, H. P. O.
  (H) 18Oct.06
✕Clegg, E. C. Lt.
  ret. pay 6Feb.07
  17Dec.13
r.e.Diggle,P.G.W. 27Apr.10
Johnson, A. B. (H)
  3May12
Kennedy, M. S. N.
  17Dec.12
Hatch-Barnwell, W.
  23June14

2nd Lieutenants. (8)
Irwin, R. S. (on prob.)
  4Mar14

Adjutant.
✕Beaty-Pownall,
  G. E., Capt.
  Bord. R. 7Mar.13
  (Capt. in Army 1July08)

Quarter-Master.
✕Austin, F. W., hon.
  capt.

THE BORDER REGIMENT—(Regtl. Dist. No. 34)—contd.

4th (Cumberland and Westmorland) Battalion.

"South Africa, 1900-02."

Drill Hall, Strand Road, Carlisle.

Hon. Colonel.

✗Cavendish-Bentinck,
Lord H. C., TD 8July93

Lt.-Colonel.

p. Donald, W. N.,
  VD (t) 8Nov.10

Majors. (2)

✗Haswell, J.F.,VD,
 (Hon. Lt. in Army
 30May01) 20Mar.11
p.s.Rigg, R. (H) 4Aug.12

Captains. (8)

Broatch, J., VD,
 hon. m. (t) 25Feb.93
p. Halton, F. W., TD
 (H) 22June98
p. Bousfield, E. ⓖ
 (H) 3Aug.01
p. Davidson, A. ⓣ 25Dec.01
p. Heelis, G. H. 20Mar.11
p.s. Lamonby, L. (H)
  4Aug.12
p.s. Crewdson, W. D.
  6July13
p. Maclaren, D. (H)
 I. of M. 28May14

Lieutenants. (8)

(p.) Richmond, T.H.
 (b) 6Aug.04
p.s.Maclaren,N.(t)26Jan.05
p.s. Errington, J.P. ⓖ
  29Aug.06

Lieuts.—contd.

p.s. Pratchitt, W. M.
  25Jan.07
p.s. Hele, J. W. 25Jan.07
p. Chance, F. S. 4May13
(p.) Story, G. A. 6July13
Banks, T. M. 6July13

2nd Lieutenants. (8)

Hoggarth, L.S. 25Nov.09
Hope, P. M. 10Jan.11
Neville, R. B. 15July12
Raikes, M. H. 15Dec.12
Baker, C. W. F. 6Feb.13
Bettison, F. H. 18Jan.14
Highet, H. 10Feb.14
Norman, J. M. 28Mar.14

Inst. of Musk.

Maclaren, D., capt.
  22Mar.09

Adjutant.

✗Meiklejon, J.R.C.,
 Lt. Bord. R., capt.
  13Apr.12

Quarter-Master.

p. Atkinson, C. E., TD,
 hon. m. 28May00

Medical Officers.

p. Symington, W.,
 M.B., TD, Surg.
  Maj. 11Nov.05
   18July91

Chaplains.

Rawnsley, Rev. Canon
 H. D., M.A., TD,
 Chapl. 1st Class
 (T.F.) (attd.) 1Apr.08
  19July84
Crosse, Rev. A.J.W.,
 B.A.,TD, Chapl.1st
 Class (T.F.)(attd.)
  16Mar.09
  16Mar.89
Morris, Rev. W. P.,
 Chapl. 2nd Class
 (T.F.) (attd.) 4Feb.14
  4Feb.99

[Uniform—Scarlet.
Facings—Yellow.]

Cadet Unit affiliated.

The Kirkby Lonsdale
 Cadet Company. }

5th (Cumberland) Battalion.

"South Africa, 1901-02."

Workington.

Hon. Colonel.

✗ℂ. Muncaster, J. F.,
 Lord, VD 20June78

Lt.-Colonel.

p.s.Dixon,G.,TD(H) 9Nov.10

Majors. (2)

p. Milburn, T. A. 10May07
p.s.✗Scoular, A. C. (Hon.
 Lt. in Army 19July,
 02) 10Nov.10

Captains. (8)

p. Soulsby, A. D. 28Mar.03
p.s. Parkin, J. (H) 28May07
 Smith, A. F. B. (H)
 I. of M. 8Aug.10
 Huck, J. 19July11
 Bewlay, H. J. (H)
  19Apr.14
 Ballantine-Dykes,
 F. H. (Lt. Res. of
 Off.) 20Apr.14

Lieutenants. (8)

p.s. Dodgson, E. H. 1Mar.09
 Lowe, E. A. 19July11
 Rigg, S. 12July12
 Spedding,W.F.12July12
 Potts, H. R. 14Sept.12
 Webb, H. C. 21May13
 Robinson, J. W.
  4Mar.14
 Adair, W. 22Apr.14

2nd Lieutenants. (8)

Longmire,F.P. 25Mar.09
Sewell, W. S. 16May12
Iredale, E. A. 16Aug.12
Jenkins, C. N. 4Dec.12
Spedding, F. B. 8May13
Graham, C. 13May13
Askew, G. G. 13May13
Franks, J. N. 13May13
Smith, H. P. 30May13

Inst. of Musk.

Smith, A. F. B.,
 capt. 1Apr.11

Adjutant.

MacDonald, T.
 W., Lt. Bord.
 R., capt. 17Nov.13

Quarter-Master.

✗Siddans, W.,
 Qr.-Mr.&Hon.
 Lt. ret. pay
 (Res. of Off.),
 hon. lt. 15Nov.13

Medical Officer.

Campbell,Rev.H.E.,
 M.A., Chapl. 2nd
 Class (T.F.) (attd.)
  28Aug.10
  28Aug.95
Curwen, Rev. S. P. I.,
 Chapl. 4th Class
 (T.F.) (attd.) 20Aug.12
Hodges, Rev. A. V.,
 M.A., Chapl. 4th
 Class (T.F.)(attd.)
  21Aug.12

[Uniform—Scarlet
Facings—Yellow.]

THE ROYAL SUSSEX REGIMENT.

Regimental District, No. **35**. [No. **10** District.]

The White (Roussillon) Plume.

"Gibraltar, 1704-05," "Louisburg," "Quebec, 1759," "Martinique, 1762," "Havannah," "St. Lucia, 1778," "Maida," "Egypt, 1882," "Abu Klea," "Nile, 1884-85," "South Africa, 1900-02."

Regular and Special Reserve Battalions.

Uniform—Scarlet. Facings—Blue. Agents—Messrs. Cox & Co.

1st Bn. (35th Foot)	.. .. Peshawar (for Egypt).	3rd Bn. (R. Sussex Mil.)	.. .. Chichester.
2nd „ (107th „)	.. .. Woking (for Devonport).		
Depôt	.. .. Chichester.	Record Office	.. .. Hounslow.

Territorial Force Battalions.

4th Bn. .. .. ; Horsham.	5th Bn.	Drill Hall, Middle Street, Hastings.
	6th „	18, Montpelier Place, Brighton.

Colonel ..	Young, Maj.-Gen. J. C., p.s.c., s. 28 Mar.14

1st and 2nd Battalions.

Lt.-Colonels. (2)
2 Montréser, B. H. 2Feb.11
1 Macnab, C. L., p.s.c., 12Aug.11

Majors. (8)
2 Cookson, M. E. 24Sept.04
Somerville, J. A. C. [i]
Mil. Attaché 8July08
28Mar.05
2 Green, E. W. B. 2Feb.07
1 Mackenzie, E. L.,
(8) 2 Osborn, W. L. 12Aug07
(Comdg. Depôt) 13July10
s. Glasgow, A. E. 2Feb.11
s. Terry, R. J. A.,
M.V.O. 12Aug.02
s. Wroughton, J. B.,
e. 18Nov.11

Captains. (14)
1 Gouldsmith, A. 17Sept.02
s. Bellamy, R., D.S.O. 17Sept.02
s. Julius, S. de V. A.,
p.s.c. [i] 15Oct.02
(3) 1 Crawley-Boevey, E. M. 17Dec.02
2 Cameron, J. S. 21Mar.03
1 Gem, G. 18July03
Villiers, E. F., D.S.O. 5Sept.04
(2) Slater, L. 27Dec.04
2 Waithman, R. H. 14Aug.04
3Feb.05
r. Willett, F. W. B. 1June05
2 Bond, C. E., D.S.O. 2Feb.07
1 Dick, R. N., p.s.c. 5Oct.07
1 Woodruffe, J.S. 14June08
1 Morphett, G. C., Adjt. 23Jan.09
(3) 2 Finké, R. F. 1Feb.09
Otter-Barry, R. B. [i] 1Feb.09
t. Hynes, B. M. 28Feb.10
1 Leachman, G. E. 19Mar.10
2 Wilkie, A. B. [L] 14Apr.11
f. 10Nov.09
1 Thorne, F. N. 1Apr.10
2 Aldridge, R. J. P. D. 1Apr.10

Captains—contd.
2 Jammett-Browne,
A. E. 1Apr.10
2 Beeton, E. C. 14Oct.10
t. Loyd, A. W. K. 8Nov.10
(2) Sleeman, J. L. 2Feb.11
1 Mitchell, T. 2Feb.11
1 Birkett, R. M. 2Feb.11
(3) 1 Impey, G. H. 14Jan.12

Lieutenants. (19)
o.o. Westall, R. C. 13May05
1 Wigley, A. B. 20May08
22Jan.06
t. Hulton, J.M.[i] 16Sept.06
2 Pelham, Hon. H. L.,
Adjt. 26Sept.08
1 Birtwhistle, J. C. D. 23Jan.09
2 Burgess, W. 1Feb.09
f.o. Downes, W. D. 14July09
1 Bridger, F. C. 24July09
1 Lamotte, L. 16Oct.09
2 Daun, E. C. 10Nov.09
2 Dashwood, V. E. C. 1Dec.09
(3)1 Lousada, E. A. 5Oct.10
1 Thomson, A. 14Oct.10
1 Apperley, W. H. W. 23Nov.10
1 du Moulin, F. L. 1Apr.11
2 Preston, E. H. 26Apr.11
w.a. Betham, R. J. A. 18Dec.11
w.a. Thompson, J. A. 14Jan.12
2 Blakeney, H. E. H. 24Apr.12
2 Panton, G. R. V. 11May12
2 Verrall, C. F. 10Nov.12
1 Pollard-Urquhart,
W. E. 15Feb.13
(3) 2 Finch, H. K. 16Apr.13
2 Orme, O. F. 11June13
1 Corban-Lucas, P. L. 16July13
18Apr.13

2nd Lieutenants. (12)
1 Malden, C. C. 4Mar.11
2 De Chair, G. H. B. 4Mar.11
1 Holderness, W.21June11
1 Hawkes, C. C. 20Sept.11
1 Christie, I. D. 19Jan.12
1 Mitchell, H. T. K. 13Mar.12

2nd Lieuts.—contd.
2 Hughes, W. S. 22May12
1 Skinner, F. S. D. 4Sept.12
2 Croft. L. R. 14Sept.12
2 Ramsay, D. G. 22Jan.13
2 Stammers, F. G. 24May13
1 Osborne, G. F. 17Sept.13
(2) Wallington, M. 25Feb.14

Adjutants.
2 Pelham, Hon. H. L., lt. 18Dec.11
1 Morphett, G. C., capt. 5Oct.13

Quarter-Masters.
1 Gilpin, G. 30Oct.11
hon. capt. 30Oct.11
2 Jones, T. A., hon. lt. 24Nov.09
r. Eastick, A., hon. lt. 18Feb.11

Special Reserve.
Lieutenant.
Turner, M. T. 5Oct.12
1Apr.10
2nd Lieutenants.
Magrath, J. S., 2Apr.13
Silvester, A. L. 6Sept.13
Hyde, H. W.
(on prob.) 18Sept.13
Shaw, C. F. 17Jan.14
Owen, A. G. L.
(on prob.) 17June14
Bowman, T. S.
(on prob.) 24June14

3rd Battalion.

(Officers serving on 11 Sept.02 in the corresponding Militia unit hold honorary Army rank equivalent to the Militia regimental rank they then held. Other officers entitled to honorary Army rank have it shown against their names.)

Hon. Colonel.
Richmond and Gordon,
C. H., Duke of, K.G.,
G.C.V.O., C.B. (Col. late Mila.), A.D.C.,
(King's Body Gd. for Scotland) 14June06
27May06

Lt.-Colonel.
p s. Alers Hankey,
C. G. H. 23Apr.13

Major.
r.e. Osborn, W. L. 13July10
p.s. Tufton, Hon. J.S.R.,
late 2nd Lt. 1 L.G. 13June13

Captains. (5)
r.e. Crawley-Boevey,
E. M. 17Dec.02
Bidder, H. F. (Q) (H) 4Feb.03
p.s. Soames, C. E., late
Lt. 8 Hrs. 24Mar.06
p.s. Wood, A., Lt. ret. pay 1Dec.07
r.e. Finké, R. F. 1Feb.09
r.e. Impey, G. H. 14Jan.12
Beynon, L. St. F.,
Lt. ret. pay (q.11Nov.12
de St. Croix, C.,
Lt. ret. pay 1Aug.13

Lieutenants. (11)
(p.s.) Boyne, L. L. 6Jan.08
r.e. Lousada, E. A. 5Oct.10
r.e. Finch, L. H. K. 16Apr.13
Churchill-Longman,
W. B. 26May13
Rowe, E. W. T. 26May13

2nd Lieutenants. (8)
Middlemiss, G. S. 25Dec.12

Adjutant.
Willett, F. W. B.,
Capt. R. Suss. R. 4Oct.11
(Capt. in Army 1June 05)

Quarter-Master.
Eastick, A., hon. lt.

THE ROYAL SUSSEX REGIMENT—(Regtl. Dist. No. **35**)—*contd.*

4th Battalion.

"South Africa, 1900-02."
Horsham.

Hon. Colonel.

p. ⚔ ✠ ᛗ. Campion,
 W. H., C.B., VD
 (Hon. Col. ret.
 Vols.) 7Feb.03

Lt.-Colonel.

p.s. Mostyn, E. H. J. D.,
 VD 14May13

Majors. (2)

p. Helme, R. M., VD,
 hon. l.c. 24Jan.03
 Hodgson, B. T., VD,
 (Q) (T) 14May13

Captains. (8)

p. Campion, W. R., TD,
 hon. m. 19Dec.94
p.s. ✠Beale, S. W. F. (H)
 (Hon. Capt. in Army
 26July02) 27Sept.02
p.s. Mathews, H. E.
 27Sept.11
p. Godman, C. R. B.
 27Apr.12
p. ✠Constable, G. S. (Hon.
 Capt. in Army 26
 Mar.02) 12Mar.13
p. Constable, B. J. L. C.
 14May13
 Kanderdine, W. H.
 16July13
 16Sept.05
 Warren, J. R. 12July13

Lieutenants. (8)

p. Duffield-Jones, E. A.
 24Sept.07
 Weekes, A. N. H.
 28Sept.10
 Mostyn, J. S. 27Apr.12
 Gray, H.J. S. 27Apr.12
 Reid, S. K. 12Mar.13
 Hankey, C. T. A.
 14May13
 Worsley, R. S. L.
 12July13
 Bevan, T. R. 15Feb.14

2nd Lieutenants. (8)

 Campbell,C.H. 22Dec.10
 Medlycott, M. 2Feb.11
 Maples, A. C. 24May11
 13Mar.09
 Loder, R. E. 27Nov.11
 Campbell,E.R. 15Feb 13
 Frank, R. J. B. 12Mar.13
 Frank, W. O'B. G.
 29May13
 Ridley, G. W. 2Jan.14
 Jebb, R. D. 14Mar.14
 7Sept.'10
 Weekes, C. R. H.3June14

Adjutant.

 ✠Hulton, J. M.,
 Lt. R. Suss. R.,
 capt. 10Nov.12

Quarter-Master.

p. Gorringe, W. H.,
 hon. maj. (H) 20June00
 29Mar.08

Medical Officers.

p. Black, Maj. G.,
 M.B., R.A.M.C.
 (T.F.)(attd.)(Hon.
 Capt. in Army
 17Jan.,01) 28Oct.13
 5May97
p. Molson, Capt. J. E.,
 M.B., R.A.M.C.
 (T.F.) (attd.)14Nov.03
 10Oct.00

Chaplains.

 ✠Southwell, Rev. Canon
 H. K., M.A., VD,
 Chapl.1stClass(T.F.)
 (attd.) 1Apr.08
 5June86
 Boyd, Rev. A. H., M.A.,
 Chapl.3rd Class(T.F.)
 (attd.) 16Mar.11
 16Mar.01

[Uniform—Scarlet.
 Facings—Blue.]

Cadet Unit affiliated.

Brighton Preparatory
Schools Cadet Corps.

5th (Cinque Ports) Battalion.

The arms of the Cinque
Ports.

"South Africa, 1900-02."

Drill Hall, MiddleStreet,
Hastings.

Hon. Colonel.

 Beauchamp, Rt.Hon.
 W., Earl, K.G.,
 K.C.M.G. 3Jan.14

Lt.-Colonel.

p. Langham, F. G., VD
 ⓦ 21Oct.11

Majors. (2)

p. ✠Ashby, J. W. F. W.,
 TD 7Jan.03
p. Langham, E. H. (Lt.
 Res. of Off.) 21Oct.11

Captains. (8)

 11Oct.02
p.s. Courthope, G. L. (t)
 11Oct.02
p.s. Dawes, E. P. 19Feb.09
p.s. Hornblower, T. B.
 16May09
 Wood, A. H. 7Oct.11
 Stewart-Jones, T. A.
 (H) 12July12
p.s. Fazan, E.A.G. 31Aug.12
 Grant, F. N. 4July13
 Barlow,P. S.(H) 3Dec.13

Lieutenants (8).

 Masters, T. A. S.
 (H) 20Aug.09
p.s. Douglas, D. G. (H)
 I. of M. 3May13
 18Sept.01
 Langham, C. R. 4July13
 Pope, R. 11Apr.14
 Aiton, J. B. 15May14

2nd Lieutenants. (8)

 Streatfeild, A. H. O.
 17Aug.12
 Bolton, G. 12Apr.13
 Brawall, E. G. 21June13
 Richardson, C. S.
 3July13
 Dawson,H,R.W.8Feb.14
 Fazan, R. 14May14
 Thomas, G. F. 27May14

Inst. of Musk.

 Douglas, D. G., lt.
 3May13

Adjutant.

 ✠Lloyd,A. W. K.,
 Capt.R.Suss.R.
 1Mar.13

Quarter-Master.

p. ✠Teed, E., Qr.-Mr.
 and Hon. Capt.
 ret. pay, hon. m.
 2Nov.01

Medical Officers.

 Waugh, P. M., M.B.,
 Surg.-Lt. 9Mar.08

Chaplains.

 Streatfeild, Rev. W.
 C., M.A., Chapl.
 4th Class (T.F.)
 (attd.) 30May10
 Cook, Rev. T. W.
 M.A., Chapl. 4th
 Class (T.F.) attd.
 10Feb.12

[Uniform—Scarlet.
 Facings—Blue.]

6th (Cyclist) Battalion.

18, Montpelier Place
Brighton.

Lt.-Colonel.

p. Clarke, C. S., VD,
 hon. c. 21Nov.11
 18Jan.99

Majors.

p. Holmes, L., TD, 2July12
 21May02

Captains. (8)

p. Johnson, C. V. 2July12
 16Mar.01
p.s. Grantham,W.W.,
 VD,hon.m. (Hon.
 Capt. in Army
 1 Dec. 00) (H) (t)
 16Apr.13
p.s. Stowell, H. O. D. (t)
 12Sept.00
p.s.Elwell, H. 4Feb.14
 3June14

Lieutenants. (5)

 Wakeford, E. F.
 7May1
 Williams, L. F. M,
 7May14
 Pope, E. H. 7May14

2nd Lieutenants. (4)

 Asser, R. A. 14Feb.13
 Blackburn, L. A.
 31Oct.13
 Fawssett, C. 27Nov.13
 Lewis, E. L. 7Mar.14
 Bennett, T. G. 1May13
 Turton, C. W. 4May14

Adjutant.

 Hynes, B.M., Capt.
 R. Suss. R. 17Jan.12

Quarter-Master.

 Goddard, N. C.,
 hon. lt. 28Sept.12

Medical Officer.

 Galt, Lt. H. M.,
 M.B., R.A.M.C.
 (T.F.) (attd.) 9Mar.14

[Uniform—Scarlet.
 Facings—Blue.]

THE HAMPSHIRE REGIMENT.
Regimental District No **37**. [No. **8** District.]

The Royal Tiger, superscribed "India,"
"Blenheim," "Ramillies," "Oudenarde," "Malplaquet," "Dettingen," "Minden," "Tournay," "Barrosa,"
"Peninsula," "Taku Forts," "Pekin, 1860," "Charasiah," "Kabul, 1879," "Afghanistan, 1878-80,"
"Burma, 1885-87," "Paardeberg," "South Africa, 1900-02."

Regular and Special Reserve Battalions.
Uniform—Scarlet.   *Facings*—Yellow.   *Agents*—Messrs. Cox & Co.

1st Bn. (37th Foot)	..	*Colchester.*	3rd Bn. (Hampshire Mil.) .. *Winchester.*
2nd „ (67th „)	..	*Mhow.*	
Depôt	..	*Winchester.*	Record Office .. .. ..*Exeter.*

Territorial Force Battalions.

4th Bn.	.. *Winchester.*	7th Bn.	.. *177, Holdenhurst Road, Bournemouth.*
5th „	.. *Carlton Place, Southampton.*	8th „	.. .. *Newport.*
6th „	.. *Connaught Hall, Portsmouth.*	9th „	.. *Hamilton House, Commercial Road, Southampton.*

Colonel .. .. ℂ. Knowles, Maj.-Gen. *Sir* C. B., *K.C.B.*, ret. pay, *p.s.c.* [R] .. 7Feb.08

1st and 2nd Battalions.

Lt.-Colonels. (2)
1Jackson, S. C. F.,
  D.S.O. [L] 24Mar.11
  bt. col. 7Sept.10
2Smith, H. C. [F]
  25Jan.13

Majors. (8)
2Leigh, E. 22July05
1Hicks, F. R., *p.s.c.* [L]
  8Aug.06
  22Aug.02
s. Williams, W. de L.,
  D.S.O., p.s.c. 3Jan.09
1Barlow, N. W. 17July09
(3)1Parker, G. H.
  (*Comdg.Depôt*)14Feb.10
2Deane, J. H. 8Oct.10
(1) Mackay, J. D. [F]
  19Apr.11
2Beckwith, A. T., *e.*
  29Dec.12

Captains. (14)
1Palk, Hon. L. C. W.
  7Feb.08
  11Nov.00
m.c.French, C. N., *p.s.c.* [l]
  14Feb.08
c.o. Andrews, A. E.
  21Sept.04
1Morley, L. C. 21Sept.04
2Addison, A. C. 21Sept.04
1Baxter, N. E., *Adjt.*
  21Sept.04
s. Allen, R. S., *p.s.c.*
  18Jan.08
  23Jan.05
1Moore, F. C. 20June06
r. Middleton, W. H.
  21July06
2Richards, J. C. F., *e.*
  21July06
t. Barton, F. St. J. 23Jan.07
2Wymer, H.J.de C.
  16Mar.07
s.a.Symes, G. S., *D.S.O.*
  [F] 9May07
(3) 2Beckett, J. D. M.
  9May07
1Connellan, P. M.
  9May07
t. Earle, F. W. 21Mar.09
s.c.Garsia, W. C. [l]
  12June09
2Parker, B. S. 12June09
2Reid, G. W., *Adjt.*
  17July09

Captains—contd.
t. Spring, T. C. 24Mar.11
(3) 2Black-Hawkins, C. C.
  R. 1Aug.11
t. Frisby, H.G.F. 1Aug.11
e.a.Mills, D. 9Aug.11
1Perkins,G.F.[l] 9Aug.11
(8) 1Unwin, L. U.[l] 9Aug.11
(1) Harland, R. W. 9Aug.11
1Johnston, R.D. 1Jan.12
t. Bowers, H. 18Dec.12
2Lockhart, J. L. 13Jan.13
t. Gribbon, H. H. 1Feb.13
2Penn-Gaskell, W.
  3Dec.13
1Corner, E. A. 22Jan.14

Lieutenants. (20)
1Atchison, F. A. 22Jan.07
2Pletts, G. S. 4May07
c.o. Venour, C. M.H.
  9May07
c.o. Foster, A. C. H. 19Oct.07
1Dolphin, E. J. W.
  9Mar.09
(3) 1Wade, E. W. N.
  13Mar.09
1im Thurn, B. B. von B.
  12June09
1Le Hunte, J. 12Feb.10
c.o.Fowle, C. H. 24Mar.11
(3) 2Berkeley, F. G. J.
  24Mar.11
2Boxall, C. L. 1Apr.11
c.o.Kent, E. M. S. 1Apr.11
2Day, O. H. L. 15July11
2Spencer Smith, R. O.
  1Aug.11
1Knocker, A.P. 9Aug.11
2Rosser, G. A. 1Nov.11
c.o. Wheeler, E. G. 20Mar.12
2Smith, C. R. 16Nov.12
2Halls, S. V. [l] 18Dec.12
c o. McMaster, P. G. W.
  13Jan.13
1Lloyd, T. M. C. 1Feb.13
1Edsell, G. L. 10Sept.13
1Cecil, V. A. 8Oct.13
c.o.Greene, H. R. [l]
  22Jan.14
2Capel, E. 22Jan.14
1Trimmer, W. D. M.
  18Mar.14

2nd Lieutenants. (12)
2Johnston,K.A. 11Oct.11
2Webb,G. V. T. 11Oct.11
2Silk, F. A. 20Dec.11
1Cowan, D. H. 2May12
1Sweet, V. 5Feb.13
2White, J. 24May13

2nd Lieuts.—contd.
1Westmorland, H. C.
  3Sept.13
1Nicholson, G. 17Sept.13
2Pakenham, C. J. W.
  10Dec.13
2Hudson, P. H. 25Feb.14
2Waddington, C. C.
  10June14
f.c.1Wadham, V. H N.
  10June14

Adjutants.
1Baxter, N. E., *capt.*
  9Aug.11
2Reid, G. W., *capt.*
  21Mar.12

Quarter-Masters.
1Hackett, F. 4Nov.05
  25Apr.00
hon. capt. 25Apr.10
r. Tarrant, E. V., *hon.lt.*
  7Sept.07
2Smith, A., *hon. lt.*
  15June12

Special Reserve.
2nd Lieutenant.
Weston, G. C. 6Dec.13

3rd Battalion.

(*Officers serving on 4 Dec.00 in the corresponding Militia unit hold honorary Army rank equivalent to the Militia regimental rank they then held. Other officers entitled to honorary Army rank have it shown against their names.*)

Hon. Colonel.
p.s.Selborne, Rt. Hon.
  W. W., Earl of,
  K.G., G.C.M.G.,
  (Hon. Col. ret.
  Mila.) (Hon. Lt.
  Col. in Army
  5 Dec. 00) ℗ 21June06
  23July04

Lt.-Colonel.
p.s. ✗Powney, C. Du P. P.,
  late Lt. G. Gds., [l]
  (H) ℗ 27Sept.13

Major.
✗Parker, G. H.
  14Feb.10

Captains. (5)
p.s.✗Humphrey, H. M. ℗
  9June02
p.s.Daniell,R.H.A. 30Apr.04
p.s.Ford, J. T.(H)(Accts.
  Office, Shanghai
  Municipal Council,
  1 Mar. 08) 29Apr.07
p.s.Cope, D. (H) 29Apr.07
r.e.✗Beckett, J. D. M.
  9May07
✗Earle,G.H.,*Capt.*
  ret. pay (H) 22Jan.10
✗Heywood, G. G.,
  Capt. ret. pay(H)
  8Jan.11
r.e.Black-Hawkins,
  C. C. R. 1Aug.11
r.e.✗Unwin,L.U.[l] 9Aug.11

Lieutenants. (11)
p.s.Sandeman, G.A.C. (H)
  6Sept.05
Twining, C.F.H.(H)
  17Nov.08
(p.s.)Wolmer, R. C., *Visct.*
  5Mar.09
r.e. Wade, E. W. N.
  13Mar.09
r.e.Berkeley, F. G. J.
  24Mar.11
Lane, E. F. 1Apr.11
Morgan, C. E. 1Apr.11
Rose, G. T. 16Sept.11
Collins, H. J. 16Sept.11
Wilson, R. E. 30June13
Wells, O. A. 30June13
Harington, H. A. B.
  30June13
Griffith, G. 17Jan.14

2nd Lieutenants. (8)
Prendergast, A. F. C. V.
  29May12
Colebrook, R. M.
  9Oct.12
Le Marchant, E.
  C. D. (on prob.)
  1Apr.14
Standen, P. E. (on
  prob.) 16May14
Collet, G. B. (on
  prob.) 3June14
Willison, A. E.
  (on prob.) 3June14

Adjutant.
✗Middleton, W. H.,
  Capt. Hamps. R.
  23Jan.14
  (Capt. in Army 21July06)

Quarter-Masters.
✗Tarrant, E. V.
  hon. lt.

THE HAMPSHIRE REGIMENT—(Regtl. Dist. No. 37)—contd.

4th Battalion.

" South Africa, 1900-02."

Winchester.

Hon. Colonel.

p.s.Cave, Sir T.S., K.C.B.,
 VD *(Col. ret. T.F.)*
 (Q) 11Apr.09

Lt.-Colonel.

p.s.Naish, W., TD (Q)
 (H) [l] 19Dec.13

Majors. (2)

p.s.Rutherford, J. A., TD
 (Q) 28July06
Footner, F. L. (Q)
 ⊛ 31Jan14

Captains. (8)

p. Stilwell, W.B.⊛ 6Feb.04
p.s.Frazer, L. (t) 30Apr.04
 Foster, H. M. 28Feb.09
 Burrell, G. P. 5Aug.11
p. Stapleton, A. F.
 ⊛St. C. (q) 25Nov.11
p.s.Howard, T. H. (H)
 (t) ⊛ [l] 5Feb.12
p. Wainwright, E. G.
 1Nov.12

Lieutenants. (8)

Spinney, E.(H)19July09
Parsons, B.E.T. 6July11
Sloley, F. J. (*Asst.
 Commr. of Police,
 S. Provs., Nigeria,*
 {1Jan.14
 {1Sept.13) 6Sept.11
North, H. F. 25Nov.11
Reeks, N. 30Apr.12
Roberts, F. W. P.
 21Apr.12
Cooper, H. F. 6July13
 8May13
Brandon,A. C.26Sept.13
Bulley,J. I. 25Apr.14
Simmons, P. E. M.
 25Apr.14

2nd Lieutenants. (8)

Osborne, H. J. 7Sept.12
Naish, W.V.J. 18Oct.12
Goddard, B. R. 25Jan.13
Macrae, C. M. 1Apr.13
Stilwell, J. G. 17July13
Lester-Garland. A. G.
 8Dec.13
Gilbert, L. A. 19Dec.13
Swanson,G.W. 14Jan.14
Harris, J. H. 26Feb.14

Adjutant.

✗Barton, F. St. J.
 Capt. Hamps. R.
 6Nov.12

Quarter-Master.

✗Andrews. D. G.,
 Qr.-Mr. *(hon. maj.)*
 ret. pay, hon. maj.
 18June12

Medical Officers.

Jones, Capt. C. E. M.,
 R.A.M.C. (T.F.)
 (attd.) 1July13
 15Jan.09
Jones, Lt. G. B. H.,
 R.A.M.C. (T.F.)
 (attd.) 5June13

Chaplains.

Ashwell, Rev. A. H.,
 M.A., Chapl. 4th Class
 (T.F.) (attd.) 1Apr.08
 17Feb.06
Gurney, Rev. A. G. H.,
 M.A., Chapl. 4th
 Class (T.F.) (attd.)
 22July09

[Uniform—Scarlet.
 Facings—Yellow.]

Cadet Unit affiliated.

Peter Symonds School
 Cadet Corps.

5th Battalion.

" South Africa, 1900-02."

Carlton Place,
 Southampton.

Hon. Colonel.

Crichton, Hon. Sir
 H.G.L., K.C.B., TD,
 Col., A.D.C., Hon.
 Lt.-Col. ret. pay
 8Feb.05

Lt.-Colonel.

Burford-Hancock, H.
 dl S. B., (Maj. Res. of
 Off.) 13Mar.12

Majors. (2)

Day, C. R. L. (t) 15May09
Bassett, J. C. 23Feb.13

Captains. (8)

p.s.Gutteridge, R. F.
 4Feb.07
p.s.Crichton, J. A. 4Feb.07
 Stevenson, A. L.
 (H) I, of M. 16Oct.11
 Silvy, W. J. 22Oct.11
 Dominy, J. C. 30Sept.13
 Hill, H. P. 1Oct.13

Lieutenants. (8)

Hoare, C. E. 22Oct.11
Thomson, R. St. C.
 3Apr.12
Burnett, F. H. 19Apr.12
Andrews, E.W.24June12
Needham. R.L. 19Dec.12
Fear, F. R. 19Dec.12
Baldwin-Wiseman,
 W. R. 30Jan.14
Firth, D. G. 12June14
Pearce, W. K. 12June14

2nd Lieutenants. (8)

Smith, S.H.G. 10Dec.12
Collins, S. H. 8Apr.14
Kitchingman, N.
 1May14

Inst. of Musk.

Stevenson, A. L., capt.
 8Oct.10

Adjutant.

✗Earle, F.W., Capt.
 Hamps. R. 1Jan.12

Quarter-Master.

p. Ruffell, G. E. M., VD,
 hon. m. 15Mar.89

Medical Officers.

p. ✗Lauder, R. E., Surg.-
 Capt. 7Feb.08
 6Aug.04
Fenton, Lt. J., M.B.,
 R.A.M.C. (T.F.)
 (attd.) 26Sept.12

Chaplains.

Matthews, Rev. C. E.,
 Chapl.3rd Class (T.F.)
 (attd.) 16Mar.11
 16Mar.01

[Uniform—Scarlet.
 Facings—Yellow.]

6th (Duke of Connaught's Own) Battalion.

" South Africa, 1900-02."

Connaught Hall,
 Portsmouth.

Hon. Colonel.

✗Field-Marshal H.R.H.
 Arthur W. P. A., Duke
 of Connaught and Stra-
 thearn, K.G., K.T.,
 K.P.,G.C.B., G.C.S.I.,
 G.C.M.G., G.C.I.E.,
 G.C.V.O., VD, Col. G.
 Gds. and A.S.C.
 and Col.-in-Chief 6
 Dns., High. L.I., R.
 Dub. Fus. and Rif.
 Brig.,Personal A.D.C.
 to the King.
 25Mar.92

Lt.-Colonel.

p. Peters, S. C., VD,
 ⊛ 13Dec.13

Majors. (2)

Wyatt, A., TD
 ⊛ (H) 1June14
Foster, M.R.W.
 24June14

Captains. (8)

p.s.Wyatt,J. R. (t) 14Mar.06
p.s.Way, E. W. 19Sept.10
p.s.Bullin, R.,⊛ 9Apr.11
p. Radwell,J.
 (attd.O.T.C.) 9Apr.11
Miller, M. R. 21Apr.12
Webb, H. J. 19Apr.14
Curtis, G. R. 1June14
Addison, A. W. N.
 24June14

Lieutenants. (8)

Fawkes, C. D. 9July13
Collet, F. C. 1Nov.13
 26June13
Blagg, F. O. 12May14
Lindsay-Young
 L. H. L. 31May14
Canning, H. G. R.
 23June14

2nd Lieutenants. (8)

Jensen, C. L. R.
 16Sept.12
Gibbings, R. G. 7Oct.12
Riddoch, J. K. 8Nov.12
 14June11
Palmer, Hon. K.
 S. A. 6Feb.13
Bagg, R. P. J. 8Feb.13
Wadeson, H. H.
 4July14

Adjutant.

Bowers, H. M., Capt.
 Hamps. R. 13Dec.12

Quarter-Master.

✗Tims, E. G. T.,
 hon. lt. 8Oct.10

Medical Officer.

Martin, Lt. G. J. M.
 R.A.M.C. (T.F.)
 (attd.) 5June13

Chaplains.

✗White, Rev. R. A. E.,
 M.A., Chapl. 3rd Class
 (T.F.) (attd.) 4Apr.10
 4Apr.00
Medlicott, Rev. R. S.,
 M.A., Chapl. 4th Class
 (T.F.) (attd.) 1Apr.08
 11July03

[Uniform—Scarlet.
 Facings—Yellow.]

Cadet Unit affiliated.
 1 C.B. Hamps.

THE HAMPSHIRE REGIMENT—(Regtl. Dist. No. **37**)—contd.

7th Battalion.

A Stirrup. In the first and fourth corners a white rose, and in the second and third a red rose.

"South Africa, 1900-02."

177, Holdenhurst Road, Bournemouth.

Hon. Colonel.

p.s.*Thomson*, J. R., VD, (Hon. Col. ret. Vols.) 28Apr.06

Lt.-Colonel.

⚔Parke, L., Maj. ret. pay (*Maj. Res. of Off.*) 3Feb.12

Majors. (2)

p. ⚔Thomson, W. R. (*Hon. Lt. in Army* 14*June*02) 6Feb.08
Smith, S. G., (*H*) ⓢ (Q) 3Feb.12

Captains. (8)

p. Gott, J. 14Nov.00
p.s.Maturin, F. H. 28Aug.07
p.s.Keene, H. 20Feb.08
p.s.Rebbeck, T. V. (*t*) 9Apr.10
p.s.Druitt, J. V. (*t*) 3Feb.12
Bacon, R. J.(*H*) *I. of. M.* 23May12
Palmer, C. W. G. 1Aug.12
Allen, L. J. S. (*H*) 8Apr.14

Lieutenants. (8)

Davenport, G. C.9Apr.10
Parke, L. S. 3Feb.12
Jenkins, R. E 1Aug.12
Druitt, G. T. ⓢ 1Aug.12
Stringer, F.W. 16Aug.13
Collins, J. C. 2Dec.13
p.s. Huth, C. F. (*late Lt.* R.Mon.R.E.Spec. Res.) (*Hon. Lt. in Army* 14*July*01)2Dec.13
Elliott, C. E. 2Dec.13

2nd Lieutenants. (8)

Last, F. B. 28Oct.12
Walkinshaw, C. C. 9Nov.12
Warner, B. M. 3Jan.13
Patmore, F. J. M. E. 8Jan.13
Malim, A. W. 4Mar.13
Smith, E. S. J. 11Mar.13
Lisby, V, C 21Jan.14
Meikle, R. 20May14

Inst. of Music.
Bacon, R. J., *capt.* 10Sept.12

Adjutant.
Gribbon, H. H., Capt. Hamps. R. 1Feb.13

Quarter-Master.

⚔Roberts, C.J., Qr.-Mr. (*hon. capt.*) ret. pay, *hon. capt.* 3Feb.13

Medical Officers.

p. Vernon, Maj. A. H., R.A.M.C. (T.F.) (attd.) 1Apr.08
Stewart, Lt. W. H.E.,R.A.M.C. (T.F.) (attd.) 14Apr.14

Chaplains.

Crick, Rev. A. C., *M.A.,* Chapl. 2nd Class (T.F.) (attd.) 5May09 5May04
Kennedy, Rev. E. J., Chapl. 3rd Class (T.F.) (attd.) 29Jan.02

[Uniform—*Scarlet.*
Facings—*Yellow.*]

8th (Isle of Wight Rifles, "Princess Beatrice's") Battalion.

"South Africa, 1900-01."

Newport.

Colonel-in-Chief.

THE KING.

Lt.-Colonel.

⚔Rhodes, J.E. (*H*) ⓢ (*Lt. Col. ret. Spec. Res.*) 23May13

Majors. (2)

⚔Davenport, S., late Capt. Rif. Brig. 26Apr.12 31May13
Wilton, H. P. 27Apr.12
Mayes, A. E. 16Oct.12

Captains. (8)

p.s.Ratsey, D. W. 1Aug.09
Clark, C. T. ⓟ 18Sept.12
⚔Lewis. E. h. (*Capt. Res. of Off.*) 4Oct.13
Raymond, G. 5Dec13
Ellery, C. L. 13Apr.14

Lieutenants. (8)

Ratsey, C. 30May10
Linington, H. A. J. 10June11
Fardell, J.G. 16Sept.11
Marvin, R. C. 9Oct.11
Read, W. F. 8Oct.12
Moore, E. 26Apr.13
Marsh, J. F. H.24May14

2nd Lieutenants. (8)

Loader, G. C. 19Feb.13
Pittis, C. S. 20Feb.13
Watkins, K. H. 1July13
White, E. S. 16Oct.13
Young-James, A. Y. 3Dec.13

Adjutant.

⚔Stone, P. V. P., Capt. Norf. R. 21Feb.13

Quarter-Master.

Medical Officers.

McKay, Lt. J. B., R.A.M.C. (T.F.) (attd.) 1July12
Read, Lt. H. W., R.A.M.C. (T.F.) (attd.) 26Feb.13

Chaplains.

Smith, Rev. Canon C., *M.V.O., M.A.,* Chapl. 2nd Class (T.F.) (attd.) 1 Apr.08 11Feb.98
Sharpe, Rev. H. E. *M.A.,* Chapl. 3rd Class (T.F.) (attd.) 21Dec.08 21Dec.96

[Uniform—*Green.*
Facings—*Black.*]

Cadet Unit affiliated.
The Ventnor Cadet Company.

9th (Cyclist) Battalion.

Hamilton House, Commercial Road, Southampton.

Lt.-Colonel.

p.s.⚔Johnson, R. A. TD,(Q)(*H*)(*Hon. Lt. in Army* 14*Apr.*01) 14Nov.11

Major.

⚔Clarke-Jervoise, Sir E. J., Bt., Capt. ret. pay (*Res. of Off.*) (Q) ⓢ 1Sept.13

Captains (8)
Perkins, A. B. ⓟ 2Feb.12
p. Willoughby, G. St. M. (*H*) (t) 5Feb.12 3Feb.04
Tyndale-Biscoe, A. A. T. ⓢ 8Feb.12
Atthill,G,DuS,(Q) 19Mar.13
13Jan.11
Rose, D'A.L.(*t*) 16Nov.10
⚔Wyllie, H. 1Nov.13
Robson, A. 8Apr.14
25Dec.12

Lieutenants (5)

Barber, C. A. 1Nov.13

2nd Lieutenants (4)

Jewell, F. N. 27Feb.12
Montefiore,L.N. [*l*] 1Feb.13
Hellyer, F. E. 2Apr.13
Campbell, I.P.F. 30Nov.13
Price, W. D. 1Dec.13
Boxer, F. R. 31Mar.14
Warris, M. W. 8Apr.14
8Nov.12
Wilkinson, A. M. 22July14

Adjutant.

Vernon Harcourt, B. F., Capt. Welsh R. 28Feb.12

Quarter-Master.

⚔Wyard, F. J., *hon. lt.* 1Apr.13

Medical Officer.

van Someren, Lt. A. G. V., *M.B.,F.R.C.S. Edin.,* R.A.M.C. (T.F.) (attd.) 1Jan.14

Chaplain.

Jephson, Rev. W. V., Chapl. 4th Class (T.F.) (attd.) 9Dec.12

[Uniform—*Scarlet.*
Facings—*Yellow.*]

THE SOUTH STAFFORDSHIRE REGIMENT.
Regimental District No. 38 [No. 6 District].

The Sphinx, superscribed "Egypt."
"Guadaloupe, 1759," "Martinique, 1762," "Monte Video," "Rolica," "Vimiera," "Corunna," "Busaco," "Badajoz," "Salamanca," "Vittoria," "St. Sebastian," "Nive," "Peninsula," "Ava," "Moodkee," "Ferozeshah," "Sobraon," "Pegu," "Alma," "Inkerman," "Sevastopol," "Lucknow," "Central India," "South Africa, 1878-79," "Egypt, 1882," "Kirbekan," "Nile, 1884-85," "South Africa, 1900-02."

Regular and Special Reserve Battalions.

Uniform—Scarlet.   Facings—White.   Agents—Messrs. Cox & Co.

1st Bn. (38th Foot) *Pietermaritzburg.*	3rd Bn. (1st K.O. Stafford Mila.)	.. *Lichfield.*
2nd „ (80th „) *Aldershot.*	4th „ (1st K.O. Stafford Mila.)	.. *Lichfield.*
Depôt .. .. .. *Lichfield.*	Record Office	*Lichfield.*

Territorial Force Battalions.

5th Bn. .. .. *Drill Hall, Walsall.* | 6th Bn. .. *Drill Hall, Wolverhampton.*

Colonel .. Tucker, Lt.-Gen. Sir C., *G.C.B., G.C.V.O.*, ret. pay [R] .. 1Sept.11
8Oct.09

1st and 2nd Battalions.

Lt.-Colonels. (2)
2Davidson, C. S. 16Oct.11
1Ovens, R. M. 1Jan.13

Majors. (8)
2Walshe, H. E. 16Oct.07
s. Jervis, S. J., *p.s.c.* [I] 18Mar.08
1Buckle, A. C. 28Dec.08
(3) 2Daukes, A. H. (*Comdg. Depôt*) 8Jan.09
1Parkin, F. H. 9June11
1Loder-Symonds, J. F 1Apr.12
1Welchman, S. C. 16Oct.11
2Routledge, P. C. L. 1Jan.13

Captains. (14)
2Boyd-Moss, L. B., *f.c.r.* 26Dec.01
s. deJoux, J. S. N. [L] *bt. maj.* 22Aug.02
21Apr.02
2James, A. H. C. 21Apr.02
(3) 1Dunlop, J. S. S. 9Feb.04
w.a. Butler, S. S. 20May08
(3) 1Morgan, R. W. 21Dec.07
18Jan.08
(2) 2Savage, M. B. 23Jan.08
2Hodgson, C. F, F. 18Mar.08
2Duckworth, R. 1Apr.08
1Bonner, S., *Adjt.* 1Apr.08
2July10
r. Collas, W. J. J. 28Dec.08
2Thomas, C. H. 8Jan.09
(3) 3Yool, G. A. 22Apr.09
1Vallentin, J.F.12June09
c.o. Taylor, B. H. W. 9Oct.09
s. Commings, P. E. C. 19Oct.09
(3) 1Savage-Armstrong, F. S. N. 19Oct.09
c.o. Leland, H. J. C., *D.S.O.* 4Dec.09
w.a. Powell, H. M. 2July10
2Kilby, A. F G. 1Apr.10
1Apr.10
1Ransford,C.G.15Nov.12
20Jan.11

Captains—contd.
1Green, C. H. 4Dec.12
2Johnson, S. G. 1Jan.13
1de Trafford, O.15Aug.13

Lieutenants. (20)
1Glover,G.deC. 30Nov.07
c.o. Keene, P. F. 21Dec.07
r. Manger, C. H. 6May08
1Adams, C. B. 6May08
1Foster, W. A. P. 12Sept.08
(3) 1Blockey, H. S.28Dec.08
2Baumann,A. B.8Jan.09
c.o. Parker, M. J. 1Apr.09
2Gunner, F. H.22Apr.09
2Chaytor, J.C., *Adjt.* 5May09
(3) 2Stephenson, L. F. 12June09
1Holmes, F. L. 14July09
c.o. Shorthose, W. J. T. 2Aug.09
c.o. Richmond, J. A. 29Sept.09
1Shore, H. K. 19Oct.09
2Dent, J. L. 1Apr.10
s.s. Naylor, R. F. B. 1Apr.10
1Morris, C. M. 1Apr.10
c.o. Dawes, G. 15Nov.11
1Crousaz, C. F.28Mar.12
2Sharpe, J. S. 1Oct.12
c.o. Hordern, A. F. 30Oct.12
w.a. Marten, M. F. 7Nov.12
2Townshend, J. S. 4Dec.12
c.o. Olive, V. G. 11Dec.12
1Moor-Radford, L. C. 1Jan.13
1Hume, C. G. 14Jan.13
1Evans, C. W. 9Apr.13
1Limbery, C.R. 12Mar.14
1Twiss, D, C. 18Mar.14
w.a. Burt, C. S. 6May14
1MacGeorge, H. W. 6May14

2nd *Lieuts.*—contd.
2Miller, R, R. O'C. 3Sept.13
1Bower, H.R.S. 17Sept.13
2Gyde, A. A. E. 17Sept.13
2Miller, G. T. 25Feb.14
1Willoughby, H. 10June14

Adjutants.
2Chaytor, J. C., *lt.* 1Mar.12
1Bonner, S., *capt.* 15Aug.13

Quarter-Masters.
1White, F. 10July01
hon. capt. 10July11
r. Brown, W., *hon. lt.* 7Mar.08
1Bradbury, S., *hon. lt.* 4Aug.09
2Hazelgrove, A., *hon. lt.* 11Sept.12

Special Reserve.
2nd *Lieutenant.*
Hill, C. H. (on prob.) 25July14

3rd Battalion.

(*Officers serving on 19 July02 in the corresponding Militia unit hold honorary Army rank equivalent to the Militia regimental rank they then held. Other officers entitled to honorary Army rank have it shown against their names.*)

Hon. Colonel.
Broun, M. A. W. (Hon. Col. ret. Mila.) (Hon. Lt. - Col. in Army 5Dec.00) 14June08
5Apr.05

Lt.-Colonel.
p.s. Jones Mitton, G (H) (b) 8Mar.11

Major.
r.e. Daukes, A. H. 8Jan.09
p.s. Timmis,T.S. 28June11

Captains. (5)
p.s. Wilson, A. E. C. 9Apr.00
p.s. Anderson, A. L. K. (H) 8June00
p.s. Lord, C. E., *hon. m.* 16Oct.00) 4July03
(Hon. Capt. in Army)
p.s. de Trafford, H. J. (H) 12May07
r.e. Morgan, R. W. 21Dec.07
Maples, K. J. (H) 4May08
r.e. Yool, G. A. 22Apr.09
r.e. Savage-Armstrong, F. S. N. 19Oct.09
Derington, W. E. (H) 6May13

Lieutenants. (11)
Yard, E. C., *Lt.* ret. pay 14July04
28July09
r.e. Blockey, H. S. 28Dec.08
r.e. Stephenson, L. F. 12June09
Rutherford, C. T. 5June11
Taunton, B. T. G. 1Mar.12
Birch, E. R. 2June12
Nixon, M. O. 24Feb.12
Robinson, F. E.14July13
Wansbrough, W. E. 14July13
Turner,J.R., T.10Sept.13
Jones Mitton, G.H.N. 10Sept.13
Fitzpatrick,D.T.F. 23Feb.14
Archer-Shee, G. 23Feb.14

2nd *Lieutenants.* (8)
Riley, R. R. 3Sept.13
Parker, G. E. (on prob.) 3Sept.13

Adjutant.
Manger, C. H., Lt. S. Staff. R. 23Jan.14
(Lt. in Army 6May08)

Quarter-Master.
Bradbury, S., *hon. lt.*

2nd *Lieutenants.* (12)
1Bean, C. R. C. 22Jan.13
1Bartlett, C.E.C. 5Feb.13
2Farwell, A. W. 24May13
2Scott, B. J. H. 3Sept.13

THE SOUTH STAFFORDSHIRE REGIMENT—(Regtl. Dist. No. 38)—*contd.*

4th Battalion.

(*Officers serving on 12 Aug.01 in the corresponding Militia unit hold honorary Army rank equivalent to the Militia regimental rank they then held. Other officers entitled to honorary Army rank have it shown against their names.*)

Hon. Colonel.

Aylesford, C. W.,
  Earl of   2Aug.08
            4Feb.99

Lt.-Colonel.

p.s.✕Bulwer, E. A. E.,
  Capt. ret.pay
  (*Res. of Off.*) 13Dec.10

Majors. (3)

✕Seckham, D. T.
  Capt. ret. pay 2July10
p.s.✕Woolf, H. G. (*Hon. Lt. in Army 21 Oct. 00*)(*H*)(*a*) 21Apr.11
p.s.✕Williams, G. A. S.,
  late Lt. R. Fus. (*H*) 6June12

Captains. (6)

p.s.✕Smith, P. E. B. F.,
  hon. m. (*H*) 4Feb.99
p.s. Kinnaird, F. J. (*H*) 4Nov.10
Arnold, S. M. (*H*) ⓣ 29Apr.12
Inglis, H. W., Lt.,
  ret. pay ⓢ 9Aug.12
Sabben, E. H.
  (*H*)(*t*) 4Jan.13
Morris, R. J.(*H*) 20June14

Lieutenants. (11)

Harman, H. A. A. F. (q)
  (*Principal, Accra Training Insfn., Gold Coast, 17Apr. 12*) 23Mar.12
Middleton, L. E. 23Mar.12
Robinson, A. (*H*)
  I. of M. 3Sept.11
            1Dec.11

2nd Lieutenants. (8).

Thomas, W. F. P. 8Oct.13
Evans, T. W. P.
  (*on prob.*) 15Apr.14
Douglas, B. F. S.
  (*on prob.*) 15Apr.14
Wollaston, J. W.
  (*on prob.*) 17June14

Inst. of Musk.

Robinson, A., *lt.* 25Apr.14

Adjutant.

Collas, W. J. J., Capt.
  S. Staff. R. 17Feb.13
  (*Capt. in Army 28 Dec.08*)

Quarter-Master.

✕Brown, W., *hon. lt.*

5th Battalion.

"South Africa, 1900-02"

Drill Hall, Walsall.

Hon. Colonel.

Dartmouth, Rt. Hon.
  W. H., Earl of, VD 1Apr.08

Lt.-Colonel.

Green, C. F. (Q) 19Feb.13

Majors. (2)

Davies, A. T. J. 19Feb.13
Griffith, S. 17June14

Captains. (8)

     Thomas, H. E. 6Aug.04
p. Burnett, W 15Sept.06
p. Hughes, F. C. 18Oct.06
p. Lees, J. 5Aug.11
p. Overend, F. L. (*H*)
  (*local capt., O.T.C.*,
  1May09) 19Aug.11
p. Lord, H. 5June12
p. Wistance, W. A. 3July12
     Lister, C. 19Feb.13
     Moore, W. E. 17June14

Lieutenants. (8)

Smith, A. A. 5Aug.11
Footner, B. M. 5June12
Smith, T. S. 16Apr.13
Pochin, H. (*H*) 17Apr.13
            13Sept.12
Cozens, L. 1Mar.14
Ivatt, H. A. 1Mar.14
Wheway, H. J. 1Mar.14

2nd Lieutenants (8)

Wilson, E. A. 25Apr.13
Hemming, F. J. 28Apr.13
Allday, S. O. 13Nov.13
Green, A. E. 31Mar.14

Adjutant.

✕Soames, G. H.,
  Capt. W. York.
  R. 1Jan.12

Quarter-Master.

Warner, R., *hon. lt.* 5Aug.11

Medical Officer.

Sydenham, Capt. F. W.,
  M.D., F.R.C.S.
  (*Edin.*), R.A.M.C.
  (T.F.) (*attd.*) 11Aug.13
            11Feb.10
✕Cooke, Lt., J. G.,
  M.B., R.A.M.C.
  (T.F.) (*attd.*) 2Jan.14

Chaplains.

Paice, Rev. A., *M.A.,*
  Chapl. 3rd Class
  (T.F.) (*attd.*) 19Mar.12
            19Mar.02
Talbot, Rev. A. T. S.,
  M.A., Chapl. 4th
  Class (T.F.)(*attd.*) 26June12

[Uniform—*Scarlet.*
Facings—*White.*]

6th Battalion.

"South Africa, 1900-02."

Drill Hall,
Wolverhampton.

Hon. Colonel.

✕Hickman, T. E.,
  C.B., D.S.O.,
  Col. ret. pay, *q.s.*
            20June09

Lt.-Colonel.

Taylor, H. (q) 21June13

Majors. (2)

Lowe, T. E.(q) 16Apr.13
Barnett, T. E. (q) 21June13

Captains. (8)

p.s. McBean, A. H. 30Apr.04
p. Law, F. W. B. 19May05
p. Holcroft, F.(*t*)22July05
p.s. Lewis, E. 12May12
p. Sims, A.G.C. (*H*) 22Aug.12
Howl, C. (*H*) 17Apr.13
Thursfield, J. H. 26May14

Lieutenants (8)

(p.s.)Adam, W. A. (*H*) 10Dec.09
(p.s.)Parkes, W. C. 14May11
(p.s.)Joynson, L. C. B, 13May12
Page, H. A. 12May12
Collisson, E. R.
            13Apr.13
Elwell, G. 1Mar.14
Sankey, S. J. 1Mar.14

2nd Lieutenants. (8)

Hanford, H. 4Apr.14
Jordan, W. A. 8May14

Adjutant.

✕Gordon, C. W. E.,
  Capt. R. Highrs. 1Oct.12

Quarter-Master.

Willner, J., *hon. lt.* 3Aug.11

Medica Officer.

Hewitt, Capt. T. H.,
  La N., R.A.M.C.
  (T.F.)(*attd.*) 18June13
            23June09

Chaplains.

Penny, Rev. A., *M.A.,*
  Chapl. 3rd Class
  (T.F.) (*attd.*) 1Apr.08
            30May96
Pratt, Rev. A., *M.A.,*
  Chapl.4th Class.
  (T.F.) (*attd.*) 17Feb.12

[Uniform—*Scarlet.*
Facings—*White.*]

Cadet Unit affiliated.
Brierley Hill Cadet Corps.

THE DORSETSHIRE REGIMENT.
Regimental District No. **39**. [No. **8** District.]

"Primus in Indis."
The Castle and Key, superscribed "Gibraltar, 1779-83," and with the Motto "*Montis Insignia Calpe*" underneath. The Sphinx, superscribed "Egypt."
"Plassey," "Martinique, 1794," "Marabout," "Albuhera," "Vittoria," "Pyrenees," "Nivelle," "Nive," "Orthes," "Peninsula," "Ava," "Maharajpore," "Sevastopol," "Tirah," "Relief of Ladysmith," "South Africa, 1899-1902."

Regular and Special Reserve Battalions.

Uniform—Scarlet.　　Facings—Grass green.　　Agents—Messrs. Cox & Co.
1st Bn. (39th Foot) .. .. Belfast. | 3rd Bn. (Dorset Mil.) .. .. .. Dorchester.
2nd Bn. (54th Foot) .. .. Poona (for Bombay).
Depôt .. .. .. Dorchester.　　　　Record Office .. .. .. Exeter.

Territorial Force Battalion.
4th Bn. .. .. .. Dorchester.

Colonel
M. Cook, Maj.-Gen. H., C.B., ret. pay　　17June10

1st and 2nd Battalions.

Lt.-Colonels. (2)
2 Rosher, H. L.　25Oct.10
1 Bols, L. J., D.S.O.,
　p.s.c. [L]　19Feb.14
　　　　　　21Feb.12

Majors. (8)
s. Clarkson, B. St. J.
　　　　　　23Jan.07
1 Roper, R. T., p.s.c.
　　　　　　19Feb.10
m.c.Cowie, H.N.R., D.S.O.,
　p.s.c.　25Oct.15
(3) 1Hannay, C. C. (Comdg.
　　Depôt)　6Jan.12
Radcliffe, F. W.,
　p.s.c.　12Oct.12
? Mercer. A.A.,e.19Nov.13
1 Saunders, C.　3 June14
2 Hope, L. C.　24June14

Captains. (14)
1 Fraser, W. A. C.
　　　　　　22Jan.02
s. Alexander, H. L.,
　p.s.c.　1Apr.04
1 Davidson, W. T. C.
　　　　　　4Oct.04
(3) 2 Kitchin, I. H. 23Jan.05
2 Utterson, H. K.
　　　　　　22Mar.05
(1) Moulton-Barrett,A.L.
　　　　　　22Mar.05
2 Herbert, G. M. 1Apr.05
2 Weldon, E. S. 29Apr.05
2 Middleton, F. 19Feb.06
1 Williams, H. S.
　D.S.C. [l]　1Apr.06
1 Hyslop, R.G.B.M.,
　p.s.c. [l]　9July10
　　　　　　9Sept.05
o.d.Jones, C. R., o. 1Apr.09
i.v. Case, H. A.　1Apr.09
(3) 2 Beveridge, H. 1Apr.09
e.a.Huddleston, H.J.
　[F]　1Apr.09
2 Roe, A. R. M., p.s.c.
　　　　　　1Apr.09
Le Marchant, H. N.
　　　　　　1Apr.09
e.a.Wheatley, M. J. 2May09
o.d.Fuller, B. M., e., o.
　　　　　　2May09

Captains—contd.
c.o.Thurston, V. B. 13June09
s. Frost, O. M. T. 19June09
r. Bullock, T. W. 25May10
1 Kelsall, J.　26May10
(3) 1 Hewitt, Hon. E. J.
　　　　　　26May10
2 Clemson, W.　26May10
t. Shute, J. V.　17Feb 12
1 Ransome, A. L., Adjt.
　　　　　　17Feb.12
1 White, O. W. 17Feb.12
s o.a. Willes, W.F.G.16June12
c.o. Priestley, A. B. 16June12
s. Rolls, S.P.A. 16June12
s. Munby, A. M. 16June12
1 Rathborne, F. H. B.
　　　　　　7Sept.12
s. Bowly, W. A. T.
　　　　　　25Dec.12

Lieutenants. (19)
1 Margetts, C. F. M.
　　　　　　24Sept.08
2 Rendall, T. S. 1Apr.09
(3) 2 Caruthers-Little,
　A. W. P.　1Apr.09
2 Yeatman,G.D. 24July09
1 Pitt, J. M.　24Oct.09
1 Partridge, R.E. 12Dec.09
c.o. Hall, A. R. 13July12
　　　　　　30June09
2 Powell, F. G., Adjt.
　　　　　　18Dec.09
g 1 George, A. K. D.
　　　　　　26May10
c.o. Collins, K. G. F.
　　　　　　23June 10
1 Algeo, W. B. 1Apr.11
s.s.Firth, C. W. M. 10Nov.11
p.d. Thwaytes,H. D. 6Dec.11
2 Miles, W. H. 4Jan.12
2 Reid, W. L. [l] 4Jan.12
c.o.Gore-Browne, E. A. R.
　　　　　　17Feb.12
(3) 1 Parkinson, J. A. F.
　　　　　　2Mar.12
1 Lilly, C. O. 10Aug.12
1 Woodhouse, G. H.
　　　　　　11Aug.12
2 Hawkins, A. E.
　　　　　　11Aug.12
1 Fraser, A. S 1Jan.13
s.o.Dudley, B. J. C. 8June13
2 Maxwell-Moffat, A.
　L. N.　11Feb.14
2 Dean, H. H. 21Mar.14
2 Cushny, D. 11July14
1 Leishman, W.A.15July14

2nd Lieutenants. (12)
2 Morley, V. S. 13Mar.12
1 Grant-Dalton, L.
　　　　　　22May12
2 Highett, C. T. 22May12
2 Stephenson, E. L.
　　　　　　4Dec.12
2 Boles, N. H. 3Sept.13
2 Baillie, H. J. 10Dec.13
2 Thomson, W. B.
　　　　　　24Jan.14
2 Simmons, D.A. 24Jan.14
2 Butcher, C. G. 10June14

Adjutants.
1 Ransome, A. L., capt.
　　　　　　10Oct.11
2 Powell, F. G., lt.
　　　　　　8June13

Quarter-Masters.
r. Kearney, J. 21Aug.95
　hon. maj. 21Aug.10
1 Gyngell, G. 19Feb.02
　hon. capt. 2Nov.10
2 Brown, A. 11May04
　hon. capt. 11May14

Special Reserve.
2nd Lieutenants.
Walker, E. B. 23Mar.12
Shannon, S. 7June13
Chapman, H. L.
　(on prob.)　5July13

3rd Battalion.

(*Officers serving on 13 July01 in the corresponding Militia unit hold honorary Army rank equivalent to the Militia regimental rank they then held. Other Officers entitled to honorary Army rank have it shown against their names.*)

Hon. Colonel.
Batten, H. C. G., hon. c.
　　　　　　2Mar.06

Lt. Colonel.
Castleman Smith, E.C.,
　C.B. (H)(t)(a) 2Mar.09

Major.
Hall, D. K. E. (Maj.
　Res. of Off.) [F]
　(Remount Service)　23Apr10
r.e. Hannay, C. C. 6Jan.12

Captains. (5)
r.e. Kitchin, I. H. 23Jan.05
p.s. Poole, E. B. (H)
　　　　　　14June08
r.e. Beveridge, H.1Apr.09
p.s. Batten, H. C. C. (H)
　　　　　　4Nov.09
p.s. Jarvis, C. S. (H)
　　　　　　18Dec.09
Chawner, L. C.,
　Capt. ret. pay 23Apr.10
r.e. Hewitt, Hon. E. J.
　　　　　　26May10
Greenhill, H. M.,
　late Lt. Dorset R.
　　　　　　6May14

Lieutenants. (11)
r.e. Caruthers-Little,
　A. W. P.　1Apr.09
Clemson, T. H. 2Sept.11
Thomas,C. (H)(Asst.
　Commr. of Police,
　Gold Coast,1Sept 13)
r.e.Parkinson, J. A. F.
　　　　　　3Feb.12
　　　　　　2Mar.12
Clarke, A. R. S. 1May13
Turner, J. R. 1May13
Burnand, G. A. 1May13
Gregory, A. L. 1May13
Clutterbuck, A.J.
　　　　　　1May13
Bishop, E. M. 1May13
King, F. D. S. 1Sept.13
Price, W. L. 10June14
d'Erf Wheeler, P.F
　　　　　　10

2nd Lieutenants. (8).
Wiltshire, L.H. 2Apr.18
Clayton, J. G.
　(on prob.)　25July14

Adjutant.
Bullock, T. W., Capt.
　Dorset R.　2Apr.13
(*Capt. in Army* 25May10)

Quarter-Master.
Kearney, J., hon. maj

THE DORSETSHIRE REGIMENT—(Regtl. Dist. No. **39**)—contd.

4th Battalion.

"South Africa, 1900-01."

Dorchester.

Hon. Colonel.

p.s. Williams, R., VD,
(*Hon. Col. ret. Vols.*)
1Dec.07

Lt.-Colonel.

p.s. Baxter, W. H., TD,
2Nov.12

Majors. (2)

Symonds, A. G., TD,
11Mar.09

Woodhouse, F. D.
2Nov.12

Captains. (8)

p. Freame, B. E., VD,
hon. m.   8Sept.88

p.s. ⚔Kitson, H. L., TD.
(*Hon. Capt. in Army*
9 *July* 01) (*H*) 14Feb.03

p. Hughes-D'Aeth, C. C.,
TD, hon. m.   1Jan.04

p.s. Lock, H. O. ⓖ 12May06

Duke, H. E.   28Feb.12

p.s. Fletcher, W. T. 15June12

p. Symes, C. W.   1July12
12July11

p. ⚔Whetham, L. (*H*)
1Jan.14

Lieutenants. (8)

(p.) Symonds, D. G.   1July11
Roper, J.   1July11
Suttill, K.   16May12
Richards, C. E. 16May12
Tucker, A. C.   1June14

2nd Lieutenants. (8)

Matthews, W. F.
13Feb.13
Royds, G. F.   21June13
Smith, F. J.   23June13
Woodhouse, H. S.
22Jan.14

Adjutant.

⚔Panton, W. F.,
Capt. Leic. R.
8Mar.13

Quarter-Master.

⚔Webb, W. A., Qr.-
Mr., (*hon. m.*) ret.
pay, *hon. m,* 2Mar.11

Medical Officers.

Paterson, Capt. A. R.,
M.D., R.A.M.C.
(T.F.) (*attd.*) 7Dec.11
28Feb.08

Walker, Capt. A.,
R.A.M.C. (T.F.)
(*attd.*)   31May12
26Aug.08

Chaplains.

Parish, *Rev. Canon*
W. O., *M.A.*, TD, Chapl.
1st Class (T.F.)
(*attd.*)   18Oct.10
18Oct.90

Gundry, *Rev.* R. H.,
B.A., Chapl. 3rd
Class (T.F.) (*attd.*)
27July10
25Aug.06

Hellins, *Rev.* E. W. J.,
Chapl. 4th Class
(T.F.) (*attd.*) 1Apr.08
10June05

[Uniform—*Scarlet.*
Facings—*Grass Green.*]

THE PRINCE OF WALES'S VOLUNTEERS (SOUTH LANCASHIRE REGIMENT).

Regimental District No. **40**. [No. **4** District.]

The Plume of the Prince of Wales. The Sphinx superscribed "Egypt."
"Louisburg," "Martinique, 1762," "Havannah," "St. Lucia, 1778," "Monte Video," "Rolica," "Vimiera,"
"Corunna," "Talavera," "Badajoz," "Salamanca," "Vittoria," "Pyrenees," "Nivelle," "Orthes,"
"Toulouse," "Peninsula," "Niagara," "Waterloo," "Candahar, 1842," "Ghuznee, 1842,"
"Cabool, 1842," "Maharajpore," "Sevastopol," "Lucknow," "New Zealand,"
"Relief of Ladysmith," "South Africa, 1899-1902."

Regular and Special Reserve Battalions.

Uniform—Scarlet. *Facings*—White. *Agents*—Messrs. Cox & Co.
1st Bn. (40th Foot) .. .. *Quetta.* | 3rd Bn. (4th R. Lancashire Mil.) .. *Warrington.*
2nd „ (82nd „) .. .. *Tidworth.*
Depôt „ .. .. .. *Warrington.* Record Office .. .. *Shrewsbury.*

Territorial Force Battalions.

4th Bn. .. .. .. *Drill Hall, Warrington.* | 5th Bn. .. .. .. *Drill Hall, St. Helens.*

Allied Regiment of Dominion of New Zealand.
9th (Wellington East Coast) Regiment.

Colonel .. .. ✠Sartorius, Maj.-Gen. E. H., *C.B., ret. pay, p.s.c.*.. 26Nov.09

1st and 2nd Battalions.

Lt.-Colonels. (2)

1Dudgeon, F. A., *p.s.o.* 28Feb.12
2Wanliss,C.[L] 27Mar.14

Majors. (8)

2Ashworth, G. 7Sept.07
1Willoughby-Osborne, A. de V. 28Feb.08
2Goren, B. R. 9Dec.08
(3)2Green, M. C. A.
(Comdg.Depôt)16May09
1Woods, C. R. S. 1Sept.11
1Herbert, H. C. 17Apr.12
s. Dawson, D'O. B. 24Apr.12
2Ewart, G. D. H. 27Mar.14

Captains. (14)

1Woods, H. K. 4June04
r. Cotton, H. T. 3Aug.04
2Ritchie, W. B. 1Dec.04
2Colvile, F. M. 19July05
 5Nov.02
m.a.Hume, W. V. 11Sept.06
,3)2Evans, B. 30May09
 22Aug.07
1Dickson, A. 24Apr.09
(3)1Robson, E. 26Apr.09
2Travis-Cook, J. D. E. 8May09
1McCarthy O'Leary, J. 8May09
(3)1Wilkins, H. J. U. 8May09
2Hutchinson, J. S. 16May09
1Anderson, L. P.23Dec.09
1Wroughton, A. C. 23Sept.13
1Nicholson, E. F. D. 27Mar.14
1Allsopp, J. B., *Adjt.*
 27Mar.14
t. Drew, F. W. M. 27Mar.14
2Charlton, F. H. 7Apr.14
2Bagley, F. A. 17June14

Lieutenants. (19)

1St. John, H.B. 1Dec.04
c.o. Shaw, G. 11Sept.06
c.o. Wesohé, E. B. 1Nov.07
t. Montgomery, W. A. M. 7Mar.08
c.o.Bell, G. H. 19Aug.08
c.o.Stretton, A. L. de C. 24Apr.09
(3)1Withers, H. H. 8May09
2Clemens, L. A., *Adjt.* 16May09
2Adams, G. 23Dec.09
(3)2Gebbie, J. F. R.
 1Jan.10
1Hammick, E. 1Apr.11
1Warner, C. T. 20Sept.11
1Killick, S. H. 11Oct.11
1Braide, R. W. 2Nov.11
1Bethune, C. F. 27Mar.12
2Hadfield, W. J. M. 7Apr.12
1Marsh, A. C. 8 Aug.12
c.o.Robinson, A. C. 4Sept.12
1Wolfe-Murray, R.A. 4Sept.12
1White, G.S.A. 16Apr.13
2Fulcher, B. V. 16July13
2Icke, J. H. T. 23Sept.13
1Barker, R. E. 24Sept.13
2Albrecht, C. E. R. 22Oct.13
1Campbell, F. E. D. 27Mar.14
2Salter, R. C. F. 7Apr.14

2nd Lieutenants. (12)

2Townend, G. A. 22Jan.13
2Hewitt, G. H. 22Jan.13
2Hewlett, C. M. 24May13
1Ward, W. D. 17Sept.13
1Ransom, R. A. 10Dec.13

2nd Lieuts.—contd.

1Macdonald, R. H. 20Dec.13
1Murray, K. M. 24Jan.14
2Burlton, W. E. N. 25Feb 14
2Sutton, F.A. 10June14
1Hislop. J.F.G. 25July14

Adjutants.

1Allsopp, J. B., *capt.* 25June12
2Clemens, L. A., *lt.* 24Sept.13

Quarter-Masters.
r. Baines, J., *hon. lt.* 25Mar.08
1Simon, T. A., *hon. lt.* 20July10
2Boast, S. T., *hon. lt.* 22Apr.11

Special Reserve.
2nd Lieutenants.
Gilmore, R. S. 25June13
Widdowson, A.J.H.R. 2July13
Berry, F. 6Aug.13

3rd Battalion.

(*Officers serving on 3Aug.01 in the corresponding Militia unit hold honorary Army rank equivalent to the Militia regimental rank they then held. Other officers entitled to honorary Army rank have it shown against their names.*)

Hon. Colonel.

✠Blackburne, R. I., C.B. (*Hon. Col. ret. Mila.*) (*Hon. Lt.-Col. in Army 4 Aug.01*) 21June06
 7Mar.08

Lt.-Colonel.

p.s.✠Vaughan, J. L.(H) 2Nov.12

Major.

r.e.✠Green, M. C. A. 16May09
p.s.✠Greg, R. A. (Q)(H) 2Nov.12

Captains. (5)

✠Herbert, L. W., Capt. ret. pay (H) 4Oct.05
r.e.✠Evans, B. 20May08
 22Aug.07
Morgan, M. H. B., Lt. ret. pay (H) 19Aug.08
r.e. ✠Robson, E. 26Apr.09
r.e. Wilkins, H. J. U. 8May09
Blackburne, G. I. 18Oct.09
p.s. Masterman, A. H.(H) 2Nov.12

Lieutenants. (11)

r.e. Withers, H. H. 8 May 09
r.e. Gebbie, J. F. R. 1Jan.10

2nd Lieutenants. (8)

Clark, W. G. 22Jan.13
Irwin, H. G. W. 14June13

Adjutant.

✠Cotton, H. T., Capt. S. Lan. R. 23Sept.13
(*Capt. in Army 3Aug 04*)

Quarter-Master.

Baines, J., *hon. lt.*

THE PRINCE OF WALES'S VOLUNTEERS (SOUTH LANCASHIRE REGT.)—
(Regtl. Dist. No. **40**)—*contd.*

4th Battalion.

"South Africa, 1900-02."

Drill Hall, Warrington.

Hon. Colonel.

Walker, J. R., late
Capt. D.of Lanc.
Own Impl. Yeo.
        7Jan.03

Lt.-Colonel.

p. ✗Fairclough, B., TD
  (*Hon. Lt. in Army*
  26 *July* 02)(Q) 17Apr.12

Majors. (2)

p.s.✗Appleton, F. M.,
  VD (*Hon. Capt. in*
  Army 26 *July* 01)⊕
          1Jan.09
✗Crosfield, G. R.
  (*Hon. Capt. in*
  Army 20Mar. 01)
  (b)(q)(H) 1Sept.12

Captains. (8)

p. Smith, R. (q) 20Feb.01
p. ✗Cary, C. F.(*Hon.*
  Lt. in Army 5*Aug.*01)
        20Feb.01
p.s.Roberts, H. G. (q)(*H*)
        16July02
Avery, P. N.(*H*) 2Apr.04
p. Layton, A. B. ⊕
        17Sept.04
p. Monks, F. R. 17July12
p.s.Fairclough, Egerton
        18Sept.12
p.s.Woods, M. 18Apr.14

Lieutenants. (8)

McClure, W. 1Feb.09
Whittle, O. L. 1Feb.09
Fairclough, Eric
        1Feb.09
(p.)Henshall, L. S. 1June09
(p.)Townroe, B. S. 1Nov.11
Skinner, A. 1Sept.12
Jones, A. S. 18Apr.14

2nd Lieutenants. (8)

Robertson,C.H.29July11
Frost, E. L. 1Nov.12
Dickson, B. T. 1Feb.13

Adjutant.

Izod, K. W., Lt.
  N. Lan. R., *capt.*
        1Nov.13

Quarter-Master.

✗ Ingram, G. H.,
  hon. lt. 4May11

Medical Officer.

p. Adams, J., M.B.,
  VD,*Surg.-Maj.*18Oct.02
        22Sept.88

Chaplain.

Bracecamp, Rev. W.,
  Chapl. 3rd Class
  (T.F.) (*attd.*) 4July13
        4July08

[Uniform—*Scarlet.*
Facings—*White.*]

5th Battalion.

"South Africa, 1900-01,"

Drill Hall, St. Helens.

Lt.-Colonel.

p. ✗Pilkington L. E.
  (*Hon. Lt. in Army*
  10 *July* 01) 9Nov.12

Majors. (2)

p. Bates, D. (*t*) 21June08
  Pilkington, W. N.
        10Nov.12

Captains. (8)

p. Caldwell, J. 20May08
p. Evans, A. L. (*t*) 18July08
p. Willcocks, A. C. (*t*)
        21June08
p. Nash, R. P. (*t*)(*H*)
        1July08
p. Lackland, L. (Q)
        8July11
p.s.Taylor,W.A.(q)⊕
        11July11
p.s.Stannard, W. L.(*t*)
        10Oct.11
p. Calland, R. 13June12
p.s.Pilkington, G. R.
        10Nov.12

Lieutenants. (8

p. Schultz, A. H. (*t*)
        1July08
p.s.Heaton, W. 7Sept.10
(p.s.)MacPhail, A. J.
        14June11
(p.s.)Dickinson, J. H.
        21Oct.11
p.s.O'Connor, J. 21Oct.11
Tennant, J. 26Oct.11
Crooks, F. ⊕ 13June12
Aukland, D. 10Nov.12
Gould, M.L.B. 22Apr.14

2nd Lieutenants. (8)

Cooper, J. A. 9May12
Cook, R. N. 9May12
Dowling, J. H. 10May12
Bullock, S. C. 20Sept.12
Lewis, A. 29Mar.13
Milligan, R. 29Mar.13
Weeks, R. M. 14June13

Adjutant.

✗Dick,J.C.,Capt.
  R. Muns. Fus.
        13May11

Quarter-Master.

Dolan, E.,*hon. lt.*1Jan.11

Medical Officers.

✗Tough, Capt. F.W.K.,
  F.R.C.S. (*Edin.*)
  R.A.M.C (T.F.)
  (*attd.*) 1Oct.11
        1Apr.08

[Uniform—*Green.*
Facings—*Scarlet.*]

THE WELSH REGIMENT.

Regimental District No. **41**. [No. **4** District.]

The Rose and Thistle on the same stalk, within the Garter. In the first and fourth corners the Royal Cypher ensigned with the Imperial Crown, in the second and third corners the Plume of the Prince of Wales.
"*Gwell angau na Chywilydd.*"
A Naval Crown, superscribed "12th April 1782."
"Martinique, 1762," "St. Vincent," "India," "Bourbon," "Java," "Detroit," "Queenstown," "Miami," "Niagara," "Waterloo," "Ava," "Candahar, 1842," "Ghuznee, 1842," "Cabool, 1842," "Alma," "Inkerman," "Sevastopol," "Relief of Kimberley," "Paardeberg," "South Africa, 1899-1902."

Regular and Special Reserve Battalions.

Uniform—Scarlet. *Facings*—White. *Agents*—Messrs. Cox & Co.

1st Bn. (41st Foot)	.. .. *Chakrata.*	
2nd ,, (69th ,,)	.. .. *Bordon, Hants.*	3rd Bn. (R. Glamorgan Mil.) .. *Cardiff.*
Depôt	*Cardiff.*	Record Office .. .. *Shrewsbury.*

Territorial Force Battalions.

4th Bn.	.. *Carmarthen.*	6th Bn. .. .. *Swansea.*
5th ,, ...	.. *Pontypridd.*	7th ,, ... li, *Newport Road, Cardiff.*

Colonel .. .. ₡. Allan, Maj.-Gen. W., ret. pay [R] 1Jan.04

1st and 2nd Battalions.

Lt.-Colonels. (2)
1Marden, T. O., *p.s.c.*
[l]   30Dec.12
2Morland, C. B.
                    22Mar.14

Majors. (8)
2Pritchard, O. B.
                    9Mar.08
(3) 2Span, H. J. B.
 (*Comdg. Depôt*)22May07
1Prothero, A. G.
                    24Sept.07
s. Ready, B. T. 26Sept.08
1Crocker, B. E. 9Jan.09
1Hoggan, G. P. 8Sept.09
1Toke, R. T. [l] [F]
                    22Mar.10
1Kerrich, J. H. 22Mar.14

Captains. (14)
(2) *Robins,* L. I. O. 16Oct.01
s. *Derry, A.,* D.S.O.
                    9Mar.02
c.o.Stevenson, G. H.
                    1June03
2Moore, W.A.G. 10Mar.04
2Ferrar, W. H., *Adjt.*
 [F]   26Mar.04
2Berkeley, C. R., *D.S.O.*
                    13May04
t. Mathias, T. G. 30Dec.04
1Broughton, G. D.
 p.s.o., o.   20May08
                    10May05
e.a.*Pridham, G. F.* 14Apr.06
t. *Vernon Harcourt, B. F.*
                    14Apr.06
r. *Lloyd, H. C. L.* 11July06
(3) 1Packe, F. E. 13Dec.06
1Torbution, C. C.
                    9Oct.07
1 *Willcox, E. L.,* Adjt.
                    25July08
(2) *Stevens, H. L.* 9Feb.10
                    4Nov.08

Captains—contd.
2Haggard, M.   1Jan.11
1Hobbs, A.H.   15May11
2Powell, P.L.W. 15May11
1Westby, E. H. H.
                   15May11
1Montgomery, R. H.
                  29July11
(3)2Hore, W. M. 1Apr.12
t. Partridge, J. E. C.
                  10Apr.12
2Rees, H. C.   12June12
2Graham, C. P. 22Jan.13
                  28July09
f.c. Picton-Warlow, V.
                   7June13
f.c. Longcroft, C. A. H.
                  13Aug.13
bt. maj. 12 Iune14
(3) 1Gwyer, C. P. 13Aug.13
f.c.Todd, G. E. 14Aug.13
t. Linton, F. H. 14Aug.13
2Lyttelton,A. G. 14Aug.13

Lieutenants. (20)
s.s.Diokinson, D. P.
                   25July08
2Evans, W. S. 26Sept.08
1Marshall, T. B. S.
                    3May10
2Carleton, C. A. S.
                   25May10
2Melville, G. D. 25May10
(3) 1Gransmore,F. W.
                   25May10
2Somerset, *Hon.* W.
                    8Dec.10
1Phillips, L.   1Jan.11
1Lloyd, G. A.   1Apr.11
s. *Huntington,*
      H. F. S.   1Apr.11
2Gilbey, J. N. 15May11
1Salmon, L. M. B.
                   29July11
(3) 2Walker, H. N. 16Aug.11
1Evan-Jones, H, G.
                   20Nov.11
1Phillips, B. T. 23Nov.11
1Brewis, G. S. 1Apr.12
1Pope, R. T.   16July12
1Monk, G. P. de B.
                    1Oct.12
1Egerton, G.W. 3Aug.13
1Dundas, D. C. H. 13Aug.13
1Whitehorne, A. C.
                   14Aug.13
2Whitty, R. X. 14Aug.13

2nd Lieutenants. (12)
1Douglas, E. M. 11Oct.11
2Partridge, G.D.11Oct.11
2Richards, E. I. G.
                   19Jan.12
1Davis, H. W. W.
                    14Feb.12
1Lomax, C. E. N.,4Sept.12
2Daniel, J. A. 4Sept.12
1Wells, F. I. P. 5Feb.13
2Owen, W.   24May13
2Corder, H. G. A.
                   l78ept.13
2Hambrough, B.T.V.B.
                   10Dec.13
2Ford, F. W.   4Feb.14
(2) Hewett, W. G. 25Feb.14
      Adjutants.
1 Willcox, E.L., *capt.*
                   28Junell
2Ferrar, W. H., *capt.*
                   2June13

Quarter-Masters.
r. Sprent. T. M.,   6Apr.04
     hon. capt, 6Apr.14
1Holt, A., *hon. lt.*
                    2July10
2Hill, R. M., *hon. lt.*
                   16Apr.13

Special Reserve.
Lieutenant.
✗Wavell, A. J. B.,
 late Lt. Welsh R.
                   31Dec.09
    FitzR.   18Jan.11

2nd Lieutenants.
Wootton, W. T.
  (*on prob.*)   7Jan.14
Vincent, J. T. C.
  (*on prob.*) 25Feb.14

3rd Battalion.

(*Officers serving on* 8Mar.02
*in the corresponding
Militia unit hold honorary
Army rank equivalent to
the Militia regimental
rank they then held. Other
officers entitled to honorary Army rank have
it shown against their
names*).

Hon. Colonel.
Plymouth, Rt. Hon.
  R.G., Earl of, C.B.
                   12July08
                   26Feb.96

Lt.-Colonel.
p.s.✗Marwood-Elton, W.
  (H)   2Apr.13

Major.
r.c. Snan, H.J.B. 22May07
p.s.✗Pope, E. A. (Q)(H)
                    2Apr.13

Captains. (5)
p.s.✗Latham, F. P., *hon.m.*
                   29Nov.09
p.s.✗Masterman, W. S.
  (H)   3May01
p.s.✗Herd, H. F.(H)(g)(a)
                   14May04
p.s.✗Kelsey, R. N. (H)
                   22Apr.05
*r.e.*Packe, F. E. 13Dec.06
r.e. Hore, W. M.   1Apr.12
*r.e.*Gwyer, C. P. 13Aug.13

Lieutenants. (11)
p. Fitzpatrick, G. R.
                   1Aug.09
r.e. Gransmore, F. W.
                   25May10
r.e. Walker, H. N. 16Aug.11
Cornelius, C. V. P.
                    5Dec.12

2nd Lieutenants. (8)
Birch, G. O.   2July13
Cocks, J. J. C.
  (*on prob.*) 21Mar.14

Adjutant.
✗Lloyd, H. C. L.,
  Capt. Welsh R.
                   27Feb.12
(*Capt. in Army* 11July06)

Quarter-Master.
Sprent, T. M., *hon. capt.*

THE WELSH REGIMENT—(Regtl. Dist. No. 41)—contd.

4th Battalion.

"South Africa, 1900-02."
Carmarthen.

Hon. Colonel.

※ⒸⒸ, ⒻⓁ. Hills-
Johnes, Lt.-Gen.
Sir J., G.C.B.
[R]   40ct.05

Lt.-Colonel.

p.s.Beddoe, A. F., VD,
(t) ⓒ   14June11

Majors. (2)

Jones, W. J.   10July12
p. Jones, W. B.   14Aug.12

Captains. (8)

p.s. Adams, J. L., TD.
   (H)   8June06
p. Williams, J. L. H.
                    6Apr.07
p.s. Lloyd, J.   4Apr.09
p.s. Bowen, A. L. 1May09
p.s. ※de Rees, J. F.
   (Hon.Lt.in Army
28Dec.02)(H) 2 Apr.12
p.s. Williams, J. R. (H)
                    2 Apr. 12
p.s. Howard, A. H. 5Oct.12
Roderick, H.B. 5Oct.12

Lieutenants. (8)

(p.s.)Bowling, W. R.
                    20Oct.08
(p.s.)Lowless, N. D. 1May09
Lewis, D. J.   14June11
John, H. E.   2Apr.12
Waddell, J. D.   30Dec.12
Griffith, R. J.   21Feb.13
                   11Aug.13
Williams, A. S.   8June13
Green, H. M.   21Jan.14

2nd Lieutenants. (8)

Dudley, W. L.   17Feb.12
Jones, H. P.   1May 12
Jones, J. D.   1 Mar.13
Jones, I. R. G.   5Apr.13
Jones, H. W. G.
                   17Apr.13
Lewis, J.   1May13
Phillips, C. A.   7June13
Williams, H. W. D.
                   15Aug.13

Adjutant.

Linton, F. H.,
   Capt. Welsh R.
                   16Oct.12

Quarter-Master.

Margrave, L., Qr.-
   Mr. (hon. lt.) ret.
   pay (Res. of Off.)
   hon. lt.   19July13

Medical Officers.

p. Evans, E., M.B., TD,
   Surg.-Maj. (Hon.
   Surg.-Lt.-Col.)
                   18Sept.02
p. Hughes, Capt. D. A.,
   R.A.M.C.   (T.F.)
   (attd.)   28July11
                   20July01
p. Williams, Capt. W.
   R.E.,MB.,R.A.M.C.
   (T.F.) (attd.) 11Oct.11
   Dick, Lt. A., R.A.M.C.
   (T.F.) (attd.) 2Dec.08

Chaplains.

Bowen, Rev. Canon
   D., B.A., TD,
   Chapl. 1st Class
   (T.F.) (attd.) 4Apr.08
                   4Apr.88
Jenkyns, Rev. E. T.,
   B.A., Chapl. 3rd
   Class (T.F.)(attd.)
                   4Feb.09
                   4Feb.99
Parry, Rev. A. W.,
   Chapl. 4th Class
   (T.F.) (attd.) 1July13
[Uniform—Scarlet.
Facings—White.]

5th Battalion.

"South Africa, 1900-02."
Pontypridd.

Hon. Colonel.

Aberdare, H. C.,
   Lord, W. (Hon.
   Lt.-Col, ret. Vols).
                   1Jan.10

Lt.-Colonel.

Morgan, M., VD, ⓒ
                   17Apr.12

Majors. (2)

Phillips, W. D., TD
                   1Apr.10
Gray, F. N. ⓒ 17 Apr. 12

Captains. (8)

p. Dowdeswell, W.
                   23Aug.05
p. Harris, D.   10Oct.06
p.s.Evans, G. A.   18Sept.07
   (H)
Southey, H. H. W.
                   4Jan.11
Robathan, D. P.
   (H)   1July14
Evans, T. A.   1July14
Evans, R. T.   1July14

Lieutenants (8)

Mander, A. O.   5Jan.11
Dowdeswell, T. R.
                   14Feb.12
Leigh, H. V.   1July14
Sandbrook, R. S.
                   1July14

2nd Lieutenants. (8)

Williams, R. L.
                   26 Apr.12
Williams, F. E.   16July12
Jones, I.   23Oct.12
Morgan, E. A.   26Feb.13
Beith, G. R. M.   22Apr.13
Evans, W, D.R.   27May13
Machon, G. C. S.
                   13June13
Phillips, T. G. I.
                   16June13
Osborne, H. E.   4June14
Llewellyn, M. H.
                   28June14

Adjutant.

Mathias, T. G.,
   Capt. Welsh R.
                   6May13

Quarter-Master.

※Evans, R. W.,
   hon. lt.   21Oct.13

Medical Officers.

p. Morgan, R. D.,
   Surg.-Capt.   1Aug.05
                   21May02
p. Cory, E. J. T.,
   M.D., Surg.-
   Capt.   1Apr.08
                   25June04

Chaplains.

Williams, Rev. F. R.,
   B.A., Chapl. 4th
   Class (T.F.) (attd.)
                   1Apr.08
                   25 Mar.05
Davies, Rev. B. T.,
   M.A., Chapl. 4th
   Class (T.F.) (attd.)
                   1Apr.08
                   12Aug.07
[Uniform—Scarlet.
Facings—White.]

6th (Glamorgan) Battalion.

"South Africa, 1900-02."
Swansea.

Lt.-Colonel

Crichton-Stuart, Lord
   N.E. (Lt. Res. of Off.)
                   8Mar.11

Majors. (2)

Thomas, J. E., VD,
   (t)   20July12
Morgan, E. M. S.
   (b)   13Dec.13

Captains. (8)

p.s.Clark, S. S., TD,
   hon. m.   2June06
p.s. Pollard, J. M. 25May07
p.s. Perry, C. (H) ⓒ 9Apr.09
p.s. Browning, R. G. S.
   (H) I. of M.   15May09
Prichard, J. S.   4Dec.12
Gibbon, J. R. (H)
                   13Dec.13

Lieutenants. (8)

Cann, H. D.   8Nov.10
Goldberg, J. M.
                   28 Apr.12
Hinton, F.A.S.   18Mar.13
                   21Apr.12

2nd Lieutenants (8)

Bevan, T. S.   28June11
Parry, T. H.   23Mar.12
Harries, H. J.   4Oct.12
Williams, D. H.   9Oct.12
Lewis, H. T.   12Apr.13
Hawkins, H.C.   14Dec.13
Langer, C.   15Dec.13
Fletcher, H.   23Apr.14

Inst. of Musk.

Browning, R. G. S.,
   capt.   27Apr.10

Adjutant.

Frisby, H. G. F.,
   Capt. Hamps. R.
                   4Mar.12

Quarter-Master.

p. Thomas, L., hon.
   m.   2May00
   capt. 2Jan.97

Medical Officers.

Isaac, Lt. C. L.,
   R.A.M.C.(T.F.)
   (attd.)   3Apr.12
                   12July05
Warren, Lt. P. T.,
   R.A.M.C. (T.F.)
   (attd.)   9June13

Chaplains.

Morgan, Rev. W.,
   B.A., Chapl. 4th
   Class   (T.F.)
   (attd.)   1Apr.08
                   20June00
Thomas, Rev. D. H.,
   [B.C.] Chapl. 4th
   Class (T.F.) (attd.),
                   28July08
Jones, Rev. J. H. W.,
   Chapl. 4th Class
   (T.F.) (attd.) 1May12
[Uniform—Scarlet.
Facings—White.]

THE WELSH REGIMENT.—(Regtl. Dist. No. 41)—contd.

7th (Cyclist) Battalion.

1, Newport Road, Cardiff.

Hon. Colonel.
p.s. *Vivian*, Sir *A. P.*,
K.C.B., VD, Col.
27Nov.95

Lt.-Colonel.

Hunter, M. H. 31Mar.14

Major,

Captains. (8)

Rankin, D. J.
(H) 1Feb.11
Green, E. E.(H) 1Jan.12
Bagley, E. H. 3June14

Lieutenants. (5)

(p.)Shaw, C. A 1June09
Stuart, J. D. 15July13
Hesketh, S. 4Jan.14

2nd Lieutenants. (4)

Hammond, A. T.
11Dec.12
Foot, J. S. 29Mar.13
Wride, H. M. 24Apr.13
Jones, H. V. E.
21Dec.13
Gay, L. J. A. 15Jan.14
Petri, C. R. 9June14

Adjutant.

✗Partridge, J. E. C.,
Capt. Welsh R.
13Aug.13

Quarter-Master.

✗Wildig, T., Qr.-Mr.
(*hon. capt.*), ret.
pay (*Res. of Off.*),
hon. capt. 8Dec.13

Medical Officers.

Costello, Lt. J, M. A.,
M.B., R.A.M.C.(T.F.)
(*attd.*) 18Mar.11
✗Rogers, Lt. W.,
M.D., R.A.M.C.
(T.F.) (*attd.*) 18Feb.12

Chaplain.

Davies, *Rev.* D. *M.A.*,
Chapl. 4th Class
(T.F.) (*attd.*) 20Aug.09

[Uniform—*Green*.
Facings—*Scarlet*.]

THE BLACK WATCH (ROYAL HIGHLANDERS).
Regimental District No. 42. [No. 1 District.]

The Royal Cypher within the Garter. The badge and motto of the Order of the Thistle. In each of the four corners the Royal Cypher ensigned with the Imperial Crown.
The Sphinx, superscribed "Egypt."

"Guadaloupe, 1759," "Martinique, 1762," "Havannah," "North America, 1763-64." "Mangalore," "Mysore," "Seringapatam," "Corunna," "Busaco," "Fuentes d'Onor," "Pyrenees," "Nivelle," "Nive," "Orthes," "Toulouse," "Peninsula," "Waterloo," "South Africa, 1846-7, 1851-2-3," "Alma," "Sevastopol," "Lucknow." "Ashantee, 1873-4," "Tel-el-Kebir," "Egypt, 1882, 1884," "Kirbekan," "Nile, 1884-85," "Paardeberg," "South Africa, 1899-1902."

Regular and Special Reserve Battalions.
Uniform—Scarlet. *Facings*—Blue. *Agents*—Messrs. Cox & Co.

1st Bn. (42nd Foot)	.. Aldershot.	3rd Bn. (R. Perth Mil.)	.. .. .. Perth
2nd „ (73rd Foot)	.. Bareilly.		
Depôt	.. .. Perth.	Record Office	.. .. Kinnoull Street, Perth.

Territorial Force Battalions.
4th Bn.	Drill Hall, Dundee.	6th Bn.	Tay Street, Perth
5th „	Arbroath.	7th „	St. Andrews.

Allied Regiment of Canadian Militia.
5th Regiment "Royal Highlanders of Canada." .. .. .. *Montreal, Quebec.*

Allied Regiment of Australian Commonwealth.
1st Battalion New South Wales Scottish Rifle Regiment .. .. *Sydney, N.S. Wales.*

Colonel-in-Chief .. .. THE KING.
Colonel .. Maxwell Lt.-Gen. Sir J. G., K.C.B., C.V.O., C.M.G., D.S.O. (R) .. 11Jan.14

1st and 2nd Battalions.

Lt.-Colonels. (2)
2Campbell, W. MacL., M.V.O. 25Feb.11
1Grant Duff, A., C.R., p.s.c. [t] 24May14

Majors. (8)
2Stewart, C. E. 15Jan.08
s. Cameron, A. R., p.s.c. 13June08
29Nov.00
(3) 1Hamilton, J. G. H., D.S.O. (Comdg. Depôt) 29Jan.09
s. Marindin, A. H., p.s.c. [L] 24May10
e.a. Harvey, W. J. St. J. [B] 5Oct.10
2Sutherland, H. H. 2Dec.10
{ 1Murray, J.T.C. 25Feb.11
w. 1Stewart-Murray, Lord G. 24May14

Captains. (14)
2Wauchope, A. G., D.S.O. 30Oct.01
1Amery, H. F. S., p.s.c. [L] [F] 17Apr.02
s. Urquhart, E. F. M. 17Apr.02
m.c. Eden, S. H. 13June03
2Robertson, F. M.B. 8Dec.03
t. Innes, S. A. 12Dec.04
2MacLeod, G. C. S. 10June08
22Aug.05
t. Grant-Suttie, G. D. 7Nov.05
1Drummond, Hon. M. C. A. 15Feb.06
s.o. Hore-Ruthven, Hon. C. M., D.S.O. 1May06
r. Bulloch, R. A. 7May06
t. Gordon, C. W. E. 24May06

Captains—contd.
s.o. Evans, L. P. 27Oct.06
(3) 2Lamb, C. C. 8Nov.06
1Green, W. 9Nov.06
(3) 2West, G. A. 2Jan.07
t. Tarleton, F. R. 15May09
m.c. Baillie-Hamilton, N. A. B. 1Oct.09
2Murray, H. F. F. 1Oct.09
2Campbell, B. 8Jan.10
d. 1Dalgliesh, C. A. de G. 8Jan.10
2Henderson, C. R. B., Adjt. 23Apr.10
(3) 1Campbell, K.J. 10Oct.10
s. Wavell, A. P., p.s.c. [L] 20Mar.13
s.o. Kedie, W.T.[L] 20Mar.13
2Forrester, R. E. 4Feb.14
1Krook, A. D. C. 2May14
1Henderson, N. G. B. 16May14
2Strahan, C. E. 21May14
s. Wallace, R. F. H., 24May14
1Skene, P.G.M. 24May14

Lieutenants. (19)
1Allan, W. D. 15July06
1Fortune, V. M. 8Nov.06
1Rowan-Hamilton, G. B., Adjt. 9Nov.06
1Chalmer, F. G. 23Jan.07
t. Bowes-Lyon, G. F. 21Apr.07
f.o. Borton, A. E. 28Nov.07
m. Sprot, J. W. L. 2Jan.09
t. Cruden, J. W. F. 8Jan.10
o.o. Ewing, J. L. S. 23Apr.10
1Anderson, F. 20June10
o.o. Warrand, A. St. J. M. 6Aug.10
(3) 1Holt, A. V. 18Sept.10
(3) 2McLeod, A. K. 1Apr.11
2Orr-Ewing, H. E. D. 19Aug.11
2Inglis, J. N. 25Sept.11
2Hamilton-Johnston, D. C. 14Feb.12
2Durie, J. A. 1Apr.12
1Anstruther, R. E. 10Apr.12

Lieutenants—contd.
c.o. Mackintosh, D. B. 28May12
1Anderson, R. C. 20Mar.13
2Denison, A. C. 14May13
s. Sutherland, A. H. C. 27Apr.14
1Rycroft, J. N. O. 28Apr.14
2Gilroy, K. R. 2May14
s. Willcocks, J. L. 16May14
1Wilson, E. H. H. J. 16May14
1Cumming, L. R. 21May14
1Edwards, W. H. C. 24May14

2nd Lieutenants. (12)
1Polson, G. W. 28Sept.11
1Rennie, J. L. 4Sept.12
2MacLeod, I. B. 4Sept.12
1Rollo, J. E. H. 4Dec.12
2Buist, S. 17Sept.13
2McMicking, N. 17Sept.13
2Stewart, W. D. MacL. 2Jan.14
2Boyd, N. J. L. 25Feb.14
2Don, R. G. 13May14
2Blair, P. E. A. 10June14
2MacRae, K. S. 10June14

Adjutants.
1Rowan-Hamilton, G. B., lt. 25Sept.11
2Henderson, C. R. B., capt. 5Jan.13

Quarter-Masters.
r. Linning, J. 26Aug.96
hon. maj. 26Aug.11
2Anderson, J., hon. lt. 28Sept.11
1Fowler, W., hon. lt. 14Jan.11

Special Reserve.
2nd Lieutenant.
McNeill, N. (on prob.) 8July14
Murdoch, T. F. (on prob.) 22July14

3rd Battalion.

(*Officers serving on 4Dec.00 in the corresponding Militia unit hold honorary Army rank equivalent to the Militia regimental rank they then held. Other officers entitled to honorary Army rank have it shown against their names.*)

Hon. Colonel.
Atholl, J. J. H. H., Duke of, K.T. 26July05
8July03

Lt.-Colonel.
×Clarke-Campbell-Preston, R. W. P. 17Feb.12

Major.
r.e. ×Hamilton, J. G. H., D.S.O. 29Jan.09
p.s. Dennistoun, A. H. O. 20Mar.12

Captains. (5)
p.s. Graham Stirling, C. H. 20Jan.94
p.s. Murray, Hon. A. D. 14July05
p.s. ×Stewart-Richardson, Sir E. A., Bt. (H) 7Feb.00
Murray, Hon. R. T. G. 19Dec.03
r.e. ×Moubray, P. L. 7May04
r.e. ×Lamb, C. C. 8Nov.04
r.e. ×West, C. C. 2Jan.07
×Boddam-Whetham, C., Capt. ret. pay (H) 14Sept.08
×Campbell, D. F., D.S.O., Capt. ret. pay 13July10
r.e. ×Campbell, K. J. 1Oct.10
×Parker, A. E., Capt. ret. pay 27Jan.12

THE BLACK WATCH (ROYAL HIGHLANDERS)—(Regtl. Dist. No. 42)—contd.

3rd Bn.—contd.

Lieutenants. (11)

p.s. Macnaghten, A. C. R. S. 19Dec.03
(p.s.) Cox, T. H. C. 18June04
Nolan, R. P. D. 2Apr.10
Bowes-Lyon, C. L. C. 2Apr.10
r.e. Holt, A. V. 13Sept.10
r.e. McLeod, A. K. 1Apr.11
Tate, A. W., late 2nd Lt. Sco. Rif. 6Jan.12
Campbell, P. K. 7Mar.13
Graham, N. 7Mar.13
Thistle, T. H. C. 7Mar.13
Maxwell, R. S. S. 19June14

2nd Lieutenants. (8)

Lumsden, D. 23Apr.13
Cooke, D. (on prob.) 21Mar.14

Adjutant.

✗Bulloch, R. A., Capt. R. Highrs. 1Jan.13
(Capt.in Army 7 May06)

Quarter-Master.

✗Linning, J., hon.maj.

4th (City of Dundee) Battalion.

"South Africa, 1900-02."

Drill Hall, Dundee.

Hon. Colonel.

The Lord Provost of Dundee for the time being.

Lt.-Colonel.

Walker, H., TD, (Q) (H) 13Mar.10

Majors. (2)

✗Tosh, E. (Hon. Lt. in Army 17June01) 18Dec.09
Muir, J. B. ⊕ (H) 16July12

Captains. (8)

p.s. Boase, E.L. (H) 10Jan.07
p. Walker, N. C. (H) 19Aug.09
Duncan, J. O. 25Oct 12
Moon, F. W. 19June14
Campbell, E.V. 12June14
Moodie, O. S. 12June14
Duncan, P. F. 12June14

Lieutenants. (8)

Gowans, S. B. 27Oct.09
Rettie, J. L. 25Jan.12
Couper, C. M. 22Feb.13
McIntyre, R.W.22Feb.13
Gray, W. B. 12June14
Robertson, W. L. 12June14
Stewart, A. J. 12June14

2nd Lieutenants. (8)

Law, I. MacK. 24Jan.12
Fraser, C. 24Jan.12
Gladstone, B. H. 30Jan.13
Miller, K. L. 30Jan.13
Robertson, J. W. H. 15Dec.13
Steven, S. H. 20Apr.14
Shepherd,D.M.20Apr.14
Sherriff, C. B. 30Apr.14

Adjutant.

✗Tarleton, F. R., Capt. R. Highrs. 5Feb.13

Quarter-Master.

✗McLachlan, D., hon. lt. 1Aug.10

Medical Officers.

p. Rogers, Maj. J. S. Y., M.B.,R.A.M.C.(T.F.) (attd.) 5Dec.07
  Whyte, Maj. G. F., M.B., R.A.M.C. (T.F.) (attd.) 7Nov.12
  17Apr.01
p. Thornton, Capt. R., R.A.M.C. (T.F.) (attd.) 8Feb.06
  25Jan.02

Chaplains.

Fergusson, Rev. A. W., B.D. [C.S.] Chapl. 4th Class (T. F.) (attd.) 15May12
McConnachie, Rev. J., M.A. [U.F.C.] Chapl. 4th Class (T.F.) (attd.) 18May12
[Uniform—Scarlet Facings—Blue.]

5th (Angus & Dundee) Battalion.

"South Africa, 1900-02."

Arbroath.

Hon. Colonel.

Strathmore and Kinghorne, C. G., Earl of 22Oct.04

Lt.-Colonel.

✗Scrymgeour-Wedderburn, H., late Capt. Gord. Highrs. 38ept.09

Majors. (2)

Glamis, P., Lord (Lt. Res. of Off.) 1Jan.10
p. Nicoll, P. S., TD 29July11

Captains. (8)

p. Dickson, J. F. jun., VD, hon. m. 22Mar.90
p. Malcolm, A. 2May00
p. Cruickshank, J., jun. 29Jan.02
p. ✗Rae, G. S. (Hon. Lt. in Army 20Sept.02) 7Nov.03
p. Guthrie, T. M., (t) 31Mar.06
p. Duncan, J. D. 5May06
p.s. Watt, A. L. (q) (H) (b) 18Nov.07
p. McNab, J. B. 29July11
p.s. Wilson, J. A. 20Jan.12
  late Lt. North'd Fus. 27Apr 12
  Wilkie, D. 6June12
  Mitchell, W. L. ⑧ 6Dec.13

Lieutenants. (8)

p. Coutts, F. 22Nov.05
  Lyell, T., (H) I. of M. 1July10
  Duke, J. McP. S. 1July10
  Arbuthnott, H. E. C. ⑧ 27Apr.12
  Wedderburn, A.H.M. 26July13
  Duke, A. W. 26July13
  Bruce, R. F. D. 26 July13
  Taylor, N. R. 1Mar.14

2nd Lieutenants. (8)

Aubertin, T. 24Dec.12
Gordon, J. W. N. 19July13
Pithie, D. 18Oct.13
McCabe, R. B. 18Oct.13
Bruce-Gardyne, L. M. 14Dec.13
Murray, J. 24Jan.14
Campbell, J. H. 19June14
Adam, G. M. 20June14

Inst. of Musk.

Lyell, T., lt. 18Apr.14

Adjutant.

Bowes-Lyon, G. F., Lt. R. Highrs., capt. 2Jan.14

Quarter-Master.

✗Hall, A., hon. lt. 15Mar.13

Medical Officer.

Morris, Lt. J. A., M.B., R.A.M.C. (T.F.) (attd.) 11July12
Thomson, Lt. J. E. G., M.B., R.A.M.C. (T.F.) (attd.) 27Dec.13

Chaplains.

Watt, Rev. H.G., D.D. [C.S.] Chapl. 3rd Class (T.F.) (attd.) 30Oct.95
Coats, Rev. W. W., D.D. [C.S.] Chapl. 4th Class (T.F.) (attd.) 1Apr.08
  22Oct.04
Stirton, Rev. J., B.D. [C.S.] Chapl. 4th Class (T.F.) (attd.) 1Apr.08
  16Aug.05
Tweedie, Rev. J. A., [U.F.C.] Chapl. 4th Class (T.F.) (attd.) 1May11
Cameron, Rev. D., B.D. [U.F.C.] Chapl. 4th Class (T.F.) (attd.) 1May11
[Uniform—Scarlet Facings—Blue.]

6th (Perthshire) Battalion.

"South Africa, 1900-02."

Tay Street, Perth.

Hon. Colonel.

p. Moncrieffe, Sir R. D., Bt., VD, Col. A.D.C. (ret. T.F.) late Lt. S. Gds. ⑧ 14Jan.14

Lt.-Colonel.

p.s. Campbell, D. C., VD 21June11

Majors. (2)

p. Colville, C. E., VD, hon. l.c. ⊕ (H) (b) 8June07
Murray-Stewart, C. 31Aug.11

Captains. (8)

p. Wylie, J. (H) 2Mar.06
p. Gibson, L. 7July06
p. Alexander, W. 8Sept.06
p.s. Pullar, G. D. (H) 17Apr.07
p. Young, T. E. 30Sept.09
  Brett, Hon. M.V.B., M.V.O., late Capt. C. Gds. 8Feb.11
p. Innes, A. 28Apr.12
p.s. Gordon, R. G. (A) 11Feb.13
  17July08

Lieutenants (8).

p.s. Strathairn, D. B., (H) (Asst. Dist. Commr., Gold Coast, 23Sept.12) 14June05
p.s. MacRosty, J., (H) 20Dec.06
  Hally, J. 18Nov.09
  Craig, J. 18Nov.09
  Gray, R. H. 31 Aug.11
  Marshall,S.H. 17Mar.12
  Campbell,W.P.10Sept12
  ✗Calder, D. B. 30Nov.13

2nd Lieutenants. (8)
Burgis, L. F. 1Mar.13
Ellis, R. B. 19July13

THE BLACK WATCH (ROYAL HIGHLANDERS)—(Regtl. Dist. No. 42)—contd.

th Bn.—contd.

Adjutant.
Oxley, R. D., Capt.
 Gord.Highrs.28Mar.14

Quarter-Master.
⚔Sadler, B., *hon. m.*
 31Mar.06

Medical Officers.
⚔Stirling, Maj. R.,
 M.D., TD, R.A.M.C.
 (T.F.) *(attd.)* 13Dec.05
 14June90
Haig, Maj. W., *M.B.,*
 R.A.M.C. (T.F.)
 (attd.) 19June12
 10Oct.00

Chaplains.
Muil, *Rev.* W. S., TD
 [U.F.C.] Chapl.
 2nd Class (T.F.)
 (attd.) 1Apr.08
 23Apr.92
Henderson, *Rev.*D.R.,
 M.A., TD, [C.S.]
 Chapl. 2nd Class
 (T.F.) *(attd.)* 28Sept.08
 28Sept.93
Ritchie, *Rev.* A., *B.D.*
 [C.S.] Chapl. 4th
 Class (T.F.) *(attd.)*
 1Apr.08
 21Mar.00
Clark, *Rev.* P. G.
 [U.F.C.], Chapl.
 4th Class (T.F.),
 (attd.) 1July09
Smith, *Rev.* H., *M.A.*
 [U.F.C.], Chapl.
 4th Class (T.F.),
 (attd.) 1Dec.09

[Uniform—*Scarlet,*
Facings—*Blue.*]

7th (Fife) Battalion.

"South Africa, 1900-02."

St. Andrews.

Hon. Colonel.
Anstruther, Sir R. W.,
 Bt., TD., (*Hon. Col.
 ret. T.F.*) 3Jan.14

Lt.-Colonel.
⚔Allen,H.M.,*D.S.O.,*
 Lt.-Col. ret. Ind.
 Army 16Nov.13

Majors. (2)
Robertson, J. W.,
 VD, 16July12
Wallace, R. (*t*) 24Nov.13

Captains (8)
p. MacDuff, P., TD,
 hon. m. 25Mar.98
p. Russell, R. 13June00
p. Macpherson, J. L.,
 TD, *hon. m.* 25Jan.02
p. Robertson, T. J.,
 TD (*H*) 5Oct.08
p.s. Guthrie, W. A. 5Oct.08
p.s. McIntosh, G. W.,
 20Dec.13
Wallace, F. T. 25June14

Lieutenants. (8)
p. Hendry, A. D. 17Apr.01
p. Maxwell, C. H.29Aug.06
p. Brown, W. B. 8Sept.06
p.s. Glen, J. F. (*H*) 25Mar.11
(p.s.) Aitken, G. 25July11
(p.s.) Gillespie, J. 10Jan.14
p.s. Smitton, C. D. 23May14

2nd Lieutenants. (8)
(p.s.) Barclay, W K.7Nov.06
Tullis, G. S. 5May09
p.s. ⚔Donaldson, J, (*t*)
 25Mar.11
 9Apr.07
Mathewson, W. G.
 19Oct.12
Graham, M. H. N.
 11Jan.13
Keir, D. R. 19July13
MacKintosh, H. C.
 16Feb.14
Westwood,A.C.20May14
Humphreys, H.
 J, 27May14

Adjutant.
⚔Baker-Carr, H. B. F.,
 Capt. Arg. & Suth'd
 Highrs. 13Sept.13

Quarter-Master.
⚔Studley, H., Qr.-Mr.
 (*hon. capt.*) ret. pay
 (*Res. of Off.*)
 hon. capt. 28Feb.12

Medical Officers.
p. ⚔Douglas,Lt. Col. C.E.
 M.D., F.R.C.S. Edin.,
 VD, R.A.M.C. (T.F.)
 (*Hon. Capt. in Army*
 27*Mar.*01) (*attd.*)
 18Oct.07
 26Feb.87
p. Dickson, Capt. D. E.,
 M.B., F.R.C.S.(*Edin.*),
 R.A.M.C.(T.F.)(*attd.*)
 1Apr.08
 20Feb.04

Chaplains.
Arnott,*Rev.*H.Y.,*B.D.,*
 [C.S.] Chapl. 2nd
 Class (T.F.) *(attd.)*
 4Sept.10
 4Sept.95
Playfair, *Rev.* P. M.,
 D.D. [C.S.] Chapl.
 3rd Class (T.F.)
 (attd.) 4Nov.09
 4Nov.99
Ray,*Rev.*J.,*M.A.*,[C.S.],
 Chapl. 4th Class
 (T.F.) *(attd.)* 1Apr.08
 22Apr.07
Miller, *Rev.*T. E., *M.A.*
 [U.F.C.] Chapl. 4th
 Class (T.F.) *(attd.)*
 1Mar.10
Todd, *Rev.* W., *M.A.*
 [U.F.C.] Chapl. 4th
 Class (T.F.) *(attd.)*
 1Mar.10

[Uniform—*Scarlet*
Facings—*Blue.*]

THE OXFORDSHIRE AND BUCKINGHAMSHIRE LIGHT INFANTRY.

Regimental District, No. **43**. [No. **7** District.]

The United Red and White Rose.
"Quebec, 1759," "Martinique, 1762," "Havannah," "Mysore," "Hindoostan," "Martinique, 1794," "Vimiera," "Corunna," "Busaco," "Fuentes d'Onor," "Ciudad Rodrigo," "Badajoz," "Salamanca," "Vittoria," "Pyrenees," "Nivelle," "Nive," "Orthes," "Toulouse," "Peninsula," "Waterloo," "South Africa, 1851-2-3," "Delhi, 1857," "New Zealand," "Relief of Kimberley," "Paardeberg," "South Africa, 1900-02."

Regular and Special Reserve Battalions.

Uniform—Scarlet. Facings—White. Agents—Messrs. Cox & Co.
1st Bn. (43rd Foot) .. .. .. Ahmednagar | 3rd Bn. (Oxford Mil.) .. .. Oxford.
2nd ,, (52nd Foot) .. .. .. Aldershot.

Depôt .. .. Oxford. | Record Office .. .. Warwick.

Territorial Force Battalions.
4th Bn. .. .. Oxford. | Buckinghamshire Bn. .. Aylesbury.

Allied Regiment of Canadian Militia.
52nd Regiment (Prince Albert Volunteers.) Prince Albert, Saskatchewan.

Allied Regiment of Dominion of New Zealand.
6th (Hauraki) Regiment.

Colonel			
ℳ.Colvile, Hon. Lt.-Gen. *Sir* F. M., *K.C.B.*, ret. pay [R] 14Sept.13			

1st and 2nd Battalions.

Lt.-Colonels. (2)
2Davies, H. R. 18Sept.11
1Lethbridge, E. A. E., *D.S.O.* 25Oct.13

Majors. (8)
2Ruck-Keene, H. L., *D.S.O.* 14Sept.07
(3) 2Darell-Brown, H. F. (*Comdg. Depôt*) 18Sept.07
1Cobb, C.H. 18Sept.07
1Hyde, A. C. 16Dec.08
2Eden, A. J. F. 18Sept.11
29Nov.00
s. Marriott Dodington, W., *p.s.c.* 28Oct.11
1Carter, L. J. 23June13
s. Pope-Hennessy,L.H.R., *D.S.O., p.s.c.* [*l*]
25Oct.13
26Mar.06

Captains. (14)
1Stapleton, F. H.,*p.s.c.* 11Sept.02
s. Clayton, E. R., *p.s.c.* 11Sept.02
r. Frith, C. H. 27Nov.02
1Forrest, C. E., *D.S.O.* 22Feb.08
t. Ballard, J. A. 28June08
1Henley, C. F. 30Oct.04
s.o.*Bayley,* A. G. 9Nov.04
f.c. *Brooke-Popham,* H. R. M., p.s.c.9Nov.04
bt. *maj,* 3June13
2Wood, H. L. 14Apr.05
s.c. Fuller, J. F. C. 21June05
w.a.*Keyworth,* R.D. 9Oct.05
*s. Weatherby,*J. T., p.s.c. 30Dec.05
2Sullivan, G. A. 28Dec.08
1 Brooke,R.R.M.28Dec.08
1Simpson, R.V. 28Dec.08
(3) 2Kirkpatrick, ℳ. H. 18Feb.09
(3)1Higgins,C.G.[*l*]18Feb.09
e.a.*Tunnard, L.* 23Jan.10

Captains—contd.
2Harden, A. H. 22Jan.10
e.a.*Pollock,* J. A. 22Jan.10
2Ponsonby, A. W. N. 22Jan.10
2Dillon, H. M. 17May10
(3) 1Logan, R. O. 19Nov.10
1Morland, W. E. T. 22Jan.14
o.c.*Parr,* B. C. 14Mar.14
s. Stephens, R. 14Mar.14
1Foljambe, Hon. J.C.W.S., *Adjt.* 14Mar.14
2Evelegh,R.C.D.[*l*]22Mar.14
t. Bartlett, *A. J. N.* 22Mar.14
f.c. *Bourke,* U.J.D. 18Apr.14
٠ Blewitt, G. 18Apr.14
2Beaufort, F. H.18Apr.14

Lieutenants. (19)
f.c.*Holt,* F. V. 11Jan.08
(3)1Sanderson,J.M. 29Jan.08
(3)2Carfrae,C.F.K.4Nov.08
1Whittall, G. E. 11Dec.08
o.o.*Portal,* J. L. 7Apr.09
2Crosse,R. B.,*Adjt.* 22Apr.09
s. Boyle, C. R. C. 19May09
2Terry, W. E. C. 4May10
1Tolson, W. G. 17May10
1Paget, B. C. T. 19Nov.10
2Worthington, R. G. 1Apr.11
1Powell, J. J. 24July11
1Plowden, G. F. 18Oct.12
1Davenport, F. M. 20Nov.12
1Courtis, J. H. 27Nov.12
2Southey, J. A. 25Feb.13
1Mundey, S. C. B. 17Apr.13
1Paris, A. C. M. 14Aug.13
2Baines, C 8. 8Oct.13
2Brett, R. J. 25Oct.13
1Wynter, F. C. W. 22Mar.14
2Owen, R.M. 18Apr.14
2Mockler-Ferryman,H. 27Apr.14

2nd Lieutenants. (12)
1Birch Reynardson, H. T. 19Jan.12
1Horan, K. 5Feb.13
2Pepys, F. 24May13
2Marshall, J. S. C. 17Sept.13
1Kearsley, J. S. 10Dec.13
2Tylden-Pattenson, A. D. 24Jan.14
2Newton-King, P. F. [*L*] 25Feb.14
1Girardot, P. C. 25Feb.14
Adjutants.
2Crosse, R.B., *lt.* 1Mar.13
1Foljambe, Hon. J. C. W. S., *capt.* 6May13
Quarter-Masters.
r. King, T. 24Nov.97
hon. *maj.* 24Nov.12
1Ivey, T. 22Sept.08
hon. *capt.* 22Sept.13
2Field, A. S. 12May09
26Feb.02
hon. *capt.* 26Feb.12

Special Reserve.
Captain.
Annesley, Hon. C. A. J., Lt. ret. pay 25Oct.13
2nd Lieutenants.
Barrington-Kennett, A. H. (*on prob.*) 5Apr.13
Button, G. T. (*H*) 4July14
16Nov.12

3rd Battalion.

(*Officers serving on* 3 *July* 01 in the corresponding Militia unit hold honorary Army rank equivalent to the Militia regimental rank they then held. Other officers entitled to honorary Army rank have it shown against their names.*)

Hon. Colonel.
ℳ.Marlborough, Rt. Hon. C. R. J., Duke of, K.G., TD. (*Lt.-Col. ret. T.F.*) 14June08

Lt.-Colonel.
Higgins Bernard, F. T. (*Q*) (*H*) 31Mar.12

Major.
p.s.Blyth, J., hon. l.c. (*H*) 5May06
p.s.Paske, G. F., hon. l.c. (*Hon. Capt. in Army* 2Nov.00) (*H*) 18Sept.06
r.e. ℳDarell-Brown, H. F. 18Sept.07

Captains. (5)
t. *Fitzwilliam,* W. C. de M., Earl, K.C.V.O., D.S.O., hon. *m.* (*Bt. Lt.-Col.* W. Rtd. R.H.A.) 11Apr.96
p.s.Barrington, Hon. W. R. S., hon. *m.* (*H*) 6Jan.91
North, A. K., *late* 2nd Lt.A.S.C. 4June02
Godsal, P. (*H*) 7June07
ℳCardwell, C. A., Capt ret. pay (*H*) ⓢ (Remount Service) 7Apr.0
Salkeld, R. E. (*Dist. Commr.,* E.Africa Prots. 12July06) 12July0
p.s.Dashwood, R. H. S., Capt. ret pay (*H*) ⓢ 1Dec.0
r.e.ℳKirkpatrick, E. H. 15Feb.0
r.e.ℳHiggins, C.G.[*l*] 15Feb.0
r.e.ℳLogan, R. O. 19Nov.1 Fitzgerald, O., Lt. ret. pay 8Mayl
Jackson, H. N., Lt. ret. pay 14Aug.1

THE OXFORDSHIRE AND BUCKINGHAMSHIRE LIGHT INFANTRY—(Regtl. Dist. No. 43)—contd

3rd Bn.—contd.

Lieutenants. (11)
Maul, H. C. (H) 12Sept.06
p.s. Tatton, R. H. G. (H) 12Sept.06
r.e. Sanderson, A. E. 29Jan.08
r.e. Carfrae, C. F. K. 4Nov.08
Turbutt, G. M. R. 5Mar.10
Spencer, A. V. (H) 5Mar.10

2nd Lieutenants. (8)
Smith, J. N. (Asst. Dist. Offr., N. Provs., Nigeria, {1Jan.14 {19Sept.10) 12July09
Humfrey, D. H. W. 2Dec.11
Fowke, C. A. F. 1Mar.12
Pendavis, H. V. 26Apr.13
Riddle, F. E. L. 1Oct.13
Hardcastle, J. B. (on prob.) 17June14

Adjutant.
⚔Frith, C. H., Capt. Oxf. & Bucks. L.I. 17Sept.12
(Capt. in Army 22Nov.02)

Quarter Master.
King, T., hon. maj.

4th Battalion.
"South Africa, 1900-01."
Oxford.

Hon. Colonel.
North, W. H. J., Lord, TD, late Lt. 1 L.G. 9Jan.95

Lt.-Colonel.
p. Stockton, A., TD, (H) 30Nov.09

Majors. (2)
p.s. Schofield, F. W. (H)(Q) 1Apr.08
p. Ovey, R. L. 30Nov.09

Captains. (8)
p.s. Rowell, R. R. S. 20Dec.05
p.s. Rose, D. M. (H) 20Dec.05
p.s. Fortescue, E. C. 1Apr.08
p.s. Fox, T. S. W. (H) 1Dec.09

Lieutenants. (8)
Dashwood, E.G. 24Dec.11
Hadden, E. W. R. 1Jan.13
Twisleton-Wykeham-Fiennes, Hon.
L. J. E. 1June13
Jones, F. B. 1Jan.14
Long, B. (H) 1Jan.14
Pickford, P. 1Jan.14
Treble, J. N. 21Jan.14

2nd Lieutenants. (8)
Taylor, F. W. (Jun. Supt., ¹ duon. Dept., Nigeria 17June14) 25July12
Jee, A. C. 1May13
Spikes, W. H. 1Nov.13
Vyner, C. J. S. 1Nov.13
Grisewood, A. A. 1Nov.13
Barton, C. J. 1Apr.14

Adjutant.
⚔Ballard, J. A., Capt. Oxf. & Bucks. L.I. 9May14

Quarter-Master.
p.s. ⚔Bridgewater, A. A., hon. m. 30Dec.05

Medical Officers.
Summerhayes, Lt. J. O. R.A.M.C. (T.F.) (attd.) (late Lt. 4 Bn. OxA & Bucks. L.I.) 28Feb.13
Gauntlett, Lt. H. L., R.A.M.C. (T.F.) (attd.) 1Apr.13

Chaplains.
Cary-Elwes, Rev. A., M.A., Chapl. 4th Class (T.F.) (attd.) 1Apr.08
14Mar.06
Smith, Rev. E. F., M.A., Chapl. 4th Class (T.F.) (attd.) 1Apr.08
28Mar.06

[Uniform—Scarlet. Facings—White.]

Cadet Units affiliated.
Cowley Cadet Corps.
Burford Grammar School Cadet Corps.

Buckinghamshire Battalion.
"South Africa, 1900-02."
Aylesbury.

Hon. Colonel.
Addington, E., Lord, VD (Hon. Col. ret. Vols.) 3Oct.08

Lt.-Colonel.
p.s. Fremantle, Hon. T. F., VD (T) (H) 24Mar.06
p. Wethered, F. O., VD 18Apr.14

Majors. (2)
Hooker, J. H. 17Oct.11
Chadwick, J., TD. 18Apr.14

Captains. (8)
p. ⚔Hawkins, L. C. (Hon. Lt. in Army 18June 01) 31Aug.01
p. Reynolds, L. L. C. 18July03
p.s. Barrett, H. L. C. 19Mar.04
Baker, A.B.L. 19June12
p.s. Crouch, L. W. (Q)(H) 19June12
p.s. Hubbard, Hon. J. G. (H) 20Sept.13
Birchall, E. V. D. 5Oct.13
Mitchell, C. J., Capt. Res. of Off. 18Apr.14

Lieutenants. (8)
Bowyer, G. E. W. 1July11
Littldale, E. H. 1July11

Lieutenants—contd.
Crouch, G. R. 19June12
Hall, P. A. (H) 17Sept.12
Reid, N. S. 17Sept.12
Jackson, G. G. 6Nov.13
Combs, H. V. 12Feb.14

2nd Lieutenants. (8)
Buckmaster, R. A. 6Dec.13
Viney, O. V. 29Jan.14
Green, B. 24June14
Simpson, G.H. 22July14

Adjutant.
Bartlett, A. J. N., Capt. Oxf. & Bucks. L.I. 25Feb.13

Quarter-Master.
⚔Powell, G., Qr.-Mr. (hon. m.) ret. pay, hon. m. 2Nov.06

Medical Officers.
p. Baker, J. C., Surg.-Capt. 25Oct.07
23Apr.04
Howard, Lt. V., R.A.M.C. (T.F.) (attd.) 29May12

Chaplain.
Wethered, Rev. O. H., M.A., TD, Chapl.2nd Class (T.F.) (attd.) 2June12
2June97

[Uniform—Dark Grey Facings—Scarlet.]

THE ESSEX REGIMENT.

Regimental District No. **44** [No. **9** District].

The Castle and Key, superscribed "Gibraltar, 1779-83," and with the motto *Montis Insignia Calpe* underneath.
The Sphinx, superscribed "Egypt." An Eagle.

"Moro," "Havannah," "Badajoz," "Salamanca," "Peninsula," "Bladensburg," "Waterloo," "Ava," "Alma," "Inkerman," "Sevastopol," "Taku Forts," "Nile, 1884-85," "Relief of Kimberley," "Paardeberg," "South Africa, 1899-1902."

Regular and Special Reserve Battalions.

Uniform—Scarlet.   Facings—White.   Agents—Messrs. Cox & Co.

1st Bn. (44th Foot)..	.. Mauritius.	3rd Bn. (Essex (Rifles) Mil.) .. .. Warley.
2nd „ (56th „)..	.. Chatham.	
Depôt	.. Warley.	Record Office .. .. .. Warley.

Territorial Force Battalions.

4th Bn.	.. Brentwood.	7th Bn. .. Walthamstow Lodge, Church Hill, Walthamstow.
5th „	.. Drill Hall, Chelmsford.	
6th „	.. West Ham.	8th „ .. .. Colchester (temp.)

Colonel.. .. .. Ventris, Maj.-Gen. F., ret. pay,(Res. of Off.) p.s.c., q.s. [R].. . 26Sept.04

1st and 2nd Battalions.

Lt.-Colonels. (2)
2Anley, F.G.[F] 23Feb.12
1Godfrey-Faussett,
  O.G., D.S.O. 29Nov.18

Majors. (8)
2Tufnell, G. M. 25Dec.07
1Rice, H. R. 8Jan.08
s. Legge, W. K., p.s.c.
  25Jan.08
1Barlow, C. W.,
  D.S.O. 23Feb.08
  22Aug.02
(3) 2Lewes, C. G. (Comdg. Depôt) 16May10
s. Stirling, Sir G. M.
  H., Bt., D.S.O. 23Feb.12
2Hobkirk, C. J. [L]
  27Nov.12
1Sammut, H. J. 29Nov.13

Captains. (14)
2Vandeleur, W. M. C.
  18Sept.04
  11May00
2Moffitt, F.W., p.s.c. [L]
  6Mar.10
  bt. maj. 22Aug.02
2Boone, C.F.de B 9Oct.00
s. Pratt, A. G. 9Oct.00
  bt. maj. 29Nov.00
s. Harding Newman, J. C.
  p.s.c. 16Apr.02
1Churchill,A.P.16Apr.02
2Halahan, A. C. [H]
  i.v Clutterbuck, A. V.
  20May08
  10May02
e.a.Daubeny, C. J. B.
  28Sept.08
i.v.Roberts-West, C. R.
  1Nov.08
2Ryan, C. I. 29Nov.04
1Wood, A. G. N., Adjt.
  14Mar.05
1Pepys, A. G. L. [I]
  20May08
  29Nov.04
2Jones, L. O. W.,
  Adjt. 26Sept.05
s. Howard, G. W.,
  D.S.O., p.s.c. 25Dec.07
f.c. Raleigh, G. H. 8Jan.08
  bt. maj. 22June14
(3) 1Sinclair Thomson,
  A. E. M 7May09

Captains—contd.
c.o.Maule, W. J. 6Mar.10
s.c. Charles, W. G. 6Mar.10
1Bowen, H. R. 25Aug.10
s. Crocker, H. E.[I] 4Jan.11
f.c. Maitland,E. M.13Jan.11
e.a.White, R. F. 23Jan.11
1Neave, R. 30Nov.11
(3) 1Thompson, R. N.
  10Apr.12
(3) 2Constable, A. T. W.
  28Sept.12
2Brodie, L. C. 2Apr.13
  18Sept.09
e.a.Pattisson,J.H.26Nov.13
r. Wilmer, G. H. 26Nov.13
t. Disney, G. 1Jan.14
1Girardot,M.H. 1Jan.14
t. Lloyd, C. G. 17Feb.14
2Scott, R. L. 17Feb.14
1Scobie, I. H. McK.
  25Apr.14

Lieutenants. (19)
1Devas, A. E. 17Jan.06
1Shepheard, P. 26July09
r. Wright, A. St.J. 27Nov.09
2Binsteed, G. C. [L]
  6Mar.10
1McMurdo, J. C. 6Mar.10
2Vance, J. 23Jan.11
1Dixon, C. R. 1Apr.11
1Ward, B. M. 25Sept.11
(1) Black, D. MacG.
  16Nov.11
c.o.Markham-Rose, K.
  28Nov.11
1Hare, R. S. M. 30Nov.11
(3) 2Pechell, P. 16Dec.11
(3) 1Meares, G. K. 16Dec.11
2Maitland, A. E. 2Jan.12
2Round,A.F.H. 28Jan.12
2Spooner, C. C. 2May12
1Revell, R. A. 11Feb.13
2Read, R.V. 26Feb.13
2Atkinson,J.V. 26Nov.13
1Cadge, F. E. 26Nov.13
1Cowley, W. G. 11Feb.14
  6Dec.13

2nd Lieutenants. (12)
2Waller,A. J. R. 19Jan.12
1Cox, L. P. 14Feb.12
1Wearne, K. M. 14Feb.12
2Smith-Masters, B. S.
  14Feb.12
2Irwin, N.M.S. 4Sept.12
2Heppel, H. M. 23Jan.13

2nd Lieuts.—contd.
1Dinan, F. C. 24May13
1Paxton, G. A. M.
  3Sept.13
1Wood, C. A. B. 3Sept.13
1Thomas, F. G. B.
  10June14
2Jones, L. O. W.,
  capt. 28Sept.12
1Wood, A. G. N., capt.
  1Nov.12
Quarter-Masters.
Freestone, S., hon. lt.
  4May10
1Ford, F. S., hon. lt.
  19Apr.13
r. Roberts, H. S., hon. lt.
  3Sept.13

Special Reserve.
Lieutenants.
✗Trewin,A. B., Lt.
  ret. pay [L] @ (Asst.
  Dist.Commr,Uganda,
  15 July 14) 27Nov.09
p.s.Howard, G. R. (H)
  8Mar.13
  19Mar.04

2nd Lieutenants.
Christy, P.A. 6Nov.12
Round, M. 12Feb.13
Shepard, J. C. M.
  7Mar.13
Johnson, G. G. F.
  15Mar.13

3rd Battalion.

(*Officers serving on 6Oct.02 in the corresponding Militia unit hold honorary Army rank equivalent to the Militia regimental rank they then held. Other officers entitled to honorary Army rank have it shown against their names.*)

Hon. Colonel.
Warwick, F. R. C. G.,
  Earl of, TD (Hon.
  Col. vet. T.F.) 13July08
  28Mar.03

Lt.-Colonel.
✗Colvin, C. H.,
  D.S.O., hon. c.,
  Capt. ret. (H) 7Feb.08

Major.
✗Blakeney, J. E. C.
  (Hon. Capt. in
  Army 4 July 01)
  (Q) (H) 2nd
  Class Resdt., N. Provs.,
  Nigeria { 1Jan.14
  { 28Sept.95)
  20May09
p.s. Penrose, E. S. (H)
  30Nov.05
p.s.Crocker, A. A. (Hon.
  Lt. in Army
  01) (H) 10June07
r.e.✗Lewes, C. G. 16May10

Captains. (5)
p.s.✗Sheffield, G. N.,
  hon. m. (H)
  (Nig. R.) 9May98
p.s.✗Stoddart-MacLellan,
  B. R. A. D., hon. m.
  (H) 20Mar.01
p.s.✗Watson, G.V.(H)
  16Apr.02
p.s.✗Rew, H. G. McK.
  (Hon. Capt. in
  Army 5 Sept. 02)
  (H)(b) 21May04
p.s.✗Lawrie, J. C, (hon.
  m.) Hon. Capt. in
  Army 10 July 01)(H)
  25Mar.05
p.s.✗Disney, J. H.,
  late 2nd Lt. Essex R.
  (H) 11Nov.05
p.s.✗Green, B. B. Capt.
  4June07
p.s.✗Mullock, S. G.
  (Hon. Lt.in Army
  2 Oct.02) (H) 20Sept.07
r.e.✗Sinclair Thomson,
  A. E. M. 7May09
✗Champion de Cres-
  pigny, C. V., Capt.
  ret. pay 19Mar.10
  17July12
✗Rose, A. H. P.,
  Capt. ret. pay 27Jan.12
✗Strickland, T. G.,
  Lt. ret. pay 8Feb.12
r.e.✗Thompson, R. N.
  10Apr.12
r.e.✗Constable, A. T. W.
  28Sept.12

| 1305 | 1306 | 1307 | 1308 |

THE ESSEX REGIMENT—(Regtl. Dist. No. 44)—contd.

3rd Bn.—contd.

Lieutenants. (11)
p.s.Kennefick, J. G. H. (H)
 (b) 1Aug.02
(p.s.)Northey, G. E. A.
  19Mar.07
Gardner, A.(H)18July10
r.e.Pechell, P. 11Dec.11
r.e.Meares, G. K. 16Dec.11
Price, V. M. 27May14
Blumenfeld, D. L.
  27May14
Spooner, W. P.
  27May14

2nd Lieutenants. (8)
Waugh, L. V. (on
 prob.) 26Feb.13
Pearce, J. P. 9Aug.13

Adjutant.
Wilmer, G. H.,
Capt. Essex R.1Jan.14
(Capt. in Army
  26Nov.13)

Quarter-Master.
✠Roberts, H. S., hon. lt.

4th Battalion.

"South Africa, 1900-02."

Brentwood.

Hon. Colonel.
✠Salisbury, Rt. Hon.
J. E. H., Marq. of,
G.C.V.O., C.B., TD,
Lt.-Col. 4 Bn. Bedf.
R., Col., A.D.C.4July88

Lt.-Colonel.
p. Meggy, A. R., VD,
 ⓣ 9Jan.13

Majors. (2)
Shepherd,W. C.13Apr.09
✠Taylor, C. H. R.
 (Hon.Lt.in Army
17Sept.01) (Lt.Res.
of Off.) 9Jan.13

Captains. (8)
p.s.Slade, H. H., hon. m.
 ⓣ 29Jan.02
p.s.Bryant, A. R. 29Jan.02
p. Harris, A. B. 29Jan.02
p.s.Dawson, C. F. 20Aug.04
 Landon, J. H. A., f.c.
  23June08
p.s.Wells, B. C. 14June09
p.s.Oliver, E. G. 28Sept.10
p. Morgan Owen, M. M.
  28Sept.10
(local capt., O.T.C. 1May09)
p.s.Gowan, J. G. (H)
 I. of M. 28Sept.10
Tyler, H. R. 9Jan.13

Lieutenants. (8)
(p.s.)Henderson, H. G.
  17Mar.08
(p.s.)Manbey, P. H. 9Jan.09
Awbery, C. L. (H)(q)
  1May11
Walker, R. H. 1May11
Crump, G. H. 20Jan.12
  6Apr.11
Booth, C. C. 4Sent.12
Calthrop, K. de S. ⓢ
  1Nov.12
Church, W. C. 13July13
Emery, G. M. 20Dec.13
Attwood, C. S. 31May14

2nd Lieutenants. (8)
Macadam, J. 4Dec.12
Copeman,H.F. 4Dec.12
Marshall, J. M. M.
  12Mar.13
Williams, S. W. 9Apr.13
Donner, F. C. 13May13
Batsford, J. F. 18Sept 13
Dale, D. D. R. 22Nov.13
New. A. W. 23Nov.13
Futcher, F. H. 28Feb.14
Chick, A. L. 27Apr.14

Inst. of Musk.
Gowan, J. G., capt.
  27Mar.13

Adjutant.
✠Rowlatt, H. N.,
Capt. Middx. R.
  7May12

Quarter-Master.
✠Mansfield, G. R.,
hon. lt. 23Mar.11

Medical Officers.
p. Aitken, Capt. J.,
M.B., R.A.M.C.
(T.F.) (attd.) 11Feb.05
  29May01
Gibson, Lt. A. J.,
M.B., R.A.M.C.
(T.F.) (attd.) 7Mar.14

Chaplains.
Whistler,Rev.W.W.,
M.A., Chapl. 2nd
Class (T.F.) (attd.)
  3June14
  3June99
Cain, Rev. C. S. Chapl.
4th Class (T.F.)(attd.)
  11May14
[Uniform—Scarlet.
Facings—White.]

Cadet Units affiliated.
Ongar Grammar School
 Cadets.
Manor Park Cadet
 Company.
Warley Garrison Cadets.
Cranbrook College (Ilford)
 Cadets.

5th Battalion.

"South Africa, 1900-02."
Association Buildings,
Market Road, Chelmsford.

Hon. Colonel.
✠ⒷⒸ. ℭ. ℌ. Wood,
Field Marshal Sir
H. E., G.C.B.,
G.C.M.G., Col.
R.H.G., p.s.c. [R]
  5Dec.79

Lt.-Colonel.
p. Welch, J.M., TD18Mar.11

Majors. (2)
p. Taylor, F. W., TD.
  7Jan.07
Ridley,W.P.N.20Sept.12

Captains. (8)
p. Turner, A. J. O. 7Jan.05
p.s.Yonge, P. C. ⓣ 7Jan.07
p. Gibbons, T. (Q) 3Mar.07
p.s.Heron, J. M. 1Dec.09
p. Wilks, G. 17Apr.12
Wilson, W. E. (H)
  13Feb.13

Lieutenants. (9)
✠Argent, H.T. 20Feb.11
Bacon, F. W. 20Feb.11
Willmott, E. D. H.
  25June13
Gould, C. A., ⓐ (H)
  25June13
Conway, L. R. O.
  25June13
Betts, L. 26Feb.14
Bright, F. G. 27June14

2nd Lieutenants. (8)
Dannatt, W. E. 21May12
Franklin, T. G. N.
  22May13
Thomson, E. G.
  24June13
Deakin, E. B., late
 2nd Lt. Res. of
 Off. 16July13
Brooks, W. H. 23Oct.13
Bellward, G. W. F.
  27Nov.13
Taylor, E. McK. 3 Jan.14
Ridley, H. L. 9Feb.14
Yonge, H. L. 14Mar.14

Adjutant.
✠Merriman, A. D. N.,
Capt. R.Ir. Rif.
  14Nov.11

Quarter-Master.
✠Nobbs, G. M., hon.lt.
  9May14

Medical Officers.
Storrs, Capt. K. S.,
M.B., R.A.M.C.
(T.F.) (attd.) 6Sept.11
  6Mar.08
Wink, Lt. C. S.,
R.A.M.C. (T.F.)
(attd.) 12July13

Chaplains.
Sacre, Rev. A. J.,
Chapl. 4th Class
(T.F.)(attd.) 1Apr.08
  13Aug.04
[Uniform—Scarlet.
Facings—White.]

Cadet Units affiliated.
Chelmsford King Edward
VI. School Cadet Corps.
Colchester Royal Grammar
 School Cadets.

6th Battalion.

"South Africa, 1900-02."

West Ham.

Hon. Colonel.
Von Pawel Rammingen,
L.A.G.L.A., Freiherr,
K.C.B., K.C.V.O., VD,
  9Feb.84

Lt.-Colonel.
Wall, R. F. (t) 25Oct.11

Majors. (2)
Oliver, H., TD ⓣ 9Aug.11
p.s.Gray, E. 25Oct.11

Captains. (8)
p.s.McDonald, G. F. H. (Q)
  26Feb.02
p.s.Clubb, E. A. 30July04
p.s.Alexander, H. P. ⓣ
  26Oct.05
p.s.Ward, B. J. 18Mar.08
p.s.Castle, P. D. (H),
  27Nov.10
p.s. Evans, G. L. (t)(H)
 I. of M. 9Aug.11
p.s. Retallack-Moloney,
H. R. (t)(H) 25Oct.11
p.s.Grant, W. F. N. (t)
  17Oct.12

Lieutenants. (8)
(p.s.)✠Walker, J. A. (t)
  18Mar.07
(p.s.)Bunch, H. W. (t)
 Culverwell, W. 14Feb.11
Nunneley, P.(H)5June11
Sly, J. M. 17Oct.12
Loftus, E. ⓢ 23Aug.13

2nd Lieutenants. (8)
Sheldon, J. L. 12Apr.13
Chapman, S. J. 3May13
Silverwood, H. F.
  1Oct.13
Taylor, K. D. 1Oct.13
Ra ner, L. B. 1Oct.13
Stenning, L. G. 1Oct.13
Hyrons, R. A. 20Nov.13
Newman, R.J. 10Dec.13
Coley, S. C. 14Feb.14
Cragg, W. T. 25Feb.14

Inst. of Musk.
Evans, G. L., capt.
  27Nov.10

Adjutant.
Disney, G., Capt.
Essex R. 16Nov.11

Quarter-Master.
Pitt, G. H., hon. lt.
  4Jan.13

Medical Officer.
Maclachlar Lt. A.
K., M.B., R.A.M.C.
(T.F.)(attd.) 3Jan.13

| 1309 | 1310 | 1311 | 1312 |

THE ESSEX REGIMENT—(Regtl. Dist. No. 44)—contd.

6th Bn.—contd.

Chaplains.
Pelly, Rev. R. A.,
 M.A., Chapl.2nd
 Class(T.F.)(attd.) 1Apr.08
 12Dec.91
Gardner, Rev. E. A.,
 Chapl. 4th Class
 (T.F.)(attd.) 1Apr.08
 11Aug.06
[Uniform—Scarlet.
Facings—White.]

Cadet Units affiliated.
1 C. B. Essex R.
The Southend High
 School Cadet Corps.
Palmer's School Cadet
 Corps.

7th Battalion.

"South Africa, 1900-02."

Walthamstow Lodge,
Church Hill,
Walthamstow.

Hon. Colonel.
Parkington, Sir J.
 R., Knt.,lateMaj.
 3 Bn. E. Surr. R.
 11Aug.00

Lt.-Colonel.
Hearn, F.W.(q)21Sept.12

Majors. (2)
Mackie, W. A.,TD,
 27Apr.12
Kemball H. F.(q)
 1July13

Captains. (8)

p.s.Johnson, W. R. (H)
 10Aug.10
p.s.Johnson, G. 18Sept.11
Ewer, G. G. (q) 28June12
Liversidge, H. E.
 (q)(H), I. of M.1July12
Maryon, J. F. 22Jan.14
Braithwaite, M. W.
 27May14
Shenstone, G. 27May14

Lieutenants. (8)

Lawrence, W., f.c.
 1May11
Clarke, R, J. 1Mar.14
Waller, F. R. 1Mar.14
Pearson, D. H. 1Mar.14
Stubbings, R.A.
 27May14
Broadberry, E. W.
 27May14
Schofield, J. 26June14

2nd Lieutenants. (8)

Jones, G. 1July13
Stammers, A. D.
 10July13
Eve, J. R. 10Sept.13
Windsor, A. C. 5Jan.14
Hearn, S. C. W.
 22Jan.14
Bailey, L. F. H. 6May14

Inst. of Musk.
Liversidge, H. E.,
 capt. 19Nov.12

Adjutant.
✗Smyly, R. J., Capt.
 N. Lan. R. 1Apr.13

Quarter-Master.

✗Oldfield, J. B.,
 Comy.of Ord. (hon.
 capt.) ret.pay, hon.
 maj. 8Jan.13

Medical Officers
Shaw, Lt.J.T.,M.D.,
 R.A.M.C. (T.F.)
 (attd.) 29Mar.13
Turtle, Lt. W. R. M.,
 M.B., R.A.M.C.
 (T.F.)(attd.) 17May13
 13Jan.13

Chaplain.
Lampen, Rev.H.D.,
 M.A., Chapl. 4th
 Class(T.F.)(attd.)
 22Mar.13

[Uniform—Scarlet.
Facings—White.]

8th (Cyclist) Battalion.

Colchester (temp).

Hon. Colonel.
✗Brooke, L. G. F.
 M., Lord,M.V.O.
 (Maj. and Bt.Lt.-
 Col.T.F.Res.) 1July10

Lt.-Colonel.
Tabor, J.C. (Q) 17July12

Major.
Ackland, W.F. 28Sept.12

Captains. (8)

p.s.Anderson, W.B.(t)
 1Oct.07
Baily, C. A. (t) 18ept.17
Innocent, H. 11June14

Lieutenants. (5)

p.s.Benham, G. C.
 18Feb.13
Dann, E. W. 7May13
Croome, W. H. 21Apr.14
 2July10

2nd Lieutenants. (4)

Parry, P. 7May12
Gibson, H. L. 16Apr.13
Attfield, C. H. 4July13
Colnett, R. D. 18Apr.14

Adjutant.
✗Needham, R.M.B.,
 Capt. Suff. R. 1Nov.12

Quarter-Master.
Nicholson, W. A.,
 hon. lt. 8June10

Medical Officer.
p. Warwick, Maj. F. J.,
 M.B., TD, R.A.M.C.
 (T.F.)(attd.) 26Feb.06
 5Aug.93

[Uniform—Scarlet.
Facings—White.]

| 1813 | 1814 | 1815 | 1816 |

THE SHERWOOD FORESTERS (NOTTINGHAMSHIRE AND DERBYSHIRE REGIMENT).

Regimental District No. **45**. [No. **6** District.]

The United Red and White Rose.

"Louisburg," "Roliça," "Vimiera," "Talavera," "Busaco," "Fuentes d'Onor," "Ciudad Rodrigo," "Badajoz," "Salamanca," "Vittoria," "Pyrenees," "Nivelle," "Orthes," "Toulouse," "Peninsula," "Ava," "South Africa, 1846-7," "Alma," "Inkerman," "Sevastopol," "Central India," "Abyssinia," "Egypt, 1882," "Tirah," "South Africa, 1899-1902."

Regular and Special Reserve Battalions.

Uniform—Scarlet. Facings—Lincoln Green. Agents—Messrs. Cox & Co.

1st Bn. (45th Foot)	..	.. Bombay (for Aden.)	3rd Bn. { (1st Derby Mil.) }.. .. Derby.
2nd „ (95th Foot)	..	.. .. Sheffield.	4th „ (R. Sherwood Foresters Mil.)
			The Barracks, Old Normanton, Derby.
Depôt	..	.. .. .. Derby.	Record Office .. .. Lichfield.

Territorial Force Battalions.

| 5th Bn. | .. | .. .. .. Drill Hall, Derby. | 7th Bn. The Drill Hall, Derby Road, Nottingham |
| 6th „ | .. | 10, Corporation Street, Chesterfield. | 8th „ .. .. Newark |

Colonel .. .. Smith-Dorrien, Gen, Sir H. L., G.C.B., D.S.O., p.s.c. [R.] s. 9June05

1st and 2nd Battalions.

Lt.-Colonels. (2)
1 Marshall, W.R. 11Feb.12
 bt. col. 26June08
2 Crofton-Atkins, O. R.
 26Feb.14

Majors. (8)

2 Leveson Gower, P.
 12May08
1 Phelps, M. P. 30Mar.11
 29Nov.00
s. Maurice, F. B., p.s.c.
 [L] 19May11
 bt. lt.-col. 10May13
1 Mortimore, C. R.
 11Feb.12
e.a. Dove, P.M. [F] 14Aug.12
(3) 2 Sadler, R. P.
 (Comdg. Depôt)
 25Dec.12
2 Taylor, R.J.F. 24Apr.13
1 Morley, L. St. H.
 26Feb.14

Captains. (14).

2 Way, B.G.V., M.V.O.
 13July00
(3) 2 Hobbs, C. J. W. 4Jan.01
s. Burnett Hitchcock,
 B.F., p.s.c. [L] 12Mar.01
2 Parkinson, C. C.,
 M.V.O. 12Sept.02
2 Frend, W. R. Adjt.
 21Sept.04
1 Castle, S. M 19July05
 29Nov.05
(3) 1 Wilkin, W. H. 20July05
f.v. Manby, G.L.H. 22Nov.05
2 Popham, R. S., D.S.O.
 22Feb.06
2 Luther, G. F. 22Feb.06
r. Wybergh, R. H. 4Apr.06
1 Webb, M. R. 1June08
s.c.o. 1 Dixon, H. B. 14June08
1 Hume, H. B. T.
 14June08
e.a. Hart, R. S. 26July08
t. Hodgson, M.K 7Dec.08
t.v. Milward, H. M. 7Dec.08
r. Harvey, C. D. 15Mar.09
(3) 1 Swinhoe-Phelan, W.
 18May09

Captains—contd.
f.c. Becke, J. H. W. 28Sept.09
t. Foster, R. T. 1Apr.10
 bt. maj. 22June14
t.v. Dumbell, C. H. 9July10
2 Wayte, A. B. 25Nov.10
2 Mathias, J. H. 5Apr.11
t. Collin, E. N. T. 28Oct.12
w.a. Fielding, G.R. 21Jan.13
f.c. Herbert, P.L. W.
 21Jan.13
1 Brownrigg, W. D. S.
 21Jan.13
2 Stackhouse, W. T.
 21Jan.13
2 Edwards, G. D. 3Aug.07
 15Mar.07
2 Schneider, C.C. 3Aug.07
c.o. Wilkinson, S. 16Nov.07
1 Sherbrooke, R. L.
 30Sept.08
1 Douglas, J. H. M.
 15Mar.09
(2) Bernard, L. A. 10Nov.09
s.s. Dammers, R. W. 1Apr.09
c.o. Ash, E. C. 1June09
1 Lang, J. A. M. 28Sept.09
r. Young, R. B. 18Oct.09
1 Dilworth, MacL. P.
 1Feb.10
(2) Needham, J. MacD.
 1Apr.10
1 Wyncoll, H. E. F.
 4May10
c.o. Maxwell, J.E.H. 9July10
(3) 2 Tower, R. B. 25Nov.10
2 Shawcross, R. R.
 24Jan.11
c.o. Earle, J. V. 17May11
1 Dobbie, G. S. 30July11
r. Murray, P. M. 18Aug.11
2 Loyd, F. F. 6Oct.11
(3) 1 Squires, R. D. 21July12
1 Stranger, R. H.,
 Adjt. 10Aug.12
1 Goodwyn, A. J. 11Sept.12
1 Chambers, G. H.
 25Oct.12
1 Mills, G. D. 21Jan.13
1 Jackson, A. H. 17Sept.13
1 Wylie, P. H. 28Mar.14
 8Dec.11

2nd Lieutenants. (12)
2 Paddock, H.L. 4Mar.11
2 Walsall, R.E.C. 20Sept.11
1 Kennedy, C.S.C.
 20Sept.11
2 Macbean, I.G. 20Sept.11

2nd Lieutenants—contd.
2 Willcox, H. B. D.
 30Dec.11
2 Orellin, W. A. W.
 14Feb.12
2 Mills, H. L. B. 4Sept.12
1 O'Dwyer, J. E.A. 5Feb.13
1 Williamson, E. M.
 3Sept.13
2 Whicher, J. D'A.
 10Dec.13
Adjutants.
2 Frend, W. R., capt.
 6Dec.12
1 Stranger, E. H., lt.
 31July13
Quarter-Masters.
2 Tomlinson, F., 20Feb.01
 hon. capt. 20Feb.11
1 Wright, J., hon. lt.
 6Oct.08
r. Ewin, A., hon.lt.10July07
r. Fielding, S., hon.
 lt. 22July14

Special Reserve.

2nd Lieutenants,
Walker, H. C. S.
 2Nov.12
Smith, H. L. C.
 (local Lt., O T.C.
 10 Dec. 13) 23Apr.13
Atkin, J. M. (on
 prob.) (attd.
 O.T.C.) 7May13
Allan, B. G. 14June13
Shaw, C. G. (on
 prob.) 21Jan.14
Smalley, W. M. (on
 prob.) 4Feb.14
Ewen, J. F. B.
 (on prob.) 4Apr.14
Peck, L. W. (on
 prob.) 15Apr.14

3rd Battalion.

(Officers serving on 4Dec.00
in the corresponding
Militia withhold honorary
Army rank equivalent to
the Militia regimental
rank they then held. Other
officers entitled to honorary Army rank have
it shown against their
names.)

Hon. Colonel.
XBC, M. Roberts, Field-
 Marshal Rt. Hon.
 F.S., Earl, K.G.,
 K.P., G.C.B., O.M.,
 G.C.S.I., G.C.I.E.,
 VD., Col. Comdt.
 R.A., Col. 1. Gds.
 [R] 26July05
 29Dec 88

Lt.-Colonel.
p.s. Heath, E. C. [l] (Q)
 (H) 7Nov.12

Major.
p.s. Wise, H. E. D.
 3Dec.12
r.e. Sadler, R. P. 25Dec.12

Captains. (5)
p.s. Reed, J. P. B. (H)
 25Jan.99
r.e. Hobbs, C. J. W.
 4Jan.01
p.s. Howorth, H. (H)
 (Hon. 2nd Lt. in
 Army21Oct.00) 3Feb.04
r.e. Wilkin, W. H.
 20July05
Meares, J. N., Lt.
 ret. pay 18Dec.07
r.e. Swinhoe-Phelan, W.
 18May09
Cattell, A.S.G., late
 Lt. Res. of Off. 25Nov.11

Lieutenants. (11)
r.e. Tower, R. B. 25Nov.10
Drury Lowe, E. N.
 25July11
r.e. Squires, E. D. 21July12

2nd Lieutenants.(8)
May, R. G. B.
 11Sept.12
Tuckett, J. R. 1Oct.12
Martin, G. C. R.
 1Oct.12
Cowgill, J. I. W.
 4Dec.12
Sowter, U. H. E.
 (on prob.) 28Mar.14

Adjutant.
Harvey, C. D.,
 Capt. Notts. &
 Derby, R. 6Mar.14
(Capt. in Army 15Mar.09)

Quarter-Master.
Fielding, S., hon. lt.

| 1317 | 1818 | 1819 | 1820 |

THE SHERWOOD FORESTERS (NOTTINGHAMSHIRE AND DERBYSHIRE REGIMENT)—(Regtl. Dist. No. 45)—*contd.*

4th Battalion.

(*Officers serving on 10May01 in the corresponding Militia unit hold honorary Army rank equivalent to the Militia regimental rank they then held. Other officers entitled to honorary Army rank have it shown against their names*).

Hon. Colonel.
Portland, Rt. Hon.
W.J.A.C.J., Duke
of, K.G., G.C.V.O.
14June08
8June89

Lt.-Colonel.
✗Hamilton A.S.,
Maj. ret. pay 1Jan.14

Majors. (3)
Graham, F., *late
Capt. Res. of Off.
(Maj. ret. Terr.
Force)* (H) 12Oct.12
✗Waddington, F. G.
(*Hon. Lt. in Army
18Oct. 00*) (H.)
1July14

Captains. (6)
p.s.Anson,G.L.(H) 21June07
de Robeck, C. R.
(*Hon. Capt. in
Army 10Oct. 00*)
25Oct.13

Lieutenants. (11)
Hudson, T. H. 7Dec.11

2nd Lieutenants. (8)
Munro-Faure, P. H.
27Jan.12
Stackhouse, J. H.
(*on prob.*) 7Feb.14
Milward. R. G.
(*on p ob.*) 22July14

Adjutant.
✗Wybergh, J. H.,
Capt. Notts. &
Derby. R. 31Aug.11
Capt.inArmy4Apr.06)

Quarter-Master.
✗Ewin, A., *hon. lt.*

5th Battalion.

"South Africa, 1900-02."
Drill Hall, Derby.

Hon. Colonel.
Devonshire, Rt. Hon.
V. C. W , Duke of,
G.C.V.O. 20May06

Lt.-Colonel.
p. Mosley, G., TD, ⊕
22June12

Majors. (2)
Lewis, G. A., TD
(Q) (H) 6Dec.09
p.s.✗Newbold, T. C.
(*Hon. Lt. in Army
30 May 01*) (H) (a)
(b) p.v.c. 22June12

Captains. (8)
p.s.✗Marsden, J. H. F.
(*Hon.Lt. in Army
26 June 02*) ⊕ (H)
⊕ 4Aug.08
p. Clay,W.H.C.(Q)17Apr.07
Checkland, B. H.
18Sept.09
p.s. Naylor,A.B.(q)12May12
p.s. Winning, T. N. (q)
⊕ 22June12
Newton, H. 17Nov.12

Lieutenants. (8)
Wragg, F. W. 23Jan.10
Kerr, J. D. 26Apr.10
(p.) Finch, L. H. 17Dec.11
Claye, H. 22June12
Hunter, J. 27July12
Stone, A. 25Jan.13
Lewes, F. H. M. 7May14
(p.) Coles, P. B. 23June14
15Feb.14

2nd Lieutenants. (8)
Fryar, M. S. 20May11
Case, R. J. ⊕ 14Feb.12
Hingston, C. V. 26Feb.12
Rudgard, H. 26June12
Jones, C. H. 29Jan.13
Stebbing, T. H. L.
21June13
Harrison, L. J. B.
1Oct.13
Rose, A. L. 29June14
16Feb.12

Adjutant.
✗Mosley, N., Capt.
N. Staff. R. 20Apr.14

Quarter-Master.
p. Wörgan, F., *hon. m.*
8Jan.07

Chaplain.
Eddison, *Rev.* F. W.,
Chapl.4th class (T.F.)
(*attd.*) 18Sept12

[Uniform—*Scarlet.*
Facings—*White.*]

6th Battalion.

"South Africa, 1900-02."
10, Corporation Street,
Chesterfield.

Hon. Colonel.
p.s. Cavendish, J. C., VD,
late Lt. R. A.,
Col., A.D.C. 2Jan.97

Lt.-Colonel.
p.s. Clayton, J. M., TD (t)
17 May12

Majors. (2)
p.s.✗ Goodman, G. D., VD
(*Hon. Capt. in Army
7Jan.02*)(*Capt.Res. of
Off.*)(Q)⊕(H)25June10
Hall, E., TD,(H) 17May12

Captains. (8)
p. Goodall, J. K., TD,
hon. m. 28Sept.97
p.s.✗Blackwall, J. E. ⊕
12Sept.03
p. Hopkins, A. J. 9Nov.06
p. Saxby, R. (b) 25Nov.11
p. Winder, B. H. (H)
⊕ 4May12
p. Heathcote, E. H.
(q) (H) I.ofM.17May12
14 Mar.06
Welch, H. 13Nov.12
Taylor,H.C.B. 26Apr.13

Lieutenants. (8)
(p.) Hills, R. (H) 29Oct.06
Darbyshire, B. 4May12
Dick, F. M. 16Nov.12
12Apr.10
Robinson, V. O.
(H) 26Apr.13
Wheatcroft, C. J.
9Aug.13
Blackwall, C. V.,
H.C. (H) 18Sept.13
Jackson, W. B. M.
17Dec 13
Taylor,E.M.B. 24June14

2nd Lieutenants. (8)
Robinson, F.B. 10Oct.11
Marshall, W. T. 4May12
Tolson, J. 11Sept.12
Jackson, H. H.18Dec.12
Davies, I. 19Mar.13
14June14
Wood, E. S. 3Dec.13
18Jan.13
Symonds, J. D. B.
17Dec.13

Inst. of Musk.
Heathcote, E. H.,
capt. 17June14

Medical Officers.
p. Shea, A. W., *Surg.-
Capt.* 1Apr.08
9Nov.06
p. Duncan, Capt. W.,
M.B., R.A.M.C. (T.F.
(*attd.*) 26Sept 10
26Mar.07

Chaplains.
Morris, *Rev. Canon*
E. E., M.A., Chapl.
2nd Class (T.F.)
(*attd.*) 4Jan.14
4Jan.90
Nixon, *Rev.* W. H.,
M.A., Chapl. 3rd
Class (T.F.)(*attd.*)
3Feb.14
3Feb.04

[Uniform—*Scarlet.*
Facings—*Lincoln Green.*]

7th (Robin Hood) Battalion.

"South Africa, 1900-02."
The Drill Hall, Derby Road,
Nottingham.

Hon. Colonel.
Portland, Rt. Hon.
W. J. A. C. J., Duke
of, K.G., G.C.V.O.
21Sept.98

Lt.-Colonel.
p.s. Birkin, C. W., TD,
6June01

Majors. (2)
p.s. Brewill, A. W., VD,
hon. l.c. (H) ⊕ 6June00
p. Wigley, G. A., TD ⊕
21May04

Captains. (8).
p.s. Payne, P. M., TD,
hon.m.(H) (Q) 6June00
p.s. Baily, B. E. 6June00
p.s. Hind, L. A. (t) (H)
4Feb.03
p.s. Lee, A. N. 4Feb.03
p.s. Spalding, E. H. (E) (t)
18June04
p. Hardstaff, J. R. (H)
18June04
p.s. Rook, W. R. (H) (q)
25June04
p. Bradwell, H. 12May06
p.s. Milner, C. W. 28Sept.07

Lieutenants. (9)
p.s.Black,G. H.(H)29Nov.07
(p.s.)Black, T. S. 29Nov.07
p.s. Cooper, L. 29Nov.07
p.s. Stubington, G. H.
(H) 18July09
Brewill, L. C. 2May11
Mellers, G.H.R.(H)
2May11
Williams, A. M.
(H) 8June13
Forman, D. P. ⊕
15Aug.13

2nd Lieutenants. (9)
McCrath, K. Y. 11Oct.09
Boot, J. C (H) 1Nov.09
Gotch, R. M. 30July11
Walker, W. E. G.
15May12
Preston, O. I. 16May12
Warren, J. C. 22Jan.13
Rook, M.
Walton, A. A. 1Jan.14
Walton, H. H. 1Jan.14

| 1321 | 1322 | 1323 | 1324 |

THE SHERWOOD FORESTERS (NOTTINGHAMSHIRE AND DERBYSHIRE REGIMENT).—(Regtl. Dist. No. **45**)—*contd.*

7th Bn.—*contd.*

Adjutant.
✗Wakefield, H. G. R., Capt. Leins. R.
[*l*]   1Sept.11

Quarter-Master.
Newham, W. H.,
hon. m.   22July05

Medical Officer.
Scott, Lt. J. W., *M.D.*, R.A.M.C.
(T.F.) (*attd.*) 19May13

Chaplain.
Hayman, *Rev.* H. T., *M.A.*, TD, Chapl. 1st Class (T.F.) (*attd.*) 22Oct.12
                      22Oct.92

[Uniform—*Lincoln Green.* Facings—*Black.*].

8th Battalion.

" South Africa, 1900-02."

Newark.

Hon. Colonel.
p. Manvers, C. W. S., Earl, VD, *late* Lt. G. Gds., Col.   27Aug.04

Lt.-Colonel.
Huskinson, C. J., TD, ⊛   16Apr.13

Majors. (2)

Fowler, G. H. (Q) (*H*)   9Dec.12

Captains. (8)
p. Tylden Wright, E. W. E.   22June98
p.s.Appleby, L. C. B. (*H*)   13Mar.10

Captains—contd.
p.s. Clarke, A. C. (*H*)   13Mar.10
p.s. Wordsworth, R. J. (*t*) (*H*)   9May10
p.s. Becher, J. P.   9May10

Lieutenants. (8)
(p.) Martyn, M. C. 26Jan.10
Cursham, F.G.14Mar.10
Allen, W. H.   18Apr 12
Smith, W. R.   1June12
                      4Nov.11
Ashwell, A. L. 1Oct.13
Lane, J. K.   1Apr.14
Davenport, C. 1Apr.14
Quibell, A. H. 1Apr.14

2nd Lieutenants. (8)
Wright, H. G. 14Feb.12
Clarke, G.   15Feb.12
Handford,H.B.S.
                13July12
Kirby, H.   1Dec.12
Turner, J, W. 15Jan.13
Pigsford, R. H. 1June13
James, E. C. A. 1Oct.13
Dobson, A. F. C. 1May14

Adjutant.
✗Collin, E. N. T., Capt. Notts. & Derby. R.   1Oct.13

Quarter-Master.
p. Sarll, W. N., TD,
hon. m.   16Jan.04

Medical Officers.
p. Johnson, Capt. F. W., *M.B.*, R.A.M.C. (T.F.) (*attd.*) 4Aug.06
                      4Feb.03
p. Stallard, H., Surg.-Capt.   27Dec.06
                      27June03

Chaplain.
Hales, *Rev.* J. P., Chapl. 4th Class (T.F.) (*attd.*) 1Mar.13

[Uniform—*Scarlet.* Facings—*Green.*]

THE LOYAL NORTH LANCASHIRE REGIMENT.
Regimental District No. **47**. [No. **3** District.]

The Red Rose.
"Louisburg," "Quebec, 1759," "Maida," "Corunna," "Tarifa," "Vittoria," "St. Sebastian," "Nive,"
"Peninsula," "Ava," "Alma," "Inkerman," "Sevastopol," "Ali Masjid," "Afghanistan, 1878-79,"
"Defence of Kimberley," "South Africa, 1899-02."

Regular and Special Reserve Battalions.
Uniform—Scarlet. *Facings*—White. *Agents.*—Messrs. Cox & Co.

1st Bn. (47th Foot)	Aldershot (for Gravesend).	3rd Bn. (3rd R. Lancashire Mil.)	Preston.
2nd „ (81st „)	Bangalore.		
Depôt	Preston.	Record Office	Preston.

Territorial Force Battalions.
4th Bn. .. .. 97, Avenham Lane, Preston. | 5th Bn. .. .. Bolton.

Colonel .. .. ᚕ. Jones-Vaughan, Hon. Maj.-Gen. H. T., C.B., ret. pay, p.s.c. [R] 31Dec.09

1st and 2nd Battalions.

Lt.-Colonels. (2)
Knight, G. C⎯ p.s.c. [l]
  4Feb.11
2Jourdain, C. E. A.,
  D.S.O. 17Dec.13

Majors. (3)
1Lloyd, W. P. 1June06
2Sanderson, W. D.
  8July08
  2June06
2Robinson, H. A.
  17Dec.09
s. Carter, A. J., D.S.O.
  14Feb.10
(3)1Bowlby, R. R.
  (Comdg.Depôt)1June10
2Braithwaite, F. J.
  4Feb.11
1Burrows, A. 16Dec.11
2Bridges, T. McG.
  17Dec.13

Captains. (14)
e.a. Woodward, F. W.,
  D.S.O. 24Dec.01
s. Newton, C. J., p.s.c.
  24Dec.01
s. James, R. E. H., p.s.c.
  24Dec.01
  bt. maj. 29July01
2Halton, E. C. 24Dec.01
2Berkeley, R. E. 24Dec.01
2Flint, S. A. 24Dec.01
  2June06
(3) 2Fairlie, J. G. 14Sept.04
r. Torbett, F. H. E.
  8Feb.05
(1) Body, G. T. 16Jan.06
(3)2Ryley, H. F. B. 5May06
s. Wells, J. B., D.S.O.,
  p.s.c. 5May06
1Fitzpatrick, H. B.
  5May06
(3)1Greenhill, F. W.,
  26June07
1Watson, H.
  27Jan.08
t. Smyly, B. J. 1June08
2Trefusis, G. R. 4June08
t. Magill, H. F. 30Mar.10
  2June08
1Helme, H. L. 17Dec.09
2Stokes, R. G. 1Jan.10
(1) Colley, A. W. 25Apr.11

Captains—contd.
1Howard-Vyse, R.
  Adjt. 25Apr.12
1Allen, J. F. 25Apr.12
1Rowley Conwy, G. S.
  1June12
(1) *Prince,* A. L. 11Sept.12
1Allason, L. T. [L]
  27Nov.12
1Wakley, B. J. 1Apr.13

Lieutenants. (19)
2Logan, R. H. 8Feb.05
2Bell, C. V. M., Adjt.
  8Feb.05
o.o. Underwood, J. P. D.,
  4Mar.05
1Mann, N. S. 6Mar.05
e.a. Sandes, C. W. W.
  16Jan.06
o.o. Dare, J. 5May06
w.a. Pease, C. 6June06
t. Izod, K. W. 13July06
o.o. Knapp, A. F. P. 1July07
(3) 1Lucey, S. T. 4June08
1Spread, E. J. W.
  20Oct.09
1Goldie, G. H. 1Jan.10
o.o. Campbell, W. A.
  19Mar.10
2Collas, D. P. J. 30Mar.10
2I'Anson, F. J. de V.
  12Apr.10
o.o. Faulknor, R. S. J.
  25June10
(3) 2Wynne, F. G. 5Oct.10
2Edwards P. A. 1Apr.11
1Loomes, H. R. 25Apr.12
1Cross, M. A. 1June12
2Cowdell, A. F. 11Sept.12
2Atkinson, G. P. 27Nov.12
1Halsted, J. G. 26Feb.13
2Watson, J. F. B.
  1Apr.13
1Cunningham, E. F.
  13Aug.13
1Robinson, E. 1Nov.13
2Anderson, W. H.
  14Jan.14
2Dickson, C. G. 15Mar.14

2nd Lieutenants. (12)
t.o. (1) Moon, T. W.
  W. W. A. N.Z.
  Staff Corps (local
  2nd lt.) 14Aug.11

2nd Lieutenants—contd.
1Batty-Smith, S. H.
  13Feb.12
1Knowles, H. L. L.
  14Feb.12
2Einem-Hickson,
  S. V. 4Sept.12
2 Withers, B. H. 4Dec.12
2Keays, R. L. C. 22Jan.13
1Rowell, W. C. 22Jan.13
2Leeb, M. E. 5Feb.13
1Collins, N. 24May13
1Calrow, W.R.L.
  17Sept.13
2Williams, G. G. R.
  24Jan.14
2Kingsley, G. C.
  10June14

Adjutants.
2Bell, C. V. M., lt.
  4Jan.12
1Howard-Vyse,R., capt.
  26Jan.12

Quarter-Masters.
Mudge, E. C., hon. lt.
  11Jan.11
2Rowley, R., hon. lt.
  10Apr.12
1Wilkinson, E., hon. lt.
  12June12

Special Reserve.
Captain.
✕Pelly, R. T.,
  Capt. ret. pay
  11 Sept.12
  1Apr.13

2nd Lieutenants.
Wallis, C. E. 18May12
Griffith, T. C. 25June13

3rd Battalion.
(*Officers serving on 15Mar.02
in the corresponding
Militia unit hold honorary
Army rank equivalent to
the Militia regimental
rank they then held. Other
officers entitled to honorary Army rank have
it shown against their
names.*)

Hon. Colonel.
✕BC, ᚕ.Roberts, Field
Marshal F.S., Rt. Hon.
Earl, K.G. K.P.,
G.C.B.,O.M.,G.C.S.I.,
G.C.I.E., VD, Col.
Comdt. R.A., Col. I.
Gds. [R] 26July08
  1Jan.03

Lt.-Colonel.
✕Cowper-Essex, T.,
  hon. c. (H) 15Sept.06

Major.
✕Harrison, P. W.,
  hon. l.c. 27June08
r.e. Bowlby, R. R. 1June10

Captains. (5)
✕Saunders-Knox-Gore,
  A. H. W., hon. m. (I)
  4Nov.93
  5Mar.12
r.e. Fairlie, J. G. 14Sept.04
r.e. Ryley, H. F. B. 5May06
p.s. Miller, E. C. (H)
  2June06
p.s. Harrison, M. C. C.
  (H)(Asst.Commr.
  of Police, Gold
  Coast, 1 July 10)
  21Mar.07
✕Crane, R. E., late Lt.
  N. Lan. R. 17June11
  Hay, G. W., Capt.
  ret. pay 9Nov.11
✕Loch, G., late Capt.,
  N. Lan. R. 5Oct.12

Lieutenants. (11)
r.e. Lucey, S. T. 4 June 08
Miller, J. H. (H)7May09
r.e. Wynne, F. G. 5Oct.10
Mason, R. C. (q)6Jan.12
Hyndson, J. G. W.
  2June13

2nd Lieutenants. (8)

Adjutant.
✕Torbett, F. H. E.,
  Capt. N. Lan. R.
  27Jan.12
(*Capt. in Army* 8Feb.05)

Quarter-Master.
✕Mudge, E. C., hon. lt.

THE LOYAL NORTH LANCASHIRE REGIMENT—(Regtl. Dist. No. 47)—contd.

1329

4th Battalion.

"South Africa, 1900-02."

97, Avenham Lane,
Preston.

Hon. Colonel.

✠Derby, Rt. Hon.
E. G. V., Earl of,
G C.V.O.,C.B.,
18June09

Lt.-Colonel.

Beckwith, H. L. (t)
29July11

Majors. (2)

✠Foley, F. W. (Hon. Lt.
in Army 21June01)
⊛(H) 2July09
Hindle, R. (H) 25Oct.11

Captains. (8)

p.s. Nickson, H, (H) ⊛
3May05
p.s. Booth, E. H. 12Oct.09
Hibbert, C. G. R.
26Apr.11
Peak, J. H. 25Oct.11
Whitfield, J. L. 19Feb.12
Crump, J. A. 18July13
Parker, H. 18July13

1330

Lieutenants. (8)

(p.)Norwood, S. B. 20Feb.13
         15Aug.03
Widdows, J. O.27Mar.13
Ord, R.⊛ 27Mar.13
Smith, W. 27Mar.13
Holt, F. R. (H) 27Mar.13
Seed, J. 1Oct.13
Rennard, E. M. 1Oct 13

2nd Lieutenants. (8)

Moore, K. H. 15Apr.12
Brindle, J. L. 1Oct.13
Gregson, E.M. 21Apr.14

Adjutant.

✠Norman, C. C.,
Capt. R. W. Fus.
17Feb.14

Quarter-Master.

p. Whitehead, H. J.,
hon. m. 4Oct.99

Medical Officers.

Derham, Capt. T. H. C.,
R.A.M.C., (T.F.)
(attd.) 1July12
         1Jan.09
Staley, Lt, J. D.,
R.A.M.C,(T.F.) (attd.)
22Jan.14

Chaplain.

Spencer, Rev. L.D.W.,
M.A., Chapl. 4th
Class (T.F.) (attd.)
1Apr.08
27Oct.06

[Uniform—Scarlet.
Facings—White.]

———

Cadet Unit affiliated.
The Arnold House School
Cadet Corps.

1331

5th Battalion.

"South Africa, 1900-02."

Bolton.

Hon. Colonel.

✠Derby, Rt. Hon.
E. G. V., Earl of,
G.C.V.O., C.B.
17May99

Lt.-Colonel.

p. Slater, J. W., VD,
⊛ 16Nov.12

Majors. (2)

✠Hesketh, G. (Hon. Lt.
in Army 21June01)
⊛ 30Oct.12
Haslam, A. H. C.
16Nov.12

Captains. (8)

p.s.✠Potter, C. K. (Hon.Lt.
in Army 16Sept.02)
25Dec.01
p.s. Boyle, R., jun. 25Dec.01
p. ✠Shaw, C. R. 30Oct.08
p. Read, P. A. O. ⊛
6Aug.04
p.s. Bouchier, C. F. 11Apr.06
p.s. Bouchier, G. J, (t)
20May07

1332

Lieutenants. (8)

Hesketh,G.M. 23Nov.10
Pilling, P. C. 24Nov.10
Hough, J. W. 24Nov.10
Entwisle, T. 1Oct.11
Makant, A. V. 1Oct.11
Grierson, W. A. (l)
1Oct.11

2nd Lieutenants. (8)

Smith, T. O. 25Feb.14

Adjutant.

✠Dann, W. R. H.,
Capt. Bedf.R. 7May13

Quarter-Master.

✠Griffiths,T.R.,Capt.
(D.O.) R.A. ret.
pay, hon. capt.
1June09

Medical Officers.

Garstang, Lt.-Col.E.M.,
M.D., VD, hon. Surg.
Col. R.A.M.C. (T.F.)
(attd.) 27Mar.01
         14May87
p. Taylor, H. J., Surg.-
Capt. 15July05
       18June02
p. Wood, J., Surg.-
Capt. 23Oct.07
       23Apr.04

Chaplain.

Elsee, Rev. H. J.,
M.A., Chapl. 3rd
Class (T.F.) (attd.)
7Mar.13
7Mar.08

[Uniform—Scarlet.
Facings—White.]

THE NORTHAMPTONSHIRE REGIMENT.
Regimental District No. **48**. [No. **9** District.]

The Castle and Key, superscribed "Gibraltar, 1779-83," and with the motto "*Montis insignia Calpe*" underneath.
The Sphinx, superscribed "Egypt."
"Louisburg," "Quebec, 1759," "Martinique, 1762," "Havannah," "Martinique, 1794," "Maida," "Douro," "Talavera," "Albuhera," "Badajoz," "Salamanca," "Vittoria," "Pyrenees," "Nivelle," "Orthes," "Toulouse," "Peninsula," "New Zealand," "Sevastopol," "South Africa, 1879," "Tirah," "Modder River," "South Africa, 1899-1902."

Regular and Special Reserve Battalions.
Uniform—Scarlet. *Facings*—White. *Agents*—Messrs. Cox & Co.

1st Bn. (48th Foot)	..*Blackdown, Farnborough.*	3rd Bn. {(Northampton and Rutland Mil.) ..}	*Northampton.*
2nd „ (58th „)	.. .. *Alexandria.*		
Depôt ..	.. .. *Northampton.*	Record Office	*Warley.*

Territorial Force Battalion.
4th Bn. .. .. "*Territorial Headquarters*," Clare Street, *Northampton.*

Allied Regiment of Dominion of New Zealand.
15th (North Auckland) Regiment.

Colonel .. .. .. Browne, Maj.-Gen. G. F., C.B., D.S.O., ret. pay, p.s.c. [R] 12Dec.10

1st and 2nd Battalions.

Lt.-Colonels. (2)
2 Prichard, C. S., D.S.O., 2June11
1 Smith, E. O. 15June13

Majors. (8)
2 Higginbotham, C. E. 2June07
1 Norman, H.H. 15June09
s. Allen, P. 11Jan.11
(3) 1Trent, G. A. (*Comdg. Depôt*) 18Mar.11
c.o. Skinner, P. C. B., p.s.c. 7Feb.12
w.a. Dobbin, L. G. W. 8Nov.12
s. Knox, H. H. S., p.s.c. 15June13
2 Drew, H.R.H. 26Nov.13

Captains. (14)
2 Mowatt, C. R. J., 17Mar.03
r. Royston-Pigott, G. A. 30Mar.03
2 Wood-Martin, J. I. (F) 2June03
w.a. Williams, F. T. 7Dec.04
c.o. Barton, C. W., D.S.O. 23Jan.05
1 Cartwright, H. 20May05
1 Gordon, R. E. 2Aug.05
c.o. Thompson, S. A. 24Sept.05
(3) 2Alston, E. A. B. 26July08
c.o. Ommanney, G. P. 1Oct.08
1 Hughes, E. L. 1Oct.08
(3) 1Russell, W. R. 1Dec.08
(3) 1Powell, D. W. 1Dec.08
e.a. Graham, C. 21Aug.09
t. Thunder, S. H. J. 21Aug.09
1 Parker, R. B. 14Feb.10
s. Hayne, S. S. 1Apr.10
(1) White, E. E. 7May10
1 Bentley, G. M. 7May10
1 Lloyd, H., *Adjt.* 15Aug.10
2 Capell, A. G. C. 20Nov.10

Captains.—contd.
s.c. Trevor, H. E. 30Nov.10
2 Robinson, L. J. 1Dec.10
2 Haldane, L. A. 11Jan.11
1 Savage, J. A. 28Mar.12
1 Hunt, G. W. 28Mar.12
c.o. Orean, T. 14June13
c.o. Roberts, C. E. 14June13
1 Dickson, B. B. 14June13
c.o. Muirhead, T.S. 15June13
2 Watts, C.H.R. 15June13
2 Power, H., *Adjt.* 15June13
2 Elston, C. D. 1Mar.14

Lieutenants. (20)
c.o. Humphrey, R. J. P. 18Mar.09
1 Robinson, G. St. G. 12Apr.09
c.o. Buckle, C.G. 30June09
(3)1 Mylne, E. C. 21Aug.09
c.o. Beattie, H. H. 15Aug.10
1 Fraser, G. M. 1Apr.11
2 Smyth, B. O. 1Apr.11
f.c. Read, A. M. 7Sept.11
21Feb.06
2 Stocker, St. J. C. 6Jan.12
2 Rastrick, U. 10Jan.12
2 Jackson, M. W. 10Jan.12
c.o. O'Brien, H. D. S. 22Jan.12
2 Beattie, S. H. 26May12
2 Lake, R. D. 27May12
w.a.1 Cobb, E. C. 27May12
1 Wauchope, C. L 27June12
2 Middleton, A. D. 12Dec.12
2 Parker, C. R. 12Dec.12
2 Coldwell, W. G. A. 19Feb.13
2 Shaw, G. T. 5Mar.13
1 Warren, E. G. 29Apr.13
1 Jervois, W. J. 14June13
1 Bacon, O. H. 8Oct.13
3July13
2 Sparrow, W.G.M. 22Oct.13
2 Sprey-Smith, S. H. 23May14
2 Lucy, R. E. 5July14

2nd Lieutenants. (12)
1 Pickering, A. C. 5Feb.13

2nd Lieuts.—contd.
2 Parker, G. A. 24May13
2 Beresford, C. Z. de la P. 3Sept.13
1 Cowley, C. S. 17Sept.13
2 Rushton, E. B. L. 10Dec.13
2 Gordon, G. D. 24Jan.14
1 Burlton, L. H. B. 24Jan.14
1 Jarvis, A. S. G. 24Jan.14
1 Gordon, C. H. 24Jan.14
1 Sherriff, A. N. 25Feb.14

Adjutants.
2 Power, H., *capt.* 20Nov.11
1 Lloyd, H., *capt.* 12Apr.12

Quarter-Masters.
2 Mayes, R., *hon. lt.* 4Nov.11
r. Walker, H. W., *hon. lt.* 3Dec.11
1 Hofman, A., *hon. lt.* 4June13

Special Reserve.
2nd Lieutenants.
Nye, A. J. (on prob.) 11Mar.14
King, F. W. (on prob.) 14Mar.14
Nobbs, H. (on prob.) 15Apr.14

3rd Battalion.
{*Officers serving on 20Sept.02 in the corresponding Militia unit hold honorary Army rank equivalent to the Militia regimental rank they then held. Other officers entitled to honorary Army rank have it shown against their names.*}

Hon. Colonel.
Stopford Sackville, S. G. (Hon. Col., ret. Mila.) 26July08
2Jan.01

Lt.-Colonel.
p.s. Westmorland, A. M. J., Earl of, Col., A.D.C. 31July07

Major.
Champion de Crespigny, G. H., *late* Lt. North'n R., *hon. l.c.* (H) 14Feb.03
r.e. Trent, G. A. 18Mar.11

Captains. (5)
Grant-Thorold, H. 18July00
p.s. O'Brien, H. H. S. (H) 10Dec.04
Coldwell, R. C., Capt. ret. pay (H) 6June06
p.s. Pigott, B. W., *late* Maj. 6 Bn. Manch R. (Hon. Capt. in Army 19 Oct. 00) (H) 14Oct.06
r.e. Alston, E. A. B. 26July08
r.e. Russell, W. R. 1Dec.08
r.e. Powell, D. W. 1Dec.08
Robinson, *Str*F. V. L., Bt., Capt. ret. pay 30Apr.12
Allott, P. B., Capt. ret. pay 7May12
4June13

Lieutenants. (11)
r.e. Mylne, E. C. 21Aug.09
Farrar, J. H. 4July10
Needham, E. J. (H) 4July10
Paget, G. G. B. 4July10
Wall, C. E. 16Oct.11

2nd Lieutenants. (8)
Nailer, H. K. F., (Asst. Dist. Offr., S. Provs., Nigeria, {1Jan.14} {(15Sept.13)} 22Feb.11
Benyon, W. W. 1Apr.11
Davison, R. (on prob.) 10Jan.14
Marshall, R. H. (on prob.) 14Mar.14
Elston, J. L. (on prob.) 18Apr.14

Adjutant.
Royston-Pigott, G. A., Capt. North'n R. 22Apr.12
(Capt. in Army 30 Mar. 08)

Quarter-Master.
Walker, H. W., *hon. lt.*

THE NORTHAMPTONSHIRE REGIMENT—(Regtl. Dist. No. **48**)—*contd.*

4th Battalion.

"South Africa, 1900-02."

"Territorial Headquarters,"
Clare Street,
Northampton.

Hon. Colonel.

p. Spencer, Rt. Hon.
C. R., Earl,
K.G., G.C.V.O.,
VD, [F] (*Hon. Lt.-Col. ret. Terr. Force*) 8Jan.13

Lt.-Colonel.

✕Barry, S.L., D.S.O.,
Maj. Res. of Off. 21Mar.14

Majors. (2)

p.s. Mulliner, A. F., VD,
hon. l.c. 5May97
p.s. Willoughby, F., VD,
hon. l.c. 13Feb.01

Captains. (8)

p. Fisher, J. W., TD,
hon. m. 17Mar.94

p. Eunson, G. S., TD,
hon. m. (H) 16Dec.96

p. Henson, A. C. (H) 6Sept.02

p.s. Brown, J. (H) 8Nov.06

p.s. Dorman, L. P. (H) 28Feb.12

p.s. Wilson, H. M. 21Jan.14

p. Wright, H. L. 7Feb.14
Wright, F. A. 6May14

Lieutenants. (8)

(p.) Edward, A. A. 9Oct.07
(p.) Butlin, N. B. 20May11
Pendered, R. D. 28Feb.12
Preston, F. H. 30July13
Yarde, C. G. E. 2Aug.13
Wyatt, J. D. 28Jan.14
Crockett, C. J. 7Feb.14

2nd Lieutenants. (8)

Bishop G. R. 1July12
Pittom, W. W. P. 21Jan.13
Marlow, S. J. 20June14

Adjutant.

Thunder, S. H. J.,
Capt. North'n Reg. 20Nov.13

Quarter-Master.

p. ✕Goacher, R., *hon. m.* 5Feb.02

Medical Officers.

✕Cogan, Lt. L. D. B.,
R.A.M.C. (T.F.)
(*attd.*) 17May12
Arthur, J., M.D.,
R.A.M.C. (T.F.)
(*attd.*) 17May12

Chaplain.

Clarke, Rev. T. G.,
M.A., Chapl. 4th
Class (T.F.)(*attd.*) 1Apr.08
21Jan.07

[Uniform—*Scarlet.*
Facings—*White.*]

Cadet Units affiliated.
King's School, Peterborough, Cadet Corps.
The Northampton School Cadet Corps.

| 1841 | 1842 | 1843 | 1844 |

PRINCESS CHARLOTTE OF WALES'S (ROYAL BERKSHIRE REGIMENT).

Regimental District No. **49**. [No. **7** District.]

The Dragon, superscribed "China."

"St. Lucia, 1778," "Egmont-op-Zee," "Copenhagen," "Douro," "Talavera," "Albuhera," "Queenstown," "Vittoria," "Pyrenees," "Nivelle," "Nive," "Orthes," "Peninsula," "Alma," "Inkerman," "Sevastopol," "Kandahar, 1880," "Afghanistan, 1879-80," "Egypt, 1882," "Tofrek," "Suakin, 1885," "South Africa, 1899-1902."

Regular and Special Reserve Battalions.

Uniform—Scarlet.   *Facings*—Blue.   *Agents*—Messrs. Cox and Co.

1st Bn. (49th Foot)	..	Aldershot.	3rd Bn. (R. Berks. Mil.)	..	..	Reading.
2nd ,, (66th Foot)	..	Jhansi.				
Depôt ..	..	Reading.	Record Office ..	..		Warwick.

Territorial Force Battalion.

4th Bn. .. .. St. Mary's Butts, Reading.

Colonel .. .. Dickson, Maj. Gen. E. T., ret. pay (*Res. of Off.*) [R] 25July13

1st and 2nd Battalions.

Lt.-Colonels. (2)

2Feetham, E. 30Apr.11
1Graham, M.D. 48ept.12

Majors. (8).

1Finch, H. M. 12Sept.06
(3)1Foley, F. W., *D.S.O.* (Comdg.Depôt)30Apr.97
2Walsh, J. G. R. 21May07
1Betty, W. R. P. K. 26Feb.08
1Maurice, D. B., *D.S.O.* 29Aug.08
2Turner, A. S. 30Apr.11
Ready, F. F., *D.S.O.*, *p.s.c.*, *e.*[1] [F] 29July11
o.o. Collins, Hon. R. H., *D.S.O.*, *p.s.c.* 4Mar.14

Captains. (14)

s. Hill, C. G., *D.S.O.* 14Mar.03
2Macdonald, A. G., *p.s.c.* 14Mar.03
2Thornton, W. B. 8May04
s. Moore, F. H., *p.s.c.* 5Aug.04
1Hunt, T. E. C., *e.* [L] 5Aug.04
2Hunt, G. P. S. 11Feb.05
1Bayley, W. K. 20May08
18Dec.07
2Harris, A. E. F. 7Jan.09
s.o. Lucas, C. H. T. 1Apr.09
s.a. Bassett, J. R. 2June09
1Collins, R. J., *p.s.c.* [L] [F] 2June09
1Bromhead, B.G.S.2June09
r. Holdsworth, A. M. 1Mar.10
1Birt, L. H. 23Apr.10
(3) 28teele, O. 31July10
o.o. Elgee, P. E. L. 1Aug.10

Captains—contd.

2Sawyer, G. H. 1Aug.10
2Fraser, A. J. 3Aug.10
(3)2Hopton, G. W. 3Aug.10
f.o. Dawes, G. W. P.30Apr.11
f.o. Murphy, C. F. De S. 3June11
1Shott, H. H., *D.S.O.* 3June11
(3)1Bird, L. W. 3June11
t. Sharpe, A. G. M. 10Apr.12
2Curtis-Raleigh, H. T. R., *e.* 4Mar.14
2Aldworth, T. R., *Adjt.* 4Mar.14

Lieutenants. (19)

o.o. Orr, E.A.B. 9Jan.08
o.o. Waters, C. L. 22Apr.08
2Radford, M. C. 5Apr.09
2Townshend, P. A. K. 7July09
3July09
1Perrott, A. H., *Adjt.* 24July09
1Hopkins, U. S. 24July09
2Moody-Ward, R. G. T. 28July09
(3)2Isaac, A. G. F. 16Feb.10
o.o. Harvey, R.B.L. 1Mar.10
(3)1Allfrey, E. M. 17July10
1Frizell, C. W. 1Aug.10
1Reeves, P. J. 3Oct.10
2Nugent, C. 30Apr.11
1Macgregor, D. A. 3June11
2Gordon, A. D. 22June11
1Fullbrook-Leggatt, C. St. Q. O. 17Aug.11
o.o. Garnett, P. N. 5Sept.11
1Wheeler, C. P. 5Feb.12
2Bagar, E. F. 10Apr.12
2Guest-Williams, W. A. 22Dec.12
2Mackwood, C. C. O. 23Feb.13
2Hodgson, G. G. 10Oct.13
1Woods, J. H. 28Jan.14
1Hanbury-Sparrow, A. A. H. 4Mar.14

2nd Lieutenants. (12)

2Saunders, A.H.20Sept.11
1Denniss, T. V. B. 20Sept.11

2nd Lieuts.—contd.

1Perkins, R. G. B. 20Sept.11
2Leslie, J. T. 9Dec.11
1Hibbert, A. P. J. 14Feb.12
1Burney, E. E. N. 22Jan.13
2Gregory, G. F. 9Apr.13
2Wood, H. R. W. 22May12
24Jan.14
1West, N. 24Jan.14
2Watson, C. G. 25Feb.14

Adjutants.

2Aldworth, T. R., *capt.* 9Sept.12
1Perrott, A. H., *lt.* 23Feb.13

Quarter-Masters.

2Lickman, H. S. 10Nov.06
hon. capt. 13Dec.13
r. Boshell, F. S., *hon. lt.* 15Feb.08
1Batt, F., *hon.lt.* 20Oct.09

Special Reserve.

2nd Lieutenants.

Wigan, Y. R. D. 28Oct.11
Suckling, W. S. (on prob.) 5July13
Moore, G. M. 5Nov.13
Rossiter, P. (on prob.) 22July14

3rd Battalion.

(*Officers serving on 18July01 in the corresponding Militia unit hold honorary Army rank equivalent to the Militia regimental rank they then held. Other officers entitled to honorary Army rank have it shown against their names.*)

Hon. Colonel,
Abingdon, M. A., Earl of, *late Lt.-Col. Mil*s. 7June08
27Oct.80

Lt.-Colonel.

p.s. Barker, F. G. 20Apr.09

Major.

r.e. Foley, F. W., *D.S.O.* 30Apr.07
North, P. W., *Capt. ret. pay* [L] (*Res. of Off.*) (*Remount Service*) 3June09

Captains. (5)

p.s. Quarry, J. S. (H) 24July10
r.e. Steele, O. 31July10
r.e. Hopton, G.W. 3Aug 10
r.e. Bird, L. W. 3June11
Harvey, R. P., *Capt. ret. pay* (*Res. of Off.*) 10Feb.12
Strange, A. F., *late* 2nd Lt. R. Berks R. (H) 22Feb.12
Morris, G. W. S., *Capt. ret. pay, o.* 16Mar.12

Lieutenants. (11)

Bishop, F. H. 4Feb.09
r.e. Isaac, A. G. F. 16Feb.10
r.e. Allfrey, E. M. 27July10
Martineau, H. M. 26Feb.12
Peters, R. H. 26Feb.12
Belcher, G. 26Feb.12
Pearson, A. G., *late* 2nd Lt. R. Berks R. 9Apr.13
Searles, G. 27Aug.13
Bennett, C. V.27Aug.13
Methven, E. B. 3Apr.14

2nd Lieutenants (8.)

Green, C. W. 1Apr.13
Getting, E. N. (on prob.) 13Jan.14
Oke, R. W. L. 3Jan.14
Hogan, R. G. R. (on prob.) 25Feb.14
McNamara, M. P. (on prob.) 13May14

Adjutant.

Holdsworth, A. M., *Capt. R. Berks. R.* 16Mar.12 (*Capt. in Army*1 Mar.10)

Quarter-Master.

Boshell, F. S., *hon. lt.*

| 1845 | 1846 | 1847 | 1848 |

PRINCESS CHARLOTTE OF WALES'S (ROYAL BERKSHIRE REGIMENT)—(Regtl. Dist. No. 49)—contd.

4th Battalion.

"South Africa, 1900-02."

St. Mary's Butts, Reading.

Hon. Colonel.

Gen. H.R.H. Prince Frederic Christian Charles Augustus of Schleswig - Holstein, K.G., G.C.V.O., VD, Personal A.D.C. to the King 29July69

Lt.-Colonel.

Pearce-Serocold, O., VD, (Q)(a)(b) 31Oct.09 bt. col. 30Apr.10

Majors. (2)

✗Clarke, R. J. (Hon. Lt. in Army 10 July 01) 18Mar.13
Hedges, F. R. 21Dec.13

Captains. (8)

p. Battcock, G. A. (t) 24Mar.10
p Bartram, C. (q)⑨ 18Dec.10
p. Aldworth, J. N. 25Apr.12
Lewis, C. A. L. 26Apr.12
Barnes, R. L. 7June13
Thorne, H. U. H. (H) 9June13
Blandy, W. E. M. (H) 27Dec.13
Forshaw, J. H., late Lt. W.I.R. 1July14

Lieutenants. (8)

Holcroft, E. S. 20Jan.12
Willink, F. A. 1July13
Attride, R. G. 1July13
Boyle, S. 1July13
Cruttwell, G. H. W. 1July13
Palmer, R. W. P. 24July13
Challenor, O.B.24Dec.13
Moore, G. 28Apr.14
Auld, S. J. M. 13May14
21 June10

2nd Lieutenants. (8)

Whittaker, R. 17Sept.13
29June10
Falcy, C. R. L. 21Oct.13
Dowson, O. J. 17Jan.14
Gedge, D. R. W. 7Feb.14
Goolden, J. H. 14May14

Adjutant.

Sharpe, A. G. M., Capt. R. Berks R. 16Feb.13

Quarter-Master.

p. Egginton, D., hon. capt. 3Mar.08

Medical Officers.

Baxter, Capt. C. B., M.B., R.A.M.C. (T.F.) (attd.) 7Dec.11
1July07
Joyce, Lt. J. L., R.A.M.C. (T.F.) (attd.) 5Jan.10

Chaplain.

Gillmor, Rev. F.J.C., M.A., Chapl. 4th Class (T.F.) (attd.) 1Apr.08
1June07

[Uniform—Scarlet.]
Facings—Blue.]

Cadet Unit Affiliated.

1st Cadet Company, 4 Bn. R. Berks. R.

| 1849 | 1350 | 1351 | 1352 |

THE QUEEN'S OWN (ROYAL WEST KENT REGIMENT).
Regimental District No. **50** [No. **10** District].

"*Quo Fas et Gloria ducunt.*"
The Sphinx, superscribed "Egypt."

"Vimiera," "Corunna," "Almaraz," "Vittoria," "Pyrenees," "Nive," "Orthes," "Peninsula," "Punniar," "Moodkee," "Ferozeshah," "Aliwal," "Sobraon," "Alma," "Inkerman," "Sevastopol," "Lucknow," "New Zealand," "Egypt, 1882," "Nile, 1884-85," "South Africa, 1900-02."

Regular and Special Reserve Battalions.
Uniform—Scarlet.   *Facings*—Blue.   *Agents*—Messrs. Cox & Co.

1st Bn. (50th Foot)	..	.. Dublin (for Kinsale).	3rd Bn. (West Kent Mil.)	.. .. Maidstone.
2nd ,, (97th ,,)	..	.. Multan.		
Depôt	.. ..	.. Maidstone.	Record Office	.. .. Hounslow.

Territorial Force Battalions.
4th Bn.   .. ..   Drill Hall, Tonbridge. | 5th Bn.   .. Drill Hall, East Street, Bromley.

Allied Regiment of Dominion of New Zealand.
1st (Canterbury) Regiment.

| *Colonel* .. .. ℭ. Leach, Maj.-Gen. Sir E., K.C.B., ret. pay [R] .. 3Apr.04 |

1st and 2nd Battalions.

Lt.-Colonels. (2)
2Pedley, S. H. 14Mar.12
1Martyn, A. 21Mar.12

Majors. (8)
1Buckle,M.P.,p.s.o.,
  p.s.c. (l) 7Mar.07
2Woulfe Flanagan,
  R. J. [l] 4Mar.08
1Pack-Beresford,C.G.
  21Mar.08
s. O'Dowda,J.W.,p.s.c.
  13Jan.09
(3)1Robinson, P. M.,C.M.G.
  (Comdg. Depôt) 17May11
s. Isacke, H.,p.s.c. [l]
  14Mar.12
bt. lt.-col. 26Nov.13
2Kitson, C. E. 21Mar.12
1Hastings, P. 21Mar.12

Captains. (14)
Nunn, T. H. C.,
  D.S.O., p.s.c. 2Aug.02
2Joslin, F. J., p.s.c.
  7Jan.03
(2)2Bonham-Carter, C.
  18Dec.07
  16Nov.01
1Lister, G. D. 9May08
s. Hildyard, R.J.T., p.s.c.
  4Jan.04
1Tulloch, R. M. G.,
  p.s.c. 20Jan.04
c.o. Hickson, L.H. 21Jan.04
1Buchanan Dunlop,
  H. D., e. 19Mar.04
e.a.Stigand, C. H. [L]
  1Apr.04
1Keenlyside, G. F. H.
  21Sept.04
m.c. Twisleton-Wykeham-
  Fiennes, J.T. 4Dec.04
(3)2Grant, A. K. 23Jan.05
t. Norman, F. H.23Jan.05
2Nelson, J. W. 3July07
  28Aug.04
(3) 1Parker, J. C. 1Sept.07
s.c.2Belgrave,H.D.18Sept.07

Captains—contd.
1White, R. L. 25Dec.07
2Ingram, C. R. 25Jan.08
t. Know, A. D'E. 21Mar.08
2Dinwiddy, M. J.
  28Mar.08
t. Johnstone, B. 7Feb.12
  28Mar.08
t. Hewitt, A. S. 18Sept.11
2Case-Morris, C. W.
  1Jan.13
2Hibbert, O. Y.,
  p.s.c. 26Mar.13
1Phillips, W. C. O.
  26Mar.13
r. Waring, H. A. 26Mar.13
e.a.Brock, R. G. C. 3Sept.13
m.c. Adams, C. F. 3Sept.13

Lieutenants. (19)
1Fisher, F. 22Jan.06
2Searight, A. K.
  [L] 12Oct.07
1Legard, G. B., Adjt.
  12Oct.07
2Graham, M. W. 25Dec.07
1Vicat, M. J. 6June14
  26May08
c.o. Yates, W. G. 13Jan.09
2Whitty, N. I. 21Jan.09
e.a.Bazley-White,
  R. B. L. 1Mar.09
2Hardy, A. E., Adjt.
  8June10
(3)1Wingfield-Stratford,
  G. E. 23Nov.10
1Johnston, D. J. 1Apr.11
(3) 2Moulton-Barrett,
  E. F. 5Apr 11
2Bredon, A. S. 18Nov.11
1Palmer, W. V. 18Nov.11
2Ford, J. B. B. 18Jan.12
2Kay, J. K. 22Jan.12
1MacNeece,W.F.,
  2Feb.12
1Newton, W. 6June12
2Wilberforce-Bell,
  P. F. 2Aug.13
2Anstruther, P. N.
  16Aug.13
  18Apr.13
2Battye, C. F. 25Feb.14
2Clarke, W. S. 11Mar.14

2nd Lieutenants (12)
2Brown,J.E.G. 20Sept.11
2Barnes, O.G.R.20Dec.11
2Howell, N. B. 14Feb.12

2nd Lieuts.—contd.
1Ames, W. K. 13Mar.12
1White,H.B.H.13Mar.12
1Broadwood, M.F.
  4Sept.12
1Gore, S. K. 4Dec.12
2Balbernie, A. G.
  10Dec.13
2Chitty, A. A. K.25Feb.14
1Dawson, W. R. A.
  10June14

Adjutants.
1Legard, G. B., lt.
  1Jan.12
2Hardy, A. E.,lt.18Mar.14

Quarter-Masters.
T. Couch, J. 26Apr.99
  hon. maj 26Apr.14
1Rogers, H. G., hon. lt.
  24Apr.12
2Grey, F., hon. lt.
  27Nov.12

Special Reserve.
2nd Lieutenants.
McCleland, N. P. K.
  25Aug.10
J. O'N. 78ept.10
  8June11
McDonagh, P.
  (on prob.) 2May14

3rd Battalion.
Officers serving on 10June01 in the corresponding Militia unit hold honorary Army rank equivalent to the Militia regimental rank they then held. Other officers entitled to honorary Army rank have it shown against their names.)

Hon. Colonel.
✠Field-Marshal H.R.H.
Arthur W. P. A.,Duke
of Connaught and
Strathearn,K.G.,K.T.,
K.P.,G.C.B.,G.C.S.I.,
G.C.M.G., G.C.I.E.,
G.C.V.O., Col. Gt. Gds.
and A.S.C., and
Col.-in-Chief R. Dub.
Fus. and Rif. Brig.,
Personal A.D.C. to
the King 2Aug.08
  2Aug.84

Lt.-Colonel.
p.s.✠Griffith-Boscawen,
  SirA.S.T.,Knt.38Sept.10

Major.
r.e.✠Robinson, P.M.,
  C.M.G. 17May11
✠Barrow, C. D. 15Oct.13

Captains. (5)
✠Beeman,A.C.31May02
✠Allfrey, C. M. (H)
  31May02
Hitchins, C. F.,
  hon. m. 7Jan.01
r.e.✠Bonham-Carter,
  C., p.s.c. 18Dec.01
  16Nov.01
r.e.✠Grant, A. K. 23Jan.05
Bonsor, R. J.,(H)
  10June05
p.s.Hall, H. S. H. H.
  (H) (Empld. in
  British N.Borneo
  25Aug.10) 10June05
r.e.✠Parker, J. C. 1Sept.07
p.s.Liebenrood,FitzH.H.
  (H) 1June08
✠Hall, G. D., Lt. ret.
  pay 22Feb.13

Lieutenants. (11)
Furber, H. A. de F.,
  late 2nd Lt.Shrops.
  L.I. (q) 11June08
  5Jan.09
(p.s.)Snelgrove, J. S. N.
  16Apr.10
r.e.Wingfield-Stratford,
  G. E. 23Nov.10
Anderson, C. R. 1Apr.11
r.e.Moulton-Barrett,
  E. F. 5Apr.11
Payton, C. M. (Empld. in
  Col. Sec.'s Office, Singapore, 3 Sept. 13)
  6Sept.11
Whitehouse, H.
  16Oct.12
Sewell, D. C. C.
  1July13

2nd Lieutenants(8)
Holloway, C. A.M.
  1Oct.13

| 1853 | 1854 | 1855 | 1856 |

THE QUEEN'S OWN (ROYAL WEST KENT REGIMENT)—(Regtl. Dist. No. **50**)—contd.

3rd Bn.—contd.

Adjutant.

✗Waring, H. A., Capt.
R.W.Kent R. 22Jan.12
(*Capt. in Army* 26Mar.13)

Quarter-Master.

✗Couch, J., *hon. maj.*

4th Battalion.

"South Africa, 1900-02."

Drill Hall, Tonbridge.

Hon. Colonel.

p.s. Williams, C. S., **VD**
(*Hon. Col. ret. Vols.*)
20Dec.06

Lt.-Colonel.

p.s.✗Watney, C. N., **TD**
(*Hon. Lt. in Army*
30May01) 4Jan.11

Majors. (2)

✗Stanhope J. R.,
Earl, late Capt.
G. Gds. (*Capt.
Res. of Off.*) ⑤
(*H*) 7Oct.09
Laurie, J. D. 21Sept.12

Captains. (8)

p. Cohen, Sir H. B., Bt.
24Sept.04
p.s.✗Carlisle, F. B. (*Hon.
Lt. in Army* 11July 01)
(*H*) 24Sept.04
p. Cohen, A. M. [L]
17June07

Captains—contd.

p.s.Robb, C. B. ⑤ (*H*)
1Feb.10
p.s.Cheale, A. R. (*H*)
1Feb.10
p.s.Henson, F. J. 4Jan.11
p.s.Smithers, H. 16May13
p.s.Kelsey, A. R. (*H*)
I. of M. 1Sept.13

Lieutenants. (8)

(p.s.)Smithers, N. 1July09
Watney, R. D. 25Apr.11
Bourne, F. C. 16May12
Norman, C. L. 16May13
Stone, F. L. 16May13
Robinson, H. I. 1Sept.13
Locket, L. G. 1Dec.13
Nash, W. 28Mar.14

2nd Lieutenants (8)

Pardington, G. E. L.
11May12
Dowling, G. 2June12
Clough, H. F. 4June13
Haslam, W. H. W.
12July13
Peareth, W. F. E.
17Sept.13
Styles, H. W. 3Jan.14

Inst. of Musk.

Kelsey, A. R., *capt.*
11May09

Adjutant.

✗Hewitt, A.S., Capt.
R.W.Kent R. 1Sept.11

Quarter-Master.

Hiland, J. H., *hon.
capt.* (Qr.-Mr.)
(Hon.Capt.)(ret.
pay)(*Res. of Off.*)
12June12

Medical Officer.

p. Vise, Maj. C., *M.D.*,
TD, R.A.M.C.(T.F.)
(*attd.*) 13Sept.05
25Feb.93

Chaplain.

Hunt, Rev. D. J. S.,
M.A., Chapl. 3rd
Class (T.F.) (*attd.*)
1Apr.08
13Jan.97

[Uniform—*Scarlet*.
Facings—*Blue*.]

Cadet Unit affiliated.
Westerham and Chipstead
Cadet Corps.

5th Battalion.

"South Africa, 1900-02."

Drill Hall, East Street,
Bromley.

Lt.-Colonel.

Frazer, F. A. 9Apr13

Majors. (2)

Willis, E. B. 9Dec.10
Clark, C. D. 9Aug.12

Captains. (8)

Hills, A. E. (*H*)
22June09
p.s.Neame, L. V. 17Dec.10
p.s.Harston, J. 19Dec.10
Satterthwaite, R. E.
(*H*) 7Oct.12
Keyes, R. 9Apr.13
Richardson, H. L. (*H*)
I. of M. 27Apr.13
Hay, J. H. 19May14

Lieutenants. (8)

Lepper, J. G. 4Oct.11
Sykes, W. E. 7Oct.12
Marshall, T. D. 1May14

2nd Lieutenants. (8)

Bennett, C. V. 20Jan.12
Stokes, C. L. L. 7June13
Hooper, A. F. 5Nov.13
Jenyns, G.C.B. 12Nov.13
Pirle, G. B. 24Jan 14
Burr, C. J. F. 4Apr.14
Brooks, L. G. 1May14
6Oct.13

Inst. of Musk.

Richardson, H. L.,
capt. 1Apr.12

Adjutant.

✗ButlerBowdon,
W.E.I., Capt. D.
of Corn. L. I. 7June11

Quarter-Master.

Cooke, J. H., *hon. lt.*
1July08

Medical Officers.

p. Jefferiss, Capt. F. B.,
R.A.M.C. (T.F.)
(*attd.*) 11Jan.07
11July03
Hamilton, Capt. J.,
R.A.M.C. (T.F.)
(*attd.*) 3Feb.12

Chaplain.

Burr, Rev. E. G.,
D.D., Chapl. 4th
Class (T.F.)
(*attd.*) 1Apr.08
27Nov.07

[Uniform—*Scarlet*.
Facings—*Blue*.]

Cadet Units affiliated.
1st Cadet (Chatham)
Company, R.M.L.I.
1 C. B. R. W. Kent R.

| 1857 | 1858 | 1859 | 1860 |

THE KING'S OWN (YORKSHIRE LIGHT INFANTRY).
Regimental District No. 51. [No. 5 District.]

The White Rose. "*Cede nullis.*"
"Minden," "Corunna," "Fuentes d'Onor," "Salamanca," "Vittoria," "Pyrenees," "Nivelle," "Orthes,"
"Peninsula," "Waterloo," "Pegu," "Ali Masjid," "Afghanistan, 1878-80," "Burma, 1885-87,"
"Modder River," "South Africa, 1899-1902."

Regular and Special Reserve Battalions.
Uniform—Scarlet.   *Facings*—Blue.   *Agents*—Messrs. Cox and Co.

1st Bn. (51st Foot) ..	.. *Singapore (for Maymyo.)*	3rd Bn. (1st West York Mil.) .. *Pontefract.*
2nd ,, (105th ,,) ..	.. *Dublin.*	
Depôt ..	.. *Pontefract.*	Record Office .. .. *York.*

Territorial Force Battalions.
4th Bn. .. .. *Wakefield.* | 5th Bn. .. .. *Drill Hall, French Gate, Doncaster*

Allied Regiment of Canadian Militia.
105th Regiment (Saskatoon Fusiliers.) *Saskatoon. Saskatchewan.*

Colonel .. Wynne, Gen. Sir A. S., *G.C.B.* (*Keeper of the Jewel House, Tower of London,* 6 Oct. 11) 4Apr.13

1st and 2nd Battalions.

Lt.-Colonels. (2)
1Marrable, A. G., *p.s.c.*
 14June12
 23July10
2Bond, R. C., *D.S.O.*
 1May14

Majors. (8)
1Withycombe, W. M.
 14June04
 22Aug.02
2Colquhoun, A. S. [L]
 19July06
(S) 2Brooke, C. R. I.
 (*Comdg. Depôt*)14June08
 29Nov.00
2Tulloch, J. B, G.,
 p.s.c. [L]   12Jan.10
Lyne, C. A. L., *p.s.o.*
 [L] [F]   7Feb.12
2Trevor, R. E. 30Apr.14
 14June12
1Boulton, R. E.,
 11Dec.12
Heathcote, C. E.
 11Nov.13

Captains. (14)
c.o. Gordon-Hall, G. C. W.,
 p.s.c. [L]   9June00
1Gowans, W.   6Apr.01
s. Riley, R. F., D.S.O.,
 p.s.c.   15Apr.01
1Warden, K. E. 17July09
 16Nov.01
s. Barker, P. F. W.
 16Nov.01
s.c. Thorp, H. W. B.
 22Mar.02
s. Deedes, C. P., D.S.O.,
 p.s.c.   14Mar.03
(S) 2Simpson, L., *M.V.O.*
 7Oct.05
1Agg, F. J. G. 22Jan.06
r. Johnson, H. C., *M.V.O.*
 26Jan.06
1Mallinson, R.   1Feb.06
2Ackroyd, C. H., *Adjt.*
 1Feb.06
2Luther, A. C. G.
 2Apr.96

Captains—contd.
2Keppel, A. R. 16June06
1Rigg, E. H.   17June06
e.a. *Postlethwaite*, F. J. M.
 19July06
s.c. Stourton, Hon. E. P. J.
 4Sept.06
2Simpson, J. E. 8Jan.07
2Gatacre, W. E. 24Sept.08
2Munby, J., *p.s.c.*
 26Apr.09
t. Littledale, H. A. P.
 [l]   1June09
(3) 1Brewis, F. B. 1June09
1Hughes, H. K.,
 Adjt.   1June09
(3) 1Chaytor, C. A.12Jan.10
t. Kaye, H. S. 19July10
t. Sullivan, G, K, 1Jan.12
1Day, M. F.   1Jan.12
1Bond, G. M. 22Jan.14

Lieutenants. (20)
d1Denison, B. N.,
 p.s.c. [L] 15Nov.05
2Rawdon, C. H, 28Jan.06
1Staveley, G. H. 7Apr.06
2Unett, W. H. de W.
1Wyley, F. J. 17June06
c.o. Symons, H. W. 4Sept.06
j.l. Carter, H.F.G. [L]
 28Sept.06
(3) 2Smyth, A. B. 20Apr.07
s.s. Orange-Bromehead,
 J. W.   10Oct.07
2Pery-Knox-Gore,
 A. E.   15May08
c.o. Kirkpatrick,
 E. R. M.   18July08
c.o. Williams, W, d'E.
 24Sept.08
c.o. Palmer, G, H. C.
 17Jan.09
(3)1Heygate, C. R. 26Apr.09
1Kent, G. H.   1June09
1Thorp, C. R. T.
 19July10
1de Hoghton, G. 1Apr.11
2Brooke, W. H. 1Apr.11
2King, C. E. D. 1Jan.12
1Lambert, E.   4Jan.12
2Reynolds, T. 22Jan.12
2Wynne, G. C. 16Apr.12
1Penny, T. F. 10Aug.12
1Bradley, E. de W. H.
 9Apr.13
1Jervois, J. A. 18Jan.14
1Law, H. A.   6May14

2nd Lieutenants. (12)
1Collis-Browne, A, U.
 20Apr.10
1Butler, C. K. 5Oct.10
2Pepys, J.   9Nov.10
2Noel, J. B.   12Apr.11
f.c.1Rabagliati, C. E. C.
 14Feb.12
2Butt, T. B.   14Feb.12
1Bowen, H. L. 24Apr.12
1Bradley Williams,
 W. P.   22May12
2Tempest, *. N, 22May12
2Hibbert, H, B. 17Sept.13
1Ritchie, A. F. 25Feb.14

Adjutants.
2Ackroyd, C. H., *capt.*
 15May14
1Hughes, H. K.,
 capt.   6Apr.14

Quarter-Masters.
1Brasier, J. C., *hon. lt.*
 14June05
r. Cocker, W., *hon.lt.*
 18Apr.10
2Bentham, A. E., *hon.
 lt.*   6Jan.12

3rd Battalion.

(*Officers serving on* 2Apr.02
*in the corresponding
Militia unit hold honorary
Army rank equivalent to
the Militia regimental
rank they then held. Other
officers entitled to honorary Army rank have
it shown against their
names.*)

Hon. Colonel.
p.s. Johnstone, M. G.,
 *D.S.O., Lt.-Col.
 ret. pay* (*Hon.
 Col. ret. Mila.*) ⊕
 28June08
 12July07

Lt.-Colonel.
Moore, F. T. T.,
 *Maj. ret. Ind. Army
 (Remount Service)*
 7Nov.13

Major.
r.e. Brooke, C. R. I.
 14June08
 29Nov.00
Heilbron, E. J. [l]
 (*Hon. Lt. in Army*
 24June01) (Q) (H)
 7Nov.13

Captains. (5)
Ellis, R. H., *late
 Lt. Yorks. L.I.*
 (H)   5Nov.04
r.e. Simpson, L., *M.V.O.*
 7Oct.05
Renny, G. M., Capt.
 ret. pay, hon. m.
 2May06
r.e. Brewis, F. B.
 1June09
r.e. Chaytor, C A. 12Jan.10
Yates, F. W. (H) (t)
 2Nov.12

Lieutenants. (11)
r.e. Smyth, A. B. 20Apr.07
r.e. Heygate, C. R.
 26Apr.09
Hayes, C. (H) 21Sept.09

2nd Lieutenants. (8)
Hunter, C.G.R. 5Aug.11
Slingsby, H. L. 25Dec.12
Carrington, W. 5Feb.13

Adjutant.
Johnson, H. C.,
 *M.V.O.,   Capt.
 Yorks. L.I.   1Oct.13
 (Capt. in Army* 28Jan.06)

Quarter-Master.
Cocker, W., *hon lt.*

THE KING'S OWN (YORKSHIRE LIGHT INFANTRY)—(Regtl. Dist. No. **51**)—contd.

4th Battalion.

"South Africa, 1900-02."

Wakefield.

Hon. Colonel.

p. Hind, E. H. VD, ⊕
(Lt.-Col. ret. T. F.)
4Feb.14

Lt.-Colonel.

Haslegrave, H. J., TD
14Dec.13

Majors. (2)

Maggs, G. E. H., TD⊕
15July11
✗Moorhouse, H. TD,
(Hon. Capt. in Army
22July02), ⊕ 14Dec.13

Captains. (8)

p.s.✗Chadwick, P. T.
(Hon. Lt. in Army
22 July 02) 23July04
p. Mayman, H., I. of M.
(H) 23July04
p. Critchley, J. P.11Apr.10
p. Newsome, G. I. (H)
15July11
Taylor, L. M. 10July12
p. Chadwick, A. C. (H)
14Dec.13
Cartwright, F. H. T.
31Mar.14
Chalker, H. C. 17June14

Lieutenants (8)

Firth, J. P. 1Oct.10
Hirst, H. 15July11
Greenwood, G. 8June12
Fraser, H. C. 10July12
Thomson, G. 11May13
Creswick, W. B.
14Dec.13
Brooke, J. S. 31Mar.14
Craik, T. E. 17June14

2nd Lieutenants. (8)

Muirhead, J.I. 15July11
Williamson, W. M.
21Feb.12
Fraser, H. G. 31Mar.13
Baines, A. R. 12June13
Plackett, C.H. 13June13
Wardley, F. 17July13
Plews, J. C. 31Mar.14

Inst. of Musk.

Mayman, H., capt.
2July10

Adjutant.

Kaye, H. S., Capt.
Yorks. L.I. 27Mar.12

Quarter-Master.

Medical Officers.

p. Mill, G. S., M.D.,
Surg.-Capt. 7Sept.06
7Mar.03

Chaplain.

Lowe, Rev. F. E.,
Chapl. 4th Class
(T.F.) (attd.) 8June14

[Uniform—Scarlet.
Facings—Blue.]

5th Battalion.

"South Africa, 1900-02."

Drill Hall,

French Gate, Doncaster.

Hon. Colonel.

p.s.✗Shaw, J. R. (Hon.
Col. ret.Spec.Res.)
(Lt.-Col, Res. of
Off.) (H) 1Jan.09

Lt.-Colonel.

p. ✗Moxon, C. C., TD
(Hon. Lt. in Army
19 June 01) 8Oct.12

Majors. (2)

✗Bradley, C. G. 17June11
Archer, J. F. 8Oct.12

Captains. (8)

p. Turner, R. F. 8Oct.06
p.s.Parkin, F. L. 9Mar.07
p.s.Walker, E. H. (H)
I. of M. 2July08
Mackenzie, T. G.
(H) 2May09
Shearman, T., jun.
(H) 21Sept.13
Walker, J. W. (H)
1July14
Taylor, A. W. 25July14

Lieutenants. (8)

Poppleton, B. E.
11Nov.10
Creyke, E. R. 5Aug.11
Jackson, A. E. B.
13July12
Beach, B. A. 27July12
Walker, N. S. (H)
18Dec.12
Tucker, A. 21Sept.13
Bentley, P. 15May14
Somerville,S.D. 1July14

2nd Lieutenants. (8)

Wadsworth, M. M.
4Apr.11
Clayton-Smith,
H. E. H. 17June12
Sandford, C. R. F. ⊕
6Sept.12
Lister, W. L. 10Oct.13

Inst. of Musk.

Walker, E. H., Capt.
11Feb.13

Adjutant.

✗Sullivan,G.K.,Capt.
Yorks L.I. 1Jan.12

Quarter-Master.

✗Barker, H., hon.lt.
3May12

Medical Officers.

p. Graham, V., Surg.-
Maj. 25Dec.12
5June01
Gray, Capt. W. J.,
R.A.M.C. (T.F.)
(attd.) 1July13
1Jan.10

Chaplain.

✗Barnes, Rev. S. R.
(Hon. Lt. in Army
26July02), Chapl.
4th Class (T.F.)
(attd.) 1Apr.08
6Oct.06

[Uniform—Scarlet.
Facings—Blue.]

| 1365 | 1366 | 1367 | 1368 |

THE KING'S (SHROPSHIRE LIGHT INFANTRY).

Regimental District No. **53**. [No. **4** District.]

The United Red and White Rose.   "*Aucto splendore resurgo.*"

"Nieuport," "Tournay," "St. Lucia, 1796," "Talavera," "Fuentes d'Onor," "Salamanca," "Vittoria," "Pyrenees," "Nivelle," "Nive," "Toulouse," "Peninsula," "Bladensburg," "Aliwal," "Sobraon," "Goojerat," "Punjaub," "Lucknow," "Afghanistan, 1879-80," "Egypt, 1882," "Suakin, 1885," "Paardeberg," "South Africa, 1899-1902."

Regular and Special Reserve Battalions.

Uniform—Scarlet.   *Facings*—Blue.   *Agents*—Messrs. Cox & Co.

1st Bn. (53rd Foot)	.. ..	Tipperary.	3rd Bn. (Shropshire Mil.) .. Shrewsbury.
2nd „ (85th „)	Trimulgherry (for Rangoon.)		
Depôt	Shrewsbury.	Record Office .. .. Shrewsbury.

Territorial Force Battalion.

4th Bn.   ..   ..   ..   *Shrewsbury.*

Colonel ..   ..   ..   Knox, Lt.-Gen. Sir C. E., K.C.B., ret. pay [R] 6Jan.07

1st and 2nd Battalions.

Lt.-Colonels. (2)

Higginson, C. P., D.S.O., p.s.c., q.s. 19Aug.13
2Bridgford, R. J., D.S.O. 11Feb.14

Majors. (8)

2Strick, J. A. 17Nov.08
2Meynell, G., p.s.c. [*l*] 6Mar.09
1Luard, E. B. 11Feb.10
1Payn, W. A., p.s.c., e. [*l*] 19Mar.10
(3) 1Smith, H.M., D.S.O. (Comdg. Depôt.) 6Mar.12
2Masefield, R. 18Sept.12
2Bailey, J. H. 19Aug.13
1Rowan-Robinson, W.J. 11Feb.14

Captains. (14)

2Wilkinson, C.A. 22Jan.02
   bt. maj. 22Aug.02
2Battye, C. W., D.S.O. 22Jan.02
2Bryant, H. G., D.S.O. 22Jan.02
2Atchison, C.E. 11Feb.02
(3) 2Rundle, A.T.C. 5Mar.05
(1) English, E. R. M. 19Aug.05
m.c.Kettlewell, H. W. 8Aug.06
1Cautley, C.H. 15Sept.06
1FitzGerald, P.F. 15Sept.06
c.o. Heard, J. R. 20May08
16Mar.07
s.c. Dorrien-Smith, E. P., D.S.O. 5Feb.08
1Miles, R. P [*l*] 6Mar.09
s.c. 2Hanbury, P.L. 6Mar.09
t. Hooper, J. C. 29Mar.09
1Groves, P. R. C. 29Mar.09
1Delmé-Murray, G.A. 17Nov.09
c.o. Murray, B. E. 9Jan.10
(3) 1Jackson, L. A. 9Jan.10

Captains—contd.

1Rogers, H. S. 9Jan.10
2Vassar-Smith, C. M. 19Mar.10
(3)(2)*Holmes à Court, R.E.* 1Apr.10

Lieutenants. (19)

e.a. Middleton, W. 3Aug.05
2Leach, F. J., *Adjt.* 19Aug.05
r. Bowen, A. P. 8Aug.06
t. Prince, P. 15Sept.06
2Winterscale, C. F. B. 22Sept.06
1Huth, P. C., D.S.O. 1Nov.06
c.o. Poyntz, R. H. 18May07
1Hoffmeister, H.A.R., *Adjt.* 8June07
1Jenings, G. P. C. 20June07
2Skinner, J. S. 18Sept.07
1Grischotti, W. 28Sept.07
1Eakin, R. A. 20May08
12Oct.07
c.o. Harris, C. D. 6Nov.07
8May07
(3) 1Colville, H. G. C. 12Mar.08
2Torin, L. H. 6Mar.09
c.o. Collins, H. S. 29Mar.09
2Fort, R. 17Nov.09
2Vyvyan, W.D. 19Mar.10
1Maunsell, F. H. R. 1Apr.10
j.c. Mansfield, W. H. C. 24July12
2Lloyd, L. J. B. 24July12
1Williams Freeman, A. P. 18Sept.12
c.o. Higgins, P. C. 15Sept.13
c.o. Lees, A.C.L.D. 15Sept.13
1Herdman, A. W. 30Oct.13
2Johnston, A. L. 26Nov.13
2Shaw, W. E. 20Feb.14
2Breffit, G. V. 28Apr.14
2Birkby, J. S. d'H. 28Apr.14
2Plowden, J. C. 29Apr.14
1Savory, F. R. E. 18July14

2nd Lieutenants. (12)

1Freeman, E. A. 8June10

2nd Lieuts.—contd.

2Marsh, C. R. C. 4Sept.12
2Hamersley, A.H. St.G. 6Nov.12
2Holman, G. 3Sept.13
2Farrer, J. O. 17Sept.13
1Perkin, T. D. 10Dec.13
2Beacall, H. 24Jan.14
1Bryans, R. 24Jan.14
1Shears, R. H. 10June14

Adjutants.

1Hoffmeister, H.A.R., *lt.* 12Jan.14
2Leach, F. J., *lt.* 14Feb.14

Quarter-Masters.

2Lewis, E. 20Mar.01
   hon. capt. 20Mar.11
r. Woodland, A. R. 21Nov.08
hon. capt. 21Nov.13
1Smith, J.W., hon. capt. 26July13

Special Reserve
2nd Lieutenants.
Charles, J.A. M. 1Oct.12
Tanner, T. C. 3May13
Richards, R. W. St. J. W. (on prob.) 10Jan.14
3May13

3rd Battalion.

(*Officers serving on 11July01 in the corresponding Militia unit hold honorary Army rank equivalent to the Militia regimental rank they then held. Other officers entitled to honorary Army rank have it shown against their names.*)

Hon. Colonel.
Meyrick, Sir T. C., Bt., K.C.B. (Hon. Col. ret. Mila.) 31May08
19Mar.02

Lt.-Colonel.
p.s. Dickin, T. 10May10

Major.
p.s. Weld-Forester, Hon. F. H. C. (H) 24Mar.06
r.e. ✕Smith, H. M., D.S.O. 6Mar.12

Captains. (5)
Wingfield, C. R. B. (H) hon. m. 4May98
p.s.✕Philips, F. G. P. (Hon. Capt. in Army 2 Nov. 00)
(H) 11Apr.00
Brooke, W. J. (H) 5Feb.02
r.e. Rundle, A. T. C. 5Mar.05
r.e.Jackson, L.A. 9Jan.10
r.e.Holmes à Court, R. E. 1Apr.10
Leslie, D. H., Lt. ret. pay 24Sept.10
Van Cutsen, E. C.L. 17Jan.14

Lieutenants. (11)
r.e. Colville, H.G. C. 12Mar.08
Mitchell, J. A. S. 12Oct.12
Hulton-Harrop, F. L. 12Oct.12
Hunt, R. E. B. 13May13
Bosvile, J. G. B. 11Mar.14

2nd Lieutenants. (8)
Parker, C. E. 1Apr.13
Whitmore, R. S. 1Oct.13
Starey, S. H. (on prob.) 7Mar.14

Adjutant.
Bowen, A. P., Lt. Shrops. LI. 29Mar.12
(*Lt. in Army 8 Aug.06*)

Quarter-Master.
✕Woodland, A. R., hon. capt.

1369	1370	1371	1372

THE KING'S (SHROPSHIRE LIGHT INFANTRY)—(Regtl. Dist. No. 53)—contd.

4th Battalion.

"South Africa, 1900-02."

Shrewsbury.

Hon. Colonel.

Anstice, Sir J. A., .
K.C.B., VD (*Hon.
Col. ret. Vols.*)
(*T*) 3Dec.04

Lt.-Colonel.

p. Howard-McLean, J.R.,
VD, *hon. c.* 29Oct.04

Majors. (2)

p. Garrett, A. N. B., TD.
 (Q) 1May04
p. ✗Harris-Edge, H. P.,
 TD 24Dec.04

Captains. (8)

p. Huntbach, W. 9July04
p.s. Cooke, J. H. (Q)
 (*H*) *I.* of *M.* 8Oct.04
 3July01

Captains—contd.

p. Hawkins, E. S. 22July05
p.s.✗Litt, W. G. 1Nov.06
p.s. Westcott, W. H,
 1Jan.10
p.s. Shearer, W. C. 1May12
 Lane, W. G. 21Apr.13
 1Feb.12
 Morris, L. H.(q)(*H*)
 25June14

Lieutenants. (8)

p.s. Haslewood, R. J. R.
 (*H*) 11June09
 Huntbach, G. W. (*H*)
 15Oct.10
 Wace. H. E. 30July11
 Burnet, J. G. 13June12
 Hughes, A. G. 18Oct.12
 Roberts, W. D. 25Jan.14
 Leake, C. F. 23Apr.14
 Symonds, K. C.
 25June14

2nd Lieutenants. (8)

Litt, E. R. 7July12

2nd Lieuts.—contd.

Peace, G. L. 1Feb.13
Greene, C. H. 17Feb.13
Marston, D.M. 1June13
Watkin, A. C. 1Apr.14
Lewis, W.B. A. 2Apr.14

Inst. of Musk.

Cooke, J. H., *capt.*
 7June11

Adjutant.

✗Hooper, J. C.,
Capt. Shrops.
L. I. 20Feb.14

Quarter-Master.

Oxley, L. J. R.,
hon. capt. 3Apr.01

Medical Officers.

p. Gwynn, Lt.-Col.
C. H., *M.D.*, VD,
R. A. M. C. (T. F.)
(*attd.*) (*hon. Surg.·
Col.*) 11Nov.11
 3Mar.80

Chaplains.

Auden, *Rev.* J. E.
M.A., Chapl. 4th
Class (T.F)(*attd.*)
 1Apr.08
 16Apr.02
Williams, *Rev.* R. W.,
Chapl. 4th Class
(T.F.) (*attd.*) 1Apr.08
 6Oct.06

[Uniform—*Scarlet*.
Facings—*Blue*.]

Cadet Unit affiliated.
Bridgnorth Cadet Company

| 1873 | 1874 | 1875 | 1876 |

THE DUKE OF CAMBRIDGE'S OWN (MIDDLESEX REGIMENT).
Regimental District No. **57**. [No. **10** District.]

The Plume of the Prince of Wales. In each of the four corners the late Duke of Cambridge's Cypher and Coronet.
"Mysore," "Seringapatam," "Albuhera," "Ciudad Rodrigo," "Badajoz," "Vittoria," "Pyrenees," "Nivelle," "Nive," "Peninsula," "Alma," "Inkerman," "Sevastopol," "New Zealand," "South Africa, 1879," "Relief of Ladysmith," "South Africa, 1900-02."

Regular and Special Reserve Battalions.

Uniform—Scarlet. *Facings*—Lemon Yellow. *Agents*—Messrs. Cox & Co.
1st Bn. (57th Foot) .. .. Woolwich. | 5th Bn. (R. Elthorne Mil.) .. .. Mill Hill.
2nd ,, (77th ,,) .. .. Malta. | 6th ,, (R. East Middlesex Mil.) .. Mill Hill.
3rd ,, ... Cawnpore. | Record Office .. Hounslow.
4th ,, ... Devonport (for Bordon).
Depot .. Mill Hill.

Territorial Force Battalions.
7th Bn. .. .. Priory Road, Hornsey. | 9th Bn. Drill Hall, Pound Lane, Willesden Green, N.W.
9th ,, .. 202a, Hanworth Road, Hounslow. | 10th ,, Stamford Brook Lodge, Ravenscourt Park, W.

Allied Regiments of Canadian Militia.
57th Regiment "Peterborough Rangers," .. .. .. Peterborough, Ontario.
77th Wentworth Regiment .. .. Dundas, Ontario.

Allied Regiment of Dominion of New Zealand.
11th Regiment (Taranaki Rifles.)

Colonel .. .. C. Kent, Hon. Lt.-Gen. H., ret. pay 30Nov.00

1st, 2nd, 3rd and 4th Battalions.

Lt.-Colonels. (4)
1 Ward, B. E. 18Sept.10
3 Stephenson, E. W. R. 17Feb.12
4 Hull, C. P. A., *t.v.* 24Feb.12
2 Hayes, R. H. 28Sept.12

Majors. (16)
1 Rowley, F. G. M. 12Dec.03
1 Ross, R. J., *p.s.c.* [l] 17Feb.04
2 Elgee, J. W. L. 24Feb.04
4 Finch, H. W. E. 22Feb.05
1 Blakeney, H. N., *D.S.O.* 27May05
3 Hall, J. H. 17Feb.08
2 Ash, W. C. C. 1Apr.09
(5)1 Ingle, W. D. [F] (*Comdg. Depôt*) 27May09
(6) 4 Bridgman, G. A. 22Sept.11
3 Hingley, S. H. [l] 17Feb.12
s. Stewart, J. F. 2Mar.12
3 Large, P. M. 27Sept.12
4 Abell, W. H. 28Sept.12
3 Poole, F. G., *D.S.O.* [l] [F] 18Dec.12
4 Davy, W. H. G. 23Jan.14

Captains. (28)
2 Ramsay, F. W. 29Mar.01
2 Thompson, B. A. 12Oct.01
1 Osborne, H. P., *p.s.c.* 12Oct.01
s. Bentley, G. W. 12Oct.01
2 Bicknell, H. P. F. 23Nov.01
Swainson, F. E. 24Mar.02
2 Heath, R. M., *D.S.O.* [F] 2Aug.02
Cochran, H. P. G. 24Sept.02
4 Oliver, G. 11May07 4Nov.02

Captains—contd.
t.v. Stewart, W. A. 4Feb.03
1 Hastings, G. H., *Adjt.* 20May08
4 Glass, H. E. L. 28May03
e.a. Percy-Smith, D.C. 17Feb.04
D.S.O. 3May04
t. Anson, H. P. R. 4July04
s. Miller, W. 18Feb.05
1 Cunningham, J. S. 11Mar.05
o.d. Sandys, E. T. F., *p.s.c.* 25Mar.05
5Nov.00
4 Newton, W. C. 19July05
16Aug.02
c.o. Stonor, W. G. 13Jan.06
(5)2 Hooper, A. H. 24Feb.12
30May05
1 Spence, H. F. 14Jan.06
t. Rowlatt, H. N. 16Jan.06
3 Hilton, H. P. 16Jan.06
(6) 4 Whiteman, J. 18Sept.06
r. Odling, W. A. 27Nov.07
2 Homan, H. L. 26Aug.09
(6) 4 Hay, C. A. 26Aug.09
r. Owen, D. C. 26Aug.09
(5)1 Samuel, W. H. 7Nov.09
4 Roy, K. J. 9Nov.10
c.o. Page, C. A. S. 14Dec.10
c.o. Goodwin, H. 21Jan.11
3 Large, H. E., *Adjt.*
21Jan.11
t. Pearson, V. L. N.
24Mar.11
s. Anwyl-Passingham, A.M.O.A.[l] 11Sept.12
3 July 11
c.o. Webb-Bowen, W.I.
6Mar.12
bt. maj. 4Sept.11
c.o. Barker, E. 6Mar.12
3 Drew, C. D. 6Mar.12
2 Wordsworth, A. G. 28Nov.01
6Mar.12
1 Skaife, A. F. 6Mar.12
3 Kitchin, C. 1Apr.12
1 Gibbons, E. S. 23Apr.12
d. Passy, L. V. 27Mar.12
(6)3 Jones, P. B. 28Sept.12
28Oct.12
3 Dawson, A. G. 27Sept.12
7Dec.10

Captains—contd
3 Scarbrough, M. C. 21Feb.13
(5)2 Tulloh, C. F. 1Jan.14
1 Gould, F. H. 22Jan.14
t. Knowles, J. E. 1Feb.14

Lieutenants. (38)
1 White, P. G. 16Jan.06
t. Dixon, J., *Adjt.* 25Apr.06
1 Evatt, G. K. K. 9May06
2 Hanley, H. A. O. 27June06
2 Fergusson, A. 11Sept.06
t. Heape, E. A. 3Apr.07
4 Sloane-Stanley, L. F. 4May07
2 Macartney, J. J. 13July07
t.v. Preston, S. 1Feb.08
(5)1 Browne, M. 11Apr.08
1 Warneford, H. W. B. 21May08
f.c. Dawes, L. 6Aug.08
c.o. Jones, W. L. 10Oct.08
4 Cartwright, H. A. 10 Apr.09
w.a. Bagley, G. O. T. 24Apr.09
4 Brown, G. L. 26Aug.09
1 Jefford, W. W. 22Sept.09
w.a. Bennett, R. D. [l] 11May10
c.o. Hardingham, R. C. 21Jan.11
(6)4 Tidbury, O. H. [l] 1Feb.11
1 Pargiter, L. L. 9Mar.11
(6) 3 Cooper-Key, A. L. 24Mar.11
4 Williams, W. E. 1Apr.11
4 Wollocombe, T. S., *Adjt.* 1Apr.11
3 Lyon, N. H. B. 1Apr.11
2 Castberg, F. A. H. [L] 19 Apr.11
1 Appelbe, E. N. 26July11
1 Welman, N. Y. L. 17Aug.11
p.d. 3 Money, H. G. 17Aug.11
2 Rowley, D. T. C. 6Mar.12
4 Robinson, A. F. E. 6Mar.12
1 Apr 12
4 Moore, R. N. 23Apr.12
3 Sichel, G. M. J. 27Apr.12

Lieutenants—contd.
p.d. Lightfoot, L. J. 7May12
3 Hilton, C. S. 1Sept.12
3 Todd, R. J. K. 8Feb.13
3 Newnham, L. A. 21Feb.13
3 Gransmore, H. 22Jan.13
t. 4 Hughman, G. S. 4June13
3 Ash, W. J. 23July13
4 Wilkinson, J. R. M. 10Oct.13
3 Row, A. W. W. 30Dec.13
2 Saville, H. B. W. 1Jan.14
(5)2 Mills, T. L. 22Jan.14
2 Harvey, C. M. 29Jan.14
2 Lindsell, R. S. 1Feb.14
3 Gordon, A. D. 9Mar.14
4 Druce, G. C. 15May14
3 Herbert, H. R. 27May14

2nd Lieutenants. (24)
1 Arnold, A. C. 4Sept.12
4 Henstock, K. P. 4Sept.12
2 Young, R. J. 4Sept.12
3 Hodding, E. M. 22Jan.13
4 Tagg, S. H. A. 5Feb.13
4 Thorp, J. R. 5Feb.13
1 Welman, L. L. 8Sept.13
2 Neumann, J. A. 3Sept.13
3 Curtler, F. M. 17Sept.13
2 Orlebar, R. E. 17Sept.13
3 Phillips, H. 17Sept.13
2 Cade, A. G. 10Dec.13
2 Belfield, E. 10Dec.13
1 Dyer, F. V. A. 24Jan.14
1 Bucknall, G. C. 25Feb.14
1 Paul, H. W. M. 25Feb.14
3 Brodie, R. H. [l] 10June14
1 Trewman, C. H. 10June14
2 Wauchope, J. B. 10June14

Adjutants.
1 Hastings, G. H., *capt.* 21Aug.11
3 Large, H. E., *capt.* 28Nov.11
4 Wollocombe, T. S., *lt.* 22Feb.13
2 Dixon, J., *lt.* 9Mar.14

| 1877 | 1878 | 1879 | 1880 |

THE DUKE OF CAMBRIDGE'S OWN (MIDDLESEX REGIMENT)—(Regtl. Dist. No. 57)—contd.

1st, 2nd, 3rd and 4th Bns.—contd.

Quarter-Masters.
3Fulcher, W. 24Mar.00
 hon. capt. 24Mar.10
r. Steed, F. S., hon. lt.
 24Nov.06
4Farrow, M. W.,
 hon. lt, 12Nov.10
r. Amor, E. H., hon. lt.
 4Feb.11
2Wiemers, H. A.,
 hon. lt. 20Aug.13
1Coman, F. A. W.,
 hon lt. 8July14

Special Reserve.
2nd Lieutenants.
Scales, E. L. 13Sept.13
Wrigley, R. (on rrob.)
 25Feb.14

5th Battalion.

(Officers serving on 18Sept.02 in the corresponding Militia unit hold honorary Army rank equivalent to the Militia regimental rank they then held. Other officers entitled to honorary Army rank have it shown against their names.)

Hon. Colonel.
p.s✘Rolleston, V. (Hon. Col. ret. Mila.)
 (Hon. Lt.-Col. in Army 16 Oct. 00) ⓖ
 2Aug.03
 10Mar.08

Lt.-Colonel.
✘Collison, C. S.,
 Capt. ret. pay
 (Res. of Off.) 2Aug.12
Major.
r.e.✘Ingle, W. D. 27May09
 Black, A. B. (H) 2Aug.12
Captains. (5)
r e✘Hooper, A. H.
 24Feb 12
 30May05
p.s.Corcoran, W. J. (H)
 ⓖ 26Mar.12
p.s.Rooke, C. P. (H)29May07
r.e.Samuel,W. H. 7Nov.09
✘Miers, M. C. C.,
 Lt. ret. pay 22Feb.12
✘Owen, H. C., Capt.
 ret. pay (Resdt.
 Magistrate, Ireland,
 28 Oct. 11) 2Apr.12
✘McClellan, F. E.,
 late Lt. Som.L.I.
 4Jan.13
r.e.✘Tulloh, C. F. 1Jan.14

Lieutenants. (11)
r.e. Browne, M. 11 Apr.08
 Venour, L. S. D, H, (H)
 (Asst.Commr.of Police,
 Gold Coast, 1 May 14)
 2Aug.08
Sheffield, W. G. F.
 10Feb.12
Wood, C. R. 8Nov.12
r.e. Mills, T. L. 22Jan.14

2nd Lieutenants. (8)
Hudleston,L.J.13July12
Avison, F. W. 28May13
Schooling, J. H.
 4June13
Lawrence, F. A. L.
 (on prob.) 1Apr.14

Adjutant.
✘Odling, W. A., Capt.
 Midd'x R. 26July11
 (Capt. in Army 27Nov.07)
Quarter-Master.
✘Amor, E. H., hon. lt.

6th Battalion.

(Officers serving on 1 Apr.02 in the corresponding Militia unit hold honorary Army rank equivalent to the Militia regimental rank they then held. Other officers entitled to honorary Army rank have it shown against their names).

Hon. Colonel.
✘C. Kent, Hon. Lt.-
 Gen. H., ret. pay,
 Col. Midd'x R.
 14June08
 14June90
Lt.-Colonel.
p.s.✘Barker, G. E. 1Sept.11
Major.
r.e.✘Bridgman, G. A.
 2Sept.11
✘King, R. F. C. (H)
 1Sept.13
Captains. (5)
p.s.✘Graves, P. H., D.S.O.
 (t) (H) 6Feb.95
p.s.Graves, C. A. H. (H)
 p.v.c. 8Nov.05
r.e.Whiteman, J. 11Sept.06
r.e. Hay, C. R. 26Aug.09
✘Willoughby, N. E. G.,
 Lt. ret. 5Sept.11
✘Iredell, S. M. L.
 Lt. ret. pay 6Sept.11
r.e. ✘Jones, P. B. 6Sept.11
 23Oct.11

Lieutenants. (11)
Josephs, L. H. O. (H)
 19Dec.08
✘Fleming, B. H. F.,
 Lt. ret. pay 3Nov.09
Williams, H. A. 1July08
r.e. Tidbury, O.H.[t] 1Feb.11
r.e. Cooper-Key, A. L.
 24Mar.11
Graham-Toler, C. B.
 1Nov.11
Sneath, C. D. 15Dec.12
Edridge-Green, H. A.
 15Dec.12
Rushton, E. R. 15Dec.12
Mortimer, M.R.
 26Feb.13
Allistone, A. B. W.
 15Apr.14
 9Sept.10

2nd Lieutenants. (8)
Coles, S. H. 10Sept.13
Willis, S. A.
 (on prob.) 3Dec.13
Adjutant.
✘Owen, D. C., Capt.
 Midd'x R. 22Dec.13
 (Capt. in Army 26 Aug. 09)
Quarter-Master.
✘Steed, F. S., hon. lt.

7th Battalion.

"Imperial Service."
"South Africa, 1900-02."
Priory Road, Hornsey.

Hon. Colonel.
Bowles, H. F. (Hon. Col. ret. Vols.)13Aug.04

Lt.-Colonel.
p.s.✘King, E J.(H)(a)(b)
 (Q) 1Nov.07

Majors. (2)
p.s.Pank, C. H., TD (H)
 (Q) 1Dec.06
King, L. R.
 (H)(b)(a)(Q) 5July13

Captains. (8)
p.s.Cranfield, S. W.
 (H)(b)(a)(Q) 9July04
p. Evors, C. A. (Q)
 8June06
p.s.King, S. (q) (H)
 (a) (b) ⓖ 9Nov.07
p.s.White, L. A. (H)
 (Q) 24Jan.08
p. Smith, S. C. M. (Q)
 18Sept.11
Reeves, S. H. (H)(q)
 23Jan12
Frost, E.G. (q) 12June12
Bower, H. A. (H)
 ⓖ (q) I. of M.
 24May13

Lieutenants.
p.s.King, H. K. (H)(b)
 8June06
Keen, A. C. ⓖ
 (q) 29June09
Eales, W. J.(t) 25July11
Cossar, J. M (t) 29Aug.11
Tully, J. K.(q) 28June12
Angas, L. L. B.31May12
Moody, E, T. (t) 1May13

2nd Lieutenants. (8)
Gillett, S.H. 17July11
Melrose, E. A. 20Dec.11
Maitland, J. K. 17Oct.12
Groser, A. G. 23Jan.13
Challen, C. P. 22Feb.13
Hurd, D. W. 22Feb.13
Tait, G. D. 13May13
Shipton, A. T. 14May13
Stacey, C. N. 10June13
Hobson, A. P. 23Jan.14
Flindt, M. H. 30July14

Inst. of Musk.
Bower, G. A. H.,
 capt. 12Oct 09

Adjutant.
✘Pearson, V. L. N.,
 Capt. Midd'x R.
 1Feb.14
Quarter-Master.
p. Hudson, J. T. H.,
 hon. m. 7Oct.02
Medical Officers.
p. Chappel, G. P., M.D.,
 Surg.-Capt. 4July03
 25Apr.00
p. Gregory, Capt. H. L.,
 M.B., R.A.M.C.
 (T.F.) (attd.) 24Aug.09
 24Feb.06
Chaplain.
Ogle, Rev. W. R.,
 M.A., Chapl. 4th
 Class (T.F.) (attd.)
 1Apr.08
 27May03

[Uniform—Scarlet. Facings—Lemon Yellow.]

Cadet Units affiliated.
Christ's College Cadet Company.
Tollington School Cadet Company.

8th Battalion.

"Imperial Service."
"South Africa, 1900-02."
202a, Hanworth Road, Hounslow.

Hon. Colonel.
p. Bott, H., V.D. Hon. Col. ret. Vols.)(Q) 7Feb.06

Lt.-Colonel.
p.s.Garner, W., TD (Q)
 12Apr.11

Majors. (2).
Dams, L. C. [l] 1Oct.11
✘Gregory, E, D. W.
 (H) 24June14

Captains. (8)
p.s.Ruston, A C. ⓖ24Dec.07
Hill, G. L. C. ⓖ (H)
 1Mar.08
Isaacson, P. de
 St. Q. (q) ⓖ(H)1Oct.11
✘South, T. (H) 1Oct.11
p.s.Woodbridge, A. H.
 (Q) 17Feb.12
 14Dec.10
Down, J. A. (Q)
 (H) 1Oct.12
✘Jones, H. C. (H)
 I. of M. 1Apr.14

Lieutenants. (8)
Peake, G. A. 1Mar.10
Greville-Smith, C. H.
 (H) 1Mar.10
Dumsday, C. 1May11
Blest, M. A. 1Nov.11
Marshall, F. P. 1July12
Avison, J. T. 1Oct.12
Buller, R. F. M. 1Apr.14

1381	1382	1383	1384

THE DUKE OF CAMBRIDGE'S OWN (MIDDLESEX REGIMENT)—(Regtl. Dist. No. **57**)—contd.

8th Bn.—contd.

2nd Lieutenants. (8)
Cranmer, A. T. 1Dec.11
Brough, J. H. 3Feb.12
White. J. D. 17Feb.12
Fane De Salis, E. W.
 11Sept.12
Mytton, P. 27Dec.12
Pears, R. 4Feb.13
Bruce, Sir M. W. S.,
 Bt. 15Feb.13

Inst. of Musk.
Jones, H. C., *capt.*
 24Mar.14

Adjutant.
Anson, H. P. R., Capt.
 Midd'x R. 2Jan.12

Quarter-Master.
p. Norwood, H. D., TD,
 hon. m. 19Oct.07

Medical Officer.

Chaplains.
Livingston-Macassey,
 Rev. E., M.A., Chpl.
 4th Class (T.F.) (*attd.*)
 1Jan.12
Battiscombe, *Rev.*
 G. C. Chapl. 4th
 Class (T.F.) (*attd.*)
 22Apr.14

[Uniform—*Scarlet.*
Facings—*Lemon Yellow*].

Cadet Unit affiliated.
Ealing Cadet Company.

9th Battalion.

"South Africa, 1900-02."

The Drill Hall,
Pound Lane, Willesden
Green, N.W.

Lt.-Colonel.
p.s. Blumfeld, J. L.
 (Q) 5Jan.10

Majors. (2)
Hewett, W. P. (Q)
 5Jan.10
Montgomerie, H. S. (Q)
 17July12

Captains. (8)
p.s.Beach, G. (Q) ⓢ
 (H) 25June04
p.s.Bartholomew, A. G. (q)
 17Dec.04
Stratton, F.C.G.ⓢ(q)
 (H) 8Mar.10
Cotton, P.V. (H) ⓢ
 I. of M. 8Mar.10
Tupper, G. W. H.
 13July12
Kenyon, H. G, 16Feb.13

Lieutenants. (8)
Mellersh-Jackson, L.
 13July12
Mellersh-Jackson, W.
 16Feb.13
Little, C. W. R.
 1May14

2nd Lieutenants. (8)
Somervell, D. B.
 14Aug.12
Fisher, C. W. 15Oct.12
Toovey, C. W. 3May13
Robinson, C. K. 27July13
Lamont, J. N. 7Mar.14
Kelly, P. S. 28Mar.14
Holt, V. 22Apr.14
Mleville, F. E. H.
 22Apr.14
Sherwood, H. 29Apr.14

Inst. f Musk.
Cotton, P. V., *capt.*
 10Feb.12

Adjutant.
✗Heape, E. A.,
 Lt.Midd'x.R.,
 capt. 15May14

Quarter-Master.
Rogers, T. G., *hon. lt.*
 11May12

Medical Officer.
p. Goullet, Maj. C. A.,
 R.A.M.C. (T.F.)
 (*attd.*) 5Dec.09
 18May98

Chaplain.
Bartholomew, *Rev.* G.
 T., *M.A.*, Chapl. 4th
 Class (T.F.) (*attd.*)
 30Jan.11

[Uniform—*Scarlet.*
Facings—*Lemon Yellow.*]

Cadet Units affiliated.

Harrow Cadet Company.
Sunbury House School
 Cadet Company.
Kilburn Grammar School
 Cadet Company.

10th Battalion.

Stamford Brook Lodge,
Ravenscourt Park, W.

Hon. Colonel.
✗Wolverton, F., Lord
 29Aug.03

Lt.-Colonel.
Johnson, C. R., TD (Q)
 27July12

Majors. (2)
Dimond, C. F. W. (Q)
 27July12

Captains. (8)
p.s.Griffiths, H. E., VD,
 hon. m. (t) 30Oct.95
p.s.✗Jarrett, C. ⓢ 13May11
p.s.✗Hosken, C. C. F.
 1Jan.12
Hohler, A. P. (Q)
 21Feb.12
White,S.H. (H) (Q)
 27July12
Overbury, J. G. (Q)
 15Aug.12
Fisher, C. J. ⓢ
 (q) 6May14
Foot, P. B. D. H.
 ⓢ (q) 6May14

Lieutenants. (8)
Ocock, W. P. 10Mar.13
Wood, R. R. 10Mar.13
Mackenzie, R. H. T.
 10Mar.13
Bagnall, H. H. 24Oct 13
Gifford, F. R. ⓢ 20May14

2nd Lieutenants. (8)
Faris Barlow,A.W.W.
 12Feb.13
Munford, C. J. H.
 15Feb.13
Bromage, J. A. R.
 22Feb.13
Coleman, R. F. 18June13
Hogben. H. F. T.
 12July13
Dolamore, A. W.
 22Sept.13
Bean, H. 10Dec 13
Sturge, E. 11Dec 13
Templer, H. E. 21Mar.14
Lisle, P. C. 27May14

Adjutant.
✗Docker, G. A. M.,
 Capt. R. Fus.
 23Apr.12

Quarter-Master.
✗Carter, A. W., *hon.
 lt.* 16July10

Medical Officer.

Chaplains.
Dennis, *Rev.* H. W.,
 M.A., Chapl. 3rd
 Class (T.F.) (*attd.*)
 1Apr.08
 12Feb.96
Hudson, *Rev.* R.,
 M.A., Chapl. 4th
 Class (T.F.) (*attd.*)
 1Apr.08
 4Aug 00

[Uniform—*Scarlet.*
Facings—*Lemon Yellow.*]

| 1885 | 1886 | 1887 | 1888 |

THE KING'S ROYAL RIFLE CORPS.
Rifle Depôt .. .. Winchester.

"*Celer et Audax.*"

"Louisburg," "Quebec, 1759," "Martinique, 1762," "Havannah," " North America, 1763-64," " Rolica," "Vimiera," " Martinique, 1809." " Talavera." " Busaco," " Fuentes d'Onor," "Albuhera," " Ciudad Rodrigo," " Badajoz," " Salamanca," "Vittoria," " Pyrenees," " Nivelle," " Nive," " Orthes," " Toulouse," " Peninsula," "Mooltan," "Goojerat " " Punjaub," "South Africa, 1851-2-3," "Delhi, 1857," "Taku Forts," "Pekin, 1860," " South Africa, 1879," " Ahmad Khel," "Kandahar, 1880," "Afghanistan, 1878-80," "Tel-el-Kebir," " Egypt, 1882, 1884." "Chitral," " Defence of Ladysmith," " Relief of Ladysmith." "South Africa, 1899-1902."

Regular and Special Reserve Battalions.
Uniform—Green.   *Facings*—Scarlet.   *Agents*—Messrs. Cox & Co.

1st Bn. (60th Foot) .. Aldershot (for Shorncliffe).	5th Bn. (Huntingdon Mil.) ..	*Winchester.*
2nd ,, (,, ,,) .. Blackdown, Farnborough.	6th ,, (R. 2nd Middlesex Mil.) ..	*Winchester.*
3rd ,, (,, ,,) .. .. Meerut.		
4th ,, (,, ,,) .. .. Gharial.		

Depôt and Record Office .. .. .. *Winchester.*

Allied Regiments of Canadian Militia.
60th Rifles of Canada .. .. .. *Moosejaw, Saskatchewan.*
63rd Regiment " Halifax Rifles " .. .. *Halifax, Nova Scotia.*

Colonel-in-Chief .. .. THE KING.

Colonels Commandant
Grenfell, Field-Marshal Rt. Hon. F. W., Lord, G.C.B., G.C.M.G., Col. 1 L. G., q.s. [R], 1st Bn. 7Aug.98
ff. Pemberton, Maj.-Gen. *Sir* W. L., *K.C.B.*, ret. pay, 4th Bn. .. 5July06
ff. Ashburnham, Hon. Maj.-Gen. *Sir* C., *K.C.B.*, ret. pay [R], 3rd Bn. .. 2May07
Hutton, Lt.-Gen. *Sir* E. T. H., *K.C.B., K.C.M.G.*, ret. pay (*Res. of Off.*)
p.s.c. [R] 2nd Bn. 3June08

Officer Commanding Rifle Depôt (also Colonel in charge of Rifle Records) } Fortescue, Col. F. A., *C.B.*, p.s.c. .. 1July12

1st, 2nd, 3rd and 4th Battalions.

Lt.-Colonels. (4)
1 Northey, E. 18Dec.11
3 Gosling, C. 18Mar.12
2 Pearce Serocold, E., p.s.c. [l] 20Aug.12
4 Sackville-West, Hon. C. J., p.s.c. [l] 1Apr.14
21Feb.05

Majors. (16)
2Philips, L. F., p.s.c. [l] 29Nov.05
22Aug.02
3Warre, H. C., D.S.O., p.s.c., 5Dec.06
s. Blore, H. R., p.s.c. 21Oct.07
29Nov.06
1Shakerley, G. C., 18Dec.07
D.S.O.
3Long, W. J. 6May08
c.o. Hordern, G. V., p.s.c. 25July05
20Aug.08
29Nov.00
(6)2Green, H. C. R. 18Sept.08
3Wyndham, W. F. G., M.V.O. [L]
2Jelf, R. G. 4Nov.10
(5)1Rennie, G. A. P., D.S.O., 12Aug.11
4Widdrington, B. F. 18Dec.11

Majors—contd.
1Armytage, G. A. 18Mar.12
(l)2Follambe, H. F. F. B. 17July12
4Majendie, B. J.20Aug.12
4Bircham, H. F. W. 14Feb.14
2Davidson, J. H., D.S.O., p.s.c. 1Apr.14
10May13

Captains. (26)
4Kay, W. A. I., p.s.c. 11Dec.01
d. 3Cathcart, A. E. 1Jan.02
1Wake, H., D.S.O., p.s.c. 1Jan.02
bt. maj. 10May15
s. Johnson, H., D.S.O., p.s.c. 7Jan.02
6)4Seymour, G. H. 7Jan.02
s. V@Price-Davies, L. A. E., D.S.O., p.s.c. 7Jan.02
2Priaulx, G. K. 22Jan.02
Legard, A. D. 14June02
(5)3Makins, G., M.V.O., 22Jan.04
t. Lomer, S. F. McI. 25July05
15July05
s. Martin, G. H., p s.c. 23Jan.05
2Acland Troyte, G. J. 28Jan.05
6)2Leith, A. R. 25Apr.05
s.c. Hawley, C. F. 23Nov.05

Captains—contd.
3Crichton, R. E., p.s.c. 11Jan.06
1Willan, F. G 2Feb.06
t. Culme-Seymour, G. 22Mar.06
3Maclachlan, A. F. C., D.S.O. 25Aug.06
3Parker-Jervis, W. S. W. 10Feb.07
3Bradford, E. A., p.s.c. 4June07
s. Howard, C. A. 19July07
(5)1Barnett, G. H. 9Oct.07
1Kelly, G. C. [L] 23Jan.08
s. Curling, B. J., p.s.c. 22Jan.08
(5)3Seymour, B. 22Jan.08
(6)4Seymour, R. H.28Feb.08
3Yeats Brown, F. V. 31Mar.08
r. Lee, G. T. 24Apr.08
1Pardoe. F. L. 23Oct.08
1Dalby, T. G. 15Oct.10
22Jan.08
s. Abadie, R. N. 27Oct.10
s. Vernon, H. A. 23Nov.10
e.a. Edwards, F. W., L. 28Nov.10
4Poë, C. V. L. 23Nov.10
r. Watson, H. W. M. 23Jan.11
4Wynne Finch, G. 12Aug.11
1Denison, E. B. 17July12
3Beaumont, Sir G. A. H., Bt. 20Aug.12
4Wingfield, C. J. T. R. 9Nov.12

Captains—contd.
m.c Soames, A. A. 28Jan.13
2Jackson, G. J. 27Mar.13
4Hunter, A. J., p.s.c. 19Apr.13
Barber, W. D. 13Feb.14
4Clements, M. L. S. 13Feb.14

Lieutenants. (40)
1Porter, H. C. M.16May05
f.o. Deedes, W. H. [L]
[E] 22Jan.06
1Evans, A. P. 22Jan.06
3Atkinson, G. M. 2Feb.06
(6)2Davis, W. J. 9May06
s.s. Willan, R. H. 10Feb.07
d. 2Bond, R. H. 27Mar.07
3Hope, J. F. B. 3Apr.07
t. Oppenheim, A. C. 4June07
t. Flower, H. J. 19July07
e.a. Clinton, W. L. 26Aug.07
4Ponsonby, H. C., Adjt. 9Oct.07
t. Mellor, J. S. 17Oct.07
2Blake, M. F. 22Jan.08
3Pearse, J. F. B 22Jan.08
t. Parish, F. W. 13Feb.08
s. Moore, L. G. 25June08
2Upton, Hon. E. E. M. J., Adjt. 8Oct.08
5)1Wakefield-Saunders, A. M. 21Oct.08
1Woods, R. H., Adjt. 23Oct.08
1Saunders-Knox-Gore, W. A. C. 28Dec.08
e.a. Bigge, Hon. J. N. 10Mar.09

O

| 1389 | 1390 | 1391 | 1392 |

THE KING'S ROYAL RIFLE CORPS—(Rifle Depôt)—contd.

1st, 2nd, 3rd and 4th Battalions—contd.

Lieutenants—contd.
2 Purcell, R. J. H. 27June09
c.o. *Butler, J. F. P.* 21Aug.09
3 *Franks, J. F., Adjt.* 16Oct.09
1 Bonham-Carter, A. L. 4May10
3 Lees, J. V. E. 8May10
1 Chaworth-Musters, P. G. 1June10
1 Gough, G. V. H. 23Nov.10
(6)4 Pleydell-Bonverie, J. E. 28Jan.11
3 Thursby, A. D. 1Apr.11
c.o.*Grattan-Bellew, C. C.* 21June11
w.a.*Dimmer, J.H.S.* 27July11
4 Ferrand, S. H. 12Aug.11
4 Curtis, H. O. 7Sept.11
(5)3 de Sales La Terrière, H. M. B. 25Nov.11
3 Cavendish-Bentinck, F. W. 30June12
2 Ellison, C. T. 17July12
1 Bourke, E. G. W. 20Aug.12
2 Jackson, B. W. 21Sept.12
3 Herbert, E. R. H. 9Nov.12
4 Lawrence, A. E. 28Jan.13
3 Shafto, E, D. 27Mar.13
4 Oxley, G. S. 19Apr.13
2 Currie, P. J. R. 7May13
1 Brocklehurst, A. H. 6June13
2 Dubs, G. R. 21June13
3 Fladgate, C. W. 1Oct.13
4 Mitchell, D. J. [l] 8Oct.13
1 H. H. Prince M, V. D. of Battenberg,K.C.V.O. 13Feb.14
4 Mackenzie, M. K. 3Mar.14
3 Macdonald-Moreton, N. C. H. 4Mar.14

2nd Lieutenants. (24)
4 Bodley, R.V. C. [l] 20Sept.11
1 Alston, J. S. 11Oct.11
2 Ormrod, M. S. 19Jan.12
1 Banon, R.A. 14Feb.12
1 Clowes,C.G.E. 13Mar.12
2 Fetherstonhaugh, R. C. 13Mar.12

2nd Lieutenants—contd.
d *Thompson,G.S,R.* 4Sept.12
4 Price-Davies, C. S. 4Sept.12
4 Eden, Hon. W. A. M. 22Jan.13
3 Walmsley, G. 5Feb.13
4 Barker, E. H. 5Feb.13
d *Forster, J.* 3Sept.13
1 Lloyd, H. C. 3Sept.13
4 King, L. H. St. A 17Sept.13
4 Campbell, E. F. 17Sept.13
3 Balfour, O. H. C. 25Feb.14
3 Crossman, W. R. M. 25Feb.14
3 Davison, S. 25Feb.14
4 Bristowe, W. P.25Feb.14
4 Pennefather,R.25Feb.14
1 H.H. Prince Leopold A.L.of Battenberg, K.C.V.O. 14Mar.14
3 *Tindall; E* V. 10June14
3 Barclay, R. H. M. 10June14

Adjutants.
1 Woods,R.H.,*lt.* 3Sept.11
4 Ponsonby, H. C., *lt.* 27June12
2 Upton, *Hon.* E.E.M.J., *lt.* 1Jan.14
3 Franks, J. F., *lt.* 1Dec 13

Quarter-Masters.
r. Judge, W. 11Feb.03
hon. capt. 11Feb.13
3 Watkins, A. C., *hon. lt.* 5Feb.08
1 Harman, A., *hon. lt.* 7July09
2 Robinson, A., *hon. lt.* 5Mar.10
4 Jones, T., *hon. lt.* 4Jan.11
r. Scutt, E., *hon. lt.* 4Mar.14

Special Reserve.
Captain.
✗St. Aubyn, E. G., Lt. ret. pay 28Sept.11
f.c. Wadham, V. H. N. 12Nov.12

2nd Lieutenants.
Butler, H. W. 22Jan.13
Wilkie, R. H. 19Feb.13
Tatham, E. T. *(on prob.)* 10Sept.13
Hope, N. 11Oct.13
Saltmarshe, P. *(on prob.)* 4Mar.14
Goad, J. F. E. *(on prob.)* 2May14
Wigan, D. G. *(on prob.)* 4 July 14

5th Battalion.

(Officers serving on 4Dec.00 in the corresponding Militia unit hold honorary Army rank equivalent to the Militia regimental rank they then held. Other officers entitled to honorary Army rank have it shown against their names.)

Hon. Colonel.
Sandwich, Col, E. G. H., Earl of, K.C.V.O., late G. Gds.(*Hon. Col.late Mila.*)(*Hon. Col. Hunts. Cydlist Bn.*) 31May08 22Feb.11

Lt.-Colonel.
✗Byron, R., *D.S.O.*, Maj. ret. pay 22Feb.13

Major.
r.e.✗Rennie, G. A. P., *D.S.O.* 12Aug.11

Captains. (5)
p.s.✗Fuge, T. W. M., *hon. m.*(*Hon. Capt. in Army* 1 Aug.01) (Labour Exchanges, Bd.of Trade 28Sept.09) 6Jan.00
r.e. ✗Makins, G., *M.V.O.* 22Jan.04
✗Lynes, W. P., Capt. ret. pay (*H*) 25Aug.06
r.e.✗Barnett, G. H. 9 Oct.07
r.e. ✗Seymour, B. 22Jan.08
✗Heseltine, G., Capt. ret. pay 3Aug.10

Lieutenants. (11)
r.e. Wakefield-Saunders, A. M. 21Oct.08
r.e.de Sales La Terrière, H. M. B. 25Nov.11
Waring, E. R. 15June14
Maynard, H. C. 15June14

2nd Lieutenants. (8)
f.c. Wadham, V. H. N. 18Sept.11
Chapel. H. 25 May 12
Chichester, B. A. 4 Mar.14

Adjutant.
✗Lee, G, T., Capt. K. R. Rif. C. 1Jan.12 (*Capt. in Army* 24Apr.08)

Quarter-Master.
✗Scutt, E., *hon. lt.*

6th Battalion.

(Officers serving on 15Oct.00 in the corresponding Militia unit hold honorary Army rank equivalent to the Militia regimental rank they then held. Other officers entitled to honorary Army rank have it shown against their names.)

Hon. Colonel.
✗Hutton, Lt.-Gen. Sir E. T. H., K.C.B., K.C.M.G., ret. pay (*Res. of Off.*), Col. Comdt. K.R.Rif.C., p.s.c. [R] 16Nov.01

Lt.-Colonel.
✗Brownlow, Hon. J. R., Maj. ret. pay (*Res. of Off.*) 1Oct.12

Major.
r.e. ✗Green, H. C. R. 18Sept.08
p.s.✗Gosling, F. R. (*H*) 12June13

Captains. (5)
r.e. ✗Seymour, C. H. N. 7Jan.02
p.s. Davies, A. R., *hon. m.* (*H*) 21Apr.03
p.s. ✗Feilden, P. H. G. (*H*) 12Mar.04
r.e. ✗Leith, A. R. 25Apr.05
p.s. Colvile, C. R. (*H*) (*a*) 2Nov.06
r.e.✗Seymour, R. H. 28Feb.08
Howard-Bury, C. K., Lt. ret. pay 21June13

Lieutenants. (11)
Forsyth-Forrest, T. R. (*H*) 11July03
r.e. Davis, W. J. 9May06
r.e. Pleydell-Bouverie, J. E. 23Jan.11

2nd Lieutenants. (8)

Adjutant.
✗Watson, H.W.M. Capt. K. R. Rif C. 1July14
(*Capt in Army* 23 Jan. 11)

Quarter-Master.
✗Judge, W., *hon. capt.*

The following Cadet Unit is affiliated to the Regiment:—
1st Cadet Battalion, The King's Royal Rifle Corps.

| 1393 | 1394 | 1395 | 1396 |

THE DUKE OF EDINBURGH'S (WILTSHIRE REGIMENT).

Regimental District No. 62. [No. 8 District.]

In each of the four corners the late Duke of Edinburgh's Cypher and Coronet.
"Louisburg," "Nive," "Peninsula," "New Zealand," "Ferozeshah," "Sobraon," "Sevastopol," "Pekin, 1860," "South Africa, 1879, 1900-02."

Regular and Special Reserve Battalion.

Uniform—Scarlet. *Facings*—Buff. *Agents*—Messrs. Cox & Co.

1st Bn. (62nd Foot) .. .. *Tidworth.*	3rd Bn. (R. Wiltshire Mil.) .. .. *Devizes.*
2nd „ (99th Foot) .. .. *Gibraltar.*	

Depôt .. .. *Devizes.*   Record Office .. .. .. *Exeter.*

Territorial Force Battalion.

4th Bn. .. .. *Fore Street, Trowbridge.*

Allied Regiment of Dominion of New Zealand.
10th (North Otago) Regiment.

Colonel .. .. ℂ. Dunne, Gen. *Str J. H., K.C.B.,* ret. pay [R.] 4Apr.98

1st and 2nd Battalions.

Lt.-Colonels. (2)
1 Hasted, A. W.   2Apr.13
2 Forbes, J. F.   19Mar.14

Majors. (8)
1 Barnes, A. A. S.   6Jan.06
2 Wyndham, J. R.   13May08
(3) 1 Brown, W. S.   27Jan.09
 (*Comdg. Depôt*)
s. Finlay, F. D., *p.s.c.*   22Aug.02
 9Feb.10
s. Evans, E., *D.S.O.*   19Mar.10
s. Wilson, A. H. H.,
 p.s.c. [l]   5Mar.13
1 Roche, T., *p.s.c.*   23July10
1 Law, C. A.   2Apr.13
  19Mar.14

Captains. (14)
1 Stoddart, F. W.   26Feb.02
1 Formby, M. L.   26Feb.02
1 Richards, M. C.   19Mar.02
2 Timmis, A. W.   13Oct.02
s. Dansey, F. H.,e.   24Aug.04
1 Blake, W. A.,*e.*   17Aug.05
s. Fisher, H. B.   17Aug.05
r. Gillson, R. M.T.   16Sept.05
2 Henslow, E. L. W.   4Nov.05
e.a. Barker, C. A.   6Jan.06
(3) 2 Makin, E. L., *p.s.c.*   29Dec.06
  17Feb.04
s. 2 Guy, R. F.   17Oct.08
2 Coddington, H. F.   1Apr.09
(3) 2 Cary-Barnard, C.D.V.   1Apr.09
(3) 1 Martin, A.V.P.   6Apr.09
1 Rowan, P. S., *Adjt.*   15Apr.09
2 Carter, C. G. M.   19Mar.10

Captains—contd.
(1) *Hern, W. S.*   14July10
1 Dawes, W. R. A.   18Jan.11
1 Davies, H. R. A.   23Jan.11
1 Mosley, W. H. [L]   25Jan.11
m. Kelly, J. U.   26Jan.11
2 Moore, C. H. E.   1Apr.11
t. Bond, C. G.   17July12
2 Le Huquet, G.   9Sept.12
2 Culver, R. P., *Adjt.*   5Oct.12

Lieutenants. (20)
f.c. Harvey, F. G.   20Oct.06
s. Wallis, H. J. F.   10Aug.07
(3) 2 Spencer, F. A.   17Oct.08
c.o. Hill, G. C.   5Mar.09
1 Mee, J. M.   1Apr.09
2 Beaver, P. S. L.   7Apr.09
c.o Segrave, H. J. [I]   17Sept.09
1 Loder-Symonds, W. C.   19Mar.10
f.c. Martyn, R. B.   29May10
(3) 1 Belcher, A. C. S.   14July10
2 Smith, R.   18Jan.11
2 Hooper, A. S.   23Jan.11
1 Broome, R. H.   25Jan.11
1 Browne, G. S.   26Jan.11
2 Ponsford, J. M.   1Apr.11
1 Bleckly, A. H.   1Apr.11
1 Goodhart, B. H.   1Apr.11
2 Ansted, D. A.   17July11
2 Geddes, W. M.   9Sept.12
1 Wand-Tetley, T. H.   5Oct.12
2 Spencer, E.   17Apr.13
2 Macnamara, G. J. P.   17Apr.13
1 Oliphant, K. J. P.   23July13
2 Grimston, H. S.   9Mar.14

2nd Lieutenants. (12)
2 Down, J. McL.   25Mar.11
1 Carrington, S. F.   25Mar.11
2 Shelford, F. L. D.   27May11
1 Rose, H. B.   20Sept.11
2 Morse, C. C   11Oct.11
1 Green, L. B.   11Oct.11
1 Lloyd, H. W. C.   19Jan.12
1 Fairchild, L.J.   22May12
2 Calley, O J.   4Dec.12
2 Fowle, M. G.   6Feb.13
2 Rogers, R. P.   10Dec.13

Adjutants.
1 Rowan, P. S., *capt.*   20Sept.11
2 Culver, R. P., *capt.*   5Oct.12

Quarter-Masters.
r. Yardley, A. J.   15Apr.99
 hon. maj. 15Apr.14
1 Cordon, W. I.   30Dec.08
 20June00
 hon. capt. 20June10
2 Hewitt, S., *hon. lt.*   18Apr.14

Special Reserve.
2nd Lieutenant.
Roseveare, H. W.
 (*on prob.*)   18Apr.14

3rd Battalion.

(*Officers serving on 11 Sept. 02 in the corresponding Militia unit hold honorary Army rank equivalent to the Militia regimental rank they then held. Other officers entitled to honorary Army rank have it shown against their names.*)

Hon. Colonel.
✕Methuen, Field-
  Marshal, P.S.,
  Lord, Maj. ret.
  pay (*Res. of Off.*)
  (*H*) Ⓢ   21Mar.14

Lt.-Colonel.
✕Heytesbury, L.,
  Lord, Maj. ret.
  pay (*Res. of Off.*)
  (*H*) Ⓢ   21Mar.14

Major.
✕Spiller, L. W.   7June13

Captains. (5)
p.s.✕Reynolds, H. C. C.
 (*H*)   19May06
r.e. Makin, E. L. *p.s.c.*   29Dec.06
  17Feb.04
Magor, A. C.,
 Capt. ret. pay   10Sept.08
  14Sept.12
r.e.✕Cary-Bernard,
 C.D.V.   1Apr.09
r.e.✕Martin, A. V. P.   6Apr.09
p.s.✕Dyer, S.B.B., *D.S.O.*
 Capt. ret. pay (*Q*)
 (*H*), *p.v.c.*   26Feb.11
✕Lambert, R.. *D.S.O.,*
 Capt. ret. pay (*Res. of Off.*)   2July13

Lieutenants. (11)
r.e. Spencer, F. A.   17Oct.08
Stewart, N. D.   14May10
r.e. Belcher, A.C.S.   14July10
Upton, A. H.
 (*Inspr. of Police,
 Cyprus, 7Jan.14*)
Richardson, E. H. B.   25Nov.11
Yockney, W. E.   2Aug.13
Cruikshank, E. O.   4July14

2nd Lieutenants. (8)
Barnes, C. H. R.   1Oct.13
Ransom, H. B.
 (*on prob.*)   24June14

Adjutant.
✕Gillson, R. M. T.,
 Capt. Wilts. R.   16Jan.12
 (*Capt. in Army* 16Sept.05)

Quarter-Master.
✕Yardley, A. J., *hon.m.*

| 1397 | 1398 | 1399 | 1400 |

THE DUKE OF EDINBURGH'S (WILTSHIRE REGIMENT)—(Regtl. Dist. No. **62**)—*contd.*

4th Battalion.

"South Africa, 1900-02."
Fore Street, Trowbridge.

Hon. Colonel.

✗Somerset, A., Duke of, TD, late Lt., 60 Ft. 13June00

Lt.-Colonel.

p.s. ✗Radnor, J., Earl of, TD (Hon. Capt. in Army 30May01), ⓣ 21Mar.08 bt. col. 22Feb.13

Majors. (2)

Armstrong, A., Capt., ret. pay (Res. of Off.) 15Mar.10
Willis, H. H., VD, 20May11

Captains. (8)

p. Randell, A. J., VD (Q)(H) ⓢ, hon. m., I. of M. 27Aug.92

p.s. Phillips, H. A. 13Feb.01

p. Vicary, G. E. 20May03

p. Bennett, C. G. (a) 3Oct.03

p.s. Morrison, D. C. A., (Q) 8Nov.05

p.s. Mackay, E. A. 5Feb.10

p.s. Blake, G. R. ⓢ 18Aug.10

p. Herbert, Hon. G. S. 5Feb.14

Lieutenants. (8)

p.s. Moulton, J. C. 4Feb.07
Hodding, C. F., late 2nd Lt. 3 Bn. Wilts R. (H) 26Oct.09

Lieutenants - contd.

(p.) Wilson, C. M. 1Feb.10
Phelps, J. W. 5Feb.10
Merewether, C. K. 17Mar.10
Pye-Smith, T. E. B. 10Nov.12
Arkell, J. G.ⓢ 25Dec.12
Carson, J. N. 17May13

2nd Lieutenants. (8)

Stanley, G. 25Nov.11
Awdry, N. J. 8Dec.11
Arkell, T. N. 25Oct.12
Harris, R. T. 1Apr.14

Inst. of Musk.

Randell, A. J., hon. m. 1Sept.09

Adjutant.

Bond, C. G., Capt. Wilts. R. 1Oct.12

Quarter-Master.

✗Taylor, A. A. hon.lt. 1Dec.11

Medical Officer

Waylen, Lt. G. H. H., R.A.M.C. (T.F.) (attd.) 24Apr.12

Chaplains.

Bodington, Ven. Archdeacon E. J., M.A., Chapl. 3rd Class (T.F.) (attd.) 7Sept.11 7Sept.01
Goddard, Rev. G. H. G., B.A., Chapl. 4th Class (T.F.) (attd.) 21July10

[Uniform—*Green*, Facings—*black*.]

THE MANCHESTER REGIMENT.
Regimental District, No. **63**. [No. **3** District.]

The Sphinx, superscribed "Egypt."

"Guadaloupe, 1759," "Egmont-op-Zee," "Peninsula," "Martinique, 1809," "Guadaloupe, 1810," "New Zealand," "Alma," "Inkerman," "Sevastopol," "Afghanistan, 1879-80," "Egypt, 1882," "Defence of Ladysmith," "South Africa, 1899-1902,"

Regular and Special Reserve Battalions.

Uniform—Scarlet.   Facings—White.   Agents—Messrs. Cox & Co.

1st Bn. (63rd Foot)	.. Jullundur.	3rd Bn. (6th R. Lancashire Mil.)	.. Ashton.
2nd „ (96th „)	.. Curragh.	4th „ (6th R. Lancashire Mil.)	.. Ashton.
Depôt .. .. Ashton-under-Lyne.		Record Office .. .. Preston.	

Territorial Force Battalions.

5th Bn.	.. Bank Chambers, Wigan.	8th Bn.	.. Ardwick, near Manchester
6th „	.. 3, Stretford Road, Hulme, Manchester.	9th „	.. Ashton-under-Lyne
7th „	.. Burlington Street, Manchester.	10th „	.. Oldham

Allied Regiment of Dominion of New Zealand.
8th (Southland) Regiment.

Colonel .. .. Barnard, Maj.-Gen. W. O., ret. pay 8Jan.04

1st and 2nd Battalions.

Lt.-Colonels. (2)
2James, H. L. 24Feb.08
          24Feb.12
1Strickland, E. P., C.M.G., D.S.O., [F] 1June14

Major. (1)
(2nd in Command.)
1Hitchins, H. W. E. 1June06
          1July01

Majors. (7)
1Crawford, J. C. 18Apr.08
2Weston, R. S. 23Sept.08
w.a.Vaughan, E. 17Feb.04
          22Aug.02
1Walker, E. J. H. 4Mar.05
s. Newbigging, W. P. E., D.S.O. 22Apr.11
(3) 2Wright, B. A., D.S.O. (Comdg. Depôt) 24Feb.12
(2) Anley, B. D. L. G., D.S.O., p.s.c. 20July12

Captains. (14)
2Dorling, F. H., p.s.c. 5Jan.01
2Truenan, C. Fitz G. H. 5Jan.01
(3) 2Hardcastle, R. N., D.S.O. 12Mar.01
1Dunlop, F. C. S. 12Mar.01
2Theobald, H. C. W., D.S.O. 13July01
1Fisher, H., D.S.O. 14July01
2Nisbet, F. S., Adjt. 14July01
1Creagh, L. 27Nov.01
1Hastings, W. C. N., D.S.O. 25Dec.01
i.v.Eddowes, W. B. 5Feb.03
(3) 1Evans, W. K. 18Dec.07
2Morley, C. 9Aug.08
(3) 1Bates, H. C. 9Aug.08
2Wymer, G. P. 1Apr.09
2Knox, H. 1Apr.09
r. Anderson, C. A. 7Dec.11
e.a.Forth, N. B. DeL. [F] 20July12
r. Stapledon, C. C. 20July12
2Fowke, M. C. 1Dec.12
2Foord, A. G. 1Dec.12

Captains—contd.
t. Holberton, P. V. 1Dec.12
1Buchan, E. N., D.S.O. 1Dec.12
1Heelis, J. R., Adjt. 1Dec.12
Tillard, A. K. D. 11Dec.12
Irwin, C. D. 11Dec.12

Lieutenants. (19)
c.o Rose, A. B. 25Oct.02
2de Putron, H. 10Nov.02
f.c.o2Mansergh, W. G. 11Nov.02
1Paulson, P. Z. 12Nov.02
c.o. Wickham, T. S. D.S.O. 12Nov.02
c.o. O'Meara, A. E. 11Dec.02
1Browne, R. G. 5Feb.03
(3) 2Ellershaw, H. 5Feb.03
1Hardingham, A. G. M. 19Aug.03
(3)1Reade, J. H. L. 3Oct.03
s.c.Bolton, C. A. 21Nov.03
2Thomas, A. F. 17Feb.04
t. Dearden, J. A. 7Feb.07
1Mair, B. V. 24Apr.07
e.a.Wright, H. T. R. S. 26Aug.07
2Sotham, E. G. 12Oct.07
2Humphrys, N. W. 18Dec.07
c.o. Musson, E. L. 12June09
1Harrison, H. G. 18July09
2Harper, J. S. 28Oct.09
w.a.Scully, A. J. 12Jan.10
f c. Freeman, W. R. 27Mar.12
c.o.Bostock, L. C. 25May12
w.a.Atkin, B. 5Mar.13
1Shipster, W. N. 3May13
1Davidson, R. I. M. 30July13
2Norman, S. 27Aug.13
1Lynch, R. F. 1Dec.13
2Vanderspar, E. R. 20Feb.14
2Albrecht, V. A. 28Apr.14

2nd Lieuts. (12)
1Parminter, R. H. R. 5Feb.13
2Smith, J. H. M. 27Sept.13

2nd Lieuts.—contd.
1Massé, C. H. 10Dec.13
1Connell, S. D. 24Jan.14
1Henderson, G. S. 24Jan.14
2Chittenden, A. G. B. 24Jan.14
2Burrows, R. F. G. 25Feb.14
2Crawhall, N. G. 25Feb.14
1Saportas, H. A. 2May14

Adjutants.
1Heelis, J. R., capt. 3May12
2Nisbet, F. S., capt. 1Dec.12

Quarter-Masters.
r. Vickers, G. E. 5Feb.02
hon. capt. 5Feb.12
2Connery, W. L., hon. lt. 27Mar.09
r. Price, H. F. W. 21Apr.09
hon. capt. 23Feb.11
1O'Brien, P., hon. lt. 4Sept.09

Special Reserve.
2nd Lieutenants.
Blane, E. R. 1July11
Sergeant, F. W. B. 10Feb.12
Wilson, A. K. 3July12
Gwyther, J. R. 20July12
Green, H. B. C. 11June10
Butler, W. E. 14June13
Balshaw, W. (on prob.) 2Aug.13

3rd Battalion.
(Officers serving on 28July02 in the corresponding Militia unit hold honorary Army rank equivalent to the Militia regimental rank they then held. Other officers entitled to honorary Army rank have it shown against their names.)

Hon. Colonel.
✕Hamilton, Gen. Sir I. S. M., G.C.B., D.S.O., Col. Cam'n. Highrs., q.s., g.,⚔.,⚔., 9Aug.08
24June05

Lt.-Colonel.
p.s.✕Oram, H. K. (H) 8Aug.12

Major.
r.e.✕Wright, B. A., D.S.O. 24Feb.12
✕Aiken, J. B. (Q) (H) 8Aug.12

Captains. (5)
✕Tillard, A. G., Capt. ret. pay 13Sept.99
4Jan.13
r.e.✕Hardcastle, R. N., D.S.O. 9Jan.01
✕Peirce, W. G. K., late Capt. Manch. Reg., ret. pay(Q)(H) ⓢ 25Dec.01
11May12
✕Thornycroft, C. M., Capt. ret. pay (Q) (H),ⓢ 5Feb.03
9Sept.11
✕Finch, W. R. E. H. (H) (Hon. Capt. in Army 6 July 01) 22Oct.04
p.s.✕Murphy, J. L. (H) 8Feb.05
p.s.Kerans, A. L., late Lt. N. Lan. R. (H) (b), ⓟ p.v.c. 22Apr.05
Anthony, G. H. (H) 12Mar.07
r.e.✕Evans, W. K. 18Dec.07
r.e.Bates, H. C. 9Aug.08

Lieutenants. (11)
r.e.✕Ellershaw, H. 5Feb.03
r.e.✕Reade, J. H. L. 3Oct.03
Brodribb, W. C. (H) 6Feb.09

THE MANCHESTER REGIMENT—(Regtl. Dist. No. 63)—contd.

2nd Lieutenants. (8)
Williamson, G. W. 20Sept.11
Dixon, G. 7Aug.12
 18May12
Miller, R. T.
 (on prob.) 26Oct.12

Adjutant.
⚔Stapledon C. C.
 Capt. Manch R. 6June14
 (*Capt. in Army 20 July 12*)

Quarter-Master.
⚔Vickers, G. E., *hon. capt.*

4th Battalion.

(*Officers serving on 30Sept.02 in the corresponding Militia unit hold honorary Army rank equivalent to the Militia regimental rank they then held. Other officers entitled to honorary army rank have it shown against their names.*)

Hon. Colonel.
⚔Derby, Rt. Hon.
 E. G. V., Earl of,
 G.C.V.O., C.B.9Aug.08
 24Dec.02

Lt.-Colonel.
⚔Jebb, J. H. M.,
 D.S.O., Maj. ret.
 pay (*Res. of Off.*) 19May13

Majors. (3)
p.s.⚔Greer, T. M. (*H*)
 (Q) p.v.o. (g) 1Apr.11
Blanch, L. K. (*H*) 30May14

Captains. (6)
p.s.⚔Moore, A. G. (*H*), (g) 22Apr.05
p.s.⚔Charlton, J. E. (*H*)
 I. of M. 5May06
Maclean, L. F. C.
 (Q) (*H*) 8Apr.10
⚔Guinness, W. E.,
 Lt. ret. pay 3May13

Lieutenants. (11)
Erskine, B. L. 1Feb.12
Laskey, F. S. [*l*] (q)
 (*H*) 1Oct.12

2nd Lieutenants. (8)
Horridge, R. 18Oct.11
Atherley, J. E. M. 20Mar.12

Inst. of Musk.
Charlton, J. E.,
 Capt. 2July14

Adjutant.
⚔Anderson, C. A.,
 Capt. Manch. R. 7Dec.11
 (*Capt. in Army 7Dec.11*)

Quarter-Master.
⚔Price, H. W., *hon. capt.*

5th Battalion.
"South Africa, 1900-02."
Bank Chambers, Wigan.

Hon. Colonel.
⚔Eckersley, N. *ff.*
 (Hon. Lt.-Col. ret.
 Spec. Res.) (*Hon.
 Capt. in Army*). 22Nov.13

Lt.-Colonel.
p.s.France, W. S., VD, *hon. c.* 23Dec.05

Majors. (2)
Fletcher, E. 23June12
⚔Darlington, H.C. (*t*)
 (*Hon. Lt. in Army 24June*01) 16Sept.13

Captains. (8)
p. ⚔Cronshaw, A.E. (*Hon.
 Lt. in Army 26July*02)
 7Jan.03
p.s.Brown, N. S. 13June03
p. Rogers, H. M. 17June05
p.s.Fletcher, C. 23Dec.05
p. Simpson, A. W. W.
 10Jan.06
p.s.Brown, F. S. 15Sept.06
p. Leech, A. C. 20Mar.13
p.s.Walker, J. S. A. (*H*)
 I. of M. 16Sept.13

Lieutenants. (8)
p. Martin, W. Y. 16Nov.06
p.s.Cherry, J. W. 16Nov.06
Wall, J. 23June10
Fletcher, S. 29June11
Hewlett, V. 20Mar.13
Woods, W. T. 10Aug.13
James, G. S. 16Sept.13
Johnson, W. G. E.
 13Nov.13

2nd Lieutenants. (8)
Ainscough, C. 9Nov.12
Johnson, A. E. 13Nov.13
Allen, G. E. 27Nov.14

Inst. of Musk.
Walker, J. S. A.,
 capt. 8Feb.12

Adjutant.
Sanders, J. M. R.
 Capt. Leins. R. 1Jan.13

Quarter-Master.
⚔Walkley, D., Qr.-Mr.
 (*hon. capt.*) ret. pay
 hon. capt. 21Jan.12

Medical Officers.
p. Roocroft, Lt.-Col. W.M.,
 VD (*hon. Surg.-Col.*),
 R.A.M.C. (T.F.)
 (*attd.*) 20Aug 04
 2Aug.84

[Uniform—Scarlet.
Facings—White.]

6th Battalion.
"South Africa 1900-02."
3, Stretford Road, Hulme, Manchester.

Hon. Colonel.
p.s.⚔Heywood, R. C. P.,
 TD, Col. T.F. Res.
 (*Hon. Capt. in Army*)(Q)(*H*) 21Jan.14

Lt.-Colonel.
p.s.Heywood, G. G. P.
 (Q)(*H*) 1Sept.11

Majors. (2)
⚔Pilkington, C. R.
 (*Hon. Lt. in Army 19Aug.*01) 24July08
p.s.Worthington, C. S. (q)
 25Feb.14

Captains. (8)
p.s.Capper. S. H. (*H*) ⊕
 25Aug.05
 bt. maj. 24Dec.13
p.s.Frank, N. G. 22Oct.06
p. ⚔Bazley, W. N. (*Hon.
 Lt. in Army* 24Oct.
 01) (q) 1Sept.11
p.s.Holt, J. (*H*) 20Dec.11
p.s.Jackson, S. F. 20July12
p. Cawley, H. T. 1June13
p.s.Bennett, J. R. 15Oct.13
Pilkington, E. F. ⓢ
 12Feb.14
Pilkington, H. B.
 24Feb.14

Lieutenants. (8)
Bolton, D. C. 18Sept.11
Kessler, E. 20Dec.11
Edgar, K. G. 14Jan.12
Blatherwick, T 7June12
Reiss, W. E. 20July12
Aldous, F. C. 12Dec.12
Heywood, A. G. P.
 1June13
(p.) Taylor, A. C. B. (*H*)
 I. of M. 19Sept.13
 25June16
Blatherwick, F. M.
 15Oct.13

2nd Lieutenants. (8)
Thomson, A. D.
 25June12
Hammick, H. A.
 25July13

Inst. of Musk.
Taylor, A. C. B., *lt.*
 6Feb.14

Adjutant.
⚔Holberton, P.V., Capt.
 Manch. R. 4Nov.11

Quarter-Master.
p. ⚔Vass, W., *hon. m.* (b)
 25July05

Medical Officer.
Norris, Capt. A. H.,
 R.A.M.C.(T.F.)(*attd.*)
 21Dec.12
 22June09

Chaplain.
Challenor, Rev. J. W.,
 TD, Chapl. 1st Class
 (T.F.) (*attd.*) 2Aug.01.11
 24Oct.91

[Uniform—Scarlet.
Facings—Yellow.]

7th Battalion.
"South Africa, 1900-02."
Burlington Street,
Manchester.

Lt.-Colonel.
Gresham, H. E., TD,
 ⊕ (*H*) 14May12

Majors. (2)
Hertz, G. B. (Q) 4Jan.11
⚔Staveacre, J. H. ⊕
 3Aug.12

Captains. (8)
p.s.Davies, H.G.(Q)28Apr.06
p. Fawcus, A. E. F. (q)
 1Mar.07
p.s.Brown, J, N. 1Mar.07
p.s.Norbury, C. 14June10
Smedley, H. 5Oct.12
Savatard, T.W. 5Oct.12
Higham, C. E. 4Dec.13

Lieutenants. (8)
p.s.Ward Jones, A. T.
 25Oct.05
Rylands, R. V. 5Jan.12
Williamson, C. H.
 5Jan.12
Eaton, H. R, (*H*)
 (*Asst. Dist. Offr.
 S. Prov., Nigeria*
 12 Jan. 14) 27Apr.12
Norbury, N. 5Oct.12
Townson, E. 22June13
Freemantle, W. G.
 22June13
Tinker, A. H. 4Dec.13

2nd Lieutenants. (8)
Thewlis. H. D.26Nov.12
Chadwick, G. 29Nov.12
Lockwood, G. S. (*H*)
 18June13
Hamilton, G. C. H.
 30Dec.13
Thorpe, J. H. 11Jan.14
Creery, W. F. 9May14

Adjutant.
Creagh, P. H., Capt.
 Leic. R. 12June11

Quarter-Master.
p. ⚔Scott, J., *hon. m.*
 (a) (b) 10Dec.04

Medical Officer.
Farrow, Capt. J, F,
 R.A.M.C. (T.F.)
 (*attd.*) 6Mar.11
 6Sept.10

Chaplain.
Kerby, Rev. E. T.,
 M.A., Chapl. 4th
 Class (T.F.)
 (*attd.*) 10Mar.14

[Uniform—Scarlet.
Facings—White.]

THE MANCHESTER REGIMENT—(Regtl. Dist. No. 63)—contd.

8th (Ardwick) Battalion.

"South Africa, 1900-02."

Ardwick, near Manchester.

Hon. Colonel.
Barlow, J., M.V.O., VD (H) (b) (Hon. Maj. ret. Vols.) 3Dec.06

Lt.-Colonel.
×Heys, W. G. TD, (Hon. Capt. in Army 20Nov.02), (t) 7Mar.14

Majors. (2)
Bentley, F. I., TD (t) 27Apr.12
p.s. Crosland, J. C. H. (Q) 7Mar.14

Captains. (8)
p.s. ×Stephenson, H. M. (Q) 8June06
p. ×Oldfield, E. G. W. 8June06
p.s. Rose, H. J. (Q) 8June06
p.s. Mandley, H. C. F. 21Apr.10
Bluhm, Q. M. 27Apr.12
Standring, D. H. 5Feb.13
Hepburn, A. J. (H) 5Feb.13
Lings, H. C. (H) I. of M. 7Mar.14

Lieutenants. (8)
Heywood, S. 16Dec.09
Moore, C. G. 27Apr.12
Robinson, F. 20Oct.12
Hall, S. 3May13
Womersley, J. W. 25May14
Marsden, R. 25May14
Marsden, A. G. 30May14

2nd Lieutenants. (8)
Wallwork, E. 28Feb.13
Lawrence, J. D. 9Apr.14
Clear, A. 3June14

Inst. of Musk.
Lings, H. C., capt. 20Jan.13

Adjutant.
×Collins, C. H. G., Capt. D. of Corn. L.I. 18Sept.12

Quarter-Master.
Stewart, W. H., hon. lt. 1May13

Medical Officer.
Nesfield, Maj. S., TD, R.A.M.C. (T.F.) (attd.) 18Feb.05 28Jan.93

Chaplain.
[Uniform—Scarlet. Facings—White.]

9th Battalion.

"South Africa, 1900-02."

Ashton-under-Lyne.

Hon. Colonel.
Wainwright, C. R., TD (Lt.-Col. ret. T.F.) 1Apr.14

Lt.-Colonel.
p.s. Wade, D. H. (Q), (H) 17July13

Majors. (2)
Garside, E. 20Apr.12
p.s. Archbutt, W. H. 17July13

Captains. (8)
p. Nowell, R. B. (Q) (H) 10June05
p. Lees, R. (H) I. of M. 26Oct.06
p. Howorth, T. E. (t) 20May09
p. Sugden, H. 6July10
p. Hamer, F. 7Dec.11
p. Platt, T. A. 20Apr.12
Woodhouse, F. 17July13
Okell, G. H. 18Oct.13

Lieutenants. (8)
Kershaw, F. W. 4Mar.11
Richardson, E. 7Dec.11
Birchenall, A. G. 13Nov.12
Stephenson, D. B. 17July13
×Makin, F. A. 24Jan.14
Handforth, G. W. 24Jan.14

2nd Lieutenants. (8)
Makir, G. 13Dec.13
Shaw, H. C. 16Feb.14
Wood, R. G. 20Feb.14
Forshaw, W. T. 13Mar.14
Hyde, F. G. 27Apr.14
Parker, J. A. 8May14

Inst. of Musk.
Lees, R., capt. 15June13

Adjutant.
×Dearden, J. A., Lt. Manch. R., capt. 12Mar.12

Quarter-Master.
×Connery, M. H., Qr.-Mr. (hon. capt.) ret. pay, hon. m. 22Apr.09

Medical Officer.
p. Hilton, Maj. A., R.A.M.C. (T.F.) (attd.) 12July11 23Aug.99

Chaplain.
Burrows, Rev. F. H., M.A., Chapl. 4th Class (T.F.) (attd.) 13May09

[Uniform—Scarlet. Facings—White.]

10th Battalion.

"South Africa, 1901-02."

Oldham.

Hon. Colonel.
p. Patterson, W., VD (Lt.-Col. ret. T.F.) 19Dec.13

Lt.-Colonel.
p.s. Rye, J. B., VD (Q) 18Dec.13

Majors. (2)
×Bamford, P. (Hon. Lt. in Army 2 June 01) (Q) 12Oct.12

Captains. (8)
p.s. ×Hardman, G. W. (Hon. Lt. in Army 6July02) 25June02
p. Wilde, L. C. 30Apr.04
p.s. Booth, A. C. 13Feb.07
p.s. Newton, G. R. (H) (Q), I. of M. 14June07
Newton, J. A. 1July11
Smethurst, R. R. 15Mar.12
Stott, G. E. 12Oct.12
Griffiths, D. E. G. 9Aug.13

Lieutenants. (8)
(p.) Leach, A. 1July08
Sutcliffe, H. 15Mar.12
Owen, G. W. 15Mar.12
Hardman, F. 8June12
Wilkinson, L. St. G. 15July13
Pochin, G. D. 9Aug.13

2nd Lieutenants. (8)
Griffiths, F. N. G. 14June12
Stott, P. 15Oct.12
Park, D. 13Feb.13
Wilde, R. W., late t.t. 9Mar.14
Clegg, J. H. 9Mar.14
Clegg, J. 9Mar.14
Emmott, J. B. 9Mar.14
Lee, A. E. 9Mar.14
Nevinson, H. K. B. 9Mar.14
Stott, J. 8Apr.14

Inst. of Musk.
Newton, G. R., capt. 9July09

Adjutant.
×de Pentheny-O'Kelly, E. J., Capt. R. W. Fus. 28Nov.13

Quarter-Master.
×Kennedy, S. E., hon. lt. 1Mar.10

Medical Officer.
Fort, Capt. H. M., M.B., R.A.M.C. (T.F.) 8June12

Chaplain.
Orton, Rev. J. W., VD. Chapl. 1st Class (T.F.) (attd.) 1Apr.08 6Dec.82

[Uniform—Scarlet. Facings—White.]

Cadet Unit affiliated.

2 C, B, Manch. R.

1413 | 1414 | 1415 | 1416

THE PRINCE OF WALES'S (NORTH STAFFORDSHIRE REGIMENT).
Regimental District No. **64.** [No. **6** District].

The Prince of Wales's Plume.   The Dragon, superscribed "China."
"Guadaloupe, 1759," "Martinique, 1794," "St. Lucia, 1803," "Surinam," "Punjaub," "Reshire,"
"Bushire," "Koosh-ab," "Persia," "Lucknow," "Hafir," "South Africa, 1900-02."

Regular and Special Reserve Battalions.
Uniform—Scarlet.   *Facings*—White.   *Agents*—Messrs. Cox & Co.

1st Bn. (64th Foot) ..	.. *Buttevant (for Cork).*	3rd Bn. (2nd K.O. Stafford Mil.)	.. *Lichfield.*
2nd ,, (98th ,,)..	.. .. *Rawal Pindi.*	4th ,, (3rd K.O. Stafford Mil.)	.. *Lichfield.*
Depôt	.. *Lichfield.*	Record Office	.. *Lichfield.*

Territorial Force Battalions.
5th Bn. .. *Drill Hall, Hanley.* | 6th Bn... .. .. *Burton-on-Trent.*

Colonel .. .. Lloyd, Maj.-Gen. T. F., ret. pay 20Aug.11

1st and 2nd Battalions.

Lt.-Colonels. (2)
2Heneker, W. C. G.,
 *D.S.O.,A.D.C,*10Apr.12
 bt. col. 24Oct.07
1deFalbe, V. W.,
 D.S.O. 14Mar.13

Majors. (8)
s. Hoskins, A. R.,
 D.S.O., p.s.c.,
 q.s.[F] *(temp.*
 Col.) 7Apr.10
 bt. lt.-col. 22Sept.10
2Fox, E. V. 22Sept.10
2Johnston, F. E.16Feb.11
(3)1Andrus, T. A.
 (Comdg. Depôt) 28June11
1Wyatt, L. J. 6Mar.12
1Leman, G. E., *p.s.c.*
 14Mar.13
2Tweedie, H. C.,
 D.S.O. 6Dec.13
2Ley, J. W. 2)Dec.1₃

Captains (14)
2Edwards, W. A. S.
 15Feb.04
1Armes, R. J., *p.s.c., e.*
 24Mar.04
2Weldon, A. S. 20Nov.05
2Beauclerk,A.N.22Jan.06
1Hume-Kelly, G. H.
 10Feb.06
1Conway, A. S. 7Apr.06
(3) 2Hughes Hallett,
 H. H., *p.s.o.* 20Feb.07
 9Nov.07
1Reid, E. B. 20Aug.08
2Giffard,J.F.[L] 30Aug.08
1Ridgway, J. H.14Mar.09
1Lyon, C. H., *p.s.c.*
 17Mar.09
1Ewald, F. C.T. 17Mar.09
2Backhouse,H. 17Mar.09
(3)2Henderson, E. E. D.
 17Mar.09
r. Koebel, F. O. 17Mar.09
1Carneyg, J 1 A pr 10
2Hodson, M.V. R., *Adjt.*
 23Jan.11
(3) 1 Bradley,R.A. 23Jan.11
t. Mosley, N. 20Mar.14
t. Anderson, C. A. W.
 20Mar.14

Lieutenants. (19)
*c.o.*Thomson, J. F. 20Nov.05
 1Lyon, P. 20Nov.05
c.o. Ogilvie, A. N. 3Oct.06
(3)1Royle, A. C. F. 20Feb.07
s. Napier, M. M. 19Feb.08
*c.o.*Fausset, H. C. 20Aug.08
r. Negus, R. E. 26Aug.08
2Stoney, H. H. 11Sept.0*
1Fraser, C., *Adjt.* 6Oct.08
1Bridges. H. C. 17Mar.09
2Punchard, A. 1Apr.09
1Hooper, A. F.A.,
 f.c.r. 25Sept.0ᶜ
1Morgan, R. F. 3Oct.09
2Robinson, H.G.20Oct.09
t. Allen, H. I. 8Jan.10
(3)2Mackenzie-Kennedy,
 K. E. B. 1Apr.10
2Havelock, B. A. J.
 1Apr.10
c.o. Lovegrove, S. J. 1Dec.10
2Gompertz, A. W. B.
 23Jan.11
1Hobart, J. W. L. S.
 19June12
2Standbridge, A. C.
 6July12
2Kennedy, G. 21Nov.12
 16Nov.07
2Tuck, S. A. 22Jan.13
*c.o.*Braum, T. P. 12May13
1Anderson, E.D.
 3Sept.13
2Vavasour, L. O.28 De a.13
1Gordon, C. F. 28Jan.14
*c.o.*Baker, A,W.H. 20Mar.14
2Meautys, P. R. 8Apr.14

Adjutants.
2Hodson, H. V. R.,
 capt. 3Oct.12
1Fraser, C., *lt.* 10Jan.14

Quarter-Masters.
r. Preston, J., 4Dec.01
 hon. capt. 4Dec.11
2Lowther, T. E.,
 hon. lt. 22June07
r. Corbett, W. J.,
 hon. lt. 22June10
1Langridge, E. J.,
 hon. lt. 26Mar.13

3rd Battalion.

(Officers serving on 28Sept.02
 in the corresponding
 Militia unit hold honorary
 Army rank equivalent to
 the Militia regimental
 rank they then held.
 Other officers entitled to
 honorary Army rank have
 it shown against their
 names.)

Lt.-Colonel.
p.s. ✕James, C. H. (H)
 31July11

Major.
r.e.✕Andrus, T. A.
 28June11
p.s.✕Falls, H. E. (H)
 19June12

Captains. (5)
p.s. Shakspeare, W.
 (Q) (H) (a) (b) 23Nov.01
p.s. Hume-Kelly, F, V.
 (H) ⓟ 21Feb.03
p.s.✕Littleton, Hon. W.
 H. (*Hon. Lt. in*
 Army 9July01) (H)
 18Mar.05
p.s.✕ Hughes Hallett,
 H. H., *p.s.c.* 20Feb.07
 9Nov.01
r.e.✕Henderson, E. E. D.
 17Mar.09
r.e.✕Bradley, R.A.23Jan.11
*p.s.*Cox, G. H. (H)
 f.c. 20 May11

Lieutenants. (11)
✕D'Arcy, L. K., Lt.
 ret. pay (H) 15May9?
 6June06
(*p.s.*)Adamson, A. G.
 19May06
r.e. Royle, A. C. F. 20Feb.07
r.e. Mackenzie-Kennedy,
 K. E. B. 1Apr.10
Harris,P.D.(H)15Feb.13
Hill, W. E. 17Apr.13

2nd Lieutenants. (8)
Chester, G. A. B.
 5Feb.13
Hughes, L. H.
 (*on prob.*) 26Apr.13
Otto, F. A. 2Aug.13
Startin, C. B. (*on*
 prob.) 7Jan.14
Magrath, M. St. L B.
 (*on prob*) 25Feb.14
Smyth, D.M. (*on*
 prob.) 4July14

Adjutant.
Negus, R. E., Lt.
 N. Staff. R. 20Feb.12
(*Lt. in Army* 26 Aug. 08)

Quarter-Master.
✕Preston, J., *hon. capt.*

4th Battalion.

(Officers serving on 11June02
 in the corresponding
 Militia unit hold honorary
 Army rank equivalent to
 the Militia regimental
 rank they then held.
 Other officers entitled to
 honorary Army rank have
 it shown against their
 names.)

Hon. Colonel.
Bill, C. (*Hon. Col.*
 rét. Mila.) 30Aug.08
 3Dec.98

Lt.-Colonel.
✕Way, B. I., Capt. ret.
 pay (*Res. of Off.*) (*a*)
 (H) [F] 30Aug.12

THE PRINCE OF WALES'S (NORTH STAFFORDSHIRE REGIMENT)—(Regtl. Dist. No. **64**)—*contd.*

4th Bn.—*contd.*

Majors. (3)

Locker, W. J., Capt.
  ret. pay (*Res. of Off.*)
  (*H*) ⓢ (Q)   5Oct.12
✗Roskell, W. J.,
  Capt. ret. pay
  (*H*) ⓢ (Q)   1Mar 13

Captains. (6)

p.s. ✗Thomas, J. C. C.
  (*H*) (*b*)   7Feb.08
p.s. ✗Ram, G. E. (*H*)
   29Nov.05
Errington, G. H., *late*
  2nd Lt. 1 D.G. (*H*)
   15Apr.08
p.s. Bankhead-Browne,
  A. E. (*H*(Q) 15Apr.08
Macleod, D., *late*
  Lt. Res. of Off.(*H*)
   9Apr.13

Lieutenants. (11)

Colville, R. N. K.
   15Aug.10
Meakin, S. A.   1Mar.13
Glascott, J.   1Mar.14
Jepson, S.   1Apr.14
Meredith, H.   1Apr.14

2nd Lieutenants. (8)

Adjutant.

✗Koebel, F. O., Capt.
  N. Staff. R.   8Jan.14
  (*Capt. in Army* 17Mar.09)

Quarter-Master.

✗Corbett, W. J., *hon. lt.*

5th Battalion.

"South Africa, 1900-02."

Drill Hall, Hanley.

Hon. Colonel.

Dobson, W. W., VD
  (*Hon.Col. ret. Vols.*)
   26May08

Lt.-Colonel.

p. Knight, J. H., VD,
  hon. c. ⓣ   15Dec.06

Majors. (2)

Blizzard. A. E. 28Oct.08
p. ✗Boote, C. E. (*Hon.*
  Capt. in Army 26
  *July*02)   12Mar.13

Captains. (8)

p. ✗Johnson, H. (*Hon. Lt.*
  in Army 18June01)
  (*t*)   7Jan.03
p. Clive, H.   6Apr.04
p.s. Griffith, J.   28Oct.08
Gamon, H. P. 19Sept.11
Barke, C. R. (*H*)
   19Sept.11
Ridgway, H.A. 6Oct.12
Wenger, F.E.[*l*] ⓢ (*H*)
   3Dec.13

Lieutenants. (8)

Wood, S. H.   10Mar.10
Worthington, G. J.
   16Aug.10
Bladen, O. C. 19Sept.11
Mason, F. E. 21Sept.11
Caddick-Adams, C.
   12Feb.13
Keary, C. R.   13Feb.13
Wedgwood, A. F.
   18Oct.13

2nd Lieutenants. (8)

Bindley, H. D. 2Apr.13
Copland, R. W.18 July13
Shelley, V. B.   7Jan.14
Dix, G. S.   8Jan.14
Brown, G. B.   4Feb.14
Aynsley, R. W. 5Mar.14
Arrowsmith,L. 13Mar.14

Adjutant.

✗Magill, H. P.,
  Capt. N. Lan. R.
   11Sept.12

Quarter-Master.

Riley, J. H., *hon. lt.*
   1Apr.08

Medical Officer.

p. Brunt, Capt. E. H.,
  R.A.M.C. (T.F.)
  (*attd.*)   29Oct.07
   5Mar.04

Chaplain.

Rabone, Rev. T. H.,
  Chapl. 4th Class
  (T.F.) (*attd.*) 1Apr.08
   18Mar.05
[*Uniform—Scarlet.*
Facings—White.]

6th Battalion.

"South Africa, 1900-02."

Burton-on-Trent.

Hon. Colonel.

p. Gretton, J., VD,
  T.F.Res., *hon.c.*
  (*Capt.Res.of Off.*)
  ⓣ   1Apr.12

Lt.-Colonel.

p. Ratcliff, R. F., VD,
   18Nov.09

Majors. (2)

Baguley, E. E. 20Sept.07
Hull, H. A.   5July13

Captains. (8)

p. Lloyd, J. F. S. 28Oct.07
p. ✗Peach, E. W. 21July08
p.s. ✗Longstaff, C. L.
  (*Hon. Capt. in*
  Army 9July01)
   25Jan.09
p.s. Jenkinson, J. 1Apr.09
p.s. Tomlinson, E. H.
  (*H*)   26Apr.10

Lieutenants. (8)

Stack, W. A.   15July09
(p.) Lyon, J. C.   15July09
p.s. Norman, F.M. 10Apr.11
   3Sept.04
Burnett, R. P. 25Nov.11
Bamford, O. J. 15Mar.13

2nd Lieutenants. (8)

Newton, B.   7Mar.11
Thoday, L. R.   2Oct.11
Bostock, H. T. 2Oct.11
Davey, H. B.   1Feb.13
Auden, J. L. 10Feb.13
p.s. Stack, J. M.(*H*)28June13
O'Sullivan, H. H.
   16Feb.14
Radcliffe, M. 23Feb.14
Shaw, R. R. S. 25Mar.14

Adjutant.

✗Anderson, C. A. W.,
  Capt. N. Staff.
  R.   12May13

Quarter-Master.

Maher, G., *hon. lt.*
   28July09

Medical Officers.

p. Fausset, H. J., *M.D.*,
  VD, *Surg.-Lt.-Col.*
  (*hon. Surg.-Col.*)
   25July03
   12Oct.78
p. Stack, Maj. E. C.,
  F.R.C.S.I.,R.A.M.C.
  (T.F.) (*attd.*) 22Oct.13
   5Mar.02

Chaplain.

Gilbert, Rev. H. W.,
  M.A., Chapl. 4th
  Class (T.F.) (*attd.*)
   1Apr.08
   23Apr.04
Uniform—Scarlet.
Facings—Blue.]

THE YORK AND LANCASTER REGIMENT.
Regimental District No. 65. [No. 5 District.]

The Royal Tiger, superscribed "India." The Union Rose.
"Guadaloupe, 1759," "Martinique, 1794,""India,1796-1819,""Nive," "Peninsula," "Arabia," "New Zealand,"
"Lucknow," "Tel-el-Kebir," "Egypt, 1882, 1884," "Relief of Ladysmith," "South Africa, 1899-1902."

Regular and Special Reserve Battalions.
Uniform—Scarlet. Facings—White. Agents—Messrs. Cox & Co.

1st Bn. (65th Foot) .. Jubbulpore.
2nd „ (84th Foot) .. Limerick (for Dublin.)
3rd Bn. (3rd West York Mil.) .. Pontefract.

Depôt .. .. Pontefract. Record Office .. .. York.

4th Bn. .. .. Territorial Force Battalions.
Sheffield, | 5th Bn. .. .. Drill Hall, Rotherham.

Allied Regiment of Dominion of New Zealand.
5th (Wellington) Regiment.

Colonel..	ᛗ. Hardy, Maj.-Gen. F., C.B., ret. pay [R] ..	..	.. 5Nov.08

1st and 2nd Battalions.

Captains—contd.
e.a. *Wauhope*, G. B. [F] 18Sept.11
t. *Williams*, R. M. 18Sept.11
t. *Jackson*, V. A. 18Sept.11
1Sharpe, C. S. 6Apr.12
2Gillam, V. A. 6Apr.12
(3) 2Mott, J. F. 1July12
1East, H. J. 22July12
2Hardy, F. K. 2Oct.12
2Horn, T. G. 14Dec.12
2Sandys, M. K. 7Apr.13
c.o. *Marwood*, A. H. L. 1Jan.14
1Collins, P. H. C. 1Jan.14

Lieutenants. (19)
(3)2Ford, V. T. R. 27Oct.08
c.o. *Rose*, R. M. T. 14Nov.08
1Bamford, E. S., *Adjt.* 1Feb.09
(3)1Bacchus, W. H. O. 17Apr.09
c.o. *Reynolds*, D. W. 1June09
2Jackson, C. B. A. 19Sept.09
c.o. *Philby*, H. P. 1Apr.10
1Judkins, L. E. H. 14Apr.10
Walker, K. P. 4Nov.10
1Gauntlett, H. G. 22May10
2Cole-Hamilton,H.A.W. 12Feb.11
2Gordon, H. F. A. 1Apr.11
16Aug.11
1Lousada, B. C. 1Sept.11
1Hardy, W. H. 4Oct.11
1Mather, J. K. 8Dec.11
w.a. *Wood*, R. P. 1July12
c.o. *Grove*, K. S. 21July12
c.o. *Murray*, G. G. 22July12
2Sim, N. E. H. 2Oct.12
1Litchfield,H. F.12Mar.13
2Cullen. W. H. 7Apr.13
2Boucher, C. B. 14May13
2Lethbridge, N. B. 1Jan.14
2Francis, R. J. 4Feb.14
2Houston, R. N. 14Feb.14
1Kent-Lemon, A. L. 6Mar.14

Lt.-Colonels. (2)
2Cobbold, E. C. 1July12
1Burt, A. G. 1Jan.14

Majors. (8)
2Clemson, W. F. 3Oct.06
1Gresson, T. T., *D.S.O.* 9Sept.08
2Halford, M. F., *p.s.c.* [l] 17Apr.06
29Nov.09
(3)2Ashton, F. E. (*Comdg. Depôt*) 2June09
1Colston, H. K. 1Jan.10
2Isherwood, F. E. B. 3May11
2Bayley, G. E. 1July12
2Robertson, E. C. 1Jan.14

Captains. (14)
o.d. *Byrne*, H. F., e., o. 16June02
s.c. *Headlam*, H. R. [F] 2Apr.03
1Wedgwood, G. H. 14June05
f.c.2Burdett, A. B. [l] *Adjt.* 1Jan.06
2Jarrett, A. V. 1Jan.06
t. *Parkinson*, T. W. 12Mar.07
1Fenning, A. E. H. 20May08
7Nov.07
1Blunt, A. St. J. 9Sept.09
(3) 1Webb, R. E. 18Nov.08
1Palmer, A. E. 1Dec.08
r. *Eardley-Wilmot*, A. 16Mar.09
12Aug.08
(3)1Pratt, G. McD. 17Apr.09
e. *Salmond*, H. A. B. 1June09

2nd Lieutenants. (12)
1Lynch, A. G. 13Mar.12
1Chamier, C. K. 4Sept.12
1Burge, C. G. 22Jan.13
2Norris, F. L. 3Sept.13
1Howard, H. C. M. 24Jan.14
2Stott, C. R. 24Jan.14
2Edye, J. H. M. 25Feb 14
2Keid, C. A. 25Feb 14
1Tayler, E. H. 20June14

Adjutants.
1Bamford, E. S., *lt.* 12Mar.13
2Burdett, A. B. [l] *capt.* 2Dec.13

Quarter-Masters.
r. *Birch*, J. 26Oct.01
hon. capt. 26Oct.11
2McGuire, E. C., *hon. lt.* 4Aug.09
1Gilliard, W. T., *hon. lt.* 23May14

Special Reserve.
2nd Lieutenants.
Taylor, S. H. (*on prob.*) 18Mar.14
Willis, R. (*on prob.*) 18Mar.14

3rd Battalion.

(*Officers serving on 23Sept.02 in the corresponding Militia unit hold honorary Army rank equivalent to the Militia regimental rank they then held. Other officers entitled to honorary Army rank have it shown against their names.*)

Hon. Colonel.
ᛗ. *Hardy, Maj.-Gen. F., C.B., ret. pay,*
Col. York & Lanc. R. [R] 2Aug.08
4Apr.88

Lt.-Colonel.
ᛗBroughton, E. C., *Maj. ret. pay* (H) 20Apr.09
Major.
r.e. ᛗAshton, F. E. 2June09
ᛗHaines, A. M., *Maj. ret. pay (Res. of Off.)* (H) 26Jan.10

Captains. (5)
ᛗWelsh. D. T. (*Hon. Lt. in Army 24 Sept. 02*) (H) 20Nov.07
r.e. ᛗWebb, R. E. 18Nov.08
r.e. ᛗPratt, G. McD. 17Apr.09
ᛗThomson, E. L., *Lt. ret. pay* 24Mar.10
ᛗKey, R.E., *Capt. ret. pay* 1Apr.10
ᛗCameron, A. C., *Lt. ret. pay* 8Mar.11
p.s. *Johnson*, R. S. (H) 17Apr.12
r.e. *Mott*, J. F. 1July12
Armitage, W. A. (H) 24Aug.12

Lieutenants. (11)
r.e. *Ford*, V. T. R. 27Oct.08
r.e. *Bacchus*, W. H. O. 17Apr.09
Ripley, C. R. 13June13
Cowley, R. B. 23June13

2nd Lieutenants. (8)
Horlington, J. 2July13
Lucas, S. (*on prob.*) 21Jan.14

Adjutant.
Eardley-Wilmot, T., *Capt.* York & Lanc. R. 9Nov.11
(*Capt. in Army 12Aug.08*)

Quarter-Master.
ᛗBirch, J., *hon. capt.*

THE YORK AND LANCASTER REGIMENT—(Regtl. Dist. No. **65**)—*contd.*

4th (Hallamshire) Battalion.

"South Africa, 1900-02."

Sheffield.

Hon. Colonel.

Vickers, T. E., C.B., VD, (Hon. Col. ret. Vols.) 26July99

Lt.-Colonel.

p. Firth, B. A., VD 1Mar.13

Majors. (2)

p. Clough, T. C., VD ⓣ (H) 1Apr.08
✗Revell-Sutton, F. (H) (Hon. Capt. in Army 1 July 08) 1Mar.13

Captains. (8)

p. Wortley, J. 1Aug.03
p. Elliot, G. (t) 19Dec.03
p. ✗Longden, E. W. 18Feb.05
  (Hon. Lt. in Army 2 Sept. 02)
p. Ellison, W. R. (H) 11Apr.06
  I. of M.
  Wilkinson, E. W (H) 15Oct.08
  Steel, H. 11May12
p.s. Marsh, J. L. 1Mar.13
p. Wilson, A. K. 25Mar.14

Lieutenants. (8)

p. Levick, C. E. 15Feb.07
p. Bedford, J. (t)ⓢ 1Apr.10
p. Burton, W. A. 1Apr.10
p. Coombe, L. J. 29Jan.13
p. Barber, H. G. 1Mar.13
p.s. Wilkinson, F. H. (H) 5July13
  Holmes, E. M. 25Mar.14

2nd Lieutenants. (8)

Fowler, W. 7June09
Firth, A. M. B. 21Sept.09
Branson, D. S. (H) 15Oct.10
Sorby, T. G. ⓢ 30Jan.12
Wortley, J. F. 31Jan.12
Boyd, A. J. 29Jan.13
Burton, T. 29Jan.13
Hewson, F. B. 21May13
Tozer, W. 24June14
Dixon, C. M. 24June14

Inst. of Musk.

Ellison, W. R., capt. 19May14

Adjutant.

✗Williams, R. M., Capt. York & Lanc. R. 22July12

Quarter-Master.

Duggan, M. J., Qr.-Mr. (hon. m.) ret. pay (Res. of Off.) hon. m. 5Feb.11

Medical Officers.

p. Newton, D. G., M.B., F.R.C.S. Edin., Surg.-Maj. 23Jan.14 9Dec.96
p. Barber, S. F., Surg.-Capt. 11Apr.03
p. Kerr, W. S., M.B., Surg.-Capt. 7May07 7Nov.03
p. Addison, C., M.D., F.R.C.S., Surg. Capt. 14Mar.14 28Mar.06

[Uniform—*Scarlet*. Facings—*White*.]

5th Battalion.

"South Africa, 1900-2."

Drill Hall, Rotherham.

Hon. Colonel.

p. Mitchell, T. W. H., VD ⓣ (Lt.-Col. ret. Terr. Force) 22Apr.14

Lt.-Colonel.

Fox, C., TD ⓣ 1Apr.14

Majors. (2)

Knight, J. E. 2Apr.08
Rhodes, H. 1Apr.14

Captains. (8)

p.s. Johnson, E. D. B. 18Aug.06
p. Smith, H. P. 16May09
p.s. Willis, C. F. (q)11Jan.10
p.s. Rhodes, S. (b) (H) 2Feb.10
  Allport, T. C. 15Feb.12
  Mallinson, A. N. 25May13
  Marsh, R. P. 23Apr.14

Lieutenants. (8)

Alderson, L. W.12Apr.10
Rideal, J. G. E.11June11
Monier-Williams, C. V. ⓢ 15Feb.12
Cheesewright, L. 16Nov.12
Fox, C. D. 9June13
Drabble, R. S. H. 21Mar.14
Hewitt, G. A. G. 31Mar.14

2nd Lieutenants. (8)

Coles, J. L. ⓢ 18May12
Colver, H. 19May12
Aizlewood, L. P. 8June12
Carr, A. G. H. 9June12
Jones, H. L. 12Mar.13

Adjutant.

✗Parkinson,T.W.,Capt. York & Lanc. R. 18Sept.11

Quarter-Master.

Barker, E. A., hon. lt. 9May10

Medical Officers.

p. Robinson, A., M.D., Surg.-Capt. 24Oct.06 28Mar.08
p. Horne, H. F., M.D., Surg.-Capt. 6May10 6Nov.06

[Uniform—*Scarlet*. Facings—*White*.]

THE DURHAM LIGHT INFANTRY.
Regimental District No. **68**. [No. **5** District.]

The United Red and White Rose.
"Salamanca," "Vittoria," "Pyrenees," "Nivelle," "Orthes," "Peninsula," "Alma," "Inkerman," "Sevastopol," "Reshire," "Bushire," "Koosh-ab," "Persia," "New Zealand," "Relief of Ladysmith," "South Africa, 1899-1902."

Regular and Special Reserve Battalions.

Uniform—Scarlet.   Facings—Dark Green.   Agents—Messrs. Holt & Co.

1st Bn. (68th Foot).. .. .. Nowshera.	3rd Bn. (2nd Durham Mil.)	Newcastle-on-Tyne
2nd „ (106th „).. .. .. Lichfield.	4th „ (1st Durham Mil.)	†Barnard Castle.
Depôt .. Newcastle.	Record Office ..	York.

Territorial Force Battalions.

5th Bn.	Drill Hall, Stockton-on-Tees.	8th Bn.	Gilesgate, Durham.
6th „	Drill Hall, Bishop Auckland.	9th „ „	Burt Terrace, Gateshead.
7th „	Livingstone Road, Sunderland.		

Allied Regiment of Canadian Militia.
106th Regiment (Winnipeg Light Infantry) .. .. .. Winnipeg, Manitoba.

Allied Regiment of Dominion of New Zealand.
2nd (South Canterbury) Regiment.

Colonel .. .. .. Upcher, Maj.-Gen. R., C.B., D.S.O., ret. pay 11Sept.08

1st and 2nd Battalions.

Captains—contd.
1Stoker, R. J. G. 2June09
2Hare, H. V. 29Mar.12
r. Coddington, H. J.
1Jan.13
1Turner, R. V. 7Apr.14
1Greenwell, W. B.,
Adjt. 7Apr.14
e.a. Hudson-Kinahan,
G. F. 27May14
2Festing, H. W. 27May14

Lieutenants. (19)
1Manger, E. V. 14July04
2Taylor, H. J. 19Oct.04
2Godsal, W. H., Adjt.
10 May05
s. St. John, Hon. R. T.
13May05
(3)1Philipps, G. W. F.
10June05
t. Hartcup, W. R. M.
7Oct.05
s. Smyth-Pigott, B. C.,
p.a.o. 23June06
1Boxer, H. C. 6Mar.07
1McCullagh, H. R.
25June08
2Congreve,C.R. 19Sept.08
c.o. Wyllie, W. T. 30Dec.08
1Gilpin, E. H. 2June09
c.o. Warren, J. F. 8Jan.10
1Smith, R. C. 29Feb.10
2Twist, W. 1Apr.10
1Churchill,J.A. 10Apr.10
1deBunsen,A.G.17July11
1Hayes, G. 4Jan.12
1Harter, J.-G. [L]4Mar.12
1Grey-Wilson, W. A.
23Oct.12
a.s. Rountree, A. N.
23 Aug.13
1Clifton, A. J. 6Sept.13
2Oct.13
1Hasted, J. O. C.
7Nov.13
(3)2Swetenham, E. 1Jan.14
2Norton, L. G. 7Apr.14

2nd Lieuts.—contd.
2Conant, N. C. P.
4Dec.12
1Lysaght-Griffin,
E. H. L. 3Sept.13
d 2Stanuell, C. M. 24Jan.14
2Beart, C. W. 25Feb.14
d 2Marshall, R. 15July14

Adjutants.
1Greenwell, W. B.,
capt. 10Apr.13
2Godsal, W, H., lt.
17 Nov.13

Quarter-Masters.
1Freel, J. 21Feb.03
hon. capt. 21Feb.13
r. Clements, T.,
hon. lt. 10May05
r. Whan, S., hon. lt.
19Mar.10
2Shea, J. P. L.,
hon. lt. 25Mar.14

Special Reserve.
Lieutenant.
Maynard, W.E. 3Jan.14
1Apr.12

2nd Lieutenants.
Bloor, V. U. 5Oct.12
Mearns, C. 1Mar.13
Baker, C. H. 9Aug.13

3rd Battalion.

(Officers serving on 3 Oct, in the corresponding Militia unit hold honorary Army rank equivalent to the Militia regimental rank they then held. Other officers entitled to honorary Army rank have it shown against their names.)

Hon. Colonel.
Londonderry, Rt.
Hon. C. S., Marq.
of, K.G.,G.C.V.O.,
C.B., VD, (Col. late
Vols.), A.D.C.30Aug.08
7June99

Lt.-Colonel.
⚔Cardiff, R. H. W.
6Jan.12

Major.
p.s.⚔Fraser, W. A., late
Capt. Ind. S.C.,
hon. l.c. (H) 8Nov.07
r.e.⚔Morant, H. H. S.
23May10

Captains. (5)
p.s.⚔Rowlandson, S. M.
(H) 29Dec.00
⚔Cochrane, G. L.,
Capt. ret. pay11Sept.01
9Apr.10
r e.⚔Cartwright, A.L.
24May02
p.s.⚔Smith, A. J. E.
(H) (b) 8Apr.06
r.e.⚔Bowers, A. H. M.
29 Jan. 09
⚔Richardson, H..
Lt. ret. pay 26Oct.10

Lieutenants. (11)
r.e Philipps, G.W.F.
10June05
⚔Wright, R.S.(Hon.
2nd Lt. in Army
4Oct.02) 1Nov.09
Smith, C. E. 10July11
r.e. Swetenham, E. 1Jan.14

2nd Lieutenants. (8)
Gilbertson, F. J.
21June11
⚔Gales, J. R. 5Oct.12
Newstead, F. L.
1Apr.13

Adjutant.
⚔Coddington, H.J.,
Capt. Durh. L. I.
1Jan.13
(Capt. in Army 1June13)

Quarter-Master.
Clements, T., hon. lt.

1429 | 1430 | 1431 | 1432

† *Letters, &c., should temporarily be addressed to Newcastle-on-Tyne.*

THE DURHAM LIGHT INFANTRY—(Regtl. Dist. No. 68)—contd.

4th Battalion.

(Officers serving on 12 June 01 in the corresponding Militia unit hold honorary Army rank equivalent to the Militia regimental rank they then held. Other officers entitled to honorary Army rank have it shown against their names.)

Hon. Colonel.
Barnard, H. de V.,
Lord 26July08
  23Dec.06

Lt.-Colonel.
p.s.✗Briggs, W. H. (H)
  22Mar.12

Majors. (3)
✗Leather, K. J. W.,
  late Lt. Durh. L. I.
  11Mar.12
p.s.✗Curling, E. S. (H)
  15Mar.12
p.s.Havelock-Allan, Sir
  H. S. M., Bt. (H)
  ⑤ 16Mar.12

Captains. (6)
p.s.Culley, G. M. G.
  (H) 20Apr.07
Hutchinson, W. R. C.
  (H) 29Apr.07
p.s.Douglas-Willan, W. G.
  18Nov.09
p.s.✗Ogden, C. A.
  (H) (g), p.v.c.,
  I. of M. 6June10
p.s.Legard, R. H. (H)
  1Mar.14

Lieutenants. (11)
Streatfeild, S. R.
  14Feb.14
Hicks, G. A. 18Feb.14

2nd Lieutenants. (8)
Vane, Hon. R. F.
  (on prob.) 22Nov.13

Inst. of Musk.
✗Ogden, C. A.
  Capt. 24May13

Adjutant.
Irvine, A. E., Capt.
  Durh. L.I. 13Nov.13
(Capt. in Army 5 June 03)

Quarter-Master.
Whan, S., hon. lt.

5th Battalion.

"South Africa, 1900-02."
Drill Hall,
Stockton-on-Tees.

Hon. Colonel.
p.s. Burdon, R., VD (Hon.
  Col. ret. Vols.) (t)
  29Sept.11

Lt.-Colonel.
p.s. Spence, G. O. (H)
  15Aug 10

Majors. (2)
Hopper, G. W. N.
  13Sept.11
Biggs, B. G. D.11May12

Captains. (8)
p. ✗Ensor, H. (Hon.
  Lt. in Army 2
  Sept.02) 4Oct.06
p. Pearson, R.W.20May08
p. Faber, H. G. (H)
  13July10
Raimes, A. L. 3Apr.12
✗Wilson, H. R.24Oct.13
Blumer, J. 21 Dec.13
Marley, W. 20May14

Lieutenants.
Pinder, F. 25Apr.10
Glasspool, R. T. B.
  1Nov.11
  1 Mar.11
Kirk, P. 3Apr.12
Wood, P. 3Aug.12
Glosg, V F. 2Apr.13
Hill, A. B. 15Feb.14

2nd Lieutenants (8)
Ropner, E. H. O. R.
  8Oct.12
Hessler, J. A. N.
  14Nov.12
Robson, W. H.26Mar.13
Moscrop, W. N. J.
  9Aug.13
Pattinson, L.A.11Jan.14
Meek, E. A. 29Jan.14

Adjutant.
✗Hartcup, W. R. M.,
  Lt. Durh. L.I., capt.
  7Nov.13

Quarter-Master.
✗Bush, T. W.,
  hon. lt. 27May13

Medical Officer.
Wilkin, Capt. H. F.,
  F.R.C.S. (Edin.)
  R.A.M.C. (T.F.)
  (attd.) 19Nov.11
  19May08

Chaplain.
Birch, Rev. J. A. G.,
  Chapl. 4th Class
  (T.F.) (attd.) 1Apr.08
  29Mar.05

[Uniform—Scarlet.
Facings—Dark Green.]

6th Battalion.

"South Africa, 1900-02."
Drill Hall,
Bishop Auckland.

Hon. Colonel.
Eden, Sir W., Bt.,
  TD, late Lt.8 Hrs.,
  late Lt.-Col. 2May96

Lt.-Colonel.
p. Watson H. C., VD,
  (Q) (H) 15July11

Majors. (2)
Hawdon,J.E.,TD4Dec.07
Wilkinson, W. (H)
  15July11

Captains. (8)
p. Petherick, J. 5Dec.00
p. Parker, J. E.(Q)5Dec.00
p. Ramsey, J. H. 4June02
p. Gray, J. 10Feb.06
p. Badcock, S. E.
  (H) 23June06
p. Cummins, A. P. (H)
  5Apr.07
p.s. Spedding, J. E.20July12
p. Townend, J. 6Aug.13

Lieutenants. (8)
(p.) Devey, W.H.D.10Feb.06
Barkas, F. G. 29Oct.09
Hanby-Holmes, E. R. ⑤
  17Aug.10
(p.) Rudd, G. W. 10June11
(p.) Monkhouse, J. T.
  20July12
Rayner, S. 1July13
Walton, F. 6Aug 13
Cleminson, C. E.
  6Aug.13

2nd Lieutenants. (8)
Park, R. D. 16May10
Thorpe, S. D. 1Feb.13
Welch, T. 6June13
Heslop, T. B. 6June13
Peberdy, R. 6June13
Wawn, C. N. 6June13
Gill, W. P. 14June13

Adjutant.
✗Jeffreys, J. W.,
  Capt. Durh. L.I.
  22Oct.13

Quarter-Master.
✗Shearwood, H.,
  hon. lt. 1June14

Medical Officers.
p. Mackay, Maj. W. M.,
  M.B., R.A.M.C.
  (T.F.)(attd.) 26Mar.14
  26Mar.02
p. Farquharson, Capt.
  A. C., M.D.,
  R.A.M.C. (T.F.)
  (attd.) 17Aug.09
  17Feb.06

Chaplains.
Barker, Rev. J. W. H.,
  B.A., Chapl. 4th
  Class (T.F.) (attd.)
  1Apr.08
  29Nov.05
Woods, Rev. F. T.,
  M.A., Chapl. 4th
  Class (T.F.)(attd.)
  1Apr.08
  17July07
Shaddick Rev. H.
  G. H., Chapl.
  4th Class (T.F.)
  (attd.) 1May12

[Uniform—Green.
Facings—Scarlet.]

7th Battalion.

"South Africa, 1900-02."
Livingstone Road,
Sunderland.

Hon. Colonel.
Boyne, G. W., Visct.,
  formerly Capt. 3 Bn.
  North'd Fus.26Apr.13

Lt.-Colonel.
✗Vaux, E., D.S.O., VD
  (Maj.ret. Vols.) (Hon.
  Capt. in Army
  12July01) 9Sept.11

Majors. (2)
p. ✗Bowman,J. B.,TD
  (Hon. Lt. in Army
  1July01) 21Jan.11
  Nicoll, J.McD., TD
  13Sept.11

Captains. (8)
p. Hines, C. W. (t) 27Jan.01
p. Spain, J. 6June03
p. Wawn, F. M. (F)
  5Dec.08
p. Priestly, W. 1Nov.08
p. Wardle, J. P., jun.
  22Feb.11
p.s. ✗Errington, J. (b)
  (H) 22Feb.11
p.s.Farrow, A. H. 27July11
Low, H. B. 18Sept.11

Lieutenants. (8)
(p.s.)Storey, M. 11Feb.10
(p.s.)Mail, M. E. 9Nov.10
Sutcliffe, T. F. 26July11
Page, T. A. 26July11
Jacks, H. 9Sept.11
Williamson, A. R.
  18Sept.11
Wood, H. H. 18Sept.11
Laing, L. 16Nov.13

2nd Lieutenants. (8)
Kirkup, P. A. 9Apr.11
Joseph, H. 1Nov.11
Carswell-Hunt,
  W. D. 7June13
Sayer, C. O. 7June13
Bell, J. A. 8June13
Bowes, A. S. 12June14

Adjutant.
✗Bergne, R. B., Capt.
  Leins. R. 1Mar.12

Quarter-Master.
Broadley, J.,
  hon. lt. 9May14

Medical Officers.
p. Milbanke, Capt.W.B.,
  M.B., R.A.M.C.
  (T.F.) (attd.) 10Mar.08
  10Sept.04
Heslop, Capt. H.L.,
  M.D., R.A.M.C.
  (T.F.) (attd.) 11July13
  11Jan.10

Chaplain.
Purvis, Rev. J. B.,
  Chapl. 4th Class
  (T.F.) (attd.) 28Apr.13

[Uniform—Scarlet.
Facings—Dark Green.]

THE DURHAM LIGHT INFANTRY—(Regtl. Dist. No. 68)—contd.

8th Battalion.
"South Africa, 1900-02."
Gilesgate, Durham.

Hon. Colonel.
Durham, Rt. Hon.
J. G., Earl of,
K.G., G.C.V.O.,
VD, late Lt. C.
Gds. 25Oct.05

Lt.-Colonel.
Blackett, W. C.
(H) ⊕ 2Oct.12

Majors. (2)
Smeddle, J. H., TD,
17Aug.10
p.s. ⨉Ritson, J. R.
(*Hon. Lt. in Army*
1*July*01)(H) 2Oct.12

Captains. (8)
d. Benson, W. A. 11Apr.06
p.s. Johnson J. B. 2May06
p. Harvey, F. G. 21July09
p.s. Bradford, T. A. 8Feb.10
p. Ritson, J. A. S. 1Jan.12
Veitch, E. H. 6Dec12
Coulson, W. H. 25May14

Lieutenants. (8)
Marshall, F. 6July10
Kirkup, E. H. 1Jan.12
Turnbull, J. 10July12
Johnson, L. V. B.
(H) 12May12
Guest-Williams, R. H.
30Aug.13
Mowlam, H. J.
30Aug.13
Blackett, G. E. 4Apr.14
Kirkup, P. 31May14
Wood, J. L. 31May14

2nd Lieutenants. (8)
Johnson, W. 26Mar.13
Leybourne, E. A.
29May13
Carpenter, F. C. H.
9June13
Brass, J. R. 11June13
Oswell, A. 26July13
Ramsay L. A. 28July13
Marshall, W. 26Jan.14
Gould, G. D. 23Mar.14
Baldwin, C W. 23Mar.14

Adjutant.
⨉Stevens, G. A.,
Capt. R.Fus. 26Apr.12

Quarter-Master.
p. ⨉Mangles, A.,
hon. capt. 26Apr.13

Medical Officers.
p. Plummer, Capt. S. W.
M.D., R.A.M.C.
(T.F.) (*attd.*) 18Apr.03
18Apr.00
Stenhouse, Lt. J.A.,
M.B., R.A.M.C.
(T.F.) (*attd.*) 9June13

Chaplains.
Taylor, Rev. E. J.,
Chapl.2nd Class
(T.F.) (*attd.*) 3Apr.10
3Apr.95
Lomax, *Rev. C., M.A.,*
Chapl. 3rd Class
(T.F.) (*attd.*) 18Apr.10
18Apr.00

[Uniform—Scarlet.
Facings—*Dark Green.*]

9th Battalion.
"South Africa, 1900-02."
Burt Terrace, Gateshead.

Hon. Colonel.
Northbourne, W. H.,
Lord 11Sept.91

Lt.-Colonel.
p. Simpson, F. R.
26July11

Majors. (2)
Henderson, A., TD,
(*Capt. Res.of Off.*)
(q) (H) ⓈＡ)15Dec.10
English, J. 12Aug.12

Captains. (8)
p. Winship, W. H. (H)
26July02
Whitfield, J. W. (H)
26July09
Hebron, A. F. (H)
19May11
p.s. ⨉Martin, W. deG.
(H) 19May11
Cole, G. T.
(H) 7June11
Bagnall, C. L. Ⓢ
3Oct.12
Bagnall, W. A. 24Oct.13
English, H. E. {24Oct.13

Lieutenants (8).
Wilkinson, A. W.
24May10
Quin, H. E. (H) 24May10
Lambert, F. J. 7June11
Gibbon, F. A. L.
10May13
Raine, J. E. 28June13
Baister, S. L. 24Oct.13
Heads, J. E. B. 17Jan.14

2nd Lieutenants. (8)
Bettison, M. H. 4Dec.12
Gatheral, R. O. 4Dec.12
Lambert, N. F. 4Dec.12
Dryden, E. Ⓢ 6Dec.12
Atkinson, H. B. 1Apr.13
Jameson, T. B. 12July13
Hopkins, C.P.I.
27July13
Williams, A. R. H.
13May14

Adjutant.
⨉Cochran, H.P.G.,
Capt. Midd'x R.
1Jan.14

Quarter-Master.
⨉Challons, P., *hon. lt.*
19Mar.13

Medical Office s.
p. Kendall, Maj. J. A.,
M.D., R.A.M.C.
(T.F.) (*attd.*) 30Apr.12
28Mar.00
Scott, Lt. J. A, C.,
M.B., R.A.M.C.
(T.F.) (*attd.*) 11June14

[Uniform—*Scarlet.*
Facings—*Dark Green.*]

THE HIGHLAND LIGHT INFANTRY.
Regimental District No. **71**. [No. **2** District.]

The Castle and Key, superscribed "Gibraltar, 1780-83," and with the motto "Montis Insignia Calpe" underneath.
The Elephant, superscribed "Assaye."
"Carnatic," "Hindoostan," "Sholinghur," "Mysore," "Seringapatam," "Cape of Good Hope, 1806," "Rolica," "Vimiera," "Corunna," "Busaco," "Fuentes d'Onor," "Ciudad Rodrigo," "Badajoz," "Almaraz," "Salamanca," "Vittoria," "Pyrenees," "Nivelle," "Nive," "Orthes," "Toulouse," "Peninsula," "Waterloo," "South Africa, 1851-2-3," "Sevastopol," "Central India," "Tel-el-Kebir," "Egypt, 1882," "Modder River," "South Africa, 1899-1902."

Regular and Special Reserve Battalions.

Uniform—Scarlet. Facings—Buff. Agents—Sir C. R. McGrigor, Bt., & Co.

1st Bn. (71st Foot)	.. Ambala.	3rd Bn. (1st R Lanark Mil.) .. *Hamilton.*
2nd „ (74th „)	.. Aldershot.	4th „ (1st R. Lanark Mil.) .. *Hamilton.*
Depôt	*Hamilton.*	Record Office .. .. *Hamilton.*

Territorial Force Battalions.

5th Bn. .. 24, *Hill St., Garnethill, Glasgow.*	8th Bn. .. .. .. *Lanark.*
6th „ .. 172, *Yorkhill Street, Glasgow.*	9th „ .. 81, *Greendyke Street, Glasgow.*
7th „ .. 69, *Main St., Bridgeton, Glasgow.*	

Colonel-in-Chief .. .. Field-Marshal H.R.H. Arthur W. P. A., Duke of Connaught and Strathearn, K.G., K.T., K.P., G.C.B., G.C.S.I., G.C.M.G., G.C.I.E., G.C.V.O., Col. G. Gds. and A.S.C. and Col.-in-Chief 6 Dns., R. Dub. Fus., and Rif. Brig. *Personal A.D.C. to the King.* .. 4Sept.01

Colonel .. .. Hildyard, Gen. Sir H. J. T., *G.C.B.*, ret. pay, p.s.c.[R] .. 30Dec.03

1st and 2nd Battalions.

Lt.-Colonels. (2)
1 Ronaldson, R. W. H. 4Nov.11
Wolfe-Murray, A. A. 18Dec.12

Majors. (8)
1 Noyes, C. E. 10Dec.05
2 Hill, E. R. 23Feb.07
(3) 2 Grahame, J. C., *D.S.O.* (*Comdg. Depôt*) 18Dec.08
s. Armstrong, E. 4Nov.11
22Aug.06
2 Prentice, R. E. S. 4Sept.12
s. Browne, A.N.E. 18Dec.12
s. Pack-Beresford, H. J. 12Feb.13
1 Murray, T. F. 19Nov.13

Captains. (14)
t.v. Singleton, H. T. C., *D.S.O.* 27Mar.01
2 Chichester, R. G. I. 27Mar.01
2 Mayne, C. R. G., *D.S.O.* [l] [F] 1Apr.01
2 Gaussen, A. W. D. 30Oct.01
2 Buist, K. L. 18Jan.07
16Dec.05
1 Pollok-Morris, T. A., *p.s.c.* 11Apr.06
2 Martin, C. T. 23Jan.07
s. Segrave, W. H.-E., *D.S.O., p.s.c.* [l] 23Jan.07
1 Walker, G. H. 6Mar.07
1 Pringle, L. G., *M.V.O.* [l] 24June08
1 Knight, G. M. 1Nov.07
r. Alston, R. C. W. 8Dec.09
(3) 1 Johnston-Stewart, H. E. H. 18Apr.10
e.a. Craigie Halkett, H.M. 11May10
e.a. Greenwood, R.C. 28Jan.11
r. Leckie-Ewing, W. C. 23Jan.11

Captains—contd.
1 Baird, R. 23Jan.11
1 Tarrant, H. S. 12Sept.11
t, Simson, J. R. 28Sept.11
2 Stevenson, H. H. MacD. 28Sept.11
(3) Halswelle, W. 28Sept.11
2 Hope, J.H., *Adjt.* 4Nov.11
(3) 2 Forbes, R. F. 12June12
1 Inglis, J., *Adjt.* 12June12
(1) Cameron, M. H. V. 4Sept.12
2 Thackeray, F.S. 18Dec.12
t, Acklom, S. 12Feb.13
t, McCallum, C.H.M. 12Feb.13

Lieutenants. (19)
2 Brodie, W. L. 19June08
2 Telfer-Smollett, A. P. D. 1July08
(3) 1 Lilburn, W. 22Jan.09
1 Campbell W. U.M. 9Apr.09
c.o. Gibson Craig, Sir A. C., Bt. 28Apr.09
1 Grant, E. M. 8Dec.09
f.c. 2 Farie, C. A. G. L H. 1Apr.10
1 Stewart, W. P. 13Apr.10
2 Dalrymple, I. D. 23Aug.11
1 Anderson, C.H.12Sept.11
2 Gerard, A. M. 28Sept.11
f.c. Mitchell, W. G. S. 4Nov.11
2 Latham, J. MacD. 12June12
1 Balfour, J. A. 4Sept.12
(3) 2 Anderson, J. F.11Dec.12
1 Pitts-Tucker, C. M. 18Dec.12
2 Hooper, C. W. 12Feb.13
2 Wallace, C. J. 18Mar.13
c.o. Loch, E. E. 11May13
v. Hayley, C. W. S. B. 17Dec.13
1 Murray-Lyon, D. M. 28Mar.14
1 Henderson, G. M. H. 29Apr.14

2nd Lieutenants. (12)
2 Fergusson, J. A. H. 14Feb.12
1 Kerr, H. R. G. 13Mar.12
A.2 Powell, R. C. H. 3Sept.12
1 Fox, M. S. 4Sept.12
1 Barry, D. D. 5Feb.13
2 MacKenzie, C. L. 24May13
1 Cowan, J. R. 3Sept.13
1 Guthrie-Smith, R. C. 3Sept.13
2 Whistler, R. A. F. 25Feb.14
1 Dixon, R. S. 25Feb.14
2 MacDonald, E. R. H. K. 10June14

Adjutants.
1 Inglis, J., *capt.* 15Oct.11
2 Hope, J. H., *capt.* 9Apr.12

Quarter-Masters.
1 Stevens, A. 19Aug.03
hon. capt. 19Aug.13
2 Taylor, J. E. 16Mar.04
hon. capt. 16Mar.14
r. Mill, W., *hon.lt.* 20June06
r. Sutcliffe, J., *hon. lt.* 21Nov.06

Special Reserve.
2nd Lieutenants.
Thomson, J. 24Feb.12
Harley, G. M. 18May12
Mylles, C. C. (*on prob.*) 25Apr.14

3rd Battalion.

(*Officers serving on 25Sept.02 in the corresponding Militia unit hold honorary Army rank equivalent to the Militia regimental rank they then held. Other officers entitled to honorary Army rank have it shown against their names.*)

Hon. Colonel.
✗ Field-Marshal H.R.H. Arthur W. P. A., Duke of Connaught and Strathearn, K.G., KT., K.P., G.C.B., G.C.S.I., G.C.M.G., G.C.I.E., G.C.V.O., Col. G. Gds. and A.S.C., and Col.-in-Chief 6 Dns., High. L.I., R. Dub. Fus. and Rif.Brig., *Personal A.D.C. to the King* 28June08
12Feb.96

Lt.-Colonel.
✗O'Dell, T. S. 11Nov.10

Major.
p.s. ✗Kindersley, A. O. I. *hon. l.c.* (H) 24Feb.03
p.s. ✗Anderson, J. F. 24Feb.06
r.e. ✗Grahame, J. C., *D.S.O.* 18Dec.08

Captains. (5)
Lyon-Campbell, C.A.M. *hon. m.* (H) 11Oct.99
p.s. ✗Outram, J. D., *hon. m.* ⑩ (H)4May00
p.s. ✗Baird, R. E. W. (H) 3Sept.04
p. ✗Jackson, T, (H) 3Sept.04

THE HIGHLAND LIGHT INFANTRY—(Regtl. Dist. No. **71**)—contd.

3rd Bn.—contd.
Captains—contd.
r.e.✗Johnston-Stewart,
  H. E. R. 13Apr.10
r.e.✗Halswelle, W.
              23Sept.11
r.e.✗Forbes, R. F. 12June12

Lieutenants. (11)
Ferrers-Guy, A. H.,
  late Lt. Res. of
  Off.   6June07
r.e. Lilburn, W. 22Jan.09
r.e. Anderson, J. F.
              11Dec.12
Craven, T. L., *late*
  Lt.Ind.Army 11June13

2nd Lieutenants. (8)

Adjutant.
✗Alston, R. C. W.,
  Capt., High. L.I.
           2Feb.14
  (Capt.inArmy 8Dec.09)

Quarter-Master.
Mill, W., *hon. lt.*

4th Battalion.

(*Officers serving on 15 Oct. 00 in the corresponding Militia unit hold honorary Army rank equivalent to the Militia regimental rank they then held. Other officers entitled to honorary Army rank have it shown against their names.*)

Hon. Colonel.
✗*Field-Marshal* H.R.H.
  Arthur W. P. A., Duke
  of Connaught and
  Strathearn, K.G., K.T.,
  K.P., G.C.B., G.C.S.I.,
  G.C.M.G., G.C.IE.,
  G.C.V.O., Col. G.
  Gds. and A.S.C., and
  Col.-in-Chief 6 Dns.,
  High. L.I., R. Dub.
  Fus., and Rif. Brig.
  Personal A.D.C. to the
  King   9Aug.08
           12Feb.96

Lt.-Colonel.
p.s.✗Jones, A. W. (*H*)
  (*Remount Service*)
           19June12

Majors. (3)
p.s.✗Gillon, A. (*Remount Service*) 1Apr.11
p.s.Rankin, W. B. 13Mar.12
Stone, H. J. 22July12

Captains. (6)
Ingle, A. C. B., *hon. m.* (*H*) 26Aug.96
p.s.✗Coghill, H. M. (*Hon. Lt. in Army* 16 Oct.00) (*H*) (*Asst. Dist. Commr., Sierra Leone*, 16 Jan.11) 16May07
✗Oppenheim, L. C. F., *Capt. ret. pay*
           25Nov.11
✗Fellows, E. G., *late Lt. A.S.C.* 25Feb.14

Lieutenants. (11)
Graham, J. G. B. P.
           6Sept.12
Russell, A. H. 4Apr.14

2nd Lieutenants. (8)
Hall, G. P. 23Aug.13
Hunter, N. B. [||
  (*on prob.*) 26Nov.13
Aston, H. S.
  (*on prob.*) 6June14

Adjutant.
✗Leckie-Ewing,
  W. C., Capt.
  High. L.I. 11May13
  (*Capt.inArmy* 23Jan.11)

Quarter-Master.
Sutcliffe, J., *hon. lt.*

5th (City of Glasgow) Battalion.

"South Africa, 1900-02."
24, Hill Street, Garnethill, Glasgow.

Hon. Colonel.
✗Hunter, Gen. Sir *A.,*
  G.C.B., G.C.V.O.,
  D.S.O., Col. R.
  Lanc. R. [R] 24June07

Lt.-Colonel.
p.s.Morrison, F. L.,
  VD, (Q) 28Sept.06
    bt. col. 24Dec.13

Majors. (2)
✗Jowitt, T. L. (*Hon. Lt.in Army* 5July02)
           5June12
Downie, A. M. 9Oct.12

Captains. (8)
p.s.Hatrick, W. L. 3May06
p.s.Macdonald, H. C.
  (*H*) (*t*) 2Aug.07
p.s.✗MacDonald, J. 2Aug.07
p.s.Neilson, J. B. 3Sept.10
Findlay, J. A. 5June12
Morton, G., jun.
           13July12
Frost, E. F. M. (*H*)
  ⑤   6Sept.13
Brand, D. E. 6Sept.13
Macfarlane, K. 1June14

Lieutenants. (8)
Townsend, R. T. 5Dec.11
Wightman, T. S. S.
           4Apr.12
          24May11
Morrison, R. H.
          10Oct.12
Currie, A. B. 2Apr.13
Buchanan, W. L.
         6Sept.13

2nd Lieutenants. (8)
Campbell, N. R. 1Mar.12
Fyfe, T. A. 9Oct.12
Moir, J. F. 16Nov.12
Leith, E. M. 16Nov.12
Miller, R. M. 30Nov.12
Milne, J. G., jun.
         6Jan.13
Malcolm, J.W. 2Apr.13
Townsend, E. T.
        17Oct.13
MacLellan, L. 17Oct.13
Main, J. W. 13Dec.13

Adjutant.
Simson, J. R., Capt.
  High. L.I. 14Feb.14

Quarter-Master.
Clark, T., *hon. lt.*
         13Oct.11

Medical Officers.
✗Kennedy, Lt. A. D.,
  M.D., R.A.M.C.
  (T.F.) (*attd.*) 27Jan.09
Dickie, Lt. D., M.B.,
  F.R.C.S. Edin.,
  R.A.M.C.(T.F.)(*attd.*)
         31Mar.11

Chaplains.
Reid, *Rev.* D. A. C.,
  B.D. [C.S.] Chapl.
  3rd Class (T.F.)
  (*attd.*) 20July11
         20July01
Harrowes, *Rev.* W.
  H., *M.A.* [U.F.C.]
  Chapl. 4th Class
  (T.F.) (*attd.*) 1May14

[Uniform—Scarlet,
  Facings—Buff.]

6th (City of Glasgow) Battalion.

"South Africa, 1900-02."
172, Yorkhill Street, Glasgow.

Hon. Colonel.
Lipton, Sir *T. J.*, Bt.,
  K.C.V.O. 21Nov.00

Lt.-Colonel.
p.s.Cochrane, J. P., VD,
         20Jan.12

Majors. (2)
Gale, W. M., TD.
         13May12
p.s.Anderson, J. (*t*) (*H*)
         13May12

Captains. (8)
p.s.Greig, P. (q) 2June06
p.s.Easson, D. E. C.
        14June07
p. Tidd, E. G. 1Apr.08
p.s.Stewart, C. 20May09
p.s.Daly, J. F. 27Apr.10
p s.Maclean, J. A. (*t*)
  (*H*) 17Apr.12
p.s.Aitken, G. J. (*H*),
  ⑤ (q) 13May12
Gemmell, S. A. (*t*)
         1Oct.13

Lieutenants. (8)
(p.s.)Miller, C. C. 27Apr.11
Daly, C. G. 18Sept.10
Smith, J. S. 17Apr.12
Thomson, R.P. 2Dec.12
McEwan, G. L. 4Apr.14
Speirs, G. P. 4Apr.14
Boyd, R. M. S. 4May14

2nd Lieutenants. (8)
Laird, G. H. R. 9May13
Wyllie, M. 26May13
Black, C. S. P. 26June13
Tidd, K. G. 1Dec.13
Murray, W. A. K. 1Dec.13

Adjutant.
Macfie, C., Capt.
  Sea. Highrs. 9Apr.13

Quarter-Master.
Boyce, T., *hon. lt.*
         20Jan.12

Medical Officers.
Martin, Lt. J. H.,
  M.B., R.A.M.C.
  (T.F.)(*attd.*) 17Oct.11

THE HIGHLAND LIGHT INFANTRY—(Regtl. Dist. No. **71**)—contd.

6th Bn.—contd.

Chaplains.
Smith, Rev. J., D.D., [C.S.] Chapl. 3rd Class (T.F.)(attd.) 6Jan.10
Dickie, Rev. W., D.D. [U.F.C.], Chapl. 4th Class (T.F.) (attd.) 22Feb.99
    1Dec.09

[Uniform—Scarlet, Facings—Buff.]

7th (Blythswood) Battalion.

"South Africa, 1900-02."

69, Main Street, Bridgeton, Glasgow.

Hon. Colonel.
Clark, W., VD (Hon. Col. ret. Vols.) 6Aug.08

Lt.-Colonel.
p.s.Galbraith, J. H., TD (t)(H) 20Dec.11

Majors. (2)
McNish, G., TD⊕4Nov.08
✕Youden, W. A., TD ⊕ (Lt. Res. of Off.) 20Dec.11

Captains. (8)
p. Murray, L. D. 14Feb.03
p.s.Laing, A. R. 22Nov.05
p.s.Douglas, W., jun. (Q)(H) ⊛ 8June06
p.s.Douglas, C.J.(t)16Nov.06
p.s.Richardson, J.(Q)(H) 24May07
p.s.Galloway, J. G.(t)(H) 20Dec.11
p.s.✕Linton, G. P.(t)(H) 29May12
p.s.Gandy, W. H.(H) 18Sept 12

Lieutenants. (8)
p.s.Craigie, J. H.,(q) (H) I. of M. 8Sept.06
(p.s.)Turner, R.(q) 26Mar.07
(p.) Watson, E. 20Dec.11
(p.) Youden, S. E 20Dec.11
McKersie,A.J.18Sept.12
Blair, A. W. 29Jan.13
Galbraith, W. B., jun. 15Nov.13
Dunlop, R. J ⊛ 18Apr.14
Weller, G. H. 18Apr.14

2nd Lieutenants. (8)
Jenkins, W. H. G. 2Apr.10
Lyle, J. A. 27Jan.12
Grieve, W. R. 5June12
Brown, J. R. 14Apr.13
Stewart, J. R. 24Apr.13
Dickson, G. 19May13
Dickson, J. R. 25May13
Macfarlane, A. J. 27Aug.13
Buchanan, E. C. 1Dec.13

Inst. of Musk.
Craigie, J. H., lt. 9Jan.14

Adjutant.
Bosanquet, G. B., Lt. Glouc. R., capt. 11Mar.14

Quarter-Master.
p. Graham. R. Y., hon. m. 18Nov.07

Medical Officers.
p. Dewar, Capt. P. M., R.A.M.C. (T.F.) (attd.) 25Aug.06
Macgregor, Lt. A. S. M., M.D., R.A.M.C. (T.F.)(attd.)25Apr.13

Chaplains.
Thomson, Rev. J., M.A. [C.S.] Chapl.3rd Class (T.F.) (attd.) 14Mar.03
    14Mar.03
Rankin, Rev. W. M., B.D. (U.F.C.) Chapl. 4th Class (T.F.) (attd.) 1Dec.09

[Uniform—Scarlet, Facings—Buff.]

8th (Lanark) Battalion.

A demi-double-headed eagle displayed.

"South Africa, 1900-02."

Lanark.

Hon. Colonel.
Stevenson, J., C.B., VD, Col., A.D.C. (Hon. Col. ret. Vols.) 22Sept.08

Lt.-Colonel.
p.s.Anderson, J., jun. 19Mar.13

Majors. (2)
Stewart, J. 15Nov.09
Shirlaw, J. 1Feb.14

Captains. (8)
p.s.Simpson, K. A. 1Apr.09
p.s.Clark, D. 16Dec.09
p.s.✕Gray, T. B. 1June11
Johnstone, J. M. 1June12
Rankin, J. S. 1June12

Lieutenants. (8)
p.s.Forrest, A. 2June06
Gilfillan, J. 1May10
Torrance, J.R. 1June11
Sommerville, D. F. 1June11
Calder, W. J. 21Feb.13
Rowbotham, J. 1Feb.14
Tennant, W. 1May14
McAuslan, P. T. 1May14

2nd Lieutenants (8)
Scott, J. 7May13
Lumsden, D. 26Nov.13
Adam, J. R. 17Feb.14
Chislett, A. R. 1July14

Adjutant.
✕McConaghey, M. E., Capt. R. Sc. Fus. 28Apr.12

Quarter-Master.
✕Griffith, H. D., hon-lt. 1May14

Medical Officers.
p. Banks, Capt. T. W., M.B, R.A.M.C., (T F.)(attd.) 22Aug.00
    4Apr.96
p. Mackinnon, Capt. W. J., M.B., R.A.M.C., (T.F.) (attd.) 2Apr.04
    3Nov.00
Paterson, Lt. R., R.A.M.C. (T.F.) (attd.) 9May01

Chaplains.
Hauxwell,Rev.F.M., TD,[C.S.]Chapl.2nd Class (T.F.) (attd.) 1Apr.08
    14June90
Brock, Rev. W. P., B.D. [C.S.] Chapl. 3rd Class (T.F.) (attd.) 1Apr.08
    26May94
Gillies, Rev. J., B.D. [C.S.] Chapl. 4th Class (T.F.)(attd.) 1Apr.08
    29Nov.05

[Uniform—Scarlet, Facings—Buff.]

9th (Glasgow Highland) Battalion.

"South Africa, 1900-02."

81, Greendyke Street, Glasgow.

Lt.-Colonel.
p.s.✕Murray, C. C., (Hon. Capt. in Army 29 Sept. 02)(t)22Nov.13

Majors. (2)
Menzies, A.D. (Q) 13Feb.14
Menzies, J. 13Feb.14

Captains. (8)
p.s.Anderson, T. A. H. (q) t.o. 3May05
o.s.Bock, H. J. R. (t) 23Dec.05
p.s.Menzies, A. H. 14Mar.06
p.s.✕Wingate, G. (Hon. Lt. in Army 13 Aug. 02) (q) 14Mar.06

THE HIGHLAND LIGHT INFANTRY—(Regtl. Dist No. **71**)—contd.

9th Bn.—*contd.*

Captains—contd.

p.s.Chalmers, J. S. (*H*)
  (*t*) *I. of M.* 25Dec.12
Young, J. G. 3Mar.13
Frew, A., jun. 1Apr.13
Coats, J. G. 13Feb.14
p.s.Reid, A. K. 15Feb.14

Lieutenants. (8)

Whitson, W. R.13May11
Todd, W. M. 2Dec.11
Coats, W. J. J. 3Dec.11
Anderson, M. 25Dec.12
Galbraith, D. J. F.
  1Apr.13
Cowie, J. A. 13Feb.14
Mackay, A. M. 15Feb.14
Armstrong, L. C,
  30Mar.14

2nd Lieutenants. (8)

Hewat, J. P. D.
  30Mar.13
McMichael, J., *jun.*⑧
  22Apr.13
Murray, A. C. 14June13
Glen, J. K. T. 13Feb.14
Raeburn, A. A. D.
  13Feb.14
MacNaughtan,A.G.
  8July14
McCosh, E. 8July14

Inst. of Musk.

Chalmers, J. S., *capt.*
  13May11

Adjutant.

Acklom, S., Capt.
  High. L.I. 27Oct.13

Quarter-Master.

Kirk, J.,*hon. lt.* 6Sept.11

Medical Officers.

p.s.*Ritchie, Capt. W.*,
  M.B., R.A.M.C.
  (T.F.) (*attd.*) 5July05
  7May02
p.s.Brown, Capt. T. D.,
  M.B., R.A.M.C.
  (T.F.) (*attd.*) 5Feb.07
p. Macphail, Lt. A.,
  R.A.M.C. (T.F.)
  (*attd.*) 14June07
  28Aug.02

Chaplains.

Scott, *Rev.* A. B.,
  B.D. [U.F.C.],
  Chapl. 4th Class
  (T.F.) (*attd.*) 1Dec.09

Maclean, *Rev.* N.,
  M.A., [C.S.], Chapl.
  4th Class (T.F.)
  (*attd.*) 1May12

[Uniform—*Scarlet.*
Facings—*Blue.*]

Cadet Unit affiliated.
1st (Glasgow Highland) Cadet Company, High.L.I.

SEAFORTH HIGHLANDERS (ROSS-SHIRE BUFFS, THE DUKE OF ALBANY'S).

Regimental District No. **72**. [No. **1** District.]

In each of the four corners the late Duke of York's Cypher and Coronet.
The motto "*Cuidich'n Righ.*" The Elephant, superscribed "Assaye."
"Carnatic," "Hindoostan," "Mysore," "Cape of Good Hope, 1806," "Maida," "South Africa, 1835," "Sevastopol," "Koosh-ab," "Persia," "Lucknow," "Central India," "Pelwar Kotal," "Charasiah," "Kabul, 1879," "Kandahar, 1880," "Afghanistan, 1878-80," "Tel-el-Kebir," "Egypt, 1882," "Chitral," "Atbara," "Khartoum," "Paardeberg," "South Africa, 1899-1902."

Regular and Special Reserve Battalions.

Uniform—Scarlet. *Facings*—Buff. *Agents*—Messrs. Cox & Co.

1st Bn. (72nd Foot) ..	.. Agra (*for Glasgow*).	3rd Bn. (Highland (Rifle) Mil.) .. Fort George.
2nd „ (78th „) ..	Shorncliffe (*for Malta*).	
Depôt	Fort George.	Record Office .. Kinnoull Street, Perth.

Territorial Force Battalions.

4th Bn.	Dingwall.	6th Bn. .. .. Elgin.
5th „	Golspie.	

Allied Regiments of Canadian Militia.

72nd Regiment (Seaforth Highlanders of Canada) .. Vancouver, *British Columbia.*
78th Pictou Regiment (Highlanders) .. .. Pictou, *Nova Scotia.*

Colonel-in-Chief .. H.R.H. L. C. E. G. A., Duke of Albany (Reigning Duke of Saxe-Coburg and Gotha), K.G., G.C.V.O. 19July05
Colonel .. .. Murray, Hon. Maj.-Gen. R. H., C.B., C.M.G., ret. pay, q s. [R] . 16Apr.14

1st and 2nd Battalions.

Lt.-Colonels. (2)
ⅾ 2Bradford, Sir E. R., Bt., p.s.c., q.s. 10June13
1Ritchie, A. B. 22Dec.13

Majors. (8)
1Vandeleur, R.S.22Dec.05
bt. lt.-col. 16July08
1Stewart, A. B. A.,
D.S.O. 22Feb.08
(3)2Gaisford, W. T.
(*Comdg. Depôt*)
25May08
s. Thomson, N. A., e. 23Jan.09
s. Arbuthnot, K. W. 10June09
22Aug.02
1Dolg, C. P. 27Mar 11
s. Marshall, F. J., p.s.c. 10June13
2Daniell, F. E. LL., p.s.c. 22Dec.13

Captains (14)
(2) Stockwell, C. I. [F] 19Mar.01
2Campion, E. 19Mar.01
2Carden. D. A. 3July01
s. Holland, L., p.s c. 31Oct.01
2Græme, D. H. [I] 23Jan.09
19Mar.01
1Thomson,W.M.22Dec.01
1Wilson, R. S 11Apr.02
1St. Clair, Hon. C.
H. M. 19Apr.02
2Baillie, H. F.", p.s.c [l] 5Aug.04
(3)1Burn, C. P. M. 15Mar.05
2Anstruther, P. G. 17Apr.05
s. Buchanan, K.G. 24Feb.06
t. Thornhill. J. E. 3Juneⅼl 24Feb.06
1Wicks, H.W. C. 4Mar.06
1Horn, R., Adjt. 21Apr.06
t. Macfie, C 27June06
2Methven, D. G. 1Apr.08
Laing, R. 28Apr.08
r. Mackenzie, S. 4May08
1Davidson,D.H.25Mar.11
(3) 1Forbes-Robertson, K. 6Apr.11

Captains—contd.
c.o.Hopkinson, J.O.3June11
(3) 2MacKenzie, K. B. 3June11
t. Gray, C.O.V. 12Oct.11
2Maclachlan, K. D. M. 8Nov.11
1Baillie-Hamilton, A. B. 8Nov.11
c.o.Schomberg, R.C.F. 15Mar.13
t. Hepburn, W. D. 15Mar.13
t.v. Gard'ner, R. D. 15Mar.13
2Spencer, N. H. M. 9Apr.13
2Hay, E. G. 16Apr.13
Lieutenants. (19)
e.a.Boyle, G. H. P. 20May08 17Jan.06
(3) 1Forsyth, F.R.G.22Feb.06 1Feb.06
1Scovell, A. M. [L] 21Apr.06
t. Anderson, F. 27June06
t. Orr, N. C. 14Jan.07
1Murray, R.A.C.15Jan.08
c.o.Kennedy, H. H. 1Apr.08
2Fraser, F. L.[L] 28Apr.08
t. Fowler, Sir J. E. Bt. 10May08
2Carr, P. W. K. 10Nov.09
(3) 2Lumsden, B. N. 13Aug.10
2Campbell, Hon.
E. O., Adjt. 28Mar.11
c.o.Fraser, F.W.I.V 3June11
1Middleton, W. A. A. 3June11
1Murray, A.C. 27June11
1Brodie, P. W 28Aug.11
2Bruce, *Hon.* B. 1Sept.11
2Burt-Marshall, D. B. 2Oct.11
1Allanby, R. H. 5June12
1Smith-Cumming,
A. M. 15Mar.13
s. Alison, G. N. 15Mar.13
2Burness, A. R. 16Apr.13
f.c.2McDonald C. Y. 11Oct.13
1Mackenzie, D. W.
A. D. 1Nov.13
1Mackenzie, D.C. 10Nov.13
1Anderson, K. A. N 29Nov.13

2nd Lieutenants. (12)
2MacWatt, N.I. 20Sept.11
1Muirhead, J. 20Sept.11
1Macandrew, I. M
McL. 21Sept.11
2Cowie, A. G. 9Dec.11
1Laurie, J. E. 14Feb.12
1Murray, A.R. 3Sept12
2Baird, C. E. 17Sept.13
2Stewart, B. 17Sept.13
1Ferrier-Kerr, W, G.
10Dec.13
2Glass, J. F 10Dec.13
2Fyfe-Jamieson,
I. N. 25Feb.14
2Dunlop, D, M. 25Feb.14
2Anderson, P. C. 25Feb.14

Adjutants.
1Horn, R., *capt.* 1May12
2Campbell, Hon. E. O., *lt.* 10May14

Quarter-Masters.
2Davidson, J. 8May01
hon. capt. 8May11
r. Reid. N., *hon. lt.*24Oct.08
1Macrae, J., *hon. lt.* 25Feb.14

Special Reserve.
2nd Lieutenants.
Williamson, A J.N.
(*attd. O.T.C.*) 31July11
Hepburn, M. A.
29Jan.13
Cameron, A.I.D. 16July13

3rd Battalion.

(*Officers serving on 11June01 in the corresponding Militia unit hold honorary Army rank equivalent to the Militia regimental rank then held. Other officers entitled to honorary Army rank have it shown against their names.*)

Hon. Colonel
✗Munro, Sir H., Bt.
(*Col. late Mila.*)(Hon.
Lt.-Col. in Army
12June01) A.D.C.

Lt.-Colonel.
78Apr.08
✗Mackenzie, A. F.,
M.V.O., Maj. ret.
pay, (Res. of
Off.) 12Aug.11
Major.
r.e.✗Gaisford, W. T.
25May08
p.s.✗Addison-Smith,
C. L. 5Oct.10
Captains. (5)
✗Mackenzie, W. F.
(H) 16Apr.02
p.s.✗Reid, W. B. J. (Q)
(H) ⑧ (g) 26Mar.04
p.s.✗Warrand, F. B.
26Mar.04
p.s.✗Grant, J. P., Capt.
ret., hom. m. 13Apr.04
r.e.✗Burn, C. P. M.
15Mar.05
Keith, R. A. L., *late*
Lt. Sea. Highrs.
5Oct.10
r.e.✗Forbes-Robertson,
K. 6Apr.11
r.e.✗MacKenzie, K.B.
3Juneⅼl
Lieutenants. (11)
r.e.✗Forsyth, F. R. G.
22Feb.08
1Feb.06
r.e.Lumsden,B.N. 13Aug.10
Perrins, J. A. D. (F)
20May12
Price, V. M. 8Aug.14

2nd Lieutenants. (8)
Mackenzie, G. M.
21Oct.11
Burn, J. R. P. (*corr. prob.*) 13June14
20May14
Adjutant.
✗Nairne, C. S., Capt.,
Sea. Highrs. 15Oct.11
(*Capt. in Army* 13Aug.10)

Quarter-Master.
✗Reid, N., *hon. lt.*

SEAFORTH HIGHLANDERS (ROSS-SHIRE BUFFS, THE DUKE OF ALBANY'S)—(Regtl. Dist. No. **72**)—*contd.*

4th (Ross Highland) Battalion.

"South Africa, 1900-02."

Dingwall.

Hon. Colonel.
⚔Stewart-Mackenzie,
J. A. F. H., Bt. Col.,
ret. pay 23Nov.08

Lt.-Colonel.
Mason MacFarlane,
D. J., TD (H)(Q)
26Feb.13

Majors. (2)
Cuthbert,T.W.16June09
p. Robertson, W. J., TD
10May14

Captains. (8)
p.s. MacKenzie, G. (Q)(H)
I. of M. 18Feb.05
p.s. Mackenzie, D. A.
6Oct.09
p.s. Munro, A. R.(Q)7Oct.09
p.s. Forbes, W. 22Jan.11
p.s. Forsyth, I. A. 6June12
p.s. Hogg, C.G. (H) 29Apr.14
p.s. Cameron, G. M.30Apr.14

Lieutenants. (8)
p.s. Mackenzie, A. 16June09
Budge, J. H. 13Mar.12
Brook, A. B. 23May12
Fraser, G. W. (H)
10Jan.13
McMillan, J. 17Feb.13
Cameron, J. 24Feb.14
Cameron, C. M. 30Apr.14

2nd Lieutenants. (8)
Macdonald,R.R.M.
16Apr.14
Dewar, W. S. 27Apr.14

Inst. of Musk.
Mackenzie, G., *capt.*
1Apr.09

Adjutant.
Fowler, Sir J. E., Bt.,
Lt. Sea. Highrs.
capt. 11Oct.11

Quarter-Master.

Medical Officer.
p. Brodie, Capt. R.,
R.A.M.C. (T.F.)
(*attd.*)
18Aug.06
3May99

Chaplains.
Dow, Rev. J., M.A., TD
[C.S.] Chapl. 1st
Class (T.F.) (*attd.*)
19July10
19July90
Mackenzie, Rev. D. F.,
B.D. [U.F.C.],Chaplain 4th class (T. F.)
(*attd.*) 16May12

[Uniform—*Scarlet*.
Facings—*Buff*.]

5th (The Sutherland and Caithness Highland) Battalion.

"South Africa, 1900-02."

Golspie.

Lt.-Colonel.
p.s. Buik, E. G., VD,
hon. c. (H)(T) 19Dec.03

Majors. (2)
p.s. Davidson, J. J. C., VD,
11June04
Sinclair, D., VD,
18June12

Captains. (8)
p.s. Dunnet, A., TD,
hon. m. 12Mar.04
p.s. Macmillan, A. L.,
TD, hon. m. 29Mar.05
p.s. Hunter, T. M. 25Apr.07
p.s. Manson, D ,TD. 1Apr.08
p.s. Menzies, J. 25Nov.11
p. Robertson,J.J. 26Nov.12
p.s.Shearer, R. 22May13
p. Harper, A., TD, 4Feb.14

Lieutenants. (8)
p.s. Milligan, D. W.20Dec.05
(p.) MacLennan, J. 1 May11
(p.s.) Cook, F. S.(H) I, of M.
1June11
p.s. Sutherland, D. ⓢ
27Apr.12
p.s. Gunn, D.W.(A)(H)
26Nov.12
(p.s.)Gunn, J. 22May13
McLeod, A. R. 31July13
(p.s.)Ritson, J. (t) 5Mar.14

2nd Lieutenants. (8)
Rutherford.G.C.2Dec.11
Macdonald, W. A.
20Jan.12
Mowat, J. D. L.14Jan.13
Gunn, J. W. 15Jan.13
Morrison, J. B. 1Mar.13
Murray, G. 16 Apr.13
Fraser, E. 14Mar.14
Barnetson, W. J.
8June14

Inst. of Musk.
Cook, F. S., *lt.*
1 Jan.11

Adjutant.
Orr, N. C., Lt.
Sea. Highrs.
capt. 1Nov.13

Quarter-Master.
p. Morrison, J., VD,
hon. m. 22June94

Medical Officers.
p. Durran, Maj. D.,
M.B.,TD, R.A.M.C.
(T.F.) (*attd.*) 29Oct.04
30May91
Simpson. Maj. J. B.,
M.D., R.A.M.C.
(T.F.) (*attd.*) 1Mar.14
18Sept.08

Chaplains.
Scott, Rev. A. B.,
M.A.,B.D.[C.S.]
Chapl.2nd Class
(T.F.) (*attd.*) 10June11
10June96
Mackenzie, Rev. J.
[U.F.C.], Chapl.
4th Class (T.F.)
(*attd.*) 1Dec.09
Soutar, Rev. A.,
M.A. [U.F.C.],
Chapl. 4th Class
(T.F.) (*attd.*) 1Feb.10
Peebles, Rev. G.S.,
B.D., [C.S.] Chapl.
4th Class (T.F.)
(*attd.*) 1Nov.12

[Uniform—*Scarlet*.
Facings—*Yellow*.]

6th (Morayshire) Battalion.

"South Africa, 1900-02."

Elgin.

Hon. Colonel.
p. Johnston, C. J., VD
(Hon. Col. ret. Vols.)
22Nov.02

Lt.-Colonel.
p. Black,W.R.,TD 8Mar.13

Majors. (2)
p. Shlach, D. A. 9Mar.09
Smith,J.G.,TD. 8Mar.13

Captains. (8)
p. Robb, A. 5May06
p.s. Doig, W. H. (H)
18Jan.08
p.s. Ramsay, A. L. ⓢ
22Apr.09
p. Mackenzie, T. R. (t)
7Dec.09
p.s. Young, R. 21June11
p. Cameron, A. 23Oct.12
p. Asher, G. W. 8Mar.13
Macdonald,W. 8June14

Lieutenants. (8)
Macpherson, A.
21June11
Legge, W. 26Dec.11
Macdonald, A. D.
26Dec.11
Grant, P. A. 25July12
Grant, R. 28Oct 12
Bothwell, J 8Mar.13
Jack, A. 20Mar.14

2nd Lieutenants. (8)
Cook, J. A. 20Feb.12
Mair, R. C, T. 20Feb.12
Petrie, W. R. 20Feb.12
Kennedy, J. A. 10Apr.12
Boyd, A. 21Aug.12
Taylor, A. P. 16Apr.13
Mackintosh, L. D.
7May13
MacDougall,J. 28Mar.14
Stewart, D. 28Mar.14

Adjutant.
⚔Anderson, F.,
Lt. Sea. Highrs.
capt. 10Nov.13

Quarter-Master.
p. ⚔Gair, S., *hon. m.*
(a)(b) 6Dec.02

Medical Officers.
p. Campbell, Maj.D, G.,
R.A.M.C. (T.F.)
(*attd.*) 20May13
16Mar.98
Stephen, Lt. J. A.,
M.B., R.A.M.C.
(T. F.) (*attd.*) 16Apr.13

Chaplains.
⚔Macpherson, Rev.
R., D.D., VD, [C.S.]
Chapl. 1st Class
(T.F.) (*attd.*) 1Apr.08
26Apr.82
MacEwen, Rev. J.,
M.A., VD, [C.S.]
Chapl. 1st Class
(T.F.) (*attd.*) 1Apr.08
26Apr.82
Sinclair, Rev. P.
M.A.,[C.S.] Chapl.
3rd Class (T.F.)
(*attd.*) 27Mar.11
27Mar.01
Hamilton, Rev. W.
[C.S.] Chapl. 3rd
Class (T.F.) (*attd.*)
27Mar.11
27Mar.01

[Uniform—*Scarlet*.
Facings—*Buff*.]

THE GORDON HIGHLANDERS.
Regimental District No. **75**. [No. **1** District.]

The Royal Tiger, superscribed "India," The Sphinx, superscribed "Egypt,"
"Mysore," "Seringapatam," "Egmont-op-Zee," "Mandora," "Corunna,"
"Fuentes d'Onor," "Almaraz," "Vittoria," "Pyrenees," "Nive," "Orthes," "Peninsula," "Waterloo,"
"South Africa, 1835," "Delhi, 1857," "Lucknow," "Charasiah," "Kabul, 1879," "Kandahar, 1880,"
"Afghanistan, 1878-80," "Tel-el-Kebir," "Egypt, 1882, 1884," "Nile, 1884-85," "Chitral," "Tirah,"
"Defence of Ladysmith," "Paardeberg," "South Africa, 1899-1902."

Regular and Special Reserve Battalions.
Uniform—Scarlet. Facings—Yellow. *Agents*—Messrs Holt & Co.

1st Bn. (75th Foot)	.. †Plymouth.	3rd Bn. (R. Aberdeenshire Mil.)	*Aberdeen.*
2nd ,, (92nd ,,)	.. *Cairo.*		
Depôt	.. *Aberdeen.*	Record Office ..	.. *Kinnoull Street Perth.*

Territorial Force Battalions.

4th Bn.	.. *Aberdeen.*	7th Bn.	.. *Banchory.*
5th ,,	.. *Peterhead.*	The Shetland Cos.	.. *Lerwick.*
6th ,,	.. *Keith.*		

Allied Regiment of Canadian Militia.
48th Regiment "Highlanders" .. .. *Toronto, Ontario.*

Colonel .. Douglas, Gen. *Sir* C. W. H., *G.C.B., q.s.* [R] 𝔸.𝔹.ℂ., *Chief of the Impl. Gen.*
Staff (1st *Mil. Member, Army Council*) 25June12

1st and 2nd Battalions.

Lt.-Colonels. (2)
1 Neish, F. H. 10Aug.11
2 Uniacke, H. P. 14Dec.11

Majors. (6)
2 Greenhill-Gardyne, A. D. [L] 2Oct.08
                22Aug.02
1 𝔹ℂGordon, W. E.
  A.D.C. 1Jan.07
  bt. col. 9Oct.11
1 Tytler, R. A. N. 14Dec.07
2 Macnab, G. R. 9Jan.08
  Gordon, A. F., *D.S.O.*,
  p.s.c. 4July08
2 Craufurd, G. S. G.,
  C.I.E., D.S.O., p.s.c.
              10Aug.11
3) 1 Simpson, C. J.
  (*Comdg. Depôt*) 14Dec.11
              22Aug.02
1 Allan, P. S., *p.s.c.*
              5July13

Captains. (14)
1 Marshall, W. M. K.
              31May00
  Booth, T. M. [L] 31Dec.00
1 Brown, P.W., *e.* 16June01
1) Baird, A. W. F.,
  D.S.O., p.s.c. [L]
              22Jan.02
  bt. maj. 22Aug.02
  Ogston, C., *p.s.c.* 22Jan.02
) Dick - Cunyngham,
  J. K., *D.S.O., p.s.c.*
              24Nov.02
  ~~Lumsden, C. E.~~ 6Feb.04
2 Stansfeld, J. R. E.,
  D.S.O., Adjt. 30May04
) Makgill-Crichton-Maitland, F. L. 25Aug.04
2 .Lockley, B. E. H. 8Sept.04
1 Mitford, W. B. J.
              16Aug.05
  McLean, G. N. 3Jan.06
2 Burnett, J. L. G. 22Jan.06
2 Sworder, F. R. F.,
              8Feb.07
2 Gordon, B. G. R. 20May08
              18Jan.08

Captains.—contd.
2 Bruce, K, H. [L] 17Oct.08
  e.a. *Craufurd, A.* 13Feb.09
  s. Campbell, R. B. 22Feb.09
(3) 2 Picton-Warlow, L.
              1Mar.10
t. Maitland, C. A. S.
              4Sept.10
r. Ross, H. A. 3June10
  1 Neish, W. 3June10
t. Burn, H. P. 6July10
e.a. Gordon, L. 6Aug.10
  1 Bell, F., *Adjt.* 18Aug.10
  2 Huggins, C. G. D.
              26Sept.10
(3) 1 Monteith, J.B.L.
              25Dec.10
(1) Fowke, G. H. S. 9Mar.11
(3) 2 Ker, A. M. 29May11
t. McClintock,S.R. 10Aug.11
  Blair, J. M., *p.s.c.*
              12Aug.11
t· Oxley, R. D. 28Mar.14

Lieutenants. (20)
2 Brooke, J. A. O. 5Aug.07
1 Taylor, T. G. 6Jan.09
d †Richmond, L. 8Feb.09
2 Carr, L.   28Feb.09
s. Davidson, E. H. 22Feb.09
1 Lyon, A. P. F. [L]
              20Mar.09
2 Fraser, J. H. 20Mar.09
2 Hamilton, J. M. 3June10
2 Blair-Cunynghame,
  R. O. 18Aug.10
2 Mackenzie, P. M.
              26Sept.10
1 Trotter, J. K. 15Oct.10
c.o. Burney, G. T. 3Nov.10
(3) 1 Hume-Gore, G. R. V.
              7Dec.10
1 Sandeman, W. A. F.
              9Mar.11
(3) 2 Maxwell, W.G. 1Apr.11
2 Latta, C. K.   10Aug.11
2 Sprot, H. M.   2Sept.11
2 Fraser, Hon. W. 22Dec.11
2 Anderson, C. E. 19June12
c.o. Murray, J. G. 2July12
1 Usher, C. M. 28Mar.14
2 Graham, A.S.B. 11July14

2nd Lieutenants. (12)
2 Doble, W. F. R.,
  f.o.r. 28Aug.11
2 Cochrane, C. 20Sept.11

2nd Lieuts.—contd.
1 Stewart, A. D. L.
              20Sept.11
1 Robertson, R. D. 11Oct.11
1 Burn, H. L. P. 14Feb.12
1 Turnbull, D. R. 13Mar.12
2 Macbean, D. G. F.
              4Sept.12
2 Bell, Q. D.   4Sept.12
2 Graham, W. J. 4Dec.12
1 Houldsworth, J. F. H.
              22Jan.13
1 Hunter Blair, D. W.
              17Sept.13
2 Boyd, J. P.   25Feb.14

Adjutants.
2 Stansfeld, J. R. E.,
  D.S.O., capt. 1Jan.12
1 Bell, F., *capt.* 22Jan.12
Quarter-Masters.
s. V℄Robertson, W.
              12May00
hon. capt. 12May10
r. MacLennan, J. 14May02
hon. capt. 14May12
2 Mackle, J., *hon. lt.*
              18Aug.10
1 Macdonald, J., *hon. lt.*
              7Oct.08

Special Reserve.
2nd Lieutenants.
Hamilton, I. B. M.
              30Aug.11
Lindsay-Young,
  E.   1Apr.13
Walker, R. J. (*on prob.*) 17Dec.13
Robertson, A. W. M.,
              7Feb.14
Griffin, C. S. J.
  (*on prob.*) 21Mar.14

3rd Battalion.
(*Officers serving on 6 July 01 in the corresponding Militia unit hold honorary Army rank equivalent to the Militia regimental rank they then held. Other Officers entitled to honorary Army rank have it shown against their names.*)

Lt.-Colonel.
Leith, A. H., *late Lt.*
Welsh R. (*H*) 2June11

Major.
p.s. Forbes, J. O. (*H*)
              14Apr.05
.e. ✕Simpson, C. J.
              14Dec.11
              22Aug.02

Captains. (5)
Duff, A. A., *C.I.E.*,
  hon. m.   8Feb.97
p s.✕Buckingham, A. W.
(*t*) (*Hon. Captain Army 31 May 01*)
  hon. m.   11Jan.02
✕Ingilby, J. U. M.,
  Capt. ret.pay (*H*)
              26Jan.07
✕Gordon-Duᵀ, L.,
  Capt.ret.pay 12Aug.09
r.e. ✕Picton-Warlow, L.
              1 Mar. 10
r.e. ✕Monteith, J. B. L.,
              25Dec.10
r.e. ✕Ker, A. M. 29May11
✕Alexander, W.,
  late Lt. Border
  Mtd. Rif. (*H*) 22Apr.12
Lieutenants. (11)
Hay, M. V. [L] 5May09
Fraser, *Hon.* A. A.
  (*Master of Saltoun*)
  (*H*)   18Oct.10
✕Murray, W. E., *late*
  Lt.Res. of Off. 18Oct.11
r.e. Hume-Gore, G. R. V.
              7 Dec.10
r.e. Maxwell, W.G. 1 Apr. 11
f.c. Cruikshank, G. L.
              1Apr.13
Watson, J. F. J.
              1Apr.13

2nd Lieutenants. (8)
Fraser, H. D. M. 1Apr.12
Macpherson, D. E.
              26Oct.12
Monteith, G. M. 1Mar.13
Forbes, M. H. O.
              1Oct.13

† *Postal Address—Crownhill S.O., Devon*

THE GORDON HIGHLANDERS—(Regtl. Dist. No. 75)—contd.

3rd Bn.—contd.

Adjutant.
✕Ross, H. A., Capt.
 Gord.Highrs.26Mar.14
 (*Capt. in Army 3 June* 10)

Quarter-Master.
✕MacLennan, J., hon.
 capt.

4th Battalion.

"South Africa, 1900-02."

Aberdeen.

Hon. Colonel.
✕Lovat, S. J., Lord,
 K.C.V.O., C.B.,
 D.S.O.,Col.A-D-C.
 (*Hon. Col. 1st & 2nd
 Lovat's Scouts*)
 (*Col. ret. T F.* 17Feb.14

Lt.-Colonel.
p. Stewart, D. B. D., VD,
 hon. c. 19Nov.06

Majors. (2)
p.s.Ogilvie, T., jun.
 11June13
p.s.Smith, G. A. 22June13

Captains. (8)
p.s.Scott, R. (*t*) 26Feb.07
p.s.Lyon, F. 7Jan.08
 Mackinnon, L, jun.
 15Apr.10
 Shirras, G. F. (*H*)
 17Sept.10
 Peterkin, C.D. 11June13

Lieutenants. (8)
(p.s.)Bennett, J. C.,
 jun. (*H*) 1Jan.08
(p.s.)Gordon, J. H. McI.
 9Jan.08
 Wilson, A. M. (*H*)
 28Oct.09
 Reid, C. (*H*) 28Oct.09
 Brander, E. W. H.
 11June13
 Johnston, A. McK. ⓢ
 7July13
 Topping, A. 28Sept.13
 Cooper, W. H. 26Feb.14

2nd Lieutenants. (8)
 Simpson, H. G.
 25July13
 Williamson, W. B.
 22Nov.13
 Watson, J. I. 14Mar.14
 Coutts, R. D. 22Apr.14
 Douglas, D. S. P.
 30Apr.14
 Falconer, D. 15July14

Adjutant.
✕McClintock, S. R.,
 Capt. Gord. Highrs.
 1Feb.13

Quarter-Master.
 Hall, J H., hon. lt.
 27Apr.11

Medical Officers.
p. Christie, Maj. J. F.,
 M.B., R.A.M.C.
 (T.F.) (*attd.*) 2Aug.12
 18July05
 Smith, Capt.F. K.,*M.B.*,
 R.A.M.C. (T.F.)
 (*attd.*) 1Nov.10
 1May07

Chaplains.
 Stewart, *Rev.* J. S.
 [U.F.C.], Chapl.
 4th Class (T.F.)
 (*attd.*) 28June09
 Leathem, *Rev.* W.
 H., *M.A.* [C.S.]
 Chapl. 4th Class
 (T.F.) (*attd.*) 14Mar.14

[Uniform—*Scarlet.*
Facings—*Yellow.*]

5th (Buchan and Formartin) Battalion.

"South Africa, 1900-01."

Peterhead.

Hon. Colonel.
✕Woolrige-Gerdon,
 J. G., Maj. (*Bt.
 Col.*) ret. pay (*Res.
 of Off.*) 11Mar.14

Lt.-Colonel.
✕Grant, A., D.S.O.,
 Capt. ret. pay
 (*Res. of Off.*) 17Apr.12

Majors. (2
p. Ferguson, W.(*t*)28July06
 p.s.Law, J., TD. 5Oct.13

Captains. (8)
p. Smith, J.T., TD, hon.
 m. (*t*) 20May08
p. Martin, D. H. 11Feb.10
p.s.Runcieman, F. S.
 18Mar.10
p.s.Reid, W. 10Apr.10
 Fowlie, C. W. L.
 27May10
p. Rennie, J., jun.29Jan.13
 McDonald, S. 17May13
p. Morrison, J., jun.
 (*H*) 5Oct.13

Lieutenants (8)
p.s.Watson, J. (*H*) 27May05
p.s.Chalmers, J. 28July06
 Mitchell, S. 1Mar.13
 Low, J. L. 1Mar.13
 Watson, W. J. 17May13

2nd Lieutenants (8)
 Gray, G. M. 1Apr.12
 21Feb.12
 Lyall, W. 10Oct.12
 Cowie, H. 16Apr.13
 Moir, G. A. C. 17Apr 13
 Buchan, G. A. B.
 15Dec.13
 Simpson, E. 12Jan.14

Adjutant.
 Cruden,J.W.F.,Lt.
 R. Highrs., *capt.*
 27Apr.14

Quarter-Master.
 Marr, J., hon. lt.
 27Nov.11

Medical Officers.
p. Wilson, Lt.-Col. R. M.,
 VD, R.A.M.C. (T.F.)
 (*attd.*) 22July96
 20May76
p. Middleton, Maj. J.,
 M.B., R.A.M.C.
 (T.F.) (*attd.*) 23Nov.10
 12Dec.94
p. Fowler, Maj. A.,
 M.D. R.A.M.C.
 (T.F.)(*attd.*) 22June12
 29July96

Chaplains.
 Johnstone, *Rev.*M.
 P. M. S., *B.D.*.TD,
 [C.S.] Chapl.2nd
 Class (T.F.)(*attd.*)
 1Apr.08
 15Dec.88
 Kemp, *Rev.* R. S.,*B.D.*,
 TD, [C.S.], Chapl.
 1st Class (T.F.)
 (*attd.*) 3Sept.12
 3Sept.92
 Halliday, *Rev.* J.
 G.,*M.A.* [U.F.C.]
 Chapl. 3rd Class
 (T.F.) (*attd.*) 18May08
 18May08
 Logan, *Rev.* W.,
 B.D. [U.F.C.]
 Chapl.4th Class
 (T.F.) (*attd.*) 1Apr.08
 Mackenzi e, *Rev.* C.
 G., *B.D.* [C.S.]
 Chapl. 4th Class
 (T.F.) (*attd.*) 1Nov.12

[Uniform—*Scarlet.*
Facings—*Yellow.*]

6th (Banff and Donside) Battalion.

"South Africa, 1900-02."

Keith.

Hon. Colonel.
p Mellis, W. A., VD ⓣ
 (*Hon. Col. ret. Terr.
 Force*) 22July11

Lt.-Colonel.
✕McLean, C., Capt.
 ret. pay (*Res. of
 Off.*) 26Jan.10

Majors. (2)
p.s.McGregor, J., TD
 (*Q*) ⓑ (*H*) 22June11
 Macdonald, W. A., TD,
 20June13

Captains. (8)
p Wilson, G. A 28Apr.06
 Gordon, J. W. 24May09
p. Dawson, J. (*t*) 6May11
 Laing, H. D. 22June11
p. Cook, J. M. 19Mar.13

Lieutenants. (8)
p.s.Cameron, J. A. S.
 24Jan.06
(p.s.)Hutcheson, J.20Nov.06
(p.s.)Smith, G. 22June11
 Paterson, J. D. 7Feb.12
(p.) Stephen, G. A. 4Dec.12
 Welch, W. B. 14Nov.13
 Cowie, J. G. 14Jan.14
 15Apr.10
(p.) Findlay, W. M. 1May14
 5July11

2nd Lieutenants. (8)
(p.) McCombie, C. 19July07
(p.) Grant, A. 19July07
 Kellas, J. 12Aug.11
 Fleming. I. G. 30Nov.11
 Walker, W.W. 21Sept.12
 Innes, J. W. 9Nov.12

Adjutant.
✕Burn, H. P.,
 Capt. Gord. Highrs.
 18Aug.13

Quarter-Master.
p. Cooper, F. W.,
 hon. m. 1Aug.10
 19May05

Medical Officers.
p. Nicol, Lt.-Col. A.,
 M.D. VD, R.A.M.C.
 (T.F.) (*attd.*) 10Mar.08
 6Nov.86
p. Taylor, Maj. J., *M.D.*,
 R.A.M.C. (T.F.)
 (*attd.*) 18Nov.07
 3July95
p. Sellar, Maj. T. A.,
 M.B., R.A.M.C.
 (T.F.) (*attd.*) 29Aug.11
 15July96
p. Nicol, Capt. J., *M.B.*,
 R.A.M.C. (T.F.)
 (*attd.*) 1Apr.08
 3Sept.92
p. Turner, Capt. E. R.,
 M.B., R.A.M.C.
 (T.F.) (*attd.*) 1Apr.08
 20Dec.02
 Murray, Capt. A. B.,
 R.A.M.C. (T.F.)
 (*attd.*) 5Dec.12
 2June08

1477	1478	1479	1480

THE GORDON HIGHLANDERS—(Regtl. Dist. No. 75)—contd.

6th Bn.—contd.

Chaplains.

Black, Rev. J., *M.A.*,
TD, [C.S.] Chapl.
1st Class (T.F.)
(attd.) 17Sept.12
    17Sept.92
Adam, Rev. P., *B.D.*,
[C.S.] Chapl. 3rd
Class (T.F.)(attd.)
    11May08
    11May98
Smith, Rev. S., *B.D.*,
[C.S.] Chapl. 3rd
Class (T.F.)(attd.)
    14Sept.08
    14Sept.98
Jack, Rev. A., *M.A.*,
[C.S.] Chapl. 3rd.
Class (T.F.)(attd.)
    6June10
    6June00
Greenlaw, Rev. J.
[C.S.] Chapl. 3rd
Class (T.F.)(attd.)
    9Jan.14
    9Jan.04

[Uniform—*Scarlet.*
Facings—*Yellow.*]

7th (Deeside Highland) Battalion.

"South Africa, 1900-02."

Banchory.

Hon. Colonel.
Huntly, C. G., Marq.
of 23Feb.76

Lt.-Colonel.
p.s.Bower, G. H., TD (Q)
    11Feb.14

Majors. (2)

Coltman, W. H. ⓣ (H)
    30June10
Bruce, R. 11Feb.14

Captains. (8)

  Dawson, J. A. 11Feb.05
p. Gregor, J. W. 27May05
p. Walker, J. W. 2Aug.07
  Riddoch, W. (A) 1Jan.11
p. Dunbar, J.C.F. 18Jan.12
  Barclay-Harvey,
  C. M. 14Aug.12
p. Braid, K.W.(H)11Feb.14

Lieutenants. (8)

p.s.Milne, J. 29Aug.06
(p.)Forsyth, W. 1Aug.09
  Adams, W. 1May10
  Falconer, R. 18Jan.12
  Mitchell, G. 3Mar.13
  Adam, R. 3Mar.13

2nd Lieutenants. (8)

Watt, A. McK. 1May11
Wimberley, E. 1Apr.12

Adjutant.
×Maitland, C. A. S.,
Capt. Gord. Highrs.
    26Mar.13

Quarter-Master.

Kennington, A. J.,
hon. lt. 1Apr.12

Medical Officers.

p. Cran, Lt.-Col. G., *M.D.*,
VD, R.A.M.C. (T.F.)
(attd.) 24June96
    9June80
p. Rannie, Maj. R., *M.B.*,
TD, R.A.M.C. (T.F.)
(attd.) 1June10
    4Apr.91
p. Mitchell, Capt. W. G.,
M.D.,R.A.M.C.(T.F.)
(attd.) 13Sept.02
    22Apr.93
p. Cruickshank, Capt. A.,
M.B., R.A.M.C.,
(T.F.)(attd.) 1Apr.08
    9Aug.02

Chaplains.

Scott, Rev. T., *M.A.*,
TD, [C.S.] Chapl.
1st Class (T.F.)
(attd.) 28Mar.14
    28Mar.94
Burnett, Rev. J. B.,
B.D., [C.S.] Chapl.
4th Class (T.F.)
(attd.) 1Apr.08
    10June05

[Uniform—*Scarlet.*
Facings—*Yellow.*]

The Shetland Companies (2)

Lerwick.

Major.
p. ×Broun, J. C. C. (H)
    10June05

Captains. (2)

p.s.Stephen, A.(H)17Sept.04
p.s.MacDougall, P. (H)
    15July05
p. Laurenson, L. 1Aug.05

Lieutenants (2).

p.s.Laing, A. L. 5May06
p.s.Ramsay, R. H. (H)
    5May06

2nd Lieutenants. (2)

Smith, A. J. 16Mar.09
Mitchell, C. E. 31Mar.09

‡ *Quarter-Master.*

p. Williamson, D.,
hon. capt. 1Apr.04

Medical Officer.

p.s.Robertson, Capt. J. F.,
M.D., R.A.M.C.
(T.F.) (attd.) 11June04
    9Mar.01

Chaplain.

Macintyre, Rev. A.,
M.A., [C.S.] Chapl.
4th Class (T.F.)
(attd.) 6Mar.12

[Uniform—*Scarlet.*]
Facings—*Yellow.*]

---

‡ This appointment is not provided for in the Territorial Force Tables of Establishments.

THE QUEEN'S OWN CAMERON HIGHLANDERS.

Regimental District No. **79**. [No. **1** District.]

The Thistle ensigned with the Imperial Crown. The Sphinx, superscribed "Egypt."
"Egmont-op-Zee," "Corunna," "Busaco," "Fuentes d'Onor," "Salamanca," "Pyrenees," "Nivelle," "Nive," "Toulouse," "Peninsula," "Waterloo," "Alma," "Sevastopol," "Lucknow," "Tel-el-Kebir," "Egypt, 1882," "Nile, 1884-85," "Atbara," "Khartoum," "South Africa, 1900-02."

Regular and Special Reserve Battalions.

Uniform—Scarlet.   *Facings*—Blue.   *Agents*—Messrs. Holt & Co.

1st Bn. (79th Foot)	.. *Edinburgh.*	3rd Bn. (Highland (Lt. Inf.) Mil.) .. *Inverness.*
2nd ,, ,, ,,	.. *Poona.*	
Depôt	*Inverness.*	Record Office .. *Kinnoull Street, Perth.*

Territorial Force Battalion.
4th Bn. .. .. *Inverness.*

Allied Regiment of Canadian Militia.
79th Cameron Highlanders of Canada .. .. *Winnipeg, Manitoba.*

Colonel-in-Chief .. .. THE KING.

Colonel .. Hamilton, Gen. Sir I. S. M., G.C.B., D.S.O., q.s., 𝔄.𝔇.ℭ. 7Dec.04

1st and 2nd Battalions.

Lt.-Colonels. (2)
2 MacEwen, D. L., p.s.c. 1Apr.12
1 McLachlan, J. D., p.s.c. [L] 9Mar.13

Majors. (8)
2 Campbell, J., D.S.O., p.s.c., e. 9Mar.05
bt. lt.-col. 21Feb 14
2 Græme, L. O. 12July09
1 Cameron, N. J. G., p.s.c., f.o.r. 3Apr.10
bt. lt.-col. 10May13
1 Sorel-Cameron, G. C. M. (*Comdg. Depôt*) 7Sept.10
1 Nicholson, A.D. 1Apr.12
2 Baird, P. T. C. 24Aug.12
s. Adlercron, R. L. 9Mar.13
1 Maitland, Hon. A. H. 13Mar.14

Captains. (14)
s. Craig-Brown, E., p.s.c., e. 7Dec.99
2 Maclean, C. W. [F] 20May08
2 Stewart, W. M.,p.s.c. 9Feb.00 6June00
1 Miers, D.N.C.C.7Mar.01
s. Sandilands, J. W., D.S.O.,p.s.c.,[I]29May01
s. Hay, S. 21Nov.01
1 Horne, A. 23Dec.01
(3) 1 Fraser, G. I. 22Jan.02
2 Fraser, P. W. N., D.S.O. 21Apr.02
r. Lumsden, H. T. 23Apr.08
2 Macpherson, A. D., *Adjt.* 28Mar.04
2 Crichton, D. E. M. M. 16Apr.04
s.c. Robertson, A. B. 26Apr.05
(3) 2 Mitford, P. H. 17May05
e.a. McCowan, W. H. 23Oct.05
2 Campbell, R. 28Oct.05
s.c. Orr, J. A. 23Oct.05
t. Campbell, C. H. 22Ja..07

Captains—contd.
(3) 2 Heathcote, J. R. C.,f.c. 1Mar.10
Trotter, R. B. 1Mar.10
t. Du𝔣, G. R. 3Apr.13
1 Mackintosh, A. H. [I] 14May10
1 Cameron, A.G. 14May10
1 Stewart-Murray, Lord J. T. 14May10
t. Erskine, Sir T. W. H. J., Bt. 11Jan.11
1 Brodie, E. J. 3May11
(1 Grieve, C. C., e. 3May11
Scovell, G. J. S. (B. S. Africa Co.) 19May11
m.c. Ramsay, G. 19May11

Lieutenants. (19)
1 Cameron, N. C. G. 5Feb.08
1 Matheson, J. S. M. 8May04
t. Dudgeon, R. M. 25Feb.05
2 Drew, J. S. 26Apr.05
2 Douglas, A.J.A.22Jan.07
2 Lampson,A.C.16May08
s Robertson, L. 11Mar.09
2 McCall, R. L. 20Aug.09
1 Meiklejohn, K. F. [L], *Adjt*. 13Sept.09
1 Johnstone, R. F. L. 2Dec.09
(3) 2 Maxwell, W.J. 1Jan.11
o.o. Baxter, G. L. 11Jan.11
2 Macduff, A. 11Jan.11
2 Methuen, H.C. 1Apr.11
2 Thomson, A. Y. G. 1Apr.11
2 Fowler, A. A. 27Apr.11
s.s. Allan, A. C. 19May11
1 Cameron, D. 6Sept.11
2 Nicholson,W.D.1Mar.12
1 Traill, S. G. [I] 4May12
2 Davidson, D.G. 6May12
s. Nicholson, A. S. 3Sept.13
2 Grant, I. C. 14Jan.14
1 Macdonald, R. M. 1May14
(3) 1 Cameron,N.K. 13May14

2nd Lieutenants. (12)
1 Stewart, R. N. 12Apr.11
1 Sprot, I. B. 27May11
2 Napier, L. R. M. 19Sept.11

2nd Lieuts.—contd.
2 Hussey-Macpherson, L. F. 19Sept.11
2 Henderson, R. A. C. 20Sept.11
1 Cameron, H. W. L. 20Sept.11
1 Cameron, A. H. 13Mar.12
1 Constable-Maxwell, I. S. J. 3Sept.12
2 Anderson, J. R. H. 9Nov.12 20Jan.13
2 Dunsmure, H. A. H. 22Jan.13
1 McLachlan, J. W. F. 17Sept.13
1 Murray,A.J.G.25Feb14
(1) Cameron,D.P.K.4Apr.14

Adjutants.
1 Meiklejohn, K. F. [L] *lt.* 13Mar.13
2 Macpherson, A. D., *capt.* 21Nov.13

Quarter-Masters.
1 Yeadon, A. P. 9Mar.96
hon. maj. 29Nov.00
2 Macdonald, D., 19Mar.04
hon. capt. 19Mar.14
r. Patrick, J. McD., hon.lt. 4Sept.12

Special Reserve.
2nd Lieutenants.
McDonald, D. P. (on prob.) 1Jan.13
Dickson, J. H. 5Apr.13
Cameron, W. 19Aug.13
Smith-Sligo, A. G. R.J. 1Dec.13
Kinmont, J. C. 9Feb 14
Mackay, G. S. (on prob.) 15Apr.14
McIntosh, R. R. (on prob.) 25Apr.14

3rd Battalion.

(*Officers serving on 4 Dec. 00 in the corresponding Militia unit hold honorary Army rank equivalent to the Militia regimental rank they then held. Other officers entitled to honorary Army rank have it shown against their names.*)

Hon. Colonel.
p.s. Mackintosh of Mackintosh, A. D. (Hon. Col. ret, Mila.) (Hon. Lt.- Col. in Army, 5 Dec.00) 2July08 8Aug.00

Lt.-Colonel.
✕ Cameron of Lochiel, D.W., Capt. ret. pay (H) ⓢ (q) 14Feb.12

Major.
r.e.✕Sorel-Cameron, G. C. M. 7Sept.10
p.s.✕Alford, H. S. L. (Capt. Res. of, Off.) (H) (q) 12June12

Captains. (5)
r.e.✕Fraser, G. I. 22Jan.02
p.s.✕Archdall, N. J. M. (Hon. Lt. in Army 3Sept.02) (H), p.v.o. 28May04
r.e.✕Mitford, P. 17May05
p.s.✕Brown, H. R., Bt. Maj. ret. pay (H) (Q) ⓖ 17May05
r.e.✕Heathcote, J. R. C., f.o 1Mar.10
p.s. Cavaye, R. J. (H) 28Jan.11
p.s. Seafield, J., Earl of (H) 29Jan.11 20Apr.08
Campbell, C. C. K. (H) 16Feb.13

THE QUEEN'S OWN CAMERON HIGHLANDERS—(Regtl. Dist. No. 79)—contd.

3rd Bn.—contd.

Lieutenants. (11)
Black, J. B., Lt.
  ret. pay 23Oct.05
r.e. Maxwell, W. J. 1Mar.10 3Sept.13
p.s ⨯Davidson, J. M., *late*
  Capt. 4 Bn, L'pool R.
  (*H*) 11Nov.11
Maclean, A. D. D.
   5May13
Maitland, *Hon.* I. C.
   11July13
Simpson, J. G. 11July13
r.e. Cameron, N. K.
   13May14
Barber, G. 30June14
Dixon, R. V. 30June14

2nd Lieutenants. (8)
Knox, W. (*on prob.*)
   3Dec.13
Blane, M. G. S.
  (*on prob.*) 16May14
Caldwell, J. H.
  (*on prob.*) 10June14

Adjutant.
Lumsden, H. T.,
  Capt. Cam'n
  Highrs. 20Oct.13
  (*Capt.in Army* 23*Apr*.03)

Quarter-Master.
Parick, J. McD., *hon.lt.*

4th Battalion.

" South Africa, 1900-02."

Inverness.

Hon. Colonel.
⨯*Ewart, Lt -Gen.* Sir
  J. S., K.C.B., p.s.c.,
  s. 10Feb.C8

Lt.-Colonel.
Campbell, E., VD.
   23Aug.13

Majors. (2)
Fraser, H., TD. 5Apr.09
⨯Campbell, J., TD,
  (*Hon. Lt. in Army*
  31*May*01) 23Aug.13
   6Jan.12

Captains. (8)
Allison, T. 5Apr.09
p.s.Macdonald, R.,
  TD 31Aug.09
p.s.Beaton, M. 31Jan.10
p. Macpherson, J.24Nov.10
p.s.⨯MacLean, R. (q)
  (*H*) 3May11
p.s.Ross, D. (*H*) 31Mar.13
p. Mackintosh,W.10Apr.13

Lieutenants. (8)
p.s.Mackenzie,D.F.10Oct.06
Mackintosh, A. J.
   4Nov.09
Campbell,J.(*H*) 5May10 16Mar.08
Cram, P. McF. 12Dec.11
p. Fraser, F. W., *late*
  Capt. 4 High.
  (Mtd.) Brig. R.G.A.
   29Jan.12
MacKenzie, N.B., jun.
   9Sept.12
Mackay, I (*H*) 31Mar.13
Leigh, J.H.(*H*)11June13
   15Mar.12

2nd Lieutenants. (8)
Ross, A. 3Apr.12
Campbell, C. 3Apr.12
Lees, A. S. 9May12
MacPherson, J. D.
   9May12
MacKenzie,M. 19Mar.13
Fletcher, A. McP.
   30Apr.13
Mackay, W., jun
   18Oct.13
Law, H. B. 11Mar.14
Shaw, W. J. 9May14

Adjutant.
Duff, G. B., Capt.
  Cam'n. Highrs.
   1Mar.13

Quarter-Master.
p. ⨯Lockie, J., *hon. m.*
   1Nov.06

Medical Officers.
p.s.Miller,Maj.A.C.,*M.D.,*
  TD, R.A.M.C.
  (T.F.) (*attd.*) 15May08
   11June92
Lindsay, Capt. R.,
  R.A.M.C. (T.F.)
  (*attd.*) 5Dec.12
   1Apr.08

Chaplains.
Macleod, *Rev.* D.,
  B.D. [C.S.] Chapl.
  4th Class (T.F.)
  (*attd.*) 1Apr.08
   28Feb.08
MacDonald, *Rev.*
  D. A. [U.F.C.]
  Chapl. 4th Class
  (T.F.) (*attd.*) 22Dec.09
MacFarlane, *Rev.* D.
  [C.S.] Chapl.4th Class
  (T.F.) (*attd.*) 22Dec.09
Bain, *Rev.* A. [U.F.C.]
  Chapl.4thClass(T.F.)
  (*attd.*) 22Dec.09

[Uniform—*Scarlet*.
Facings—*Blue.*]

THE ROYAL IRISH RIFLES.
Regimental District No. **83**. [No. **11** District.]

The Harp and Crown, with the Motto "*Quis Separabit.*"
The Sphinx, superscribed "Egypt."

"India," "Cape of Good Hope, 1806," "Talavera," "Bourbon," "Busaco," "Fuentes d'Onor," "Ciudad Rodrigo," "Badajoz," "Salamanca," "Vittoria," "Nivelle," "Orthes," "Toulouse," "Peninsula," "Central India," "South Africa, 1899-1902."

Regular and Special Reserve Battalions.

Uniform—Green.	Facings—Dark Green.	Agents—Messrs. Cox & Co.
1st Bn. (83rd Foot) .. Aden (for *Tidworth*)	3rd Bn. (Royal Antrim Mil.)	.. .. *Belfast.*
2nd „ (86th „) .. Tidworth (for Malta)	4th „ (Royal North Down Mil.)	*Newtownards.*
	5th „ (Royal South Down Mil.)	*Downpatrick.*

Depôt .. .. .. Belfast.   Record Office .. .. Dublin.

Colonel .. .. .. Burnett, Gen. Sir C. J., K.C.B., K.C.V.O., ret. pay, p.s.c. [R] .. 15Mar.14

1st and 2nd Battalions.

Lt.-Colonels. (2)
1 Laurie, G. B. 28Oct.12
2 Bird, W. D., *D.S.O.*, *p.s c.* [l] 24Sept.13
18Dec.09

Majors. (8)
1 Weir, A. V. 21July06
1 Baker, O. C. 22Sept.06
(3) 2 Bradford, E. C. (*Comdg. Depôt*) 30Dec.08
22Aug.02
1 Wright, H. C. 2Nov.11
2 Spedding, C. R., *D.S.O.* 2Nov.11
2 Daunt, R. A. C., *D.S.O.* 5Sept.12
1 Alston, J. W. 28Oct.12
2 Charley, H. R. 17Sept.13

Captains. (14)
s. Sprague, L. C., *p.s.c.* [L] 10Dec.02
e.a. Macnamara, C. C. 10Dec.02
t. Merriman, A. D. N. 20May06
5Feb.08
s. Stevens, R. W. M., *p.s.c.* 2Jan.04
Dunn, E. G., *p.s.c.* 16Jan04
(3) 1 Dixon, C. S. 18July04
(3) 1 Rodney, L.G.B. 16June06
2 Bowen-Colthurst, J.C., [L] 21Dec.07
r. Lanyon, W. M. 7Feb.08
1 Biscoe, A. J. 28June08
e.a. *Maynard, P. G. W.* 28June08
2Soutry, T.L. B. 28June08
1 Cinnamond, C. H. L., *e.* 28June08
s. Cooke-Collis, W.J.N., *e.* 28June08
2 Goodman, H. R. 28June08
(3) 2 Eastwood, W. 28June08
2 Master, C. L. 28June08
1 Gifford, H. L., *e.* 8Aug.08
9Oct.01
2 Becher, C. M. L. 22Jan.09
Reynolds, T. J. 15May09

Captains—contd.
(2) Haskett-Smith, W. J. J. S. 8Mar.10
1 Whelan, J. P. 8Mar.10
e.a. Forbes, Hon. B. A. 8Mar.10
2 Durant, H. N. 11Mar.10
1 O'Sullivan, A. M. 11Mar.10

Lieutenants. (19)
1 Tee, C. C. 27Apr.07
1 Martyr, J. F. 27Apr.07
t. Scott, G. C. 28Apr.07
f.c. 1 Ludlow-Hewitt, E. R. 24Sept.07
1 Graham, F.R.W. 5Dec.07
s. Hutcheson, N. H. 21Dec.07
(3) 1 Mansergh, R. O. 7Feb.08
1 Galwey, A. W. 28June08
1 *Wright, A. O'H., Adjt.* 22Jan.09
2 Peebles, A. E. 1Apr.09
2 Dillon, S. S., *Adjt.* 22Apr.09
2 Varwell, R.P. 23May14
1Apr.09
r. Knox, U. A. F. 1Aug.09
(3) 2 Hutcheson, R. B. 1Jan.10
1 Newport, C. J. 5Jan.10
2 Thomas, E. M. 8Mar.10
c.o. Umbers, T. R. 27Jan.12
24Oct.08
1 Browne, D. A. 8Mar.10
s.s. How, W. F. 1Apr.10
1 Foley, J. W. 7June10
1 Gartlan, G. I. 11July10
1 Gavin, E. Fitz A. 15Apr.13
c.o. Cowley, V. L. S. 24Jan.14
c.o. Clements, G. S. 4Feb.14
c.o. Rodwell, R. M. 4Feb.14
2 Norman, G. S. 11Feb.14
2 Whitfeld, A. N. 17Mar.14
2 Dawes, C. R. B. 27May14

2nd Lieutenants. (12)
2 Teele, W. B. 9Apr.10
2 Swaine, H. P. 5Oct.10
2 Matthews-Donaldson C. L. G. 25Mar.11
1 Burges, W. A. 20Apr.10
(to take precedence from 20 Apr. 11.)
1 Adeley, G. G. 11Jan.13
2 Innes-Cross, S. M. 5Feb.13
2 Lorie, R. H. 10June14

Adjutants.
1 Wright, A. O'H., *lt.* 1Jan.13
2 Dillon, S. S., *lt.* 27Nov.13

Quarter-Masters.
r. Henderson, A. 15Apr.96
hon. maj. 15Apr.11
r. Templeton, G. 17Sept.02
hon. capt. 17Sept.13
1 Foster, H. W. 21Oct.08
hon. capt. 21Oct.13
r. Edwards, G. W., hon. lt. 30Mar.10
2 Clark, W., hon. lt. 25Apr.14

Special Reserve.

2nd Lieutenant.
Sullivan, H. R. F., *late* 2nd Lt. R. Ir. Rif. 22July12
24June14

3rd Battalion.

(*Officers serving on 1 Nov.00 in the corresponding Militia unit hold honorary Army rank equivalent to the Militia regimental rank they then held. Other officers entitled to honorary Army rank have it shown against their names.*)

Hon. Colonel.
× *Wilson, Maj.-Gen. H.H.*, C. B. D,S.O *p.s.c.* (*Dir. of Mil. Opns.*) 16Nov.12

Lt.-Colonel.
p.s. McCammond, W.E.C. 6Dec.12

Major.
r.e. Bradford, E. C. 30Dec.08
22Aug.02
p.s. × McFerran, E.M.G. (*H*) 19Dec.12

Captains. (5)
p.s. × Rosborough, J. (*Hon. Capt. in Army* 18 *Oct.* 00) (*H*) 18May02
r.e. Dixon, C. S. 18July04
p.s. Jonsson, A. T. 1Oct.04
p.s. × Chatterton, E. V. H. 5Aug.05
p.s. × Heslip, I. (*H*) (*Asst. Commr. of Police, Sierra Leone*, 7Oct.10) 5Aug.05
r.e. × Rodney, L. G. B. 16June06
p.s. × Samman, J.G.S.W. 16July06
(*Hon. 2nd Lt. in Army* 4 *Oct.* 02) (*H*) 15Dec.07
McLaughlin, N. 21Jan.08
r.e. × Eastwood, W. 28June08

Lieutenants. (11)
p.s. Curran, J.P.C. (*H*) 1Jan.08
r.e. Mansergh, R. O. 7Feb.08
r.e. Hutcheson, R. B. 1Jan.10
(p.s.) Mulcahy-Morgan, E. S. (*H*) 7Apr.10
Popplewell, H. E. (*Asst. Dist. Commr., E. Africa Prote.*, 8 *Dec.* 10) 20Dec.13
Finlay, F. L. 20Dec.13

2nd Lieutenants. (8)
Magenis, R. H. C. 1Feb.08
28May14

Adjutant.
× Reynolds, T. J., Capt. R. Ir. Rif. (*Capt. in Army* 15 *May* 09)

Quarter-Master.
× Edwards, G. W., hon. lt.

THE ROYAL IRISH RIFLES—(Regtl. Dist. No. 83)—contd.

4th Battalion.

(*Officers serving on 19Oct.00 in the corresponding Militia unit hold honorary Army rank equivalent to the Militia regimental rank they then held Other officers entitled to honorary Army rank have it shown against their names.*)

Hon. Colonel.

Londonderry, Rt. Hon. C. S., Marq. of, K.G., G.C.V.O., C.B., VD (Col. late Vols.), A.D.C. 28June08
 26Mar.02

Lt.-Colonel.

Findlay, F. (*H*) hon. c. 2Dec.08

Majors. (3)

p.s.✗Reeve, H. W. (*Hon. Capt. in Army20Oct.02*) (*H*) (*b*) 1Apr.11
✗Eckford, P. G. W., Capt. ret. pay (*Res. of Off.*) 1Dec.11
Syer, H. B. 13Aug.13

Captains. (6)

✗Burgoyne, G. A., Capt. ret. pay 7May10
 17July12
Gaussen, H. A., *late* Capt. 3 Bn. R. Ir. Rif. 26Apr.11
Hall-Thompson, S. H. 8Nov.13
Monro, E. W. C., Capt. ret. pay (*Res. of Off.*) (*H*) ⑤ 21Feb.14
Drought, J. B. A., Lt. ret. pay (*H*) 2May14

Lieutenants. (11)

p.s. Algeo, L. W. A. 5Dec.08
✗Thompson, W. O., *late* 2nd Lt. Conn. Rang. 29Dec.09
Jeffares, R. T. 20Feb.13
La Nauze, G. M. 20Feb.13
Rea, V. T. T. 20Feb.13
Browne, L. 20Feb.13
Howard, W. E. S. 13June14

2nd Lieutenants. (8)

La Nauze, W. (*on prob.*) 20May14

Adjutant.

Knox, U. A. F., Lt. R. Ir. Rif. 4Feb.14
(*Lt. in Army* 1Aug.09)

Quarter-Master.

✗Templeton, G., hon. capt.

5th Battalion.

(*Officers serving on 24July02 in the corresponding Militia unit hold honorary Army rank equivalent to the Militia regimental rank they then held. Other officers entitled to honorary Army rank have it shown against their names.*)

Hon. Colonel.

Hill, Rt. Hon. Lord A. W., *late* Cornet and Sub-Lt., 2 L.G. 28June08
 5Apr.02

Lt.-Colonel.

p.s.✗McCammon, T. V. P. 22Jan.13

Majors. (3)

p.s.✗Hardy, W. A. 22Jan.13
p.s. Leathes, C. de M. (*H*) 27June13
Fitzmaurice, A. J. W. (*H*) 2May14

Captains. (6)

p.s.Campbell, J. C. (*H*) 12May06
p.s.Ferguson, J. A. (*H*) ⑦ 17Mar.06

Captains—contd.

✗Smyth, C.D., Capt. ret. pay 28June13
Mockett, G. (*H*) 2May14
✗Ross, A. J. (*H*) ⑧ 7June14

Lieutenants. (11)

✗Chatterton, G. A., Lt. ret. pay 12Apr.06
 2Apr.10
Lowry, G. 19Apr.13

2nd Lieutenants. (8)

Heron, C. 12June12
Morton, T. M. (*Jun. Admin. Offr., late Africa,*27Apr.14) 2July13
Butler J. H. (*on prob*). 25July14

Adjutant.

Lanyon, W. M., Capt. R. Ir. Rif. 1Nov.13
(*Capt. in Army* 7Feb.08)

Quarter-Master.

✗Henderson, A., hon. maj.

PRINCESS VICTORIA'S (ROYAL IRISH FUSILIERS).
Regimental District No. **87**. [No. **11** District.]

The Plume of the Prince of Wales. In the first and fourth corners Princess Victoria's Coronet, in the second an Eagle with a Wreath of Laurel, in the third the Harp and Crown.
The Sphinx, superscribed "Egypt."   "*Faugh-a-Ballagh.*"

"Monte Video," "Talavera," "Barrosa," "Java," "Tarifa," "Vittoria," "Nivelle," "Niagara,"
"Orthes," "Toulouse," "Peninsula," "Ava," "Sevastopol," "Tel-el-Kebir," "Egypt, 1882-1884,"
"Relief of Ladysmith," "South Africa, 1899-1902."

Regular and Special Reserve Battalions.

Uniform—Scarlet.   *Facings*—Blue.   *Agents*—Messrs. Cox & Co.

1st Bn. (87th Foot) .. *Shorncliffe (for Jersey.)*	3rd Bn. (Armagh Mil.)	*Armagh.*
2nd „ (89th „) .. *Quetta (for Madras.)*	4th „ (Cavan Mil.)	*Cavan.*
Depôt .. .. .. *Armagh.*	Record Office	*Dublin.*

Colonel-in-Chief .. .. THE KING.
Colonel .. .. .. Stevenson, Maj.-Gen. T. R., C.B., ret. pay 14Sept.99

1st and 2nd Battalions.

Lt.-Colonels. (2)

1 Churcher, D. W., p.s.c.   14Sept.10
2 Wood, P. R. [F]   14Mar.13

Majors.

1 Burrowes, A. R., p.s.c.
 [l]   10Nov.06
2 Conyers, C.   5Jan.09
2 Greer, F. A.   19Mar.10
2 Gould, P.   16July10
    22Aug.02
1 Gray, R. A.   14Sept.10
1 Phibbs, W. G. B.   4Jan.11
    22Aug.02
2 Holmes, H. B.   14Mar.13
s Knight, H. L., p.s.c.
    21 Jan.14

Captains. (14)

2 MacGregor, A. H. C.   14May02
(3) 1 Shuter R. G., D.S.O.   (*Comdg. Depôt*)
    8Jan.08
    23 Nov.01
s. Kentish, R. J.   1Aug.02
1 Carbery, M. B. C.   17Feb.03
c.o. Gibbon, C. M., p.s.c.   19Dec.03
(3) 1 Jeudwine, R. W. R.   14Sept.06
Wortham, H. C. W. H., Adjt.   19Sept.06
2 Furnell, M. J.   19Sept.06
t. Orpen-Palmer, H.B.H.   [l] 20May08
    23Feb.07
1 Atkinson, Hon. F. W.   8Sept.09
(3) 2 Johnson, F. W. E.   1Feb.10

Captains—contd.

2 Dobbs, R. C.   11June10
r. Meares, C. F.   16July10
2 Incledon-Webber, A. B.   18Aug.10
r. Findlater, W. A. V.   23Jan.11
c.o. Gordon, J. G.   17Apr.12
e.a. O'Farrell, E. H. M.   17Apr.12
1 Bull, G.   3Aug.12
2 McCarthy O'Leary, H.W.D., Adjt.   3Aug.12
1 Yates, H. W. M.   14Mar.13
2 O'Hara, O.   26Mar.13
(3) 2 MacGillycuddy, D. De C. C.   7May13
Gregg, W.T.H.   7June13
1 Hill, G. V. W.   7June13

Lieutenants. (19)

s.s. Wright, G. M. H.   12Feb.09
1 Olphert, A. V.   15May09
1 Stokes, H. F.   25July09
1 O'Brien, J.C.P.   17Nov.09
s. Davison, D.A.   22Dec.09
(3) 1 Kelly, P. E.   16July10
c.o. Penn, P.   18Aug.10
(3) 2 Power, R. P.   14Sept.10
1 Penrose, E. J. McN.   4Mar.11
1 Herrick, H. E.   4Mar.11
2 Hennessy, G. T.   11Mar.11
s. Elton, G. D. C.   21Oct.11
2 Kellie, G. J. D.   15Apr.12
2 Jones, B. I.   17Apr.12
2 Wilson, E. R.   3Aug.12
2 Angell, J.   8Aug.12
f.c. Allen, D.L. [l]   16Aug.12
f.o. Mulcahy-Morgan, T. W.   15Jan.13
2 Kavanagh, H. R.   14Mar.13
2 Verschoyle, W. A.   26Mar.13
2 Hatch, W.L.R.   16Apr.13
2 Emerson, K. A.   7June13
2 Sheridan, D. J.   18Sept.13
1 Wakefield, R. O. B.   14Jan.14

2nd Lieutenants. (12)

2 Hodges, J. F.   13Feb.12
2 Faris, A. P.   4Sept.12
1 O'Donovan, M. J. W.   5Feb.13
1 Cockburn, G. E. G.   5Feb.13
1 Tuely, C. S.   5Feb.13
1 Barefoot, G W. N.   3Sept.13
2 MacMullen, H. A.   3Sept.13
2 Egerton, R.   3Sept.13
1 Liesching, W. H.   17Sept.13
2 Morgan, S. P. M.   17Sept.13
1 Massy-Westropp, J. F. R.   10Dec.13

Adjutants.

1 Wortham, H.C.W.H., capt.   18Jan.12
2 McCarthy-O'Leary, H.W.D., capt.   5Oct.13

Quarter-Masters.

2 Shannon, J.,   12Dec.00
    hon. capt.   12Dec.10
r. McDonnell, P.   3Apr.09
    23June00
r. Wallace, R., hon. lt.
    hon. capt.   6Jan.12
1 Bunting, T. E.,   hon. lt.   4Jan.13

Special Reserve.

Captain.

p.s. Wilson-Slator, H. B.   (H) 2 Dec. 06
    24 Jan. 14

2nd Lieutenants.

McErvel, J.H.   6Jan.12
Gaffkin, P. J.   12Apr.13
    18Feb.11
Samuels, A. M.   2July13

3rd Battalion.

(*Officers serving on 4 Dec. 00 in the corresponding Militia unit hold honorary Army rank equivalent to the Militia regimental rank they then held. Other officers entitled to honorary Army rank have it shown against their names.*)

Hon. Colonel.

Gosford, A. B. S.,
Earl of, K.P.   12July08
    4Mar.99

Lt.-Colonel.

p.s. Lidwill, R. A.   20Jan.12

Major.

Swettenham, G. K.,
D.S.O., Maj. ret. pay
(*Res. of Off.*)   12Feb.13

Captains. (5)

r.e. ⚔Shuter, R. G., D.S.O.   8Jan.08
    23Nov.01
p.s. ⚔Cross, P. W. (*Hon. Capt. in Army* 6 July 02) (H)   14May04
p.s. Carron-Roberts, T. J.   (H)   6Mar.05
r.e. ⚔Jeudwine, R. W. R.   14Sept.06
r.e. ⚔Johnson, F. W. E.   1Feb.10
r.e. ⚔MacGillycuddy, D. De C. C.   7 May 13

Lieutenants. (11)

p.s. Stewart, W. (H) 6Apr.07
r.e. Kelly, P. E.   16July10
r.e. Power, R.P.   14Sept.10
MacIlwaine, E. M.   22Aug.12
Fforde, E. H.   22Aug.12
Crymble, C. R.   22Aug.12

PRINCESS VICTORIA'S (ROYAL IRISH FUSILIERS)—(Regtl. Dist. No. **87**)—contd.

3rd Bn.—contd.

2nd Lieutenants (8)

Millar, A J   25May12
Montgomery, W. N.   25May12
Wadden, G.   19Feb.13

Adjutant.

✗Meares, C. F., Capt. R. Ir. Fus.   3Nov.13
(Capt. in Army 16July10)

Quarter-Master.

Wallace, R., hon. lt.

4th Battalion.

(*Officers serving on 19 Oct. 00 in the corresponding Militia unit hold honorary Army rank equivalent to the Militia regimental rank they then held. Other officers entitled to honorary Army rank have it shown against their names.*)

Hon. Colonel.

p s.Hodson, Sir R. A., Bt. (Hon. Col. ret. Mila.) (Hon. Lt.-Col. in Army 20 Oct.00) (H)   2Dec.06

Lt.-Colonel.

p.s.Madden, J. C. W. (Hon. Capt. in Army 21 Oct.00) ⓟ (H)   2Dec.12

Majors (3).

p.s.Stoney, L. S. (H)15May12

Captains. (6)

p.s.Malley, V. F. F. (H)   3Feb.97   25Nov.93

p.s. Clements, S. U. L. (H) (Nigerian Rly., Nigeria, 24 Apr. 12)   6June04

p.s.Vanston, H. W. F. M. (H)   3Dec.13

Lieutenants. (11)

McVeagh, F. A.   13Mar.13
Rogers, O. C. F.   20Dec.13
West, A. F.   20Dec.13

Lieuts.—contd.

Patterson, D. K.   20Dec.13
Tougher, R.A.   20Dec.13

2nd Lieutenants. (8)

Browne, C. E. (on prob.)   18Feb.14
Buchanan, J. H. (on prob.)   24June14
Harvey, W. J. (on prob.)   24June14

Adjutant.

✗Findlater, W.A.V., Capt. R. Ir. Fus.   12Oct.12
(Capt. in Army 23Jan.11)

Quarter-Master.

✗McDonnell, P., hon. capt.

THE CONNAUGHT RANGERS.
Regimental District No. **88.** [No. **12** District.]

The Harp and Crown, with the motto "*Quis separabit.*" The Elephant. The Sphinx, superscribed "Egypt."

"Seringapatam," "Talavera," "Busaco," "Fuentes d'Onor," "Ciudad Rodrigo," "Badajoz,"
"Salamanca," "Vittoria," "Pyrenees," "Nivelle," "Orthes," "Toulouse," "Peninsula,"
"Alma," "Inkerman," "Sevastopol," "Central India," "South Africa, 1877-8-9,"
"Relief of Ladysmith," "South Africa, 1899-1902."

Regular and Special Reserve Battalions.

Uniform—Scarlet. *Facings*—Green. *Agents*—Messrs. Cox & Co.

1st Bn. (88th Foot) .. Ferozepore (*for Agra*).	3rd Bn. (Galway Mil.)	
2nd ,, (94th ,,) .. Aldershot.	4th ,, (Roscommon Mil.) .. .. Galway.	
		.. Boyle.
Depôt .. .. .. Galway.	Record Office .. .. .. Cork.

Colonel .. .. Dalrymple, Maj.-Gen. W. L., *C.B.*, ret. pay, p.s.c. [R] .. 20Jan.12

1st and 2nd Battalions.

Lt.-Colonels.
2Abercrombie, A. W., p.s.c. 15Nov.11
1Ravenshaw, H. S. L. 16July14

Majors. (8)
1Murray, S. J. [L] 22Sept.08
2Sarsfield, W. S. 5Dec.08
1Hamilton, W.A.16July10
1Deacon,H.R. G.4Mar.11
s. White, W. A., p.s.c.[t] 15Nov.14
bt. lt.-col. 21Feb.14
(3)2Jourdain, H. F. N. (Comdg. Depôt) 10Apr.12
2Alexander, W. N. S. 4Mar.14
2Hutchinson, H. M., D.S.O. [I] [F] 3June14

Captains. (14)
2Yeldham, E., *Adjt.* 19Jan.04
r. MacSwiney, J. C. 16Apr.04
1Hack, C E. 17May04
t. Thompson, O. 29Nov.05
2De Hochepied Larpent, L. W. P. 24June08
(3) 2Comyn, L. J. 27Jan.06
1Payne, R. L. 8Feb.06
(3)1Truell, E.G.S. 18Jan.08
4Apr.06
r. Lloyd, O. P. 21Apr.06
1Wratislaw, J. M. B. 22June07
1Eames, T. B. G. F. 18Feb.09
e.a.Joyce, P.C. [F] 8May09
s.c. Davis. H. J. N. 8May09
s. 2Kinsman, F. F. I. 8May09
2O'Sullivan, C. J. 14July09
1Underhill Faithorne, C. F. 14July09
c.o. Wickham, M. H. C. De C. De B. 23Dec.09

Captains—contd.
3) 1Nolan-Ferrall, H. J. 23Dec.09
2Ruttledge, T. G., *e*. 8Feb.10
m.o. Atkinson, Hon. *H. R.* 16July10
1Eyre, R. G. 23Jan.11
2Hamilton, E.G. 28Jan.11
2Roche, W. W. 1Apr.11

Lieutenants. (19)
c.o. Leader, F. W. M. 30Dec.05
1Callaghan, G. F.8Feb.06
1Foster, T. F. V.18Feb.06
1Armstrong-Lushington-Tulloch, G. De M. 7Apr.06
2Fraser, J. 11Apr.06
1Moutray, A. G. 21Apr.06
c.o. Maling, H. B. W.3Aug.07
1George, F. R., *Adjt.* 2Jan.09
1Robertson, H.G. 5Jan.09
t. Markwick,H.W. 4Feb.09
2Barker, W. G. S. 17May13
27Feb.09
1Hume, J. E. 6Apr.11
8May09
t. Walsh, C. H. 6Oct.09
1Von Stieglitz, F. L. 20Oct.09
w.a.Massy, G. J. B. E. 23Dec.09
2Henderson, R. M. H. 8Feb.10
2Fenton, G. R. 8Feb.10
(3) Irwin, H. Q. 23Mar.10
c.o.Fell, M. E. 1Apr.10
c.o.Howard, S. W. 23Jan.11
2Blacker, C. F. 28Jan.11
1Irvine, C. T. C. 11Feb.11
2Ovens, J. R. 7June11
c.o. Cooke, H. H. A.28Aug.11
f.c. Small, F. G. 23Dec 11
1Thomas, R. I. 23Oct.12
(3)2Lewis, S. H. 26Mar.13
1Anderson, A. L. B. 17Apr.13
c.o Steuart, N. K. 30July13
1Abbott, G. D. 9June14

2nd Lieutenants. (12)
1Morris, E. W. 4Mar.11
c.o. Burke, R.V. 25Mar.11
t 3de Stacpoole, M. A. 20Sept 11
2Benison, R. B.20Sept.11
2Turner, C. A. C. 14Feb.12

2nd Lieuts.—contd.
2Spreckley. R. L 5Feb.13
1Hewitt, H. T. 5Feb.13
2Brook, G. R. C. 17Sept.13
2Allen, G. 17Sept.13
1Dennys, C. H. M. 24Jan.14
2Hardy, J. L. 24Jan.14
2Lentaigne, V. A. 24Jan.14

Adjutants.
2Yeldham, E.,*capt.* 5Feb.12
1George, F. R., *lt.* 9June14

Quarter-Masters.
r. Smyth, C. 23Dec.99
hon. capt. 23Dec.02
r. Rafferty, J. 23Apr.02
hon. capt. 23Apr.12
1Gorman, J. T., *hon. lt.* 8Mar.11
2Dryden, C. F., *hon. lt.* 22Nov.13

Special Reserve.

2nd Lieutenants.
Beard, A. S. 25Dec 12
de la Cour, F. R. S. (on prob.) 14Mar.14
Latham, W. P. F. 24June14
3Apr.14

3rd Battalion.

(*Officers serving on 17 Oct. 00 in the corresponding Militia unit hold honorary Army rank equivalent to the Militia regimental rank they then held. Other officers entitled to honorary Army rank have it shown against their names.*)

Hon. Colonel.
Daly, J. A. (Hon. Col. ret. Mila.) 2Aug.08
11July91

Lt.-Colonel.
Lewin, A. C., *D.S.O.*, *Capt. ret. pay* 6Aug.13

Major.
Digan, A. J., D.S.O. (*Hon.Capt.in Army* 7Nov.00) (*H*) (*I*) 22Dec.09
1July07
r.e. Jourdain, H. F. N. 10Apr.12

Captains. (5)
p.s.Tighe, T. (*hon. Lt. in Army* 6 July 01) (*H*) 19Mar.04
p.s. Clifford, T. R. B. (a) 14May04
Campbell, M. I. M. (*Hon. Lt. in Army* 23Sept.02) 20June04
Blockley, A. W. (*H*) 5Apr.05
r.e. Comyn, E. J. 27Jan.06
r.e. Truell, E.G S 18Jan.08
4Apr.06
King, W. H., *Capt.* ret.pay(*Dep.Asst. Dir. of Rents.,* Irish Comd.) 19Sept.08
r.e. Nolan-Ferrall, H. J. 23Dec.09
O'Brien, W.D., *Capt.* ret. pay 28Jan.11

Lieutenants. (11)
Whyte, A.W.P.T., *Lt. ret. pay* 8Feb.07
20Aug.13
p.s.de Stacpoole, G. B. (*H*) 20May07
r.e. Irwin, H. Q. 23Mar.10
Lambert, W. P., *late 2nd Lt. Conn. Rang.* 7Sept.12
r.e. Lewis, S. H. 26Mar.13
Foott, F. D. 1Oct.13

2nd Lieutenants. (8)
Jackson, J. L. 2Apr.13
Aveling, L. N.30June13
Gibson, F. M. S. (on prob.) 8Nov.13

Adjutant.
Lloyd, O. F., *Capt.* Conn. Rang. 20Sept.11
(*Capt. in Army* 21Apr.06)

Quarter-Master
Rafferty, J., *hon. capt.*

THE CONNAUGHT RANGERS—(Regtl. Dist. No. **88**)—contd.

4th Battalion.

(*Officers serving on 5July01 in the corresponding Militia unit hold honorary Army rank equivalent to the Militia regimental rank they then held. Other officers entitled to honorary Army rank have it shown against their names.*)

Lt.-Colonel.

✠Hammond, D. T., C.B., Hon. Lt.-Col. ret. pay, hon. c. (*H*)   8Nov.99

Majors. (3)

p.s.Harrison, R. W. G., hon. l.c., p.v.c. (*H*)   2May07
p.s.Bellew, *Sir* H. C. G., *Bt.* (*H*) ⊕ (*a*) (*b*)   28June08
p.s.✠Grimshaw, W. A. H. (*H*)(*a*)   18June13

Captains. (6)

p.s.✠Brooke, H. H. (*H*)   1Nov.03

p.s.Wickham, E. T. F D1 C. de B. (*H*) [*l*]   26Mar.04

p.s.Jackson, F. H. (*H*)   14Oct.05

p.s.✠Hughes, C. J. (*Hon. 2nd Lt. in Army 6 July* 01) (*H*) 19May06

p.s.✠Saker, R. (*H*)14Feb.07

p.s.✠Goode, H.R. (*H*) c.o.(*Asst.Commr. of Police,S.Provs. Nigeria,* { 1Jan.14
{ 10Jan.12)   7Oct.07

p.s.Ingham, J. P. M. (*H*)   21Nov.08
    1Jan.08

Lieutenants. (11)

p.s.Saker, F. H. (*H*)   11June06

p.s.Wickham, A. T. C. (*H*)(*a*)(*b*)   7Oct.07

Cooke, I. A. S. 14May10

Power, A. F. R.   2Aug.11

McKeon, F. T. (*Asst. Commr. of Police, SierraLeone,*1May14)   2Aug.12

Keating, P. W. 1May14

Kenny, M. J.   1May14

2nd Lieutenants. (8)

Belemore, R. A. (*on prob.*)   3Dec.13
McKay, H. D. (*on prob.*)   4Feb.14
Maguire, W. R. (*on prob.*)   18Feb.14
Battersby, A. W. (*on prob.*)   25Mar.14

Adjutant.

✠MacSwiney, J. C. Capt. Conn. Rang.   2Apr.12

(*Capt. in Army* 16Apr.04)

Quarter-Master.

Smyth, C., *hon. capt.*

PRINCESS LOUISE'S (ARGYLL AND SUTHERLAND HIGHLANDERS).
Regimental District No. 91. [No. 1 District.

A Boar's Head, with the motto "*Ne obliviscaris*" within a Wreath of Myrtle, and a Cat with the motto "*Sans Peur*" within a Wreath of Broom, over all the label as represented in the arms of the Princess Louise, and surmounted with Her Royal Highness's Coronet. In each of the four corners the Princess Louise's Cypher and Coronet.

"Cape of Good Hope, 1806," "Rolica," "Vimiera," "Corunna," "Pyrenees," "Nivelle," "Nive," "Orthes," "Toulouse," "Peninsula," "South Africa, 1846-7, 1851-2-3," "Alma," "Balaklava," "Sevastopol," "Lucknow," "South Africa, 1879," "Modder River," "Paardeberg," "South Africa, 1899-1902."

Regular and Special Reserve Battalions.
Uniform—Scarlet.   *Facings*—Yellow.   *Agents*—Messrs. Cox & Co.

1st Bn.	(91st Foot) ..	Dinapore (for Ferozepore).	3rd Bn. ..	(Highland Borderers Mil.)..	Stirling.
2nd ,,	(93rd ,,) ..	Fort George (for Tidworth).	4th ,, ..	(R. Renfrew Mil.) ..	.. Paisley.

Depôt .. .. .. Stirling.   Record Office .. Kinnoull Street, Perth.

Territorial Force Battalions.

5th Bn. ..	Drill Hall, Finnart Street, Greenock.		8th Bn. ..	.. .. ..	Dunoon.
6th ,, ..	66, High Street, Paisley.		9th ,, ..	.. ..	Hartfield, Dumbarton.
7th ,, ..	.. .. .. Stirling.				

Allied Regiment of Canadian Militia.
91st Regiment (Canadian Highlanders) .. .. Hamilton, Ontario.

Colonel-in-Chief .. H.R.H. the *Princess* Louise, *Duchess of* Argyll.
Colonel .. Boyes, Maj.-Gen. J. E., C.B., ret. pay [R] .. .. 20 Mar. 07

1st and 2nd Battalions.

Lt.-Colonels. (2)
2 Moulton-Barrett, H. P.   27 June 11
1 Henderson, H. L.   12 Dec. 11

Majors. (8)
1 Gore, R. C.   12 Dec. 07
(3) 2 Kirk, H. B.
(Comdg. Depôt) 2 Sept. 09
s. Malcolm, N., D.S.O.,
p.s.c. [L]   20 Aug. 10
    18 Dec. 09
s. Dundas, F. C., p.s.c. [L]   18 Apr. 11
2 Marshall, K. F. C.   27 June 11
1 Tweedie, W. J. B.   12 Dec. 11
2 Maclean, A. H.   25 May 12
c.o. Glasfurd, D. J., p.s.c.   20 Sept. 13

Captains. (14)
t. Baker-Carr, H. B. F.   3 July 13
    11 Jan 00
2 Hyslop, H. H. G.   13 Apr. 01
r. Elphinston. A.   28 May 01
(3) 1 Cox, R. J. P.   3 July 01
s. Maclean, C. A. H.   28 Dec. 01
    bt. maj. 21 Feb 14
t. Watson, I. W.   28 Feb. 02
s. Clarke, A. L. C.,
    p.s.c. [L]   27 Aug. 04
s. Muir, G. W.   27 Aug. 04
s.c. Thorpe, G.   5 Oct. 04
1 M. Mackay, J. F.   20 May 08
    8 May 07
Neilson, W. G.,
    D.S.O.   16 July 07
(3) 2 Thomson, H.M.   19 Oct. 07
m.c. Wheatley, L. L.,
    D.S.O.   22 July 08
    22 Jan. 05
e.s. Kennedy, J.   28 Apr. 09
(3) 1 Sceales, G. A. McL.   28 Apr. 09

Captains—contd.
s.c. Lang, B. J.   28 Apr. 09
    2 Fraser, J. A.   28 Apr. 09
1 Sandeman, M. G.
    20 May 09
1 Maclean, A. J. H.
    20 May 09
s. Scott, J. C.   20 May 09
2 Thorburn, A.B.   20 May 09
s. Laird, K. M., p.s.c.
    25 Aug. 09
2 Henderson, W. A.
    5 Sept. 10
t. Campbell, J. A. L.
    5 Sept. 10
2 Bruce, Hon. R.
    (Master of Burleigh)
    [F]   10 Sept. 10
Forbes, R. R.
    (Comdt., Detention Barracks)   10 Sept. 10
2 Walker, C.C.   26 Mar. 11
2 Kennedy, A.E.,e.
    10 July 12
t. James, C. P.   1 Feb. 13
1 MacEwen, N. D. K.
    1 Feb. 13
1 Sprot, M. W. R.   4 Sept. 13
e.a. Maclaine, R.G.   13 Sept. 13
1 Porteous, D.   13 Sept. 13
r. Couper, J. R.   20 Sept. 13
t. Thomson, N.   7 Feb. 14
1 Wilson, A. R. G. 21 Mar. 14

Lieutenants. (19)
2 Stirling, A.   18 Mar. 08
(3) 2 Purves, H. deB. 5 Dec. 08
1 Boyle, A. R., Adjt.
    17 Mar. 09
2 MacLean, A. K. 1 Apr. 09
o.o. Colquhoun, A. G. C.
    28 Apr. 09
f.c. 2 Crosbie, D.S.K. 5 May 09
(3) 1 Lumsden, W.V. 20 May 09
1 Patten, C. H.   6 Aug. 09
o.o. Bennett, N. C.   25 Aug. 09
1 Gilkison, J.D.   25 Mar. 10
1 Young, J. F.   1 Apr. 10
2 Clark, H. J. D.
[l] Adjt.   5 Sept. 10
2 Burt-Marshall,
    W. M.   10 Sept. 10

Lieuts.—contd.
Irvine, J. L. G. 17 June 11
2 Campbell, W. G.
    [l]   24 Feb. 12
1 Holford Walker, A.
    4 May 12
1 Purvis, C. B. 25 May 12
2 Aytoun, R. M. G.
    10 July 12
2 Connal Rowan, G. F.
    31 July 12
2 Johnstone, C. C. G.
    4 Sept. 13
1 Mackay, T.   20 Sept. 13
2 St. Clair, W. F. 21 Mar. 14
2 Rose, J. C. R.   1 Apr. 14
2 Aitken, J. C.   23 Apr. 14
2nd Lieutenants. (12)
1 Stirling, R.   14 Feb. 12
1 Steel, J. C.   14 Feb. 12
1 Ritchie, A. MacD.
    4 Sept. 12
1 Clarke, M. C. C. 4 Sept. 12
1 Greenfield, K. H.
    4 Sept. 12
1 Denny, P. A.   22 Jan. 13
2 Campbell, C.L. 22 Jan. 13
2 Boyd, C. L.   17 Sept. 13
1 Pearetth, W.M. 24 Dec. 13
1 Fetherstonhaugh,
    J. L.   24 Jan. 14
1 Stewart, I. MacA.
    25 Feb. 14
1 Campbell, H. A.
    2 May 14
Buchanan, E. P.
    10 June 14

Adjutants.
2 Clark, H. J. D.
    [l] lt.   1 Apr. 14
1 Boyle, A. R., lt. 1 Apr. 14

Quarter-Masters.
r. Scott, J. J.   19 Sept. 00
    hon. capt. 19 Sept. 10
r. Potter, T., hon. lt.
    18 Mar. 08
2 Clayton, T. H.,
    hon. lt.   11 Mar. 11
1 Heatly, J., hon. lt.
    14 Oct. 11

Special Reserve.

2nd Lieutenants.
McKean, J.   14 Feb. 12
Anderson, P.   5 Mar. 13

3rd Battalion.

(*Officers serving on 23 Sept. 02 in the corresponding Militia unit hold honorary Army rank equivalent to the Militia regimental rank they then held. Other officers entitled to honorary Army rank have it shown against their names.*)

Lt.-Colonel.
p.s.✕Fergusson, H. C.,
    Maj. ret. pay
    (Res. of Off.) 31 Oct. 09

Major.
r.e. ✕Kirk, H. B.   2 Sept. 09
p.s.✕Rouse, M. E.
    (Hon. Capt. in
    Army 5 Dec. 09)
    (H) ⑤   15 June 13
Captains. (5)
r.e.✕Cox, R. J. P.   3 July 01
r.e.✕Ure, J. A. (H) 1 Nov. 06
r.e.✕Thomson, H. M.
    19 Oct. 07
r.e.✕Sceales, G. A. McL.
    28 Apr. 09
Moorhouse, S., Lt.,
    ret. pay.   5 Oct. 10
✕Ripley, Str F. H.,
    Bt., late 2nd Lt.
2 L.G.   17 May 11
Long, A.de L. ⑤
    (H)   25 Dec. 12

PRINCESS LOUISE'S (ARGYLL AND SUTHERLAND HIGHLANDERS)—(Regtl. Dist. No. **91**)—*contd.*

3rd Bn.—*contd.*

Lieutenants. (11)
r.e.Purves, H. de B.5Dec.08
r.e. Lumsden,W.V. 20May09
Macpherson,K.I.,
 late Lt. Arg. &
 Suth'd Highrs.
    1Nov.11
    4Dec.12
Hutchison, G. S.,
 late 2nd Lt. Res.
 of Off. (Empld.
 with Rhodesian
 Def. Force 18Mar14)
    19Apr.13
Fairlie, N. E. 26Apr.13
p.s.✠Warren, C.A.R.,
 late Capt. (H.)
    18June13

2nd Lieutenants. (8)
Colquhoun, A. R.
    9Aug.11
Liddell, J. A. 1June12
Elliot, R. B. 25Jan.13
    1Apr.12
Higginbotham, H.C.
    5Mar.13
Lothian, M. P.
 (on prob.) 13Dec.13
Erskine, J. F. A.,
Lord(onprob.)25Feb.14

Adjutant.
✠Elphinston, A.,
 Capt. Arg. &
 Suth'd Highrs.
    23Feb,12
(*Capt. in Army* 28 May 01)

Quarter-Master
✠Potter, T., *hon. lt.*

4th Battalion.

(*Officers serving on 6 Aug.01
in the corresponding Militia unit hold honorary
Army rank equivalent to
the Militia regimental
rank they then held. Other
officers entitled to honorary Army rank have it
shown against their
names.*)

Hon. Colonel.
✠Dick, A. C. D., C.B.
 (Hon.Col.ret.Mila.)
 (*Hon. Lt.-Col. in
 Army*7 Aug.01) 2Aug.08

Lt.-Colonel.
✠Wilson, G. T. B.,
 Maj. ret. pay (Res.
 of Off.) 9Oct.12

Majors. (3)
✠Richardson, F. J.,
 D.S.O., Capt. ret.
 pay (Res. of Off.)
 (*Dep. Asst. Dir. of
 Remts., E. Comd.*)
    23Sept.11
✠Gilligan, G. G.,
 (H) 11Jan.13

Captains. (6)
✠Sotheby, H. G.,
 M.V.O. 4Feb.02
p.s.Douglas-Campbell,
 A. (H) 10Jan.08
✠Cuningham, F. G!G.,
 Capt. ret.pay 20May09
    18June13
Gilmour, A. C., Lt.
 ret. pay 4Jan.13
p.s.Nicol,R. J. (H) 11Jan.13
p.s.Chrystal, R. A. (H)
    11Jan.13
Wardlaw Ramsay,
 A.B. (Asst.Inspr.,
 Bd. of Agriculture
 and Fisheries
 1 Aug. 11) 29July13
✠Boddam-Whetham,
 A, C., late Lt. Res.
 of Off. (Hon, 2nd Lt.
 in Army, 9 July 01)
    22Oct.13

Lieutenants. (5)
Thomson, J. C. H.
    1July12
Cunningham, J. C.
    30June13

2nd Lieutenants. (8)
Paterson, W. H. 1Oct.13
Thomas, D. C. W.,
 late 2nd Lt. A.S.C.
    4Apr.14

Adjutant.
✠Couper, J. R.,
 Capt. Arg. &
 Suth'd Highrs.
    6Mar.14
(*Capt. in Army* 20Sept.13)

Quarter-Master.
✠Scott, J, J., *hon. capt.*

5th (Renfrewshire) Battalion.

"South Africa, 1900-02."
Drill Hall, Finnart Street,
Greenock.

Hon. Colonel.
Stewart, Sir H. S.,
 Bt. 12Mar.04

Lt.-Colonel.
✠McIntyre, H. D.,
 Bt. Col., ret. Ind.
 Army 27Apr12

Majors. (2)
p. Fisher, W. A., TD (*t*)
    5May09
Prentice, W,G., TD
 (*t*)(H) 10July12

Captains. (8)
p.s.Clapperton-Stewart,
 R. A. (*t*) 14May04
p.s.Lyle, F. (*t*) 12July05
p.s.Agnew, J. (*t*) (H)
    28Jan.08
p.s.Main, D. M. 13May09
 Kerr, J. 25Mar.11
p.s.Agnew, A. (*t*) 20Jan.12
 Duncan, D. 10July12
Nesmith, J. 13July12

Lieutenants. (8)
(p.s.)Hewison, H. M.
    9Apr.11
(p.s.)Lang, W. B. 9Apr.11
McKirdy, R. F. 20Jan.12
Campbell, W.M. 29Oct.12
Fleming, M. J. H.
    30Oct.12
Brown, R. 22Apr.14
2nd Lieutenants. (8)
Rowan, J.L. 13May11
Leitch, E. 7Oct.11
Macdougall, R. McI.
    25Dec.12
Carmichael, R. H. M.
    11Mar.13
Blake, G. 12Mar.13
Thompson, R. R.
    28June13
Nicol, A. 16Jan.14
Beveridge, T. B.
    1June14

Adjutant.
✠Laing, R., Capt.,
 Sea. Highrs. 4July11

Quarter-Master.
✠Watson, W. J.
 (*hon. lt,*) 1July12

Medical Officers.
p. Philip, Lt.-Col. J. C.
 M.B.,VD,R.A.M.C.
 (T.F.) (*attd.*) (*hon.
 Surg.-Col.*) 30Dec.05
    5Dec.85
p Leitch, Maj. J. A.,
 M.B., R.A.M.C.
 (T.F.) (*attd.*) 23Mar.08
    26Feb.96

Chaplains.
Beveridge,Rev.W.W.,
 TD [U.F.C.] Chapl.
 1st Class (T.F.)
 (*attd.*) 19Apr.90
    19Apr.90
Service, Rev. W. J. N.,
 B.D. [C.S.] Chapl.
 4th Class (T.F.)
 (*attd.*) 1Apr.08
    5Mar.04
Young, Rev. H., M.A.
 [U.F.C.] Chapl. 4th
 Class (T.F.) (*attd.*)
    1Apr.08
    15Jan.05
[*Uniform—Scarlet.
Facings—Yellow.*]

6th (Renfrewshire) Battalion.

"South Africa, 1900-02."
66, High Street, Paisley.

Hon. Colonel.
p. Glen-Coats,Sir T.G.,
 Bt., C.B, VD, (Hon.Col.
 ret. Vols.) 13June03

Lt.-Colonel.
p. ✠Cook, J.,VD (*Hon.
 Capt. in Army*
 19June01) ⓣ 18Dec.06

Majors. (*2*)
p.s.Stewart, J. S.,
 TD 26Nov.07
Barr, J. C. (*t*) 18June10
Captains. (8)
p.s.Stewart, R., TD,
 hon. m. 27Mar.01
p.s.Fraser, J. C. 19Mar.04
    25Dec.01
p.s.✠Hepburn,W.McK.
    1Nov.05
p.s.Haldane, R. H. B.
    11Apr.06
p. Locke, H K. (H)
    28Apr.06
p.s.Coats, S. 8Sept.06
p.s.Swan, J, H. C. 15Mar.07
p.s.✠Gardner, A. (*t*)12May10
p.s.McHaffie, H. McC.
 (H) 18June10

Lieutenants. (8)
p.s.McLardie, A. (*H*)
    8Sept.06
(p.s.)Craig, A. 23Feb.10
(p.s.)Gillespie, W. 12Apr.10
(p.s.)Brown, J. H. 27May10
(p.s.)MacRobert, J. (*H*)
    13June10
Lang, F. M. 24Feb.12
Robertson, D. N.
    24Feb.12

2nd Lieutenants. (8)
Drybrough,D.N.5Feb.11
Shanks, J.A.G. 1Mar.11
Paton, J. S. 15Nov11
Harvie, R. 20Jan.12
Spence, J. ⓣ 14Feb.12
Hardie, S. J. L. 1July13
Clement,A.M. 23Sept.13
Milne, R. S. 20Feb.14

Adjutant.
✠Watson, I. W.,
 Capt. Arg. &
 Suth'd. Highrs.
    1Nov.13

Quarter-Master.
Thomson, J. A.,
 hon. lt. 18July14

Medical Officers.
p. ✠Donald, Maj., H.C.,
 M.B., TD, R.A.M.C.
 (T.F.) (*attd.*) 26Mar.04
    13Feb,92
p. Stevens, Maj. J.B.,
 M.B., T.D., R.A.M.C.
 (T.F.) (*attd.*) 4Oct.11
    17Mar.94
p. Herbertson, Capt.
 J. C., R.A.M.C.
 (T.F.) (*attd.*) 19Mar.07
    19Sept.03

Chaplains.
Barr, Rev. N., M.A.
 [C.S.] Chapl. 4th
 Class (T.F.) (*attd.*)
    1Apr.08
    14Dec.98
Langlands, Rev. F.D.,
 B.D. [C.S.] Chapl.
 4th Class (T.F.)
 (*attd.*) 1Apr.09
Marr, Rev. J., B.D.
 [U.F.C.] Chapl.
 4th Class (T.F.)
 (*attd.*) 1Dec.09
[*Uniform—Scarlet.
Facings—Yellow.*]

P

7th Battalion.

"South Africa, 1900-02."
Stirling.

Hon. Colonel.
Mar and Kellie, W. J. F.,
Earl of, K.T., (King's
Body Gd. for Scot-
land) 5Aug.96

Lt.-Colonel.
p.s.Craig, J., TD 18Sept.06

Majors. (2)
p.s.Ferguson, F. D.,
TD, hon l.c. ⊕ 1Jan.07
p.s.Tullis, J, K. 19Mar.07
p.s.✗Ross, C. W. L.
(Hon. Lt. in
Army 6May02)
(B) 20Mar.08
p.s.King, A. B. ⊕ 25May11

Captains. (8)
p.s.Black, A. (q) (H)
22May01
p.s.Jones, J. F. (t) 17Dec.04
p.s.Frew, D. (t) 17Dec.04
p.s.Philp, J. 10May05
p. Moodie, P. T. 7Dec.06
p.s.Tullis, R. R. 31Mar.09
p.s.Archibald, J. R. 1Feb.12
p.s.Murdoch, J. 14Sept.12
8July09

Lieutenants. (8)
(p.s.)Frew, W. 5Apr.07
p.s.Thomson, A. D. (b)
1Apr.10
(p.s.)McCracken, W.
26June10
(p.s.)Scott, J,M.(H) 1Jan.12
Wilson, J, M. C.
(local Capt. O.
T.C.16 Sept. 12) 1Jan.12
(p.)Stein, A. (H) 1Jan.12
Anton, N. 1June13

2nd Lieutenants. (8)
Mitchell, A. W. S.
5Dec.11
Whyte, J. 1Feb.12
Stewart, W. 6Dec.12
Wright, V. O. 6Dec.12
Robertson,D.I. 26May13
Falconer, W. K., jun.
20Sept.13
Moir, A. G. 12May14
Sherriff, J. G. 3June14

Adjutant.
Thomson,N.,Capt.
Arg. & Suth'd
Highrs. 27Feb.14

Quarter-Master.
p. Watters, L.G.,hon.
capt. 1July08
Medical Officers.
p. Dyer, Maj. E. E.,
M.B., R.A.M.C.
(T.F.) (attd.) 5July11
29Nov.99

Chaplains.
Murray, Rev. G., B.D.,
TD,[C.S.] Chapl.
2nd Class (T.F.)
(attd.) 1Apr.08
6Aug.90
Fairley, Rev. J.,
[C.S.] Chapl. 4th
Class (T.F.)(attd.)
1Apr.08
5Oct.04

Chaplains—contd.
Aitken, Rev. J.,
[U.F.C.], Chapl.
4th Class (T.F.)
(attd.) 1Apr.08
17Dec.04
Brown, Rev. W., B.D.,
[C.S.], Chapl. 4th
Class (T.F.)(attd.)
1Apr.08
24Dec.04
Arnott, Rev. J., M.A.
[U.F.C.], Chapl.
4th Class (T.F.)
(attd.) 1June09

[Uniform—Scarlet.
Facings—Yellow.]

8th (The Argyllshire) Battalion.

"South Africa, 1900-02."
Dunoon.

Hon. Co'onel.
Argyll, N. D., Duke of
22July14

Lt.-Colonel.
✗Campbell, J., Capt.
ret. pay (Res. of Off.)
14Feb.12

Majors. (2)
Brown,T.L.,TD, 24Jan.08
p.s.✗Pender, J. (b)(Q)
7Nov.13

Captains. (8)
p. Henderson, J. S.
(H) 25Feb.05
p. Cunningham, R.Y.
5Apr.05
Duncan, G.M. 17Dec.10
p. MacArthur, A. 15Oct 12
Rogerson, A. W.
25Feb.14
Macnicol, R. R.25Feb.14

Lieutenants. (8)
Campbell, A. 19May11
Campbell,N.D.11Nov.11
MacGregor, D.18Sept.12
Chalmers, R. 9June13
Owen, O. A. 14Feb.14
Lauder, J. C. 20Apr.14
Mactaggart, M. A.
20Apr.14
Campbell, J. MacL.
20Apr.14

2nd Lieutenants. (8)
Macdonald, J. V. F.
16June11
Phillimore, H. B.
16Oct.12
Taylor, J. 17May13
McIntyre, A.C. 17May13
Maiden, A. McD.
4June13
Munro, H. A. 3Oct.13
Sandison, A. J. 15July14

Adjutant.
✗Campbell, J.,A.L.,
Capt. Arg. &
Suth'd Highrs.
16Oct.12

Quarter-Master.
✗Lockie,A.,hon.lt.
2June11

Medical Officers.
p. ✗Brown, Maj. J.P.,
M.B., R.A.M. C.
(T.F.) (attd.) 13Apr.11
20July98
Henderson, Lt. G.,
R.A.M.C. (T.F.)
(attd.) 6Nov.13
Chaplains.
Howie,Rev. W.,B.D.
[C.S.], Chapl. 4th
Class (T.F.)(attd.)
1Dec.09
McPhail, Rev. W.,
[C.S.] Chapl. 4th
Class (T.F.)(attd.)
1Dec.09
Stewart, Rev. D. C.,
[U.F.C.] Chapl.
4th Class (T.F.)
(attd.) 1Dec.09

[Uniform—Scarlet.
Facings—Yellow.]

Cadet Unit affiliated.
Dunoon Grammar School
Cadet Corps.

9th (The Dumbartonshire) Battalion.

"South Africa, 1900-02."
Hartfield, Dumbarton.

Hon. Colonel.
p. Denny, J. McA.,
VD (Hon. Col.ret.
Vols.) 7Feb.03

Lt.-Colonel.
Leith-Buchanan, Sir A.
W.G.T. Bt. 4Mar.11

Majors. (2)
✗Gardner,T. K.(Capt.
Res. of Off.) (Hon.
Capt. in Army
27 June 01) 3July12

Captains. (8)
p. Turnbull, S. K. 28July06
p. McBride, D., TD 20Apr.
31Jan.10
p.s.MacBain, J. C.
(q) 7Jan.11
p.s.Denny, A. C. 20July12
Brown, A. G. 24Jan.13
p.s.MacConnell, L. S.
20Sept.13
p.s.Brown, A. S. 21Dec.13
Gordon, T. 19Mar14

Lieutenants. (8)
p. Napier, J. 15Dec.10
(p.s.)Baird, W. M. 20June12
(p.s.)McGee,D.jun, 20July12
Denny, W. 8Jan.13
Findlay, R. S. 24Jan.13
Erskine,J.A.D. 24Jan.13
Jackson, J. 21Dec.13
Ross, W. C. 19Mar.14

2nd Lieutenants. (8)
Kirsop, P. A. 18Dec.12
Belfrage, A. G. 28Mar.13
Anderson,A.D.MacA.
7Apr.13
Hutton, F. R. H.
16June13
Leith-Buchanan,
A. W. G. 27Apr.14
Bonnar, J. C. 28Apr.14

Inst. of Musk.
Ure, I., capt. 7Feb.13

Adjutant.
✗Gray,C.O.V.,Capt.
Sea. Highrs. 8May12

Quarter-Master.
p. Kerr, J. S., hon.
capt. 25Dec.08

Medical Officers.
p. Armstrong, Maj.
W. B., M.B.
R.A.M.C. (T.F.)
(attd.) 11Jan.12
13June00
p. Allan, Capt.J., M.B.,
R.A.M.C. (T.F.)
(attd.) 7Oct.09
7Apr.06

Chaplains.
Goldie, Rev. W. McL.,
[C.S.], Chapl. 2nd
Class (T.F.) (attd.)
10July10
10July95
Inch, Rev. A. S.,
M.A., [U.F.C.],
Chapl. 4th Class
(T.F.) (attd.) 17May09
Macmorran, Rev.
R. S., M.A.
[U.F.C.] Chapl.
4th Class (T.F.)
(attd.) 1Dec.13

[Uniform—Scarlet.
Facings—Yellow.]

THE PRINCE OF WALES'S LEINSTER REGIMENT (ROYAL CANADIANS).

Regimental District No. **100** [No. **12** District.]

The Plume of the Prince of Wales. In each of the four corners a Maple Leaf.
"Niagara," "Central India," "South Africa, 1900-02."

Regular and Special Reserve Battalions.

Uniform—Scarlet. Facings—Blue. Agents—Messrs. Cox & Co.

1st Bn. (100th Foot)	Fyzabad.	3rd Bn. (King's County Mil.)	..	Birr.
2nd „ (109th „)	Cork(for Buttevant).	4th „ (Queen's County Mil.)	..	Maryborough.
Depôt	Birr.	5th „ (Royal Meath Mil.)	..	Drogheda.
		Record Office	..	Cork.

Allied Regiment of Canadian Militia.

100th Winnipeg Grenadiers, ... Winnipeg, Manitoba.

Colonel	Prior, Maj.-Gen. G. U., ret. pay, p.s.c. [R]	.. ..	5July10

1st and 2nd Battalions.

Captains—contd.
s.c.Dill, J. G. 12July11
t. Seagrim, A. H. [L] 27Oct.11
 20Feb.09
c,o, Massy, H. P. 3July12
t. Bergne, R. B. 3July12
2Dix, S. H. 3July12
t. Scott, G. B. 13Aug.12
1Heenan, M. C. 21Sept.12
r. Gaye, H. W. 21Sept.12
1Adams, J. G. 21Sept.12
1Bates, W.G.H.21Sept.12
2Orpen-Palmer. G. de M. H. 5Mar.13
1Deane, T. B. N. 7May13
t. Sanders, J. M. B. 12Nov.13

Lt.-Colonels. (2)
1White, S. R. L., D.S.O. 23May11
2Reeve,W.T.M. 13Aug.12

Majors. (8)
1Rooke, G. H. J.20Dec.05
(3)2Craske, J., D.S.O.
 [Comdg. Depot] 11May07
1Sharp, A.G.G.23 May 07
2Bullen-Smith, G. M. 20Mar.09
1Dugan, F. R. 23May11
 29Nov.09
s. Legge, R. F., e. 12July11
(2)Cochrane, J. K.,
 p.s.c. 3July12
2Mather, J. D. 13Aug.12

Lieutenants. (19)
2Macartney, J. V.
 [l] 23May08
(2)D'Arcy-Irvine, C. W. 5Oct.08
1Greville, G. G. F. F. 13Feb.09
2Hamilton, C. S. 20Mar.09
1Meredite, J. V. 1Apr.09
3lde Stacpoole, E. H. M. 4Oct.10
2Daly, L D. 1Apr.10
2Caulfeild, W.S.,Adjt. 1Apr.10
f.c. Small, R. G. D. 1Apr.10
w.a. Venour, V. W. H. 13Apr.10
c.o. Lecky, A. 7Oct.10
t. Westmacott, S. R. 24Jan.11
(3)2Andrews, H. W. 27Mar.12
1Murray, T. D. 17Apr.12
1Mackenzie, R. A. H. 3July12
f.c.1Lindop,V.S.E.13Aug.12
1Cavendish, F. G. 21Sept.12
2Gaitskell,C.E. 1Jan.13
2O'Conor, R. D. 1Jan.13
2Murphy, A. D. 5Mar.13
2Cormac-Walshe,E. J. 7May13
1Pemberton, A.J. H. 14May13
2Morrogh,W.F. 9Sept.13
1Bailey, G. B. 5Nov 13
1Palin, A. C. S. 2May14
 18Apr.13

Captains. (14)
1Taylor, G. A. 12Aug.00
2Maffett, H. T. 12Aug.00
(2)Whitton, F. E.,
 p.s.c. [L] 12Aug.00
2Heneker,F.C. 14Nov.00
1Jones, B. J. 19Dec.00
t. Wakefield,H.G.R. [l] 20Nov.01
i.v. Raynsford, R. M. 27May03
r. Orpen-Palmer, R.A.H. 23Jan.04
2Montgomerie, W. G., e. 19Apr.05
 28Nov.05
1Weldon, H. W., Adjt. 23Jan.06
s. Boyd, G. F., D.S.O.,
 p.s.c. 19Mar.04
(3)Markes, J. C. 24June08
 26Oct.04
r. Burnand, N.G. 20Mar.09
s. Brooke,N.P. [L] 3May09
2Currey, R. G. T. 3May09
t.v. Wildblood, E. R. 3May09
(3)2Harman, C. 3July09
m.c.Ussher. B. 1Apr.10
2Smyth, R. R. 1Apr.10
v. Gray, R. W. 1Apr.10
(3)1Riall, B. C. 7Oct.10

2nd Lieutenants. (12)
1Otway, H. F. 19Jan.21
1Battersby, T. E. M.
 5Feb.13
1Whitty, J. L. 5Feb.13
2Young, G. N. G.
 17Sept.13
1Rogers, C. R. de W.
 24Jan.14
2Berne, H. C. 24Jan.14
1Budgen,W. D. 10June14
1Jennings, A. J. 11July14

Adjutants.
. 2Caulfeild, W. S., lt.
 3May12
1Weldon, H.W., capt. 4Oct.12

Quarter-Masters.
?. Hayes, D., hon. lt.
 4Sept.09
1Kelly, W., hon. lt.
 16Oct.09
r. Hardie, J., hon. lt.
 18Jan.13
r. Evans, W., hon. lt.
 2May14
2Squire, H. O., hon. lt. 18July14

3rd Battalion.

(Officers serving on 26 May02 in the corresponding Militia unit hold honorary Army rank equivalent to the Militia regimental rank they then held. Other officers entitled to honorary Army rank have it shown against their names.)

Hon. Colonel.
Cosby, R. G., late Lt. 6 Dns. (Hon. Col. late Mila.) 12July08
 4Nov.93

Lt.-Colonel.
XCanning, A., Maj. ret. pay (Res of Off.) 6Aug.12

Major.
XReed, W. B., hon. l.c. (Hon. Maj. in Army 7 Nov. 00) 29Sept.00
r.e.XCraske, J., D.S.O.
 11May07

Captains. (5)
p.s.Alexander, J. W. F.
 (Hon. Lt. in Army 4July01) 17Oct.03
r.e.XMarkes, J. C. 24June08
 26Oct.04
p.s.XAdcock, St. J. (b) (H) 2May06
Robinson, G. W.,
 p.v.c. (b) 1Aug.06
 5May09
r.e.XHarman, C. 3July09
Freeman, F. F. (H)
 (I) (Hon. Lt. in Army 10Oct.00) 14May10
r.e.XRiall, B. C. 7Oct.10
 20Apr.03
p.s. Alcock, G. A. C. (H) 25Jan.13
 2Apr.07

Lieutenants, (11)
(p.s.)Saunders, F, G. (H) 3June07
r.e. de Stacpoole,
 E. H. M. 4Oct.09
Marshall,G. K. 1Jan.10
Barry, C. C. E)16Dec.11
Goodbody, T. P.
 16Dec.11
r.e.Andrews, H. M.
 27Mar.12

2nd Lieutenants. (8).
Woods, C. E. 8Nov.11
FitzGerald, G. V.
 3July12
O'Brien, J. J. 21Dec.12
Walmisley, E. K.
 (on prob.) 4Jan.13
Poiguand, G. C. I.
 (on prob.) 1Apr.13
Algeo, N. 17May13

Adjutant.
XGaye, H. W., Capt. Leins. R. 1Feb.12
 (Capt. in Army 21Sept.12)

Quarter-Master.
XHayes, D., hon. lt.

THE PRINCE OF WALES'S LEINSTER REGIMENT (ROYAL CANADIANS)—(Regtl. Dist. No. 100)—contd.

4th Battalion.

Officers serving on 6 July 01 in the corresponding Militia unit hold honorary Army rank equivalent to the Militia regimental rank they then held. Other officers entitled to honorary Army rank have it shown against their names.

Hon. Colonel.
Brooke, G. H., Adjt. ret. pay 12July08
 17Oct.00

Lt.-Colonel.
✗Weldon, Sir A. A., Bt., C.V.O., D.S.O.
 12July08

Majors. (3)
✗Willington, T. E. W. (H) 12July08
✗Hamilton, W. D. (H) 18Dec.13

Captains. (6)
p.s.Hamilton, M. W. C. (H) 27May06
p.s.Savage-Armstrong, J. R. S. (H) 12July08

Captains—contd.

de la Poer, J. W. R., Lt. ret. pay 28Apr.09
p.s.✗van Cutsem, R. E. G. (H) 1Nov.12
✗Persse, A. F., late 2nd Lt. 14 Hrs. (H) .13Sept.13
 2Apr.06

Lieutenants. (11)
Crowe, A. F. H.
 25May10
 13Jan.06
Bowen-Colthurst, R. McG. 21Mar.12
Goodbody, H. E. (Asst. Commr. of Police, Gold Coast, 4June13)
 1Aug.12

2nd Lieutenants. (8)

Adjutant.
✗Burnand, N. G., Capt. Leins. R.
 4May12
(Capt. in Army 30 Mar.09)

Quarter-Master.
Hardie, J., hon. lt.

5th Battalion.

(Officers serving on 19 Oct. 00 in the corresponding Militia unit hold honorary Army rank equivalent to the Militia regimental rank they then held. Other officers entitled to honorary Army rank have it shown against their names.)

Hon. Colonel.
Pepper, C. (Hon. Col. ret.Mila.)(Hon.Lt.-Col. in Army20Oct.00)
 12July08
 16Apr.04

Lt.-Colonel.
p.s.Farrell, E. F. J. J. (H) 10July12

Majors. (3)
McDonnell, J. (H) ⊕
 20May11
✗Jameson, E. J., late Capt.14 Hrs., ret. pay 20May11
✗Metge, R. H., Capt, ret. pay (H) 19Dec.12

Captains. (6)
✗Murphy, E. H., Capt., ret. pay 1Feb.11
 7May13
✗Russell, N. H. C., Capt. ret.pay 11Nov.11
Gilliat, R. H. C.
(b) (H) 10Oct.12
Radcliff, H. T. (H)
 10Feb.13
Woods, C. J. (H)
 1Aug.13
Farrell,C.J.(H) 1June14

Lieutenants. (11)

Farrell, J. A. J. 1June10
Butler, J. D. 12June11
O'Morchoe, K. G.
 1Aug.13
Henry, W. A. D. 2Apr.14
Mackay, C. 1June14

2nd Lieutenants. (8)
Leathley, F. 4Oct.13

Adjutant.
✗Orpen-Palmer, R. A. H., Capt. Leins. R. 5Oct.11
(Capt. in Army 23 Jan. 04)

Quarter-Master.
Evans, W., hon. lt.

THE ROYAL MUNSTER FUSILIERS.
Regimental District No. **101** [No. **12** District].

A Shamrock.   The Royal Tiger.

"Plassey," "Condore," "Masulipatam," "Badara," "Buxar," "Rohilcund, 1774," "Sholinghur," "Carnatic," "Rohilcund, 1794," "Guzerat," "Deig," "Bhurtpore," "Ghuznee, 1839," "Affghanistan, 1839," "Ferozeshah," "Sobraon," "Chilianwallah," "Goojerat," "Punjaub," "Pegu," "Delhi, 1857," "Lucknow," "Burma, 1885-87," "South Africa, 1899-1902."

Regular and Special Reserve Battalions.

Uniform—Scarlet.	Facings—Blue.	Agents—Messrs. Holt & Co.	
1st Bn. (101st Foot)	Rangoon (for Poona.)	3rd Bn. (Kerry Mil.)	Tralee.
2nd „ (104th „)	Aldershot.	4th „ (South Cork Mil.)	Kinsale.
Depôt	Tralee.	5th „ (R. Limerick County Mil.)	Limerick.
		Record Office .. Cork.	

Allied Regiments of Canadian Militia.
101st Regiment, "Edmonton Fusiliers" .. Edmonton, Alberta.
104th Regiment (Westminster Fusiliers of Canada) .. New Westminster, British Columbia.

Colonel .. .. Miles, Lt.-Gen. Sir H. S. G., G.C.B., C.V.O., p.s.c. [R] s, .. 21May12

1st and 2nd Battalions.

Lt.-Colonels. (2)
1 Tizard, H. E. 11Mar.13
2 O'Meagher, J. K. 23July13

Majors. (8)
1 Bent, A. M. 9Dec.08
2 Charrier, P. A [L] 11Mar.09
(3) 2 Worship, V. T., D.S.O. (Comdg. Depôt) 23July09
1 Rickard, V. G. H. 24July09
s. Thomson, E. P. 17Feb,12
1 Monck-Mason, R. H. 11Mar.13
2 Day, F. I. 4June13
1 Hutchinson, W. A. 23July13

Captains. (14
1 Jarrett, C, C.H.B.14Jan.02
t. Carroll. H. A. 13Mar.05
(3) 1Gorham, A. 23May06
(3) 2 Ryan, G. J., D.S.O. [F] 9June06
bt. maj. 7Nov.08
2 Simms, G. N., M.V.O. 9June06
2 Jervis, H. S., p.s.c. 30July06
2 Woods, G. A. 20May08
27Oct.06
1 Hall, C. R. 18Sept.07
2 Wise, D., Adjt. 24Dec.07
2 Rawlinson, C. R. 24Dec.07
t. Dick, J. C. 13June08
2 Conway, E.P. 2Aug.08
s. Aspinall, C. F., p.s.c. 2Aug.08
2 Barrett, P. G. 2Aug.08
s. Dillon, E. FitzG., p.s.c. 28Sept.08
1Aug.05
s. Braine, H. E. R. R., p.s.c. 1Mar.10

Captains—contd.
1 Geddes, G. W. 1Mar.10
r. West, A. B. 9Mar.10
(3) 1 O'Brien,H.C.H. 1Apr.10
r. Crosbie, W. McC. 1Apr. 10
r. Stubbs, T. T. 23July13
1 Henderson, E. L. H., Adjt. 23July13
m.c.Tonson Rye, H. B.
1 Wilson, H. S. 19Sept.13
1 Considine, J. W. 30Oct.13
2 Emerson, W. 12Mar.14

Lieutenants. (19)
2 Gower, E. W. 20May08
14Dec.07
2 Chute, C. F. T. 9Feb.08
1 Williams, C. R. 2Aug.08
c.o. Latham, J. 2Aug.08
c.o. Critchley-Salmonson, A. C. B. 16Sept. 09
Deane-Drake, C. J. V. 14Sept.09
f.c.Roche, H. J. A. 1Mar.10
1 Filgate, T. W. 8Mar.10
2 Banning, P. S. 8Mar.10
2 O'Malley,T.F. 12Mar.10
6Jan.09
1 Kane, R. R. G. 14Mar.10
c.o.Kilkelly, J.G.J. 1Apr.10
1 Dorman, E. C. 1Apr.10
1 Lane, R. 26July10
(3) 2 Whateley,S.W.26July10
(3) 1 Pemberton, O. 26July10
1 Tomlinson, T. S. 26July10
1 O'Brien, J. F. 18Sept.13
1 Pollard, G. E. G. 18Sept.13
1 Nightingale, G. W. 5Mar.14
1 Russell, F. X. 12Mar.14
w.a.Holt, H. B. 22Apr.14
f.c. Shekleton, A. 22Apr.14
2 l'hayre, C. F. 22Apr.14
2 Moseley, R. A. D. 28Apr.14

2nd Lieutenants. (12)
1 Lee, F. J. F. 5Oct.02
1 Prendergast,G.R. 4Mar.11
2 Awdry, C. E.V.17Sept.13
2 Brereton, W. M. L. 25Feb.14
1 Sulivan, P. H. 25Feb.14
1 Waldegrave, F. S. 11Mar.14
2 Crozier,J.C.B. 10June14
Adjutants.
1 Henderson, E. L. H., capt. 5Nov.11
2 Wise, D., capt.18Nov.12
Quarter-Masters.
r. Forsdick, W. H. 28July97
hon. maj. 28July12
r. O'Connor, J. 22Jan.98
hon. maj. 22Jan.13
1 Baxter, F. T. 6Dec.02
hon. capt. 16Dec.11
r. Connors, M., hon. lt. 18Jan.05
2 Devanney, P., hon.lt. 28Sept.10

Special Reserve.

Lieutenant.
Styles, T. E., Lt. ret. pay (H) 9June06
22Apr.14
2nd Lieutenant.
Newson, H. A. 12Mar.13

3rd Battalion.

(Officers serving on 18Oct.00 in the corresponding Militia unit hold honorary Army rank equivalent to the Militia regimental rank they then held. Other Officers entitled to honorary Army rank have it shown against their names.)

Hon. Colonel.
Kenmare, V. C., Earl of, C.V.O. 2Aug.08
27Dec.02

Lt.-Colonel.
p.s.×Brasier-Creagh, R. S. (Hon. Maj. in Army 1Aug.01)(H) 28Dec.12

Major.
p.s.×Clerke, A. W., D.S.O., hon. l.c. (Hon. Capt. in Army 1Aug. 01) (H) 28Sept.08
r.e.×Worship, V. T., D.S.O. 23July09

Captains. (5)
Leslie, C. R., hon. m. (H) 30May98
p.s.Leeson-Marshall, M. R. (H) 28Mar.00
p.s.Goodlake, T. J. (H) 18May08
r.e.×Durand, F. W. (F) (H) (Q) 10Feb.06
r.e.×Gorham, A. 23May06
r.e.×Ryan, G. J., D.S.O. 9June06
bt. maj. 7Nov.08
p. Foley, R. P. (H)27May07
p.s.Humphreys, W. M. H. (H) (a) (b) 28Sept.08
r.e.×O'Brien, H. C. H. 1Apr. 10

Lieutenants. (11)
(p.s.)Meredith, W. J. 28May06
r.e.Whateley, S. W. 26July10
r.e.Pemberton, O. 26July10
(p.s.)Power, A. G. 18Sept.10
Smyth, J. H. G. (H), (Asst. Dist. Offr., N. Provs., Nigeria,12Jan.14) 14Feb.11
Eagar, W. G. M. 26Apr.11

THE ROYAL MUNSTER FUSILIERS—(Regtl. Dist. No. **101**)—contd.

3rd Bn.—contd.

2nd Lieutenants. (8)
MacGillycuddy, A. J. 18Nov.11
Knight, A. A. A. 13July12
Thomas, R. W. 21June13
Howe, J. G. 21June13

Adjutant.
✗Crosbie, W. McC., Capt. R. Muns. Fus. 1Apr.12
(*Capt. in Army* 1Apr.10)

Quarter-Master.
✗O'Connor, J., hon. maj.

4th Battalion.

(*Officers serving on 31 Mar. 02 in the corresponding Militia unit hold honorary Army rank equivalent to the Militia regimental rank they then held. Other officers entitled to honorary Army rank have it shown against their names.*)

Hon. Colonel.
✗O'Donovan, M. W., C.B. (*The O'Donovan*) (*Lt.-Col. & Hon. Col. ret. spec. Res.*) 17June14

Lt.-Colonel.
✗Soden, G. W. C. (*H*) 17Jan.14

Majors. (3)
p.s ✗MacCarthy Morrogh, D. F. (*H*) 3Sept.09

Captains. (6)
✗Meade, R. J. (*H*) 24Jan.08
p.s.✗King, A. E. (*H*), p.v.c. 18July03
p.s.Hutchins, R. (*H*) 5Sept.03
p.s.Maunsell-Eyre, R. H. 22Oct.04
p.s.✗Purdon, B. H. (*H*) (a) 20July11

Lieutenants. (11)
Hawkes, M. W. L. (*H*) 7June10
King, L. S. (*H*) 7June11
King, C. S. 22Aug.12
Eustace, T. G. 2Aug.13

2nd Lieutenants. (8)

Adjutant.
✗West, A. B., Capt. R. Muns. Fus. 19Sept.13
(*Capt. in Army* 9Mar.10)

Quarter-Master.
✗Forsdick, W. H., hon. maj.

5th Battalion.

(*Officers serving on 8 Oct. 01 in the corresponding Militia unit hold honorary Army rank equivalent to the Militia regimental rank they then held. Other officers entitled to honorary Army rank have it shown against their names.*)

Hon. Colonel.
✗Dunraven and Mount-earl, Rt. Hon. W. T., Earl of, K.P., C.M.G. (*Hon. Capt. in Army* 26July01) 2Aug.08 25Aug.97

Lt.-Colonel.
p.s.✗Stopford, J. W. (*H*)(a)(b) p.v.c. 2Dec.11

Majors. (3)
p.s.✗Stacpoole, J. W. (*H*) 19Jan.11
p.s.✗Thackwell. E. H. R., late Lt. E. Lan. R. (*H*) 7May13

Captains. (6)
p.s.✗Beamish, W. E. (*H*) (*Supt. of Prisons, N. Provs.,* { 1Jan.14 *Nigeria,* { 15May09) 29Sept.06
✗Travers, H. M., Capt. ret. pay (*H*) 6Nov.07
p.s.Mackesy, J. P. T. 28Oct.08
Arthur, C. W. A (*Hon. 2nd Lt.in Army* 7Nov.00) 6May11
✗Keogh-Cullen, E., Lt. ret. pay 2June13
p.s. ✗Fitz-Patrick, J. E. (*H*) 21Sept.13

Lieutenants. (11)
Gloster, J. FitzG. 20May10
Massy, L. H. (*Asst. Commr. of Police, Gold Coast,* 8 *Jan.* 12) 1Feb.11
Place, H.L. (*H*) 1June12

2nd Lieutenants. (8)
Delmege, J. C. R. 17May11
Sullivan, A. H. (on prob.) 11July14

Adjutant.
✗Stubbs, T. T., Capt. R. Muns. Fus. 14Sept.13
(*Capt. in Army* 23 *July* 13)

Quarter-Master.
✗Connors, M., hon. lt.

THE ROYAL DUBLIN FUSILIERS.
Regimental District No. **102** [No. **11** District.]

The Royal Tiger, superscribed "Plassey," "Buxar," and with motto "*Spectamur Agendo*" underneath. The Elephant, superscribed, "Carnatic," "Mysore."
"Arcot," "Condore," "Wandiwash," "Pondicherry," "Guzerat." "Sholinghur," "Nundy Droog," "Araboyna." "Ternate," "Banda," "Seringapatam," "Kirkee," "Maheidpoor," "Beni Boo Alli," "Ava," "Aden," "Mooltan," "Goojerat," "Punjaub," "Pegu," "Lucknow," "Relief of Ladysmith." "South Africa, 1899-1902."

Regular and Special Reserve Battalions.
Uniform—Scarlet. Facings—Blue. Agents—Sir C. R. McGrigor, Bt. & Co.

1st Bn. (102nd Foot)	.. Madras (for Quetta).	3rd Bn. (Kildare Mil.) .. Naas.
2nd ,, (103rd ,,)	.. Gravesend (for Shorncliffe).	4th ,, (R. Dublin City Mil.) .. Dublin.
Depôt	.. Naas.	5th ,, (Dublin County Mil.) .. Dublin.
		Record Office .. .. Dublin.

Colonel-in-Chief — Field-Marshal H.R.H. Arthur W. P. A., *Duke of* Connaught and Strathearn, K.G., K.T., K.P., G.C.B., G.C.S.I., G.C.M.G., G.C.I.E., G.C.V.O., Col. G. Gds. and A.S.C., and Col. in Chief 6 Dns., High. L.I. and Rif. Brig., *Personal A.D.C. to the King* 7Nov.03

Colonel - Cooper, Hon. Maj.-Gen. C. D., C.B., ret. pay - 13Mar.10

1st and 2nd Battalions.

Lt.-Colonels. (2)
2 Mainwaring, A.E. 5Mar.12
1 Rooth, R. A. 7June14

Majors. (8)
(3)2 Loveband, A. (*Comdg. Depôt*) 10Apr.07
1 Fetherstonhaugh, E. 5Mar.08
s. Romer, C. F., *p.s.c.* 29Nov.00
bt. lt.-col. 10May13
2 Shewan, H.M., *D.S.O.* 7June10
s. Higginson, H. W. 5Mar.12
s. Cory, G. N., *D.S.O.*, *p.s.c.* 25Jan.13
c.o. Maclear, P., *p.s.c.* 19Feb.13
7Apr.14
c.o. Perreau, C. N. 28Sept.01
7June14

Captains. (14)
(3)2 Magan, A. T. 18Jan.06
3Mar.00
2 Higginson, G.S. 26Oct.01
1 Molesworth, E. A. 26Oct.04
1 Grimshaw, C. T. W., D.S.O., *Adjt.* 14July04
s. Renny, L. F., *p.s.c.* 16July06
s.c. Haskard, J. McD.[*l*] 16July06
2 Clarke, N.P.[*l*] 20May08
23Apr.05
r. Jeffreys, R. G. B. 28Dec.05
2 Frankland, T. H. C., *p.s.c.*, *f.c.r.* 18May08
1 Brodhurst-Hill, A. 21June08
c.o. Moore, A., *D.S.O.* 21June08
2 Conlan, R.L,H. 21June08
2 Wheeler, S. G. de C. 21June08

Captains—contd.
2 Supple, W. H., *o.* 17July08
(3)1 Smithwick,S.G.17July08
r. Weldon, K. C. 22Jan.09
r. Smith, E. St. G. 23May10
t. Tredennick, J. P. 7June10
c.o. Knox. R. F. B. 23Jan.11
m.c. Maclear, B. 4Feb.11
m.c. Robinson, J. P. B. 4Feb.11
t. Seymour, E. F. E. 1Mar.12
1 Higginson, W. F. 5Mar.12
1 Johnson. A. M 24Apr.12
(3)1 Hoey, C. B. R. 24Apr.12
1 Crozier, H. C. 1Feb.13
1 French, D. 19Feb.13
1 Molony, A. W. 1Apr.13
1 Mood, J. M. 2Aug.13
2 Trigona, A. S. [*l*] 15Apr.14
2 Preston,A.J.D. 7June14

Lieutenants (19).
c.o. Wilson, D. E. 18July08
2 Watson, R. M., *Adjt.* 18Dec.09
1 Anderson, D. V. F. 24Dec.09
1 Grove, J. R. W. 1Apr.10
(3)1 Carew, R. J. H. 1Apr.10
2 Vernon, J. A. 23May10
1 Dobbs, J. F. K. 7June10
1 Dunlop, G. M. 15June10
2 Leahy, T. J. 22June10
1 Floyd, H. M. 12Nov.10
c.o. Law, R. 22Jan.11
f.c. Corballis, E. R. L. 1Mar.12
1 Philby, D. S. 5Mar.12
1 Shine, J.O. W. 4Apr.12
2 West, C.H.L'E 12Feb13
c.o. Maunsell, E. R, L. 19Feb.13
1 Lanigan-O'Keefe, F. S. 1Apr.13
2 Braddell, W. H. 2Aug.13
c.o. Priest, C. D. 10Sept.13
2 Shadforth, H. A. 13Sept.13
1 Bernard, R. 12Nov.13
1 Bagley, A. B. 15Apr.14
1 O'Hara, H. D. 29Apr.14
2 Massy-Westropp, R. F. H. 7June14

2nd Lieutenants. (12)
1 Carruthers, C. G. 26July13
1 Boustead, L. C. 8Sept.13
2 Bush, R. O. C. 8Sept.13
1 deLusignan, R. 8Sept.13
2 Dickie, J. MacN. 24Jan.14
2 Macky, F. C. S. 25Feb.14
1 Corbet, R.V.C. 25Feb.14
2 McGuire, R. 25Feb.14
2 Kennedy,'.A. St. C. 10June14

Adjutants.
1 Grimshaw, C. T. W. D.S.O., *capt.* 28Dec.11
2 Watson R. M., *lt.* 12Feb.13

Quarter-Masters.
2 Burke, J. 1Mar.01
hon. capt. 1Mar.11
r. Holloway, L. 28Nov.03
hon. capt. 28Nov.13
1 Kennedy, M. J., *hon. lt.* 7May10
r. Armstrong, C. W., *hon. lt.* 6Sept.11
r. Williams, A. R., *hon. lt.* 8Mar.13

Special Reserve
2nd Lieutenants.
Dunlop,J.G.M. 7Sept.10
3June11
Goff, R. A. J. 18May12
Taylor, J. A. H. 20July12

3rd Battalion.

(*Officers serving on 18 Oct. 00 in the corresponding Militia unit hold honorary Army rank equivalent to the Militia regimental rank they then held. Other officers entitled to honorary Army rank have it shown against their names.*)

Hon. Colonel.
Lawless, Hon. E. (*Hon. Col. ret. Mila.*) 21June08
8July96

Lt.-Colonel.
Lindsay, W. C., M.V.O. 18Mar.14

Major.
r.e.✗Loveband, A. 10Apr.07
p.s. Keogh, E. J. L. 18Mar.09

Captains. (5)
r.e.✗Magan, A. T. 18Jan.08
3Mar.00
p.s.✗Johnson, R. D. (H) 7Oct.05
r.e.✗Smithwick, S. G. 17July08
✗Rankes, E. N., Capt. ret.pay12Sept.08
4Dec.12
p.s. Harold-Barry, J. 13July10
r.e.✗Hoey, C. B. R. 24Apr.12

Lieutenants. (11)
r.e. Carew, R. J. H. 1Apr.10
Robinson, W. M. 1July12
Hall, J. R. F. 8July13
French, C. S. 10Oct.13

2nd Lieutenants. (8)
Hallowes, P. C. (*on prob.*) 26Feb.13
Denning, R. E. V. 2July13
Webb, C. St. L. (*on prob.*) 4Feb.14
Magill, R. (H) (*on prob.*) 17June14

Adjutant.
✗Jeffreys, R.G.B., Capt. R. Dub. Fus. 13Jan.14
(*Capt. in Army 28Dec.05*)

Quarter-Master.
✗Holloway, L., *hon. capt.*

THE ROYAL DUBLIN FUSILIERS—(Regtl. Dist. No. **102**)—contd.

4th Battalion.

(*Officers serving on 4 Oct. 02 in the corresponding Militia unit hold honorary Army rank equivalent to the Militia regimental rank they then held. Other officers entitled to honorary Army rank have it shown against their names*).

Lt.-Colonel.

✗Hackett, M. C.,
hon.c,(*H*) 30Apr.07

Majors. (3)

p.s.✗Meldon, J. A.(*H*)
(*Chief of Police and Comdt. Local Forces, St. Vincent*, 4June1913)
10June06
✗Beddoes, H. R.,
Bt. Maj. ret. pay
(*Capt. Res. of Off.*)
hon. l.c. (*H*)
(*Labour Exchanges and Unemplt. Insce., Bd. of Trade*,
11Nov.12) 1May07

Captains. (6)

p.s.✗Dunn, W. B., (*Hon. Capt. in Army* 16
Oct. 00) (*H*) 1July10
Dickie, T, W.(*H*) 24June12
Lees, A.G H.(*H*) 24June12
Weir, E. W. B.,
Lt. ret. pay 24Sept.13

Lieutenants. (11)

p.s.✗Jenings, U. C.
16Apr.02
Maunsell, D. S.
1Dec.11
Tippet, H. C. C.
(*H*) *I. of M.* 1Dec.11
Tyndall, J. C. 20Apr.12
Malcolmson, W. H.
W. B. 20Apr.12
Colles, A. G. 20Apr.12
Persse, D.E. 20Apr.12
Peggs, J. H. 19June13
Long, G. B. 13Dec.13
1May11
Maunsell, E. F. T.
23Jan.14
Radcliff, E. F. (*H*)
6May14

2nd Lieutenants. (8)

Hayes, H. J.;(*H*) 4Jan.13
Carroll, J. F. J.
23Apr.13
McLoughlin, J. P.
28May13
Lunn, J. S 16July13
MacSweeny, M. C.
(*on prob.*) 7Feb.14
Porritt, C. A.
(*on prob.*) 21Mar.14
Killingley, H. G.
(*on prob.*) 15Apr.14

Inst. of Musk.

Tippet. H. C. C.
lt. 16Apr.13

Adjutant.

✗Weldon, K. C., Capt.
R. Dub. Fus. 12Mar.12
(*Capt. in Army* 22Jan.09)

Quarter-Master.

Williams, A. R., *hon.lt.*

5th Battalion.

(*Officers serving on 25 Feb. 02 in the corresponding Militia unit hold honorary Army rank equivalent to the Militia regimental rank they then held. Other officers entitled to honorary Army rank have it shown against their names*).

Hon. Colonel.

Meath, Rt. Hon. R.,
Earl of, K.P, (*t*)
21June08
9July87

Lt.-Colonel.

p.s.✗Macnamara, F. H.,
(*H*) *p.v.c.* 16Feb.13

Majors (3)

p.s.Browne, L. M. (*Hon. Lt. in Army* 6 July
01) (*H*) (*a*) (*b*) 7July10

Captains. (6)

✗Swifte, L. C. 14Nov.03
p.s.✗O'Carrol, F. W. J.
(*H*) 14Nov.03
p.s.✗Robinson, R. H. St.
C, C. (*H*) 14Nov.03
✗O'Brien, A.K.H.
Capt., ret. pay 3Apr.07
7Dec.12
p.s.✗Popham, F. S. (*H*)
8June09
p.s.Bourke, B. W. (*H*)
24Feb.12

Lieutenants. (11)

✗Wodehouse, A. H.,
Lt. ret. pay(*H*)4Feb.05
18Dec.09
Longfield, W. B. M.
26Mar.09
Barton, C. M.
(*Magistrate
E. Afr. Prot.*
{ 1Apr.14
{ 28*Apr*.13) 1Aug.11
Macnamara, C. R.
27June12
White, E.R.K. 27June12
Thornhill, H. E. B.
28Nov.12
Jameson, M. E. F. B.
28Nov.12
Moran, G. C. 24Apr.13

2nd Lieutenants. (8)

Finlay, R. A. 7June13

Adjutant.

✗Smith, E., St. G.,
Capt. R.Dub.Fus.
1May12
(*Capt. in Army* 23May10)

Quarter-Master.

✗Armstrong, C.W.,
hon. lt.

THE RIFLE BRIGADE (THE PRINCE CONSORT'S OWN).
Rifle Depôt .. .. Winchester.

"Copenhagen," "Monte Video," "Roliça," "Vimiera," "Corunna," "Busaco," "Barrosa," "Fuentes d'Onor," "Cuidad Rodrigo," "Badajoz," "Salamanca," "Vittoria," "Pyrenees," "Nivelle," "Nive," "Orthes," "Toulouse," "Peninsula," "Waterloo," "South Africa, 1846-7, 1851-2-3," "Alma," "Inkerman," "Sevastopol," "Lucknow," "Ashantee, 1873-4," "Ali Masjid," "Afghanistan, 1878-9," "Burma, 1885-87," "Khartoum," "Defence of Ladysmith," "Relief of Ladysmith," "South Africa, 1899-1902."

Regular and Special Reserve Battalions.

Uniform—Green.   *Facings*—Black.   *Agents*—Messrs. Cox & Co.

1st Bn. (Rifle Brigade) .. *Colchester (for Belgaum).*	5th Bn. (Q.O. R. Tower Hamlets Mil.)	Winchester.
2nd „ („ „) .. *Kuldana (for Colchester).*	6th „ (K.O. „ „ „)	Winchester.
3rd „ („ „) .. *Cork.*		
4th „ („ „) .. *Dagshai (for Peshawar.)*		

Depôt and Record Office .. .. Winchester.

Allied Regiment of Canadian Militia.
6th Regiment "The Duke of Connaught's Own Rifles."   Vancouver, British Columbia.

Colonel-in-Chief.
Field-Marshal H.R.H. Arthur W. P. A., Duke of Connaught and Strathearn, K.G., K.T., K.P., G.C.B., G.C.S.I., G.C.M.G., G.C.I.E., G.C.V.O. Col. G. Gds. and A.S.C., and Col.-in-Chief 6 Dns., High. L.I., and R. Dub. Fus., *Personal A.D.C. to the King.*   29May80

Colonels Commandant.
Swaine, Maj.-Gen. Sir L. V., K.C.B., O.M.G., ret. pay [R]	3rd Bn.	19Nov.08
Lyttelton, Gen. Rt. Hon. Sir N. G., G.C.B., G.C.V.O., ret. pay [R]	4th Bn.	29Mar.12
Howard, Maj.-Gen. Sir F., K.C.B., C.M.G., ret. pay [R]	2nd Bn.	19July13
C. Att. Nicholl, Maj.-Gen. C. R. H., ret. pay	1st Bn.	19Aug.13

Officer Commanding Rifle Depôt (also Colonel in charge of Rifle Records) } Fortescue, Col. F. A., C.B., p.s.c. .. 1July12

1st, 2nd, 3rd and 4th Battalions.

Lt.-Colonels. (4)
1 Biddulph, H. M., p.s.c. [L] 16Dec.11
3 Alexander, R. 15Oct13
4 Thesiger, G. H., C.B., C.M.G., p.s.c. [l] 1Dec.13
   bt. col. 29Nov.06
2 Stephens, R. B., p.s.c. [l] 24Mar.14

Majors. (16)
2 Harman, G. M. N., D.S.O. 26June07
3 Henniker, C. H. C., Lord 16Dec.07
1 Paley, G., p.s.c. [l] 8July08
2 Bright, R. G. T., C.M.G., e. [F] 19Dec.08
  17Dec.99
3 Boden, A. D. 6Mar.09
2 Percival, C. V. N., [F] 15Oct.09
(6) 3 Heriot-Maitland, J. D., D.S.O. 1Dec.09
4 King, A. M. 23Dec.09
3 Maclachlan, R. C. (Comdg. Oxford Univ. Contgt. O.T.C.) 26Jan.10
Grogan, Sir E. I. B., Bt., p.s.c. [L] Mil. Attaché 24Mar.10

Majors—contd.
2 Rickman, S. H. 16Dec.11
1 Salmon, G. N. 3July12
s. Burnett-Stuart, J. T., D.S.O., p.s.c. [l] 4Oct.13
s. Cooke, B. H. H., p.s.c. [L] 15Oct.13
s. Hollond, S. E., p.s.c. 1Dec13
4 Harington, J. 24Mar.14

Captains. (26)
Cuninghame, Sir T.A.A.M., Bt., D.S.O., p.s.c., Mil. Attaché 18Jan.02
s. Paley, A.T., p.s.c. 18Jan.02
s. Grant, R. F. S., D.S.O., M.V.O., p.s.c. [l] 8Mar.04
s.c. Seymour, W.W. 27Apr.04
s. Davies, W. E. 29Apr.04
(6) 4 Buxton, J. L. 14May04
s. Solly-Flood, R. E. 28July04
t. Gathorne-Hardy, Hon. N. C. 24June08
s.c. 2 Powell, E. B. 23Jan.05
3 Pitt-Taylor, W. W., D.S.O., p.s.c. 23Jan.05
m.c. Riddell, E. P. A. 24June08
9Feb.05
4 Wollaston, F. H. A. 27Feb.05

Captains—contd.
1 Nugent, F. H. 8Mar.0
4 Helyar, M. H. 30May05
(5) 1 Sturgis, H. R. 4Dec.05
s. Lindsay, G. M. 15Dec.06
2 Verney, R. 2Apr.08
s. Wilson, H. M. 2Apr.08
  Jenkinson, J. B., p.s.c. 6May08
3 Weld-Forester, Hon. E. A. C. 10May08
3 Somerville, H. F. 8July08
s.c. Spencer, J. A. W. 22Oct.09
4 Hargreaves, A. K. 22Jan.10
s. Buller, H. C. 22Jan.10
3 Meade-Waldo, E. R. 23Mar.10
m.c. Follett, R. S. 15Apr.10
r. Baring, T. E., e. 14Oct.10
r. Burrowes, R. P. 27Oct.10
4 Prescott-Westcar, W. V. L. 8Dec.10
3 Starkey, J. H. 15Dec.10
(6) 3 Pryce, H. B. M. 18Jan.11
1 Lane, G. E. W. 22Jan.11
2 Sloggett, A. J. H. 22Jan.11
t. Prittie, Hon. H.C. O'C. 15Feb.11
1 de Moleyns, R.P.A. 15Feb.11

Captains—contd.
1 Ovey, D. 3Mar.11
t. Crosbie, J.P.G. 14June11
s. Tod, A. A. 29July11
t. Sladen, G. C. 3Oct.11
s. Davies, C. M., p.s.c. 6Oct.11
f.c. Pigot, R. 23Dec.11
t. Morris, T.H. P. 20Jan.12
e.a. Ritson, C. W. 22Jan.12
3 Scott, H. V. 8Feb.12
4 Sherston, S. A. 13Mar.12
2 Walpole, R. S. H. 25May12
s.c. Bernard, D. J. C. K. 25May12
t. Dimsdale, E. C. 2Aug.12
o.o. Leeke, R. H. 1Feb.13
s. Downes, O. C. 1Feb.13
e.a. Jones-Vaughan, H. T. C. 1Feb.13
1 Wingfield, Hon. M. A., D.S.O. 1Feb.13
2 Whitaker, H. 21Sept.13
1 Liddell, G. W., Adjt. 21Sept.13
(6) 4 Burton, R. C. 4Oct.13
1 Brownlow, G. J. 4Oct.13
r. Railston, H. G. M. 4Oct.13
o.o. Drummond, S. H. 30Oct.13
s. Richardson, H. S. C. 16Dec.13
1 Toynbee, G. P. R. 21Feb.14
4 Cole, J. J. B. 16Apr.14
3 Leslie, N. J. B. 1May14

THE RIFLE BRIGADE (THE PRINCE CONSORT'S OWN)—(Rifle Depôt)—contd.

1st, 2nd, 3rd, and 4th Bns.—contd.

Lieutenants. (40)
s. Hopwood, R. G. 22Oct.09
4Kennedy, P. A. 30Dec.09
1Morgan-Grenville, Hon. R. G. G., (Master of Kinloss) 22Jan.10
2Riley, H. L. 9Feb.10
f.c. Boyle, Hon. J.D. 23Mar.10
4Moore-Gwyn, H.G., Adjt. 15Apr.10
3Meysey-Thompson, Hon. C. H. M., Adjt. 14Oct.10
1Sutton-Nelthorpe, O. 27Oct.10
2Fellowes, R. T. 1Jan.11
(6) 3Parker, W. M. 18Jan.11
3Swan, C. F. T. 22Jan.11
4Selby-Smyth, M. B. 23Jan.11
2Fitzherbert-Brockholes, T.J., Adjt. 15Feb.11
(5)1Stewart, W. R. 3Mar.11
f.c. Cholmondeley, R. 1Apr.11
4Mostyn-Owen, R. A. 1Apr.11
2Durham, E. 14June11
c.o.Paget, L. B. 11July11
3Cavendish, A. L. C. 23Sept.11
3Alexander, M. 3Oct.11
1Micklem, J. 6Oct.11
s. Eastwood, T. R. 11Nov.11
3Godolphin Osborne, M. 23Dec.11
1Coryton, J. T 3Jan.12
(5) 2Gull, F. W. L. 4Mar.12
4Collins, R.L.H. 23Mar.12
2Bridgeman, R. O. 23Mar.12
(6) 4Reeve, J.T.W. 23Mar.12
4Campbell,H.F. 8May12
3Morgan-Grenville, Hon. T. G. B. 25May12
4Edwards, B.M.M. 17July12
4Stopford Sackville, L.C. 2Aug.12
2Mansel, R. C. 6Nov.12
4Alston. W. H. S. 13Jan.13
3Prideaux-Brune, D. E. 1Feb.13
3Congreve, W, La T. 1Feb.13
2Peyton, H. S. C. 16Mar.13
2Leigh, E. H. 17Apr.13
1Foljambe, W. S. 17Apr.13
3Landale, D. B. 17Apr.13
4Kewley, E. R. 17Apr.13
1Williams, E. S. R. 17Apr.13
2Stopford. M. G. N. 1Sept.13
4Calvert. J. D. 16Apr.14
2Earle, G.F. 29Apr.14
3Wolseley-Jenkins, C. W. 1May14

2nd Lieutenants. (24)
1Barclay, G. W. 19Jan.12
1Graham, O. B. 19Jan.12
2McGrigor, C. C. 14Feb.12
4Hargreaves. R. C. 14Feb.12
2Chichester-Constable,R.C.J. 22May12
2Bulkeley-Johnson, V. F. 3Sept.12
1Cartland,G.T. 4Sept.12
2Lawrence, G. St. P. 4Sept.12
3Dunlop, G. R. 4Sept.12
2Pilcher, T. P. 4Sept.12
1Prioleau, R. U. H. 4Dec.12
1Tennyson, Hon. L. H. 25Dec.12
1Aug.11
1Hunter, H. J. F. 5Feb.13
4Burn, A. H. P. 3Sept.13
4Burnell, A. C. 17Sept.13
1Winter, C. E. 17Sept.13

Adjutants.
1Liddell, G. W., capt. 17July12
3Meysey-Thompson, Hon. C. H. M., lt. 15Sept.13
4Moore-Gwyn, H. G., lt. 15Dec.13
2Fitzherbert-Brockholes, T.J. lt. 21Feb.14

Quarter-Masters.
2Alldridge, J. H., hon. lt. 8Nov.05
r. Walter, J., hon. lt. 10Feb.06
3Eastmead, L., hon. lt. 28May10
4Worthing, H. E., hon. lt. 25Sept.12
r. Ayers, A. E., hon. lt. 9Aug.13
1Mitchell, G. 18Oct.13
hon. lt. 19Feb.10
hon. lt. 19Feb.10

Special Reserve.

Lieutenant.
Glyn, R. G. C., late Lt. Res. of Off. 16July13
24Aug.09

2nd Lieutenants.
Sherston, G. W. 11Jan.13
Baird, R. D. 26Feb.13

5th Battalion.
(Officers serving on 3 Oct.02 in the corresponding Militia unit hold honorary Army rank equivalent to the Militia regimental rank they then held. Other officers entitled to honorary Army rank have it shown against their names).

Hon. Colonel.
✗Lyttelton, Gen. Rt. Hon. Sir N. G., G.C.B., G.C.V.O., ret. pay, Col. Comdt. Rif. Brig. [R] 14 Aug. 11

Lt.-Colonel.
✗Talbot, F. G., D.S.O., Maj. ret. pay, (Q) (H) 1Apr.13

Major.
r.e. ✗Harrison,C.E.12Apr.04
r.e. ✗Wood, D. 14May04
r.e. Sturgis, H.R. 4Dec.05
p.s. ✗de la Chapelle, X. R. A. (Hon, Capt in Army 9Oct.01) (Q) (H) 12Nov.07
r.e. ✗Byrne, G. B., Capt. ret. pay (Res.of Off.) (H) 13Nov.07
20May12
p.s. Parkyn, H. G. (Q) (H) 1Jan.08
p.s. Watts, S. J. (Q) (H) 25Apr.08
r.e. Frittie, Hon. F. R. D. 16May08
✗Sarel, W. G. M., Lt. ret. pay (q) (H) 4Sept.09
✗Blacker, F. St. J., Capt. ret. pay(q)(H) 8Oct.10
✗Gilliat, O. C. S., Capt. ret. pay (q) (H) ⓑ 6Sept.11
Rickards, A. K. (q) (H) (Asst. Commr. of Police, N.Provs., { 1Jan.14 Nigeria, {10June13) 29June09
Lascelles, Hon. E. C. late Lt. Rif. Brig. 23Jan.11
22Feb.13
r.e. Stewart, W. R. 3Mar.11
Orr, J. E. (H) 22May11
r.e. Gull, F. W. L, 4Mar.12
Campbell,G.V. 23Apr.13

2nd Lieutenants. (8)
Crawford-Kehrmann, J. 20July12
Grinnell-Milne,D.W. (on prob.) 13Dec.13
Daniell. A. S. L. (on prob.) 3June14

Adjutant.
Railston, H. G. M., Capt. Rif. Brig. 16Mar.13
(Capt.in Army 4Oct.13)

Quarter-Master.
✗Walter, J., hon. lt,

6th Battalion.
(Officers serving on 18 Oct.00 in the corresponding Militia unit hold honorary Army rank equivalent to the Militia regimental rank they then held. Other officers entitled to honorary Army rank have it shown against their names).

Hon. Colonel.
Somerset, Sir A, P, F, C., K.C.B., late Lt. 13 Ft. 28June08
18June92

Lt.-Colonel.
✗Dawson, E. A. F., Maj. ret. pay (Res. of Off.) (H) 10Nov.11

Major.
r.e. ✗Heriot-Maitland, J. D., D.S.O. 1Dec.09
p.s. Cowell.A.V.J.[I]Capt. late Rif. Brig., (Capt. Res. of Off.) (H) (b) ⓑ (Q) 30Oct.11

Captains. (5)
✗Bell, M, E., Capt. ret. pay (Res. of Off.) 9Aug.09
18Nov.09
r.e. ✗Buxton, J. L.14May04
✗. ✗Thornton, L. H., Capt. ret. pay ⓑ (H)(Q)19Sept.06
✗Dorrien-Smith, A. A., D.S.O., Capt. ret. pay 15Dec.06
p.s. ✗Haig, R., Capt. ret. pay (H) 6Apr.07
✗Turner, B. A., D.S.O., Capt. ret. pay 3July09
r.e.✗Pryce, H. B. M. 18Jan.11
✗Dick-Cunyngham, G. A., Capt. ret. pay 18Jan.11
✗Robertson,Hon.E.B. F., Capt. ret. pay 26July11
r.e. Burton, R. C. 4Oct.13

Lieutenants. (11)
r.e. Parker, W. M. 18Jan.11
Bowle-Evans, W. [l] (Hon. Attaché, Tokio, 10 Apr. 13) 25May11
r.e. Reeve, J. T. W. 23Mar.12

2nd Lieutenants. (8)
Jameson, T. O. 20Nov.12
Skeggs, R. O. (on prob.) 3Sept.13
Townshend, F, C. (on prob.) 27Sept.13
Hardinge,Hon.H.R. (on prob.) 11Feb.14
Smith, J. H. (on prob.) 14Feb.14
Ellis, A. E. P. (on prob.) 21Feb.14

Adjutant.
✗Burrowes, R. P., Capt. Rif. Brig. 17Nov.11
(Capt. in Army 7Oct.10)

Quarter-Master.
✗Ayers, A. E., hon. lt.

Infantry. Territorial Force.

THE MONMOUTHSHIRE REGIMENT.

1st Bn. .. .. .. Stow Hill, Newport.
2nd Bn. .. .. Osborne Road, Pontypool.
3rd Bn. .. .. .. Abergavenny.

1st Battalion.

"South Africa, 1900-02."
Stow Hill, Newport.

Hon. Colonel
✠Tredegar. C. C. E.,
Visct. (*Hon. Lt -
Col. ret. Mila.*) 8Mar.14

Lt.-Colonel,
p.s, Smith, C. H., VD,
(t)(H) 18Mar.11
Majors. (2)
p.s. ✠Robinson,C.L., TD,
(Hon. Capt. in
Army 7 May 2),
hon. l.c. (H) 5Sept.06
p.s.Birrell Anthony, H.
A., VD, 6June11
Captains. (8)
Williams, E. S.,(t)(H)
5Sept.06
p. Evill, C. A. (t) 16May09
p. Perry, B. L. (H) 8Oct.10
p. Edwards, H. T. (H)
8Apr.11
Llewellin. L. C.(H)
21Feb.12
Rowe, J. L.(H)18Feb.13
p. Williams, O. M.(H)
18Feb.13
I. of M. 18Feb.13
Llewellin,M.C.(H)
18Feb.13
Hepburn, W. C. 9Oct.13

Lieutenants. (8)
Francis,G,L,B.15Dec.11
Stanton, C. W.
(H) 21Feb.12
Murphy, D,G.C. 5Apr.13
2nd Lieutenants. (8)
Llewellin, E. C. 1Apr.13
Thompson,H. C R.
2Apr.13
Thomas, R. C. L.
3Apr.13
Bailey, C. H. 25Apr.13
Evans, A. L. 15May13
Cayley, C. 12Jan.14
Inst. of Musk.
Williams, O. M., *capt.*
20Jan,09

Adjutant,
Dimsdale, E. C.,
Capt. Rif. Brig.
27Oct.13

Quarter-Master.
Martin, R. H., *hon. lt.*
10Apr.10
Medical Officers.
✠Ingram, Capt. P.C.P.,
M.B., R.A.M.C.(T.F.)
(*attd.*) 30Sept.12
30Mar.09
Chaplain.
Llewellyn-Jones, *Rev.*
D.E., Chapl. 4th class,
(T.F.)(*attd.*) 7Nov.12
[Uniform—Green. Facings
—Black.]

Cadet Unit affiliated.
1 C.B. Mon. R. (1 Co.)

2nd Battalion.

"Gwell angau na gwarth."
"South Africa, 1900-02."
Osborne Road, Pontypool
Hon. Colonel,
Hanbury, J. C. 29Oct.92
Lt.-Colonel,
B., *M.V.O. Lt. ret.
pay (Res. of Off.)*
27Apr.12
Majors. (2)
Jenkins, J. C. 29May11
p.s,Graham, D. W.(*Maj.
ret.T.F.*)(*formerly
2nd Lt. R,Highrs.*)
1Jan.13
Captains. (8)
p. Broackes, J. G. 1Apr.08
Hobbs, R.A.(H)8Feb.12
Edwards, A.H.
(H) 20Nov.13
Thomas, J. G. 18Feb.14
Lieutenants (8)
Jenkins, E.D.T.20Apr.11
Watkins. I. E. M.
(H)⑧(t) 8Feb.12
Watkins, V.H. 8Feb.12
Edwards, E. 9Feb.14
Taylor, J. W. (H)
I. of M. 10Feb.14
Walters, H. J. 11Feb.14
Hockaday, P. 29Apr.14

2nd Lieutenants (8)
Bowen. A. W. 23Jan.13
Dart. L. V. 1Apr.13
Sale, A. C. 2Apr.13
Jacob, J. H. 28May13
Williams,W.J. 10June13
James, W. N. 3Aug.13
Williams, B.A.15Sept.13
Cox, G. 25Mar.14
Inst. of Musk,
Taylor, J. W., *lt,*
29Sept.13
Adjutant,
Rolls, S. P. A., Capt.
Dorset R.. 2Mar.12
Quarter-Master.
p. ✠Sale, A., *hon m,*
6Sept.99
Medical Officers.
Mason, Lt. G. W.,
R.A.M.C. (T.F.)
(*attd.*) 2Apr.13
Chaplain.
Morgan, *Rev.* E., *B.A.*,
Chapl. 3rd Class,
(T.F.) (*attd.*) 20Dec.12
20Dec.02
[Uniform—Scarlet,
Facings—Green,]

Cadet Units affiliated,
1 C.B. Mon. R.
(3 Cos.)

3rd Battalion.

On a mount the Red Dragon
segreant. In each of the
four corners a Leek.
"South Africa, 1900-02,"
Abergavenny.
Hon. Colonel.
✠Herbert, *Hon.* Maj.-
Gen. Sir I. J. C.,
Bt., C.B., C.M.G.,
ret. pay, p.s.c. [R.]
27Apr.09
Lt.-Colonel,
p. Ford, P. B., TD,
(H) 24Mar.14

Majors (2)
Fawckner, E. H. (Q)
1Aug.11
Bishop,J.G.(Q)24Mar.14

Captains (8)
P. Lewis, W. A. 26Nov.04
p.s.Jacob, J. R. 23Nov.07
p.s.Williams, L.T.C.1Apr08
p.s.Steel, O. W. D.
(H) *I. of M.* 12July11
Coxon, H., *late
Maj. 1 Newc.-
on-Tyne R.G.A.
(Vols.)* 29May14
Lieutenants (8)
Routledge,W.(q)1Feb.10
Lancaster, J. 1Feb.10
Walbeoffe-Wilson,W,
25May11
Gattie, K. C. D. (q)
1Dec. 11
Gorman, B, M. P.,(q)
1July12
Lewis, R. A 21Sept.12
2nd Lieutenants (8)
Martin, C. H. G.
(H) 5June12
12Oct.09
Gregson, W. 1Apr.13
Jones, J.M. 7June13
Bennett, G. 23June13
Reed, C. S. 14June13
Nyhan, C. 4June14
Abbott, W. P. 4June14
O'Connor, E.J.27June14
Inst. of Musk,
Steel, O. W.D.,
capt. 7Apr.09
Adjutant,
✠Smithers, H. O. H.
Capt. Bedf.R,14Nov.12
Quarter-Master.
✠Fry, A. A., *hon. lt.*
11July10
Medical Officer.
Phillips, *Rev.* J. R.,
M.A., Chapl. 2nd
Class (T.F.) (*attd.*)
20Nov.12
20Sept.97
Williams, *Rev.* W. C.,
M.A., Chapl. 4th
Class (T.F.) (*attd.*)
1Apr.08
21Sept.98
[Uniform—Scarlet,
Facings—Green,]

Cadet Units affiliated.
1 C.B. Mon. R.
(2 Cos,)

THE CAMBRIDGESHIRE REGIMENT.

A Castle, thereon an escutcheon of the Arms of Ely.
1st Bn. .. .. 14, *Corn Exchange Street, Cambridge*.

1st Battalion.

"South Africa, 1900-01."

Hon. Colonel,

✠French,Field-Marshal
Sir J.D.P., G.C.B.,
G.C.V.O., K.C.M.G.,
Col. 19 Hrs. and Col.-
in-Chief R. Ir. Regt.
[R] 22Apr.09

Lt.-Colonel,
p.s.Tebbutt, L. (Q) (H)
29July11

Majors (2)
Copeman, C. E. F.
29July11
Archer, G. I,, (Q)
16Dec.11

Captains (8)
p.s.Bowes, G. B. (H)
13Dec.05
p.s.Staton, H. H., 28Sept.12
6Sept.02
p.s.Saint, E. T. 5Apr.13
Sindall, R. E. 23June13
Sindall, W. T. 3Dec.13

Lieutenants. (8)
Clayton, M. C. 16Aug.11
Symonds, F. G. 20Oct.12

2nd Lieutenants. (8)
Tebbutt, O. N. 12Sept.12
Tebbutt, R. J. 30Sept.12
Formby, T. H. 27Nov.12
Keenlyside,C.A.H.
24Feb.13
Saunders,E.W. 6Mar.13
Smalley, J. D. 10Mar.13
Ollard,J. W.A.A.9Apr.13
McMicking, G.T.G.
29Oct.13
West, W. M. 28Mar.14
de Cerjat, C. S. 4Apr.14

Adjutant
Littledale, H. A.P.,
Capt. Yorks. L. I.
4Oct.13

Quarter-Master.
Verrinder, H. E.,
hon lt. 26May06
Medical Officers.
Ellis, Lt. R., *M.B.,*
R.A.M.C. (T.F.)
(*attd.*) 9May14
Chaplains.
✠Crookham, *Rev.* W.
T. R. Chapl. 2nd,
Class (T.F.) (*attd.*)
8Jan.14
15Jan.09
Whittington, *Rev.* F.
B., Chapl. 4th
Class (T.F.) (*attd.*),
21Feb.09
1Apr.08
[Uniform—Scarlet.
Facings—Blue.]

Infantry. Territorial Force.

THE LONDON REGIMENT.

1st Bn.	Handel Street, Bloomsbury, W.C.		15th Bn.	Somerset House, Strand, W.C.
2nd ,,	9, Tufton Street, Westminster, S.W.		16th ,,	Queen's Hall, 58, Buckingham Gate, Westminster, S.W.
3rd ,,	21, Edward Street, Hampstead Road, N.W.		17th ,,	66, Tredegar Road, Bow, E.
4th ,,	112, Shaftesbury Street, City Road, N.		18th ,,	Duke of York's Headquarters, Chelsea, S.W.
5th ,,	130, Bunhill Row, E.C.			
6th ,,	57a, Farringdon Road, E.C.		19th ,,	76, High Street, Camden Town, N.W.
7th ,,	24, Sun Street, Finsbury Square, E.C.		20th ,,	Holly Hedge House, Blackheath, S.E.
8th ,,	130, Bunhill Row, E.C.		21st ,,	4, Flodden Road, Camberwell, S.E.
9th ,,	56, Davies Street, Berkeley Square, W.		22nd ,,	2, Jamaica Road, Bermondsey, S.E.
10th ,,	49, The Grove, Hackney, N.E.		23rd ,,	27, St. John's Hill, Clapham Junction, S.W.
11th ,,	17, Penton Street, Pentonville, N.			
12th ,,	Chenies Street, Bedford Square, W.C.		24th ,,	71, New Street, Kennington Park Road, S.E.
13th ,,	Iverna Gardens, Kensington, W.			
14th ,,	59, Buckingham Gate, Westminster, S.W.		25th ,,	Fulham House, Putney Bridge, S.W.
			26th ,,	Duke's Road, Euston Road, W.C.

1st (City of London) Battalion, The London Regiment, (Royal Fusiliers).

The Arms of the City of London.

In each of the four corners the United Red and White Rose ensigned with the Imperial Crown, within the Garter.

"South Africa, 1900-02."

Handel Street, Bloomsbury, W.C.

Hon. Colonel.
Jessel, H. M., late
Capt. 17 Lrs. (Hon. Maj. ret. Impl. Yeo.)
2Dec.05

Lt.-Colonel.
p.s. Crowe, P. B. G. O.,
vD, hon. c. (Q) [L]
3Mar.07

Majors. (2)
p.s.Taylor, C. E. W.
TD, (H) ⊕ 19Dec.03
p.s.✗Mercer, E. B. (Hon. Capt. in Army 26 Aug., 02) 3Mar.07

Captains. (8)
p.s.Smith, D. V. ⊕ 2Aug.01
p.s.Glover, W. R. ⊕ 16Jan.04
p.s.Jones, W. H. 7Jan.05
p.s.Glover, R. B. G. 3Mar.07
Mouat, G. M. D. 2Mar.09
p.s.✗Lyle, A. A. (Hon Lt. in Army 10July 02) ⊕ 1Nov.10
Marchment, A. F. (H) I. of M. 23July12
Tatham, C. K. 25July13

Lieutenants. (9)
Baelz, E. F. W. 1Sept.11
Crosthwaite, J. D. 18Sept.11
Brooks, C.J.(H) 1Mar.13
Seaverns, J. H. 1May13
Bowen, R. G. B.16July13
Woodthorpe, J. S. 25July13
Boyton, H. J. 1Jan.14
Crowe, H. B. 1Jan.14

2nd Lieutenants. (8)
Higgins, E. L. 28Apr.13
Dicke, R.E.H. 11June13
Jacks, M. 15Dec.13

Inst. of Musk.
Marchment, A. F., capt. 24Mar.11

Adjutant.
✗Rayner, W. B. F.,
Capt. R. Fus. 11May14

Quarter-Master.
p. Ibbs, T. C., hon. capt. 3Feb.08

Medical Officers.
p. Hardwicke, Capt. L. C. V., M.B., R.A.M.C., (T.F.) (attd.) 22Jan.09
✗Meggitt, Capt. H., R.A.M.C. (T.F.) (attd.) 25Mar.12

Chaplain.
Shedden, Rev. R. G., M.A., Chapl. 4th Class (T.F.)(attd.) 24Aug.09

[Uniform—Scarlet, Facings—Blue.]

2nd (City of London) Battalion, The London Regiment, (Royal Fusiliers).

The Arms of the City of London.

In each of the four corners the United Red and White Rose ensigned with the Imperial Crown within the Garter.

"South Africa, 1900-02."

9, Tufton Street, Westminster, S.W.

Hon. Colonel.
p. Carlebach, P., ᴛᴅ (Lt.-Col. ret. T. F.) (Capt. Res. of Off.) 17 Dec.10

Lt.-Colonel.
p.s.Marler, E. L., ᴛᴅ 17Dec.10

Majors. (2)
Hogan, E. J. ⊕ 29Oct.10
Attenborough,
J. (H) 17Dec.10

Captains. (8)
p.s.Stacey, G. A. 25Feb.05
p.s.Scott, M. F. ⊕ (H) (Q) 22May07
p.s.Davies, E. O. 1Apr.08
30Jan.08
p.s.Guttmann, C. J., (Q) 30July10
Heumann, R. 1May11
Houlder, A. G. (Q) 26July12
Marians, R. I. (H)
I, of M. 6Feb.13
Marno,C.L.V. 19July13

Lieutenants. (8)
(p) Curwen, W. J. H., late
Lt. 2 V.B. R. Fus., s. 28July12
Inglis, L. H. R. 28July12
Rees, J. D. 15July13
Sneath, R. E. F. 29July13
Handyside, P. J. A. 7Oct.13

2nd Lieutenants. (8)
Moon, F. J. T. 12May09
Emanuel, O. 1Jan.13
Everitt, H. W. 10Apr.13
Bate, E. E. H. 24Dec.13

Inst. of Musk.
Marians, R. I., capt. 15July12

Adjutant.
✗Westley, J. H. S.,
Capt.York.R.28Sept.11

Quarter-Master.
Warrener, J., Qr.-Mr. (hon. capt.) ret. pay 11May12

Medical Officers.
McHoul, Lt. J., R.A.M.C. (T.F.) (attd.) 19Oct.08

Chaplain.
Bell, Rev. W. G., B.A., Chapl. 4th Class (T.F.) (attd.) 27Apr.09

[Uniform—Scarlet, Facings—Blue.]

---

* On all ceremonial occasions the addition (City of London) or (County of London) battalion should be added to the short title of the London Regiment.

| 1573 | 1574 | 1575 | 1576 |

Infantry. Territorial Force.

London Regt.—*contd.*

3rd (City of London) Battalion, The London Regiment, (Royal Fusiliers).

The Arms of the City of London.

In each of the four corners the United Red and White Rose ensigned with the Imperial Crown within the Garter.

"South Africa, 1900-02."

21, Edward Street, Hampstead Road, N.W.

Hon. Colonel.
Parsons, Sir H. J. F., Knt. 4Nov.10

Lt.-Colonel,
p.s.✕Howell, A. A. (*Hon. Capt. in Army* 1Dec.00) 8Mar.10

Majors. (2)
Beresford, P. W. 16Aug.10
✕Samuel, F. D. (*H*)(*b*) 9Nov.10

Captains. (8)
p. Pulman, H. R. S. 22Sept.06
p.s. Moore, H. A. 4Mar.08
Reeves, G. N. 1July10
✕Livingstone, G. (Q) 24Jan.11
Noël, E. A. 24Jan.11
p. Prance, H. W. 2Sept.12
 3Dec.08
Agius, A. V. L. B. 1May13
Cornelius-Wheeler, F. 5Dec.13

Lieutenants. (8)
Wolter, H. F. 1June11
Jenkins, F. C. 1June11
Noël, E. V. 1June11
Clermont, A. 2Sept.12
 18Aug.10
Agius, A. J. J. P. 12Apr.13
Rochford, C. E. 14Feb.14
Moreing, A. C. 14Feb.14
Edwards, G. H. 14Feb.14

2nd Lieutenants. (8)
Sutcliffe, R. D. 2June13
Crichton, C. A. W. 3June13
Sorley, G. M. 9June13
Page, C. J. ⓢ 10June13
Stephens, J. L. 1July13
Clarke, H. F. 4May14
Reeves, E. J. 23June14

Adjutant.
Hawes, G. E., Capt. R. Fus. 1Apr.12

Quarter-Master.
✕Brown, G., *hon. lt.* 26June14

Medical Officers.
p. Robinson, Maj. J., R.A.M.C. (T.F.) (*attd.*) 16Nov.07
 11Sept.95
Gregg, Lt. E. A., R.A.M.C. (T.F.) (*attd.*) 12Feb.12

Chaplain.
Corbett, Rev. F. St. J., *M.A.*, Chapl.3rd Class (T.F.) (*attd*) 30May12
 30May02
Sandberg, Rev. W. B., *M.A.*, Chapl. 4th Class (T.F.) (*attd.*) 31May11

[Uniform —*Scarlet.*
Facings—*Blue.*]

4th (City of London) Battalion, The London Regiment, (Royal Fusiliers).

The Arms of the City of London.

In each of the four corners the United Red and White Rose ensigned with the Imperial Crown, within the Garter.

"South Africa, 1900,"

112, Shaftesbury Street, City Road, N.

Hon. Colonel.
✕Œ. Moncrieff, Lt.-Gen. G. H., VD, ret. pay, Col. R. Scots [R] 24July86

Lt.-Colonel,
Botterill, G. P. 4Feb.14

Majors. (2)
Burnett, L. T. (*H*)(*b*)(*q*) 18Oct.13

Captains. (8)
p.s. Jackson, R. J. J. 27Jan.08
p.s. Vine, G. H. M. 23Feb.08
p.s. Duncan-Teape, H. J. T. 17June12
p.s. Arthur, R. N. 21July12
Cart de Lafontaine, H. P. L. 5Oct.12
Moore, W. 18Oct.13

Lieutenants. (8)
Clark, W. G. 17Aug.12
Saunders, C. R. E. 5Oct.14
Elliott, S 14Feb.12
Edwards, V. W. 2Apr.14
Grimwade, F. C. 2Apr.14
Stanham, H. G. 30May14
Stedman, P. B. K. 30May14
Parkhouse, H. 10June14

2nd Lieutenants. (8)
Weathersbee, H. W. 5Nov.13
Long, A. L. 19Mar.14
Sykes, J. T. 26May14
Herring, R. L. 4July14

Adjutant.
✕Scott, G. B., Capt. Leins. R. 17Jan.14

Quarter-Master.
Tomsett, E. S., *hon. lt.* 16Dec.13

Medical Officers.
p. Pratt, Maj. J. D., M.D., TD, R.A.M.C. (T.F.) (*attd.*) 2Dec.02
 16Aug.90
p. Dutch, Maj. H., TD, R.A.M.C. (T.F.) (*attd.*) 22July05
 20May93
p. Parr, Maj. J. F. F., R.A.M.C. (T.F.) (*attd.*) 28May12
 7Nov.00

Chaplains.
Sheppard, Rev. Canon E., K.C.V.O., D.D., Chapl. 4th Class (T.F.) (*attd.*) 1Apr.08
 26June01
Bourchier, Rev. B. G., *M.A.* Chapl. 4th Class (T.F.) (*attd.*) 4 Apr.14

[Uniform—*Scarlet.*
Facings—*Blue*].

Infantry. Territorial Force.

London Regt.—contd.

5th (City of London) Battalion, The London Regiment, (London Rifle Brigade).

"South Africa, 1900-02."
130, Bunhill Row, E.C.

Lt.-Colonel.
✗Cairns, W. D., Earl,
(Hon. Maj. in Army,
21Oct.00)(Hon.Lt.-Col.
ret. Mila.) (In command) 9Dec.12
p.s. ✗Matthey,C.G.R., vD,
hon. c. (Hon. Capt. in
Army 1 Dec.00)(T) 16Apr.02

Majors. (2)
King, N. C.,TD,(Q)22July12
Captains. (8)
p.s.Bates, A. S. (t) 13Nov.01
p.s.Soames, M. H. 1Aug.08
p.s.MacGill,C.G.H.,
M,V,O. (H) 2Dec.08
p.s.Bowers, S. 9July10
p.s.Husey, R. H. 26Nov.12
Thompson, C. H. F.
18Sept.13
MacGeagh, H. D. F.
18Sept.13
Somers-Smith, J. R.
9June14

Lieutenants. (8)
Otter, R. E. 17Oct.10
Biscoe, V. F. 18May12
Warner, B. A. (Asst.
Dist.Commr., Uganda,
13 May 12) 9July12
Bewsher, F. W. 9July12
Robinson, J. G.26Nov.12
Morrison,G.H.18Sept.13
Large, E. L. 9Apr.14
de Cologan, A. T. B.
(H) 9Apr.14

2nd Lieutenants. (8)
Cholmeley, G.H.6Dec.13
Forbes, K. 2Jan.14
Furze, C. 18Feb.14
25Aug.11
Cartwright, G.H.G.M.
19Feb.14
Long, C. W. 9June14

Adjutant.
Oppenheim, A. C.,
Lt. K. R. Rif. C.,
capt. 1Jan.13

Quarter-Master.
Petersen, J. R. S.,
hon. lt. 29Apr.14

Medical Officers.
Ducat, Maj. A. D.,
M.B., TD,
R.A.M.C. (T.F.)
(attd.) 31Mar.08
25Dec.95
Price, Lt. F. W., M.B.,
R.A.M.C. (T.F.)
(attd.) 28Sept.10

Chaplain.
London, Rt. Hon.
and Rt. Rev. A. F.,
Lord Bishop of,
D.D., LL.D., Chapl.
1st Class (T.F.)
(attd.) 1Apr.08
15May01
[Uniform—Green.
Facings—Black.]

Cadet Unit affiliated.
Coopers' Company's
School Cadet Corps.

6th (City of London) Battalion, The London Regiment, (Rifles).

"South Africa, 1900-02."
57a, Farringdon Road,E.C.

Hon. Colonel.
✗ⒸⒸ. ℳ. Roberts, Field-
Marshal Rt. Hon. F. S.
Earl,K.G.,K.P.,G.CB.,
O.M.,G.C.S.I.,G.C.I.E.
vD, Col. Commdt. R.
A., Col. I. Gds. [R]
24Sept.87

Lt.-Colonel.
✗Moore, G. D. M.,
Maj.ret. pay 27Sept.12

Majors. (2)
p.s.Lockett, E. T. Ⓒ 9Oct.05
Stokes, E. 1Feb.13

Captains. (8)
p.s.Myer, E. A. 23Nov.01
p.s.Mildren, W. F. 18Nov.02
p.s.Schwersee, M. H.
(H) 24Mar.03
p.s.Boothby, R. C. 14Nov.06
p.s.Tucker, F.G.(H) 8Dec.08
p.s.Phillips, E. L. 22Jan.09
p.s.Cotton, M.A.F. 1Feb.13

Lieutenants. (8)
Lyon, W. R. (H) (Asst.
Dist. Commr., Sierra
Leone, 27 Nov.12)
7July10
Valentine, G. 9Mar.11
Powell, G,N,F. 25July12
Myer, H. D. 23 Sept.12
Hughes, M. W. 8Jan,13
Ashby, G. W. 1Feb.13
Cooke, S. T. 7Mar.14
Hughes, W. 9May14

2nd Lieutenants. (8)
Sherrin, F. J. 12Feb.13
Kinsley, L. H. 26Apr.13
Wardhaugh, T.W.
20Oct.13
Lester, A. M. 7Mar.14
Neely, G. H. 17Mar.14
Löwy, J. E. 7May14
McLaughlin, E. C.
10June14

Adjutant.
✗Seagrim, A. H., [L]
Capt. Leins. R.
5Mar.13

Quarter-Master.
Thomas, F. H. H.,
hon. lt. 20May11
Cavanagh, B. G.,
hon. lt. 6June14

Medical Officer.
✗Collen, Lt. G. D.,
M.D., R.A.M.C.
(T.F.) (attd) 16Dec.09
✗Bate, Lt. J. B., M.D.,
R.A.M.C. (T.F.) (attd.)
17 June 11

Chaplain.
Wilkinson, Rev.
A. E., Chapl.
4thClass(T.F.)
(attd.) 27Feb.13
[Uniform—Green.
Facings—Scarlet.]

Cadet Unit affiliated.
1st Cadet Company 6 Bn.
Lond. R.

7th (City of London) Battalion, The London Regiment.

A representation of St.
Paul's Cathedral.
"South Africa, 1900-02."
24, SunSt, FinsburySq., E.C.

Hon. Colonel.
p. Stevenson, E. C., vD(Hon.
Col.ret.Vols.)(t)15Oct.04

Lt.-Colonel.
Hood, G. A. A., Visct.,
p.s.c. (l) Maj.ret. pay
(Res. of Off.) (In command) 27Nov.12
p.s.Faux, E., vD, hon. c.
1Dec.04

Majors. (2)
p. ✗Berkeley, C.W.,TD.,
hon.l.c.(Hon. Capt.
in Army 1Dec.00)
(Q) 12Nov.04

Captains. (8)
p.s Enoch, C. D.[l]
Ⓒ 17Nov.97
p.s. Barnes, H. D. 20June00
p.s. Casson, W. (t) 6Jan.03
p.s. Laurie, A.D. (Q) 7Apr.03
p.s. Prince, A. G. ✗Feb.07
Hosking, S. L. (Q)
1Jan.12
Green, C J.S.(Q)29Feb.12
King-Church, C. E.
(H) I, of M. 30Apr.14

Lieutenants. (8)
Green, H. S.(q)1Aug.11
Holtzapffel, J. G. H.
1Aug.11
Fletcher,J.H.B.
Ⓒ (t) 1Jan.12
Davis, F. M. 1Feb.13

Lieutenants—contd.
Tims, R. D. M. 1June14
Head, H. G. 1June14
Ward, D. E. 1June14
Rushworth,H.M.
1June14

2nd Lieutenants. (8)
Rushworth, T. 16Oct.13
Head, J. L. 16Oct.13
Ferguson, A. A.10Dec.13
Smith, A. J. 20Dec.13
Smith, W. S. 20Dec 13

Inst. of Musk.
King-Church, C. E.,
capt. 1Oct.13

Adjutant.
Foster, R. T., Capt.
Notts. & Derby.R.
1Dec.11

Quarter-Master.
Roche, G. D., hon. lt.
20Oct.09
Medical Officers.
Hayes, Lt. J. G.,
R.A.M.C. (T.F.)
(attd.) 30May13
Chaplains.
Smith, Rev. H. R. C.,
D.D., TD, Chapl. 3rd
Class (T.F.) (attd.)
27May10
27May93
[Uniform—Scarlet.
Facings—Buff.]

8th (City of London) Battalion, The London Regiment, (Post Office Rifles).

"Egypt, 1882."
"South Africa, 1899-1902."
130, Bunhill Row, E.C.

Hon. Colonel.
H. H. AdolphusC,A.A.E.,
G.P.L.L., Duke of Teck,
G.C.B., G.C.V.O.,
C.M.G., Bt. Lt.-Col.
1 L. G., Personal
A.D.C. to the King,
19July12

Lt.-Colonel.

✗Liverpool, A. W. de B.
S., Earl of, G.C.M.G.,
M.V.O.,Maj.ret.pay
(Maj. Res. of Off.) Ⓒ
(Q),(H), (a) 30Oct.11

Infantry. Territorial Force.

London Regt.—contd.
8th Bn.—contd.

Majors (2)

✗Labouchere, F. A.,
 TD. (*Lt. Res. of Off.*)
 1Apr.13
Hood, E., TD 15July14

Captains. (8)

p.s.✗McClintock,
 H. F., hon. m. (t)
 9Aug.02
p.s.✗Preece,P.J.,TD(*Hon.
 Capt. in Army* 1June
 02) (*Lt. Res. of Off.*)
 hon. m. (t) 9Dec.02
p.s. Chaytor, A. H. 18Dec.05
p.s.✗Owen, F. 18Dec.05
p.s. Maxwell, A. 20Jan.08
p.s. Little, D'A. H. (*H*)
 3July09
p.s. Wynne, H. (*H*) 5July11
Davie, B.G. 5July11
Reynolds, L. G. S.
 15July14

Lieutenants. (9)

Milne, D. D. 1June10
King, H. H.Ⓢ 4Feb.11
West, L. R. E. 1May11
Barnes. G. G. 1May11
Gore Browne,E.15Jan.12
Dale, J. A. 30 Sept.12

2nd Lieutenants. (8)

s. Hatfield, R. B. 1Jan.12
Russell,D L.(*H*)13Mar13
Powell, E B. 29July13
Blight, E. C. 24Dec.13
MacLehose, N. C.
 24Dec.13
Vince, W. B. Ⓢ 23Jan.14

Adjutant.

✗Morris, T. H P.,
 Capt. Rif. Brig.
 1Dec.13

Quarter-Master.

p. ✗Williams, W., hon.
 m. 12Feb.06

Medical Officers.

Beard, Capt. T.,
 R.A.M.C. (T.F.)
 (*attd.*) 21Jan.05
Hadden, A. R. 27Mar.11
 21Dec.01

Chaplain

Pearce, Rev. Canon
 E.H., *M.A.*, Chapl.
 3rd Class (T.F.)
 (*attd.*) 1Apr.08
 4Aug.97
Hine-Haycock, Rev.
 T. R., *M.A.*, Chapl.
 4th Class (T.F.)
 (*attd.*) 1Jan.13

[Uniform—*Green.*
Facings—*Black*].

9th (County of London) Battalion, The London Regiment, (Queen Victoria's Rifles).

"South Africa, 1900-02."

56. Davies Street, Berkeley Square, W.

Hon. Colonel.

✗Campbell, Lt.-Gen.
 W. P.. C.B. 22Nov.13

Lt.-Colonel.

p. ✗Shipley, R. B., TD.
 (*Hon.Capt.in Army*
 1Dec.00,(*t*)(*H*) 11Dec.12

~~R Berry 16 Sept~~ ~~Col of Roll~~ p.
 ~~Majors. (2)~~ ~~1914~~

Dickins, V, W. F., VD
 (*Lt. Res. of Off.*) Ⓖ
 (Q) (*H*) 11Dec.12
Lees, T, P. (Q) 15Aug.13

Captains. (6)

p.s.Shea, S. V. (Q)(*H*),
 I. of M. 8Dec.06
p.s.Sampson, S. J. M.
 (*H*) (*Q*) 5Feb.07
p.s.Flemming, H.(q)
 23 Jun12
p.s.Cox, R. W. (t) 11Dec.12
p.s.Warren, R. G. 25Jan.13

Lieutenants. (8)

Cox, H. E. L. 4Mar.11
Lindsey-Renton,
 R. H. (*H*) 23 June 12
Bolton, F. W.
 (*H*) 1Nov.12
Fargus, F.B.A.11Dec.12
Hunter, J.E.A. 25Jan.13
Fazakerley-Westby,
 G. B. J. 23July13

2nd Lieutenants. (8)

Hamilton, E. W.
 15July12
Andrews, J. C. 1Sept.12
Rashleigh, H. P.
 Ⓢ 16Nov.12
Cowtan, A. L. 16Nov.12
Johnson,K.W. 22May13
Hunter, J. B. 30June13
Nichols, J. 1Oct.13

Inst. of Musk.

Shea, S. V., *capt.*
 18Mar.10

Adjutant.

✗Culme-Seymour, G.,
 Capt. K.R.Rif.C.
 1Jan.13

Quarter-Master.

✗O'Shea, T., Qr.-Mr.
 (*hon. m.*) ret. pay,
 hon. m. 2Jan.11

Medical Officers.

p. Roe, Capt. W, F.,
 R.A.M.C. (T.F.)
 (*attd.*) 9Mar.07
 9Sept.03
p. Macfee, Capt. W. G.,
 R.A.M.C. (T.F.)
 (*attd.*) 4June07
 4 Dec.03

Chaplain.

Sinclair, Rev. R. B.,
 M.A., Chapl. 4th
 Class (T.F.) (*attd.*)
 1 Apr.08
 13Aug.02

[Uniform—*Green.*
Facings—*Scarlet.*]

10th (County of London) Battalion, The London Regiment (Hackney).

49, The Grove, Hackney,
 N.E.

Hon. Colonel.

Fenton-Jones, W. F.
 17Oct.12

Lt.-Colonel.

p.s. Cobbett, G. T. B.,
 VD,hon. c.(Q) 21Sept.12
 15Nov.06

Majors. (2)

Walker, E. J. (q)17Oct.12
Kittoe, M. F. M.
 S. (Q) 17Oct.12

Captains (8)

p.s. Ford-Moore, A.P.
 (*Hon. Maj. ret. Vols.*),
 hon. m. (Q) 17Oct.12
 5Apr.11
Mann, T.B.D. 17Oct.12
 (*H*) *I. of M.* 25Jan.12
Fenton-Jones, J. C.
 17Oct.12
Cowley,G.E. (Q) (*H*)
 4Mar.13
 10Dec.11
✗Russell,W.P.M,5Apr13
Clarke, F.A.S.Ⓔ27Oct.13
Walser, A. A. Ⓔ27Oct.13
Edmonds, A.G.
 (*H*) 14Feb.14

Lieutenants. (8)

Isard, C. B. 15July13
Scrivener,A.W.24Nov.13
Turner, S. 24Nov.13
Hurrell,C.J.R. 3Dec.13
Cobbett, S. T. 3Dec.13
Prestige,H.H.C.3Dec.13

2nd Lieutenants. (8)

Hertslet, W.E. 10May13
Pullar, L. J. L 10May13
Hinde, H. P. 6June13
Farmar,C.H.B.12Nov.13
Douglas, G. A. P.
 12Nov.13
Williams, R. W. 2Jan.14
 18Dec.12
Glover. H. J. 6July14
Prior, L. P. 6July14
Betbeder, G. L.29July14

Inst. of Musk.

Mann, T. B. D.,
 capt. 2Jan.14

Adjutant.

✗Prittie, Hon. H.C.
 O'C., Capt.
 Rif. Brig. 23Nov.12

Quarter-Master.

✗Bass, W., Qr.-
 Mr. (*hon. capt.*)
 ret. pay, hon. capt
 17Oct.12

Medical Officers.

✗Morcom Harneis,Lt.
 T. W., R.A.M.C. (T.F.)
 (*attd.*) 17Oct.12

Chaplain.

Rainforth, Rev. J. D.,
 B.A., Chapl. 4th
 Class (T.F.) (*attd.*)
 9Nov.12

[Uniform—*Scarlet.*
Facings—*White.*]

| 1585 | 1586 | 1587 | 1588 |

Infantry. Territorial Force.

London Regt.—contd.

11th (County of London) Battalion, The London Regiment, (Finsbury Rifles).

"South Africa, 1900-02."

17, Penton Street, Pentonville, N.

Hon. Colonel.
Penton, F. T., VD, late Capt. 4 D.G. 4Apr.83

Lt.-Colonel.
p.s.✗Byrne, S. C., TD (Hon.Capt.in Army 1Dec.00) (Lt. Res. of Off.)(H) 27May14

Maurice H Grant 16 Sep/14
Late of Battⁿ

Majors (2).
Davis, W. R. (H) 13Aug.13

Captains (8).
p.s. Shearsmith, H. W. (H) 24Oct.00
p.s. Tasker, R. I. 12Apr.02
p.s. Murray, W. 18Feb.04
p.s. Dawes, E. J. (H)9July04
p.s. Davis, G. F. ⑱(H) 15May05
p. Day, H. J. L. 4May13
Lewer, A. J. (Q) (H) 10May13
✗Windsor, A. H., I. of M. 13Aug.13

Lieutenants. (8)
(p.) Garraway,F.H.14July09
(p.) Collins, H. A. D. (q) 14July09
Lewthwaite, A. T. 15July11
Tattersall, P. C. P. 10May13
Phillips, P. H. 15July13
Hooper, G. M. 13Aug.13

2nd Lieutenants. (8)
McBride, F. C. 7Oct.13
Maxwell, J. 24Jan.14
Comber, W. G. 9May14
Ground, E. G. 9May14
Kitby, G. S. 15May14
Harding, A. F. 15May14
Hunt, W. 3June14

Inst. of Musk.
✗Windsor, A. H., capt. 1Apr.09

Adjutant.
✗Crosbie, J. P. G., Capt. Rif. Brig. 18Nov.12

Quarter-Master.
✗Tutin, T. A., hon. lt. 7Feb.12

Medical Officers.
p. Malcolm, Capt. W. A., M.B., R.A.M.C.(T.F.) (attd.) 21Apr.06 21Oct.02
p. Smelt, Capt. C. A. C., M.B., R.A.M.C.(T.F.) (attd.) 27Nov.06 24Feb.13

Chaplain.
Must, Rev. H., Chapl. 4th Class (T.F.) (attd.) 15Feb.11

[Uniform—Green. Facings—Scarlet.]

12th (County of London) Battalion, The London Regiment, (The Rangers).

"South Africa, 1900-02."

Chenies Street, Bedford Square, W.C.

Hon. Colonel.
Woodall, Sir C., Knt. 9Nov.08

Lt.-Colonel.
p. Wilton, T., TD ⑱ 8Apr.11

Majors (2)
p.s. Bayliffe, A. D., TD. 8July12
Syms, A. G. E. ⑱ 17Sept.12

Captains (8).
p.s.✗Challen, H. G. 28Aug.06
p.s.✗Hoare, V. R. (q) 25Feb.09
 2Nov.06
p.s. Wilson, K. R. 11May09
Foucar, J. L. 7May10
Jones, L. F. 2Dec.11
Freeman, R. C. ⑱ 5Dec.12
Edgell, J. 5Dec.12
Parker, J. E. (H) I. of M. 14June13

Lieutenants. (8)
Tucker, G. S. 20Aug.10
Arbuthnot, A. H. 2Aug.11
Studd, L. F. 7May12
Tattersall, S. E. V. 7May12
Worthington, W.G. (H) 5Dec.12
Hardy, C. 14June13
Wyatt, G. M. G. 12Nov.13
Stein, L. J. 4Feb.14

2nd Lieutenants. (8)
Wilton, N. 10Oct.12
Wightwick, H. W. 21Nov.12
Hunter, R. W. 19Feb.13
Balfour, G. A. 14Apr.14
Perkins, H. O. 8June14
 19June13
Walford, L. N. 8July14

Inst. of Musk.
Parker, J. E., capt. 17Dec.13

Adjutant.
Venning, W. K., Capt. D. of Corn. L.I. 1Jan.12

Quarter-Master.
✗Davies, W. H., Qr.-Mr. (hon. capt.) ret. pay, hon. capt. 4Jan.14

Medical Officers.
p. Ehrmann, Maj. A., R.A.M.C. (T.F.) (attd.) 9Jan.11
 24May99
Denne, Lt. F. V., R.A.M.C. (T.F.) (attd.) 16Mar.11

Chaplain.
Morrow, Rev. W. E. R., M.A., Chapl. 4th Class (T.F.) (attd.) 18Nov.13

[Uniform—Green. Facings—Scarlet.]

13th (County of London) Battalion, The London Regiment, (Kensington).

The arms of Kensington, "Quid nobis ardui."

"South Africa, 1900-02."

Iverna Gardens, Kensington, W.

Hon. Colonel.
✗Turner, Maj. Gen. Sir A. E., K.C.B., ret. pay [R] q.s., Col. Comdt. R.A. 29Nov.06

Lt.-Colonel.
p. Lewis, F. G., TD ⑱ 2Feb.10
R. J. McLean, T.F.R.Oseme

Majors (2).
p.s ✗Stafford, H. J. 14 Sh/14
(Hon.Capt.in Army 31Aug.02) (t) (a) (b) (H) 1Nov.07
Campbell, H. 17Sept.13

Infantry. Territorial Force.

London Regt.—*contd.*

13th Bn.—*contd.*

Captains (8).
p. Prismall, A. (q) (*H*) 10Dec.07
p.s. Parnell, E. L. (*H*) 1Aug.08
p.s. Thompson, G. 22Jan.11
Barnett, H.W. 20Jan.12
p.s. Kimber, E. G. (*t*) (*H*) 1Nov.12
15Nov.99
Herne, A. C. 18Apr.14
Dickens, C. C. 20Apr.14

Lieutenants. (8)
Whitty, H. N 1Feb.10
Herbert, R.B. ⑤ 10June12
Keen, E. B. 1Apr.13
Howard, C. N. C. 4May13
Fox, C. J. 1Oct.13
Macgregor, R. M. 4July14

2nd Lieutenants. (8)
Bamber, M. C. K. 20May13
Field, E. V. 12July13
Hall, G. L. D. 12July13
Burn, W. G. 12July13
Sewell, N. O. 12July13
Cohen. L. L. 2Nov.13
Strong, C. C. (*late 2nd Lt. Res. of Off.*) 6Dec.13
Kindersley, B. J. F. C. 6Dec.13
Venables, C. 8Apr.14
Leigh-Pemberton, T. E. G. 12May14

Adjutant.
Thompson, G., Capt. Conn. Rang. 1Jan.13

Quarter-Master.
✗Ridley, A., *hon. lt.* 1June11

Medical Officers.
Colebrook, Capt, L., M.B., R.A.M.C. (T.F.) (*attd.*) 3Apr.14
3Oct.10

Chaplain.
Pennefather, Rev. Preb. S. E., *M.A.,* Chapl. 3rd Class (T.F.) (*attd.*) 17Aug.08
17Aug.98

——

Cadet Units affiliated.
Kensington and Hammersmith Navy League Boys' Brigade.

St. Peter's Cadet Company.

[Uniform—*Grey.*
Facings—Scarlet.]

14th (County of London) Battalion, The London Regiment (London Scottish).

In front of a circle inscribed with the motto, "Strike Sure," St. Andrew's Cross surmounted by a lion rampant.

"South Africa, 1900-02."

59, Buckingham Gate, Westminster, S.W.

Lt.-Colonel.
p.s. Malcolm, G. A., TD (*t*) 15Feb.11

John N Grey Col of Bath 16/9/14

Majors. (2)
✗Green, B. C., TD, (*Hon.Capt.in Army* 18Aug.02) 1Jan.10
✗Torrance, J. H. (*Hon. Lt. in Army* 26July01) 18Aug.11

Captains. (8)
p.s. Lindsay, J.H.(Q)17Feb03
p.s. Lindsay F. H. (*t*) 27Nov.05
p.s. Clowes, G. C. K. (*p*) 4Dec.05
p.s. Monro, E. G. (*t*) 1Jan.10
p.s. White, J. S. (*t*) 1Nov.12
p.s. ✗Dunsmore, R. (*t*) 1Jan.14
p.s. Cartwright, H. S. (*t*) 8Jan.14
p.s. Low, C. J. (*t*) 15Apr.14

Lieutenants. (8)
p.s Alexander, R. D. T. 4Dec.05
(p.s.) Downie, F. 1Jan.10
Henderson, I. M. 13Sept.11
(p.) Paterson, J. 18Sept11
Stebbing, H.E. 1Nov.12
(p) Parker Smith, A. C. H. 1Nov.13
Blaikie, A. 1Jan.14
Stirling, E. M. 8Jan.14
Farquharson, J. C. L. 8Jan.14
Lindsey-Renton, L. S. ⑤ 15Apr.14

2nd Lieutenants. (8)
Ker Gulland, R. G. (*H*) I. of M. 24July10
Taylor, C. C. 25Nov.11
Grant, D. L. 6Dec.11
Young, W. A. 27Apr.12
Palmer, H. C. 27Apr.12
Anderson, W. H. 19Mar.13

Inst. of Musk.
Ker Gulland, R. G., 2nd lt. 15Apr.12

Adjutant.
Campbell, C. H., Capt. Cam'n Highrs. 3Feb.13

Quarter-Master.
✗Webb, W.E., Qr.-Mr. (*hon. capt.*) ret.pay, hon. capt. 21May14

Medical Officers.
✗Macnab, Lt. A., M.B., F.R.C.S. R.A.M.C.(T.F.) (*attd.*) 1Mar.11

Chaplain.
Fleming, Rev. A., *M.A., D.D.* [C.S.], Chapl. 4th Class (T.F.) (*attd.*) 1Apr.08
3Nov.00

[Uniform—*Grey,*
Facings—*Blue.*]

15th (County of London) Battalion, The London Regiment (Prince of Wales's Own, Civil Service Rifles).

"South Africa, 1900-02."

Somerset House, Strand, W.C.

Lt.-Colonel.
p.s. Hayes, R. G.,TD (*t*) 11Apr.12

Majors. (2)
Chew, R. (q) 11Apr.12
Strange, E. F., TD (*H*) 6June13

Captains. (8)
p.s. Kirkby, W. T. ⑤ (*t*) 1Apr.08
p.s. Saunders, A. E. (*H*)(*t*) 1Apr.08
p.s. ✗Newson, W. F. K. ⑤ 9Feb.12
p.s. Bell, A. D. (*H*) 9Feb.12
Warne, H. F.M. ⑦ 16Mar.12
p.s. ✗Oliver, A. A. (*t*) 11Apr.12
Higginbottom, H. E. 12Mar.13
Tarver, F. F. 6June13

Infantry. Territorial Force.

London Regt.—contd.
15th Bn.—contd.

Lieutenants. (8)

Coles, E. A. (H)
  I. of M. 9Feb.12
✗Adamson, T.L. 9Feb.12
✗Trembath, A. E.
  (*Hon. Lt. in Army* 7Feb.03) 9Feb.12
Kinsman, J. C. P. 16Mar.12
Gaze, A. W. 15July13
Roberts, A. 15July13
Radice, F. R. 4July14
Crofts, H. M. 4July14

2nd Lieutenants. (8)

Gaze, G. A.⑤ 26June12
Lewis, H. T. 31Jan.13
Gold, R. J. S. 8Feb.13
Davies, L. 3May13
Stokes, G. E. 14June13
Chalmers, R. 13May14
Benké, A. C. M. 22July14
Sharratt, T. H. 29July14

Inst. of Musk.
Coles, E. A., *lt.* 8July12

Adjutant.
Parish, F. W., Lt.
K. R. Rif. C.,
capt. 22Nov.13

Quarter-Master.
Clark, W. H. D.,
hon. lt. 2Feb.10

Medical Officers.
Branthwaite, R. W.,
Surg.-Capt. (C)
  2Apr.04
  31July05
Hamill, Lt. J. M.,
R.A.M.C (T.F.)
(*attd.*) 6Aug.13

Chaplain.
Henson, *Very Rev.*
H. H., D.D. (*Dean of Durham*) Chapl.
4th Class (T.F.)
(*attd.*) 8July10

[Uniform—*Grey.*
Facings—*Blue.*]

Cadet Unit affiliated.
2nd (Civil Service) C. B.
Lond. R.

16th (County of London) Battalion, The London Regiment, (Queen's Westminster Rifles).

"South Africa, 1900-02."

Queen's Hall, 58, Buckingham Gate, Westminster, S.W.

Lt.-Colonel.
Shoolbred, R., TD,
(q) 15Feb.11

*Crawfurd A G Clerk
Lt Col of Battn 16/9/14*

Majors. (2)
✗Cohen, J. W., TD (t)
  ⑥ (*Hon. Lt. in Army* 1 Dec. 00)
  15Feb.11
p.s.✗Tyrwhitt, N. B., *hon. m.* (*Capt. Res. of Off.*) ⑥ (q) 28Nov.11

Captains. (8)
p s.Dodd, E. A., TD,
  hon. m. 4July00
p.s.Glasier, E.B.(t)29Aug.03
p.s.✗Lambert, G. H. ⑥ 21Mar.05
p.s.Low, S. (t) ⑥ 25Oct.09
p.s.Henriques, J.Q. 1Nov.10
p.s.Challis, L. S. (H) 20Jan.12
p.s.Whitmore, J. B.29July14

Lieutenants. (8)
(p.s.)Cox, E. G. H. 17Jan.10
(p.s.)Townsend-Green, H.R.
  1Nov.10
James, C. de B. 20Jan.12
Hoskyns, O. P. L.
  23Mar.12
Waley, E. G. S.26June12
Glasier, P. M. 9Aug.13
Savill, S. R. 29July14

2nd Lieutenants. (8)
Townsend Green, S.L.
  1Nov.11
Corlett, H. D. 27Apr.12
Baber, J. B. 1Nov.12
Green, J. A. 19July13

Adjutant.
Flower, H. J., Lt.
K. R. Rif. C.,
capt. 23Nov.13

Quarter-Master.
p. Pridmore, A. S.,
TD, *hon. m.* 12Apr.07

Medical Officers.
p. Morris, Capt. C.
A., C.V.O., M.B.,
R.A.M.C., (T.F.)
(*attd.*) 30Apr.02
  4Feb.99
Rowntree, Lt. C.W.,
M.B., F.R.C.S.18Feb.14
  18Nov.11

Chaplain.
Ryle, *Rt. Rev. Bishop*
H. E., C.V.O., D.D.,
Dean of Westminster,
Chapl.1st Class (T.F.)
(*attd.*) 1Apr.06
  21Jan.05

[Uniform—*Grey.*
Facings—*Scarlet.*]

Cadet Unit affiliated.
The Queen's Westminster
Cadet Corps.

17th (County of London) Battalion, The London Regiment, (Poplar and Stepney Rifles).

"South Africa, 1900-02."
66, Tredegar Road, Bow, E.

Hon. Colonel.
p. Bryan, W. B., VD,
hon. c. 27June03

Lt.-Colonel.
Godding, J. 19Mar.13

Majors. (2)
Newman, T. G. W., TD
  16Aug.13
Oxley, F. J. (Q) 4Feb.14

Captains. (8)
p.s.Bubbers, W. R.
(b)(H) 21May08
Evans, F. E. 4Dec.13
Bawden, V. C. (H) 4Dec.13
Grimwood, F.R. 4Dec.13
Wheatley, A.(H)
  I. of M. 4Dec.13
Lieutenants. (8)
(p.)Hands, A.S. 1Oct.09
Caldwell, H. H. 1Apr.12
Hatch, W. E. J. 16July13
Daniels, R. J. 16July13
Piercy, W. A. 4Dec.13
Thompson, F.S. 4Dec.13
Downes, P. W. 20Nov.13
✗Allen, F. J. 2May14
2nd Lieutenants. (8)
Walters, A. B. 19Mar.13
O'Brien, K.R. 15Apr.13
Chandler, E. A. B.
  25Apr.13
Clarke, H. M. 9May13
Medwin, T. 17May13
Rylett, S. H. 1June13
Wright. H. C. 5July13
Crofts, F. W. 23Jan.14
Martin, C. G. 1May14
Withers, H. D. 5May14
Carpenter, R. L.6May14
Clarke, W. A. 13June14
Robb, T. D. 22June14
Inst. of Musk
Wheatley, A., *capt.*
  25Aug.13

Adjutant.
✗Collison-Morley, H.
D., Capt. E. Kent R.
  15Dec.11

Quarter-Master.
p. Evans, F., TD, *hon. m.*
  23Apr.02
capt. 27Feb.01
p.s.Swain, Maj. J. S.,
R.A.M.C. (T.F.)
(*attd.*) 23Oct.10
  29Mar.99
White, Lt. F. H.,
R.A.M.C.(T.F.)
(*attd.*) 17Apr.14
Chaplain.
Mason, *Rev. Preb.*
H. A., Chapl.
2nd Class (T.F.)
(*attd.*) 24Apr.12
  24Apr.97

[Uniform—*Green.*
Facings—*Black.*]

Infantry. Territorial Force.

London Regt.—contd.

18th (County of London) Battalion, The London Regiment, (London Irish Rifles).

Within a wreath of shamrock leaves the Harp and Crown.

"South Africa, 1900-02."

Duke of York's Headquarters, Chelsea, S.W.

Hon. Colonel.
× Field · Marshal H.R.H. Arthur W. P. A., Duke of Connaught and Strathearn, K.G., K.T., K.P., G.C.B., G.C.S.I., G.C.M.G., G.C.I.E., G.C.V.O., VD, Col. G.Gds. and A.S.C. and Col.-in-Chief 6 Dns., High. L.I., R Dub. Fus., and Rif.Brig., Personal A.D.C. to the King 30June71

Lt.-Colonel.
p.s. ×Concanon, E. G., D.S.O., TD (Hon. Lt. in Army 1Dec.00) 5Nov.13

Majors. (2)
p. Mathews, W. J., TD (t)(H) 22Dec.10
Allen, J. S. 5Nov.13

Captains. (8)
p.s. Healy, H. M., TD, hon. m. 27Jan.03
p.s. Kimmitt, R. R., late Capt.5 Bn.R.Muns. Fus. (H), I. of M. 2Nov.09
Beresford, C. 28June12
de Montmorency, J.H.B.(A sst.Dist. Offr., S. Provs. Nigeria, 12Jan.14) 15May13
×Ommanney, C. C. (Hon. Lt. in Army 2 Sept. 02) (Lt. Res. of Off.) ⊛ 15May13
Frisby, P. S. 15May13
Curtis, R. W. 18Apr.14

Lieutenants. (8)
Trinder, J. R. 30May12
Law, R. D. 21July12
Hobbs, R. V. H. 24Oct.12
p.s. Barnes, H. (H) 1June13
Harrison, J.C. 21Aug.13
Willock, G. C. B. ⑤ 27Nov.13
Macreight, A. W. J. 14Feb.14

2nd Lieutenants. (8)
Hutchinson, S. J. 13July12
Litton, E. L. 11Nov.12
Bainsmith, B. 17June13
Shore, B. C. G. 10July13
Dale, T. E 14Jan.14
Dale, B. G. 16Jan.14
Rich, J. H. B. 27Apr.14
Steele, E. 24June14

Inst. of Musk.
Kimmitt, R. R., capt. 13Nov.13

Adjutant.
Hamilton, A.P., Lt. R.W.Surr.R., capt. 25Apr.14

Quarter-Master.
Webb, P. L., hon. lt. 7Mar.12

Medical Officer.
p. Spooner, Capt. C.A., R.A.M.C. (T.F.) (attd.) 4Dec.08 5June05

Chaplains.
Selwyn, Rev. W.M., Chapl.4th Class(T.F.) (attd.) 15Mar.11
St.John, Rev.S.B.M. (R.C.) Chapl. 4th Class (T.F.) (attd.) 18Feb.13

[Uniform—Green. Facings—Light Green.]

19th (County of London) Battalion, The London Regiment, (St. Pancras).

The figure of St. Pancras. "South Africa, 1900-02."

76, High Street, Camden Town, N.W.

Hon. Colonel.
Brown, Sir W. J., K.C.B., VD (Hon. Col. ret. Vols.)10May99

Lt.-Colonel,
p.s. Cattell, G. T., TD (Q) (H) 1Apr.08

Majors. (2)
p. Hall, W. G. C. (H) (Q) 1Mar.09
×Kennard, A. C. H., Capt. ret. pay (Res. of Off.) 19Mar.13

Captains. (8)
p.s. Bantick, S. H. 8Feb.07
p.s. Bantick, C. J. (H) I. of M. 13Mar.09
Davis, E. J. ⑫ (H) 18Sept.10
Danby, L. J. (H) 22Feb.11
etson, G. ⑫ 19Sept.11
p.s.× Kershaw, H. V. (Q) (Asst. Accountant, Rly., Uganda, 23Oct.12) 17Apr.12
Riley, A. C. 16May13

Lieutenants. (8)
Haskins, S. C. 19Sept.11
Newman, A.D. 19Sept.11
Davis, L. J. 13June12
De Meza, J. ⑧ 20Nov.12
Pommerol, J. G. L. (L) 9July14
Pass, J. A. 9July14
Bantick, R.A.J. 9July14
Jackson, S. R. 9July14

2nd Lieutenants. (8)
Fox, H. 26July11
Raynor, R. O. 7Jan.13
Hanewinkel, E. E. 15June11
Frank, J. L. ⑧ 22Apr.13 4Apr.13
Pusch, F. L. 9May13
Hore, K. S. 18June14

Inst. of Musk.
Bantick, C. J., capt. 29Mar.11

Adjutant
Needham, D. A. F., Capt. R. Fus. 6Mar.14

Quarter-Master.
Rosam, W. R., hon. lt. 1June12

Medical Officer.
Hanks, Capt. A. G.T., R.A.M.C. (T.F.) (attd.) 6Oct.13 6Apr.10

Chaplain.
Metcalfe, Rev. E. L., M.A., Chapl.4th Class (T. F.)(attd.) 1Apr.08 8Feb.07

[Uniform—Scarlet, Facings—Green.]

20th (County of London) Battalion, The London Regiment, (Blackheath and Woolwich).

"South Africa, 1900-02."

Holly Hedge House, Blackheath, S.E.

Lt.-Colonel.
p. Christmas, H. A. ⊛ 8Apr.11
Majors. (2)
Pownall, A. (q) 8Apr.11
p. Dodd, A. J. ⑫ (H) 4Dec.12

Captains. (8)
p s. Fitzgerald, E. (H) I. of M. 1May09
Bentley, F.C.(Q)(H) (attd O.T.C.) 3May09
p.s. Cook, J. O, 6Aug.10
Edwards, G. J. 7Oct.11
Hefford, C. R. 20Jan.12
Hooper, B. L. 20July12
p.s. Franklin, A. H. (late Capt. 1 V.B. Essex R.) (H) 17Dec.13

Lieutenants. (8)
Dyer, W. F. 4Dec.c0
Bell, J. J. 20Dec.11
Honeybourne, H. C. 26June12
Cowie, A. G. (Empld. in British N. Borneo, 5Oct.11) 20July12
Escombe, W. M. L. 20July12
Goodwin, H.T. 15July13
Williams, G. 22Nov.13

2nd Lieutenants. (8)
Stanger, P. J. 1July14

Inst. of Musk.
Fitzgerald, E., capt. 1Feb.12

Adjutant.
×Norman, E. H., Capt.R.W.KentR. 21Jan.14

Quarter-Master.

Medical Officer.
Matthews, Capt. S. R. R., R.A.M.C.(T.F.) (attd.) 1Nov.12 1May09

Chaplain.
Kendall, Rev.J.F., M.A., Chapl.4th Class (T.F.) (attd.) 13Apr.14

[Uniform—Scarlet, Facings—Black.]

Infantry. Territorial Force.

21st (County of London) Battalion, The London Regiment (First Surrey Rifles).

"South Africa, 1900-02."
4, Flodden Road, Camberwell, S.E.

Hon. Colonel.
p. *Villiers, E.*, VD, Col., A.D.C. (H) (Hon. Col. ret. Vols.) 2Dec.02

Lt.-Colonel.
Tomlin, M. J. B. (Hon. Maj. ret. Mila.) 30June11

H. S. Coldicott late Batt. 10/9/14

Majors (2).
Fletcher, B. 3Sept.11
Morris, W. F. 9Aug.12

Captains (8).
p.s.✗Richards, H. P. (†) 8Oct.08
Heslop, C. W. B. (Q) 9June09
Saffery, W. H. (H) 6May11
Hutchence, A. (H) 9Dec.11
I. of M.
Leman, H. C. (†) 27Apr.12
Wright, S. (H) 7Dec.12
Crowe, E. G. 5Apr.13
Walford, Q. 26Apr.13

Lieutenants. (8)
Bratt, L. A. 10Dec 11
Drake, H.W. 1Dec.12
(Asst. Auditor, Nigeria 4July14)
Heppell, T. R. 23Nov.13
Mobberley, G. M. 24Nov.13
Smith, H. T. 25Nov.13
Puckle, R. A. 26Nov.13
Waghorn, H.C. 11May14

2nd Lieutenants. (8)
Spencer, E. E. 21May13
Pidsley, W. G. 9Sept.13
Camm, G. F. 17Oct.13
Hull, L. H. R. 13Dec.13
Bloy, A. W. B. S. F. 15Dec.13
Fritsch, H.F.R. 18Feb.14
Brown, S. D. 23Feb.14
Savel, R. 26Mar.14
Moberly, A. H. 8Apr.14

Inst. of Musk.
Hutchence, A., *capt.* 5Nov.12

Adjutant.
✗Kennedy, H.B.P.L., Capt. K.R. Rif. C. 1Sept.13

Quarter-Master.
p. p.s. Durham, G. A., TD, hon. maj. 26June01
capt. 26June01

Medical Officers.
Robinson, Lt. H. H., R.A.M.C. (T.F.) (attd.) 25Apr.14

Chaplain.
Southwark, Rt. Rev. H. M., Lord Bishop of, D.D., Chapl. 1st Class (T.F.) (attd.) 20Dec.11

[Uniform—Green. Facings—Scarlet.]

Cadet Unit affiliated.
South London Cadets.

22nd (County of London) Battalion, The London Regiment, (The Queen's).

The Paschal Lamb.
"South Africa, 1900-02."
2, Jamaica Road, Bermondsey, S.E.

Hon. Colonel.
p.s. Bevington, R. K., VD, ✠ ⑤ (Lt.-Col. ret. T.F.) 25Feb.14

Lt.-Colonel.
p. Previté, E. J., VD, ⑤ 1June09

Majors (2).
Bathurst, H. M. (Q) 25Jan.12

Captains. (8).
p.s. Gunnis, A. A. (Q) 1May09
p.s. Mayhew, E. W. (H) 6Jan.04
Turner, H. C. (H) ⑥ 1June09
Boosey, L. A. 25Jan.12
Bowen, A. E. (H.) ⑤ 25Jan.12
Green, F. M. 22Apr.12
Woolley, E. J. 1May13
Cork, R. P. 1May13

Lieutenants (8).
Austin, E.R. 1Sept.10
Ewen, R. M. 15June11
Hayward, R. F. 1Feb.12
Hall, R. A. 1May13
Green, H. E. 1May13
Austin, E. (H) 1May13

2nd Lieutenants (8).
Ratton, W. H. 13July12
Boosey, N. C. 15Mar.13
Pattle, T. F. C 24Jan.14
Lendon, W. W. 1Feb.14
Bare, A. R. 13May14

Adjutant.
✗Tredennick, J. P., Capt. R. Dub. Fus. 1Mar.12

Quarter-Master.
Johnson, H. S. (Hon. maj. ret. T.F.), hon. m. 24Jan.14

Medical Officer.
Hills, Lt. T. W. S., R.A.M.C. (T.F.) (attd.) 24Jan.14

Chaplain.
Wilson, Rev. F. R., Chapl. 4th Class (T.F.) (attd.) 1Mar.10

[Uniform—Scarlet. Facings—Blue.]

23rd (County of London) Battalion, The London Regiment.

An annulet ensigned with a cross patée and interlaced with a saltire conjoined in base "Loyalty unites us.",

"South Africa, 1900-02."

27, St. John's Hill, Clapham Junction, S.W.

Hon. Colonel.
p.s. Thomson, B. T. L., VD, ✠ (Hon. Col. ret. T.F.) 10Feb.12

Lt.-Colonel,
✗Montagu Douglas Scott, Lord H.A., D.S.O. (Capt. Res. of Off.) 14Dec.10

Majors, (2)
✗Kayser, F., 3Aug.13
late Lt. 1 D.G. 3May08

Captains. (8)
p.s Cornford, R. G. (H) 23Sept.07

Captains—contd.
p.s. Hargreaves, T. C. (H) (Examiner of Accounts, Uganda, 9Jan.12) 14July10
Streatfeild, H.S.J., late Lt. G. Gds. 14Dec.10
Alexander, Sir L. C. W., Bt., late Lt. G.Gds. ⑤ 22Mar.11
Clark, A. J. (H) 20May11
p.s. Fearon, A. T. 23Dec.11
Wilkins, V. S. D. A. 1June13
VanGelder, L. 27Oct.13
Phillips, G. C. 9Mar.14
Johnson, F. J. 21Apr.14

Lieutenants. (8)
Grindel, R. S. M.
(H) I, of M. 20Dec.05
Rees, V. O. 27Oct.13
Robertson, O. J. ⑤ 27Oct.13

2nd Lieutenants. (8)
Ward, D. C. L. 26July11
Edwards, H. C. S. P. 3Apr.13
Johnson, D. G. 21May13
Entwisle, F. 18Oct.13
Thomas, R.W. 5Nov.13
Clinton, L. S. 19Nov.13
Rowley, C.A.C. 13Jan.14
Berry, R. A. 1Apr.12
Saw, A. 19Feb.14
Hemingway, J. D. V. 22Apr.14
1June14

Inst. of Musk.
Grindel, R. S. M., capt. 15Jan.14

Adjutant.
✗Thornhill, J. E., Capt. Sea.Highrs. 15Mar.13

Quarter-Master.
p. ✗Nightingale, G. C. hon. m. 1July07

Medical Officers.
p. Martin, Capt. C. J., M.B., R.A.M.C. (T.F.) (attd.) 12Feb.02
25Jan.99

Chaplain.
Pegg, Rev. H. F., M.A., Chapl.4th Class (T.F.) (attd.) 30Nov.12

[Uniform—Scarlet. Facings—White.]

Cadet Unit affiliated.
St.Thomas's (Wandsworth) Cadet Corps.

| 1605 | 1606 | 1607 | 1608 |

Infantry. Territorial Force.

London Regt.—contd.

24th (County of London) Battalion, The London Regiment, (The Queen's).

The Paschal Lamb.

"South Africa, 1900-02."

71, New Street, Kennington Park Road, S.E.

Hon. Colonel.
Faunce-De Laune, A. 1Apr.08

Lt.-Colonel.
✗Simpson, W. G., Capt. ret. 12Dec.10

Majors. (2)
p.s.✗Carr, G. A. B. (Hon. Lt. in Army 6 Aug. 01) (H) 3May05
Parker, W. (t) 1Apr.10

Captains. (8)
p.s. Phillips, A. E., VD, hon. m. 29May00
p.s.✗Garrard, P. (Hon. Lt. in Army 3 Feb. 08) (H) 20Dec.05
p.s. Gill, F. M. 26Dec.09
p.s. Dewsbury, H. B, 14Apr.10
p.s. Harley, J. T. (H) I. of M. 18Sept.10
p.s. Nadaud, H. L. F. B. 22Mar.11
p.s. McAnally, J. A. 19July11
Bee, A. R. 20May13
Millner, G. E. (L) 3Dec.13
p.s. Armstrong, R. C. (q) 2June14
20June12

Lieutenants. (8)
p.s. Holliday, R. J. 9June10
Galer, F. B. 22Mar.11
Herivel, W. J. 26July11
Galer, R. V. 12Aug12
Morrison, W.H.S., 8Feb.13
Rees, A. E. 20May13
Wheater, S. 3Dec.13
Palmer, A. L. 1July14

2nd Lieutenants. (8)
Poland, F. R. 18Dec.12
Kelly, T. A. 31Dec.13
Devane, J. B. 7Jan.14
Fowler, J. B. 11Feb.14
Misquith, O. G. 26May14

Inst. of Musk.
Harley, J. T., capt. 26June12

Adjutant.
✗Maude, C. G., Capt. R. Fus. 19Feb.12

Quarter-Master.
p. Hargan, F. G., hon. m, 1Dec.97

Medical Officer.

Chaplain.
Conybeare, Rev. W. J., Chapl. 4th Class (T.F.) (attd.) 15Aug.11

[Uniform—Scarlet.
Facings—Blue.]

25th (County of London) Cyclist Battalion, The London Regiment.

Fulham House, Putney Bridge, S.W.

Hon. Colonel.
p.s. Smith, G., TD ⓢ (t) (Lt.-Col. ret. T.F.) 16Apr.13

Lt.-Colonel.
Churchill, A. (H) ⓢ 16Apr.13
E J Smith Lt Col of Bedrs 16/9/14

Major. (1)
p. Barrett, A. W. (q) 26Apr.13

Captains. (8).
p.s. Trapmann, A. H. (H) 15Feb.07
p.s. Easton, M. H. 1June08
p.s. Swinnerton, H. 1June08
p.s. Stafford, W. S. 1July09
Stapleton, N. (H) 26July11
Shaw, W. H. 1July12
Paget, C. N. 1Apr.13
Long, E. W. 1Apr.14
Turnour, G. A. 1June14

Lieutenants. (5)
Barnett, E. B. 1Mar.14
Blunden, H. G. 1Apr.14

2nd Lieutenants. (4)
Pollard, H. B. C. 9May12
Gillett, N. C. 22Feb.13
Collins, V. F. C. 25May14
McC.

Adjutant.
✗Seymour, E. F. E., Capt. R. Dub. Fus. 7Apr.13

Quarter-Master.

Medical Officers.
Hoyten, Capt. W. J., R.A.M.C. (T.F.) (attd.) 21Oct.12
Churchill, Lt. J. H. R.A.M.C. (T.F.) (attd.) 13Nov.12
21Apr.09

Chaplain.
Belcher, Rev. R. H., M.A., Chapl. 4th Class (T.F.) (attd.) 1Nov.09

[Uniform—Grey.
Facings—Scarlet.]

28th (County of London) Battalion, The London Regiment (Artists Rifles).

"South Africa, 1900-01."
Duke's Road, Euston Road, W.C.

Hon. Colonel.
p. Edis, R. W., C.B., VD, (Hon. Col. ret. Vols.) 16Dec.02

Lt.-Colonel.
p.s. May, H. A. R., VD, (T) 13Jan.03
n C House late of Rob 16/9/1

Majors. (2)
Chatfeild Clarke, S., VD (Q) 1Apr.08
✗Edlmann, H. E., TD, (H), (Q) (Hon. Lt. in the Army 11 Sept. 01) 9Dec.12

Captains. (8)
p.s. Higham, S. S., VD, hon. m, (Q) 30May00
p.s.✗Scharlieb, H. J., C.M.G., TD, hon. m. (Q) 1Dec.06
p.s. Innes, C. G. D., TD (H) (q) I. of M. 29May09
p.s. Edwards, H. P. (q) 31May09
p.s. West, W. G., TD (H) 4Sept.09
p.s.✗Greenwood, C. F. H. (H) (Q) 23Jan.10
p.s. Keene, A. V. ⓟ 7Jan.11
p.s.✗Austen, E. E. (q) 9Dec.12

Lieutenants. (8)
p.s. Croft, B. (q)(H)28May06
p.s. Neame, A. J. 4Sept.09
(p.s.) Roydes, A. F. 4Sept.09
Neighbour, S. W. (q) 13July10
Bare, A. E. (q) 7July10
Ostle, H. K. E. 9Dec.12
Simmons, F. K. (q) 18Dec.12
Thompson, A. R. 20Dec.13

2nd Lieutenants. (8)
Hall, A. W. 4Mar.11
Gilks, H. L. 23 Oct.12
Burmann, R. M. 23Oct.12
Tyer, A. A. 5Mar.13
Money, D. F. 5Mar.13
Fairtlough, G. H. 24June14
Rickatson, H. C. 24June14

Inst. of Musk.
Innes, C. G. D., TD, capt. 25Feb.10

Adjutant.
✗Blackwood, A. P., Capt. Bord. R. 20Oct.12

Quarter-Master.
Smith, J. A., hon. lt. 8July14

Medical Officers.
p.,p.s. de Segundo, Maj. C. S., M.B., VD, R.A.M.C. (T.F.) (attd.) 2July09
15Dec.07
Jones, Capt. D. W. C., R.A.M.C. (T.F.) (attd.) 26Apr.13
26Oct.09

[Uniform—Grey.
Facings—White.]

Infantry. Territorial Force.

INNS OF COURT OFFICERS TRAINING CORPS.

"South Africa, 1900-01."

10, Stone Buildings, Lincoln's Inn, W.C.

Hon. Colonel.
※ⒸⒸ.⚙.*Wood, Field-Marshal* Sir H. E., G.C.B., G.C.M.G., Col. R.H.G., p.s.c.
[R.] 15Nov.99

Lt.-Colonel.
p.s.Errington, F. H. L., VD,(Q) 29Mar.13

Major.
Mead, C. W., TD (*H*) Ⓖ
 1Apr.08

---

1 Sqn. Cav.
Major.
※Elphinstone, L., *H*, (*H*)(Q) 29Mar.13

Captain.
Moore,E.D.(q) 29Mar.13

Lieutenants. (2)
Wood-Hill, C. 1Sept.11
Field, W. R. 29Mar.13

2nd Lieutenants. (2)
Leveson-Gower, W. G. G. 11Oct.11
Robinson, J. F. M.
 3May13

---

3 Cos. Inf.
Major.
Hav, J. A., TD (*H*)
 Ⓖ(*t*) 1Apr.08

Captains, (2)
p. Kenyon, Sir F. G.,
 K.C.B. 27Mar.12
McLean, A.(*H*)
 I. of M. 27July12

Lieutenants. (6)
Holland,H.W. 1Sept.11
Bergne, E.& C. 28Oct.11
O'Brien, R. F. C.
 (*H*) 28Feb.12
Butler, H. B. 27Mar.12
Malkin, H.W. 27July12
Clark, A. N. 16Apr.13

2nd Lieutenants. (6)
Trench, C. R. C.
 1Apr.12
Negus, R. E. 5June12
Willink, G. O. W.
 16Apr.13
Gray, J. N. 15Nov.13

Inst. of Musk.
McLean, A, *capt.*
 10Oct.12

Adjutant.
(*attd. to Gen. Staff.*)
※Rainsford-Hannay, J.
 Capt. R.W. Surr. R.
 27 Jan.13

Quarter-Master.
※Holbourn, W., Qr.-
 Mr.(*hon. maj.*) ret.
 pay, *hon. maj.*1Mar.12

Medical Officers.
Cane, Capt. L. B., M.D.,
 R.A.M.C. (T.F.)
 (*attd.*) 22May12
 15Sept.08
Rice-Oxley, Capt,D. G.,
 M.B., R.A.M.C.(T.F.)
 (*attd.*) 19Nov.12
 19May09

Chaplain.
Williams, *Rev.* H.,
 M.A., Chapl. 4th
 Class (T F.)(*attd.*)
 1Apr.08
 12June07

[Uniform-Cavalry—*Blue,*
 Facings—*Green.*
Infantry—*Grey.*
 Facings—*Scarlet.*]

THE HERTFORDSHIRE REGIMENT.

A Hart lodged, in water.

1st Bn .. .. Hertford.

1st Battalion.

"South Africa, 1900-02."

Hon. Colonel.
p.s.Brownlow, Rt. Hon.
 A. W. B., Earl, VD,
 late Ens. & Lt. G
 Gds., Col., *A.D.C.*
 9Mar.01

Lt.-Colonel.
※Hampden, T. W.,
 Visct. Maj. ret.
 pay (*Res. of Off.*)
 12Feb.13

Majors (2)
Gripper, B. J., VD,
 hon. l.c. Ⓖ *t.a.*25July00
Baker, H., VD,
 Ⓖ 7May12
Croft, H. P. 14Feb.14

Captains. (8)
p.s.*Jones, E. M.* (*q*) (*H*)
 (local Maj., *O.T.C.*
 19 Feb. 13) 25Mar.05
p.s.※Page, F. (*t*) 29Mar.11
p.s *Mitchell,H. C. B,*
 (*t*) 7Jan.12
p.s.Kennedy, C. C. M.
 15Mar.12
p.s.Gough,J. B, T,(q)(*H*)
 7May12
Daniell, J. C. 26June13
Boyd, A. C. (*H*)
I. of M. 14Feb.14

Lieutenants. (9)
p. Pawle, J. 13July07
p.s.*Wightman, C. F* Ⓖ
 1Nov.09
p.s.Clerk, A. G. 1Mar.11
Longmore, P. E. Ⓖ
 7Jan.12
Smeathman, L. F. (*H*)
 10July12
Sanders, R. O. 16Apr.13
Bates, E. C. 12Nov.13
Pawle, H. 12Nov.13

2nd Lieutenants (8)
Palmer, V. H 16Dec.11
Ransom, J. 15Mar.12
Times, W. O. 8May12
Whitfield,G. E.15May12
Brown, G. M. 19June12
 16July10
Snowden, H. J.
 21June13
Daish, A. J. 10July13
Bevan, J. H. 8Oct.13
Gripper, *B. J. N.*
 12Nov.13
Le Mare, H. J. 27Feb.14

Inst. of Musk.
Boyd, A. C., *capt.*
 14June11

Adjutant.
Gathorne-Hardy,
 Hon. N. C., Capt.
 Rif. Brig. 8Feb.12

Quarter-Master.
Barber, T., TD, hon. m.
 19Aug.06

Medical Officers.
p. Rudyard, Capt. H. A.,
 R.A.M.C. (T.F.)
 (*attd.*) 27Aug.98
 24July95

Chaplains.
Crofton, *Rev.* W. d'A,
 M.A., TD, Chapl. 1st
 Class (T.F.) (*attd.*),
 16Feb.09
Gainsford, *Ret.*G.B., TD,
 M.A., Chapl.3rdClass
 (T.F.) (*attd.*) 1Apr.08
 26Feb.96

[Uniform—*Scarlet,*
Facings—*White.*]

Cadet Units affiliated.
2nd Hertfordshire (Watford
 Scouts) Cadet Company.
3rd Hertfordshire Cadets
 (Stortford School)
4th Hertfordshire Cadets
 (St. George's School)

Infantry. Territorial Force.

THE HEREFORDSHIRE REGIMENT.

A Lion passant guardant holding in the dexter paw a sword.

"*Manu forti.*"

1st Bn. .. .. *The Barracks, Hereford.*

1st Battalion.

"South Africa, 1900-02."

Hon. Colonel.

p. Heywood, T., VD, *late Capt.* 16 Lrs., *hon. c.*
    28July93

Lt.-Colonel.

p.s. Gilbert-Harris, J. H.
(Q)   27Apr.12

Majors. (2)

Wood-Roe, W. B. TD, ⊕
    22June12
Carless, W.T.⊕25July12
Drage, G.,Maj.ret.
  R. Mar. [L] 10Dec.13
⚔Pateshall, H. E. P.,
  Capt. ret. pay (*Res.*
  of Off.)   26Mar.14

Captains. (8)

p.s. *Boulton, A. H. (H)*
  I. of M. 28Mar.09
p.s. *Yates, R.G.(Q)*31Aug.10
Green, A.L.B. 1Mar.11
⚔Holman, A. V.
    25July11
Greenly, J. H. M.
    1Oct.13

Lieutenants. (8)

Capel, E. A. 19Nov.09
Speer, F. A.(*H*) 1Oct.11
Rogers, E. T. P. 1Dec.11
Nott, F. T. (⑤)(*H*)(q)
    1Dec.11
Wallis, O. B. 1Dec.11
Baily, R.E.H. 9Mar.13

2nd Lieutenants. (8)

Sale, R. C. (*H*) 1June12
Smith, M. V. 13June12
Barker, F. G. 18Dec.12
Burlton, R. F. 3Mar.13
Hamlen-Williams,
  D. W. 25May13
Carver, F. T. 10June13

Inst. of Musk.

Boulton, A. H.,
capt. 1July09

Adjutant.

⚔Prince, P., Lt.
Shrops. L.I.,
capt. 30Oct.13

Quarter-Master.

Roberts, R.W., *hon.*
lt. 13Dec.13

Medical Officers.

p. Macmullan, Capt.
  J. N., R.A.M.C.
  (T.F.) (*attd.*) (*t*)
    1Nov.06
    1Aug.03

Chaplain.

Cope, Rev. A. N.
M.A., Chapl. 4th
Class (T.F.) (*attd*).
    1Apr.13

[Uniform—*Scarlet.*
Facings—*Grass Green.*]

THE NORTHERN CYCLIST BATTALION.

Drill Hall, Hutton Terrace, Sandyford Road, Newcastle-on-Tyne,

Hon. Colonel.

Blake, Sir F. D., Bt.
(Hon. Col. Unattd.
List, Spec Res.)
(Hon. Col. ret.
Mlta.) (Hon. Capt.
in Army 12 Oct. 00)
    8Jan.13

Lt.-Colonel.

, Collis, A. J. ⊕ (Q)
    5July11

Major.

Boss, T. G. (*H*) 2Aug.12

Captains. (8)

p.s. Boss, J. G. 1May11
Harrison, P. S. 1Apr.13
Crawford, G. 20Aug.13
Arrowsmith, J. (*H*)
  I. of M. 2Feb.14
Kirby, B. La S.
    17Apr.14

Lieutenants. (5)

Hogarth, J. W. 2Mar.12
Balfour, F. D. 17Apr.14
Hill, W. 17Apr.14
Keenlyside, T. H.
    17 Apr. 14
Brunskill, J. H.
    17Apr.14

2nd Lieutenants. (4)

Dodds, J. W. 28Jan.13
Boss, T. H. 13May13
Phorson, R.M. 13June13
Newnam, P. E. 5July13
Moor, W. J. 11Apr.14
Balfour A. M. 21May14

Inst. of Musk.
Arrowsmith, J., *capt.*
    20Oct.13

Adjutant.
⚔Spring, T. C.,
Capt. Hamps.
R. 1Apr.12

Quarter-Master.

⚔Simpson, W. C., *hon.*
lt. 18Dec.11

Medical Officers.

Threlfall, Capt. E. N.,
M.D., R.A.M.C.
(T.F.) (*attd.*) 1July12
    1Jan.09
Anderson, Lt. J.,
M.B., R.A.M.C.
(T.F.) (*attd.*) 31Jan.14

Chaplain.

[Uniform—*Scarlet.*
Facings—*Green.*]

Infantry. Territorial Force.

THE HIGHLAND CYCLIST BATTALION.

"South Africa, 1900-2."

Kirkcaldy.

Hon. Colonel.
Breadalbane, Rt. Hon. G., Marq. of, K.G., Col. A.D.C., Lt.-Col. ret. T.F.) (*King's Body Gd. for Scotland*) 30July13

Lt.-Colonel.
Rothes, N. E., *Earl of, late Capt.* Fife R.G.A. (Mila.) 1 Sept. 11

Major.
Stewart, H. R. 22Aug.12

Captains. (8)
p.s. Forbes, S. A. 1Apr.10

Captains—contd.
Keiller, J. M. R. (H) 1Dec.11
p.s. Hotchkis, J.N. (A)(H) *Hon. Lt. in Army 9 Aug.* 01) *hon. m.* 20Jan.12
9Apr.01
Cairncross, J.C. 11Feb.13
Cox, J. A. 11Feb.13
Guild, A. M. 24June14

Lieutenants. (5)
Lockhart, R.B.(H) 9June13
Thom, J. A. 9June13
McKillop, J. 9June13
Muirhead, L.I.F. 9June13
Wightman, J. 24June14

2nd Lieutenants. (4)
Ferguson, H. S. 2Apr.13 p.
French, H.J. 12Nov.13
Somerville, D. B. 12Dec.13
Oswald, W. J. 12Dec.13
Dick, W. 14Jan.14
Lockhart, G. B. 25Feb.14
Stewart, C. J. 28June14

Adjutant.
Innes, S. A., Capt. R. Highrs. 28Sept.11

Quarter-Master.
Douglas, G.R.P., *hon. lt.* 1July11

Medical Officer.
Paton, Maj. E. L., M.B., R.A.M.C. (T.F.) (*attd.*) 7Sept.08
17Feb.97

Chaplain.
Davidson, Rev. R. S., B.D. [C.S.], Chapl. 2nd Class (T.F.) (*attd.*) 24Feb.12
24Feb.97

[Uniform—*Grey*. Facings—*Scarlet*.]

THE KENT CYCLIST BATTALION.

Drill Hall, Tonbridge.

Hon. Colonel.
Streatfeild, Bt. Col. H., C.V.O., C.B., ret. pay, Eq. (*Equerry to Queen Alexandra*, 7May10) 25Mar.09

Lt.-Colonel.
Egginton, J. 2July13

Major.
Parkinson, T.F. (H) (Q) 2July13

Captains. (8)
Shaw, H. W. 21Apr.09
Moore, W. G. 27Mar.12
Robinson, W. H. 20Feb.13
Oldendorff,A.J.A. (S) 1Oct.13
4Oct.11
Warner, K. C. H. (H) 2June14

Lieutenants. (5)
Powell, G. F. W. 20Nov.12
Pilditch, I. 17Mar.13
Walmsley, E.S. 24June13
Donald, S. B. 15Apr.14

2nd Lieutenants. (4)
Allan, A. M. 27Nov.12
Dunn, G. L. 3Jan.14
Sankey, G.B. 4Feb.14
Boulter, F. H. 4Feb.14
Phillips, C. S. 14Mar.14
Jenyns, R. F. 18Apr.14

Adjutant.
Knox, A. D'E., Capt. R. W. Kent R. 1Nov.12

Quarter-Master.
Bain, K. D., *hon. lt.* 19Mar.14

Medical Officer.
Bunting, Lt. G. L., M.D., R.A.M.C. (T.F.) (*attd.*) 6Mar.12

Chaplain.
Hassard-Short, Rev. F. W., M.A., Chapl. 4th Class (T.F.) (*attd.*) 11June10

[Uniform—*Scarlet*. Facings—*Black*.]

THE HUNTINGDONSHIRE CYCLIST BATTALION.

St. Mary's Street, Huntingdon.

Hon. Colonel.
Sandwich, Col.E.G.H., Earl of, K.C.V.O., *late* G. Gds. (*Hon. Col.* 5 Bn. K. R. Rif. C.) (*Hon. Col. late Mila*) 27Feb.14

Lt.-Colonel.
Herbert, E. R. 27Feb.14

Major.

Captains (8)
p.s. Cook, S. G. 27Feb.14
7Jan.05
Barkley, M. 27Feb 14
Lowe, A. R. 27Feb.14
Longbourne, H. R. 27Feb.14
Musk, J. C. S. 27Feb.14

Lieutenants (5.
Hunnybun, K. 27Feb.14
Day, G. L. 27Feb.14
Warwick, J. D. B. 27Feb.14
2May13
Rowe, C. W. 27Feb.14
2May13

2nd Lieutenants (4)
Hankin, J. H. I. 27Feb.14
Mellows, A. H. 20May14
Gardner, J. M. S. 20May14

Adjutant.
Drew, F.W.M., Capt. S. Lan. R. 7Apr.14

Quarter-Master.

Medical Officer.
Garrood, Lt. J.R., M.D. R.A.M.C. (T.F.) 27Feb.14

Chaplain.
Knowles, Rev. K. D., Chapl. 4th Class (T.F.) (*attd.*) 5June14

[Uniform—*Scarlet*. Facings—*White*.]

THE WEST INDIA REGIMENT.

"Dominica," "Martinique, 1809," "Guadaloupe, 1810," "Ashantee, 1873-4," "West Africa, 1887, 1892-3-4," "Sierra Leone, 1898."

Uniform—Scarlet. *Facings*—White. *Agents*—Messrs. Cox & Co.

1st Bn. (1 W. I. R.)	*Sierra Leone (for Jamaica).*
2nd „ (2 W. I. R.)	*Jamaica (for Sierra Leone).*

Colonel	Hallowes, Maj.-Gen. H. J., ret. pay [R] .. 1Dec.10

Lt.-Colonels. (2)

1 Hill, H. A.   3Feb.10 / 4Feb.11
2 Barchard, A. E.   8July11

Majors. (6)

1 Liston, F. A.   8Jan.02 / 15Aug.00
w.a.Cowie, E. L.   16July04
2 Long, C. W.   3Feb.06
1 Litchford, R.   11Jan.11
1 Faunce, B.   4Feb.11 / 17Apr.02
2 Bliss, J. P.   8July11

Captains. (10)

2 Lawrenson, R. R.   27Aug.98
2 Pomeroy, E. J.   4Jan.99
c.o. Martin, A. T. de M.   15Dec.99
1 Carleton, C. E. W.   16Jan.09
1 Hill, C. W.   1Apr.10

Captains—contd.

c.o.1 Hart, J. G. V.   8July11
1 Ogle, E. C.   8July11
2 Poë, J. H. L.   31Oct.13
2 Norton, A. E.   10Oct.13
2 Nicholson, T. B.   4Nov.13
1 Collins, R. G.   4Nov.13
2 Biscoe, J. S.   8Nov.13
1 Thelwall, H. W.   12Nov.13

Lieutenants (20)

1 Miller, E. M.   10Feb.02
2 Leader, R. R., *Adjt*,   19Oct.04
1 Woolnough, F. W.   22Oct.04
t. Groom, G. B.   17Mar.06
w.a. Pridham, C. H. B.   30Oct.06
2 Buchanan, J. C.   16Feb.07
f.c. Glanville, H. F.   6Nov.07

Lieuts.—contd.

1 Furber, A. M., *Adjt*.   16Jan.09
w.a. Jones, L. J.   16Jan.09
f.c. Lewis, R. E.   6Mar.09
w.a. Minniken, H. J.   11May09
1 Sharp, P. C.   1Apr.10
1 Cranko, A. C. W.   1Apr.10
c.o. Porter, H. C. V.   4July10
w.a. Tomlins, A. W. G.   15May11
1 Torrens, G. L.   8July11
w.a. Griffiths, T. R. H.   2Aug.11 / 25Jan.11
w.a. Garbett, H. G.   27Sept.11
2 Ottley, L. E.   4Oct.11
w.a. Macpherson, E. R.   20Jan.12 / 1Apr.10
2 Ramsden, W. H. C.   2Oct.12
w.a. Walker, W. E.   1Jan.13
1 King, F. H.   1Jan.13
1 Kirkland, J. V.   31Oct.13
1 Tinney, L. H.   4Nov.13

Lieuts.—contd.

2 Bear, E. A. M.   29Dec.13
1 Howard, A. W.   29Dec.13
1 Fink, R. H. L.   6Feb.14
2 Holloway, F. A. B.   27May14
1 Larnder, E. M.   5June14
2 Donovan, R. B.   5June14

2nd Lieutenants (9)

2 Green, V. C.   10Dec.13
1 Procter, T. G.   24Jan.14
2 Ottley, K. C. G.   25Feb.14
2 Hatten, J. C.   10June14

Adjutants.

1 Furber, A. M., *lt.*   3Oct.13
2 Leader, R. R., *lt.*   19Mar.14

Quarter-Masters.

1 King Church, J. E., *hon. lt.*   16May06
2 Price, S. H., *hon. lt.*   16June06

THE ARMY SERVICE CORPS.

Uniform—Blue. *Facings*—White.
Agents—*Sir* C. R. McGrigor, Bt., & Co., 39, Panton Street, Haymarket, S.W.

Officer in charge of Records - - -	Carter, Col. E. E., *C.M.G., M.V.O., p.s.c., e.*
	Woolwich Dockyard 15Dec.13
Assistant to Colonel in charge of Records -	Grapes, Hon. Capt. J., Qr.-Mr. ret. pay 1Oct.06

Stations of the Head Quarters of Companies.

Horse Transport Companies.	Horse Transport Companies.—contd.	Horse Transport Companies.—contd.	Mechanical Transport Companies.—contd.
1 Co. Aldershot (Transport Depôt)	21 Co. Devonport	42 Co. Pretoria	60 Co. Aldershot
2 „ Woolwich (Transport Depôt)	22 „ Bulford	43 „ Potchefstroom	61 „ Aldershot
3 „ Bradford (Transport Depôt)	23 „ Curragh		62 „ Portsmouth
4 „ Dublin	24 „ York	*Mechanical Transport Companies.*	63 „ Bulford
5 „ Woolwich	25 „ Woolwich		64 „ Bulford
6 „ Curragh	26 „ Aldershot	45 Co. Devonport	65 „ Chatham
7 „ Aldershot	27 „ Aldershot	46 „ Woolwich	
8 „ Edinburgh	28 „ Aldershot	47 „ Woolwich	
9 „ Aldershot	29 „ Portsmouth	48 „ Dublin	
10 „ Aldershot	30 „ Devonport	49 „ Curragh	
11 „ Kensington Bks., London	31 „ Aldershot	50 „ Fermoy	*Supply Companies.*
12 „ Portsmouth	32 „ Shorncliffe	51 „ Curragh	"A" Co. Aldershot (Supply Depôt)
13 „ Bordon	33 „ Belfast	52 „ Aldershot (M. T. Depôt).	"B" „ Gosport
14 „ Woolwich	34 „ Devonport	53 „ Aldershot	"C" „ Aldershot
15 „ Bulford	35 „ Aldershot	54 „ Aldershot	"D" „ Curragh
16 „ Aldershot	36 „ Aldershot	55 „ Bulford	"E" „ Woolwich
17 „ Cork	37 „ Curragh	56 „ Bulford	*Remount Companies.*
18 „ Kensington Bks., London	38 „ Dover	57 „ Aldershot	"AA" Co. Woolwich
19 „ Dublin	39 „ Gibraltar	58 „ Aldershot	"BB" „ Dublin
20 „ Aldershot	40 „ Malta	59 „ Aldershot	"CC" „ Lusk
	41 „ Cairo		"DD" „ Dublin (*temp.*)

Colonel -	Field-Marshal H.R.H. Arthur W. P. A., *Duke of* Connaught and Strathearn, K.G., K.T., K.P., G.C.B., G.C.S.I., G.C.M.G., G.C.I.E., G.C.V.O., Col. G. Gds., and *Col.-in-Chief* 6 Dns., High. L.I., R. Dub. Fus., and Rif. Brig., *Personal A.D.C. to the King* - - - - - 28Sept.02

Removed from the Corps and still on the Active List.

General Officers.

Heath, Maj.-Gen. 1Mar.07
C. E., *C.V.O., C.B.*
Clayton, Maj.-Gen. Pretoria 2Apr.09
F. T., *C.B., s.*
Landon, Maj.-Gen. War 1Apr.13
F, W. B., *C.B.* (*Dir.* Office
of Transport and Movements)

Colonels.

Koe, F. W. B., *C.B., s.* Chester 3Aug.04
Gilpin, F.C.A., *C.B.* 2July05
Foster, T. D., *C.B.,* Horse Guards,
M.V.O., *e.* (*Inspr. S.W.* 29Nov.06
of A.S.C.) (*temp. Brig.-Gen.*)
Long, S. S., *C.B.* War 13Dec.06
(*Dir. of Supplies* Office
and Quartering)
(*temp. Brig.-Gen.*)
Hobbs, P. E. F., 2Apr.08
C.M.G.
Bramhall, E. A. *Malta* 3Sept.08

Removed from the Corps and still on the Active List—contd.

Colonels—contd.

Ludlow, E. R. O. *York* 15Oct.08
p.s.c., s.
King, *Sir* C. W., *Woolwich* 1Jan.09
Knt., M.V.O. *Arsenal*
Jack, R. R. H., *S. Africa* 7May09
C.M.G.
Sargent, H. N., *Aldershot* 27Oct.09
D.S.O.
Parker, B. J. W. T., War 4Oct.11
s. Office
Long, A., *D.S.O.* *Salisbury* 4Oct.11
Moore, J. S., *s.* *Dublin* 6June12
Boyce, W. G. B., *E. Comd.* 30Oct.12
D.S.O *London*
Carter, E. E., *Record* 16Dec.13
C.M.G., M.V.O., *Office*
p.s.c., e.

Lieutenant-Colonel.

Phelps, A. *Salisbury* 8Nov.09

Lieutenant-Colonels (22).

Welman, A. P. *Belfast* 15Oct.09
Thring, E. C. *Chester* 1Apr.10

Lieut.-Colonels—contd.

Seccombe, A. K. *Malta* 1Aug.10
D.S.O. [F]
Ryan, C. M., *S. R. Depôt,* 15Oct.10
D.S.O. *Woolwich*
Dodgson, C. S. [L] *Woolwich* 1Nov.10
Conway-Gordon, *Edinburgh* 1Jan.11
G., *e.*
Grey, C. W. *Pretoria* 1Jan.11
Ward, E. I. *Egypt* 9June11
Taylor, E. F., *e.* *Dublin* 27Oct.11
Ford, R., *D.S.O. Aldershot* 27Oct.11
Wilson, F. M. *Trg. Establt.* 7Nov.11
Aldershot
Black, J. C. L. *Gibraltar* 20Feb.12
Courtney, E. A. *Devonport* 1Apr.12
W., *e.*
Gillespie, E. C. F., *e. Curragh* 25July12
Taylor, F. P. S. *Dover* 23Oct.12
Scott, P. C. J., *e.* [l] *Chatham* 1Feb.13
Longmore, J. C. G. *Bulford* 15Feb.13
Master, A. G. *York* 26Sept.13
Berry, R. G. J. J. *Portsmouth* 21Nov.13
Vawdrey, G., *e. Colchester* 15Dec.13
Armstrong, *Cork* 15Dec.13
W. M. H.
Atkins, R. K. C. *London* 18Dec.13
10May13

Army Service Corps.

Majors (62).

Davies, H. Cork 1Apr.02
Harrison, J. M., Newcastle-on-Tyne 19Dec.03
Lewis, C. H. Bordon 20Sept.04
Swabey, W. S., Preston 1Aug.05
e. [F] 26June02
James, M. R. de B, E.Comd., 1Aug.05
London
Delavoye, A. E., e. Dublin 3Sept.05
29Nov.00
Burne, R. O. Sierra Leone 15Oct.05
Christopher, London 1Nov.05
C. D., e.
Atkinson, F. S. York 1Jan.06
Morgan, J. W. M. Chester 3Mar.06
Brooke, H. F. Aldershot 7May06
Pigott, G. E., Devonport 27Oct.06
D.S.O.
Norrington, Londonderry 3Nov.06
F.C.S., e.
Puckle, J. Chatham 12Dec.06
D.S.O., e.
Davies, P. M., e. Salisbury 20Feb.07
Howard, F.J. L.Trg.Estabt.,16Mar.07
[F] Aldershot 14Mar.00
Hazelton, P. O., Shorncliffe 1Apr.07
e.
Brooke, E. W. Portsmouth 22May07
Cannot, F. G. E., Trg. 28Oct.07
e., [L] Estabt., Aldershot
Mears, E. L. Singapore 21Jan.08
Bernard, W. K., Bulford 1Feb.08
e.
Russell, H. J., Trg. Estabt.
e. [l] Aldershot 6June08
Burrard, H. G., e. Gibraltar 26Sept.08
Duffus, F. F., e. Bulford 21Nov.08
Davies, G. F., e Bradford 19Dec.08
Moores,C.F., D.S.O., War 12Jan.09
p.s.c., e., [l] s. Office
Johnson, T. P. Woolwich 4July09
Liddell,A.R.,e. Bermuda 6Oct.09
Wilder, H. C. 52 Co., 15Oct.09
Aldershot
Scott, E. W. W. Egypt 3Nov.09
Coulson, J., e. Edinburgh 16July10
Watling, C. E. Capetown 1Aug.10
Parsons, D., e. Fermoy 3Sept.10
Lecky, J. G. Dublin 15Oct.10
Fitzwilliams, Hong Kong 1Nov.10
E., C. L.
Evans, E. G. Dover 1Jan.11
Young, J. M., e. Aldershot 13Jan.11
Tarver, W. K., War Office 14Jan.11
e. s.
Wood, E. [l] 42 Co., 9June11
Pretoria
Grose, D. C. E., e.Jamaica 27Oct.11
Chatterton, Gibraltar 27Oct11
F. B. M., e.
Carey, H. W. W. O.
Potchefstroom 7Nov.11
Wright, H. S. Woolwich 20Feb.12
Airey, R. B., e. N. China 1Apr.12
Striedinger, O., e. Mauritius 3Apr.12

Majors—contd.

Moore, M., e. Curragh 25July12
Lord, F. B., e. Ceylon 11Sept.12
Richards, H.A.D. Pembroke 7Oct.12
Dock 26June02
Anderson, N. G., Curragh 23Oct.12
D.S.O., p.s.c., s.
McNalty, C. E. I., Dublin 21Jan.13
e. 2Jan.01
Mears, T. I. N., s. Pretoria 15Feb.13
Lea, P. G. P., e. 17 Co., Cork 26Sept.13
Reid, F. J., e. Malta 20Sept.13
Barton, W. H., e. Lichfield 21Nov.13
Cracroft, H., e. Aldershot 15Dec.13
Russell, H. D., Aldershot 15Dec.13
D.S.O. (temp.)
Beadon, L. R. Mil. Coll. 18Dec.13
Bingham,C.H.M.Singapore 3Jan.14
p.s.c., e., s.
Johnson, H. A. Aldershot 2Feb.14
Northen, A. Aldershot 28Mar.14
Stringer, F. W., s.War Office 25Apr.14
Scott-Elliot, W., Belfast 22July14
e.

Captains (146).

Parker, W. M., e. London 1Feb.05
Hills, C. E., e. [F] Lichfield 1Apr.02
Gibb, E., D.S.O.,Trg.Estabt. 1Apr.02
Aldershot,
bt. maj. 18Jan.11
Buller, J. D., e. "C" Co., 1Apr.02
Aldershot
Galloway,A.G. Canterbury 1Apr.02
e. [F]
Jesse, J. L. Devonport 7Apr.02
Molony, W. W. Capetown 13May02
Rivis, T. C. L., e. Pembroke 27Aug.02
Dock
Stewart, H. A., t. Glasgow 27Aug.02
Christie, W. E. T., e. Malta 2Oct.02
Browne, J. C., Aldershot 15Oct.02
e. [F]
Crosse, W. C. 40 Co., Malta 15Oct.02
Terry, C. E. Netley 20Oct.02
3Sept.02
Shinkwin, I. R.S.,e. S. R. 7Jan.03
Depôt, Woolwich
Collum, H. W. A. War Office 7Jan.03
[F] (temp.)
Kelly, W.H.F., t. Exeter 7Jan.03
Crawley, R. P., Guernsey 20Feb.03
M.V.O.,e.
Annesley, C. R. T. E Co., 1Apr.03
Woolwich
Cutbill, R. H. L. "B" Co., 18Feb.04
Gosport
Huskisson, W. G. e.a. 18Feb.04
Beddy, B. L., e. Hounslow 18Feb.04
Lucas,C.F., e. 10 Co., 18Feb.04
Woolwich
Percival, H. F. P., Staff 18Feb.04
D.S.O. [L] s. Coll.
Mackenzie, K.D.,No.1 Depôt 18Feb.04
e. Co., Aldershot
Hayter, H. R. Aldershot 18Feb.04
Worsley, R. S., e., e.a. 9June04
Anderson,A.,U.,e. 13 Co. Bordon 20Sept.04
Anderson, A. J. 21Sept.04
Macleod, C. W., Adjt. 1Oct.04
Woolwich
Courtney R. W., e. Parkhurst 1Oct.04

Captains—contd.

Sykes, H. E. York 1Oct.04
Law, W. H. P., s. Warwick 1Oct.04
Jellicoe, R. C., e. Warley 1Oct.04
De la Pryme,P.C., e. Queens- 1Oct.04
town
Donovan, S. J. A Co. 1Oct.04
Aldershot
Stokes,H.W.P. 6Co.,Curragh 1Oct.04
McAllister, E. J. Dundalk 1Oct.04
Delavoye. F. B. Aldershot 1Feb.05
Reid, H. G., e., New Zealand 1Feb.05
c.o.
Caddell, H. M.Trg.Estabt., 1Feb.05
Aldershot
Harvey,G.H.,e. Trg.Estabt., 1Feb.05
Aldershot
Barbor, R. D., Portsmouth 1Feb.05
p.s.c.
Jones, H. A., t. Ilford 1Feb.05
Page, L. M. S. Portsmouth 1Feb.05
Pearse, W. P. t.a. 1Feb.05
Fessenden, J. H. 25 Co., 1Feb.05
Woolwich
Coke. J. D'E. Fitz-E 1Feb.05
Norwich
Hutchinson, T. M. War 1Feb.05
(Sec.. Mech. Trans. Office
Commee. 20 June 14)
Foster, H. N., e. War Office 1Feb.05
Berger, A. Bermuda 1Feb.05
Woods, B. J. G. Exeter 1Feb.05
Slaughter, R. J., e., t. 1Feb.05
Manchester
Cameron, D, C. 8 Co. 15Mar.05
p.s.c. [l] Edinburgh
Cox, C. E. e.a. 1Aug.05
St.Clair,C.H.D. 26 Co., 1Aug.05
Aldershot
Macdonald, H. Malta 1Aug.05
Lever, H. R. London 1Aug.05
Leland, F.W.G.Birmingham 1Aug.05
Wright, F, W. 18Co.London 1Nov.05
Harding, G 4 Co. Dublin 1Nov.05
Furneaux, C. H. 24 Co., 1Nov.05
York
Hollins, W. T., e. 28 Co., 1Nov.05
Aldershot
Lawson, H. S. 38 Co. Dover 1Nov.05
Noverre, A. K. 49 Co., 1Nov.05
Curragh
Nunn, C. H. N. Pretoria 1Nov.05
Allin, H.C., e. 19 Co., Dublin 1Jan.06
O'Hara,E.K. Clonmel 1Jan.06
Hull, C. R. I. Weymouth 1Apr.04
29May06
MacCall, G. F., e. 30 Co., 30Apr.06
Devonport
Marks, W. O. 30Apr.06
Dartnell, G. B. 32 Co., 30Apr.06
Shorncliffe
Maconochie-Welwood. 30Apr.06
W. A. M. G. Bulford
Traill, E. F. T. Aldershot 30Apr.06
Dyer, H. G. London 30Apr.06
Cockshott, A. M. 63 Co., 30Apr.06
Bulford
Dickey, O. B. R. Aldershot 1May06
Thwaites, G., e. e.a. 1May06
Falkner, E. F Bulford 1May06
McNalty, A. G. P., s. Egypt 1May06
Herring Cooper, Khartoum 1May06
W. W., D.S.O.
Hunt, G. V. Newcastle-on-Tyne 1May06

Army Service Corps.

Captains—contd.

Robinson, A. C., c.o.   *New Zealand* 1Aug.06
Lambert, M. L.   *Cairo* 10Nov.06
B. H., [l]
Byng, A. S.   *Salisbury* 10Nov.06
Bennett, T. E., *e.* 34 Co., 10Nov.06
   Devonport
Oakes, D. M.   *Ceylon* 10Nov.06
Upton, C. D. E., *e. Bulford*
   10Nov.06
Elliott, W.   *Cyprus* 10Nov.06
Humphreys, A. S. *Brighton* 21Jan.13
   1Nov.05
Sydney-Turner, *Leeds* 10Nov.06
 C. G. R., *e.*
White, *W. N.* [l] *t.* *York* 10Nov.06
Wilson, A. M. 48 Co., *Dublin* 10Nov.06
Sayers, L. D. W., *e. Athlone* 10Nov.06
Marsh, J. T,   *c.o.* 23Mar.07
   12Dec.03
Roberts, A.H.,*e.,t. Southport* 1May07
Alexander, A. W. *Gibraltar* 1May07
Hamilton, J. A. *N. China* 1May07
Blencowe, E. P., *e. Warwick* 1May07
Johnson, F. E.   31 Co., 1May07
   Aldershot
Fraser, P. B.   *Cork* 1May07
Lawson, J. L., *e., t.* 18Dec.07
   Woolwich
Brancker, S.D. *Leicester* 13June08
[L] *t.*   21June07
Crocker, C. H. C. 23 Co., 22June08
   Curragh
Canny, J. C. M. 39 Co., 22Sept.08
D.S.O. *Gibraltar* 13June08
De Brath, H. *Pietermaritz-* 17Feb.09
   burg
Coventry, C. *Ceylon* 4July09
Larken, P. M.   e.a. 1Oct.09
Roe, W. E.   21 Co., 1Oct.09
   Devonport
Ainslie, M. *Capetown* 15Oct.09
Horton, C.W., *t. Newcastle* 31Oct.09
Jackson R. R. B., *e.* 31Dec.09
   Hounslow
Holden, A. H. S. 29 Co., 8Jan.10
   Portsmouth
Boyd, C. T. 35 Co., *Aldershot* 1Nov.10
Browne, W. T. R. *Belfast* 18Nov.10
Bell, J. A. D., *e.* 47 Co., 18Nov.10
   Woolwich 19Dec.10
Herklots, A., *e.* 59 Co. 10Dec.10
   Aldershot
Hutohins, S.   e.a. 21Dec.10
Hazlerigg, T. *Bulford* 1Jan.11
Walker, C. B., *e. Colchester* 1Jan.11
Blamey, E. H. 52 Co. 1Jan.11
   Aldershot
Morgan, C. R. F. 9 Co., 1Jan.11
   Aldershot
Iredell, J. S. *Colchester* 1Jan.11
Scott, M. de B.[l], 15 Co.
   Bulford
Blunt, G. C. G.   *Malta* 1Jan.11
Savage, G. T. *Trg. Establt.,* 1Jan.11
   Aldershot
Alleyne, C. F. *Colchester* 1Jan.11
Robinson, W. P. 62 Co., 1Jan.11
   Portsmouth
Bearne, L.C. 65 Co., *Chatham* 1Jan.11
Wakelin, *A. B., i.a.* 1Jan.11
Organ, C. A. *Trg. Establt,* 1Jan.11
   Aldershot
Lloyd, L. H. 41Co., *Cairo* 1Jan.11
Humphreys, G. N. *Alexandria* 1Jan.11

Captains—contd.

Crawley-Boevey, *Aldershot* 14Jan.11
C. A.
Weston, J. L., *t. Perth* 21Jan.11
Watson, A.H.K.*Hong Kong* 13Apr.11
Pery-Knox-Gore, 46 Co., 31May11
A. F. G.   *Woolwich*
Doran, J.C.M.,*t.Birmingham* 9June11
Moores, F. G. G. *Jamaica* 28June11
Giles, S. E, H.   e.a. 22July11
Swayne, T. E. G. 9 Co., 22July11
   Aldershot
Goldsmith, G.E. 56 Co., 2Aug.11
   Bulford
Peyton, J. H. B. *Limerick* 28Sept.11
Falle, P. V. Le G. *Trg.* 27Oct.11
[L] *Adjt.* *Establt.*
   Aldershot
Morris, J. H. *Jersey* 7Nov.11
Cotgrave, T. S. "D" Co., 16Dec.11
   Curragh
Inglefield, L. D. *Aldershot* 22Dec.11
Rose, H.de M. 50Co.,*Fermoy* 20Feb.12
Campbell, R. M., *s.* War 21Feb.12
   Office
Royston-Pigott, W.M. *Lusk* 23Feb.12
Hamilton, N.C., *New* 9Mar.12
c.o.   *Zealand*
Peterson, G. L. *Jamaica* 23Mar.12
Holbrook, A. E., *t. Hereford* 4Apr.12
Redfern, A. F., c.o. 19Apr.12
   11Aug.09
Milsom, C. F. *Glasgow* 4May12
Burton, C. *Perth* 4May12
Hay, C. O. 43 Co., 8May12
   Potchefstroom
Dyer, B.A.S. *Potchefstroom* 24May12
Coleman, G. B., *t. London* 9June12
Davis, C. L. 3 Depôt Co. 24July12
   Bradford
Edwards, C. W. *Aldershot* 12Sept.12
MacGwire, J. E. 11 Co., 12Sept.12
   London
Goldney, P. C. *Egypt* 10Oct.12
de Smidt, A. *Sierra Leone* 7Oct.12
G. C.
Gill, G. H. *Tidworth* 15Oct.12
Godfray, J. C. L. 45 Co. 25Oct.12
   Devonport
Gaskell, F. T. L. *London* 30Oct.12
[L]   *(temp.)*
Cooke, C. F. *Mauritius* 30Nov.12
Prescott-Roberts, P. A.
   Aldershot 14Jan.13
Vyvyan, P.H.,*No.2 Depot Co.* 29Jan.13
N. N.   *Woolwich*
Puckle, F. K. *Singapore* 15Feb.13
Stanley, T. A. *Aldershot* 6Mar.13
Biddulph, A. L, N. 28 Co.,
   Aldershot 21Aug.13
Shelton, R. *Curragh* 1Sept.13
Barnes, F. P. *Aldershot* 21Nov.13
Phillimore, P. G. *Aldershot* 22Nov.13
   24Dec.11
Smyth, F.W 7 Co., *Aldershot* 6Dec.13
Milner-Jones, *Hong Kong* 15Dec.13
F.E.M.
Badcock, G. E. 10 Co., 15Dec.13
   Aldershot
Unwin, E.F., *f.c.r. London* 18Dec.13
Hamersley, J. *Dublin* 19Dec.13
St. G.
Dawes, F. R. *Tientsin* 25Apr.14
Harvey, J. A. *Curragh* 2May14
Fraser, C. L. B. *London* 4July14
Young, G. M. *Dublin* 29July14

Lieutenants and 2nd Lieuts.
(163).

Lieutenants.

Hart, C. H. *Aldershot* 27Jan.07
   29Mar.05
Corfield, F. A. *Jamaica* 27Jan.07
Airey, R. M. *Khartoum* 6May07
Campbell, G. A. *Belfast* 20May07
Wright, H. H.,
c.o. *New Zealand* 4June07
Morton, R. B. *Chester* 4June07
Crawford,H.A.B.*Portsmouth*3Aug.07
   6Sept.05
Clifton-Shelton, A. *Inverness* 6Aug.07
Warren, T. R. P. 53 Co., 16Aug.07
   Aldershot
Fitzherbert, E H. *Alder-* 16Aug.07
   shot
Cunningham, *Alexandria* 16Aug.07
D. W.
Seth-Smith,H.G. *Malta* 16Aug.07
English, W. J. *Ports-* 27Oct.07
   mouth
Archibald, G.K. *Manchester* 22Nov.07
Johns, A. W. *Sierra Leone* 22Nov.07
Saunders O'Mahony,
C. C. *Aldershot* 29Nov.07
Blount-Dinwiddie, *Edin-* 24Jan.08
J.   *burgh*
Whitaker, A.P.D. *Aldershot* 24Jan.08
Bennett, W. de C. *Fermoy* 24Jan.08
Saulez, A. G. "O" Co., 3Feb.08
   Aldershot
Reynell. G. M. *Bradford* 1Apr.08
Studdert, R. *Devonport* 1Apr.08
Toynbee, G. E. *Portsmouth* 5Aug.08
Solomon, H. J. *Kensington* 1Oct.08
   Bks., London
Williams, N. J. *Aldershot* 24Jan.09
Otway, W. G. *Cork* 23May09
Boutflower, G. i.a. 23May09
Ryan, T. W. *Potchefstroom* 28May09
Fasken, J. E. *Egypt* 23May09
Hewson, F.L. 51Co., *Curragh* 1June09
Snowden-Smith,
R. T. *Manchester* 29Aug.09
Hall, H. G. L. *Malta* 29Aug.09
Brander, M. S. *Trg. Establt.,* 29Aug.09
   Aldershot
Carter, L. A. L. *Chatham* 29Aug.09
St. John, O. C. *Aldershot* 1Oct.09
   29Nov.07
Macdonald, F. *Potchef-* 1Oct.09
   stroom
Garstin, J. L. e.a. 1Oct.09
Barrett, F. H. H. i.a. 14Dec.09
Holbrook, C. V. *London* 16Jan.10
Robinson, L.G. 16Jan.10
Carolin, G. I. *Perth* 16Jan.10
Craig, N. L. *Dublin* 27Jan.10
Tweedie, J. M. *York* 2Feb.10
Wintle, N. *Malta* 2Feb.10
Wright, G. T. *N. China* 2Feb.10
Loveband, R.D. *Pretoria* 2Feb.10
Haddon-Smith, H. B. 2Feb.10
Beuttler, V. O. *Bulford* 2Mar.10
Beadon, R. H. *Pretoria* 29May10
Russell, R. V. *Pretoria* 29May10
Gardner, H. A. C. *Egypt* 29May10
Hazlerigg, G. M. c.o. 1Oct.10
   22Jan.08
Goldney, C. Le B. *Trg. Establt.,*10Oct.10
   Aldershot 23Oct.10
Berkeley, M.H.F., *Curragh* 10Oct.10
   26Apr.09
O'Flynn, *Capetown* 9Oct.10
A. J. G.D., [l]

Army Service Corps.

Lieutenants—contd.

Buller, W. T. M	Curragh 11Dec.10
Apthorpe, C. K.	Devonport 25Oct.11
	8May08
Dunphy, L.O.A.	Fermoy 11Dec.10
Aylmer, R. M.	Woolwich 8Feb.11
Verschoyle, H. P. C.	Gibraltar 8Feb.11
Mayne, R. C.	Bulford 8Feb.11
Barrett, B. B.	Aldershot 11May11
Morrison, S. W.	Bulford 27May11
Frisby, M. A.	Aldershot 27May11
Moore, T. C. R.	Pretoria 4July11
Langmaid.T.J.R.	Chatham 19Sept.11
Custance, C. N.	c.o. 19Sept.11
Allden, S. G.	Bulford 19Sept.11
Raymond, H. P.	Chatham 19Sept.11
Gibbs, S. G., c.o.	Australia 1Oct.11
	1July05
Carter, J. L. G.	Aldershot 1Oct.11
	7Dec.08
Laird, A. H. R. M.	Curragh 1Oct.11
	15Dec.09
Pereira, A. B. P.	Woolwich 1Oct.11
	22Jan.10
Beall, F. W.	Aldershot 6Jan.12
Hodder, G. E.	Egypt 27Jan.12
Tudor, C. L. St.J.	Aldershot 6Feb.12
Armstrong, J. C.	Aldershot 15Sept.12
	(temp.)
McWatters, H. V.	Woolwich 15Sept.12
McCaskill, K. D. F.	Aldershot 1July14
	6Feb.12
Parkin, H. D.	London 2Oct.12
	18Sept.09
Dalton, M. N.	Dover 2Oct.12
	1Apr.10
Hacker, E.S.	Aldershot(temp.) 2Oct.12
	1Apr.11
Pinder, E. C.	Aldershot(temp.) 2Oct.12
	16Sept.11
Warren, W.R.V.	Aldershot 2Oct.12
	19May12
Brain, A. H.	Shorncliffe 8Dec.12
Watson, H. N. G.	Devonport 8Dec.12
Holden, U. S.	Bulford 8Dec.12
Howard, W. E. W.	Aldershot 23Feb.13
	(temp.)
Butterworth, A. B.	Woolwich 23Feb.13
Growse, R. H.	Dublin 23Feb.13
Reckitt, J. T.	Aldershot 23Feb.13
Verney, R.H., f.c.	28May13
Thompson, G.	Devonport 28Sept.13
Humphreys, L.G.	Aldershot 8Sept.13
Mellish, H. T.	Woolwich 8Sept.13
Drysdale, J. E.	Aldershot 6Sept.13
	23Oct.12
White, E. S.	Aldershot 1Oct.13
	1Apr.10
Simpson, G.	Portsmouth 1Oct.13
	1Dec.10
Owen, J. W.	Devonport 1Oct.13
	19Mar.11
Lawson, W. D.	Belfast 1Oct.13
	12July11
Thomson, J. B.	Aldershot 6Oct.13
	17Nov.11
Langmaid, C. W. E.	Aldershot 7Dec.13
Spafford, P. L.	Aldershot 7Dec.13
Beale-Browne, G. A.	Aldershot 7Dec.13 (temp.)

Lieutenants—contd.

Aylwin-Foster, E. W. F.	Aldershot 14Jan.14 (temp.)
Spencer, F. A.	Aldershot 3Feb.14
Hedges, K. M. F.	Aldershot 3Feb.14
Sealy, P. T.	Aldershot 3Feb.14
Jenkins, A.De B.	Cork 4Feb.14
Stubbs, J. B.	Curragh 4Feb.14
bruce, M. J. H.	Leyland 11Feb.14
Cope, E. B. K.	Dublin 27May14
Lowdell, A. D.	Bulford 27May14
Humphries, E. D. M	London 27May14
Croker, C.	Curragh 27May14

2nd Lieutenants.

Cuffe, W. P. de L.	Aldershot 23Aug.11
McLennan, J. L.	Shorncliffe 30Aug.11
Barbor, J. H.	Aldershot 8Sept.11
Gale, H. M.	Woolwich 8Sept.11
Brooke Murray, K. A.	Woolwich 8Sept.11
Rowcroft, E. B.	Aldershot 9Sept.11
Henderson, H.P.	Dover 9Sept.11
Howard, H.J.M.	Curragh 9Sept.11
Birch, E. N. W.	Aldershot 9Dec.11
Clarke, W. H.	Woolwich 19Jan.12
Godley, F. W. C.	Aldershot 7Feb.12
Smith, R. H.	Bulford 7Feb.12
Courtenay, H.A.	Aldershot 7Feb.12
Nichols, F. P. R.	Gosport 7Feb.12
Tapp, H. A.	Devonport 7Feb.12
Davis, O. E.	Portsmouth 7Feb.12
Turnbull, D.	Bulford 22May12
Vance, C. H.	Aldershot 22May12
Stewart, M. S.	Portsmouth 22May12
Flook, W. H.	Aldershot 38Sept.12
Field, J. T.	Woolwich 38Sept.12
Keays, C. A.	Bulford 48Sept.12
Arden, P. A.	Bulford 48Sept.12
Boileau, D. W.	Aldershot 48Sept.12
Daubeny, M. P.	Devonport 48Sept.12
G, J.	
Fleming, P. B.	Woolwich 48Sept.12
Martin, C. J.	Woolwich 4Dec.12
Frazer, H. F.	Dublin 4Dec.12
Stewart, G. D.	Dublin 5Feb.13
Clover, B.	Aldershot 5Feb.13
Fuller, G. F.	Portsmouth 5Feb.13
Campbell, D. F L.	Aldershot 5Feb.13
Hawkins, H.J.C.	London 24May13
Collins, A.F.St.C.	York 24May13
Cockburn, C.	Woolwich 26July13
Butler, H. B. B.	Woolwich 26July13
Lynn, J. A. G.	Woolwich 17Sept.13
Longridge, T. E.	Woolwich 17Sept.13
Unwin, E. B.	Woolwich 17Sept.13
Fleming, N. (l),	Devonport 1Oct.13
Lt. L'pool R. (on prob.)	
	lt. 2Nov.12
Walker, H. N. B., Aldershot 1Oct.13
Lt. W. Rid. R. (on prob.)	
	lt. 16July13
Rountree, A. N.	Aldershot 1Oct.13
Lt. Durh.L.I. (on prob.)	
	lt. 3Aug.13
Chapman, M. T.	Bradford 4Oct.13
Cadic, H. M.	Aldershot 9Oct.13
Heriot-Hill, E. D. M.	Woolwich 10Dec.13
Richardson, T. W.	Woolwich 24Jan 14
Collings, W. d'A.	Woolwich 24Jan.14
Rowlandson, J.M.	Woolwich 24Jan.14
Whitcombe, P. S.	Woolwich 10June14

Quarter-Masters. (70)

Gleeson, A. F.	War Office 8Mar.95
	hon. maj. 28Sept.06
Staff, F. W.	Chatham 25May98
	hon. maj. 25May13
Wilson, T.	Pietermaritzburg 27Sept.99
	hon. capt. 27Sept.09
Farraday, W.	Malta 27Sept.99
	hon. capt. 22Aug.02
Guerin, C. J.	Dover 27Sept.99
	hon. capt. 27Sept.09
Walsh, J. P.	Bristol 27Sept.99
	hon. capt. 22Aug.02
Bamford, C. W.	Brighton 11Oct.99
	hon. capt 11Oct.09
Donnelly, J.J.G.	Newbridge 11Oct.99
	hon. capt. 11Oct.09
Barron, A.	Chester 22Nov.99
	hon. capt. 22Nov.09
Rose, A. G.	Woolwich 3Feb.00 Arsenal
	hon. capt. 3Feb.10
Caddy, J.	Woking 3Feb.00
	hon. capt. 3Feb.10
Bennett, W. J.	Bedford 26May00
	hon. capt. 26May10
Harlow, G.	"A.A." Co., 29Nov.00 Woolwich
	hon. maj. 27Nov.12
Duggan, J.	Liverpool 29May01
	hon. capt. 29May11
Browne, W. D.	Gravesend 29May01
	hon. capt. 29May11
Eady, F. O.	Woolwich 29May01
	hon. capt. 29May11
Wade, W. J.	Portsmouth 29May01
	hon. capt. 29May11
Walsh, E.	Warwick 29May01
	hon. capt. 17July01
McCallum, D.	Edinburgh 17July01
	hon. capt. 17July11
Kelly, H. A.	Hounslow 17July01
	hon. capt. 17July11
Feherty, W.	Chelsea Bks., 22Aug.02
	hon. capt. 22Aug.02
Hebb, J. A.	Gosport 22Aug.02
	hon. capt. 22Aug.12
Wildman, S. B.	Dublin 22Aug.02
	hon. capt 22Aug.12
O'Keefe, J. M., hon. lt.	Curragh 14Dec.04
Frost, R. H., hon. lt.	Shorncliffe 8Aug.05
Fairfield, V.H., hon. lt.	Bermuda 28 Sept 06
Barron, W. W., hon. lt.	Devonport 3Oct.06
Warner, F.M.C., hon. lt.	Bulford 15Dec.06
Batchelor, J. W., hon. lt.	Preston 2Jan.07
Lovell, G. M., hon. lt.	York 23Jan.07
Mitchell, F., hon. lt.	27Mar.07
Stevens, A., hon. lt.	Glasgow 14Dec.07
Derbyshire, F., hon. lt.	Gibraltar 3June08
Ayres, C. J., hon.lt.Capetown 3June08
Thynne, A. C., hon.lt.	Newcastle-on-Tyne 15July08
LeWarne, A., hon. lt.	Potchefstroom 14Nov.08
Elson, A., hon. lt.	London 24Mar.09

Army Service Corps.

Quarter-Masters—contd.	Quarter-Masters—contd.	Riding Masters (3).
McLeod, D., *hon. lt.* Aldershot 5May09	Smith, S. J., *hon. lt.* Aldershot 21Feb.14	Sinfield, T. Woolwich 29Nov.00 *hon. capt.* 29Nov.10
Haslop, J., *hon. lt.* Sheerness 28July09	Durainville, C. *hon lt.* Tidworth 11Mar.14	Sadler, H., *hon.lt.* Aldershot 4Jan.05
Calvey, C., *hon. lt.* Belfast 3Nov.09	Banks, S., *hon. lt.* 13June14	Stanton, F. W., Bradford 6June08 *hon. lt.*
Morris, G. C., *hon. lt.* Aldershot 24Nov.09	**Adjutants.**	
Dudley. E., *hon. lt.* Aldershot 22Jan.10	Falle, P. V. Le G. (L) *capt.* Aldershot 1Apr.17	
Way, F., *hon. lt.* Aldershot 29Jan.10	Browne, J. C., *capt.* Aldershot 16Oct.13	
Camfield, C. N., *hon. lt.* Pretoria 4May10	Macleod, C. W., *capt.* Woolwich 1Dec.13	
Bayman, F. J., *hon. lt.* Malta 28May10	**Inspectors of Subsidized Transport Vehicles.**	**Retired Officer Temporarily Employed.**
Owen, J., *hon. lt.* Aldershot 4June10	*Chief Inspector.*	Woods, Hon. Woolwich 5Jan.07 Capt. J. C., Dockyard Qr.-Mr. ret. pay
Adams, R. F., *hon.lt.* Woolwich 10Sept.10	Foster, H. N., e., War Office 1Oct.11 *capt.*	
Williams, F. E., *hon. lt.* Hong Kong 3Dec.10	*Inspectors.*	
Burdett, F. W., *hon. lt.* Pretoria 14Dec.10	Lever, H, R., *capt.* London 1Oct.11	
Bate, H., *hon. lt.* Pretoria 4Jan.11	Snowden-Smith, Manchester 17Aug.12 R. T., *lt.*	
Franks, W., *hon.lt.* Bordon 27May11	Holbrook, C. V., *lt.* London 1May12	
Lawrence, J., *hon. lt.* War Office 23Aug.11	Hunt, G. V., *capt.* Newcastle-on-Tyne 1Feb.13	
Kennedy, F. J. *hon. lt.* Singapore 27Jan.12	Archibald, G. K., Manchester 9Oct.13 *lt.*	**District Barrack Officers.**
Bagg, L. C., *hon. lt.* Aldershot 24Feb.12	Leland, F. Birmingham 1June14 W. G., *capt.*	Wyncoll, Bt. Col. London 24Apr 05 C. E., ret. pay
Hallett, E. U., Pembroke 22June12 *hon. lt. Dock*	**Inspectors of Mechanical Transport (6).**	Roberts, Bt. Col. Chester 20May07 A. N., ret. pay *(Lt.-Col. Res. of Off.)*
Laurie, W., *hon. lt.* Salisbury 12Oct.12	*Chief Inspector.*	
Paul, E., *hon. lt.* Egypt 5Feb.13	Donohue, W, E., Aldershot 1Aug.07 M.I. Mech. E. *hon. maj.* 14Apr.03	Collard Col. A. W., Dublin 12Dec.08 ret. pay
Harris, W. J., *hon. lt.* Aldershot 5Feb.13	Assoc.M.Inst.C.E.	
Russell, H., *hon.lt.* Cork 19Apr.13	*2nd Class.*	Hill, Bt. Col. R.E., York 1Nov.11 ret. pay *(Res. of Off.)*
White, W.J., *hon.lt.* Woolwich 19Apr.13	Owen, A. D. Aldershot 1Oct.07 *hon. capt.* 19May06	
Johnson, J. R., *hon. lt.* Woolwich 3May13	*3rd Class.*	Lynn, Bt. Col. S. Aldershot 1July13 H., ret. pay
Webb, T., *hon. t.* Bradford 10May13	Mackie, J. C., Aldershot 26Oct.10 *hon. lt. (on prob.)*	
Blay, J. A., *hon.lt.* Dublin 4June13	Smith. A. T. F. Aldershot 14Feb.14 *hon. lt (on prob.)*	Welch, Col. G.O., Edinburgh — C.B., ret. pay *(Res.of Off.)*
Williams, C. J., *hon. lt.* Malta 20Sept.13	Hoare, H. G., Aldershot 14Feb.14 *hon. lt.(on prob.)*	Phelps, Lt.-Col. A. 18Dec.13 Salisbury
Neville, F. F., *hon. lt.* Aldershot 8 Nov.13		
Wadler, G. C., *hon. lt.* Weedon 10Jan.14		
Morris, S., *hon. lt.* Curragh 7Feb.14		

ARMY SERVICE CORPS.
SPECIAL RESERVE.
Captains.

Teeling, B. L. C., Capt. ret. pay [l] E. Comd. 28June11

Matteson, L., Capt. ret. pay .. E. Comd. 21Feb.12

Bayldon, O. H., *late* Capt. A, Motor Res., Mech. Trans. .. .. Aldershot Comd. 14May13

✗Beattie, A. E. (*Hon.* 2nd *lt. in Army* 21 Oct. 00) (on prob.) Aldershot Comd. 7Jan.14
23July04

Lieutenants.

✗Fenwick, N.A. F., Lt. ret. pay .. S. Comd. 7Mar.01
10July09

Mayers, F. H. A. .. .. .. E. Comd. 1Aug.13

2nd Lieutenants.

Bannerman, S. Sco. Comd. 13July10
C. F.

Glen, H. R. Mech. Trans., Aldershot Comd. 21June13

Harte, M. J. Irish Comd. 11Mar.14 (on prob.)

Jackson, T. S. Sco. Comd. 19July11

Baerlein, O. F. E. Comd. 25June13 (on prob.)

Wilson, L. (on prob.) E.Comd. 18Apr.14

Moran, J. W. Irish Comd. 10Apr.12

Painton, W. London 23May14 (on prob.)

Shaw, D. G. Irish Comd. 8May12 (attd. O.T.C.)

Burke, W. M. Sco. Comd. 13Aug.13 (on prob.)

Barnes, G. V. W. London 17June14 (on prob.)

Hannington, G.J. Mech. Trans. Aldershot Comd. 15Mar.13

Cole, E. R. Mech. Trans., Aldershot Comd. 3Dec.1

Beckett, E. A. Irish Comd. 17June14 (on prob.)

Rendell, H. T. Mech. Trans. Aldershot Comd. 19Mar.13

Dobbs, C. E. S. Irish Comd.10Jan.1 (on prob.)

Grant, A., *late* 2nd Lt. Ind. Army Res. of Off. (on prob.) Aldershot Comd, 29July14

Brown, E. E. N. Comd. 3May13

Martin, W. J. Mech. Trans., Aldershot Comd. 4June13

Rushton, G. W. London 18Feb.1 (on prob.)

ARMY SERVICE CORPS.
TERRITORIAL FORCE.

(Dates shown prior to 1st April, 1908, are those of the officers' corresponding rank in a late unit of the Volunteer Force.)

I. Mounted Brigade Transport and Supply Columns.
II. Divisional Transport and Supply Columns.

I. MOUNTED BRIGADE TRANSPORT AND SUPPLY COLUMNS.

[*The order of precedence of columns is denoted by numerals in brackets.*]

Eastern.
[12]
(1 *Company.*)
Market Road, Chelmsford.

Captains (2)
Toton, E. J. (b) 22June08
Dawson, N. J. 1May14

Lieutenant.
Spencer-Phillips, J. C.
1May14

2nd Lieutenant.

Highland.
[1]
(1 *Company.*)
Drill Hall, Academy Street, Inverness.

Captains (2)
p.s MacKintosh, J. K. ⓢ
(A) (a)   23Aug.05

Lieutenant.
p.s. Forsyth, A. R. (A) (b)
20Dec.06

2nd Lieutenant.
Maxwell, W. 1Jan.13
MacEwen, G. MacE.
17Feb.14

London.
[14]
(1 *Company.*)
Calthorpe Street, W.C.

Captains (2)
p.s Hayward, W. G.
(*Capt. Res. of Off.*) ⓔ (H) 12Dec.06
1Apr.08
Cook, J. W. D. 1July14

Lieutenant.
Cox, E. S.   1July14

2nd Lieutenant.

Lowland.
[2]
(1 *Company.*)
The Drill Hall, Brandon Terrace, Edinburgh.

Captains. (2)
Bruce, J.   1July10
23Apr.09

Lieutenant.
Harvey, G. T. 1June12

2nd Lieutenant.
Bruce, A. C. A. 27Apr.10
Ritchie, C. D. 26June12
Chaplain.
Pagan, Rev. G. L.,
B.L. (C. S.) Chapl.
4th class (T.F.)
(attd.)   1May12

North Midland.
[7]
(1 *Company.*)
11, The Magazine Leicester.

Captains (2)
Briggs, O W. H. 7Dec.11
Briggs, A. E. 3May14

Lieutenant.
Cooper, R. T. 3May14

2nd Lieutenant.
Hearth, C.H. 2Apr.13

1st South Midland.
[8]
(1 *Company.*)
New Drill Hall, Taunton Road, Sparkbrook, Birmingham.

Captains (2)
Ash, F. (a) (b) 25June08
Moody, A. H. (b)
27Nov.12

Lieutenant.
King, A. A. (a) 27Nov.12

2nd Lieutenant.
Blakemore, P. W. B.
21Dec.11
Checkland, L. W. 15Oct.13

2nd South Midland.
[9]
(1 *Company.*)
Yeomanry House, Castle Hill, Reading.

Captains. (2)
Troup, A. G. 13Feb.09
Smith-Hughes, T.
1Nov.11

Lieutenant.
Troup, L. G. 27Dec.12

2nd Lieutenant.
Hatt, R. C. 20July12

Notts. & Derby.
[6]
(1 *Company.*)
Drill Hall, Chesterfield.

Captains. (2)
Tristram, U. H.,
late Capt. 14
Hrs. (Remount Service.) 1July08
Tylden-Wright,H.
1July08

Lieutenant.
Mills, R. N. F. 1July08

2nd Lieutenant.
✕Penrose, J. D.
(Hon. 2nd Lt. in Army 5 Oct. 02)
4Jan.12
Adamthwaite, J. W. E.
27Nov.12

South Eastern.
[13]
(1 *Company.*)
Croydon.

Captains. (2)
Docking, S. R. 22Mar.11

Lieutenant.
Hacking,F.L. 17Apr.12

2nd Lieutenant.
Curtis, W. 16May12
Needham, E. S. 8Apr.14

South Wales.
[4]
(1 *Company.*)
7, Rutland Street, Swansea.

Captains (2)
p. Isaac, G. G. (b) 2July05
Harries, J.   21 May 12

Lieutenant.
Taylor, E. J. 1Dec.12

2nd Lieutenant.
Randell, F W. 23Apr.13

1st South Western.
[10]
(1 *Company.*)
The Armoury, Tisbury, Wiltshire.

Captains (2)
Alexander,W.H.R.
4Feb.14
Lieutenant.
Blake, G. H. 26Apr.11
2nd Lieutenant.
Carter, H. T. 22Apr.14
Harman, E. L.
H. B.   13May14

2nd South Western.
[11]
(1 *Company.*)
Drill Hall, High Street, Weston-super-Mare.

Captains (2)
p. Boyle, M. (b) 3Oct.0˙
23Apr.02
Tucker, W. K. (b)
1Dec.11

Lieutenant.
2nd Lieutenant.

Welsh Border.
[3]
(1 *Company.*)
79a, Harrowby Rd., Birkenhead.

Captains (2)
p.s. ✕McLean,J.L.,TD,
hon.m.(Hon.Lt.in Army 27 Aug. 02)
(H)   23Aug.02
p. Newell, L. M. (t) 4Feb.07

Lieutenant.
Young, H. O. 5Mar.13
1Jan.10

2nd Lieutenant.
Deacon, V. 17Dec.13
Law, E. S. 16May14

Yorkshire.
[5]
(1 *Company.*)
Lumley Barracks, York.

Captains. (2)
✕Brown, J., I.S.O.,
late Gambia Art.
(Vols.)   7Apr.12
Landon, J. W. B.
14Feb.13

Lieutenant.
2nd Lieutenant.
Harland, C. S. 24Jan.14

| 1658 | 1659 | 1660 | 1661 |

Army Service Corps. Territorial Force.

II. DIVISIONAL TRANSPORT AND SUPPLY COLUMNS.
[*The order of precedence of columns is denoted by numerals in brackets.*]

East Anglian.
[25]

156, High Road, Ilford.

Hon. Colonel.
✗Landon, Maj.-Gen. F. W. B., C B. (*Dir. of Transport and Movements*) 8June14

Lt.-Colonel.
✗Probert, W. G. (*hon. Capt. in Army* 28Sept.02) (*Hon. Maj. ret., Spec. Res.*) 27Apr.12

Major.
Marchbank, W. G. (*a*) 1Dec.11
 25 Jan.11

Adjutant.
Jones, H. A., Capt. A.S.C. 21Oct.12

Medical Officers.
Anderson, Lt. C. E., R.A.M.C. (T.F.) (*attd.*) 2July13

Chaplain.
Colchester, *Rt. Rev.* R. H., *Lord Bishop of, D.D.*, Chapl. 1st Class (T.F.) (*attd.*) 20July09

East Anglian Divisional Co.
(*Hd.-Qrs.*)

156, High Road, Ilford.

Major.
p. ✗Soper, F. P. P. (*Hon. Lt. in Army* 28Sept.02) (*Q*) (*a*) (*H*)(*b*), *p.v.o.* 9Dec.11

Captains. (2)
p. Dixon, R. H., VD, *hon. m.* (*a*) 20Oct.06
✗Franklin, P. C. (*Q*) 22Feb.12

Lieut. and 2nd Lieut. (2)

Lieutenant.
Robertson, D. G. 10Mar.13

2nd Lieutenant.
Elms, A. 12Oct.12

Norfolk & Suffolk Brigade Co.

King's Lynn, Norfolk.

Captains. (2)
Hawkins, E. R. (*b*) 15July10

Lieut. and 2nd Lieut. (2)

Lieutenant.
Rodwell, H. 11Jan.11

2nd Lieutenant.
Clark, A. C. 20Dec.13

East Midland Brigade Co.

Northampton.

Captains. (2)
p.s.Church, L. H. 15July10

Lieut. and 2nd Lieut. (2)

Lieutenant.
Dawson, B. N. 1Sept.13

2nd Lieutenant.
Dawson, C. 27Jan.12
Phipps, R. T. 18Apr.14

Essex Brigade Co.

Bay Lodge, The Green, Stratford, E.

Captains. (2)
p.s.✗Rust, W. T. C. (*q*) 26Mar.09
Bray, R. B. 9Dec.11

Lieut. and 2nd Lieut. (2)

Lieutenant.
Marchand, V. W. I. 22June10
Ketley, W. J. B. 12Mar.13
Ross, R. E. 1Apr.14

2nd Lieutenant.

Highland.
[15]

Drill Hall, Tay Street, Perth.

Hon. Colonel.
Sempill, J., Lord, Capt. ret. pay 1Apr.13

Lt.-Colonel
Henderson H. D., VD (*a*) 1Apr.14

Major.

Adjutant.
Weston, J. L., Capt. A.S.C. 21Nov.11

Chaplain.
Lee, *Rev.* W. E., *M.A.* [C.S.] Chapl. 4th class (T.F.) (*attd.*) 1June12

1st (*Head-quarters*) Co.

Drill Hall, Tay Street, Perth.

Major.

Captains. (2)
Gray, W. (*a*) 18Jan.09
Taylor, E. N.(*a*)18Jan.09

Lieut. and 2nd Lieut. (2)

Lieutenant.
Taylor, D. 1Sept.11
Archbold, S. 13Mar.13

2nd Lieutenant.
McIntosh, J. McG. H. 6June14

Medical Officer.
Taylor, Maj. W. A., M.B., R.A.M.C. (T.F.) (*attd.*) 30Oct.12
 26July99

2nd Co.

St. John Street, Stirling.

⸮Major.
MacGregor, A. (*a*) 5Jan.13

Captains. (2)
p.s.Wilson, H. (A)(*a*) 1July11

Lieut. and 2nd Lieut. (2)

Lieutenant.
Meiklejohn, R. (*a*) 12Nov.09
Ritchie, G. M. 13Mar.13

2nd Lieutenant.
McCulloch, R. C. S. 4Dec.13

3rd (*Gordon Brig.*) Co.

Territorial Barracks, Fonthill Road, Aberdeen.

Captains. (2)
Nicol Smith, A. G. 1Apr.11

Lieut. and 2nd Lieut.

Lieutenant.
Watt, C. 1June11
Lorimer, J. V. 13Mar.13

2nd Lieutenant.
Macdonald, H. R. 12June13

4th Co.

Drill Hall, Dundee.

Captains. (2)
Cochrane, C. W. 16June08
✗Glass, D. 1July12

Lieut. and 2nd Lieut. (2)

Lieutenant.

2nd Lieutenant.
Black, D. 5June12
Russell, J. 10May13
Fraser, A. C. McK. 29May13

⸮ This rank is not provided for in the Territorial Tables of Establishments.

| 1662 | 1663 | 1664 | 1665 |

Army Service Corps. Territorial Force.

Divl. T. and S. Cols.—contd.

Home Counties.
[26]
Hounslow.
Hon. Colonel.
✗Leconfield, C. H., Lord (Hon. Col. ret. T.F.) 18Apr.10
Lt.-Colonel.
Martin, A. H., TD ⊕ (H), (a), (b) 14Dec.08
bt. col. 22Feb.13
Major.
p. Maynard, S. T. 1Jan.10
29Jan.07
Adjutant.
✗Beddy, B. Lt. A S.C. 16Apr.13

Home Counties Divisional Company (Hd.-Qrs.)
Drill Hall, 117, Gloucester Road, Brighton.
Major.
Cox, R. J. 27Feb.13
Captains (2)
Lieut. and 2nd Lieut. (2).
Lieutenant.
Stoner, P. B. 1Nov13
2nd Lieutenant.
Jay, R. B. 4Jan.13

Surrey Brigade Co.
259, Walton Road, Woking.
Captains (2)
Allen, C. G. 15Feb13
19Feb.09
Sharpley, R. 1Jan.14
Lieut. and 2nd Lieut. (2)
Lieutenant.
2nd Lieutenant.

Kent Brigade Co.
Drill Hall, Union Street, Maidstone.
Captains (2)
p.s. Lattimer, E. 19Dec.06
Cox, F. T. 15Feb.14
Lieut. and 2nd Lieut. (2)
Lieutenant.

2nd Lieutenant.
Fletcher, H. 27July13

Middlesex Brigade Co.
The Barracks, Barnet.
Captains. (2)
Medcalf, S. A. 26Oct.11

Lieut. and 2nd Lieut. (2)
Lieutenant.
Tufnell - Klug, M. W. T. 1July13
2nd Lieutenant.
Craxton, T. W. H. 14Mar.14

East Lancashire.
[18]
Hulme Barracks, Manchester.
Hon. Colonel.
✗Ellesmere, J. F. G. S., Earl of, M.V.O. (Lt.-Col, 3 Bn. R. Scots) 1Sept.09
Lt.-Colonel.
Needham, J. G. (b) 4Dec.13
Major.
England, A. 9Mar.11
Adjutant.
✗Slaughter, R. J., Capt. A.S.C. 30Apr.12
Medical Officer.
p. Smithard, Maj. W. R. N., M.B., R.A.M.C. (T F.) (attd.) 17Mar.14
21Dec.01

East Lancashire Divisional Co. (Hd.-Qrs.)
Hulme Barracks, Manchester.
Major.
Captain (2)
Sykes, G. A. 26Nov.10
Lieut. and 2nd Lieut. (2)
Lieutenant.
Clark, F. E. 16Nov.12
Knowles, E. M. 10Dec.13
2nd Lieutenant.
Brocklehurst, J.G. 17Mar14

Lancashire Fusiliers Brigade Co.
Hulme Barracks, Manchester.
Captains. (2)
Gillibrand, A.(b)1Feb.14
Ison, F. H. 25Feb.13
Lieut. and 2nd Lieut. (2)
Lieutenant.
Reynolds, H. J. B. 3Dec.13
2nd Lieutenant.
Porter, T. Y. 27Mar.12
Prestwich, J. 16Mar.14

East Lancashire Brigade Co.
Rawtenstall.
Captains (2)
p. ✗Kenyon, H. M. (b) 30July04
p.s. Lyle, J. C. (a)(b) 9July11
10Nov.05
Lieut. and 2nd Lieut. (2)
Lieutenant.
Hodgson, T. B. 5Feb.13
10May10
2nd Lieutenants

Manchester Brigade Co.
Hulme Barracks, Manchester.
Captains. (2)
Howard, F. 2Feb.10
Lieut. and 2nd Lieut. (2)
Lieutenants.
Holland, R. L. 15Nov.11
1Jan.10
Ball, F. 5June12
2nd Lieutenant.
Lacey, F. H. 16Feb.14

West Lancashire.
[17]
Southport.
Hon. Colonel.
✗Derby, Rt. Hon. E. G. V., Earl of, G.C.V.O., C.B. 1Apr.08
Lt.-Colonel.
p.s. Lomas, A.D., TD 1Apr.08
Major.
Atherton, G. B. 13May11
Adjutant.
✗Roberts, A. H., Capt. A.S.C., e. 13May14
Medical Officers.
Reid, Maj.J. R., TD, R.A.M.C., (T.F.) (Hon. Maj. ret. Vols.) (attd.) 1May08
Edmiston, Lt. J. F., M.B., R.A.M.C., (T.F.) (attd.) 3June12

West Lancashire Divisional Co. (Hd.-Qrs.)
Drill Hall, Manchester Road, Southport.
Major.
Captains (2)
Gibson, W. R. 5Dec.12
Taylor, K. F. 6Dec.12
Gregson, W. 19Mar.13
Lieut. and 2nd Lieut. (2)
Lieutenant.
Parker, J. W. 10Oct.11
2nd Lieutenant.
Gibbs, C. E. 1June13
Hinchliffe, W. G. E. 20Apr.14
[l] 20Mar.12

North Lancashire Brigade Co.
Tramway Road, Aigburth, Liverpool.
Captains (2)
Lieut. and 2nd Lieut. (2)
Lieutenant.
Barton, J. W. 18Feb.13
Baron, R. 8Apr.14
2nd Lieutenant.
Ronald, R. S. 21Jan.14

Liverpool Brigade Co.
Tramway Road, Aigburth, Liverpool.
Captains (2)
Lansdale, E.E.(a)1June10
Carter, H. (b) 1Oct.11
Lieut. and 2nd Lieut. (2)
Lieutenant.
Thomas, W. A. 30Apr.13
2nd Lieutenant.
Taylor, W. W. 1May13
Inglis, A. G. 1June14

South Lancashire Brigade Co.
46, Legh St., Warrington.
Captains (2)
p.s. Picton, J. T. 1Apr.08
p. Roberts, R. McM. (a) 1Apr.06
Lieut. and 2nd Lieut. (2)
Lieutenant.
Fairclough, H. 1Oct.10
Richardson, J. S. 1Feb.12
2nd Lieutenant.

1st London.
[27]
Charles Street, Plumstead, S.E
Hon. Colonel.
Dunn, Sir W. H., Knt. 1Jan.09
‡ Colonel.
✗Kearns, T. J., C.B., Rdg.-Mr. (hon. capt.) ret. pay (Rdg.-Mr. Res. Off.) (a) (b) 1Apr.08
Lt.-Colonel.
Davies, E. R. (a)·(b) 1Apr.08
Adjutant.
✗Lawson, J. L., Capt. A. S. C., e. 21Apr.13
Medical Officers.

Chaplain.
Pickering, Rev. A. M., M.A., Chapl. 4th Class (T.F.) (attd.) 30Sept.11

‡ This rank is not provided for in the Territorial Force Tables of Establishments.

Q

Army Service Corps. Territorial Force.

Divl. T. and S. Cols.— *contd.*

1st London Divisional Co.
(Hd.-Qrs.)
Charles Street, Plumstead, S.E.
Major.
Allen, L. A. (a)(b) 1Apr.09
Captains (2)
Young, R. V. C. (b) 19May11
Lieut. and 2nd Lieut. (2)
Lieutenant.
Norman, R. G. 7Aug.12
Reynolds, W. P. K. 16Nov.13
2nd Lieutenant.

1st London Brigade Co.
Charles Street, Plumstead, S.E.
Captains (2)
Kearns, R. A.
E. H. (a)(b) 9Aug.10
Falkner, F. N. 19Apr.08
18Oct.13
Lieut. and 2nd Lieut. (2)
Lieutenant.
Quin, L. M. 16Nov.13
Williams, C. G. 14Feb.14
2nd Lieutenant.

2nd London Brigade Co.
Charles Street, Plumstead, S.E.
Captains (2)
Clough, C. E. (a)(b) 19May11
Robertson, J. A. 5Dec.12
Lieut. and 2nd Lieut. (2)
Lieutenant.
Vincent Poore, E. 15Nov.13
2nd Lieutenant.
Reeves, M. G. 22Apr.14

3rd London Brigade Co.
Charles Street, Plumstead, S.E.
Captains (2)
Newton, E. H. 19Oct.13
Lieut. and 2nd Lieut. (2)
Lieutenant.
2nd Lieutenant.
Davies, K. C. J. 3May13
Bune, J. G. 2Mar.14

2nd London.
[28]
Duke of York's Headquarters, Chelsea, S.W.
Hon. Colonel.
Ward, Col. Sir E. W.
D., Bt., K.C.B., K.C.V.O., ret. pay, late Permt. Under Sec. of State for War 12Dec.08

Lt.-Colonel.
Blyth, C. F. T., TD, (Q) 15May12
Major.
Galbraith, W. C. (b) 1June12
Adjutant.
✗Coleman, G. B., Capt. A.S.C. 1Apr.12
Medical Officer.
p. Bourke, Maj. E. U. F.
Mac W., R.A.M.C. (T.F.)(attd.) 28Sept.08
24Feb.97

2nd London Divisional Co.
(Hd.-Qrs.)
Duke of York's Headquarters, Chelsea, S.W.
Major.
Maurice, A. J. (H)⊕ 18Dec.12
Captains (2)
Lieut. and 2nd Lieut. (2)
Lieutenant.
Kenyon, G. M., late Lt. A. Motor Res. 4Aug.12
Smith, F. E. 1Apr.12
3June13
2nd Lieutenant.
✗Wigginton, J. H. B. 15Feb.13
Fleming, T. V. 18Dec.13

4th London Brigade Co.
Duke of York's Headquarters, Chelsea, S.W.
Captains (2)
Lieut. and 2nd Lieut. (2)
Lieutenant.
Townend, R. 12Nov.13
D. G. 5June13
2nd Lieutenant.
Wood, A. L. S. 22Jan.13

5th London Brigade Co.
Duke of York's Headquarters, Chelsea, S.W.
Captains (2)
Robertson, W. 16Jan.14
18May10
Lieut. and 2nd Lieut. (2)
Lieutenant.
Masters, E. A. 2June13
2nd Lieutenant.
Wills, T. E. 15Jan.13
Smith, E. T. 22Jan.13

6th London Brigade Co.
Duke of York's Headquarters, Chelsea, S.W.
Captains (2)
Maude, A. H. (b) 1Apr.12
✗Crispin, E. H. (b) 15May12
Lieut. and 2nd Lieut. (2)
Lieutenant.
van Homan, B. 18Sept.13
2nd Lieutenant.
Whiffen, S. W. 1Dec.13

Lowland.
[16]
22, Lochburn Road, Maryhill, Glasgow.
Hon. Colonel.
✗Fergusson, Maj.-Gen. Sir C., Bt., C.B.
M.V.O., D.S.O., s.[F] 24Sept.08
Lt.-Colonel.
Matthew, J. S., TD. 1Apr.13
Major.
Adjutant.
✗Stewart, H. A., Capt. A. S. C. 1Aug.11
Medical Officers.
p.s.,p.s. Jamieson, Maj. J. B., TD (t) R.A.M.C. (T.F.)(attd.) 31July09
19Nov.04
Brand, Lt. G. B.
M.B., R.A.M.C. (T.F.)(attd.) 15May11
Chaplains.
Pagan, Rev. G. L.,
B.D. (C.S.), Chapl. 4th Class (T.F.) (attd.) 1May12
Thomson, Rev. P. D.,
M.A. (U.F.C.) Chapl. 4th Class (T.F.) (attd.) 1June14

1st (Headquarters) Co.
22, Lochburn Road, Maryhill.
Major.
Graham, J. McG. (b) 19May13
Captains (2)
Lieut. and 2nd Lieut. (2)
Lieutenant.
Heilbron, I. M. 11Jan.13
2nd Lieutenant.
Shirlaw, N. M. 6May13
Walker, G. C. 29Apr.14

2nd Co.
The Drill Hall, Brandon Terrace Edinburgh.
Captains (2)
Lieut. and 2nd Lieut. (2)
Lieutenant.
Grieve, J. 3Apr.13
Deas, P. B. 31Mar.14
2nd Lieutenant.
Gallie, D. A. 3May13

3rd (Scottish Rifle Brigade) Co.
Drill Hall, Motherwell.
Captains (2)
p.s. Clarke, R. (a) 1Apr.08
Lieut. and 2nd Lieut. (2)
Lieutenant.
McFarlane, J. S. 31Mar.14
Wilson, J. 31Mar.14
2nd Lieutenant.
Moore, W. C. 19Mar.14

4th (Highland Light Infantry Brigade) Co.
Gilbert Street, Yorkhill, Glasgow.
Captains (2)
Wordie, W. (a)(b) (Q) 8Apr.11
Lieut. and 2nd Lieut. (2)
Lieutenant.
Goldie-Morrison, W. D. 31Mar.14
Macdonald, R. G. 31Mar.14
2nd Lieutenant.
Cullen, W. G. 28Apr.14

North Midland.
[22]
7, Magazine Square, Leicester.
Hon. Colonel.
Dartmouth, Rt. Hon. W. H., Earl of, VD, 1Apr.08
Lt.-Colonel.
Wright, A. E. (a)(b) 17Apr.12
Major.
Jones, H. W. (a) 27Apr.14
1June13
Adjutant.
✗Brancker, S. D., [L] Capt. A. S. C. 11Jan.12
Medical Officer.
McAllister-Hewlings, Capt. W. F., R.A.M.C. (T.F.)(attd.) 16Mar.11
Chaplain.

North Midland Divisional Co.
(Hd.-Qrs.)
Drill Hall, Handsworth, Birmingham.
Major.
Reading, L. G. 1Feb.09
Captains (2).
Pemberton, R. T. (a) 1Feb.11
Smith, S. 1June13
Lieut. and 2nd Lieut. (2)
Lieutenant.
2nd Lieutenant.
Shaughnessy, H. 18June13

Army Service Corps. Territorial Force.

Divl.T.& S.Cols.—contd.
North Midland—contd.

Lincoln and Leicester Brigade Co.
19, Magazine Square, Leicester.
Captains (2)
Williams, A. T. (b) 18May11
Lieut. and 2nd Lieut. (2).
Lieutenant.
✠Tomlinson, R. 3May13
Fowler, E. G. 12July13
2nd Lieutenant.
Cawdell, P. R. 30June13

Staffordshire Brigade Co.
Drill Hall, Handsworth.
Captains (2).
Clark, C. H. (a) 4Dec.12
Best, J. A. 18June13
Lieut. and 2nd Lieut. (2).
Lieutenant.
2nd Lieutenant.
Court, W. A. 29May13

Notts and Derby Brigade Co.
Drill Hall, Derby Road, Nottingham.
Captains (2).
Potter, W. A. 30Sept.12
Lieut. and 2nd Lieut. (2).
Lieutenant.
Davis, F. P. 1Jan.14
2nd Lieutenant.
Armitage, S. C. 7Nov.12

South Midland.
[23]
Aston, Birmingham.
Hon. Colonel.
✠Hamilton, Gen. Sir I. S. M., G.C.B., D.S.O., Col. Cam'n Highrs., q.s., 𝔄.𝔇.ℭ. 1Jan.09
Lt.-Colonel.
Collis, C. H., VD (b) bt.-col. ⓣ 1July08 6Jan.12
Major.
,s.✠Whitcombe, R. H., jun., VD (Hon.Capt. in Army 10July01) 1Apr.08
Adjutant.
✠Doran, J. C. M., Capt. A.S.C. 1Apr.14

Medical Officer.
Chaplain.

South Midland Divisional Co.
(Hd.-Qrs.)
Aston, Birmingham.
Major.
Pearson, F. S. (q) 1Apr.08
Captains (2),
Lieut. and 2nd Lieut. (2).
Lieutenant.
Godrich, A. E. 28July08
Grinsell, G. H. 1July11
Huxley, J. E. 1July13
2nd Lieutenant.
Ham, P. S. 1June14

Warwickshire Brigade Co.
Court Oak House, Harborne, Birmingham.
Captains (2).
p.s. Wright, J. A. C. (b) 1Apr.08
Bradbury, J. F. 21June13
Lieut. and 2nd Lieut. (2).
Lieutenant.
Walker, G. S. 18Sept.10
Odgers, R. B. 25Mar.13
2nd Lieutenant.

Gloucester and Worcester Brigade Co.
Wallbridge, Stroud, Glos.
Captains (2).
p.s. Ball, J. R. M. (b) 18Aug.06
Marshall, M. H. (a) (b) 1Nov.08
Lieut. and 2nd Lieut. (2).
Lieutenant.
Ball, A. K. M. 1Sept.10
2nd Lieutenant.
Humphreys, L. M. 1Sept.13

South Midland Brigade Co.
Drill Hall, Taplow, Bucks.
Captains (2).
p.s.✠Barron, C. A. (Hon. Lt. in Army 18June01) (a) 28May02
Lieut. and 2nd Lieut. (2)
Lieutenant.
Stanley, R. B. 1Nov.13
Stanley, H. C. 1Nov.13
2nd Lieutenant.
Clark, J. E. 1May13

Northumbrian.
[20]
St. George's Hall, Newcastle-on-Tyne.
Hon. Colonel.
p. Erskine, H. A., C.B., VD, ⓣ (Hon. Col. ret. T.F.) 7Feb.14
Lt.-Colonel.
Major.
Dowling, T. (a) 15Nov.11
Adjutant.
✠Horton, C. W., Capt. A.S.C. 23Nov.11
Medical Officer.
Livingstone, Capt. T. H., M.D., F.R.C.S. (Edin.) R.A.M.C. (T.F.) (attd.) 20June10 1Mar.09
Chaplain.
Boot, Rev. Canon A., M.A., Chapl. 4th Class (T.F.) (attd.) 1Mar.09

Northumbrian Divisional Co.
(Hd.-Qrs.)
Angus Hall, Gateshead.
Major.
p. Pinkney, E. W. R. (b) 8Sept.06
Captains (2).
p.s. Millican, H. C. (A) 1Nov.08 13Feb.08
Lieut. and 2nd Lieut. (2).
Lieutenant.
Angus, M. S. 24May11
Ramsey, W. J. 24May12
2nd Lieutenant.

Northumberland Brigade Co.
St. George's Drill Hall, Newcastle-on-Tyne.
Captains (2).
✠Ager, F. G. 22May12
Lieut. and 2nd Lieut. (2).
Lieutenant.
Clark, E. G. 25May12
2nd Lieutenant.

York and Durham Brigade Co.
Walton Street, Hull.
Captains (2).
Lieut. and 2nd Lieut. (2)
Lieutenant.
Walker, C. (b) 1May08
2nd Lieutenant.
Cooper, J. S. 22Dec.10
Hay, W. 1Feb.13

Durham Light Infantry Brigade Co.
Drill Hall, Green, Sunderland.
Captains (2).
Hudson, R. C. (b) 25Apr.09
Dent, A. 23May13
Lieut. and 2nd Lieut. (2).
Lieutenant.
McLaren, J., jun. 1July10
Wigham, J. R. 31July10
2nd Lieutenant.

West Riding.
[21]
Harewood Barracks, Woodhouse Lane, Leeds.
Hon. Colonel.
✠Scarbrough, Col. A. F.G.B., Earl of K.C.B., TD, A.D.C. 8Dec.08
Lt.-Colonel.
Chambers, J. C., VD (t) (H) (a) 28May06
Major.
✠Haigh, B. (a) 21July11
Adjutant.
✠White, W. N., Capt. A.S.C. 1Jan.12
Medical Officers.
Hughes, Lt. G. S., M.B., F.R.C.S., R.A.M.C. (T.F.) (attd.) 2Dec.08
Haddow, Lt. A. C., M.B., R.A.M.C. (T.F.) (attd.) 15May14
Chaplain.
Sullivan, Rev. A. M., Chapl. 4th Class (T.F.) (attd.) 24Apr.14

Q 2

Army Service Corps. Territorial Force.

Div. T. and S. Cols.—contd.

West Riding—contd.

West Riding Divisional Co. (Hd.-Qrs.)
Lumley Barracks, Burton Stone Lane, York.

Major.

Captains (2).
Wilberforce, H. H. 1July12
Scott, F. G. (a) 17June14

Lieut. and 2nd Lieut. (2).
Lieutenant.
Pearson, R. T. 14June14
2nd Lieutenant.
Procter, A. K. 5July13
Mills, G. H. 24June14

1st West Riding Brigade Co.
Harewood Barracks, Woodhouse Lane, Leeds.
Captains (2).
Stonehouse, E. C. (a)
[l] 16June10
Reynolds, P. R.
24June14
2July12
Lieut. and 2nd Lieut. (2).
Lieutenant.
Hall, D. C. 7Apr 14
2nd Lieutenant.
Mantle, C. A. 6Feb.14

2nd West Riding Brigade Co.
Harewood Barracks, Woodhouse Lane, Leeds.

Captains (2).
Kitson, H. V. (a)
16June10
Montgomery, C. E.
26June14
Lieut. and 2nd Lieut. (2).
Lieutenant.
Milner, J. 9Oct.13
2nd Lieutenant.

3rd West Riding Brigade Co.
Leeds.

Captains (2)
Cameron, W. S. (a)
16June10
Shaw, F. H. 6June13
Lieut. and 2nd Lieut. (2)
Lieutenant.
Clayton, W. B. 24Oct.12
2nd Lieutenant.
Kitson, W.F.C.30Jan.14
Simpson, J. R. 23Feb.14

Welsh.
[19]
The Barracks, Hereford.

Hon. Colonel.
Cotterell, Sir J. R. G., Bt. 10Nov.08

Lt.-Colonel.
Leather, F. H., TD (t)
(H) (a) (b) 3May13

Major.

Adjutant.
✗Holbrook, A. E.,
Capt. A.S.C.
12Sept.12

Medical Officer.
Southam, Lt. S.,
R.A.M.C.(T.F.)
(attd.) 3Jan.14

Chaplain.
Lushington, Rev.
P. A., M.A.,
Chapl. 4th
Class (T.F.)
(attd.) 1Apr.12

Welsh Divisional Co. (Hd.-Qrs.)
Weobley, Herefordshire.

Major.

Captains (2)
p.s.Caddick, E. W. (a)
1Apr.08
27Sept.05
Hill, J. A. 19Jan.12

Lieut. and 2nd Lieut. (2)
Lieutenant.
Vaughan, C. H.
28Aug.12
James, H. G. 21Feb.14
2nd Lieutenant.
Power, K. F. M. 1Mar.10
Thynne, H. S. 2Apr.14

Cheshire Brigade Co.
73a, Harrowby Road, Birkenhead.

Captains (2)
Norbury, F. H. (a)
4Feb.07
Hughes, R. T. 1Feb.14
Lieut. and 2nd Lieut. (2)
Lieutenant.
Hime, H. 12Dec.13
14Dec.09
Wattleworth, J.
18June14
2nd Lieutenant.

North Wales Brigade Co.
Ruthin.

Captains (2)
Gettins, J. H. 8Apr.14

Lieuts. and 2nd Lieuts. (2)
Lieutenant.

2nd Lieutenant.

Welsh Border Brigade Co.
Ystrad, Rhondda, Glamorgan.

Captains (2)
p. Dyke, R. C., VD,
hon. m. 6Dec.99
Broome, W. J. (a)
28Sept.08

Lieut. and 2nd Lieut. (2)
Lieutenant.

2nd Lieutenant.
Davies, E. H. 9 Oct.12

Wessex.
[24]

14, Oxford Road, Exeter.

Hon. Colonel.
Clifford, L. H. H.,
Lord, VD, Col.,
A.D.C. 23Dec.09

Lt.-Colonel.
Cooper, H. L., TD (a)
(b) 1Nov.09

Major.
Pollock, E. H. (a) (b)
1Mar.10

Adjutant.
✗Kelly, W. H. F.,
Capt. A.S.C. 1Oct.13

Medical Officer.

Wessex Divisional Co. (Hd.-Qrs.)
Andover, Hants.

Major.

Captains (2)
Holman, K. R. C. (b)
8Mar.12
Wetherall, G. C.
21Feb.12
1June12

Lieut. and 2nd Lieut. (2)
Lieutenants.
Clarke, J. T. P. 1Oct.12

2nd Lieutenant.
Henshaw, F. 20Aug13

Devon and Cornwall Brigade Co.
Mutley Barracks, Plymouth.

Captains (2)
p. Collier, M. C.
(a) (b) p.v.c. 20Oct.02
Shorto, H. G. 1Apr.08

Lieut. and 2nd Lieut. (2)

Lieutenant.
Gould, H. C. 10Sept.09
Johns, R. A. P. 29Mar.11

2nd Lieutenant.

South Western Brigade Co.
Bridgwater, Somerset.

Captains (2)
p. Peace, A. H., TD,
hon. m. (b) (H) 4July00
Gregory, H. M. 25Oct13

Lieut. and 2nd Lieut. (2)
Lieutenant.
Foley, F. Y. 6June14

2nd Lieutenant.

Hampshire Brigade Co.
The Drill Hall, Redan Hill, Aldershot.

Captains (2)
p.s.Atkinson, J, (Q)
(H) (a) (b) 13June03
Simpkins, W, (S)
29Mar.11

Lieut. and 2nd Lieut (2).
Lieutenant.
Phillips,T.K.(q) 1Oct.11

2nd Lieutenant.
Potter, G. J. R. 1May14

ARMY MEDICAL SERVICE.

Agents.. .. .. Messrs. Holt & Co., 3, Whitehall Place, S.W.

ROYAL ARMY MEDICAL CORPS.

Within a laurel wreath surmounted by a crown the rod of Æsculapius with a serpent entwined.
"*In Arduis Fidelis.*"

Uniform—Blue. *Facings*—Dull Cherry.

Officer in charge of Records .. .. .. Thomson, Lt.-Col. J., *M.B., Aldershot* .. 1July13

Stations of the Head-Quarters of Companies.

1 Co. Aldershot.	10 Co. Chatham.	19 Co. Chester.	28 Co. Gibraltar.
2 ,, Aldershot.	11 ,, Shorncliffe.	20 ,, Tidworth.	29 ,, Jamaica.
3 ,, Aldershot.	12 ,, Woolwich.	21 ,, Netley.	30 ,, Malta.
4 ,, Netley.	13 ,, Edinburgh.	22 ,, Wynberg.	31 ,, Mauritius.
5 ,, Netley.	14 ,, Dublin.	23 ,, Roberts' Heights,	32 ,, Singapore.
6 ,, Cosham.	15 ,, Belfast.	Pretoria.	33 ,, Cairo.
7 ,, Devonport.	16 ,, Cork.	25 ,, Bermuda.	34 ,, Woolwich.
8 ,, York.	17 ,, Curragh.	26 ,, Ceylon.	35 ,, London (Grosvenor
9 ,, Colchester.	18 ,, London.	27 ,, Hong Kong.	Road, S.W.)
	(Rochester Row, S.W.)		

Depôt Companies :—A, B, C Aldershot.

Removed from the Corps and still on the Active List.

Surgeon-General (ranking as Lieutenant-General).
Sloggett, Sir *War Office* 1June14
 A. T., Knt., C.B., C.M.G.,
 K.H.S. [F] (*Dir.-Gen.*)

Surgeon-Generals (ranking as Major-Generals).
Whitehead, H. R., *E. Comd.* 21Jan.09
 C.B., F.R.C.S.
MacNeece, J. G., *S. Comd.* 23Apr.10
 C.B. [F]
Corker, T. M., *Ootacamund* 11Dec.11
 M.D., K.H.P.
Ve Babtie, W., C.B., *Army* 11Dec.11
 C.M.G., M.B.,   *Hd.-Qrs.,*
 K.H.S. s.   *India*
Bruce, Sir D., Knt., *Nyasaland* 1Apr.12
 C.B., F.R.S., M.B.,
 F.R.C.P., c.v.
Anderson, L. E., *Irish Comd.* 4May12
 C.B.
Hathaway,   *Darjeeling* 15Oct.12
 H. G., C.B.
Bedford, W. G. A., *Pretoria* 1Jan.14
 C.M.G., M.B.
Ford, R. W., *N. Comd.* 1June14
 D.S.O.
Woodhouse, T.P. *Aldershot* 14July14
     Comd.
Macpherson, *War Office* 14July14
 W.G.,C.M.G., M.B.,
 K.H.P. [F].

Colonels.

Porter, R., *M.B.* 14Jan.10

Removed from the Corps and still on the Active List—contd.

Colonels—contd.
O'Keeffe, M.W., *M.D.* 23Apr.10
O'Donnell, T. J., 7July10
 D.S.O.
Sawyer, R. H. S., *Dublin* 3Aug.10
 M.B., F.R.C.S.I. [L]
Culling, J. C. *Chester* 8Aug.10
Birrell, W. G., *Dover* 15Mar.11
 M.B.
Jencken, F.J., *Colchester* 12May11
 M.B.
Treherne, F.H., *Mussoorie* 13June11
 F.R.C.S. *Edin.*
Barratt, H. J. *Ranikhet* 20Oct.11
Trevor, H. O. *Cork* 26Oct.11
Pike, W. W., *Abbottabad* 9Nov.11
 M.B., F.R.C.S.I.
Irwin, J.M., M.B. *Hong Kong* 11Dec.11
Nichol, C. E., *Jubbulpore* 9Mar.12
 D.S.O., M.B.
Westcott, S., *Portsmouth* 20Mar.12
 C.M.G.
Skinner, B .M., *Comdt.* 4May12
 M.V.O.   *R. A. M. Coll.*
Kirkpatrick R., *Darjeeling* 21May12
 C.M.G., M.D.
Lynden-Bell, E. *London* 19 Sept, 12
 H. L., M.B.
Firth, R. H.. *Cherat* 13Nov.12
 F.R.C.S.   10Nov.09
Tate, A. E. *Bangalore* 31Dec.12
Faunce, C. E. *Woolwich* 26Jan.13
Geddes, B. J., *Devonport* 5Feb.13
 D.S.O., M.B.
Sloggett, H. M. *Belfast* 27Mar.13
Maher, J.   *Gibraltar* 13Sept.13
Hunter, G. D., *Allahabad* 15Sept.13
 D.S.O. [F]
Thompson, H.N.,*Edinburgh*17Nov.13
 D.S.O., M.B.

Removed from the Corps and still on the Active List—contd.

Colonels—contd.
Manders, N. *Cairo* 21Dec.13
Birt, C.   *Bombay* 1Jan.14
Henderson, R.S.F., *Quetta* 2Jan.14
 M.B., K.H.P.   22Nov.10
Russell, M. W. *Malta* 14Jan.14
Reilly, C. C. *Chatham* 23Apr.14
Hickson, S., *War Office* 7July14
 M.B., K.H.S.,   2Jan.13
 Inspr. of Med.
 Services
Jones, F. W. C., *Tidworth* 14July14
 M.B.

Lieutenant-Colonels.

[*In the case of the senior officers the first date is that of selection for increased pay under Article 358 of the Royal Warrant.*]

Winter, T. B. *Canterbury* 14Dec.09
     2Feb.04
Haines, H. A., *Chatham* 18Feb.11
 M.D.   31Jan.05
Lilly, A. T. I. *Colaba* 15Mar.11
     31Jan.05
Caldwell, R. *Portsmouth* 6Apr.05
 F.R.C.S. [l]   31Jan.11
Fletcher, B. J., *Rawal* 12May11
 M.B.   *Pindi* 30May05
Meek, J., *M.D. Cosham* 7June11
     30May05
Swan, W. T., *Chester* 13June11
 M.B.   30May05
Macleod, R.L.R.,*Devonport* 26Oct.11
 M.B.   30May05

Royal Army Medical Corps.

Lieut.-Colonels -contd.

Adams, G. G.,*Secunderabad* 2Nov.11
                       30May05
Shine, J. M. F., *Nowshera* 4Nov.11
M.D.   30May05
Ferguson, N. C.,   *York* 9Nov.11
C.M.G., M.B.   30May05
Hall, R. H., *M.D.* *Tidworth* 22Jan.12
                       30May05
Cree, G.   *Bordon* 9Feb,12
                       30May05
Philson, S. C.   *Lucknow* 19Feb,12
                       30May05
Allen, S. G. [L]   *Gibraltar* 1Mar.12
                       1Aug.05
Green, J. S., *M.B.*   *Fermoy* 9Mar.1"
                       22Oct.07
                       1Aug.05
Gordon, P. C. H.   *Jersey* 20Mar.12
                       1Aug.05
Nash, L. T. N. *Hounslow* 4May12
                       1Aug.05
O'Halloran, M., *Edinburgh* 8May12
M.D.   1Aug.05
Daly, J. H.   *Belfast* 21May12
                       1Aug.05
Rowan, H. D.,   *Dublin* 8June12
M.B.   1Aug.05
Carr, H., *M.D.*   *Ambala* 14Aug.12
                       1Aug.05
Daly, T,   *Chester* 9Sept.12
                       1Aug.05
Sexton, M.J., *M.D* *Wynberg*11Sept.12
                       1Aug.05
Cree, H. E.   *Sialkot* 18Sept.12
                       1Aug.05
Starr, W. H.   *Lichfield*19Sept.12
                       1Aug.05
Sutton, A. A.,   *Training* 13Nov.12
D.S.O. Establt., Aldershot 1Aug.05
Yarr, M. T.,   *London* 23Nov.12
F.R.C.S.I.   30Jan.06
Melville, C. H.,   *Tidworth* 31Dec.12
M.B.   30Jan.06
          bt. col. 24Feb.12
Wilson, J.B., *M.D.* *Jamaica* 6Jan.13
                      30Jan.06
Gordon-Hall, *Hong Kong* 26Jan.13
F. W. G., *M.B.*   30Jan.06
Kennedy, A.   *Netley* 5Feb.13
                      30Jan.06
Elkington,H.P.G.*Shorncliffe*13Feb.13
                      30Jan.06
Adamson, H. M., *Belgaum* 27Mar.13
M.B.   20Jan.06
Lavie, T. G.   *Malta* 7May13
                      30Jan.06
Burtchaell, C. H., *War* 25May13
M.B., s.   *Office* 28July06
Gerrard, J. J., *W. Africa* 25May13
M.B.   28July06
Davidson, J. S.,   *Agra* 20Aug.13
M.B.   28July06
Fallon, J.   *Chakrata*15Sept.13
                      28July06
MacDonald, C. J., *Tientsin* 17Nov.13
M.D.   28July06
Wright, R. W.   *Mhow* 21Dec.13
                      28July06
Eckersley, E.,   *Quetta* 1Jan.14
M.B.   28July06

Lieut.-Colonels—contd.

O'Callaghan, D.   *Dover* 2Jan.14
M,   28July06
Donaldson, J.   *Jubbulpore* 3Jan.14
                       28July06
Barefoot, G. H.   *London* 14Jan.14
                       28July06
Newland, F. R., *Colchester* 4Feb.14
M.B.   28July06
Windle, R. J., *M.B. Poona* 25 Feb.14
                       28July06
Russell, J. J.,   *Salisbury* 20Apr.14
M.B.   28July06
Whaite, T. Du B., *Lahore* 28Apr.14
M.B.   28July06
Knaggs, H. T.,   *Cairo* 23Apr.14
M.B.   28July06

Berryman, W. E. *Woking* 31Jan.05
Morris, A. E., *M.D.* *Cork* 30May05
Blackwell, C. T.,*Hyderabad*30May05
M.D.
Lane, C. A., *M.B.* *Madras* 1Aug.05
Brown, H. H.,   *Newcastle-* 30Jan.06
M.B.   *on-Tyne*
Donegan,J,F.*Secunderabad* 28July06
Marks,G. F. H., *Dalhousie* 28July06
M.D.
Holyoake, R.   *Kamptee* 28July06
X Le Quesne, *Gravesend* 7July14
F. S.   28July06
Penton, R. H.,   *Ranikhet* 22July14
D.S.O. [F]   28July06
Bate, A. L, F, *Woolwich* 28July14
Morgan, F. J.   *R Arsenal* 12May11
                 Woolwich
Horrocks, W.H.,*Lond.Dist.* 19 May 11
M.B. (Member *bt. col.* 20May11
of Advisory Board)
Hale, C. H.,   *Sialkot* 7June11
D.S.O.
Thurston, H.C., *Aldershot*13June11
C.M.G.
Scott, B. H.   *London* 21June11
Julian, O. R. A., *R. Hosp.,* 21June11
          C.M.G   *Chelsea* 16July06
Burnside,E.A. *Bangalore* 3July11
McCulloch, T.,   *Netley* 29July11
M.B.
Macdonald, S., *Salisbury* 29July11
M.B.
Holt, M. P. C., *Aldershot* 29July11
D.S.O.   *bt. col.* 4July14
Gray, W. L.,   *Jullundur* 2Aug.11
M.B.
Browne, E. G.   *Peshawar* 2Aug.11
Morgan, J. C.   *Glasgow* 30Aug.11
Pocock, H. I.   *Murree* 2Oct.11
Elliott, C. R.,   *Jhansi* 26Oct.11
M.D.
Young, C. A.   *Chatham* 2Nov.11
Bullen, J. W.,   *Strensall* 2Nov.11
M.D.
Inniss, B. J.   *Delhi* 2Nov.11
Clark, S. F.,   *Chester* 4Nov.11
M.B.
Hassard, E. M.   *Karachi* 9Nov.11
Leishman, *Sir,*W. B.,   11Dec.11
Knt., F.R.S., M.B., bt.col., 15Oct.12
F.R.C.P., K.H.P.
(*Member of Advisory board*)

Lieut.-Colonels—contd.

Thomson, J., *Record Office,* 11Dec.11
M.B.   *Aldershot*
Rawnsley,G.T.,t. *Monchester* 22Jan.12
Blenkinsop, A. P.   *Simla* 22Jan.12
                       4May10
Girvin, J.   *Curragh* 9Feb.12
Luther, A. J. *Potchefstroom* 19Feb.12
Hallaran, W.,   *Bareilly* 1Mar.12
M.B.
Moores, S. G.   *Warley* 9Mar.12
Beach, T. B.   *Alexandria* 10Mar.12
Healey, C. W. R. *Woolwich* 20Mar.12
Austin, J. H. E. *Edinburgh* 4May12
Mould, W. T.   *Fyzabad* 8May12
Bewley, A. W.   *York* 15May12
Copeland, R. J.,   *York* 10Sept.12
M.B.   30Jan.12
Stone. C.A., *M.D. Parkhurst*21May12
Winter, H. E.   *Colaba* 8June12
Way, L.   *Ferozepore* 8June12
Smith, F., *D.S.O.*   *Dublin* 14Aug.12
                   bt. col., 4Sept.12
McLoughlin, *Winchester* 11Sept.12
G. S., *D.S.O.,*
M.B. [F]
Beveridge, W. W. O., *R.A.M.* 18Sept.12
D.S.O., M.B. Coll.
Mawhinny, R. J. *Nasirabad* 11Oct.12
W.
Bray,G.A.T., *R.Hosp.Chelsea* 13Nov.12
Forde, B., *M.B.*   *Buford* 30Nov.12
Ferguson, J. D., *Straits* 31Dec.12
D.S.O. [F]   *Settlements*
Connor, J. C.,   *Dublin* 4Jan.13
M.B.
Hardy, F. W., *Allahabad* 26Jan.13
M.B.
Shanahan, D. D.   *London* 5Feb.13
Whitestone,   *Hilsea* 13Feb.13
C. W. H., *M.B.*
Dalton, C.   *Dublin* 7May13
Robinson, O. L.   *R.A.M.* 25May13
                       Coll.
Gibbard, T.W.,   *London* 20Aug.13
M.B., K,H.S.   14Aug.12
                 bt. col 14July14
Buist, H. J. M.,   *Pretoria* 22Aug.13
D.S.O., M.B.
Stanistreet,G.B., *War Office* 13Sept.13
M.B., s.
Hardy, W. E.   *Calcutta* 13Sept.13
Brogden, J. E.   *Malta* 5Sept.13
Tate, G. W., *M.B. Bermuda* 7Oct.13
Falchnie, N., *M.B. Preston* 13Oct.13
Begbie, F. W.   *Maymyo* 17Nov.13
Jameson, J. C., *Woolwich* 21Dec.13
M.B.
Pilcher, E. M.,   *R.A.M.* 1Jan.14
D.S.O.,M.B.,   Coll. 26Nov.13
F.R.C.S.*
Beyts, W. G.   *Rurki* 1Jan.14
Dunn, H. N., *M.B.* *Netley* 4Feb.14
[F]
Withers, S. H.,   *Dagshat* 25Feb.14
M.B.
Morphew, E. M.   *Bury* 20Apr.14
Tyacke, N., *M.B. Devonport* 21Apr.14
Hennessy, J., *M.B. Ahmed-* 7July14
                     nagar
Mitchell, L. A., *Aldershot* 14July14
M.B.

Royal Army Medical Corps.

Majors.

Smithson, A. E., M.B. — Dublin 29July02
Powell, E. E. — Ambala 31Jan.03
Graham, W. A., S. J. — Neemuch 31Jan.03
MacCarthy, I.A.O. Woolwich 28July03
Martin, C. B., M.B. — R. Mil. Coll. 30Jan.04
Lawson, C. B., M.B. — Shorncliffe 30Jan.04
Kelly, J. F. M., M.B. — Colchester 30Jan.04
Crawford, G. S., M.D. [F] — Dublin 30Jan.04
Alexander, J. D., M.B. — Jubbulpore 30Jan.04
Hinge, H. A. — Aldershot 27July04
McNaught, J.G., M.D. [l] — Aldershot 27July04
Bray, H. A. [F] — e.a. 27July04
McDermott, T., M.B. — Woolwich 27July04
Slayter, E. W., M.B. — Cahir 27July04
Thurston, H. S. — Dublin 27July04
More, L.P., M.B. — Wellington, Madras 27July04
Jones, T. P., M.B. — Pembroke Dock 27July04
Thompson, A.G., M.B. — Tidworth Park 27July04
Moore, G. A., M.D. — Aldershot 27July04
Lewis, R. C. — Gibraltar 27July04
O'Reilly, H. W., H., M.B. — Secunderabad 27July04
Condon, E.H., M.B. — Meerut 27July04
Read, H. W. K. — Rangoon 27July04
Mangin, F. M. — Poona 30July04
Pollock, C.E. [L] — W. Africa 30July04
Taylor, W. J., M.B. — 30July04
Longhurst, B. W. — Sabathu 30July04
Buswell, F. E. — Jubbulpore 30Oct.04
Symons, F. A., M.B. — Gosport 30Oct.04
Samman, C. T. — Kamptee 30Jan.05
Goodwin, T.H., J. C., D.S.O. — Devonport 30Jan.05
Keble, A. E. C., t. — Perth 30Jan.05
Collins, D. J., M.D. — Kirkee 30Jan.05
Anderson, J.B. — Southampton 30Jan.05
McMunn, J. R. — Netley 29Apr.05
Prynne, H.V., F.R.C.S. — R. Mil. Acad. 29Oct.05
Master, A. E., M.B. — Windsor 29Oct.05
Dansey-Browning, G. [F] — Gibraltar 29Oct.05
Clark, E.S., M.B. — Jhansi 29Oct.05
Barnett, K.B., M.B., F.R.C.S.I. — Lydd 29Oct.05

Majors—contd.

Fox, A. C. — Dublin 29Oct.05
Green, S.F. St. D., M.D. — Quetta 29Oct.05
Tibbits, W., M.B. — Multan 29Oct.05
Boyle, M., M.B. — Jersey 29Jan.06
Evans, P., M.B. — Devonport 29Jan.06
Morgan, C. K., M.B. — Training Estabt., Aldershot 29Jan.06
Buist, John M., M.B. — Netley 29Jan.06
Thom, G. St. C., M.B., t. — Glasgow 29Jan.06
Silver, J. P., M.B. — Tipperary 28July06
Harrison, W. S., M.B. — Jamaica bt. lt. col. 29July06 4July14
Howell, H. A. L. — R.A.C.Factory, Pimlico 29July06
Lawson, D. — Mauritius 29Oct.06
Steel, E. B., M.B. — Exeter 29Oct.06
Profeit, C. W., M.B. — London 29Oct.06
Kiddle, F., M.B. — Colchester 29Oct.06
Staddon, H. E. — Rawal Pindi 29Oct.06
Perry, S. J. C. P., F.R.C.S.I. — Lebong 29Oct.06
Smith, L. F., — Aden 29Jan.07
Blackham, R. J., C.I.E. — Jutogh 29Jan.07
Grattan, H. W. — Naini Tal 29Jan.07
Grech, J. — Warrington 29Jan.07
Killery, St. J. B. — Lucknow 1Mar.07
Fairrie, S. H., M.B. — Shoeburyness 29Apr.07
Maurice, G. T. K. — Tidworth 29Apr.07
Gunter, F. E., M.B. — R. Mil. Coll. 29Apr.07
Campbell, J. H., D.S.O. — London 29Apr.07
Forrest, J. V., M.B. [L] s. — War Office 29July07
Statham, J. C. B. — W. Africa 29July07
Hayes, E. C. — Cosham 29July07
Birrell, E. T. F., — London 29July07
Bliss, E. W. — Tidworth 29Oct.07
Probyn, P. J., D.S.O., M.B. — Leeds 29Oct.07
Hooper, A. W., — Shorncliffe 29Oct.07
Waring, A. H. [L] — Gosport 29Jan.08
Ward, W. A. — Bulford 29Jan.08
Cochrane, E. W. — Aldershot 29Jan.08
W., M.B.
Morris, A. H. — Malta 29Jan.08
Archer, S. A. — Dundalk 22Jan.08
Clements, E.W., M.B. — Cork 29Jan.08

Majors—contd.

MacDougall, A.J., M.B. — Athlone 29Apr.08
Swabey, M. — St. Thomas' Mount 29Apr.08
Riddick, G. B. — Aldershot 29July08
Hewetson, H. — Mill Hill 29July08
Stammers, G.E.F. — Quetta 29July08
Wanhill, C. F. — Mhow 29July08
Hudleston, W. E. — Portsmouth 29July08
Corkery, M. P. — Fermoy 29July08
Addams Williams, L. — Quetta 28Oct.08
Rattray, M., MacG., M.B. — Woolwich 28Oct.08
Clarke, T. H. M., C.M.G., D.S.O., M.B. — R. Hosp., Kilmainham 28Jan.09
Marriott, E. W., P. V. — Mullingar 28Jan.09
Cummins, S.L., M.D. [F] — R.A.M.Coll. 28Jan.09
MacKessack, P. — London 28Jan.09
Norrington, H. L. W. — Scutari 28Jan.09
McCarthy, J. McD., M.B. — Ambala 28Apr.09
Poe, J., M.B. — Shorncliffe 28Apr.09
Stallard, H. G. F. [F] — Mhow 28Apr.09
Brodribb, E. — Scutari 28Apr.09
Bowen, A.W.N. — Curragh 28July09
DG Nickerson, W. H. S., M.B. — Rawal Pindi 28July09
Browne-Mason, H. O. B. — Poona 28July09
Penny, F. S., M.B. — Limerick 28July09
Watts, B. — London 28Oct.09
Martin, H. G. — Dublin 28Oct.09
Carroll, F. F., M.B. [F] e.a. — 28Oct.09
Macpherson, J., D. G., M.B., t. — Liverpool 28Oct.09
Gwynn, W. F. — Dublin 28Oct.09
O Grady, S. deC., M.B. — Deepcut 28Oct.09
Young, A. H. O. — Jullundur 28Oct.09
Bourke, E. A. — Cardiff 28Oct.09
Lowsley, M. M. — Kasauli 28Oct.09
Ross, N. H., M.B. — Fyzabad 28Oct.09
DG Inkson, E. T., t. — Exeter 28Jan.10
Collingwood, P. H. — Devonport 28Jan.10
O'Gorman, C. J., D.S.O. — Barrackpore 28Jan.10
Fuhr, R. S. H., D.S.O. — R. Arsenal, Woolwich 28Jan.10
Barrow, H. P. W., s. — War Office 28Jan.10
Harvey, D., M.D. — R.A.M. Coll. 28Jan.10
Archer, G. J. S., M.B. — Netley 27Apr.10
Hall, S. O. — Rangoon 27Apr.10
Weld, A. E. — Malta 27Apr.10
Gallie, J.S. — Caterham 27Apr.10
Heffernan, F.J.C., F.R.C.S.I. — Mhow 27Apr.10

Royal Army Medical Corps.

Majors—contd.

Herrick, H. *Holywood* 27Apr.10
Cowan, J., *M.B. Fachmarhi* 27Apr.10
O'Flaherty, A. R. *Kasauli* 27Apr.10
Walton, H. B. G. *Ranikhet* 27Apr.10
Crisp, G. B. *Hong Kong* 27July10
Mainprise, C. W. *Kuldanna* 27July10
Scott, A. L. *Ahmednagar* 28July10
Goddard, G. H. *Brighton* 28July10
Hodgson, J. E. *York* 28Oct.10
Fell, M. H. G. *Aldershot* 28Oct.10
Winkfield, W. B. *Maymyo* 28Oct.10
Leake, J. W. *Dover* 28Oct.10
Houghton, J.W.H., *Meerut* 28Oct.10
 M.B.
Goldsmith, G. M. *Dublin* 28Oct.10
 M.B.
Lloyd, R. H. *Dagshai* 28Oct.10
Sloan, J. M., *Lahore* 28Oct.10
 D.S.O., M.B.
Packer, H. D. *Karachi* 28Oct.10
Humphry, L. *Chatham* 28Oct.10
Ashe, F. *Secunderabad* 28Oct.10
Gill, J. G. *Tidworth* 28Jan.11
Lauder, T. C., *Kinsale* 28Jan.11
 M.B.
Curme, D. E. *Pontefract* 28Jan.11
Taylor, H. S. *Fort George* 28Jan.11
Brakenridge, F. J. *Oxford* 28Jan.11
 [F]
Rutherford, N. *Cork* 28Jan.11
 J. C., *M.B.*
Ormsby, G. J. A., *Dublin* 28Jan.11
 M.D.
Palmer, H. K. *Cosham* 28Jan.11
Palmer, F. J. *Mhow* 28Jan.11
Crawford, V. J. *Hilsea* 28Jan.11
Webb, A. L. A. *Edinburgh* 28Jan.11
Ensor, H., *D.S O.,Woolwich*28Jan.11
 M.B. [F]
Cunningham, *Mussoorie* 27Apr.11
 R. A., *M.B.*
Delap, G. G., *Pretoria* 27Apr.11
 D.S.O.
Simson, H. *Muttra* 27Apr.11
Blackwell, *War Office* 27Apr.11
 W. E., s.
Nicholls, H. M., *Edinburgh* 27Apr.11
 M.B.
Chopping, A. *Netley* 27Apr.11
Butler, S. G. *Curragh* 27Apr.11
Prescott, J. W., *Portland* 27Apr.11
 D.S.O.
Wroughton. *Maidstone* 20Sept.11
 A. O. B.   28Oct.10
Falkner, P. H., *Purfleet* 27Apr.11
 F.R.C.S.I.
Douglas, H. *Cairo* 27Apr.11
 E. M., *D.S.O.*
Ellery, E. E. *Cairo* 27Apr.11
Langstaff, J. W. *London* 27Apr.11
Wood, L. *Quetta* 27Apr.11
Fawcus, H.B., *Aldershot* 27Apr.11
 M.B.
Sewell, E. P., *Ceylon* 27Apr.11
 M.B.

Majors—contd.

Harrison, L. W., *London* 17May11
 M.B.
Morton, H. M., *Glasgow* 17May11
 M.B.
Babington, M. H. *London* 17May11
Roch, H. S. *Pretoria* 17May11
Harvey, F. *Colaba* 17May11
Hime, H. C. R., *Wellington* 4June11
Cumming, C. C., *Malta* 4June11
 M.B.
Evans, C. R. *Malta* 4June11
Norman, H. H., *Woolwich* 21July11
Woodside, W. A. *Agra* 27July11
Winslow, L. F. F. *Sheffield* 27July11
Elsner, O. W. A. *Pieter-* 27July11
 maritzburg
Seeds, A. A., *Rawal Pindi* 27July11
Anderson, H. S. *Buttevant* 27July11
 [F]
LLoyd, L. N., *D.S.O. Preston* 27July11
MacKenzie, T. C. *Richmond,* 27July11
 D.S.O. [F], t. *Yorks.*
Connolly, E. P. *Murree* 27July11
Bond, J. H. R. *Naini Tal* 27July11
rvine, F. S., *R.A.M. Coll.* 17Aug.11
 M.B.
Richards, F. G. *Queenstown* 17Aug.11
Knox, E. B., *Norwich* 17Aug.11
 M.D.
Matthews, J. *York* 17Aug.11
O'Reilly, P. S. *R. Arsenal,* 17Aug.11
 Woolwich
MacLaughlin, *Bellary* 4Sept.11
 A. M., *M.B.*
Hartigan, J. A. *Tientsin* 4Sept.11
Martin, J. F., *Aldershot* 4Sept.11
 M.B.
McDonnell, E., *Shorncliffe* 4Sept.11
 M.B.
Safford, A. H. *Colchester* 4Sept.11
Fielding, T. E., *Devonport* 25Oct.11
 M.B.
Straton, C. H. *Pretoria* 25Oct.11
Cuthbert, J. M. *Edinburgh* 25Oct.11
 M.B.
Brown, R. T., *Darjeeling* 25Oct.11
 M.D.
Siberry, E. W. *London* 17Nov.11
Wingate, B. F. *London* 17Nov.11
West, J. W., *M.B. Rawal* 29Nov.11
 Pindi
Smith, C. S., *M.B. Dum Dum* 4Dec.11
Carlyon, A. F. *Mauritius* 4Dec.11
Croly, W. C. *Mount Abu* 4Dec.11
Henderson, *Portsmouth* 21Dec.11
 P. H., *M.B.*
Spiller, W. M. H., *Cawn-* 21Dec.11
 pore
Jameson, A. D. *Peshawar* 21Dec.11
Burke, B. B. *Dover* 21Dec.11
Fry, W. B. *Woolwich* 21Dec.11
Douglass, P. C. *Nowgong* 21Dec.11
Baker, W. L. *London* 25Jan.12

Majors—contd.

Cotton, F. W. *Nasirabad* 25Jan.12
Parry, F. M., *Mauritius* 25Jan.12
 M.B.
Dennis, B. R., *London* 25Jan.12
 M.B.
Adye-Curran, *Cosham* 25Jan.12
 W. J. P.
Powell, J., M. B. [F] e.a. 25Jan.12
Bennett, W., *M.B. Maymyo* 25Jan.12
Biggam, T., *Bordon* 25Jan.12
 M.B.
Bartlett, B. S. *Lahore* 25Jan.12
Hyde, D. O., *M.B.*, t. *York* 25Jan.12
Hamerton, *Colchester* 25Jan.12
 A. E., *D.S.O.*
Houghton, G. J. 25Jan.12
Churton, J. G. *Bangalore* 25Jan.12
Waring, A. D., *Gosport* 25Jan.12
 M.B.
Weston, A. F. *Jamaica* 25Jan.12
Dorgan, J., *M.B, Hong Kong* 25Jan.12
Furnivall, C. H. *Karachi* 25Jan.12
FitzGerald, *Dover* 25Jan.12
 Fitz G. G.
Lauder, F. P. *Tralee* 29Feb.12
Tobin, J. *Gibraltar* 29Feb.12
Murphy, J. P. J., *Potchefs-* 21Mar.12
 M.B. *troom*
Greenwood, A. R. *Alder-* 21Mar.12
 shot
Bennett, W. L., *Halifax* 21Mar.12
 M.B., F.R.C.S. Edin.
Argles, R. L. *Ferozepore* 25Apr.12
Foster, J. G., *Kirkee* 25Apr.12
 M.B.
Walker, F.S., *Fort Camden,* 25Apr.12
 F.R.C.S.I. Queenstown Harb.
Purser, L. M., *Ranikhet* 25Apr.12
 M.B.
McLennan, F., *Aberdeen* 25Apr.12
 M.B., t.
Robinson, J. H. *Peshawar* 25Apr.12
Fleming, C. E., *Pretoria* 14May12
 M.B.
Lelean, P. S., *R.A.M.Coll.* 14May12
 F.R.C.S.
Johnson, J. T., *M.D. Naini Tal* 14May12
Goodwin, W. R. P. *Landour* 14May12
Steele, W. L. *Tidworth* 29May12
Riach, W., *M.D. London* 29May12
Kennedy, J. C., *Lebong* 29May12
 M.D.
Parsons, A. R. C. *Edin-* 29May12
 burgh
Powell, E. W. *Ballincollig* 29May12
Carr, C. H., *M.D. Tidworth* 30May12
Bennett, E. *Deolali* 30May12
Adderley, A. C. *Wynberg* 30May12
Worthington, Sir *Canada* 30May12
 E. S., Knt., M.V.O.
Ronayne, C. R. L., *Gibraltar* 21June12
Baillie, G., *M.B. Colchester* 21June12
Thorpe, L. G. *St. Thomas* 21June12
 Mount
Crosthwait, *Ambala* 21June12
 W. S.
Ellery, R. F. *Bareilly* 21June12

Royal Army Medical Corps.

Majors—contd.

Popham, R. L. *Nowshera* 21June12
Bransbury, *Belgaum* 29July12
H. A.
Hull, A. J., *London* 29July12
F.R.C.S.
Whelan, J. F., *M.B. Poona* 14Aug.12
Power, W. M. *Chatham* 14Aug.12
Brunskill, J. H., *Dublin* 29Aug. 12
M.B.
Duffey, A. C., *Rawal Pindi* 29Aug. 12
M.D.
Myles, C. D., *Chester* 29Aug.12
M.B.
Davidson, H. A.. *Straits* 29Aug.12
M.B. *Settlements*
Bateman, H. R. *Shorncliffe* 29Aug.12
Pinches, H. G. *Dover* 29Aug.12
Sparkes, W. M.B. *W.Africa* 29Aug,12
Smith, S. B., *Belfast* 29Aug.12
M.B.
Skinner, R, McK. *Calcutta* 2Oct.12
Clarke, J. B., *Colchester* 14Oct.12
M.B.
Falkner, M. W., *Bermuda* 29Oct.12
F.R.C.S.I
Woodley, R. N., *t. Cardiff* 29Oct.12
Parkes, E. E., *Jubbulpore* 29Oct.12
M.B.
Cowey, R. V. *Bulford* 29Oct.12
Rowan-Robinson *Bermuda* 29Oct.12
F. E., M.B.
Bostock, J. S., *Aldershot* 29Oct.12
M.B.
Mitchell, A. H. *Dover* 29Oct.12
McN.
Waters, W. J. *Tientsin* 14Nov.12
Shea, H. F., *M.B. Kasauli* 14Nov.12
L'Estrange, *Londonderry* 14Nov.12
E. F. Q.
Unwin, T. B., M.B. 14Nov.12
Gibson, A. W. *Dalhousie* 29Nov,12
Hunt, R. N., *M.B. Cairo* 29Nov.12
Howley, H.E.J.A.*Dinapore* 29Nov.12
Fawcett, R. F. M. *Dublin* 29Nov,12
Jones, J. L. *Wellington* 29Nov,12
Potter, T. J. *Cairo* 27Dec.12
Foulds, M. F. *Belfast* 9Jan.13
Sheehan,G.F. *Cawnpore* 29Jan.13
Ryan, E. *Aldershot* 29Jan.13
Barbour, J. H., *London* 29Jan.13
M.B.
Wilson, R. C., *M.B.Gibraltar* 3Feb.13
Winder, J. H. R., *Aldershot* 27Feb.13
M.D.
Hyde, P. G., *M.B. Ceylon* 27Mar.13
Lamballe, F. W., *Maymyo* 27Mar.13
M.B.
Beatty, M. C., *Devonport* 27Mar.13
M.B.
Ritchie, T. F. *M.B. London* 27Mar.13
Williamson, *Singapore* 27Mar.13
A. J., M.B.
Aylen, E. V. *Barian* 27Mar.13
Davis, W. *Naini Tal* 27Mar.13
Harding, D. L., *Mullingar* 26Apr.13
F.R.C.S.I.
Thomson, C. G. *Glencorse* 3May13
Ffrench, E. G., *London* 28May13
M.D., F.R.C.S. Edin.
McMunn, A. *Hong Kong* 25June13
Sampey, A. W. *Wellington* 27June13
Rogers, H.,*M.B. Malta* 27June13

Majors—contd.

Long, H. W., *Netheravon* 27June13
M.B.
Irwin, A. W. A. *Cork* 1July13
Adye-Curran, S. M. *Stalkot* 26July13
Cotterill, L.,*M.B. Cherat* 5Dec.13
Harvey,W. J. S. *Jamaica* 14Jan.14
Craig, B. A., *t. Newcastle* 29Jan.14
Smallman, A. B., *Aldershot* 1Mar.14
M.D., s. 10May13
Tyndale, W. F., *Devonport* 1Mar.14
C.M.G., M.D.
Ellis, W. F. *Aldershot* 1Mar.14
Ainsworth, R. B. *Tidworth* 1Mar.14
M.B.,[L]
Skelton, D.S., f.o. *Zanzibar* 1Mar.14
Easton, P. G. *Aldershot* 1Mar.14
Rutherford, R., *Cardiff* 1Mar.14
M.B.
Davidson, P., *Aldershot* 1June14
D.S.O., M.B.
Mackenzie, J., *Dinapore* 1June14
M.B.
Walker, N. D., *Quetta* 1June14
M.B.
Hayes, A. H. *Ambala* 1June14
Crossley, H. J. *Bareilly* 1June14
Storrs, R. *Winchester* 1June14
Foster, R.L.V., *Crown Hill* 1June14
M.B.
Clarke, F. A. H. *Lebong* 1June14
Reed, G. A, K.H. *Aldershot* 1June14
Conway, J. M. H., *Leeds* 1June14
F.R.C.S.I., t.
Meadows, S. *Tidworth* 1June14
M. W.
Browne, W.W. *Ahmednagar* 1June14
Kelly, W. D. C., *Pretoria* 1June14
M.B.
Harding, N. E. J., *London* 1June14
M.B.

Captains.

Seccombe, J.W.S. *Topsham* 1Mar.06
Bagshawe, H. V. *Cairo* 1Mar.06
Franklin, R. J. *Ferozepore* 1Mar.06
Bell, J. G., M.B. *Straits* 31July06
Settlements
Winder, M. G. *Jamaica* 31July06
Dawson,F.W.W.,*Jullundur* 31July06
M.B.
Gatt, J. E. H., *Murree* 31July06
M.B.
Coates, T. S., *Meerut* 31July06
M.B.
Wood, A. E. B., *Tientsin* 31July06
J. C., M.B.
Carmichael, *Malta* 31July06
Bridges, R.H.t.*Manchester* 31July06
Webster, *Neemuch* 31July06
J. A. W.
Lambert, F. C. *Poona* 31July06
Meldon, J. B., *Gibraltar* 31July06
M.B.
Wilmot, R. C. *Hythe* 31July06
Holden, C. W. *E. Comd.* 31July06
Kelly, H. B., *Currach* 31July06
Pennefather, E. M. *Multan* 31July06
Brown, G. H. J. *Aberdeen* 31July06
M.B.

Captains—contd.

Dunbar, B. H. V., *Belfast* 31July06
M,D
Ahern, D. *Currach* 31July06
Carmichael, *Cliffden* 31July06
D.G., M.B.
Crawford, J.M.M., *Ipswich* 31July06
F.R.C.S.I. t.
Bramhall, C. *Birmingham* 31July06
Harty, T. E. *W. Africa* 31July06
Duguid, J. H., *Bellary* 31July06
M.B.
Stack, H. T., *Ranikhet* 31July06
M.B.
Patch, B. G. *Kirkee* 31July06
Hughes, *Plymouth* 31July06
G, W. G. [F]
Gray, A. C. H., *R.A.M.Coll.* 28Feb.07
M.B.
Watson, D. P., *Currach* 28Feb.07
M.B.
Dudding, T. S. *Belgaum* 28Feb.07
Powell, J. E. *Hilsea* 28Feb.07
Ievers, O., M.B. *Shorncliffe* 28Feb.07
MacNicol, R. H., *Malta* 28Feb.07
M.B.
Fawcett, H.H.J.J., *tMaidstone* 28Feb.07
Pallant, S. L. *Netley* 28Feb.07
Sylvester-Bradley, *Exeter* 28Feb.07
C. R. t.
Lewis, S. E., *Devonport* 28Feb.07
M.B
Kempthorne, G.A.*Tregantle* 28Feb.07
McEntire, J. T., *Tralee* 28Feb.07
M.B.
Dunkerton, N.E.t. *London* 28Feb.07
Hanafin, P. J. *Dublin* 28Feb.07
Richmond, J. D. *Edinburgh* 28Feb.07
M.B.
Glanvill, E.N. *M.B.Newcastle* 28Feb.07
Wetherell, M. C., *Fethard* 28Feb.07
M.B.
Hildreth, H.C., *Fermoy* 28Feb.07
F.R.C.S., Edin.
MacDowall, W. *W. Africa* 28Feb.07
MacD.
Collins, R. T. *Glasgow* 28Feb.07
Wright, T. J. *Training* 28Feb.07
Estabt., Aldershot
Osburn, A. C. *Netley* 28Feb.07
Rugg, G. F. *Peshawar* 30July07
Thomson, D. S. B.,*M.B.*,s.a. 30July07
Fairbairn, J., *Sco. Comd.* 30July07
M.B.
Anderson, R. G, [F] s.a. 30July07
Douglass, J. H., *W. Africa* 30July07
M.D.
Lewis, R. R. 30July07
Otway, A. L., *Portsmouth* 30July07
M.B.
Turner, C. H. *Dublin* 30July07
Whitehead, E.C., *Dinapore* 30July07
M.B.
Vaughan, W. F. H. *Malta* 30July07
Hole, R.B..M.B. t. *Glasgow* 30July07
Lucas, T. C.,M.B.,*i.Bombay* 30July07
Cathcart,G.E. *Jubbulpore* 30July07
Wiley, W., M.B. *Dover* 30July07
Harding, H., *Warley* 30July07
M.B.
Turnbull, J. A. *Jubbulpore* 30July07
Grant, M.F.,*M.D.*, *London* 30July07
Johnstone, D.P. *Jhansi* 30July07
Moore, E.H.M.*Shoeburyness* 30July07

Royal Army Medical Corps.

Captains—contd.

Ahern, M.D.   Bermuda   30July07
Garland,F.J.,M.B.,   Colchester   30July07
Meaden, A. A.   Colchester   30July07
Cahill, R. J., M.B.   Belfast   30July07
Bowie, S. C.   Newbridge   30July07
Connell, H. B.   Liverpool   30July07
Arthur,A.S., PembrokeDock   1Oct.07
M.B.
Byam, W. [F]   e.a.   30Jan.08
Ryley, C.   Bermuda   30Jan.08
Dwyer,P.,M.B.   Dublin   30Jan.08
Davy, P. C. T.,   Aldershot   30Jan.08
M.B.
Wilson, H. T.   Chatham   30Jan.08
Hallowes, R. C.,   Holywood   30Jan.08
M.B.
Campbell, J. H.,   Edinburgh   30Jan.08
M.B.
Harvey, G. A. D.   e.a.   30Jan.08
Winckworth,   Quetta   30Jan.08
H. C. [F]
Russell, B. W.,   Kasauli   30Jan.08
M.D.
Sidgwick, H. C.,   Woolwich   30Jan.08
M.B.
Sinclair,M.,M.B.   London   30Jan.08
Painton, G. R.   E. Comd.   30Jan.08
Low, N.   Colchester   30Jan.08
Fraser, A. N.,   Singapore   30Jan.08
M.B.
Cordner,R.H.L.   Aldershot   30Jan.08
Carter, H. St. M.,   Aldershot   30Jan.08
M.D.
Frost, A. T., M.B.   Poona   30Jan.08
Doig,K.A. C.   Chakrata   30Jan.08
LloydJones,P.A.,   Aldershot   30Jan.08
M.B. [F]
Millar, C. R.   Cork   30Jan.08
Maughan, J. St. A.   Exeter   30Jan.08
Thurston,L.V.   Aldershot   30Jan.08
Gater, A. W,   Winchester   30Jan.08
Lynch, J. P.   Canterbury   30Jan.08
Thomson, C. P.,   Egypt   31July08
M.D., f.o.
Heron, G. W., f.o.   Egypt   31July08
Buchanan,   Netley   31July08
R. J. B.
Churchill,G.B.F.IrishComd.31July08
Wallace, G. S.,   Bellary   31July08
M.B.
Coppinger, C. J.,   R.A.M.   31Mar.11
M.B.   Coll.   1Feb.08
Meredith, P. G.,   Ceylon   31July08
M.B.
Roberts, F. E.   Shorncliffe   31July08
White, R. K.   Aldershot   11July10
  1Feb.08
Gibbon, T. H.,   Dublin   31July08
M.D.
Hoar, J. E.   Sheerness   31July08
Beadnell,H.O.M. Tidworth   17Jan12
  30Jan.08
Booth,E.B., M.D. W.Africa   31July08
Thompson, R.J.C. Chatham   31July08
[P]
Lithgow,E.G.R.f.o. Upavon   31July08
Power,P., M.B. Poonamallee   31July08
Pascoe, J. S.   Woolwich   31July08
O'Brien, C. W.   Pirbright   31July08
Richard, G. H.   Weedon   25July10
  30Jan.08
Tabuteau,G.G.   Cork   31July08

Captains—contd.

Rahilly,J.M.B., Shorncliffe   31July08
M.B.
Humfrey,   Secunderabad   31July08
R.E., M.B.
Maydon, W. G.,   Liverpool   31July08
M.B., t.
Ormrod, G.,   W. Africa   31July08
M.B.
Anderson,   W. Comd.   31Jan.09
J. A., M.B.
Browne, C. G.   S. Comd.   31Jan.09
Sherren, H. G.   London   31Jan.09
Emerson,   Leicester   31Jan.09
H. H. A., M.B.
Lewis, R. P.   Aldershot   31Jan.09
Graham, J. H.,   Cosham   31Jan.09
M.B.
Benson, W.,   Aldershot   31Jan.09
M.B. [L]
Ferguson, G. E.   York   31Jan.09
Fawcett,   Secunderabad   31Jan.09
C. E. W. S., M.B.
Rose, A. M.,M.B. Longmoor   31Jan.09
Rees, G. H.,   E. Comd.   31Jan.09
M.B.
Scatchard,   Aldershot   31Jan.09
Symons,V. H.   Seaforth   31Jan.09
Anthonisz,E.G.   S. Comd.   31Jan.09
Bryden, R. A.   Fleetwood   31Jan.09
Moss, E. L.   Portsmouth   31Jan.09
Irvine, A. E. S.   S. Comd.   31Jan.09
Moriarty, T. B. Lond. Dist.   31Jan.09
Ritchie, M.B.H., Colchester   31Jan.09
Weston, W. J.   E. Comd.   31Jan.09
Cromie, M. J.   W. Africa   31Jan.09
Potts, E. T.,   Cosham   31Jan.09
Ware, G. W. W.,   Kilkenny   31Jan.09
M.B.
McConaghy, W.   Woolwich   31Jan.09
Nimmo, W. C.   Aldershot   31Jan.09
Wyatt, C. J.,   31Jan.09
M.B.
Keane, M.   Calicut   31Jan.09
White, C. F.   Dublin   31Jan.09
M.B.
Sampson, F.C.,   Woolwich   31Jan.09
M.B.
Blackwell,T.S.   Colchester   31Jan.09
Smyth, R. S.,   IrishComd.   31Jan.09
M.B.
Priestley, H. E.   S. Comd.   31Jan.09
Marett, P. J. [l]   Malta   31Jan.09
Stewart, H.,   Irish Comd.   31Jan.09
M.B.
Dunne, J. S.,   S. Comd.   1Mar.09
F.R.C.S.I.
O'Carroll, A.D.,   Aldershot   1Mar.09
M.B.
Drew, C. M., M.B.   e.a.   30July09
Sutcliff, A.A., M.B. Chester   30July09
Cummins, A. G., M.B.   e.a.   30July09
Littlejohns, A.S.   E. Comd.   30July09
Galwey, W. R., Wellington   30July09
M.B.
Archibald,R.G.,M.B.[F] e.a.   30July09
McCammon,   Irish Comd.   30July09
F. A., M.B.
De la Cour, G.,   E. Comd.   30July09
M.B.
Egan, W.,M.B. Irish Comd.   30July09
Tate, R. G. H.,   Dublin   30July09
M.D.
Dawson, A.,   E. Comd.   30July09
M.B.

Captains—contd.

Forrest, F.   Irish Comd.   30July09
Williams, A. S.   N. Comd.   30July09
Honeybourne,   S. Comd.   30July09
V. C.
Edmunds, C. T.   Bulford   30July09
Johnson, V. G.   S. Comd.   30July09
Morris,C.R.M., Irish Comd.   30July09
M.B.
Newman,   Irish Comd.   30July09
R. E. U., M.B.
Paine, E.W.M.   S. Comd.   30July09
Howell, F.D.G.   E. Comd.   30July09
Sampson, P.   S. Comd.   30July09
Dill, M. G., M.D.   Ayr   30July09
Grogan, J. B.   E. Comd.   30July09
O'Neill, E. M.,   W. Comd.   30July09
M.B.
Edwards, G. B.   Shorncliffe   30July09
Scott, J. W. L,   Aldershot   30July09
Smales, W. C.   S. Comd.   30July09
Bond, A. H.   S. Comd.   30July09
Leslie, T. C. C.   Allahabad   30July09
O'Grady, D. de C. Chatham   30July09
Gibson, L. G. [f]   Amritsar   30July09
Stewart, P.S.,M.B.Tidworth   30July09
Sexton,T.W.O.   E. Comd.   30July09
Vidal, A. C.   Aldershot   29Aug.09
Robinson,   Lond. List.   4Oct.09
T. T. H., M.B.
Stevenson,   S. Comd.   30Jan.10
G. H., M.B.
Forsyth,W.H., Irish Comd.   30Jan.10
M.B.
Amy, A. C.,M.D.   Preston   30Jan.10
Heslop, A. H.,   Aldershot   30Jan.10
M.B.
Mitchell, W..M.B. Wrexham   30Jan.10
Elliot, E.J., M.B.   Ashton   30Jan.10
Gibbon, E., M.B.   e.a.   30Jan.10
Leslie, R. W. D.   Aldeney   30Jan.10
Lathbury, E. B.   Kilworth   30Jan.10
Scaife, C., M.D.   Leeds   30Jan.10
Corbett, D. M.,   Wrexham   30Jan.10
M.B.
Lochrin, M. J.   Aldershot   30Jan.10
Caddell, E. D.,   London   30Jan.10
M.B.
Johnson, B., M.B. Limerick   30Jan.10
Lunn, W.E.C.,   Aldershot   30Jan.10
M.B.
Foster, J. R.   Dublin   30Jan.10
Benett, A. M.   Newport   30Jan.10
Bracken, G. P. A. Lichfield   30Jan.10
Bradish, F. L.   Curragh   30Jan.10
Bennett,J. A.,M.B. Youghal   30Jan.10
Bell, W, J. E.,   London   30Jan.10
M.B.
Bowie, C. W.   Enniskillen   30Jan.10
Howell, H. L.   Kirkee   30Jan.10
Loughnan,   Hounslow   30Jan.10
W. F. M.
Browne, T. W.   Cork   30Jan.10
Thompson, W.I., Aldershot   30Jan.10
M.B.
MacCarthy,D.T., Mandalay   30Jan.10
M.B.
Phelan, E. C., Londonderry   30Jan.10
M.B.
O'Keeffe,J.J.,M.B. Chatham   30Jan.10
Kavanagh,   E. Comd.   30Jan.10
E. J., M.B.

Royal Army Medical Corps.

Captains—contd.

Jacob, A. H.	*N. Comd.*	30Jan.10
Cooke, O. C. P.	*Queenstown*	7Mar.10
Denyer, C. H.	*Winchester*	7Mar.10
Beaman, W. K.	*York*	28July10
Cassidy, C., M. B. [F]	e.a.	28July10
Fraser, A. D.,	*Netley*	28July10
M.B		
Irvine-Fortescue, A.,	*j.l.*	28July10
M.B.		
Gibson, H. G.	*E. Cmmd.*	28July10
Field, S.	*Fort Carlisle,*	28July10
Queenstown Harbour		
Chapman, F. H. M.	*Delhi*	28July10
Perry, H. M. J.	*Devonport*	28July10
Wood, J. L.	*Richmond,*	28July10
	Yorks.	
Turner, F. T.	*Dorchester*	28July10
Leahy, M. P.,	*Lond. Dist.*	28July10
M.B.		
Boyd, J. E. M.	*Ferozepore*	28July10
Mackenzie, D. F.,	*Meerut*	28July10
M.B.		
O'Connor, R. D.	*Sheffield*	28July10
McEwen, O. R.	*London-*	28July10
	derry	
Boyce, W. W.	*Ewshott*	29June14
		30Jan.10
Wilson, M.O., *M.B. Sheerness*	28July10
Langrishe,	*Spike Island,*	28July10
J. du P., *M.B., Queenstown*		
	Harbour	
Scott, T. H.,	*Bradford*	28July10
M.B.		
Rudkin, G. F.	*Kilbride*	28July10
Andrews, L. A. A.	*York*	28July10
Gurley, J. H.	*Netley*	28July10
Elliott, A.C., *M.B. Colchester*	28July10
Purdon, W. B., *M.B. Belfast*	28July10
Casement, F.,	*Edinburgh*	28July10
M.B.		
Middleton, E. M.	*Chatham*	28July10
Carruthers, V. T.,	*Norwich*	28July10
M.B., F.R.C.S. Edin.		
Farebrother,	*Meiktila*	28July10
H. W.		
Howlett, A. W.,	*Bordon*	29July18
M.B.		27July10
Dawson, G. F.,	*Bareilly*	29Jan.11
M.B.		
Phillipu, T. McC., *Allahabad*	29Jan.11
M.B.		
Byatt, H. V. B.	*Karachi*	29Jan.11
Dickson, H. S.	*Gibraltar*	29Jan.11
Todd, R.E., M.B., *f.o. Egypt*	29Jan.11
Petit, G.	*Benares*	29Jan.11
Stuart, F. J., *M.B. Meerut*	29Jan.11
Gibson, H.	*Kamptee*	29Jan.11
O'Farrell, W. R.	e.a.	29Jan.11
Renshaw, J.A.	*Wellington*	29Jan.11
O.A. T., *M.B,*		
Conyngham,	*Mhow*	29Jan.11
McGrigor, D. B.,	*Landour*	29Jan.11
Gregg, R. G. S.,	*Aden*	29Jan.11
M.B.		
Spong, W. A., *M.B. Karachi*	29Jan.11
Carson, H. W., *M.B. Khanspur*	29Jan.11
Hart, H.P., *M.B. Cannanore*	29Jan.11
Dowling, F. T., *Nowshera*	29Jan.11
M.B.		
Dickinson,	*Dublin*	29Jan.11
R. F. O'T.		
Hingston, J. C. L. *Rangoon*	29Jan.11
Jones, A. E. B., *Bangalore*	29Jan.11
M.D.		
Odlum, B.A., *Bloemfontein*	29Jan.11
c.o.		
Hendry, A., *M.B. Satara*	29Jan.11

Captains—contd.

O'Brien Butler,	*Kildare*	29Jan.11
C. P.		
Lloyd, J. R.	*[Aden*	29Jan.11
Grant, J. F., *M.B. Maymyo*	29Jan.11
Coppinger, F. R.,	*[India*	15July14
	1Feb.11
James, J., *M.B.*	*E. Comd.*	4Aug.11
Suhr A.C.H., *Straits Settle-*	4Aug.11
M.B.	*ments*	
Ellcome, J. E.	*Nowgong*	4Aug.11
Keane, G. J., *M.D.*	c.o.	4Aug.11
Blake, H. H.,	*Cherat*	4Aug.11
M.B.		
Dickson, R. M.,	*Lucknow*	4Aug.11
M.B.		
Worthington, F., *Gravesend*	4Aug.11
M.B.		
Bradley, F.H.,	*Allahabad*	4Aug.11
M.B.		
Stevenson, A.L., *Secundera-*	4Aug.11
M.B.	*bad*	
Varvill, B.	*Mhow*	4Aug.11
Houston, J.W., *M.B. Peshawar*	4Aug.11
Shepherd, A.,	*Mandalay*	4Aug.11
M.B.		
Dunn, W. J.,	*Thayetmyo*	4Aug.11
Dalgliesh, F. B. *Jubbulpore*	4Aug.11
Leckie, M.	*Tidworth*	4Aug.11
Walker, S.G., *M.B. Cawnpore*	4Aug.11
Harding, C. E. L.,	*Aden*	4Aug.11
M.B.		
Hewson, F. P.,	*Karachi*	4Aug.11
F.R.C.S.I.		
Foster, A. L.	*Aden*	4Aug.11
Rigby, C. N.	*Colaba*	4Aug.11
Wells, A. G.	*Inverness*	4Aug.11
Fraser, A. E. G.	*Hounslow*	4Aug.11
Barney, W. H.S.	*Solon*	4Aug.11
Kelly, C.,	*Woolwich*	5Jan.13
M.D.		30Jan.10
Eves, T. S., *M.B. Lucknow*	4Aug.11
Murphy, L.	*Cawnpore*	4Aug.11
Davis, A. H. T.	*Poona*	4Aug.11
McCombe, J.S., *Secunderabad*	4Aug.11
M.B.		
Tobin, W. J.	*Nasirabad*	4Aug.11
McQueen, C.	*S. Comd.*	4Aug.11
O'Kelly, R.	*Delhi*	4Aug.11
Ryles, C., *M.B. Alderney*	1Feb.12
Buist, D. S., M.B	e.a.	1Feb.12
Marshall, T. E., M.B. [F] *Cork*	1Feb.12
Pollard, A. M., *Colchester*	1Feb.12
Collet, G.G., *M.B. Meerut*	1Feb.12
Clarke, C., *M.B.*	*Malta*	1Feb.12
F.R.C.S.		
Vaughan,	*Okehampton*	1Feb.12
E. W., *M.B.*		
McNeill, A. N. R.,	*Lichfield*	1Feb.12
M.B.		
Wright, A. R.,	*Malta*	1Feb.12
Nicholls, T. B., *M.B. Cyprus*	1Feb.12
Jones, J. B., *M.B. Muttra*	1Feb.12
Clark, J. A., *M.B.*	e.a.	1Feb.12
Saunders, S. McK.	e.a.	1Feb.12
Mitchell, T. J., *M.B Sabathu*	1Feb.12
MacArthur D.H.C., *Sab-*	1Feb.12
M.D.	*athu*	
Parkinson, G.S.	*S. Comd.*	1Feb.12
Gall, H.	*Gharial*	1Feb.12
O'Rorke, C. B., *Darjeeling*	1Feb.12
M.B.		
Byrne, A. W , *M.B.*	*Lahore*	1Feb.12
Startin, J.	*Satara*	1Feb.12
Sherlock, C.G., *M.D. Lahore*	1Feb.12
Stack, G. H.	*Aldershot*	1Feb.12
Leeson, H. H.,	*Khartoum*	1Feb.12
Kyle, S.W., *M.B Jubbulpore*	1Feb.12

Captains—contd.

Lane, J. W., *M.D. Dalhousie*	1Feb.12
Wright, W. G.	*Gibraltar*	1Feb.12
McCreery, A.T., *J Mhow*	1Feb.12
M.B.		
Ranken, H. S., *M.B.*	e.a.	30July12
Manifold, J. A., *Bermuda*	30July12
M.B.		
Dykes, S. S., *M.B. Dum Dum*	30July12
O'Riordan, W.H. *RawalPindi*	30July12
Benson, C.T.V.	*Madras*	30July12
MacArthur, W.P., *Mauritius*	30July12
M.D., F.R.C.P.I.		
Priest, R.C., *M.B. Allahabad*	30July12
Tomlinson, P. S.	*Rurki*	30July12
Cunningham,	*Murree*	30July12
F. W. M., *M.D.*		
Parsons-Smith, E. M.	e.a.	30July12
Stirling, A. S.	*Cairo*	30July12
M.B.		
Taylor, G. P., *M.B., Pretoria*	30July12
Paris, R. C.	*Quetta*	30July12
Bevis, A. W.	*W. Comd.*	30July12
Lambkin, E. C., *Hong Kong*	30July12
M.B.		
McSheehy, O.W., *Pietermar-*	30July12
M.B.	*itzburg*	
Williamson,	*Simonstown*	30July12
M. J., *M.B.*		
Franklin, C.L.,	*Capetown*	30July12
M.B.		
White, M., *M.B.*	*Shwebo*	30July12
Roche, J. J. D.,	*Gibraltar*	30July12
M.B.		
Joynt, H. F.,	*Wynberg*	30July12
M.B.		
Winder, A.S.M.,	*Sitapur*	30July12
M.B.		
Edwards, H. R.	*Pretoria*	30July12
Yourell, J.R., *M.B. Rangoon*	30July12
Elvery, P. G. M.	*Cairo*	30July12
Beckton, J.H., *RawalPindi*	30July12
Rennie, W. B., *Hyderabad*	30July12
M.B.		
Nolan, R. H.	*Lond. Dist.*	30July12
Mathieson, W.	*Pretoria*	30July12
Dive, G. H.	*Peking*	31Jan.13
Hayes, L.C., *M.B. Bermuda*	31Jan.13
Gale, R., M.B., *f.o. Egypt*	31Jan.13
Jones, A. G., *Rawal Pindi*	31Jan.13
M.B.		
Comyn, K. M.D., *Gibraltar*	31Jan.13
Laing, F.R., *M.B. Lucknow*	31Jan.13
Cane, A. S.	*Purandhar*	31Jan.13
Weddell, J. M.	*Fyzabad*	31Jan.13
Nicol, C.M., *M.B. Alexandria*	31Jan.13
O'Connor, A. P., *Khartoum*	31Jan.13
M.B. [L]		
Dickson, T.H., *M.B. Ranikhet*	31Jan.13
Robertson, H.G., *Scutari*	31Jan.13
Stanley, H.V., *M.B. Gibraltar*	31Jan.13
M.B.	e.a.	31Jan.13
Field, P. C.	e.a.	31Jan.13
Davies, R M.,	*Pretoria*	31Jan.13
Kinkead, R.C.G.	*Potchef-*	31Jan.13
M.B.	*stroom*	
Stoney, E. C.,	*Maymyo*	31Jan.13
M.B.		
Stallybrass,	e.a.	31Jan.13
T. W., *M.B.*		
Hutchinson, *Potchefstroom*	31Jan.13
V. P.		
Gilmour, J.	*Egypt*	28July13
M.B., F.R.C.S. Edin., *f.o.*		
Treves, W.-W., *M.B., Egypt*	28July13
F.R.C.S., f.o.		

Royal Army Medical Corps.

Captains—contd.

Simson, J. T., M.B. e.s. 28July13
Robb, C., M.B., f.o. Egypt 28July13
M.B.
Gaunt, E. T., Malta 28July13
M.B.
Harold, C. H. H., Dagshai 29Jan.14
M.D.
Fyffe, E.L., M.B. Poona 29Jan.14
Bridges, R. F., Peshawar 29Jun.14
M.B.
Hallinan, T. J., Kalabagh 29Jan.14
M.B.
Monteith, H. G. Hong Kong 29Jan.14
Bowie, J. D., Alexandria 29 Jan.14
M.B.
Stringer, C. H. Jamaica 29Jan.14
Chambers, G.O. Alexandria 29Jan.14
Gaunt, J. K., M.B. Malta 29Jan.14
Way, L. F. K. Wynberg 29Jan.14
Biggar, B., M.B. Cairo 27July14
Finny, C.M., Upper Topa 27July14
M.B.
Kidd, J. D., Secunderabad 27July14
Steven, W.S.R., Karachi 27July14
M.B.
Wilson, G., Secunderabad 27July14
M.B.
Cane, E. G. S. Colaba 27July14
Robinson, F. A., Nasirabad 27July14
M.B.
Frost, W. A., M.B. Kamptee 27July14
Reynolds, D., M.B. Sialkot 27July14
Seaver, C. D. K. Dalhousie 27July14
Levack, J.S., M.B. Nowshera 27July14
Graham, W. T., Calcutta 27July14
M.B.
Bisset, W., M.B. Dagshai 27July14
Weston, T. A., Lucknow 27July14
M.B.
Fretz, W. L. E., Peshawar 27July14
M.B.
Hayes, P., M.B. Bangalore 27July14
Brett. P. M. J., e.a. 27July14
M.B.
Archer, T. C. R. S. China 27July14

Lieutenants

Spence. B. H. H., M.B. e.a 28July11
Laird, W. B. Bangalore 28July11
Davidson, R., Meerut 28July11
M.B.
Blackmore, H. S. Bangalore 28July11
Elliott, J. M., Rawal Pindi 28July11
M.B.
Skrimshire, Madras 28July11
F. R. B.
Bruce, D. W., M.B. Multan 28July11
Osmond, T. E Lucknow 28July11
Vivian, R. T. Secunderabad 28July11
Cowen. E. G. H., Chakrata 28July11
M.B
Buckley, L., M.B. Gharial 28July11
Webster, W. L., Cairo 28July11
M.B.
Allnutt, W., Poona 28July11
Sykes, S. P., Khyra Gali 28July11
M.B.
Todd, H. C., Secunderabad 28July11
Davies, A. M., Allahabad 28July11
Wells, H. J. G., Rawal Pindi 28July11
M.B.
Deane, E. C. Meerut 28July11
Tamplin, F. S. Gibraltar 28July11
Hudleston, I. R. Jamaica 28July11
Stewart, W., M.B. Chakrata 28July11
MacIlwaine, Quetta 28July11
A .G. J.
Heale, A. S. Campbelltown 28July11
Biggam, A. G., Lahore 1Feb.11
M.B.

Lieutenants—contd.

Mallam, R. K., Ambala 26Jan.12
M.B.
McNaughtan, W., Quetta 26Jan.12
M.B.
Large, D. T. M., M.B. Mhow 26Jan.12
Pratt, W. W.. Nasirabad 26Jan.12
M.B.
Christie, W. F., Straits 26Jan.12
M.B. Settlements
Burnett, M. Belgaum 26Jan.12
Hood, A., M.B. Agra 26Jan.12
Strachan, E. A. Ranikhet 26Jan 12
M.B.
Blaikie, C. J. Bangalore 26Jan.12
Frobisher, Barrackpore 26Jan.12
J. H. M., M.B.
Stevenson, Ambala 26Jan.12
W.B., M.B.
Ritchie, J. L., Murree 26Jan.12
M.H , F.R.C.S.
Richardson, Jubbulpore 26Jan.12
D. T., M.B.
Wynne, O. W. J. Allahabad 26Jan.12
Ingoldby, C.M. Jullundur 26Jan.12
Higgins, S. J. Lucknow 26Jan.12
Blake, G. A , M.B. Fyzabad 26Jan.12
With, P. A. Bangalore 26Jan.12
Little, C. J. H., M.B. Sialkot 26Jan.12
Barry, S. J. Poona 26Jan.12
Vint, R. W., M.B. Agra 26Jan.12
L'Estrange, Mauritius 26Jan 12
H. R
Allott, H. W. L. Bareilly 26Jan.12
Smith, E. P. A., Lucknow 26Jan.12
M.B.
Price, B., M.B. London 26Jnly12
Wigmore, J.B.A. Aldershot 26July12
Hare, J., M.B. Belfast 26July12
Flood, R. A., M.B. Woolwich 26July12
Lang, E C , M.B. Curragh 26July12
Corbett, W. V. Pirbright 26July12
Poole, L. T., M.B. York 26July12
Balfour, T.H., M.B. Stirling 26July12
Huggan, J. L., M.B. London 26July12
Cowtan, F. C. Woolwich 26July12
Jones, J. C., M.B. London 26July12
Porter, R.E., M.B. Limerick 26July12
Shields, H. J. S., Caterham 26July12
M.B.
Power, P. M. J. Gosport 26July12
Whitby, E.V., M.B. Fermoy 26July12
Russell, E. U. Woolwich 26July12
Shaw, R. G., M.B. Curragh 26July12
Stevens, N. W., Woolwich 26July12
M.B.
Phillipps, R. B. Cork 26July12
Urquhart, A. L., R.A.M. 26July12
M.B. Coll.
Whitehead, N.T., Woolwich 26July12
M. B.
Sproule, Rollestone Camp 26July12
J. C.
Martyn, A. F. C. Egypt 26July12
Allison, G. F. York 26July12
Carlyle, R.C., M.B. Malta 26July12
Tepper, J.E. Larkhill Camp 26July12
Dunbar, J., M.B. Calcutta 26July12
Panton, N. F., Mhow 26July12
M.B.
Beddingfield, H., Woolwich 24Jan.13
M.B.
Davidson, F. C., Glasgow 24Jan.13
M.B.
O'Connell, J. F., Aldershot 24Jan.13
Large, S. D. Edinburgh 24Jan.13
Helm, C. Dublin 24Jan.13

Lieutenants—contd.

Bell, W. O. W., Longmoor 24Jan.13
M.B.
Crocket, J., M.B. Edinburgh 24Jan.13
Sealy, H. N. Belfast 24Jan.13
Jackson, A. Dublin 24Jan.13
Beddows, E. C. Curragh 24Jan.13
Dyas, G. E. (on prob.) 4Jan.13
  London Dist.
Thornton, C. V., Curragh 24Jan.13
M.B.
Rowe, J., M B. Deepcut 24Jan.13
Croker, W. P , M.B. Newry 24Jan.13
Bridges, A. B H. London 24Jan.13
Brown, A. G , M.B. Curragh 24Jan.13
Warburton, P. D. (on prob.) 24Jan.13
  Aldershot
Hemphill, R., M.B. Netley 24Jan.13
Smith, S H. Woolwich 24Jan.13
Wade, E W., M.B.(on prob.) 25July13
Woodhouse, B. (on prob.) 25July13
Morrison, W. K., (on prob.) 25July13
M.B.
Percival, E., M.B. (on prob.) 25July13
Rankin, H. C. D., Aldershot 25July13
M.B.,
Thompson, T. O., (on prob) 30Jan.14
M.B.,
Linzell S.J., M.B. (on prob.) 30Jan.14
Shore, L. R. (on prob.) 30Jan.14
Gill, J. G. M.B. (on prob.) 30Jan.14
  Aldershot
Stubbs, J. W. C., (on prob.) 30Jan.14
M.B. S. Comd.
Hattersley, S. (on prob.) 30Jan.14
M., M.B. Aldershot
Rintoul. D. W., (on prob.) 30Jan.14
M.B. E. Comd.
Watson, A., M.B. (on prob.) 30Jan.14
  Irish Comd.
Lothian, N.V., M.B.(on prob) 30Jan.14
  Irish Comd.
Breen, T. F. P., (on prob.) 30Jan.14
M.B. Aldershot
Gwynne, J. (on prob.) 30Jan.14
FitzG., M.B : Lond. Dist.
Menzies, A.J.A., (on prob.) 30Jan.14
M.B. Lond. Dist.

Adjutant.

Quarter-Masters.

Short, J.B., [F] 14Co., Dublin 12Sept.94
  hon. maj. 12Sept.04
Hasell, H. G. Malta 17Apr.95
  hon. maj. 17Apr.10
Spackman, H.10Co., Chatham 4Oct.99
  hon. capt. 4Oct.09
Chalk, A. J. 35 Co. London 18Nov.99
  hon. capt. 18Nov.09
Green, J. York 18Nov.99
  hon. capt. 18Nov.09
Woolley, H. 7 Co., Devonport 13Dec.99
  hon. capt. 13Dec.09
Offord, E. P. 6Co., Cosham 8Feb.00
  hon. capt. 8Feb.10
Audus, H. J. F. 8Feb.00
  Tidworth
  hon. capt. 8Feb.10
Wilson, A Southampton 17Mar.00
  hon. capt. 17Mar.10
Glover, H. W. 19 Co., Chester 17Mar.00
  hon. capt. 17Mar.10
Exton, T. Dover 23May00
  hon. capt. 23May10
Crookes, F. Woolwich 23May00
  hon. capt. 29Nov.00

Royal Army Medical Corps.

Quarter-Masters—contd.
Cowan, R. R. 2 Co. *Aldershot* 30May00 *hon. capt.* 30May10
Wakefield, H.P. *Tidworth* 23June00 *hon. capt.* 23June10
Wheeler, A. *Shorncliffe* 23June00 *hon. capt.* 23June10
Lunney, A. Co., *Curragh* 16Feb.01 *hon. capt.* 16Feb.11
Archibald, W. N. *Netley* 13Mar.01 *hon. capt.* 13Mar.11
Gillman, J., *Depôt, Aldershot* 11Jan.02 *hon. capt.* 11Jan.12
Osborne, J. W., *Colchester* 18Mar.08 *hon. lt.*
Saunders, E. V., 16 Co., *Cork* 25Sept.09 *hon. lt.*
Wilson, J., *War Office* 20Nov.09 *hon. lt.*
Kinsella, C. W., *Egypt* 26Jan.10 *hon. lt.*

Quarter-Masters—contd.
Clark, J., *Woolwich* 18May10 *hon. lt.*
Newland, E. W., 30 Co., *Malta* 22Oct.10 *hon. lt.*
Tait, A. F., 1 & 3 Cos., *Aldershot* 18Feb.11 *hon. lt.*
McColgin, T. E., *S. Africa* 4Mar.11 *hon. lt.*
Smith, C. H., *Tientsin* 4Mar.11 *hon. lt.*
Spencer, W. T., *Gibraltar* 24June11 *hon. lt.*
Cooper, C. H., *Hong Kong* 19July11 *hon. lt.*
Downing, R. N., 12 & 34 Cos., 4May12 *Woolwich hon. lt.*
Conway, T. D., *Devonport* 11Sept.12 *hon. lt.*
Buckley, E. J., *Dublin* 4Jan.13 *hon. lt.*

Quarter-Masters—contd.
Green, R. H., *hon. lt. Egypt* 5July13
Collard, F. E., 8 Co., *York* 6Aug.13 *hon. lt.*
Packard, J. T., 18 Co., 12Nov.13 *hon. lt. London*
Jones, L., *hon. lt.* 13 Co., 7Feb.14 *Edinburgh*
Woollard, J., *hon. lt.,* 18Feb.14 *S. Africa*
Ward, E. E., *hon. lt.,* 15 Co., 18Feb.14 *Belfast*
Lowe, W. E., 4, 5 & 21 Cos., 26Apr.14 *hon. lt. N-tley*
Escott, E. W. J., *hon. lt., Netley*
Ward, H. A., *Aldershot* 11July14 *hon. lt.*
Grenfell, T., *hon. lt., Dublin* 25July14

Retired Officers of the Royal Army Medical Corps, Regular Army and Special Reserve, and of the late R.A.M.C. Militia, who are employed.

REGULAR ARMY.

Officers not liable to be recalled to service.

Kay, Lt.-Col. A. G., *M.B., Clifton, Bristol.*
Charlesworth, Lt.-Col. H., *C.M.G., Nottingham.*
Browne, Lt.-Col. A. W., *Armagh.*
Battersby, Lt.-Col. H. L., *Ipswich.*
Woods, Lt.-Col. C. R., *M.D., F.R.C.S.I., Birr.*
Bourke, Lt.-Col. U. J., *Hamilton.*
Coutts, Lt.-Col. G., *M.B., Chichester.*
Rowney, Lt.-Col. W., *M.D., Manchester.*
Poynder, Lt.-Col. G. F., *Bedford.*
Barnes, Lt.-Col. R. W., *Dorchester.*
Trewman, Lt.-Col. G. T., *M.B., Reading.*
Archer, Lt.-Col. T., *M.D., Lydd.*
Riordan, Lt.-Col. J., *M.B., Clonmel.*
Clements. Lt.-Col. W. G., *Christchurch.*
Osburne, Lt.-Col. J., *Galway.*
Duncan, Lt.-Col. S. E. *Shrewsbury.*
Myles, Maj. E. H., *M.B., Guernsey.*
Nichols, Lt.-Col. F. P., *M.B., Taunton.*
McCormack, Maj. R. J., *M.D., Omagh.*
Thomson, Lt.-Col. W. B., *Northampton.*
Burke, Maj. J. F., *Penally.*
Robinson, Surg.-Lt.-Col. G. S., *Eastbourne.*
Butterworth, Maj. S., *Carlisle.*
Power, Maj. R. I., *Waterford.*
McCreery, Lt.-Col. B. T., *M.B., F.R.C.S.I., Perth.*
Mosse, Lt. Col. C. G. D., *F.R.C.S.I., Guernsey.*
Morris, Lt.-Col. W. G., *Scarborough.*
Tuckey, Lt.-Col. T. B. A., *Detention Barracks, York*
Gubbin, Lt.-Col. G. F., *Dep. Asst. Dir. of Med. Services, 1 Lond. Div.*
Haywood, Lt.-Col. L., *M.B., Dep. Asst. Dir. of Med. Services, S. Mid. Div.*
Wight, Lt.-Col. E. O., *Dep. Asst. Dir. of Med. Services, Home Cos. Div.*
Spence, Maj. A. E. C., *M.B. Warwick.*
Baird, Lt.-Col. A., *M.B., F.R.C.S. Edin., Worcester*
Beevor, Lt.-Col. W. C., *C.M.G., M.B., Dep. Asst. Dir. of Med. Services, N. Mid. Div.*
Holmes, Maj. C. J., *M.D., F.R.C.S.I., Lancaster.*
Reilly, Maj. C. W., *M.D., Great Yarmouth.*
Allport, Maj. C. W., *M.D., Bodmin.*
Butt, Col. E., *F.R.C.S.I., Dep. Asst. Dir. of Med. Services, 2 Lond. Div.*
Turner, Lt.-Col. W., *Dep. Asst. Dir. of Med. Services, Welsh Div.*

Officers belonging to the Reserve of Officers.

Peeke, Maj. H. S., *Derby.*
Greig, Lt.-Col. F. J., *Stirling.*
Kearney, Lt.-Col. J., *M.D., Landguard Fort.*
Whitty, Lt.-Col. M. J., *M.D., Liverpool.*
Nicolls, Lt.-Col. J. M., *M.B., Detention Bks., Cork.*
Dowman, Lt.-Col. W. S., *Kingston-on-Thames.*
Wade, Maj. G. A., *M.D., F.R.C.S.I., Horfield.*
Davoren, Maj. V. H. W., *Bury St. Edmunds.*
Hosie, Lt.-Col. A., *M.D., Sandown.*
Trotter, Maj. W. J., *Naas.*
Scanlan, Lt.-Col. A. De C., *Guildford.*
Duggan, Maj. C. W., *M.B., Lincoln.*
Jackson, Maj. R. W. H., *M.D. [I], Weymouth.*
Austin, Lt.-Col. H. W., *Fort Stamford.*
Freeman, Maj. E. C., *M.D., Dep. Asst. Dir. of Med. Services, E. Anglian Div.*
Chambers, Maj. A. J., *Lichfield.*
Williams, Maj. E. M., *Leicester.*
Mansfield, Maj. O. S., *M.B., St. Peter's, Jersey.*
Hopkins, Maj., C. H., *Devizes.*

OFFICERS OF SPECIAL RESERVE AND LATE MILITIA.

Ranson, Capt. W., *F.R.C.S.Edin., R.A.M.C., Spec. Res., Beverley.*
Thomas, Capt. T. P., *late R.A.M.C (Mila.), R.A.M.C. (T.F.), Brecon.*
McAllum, Maj. S. G., *M.D., R.A.M.C., Spec. Res. (Hon. Lt. in Army), Berwick.*

ROYAL ARMY MEDICAL CORPS.
SPECIAL RESERVE.
No. 18 Field Ambulance.
Upper Chorlton Road, Manchester.

Lieutenant-Colonel.
✗Watson, A. A., VD,
  Lt.-Col. R.A.M.C.(T.F.)
  (Hon. Maj. in Army
  25 Sept. 02) 1May14

Majors (2).
Captains and Subalterns (6).

Captains.
p. ✗Roberts, C., Capt.
  1 E. Lan. Fd. Amb.,
  R.A.M.C. (T.F.) .. 7Mar.10

Captains—contd.
p. Smeeth, H. G., M.D.,
  Capt. 1 E. Lan. Fd.
  Amb., R.A.M.C.(T.F.) 7Mar.10

Loudon, A. W. B.,
  M.D., Capt. 2 E. Lan
  Fd. Amb., R.A.M.C.
  (T.F.) .. 24Apr.14

Lieutenants.

Quarter-Master.

Dugdale, H., Qr.-Mr.
  (Hon.Lt.) 3 E.Lan.Fd.
  Amb.,R.A.M.C.(T.F.),
  hon. lt. 7Mar.10

Supplementary Officers.

Majors.

p.s. ✗Steele, W. K. (Hon.
  Capt. in Army1Mar.03) 6Apr.08

p.s. ✗Clerke, J. (Hon. Capt.
  in Army 1Apr.03) .. 11Jan.11

p.s. Dalby, H. E. (Hon.Capt.
  in Army 1Apr.03) .. 28Mar.12

p.s. Graham, J. H. P. (Hon.
  Lt. in Army 1Apr.03) 11Apr.12

p.s. ✗McAllum, S. G., M.D.
  (Hon.Lt.inArmy1Mar.03)15May13

p.s. Best, W. H. G. H. (Hon.
  Lt. in Army 1Mar.03)
  (Provincial Med.Offr.,
  S. Provs., Nigeria,
  { 1Jan.14
  { 30Apr.02) 30Apr.14

p.s. ✗Furness, J. C. (Hon.
  Lt. in Army 1Mar.03)18June14

Captains.

✗Lane, G. (Hon. Lt. in
  Army 1Mar.03) (Med.
  Offr., Uganda,
  { 2Dec.04
  { 30Sept.02)30Mar.06

p.s. McCarroll, J. C., M.B. 18Aug.08
p.s. Stirling, R.J. 10ct.09
p.s. Ranson, W., F.R.C.S. Edin.
  (Lt.-Col. 3 North'bn. Fd.
  Amb.,R.A.M.C.,T.F.) 26Nov.09

Browne, W. M., late Lt.
  A. Med. Res. 1Aug.10

Nicoll, C. V., late Lt. A.
  Med. Res. 1Nov.10

Murphy, J. F., M.B., late
  Capt. A. Med. Res. 1Nov10
  .. .. .. 1May14

Taylor, M. R., M.B., late
  Capt. A. Med. Res. 1Nov.10
  .. .. .. 1May14

Usmar, G. H.. late Lt.
  R.A.M.C. 24Feb.12
McLaughlin,J. N.,M.D. 1Sept.12
Robertson, R.T.C., M.B. 1Sept.12
McCutcheon,J.G., M.B. 1Sept.12
Magill, R., M.B. .. 7Dec.12
Darling, W., M.B.,
  F.R.C.S. Edin. (local
  Capt.,O.T.C. 1 Oct.10).. 11Feb.13
Darling, J. M., M.B.
  F.R.C.S. Edin... .. 11Feb.13
Habgood, A. H. .. 22Mar.13
McCarthy,W.H.L.,M.D. 17May13
Inkster, J., M.D. .. 24May13
Dale, A. R. 29May13
MacKinnon, R., M.B... 7June13
Dickson, I. D., M.B. ..17June13
Sandeman, C. S., M.B. 17June13
Mathew, P. W. .. 30June13

Ward, G. R. 8July13
Shand, G. E., M.B. .. 20July13
✗Steward, S. J., M.D... 28July13
Macfadyen, D., M.B. 26Aug.13
Page,C.M.,M.B.,F.R.C.S.14Sept.13
Randall, G. F. ..19Sept.13
Holland, E. T. ..28Sept.13
Hall, J. C., M.D. ..30Sept.13
Biden, W. M., M.B. ..30Sept.13
Ruthven, M. W., M.B... 31Oct.13
Lindsay, T., M.B. .. 12Nov.13
Trist, J. R. R. .. 30Nov.13
Court, A. C., M.B. .. 17Dec.13
Walshe, S. J. A. H.,M.B. 15Feb.14
Stevenson, G. H., M.B. 1Mar 14
Gardner, W. R., M.B. .. 18May14
Hamilton, E. S. B.,
  M.B. 29June14
Crymble, W. 13July14

Lieutenants.

McEwen, T. 13Aug.09
Guthrie, T. E., M. .. 17Dec.09
MacGlashan, K. B., M.D.,
  F.R.C.S., Edin. 1Feb.10
Williamson, J. B., M.B. 12Feb.10
Johnson, C., M.B. .. 25May10
Roth, P. B., M.B. .. 28May10
Bell, J. H., M.B... .. 21June10
Adams, J., M.B. ..19Sept.10
Lumsden, F. W., M.B. 18Oct.10
Charnock, J. P., M.B. 28Oct.10
Hamilton, J. O., M.B. 9Nov.10
Linnell, R. McC. .. 6Jan.11
Bignold, C. A., M.B. .. 17Jan.11
Routh, L. M. 6Feb.11
Taylor, L.W. O., M.B... 17Mar.11
Fisher, R. 27Mar.11
Priestley, P. T. 30Mar.11
Aubrey, G. K. 31Mar.11
Brown, H. H., M.B. .. 1Apr.11

Vellacott,H. F.,F.R.C.S. 24Apr.11
Shaw, J. J. McI., M.B. 29Apr.11
Greenwood, R. A., M.B. 2June11
Button, P. N. 19June11
Carlton, C. H. 31July11
Power, D'A. .. 7Aug.11
McLean, W. F., M.B. .. 8Oct.11
Beath, R. M., M.B. .. 25Oct.11
Walker, T., M.B. .. 31Oct.11
Dowse, W. 1Nov.11
Walker, W. Mc N., M.B. 1Nov.11
McCullagh, W. Mc K. H.,
  M.B. 1Nov.11
Rollinson, H. D., M.B. 3Nov.11
Armstrong, S. R., M.B. 8Nov.11
Gray, J. W., M.B. .. 27Dec.11
Miller, S. 11Jan.12
Miller, W. A., M.B. .. 19Feb.12
Lyon, D. M., M.B. .. 4Mar.12
Hayman, J. R. 13Mar.12
Wilson, E. A., M.B. .. 13Mar.12
Green, R. 22Mar.12
Brown, A. J. 29Mar.12

Tasker, L. S. B., M.B. 30Apr.12
Dickson, R. C., M.B... 6May12
Cormack, R.P. .. 15May12
Gilmour, D., M.B. .. 15May12
Hills, H., M. 16May12
Nelson, T. S. 4June12
Grant, G. B., M.B. .. 4June12
Ward, J. H., M.B. .. 10June12
Leary, G. F. V., M.B. ..11June12
Hepple, R. A., M.B. .. 12June12
Walker, J., M.B. .. 12June12
Aitchison, R. C. .. 27June12
Wilson, O., M.B. .. 1July12
Campbell, J., M.B. .. 1July12
Les, E. T. R. 3July12
Campion, R. B. .. 5July12
Morse, C. G. H. .. 16Sept.12
✗Nelson, M. K. .. 15Oct.12
Wright, S. 17Oct.12
Jefferson, F., M.B. .. 17Oct.12
Goldie, R. D., M.B. .. 17Oct.12

Royal Army Medical Corps. Special Reserve.

Lieutenants—contd.

Tyrrell, W., *M.B.*	18Oct.12
Davidson, W. C., *M.B.*	22Oct.12
d'Avray, A. D.	5Nov.12
McCutcheon, A. M.	26Nov.12
Tobias, W. O.	1Dec.12
Perry, A. C. (*on prob.*)	2Dec.12
Hampson, T., *M.B.*	14Jan.13
Laird, W. J. A.	23Jan.13
Gossip, J., *M.B.*	30Jan.13
Pridham, J. A.	6Feb.13
Waddell, I. L.	14Feb.13
Evans, H., *M.B.*(*on prob.*)	15Feb.13
Hyde, W. S.	20Feb.13
Burke, E. T.	25Feb.13
Johnston, W. H.	26Feb.13
Sinderson, H. C., *M.B.*	6Mar.13
McCurry, W. T.	11Mar.13
Gibbons, G. F. P.	29Mar.13
Cesari, S. F. M., *M.B.*	8Apr.13
Rafter, J., *M.B.*	9Apr.13
Foster, F. G., *M.B.*	12Apr.13
Elliott, W. E., *M.B.*	12Apr.13
McElney, R. G.	15Apr.13
Griffith, H. S.	21Apr.13
Moore, F. O. L., *M.B.*	22Apr.13
Wagstaffe, W. W., *M.B.*	24Apr.13
Atkinson, C.	26Apr.13
McClurkin, T.	30Apr.13
King, D. R.	1May13
Young, G.	1May13
Dun, T. I.	2May13
Ward, H. K., *M.B.*	2May13
Maltby, H. W.	6May13
Inglis, M. P.	12May13
Fraser, A. D.	14May13
Brown, B. W., *M.B.* (*on prob.*)	17May13
Kelly, T. J., *M.B.*	26May13
Tomory, K. A. M.	27May13
Taylor, J., *M.B.*	27May13
Crow, H. P.	27May13
Mackie, D.	27May13
Mulholland, H. H., *M.B.*	26May13
Finlay, J. J.	4June13
Kennedy, A. P. (*on prob.*)	6June13
Taylor, R. (*on prob.*)	9June13
Tulloch, F. L., *M.B.*	16June13
Haines, G. H.	17June13
Bird, W.	19June13
Gwynne-Jones, H.	20June13
Meenan, J. F. W.	27June13
Elliott, T. W. E.	7July13
Montgomery, R., *M.B.*	11July13
Slaughter, C. A. (*on prob.*)	14July13
Pepper, G. E.	18July13
Lethem, W. A., *M.B.*	20July13
Hoyland, S. W. (*on prob.*)	25July13
Grellier, E. F. W.	21Aug.13
Stewart, C. M. (*on prob.*)	1Sept.13
Rook, H. C.	4Sept.13
Armour, D. J., *F.R.C.S.*	22Oct.13
Griffin, S. (*on prob.*)	21Nov.13
Baird, J. H. (*on prob.*)	28Nov.13
Hairsine, O. (*on prob.*)	29Nov.13
Graham, T. O., *M.D., F.R.C.S.I* (*on prob.*) (*attd. O.T.C.*)	4Dec.13
Cole, G. A. (*on prob.*)	14Dec.13
Wylie, T. W., *M.B.*	19Dec.13
Gibson, A. J., *M.B.*	22Dec.13
Clausen, R. J., *M.B.* (*on prob.*)	9Jan.14
Harkness, J. W. P. (*on prob.*)	24Jan.14
Picken, A. (*on prob.*)	24Jan.14
Dempster, D. (*on prob.*)	26Jan.14
O'Kelly, R. (*on prob.*)	26Jan.14
Macphee, E. S., *M.B.*	26Jan.14
Young, T. (*on prob.*)	28Jan.14
Cassells, A. C. (*on prob.*)	29Jan.14
Whittingham, C. A. (*on prob.*)	31Jan.14
Huban, J. P. (*on prob.*)	2Feb.14
Beveridge, J. O'S. (*on prob.*)	2Feb.14
Shields, A. F. L. (*on prob.*)	5Feb.14
McKibbin, F. (*on prob.*)	5Feb.14
Davie, T. M. (*on prob.*)	5Feb.14
MacCormack, C. McN. (*on prob.*)	5Feb.14
Clarke, A. R. F. (*on prob.*)	17Feb.14
Davies, E., *M.B.* (*on prob.*)	19Feb.14
Horne, A. J. (*on prob.*)	20Feb.14
MacDonald, G. A. (*on prob.*)	20Feb.14
Walker, J. H. C. (*on prob.*)	21Feb.14
Ronaldson, J. G., *M.B.* (*on prob.*)	23Feb.14
Forgan, R. (*on prob.*)	4Mar.14
Menzies, T. (*on prob.*)	9Mar.14
Horton, R. L., *M.B.* (*on prob.*)	13Mar.14
Pedler, H. C. G. (*on prob.*), *late Surg-Lt.* 1 L. G.	18Mar.14
Blair, R. G. (*on prob.*)	24Mar.14
Warrington, T.	25Mar.14
O'Brien, J. (*on prob.*)	26Mar.14
Alston, J. (*on prob.*)	6Apr.14
McIntosh, C. R., *M.B.*	8Apr.14
Cameron, J. (*on prob.*)	9Apr.14
Brash, J. C., *M.B.* (*on prob.*)	17Apr.14
Jebb, A. C. (*on prob.*)	24Apr.14
O'Driscoll, J. A. (*on prob.*)	27Apr.14
Macnaughton, F. G. (*on prob.*)	29Apr.14
Chesney, W. McM., *M.B.* (*on prob.*)	30Apr.14
Pirrie, I. M, *M.B.* (*on prob.*)	4May14
Rowbotham, E. S. (*on prob.*)	6May14
Melvin, J. (*on prob.*)	7May14
Walker, W., *M.B.* (*on prob.*)	7May14
Marr. D. M. (*on prob.*)	8May14
Norrie, F. H. B. (*on prob.*)	9May14
Cumming, R. S. (*on prob.*)	9May14
Firth, I. G. M. (*on prob.*)	9May14
Myles, R. B. (*on prob.*)	9May14
Sandison, J. F. W. (*on prob.*)	11May14
Lawrence, R. D. (*on prob.*)	12May14
Orme, J. McC. (*on prob.*)	13May14
Walsh, E. (*on prob.*)	14May14
Jepson, W. B. (*on prob.*)	16May14
Mollan, F. R. N. (*on prob.*)	20May14
Dawson, W. S. (*on prob.*)	20May14
Evans, G. I. (*on prob.*)	20May14
Perkins, G. (*on prob.*)	30May14
Evans, I. D., *M.B.* (*on prob.*)	21May14
Murray, D. H. (*on prob.*)	25May14
Clarke, T. W. *M.B.* (*on prob.*)	26May14
Annesley, F. D. (*on prob.*)	26May14
Thompson, W. A. (*on prob.*)	2June14
Rossdale, G. H. (*on prob.*)	3June14
Cullenan, J. (*on prob.*)	4June14
Fisher, A. G. (*on prob.*)	5June14
Suttie, I. D., *M.B.* (*on prob.*)	15June14
Bazett, H. C., *M.B., F.R.C.S.* (*on prob.*)	19June14
Bryars, W. (*on prob.*)	7July14
Chesney, G. (*on prob.*)	7July14

ROYAL ARMY MEDICAL CORPS.
TERRITORIAL FORCE.

The names of Officers attached to Units other than Medical Units are shewn under those Units. Where two dates appear against the name of a Medical Officer attached to a Unit or borne on the Unposted List, the earlier date is that of his first appointment.

The names of Officers of the late Royal Army Medical Corps (Volunteers) not yet gazetted to the Territorial Force are shewn on page 1774.

[Dates shown prior to 1 April 1908 are those of the Officers' corresponding rank in a late unit of Volunteer Force.]

   I. Field Ambulances.
      a. Mounted Brigade Field Ambulances.
      b. Field Ambulances.

  II. General Hospitals.

  II. Sanitary Service.
      a. Sanitary Companies.
      b. Sanitary Officers.

 IV. Clearing Hospitals.

  V. Schools of Instruction.

1.a. MOUNTED BRIGADE FIELD AMBULANCES.

[The order of precedence of units is denoted by numerals in brackets.]

Eastern.
[12]
Drill Hall, Grove Road, Luton, Beds.
Lt.-Colonel.
p. Cross, E. J., *M.D.* 7Dec.12
Major.
Captains and Subalterns and Transport Officer (4).
Captain.
Archibald, W., *M.D.* 2July12
Lieutenants
Sharp, C. G. K., *M.B.* 5Nov.12
Transport Officer.
Ashurst, J., *hon. lt.,* 16June09

Highland.
[1]
Drill Hall, Rose Street, Inverness.
Lt.-Colonel.
Major.
Captains and Subalterns and Transport Officer (4).
Captain.
p. Mackenzie, J, W., *M.D.* 28Jan.09
Lieutenants.
Mitchell, L.M.V., *M.B.*
   27Jan.12
Lee, A. F., *M.D.* 8Mar.12
Middleton, G. G., *M.B.* 1Apr.13
Broadfoot, J., *M.B.* 1May14
Transport Officer.

London.
[14]
3, Henry Street, Gray's Inn Road, W.C.
Lt.-Colonel.
p. ✗Stonham, C., *C.M.G.* (Hon. Maj. in Army) 2May01 1Apr.08
Major.
p. Cooke, M. A., TD 20June09
   20June08
Captains and Subalterns and Transport Officer (4).
Captains.
p. Thomas, W. P., *M.D.* 27Sept.09
   21Nov.07
p. Dixon, J. H., *M.D.* 1July12
   5May08
Beadles, H. S. 5Sept.12
Findlater, A., *M.D.* 7Dec.12
Lieutenants.

Lowland.
[2]
Yorkhill Parade, Yorkhill, Glasgow.
Lt.-Colonel.
p.s. Thomson, H. W., *M.D.* 27Apr.12
Major.
p.s. ✗Bruce, J., *M.D.* 10June13
Captains and Subalterns and Transport Officer (4).
Captains.
p. Gracie, F. M., *B.* 22Apr.07
p.s. Anderson, R. Y., *M.B.* 15Oct.07
Lieutenant.
Muir, A. R., *M.B.* 7Feb.13
Forrest, H., *M.B.* 12Mar.13

North Midland.
[7]
Drill Hall, Nineveh Road, Handsworth, Birmingham.
Lt.-Colonel.
Major.
Goodwin, A. C., *M.B., F.R.C.S.* 3June14
Captains and Subalterns and Transport Officer (4).
Captain.
Buchanan, T. G., *M.B.* 28Apr.13
Transport Officer.
Bishop, S. H., *hon. m.* 1Apr.08
Qr.-Mr. 20June08
Chaplain.

Notts & Derby.
[6]
Derby Road, Nottingham.
Lt.-Colonel.
Major.
p. ✗Tweedie, A. R., *F.R.C.S.* 14Mar.14
Captains and Subalterns and Transport Officer (4).
Captains.
Fisher, W. H., *M.D.* 1Apr.12
p.s.Mulhall, A. T., *F.R.C.S.I.* 15Feb.13
   15June10
Lieutenants.

South Eastern.
[13]
The Drill Hall, Victoria Road, Margate.
Lt.-Colonel.
p. Burgess, P. C. 24Nov.10
Major.
Captains and Subalterns and Transport Officer (4).
Captain.
Treves, F. B., *M.B.* 8Dec.11
Lieutenants.
Transport Officer.
Williams, S.R.T.A.M., *hon. lt.,* 1Apr.08

1st South Midland.
[8]
The Barracks, Great Brook Street, Birmingham.
Lt.-Colonel.
Stephen, W. H., *M.B.* 21June12
Major.
Captains and Subalterns and Transport Officer (4).
Captains.
Forrest, T. H., *M.B.* 31Jan.12
Spring, D. M., *M.B.* 30Apr.13
Lieutenants.
Buchanan, D., (Med. Offr., Straits Settlements, 25 May 12) 8May09
Leggat, A. 19July13
Torrance, W.T. 1Mar.14
Transport Officer.
Heeley, F. P. R., *hon. lt.,* 8Mar.12

| 1718 | 1719 | 1720 | 1721 |

Royal Army Medical Corps. Territorial Force.

Mtd. Brigade Field Ambulances—contd.

2nd South Midland.
[9]

Stony Stratford, Bucks.

Lt.-Colonel.
Deyns, C. J. 1Apr.12

Major.

Captains and Subalterns and Transport Officer. (4)
Captain.
Moore, A. W., *M.B.* 13Nov.11
Buxton, G. W. 18Nov.11

Lieutenants.

Transport Officer.
Bull, W. E. H., *hon. lt.* 20May08

South Wales.
[4]

The Barracks, Hereford.

Lt.-Colonel.
p. Raywood, J. R. I. Dec.10

Major.
p. Harrison, J. McK., *M.B.* 25Mar.12
p. Griffiths, J. 13May13

Captain and Subalterns and Transport Officer. (4)
Captains.

Lieutenants.
Browne, J. 23Nov.12

Transport Officer.
Thomas, T., *hon. lt.* 15Oct.08

1st South Western.
[10]
Drill Hall, Church Place, Swindon.
Lt.-Colonel.
Major.
Haydon, T. H., *M.B.* 18Dec.12
Captains and Subalterns and Transport Officer. (4)
Captain.
Burton, J. C. 16Nov.11
p. French, A. W. 5Nov.13
3Dec.04
Lieutenants.
Savage, A. H., *M.B.* 20Apr.12
Transport Officer.
James, R. G., *hon. lt.* 19May14

2nd South Western.
[11]
Frome.
Lt.-Colonel.
Cary, A. 7Aug.12
Major.
Benson, J. R., *F.R.C.S.,* p
late Lt. A. Motor Res. 15Mar.14
Captain and Subalterns and Transport Officer. (4)
Captain.
Waterhouse, R., *M.D.* 15Oct.13
15Apr.10
✗Dupont, J. M., *M.D.* 16May14
✗Parnett. H. N., *F.R.C.S. (Edin.)* 16May14
Lieutenants.
Transport Officer.
Cooper, J. B., *hon. lt.* 27Sept.13

Welsh Border.
[3]
Thomas Street, Chester.
Lt.-Colonel.
Hamilton A.G.18July13
Major.
Captains and Subalterns and Transport Officer. (4)
Captain.
Orton, D. C. L. 5Sept.10
Lieutenants
Gerrard, R. F. 12Apr.12
Transport Officer.
Cockrill, R. G., *hon. lt.* 1Apr.12

Yorkshire.
[5]
Drill Hall, Vicarage Street, Wakefield.
Lt.-Colonel.
Clayton, W. K. 1Jan.11
Major.
Captains and Subalterns and Transport Officer.
Captains.
p. Hammerton, G. H. L. 10Apr.07
Hepple, J. 1July12
Lieutenants.
Downie, J., *M.B.* 24Jan.14
Ellis, E. D. 14Mar.14
Transport Officer.
Greenwood, E. A., *hon. lt.* 2June09

1.b. FIELD AMBULANCES.
[The order of precedence of units is denoted by numerals in brackets.]

East Anglian Division.

Hon. Colonel.
Marsh, H., *F.R.C.S.* 1Oct.08
———

1st East Anglian.
[31]
Drill Hall, Woodbridge Road, Ipswich.

Lt.-Colonel.
Gostling, E. V. 8Apr.14

Majors.(2)

Captains and Subalterns and Transport Officer. (6)
Captains.
Hetherington, G. M. 23Dec.11
Ennion, O. R. 30June12
Young, A. C. 23July12
Lieutenants.
Searle, C. F., *M.B.* 13Aug.13
Transport Officer.
Harris, F., *hon. lt.* 15Mar.13
Quarter-Master.
Rice, W. J., *hon. lt.* 6May08
Chaplain.
Titcombe, Rev. J. C., Chapl. 4th Class (T.F.) (attd.) 10Mar.09

2nd East Anglian.
[32]
44, Bethel Street, Norwich.

Lt.-Colonel.

Majors (2)
p. Masson, G. B. 10Oct.10
p. Bremner, J. M. G., *M.B.* 5Nov13
Captains and Subalterns and Transport Officer. (6)
Captains.
Phillips, R., *M.B.* 21May12
Boswell, D. W., *M.D.* 2July12

Lieutenants
Flynn, T. A. 5May12
Morgan, B. B., *M.D.* 18Apr.14
1Apr.12
Hinde, E. B. *M.B.,F.R.C.S. (Edin.)* 20Apr.14

Transport Officer.
Edwards, E. J., *hon. lt.* 17June11

Quarter-Master.
Mason, R. S., *hon. lt.* 17June11
Transprt.Offr.16Oct.08

Chaplain.
Titcombe, Rev. J. C., Chapl. 4th Class (T.F.) (attd.) 10Mar.09

1722 | 1723 | 1724 | 1725

Royal Army Medical Corps. Territorial Force.

Field Ambulances—contd.
3rd East Anglian.
[33]
Walthamstow Lodge,
Church Hill,
Walthamstow.
Lt.-Colonel.
p. Challis, H. T., *M.D.*,
VD 20June10
Majors (2)
p. Oldfield, J., *M.B.*
6Jan.10
Captains and Subalterns and Transport Officer. (6)
Captains.
✗Pooler, J. R., *M.B.*
24June12
Turtle, J. 27July12
Cowell, W. I. 10Nov.13
Graham, A., *M.B.*
7Jan.14
Roberts, W. R. S.,
M.B. 1May14
Lieutenants.
Brander, W., *M.D.*
22Oct.12
Transport Officer.
Beamand, A. W.,
hon. lt. 27Apr.12
Qr.-Mr. 1Aug.10
Quarter-Master.
Taylor, F. T.,
hon. lt. 17July12

Highland Division.
Hon. Colonel.
Ogston, Sir A., K.C.V.O.,
M.D., LL.D. 1Apr.08

1st Highland.
[1]
Territorial Barracks,
Fonthill Road, Aberdeen.
Lt.-Colonel.
p. Fraser, T., *M.B.*
1Nov13
Majors (2)
Captains and Subalterns and Transport Officer. (6)
Captains.
p. Howie, P., *M.B.*14Sept.09
Robertson, J., *M.D.*
14Oct.11
Kellas, A., *M.B.* 2Aug.12
Fiddes, J. D., *M.B.*
10Dec.12
Lieutenants.
Quarter-Master.
Prosser, A. A.,
hon. lt. 1May10
Chaplain.
Smith, Rev. J., *M.A.*,
B.D.,T.D.[C.S.]Chapl.
1st Class (T.F.)
(attd.) 8June09
8June89

2nd Highland.
[2]
Territorial Barracks,
Fonthill Road, Aberdeen.
Lt.-Colonel.
p. Ogston, A., *M.B.*12Feb.12
Majors (2)
Captains and Subalterns and Transport Officer. (6)
Captains.
p. Noble, J. D., *M.B.*
28Dec.06
27June03
MacIntosh, J. F., *M.B.*
14Oct.11
Lieutenants.
Cameron, C., *M.B.*
1Apr.11
Grant, A. R., *M.B.*
28Jan.14
Transport Officer.
p. Duthie, D. H., hon. lt.
2Feb.09
Qr.-Mr. 7Apr.06
Quarter-Master.
p. Munro, J. M., hon. lt.
6Feb.09
Chaplain.
Smith, Rev. J., *M.A.*,
B.D., Chapl. 1st Class
(T.F.) (attd.) 8June09
8June89

3rd Highland.
[3]
Dudhope, Drill Hall,
Brown Street, Dundee.
Lt.-Colonel.
p. Foggie, W. E.,
M.D. 19May13
Majors and Captains and Subalterns and Transport Officer. (6)
Captains.
p. Kidd, A. E., *M.B.*
12June07
p. Miller, G. W., *M.B.* ⓣ
24June08
Smith, J. M., *M.B.*,
1Oct.11
Hunter, J. E., *M.B.*,
10Oct.11
Gorrie, H. J. 10Mar.13
Robertson, W. L.,
M.B., F.R.C.S.
(Edin.) 19Apr.14
Transport Officer.
Tait, J. 12July13
capt. 30Dec.12
Quarter-Master.
p. Dunn, J., hon. m.
(t) 18Feb.05
Chaplain.
Lang, Rev. M. B.,
B.D., [C.S.], Chapl.
2nd Class (T.F.)
(attd.) 11May11
11May96

Home Counties Division.
Hon. Colonel.
Evatt, Surg.-Gen.
G. J. H., C.B.,
M.D., ret.pay [R.]
27Apr.08

1st Home Counties.
[34]
The Palace, Maidstone.
Lt.-Colonel.
p. Rogers-Tillstone,
J. M. 1Apr.12
Majors (2)
Captains and Subalterns and Transport Officer. (6)
Captains.
p. Ward, J. 1Feb.10
Potts, G., F.R.C.S.
(Edin.) 11Aug.12
Lieutenants.
Peyton, T. H. 3Mar.11
Johnston, D. M., *M.B.*
18Jan.13
Greene, C. W., *M.B.*,
F.R.C.S. 15Mar.13
Killick, C., *M.D.*,
F.R.C.S. 21Feb.14
Transport Officer.
Beale, R. W., hon. lt.
19Nov.13
Quarter-Master.
Okill, H. C., hon. lt.
4Oct.09
Chaplain.
Hardcastle, Rev. E. H.,
Chapl. 4th Class
(T.F.) (attd.) 1Dec.09

2nd Home Counties.
[35]
Drill Hall, Ashford,
Kent.
Lt.-Colonel.
p. Hamilton, D. L.,
F.R.C.S. Edin.
17June11
Majors (2)
Captains and Subalterns and Transport Officer. (6)
Captains.
Flint, W. H. 8Dec.11
✗Willan, G. T. 8Oct.12
Alston, W. E., *M.D.*
20June14
1Jan.13
Lieutenants.
Billings, B. R. 27Jan.12
1Mar.11
Transport Officer.
Hamilton, J. L.,
hon. lt. 5Jan.10
Quarter-Master.
Harris, G. W.,
hon. lt. 6Apr.10
Chaplain.
Railton, Rev. D.,
Chapl. 4th Class
(T.F.) (attd.) 2Dec.11

3rd Home Counties.
[36]
24, Claremont Road,
Surbiton, Surrey.
Lt.-Colonel.
p. Edsell, G. A., *M.D.*
22Oct.11
Majors (2)
Captains and Subalterns and Transport Officer. (6)
Captains.
Coad, S. A. 22Feb.12
Mackenzie, H. G. G.,
M.D. 23Apr.13
✗Barkley, J., late
Lt. R.A. M.C. 3Feb.14
Houchin, E. A. 12Apr.14
Lieutenants.
Brewer, A. H. 2May13
Keogh, F.E.H. 13June13
Merrick, H.T.N.,
M.B. 4Mar.14
Transport Officer.
✗Devlin, T., hon. lt.
24May09
Quarter-Master.
✗Hewitt, M.,
Qr.-Mr. (hon.
capt.) ret. pay
hon. m. 21July09
Chaplain.
Macnutt, Rev. Canon
F. B., *M.A.*, Chapl.
4th Class (T.F.)
(attd.) 3Mar.11

East Lancashire Division.
Hon. Colonel.
Coates, W., C.B., VD.
(Col. ret. T.F. Res.)
12Nov.13

1st East Lancashire.
[10]
Upper Chorlton Road,
Manchester.
Lt.-Colonel.
p Parker, H. G.,
F.R.C.S.Edin.11Nov.12
Majors (2)
p. Bentley, W. L. 1Apr.08
20May11
Captains and Subalterns and Transport Officer (6)
Captains.
p. †✗Roberts, C. 19Mar.07
p. †Smeeth, H. G., *M.D.*
4July08
p. Fitzgerald,G.W14May10
4July08
Postlethwaite, J. M.
2Aug.13
Ramsbottom, A.,
M.D., late Capt.
2W.Gen.Hosp.14Nov.13
Lieutenants.
Douglas, W. R. 12Dec.07
Quarter-Master.
Bramwell, T.,
hon. lt. 10Apr.13
Chaplain.
Kent, Rev. J. E.,
M.A., Chapl. 4th
Class (T.F.) (attd.)
31July09

† Supernumerary whilst serving with No. 13 Fd. Amb., R.A.M.C., Spec. Res.

Royal Army Medical Corps. Territorial Force.

Field Ambulances—contd.

2nd East Lancashire.
[11]
Upper Chorlton Road, Manchester.
Lt.-Colonel.
p. Pritchard, W. B. 18Nov.11
Majors (2),
Captains and Subalterns and Transport Officer. (6)
Captains.
p. ✗Ashton, G., *M.D.* 5May06
p. Callam, A. 28Sept.09
p. ✗Pritchard, H.W. 7Mar.10
Munro, W. F., *M.B.* 22Nov.07
Redmond, C. H. S., *M.B.* 23Sept.11
Loudon, A. W. B., *M.D.* 1Nov.13
Lieutenants.
Purves, W. J. 21Dec.10
Webster, C. A. 16May14
Transport Officer.
Steell, J. W. G., *hon. lt.* 27Mar.13
Qr.-Mr. 28Sept.10
Quarter-Master.
p. Pritchard, S., *hon. capt.* 14May02

3rd East Lancashire.
[12]
Upper Chorlton Road, Manchester.
Lt.-Colonel.
p. Steinthal, W. M. 1Mar.13
Majors (2).
p. Matthews, W. R., *M.B.* 1Apr.08
Captains and Subalterns and Transport Officer. (6)
Captains.
Cox, E.H., *M.B.* 14Nov.13
Lieutenants.
Jones, K. W., *M.D.* 11Feb.12
Reid, W.J., *M.B.* 1Apr.13
Lund, J. K. 2July13
Johneon, A.M., *M.D.* 16Mar.14
Quarter-Master.
†✗Dugdale, H., *hon. lt.* 1Dec.08
✗Hartshorn, A. H., *hon. lt.* 7Mar.10

West Lancashire Division.
Hon. Colonel.
Glynn, T. R., *M.D.*, 13Aug.13

1st West Lancashire.
[7]
Tramway Road, Liverpool, S.
Lt.-Colonel.
p. O'Hagan, J. J., *M.B.*, *F.R.C.S.I.* 5June12
Majors (2).
Captains and Subalterns and Transport Officer. (6)
Captains.
Lindsay, C. H., *M.D.* 25May11
MacFall, J. E. W., *M.D.* 1Oct.11
Taylor, R. S., *M.B.*, *F.R.C.S.(Edin.)* 1Oct.11
Simpson, A. P. H. 1Oct.11
Lieutenants.
McCausland, S. 1June14
Transport Officer.
Leonard, R. M., *hon. lt.* 6Mar.12
Quarter-Master.
Fraser, C.F., *hon. lt.* 14Feb12

2nd West Lancashire.
[8]
14, Harper Street, Liverpool.
Lt.-Colonel.
Stevenson, T., *M.D.*, TD 1Apr.12
Majors (2)
Blackledge, W.T., *M.B.* (late Capt. 3 W. Lan. Brig. R. F. A.) 27July12 28Sept.11
Captains and Subalterns and Transport Officer. (6)
Captains.
Hawksley, W. L., *M.B.* 1Oct.11
Macdonald, W., *M.B.* 1Oct.11
Williams, O. H., *M.B.* 23Dec.11
Simpson, G. C. E., *M.B.*, *F.R.C.S.* 4Apr.13
Lieutenants.
Pierce, W. R., *M.D.* 22May12
Roberts, J. F., *M.B.* 24July13
Transport Officer.
Kilburne, G., *hon. lt.* 27Apr.12
Quarter-Master.
Bennett, J., *hon. lt.* 12July13

3rd West Lancashire.
[9]
Croppers Hill, St. Helens (for 2 Sections).
Kendal (for 1 Section).
Lt.-Colonel.
p. Gullan, A. G., *M.D.*, *F.R.C.S.* 8Apr.14
Majors (2).
Captains and Subalterns and Transport Officer. (6)
Captains.
✗Merrick, A. A. W., *F.R.C.S.(I.)* 1Oct.11
Coffey, R. 4Dec.12
Lieutenants.
Dick, M.I., *M.B.* 15Dec.11
Hauxwell, F., 12Mar.13
M.B.
Frew, R. D. B., *M.D.* 27Apr.12
Transport Officer.
Saywell, J. R., *hon. lt.* 3June13
Quarter-Master.
Jukes, E. J., *hon. lt.* 1Apr.08

1st London Division.
Hon. Colonel.
p. Cantlie, Hon. Surg.-Col. J., *M.B.*, *F.R.C.S.*, VD. 5Mar.04

1st London (City of London).
[37]
Duke of York's Head-Quarters, Chelsea, S.W.
Lt.-Colonel.
p.s.✗Sleman, F.R., *M.D.*, VD. (Hon. Capt. in Army 1Dec.00) 1Apr.08
Majors (2).
p. ✗St. Vincent-Ryan, E. W. (Hon. Capt. in Army 1Dec.00) 9Jan.09
Captains and Subalterns and Transport Officer. (6)
Captains.
p.s.✗Elliot, A., *M.D.* 17June08
p. Rowse, E. L., *M.D.* 1Oct.11
✗Fitzwilliams, D.C.L., *M.D.*, *F.R.C.S.* 3July13
Lieutenants.
Williams, A. D. J. B. (Proby. Med. Offr., E. Africa Prote., 1May12) 7Sept.11
Griffith, A. D., *M.B.*, *F.R.C.S.* 22Nov.11
Gauntlett, E. G., *M.B.*, *F.R.C.S.* 28Oct.12
Donaldson, E. 11July14
Quarter-Master.
✗Mount, A. B., *hon. lt.* 7July09

2nd London (City of London).
[38]
Duke of York's Head-Quarters, Chelsea, S, W.
Lt.-Colonel.
p.s. Sharpe, W.S., *M.D.*, TD. 17July12
Majors (2),
p. Montgomery-Smith, E. C. 14Nov.12
Captains and Subalterns and Transport Officer. (6)
Captains.
p. Humphreys, F. R. 1Oct.11
Bickerton, R. E., *M.B.* 13Oct.12
Rawes, L. 4Dec.13
Lieutenants.
Harwood, L. A. 2June13
Pinto-Leite, H. 16June13
Transport Officer.
Turner, F. S., *hon. lt.* 30Nov.09
2July09
Quarter-Master.
p. Knights, A. J. H., *hon. capt.* 1Apr.08

3rd London (City of London).
[39]
Duke of York's Head-Quarters, Chelsea, S.W.
Lt.-Colonel.
p. Whait, J.R., *M.B.* 1Apr.12
Majors (2)
p. Waggett, E.B., *M.B.* 3Feb.10
Captains and Subalterns and Transport Officer. (6)
Captains.
p.s.✗Lawson, G. L., late Surg. Capt. 6 Regt. Impl. Bushmen, N.S. Wales 22Aug.08
p. Fairbank, H. A. T., *F.R.C.S.* 30Aug.10
Potter, B. E., *M.B.* 12Nov.12
Vick, R. M. 22May13
Lieutenants.
Robbins, H. 10July12
Barnsley R.E. 13Mar.13 22July12
Taylor, J., *F.R.C.S.* 24June14
Quarter-Master.
✗Kemp, J. W., *hon. lt.* 28May10 22July06

† Supernumerary whilst serving with No. 18 Fd. Amb., R.A.M.C, Spec. Res.

Royal Army Medical Corps. Territorial Force.

Field Ambulances—contd.

2nd London Division.

Hon. Colonel.
Keogh, Sir A.,
K.C.B., M.D.,
F.R.C.P., Surg.-
Gen. ret. pay 3Dec.13

4th London. [40]
School of Ambulance,
Brookhill Road, Woolwich.
Lt.-Colonel.
p. Greenway, A. S.,
M.D., TD 1Apr.08
Majors (2).
p. Jerman, A. E. 18June13
Captains and Subalterns and Transport Officer (6).
Captains.
Thompson, P. W. 24Apr.12
Holmes, J. R., M.B., 26Apr.12
Cowie, W., M.B. 7Oct.12
Lieutenants.
Williamson, A. J.,
M.B., 19June13
 21Apr.11
Transport Officer.
Messent, A. J.,
hon. capt. (b)15Apr.05
Qr.-Mr. 9July04
Quarter-Master.
p. Ekins, J. P.,
hon. capt. 20July01

5th London. [41]
159, Greenwich Road, S.E.
Lt.-Colonel.
p. Dowsett, E. B. 18May12
Majors (2).
Captains and Subalterns and Transport Officer (6)
Captains.
p. Corfe, R. 1Dec.10
p. Macaulay, W. C.,
M.B. 13June11
Steadman, S. F. St. J. 19Aug.12
Lieutenants.
Annis, E. G. 30July12
Hill, W. B., M.D., 17Feb.14
Sandilands, J. E.
M.D. 4Apr.14
Transport Officer.
p.s. Hardcastle, B.,
hon. m. (b) 1Apr.08
Qr.-Mr. 7July06
Quarter-Master.
p. Naylor, A. J.,
hon. capt. 18June02

Chaplain.
Money, Rev. W. T.,
M.A., Chapl. 4th
Class(T.F.) (attd.)
 16Dec.13

6th London. [42]
Duke of York's Head-Quarters, Chelsea, S.W.
Lt.-Colonel.
p.s. O'Connor, W. M.,
M.D., late Maj.
R.A.M.C.(Mils.)
(Hon. Maj. in Army
 1Apr.08) 31Mar.13
Captains and Subalterns and Transport Officer (6).
Captains.
✗Dawson, H. K., M.D.
 6Jan.13
Minett, E. P. 11Feb.13
Lieutenants.
Ryan, J. E., M.D.
 1June13
 1Feb.11
Price, P. S. 2June13
Coleman, F. 13Oct.13
 6Feb.13
Transport Officer.
Toms, C. B., hon. lt.
(b) 22Feb.09
Quarter-Master.
Ramsay, W., hon. lt.
 10Mar.13

Lowland Division.

Hon. Colonel.
p. Goff, B., M.D., VD,
hon. c. 26June01

1st Lowland. [4]
Yorkhill Parade,
Yorkhill, Glasgow.
Lt.-Colonel.
p.s. Edington, G. H., M.D.,
F.F.P.S. 27Jan.12
Majors (2).
Captains and Subalterns and Transport Officer (6).
Captains.
p.s. Bryce, W., M.D.1June07
p. Murray, W. C., M.B.
 25Dec.07
p. Leitch, J. W. 1Apr.08
Lieutenants.
Mackenzie, W. F.,
M.B. 18Feb.11
MacInnes, N.,
M.B. 19June11
Downes, A. D.,
M.B. 12Dec.13
Gunn, W. C., M.B.
 31Jan.13
Taylor, R. S.,
M.B. 19Feb.14
Quarter-Master.
p. ✗Kenny, J., hon. m.
 7Feb.06

Chaplain.
Adamson, Rev. T.,
D.D., [U.F.C.],
Chapl. 2nd Class
(T.F.) (attd.) 29July11
 29July96

2nd Lowland. [5]
Yorkhill Parade,
Yorkhill, Glasgow.
Lt.-Colonel.
Moffat, A. D., M.D.,
TD 1Apr.08
Majors (2).
p.s. McKie, J., M.B.
 1Apr.08
p.s. Dunning, M., M.B.
 5Apr.13
Captains and Subalterns and Transport Officer (6).
Captains.
p.s. Burns, W. A. 1May07
p.s. Aitken, J. A. H., M.B.
 28Oct.09
p. ✗Shannon, D., M.B.
 18Sept.10
p. Watson, A. M., M.B.
 7Nov.11
Lieutenants.
MacPhail, D. H.4Jan.11
Manson, W. H., M.D.
 17Feb.14
Quarter-Master.
Macdonald, J., hon. lt.
 12Mar.13
Chaplain.
Macmillan, Rev.
D., D.D.,[C.S.]
Chapl. 4th Class
(T.F.)(attd.) 13May12

3rd Lowland. [6]
Easter Road Barracks,
Edinburgh.
Lt.-Colonel.
p.s. Ross, A. A., M.B.
 15Aug.08
Majors (2).
p. McIntosh, A. M.,
M.B. 1Apr.09
Captains and Subalterns and Transport Officer (6).
Captains.
p. ✗Pirie, J. H. H.,
M.D. 1Oct.09
(Pathologist &
Asst.Bacteriologi-t,
E. Africa Prote.
{10 June 13})
p. Leebody, H. A.,
M.B. 19Nov.09
p.s. Keay, J. W., M.D.
 1June10
Young, J., M.B.,
F.R.C.S.(Edin.)8Aug.13
Lieutenants.
Brown, A. J. 10Apr.13
Barnetson, R. B.,
M.B. 29Apr.14
Quarter-Master.
✗Macintosh, P., Qr.-
Mr. (hon. capt.) ret.
pay, hon. maj. 12Oct.09

North Midland Division.

Hon. Colonel.
Luce, R. H., M.B.,
F.R.C.S., VD.
Col. T.F Res. 5Nov 13

1st North Midland. [22]
91, Siddals Road, Derby.
Lt.-Colonel.
Majors (2)
p. ✗Wraith, E.A.19Nov.13
Captains and Subalterns and Transport Officer (6).
Captains.
Barron, T. A. 10Jan.12
Bremner, F. R.,
M.B. 2Apr.12
Kewley, A. G. 24May12
Dawson, H. G. W.,
M.B. 7Apr.13
Lieutenants.
Grieve, J. C., M.B.
 1Jan.14
Transport Officer.
✗Piggin, H. A.,
hon. lt. 1May14
Quarter-Master.
Moreton, W. M.,TD,
hon. m. 21May08

2nd North Midland. [23]
Oxford Street, Leicester.
Lt.-Colonel.
Majors (2)
Riddett, A. J. 7Feb.14
Captains and Subalterns and Transport Officer (6).
Captains.
West, R. M., M.D.,
late Capt. 5 N. Gen.
Hosp., R.A.M.C.
 9Dec.12
Lieutenants.
Cowper, C. M. 17Oct.11
Turner, A. C. F.,
M.B. 20Oct.12
Transport Officer.
Read, T., hon. lt.
 23Nov.12
Quarter-Master.
Spibey, T., hon.
capt. 1Apr.08

Royal Army Medical Corps. Territorial Force.

Field Ambulances—contd.

3rd North Midland.
[24]
The Deanery, Stafford Street, Wolverhampton.
Lt.-Colonel.
p. ⨯Dent, H H.C., *M.B.*, F.R.C.S. 5Sept.11
Majors (2)
Captains and Subalterns and Transport Officer. (6)
Captains.
Hodder, A. E., *M.B.* 24Mar.11
Stidston, C. A., *M.D.* 7June13
Strange, E. W., *M.D.* 24June13
Miller, J. 27Aug.13
5Nov.11
Lieutenants.
Harris, J. C. 1Oct.11
Lee, C. S. 19Feb.13
Boyd, W., *M D*, 27Nov.13
Haycraft, G. F. 1May14
Transport Officer.
Hinde, W. H., *hon lt* 6May11
Quarter-Master.
King, J., *hon. lt.* 13Apr.08

South Midland Division.
Hon. Colonel.
Osler, Sir W., Bt., M.D., LL.D.,F.R.S. 21Sept.08

1st South Midland.
[25]
The Barracks, Great Brook Street, Birmingham.
Lt.-Colonel.
⨯Howkins, C. H. 22Aug.10
Majors (2)
Captains and Subalterns and Transport Officer. (6)
Captains.
Sturrock, W.M., *M.B.* 1Oct.11
McCall, W., *M.B.* 1Oct.11
Boeddicker, H. F. W., *M.B.* 1Jan.13
Boome, E. J., *M.B.* 19Aug.13
Lieutenants.
McCready, H.E., *M.D.* 31Jan.14
Transport Officer.
Dawes, G. H., *TD*, *late Lt. N. Mid. Div. T.& S. Col. A.S.C.,* (*hon. m.*) (*b*). 12Oct.11
Quarter-Master.
Kimpton, W. H., *hon. capt.* 5Aug.12
1Apr.08
Chaplain.
Gillingham, Rev. F. H., Chapl. 4th Class (T.F.)(*attd.*) 18Sept.11

2nd South Midland.
[26]
The Barracks, Great Brook Street, Birmingham.
Lt.-Colonel.
p. Craig, G. W. 1Oct.13
Majors (2)
Captains and Subalterns and Transport Officer. (6)
Captains.
Holland, W. A. L. 1Oct.11
Hobling, J. H. 1Oct.11
Lieutenants.
Dale, J. *M.B.* 1May12
Transport Officer.
Yates, J. H., *late Capt. 1 V.B. S. Staff. R., h m. m.* 1Apr.08
Quarter-Master.
Wright, S. C., *hon. lt.* 1May11

3rd South Midland.
[27]
Colston Fort, Montague Place, Kingsdown, Bristol.
Lt.-Colonel.
p. Young, J., *M.D.* 5Mar.13
Majors (2)
Rogers, B. M. H. *M.D.* 16May14
Captains and Subalterns and Transport Officer. (6)
Captains.
Mather, J. S. 1Oct.11
Green, T.A., *M D*, 1Oct.11
Moxey, P. 1Feb.13
1Oct.11
Lieutenants.
Herapath, C. E. K., *M.B.* 1Apr.11
Williamson, G.S. 5Oct.11
1Nov.09
Rintoul, D. W., *M.B.* 1June13
Harty, J. P. I., *M.B.* 1Apr.14
Smythe, H. J. D. 18June14
Quarter-Master.
Lambert, H., *hon. lt.* 1Apr.08
Chaplain.
Alford, Rev. Canon J. G., *M.A.*, VD, Chapl. 1st Class (T.F.) (*attd.*) 1Jan.10
11Dec.78

Northumbrian Division.
Hon. Colonel.
Blandford, J.W., VD, (*Col. ret.* A. Med. Serv. (T.F.) 12Nov.13

1st Northumbrian.
[16]
Drill Hall, Hutton Terrace, Newcastle-on-Tyne.
Lt.-Colonel.
Majors.
p. Hawthorn, F., *M.D.* 13Dec.13
Captains and Subalterns and Transport Officer. (6)
Captains.
Gover, J. M. 1Oct.11
Milne, J. P. 25Oct.11
Simpson, W. 25Oct.11
Spencer, G. H. 2Nov.11
Lieutenants.
Kitching, E. B. 5Mar,13
23Feb.12
Craven, J. W., *M.B.* 22Mar.13
Badenoch, R.G., *M.B.* 28Apr.14
Quarter-Master.
p. Greenwood, N., *hon. lt.* 7May08
Chaplain.
Wilkinson, Rev. J., *M.A.*, Chapl. 1st Class (T.F.)(*attd.*) 7Apr.14
7Apr.94

2nd Northumbrian.
[17]
Larchfield Street, Darlington.
Lt.-Colonel.
p. Blandford, L. J., *M.D.* 9July10
Majors (2)
Captains and Subalterns and Transport Officer. (6)
Captains.
p. Cameron, D. A., *M.B.* 8May09
Haig, D.V., *M.D.*, 30July11
Fisher, D. L., *M.B.* 31July11
McCullagh, A. C. W., *M.B.* 3Dec.12
Ellis, H. D., *M.B.* 3Dec.12
Lieutenants.
Lawrence, A. C. C. 8Sept.13
Wilson, W. M., *M.B.* 27Sept.13

Transport Officer.
Green, H. W., *hon. lt.* 21Aug.13
Quarter-Master.
Lyall, E., *hon. lt.* 1Apr.09

3rd Northumbrian.
[18]
Wenlock Barracks, Walton Street, Hull.
Lt.-Colonel.
p.s. Ranson, W., F.R.C.S., Edin. (*Capt. R.A.M.C., Spec. Res.*) 8Feb.13
Majors (2)
Captains and Subalterns and Transport Officer. (6)
Captains.
p. Appleton, O. L. 9Aug.10
p. Ash, P. R. 19Aug.10
Thompson, W. A. 1July12
Archdale, M.A., *M.B.* 24Sept.12
Lieutenants.
Perl, A. F., *M.B.* 14 Jan.11
Transport Officer.
Brown, G. W., *hon. lt.* 30Nov.08
Quarter-Master.
Cohen, M., *hon. lt.* 10Dec.08

West Riding Division.
Hon. Colonel.
Birch, de B., C.B., M.D., VD (*Col. ret. A. Med. Serv* (T.F.) 5Nov.13

1st West Riding.
[19]
Harewood Barracks, Woodhouse Lane, Leeds.
Lt.-Colonel.
p.s. ⨯Sharp, A. D. 24Jan.11
Captains and Subalterns and Transport Officer. (6)
Captains.
p. Stewart, A. B. S. 15Feb.10
Ewing, J. 1Oct.11
Lister, W. 21Feb.12
Lieutenants.
Pope, H. B. 2June13
Goode, H.N., *M.B.*, F.R.C.S., (*Edin.*) 9Dec.13
Transport Officer.
p. Gardner, W., *TD*, *hon. m.* 1Apr.08
Quarter-Master.
Ross, C. T., *hon. lt.* 9July08
Chaplain.
Phillips, Rev. J. F., *M.A.*, Chapl. 3rd Class (T.F.)(*attd*) 1Apr.08
9Mar.99

| 1738 | 1739 | 1740 | 1741 |

Royal Army Medical Corps. Territorial Force.

Field Ambulances— *contd.*

2nd West Riding.
[20]
Harewood Barracks, Woodhouse Lane, Leeds.

, *Lt.-Colonel.*
p. Young, W. Mc G., *M.D.* 1Apr.11

Majors (2)

Captains and Subalterns and Transport Officer. (6)

Captains.
Collinson, H., *M.B.* 1Apr.08
Whalley, F., *M.B.* 1Apr.08
Eames, C. W., *M.D.* 1Jan.12
Dobson, F. G., *M.B.* 13May13

Lieutenants.
Dixon, R. G., *M.B.* 1Nov.13

Quarter-Master.
p. Boswell, J., *hon. capt.* 7Feb.06

Chaplain.
Phillips, *Rev.* J. F., *M.A.*, Chapl. 3rd Class (T.F.) (*attd.*) 9Mar.08

3rd West Riding.
[21]
Brook House, 2, Gell Street, Sheffield.

Lt.-Colonel.

Major
✗Hadley, F. A., F.R.C.S. (*Hon. Capt. in Army* 2June01 15Nov.11
Stokes, J. W. 11Feb.14

Captains and Subalterns and Transport Officer. (6)

Captains.
Mackinnon, J. 1Oct.11
Finch, E. F. 6Oct.11
p. Murray, C. G. 10Oct.11
Skinner, E. F. 11Oct.11

Lieutenants.

Quarter-Master.
✗Jones, E. T., *hon. lt.* 6June14

Welsh Division.
Hon. Colonel.
Williams, Sir J., Bt., G.C.V.O., M.D. 21Sept.08

1st Welsh.
[13]
Ebbw Vale, Mon.
Lt.-Colonel.
Davies, J. W., VD. 1Apr.08
Majors (2)

Captains and Subalterns and Transport Officer. (6)

Captains.
p. Donovan, T. 12Dec.08
O'Sullivan, J. 19June11
Buckner, J. 1Oct.11
McGinn, P. J. 21July12
Connellan, E. V. 1Aug.13

Lieutenants.

Transport Officer.

Quarter-Master.
Bull, E., *hon. lt.* 19Mar.10

Chaplain.
Williams, *Rev.* H.S.F., B.A., Chapl. 4th Class (T.F.) (*attd.*) 13July10

2nd Welsh.
[14]
15, Newport Road, Cardiff.
Lt.-Colonel.
p. ✗Sheen, A. W., M.D. 1Feb.09
p. Collins, E. T. 10July13
Majors (2)

Captains and Transport Officer. (6)

Captains.
p. ✗White, C. R., M.B. 12June07
p. Samuel, H. T. 1Apr.08
Dunbar, H. J., M.B. 22Apr.12
Rhys, O. L., M.D. 25Mar.13

Lieutenants.
Devereux, A. C., M.B. 11July11
Wallace, J., M.B. 10July13
Shaw, A. F. B., M.B. 8Dec.13
Myles, C.W.C., M.B., *late Lt.* R.⊃.M.C., Spec. Res. 7Jan.14
Davies, I. J., M.D. 16Feb.14

Transport Officer.
Culley, A. C., *hon. lt.* 14Oct.08

Quarter-Master
Nicholas, J., *hon. lt.* 29Apr.09

Chaplain.
Price, *Rev.* C. L., M.A., Chapl. 3rd Class (T.F.) (*attd.*) 1Apr.08 26May97

3rd Welsh.
[15]
The Drill Hall, Swansea.
Lt.-Colonel.
p.s. Jones, A. L. 1Apr.08

Majors. (2)

Captains and Subalterns and Transport Officer. (6)

Captains.
p. Chiles-Evans, D. B. 12Dec.08
Evans, D. E., M.B. 25Dec.11
Brice, E. 25Dec.11
Jones, G. D. E., M.D., F.R.C.S. 7Jan.12

Lieutenants.
Quick, H. E., M.B., F.R.C.S. 15May12

Transport Officer.
Ackland, W. J., *hon. lt.* 19Apr.14 10June10

Quarter-Master.
Thomas, A., *hon. lt.* 19Apr.14

Wessex Division.
Hon. Colonel.
✗Treves, Sir F., Bt., G.C.V.O., C.B., F.R.C.S. 21Sept.08

1st Wessex.
[28]
71, Holloway Street, Exeter.
Lt.-Colonel.
p. Pickard, R., M.D. 29Mar.10

Majors (2)
p. Sayres, A.W.F. 22Mar.12

Captains and Subalterns and Transport Officer. (6)

Captains.
Duncan, T., M.B. 5Nov 11
Hawker, G.P. D., M.B. 5Nov.11
Eager, R., M.B. 5Nov.11

Lieutenants.
Roper, F. A., M.B. 22Apr.13

Transport Officer.
Squire, E. F., *hon. lt.* 1Feb.09

Quarter-Master.
p. Maunder, J. H., *hon. lt.* 5May08

Chaplain.
Prince, *Rev.* J. H., Chapl. 4th Class (T.F) (*attd.*) 1Apr.09

2nd Wessex.
[29]
Drill Hall, Millbay, Plymouth.
Lt.-Colonel.
p. Soltau, A. B., M.D. 1Apr.10

Majors. (2)

Captains and Subalterns and Transport Officer. (6)

Captains.
p. Whitmore, F. C. 3Mar.09
p. Crowther, C. R., M.B. 25Dec.11
Blackwood, W., M.B. 30July12
Puddicombe, T. P. 27Oct.12
Macnair, D., M.D. 3June13

Lieutenants.

Transport Officer.
Miller, F. J., *hon. lt.* 14May10

Quarter-Master.
Garland, G. S., *hon. lt.* 25June08

Chaplain.
Baker, *Rev.* J. P., M.A., Chapl. 4th Class (T.F.) (*attd.*) 28Apr.13

3rd Wessex.
[30]
Portsmouth.
Lt.-Colonel.
p. Brook, H. D., VD 18Aug.09

Majors. (2)
✗Milne-Thomson, A., *late Surg.-Maj.* 9 N. Zealand Mtd. Rif., S.A.F.F. 11Apr 12

Captains and Subalterns and Transport Officer. (6)

Captains.
Stokes, F. E. 19Nov.11
Alderson, E., M.D. 16Dec.12
Bird, E. B. 23May13

Lieutenants.
Maybury, A. V., M.B. 1Mar.12
Plummer, E. C. 5Sept.13

Transport Officer.
Larman, H., *hon. lt.* 4Oct.09

Quarter-Master.
Hearn, C. W., *hon. lt.* 25May10

Royal Army Medical Corps. Territorial Force.

II. GENERAL HOSPITALS.

[The order of precedence of units is denoted by numerals in brackets.]

1st Eastern.

[18]

39, Green Street, Cambridge.

‡*Colonel.*
Griffiths, J., *M.D.,*
TD. 6May08
Lt.-Colonel.

Major.
p. Webb, F. E. A. 6May08

Quarter-Master
Porter, R. H., *hon. lt.* 5Apr.11

Officers whose services will be available on mobilization.

Lt.-Colonels.
Allbutt, Sir T. C., *K.C.B., F.R.S., M.D.,* 6May08
Wherry, G. E., *M.B., F.R.C.S.* 6May08
Bradbury, J. B., *M.D.,* 6May08
Deighton, F., *M.B.* 6May08

Majors.
Humphry, L., *M.D.* 6May08
Cooke, A., *M.B., F.R.C.S.* 6May08
Jones, E. L., *M.D.* 6May08
Burton-Fanning, F. W., *M.D.* 6May08
Ballance, H. A., *M.D., F.R.C.S.* 6May08
Wright, J. A., *M.D.* 6May08
Hichens, P. S. *M.D.* 6May08
Milligan, R. A., *M.D.* 6May08

Captains.
Brown, H. H., *M.D.* 6May08
Gutch, J., *M.D.* 6May08
Graham, J. C. W. 6May08
Rogers, G. F., *M.D.* 6May08
Haynes, G. S., *M.D.* 6May08
Nicholson, B. H., *M.B.* 6May08
Malden, W., *M.D.* 6May08
Curl, S. W, 6May08

2nd Eastern.

[19]

117, Gloucester Road, Brighton.

Lt.-Colonel.

Major.
p. Booth, J. A. 12July13

‡*Lieutenant.*
Walker, H. J., *F.R.C.S. (Edin)* 18July13

Quarter-Master.
Briscoe, T. F. H., TD, *hon. m. (H)* 27Apr.08

Officers whose services will be available on mobilization.

Lt.-Colonels.
Hobhouse, E., *M.D.,* 27Apr.08
Jowers, R. F., *F.R.C.S.* 27Apr.08
Maynard, E. F., *M.D.,* 21May11
Paley, F. J., *M.D.* 21May11

Majors.
Broadbent, W., *M.D.,* 27Apr.08
Griffin, W. W., *M.B., F.R.C.S.* 27Apr.08
Hall D. G., *M.D.,* 27Apr.08
Buck, A. H., *F.R.C.S. (Edin.)* 27Apr.08
Bailey, C. F., *M.D.,* 27Apr.08
Ionides, T. H., *M.B., F.R.C.S.* 27Apr.08
Bushnell, F. G., *M.D.* 21May11
Bowring, W. A., *F.R.C.S.* 21May11

Captains.
Whittington, E., *M.D.* 27Apr.08
✗Braley, W. H., *M.D.* (Hon. Lt. in Army 1 Dec. 00) 27Apr.08
Taylor, H. H., *F.R.C.S.* 27Apr.08
Gervis, H., *M.B.* 27Apr.08
Morgan, G., *F.R.C.S. (Edin.)* 27Apr.08
Benham, C. H., *M.D.,* 27Apr.08
Parry, L. A., *M.D., F.R.C.S.* 27Apr.08
Colcutt, A. M., *M.B.* 27Apr.08
Sanderson, R., *M.B.* 27Apr.08

Captains—contd.
Shardlow, J., *M.B.* 27Apr.08
Hutchison, A. J., *M.B.* 27Apr.08
Chadborn, C. N. 27Apr.08
Bate, A. G. *M.B., F.R.C.S.(Edin.)* 27Apr.08
Rigby, M. N. J. 27Apr.08
Daldy, A. M., *M.D.* 27Apr.08
Nash, R. P. 27Apr.08
Wood, W. R. 27Apr.08
✗Fletcher, H. N., *F.R.C.S. Edin.* 4Oct.11
Hutchinson, F.A.S. *M.D.* 4Oct.11

1st London
(City of London.)

[20]

Duke of York's Head-Quarters, Chelsea, S.W.

Lt.-Colonel.
p. Atkinson, W. A., *M.D.,* TD. 17Mar.13

Major.
‡ *Captain.*
p. Oswald. R. J. W. 22May13

Quarter-Master.
p.s. Purcell, H.E.L., *hon. m.* 20July98

Officers whose services will be available on mobilization.

Lt.-Colonels.
Bowlby, Sir A. A., *Knt., C.M.G., F.R.C.S.* 20June14
Herringham, Sir W. P., Knt., *M.D. (local Lt.-Col., O.T.C.* 3 *Apr.* 14) 20June14

Majors.
Lockwood, C. B., *F.R.C.S.* 31July08
✗Tooth, H. H., *C.M.G., M.D.* 31July08
Power, D'A., *M.B., F.R.C.S.* 31July08
Garrod, A. E., *M.D.* 31July08
Waring, H. J., *M.B., F.R.C.S.* 31July08
Calvert, J., *M.D.* 20Feb.09
Eccles, W. McA., *M.B., F.R.C.S.* 13Mar.09

Captains.
✗Fletcher, H. M., *M.D.* 31July08
Bailey, R. C., *M.B., F.R.C.S.* 31July08
Drysdale, J. H., *M.D.* 31July08
Rawling, L. B., *M.B., F.R.C.S.* 31July08
Horton-Smith-Hartley, P., *C.V.O., M.D.* 31July08
Gask, G. E., *F.R.C.S.* 31July08
Androwes, F. W., *M.D.* 25May09
Brown, W. L., *M.D.,* 25May09

2nd London
(City of London.)

[21]

Duke of York's Head-Quarters, Chelsea, S.W.

Lt.-Colonel.
p. Callender, E. M., *M.D.,* TD. 13Mar.12

Major.

Quarter-Master.
p. Spratley, T. J., *hon. lt.* 1Apr.08

Officers whose services will be available on mobilization.

Lt.-Colonels.
Warner, F., *M.D., F.R.C.S.* 23Dec.08
Sharkey, Sir S. J., *Knt., M.D.* 23Dec.08
Makins, G. H., *C.B., F.R.C.S.* 23Dec.08
White, W. H., *M.D.* 9Nov.09

Majors.
Moullin, C. W. M., *M.D., F.R.C.S.* 23Dec.08
Acland, T. D., *M.D.* 23Dec.08
Eve, Sir F. S., *Knt., F.R.C.S.* 23Dec.08
Pitt, G. N., *M.D.* 23Dec.08
Battle, W. H., *F.R.C.S.* 23Dec.08
Shaw, L. E., *M.D.* 23Dec.08
p. Symonds, C. J., *M.B., F.R.C.S.* 23Dec.08
Hawkins, H. P., *M.D.* 9Nov.09

---

‡ This rank is not provided for in the Territorial Force Tables of Establishments.

Royal Army Medical Corps. Territorial Force.

General Hospitals—contd.
2nd London—contd.

Captains.
Lane, Sir W. A., Bt.,
  M.B.,F.R.C.S. 23Dec.08
Smith, F. J., M.D.,
  F.R.C.S. 23Dec.08
Ballance C. A.,
  M.V.O., M.B.,
  F.R.C.S. 23Dec.08
Hadley, W. J., M.D.,
  F.R.C.S. 23Dec.08
Fenwick, E. H.,
  F.R.C.S. 23Dec.08
Mackenzie, H. W. G.,
  M.D. 23Dec.08
Dunn, L. A., M.B.,
  F.R.C.S. 23Dec.08
Turney, H. G., M.D.,
  F.R.C.S. 23Dec.08
Hutchinson, J., jun.,
  F.R.C.S. 23Dec.08
Dawson, Sir B.,
  K.C.V.O.,M.D.23Dec.08
Robinson, H. B.,
  M.D.,F.R.C.S.23Dec.08
Head, H., F.R.S.,
  M.D. 23Dec.08
Perkins, J. J., M.B.,
  23Dec.08
Steward, F. J.,
  F.R.C.S. 23Dec.08
Colman, W. S.,
  M.D. 23Dec.08
Fagge, C. H., M.B.,
  F.R.C.S. 23Dec.08
Fawcett, J., M.D.,
  F.R.C.S. 23Dec.08
Rowlands, R. P.,
  M.B.,F.R.C.S.23Dec.08
Rigby, H.M., M.B.,
  F.R.C.S. 19Mar.10

3rd London
[22]
Henry Street, Gray's Inn Road, W.C.

Lt.-Colonel.
Bruce-Porter, H. E. B.
  formerly Surg.-Capt.
  A.Med.Staff 12May13

Major.
Miller, F. R. 7Jan.14

Quarter-Master.
Fish, W. A.
  hon. lt. 17May15

Officers whose services will be available on mobilization.

Lt.-Colonels.
Fowler, Sir J. K.,
  K.C.V.O., M.D.,
  F.R.C.P. 2Dec.08
Godlee, Sir B. J.,
  Bt.,K.C.V.O.,M.B.,
  F.R.C.S. 2Dec.08

*Lt.-Colonels—*contd.
Phillips, S. P., M.D. 5Dec.09
Pasteur, W., M.D., 21Feb.12
  F.R.C.P.

Majors.
Gould, Sir A. P.,
  K.C.V.O., M.B.,
  F.R.C.S. 2Dec.08
Bradford, Sir J. R.,
  K.C.M.G.,F.R.S.,M.D.,
  2Dec.08
Mayo Robson, A. W.,
  F.R.C.S. 2Dec.08
Luff, A. P., M.D. 2Dec.08
Barker, A. E. J., F.R.C.S.
  2Dec.08
Martin, S. H. C., M.D.
  5Dec.09
Pollard, B., M.B., F.R.C.S.
  21Feb.12
Wynter, W. E., M.D.,
  F.R.C.S. 21Feb.12

Captains.
Lane, J. E., F.R.C.S.2Dec.08
Voelcker, A. F., M.D.,
  2Dec.08
Bland-Sutton, Sir J.,
  Knt.,F.R.C.S. 2Dec.08
Johnson, R., M.B.,
  F.R.C.S. 2Dec.08
Russell, J. S. R., M.D.,
  2Dec.08
Murray, J., M.B., F.R.C.S.
  2Dec.08
Wethered, F. J., M.D.,
  2Dec.08
Shaw, H. B., M.D.,
  F.R.C.P.,F.R.C.S. 2Dec.08
Kellock, T. H., M.D.,
  2Dec.08
Poynton, F. J. M.D.2Dec.08
Low, V. W., M.D.,
  F.R.C.S. 2Dec.08
Harris, W., M.D. 2Dec.08
Handley, W. S., M.D.,
  F.R.C.S. 2Dec.08
Broadbent, Sir J. F.
  H., Bt., M.D. 2Dec.08
Horsley, Sir V. A. H.,
  Knt., F.R.S., M.B.,
  F.R.C.S. 13Feb.10
✕Smith, S. M., M.B.,
  F.R.C.S. 18Mar.12
Willcox, W.H.,M.D.,
  F.R.C.P. 18Mar.12
Thomson, H.C.,M.D.,
  F.R.C.P. 25Mar.12

4th London.
[23]
Duke of York's Headquarters, Chelsea, S.W.

Lt.-Colonel.
p. ✕Thorne, A., M.B.,vD,
  hon. Surg-Col. (Hon.
  Capt. in Army 1Dec.00)
  19Feb.06

Major.
Biggs, G. N. M.B.
  26Feb.09

Quarter-Master.
p. ✕Boxall, J., hon. capt.
  26Feb.09

Officers whose services will be available on mobilization.

Lt.-Colonels.
Tirard, N. I. C.,
  M.D. 2Dec.08
✕Cheyne,Sir W.W.,
  Bt., C.B., M.B.,
  F.R.C.S. 16Nov.12
Dalton, N., M.D.
  16Nov.12
Turner, G. R.,
  F.R.C.S. 16Nov.12

Majors.
Boyd, S., M.B.,
  F.R.C.S. 2Dec.08
Hebb, R. G.,
  M.D. 2Dec.08
Tubby, A. H.,
  M.B., F.R.C.S. 2Dec.08
Mott, F. W.
  M.D. F.R.C.P.,F.R.S.
  27Jan.12
Spencer, W. G.,
  M.B.,F.R.C.S.16Nov.12
Turner, W. A., M.D.
  16Nov.12
Carless, A., M.B.,
  F.R.C.S. 16Nov.12
Galloway, J.,
  M.D.,F.R.C.S.16Nov.12

Captains.
Burghard, F. F.,
  M.D., F.R.C.S. 2Dec.08
Gossage, A. M.,
  M.B. 2Dec.08
Waterhouse, H. F.,
  M.D.,F.R.C.S. 2Dec.08
Ogle, C., M.D. 2Dec.08
Crawford, R. H. P.,
  M.D. 2Dec.08
✕Gibbs, C., F.R.C.S.
  2Dec.08
Latham, A., M.D.,
  F.R.C.P. 2Dec.08
✕Turner, W., M.B.,
  F.R.C.S. 2Dec.08
Hunter, W., M.D.
  2Dec.08
Jaffrey, F., F.R.C.S.
  2Dec.08
Bosanquet, W. C.,
  M.D. 2Dec.08
✕Evans, A. H.,
  M.D.,F.R.C.S. 2Dec.08
Collier, J. S., M.D.,
  2Dec.08
Pendlebury, H.S.,
  M.B., F.R.C.S. 2Dec.08
p. Stewart, J. P., M.D.,
  F.R.C.P. 29Feb.12
Spriggs, E., M.D.,
  F.R.C.P. 9Jan.13
Carling, E. R., M.B.,
  F.R.C.S. 31Jan.13
Clogg, H. S., M.B.,
  F.R.C.S. 3Feb.13
English, T. C., M.B.,
  F.R.C.S. 4Mar.13

1st Northern.
[8]
Drill Hall, Hutton Terrace
Newcastle-on-Tyne.

Lt.-Colonel.

Major.
Gowans, T., M.B.
  1Apr 12
Pybus, F. C., M.B.,
  F.R.C.S. 8Feb.13

Quarter-Master.

Officers whose services will be available on mobilization.

Lt.-Colonels.
Martin, A. M., M.B.,
  F.R.C.S. 11Jan.11
Beattie, T., M.D.
  16July13
Hume, W. E., M.D.
  16July13

Majors.
Richardson, W. G.,
  M.B.,F.R.C.S.30Mar.09
Bolam, R. A., M.D.
  30Mar.09
Arnison, W. D., M.D.
  30Mar.09
Wardale, J. D., M.B.
  30Mar.09
Lyle, R. P. R., M.D.
  30Mar.09
Leech, J. W., M.D.,
  F.R.C.S. (Edin.)
  11Jan.11
Turner, G. G., M.B.,
  F.R.C.S. 16July13
Parkin, A., M.D.,
  F.R.C.S. 16July13

Captains.
Hall, G., M.D. 30Mar.09
Allison, T. M., M.D.
  30Mar.09
Stewart, J. C., M.B.
  30Mar.09
Whillis, S. S., M.B.
  30Mar.09
Patterson, D. W.,
  M.B. 30Mar.09
Slade, H. J., M.B.
  30Mar.09
Markham, M. H.,
  M.B. 30Mar.09
Seymour, W., M.B.
  30Mar.09
Armstrong, F. G.,
  M.B., 12May11
Heslop, J. W. 31May12
  5Oct.11
Wilson, W. F.,
  M.B. 9Aug.13

Royal Army Medical Corps. Territorial Force.

General Hospitals—contd.

2nd Northern.
[9]
Harewood Barracks,
Woodhouse Lane, Leeds.

Lt.-Colonel.

Major.
Dobson, J. F.,
M.B., F.R.C.S. 1May12
Coupland, J. A.,
M.B., F.R.C.S. 1May12

Quarter-Master.
Sedgwick, C. H.,
hon. lt. 14Dec.08

Chaplain.
Phillips, Rev. J. F.,
M.A., Chapl. 3rd
Class (T.F.) *(attd.)*
9Mar.08

Officers whose services
will be available on
mobilization.

Lt.-Colonels.
Churton, T., *M.D.*
14Oct.08
Teale, T. P.,
M.B., F.R.C.S.,
F.R.S. 14Oct.08
Barrs, A. G., *M.D.*
14Oct.08
Littlewood, H.,
F.R.C.S. 14Oct.08

Majors.
Griffith, T. W.,
M.D. 14Oct.08
Knaggs, R. L.,
M.D., F.R.C.S. 14Oct.08
Moynihan, Sir B. G. A.,
Knt., M.B., F.R.C.S.
14Oct.08
Grünbaum, A. S. F.,
M.D.
Walker, H. S.,
F.R.C.S. 14Oct.08
Telling, W. H. M.,
M.D. 14Oct.08
Thompson, W.,
F.R.C.S. 14Oct.08
Watson, G. W.,
M.D. 14Oct.08

Captains.
Whitehead, A. L.,
M.B. 8Aug.01
Braithwaite, L. R.,
M.B., F.R.C.S. 1May10
Veale, R. A., *M.D.,*
28Mar.12

3rd Northern.
[10]
Sheffield.

Lt.-Colonel.
p. Connell, A. M.,
F.R.C.S.(Edin.) 20Feb.14
Major.
‡ *Captain.*
✗Pooley, G.H., *F.R.C.S.*
30July13
1Feb.12
Quarter-Master.
Stout, D., *hon. lt.* 5Mar.09

Officers whose services
will be available on
mobilization.
Lt.-Colonels.
Burgess, D., *M.B.*
2Jan.09
Porter, W. S., *M.D.*
18Apr.09
White, J. S., *M.D.,*
F.R.C.S. 17May13
5Mar.09
Majors.
Hall, A. J., *M.D.* 2Jan.09
Wilkinson, G., *M.B.,*
F.R.C.S. 2Jan.09
Naish, A.E., *M.B.* 2Jan.09
Hallam, A. R.,
M.D. 20Nov.09
Beattie, J. M., *M.D.*
2Jan.11
Riseley, S., *M.D.* 3Jan.11
Captains.
Nutt, W.H., *M.D.* 2Jan.09
Simpson, G. S.,
F.R.C.S. 2Jan.09
Wilson, A. G., *M.B.,*
F.R.C.S. 2Jan.09
Barnes, A. E., *M.B.*
1Feb.12
Williams, H. J. E. H.
1Feb.12
Vincent, W. J. N.,
M.B. 1Feb.12

4th Northern.
[11]
6b, Guildhall Street,
Lincoln.

Lt.-Colonel.
Brook, W. H. B.,
M.D., F.R.C.S. 3Nov.08
Major.
Lambert, F. S. 3Nov.08
Quarter-Master.
Dickinson, J. E.,
hon. lt. 3Nov.08

Officers whose services
will be available on
mobilization.
Lt.-Colonels.
Brook, C. 14Oct.08
Harrison, C., *M.D.*
14Oct.08
Grimoldby, G. H.
14Oct.08
Stephenson, G. S.,
M.D. 14Oct.08

Majors.
Carline, W. A.,
M.D. 14Oct.08
Sympson, E. M.,
M.D. 14Oct.08
Daman, T. W. A.,
M.B. 14Oct.08
Westlake, A., *M.B.*
14Oct.08
Turner, C. B. 14Oct.08
Watkins, D. J. G.,
M.B. 3Nov.08
Genney, F. S.,
M.B. 1Aug.12
Clements, E. C. 6June14

Captains.
Chapman, O. H.,
M.D. 14Oct.08
Shipman, G. A. C.,
M.B. 14Oct.08
McFarland, B.,
M.D. 14Oct.08
Burgess, A., *M.D.*
14Oct.08
Pratt, A. A., *M.D.*
14Oct.08
South, R. E. E. 14Oct.08
Wilson, R. A.,
M.D. 14Oct.08
Miller, A., *M.B.* 14Oct.08
Giles, O. 14Oct.08
Passmore, J. E. S.
14Oct.08
Withers, F. E. 14Oct.08
Winter, E. S. 3Feb.09
Higgins, W. R., *M.B.*
3Feb.09
Revill, G.L.H. 3Feb.09
Alcock, F., *M.D.*
14Feb.10
Coleman, C. J.,
M.D. 11Dec.11
Lowe, G. J. R. (t.)
(H) 27Feb.12
Yates, A. L., *M.D.*
3Apr.12
Rainforth, J. J.,
M.B., F.R.C.S.
1May14

5th Northern.
[12]
Leicester.

Lt.-Colonel.

Major.
Harrison, L. K., *M.B.*
24Feb.09
Quarter-Master.
Barfield, G. E.,
hon. lt. 31July08

Officers whose services
will be available on
mobilization.
Lt.-Colonels.
Franklin, G. C.,
F.R.C.S. 30Sept.08
Pratt, R., *M.D.*
30Sept.08
Douglas, C., *F.R.C.S.*
30Sept.08

Majors.
Sevestre, R., *M.D.*
30Sept.08
Crosby, T. V., *M.D.*
30Sept.08
Davies, J. T. H., *M.D.*
30Sept.08
Blakesley, H. J.,
30Sept.08
Marriott, C. E., *M.B.,*
F.R.C.S. 30Sept.08
Sloane, J. S., *M.B.,*
F.R.C.S. 30Sept.08
Slight, J. D., *M.D.*
30Sept.08
Stewart, R., *M.D.*
24Feb.09

Captains.
Waite, J. E., *M.B.*
30Sept.08
Carter, F. B., *M.D.,*
F.R.C.S. 30Sept.08
Lilley, E. L., *M.B.,*
F.R.C.S. 30Sept.08
Young, R. R., *M.B.*
30Sept.08
Patrick, J. W., *M.D.*
30Sept.08
Phillips, E. V. 30Sept.08
Smith, S. F. 30Sept.08
Michell, R. 30Sept.08
Bennett, F. W., *M.D.*
30Sept.08
Henry, R. W. W.,
30Sept.08
Gibbons, W. E., *M.D.*
30Sept.08
Fagge, R. H. 30Sept.08
Stamford, R. B.,
F.R.C.S. (Edin.)
30Sept.08
Holmes, W. M., *M.B.*
30Sept.08
Cumberlidge, W. I.
F.R.C.S. 4Dec.12

1st Scottish.
[1]
Aberdeen.

Lt.-Colonel.
p. Mitchell, P., *M.D.*
1Aug.12
Major.
‡ *Captain.*
p. Smart, J., *M.B.* 15Oct.12
27Dec.06
Quarter-Master.
Callan, J., *hon. capt.*
1Apr.08

Officers whose services
will be available on
mobilization.
Lt.-Colonels.
p. Marnoch, J., *M.B.*
27June08
p. Lister, A. H., *M.B.*
22May10
p. Mackintosh, A. W., *M.D.*
25 Feb.11
Booth, J. M.,
M.D. (Lt.-Col. ret. T.F.)
20Dec.12

---
‡ This rank is not provided for in the Territorial Force Tables of Establishments.

Royal Army Medical Corps. Territorial Force.

General Hospitals—contd.

1st Scottish—contd.

Majors.
McKerron, R. G., *M.D.*
 27June08
Gray, H. McI. W., *M.B., F.R.C.S. (Edin.)*
 27June08
Gibb, G., *M.B.* 27June08
Galloway, A. R., *M.B.*
 27June08
Usher, C. H., *M.B., F.R.C.S. (Edin.)*
 27June08
Pirie, W. R., *M.B.*
 27June08
Geddie, D. W., *M.B.*
 27June08
Milne, J. W., *M.D.* 20Dec12

Captains.
Levack, J. R., *M.B.*
 27June08
Peterkin, H., *M.B.*
 27June08
Crombie, J.M.F., *M.B.*
 27June08
Stalker, A. M. *M.D.* 20Dec.12
Whyte, J. M., *M.D.* 20Dec.12
Don, A., *M.B., F.R.C.S. Edin.* 20Dec.12
Kerr, C., *M.B.* 20Dec.12
Low, A.P., *M.B.* 20Dec.12
Falconer, A. W., *M.B.* 20 Dec.12
Colt, G. H., *M.B., F.R.C.S.* 20Dec.12
Mitchell, A., *M.B.* 20Dec.12
McGillivray, A., *M.B.* 20Dec.12
Duncan, G. M., *M.B.* 20Dec.12
Souter, W. C., *M.D.* 20Dec.12
Johnston, J., *M.B.* 20Dec.12
Brown, W., *M.B.* 20Dec.12
McQueen, J. M., *M.B.* 20Dec.12

2nd Scottish.
[2]
4, Lindsay Place, Edinburgh.

Lt.-Colonel.
Fayrer, Sir J., Bt., *M.D., F.R.C.S. Edin.*,
Lt.-Col. ret. pay
 19Oct.12

Major.
¿*Captain.*
Graham, D. J., *M.D., F.R.C.P.* 9Apr.14
 3Jan.12

Quarter-Master.
Baker, W. C., *hon. lt.*
 3Apr.12

Officers whose services will be available on mobilization.

Lt.-Colonels.
Cotterill, J. M., *M.B., F.R.C.S. (Edin.)* 21July08

Lt.-Colonels—contd.
Cathcart, C.W., *M.B., F.R.C.S.* 21July08
Philp, Sir R. W., *Knt., M.D.* 15Sept.11
Caird, F. M., *M.B., F.R.C.S. (Edin.)*
 9Apr.14

Majors.
Russell, W., *M.D.* 21July08
Berry, G. A., *M.B., F.R.C.S. (Edin.)* 21July08
Brown, J. J. G., *M.D.* 21July08
Hodsdon, J.W. B., *M.D., F.R.C.S. (Edin.)* 21July08
Gulland, G. L., *M.D.* 21July08
✗Wallace, D., *C.M.G., M.B., F.R.C.S. (Edin.)*
 21July08
Comrie, J. D. 22July09
Boyd, F. D., *C.M.G., M.D.* 15Sept.11

Captains.
Stiles, H. J., *M.B., F.R.C.S. (Edin.)* 21July08
Fleming, R. A., *M.D.* 21July08
Thomson, H. A., *M.D., F.R.C.S. (Edin.)* 21July08
Langwill, H. G., *M.D.* 21July08
Miles, A., *M.D., F.R.C.S. (Edin.)*
 21July08
Rainy, H., *M.D.* 21July08
Turner, A. L., *M.D., F.R.C.S. (Edin.)* 21July08
Watson, D. C., *M.D.* 21July08
Guy, W., *F.R.C.S. (Edin.)* 21July08
Ritchie, W. T., *M.D.* 21July08
Dowden, J.W., *M.B., F.R.C.S. (Edin.)* 21July08
Bramwell, B., *M.B.* 21July08
✗Skirving, A. A. S., *C.M.G., M.B., F.R.C.S. (Edin.)*
 21July08
Cattanach, J. D., *M.B.* 21July08
Chiene, G. L., *M.B., F.R.C.S. (Edin.)* 21July08
Matthew, E., *M.B.* 21July08
Stuart, W. J., *M.B., F.R.C.S. (Edin.)*
 21July08
Eason, J., *M.D.* 21July08
Carmichael, E. W. S., *M.B., F.R.C.S. (Edin.)*
 21July08
Simpson, J. W., *M.D.* 15Sept.11

3rd Scottish.
[3]
Yorkhill Parade, Yorkhill, Glasgow.

Lt.-Colonel.
p. Hay, A. G., *M.D.*
 19Apr.12

Majors.
p.s.Riddell, B., *M.D.*
 9May12

Quarter-Master
p.✗Lee, W., *hon. m.* 9Jan.13
 12Jan.96

Officers whose services will be available on mobilization.

Lt.-Colonels.
Gemmell, S., *M.D.*
 3July08
Stockman, R. *M.D.*
 3July08
Muir, R., *M.D.* 3July08
Dalziel, T. K., *M.B.*
 16Dec.12

Majors.
Rutherfurd, H., *M.B.*
 3July08
Nicoll, J. H., *M.B.*
 3July08
Hunter, W. K., *M.D.*
 3July08
Cowan, J. M., *M.D.*
 3July08
Downie, J. W., *M.B.*
 3July08
Ramsay, A. M., *M.D.*
 3July08
Macartney, D., *M.D.*
 3July08
MacLennan, W., *M.B.*
 16Dec.12

Captains.
Laurie, J. E., 3July08
Ness, R. B., *M.B.*
 3July08
Johnston, J. McC., *M.D.* 3July08
Carslaw, J., *M.B.*
 3July08
Towart, J. 3July08
Morton, J., *M.B.* 3July08
Young, A. A., *M.B.*
 3July08
Christie, W. W., *M.D.*
 3July08
MacLennan, A., *M.B.*
 3July08
Fortune, E. G., *M.B.*
 3July08
McClure, J. C., *M.B.*
 3July08
Fullarton, R., *M.B.*
 3July08
Gilchrist, J., *M.D.*
 3July08
Edwards, A. H., *M.B., F.R.C.S. (Edin.)*
 3July08
Taylor, M. L., *M.B.*
 3July08
Gracie, J., *M.B.* 3July08
Findlay, J., *M.B.* 3July08
Cuthbert, C. C., *M.D.*
 3July08
Harrington, A. W., *M.D.* 3July08

4th Scottish.
[4]
Yorkhill Parade, Yorkhill, Glasgow.

Lt.-Colonel.
Napier, A., *M.D.*, VD, *hon. Surg.-Col.*
 (*Hon. Surg.-Col.*
 ret. Vols.*) 22Mar.09
 3July08
MacGregor, D. O., *M.B.* 24June08

Quarter-Master.
Conacher, P. A., *hon. lt,* 24June08

Officers whose services will be available on mobilization.

Lt.-Colonels.
Renton J. C., *M.D.*
 3July08
Barlow, J., *M.D., F.R.C.S.* 3July08
Middleton, G. S., *M.D.*
 3July08

Majors.
Parry, R. H., *F.R.C.S. (Edin.)*
 3July08
Pringle, J. H., *M.B., F.R.C.S. (Edin.)*
 3July08
Monro, T. K., *M.D.*
 3July08
Andrew, J. G., *M.B.*
 3July08
Anderson, J. B. McK., *M.B.* 3July08
Fergus, A. F., *M.D.*
 3July08
Love, J. K., *M.D.* 3July08
p. ✗Young, A., *M.B.*
 24Sept.12
 1Apr.08

Captains.
Hamilton, J., *M.B.*
 3July08
McGregor, A. N., *M.D.*
 3July08
Kelly, A. B., *M.D.*
 3July08
Tindal, A. S., *M.D.*
 3July08
Russell, D. W., *M.B.*
 3July08
Lamb, D., *M.B.* 3July08
Maclean, J., *M.B.* 3July08
Buchanan, G. B., *M.B.* 3July08
Walker, H., *M.B.* 3July08
Macrae, F., *M.B.* 3July08
Mackay, E., *M.B.* 3July08
Macewan, J. A. C., *M.B.* 3July08
Holmes, J. D., *M.B.*
 3July08
Henderson, J., *M.D.*
 3July08
Chalmers, J. R., *M.B.*
 3July08
Fraser, A., *M.B.* 3July08
Fyfe, D., *F.R.C.S. (Edin.)* 3July08
Barr, J. S., *M.B.* 3July08
Tomkinson, J. G., *M.D.* 3July08
Carslaw, R. B., *M.B.*, (b) 7May12
 7Oct.09

¿ This rank is not provided for in the Territorial Force Tables of Establishments.

Royal Army Medical Corps. Territorial Force.

General Hospitals— contd.

1st Southern.
[13]

The Barracks, Great Brook Street, Birmingham.

Lt.-Colonel
Marsh, F., *F.R.C.S.*
 3July08

Major.
Sawyer, J. E. H., *M.D.* 3June08

Quarter-Master.
Bennison, E. C., *hon. lt.* 1Apr.12

Officers whose services will be available on mobilization.

Lt.-Colonels.
Saundby, R., *M.D.* 3July08
Barling, H. G., *F.R.C.S.*, 3July08
Simon, Sir R. M., *Knt.*, *M.D.* 5Aug.08
Haslam, W. F., *F.R.C.S.* 5Apr.13

Majors.
Kauffman, O. J., *M.D.* 3July08
Morrison, J. T. J., *F.R.C.S.* 3July08
Short, T. S., *M.D.* 3July08
Stanley, J. D., *M.D.* 3July08
Leedham-Green, C. A., *M.D., F.R.C.S.* 3July08
Russell, J. W., *M.D.* 5Aug.09
Heaton, G., *F.R.C.S.* 5Apr.13

Captains.
Emanuel, J. G., *M.D.* 3July08
Billington, W., *F.R.C.S.* 3July08
Barnes, A. S., *M.D.* 3July08
Lucas, A., *F.R.C.S.* 3July08
Mackey, L. G. J., *M.D.* 3July08
Gamgee, L. P., *F.R.C.S.* 3July08
Wynn, W. H., *M.D.* 3July08
Barnes, F., *F.R.C.S.* 3July08
Young, J. M., *M.B.* 3July08
McCardie, W. J., *M.B.* 24Sept.08

2nd Southern.
[14]

Colston Fort, Montague Place, Kingsdown, Bristol.

Lt.-Colonel.
Bush, J. P., *C.M.G.* 1Apr.08

Major.
Quarter-Master.
Nichols, F. C., *hon. lt.* 25Oct.11

Officers whose services will be available on mobilization.

Lt.-Colonels.
Smith, R. S., *M.D.* 30Sept.08
Board, E. C. 30Sept.08
Clarke, J. M., *M.D.* 30Sept.08
Smith, G. M. 30Sept.08

Majors.
Prowse, A. B., *M.D., F.R.C.S.* 30Sept.08
Swain, J., *M.D., F.R.C.S.* 30Sept.08
Parker, G., *M.D.* 30Sept.08
Morton, C. A., *F.R.C.S.* 30Sept.08
Williams, P. W., *M.D.* 30Sept.08
Lansdown, R. G. P., *M.D.* 30Sept.08
Walker, C. H., *M.B., F.R.C.S.* 30Sept.08
Ackland, W. R. 30Sept.08

Captains.
Edgeworth, F. H., *M.B.* 30Sept.08
Firth, J. L., *M.D., F.R.C.S.* 30Sept.08
Symes, J. O., *M.D.* 30Sept.08
Carwardine, T., *M.B., F.R.C.S.* 30Sept.08
Taylor, J. 30Sept.08
Kyle, H. G., *M.B.* 30Sept.08
Coombs, C. F., *M.D.* 30Sept.08
Mole, H. F., *F.R.C.S.* 30Sept.08
Williams, E. C., *M.B.* 30Sept.08
Groves, E. W. H., *M.D., F.R.C.S.* 30Sept.08
Fortescue-Brickdale, J. M., *M.D.* 30Sept.08
Stack, E. H. E., *M.B., F.R.C.S.* 30Sept.08
Freeman, J., *M.D., F.R.C.S. (Edin.)* 30Sept.08
Dacre, J. 30Sept.08
Lucas, J. J. S., *M.D.* 30Sept.08
Harris, H. E., *M.B., F.R.C.S.* 30Sept.08
Cotton, W., *M.D.* 30Sept.08
Hill, H., *M.D.* 30Sept.08
Stock, W. S. V., *M.B.* 30Sept.08
Adams, P. E. H., *M.B., F.R.C.S.* 1Jan.14

3rd Southern.
[15]

Oxford.

Lt.-Colonel.
Ranking, G. S. A., *M.D., late Ind. Med. Serv.* 15Mar.09

Major.
Foster, E. C. M. 15Mar.09

Quarter-Master.
Symonds, J. C., *hon. lt.* 1Mar.10

Officers whose services will be available on mobilization.

Lt.-Colonels.
Freeman, W. R., *M.D., F.R.C.S.* 3Mar.09
Hawkins, F. H., *M.D.* 3Mar.09
Maurice, W. J., *M.B.* 3Mar.09
Symonds, H. P., *F.R.C.S. (Edin.)* 3Mar.09

Majors.
Abram, G. S., *M.B.* 3Mar.09
Collier, W., *M.D.* 3Mar.09
Dodds-Parker, A. P., *M.B., F.R.C.S.* 3Mar.09
Guilding, L. M., *M.B.* 3Mar.09
Mallam, E., *M.D.* 3Mar.09
Price, J. A. P., *M.D.* 3Mar.09
Waters, W. A. P., *M.D.* 3Mar.09
Whitelock, R. H. A., *M.D., F.R.C.S.* 3Mar.09

Captains.
Bevers, E. C., *M.D.* 3Mar.09
Clarke, H. M., *M.B.* 3Mar.09
Clowes, N. B. 3Mar.09
Counsell, H. E., *F.R.C.S.* 3Mar.09
Coventon, C. A. 2Mar.09
Duigan, W., *M.B.* 3Mar.09
Foster, W. J., *F.R.C.S.* 3Mar.09
Freeborn, J. C. R. 3Mar.09
Gibson, A. G., *M.D.* 3Mar.09
Holden, G. H. R., *M.D.* 3Mar.09
Humphry, R. E. 3Mar.09
Murrell, G. F., *M.B.* 3Mar.09
Prowse, W. B., *M.B.* 3Mar.09
Ritson, R. 3Mar.09
Sankey, R. H., *M.B.* 3Mar.09

Captains—contd.
Secretan, W. B., *M.B., F.R.C.S.* 3Mar.09
Turrell, W. J., *M.D.* 3Mar.09
Waterhouse, A. T., *M.B.* 3Mar.09
Ormerod, A. L., *M.D.* 10July09

4th Southern.
[16]

Territorial Buildings, Millbay, Plymouth.

Lt.-Colonel.
Webber, H. W., *F.R.C.S. (Edin.)* 27Jan.12

Major.
Wilson, W. C., *M.D.* 29Jan.12

Quarter-Master.
Briggs, H. B., *hon. lt.* 7May14

Officers whose services will be available on mobilization.

Lt.-Colonels.
Davy, H., *M.D.* 29Sept.08
Domville, E. J. 29Sept.08
Fox, E. L., *M.D.* 29Sept.08
Square, J. E., *F.R.C.S.* 29Sept.08

Majors.
Mortimer, J., *M.B.* 29Sept.08
Roper, A. C., *F.R.C.S. (Edin.)* 29Sept.08
Davis, A. N. 29Sept.08
Woollcombe, W. L., *F.R.C.S. (Edin.)* 29Sept.08
Rutherford, R. L., *M.D.* 29Sept.08
Lucy, R. H., *M.B., F.R.C.S.* 29Sept.08
Coombe, R., *M.D., F.R.C.S.* 29Sept.08
Gill, J. W., *M.D.* 29Jan.12

Captains.
Bean, C. E., *F.R.C.S. (Edin.)* 29Sept.08
Dawe, J. H., *M.B.* 29Sept.08
Aldous, G. F., *F.R.C.S. (Edin.)* 29Sept.08
Solly, R. V., *M.D.* 29Sept.08
Andrew, H. 29Sept.08
Saunders, E. G. S., *M.D.* 29Sept.08
Hamilton, W. C., *M.B.* 29Sept.08
Pethybridge, W. L., *M.D.* 29Sept.08
Arnold, G. J., *F.R.C.S.* 29Sept.08
Sandford, G. C., *M.D.* 29Sept.08
Horton, T., *M.D.* 29Sept.08

Royal Army Medical Corps. Territorial Force.

General Hospitals— *contd.*

4th Southern—*contd.*
Captains—contd.
Lindsey, C. D., *M.D.* 29Sept.09
Dyball, B., *M.B.,*
F.R.C.S. 29Sept.08
Lander, C. L., *M.B.* 29Sept.08
Roberts, G. A.,
F.R.C.S. 29Sept.08
Smith, E. G. 29Sept.08
Robinson, G.C.S.,
F.R.C.S. 3Dec.12
Pinker, H. G. 21Oct.13

5th Southern.
[17]
Connaught Drill Hall, Gosport.
Lt.-Colonel.

Major.
Kyffin, J. 28Sept.10
Quarter-Master.
Blake, L. N., *hon. lt.* 23Aug.10

Officers whose services will be available on mobilization.
Lt.-Colonels.
Childe, C. P., *F.R.C.S.* 21July08
Sparrow, G. G., Surg.-Lt.-Col. & Hon. Surg.-Col., ret. Vols. 21July08
Shettle, H. W. 21July08
Robertson, J. R. S., *M.B.*, late Surg. A.M.D. 1May11
Majors.
Ford, A. V. 21July08
Phillips, J., *M.B.*21July08
Keele, J. R. 21July08
Aldridge, N. E.,
M.B. 21July08
Routh, C. F., *M.D.* 21July08
Purvis, W. P., *M.D.*,
F.R.C.S. 21July08
Ward, H. P., *M.B.* 21July08
Forde, T. A. M. 1May11
Captains.
Goss, S. 21July08
Cowen, G. H., *M.B.*,
F.R.C.S. 21July08
McEldowney, W. P.,
M.B. 21July08
Ridout, C. A. S.,
*M.B., F.R.C.S.*21July08
Leon, J.T., *M.D.* 21July08
Burrows, H., *M.B.*,
F.R.C.S. 21July08
Fraser, J. H. P.,
M.B. 21July08
Wright, J. L. 21July08
Taylor, E. J. D.,
M.B. 21July08

Captains—contd.
Holmes, T., *M.D.*21July08
Hughes, S., *M.B.*21July08
Saunders, C. H., *M.B.* 21July08
O'Meara, W. P. 21July08
Dove, R.A., *M.B.*21July08
Power, A. W. 21July08
McDougall, J. T. M. 21July08
Lamplough, C., *M.D.* 21July08
Way, M. H. 21July08
Wood, M. D., *M.D.* 4Jan.12

1st Western.
[5]
73 Shaw Street, Liverpool.
Lt.-Colonel.
Gemmel, A. B. 20Aug.13
Major.
Rundle, C., *M.D.*7Feb.14
Quarter Master
Naldrett, A.,
hon. lt. 1May09

Officers whose services will be available on mobilization.
Lt.-Colonels.
Parker, R., *M.B.*,
F.R.C.S. 7July08
Barr, Sir J., *Knt.*,
M.D. 7July08
Alexander, W., *M.D.*,
F.R.C.S. 7July08
✗Ross, Sir R.,*K.C.B.,*
F.R.S., F.R.C.S., Maj. ret. Ind.Med.Serv. 12Nov 13
Majors.
Paul, F. T., *F.R.C.S.* 7July08
Bushby, T., *M.B.*7July08
Jones, R., *F.R.C.S.*
(Edin.) 7July08
Murray, R. W.,
F.R.C.S. 7July08
Bradshaw, T. R.,
M.D. 7July08
Browne, A.,
*F.R.C.S.(Edin.)*7July08
Utting, J. 7July08
Davidson, P., *M.B.* 12Nov.13
Captains.
Logan, J. R. 7July08
Hunt, J. M., *M.B.* 7July08
Larkin, F. C. 7July08
Permewan, W.
M.D., F.R.C.S. 7July08
Douglas-Crawford,
D., *M.B., F.R.C.S.* 7July08
Roberts, J. L., *M.D.*,
F.R.C.S. 7July08
Holland, C. T. 7July08
Buchanan, R. J.
McL., *M.D.* 7July08
Bickersteth, R. A.,
M.B., F.R.C.S. 7July08
Warrington, W. B.,
M.D. 7July08

Captains—contd.
Fingland, W. 7July08
Armstrong, H.,
M.D. 7July08
Hay, J., *M.D.* 7July08
Armour, T. R. W.,
M.B. 7July08
Kelly, R. E., *M.D.*,
F.R.C.S. 7July08
de Boinville, V. C.,
M.D. 7July08
Morgan, L. A.,
M.B. 22Sept.09
Monsarrat, K. W.,
M.B. 28Dec.11
✗Evans, A. J.,
F.R.C.S. (*Edin.*)
12Nov.13
14July09

2nd Western.
[6]
Manchester.
Lt.-Colonel.
✗Smith, J. W., *M.B.*,
F.R.C.S. (Hon. Lt. in Army 6Nov.00)
22June12
1Apr.08
Major.
Westmacott, F. H.,
F.R.C.S. 28Feb.09
Quarter-Master.
Wild, F. B., *hon. lt.* 3Mar.09

Officers whose services will be available on mobilization.
Lt.-Colonels.
Southam, F. A., *M.B.*,
F.R.C.S. 2July08
Thorburn, W., *M.D.*,
F.R.C.S. 28Feb.09
Majors.
Griffith, A. H., *M.D.*,
F.R.C.S.(*Edin.*)2July08
Reynolds, E. S., *M.D.* 2July08
Milligan, *Sir* W.,
Knt., M.D. 2July08
Wild, R. B., *M.D.*2July08
Cox, J. J., *M.D.*,
F.R.C.S.(*Edin.*)9Jan.09
Burgess, A. H., *M.B.*,
F.R.C.S. 22Jan.13
Ray, J. H., *M.B.*,
F.R.C.S. 22Jan.13
Murray, G. R., *M.D.* 22Jan.13
Captains.
Wilson, A., *F.R.C.S.* 2July08
Williamson, R. T.,
M.D. 2July08
Telford, E. D.,
F.R.C.S. 2July08
Cunliffe, E. N., *M.D.,* 2July08
Wrigley, P. R.,
F.R.C.S. 2July08

Captains—contd.
Melland, C. H., *M.D.* 2July08
Bythell, W. J. S.,
M.D. 2July08
Moore, F.C., *M.D.*2July08
Marsden, E. W., *M.D.* 2July08
Wright, G., *M.B.*,
F.R.C.S. 2July08
Loveday, G. E., *M.B.* 2July08
Wharton, J., *M.D.* 2July08
Sellars, A., *M.D.*2July08
Hooton, W. A. 2July08
Donald, A., *M.D.* 6Mar.10
Rayner, H. H., *M.B.*,
F.R.C.S. 20Jan.12

3rd Western.
[7]
15, Newport Road, Cardiff.
Lt.-Colonel.
p. Hepburn, D., *M.D.*,
VD, *Surg.-Lt.-Col.*
(hon. *Surg.-Col.*)
14Oct.08
Major.
Maclean, E. J., *M.D.*, 11Mar.09
Quarter-Master.
Purnell, G. D., *hon. lt.* 15Mar.09
Officers whose services will be available on mobilization.
Lt.-Colonels.
Vachell, H. R., *M.D.* 30Dec.08
Wallace, T., *M.D.* 30Dec.08
Lancaster, E. Le C.,
M.B. 30Dec.08
Marsh, O. E. B.30Dec.08
Majors.
Griffiths, P. R., *M.B.* 30Dec.08
Stevens, W. M., *M.D.* 30Dec.08
Lewis, C., *M.D.*30Dec.08
Paterson, D. R.,
M.D. 30Dec.08
Broad, B. W., *M.B.* 30Dec.08
Howell, A.,
F.R.C.S. 30Dec.08
Brook, W. F.,
F.R.C.S. 30Dec.08
Captains.
Griffiths. C. A.,
F.R.C.S. 30Dec.08
Elsworth, R. C.,
*M.D.,F.R.C.S.*30Dec.08
Schölberg, H. A.,
(I) 30Dec.08
Greer, W. J., *F.R.C.S.* 30Dec.08
Thomas, T. M., *M.D.*,
F.R.C.S. 30Dec.08
Nicholson, W. 30Dec.08
Reid, E. 24June08
1Apr. 08
p. Thomas, F.G. 5July11

Royal Army Medical Corps. Territorial Force.

III. SANITARY SERVICE.
a. Sanitary Companies.

1st London (City of London).
Duke of York's Head-Quarters, Chelsea, S.W.

Major.
p. Bryett, L. T. F., *M.D.*, TD .. 21Jan.08

Captains. (2)
Fremlin, H. S. 24May12
Grounds, J. 4Dec.13

Subalterns. (2)

Lieutenants.

2nd London.
Duke of York's Head-Quarters, Chelsea, S.W.
(Right Wing.)

Major.
Goddard, C. E., *M.D.* 2July13
 .. .. 3July11

Captains. (2)
Martin, A. J., *M. Inst. C.E.* .. 26Oct.12

Subalterns. (2)

Lieutenants.
Cave, P. N., *M.D.* 9Jan.12
Caley, F. G., *M.B.* 14June12
Slowan, W. J. M., *M.D.* 9June14

b. Sanitary Officers.

Sanitary Officers.

Officers whose services will be available on mobilization.

Lt.-Colonels. (6)
Newsholme, A., *C.B.*, *M.D.* 22Aug.08
Collingridge, W., *M.D.*, late Surg.-Lt.-Col. R.A.M.C. (Mila.) 2Jan.09
Davies, D. S., *M.D.*, late Surg.-Col. 1 Glouc. R. G.A. (Vols.) 2Jan.09
Gibb, R. S., *M.B.*, late Surg.-Lt. Col., 2 V.B. K. O, Sco. Bord. 2Jan.09
Hay, M., *M.D.* 2Jan.09
Murphy, Sir S.F., Knt. 2Jan.09
Stevens, W. G., late Surg.-Lt. Col., 2 V.B. Arg. and Suth'd High'rs. 2Jan.09
Woodhead, G. S., *M.D.*, VD 2Jan.09

Majors. (40)
Barwise, S., *M.D.* 2Jan.09
Boobbyer, P., *M.D.* 2Jan.09
Bruce, W., *M.D.* 2Jan.09
Collins, H. B., late R.N. 2Jan.09
Doble, D. R., *M.D.*, *F.R.C.S. Edin.* 2Jan.09
Handford, H., *M.D.* 2Jan.09
Hope, E. W., *M.D.* 2Jan.09
Jones, H. 2Jan.09
Kelly, T. W. G., *M.D.*, late Capt. R.A.M.C.(Mila.) (Hon. Capt. in Army 1 Mar. 08) 2Jan.09
Kenwood, H. R., *M.B.* 2Jan.09

Majors—contd.
Littlejohn, H. H., *M.B.*, *F.R.C.S. Edin.* 2Jan.09
McVail, J. C., *M.D.* 2Jan.09
Mussen, A. A., *M.D.* 2Jan.09
Niven, J., *M.B.* 28Dec.08
 2July08
✗O'Connor, J. E., *M.B.*, late Capt. R.A.M.C. (Mila.) (Hon. Capt. in Army 1 Mar. 08) 2Jan.09
Pattin, H. C., *M.D.* 2Jan.09
Permewan, A. E., *M.D.* 2Jan.09
Stott, H. 2Jan.09
Symons, W. H., *M.D.* 2Jan.09
Taylor, G. C., *M.D.* 2Jan.09
Tew, J. S., *M.D.* 2Jan.09
Thresh, J. C., *M.D.* 2Jan.09
Walford, E., *M.D.* 2Jan.09
Willoughby, W. G., *M.D.* 2Jan.09
Parkes, L. C., *M.D.* 24Mar.09
Howarth, W.J., *M.D.* 7May13
 2Jan.09

Captains. (60)
Barclay, W. B. 2Jan.09
Beach, H. W. 2Jan.09
Belding, D. T. 2Jan.09
Bowen-Jones, L. M. 2Jan.09
Brown, W. F., *M.B.* 2Jan.09
Cameron, J. A., *M.D.* 2Jan.09
Carrington, G. H. 2Jan.09
Connon, M., *M.D.* 2Jan.09
Coutts, F. J. H., *M.D.* 2Jan.09

Captains—contd.
Crocker, J. H., *M.D.* 2Jan.09
Dawson, J., *M.B.* 2Jan.09
Dick, G., *M.B.* 2Jan.09
Duncan, A., *M.B.* 2Jan.09
Dunn, R. A., *M.D.* 2Jan.09
Fison, E. T., *M.D.*, *F.R.C.S. (Edin.)* 2Jan.09
Forbes, D., *M.D.* 2Jan.09
Graham, J. T., *M.B.* 2 Jan.09
Graves, T. W. 2Jan.09
Griffith, A., *M.D.* 2Jan.09
Hall, A.J., *M.D.* 2Jan.09
Havard, D., *M.D.* 2Jan.09
Hislop, J. A., *M.D.* 2Jan.09
Jones, R., *M.D.* 2Jan.09
Ledingham, A., *M.D.* 2Jan.09
Lewis, W. C. 2Jan.09
McCleary, G. F., *M.D.* 2Jan.09
McCrindle, J. D., *M.B.* 2Jan.09
Macdonald, C. R., *M.D.* 2Jan.09
McGregor, A. J., *M.D.* 2Jan.09
Mackie, W., *M.D.* 2Jan.09
Munro, A. C., *M.B.* 2Jan.09
Murray, J., *M.B.* 2Jan.09
Nash, J. T. C., *M.D.* 2Jan.09
Paterson, M., *M.D.* 2Jan.09
Peck, H., *M.D.* 2Jan.09
Peterkin, G., *M.D.* 2Jan.09
Phillips, F. B. W., *M.D.* 2Jan.09

Captains—contd.
Prangnell, J. T., *M.D.* 2Jan.09
Pringle, A. M. N., *M.B.* 2Jan.09
Rees-Jones, E. W., *M.D.* 2Jan.09
Rennet, D., *M.D.* 2Jan.09
Robb, A., *M.D.* 2Jan.09
Robertson, W., *M.D.* 2Jan.09
Robinson, T. 2Jan.09
Rogerson, T., *M.B.* 2Jan.09
Ross, J. M., *M.B.*, *F.R.C.S. (Edin.)* 2Jan.09
Rutherford, T., *M.B.* 2Jan.09
Scurfield, H., *M.D.* 2Jan.09
Snell, E. H., *M.D.* 2Jan.09
Streeten, F. E. 2Jan.09
Templeman, C., *M.D.* 2Jan.09
Thomas, A. E., *M.B.* 2Jan.09
Travis, G. L. 2Jan.09
Watt, J.P., *M.B.* 2Jan.09
Whelan, L. T., *F.R.C.S.I.* 2Jan.09
Williams, J. H., *M.D.* 2Jan.09
Wilson, J. T., *M.D.* 2Jan.09
Yule, R. M., *M.D.* 2Jan.09
Yunge-Bateman, M. G. 2Jan.09
Butler, W., *M.B.* 5June09
Fegen, C. M. 7Jan.10
✗Dunne, A. B., *M.B.* 21Dec.12
 17Feb.12
Hunter, H. 14Feb.13
Dundas, J., *M.B.* 9Apr.12
Francis, T. E., *M.D.* 1Sept13
Buchan, J. J., *M.D.* 7Jan.14

Royal Army Medical Corps. Territorial Force.

IV. CLEARING HOSPITALS.

[The order of precedence of units is denoted by numerals in brackets.]

*East Anglian.
[11]
Ipswich.

Lt.-Colonel.

§ *Major.*
p.s. ✗Warracle, J. S., *M.D.* 25June14
                                    29Jan.13

Captain.

§ *Lieu'enant.*
Redpath, W., *M.B.* 1ªJuly14

Quarter-Master.

*Highland.
[1]
Aberdeen.

Lt.-Colonel.
p. Kelly, F., *M.D.* 1Nov.13
                                    22May10

Captain.
p. Rorie, D., *M.D.* 1Nov.13
                                   12Dec.03

Quarter-Master.
Gibbon, A., *hon. lt.* 7Jan.14

*Home Counties.
[12]
Surbiton.

Lt.-Colonel.

Captain.

Quarter-Master.
✗Masters, E. F., *hon. lt.* 6May14

*East Lancashire.
[4]
Manchester.

Lt.-Colonel.

Captain.

§ *Lieutenant.*
Wolstenholme, T. B., *M.B.* 8Apr.14

Quarter-Master.
Anderton, J. E. H., *hon. lt.* 6Apr.14

*West Lancashire.
[3]
Kendal.

Lt.-Colonel.
p. Cockill, W. B., *M.D.*, TD. 1Dec.13
                                    19Mar.13

Captain.

Quarter-Master.
Hunter, H. G., *hon. lt.* 8Apr.14

*1st London.
[13]
Duke of York's Head-Quarters, Chelsea, S.W.

Lt.-Colonel.
p.s.Lyon, A. B., *M.D.*, TD 28Nov.13

Captain.

Quarter-Master.
Withers, C. H., *hon. lt.* 16Jan.14

*2nd London.
[14]
Duke of York's Head-Quarters, Chelsea, S.W.

Lt.-Colonel.
✗Monk, C., Lt.-Col. ret. Ind. Med. Serv. 6Mar.14

Captain.
Higgs, F. W., *M.D.* 29Jan.14
                                10ct.12

Quarter-Master.
Monkhouse, J. A., *hon. lt.* 25Mar.14

*Lowland.
[2]
Glasgow.

Lt.-Colonel.
p.s.Shaw, P. F. 1Nov.13

Captain.

§ *Lieutenant.*
Fleming, G. B., *M.B.* 1Nov.13
                                22Sept.11

Quarter-Master.
✗Law, J., *hon. lt.* 3Dec.13

---

* Unit not yet recognized by the Army Council.
§ This rank is not provided for in the Territorial Force Tables of Establishments.

Royal Army Medical Corps. Territorial Force.

Clearing Hospitals—*contd.*

*North Midland.
[8]
Leicester.
Lt.-Colonel.
p. Peake, W. P. 21Jan.14
5Nov.09

Captain.

Quarter-Master.
Stokes, J. T., *hon. lt.* 13May14

*South Midland.
[9]
Birmingham.
Lt.-Colonel.
Barling, S. G., *M.B., F.R.C.S.* 7Jan.14

Captain.
Goodwin, B. G., *F.R.C.S., late Lt. R.A.M.C.*
4Dec.13

Quarter-Master.
Taylor, D. P., *hon. lt.* 29Jan.14

*Northumbrian.
[6]
Newcastle.
Lt.-Colonel.
p.s ⚔Clay, J., *M.B., F.R.C.S. (Hon. Lt. in Army* 8 June 02) 20Dec.13
9July10

Captain.
Harkness, W. T., *M.B.* 14Mar.14
21Feb.12

Quarter-Master.

*West Riding.
[7]
Leeds.
Lt.-Colonel.
p. Wear, A. E. L., *M.D.* 21Jan.14
1Apr.08

Captain.
Darlow, F., *M.B.* 11Feb.14
24Jan.12

Quarter-Master.

*Welsh.
[5]
Cardiff.
Lt.-Colonel.
p. Green, C. T. 12Nov.13

§ *Major.*
p. Bird, A. 28Mar.14

Captain.

Quarter Master.
Lougher, G. R., *hon. lt.* 30Mar.14

Wessex.
[10]
Exeter.
Lt.-Colonel.

§ *Major.*
Ellis, C. I., *M.D.* 25Mar.14

Captain.

§ *Lieutenant.*
Iles, A. J. H. 9June14

Quarter-Master.
Warren, S. V., *hon. lt.* 20May14

---

* Unit not yet recognized by the Army Council.
§ This rank is not provided for in the Territorial Force Tables of Establishments.

| 1774 | 1775 | 1776 | 1777 |

Royal Army Medical Corps. Territorial Force.

V.—SCHOOLS OF INSTRUCTION (14).

District.	Address.	Adjutant.
No. 1 (Highland Division)	Territorial Barracks, Fonthill Road, Aberdeen.	✗McLennan, Maj. F., *M.B.*, R.A.M.C. .. 1Nov.11
No. 2 (Lowland Division)..	Yorkhill Parade, Yorkhill, Glasgow	✗Hole, Capt. R. B., *M.B.*, R.A.M.C. .. 1Nov.11
No. 3 (East Lancs. Division)	Upper Chorlton Road, Manchester	Bridges, Capt. E. H., R.A.M.C. .. 1Nov.11
No. 3 (West Lancs. Division)	14, Harper Street, Liverpool	Maydon, Capt. W. G., *M.B.*, R.A.M.C. .. 12Nov.13
No. 4 (Welsh Division)	15, Newport Road, Cardiff	✗Woodley, Maj. R. N., R.A.M.C. .. 1Nov.11
No. 5 (West Riding Division)	Harewood Barracks, Woodhouse Lane, Leeds.	Conway, Capt. J. M. H., *F.R.C.S.I.*, R.A.M.C. 1Nov.11
No. 5 (Northumbrian Division)	Drill Hall, Hutton Terrace, Newcastle-on-Tyne	Craig, Maj. B. A., R.A.M.C. 1Mar.12
No. 6 (North Midland Division)	Oxford Street, Leicester	Emerson, Capt. H. H. A., *M.B.*, R.A.M.C. .. 1Nov.11
No. 7 (South Midland Division)	The Barracks, Great Brook Street, Birmingham	Bramhall, Capt. C., R.A.M.C. .. 1Nov.11
No. 8 (Wessex Division)	Lennards Buildings, Goldsmith Street, Exeter	✗Sylvester-Bradley, Capt. C. R., R.A.M.C. .. 1Nov.11
No. 9 (East Anglian Division)	Drill Hall, Woodbridge Road, Ipswich	✗Crawford, Capt. J. M. M., *F.R.C.S.I.*, R.A.M.C. 1Nov.11
No. 10 (Home Counties Division)..	The Palace, Maidstone..	Fawcett, Capt. H. H. J., R.A.M.C... .. 19Oct.11
London { (1st London Division)	Duke of York's Head-Quarters, Chelsea, S.W.	Grant, Capt. M. F., *M.D.*, R.A.M.C. 1Nov.11
London { (2nd London Division)	Duke of York's Head Quarters, Chelsea, S.W.	✗Dunkerton, Capt. N. E., R.A.M.C. .. 1Mar.13

For attachment to Units other than Medical Units.

(*Unposted.*)

p. Bryden, Maj. R. J., VD, R.A.M.C. (T.F.)   9Aug.02   Home Cos.   2July87   Div.

p. Farquharson, Maj. J. D., *M.B.*, TD, R.A.M.C. (T.F.)   25Dec.07   North'bnDiv.   25Dec.95

p. Ker, Maj. C. B., *M.B.*, R.A.M.C. (T.F.)   1Apr.08   Low. Div.   27Feb.95

p. ✗Herrington, Capt. E. W. (*Hon. Lt. in Army* 19*July*02) R.A.M.C.(T.F.)   27Jan.03   1 Lond. Div.   17Jan.00

Supernumerary for service with the Officers Training Corps.

Roderick, Maj. H. B., *M.D.* ..   4July13
Sturrock, Capt. W. D., *M.D.* .. 1Feb.08
Gray, Capt. A. M. H., *M.D.* .. 5Dec.10
Johnson, Capt. A. E., *M.B.* .. 27July12
Rutherford, Capt. N. C., *M.B.*, *F.R.C.S.* 12Feb.14   15Oct.12
Layton, Capt. T. B. 3July14

Wilson, Lt. W. J., *M.B..* 25May11
Williamson, Lt. G. A., *M.D.* .. 13July12
Alderson, Lt. G. G. 8May13
Griffith, Lt. H. K., A..B., *late Lt. 9 Bn. Lond. R.* .. 23July13
Mitchiner, Lt. P. H., *M.B.*, *F.R.C.S.* .. 4Mar.14

OFFICERS OF THE LATE R.A.M.C. (VOLS.) NOT YET GAZETTED TO THE TERRITORIAL FORCE.

Western Command, Manchester Companies.

Transport Officers.

p. Wattleworth, G. R. 7May04
p. Stoddard, C. G .. .. ..4Aug.05   Qr.-Mr. 28Nov.03

ARMY VETERINARY SERVICE.

Uniform—Blue. *Facings*—Maroon.
Agents—Messrs. Holt & Co., 3, Whitehall Place, S.W.

Director-General.—Pringle, Maj.-Gen. (hon.) R., C.B., D.S.O., Col., ranking as Maj.-Gen. 15 Oct. 10 16, *Victoria St., S.W.*

ARMY VETERINARY CORPS.

Officer in charge of Records .. Larnder, Lt.-Col. E. W. .. .. .. *Woolwich.*

Removed from the Corps as Colonels and still on the Active List.

Rutherford, 17May07 *S. Comd.* C., C.B., C.M.G., F.R.C.V.S.
Hazelton, E. 15Oct.07 *H.-Q., India* H., F.R.C.V.S.
Blenkinsop, L. 15Mar.08 *Lucknow* J., D.S.O.
Nuthall, C. E. 4June10 *H.-Q., S. Africa*
Moore, J., 15Oct.13 *Aldershot* F.R.C.V.S. *Comd.*
Butler, E.R.C., 25Apr.14 *E. Comd.* F.R.C.V.S. 18Jan.11

Lieutenant-Colonels.

Taylor, E. 4June10 *Dublin*
Larnder, E.W. 15Oct.10 *Woolwich*
Newsom, A.C. 16Nov.12 *Rawal Pindi*
Eassie, F., 4Oct.13 *Ootacamund* D.S.O.
Smith, W. D. 15Oct.13 *Curragh* [F]
Sawyer, H. T. 25Apr.14 *N. Comd.*

Majors.

Stratton, F.C. 5Mar.05 *Aldershot*
Cranford, R.L., 22Oct.05 *Bangalore* F.R.C.V.S.
Williams, G.M. 7Jan.06 *Woolwich*
Wilson, F. W., 7Jan.06 *Deepcut* F.R.C.V.S.
Tatam, W. J. 18Feb.06 *Cairo*
Axe, H. J. 3Feb.07 *Exeter*
Martin, E.E., 3Feb.07 *A. V. Sch.* F.R.C.V.S.
Hunt, F. D. 3Feb.07 *Ahmednagar*
Shore, W. F. 25July09 *Saharanpore*
Hunt, F. W. 20Mar.10 *Tidworth*
Edwards, 12June10 *Canterbury* W. B.
Rudd, T. W. 28Aug.10 *Mhow*
Holmes, R. 28Sept.10 *Colchester* H., F.R.C.V.S.
Carr, F. U. [F]16May11 e.a.
Anthony, W.S. 14Oct.11 *Poona*
Lenox-Conyng- 5Jan.12 *Curragh* ham, H.M., F.R.C.V.S.
Wood, W. A. 7July12 *Lahore*
Bolton, D. 29Sept.12 *Shorncliffe*
Harris, P. J. 2Dec.12 *Potchefstroom*
McGowan, J. 22Jan.13 *Ambala* A. B.
Cochrane, R.C., 9Mar.13 *Woolwich* F.R.C.V.S.
Todd, A. G. 2Apr.13 (*Asst.Dir.* 18Jan.11 *Gen.) War Office.*
Bartlett, E. B. 19May13 *London*

Majors—contd.

Conder, G. 6July13 *Bulford*
Williams, A. J., 6July13 *Secunderabad* F.R.C.V.S.
Griffith, J. J., 24Aug.13 *Newbridge* F.R.C.V.S.
Olver, A., 8Mar.14 *Pretoria* F.R.C.V.S. [F]
Brown, E. 2June14 *Gibraltar*

Captains.

Aitken, J.J. 13Apr.06 *Pretoria*
Deacon, A. F. 13Apr.06 *Pretoria*
Dalgleish, A.J.13Apr.06 *Potchefstroom*
Welch, H. C. 13Apr.06 *Bulford*
Fisher, O. S. 13Apr.06 *Camberley*
Gamble, H. 13Apr.06 *Cahir* F.R.C.V.S.
Lake, B. L. 13Apr.06 *Bordon*
Knott, G. P.[F]13Apr.06 e.a.
Jackson, 2Nov.06 *Edinburgh* G. T. T.
Love, W. C., 2Nov.06 *Hosur* F.R.C.V.S.
Swanston A. 2Nov.06 *Colchester* N. M.
Steel, C. E. 2Nov.06 *Lahore*
Gillett, E. S. 2Nov.06 *Simla*
Beatty, P. V. 2Nov.06 *Rawal Pindi*
Porteous, R. 2Nov.06 *Jhansi*
Orton, E. C. 2Nov.06 *Meerut*
Glasse, M. 15Apr.07 *Simla* St. G.
Nicol, W. H. 15Apr.07 *Multan*
Probyn, R. S. 15Apr.07 *Allahabad*
Mosley, H. S. 15Apr.07 *Aldershot*
Roberts, N.d'E.4Mar.08 *Babugarh*
Fail, F. 16May08 e.a.
Moore, F.A.S 16May08 e.a.
Ludgate, W. 16May08 *Bareilly*
Plunkett, R.A, 16May08 *Fyzabad*
Jelbart, W.A. 16May08 *Maymyo*
Nicholas, J. 16May08 *Quetta*
Pallin, S. F.G. 16May08 *Malta*
Tapley, J.J.B. 16May08 e.a.
Allen, H. 16May08 *Lyallpore*
Oliver, E. S. 16May08 e.a.
Greenfield, H. 16May08 *N. China*
Schofield, W.E.16May08 *Peshawar*
Webb, E. C., 16May08 e.a. F.R.C.V.S.
Wadley, E. J. 16May08 *Aldershot*
Steevenson, 16May08 *Ambala* J.R.
Neale, W.W.R.16May08 *Remt. Duty*
Gibbs, H. E. 16May08 *Cairo*
Matthews,R.C.16May08 *Jhansi*
Ryan, H. T., 22July08 *Ballincollig* F.R.C.V.S.
Leaning, A. 16Nov.09 *Muttra*
Argyle, E. P. 23Jan.09 *Netheravon*
Macdonald, D. 6Feb.09 *Meerut*
Holness, H. J. 6Feb.09 *Neemuch*

Captains—contd.

Thompson, 6Feb.09 *Nowshera* A. J.
O'Rorke, F.C., 6Feb.09 *Remt. Duty* F.R.C.V.S.
Nicholas, T. A. 6Feb.09 e.a.
Kirby, H. 11May09 *Leeds*
Burridge, T.E. 3Sept.09 *Remt. Duty*
Verney, L. M., 3Sept.09 *Canterbury* F.R.C.V.S.
Thomas, F. 8Sept.09 *Saugor* W. H.
Dibben, H. C. 18Oct.09 *Kirkee*
Edgar, A. 4Feb.10 *Dundalk*
Williams, H.M. 4Feb.10 *Rawal Pindi*
McKenzie, K. 4Feb.10 *A.V. Sch.* McL.
Nimmo, J. S. 4Feb.10 *Remt. Duty*
Ashmead- 4Feb.10 e.a. Bosley, J.
Russell, E. C., 7Mar.10 *Quetta* F.R.C.V.S.
Daniels, L. 26Aug.10 e.a.
Anderson, 26Aug.10 e.a. A. C.
Dale, W. J. 26Aug.10 *Aldershot*
Hodgkins, 26Aug.10 *Dublin* J. R., F.R.C.V.S.
Simpson, W.H.26Aug.10 *Woolwich*
Walker, W. H. 3Feb.11 e.a.
Horner, A. L. 3Feb.11 *Rawal Pindi*
Mellard, R. W. 3Feb.11 *Aldershot*
Andrews, J. O. 3Feb.11 *Remount Duty*
Audas, R. S. 3Feb.11 e.a.
Macauley, W.I. 6Mar.11 *Aldershot*
Harrison, J. 12May11 *Sargodha*
Bone, T. 12May11 *Fermoy*
Dixson L. L. 5Sept.11 *Brighton*
Taylor, W. H. 5Sept.11 *Longmoor*
Rowston, W.N. 5Sept.11 *Curragh*
Leckie, V. C. 5Sept.11 *Hounslow*
Lawrie, A. S. 11Oct.11 *Remt. Duty*
Hodgins, A. 13Feb.12 *Woolwich*
Stewart, H. A. 13Feb 12 *Aldershot*
Stewart, H.C. 13Feb.12 *Hilsea*
Lishman, T. 13Feb.12 *Aldershot*
Tindle, R. 13Feb.12 *Tidworth*
Black, S. 13Feb.12 *Kildare*
Bone, H. 23May12 *Norwich*
Roche-Kelly, F.R. 28Aug.12 e.a.
O'Kelly, J.W. 28Aug.12 *Mona*
Devine, E. J. 28Aug.12 *Aldershot*
Walsh, M. P. 28Aug.12 *Curragh*
Hearne, E. 28Aug.12 *Potchefstroom*
Tillyard, G. E. 9Sept.13 *Pretoria*
Hilliard, J. J. 9Sept.13 *Secunderabad.*
Jarvis, B. A. 9Sept.13 e.a.
Gooderidge, 9Sept.13 *Sialkot* R. A.
Bright, W.F.L. 9Sept.13 e.a.
Murray, C. A. 7Oct.13 *Sialkot*
Bowhay, A. B. 20 Oct.13 *Jubbulpore*

1781 | 1782 | 1783-6
Army Veterinary Corps.

Lieutenants.

Malone, P. J.	5Jan.10	*Mona*
Bett, R. F.	5Jan.10	*Bangalore*
Carey, P. D.	5Jan.10	e.a.
Turner, E. G.	5Jan.10	*Hyderabad*
Godwin, G. W.	5Jan.10	*Rawal Pindi*
Soutar, J. J. M.	29Jan.10	e.a.
McCartney, W.	3Sept.10	e.a.
St. J. F.		
Doyle, E. C.	3Sept.10	*Nasirabad*
Higgins, R.H.C.	3Sept.10	*Lahore*
Nicholl, E. McK.	3Sept.10	*Bangalore*
Thwaytes, R. C. G.	3Sept.10	*Lucknow*
Thomas, W. H.	15Feb.11	*Quetta*
Body, B. R.	15Feb.11	*Campbellpore*
Kelly, G. A.	15Feb.11	*Secunderabad*
Steevenson, G. F.	16Sept.11	*Secunderabad*
Hayes, F. B.	16Sept.11	*Ambala*
Hogg, F.	16Sept.11	*Lucknow*

Lieutenants—contd.

Golding, G. V.	17Feb.12	*Nowshera*
Lewis, H. D.	17Feb.12	*Meerut*
Beck, D'A. S.	17Feb.12	*Kirkee*
Stephenson, H.	17Feb.12	*Mhow*
Shea, T. L.	17Feb.12	*Lahore*
Irwin, H.E.A.L.	21Sept.12	*Bulford*
Davis, T. J.	21Sept.12	*Aldershot*
Going, J.	5Oct.12	*York*
Walker, U. W. F.	4Dec.12	*Woolwich*
Davenport, C.	27Sept.13	(on prob.)
Marriott, S. W.	27Sept.13	(on prob.)
Weir, F. J.	27Sept.13	(on prob.)
Smith, J.	27Sept.13	(on prob.)
Stewart, C. M.	7Feb.14	(on prob.)
Williamson, G.	7Feb.14	(on prob.)
Ellison, J. R.	7Feb.14	(on prob.)

Quarter-Master.

Campey, T. E., 18Mar.08 *Woolwich, hon. lt.*

Stations of the Sections of the Army Veterinary Corps.

Sections.	Officer Commanding.	Station.
1 and 2	Mosley, Capt. H. S.	Aldershot
3 ,, 4	Williams, Maj. G. M.	Woolwich
5 ,, 6	Conder, Maj. G.	Bulford
7 ,, 8	Lenox-Conyngham, Maj. H. M., F.R.C.V.S.	Curragh
9	Olver, Maj. A., F.R.C.V.S.	Pretoria
10	Harris, Maj. P. J.	Potchefstroom
11	Holmes, Maj.R.H. F.R.C.V.S.	Colchester
12	Williams, Maj. G. M.	Woolwich
13	Williams, Maj. G. M.	Woolwich
	Depôt, Woolwich.	

ARMY VETERINARY CORPS.
SPECIAL RESERVE.

Lieutenants.

Mattinson, A.B., F.R.C.V.S.	21July09	
Faithfull, T. J.	22Feb.11	
Lowry, H. C.	4Mar.11	
Henderson, W.W. (Vety. Offr., E. Africa Prote. 15July13)	25Mar.11	
Lindsay, P. T.	25Mar.11	
Tabuteau-Herrick, H. G.	22Apr.11	
Riley, P. B.	23Sept.11	
Stirling, R. F., F.R.C.V.S., late Lt. A.V.C.	2Oct.11	
McKenzie, W. J. E.	2Aug.13 / 4Oct.11	
Jones, S. K.	8Nov.11	
Armfield, J. M.	9Mar.12	
Keppel, J. J. G.	11May12	
Mathias, A. S. (Vety. Surg., Straits Settlements, 22Mar.13)	28Aug.12	
Sneyd, F.B., late Lt. A.V.C.	16Oct.12 / 13Dec.13	
Rae, J.	14Dec.12	
Holmes, S. E.	5Feb.13	
Williamson, D. R.	12Feb.13	
McMenamin, J. A.	3Mar.13	
Wheeler, R. C. (Vety. Offr., E. Africa Prote. 17July13)	3Mar.13	
Phipps, W. E.	3Mar.13	
Halstead, W., late Lt. A.V.C.	14June13	
Moore, R. (on prob.)	9July13	
Roche, F.	15July13	
Little, E. S.	7Sept.13	
Lawson, M. R.	4Oct.13	
Dimes, D. H.	8Oct.13	
Mills, J. J.	28Mar.14	
Sewell, E.	4Apr.14	

ARMY VETERINARY CORPS.
TERRITORIAL FORCE.

[Dates shown prior to 1 April, 1908, are those of the officers' corresponding rank in a late unit of the Volunteer Force.]

Lt.-Colonels.

	Elphick, G., TD	..21June99	
	Plomley, W., TD	..5Nov.04	North'n D v.
	Porritt, A., TD	..27May05	Home Cos. Div.
	Johnson, E.D., TD	..23Jan.07	W. Lan. Div.
p.	Dickinson, J.G.B., TD	..13Feb.07	N. Mid. Div.
	Dixon, W. G., TD (Hon. Vety.-Lt. in Army 6 Mar. 01)	..23Aug.07	W. Lan. Div.
p.	Coe, J.W., F.R.C.V.S., TD	15Jan.09	N. Mid. Div.
p.	Storrar, D.M., F.R.C.V.S., TD	..1Jan.10	Welsh Div.
p.s.	Franklin, E.	..30Apr.14	S. Mid. Div.

Captains.

	Channon, J.S.	..9Jan.01	Home Cos. Div.
p.	Logan, W.	..30Mar.03	High. Div.
	Elliott, R.	..24Sept.04	2 Lond. Div.
p.s.	Todd, J. A.	..1May05	Welsh Div.
	Harrison, H. C.	..17June05	Welsh Div.
	Perry, E. M.	..5July05	Home Cos. Div.
p.s.	Hobson, T.H., F.R.C.V.S.	18Oct.05	N. Mid. Div.
p.	Peddie, J.	..13Dec.05	High. Div.
p.s.	Golledge, C. H.	..24Jan.06	Wessex Div.

Captains—contd.

p.	Taylor, F. J.	..11Aug.06	2 Lond. Div.
p.	Green, R. L.	..2Nov.06	S. Mid. Div.
p.s.	Harrison, W. L., F.R.C.V.S.	..18July07	1 Lond. Div.
p.	Connell, J. A.	..28Oct.07	N. Mid. Div.
p.s.	Dayer Smith, P. W.	..4Nov.07	2 Lond. Div.
p.s.	Anderson, R. G.	..30Mar.08	High. Div.
	Awde, W., F.R.C.V.S.(A)	1Apr.08	North'n Div.
p.	Abson, J., F.R.C.V.S.	..1Apr.08	W. Rid. Div.
p.s.	Hibbard, T.	..6May08	Home Cos. Div.
	Nelder, W. B.	..6May08	Wessex Div.
	Simpson, P. J.	..1Dec.08	S. Mid. Div.
	Parks, E. W.	..12Jan.09	E. Ang. Div.
	Baxter, C., p.v.c.	..28Feb.09	Wessex Div.
p.s.	Davey, G. M.	..24Mar.09	W. Lan. Div.
	Still, J. E. L.	..10Apr.09	Home Cos. Div.
p.s.	Spreull, A.	..18July09	High. Div.
	Hamilton, D.	..3May10	Low. Div.
p.	Lewis, R. N.	..17June10	High. Div.
	Adamson, J., p.v.c.	..9July10	E. Lan. Div.
p.s.	Edwards, F. G.	..10Feb.11	Welsh Div.
	Barnes, W. G. (Hon. Vety.-Lt. in Army 23Aug. 02)	..15Feb.11	1 Lond. Div.

Army Veterinary Corps. Territorial Force.

Captains—contd.

Jones, J. L. C...	..18Aug.11	W. Rid. Div.
✗Pawlett, F. W.	..7Dec.11	W. Rid. Div.
Williams, S. J. ...	..30July12	2 Lond. Div.
Tagg, J.	..19Dec.12	E. Ang. Div.
Rankin, J. F. ..	..14Mar.13	E. Lan. Div.
Bennett, F. P., p.v.c.	..27June13	Wessex Div.
Rawlins, R. ..	..1July13	Wessex Div.
Lloyd, T. W. ..	..3July13	Wessex Div.
Ascott, W. ..	..11July13	Wessex Div.
Coleman, J. C...	..11Aug.13	Wessex Div.
✗Gresham, F. B. ..	..16Jan.14	N. Mid. Div.
Neill, C. E. ..	..12Feb.14	W. Lan. Div.
Wragg, W. G. ..	..1Mar.14	Home Cos. Div.
✗Rold,A.W., F.R.C.V.S.	12Mar.14	Home Cos.Div.
McArthur, J. ..	..4May14	E. Ang. Div.
✗Fyrth,W., late Vety.- Capt. Natal Vety. Corps	..3June14	Wessex Div.
Crapp, A. ..	..14June14	1 Lond. Div.

Lieutenants.

Carless, W. S. ..	..9Mar.01	S. Mid. Div.
Williams, R. D.	..20Sept.01	Welsh Div.
Storie, J., TD ..	..5Oct.01	Low. Div.
Davidson, D. S.	..9May03	Low. Div.
✗Anthony, H. ..	..26May08	Welsh Div.
Ridley, J. J. ..	..5June03	W. Rid. Div.
Drabble, C. ..	..18July03	W. Rid. Div.
Tuson, W. V., TD. ..	..9July04	Welsh Div.
Seldon, E. E. ..	..29Aug.06	S. Mid. Div.
Henderson, G. ..	..26June07	Low. Div.
Walker, A. ..	..29Nov.07	W. Lan. Div.
Hartley, C., jun., F.R.C.V.S. 27Mar.08		N. Mid. Div.
Weir, G. W. ..	..1Apr.08	Low. Div.
Weir, D. ..	..1Apr.08	Low. Div.
Peele, H. ..	..28Apr.08	North'n Div.
Soulsby, J. ..	..1May08	W. Lan. Div.
Macgregor, W. A.	..26June08	Low. Div.
✗Batt, A. E. G. ..	..4July08	Wessex Div.
Abson, P. ..	..14Sept.08	W. Rid. Div.
Elphick, H. S. ..	..26Sept.08	North'n. Div.
✗Symes, T. J. C. ..	..11Dec.08	Wessex Div.
✗Beilby, R. E...	..25Jan.09	W. Rid. Div.
Foster, A. N., F.R.C.V.S.	9Mar.09	W. Rid. Div.
Prudames, W. C.	..1Apr.09	E. Ang. Div.
Barron, W. K. ..	..16Apr.09	W. Lan. Div.
✗Crone, J. R. ..	..10May09	North'n. Div.
McIntyre, P. ..	..20May09	Low. Div.
Bowden, J. S. ..	..27May09	Welsh Div.
Fearnside, J. A. ..	..13Aug.09	High. Div.
Chatterley, D. R. (Empld. with British S. Africa Co, 1Sept.11)..	..17Aug.09	
Cade, W. J. ..	..17Sept.09	S. Mid. Div.
Bradbury, H. J. A.	..2Oct.09	Wessex Div.
Sadler, M. T. ..	..1Jan.10	N. Mid. Div.
Gillies, J. ..	..12Feb.10	Low. Div.
✗Evershed, P. M.	..19Mar.10	N. Mid. Div.

Lieutenants—contd.

Richardson, J. M.	..22Apr.10	Home Cos. Div.
Young, T. D.	..11May10	1 Lond. Div.
Curtis, A. J. ..	..1June10	Welsh Div.
Dixon, J. A. ..	..16June10	W. Rid. Div.
Wall, R. F. ..	..22July10	2 Lond. Div.
Ewin, C. A. A.	..8Aug.10	Home Cos. Div.
McIntyre, G.	..19Aug.10	E. Ang. Div.
Jürgensen, W. N.	..3Sept.10	E. Ang. Div.
McVean, H. ..	..6Sept.10	High. Div.
Hill, J. ..	..7Sept.10	Welsh Div.
Powell, H. E. ..	..18Oct.10	N. Mid. Div.
Heyes,J.P.,F.R.C.V.S.	18Nov.10	E. Lan. Div.
Standley, H. P.	..17Feb.11	E. Ang. Div.
Thomson, J. H.	..23Feb.11	High. Div.
Blakeway, J.	..24Feb.11	S. Mid. Div.
Saunders, A. G.	..18Mar.11	Wessex Div.
✗Hepburn, W.	..10May11	High. Div.
✗Powell, J. C. S.	..15May11	Wessex Div.
Aulton, R. M.	..16May11	N. Mid. Div.
Lloyd, L. W. W.	..19May11	Welsh Div.
Chadwick, C. R.	..10Oct 11	High. Div.
Duncan,A.C.,F.R.C.V.S.I. 23Dec.11		S. Mid. Div.
✗Lornie, W. S.	..20Jan.12	High. Div.
Castle, A.F.,F.R.C.V.S.	8Apr.12	E. Ang. Div.
Thrale, P. R. A.	..15May12	Home Cos. Div.
Martin, E. S.	..15May12	Wessex Div.
McGregor, J. G.	..7June12	Low. Div.
Heath, F. E.	..10Aug.12	S. Mid. Div.
Jordan, W. D.	..24Aug.12	Welsh Div.
Wright, J. R.	..1Sept 12	E. Lan. Div.
Drinkwater, F. W. C.	1Sept.12	Wessex Div.
Williams, W. D.	..1Sept.12	Welsh Div.
Morgan, P. S.	..1Sept.12	Welsh Div.
Cartwright, C. W.	..1Sept.12	Welsh Div.
Thomson, T.	..1Sept.12	N. Mid. Div.
Williams, R. W.	..1Sept.12	Welsh Div.
Jones, J. H. ..	..9Sept.12	Welsh Div.
Over, R. H. H.	..21Oct.12	S. Mid. Div.
Berry, E. ..	..30Jan.13	Wessex Div.
Jones, V. P. ..	..20Feb.13	S. Mid. Div.
Henson, G. E.	..1Mar.13	S. Mid. Div.
Tait, J. W. ..	..31Mar.13	Low. Div.
Bishop, G. H.	..25Apr.13	S. Mid. Div.
Bogue, J. Y.	..25June13	S. Mid. Div.
Bartrum, V. A.	..22Oct. 13	Welsh Div.
Palmer, R. B.	..11Nov.13	S. Mid. Div.
McCall. J. R.	..17Nov.13	Low. Div.
Crabb, D. R.	..5Dec.13	Low Div.
Bagshaw, T.	..16Dec.13	S. Mid. Div.
✗Hines, A. J. ..	..6Jan..14	N. Mid. Div.
Cocksedge, T. A. B...	7Jan.14	Wessex Div.
Moon, F. J. ..	..20Mar.14	Welsh Div.
Robb, A., jun.	..6May14	Low. Div.
Thomson, W. G.	..18May14	N. Mid. Div.
Routledge, A. R.,F.R.C.V.S. 25May14		N. M'd. Div.
Shaw, J. A. ..	..13June14	N Mid. Div.

Officers of the Army Veterinary Department transferred to the Indian Civil Veterinary Department.

Colonels.

Name	Date	Post
Pease, H. T., C.I.E.	3Sept.10	Principal, Punjab Vety. Coll.
Evans, G. H., C.I.E.	10Feb.13	Burma, Rangoon

Lieutenant-Colonels.

Name	Date	Post
Maxwell, H. M., F.R.C.V.S.	7Dec.09	Poona
Farmer, J., F.R.C.V.S.	28Feb.10	Punjab

Majors.

Name	Date	Post
Smith, A., F.R.C.V.S.	21June08	Principal, Vety. Coll., Calcutta
Baldrey, F.S.H., F.R.C.V.S.	28Feb.09	Central Provinces

Majors—contd.

Name	Date	Post
Waller, G. K., C.I.E.,F.R.C.V.S.	25July09	Professor, Vety.Coll.,Punjab
Holmes, J. D. E., C.I.E.	28Aug.10	Muktesar
Dawson, W.O.C.	4Mar.11	Central Provinces

R

1789 | 1790

ARMY CHAPLAINS' DEPARTMENT.

Agents:—Sir C. R. McGrigor, *Bt.,* & Co , 39, Panton Street, Haymarket, S.W.

Note.—Presbyterian Chaplains are distinguished by the letter [P]. Chaplains after whose names the letters [RC] appear belong to the Roman Catholic Church.
Where two dates are shown, the earlier is the date from which service reckons towards retired pay under Article 540, Royal Warrant, 20 Aug. 13.

Chaplain General, ranking as Major-General.

Taylor Smith, *Rt. Rev. Bishop* J., *C.V.O., D.D.* 1 Nov.01

Chaplain to the Forces (1st Class), ranking as Colonels.

Simms, *Rev.* J. M., *D.D.* K.H.C. [P]	16Nov.03 *Aldershot*		Oliver, *Rev.* R.J.D., *M.A.*	29Nov.10 *Shorncliffe*
Dowding, *Rev.* W. B.	9Apr.05 *Parkhurst*		Hordern, *Rev.* A. V. C.	29Nov.10 *Colchester*
Gedge, *Rev.* A.A.L., *M.A.*	29Nov.05 *Preston*		Jaffray, *Rev.* W. S. [P]	29Nov.10 *Malta*
Matthews, *Rev.* L. J. [RC]	29Nov.05 *Gibraltar*		Tuckey, *Rev.* J. G. W., *M.A.*	29Nov.10 *Woolwich*
Borsble, *Rev.* W. F., *M.A.*	29Nov.05 *Pretoria*		Keatinge, *Rev.* W. [RC]	29Nov.10 *Cairo*
Norman-Lee, *Rev.* F.B.N., *M.A.*	28Mar.06 *Winchester*		Blackbourne, *Rev.* J., *M.A.*	29Nov.10 *Aldershot*
Wilkin, *Rev.* S. W. W.	1Oct.07 *York*		Jones, *Rev.* M., *D.D.*	1Dec.10 *Gosport*
Haines, *Rev.* W. C.	5Nov.07 *Dover*		Little, *Rev.* H., *B.A.*	25Feb.11 *Cairo*
Moseley, *Rev.* R., *M.A.*	1Feb.10 *Chelsea Hosp.*		Brough, *Rev.* J., *M.A.*	8Sept.11 *Newbridge*
Hatton, *Rev.* J. A., *M.A.*, *B.D.*	1June10 *Curragh*		Baines, *Rev.* C. F., *M.A.*	30Dec.11 *Dublin*
Churchward, *Rev.* M. W., *M.A.*	19Sept.10 *London*		Hill, *Rev.* F. A., *B.A.*	26June12 *Shoeburyness*
Ward, *Rev.* W. J., *B.D.*	10Oct.10 *Cork*		Day, *Rev.* E.R., *M.A.*	26June12 *Lichfield*
Pulling, *Rev.* E. H.	27Nov.10 *Portsmouth*		Norris, *Rev.* E.W.M.,*M.A.*	19Aug.12 *Chatham*
Macpherson,*Rev.* E. G. F., *B.A.*	29Nov.10 *Devonport*		Bickerstaffe-Drew, *Rev.* F. *B.D.* [RC]	1Feb.13 *Salisbury Plai*
			Benoy, *Rev.* J., *M.A.*	9July13 *Aldershot*
			Bird, *Rev.* J. T., *M.A.* [P]	26July13 *Glasgow*
			Wetherall, *Rev.* A. G. M.	26Apr.14 *Dover.*

Chaplains to the Forces (2nd Class) ranking as Lieut.-Colonels.

Witt, *Rev.* A. R., *M.A.*	28May10 *Canterbury*		Rogers,*Rev.*S.F.H.[l] [RC]	23June13 *Aldershot*
Jellicoe, *Rev.* F. J. P.	25Mar.11 *Chatham*		Lane, *Rev.* D. P. [RC]	7Jan.14 *Devonport*
Nash, *Rev.* R. H. [L] [RC]	18May13 *S. Africa*			

Chaplains to the Forces (3rd Class) ranking as Majors.

Forrest, *Rev.* W. [RC]	5Aug.09 *Shorncliffe*		Ensell, *Rev.* C. S., *B.A.*	2July11 *Netley*
Moreton, *Rev.* T. P., *M.A.*	11May10 *Gibraltar*		Brook, *Rev.* T., *B.D.,LL.D.*	27Sept.11 *Cairo*
Cowper, *Rev.* J. J. M. *M.A.* [P]	1July10 *Egypt*		O'Rorke, *Rev.* B. G. *M.A.*	16Nov.11 *Bordon*
Goudge, *Rev.* T. S., *B.A.*	1July11 *Dublin*		Webb-Peploe, *Rev.* H. M., *M.A.*	15July12 *Caterham*
Dawes, *Rev.* A. W., *B.A.*	1July11 *Dover*		Radford, *Rev.* C. I.	17Dec.12 *Gibraltar*
Peacock, *Rev.* C. A., *M.A.*	1July11 *Woolwich*		Read, *Rev.* F. P., *M.A.*	13Feb.13 *Gibraltar*
Hales, *Rev.* J. T.	1July11 *Tidworth*		Fleming, *Rev.* H. J., *M.A.*	21Feb.13 *R. Mil. Acad.*
Colbeck, *Rev.* G. H.	1July11 *Hilsea & Cosham*		Mitchell, *Rev.* P. R., *M.A.*	21Feb.13 *Tower of London*
Hanson,*Rev.* R.E.V.,*M.A.*	1July11 *Malta*			
Baynham, *Rev.* J. H.,*M.A.*	2July11 *Deepcut*			

Army Chaplains' Department.

Chaplains to the Forces (3rd Class) ranking as Majors—contd.

Findlay, Rev. J. L. O. B.	22Feb.13 Bermuda	Dey, Rev. J. [RC]	7Aug.13 Aldershot
Drury, Rev. W., M.A.	22Feb.13 Crownhill, Plymouth	Campbell, Rev. J. [P]	10Oct.13 London
Searle, Rev. G., M.A.	22Feb.13 Mauritius	Moth, Rev. J. C. [RC]	12Feb.14 Potchefstroom
Carey, Rev. D. F., M.A.	22Feb.13 Jamaica.	Davies, Rev. H. J., B.A.	14Feb.14 Pretoria.
Hughes, Rev. L. A., M.A.	22Feb.13 Tidworth	King, Rev. F. J., M.A.	14Feb.14 Plymouth
Anderson, Rev. F. I., M.A.	22Feb.13 Shorncliffe	Parry-Evans, Rev. J. D. S.	14Feb.14 Aldershot
Stewart, Rev. F. W M.A. [P]	21Apr.13 Edinburgh	Ennis, Rev. A. D. L., M.A.	14Feb.14 Wellington Barracks
Yeoman, Rev. A. R., M.A. [I] [P]	24July13 Shorncliffe	Blackburne, Rev. H. W., M.A.	14Feb.14 R. Mil. Coll.
		Bradley, Rev. P. [RC]	8Apr.14 Netley

Chaplains to the Forces (4th Class), ranking as Captains.

Avent, Rev. E., M.A.	1Jan.04 Dublin. 10Oct.04	Webster, Rev. F. G. D., M.A.	6Aug.08 Potchefstroom. 14Dec.08
Dunphy, Rev. J. [RC]	4July02 Malta. 26Oct.04	Pegg, Rev. W. H. F., B.A.	19Apr.09 Warley. 10May09
Meeke, Rev. H. C., M.A. [P]	4Jan.05 Crownhill.	Marshall, Rev. H. G., M.A.	12Feb.09 Singapore. 8July09
Morrison, Rev. D. A., M.A. [P]	12Jan.05 Aldershot.	Jarvis, Rev. A. C. E.	24June09 Portsmouth. 8July09
Winnifrith, Rev. D.P., M.A.	1June04 Dublin 22May05	Marshall, Rev. H., M.A.	6July09 Malta. 8July09
Rowan, Rev. B. W., B.A.	14May04 Bulford. 17May06	Holmes, Rev. R. H.	20Sept.09 Alexandria. 24Feb.10
Smithwick, Rev. F. F. S., B.A.	24June04 Woking. 27Sept.06	Green, Rev. E. W., M.A.	1Jan.10 Cairo. 28July10
Campbell, Rev. E. F., B.A.	1May06 Bulford. 4Oct.06	Fitch, Rev. E. A.	7Apr.10 Pretoria. 28July10
Thorold, Rev. E. H., M.A.	7Aug.06 Aldershot. 24Dec.06	Parker, Rev. H. L., B.A.	15Apr.10 Malta. 28July10
Burrough, Rev. J., M.A.	15Oct.06 Hounslow 24Dec.06	Alford, Rev. C. S. L., M.A.	29Apr.10 Malta. 28July10
Walker, Rev. F. J., M.A. B.D.	1Feb.07 Tientsin. 21Apr.07	Edmonds-Smith, Rev. E., M.A.	1Oct.10 Scutari, Albania. 14Nov.10
Williams. Rev R.C.L., B.A.	1July07 Duke of York's School. 20Oct.07	Connor, Rev. J. M., M.A., [P]	19Dec.04 Dublin. 19Dec.10
Tobias, Rev. M., B.A.	15Nov.06 Malta. 8Jan.08	Guinness, Rev. P.W., B.A.	16Jan.11 Curragh. 5Mar.11
Beardmore, Rev. C. L. H., M.A.	14Sept.07 Wynberg. 8Jan.08	Hunt, Rev. C. L. C., B.A.	1Jan.11 Hong Kong. 30Apr.12
Miller, Rev. W. H. L., B.A.	18Oct.07 Malta. 8Jan.08	Walkey, Rev. J. R., M.A.	17Apr.11 Woolwich. 4May12
Gell, Rev. E. A. S., M.A.	15Mar.08 Colchester. 18Apr.08	Edlin, Rev. A. H. C., M.A.	11Jan.08 Millbank. 6Nov.12
Martin, Rev. E W., B.A.	1May07 Colchester. 6July08	Paterson, Rev. W. R., M.A., [P]	28Feb.08 Curragh. 19Apr.13
		Kinnear, Rev. J. C., M.A.	1Oct.11 Woolwich. 5Oct.13
		Gibb, Rev. J. H. O., B.A.	20Oct.11 Tidworth. 26Oct.13
		McCready, Rev. M.P., M.A.	1Oct.12 Shorncliffe. 16Nov.13

Temporary Roman Catholic Chaplains.

Grobel, Rev. P.	..	25Dec.09 Bulford
Molony, Rev. J. P.	..	1Oct.10 Aldershot
O'Reilly, Rev. J.	..	17Oct.11 Aldershot
Flynn, Rev. W. J.	..	10Jan.13 Aldershot

Army Chaplains' Department.

Acting Army Chaplains.
(Only Clergymen giving their whole time to the Troops are shown in this list.)

Church of England.

Archdale, Rev. M., B.A.	.. Belfast.		Lamb, Rev. P. C. C., B.A.	.. Dublin.
Bate, Rev. E. Y., M.A.	.. York.		Ma'aher, Rev. H. T., M.A.	.. Aldershot.
Bour hier, Rev. W, La R., B.A.	.. Curragh.		Oldfield, Rev. H. D.	.. Woolwich.
Chadwick, Rev. C. E., M.A.	.. Aldershot.		O'Malley, Rev. J. J. E., B.A.	.. Bordon
Farren, Rev. W. M. A., M.A.	.. Aldershot.		Shewell, Rev. M. W., M.A.	.. Aldershot.
Griffin, Rev. J. W. K., M.A.	.. Shorncliffe.			

Presbyterian.

✗Archibald, Rev. W. F., M.A.	.. Colchester.		Farquhar, Rev. H., B.D.	.. Dover.
Cairns, Rev. J., VD	.. Woolwich.		✗Howe, Rev. G. B.	.. Potchefstroom.
Connan, Rev. D. M., M.A.	.. Tidworth.		Lynn, Rev. J., B.A., B.D.	.. Aldershot.
Duncan, Rev. J., M.A.	.. Caterham.		Metcalfe, Rev. W., B.D.	.. Shoeburyness.

Roman Catholic.

Bloomfield, Rev. J.	.. Colchester.		Hockran, Rev. D.	.. Alexandria.
Egan, Rev. J.	.. Cairo.		Mason, Rev. S.	.. Woking.
Hessenauer, Rev. J.	.. Chatham.		Murphy, Rev. W.	.. Curragh.

Wesleyan.

Armstrong, Rev. I.	.. Plymouth & Devonport.		Peverley-Dodd, Rev. H.	.. Malta.
			Philpott, Rev. H. J.	.. Cairo.
Cape, Rev. A. T.	.. Shorncliffe.		Raw, Rev. A. E.	.. Salisbury Plain.
Hall, Rev. R.	.. Chatham.		Sackett, Rev. A. B.	.. Gibraltar.
Kelly, Rev. J. D.	.. Curragh.		Sarchet, Rev. W. H.	.. Portsmouth.
✗Laverack, Rev. J.	.. Netley.		Sharpley, Rev. W. T.	.. Bordon & Longmoor.
✗Lowry, Rev. E. P. (Hon. Chaplain to the Forces, 1st Class)	Aldershot.		Thorpe, Rev. T. J.	.. Woolwich.
Morrow, Rev. A. W.	.. Aldershot.		✗Watkins, Rev. O. S. (Hon. Chaplain to the Forces, 3rd Class)	London.

Baptist and Congregationalist.

Kemp, Rev. F. G.	..			.. Aldershot.
Seeley, Rev. J.	..			.. Woolwich.

CHAPLAINS' DEPARTMENT.
TERRITORIAL FORCE.

The names of Chaplains of the Territorial Force who are attached to units are shewn thereunder.

Where two dates appear against the name of a Chaplain under a unit, the earlier is that of his first appointment.

Honorary Chaplains.

Chester, Rt. Rev. F. J., Lord Bishop of, D.D.	5Mar.10		Barker, Very Rev. W., D.D., VD, Dean of Carlisle	5July11
Hannah, Very Rev. J. J., M.A., VD, Dean of Chichester	5Mar.10		Brownrigg, Very Rev. J. S., M.A., VD, Dean of Bocking	5July11
Wace, Very Rev. H., D.D., Dean of Canterbury	5Mar.10		Lister, Rev. Canon T. L., M.A., VD	5July11
Dangar, Rev. Preb. J. G., D.D., VD	5Mar.10		Clarke, Rev. A. D., M.A., VD	5July11
Shickle, Rev. C. W., VD	5Mar.10		Kingston, Rev. J., LL.D., VD, Chaplain R.N. ret. pay, G.H.P.	5July11
MacLeod, Very Rev. D., D.D. [C.S.]	5Mar.10		Pilkington, Rev. J. G., M.A., TD	5July11
✗Cameron, Rev. T. A., M.A. VD [C.S.]	5Mar.10		Lang, Rev. G., VD [C.S.]	5July11
Henderson, Rev. A., D.D., TD [U.F.C.]	5Mar.10		Blair, Rev. W., D.D., VD [U.F.C.]	5July11
Cairns, Rev., J., VD [E.P.]	5Mar.10		Winchester, Rt. Rev. E. S., Lord Bishop of, D.D., TD (2nd Cl. Chapl. ret. T.F.)	4Sept.12
✗Brindle, Rt. Rev. R., Bishop, D.S.O., Chaplain 1st Class ret. pay [R] [R.C.]	5Mar.10		Bath and Wells, Rt. Rev. G. W. Lord Bishop of, D.D.	17Sept.13
Currie, Very Rev. E. R., D.D., VD, Dean of Battle	5July11		✗Bateson, Rev. J. H. [W]	11Oct.13
Roberts, Very Rev. W. P., D.D., Dean of Salisbury	5July11			

Unattached.

Adler, Rev. M., B.A. [J], Chaplain 4th Class	22June09
Lyon, Rev. W. T., B.A., Chaplain 4th Class	22Nov.10
Walters, Rev. A. H. [W], Chaplain 4th Class	27June12

STAFF FOR ROYAL ENGINEER SERVICES.

Uniform—Blue. *Facings*—Bright Blue. *Edgings*—Scarlet.

[*N.B.—The seniority of Officers, appointed after open competition, is governed by the order of merit assigned to them by the Civil Service Commissioners.*]

Chief Inspector of Works.

Kingston, W., *B.E., M.Inst. C.E.* 29Apr.14 *War Office.*
hon. lt.-col. 29Apr.14

Superintending Inspectors of Works.

Bartholomew, W. B.	1Apr.07	*Aldershot.*		Elto , H. A., *F.S.I.*	1Apr.07	*London, E.C.*
	hon. maj. 1Apr.07				hon. maj. 1Apr.07	
Raves, B. A., *F.S.I., Assoc. M.Inst.C.E.*	1Apr.07	*Salisburgh.*		Emery, A. J., *F.S.I.*	1Apr.07	54, *Victoria St., S.W.*
	hon. maj. 1Apr.07				hon. maj. 1Apr.07	
Greenwood, J., *F.S.I.*	1Apr.07	*Lond. Dist.*		Coleman, T. E.	7Mar.08	*Lond. Dist.*
	hon. maj. 1Apr.07				hon. maj. 11May07	
Gregory, A., *F.S.I.*	1Apr.07	4, *Victoria St., S.W.*		Bridges, E. J., *A.R.Inst.B.A.*	29Apr.14	*Salisbury.*
	hon. maj. 1Apr.07				hon. maj. 18May07	

Inspectors of Works.

Galbraith, S. H., *M.A., B.E., F.S.I.*	1Apr.07	*Netley.*		Spriggs, C. W.	1Apr.07	*Singapore*
	hon. maj. 18May07				hon. maj. 8July14	
Addenbrooke, J. S., *A.R.Inst.B.A.*	1Apr.07	*Edinburgh.*		Sayer, G. W., *F.S.I.*	1Apr.07	*Chester.*
	hon. maj. 18May07				hon. capt. 1Apr 07	
Hammond, R. W., *F.S.I.*	1Apr.07	*Dublin.*		Addenbrooke, W. H. S.	1Apr.07	54, *Victoria St., S.W.*
	hon. maj. 18May07				hon. capt. 1Apr.07	
Pearse, S.	1Apr.07	*Chatham.*		Bradshaw, J. B., *Assoc.M.Inst.C.E.*	1Apr.07	*Weymouth.*
	hon. maj. 18May07				hon. capt. 1Apr.07	
Child, H. J., *F.S.I.*	1Apr.07	*Tidworth.*		Raves, B. A., *Assoc.M.Inst.C.E.*	1Apr.07	*Canterbury.*
	hon. maj. 14June08				hon. capt. 1Apr.07	
Moxon, H. W., *F.S.I.*	1Apr.07	*Colchester.*		Carruthers, E. S.	1Apr.07	*Pembroke Dock.*
	hon. maj. 14June08				hon. capt. 1Apr.07	
Morris, G. J.	1Apr.07	*Portsea.*		Knight, H. St. J., *F.S.I.*	1Apr.07	*Weedon.*
	hon. maj. 14June08				hon. capt. 1Apr.07	
Boxshall, H. E., *F.S.I.*	1Apr.07	*Sandhurst.*		Bagot, L. B., *F.S.I., Assoc.M.Inst.C.E.*	1Apr.07	*Bristol.*
	hon. maj. 14June08				hon. capt. 1Apr.07	
Gates-Warren, G. G., *Assoc. Inst.C.E.(I.)*	1Apr.07	*Dover.*		Walmsley, A. T., *F.S.I.*	1Apr.07	*Lichfield.*
	hon. maj. 14June08				hon. capt. 1Apr.07	
Rogers, A. M., *F.S.I.*	1Apr.07	*Fermoy.*		Bryant, G. H., *F.S.I.*	1Apr.07	*Bulford.*
	hon. maj. 14June08				hon. capt. 1Apr.07	
McEwen, J.	1Apr.07	*Belfast.*		Taylor, E. C., *F.S.I.*	1Apr.07	*Devonport.*
	hon. maj. 11Mar.11				hon. capt. 1Apr.07	
Caws, B. F., *Assoc. M.Inst.C.E.*	1Apr.07	*Jamaica.*		Bone, E. J.	1Apr.07	*Norwich.*
	hon. maj. 11Mar.11				hon. capt. 1Apr.07	
Wenborn, S. T., *F.S.I.*	1Apr.07	*Hong Kong.*		Earle, F., *A.R.Inst.B.A.*	1Apr.07	*Newcastle-on-Tyne.*
	hon. maj. 15Mar.11				hon. capt. 1Jan.09	
Stanbury, W. H., *A.R.Inst.B.A.*	1Apr.07	*Woolwich*		Nicholls, E. A.	1Apr.07	*Bulford.*
	hon.maj. 25Mar.11				hon. capt. 1Jan.09	
Billingham, J. A. L., *F.S.I.*	1Apr.07	*Ceylon.*		Harrison, S. W.	1Apr.07	*Preston*
	hon. maj. 1July12				hon. capt. 13Apr.10	
Humphrey, W. C.	1Apr.07	*Hong Kong.*		Barkshire, C. R.	1Apr.07	*Gibraltar.*
	hon. maj. 7July12				hon. capt. 6Oct.10	
Chapell, C. H.	1Apr.07	*Malta.*		Critchlow, J.	1Apr.07	*Gosport.*
	hon. maj. 17July13				hon. capt. 8Dec.10	
Rea, J. T., *F.S.I.*	1Apr.07	*York.*		Roberts, S., *F.S.I.*	1Apr.07	54, *Victoria St., S.W.*
	hon. maj. 24July13				hon. capt. 1May11	
Wright, G. J., *F.S.I.*	1Apr.07	*Exeter.*		Coad, H. E., *Assoc.M.Inst.C.E.*	1Apr.07	*Bermuda.*
	hon. maj. 8Sept.13				hon. capt. 7Nov.11	
Pownall, W. E.	1Apr.07	*S. Africa.*				
	hon. maj. 23Nov.13					
Rogers, C. P., *F.S.I.*	1Apr.07	*Curragh.*		Hewitt, F. T. B., *F.S.I*	1Apr.07	*Dublin.*
	hon. maj. 12Jan.14				hon. capt. 17Aug.12	
Chapman, G. J., *F.S.I., Assoc.M.Inst.C.E.*	1Apr.07	*Hounslow.*		Short, E. W. G., *F.S.I.*	1Apr.07	*S. Africa.*
	hon. maj. 26Jan.14				hon. capt. 10Dec.12	

Serving under a previous Warrant.

Surveyor 2nd Class.
(*Ranking as Captain.*)

Burns, G. J. .. 10May98 *Woolwich Arsenal.*

| 1799 | 1800 | 1801 |

QUEEN ALEXANDRA'S IMPERIAL MILITARY NURSING SERVICE.

(*Established by Royal Warrant dated 7th March, 1902.*)

On a cross pattee (as borne in the Royal Arms of Denmark), surmounted by an Imperial Crown, the letter A within a circle, and surrounded by an oval band bearing the inscription, "Queen Alexandra's Imperial Military Nursing Service."
"*Sub Cruce Candida.*"
Uniform, Grey. Facings, Scarlet.

Note.—Where two dates are shown, the second is that of appointment to the Army Nursing Service.

President.
QUEEN ALEXANDRA.

Matron-in-Chief.
Becher, *Miss* E. H., *R.R.C.*   5Apr.10   *War Office.*

Principal Matrons.
McCarthy, *Miss* E. M., *R.R.C.*   5Apr.10   *War Office*
Oram, *Miss* S. E., *R.R.C.*   19June11   *S. Africa*
                                     1May 86

Matrons.

Blakely, *Miss* M. M.   21Apr.14   *Cork*
Bond, *Miss* A. S., *R.R.C.*   5Mar.07   *Alexandria*   27Jan.92
Cox, *Miss* A. L.   14Jan.04   *Devonport*
Cox, *Miss* E. A.   1 Dec.07   *Pretoria*   1Nov.97
Dods, *Miss* J.E.   1Feb. 11 *Shorncliffe*
Hoadley, *Miss* J., *R.R.C.*   5Mar.07   *Malta*   7Sept.93
Hodgins, *Miss* F. M.   1Mar.11   *Dublin*
Humphreys, *Miss* E. C.   12Nov.11   *Gibraltar*

Jones, *Miss* B.I.,   12Feb.03   *Chatham*   *R.R.C.*
Lamming, *Miss*   21July11   *Cairo*   S.
Mark, *Miss* M.   20Oct.10   *Curragh*   10Oct.98
Martin, *Miss* E. J., *R.R.C.*   5Mar.07   *London*   2Aug.93
Murphy, *Miss* A. A.   15July09   *Wynberg*   23May94
Nixon, *Miss* A., *R.R.C.*   1Dec.07   *Woolwich*   1Oct.94
Osborne, *Miss* R.   17Oct.11   *York*
Rannie, *Miss* M.L.   29June03   *Netley*

Reid, *Miss* H. W.   14Oct.03   *Colchester*
Richards, *Miss* G. M.   14Mar.04   *London*
Smith, *Miss* A. B., *R.R.C.*   30Mar.03   *Aldershot*
Steen, *Miss* L. E. C.   21May10   *Tidworth*   13Mar.97
Stewart, *Miss* L. M., *R.R.C.*   17Feb.03   *Dover*   16Dec.89
Tulloh, *Miss* L. W., *R.R.C.*   11Jan.06   *Hounslow*   13Sept.87
Willetts, *Miss* I. G.   1Nov.10   *Hong Kong*
Wilson, *Miss* M., *R.R.C.*   17Feb.03   *Cosham*   12Oct.97

Sisters.

Allen, *Miss* G. M.   21June06   *Wynberg*
Allsop, *Miss* K.A.   6Dec.06   *Gibraltar*
Ayre, *Miss* A.   19June11   *Netley*
Barbec, *Miss* E.   10Nov.06   *Aldershot*
Barker, *Miss* A.   30Mar.03   *Hong Kong*   9May98
Barton, *Miss* M.   1May11   *Aldershot*
Beamish, *Miss* S. O.   1July09   *Tidworth*
Belcher, *Miss* L.   6Dec.06   *Gibraltar*
Bills, *Miss* S. K.   10Apr.05   *London*
Bilton, *Miss* C. T.   6Dec.06   *Gibraltar*
Blew, *Miss* N.   21June06   *Hong Kong*
Bond, *Miss* M.M.   9Aug.04   *London*
Byers, *Miss* A.F.   9Aug.04   *Edinburgh*
Cameron, *Miss* A. B.   1Dec.07   *York*
Cheetham, *Miss* E. C.   12Feb.03   *Woolwich*
Clements, *Miss* M.   8Dec.06   *Potchefstroom*
Close, *Miss* E. J. H.   21July11   *Cosham*
Congleton, *Miss*   21Apr.14   *London*
Dalton, *Miss* J. G.   10Apr.12   *Shorncliffe*
Daly, *Miss* S. N.   28Jan.09   *Cosham*
Darnell, *Miss* E.B.   1Sept.12
Davis, *Miss* M.   20Oct.10   *Curragh*
Denne, *Miss* E. M.   9Aug.04   *R.Mil.Coll.*

de Stourdza-Zrinyl, *Miss* F. G. P.   15Aug.05   *Netley*
Drage, *Miss* H M.   15Aug.05   *Colchester*
Fairchild, *Miss* E. M.   21June06   *Woolwich*
Fox, *Miss* E. C.   10Nov.06   *Curragh*
Gardner, *Miss* J. S. G.   28Oct.11   *Aldershot*
German, *Miss* M.   4Nov.11   *Netley*
Grierson, *Miss* M. E. M.   21June06   *Khartoum*
Harding, *Miss* M. E.   17Feb.03   *Pretoria*   3Mar.98
Hare, *Miss* H.A.   28Dec.06   *Pretoria*
Harris, *Miss* M. L.   10Nov.04   *London*
Hartigan, *Miss* H.   1July09   *London*
Hay, *Miss* E. H.   29Oct.04   *Cork*
Hepple, *Miss* M. J.   16June10   *London*
Hordley, *Miss* E. H.   21Oct.03   *London*
Howe, *Miss* G.A.   16Oct.11   *London*
Jacob, *Miss* G. S.   15July07   *Dublin*
Johnson, *Miss* C. V. S.   1Oct.13   *Dublin*
Johnston, *Miss* M. C.   1July09   *Aldershot*
Jones, *Miss* O. W.   27May11   *Aldershot*

Kaberry, *Miss* M.L.   7Nov.10   *Malta*
Keene, *Miss* E. J. M.   29Oct.04   *Devonport*
Knowles, *Miss* G.   10Apr.05   *Hounslow*
Lang, *Miss* E. M.   1Dec.07   *Aldershot*
Lees, *Miss* C. G.   20Dec.10   *Aldershot*
Lyde, *Miss* E.M.   8June06   *Aldershot*
McAllister, *Miss* E. L.   8June06   *Netley*
McCreery, *Miss* M. O'C.   10Nov.06   *Netley*
Mackay, *Miss* C.   10Apr.05   *R. Mil. Acad.*
Mackay, *Miss* L. E.   10Nov.04   *London*
Makepeace, *Miss* M. R.   17Feb.03   *Malta*   15Oct.94
Manfield, *Miss* F. E.   12Nov.11   *Cairo*
Massey, *Miss* W. G.   10Apr.05   *Edinburgh*   10Jan.01
Medforth, *Miss* M.E.   21Mar.14   *Aldershot*
Michell, *Miss* D. M. C.   24Apr.08   *Cairo*
Minns, *Miss* E. J.   1Dec.07   *Tidworth*
Mowat, *Miss* A. C.   7Nov.10   *Aldershot*
Murphy, *Miss* J.   28Jan.09   *Alexandria*
Neville, *Miss* M. E.   10Nov.06   *Cairo*

Queen Alexandra's Imperial Military Nursing Service.

Sisters—contd.

Newman, Miss M. C. E. 1Feb.11 *Netley*
Pagan, Miss A.M. 5Aug.05 *Devonport*
Pedler, Miss M. 16Feb.04 *Chatham*
Perkins, Miss B. F. 8June06 *Dublin*
Phillips, Miss A. M. 12July12 *Dublin*
Potter, Miss M.L. 16Feb.04 *Tidworth*
Potter, Miss W. 17Feb.03 *Dublin* 16Nov.97
Ram, Miss M.S. 21June06 *Potohefstroom*
Rentzsch, Miss E. M. 1July09 *Colchester*
Richards, Miss S. 16June10
Richardson, Miss M. E. 15Aug.05 *Pretoria*
Roberts, Miss F. N. 28Dec.06 *Hong Kong*
Robinson, Miss E. M. 10Nov.06 *Aldershot*
Roscoe, Miss K. 9June08 *Cosham*

Rowe, Miss A. 6Dec.06 *Gibraltar*
St. Quintin, Miss E. 1Aug.07 *London*
Saunder, Miss D. J 6Dec.06 *Malta*
Smith, Miss G.M. 8June06 *Woolwich*
Smith, Miss M. 29July04 *Tidworth*
Smyth, Miss S. 29Oct.04 *Cosham* 25Mar.02
Steele, Miss P. 28Dec.06 *Pretoria*
Steenson, Miss M. 24Nov.03 *Curragh*
Steer, Miss A.A. 31May11 *Aldershot*
Stronach, Miss C. G. 9Aug.04 *Curragh*
Suart, Miss H. 27June03 *R. Arsenal, Woolwich*
Taylor, Miss D. M. 29Oct.04 *Colchester*
Todd, Miss E. M. E. 17Feb.03 *London* 23June98
Toller, Miss L.M. 15Aug.05 *Netley*
Tosh, Miss F. M. 1Mar.11 *Dublin*

Tripp, Miss D. D. 17Feb.03 *Tidworth* 6Oct.94
Tunley, Miss M. M. 16Feb.04 *Aldershot*
Walker, Miss A. L. 29Oct.04 *Woolwich* 1Apr.01
Walker, Miss M. 10Nov.04 *Dublin*
Wilkin, Miss M. E. 15July07 *Shorncliffe*
Willes, Miss A. 15Aug.05 *Devonport*
Williams, Miss C. M. 21Aug.12 *Dublin*
Williams, Miss M. B. 16June10 *London*
Williams, Miss M. S. 8Apr.12 *Dublin*
Wilson, Miss A. A. 9Aug.04 *Dover*
Wilson, Miss J. W. 17Feb.03 *Woolwich* 1July95
Wohlmann, Miss A. B. 28May03 *Chatham*
Woodhouse, Miss M. D. 17Oct.11 *Shorncliffe*
Worthington, Miss M. 10Apr.05 *Woolwich* 9May99

Staff Nurses.

Ahern, Miss A. M. 7July11 *Netley*
Alban, Miss A. D. M. 23Sept.13 *Aldershot*
Barrow, Miss E. J. 1Apr.08 *Cork*
Bentley, Miss G. L. 1Aug.10 *Aldershot*
Best, Miss D. M. 7Jan.13 *Woolwich*
Bird, Miss V.L.W. 1Mar.11 *Tidworth*
Black, Miss E. B. 25Feb.09 *London*
Blakely, Miss J. L. 1July10 *Netley*
Bonallo, Miss M. V. 8Feb.12 *Devonport*
Bond, Miss E. W. 8Mar.12 *Aldershot*
Bradley, Miss A. 25Feb.11 *York*
Branson, Miss M. J. 19June08 *Cork*
Brewer, Miss K.C.P.H. 3Mar.09 *Dublin*
Brown, Miss M. 1July13 *London*
Bulfin, Miss E. 7July11 *Aldershot*
Buyers, Miss A. I. 1July08 *Curragh*
Carleton, Miss R.C.S. 12Nov.10 *Devonport*
Carruthers, Miss I. 10June13 *Cosham*
Casswell, Miss M. R. 2Apr.13 *York*
Casswell, Miss M. T. 23Mar.10 *Devonport*
Caulfeild, Miss G. H. 20Jan.08 *Curragh*

Charles, Miss A.M.E.C. 1Apr.13 *Cosham*
Cochran, Miss A. M. 21Feb.13
Cole, Miss E. H. 15Jan.13 *Tidworth*
Collins, Miss E.M. 25May10 *Netley*
Collins, Miss E.R. 5Jan.07 *Cairo*
Corbishley, Miss M. C. 1Aug.10 *Colchester*
Craig, Miss F.C. 29Aug.07 *Cairo*
Davies, Miss E. H. 28Jan.07 *Edinburgh*
Davies, Miss E.M. 1Jan.13 *Woolwich*
Davies, Miss S.F. 2Nov.08 *Aldershot*
Davis, Miss M. E. 28Dec.10 *Devonport*
Dempster, Miss 20July11 *Colchester*
Dickinson, Miss K.D.G. 10July13 *Aldershot*
Eardley, Miss W. E. 18May09 *Shorncliffe*
Esden, Miss A. H. 13Jan.09 *London*
Evans, Miss M.E. 1Apr.11 *Hounslow*
Fawcett, Miss K. F. 10Dec.06 *Cairo*
Featherstonhaugh, Miss A. E. 27Mar.12 *London*
Fielding, Miss A.L. 18Sept.13 *Colchester*
Findlater, Miss J. 25Oct.09 *Aldershot*
Foley, Miss M. G. C. 1May09 *Woolwich*
Forrest, Miss E. V. 4Aug.08 *London*

French, Miss E. J. 1Nov.09 *Shorncliffe*
Gambardella, Miss C. M. 2Aug13 *Chatham*
Gedye, Miss W.M. 1Jan.09 *Dublin*
Gibb, Miss C.C.M. 1Jan.07 *Netley*
Graham, Miss M. H. 23Aug.07 *Cairo*
Griffin, Miss C. I. 24June12 *Cosham*
Griffiths, Miss E. 15Oct.10 *Aldershot*
Hale, Miss M. 11Nov.11 *Aldershot*
Hall, Miss E. L. 1Apr.13 *London*
Halloran, Miss W. 1July09 *Dover*
Harries, Miss C. E. A. 1Apr.07 *Wynberg*
Harvey, Miss E.A. 1Mar.06 *York*
Hodson, Miss C. M. 1Nov.07 *Gibraltar*
Holmes, Miss F. R. 1July12 *Woolwich*
Holmes, Miss K. H. M. 12Feb.08 *London*
Horne, Miss G. St. G. 15Oct.10 *London*
Hughes, Miss G. 16Jan.08 *Cairo*
Humfrey, Miss I. D. 4July08 *Chatham*
Isaacson, Miss D. C. 1Sept.10 *Netley*
Jackson, Miss B. 29Aug.10 *Chatham*

Queen Alexandra's Imperial Military Nursing Service.

Staff Nurses—contd.

James, Miss L. E., 3Nov.10 Tidworth
Johnston, Miss I. M., 13Feb.07 Alexandria
Jones, Miss G. M. 1July12 Woolwich
Jordan, Miss N. I. 10July08 Tidworth
Killery, Miss E. S. 1Jan.10 Dover
Kinkead, Miss I. E., 20Sept.13 Aldershot
Lee, Miss A. 9Dec.07 Malta
Levay, Miss E. B. 3Oct.08 Edinburgh
Long, Miss E. M. 22Sept.11 London
Lowe, Miss E. 25Jan.10 Curragh
Lowe, Miss K. 7Dec.07 Hong Kong
McBride, Miss M. 6Aug.07 Pretoria
McCabe, Miss M. A. 1Nov.07 Hong Kong
McClelland, Miss F. 8Apr.08 Dublin
McCormick, Miss M. 10Mar.10 Hounslow
Macgregor, Miss D. J. 1Nov.10 Aldershot
Macpherson, Miss F. 1May07 Wynberg
McPherson, Miss J. D. C. 1Jan.10 London
Macrae, Miss C. 13Feb.07 Gibraltar
MacRae, Miss C. MacK. 20Apr.07 Gibraltar
Martin, Miss D. M. 22Sept.13 Aldershot
Mathews, Miss K. M. 10Feb.08 Netley
Molloy, Miss N. 15Nov.09 Dublin
Moore, Miss E. M. 6Dec.10 Dublin
Newman, Miss V. S. 1Nov.10 Chatham
Nicholson, Miss M. 4Jan.12 London
Nunn, Miss A. E. 8Jan.07 Devonport

Nye, Miss B. M. 13Mar.07 Cairo
O'Connell, Miss E. E. 26Sept.12 Cosham
Parke, Miss N. 1June07 Potchefstroom
Parker, Miss E. K. 2July07 Malta
Parker, Miss L. A. 21Jan.13 London
Pattullo, Miss A. M. 2Dec.12 Aldershot
Paynter, Miss G. H. C. 9Mar.06 Curragh
Pearce, Miss C. M. 19June08 Aldershot
Pearse, Miss P. A. 18Nov.12 Tidworth
Plimsaul, Miss A. L. 25Feb.09 Colchester
Rice, Miss A. M. 1July11 Shorncliffe
Riddall, Miss E. S. 4Sept.12 Devonport
Riddell, Miss M. J. 24Apr.13 Cosham
Roberts, Miss M. M. 15Feb.11 London
Robinson, Miss C. L. A. 21Oct.12 Aldershot
Roe, Miss M. A. 21Nov.08 Cork
Rooke, Miss R. M. 25Nov.09 Dublin
Roy, Miss C. M. 3Aug.09 Devonport
Rutherford, Miss E. A. 17July07 Hong Kong
Sandbach, Miss C. 12Jan.12 Tidworth
Schafer, Miss E. 15Sept.09 Cosham
Seale, Miss A. 21Jan.13 Aldershot
Sellar, Miss G. H. 16Dec.06 Alexandria
Shearer, Miss A. 16Dec.13 Aldershot
Skinner, Miss K. F. G. 1Jan.07 Khartoum
Slaney, Miss C. 8Nov.12 Aldershot
Smith, Miss B. E. 18 Nov.11 Tidworth
Smith, Miss M. B. 1Jan.13 Aldershot
Smith, Miss M. E. 1Jan.07 Hong Kong
Smyth, Miss M. H. 3Mar.07 Pretoria

Steen, Miss A. E. M. 16Jan.08 Malta
Stephenson, Miss E. F. 1Apr.12 London
Stevens, Miss C. A. 24Feb.12 Curragh
Stewart, Miss K. J. 3Aug.09 Dover
Stewart, Miss M. E. 9Mar.09 Dublin
Stinton, Miss O. F. 20Jan.09 Curragh
Stuart, Miss J. A. M. 17June09 Dublin
Taunton, Miss I. J. 15Nov.10 Dublin
Tawney, Miss M. C. 10July08 Gibraltar
Teevan, Miss A. C. W. 13Jan.09 Woolwich
Temperley, Miss G. F. V. 25Oct.09 Colchester
Thompson, Miss C. V. E. 18Apr.11 London
Todd, Miss J. 20Jan.10 London
Townend, Miss C. R. 15Feb.08 Netley
Watkins, Miss G. M. 16Apr.09 Dublin
Watson, Miss J. F. 20Apr.11 Shorncliffe
Weir, Miss A. 18Jan.07 Malta
Whittall, Miss E. M. 1Feb.11 Aldershot
Whyte, Miss I. M. 17Oct.10 Aldershot
Willes, Miss M. 1June07 Pretoria
Williams, Miss M. 1June12 Aldershot
Wilson, Miss A. P. 25Mar.07 Potchefstroom
Wolseley, Miss H. V. B. 22Oct.07 Pretoria
Wood, Miss M. 1Feb.12 London
Wooler, Miss S. W. 18Jan.07 Cairo
Yockney, Miss E. A. B. 23Aug.07 Malta

www.ingramcontent.com/pod-product-compliance
Lightning Source LLC
Chambersburg PA
CBHW070934180426
43192CB00039B/2176